The Shell Guide to England

Cover picture: Kentish oast-houses. From a painting
by Rowland Hilder

The Shell Guide to

England

Edited by John Hadfield

Preface by J. B. Priestley

Introductory essays by

John Arlott
Phyllis Bentley
Ronald Blythe
Ivor Brown
Richard Church
Olive Cook
Phil Drabble
Peter Fleetwood-Hesketh
H. L. V. Fletcher
G. E. Fussell
Geoffrey Grigson
Miles Hadfield

Jacquetta Hawkes
Paul Jennings
Barbara Jones
James Lees-Milne
John Lewis
Jack Longland
Laurence W. Meynell
L. T. C. Rolt
Anne Scott-James
Thomas Sharp
Sir John Summerson
Maurice Wiggin

Gazetteer entries by

Therese Appleby · Gerald Barry · Nigel Batley
Euan Bowater · Sybil Burnaby · Judy Cowell
Frances Howell · Betty James · John and Anne Mason
Michael Webber · J. B. Willan · Ellen Wilson

Published by Michael Joseph
in association with Rainbird Reference Books

First published in 1970 by
Michael Joseph Ltd
52 Bedford Square
London WC1B 3EF
in association with
Rainbird Reference Books Ltd
36 Park Street, London W1Y 4DE
who designed and produced the book

Reprinted 1979

ISBN 0 7181 4032 X

House Editor: George Speaight
Assistant Editors: Raymond Kaye, Gillian Robinson,
Gabrielle Wilson
Cartographer: John Flower
Picture Research: Patricia Vaughan, Frances Latty
Designer: Gwyn Lewis

It was printed and bound by Jarrold and Sons Ltd, Norwich

The maps on pages 921–36 are based on the Ordnance Survey
Map with the sanction of H.M. Stationery Office (Crown
Copyright reserved)

Contents

Colour Plates

Editor's Foreword

This book is the fourth in a series of Shell *Guides* to the British Isles. It differs in several respects from the earlier volumes on Scotland, Ireland and Wales. The area covered is much larger: England comprises more than 50,000 square miles, often densely populated, as against less than 30,000 sparsely populated square miles in Scotland, some 32,000 square miles in Eire and Northern Ireland, also thinly populated, and less than 7,500 square miles in Wales.

Although it was a herculean task, it was possible for one author to encompass Scotland, and for two pairs of authors to compile the volumes on Ireland and Wales. In view of its relative size and number of towns and villages it was too much to expect a single author, or even two, to tackle the whole of England.

Moreover, in each of the three countries already covered there are national characteristics – of racial origin, history, language, even of scenery and architecture – which make for a certain unity and comprehensibility. Despite conflicts of interest between Highlands and Lowlands, or between Eire and Ulster, a Scotsman is unmistakably a Scotsman, and an Irishman – from north or south – has the map of Ireland on his face and the sound of Synge in his voice. But what are the distinctively *English* characteristics of an Englishman? Apart from the use of the same basic language there is as much difference between a Yorkshireman and a Cockney, or between a Cornishman and a Geordie, as there is between a Welshman, an Irishman and a Scot. And their environments, their local landscapes and ways of life, are equally varied. Admass, standardized education and TV are breaking down the differences, but they are still there. A supporter of Everton or Liverpool football clubs is more conscious of being a man of Merseyside than of being English. The same sense of local identity goes for a Cornishman, a Fenman or an East Anglian.

This regional individuality, which is often related to variations of landscape, agricultural or industrial background, or the form and material of the houses which people live in, still survives sufficiently for us to have to call on local writers to sum up the characteristics of each region. It is not easy to find an all-round, representative, English author, except possibly that cosmopolitan but dyed-in-the-Bradford-wool Yorkshireman who writes the Preface to this book. For this reason, this Shell *Guide* is a symposium – a work to which several people have been invited to contribute, each according to his "roots".

The introductory chapters are written for the most part by specialists in their fields, and it is hoped that they provide a certain amount of solid historical, topographical, botanical and architectural information. But their aim is primarily to set the scene, to alert the reader, the traveller, the tourist, the weekend motorist, to standards of judgment, comparison and interest which he or she may apply to things observed. The purpose of this book is to enable England to be enjoyed – but enjoyed with reasonable discrimination, a due sense of the past, and an eye for what used to be called "the Picturesque" rather than the conventional "tourist's

attraction". As a further change from the conventional guide-book, these introductory chapters – and some of the regional essays – are illustrated not with colour
photographs but with paintings and watercolours by artists who have had a special
feeling for the English scene.

The area covered by the gazetteer includes the whole of the mainland of England.
The Scilly Isles and the Isle of Man are excluded. The country has been divided
into eleven regions, within each of which the places of interest are arranged in
alphabetical order.

After the name of the place in the gazetteer comes the name of the county in
italic type, and then a map reference within brackets. The map reference refers to
the map section at the end of the text. The first figure in the map reference refers
to the page in the map section; the following group of letters and figures indicates
the position of the place according to the National Grid reference system. Thus,
for example, the reference for Amberley is 6–TQ0313; this means that Amberley
will be found on page 6 of the map section, within the 100-kilometre square TQ, 3
kilometres east and 13 kilometres north of the south-west corner of the square.
As the National Grid is shown on the maps in the map section, it will in practice
be found a simple matter to identify on the map every entry in the gazetteer.

In London a different system has been employed. Places in Outer London will
be found on the appropriate area map of England by means of the system described
above. Places in London are numbered in a single numerical series, grouped in the
areas into which London is divided, and are shown on the special London map on
page 16 of the map section.

Cross references in the gazetteer to places which are themselves described in
other gazetteer entries are printed in small capitals. In some cases the description
of a place of comparatively minor importance is included under the gazetteer
entry of a larger or more important place in its vicinity. In these cases, the name of
the additional place thus described is printed in bold type, to give it emphasis.

Particulars are not given of times of opening of museums, country houses,
gardens, etc.; nor are prices of admission, or other details that are liable to change.
The traveller is advised to furnish himself with one of the annual guides to houses
and other properties open to the public as a complement to this book.

The Index lists in one alphabetical sequence all the entries and sub-entries in the
regional gazetteers.

As General Editor of the book I want to pay tribute to my colleague George
Speaight, who has organized and supervised the formidable task of compiling the
gazetteer, and to Raymond Kaye and Gillian Robinson, who have performed
wonders in checking, revising, correlating and arranging so vast an assemblage of
facts. Thanks are also due to the County Librarians of almost all the counties in
England, who have read and checked the entries relating to their areas. All the
contributors to the gazetteer owe a great debt to the pioneer work of Sir Nikolaus
Pevsner in recording the architectural heritage of individual counties in his
magnificent series, *The Buildings of England.* They also wish to acknowledge the
help and guidance they have derived from the many published volumes in the
series of *Shell County Guides.*

Like any other guide-book this must inevitably be far from perfect. Although
every effort has been made to provide accurate and up-to-date information, the
editor will welcome any corrections or suggestions for improvement for future
editions that readers may care to send.

                                                                        J.H.

Preface

ON ENGLAND

J. B. PRIESTLEY

Out of a little stir of memories, from about forty years ago, that old German has returned to me. We were fellow passengers on a veteran tub out of San Francisco and bound for New Zealand. But she called at Papeete, Tahiti, where I was going. I cannot remember where the old German was going, but I know where he had been – and that was almost everywhere. Leisurely and not too expensive world travel was his way of life. (Does the type still exist? I doubt it.) Rolling easily down the Pacific, which day after day would look like moving dark-blue marble with thin foam its veins, the old German and I would talk for hours at a stretch. Finally I chanced to ask what was the most beautiful country he had ever seen. Very seriously, not trying to please me, he said "England".

You might say that even in those days I was getting around. Since then, perhaps anxious somewhere in the dark of my mind to out-travel that old German, I have got around more and more. A holiday painter, sketching in gouaches as other people take colour photographs, I have taken out tubes, brushes and (with any luck) Ingres paper in Marrakesh, Samarkand, Jaipur, Hong Kong, in Martha's Vineyard, New England, and Death Valley, California, in Cuernavaca, Yucatan and the dense jungle of northern Guatemala, along the desert coast of Peru and among the lakes and volcanoes of southern Chile, and have landed in the black howling night of the Aleutians and in the dazzling daylight of Alice Springs, Australia. But enough – though there is plenty more – or it will be all mere boast and brag!

The point is, I have now probably travelled at least as far as that old German, and I am ready to reply as he did – "England". But only, of course, what we have left of it. And between the England that German had seen and admired and the England we see now there stands, like a mountain of trash, the dreadful legacy of the 'thirties, surely the most determinedly tasteless of all our decades. I am staring now at a volume I found on one of the top shelves in my library. It is called *The Beauty of Britain*, was published bang in the middle of those 'thirties, and I wrote an Introduction to it. There, I have just discovered to my astonishment, I called attention to the Council for the Preservation of Rural England, that very C.P.R.E. (the name is the worst thing about it) for which I have made a public speech or two in the West Midlands. It was certainly not winning then. Is it winning now? Here and there I think it is, but what I like to call the "Evil Principle", which haunts planners and surveyors and inspires them to pull down only charming old houses or rows of cottages to make way for the motor road, is hard at work among us.

Mind you, we do not see everything as we did in 1935, when I wrote that other Introduction. For example, when I return now to my native West Riding it is not the old mills and the steep Victorian streets surrounding them that offend my eye. No, it is the occasional new factories and blocks of flats, all glass and glitter and California, that annoy me – so many swaggering invaders. The old familiar scene, belonging to my boyhood, begins to look so much industrial archaeology, and I feel that at any time now my wife and her colleagues will begin to explore it, removing samples to distant museums.

We may not have done our best to ruin our enchanting country, but we have undoubtedly had a devil of a good try. Any readers who question this should do what we did a few years ago, when we went by road from Brighton to Portsmouth Harbour, on our way back to the Isle of Wight. I do not think any other people in Europe would have done what we have done to that coastline. Ranging from the tasteless to the peculiarly horrible, it is one long monument to the Evil Principle. When we can afford to get round to it, the whole thing should be bulldozed back into the ground, like another Carthage. So please remember, before it is too late, the C.P.R.E.

But now let us – as that curious American song had it – "accentuate the positive". To begin with, I claim there is a magical element in England and the English (unruined) scene. And if I can believe this, after having lived here since 1894, then few others should doubt it. The magic starts in the astonishing difference between the geographical size of England and her *real size*. She is just pretending to be so small. Once you have made her acquaintance, letting her see that you find her attractive, then you discover there is more and more of her. I have already mentioned the Isle of Wight, and now I offer it as a perfect illustration of what I mean. Any man from America or Australia might take one glance at the island as something on a map, and then decide to give it a couple of hours. But you can spend days and days and days exploring the Isle of Wight, which, if you are really interested, begins magically enlarging itself for you.

England is like that, only of course on an immensely larger scale. There are whole regions I cannot pretend to know, even after living in this country so long. They remain in my imagination like mysterious provinces. I have passed through them, of course, but I do not really *know* them. So much of England is *round the corner*. (I shall return to this later.) I can offer the usual rational explanations. First, we have an astonishing variety of scene and landscape in comparatively small areas, packed like boxes of Japanese toys. Secondly, we have a lot of history on show. Here you wander not only along little winding roads, determined to slow you up, but also down through the centuries, even back to the Romans. (How many overseas tourists go north to see the Wall, the furthest outpost of the Roman Empire, and one of the most romantic sights in all Europe?) But even so, there remains something inexplicable here – the magical enlargement.

Take our mountains, up in the Lake District, where in the early 'twenties I spent much time, scrambling up and down every one of their peaks. On paper they are a joke, just so many hills. Go up there and you find they are real mountains, capable of killing you if you are too careless. A Swiss guide, taken there for the first time, allotted two days to climbing one of them, when in fact only two or three hours were needed. The magical element had deceived him. It deceives us, too. Just lately there has been a lot of archaeological digging to find King Arthur's Camelot. But it would not surprise me if somebody decided to follow some tiny overgrown lane and then found that at the end of it Camelot was still there, with nettles thick around a dusty Round Table.

In large countries you can go two hundred miles along one valley, three hundred miles across one monotonous plain. These are countries for which the jets were invented. Fly – and get done with them. Even the English should not fly over England. The magical element vanishes; the soul of the country does not reveal itself. Among so much that will be missed is the wonderful relationship here between Man and Nature. They are not in conflict as they tend to be in huge countries, where Nature is permanently hostile to Man and tries to drive him out with blizzards, dust storms, hurricanes and tornadoes. English weather is often abused, chiefly because it is changeable, does not offer sufficient sunlight, has too many grey days. So the foolish people rush abroad, to cook their bodies day after day. But it is this hazy weather, avoiding the glare of strong sunlight, that has given us the best watercolour painters in the world, trying to capture the delicate shades and the harmonious tones of this unique landscape. Why do I go away to try again to paint what I see? Because I know I am not good enough for the vague enchantments of the English scene, with its harmonious relationships, its tender variety.

I make one grand exception, faulty as I am. I keep returning to the Yorkshire Dales, which I believe to be the most rewarding, the most satisfying countryside in the world, from the bold and challenging uplands of the moors down to the fresh foliage, the sparkling trout streams, the white-washed old villages and their little bridges. And a man must linger here and not go tearing through it, thinking he is seeing everything when he is seeing nothing. Do not, I beg you – and now I am directly addressing overseas visitors – turn yourself into the victim of some ambitious itinerary that rushes you from one "high spot" to the next, doing six cathedral cities in a day. Better, far better, to take your car to one centre – it could be in the Cotswolds, East Anglia, the West Country, the Yorkshire Dales or the Lake District – and then do some leisurely exploring at twenty miles an hour. Only in this way can the magical element work for you, for ever enlarging and deepening your interest, taking you where you must not fail to go – *round the corner*.

The Beginnings

JACQUETTA HAWKES

Where can one begin the history of England? If one keeps to the name and looks no further back than the coming of the Anglo-Saxons, then millennia of creative history, scores of most visitable monuments, will be lost. If, on the other hand, one begins to follow the relationship between the people and the land on which they lived, then one will soon be travelling back through geological aeons towards the flames and particles of the birth of the solar system.

Plainly it is necessary to be practical. The most practical point at which to begin a guide-book would seem to be when men first left monuments worth being guided to. In England that time was rather over 5,000 years ago – unless one includes those few caves hallowed by having given shelter to Old Stone Age hunters.

Yet, before reaching men and monuments, some account of the countryside itself is justified. All landscape is, after all, historical: the creation first of the slow interplay of titanic natural forces, later modified, for better and for worse, by the hand of man. The geological foundations of the landscape have had an irresistible influence on where and how men have lived and on the character of their monuments.

In comparison with the rest of the United Kingdom, England is, of course, a soft and low-lying country, relatively young in terms of geological time. Within the last million years much of East Anglia and the Midlands was blanketed with clays, sands, gravels and loams left by ice-sheets and glaciers. Great stretches of these lands formerly supported oak and other deciduous forest, with such a formidable undergrowth of thorn and bramble that prehistoric man left them well alone. In the gravel terraces of the Thames and other river valleys of southern England lie the flint implements of the primitive hunters who lived during the warmer intervals of the Ice Age. There, too, lie the fossil bones of the elephants, rhinoceros and hippos that were their contemporaries. In a gravel pit by the lower Thames at Swanscombe fragments of a human skull were found. These are the earliest known human remains in Britain, dating back about a quarter of a million years. Swanscombe Man is recognized as one of the direct ancestors of *Homo sapiens* – as an examination of his famous skull (now in the Natural History Museum, South Kensington) will clearly show.

Away from the gently undulating Midland Plain there is no part of lowland England that is not agreeably broken by hills. Most characteristic, perhaps, are the chalk downs with their smooth, rounded polls. From the nodal point of Salisbury Plain and the hills of the White Horse, one line runs south-west into Dorset and another connects with the best known of all the chalk hills, the South Downs that end in the splendid cliffs of Beachy Head and the North Downs that give us the white cliffs of Dover. A third limb of the chalk stretches north-eastward as the Chilterns, the Gog Magog Hills of Cambridgeshire and the Norfolk Edge. Across the Wash it reappears in much greater bulk and beauty as the Lincolnshire and Yorkshire Wolds.

Running parallel with the chalk along its western side are the older, harder limestone hills. In Dorset the formation is broken up, but has created the beauty spot of Lulworth Cove as well as the Purbeck Hills and the Isle of Portland. In Portland it yields the finest building stone in Britain, much of it quarried to rebuild London after the Great Fire. The line of the limestone becomes clearly marked with the beginning of the Cotswold Hills near Bath. Here again is good building stone, already appreciated by the Romans when they made the original baths. The Cotswolds, extending north-eastward to within a few miles of Stratford-upon-Avon, show man and nature working together in sweetest harmony.

Beyond the Cotswolds the limestone can be followed along battle-renowned Edgehill, the miniature Dasset Hills, through Northamptonshire and Rutland to the spine of Lincoln Edge. This spine is hardly more than wide enough to carry Roman Ermine Street on its way to York. After this the limestone is almost buried by the chalk Wolds, but comes out again boldly, mixed with grittier sandstone, to reach 2,000 feet along the lovely western part of the North Yorkshire moors.

When seeing these downs and hills through car windows, much more when walking among them, it can add to one's pleasure to think of their substance being laid down in the days of the great reptiles.

In the oceans and lagoons where the limestone and later the chalk were forming, shoals of fish were preyed on from below by giant ichthyosaurs, from above by twenty-foot pterodactyls. On land dinosaurs of all shapes and sizes, some ferocious carnivores, others mild vegetarians, were the supreme form of life. In a rich vegetation of gingkos, archaic conifers, fern and maidenhair trees, flapped the first birds, still half reptilian. As the snowy chalk precipitated, it was probably sponges or some other simple form of marine life that produced those beds of flint nodules that so often show as black bands in cliffs and chalk-pits. Some hundred million years later they were to be mined by late Stone Age man as the finest raw material for his tools.

It will by now have become apparent that as one drives westward across England one is also driving further and further back into geological time. This ageing of the landscape is continued beyond the limestone belt by the New Red Sandstone that runs up the western side of England from Devon, through the west Midlands, to the far north of Cumberland. This rock was formed not on sea-beds but in arid heat. It is the red of desert sands that glows so warmly in Devon soil and which gives a ruddy complexion to so many buildings in the north-west.

In their day these desert sandstones formed against rock so ancient that some existed before life itself had taken any recognizable shape. The ancient moors and mountains comprise Wales and Scotland. England's share is smaller, yet in the south-west peninsula with its cliffs and moorland, in the Mendips, the Welsh border land, the Lakeland mountains and the great Pennine Chain, she has enough to provide her with some height, some rugged wildness, where old ways and peoples have held out against the sharpness of change.

While the forested lowlands were left to the wild beasts, the hills and the milder slopes of the ancient highlands were relatively more open and attractive for human settlement. Their lighter woodland could be cleared with axes of stone or bronze, helped out by burning. From the time when farming was first introduced it was these areas that were most populous – and it is therefore in these areas that the greatest concentrations of prehistoric remains are to be seen today.

It is not chance that three of the finest prehistoric monuments in Britain – and indeed in Europe – were raised in the heart of the chalk downlands of Wiltshire. Stonehenge, the Avebury circles and Silbury Hill are near the centre point of the

whole upland system. They would have been places of ready access for the tribesmen of all the radiating chalk and limestone ridges, and of the Mendips and the
South-west. Men and ideas moved freely on the upland trackways.

The earliest men to inhabit the country made little more impression upon it
than the animals they hunted. Swanscombe Man and his successors for an immensely long time are known to us only from their tools and their bones. During
the last glacial age, however, the hunters took to living in caves and these dwellings
do help to make their existence seem nearer and more real. Britain was bitterly
cold and could not support large or prosperous communities, such as those that
created the marvellous works of art found in France and Spain. There are, however,
two places in England where the Old Stone Age has some imaginative life in it –
Cheddar Gorge in the Mendips and Cresswell Crags in Derbyshire. The earliest
cave dwellers (at Cresswell only) were almost certainly of the low-browed
Neanderthal breed, but they were succeeded some 30,000 to 40,000 years ago by
men of modern type, skilled hunters with brains quite as good as our own. Among
the occupation rubbish in one of the Cresswell caves was a bone engraved with a
horse's head. Although this sketch is a poor thing if set beside the French and
Spanish treasures, it is good enough to suggest what the Cresswellians might have
accomplished in easier conditions.

At this time Britain was a promontory of north-western Europe. About 10,000
years ago, however, the ice-sheets and glaciers began to melt back towards their
present positions, and the release of enormous quantities of water raised the sea
level. By about 6000 B.C. the North Sea had been formed, and the landbridge with
France severed. Britain had become an island. The warmer climate allowed the
spread of trees and the hunters had to adapt to forest conditions. They became
skilled with bow and arrow, and as fishermen and carpenters. We can picture small
groups living in huts on river banks, by lakes, their dug-out canoes moored nearby.
Others hunted on the moors and others again took to a beachcombing life by the
seashore.

It is impossible to guess how long the islanders would have continued to live
in this quite efficient but mute and inglorious manner if they had not been roused
by the arrival of foreign immigrants. The first of these newcomers crossed from
northern France – their material culture had much in common with that of the
earliest Swiss Lake dwellers. A little later other settlers, probably hailing from
Brittany or still further south, settled up the western coasts of Britain all the way
from south-west England to the Orkneys. All these people are likely to have
crossed in oxhide boats akin to Irish curraghs. They certainly arrived, men, women
and children together, and brought with them breeding livestock and supplies of
seed corn. They also brought with them a knowledge of the art of potting.

These revolutionary events took place during the second half of the fourth
millennium B.C. They mark the beginning of the New Stone Age in Britain. Since
the beginning of human time mankind had been wholly dependent on what nature
had to offer. Now there was to be a fundamental change in the economic basis of
society. Although the men did not entirely give up hunting, nor women the culling
of wild fruits and vegetables, their main economic concerns were henceforward
to be with domestic flocks and herds and the cultivation of wheat and barley.

For those who want to visit prehistoric monuments, the most important result
of the revolution lies in the fact that it brought about a sudden increase in man's
creative activity. This was partly due to better food supplies supporting much
larger communities. But it must also have been due to a tradition derived, however

tenuously, from the higher civilizations now flourishing in the Eastern Mediterranean and beyond. These Stone Age farmers had already been imbued with the idea that they could enhance the power of their religious rites by providing them with monumental settings.

They did, it is true, put considerable labour into building for practical purposes. They made roughly circular embankments, probably mainly used for the management of cattle, of a type known to archaeologists as causewayed camps. Then on Dartmoor and elsewhere in the south-west "hut circles" of quite sizable stones represent dwellings with substantial foundations. Both labour and organization were needed to sink shafts and drive galleries into the chalk to obtain fresh flint for their axes. (The best known group of flint mines is at Grimes Graves in Norfolk, but there are several of them also in Sussex and the southern Chilterns.) Yet their greatest and most imaginative efforts went into sacred buildings and particularly into making monuments for the dead.

Everyone who is at all familiar with the downlands of England will have noticed the burial mounds that so often stand out conspicuously against the sky. The oldest of these were raised by the farmers of the New Stone Age. They are easily distinguished by their long, narrow form – originally often wedge-shaped, although the angles have been rounded by time. The largest are as much as 300 feet in length. The broader and higher end usually pointed eastward, and it was here that the burials were made. There was always more than one corpse, sometimes over twenty. Men, women and children were interred in them without discrimination, but it seems that such burial was probably reserved for the families of chiefs. Long barrows are commonest on the Wessex chalk – there is a beauty at the Winterbourne crossroads near Stonehenge. But they are also to be seen on the South and North Downs, the Lincolnshire and Yorkshire wolds and the North Yorkshire moors.

Although their sheer size makes these barrows impressive, they are far less spectacular than the megalithic tombs that were built by the settlers along the western coasts. In megalithic funerary architecture the burial chamber is formed of huge blocks of stone, the spaces between them often filled with drystone walling. In Britain the chambers are usually also roofed with big slabs, but occasionally with corbelled vaults. They were made dark and cave-like by a covering mound – either round or elongated. Like the family vaults of recent times, they could be reopened to admit a succession of burials. Perhaps the dead were consigned to these dark chambers in the hope of rebirth through the Mother Goddess.

England has not so many megalithic tombs as Wales, nor such splendid ones as Ireland and Scotland; yet in Cornwall and the Cotswolds – with a few notable outliers further east – there are plenty that are well worth seeing. Wind and rain have denuded most of the Cornish tombs so that the stones stand out starkly in the bare landscape. In the Cotswolds the chambers are hidden in long cairns. At Hetty Pegler's tump one can enter through the low portal to find the chamber just as it was when it was in use 4,000 years ago. Here is the earliest architecture in England.

While the immigrant farmers were spreading about the country, what was happening to the native population of hunters and fishers? At first they were dominated by the superior culture while at the same time learning from it. They were soon keeping domestic animals and making pots. They seem also to have played some part in flint-mining and the trade in flint and polished stone axes. Then, as the centuries went by, these old stocks began to reassert themselves, and

Stonehenge. Watercolour drawing by John Constable, c. 1835

in the end it was they rather than the immigrant population who made the greater contribution to the succeeding Bronze Age.

These native peoples were the originators of a type of monument, unique to Britain, that had a very splendid future before it. This is the "henge", a variety of sanctuary named after the genuine folk name of Stonehenge itself. The henges built towards the end of the New Stone Age were quite simple affairs. A bank and ditch, nearly always circular, enclosed a sacred area where there was sometimes a ring of ritual pits, sometimes rings of standing stones or posts. The best known example is the enclosing bank and ditch with the Aubrey holes at Stonehenge. These represent the first stage of a monument that was to be elaborated over many centuries.

The further development of henge architecture was probably due to the conquest of Britain by the Beaker Folk. This name is something of a joke, but is too well established to be given up. Though they came in various groups with differing cultural traditions, they were on the whole a physically strong and warlike people, archers and wielders of shapely stone battle axes. The Beaker Folk began to arrive before bronze had come into use in Britain, but as their enterprise helped to stimulate its introduction it is convenient to relate their conquest with the beginning of the Bronze Age. This was in about 1800 B.C.

The Beaker Folk certainly played a major part in the building of what is in some ways the most fascinating prehistoric monument in Britain: the great henge of Avebury. The enclosing bank and ditch are enormous – most of the present-day village stands inside them – and the sarsen stones of the several internal circles and the long processional avenue are on a corresponding scale. (Nearby, as well as the huge mound of Silbury Hill, there is a causewayed camp, the West Kennet megalithic tomb and a variety of barrows. There is no better place for an excursion into prehistory.) At Stonehenge the Beaker Folk had a hand in the second main stage of construction. This was when the "blue-stones" were transported all the way from the Prescelly hills in Wales. The much larger sarsen circle and trilithons were added in about the fifteenth century B.C., when foreign trade and pastoralism had made Wessex very prosperous.

Although Avebury and Stonehenge dwarf the rest, there are several other henges in England that are well worth seeing. One is Arbor Low in Derbyshire; there are the fine though stoneless Knowlton circles in Dorset, while in Maumbury Rings near Dorchester, in the same county, there is the oddity of a henge converted by the Romans into an amphitheatre.

Circles of standing stones without embankments must be distinguished from the henges. It is true that they, too, must have been sacred places intended for ritual use, and that they date from the Bronze Age – although they probably outlasted the true henges. Their distribution, however, is quite different, so that they cannot have been raised by the same people. Most of them are to be seen on moors in the ancient highland country. There are a few on Exmoor, many on Dartmoor and Bodmin Moor in the south-west. In this region, but off the moorland, there is a remarkable group of circles and alignments at Stanton Drew, Somerset. Of those in the North-West the most appealing is Castlerigg near Keswick. Keats visited this circle and probably had it in mind when in *Hyperion* he wrote of a "dismal cirque of Druid stones, upon a forlorn moor . . .". The Rollright circle between Stratford-upon-Avon and Oxford is in distinguished isolation so far to the east.

Standing stones, or menhirs, are sometimes found associated with stone circles, sometimes in isolation or in small groups. Like the circles themselves, they are most numerous on the moorlands of the south-west and north. The finest examples are both in Yorkshire, the Devil's Arrows at Boroughbridge and the standing stone in the churchyard at Rudston, on the Wolds. It is over twenty-five feet high – taller than any upright at Stonehenge.

The Beaker Folk were certainly involved in the building of the complex English henges and probably to some extent with the raising of stone circles. They affected our prehistoric landscapes even more extensively by the monuments they raised for their dead. All over England the old practice of building long barrows or megalithic tombs for family or communal burial came to an end. The warrior Beaker Folk brought with them from northern Europe the custom of individual burial under a circular mound. The round barrow became the usual form of tomb for the whole of the Bronze Age and by far the commonest form of field monu-ment. There are over 4,000 still to be seen in Wessex alone – and great numbers must have been destroyed.

On the chalk hills these barrows are shaped with extreme precision; on moors and in other stony country they have the looser form of piled cairns. The Beaker Folk themselves usually raised simple mounds shaped like soggy puddings (but known as bowl barrows) with a ditch immediately outside the mound. Later the same prosperous Wessex pastoralists who added the sarsens to Stonehenge devised more elaborate barrows. The most easily distinguished are the bell barrow, in which a level space was left between the mound and the ditch, and the disc barrow, in which the mound was very small, the main features being a ditch with a neat bank outside it. Round barrows of all types crowd round Stonehenge, for just as the great men of today may hope for a Westminster Abbey funeral, the great of the Bronze Age sought to be buried beside their noblest sanctuary. Several of these barrows covered richly furnished graves. One of the most princely was that of the Bush Barrow on Normanton Down, where a powerfully built warrior had been buried with his bronze weapons, gold ornaments and a sceptre.

Although there are some mounded Iron Age burials in Yorkshire, one can be reasonably sure that any round barrow on an upland site dates from the Bronze Age. On the other hand a rather steep-sided barrow on a low-lying site may possibly be Roman – Holborough Knob in Kent and the Six Hills at Stevenage, Hertford-shire, being good examples out of the hundred or so that are known. More rarely still the Anglo-Saxons and Vikings made burial mounds. Of these far and away the most famous is the group at Woodbridge, Suffolk, which included the treasure-filled Sutton Hoo ship burial.

The latter part of the Bronze Age saw great advances in both agriculture and metallurgy, but it was not a period that has left any conspicuous field monuments. They are not to be found again until well after the beginning of the Iron Age in the sixth century B.C. This was a time of stress on the Continent when various Celtic-speaking peoples migrated to Britain. The first to cross were still living within the native tradition of prehistoric Europe, but the culture of those who followed after 300 B.C. had been affected by their contacts with the Greek world. Then towards the very end of the second century there were several incursions by Belgic tribes who carved out kingdoms for themselves in south-eastern and southern England. It was the Belgae who first brought Britain into the light of history. Their powerful princes were in touch with Rome, they imported Roman luxuries, issued inscribed coin – and yet, when the time came, put up the fiercest resistance to the Roman legions.

The Celtic aristocracy was much given to inter-tribal warfare. If it were not already known from Roman history, their warlike ideals would be proved by the fact that the finest work of Celtic artists was lavished on splendid helmets, shields, weapons and accoutrements for war chariots. They are also manifest in the massive hill-forts which were their great contribution to the English landscape. Now for the first time most labour was given not to sacred buildings and tombs, but to military fortification.

Hill-forts come in endless variety. The older ones mostly had a single bank and ditch following the natural contours. Later the ramparts might be increased to two or three, and the entrances were strengthened by hornworks and other in-genious devices. Most of the larger hill-forts cover from 15 to 20 acres, but Wessex has larger ones – up to the 46 acres of Maiden Castle, Dorset, much the largest and most elaborate of them all. When looking at the earthen ramparts of today it should be remembered that they were originally faced with vertical walls of wood, chalk or turf, while the ditches were far deeper. In the highland country the ram-parts were built of stone blocks – as can still be seen for example at the fort on towering Ingleborough in Yorkshire, or in the small but immensely strong Chun Castle above Land's End.

All these Iron Age strongholds were essentially defensive in purpose. They were intended as refuges for men and beasts in times of stress – whether due to invasion or inter-tribal fighting. For many of them, including Maiden Castle, their last defence was against the Roman legions.

This is no place to attempt an account of the Roman conquest or of Roman Britain. It is in all the history books. From the point of view of field monuments the most significant distinction is between the military zones in the west and north and the usually peaceful civilian lowlands. Many of the well-to-do Roman Britons lived on large agricultural estates in the comfortable country houses we have come to call Roman villas. There are so many across southern England that selection is difficult. Perhaps the best of all is at Fishbourne, near Chichester; then Bignor, also in Sussex, is an old favourite. Lullingstone in Kent is of great interest, and so too, away to the west, is Chedworth in the Cotswolds.

The introduction of Mediterranean-style town life was the most important of Roman innovations, and ruins of town walls and public buildings form the other main category of civilian monuments. They still stand in many existing cities – for instance in the City of London itself, in St Albans, Cirencester, Lincoln and York. Perhaps Colchester is even more remarkable, for there, as well as striking remains of the first capital of the Roman province, one can see the earthworks of the earlier Belgic capital, and what may be the tomb of its most famous ruler – King Cymbeline.

Lowland England has some fine though late military remains in the Forts of the Saxon Shore built against barbarian raiders. The best are at Burgh Castle near Yarmouth, Richborough in Kent, and Pevensey in Sussex. Nearly all the great military works, however, are in the west and north, where garrisons had to be maintained all through the four centuries of Roman rule. Remains of the legionary fortress that served as the base for holding down the Celtic tribes of Wales are to be found at Caerleon in Monmouthshire. England's finest Roman monument is, of course, Hadrian's Wall, the strongly manned frontier held against unconquered Scotland. It has a dozen sites worth visiting, but to understand and enjoy it one should walk its whole length from sea to sea. Up there on the frontier it is not hard to imagine the collapse of the Roman province before the barbarian attacks: Scots and Picts and their allies in the north, Angles, Saxons and Jutes in the south. But that is another story – the beginning of the story of medieval England.

The Agricultural Heritage

G. E. FUSSELL

The English rural scene as it exists today, with all its variations in different parts of the country, is the result of thousands of years of work. Farmers of former days have left their indelible mark upon the countryside, from the tiny hill farms of prehistoric man that can still be traced on Dartmoor and the Sussex Downs to the "factory farming" enterprises of today.

Nature, however, places severe restraint upon man's farming and indeed upon the appearance of the land. Climate, elevation, slope, dry uplands, wet and marshy lowlands, are elements in the fashioning of farm work, and consequently upon the appearance of the man-made, as opposed to the original, countryside. Today most of the landscape has been so much worked over by man that it is difficult to imagine what it looked like before this human interference. The scene has always been in a state of flux, even before man began to work upon it, but in historic times our land has been more modified by human activity than by natural forces, although coast erosion, with a trifle of compensating lift at some places, has made some changes.

The most marked changes were made by farmers during the thousand years after A.D. 900. In the midland arable area which runs from the East Riding to Dorset, right across the country, these changes fall into three stages. Traces of the first can still be seen in some of these counties, as they can also in Gloucestershire. It was the laying out of the farm lands in the acre strips of the open fields, one example of which is being preserved by the Ministry of Agriculture at Laxton, Nottinghamshire. Other remnants of the system can be seen at Haxey and Epworth in the Isle of Axholme, and fragments at Braunton, in Devon. Each man's farm was made up of pieces of land scattered amongst those of his neighbours in two or three great fields, which were often several hundred acres in extent. The boundary between each piece was either a drainage furrow, a balk, a track or way giving access to the different pieces, or an occasional wider path forming an unmade road. The great stretches of arable were unfenced except for temporary obstacles to prevent grazing cattle from trespass. The villages of the Vale of White Horse and some of those in Lincolnshire had only two arable fields. These were on the lower slopes, and lay between the wet riparian meadows and the dry grazing of the upper downs; they were formed of intermixed semi-rectangular pieces. The farmed fields everywhere were surrounded by large areas of uncultivated land. The farm-houses and cottages were lined along a village street and grouped round the church and manor house.

This was the general appearance of the countryside where the major occupation was the production of cereal crops, although that main activity was usually combined with some stock breeding, horses, cattle, sheep, pigs and poultry. All this area remained in much the same state for many centuries, minor changes excepted. For example, some villages lost their entire population in the Black Death in the fourteenth century and became desolate. Others were depopulated by the lords for the sake of sheep grazing at a slightly later date. Occasionally a progressive and ambitious farmer got together a few adjacent pieces of land and fenced them to form a field within a field. In some places these changes were substantial but in others they took place very slowly.

The next stage was a major alteration in farm lay-out, made at a much more rapid rate between about 1760 and 1845, some six million acres being affected. This is only a fraction of the whole country, but the area most changed was the midland arable area, and consequently a most important part of the country's surface. As I have said, the enclosure and redistribution of the open fields and waste had been going on slowly in a limited way for a long time. Some great spaces of open field had been surveyed and re-arranged into hedged fields more or less square or rectangular in shape. This process was enormously accelerated as the so-called agricultural revolution gathered momentum, a revolution that provided the opportunity of growing fodder crops alternately with food crops and so enabled more and better livestock to be kept. The necessities of this new, or at least modified, system of farming caused new hedges to be planted, or, in the Cotswold country, dry-stone walls to be built so that the stock could be kept in the selected field to graze. Over much of the Midlands these fields are still in being. Some have been put down to grass, and in these traces of the old ridge and furrow can still be seen. This ridge and furrow is especially clear in some parts of Gloucestershire. A caveat must be issued here. Only where the old ridge and furrow crosses from one field to the next in spite of the relatively new hedges can it be assumed that once upon a time they were part of holdings dispersed about an open field. This is a part of England's agricultural heritage that is worth while looking for when travelling through the Midland counties and some others.

A good deal of the arable of the Midlands and indeed elsewhere was turned over to grass in the depression of the last twenty-five years of the nineteenth century. This did not change the shape of the fields, but developments during and after the two wars have done this on a large scale. First, the root break has given place to sugar beet, not completely, of course, but to a large degree. Potatoes, too, have been grown on a greater area. Second, the effective use of massive modern agricultural machinery demands large fields so a great many of the carefully created and main-tained hedgerows of the eighteenth century have been rooted out, ditches filled and covered drains substituted, and huge fields have once again come into being. Much of the countryside has become similar, though on a lesser scale, to the great wheat fields of the former prairie in Canada and the U.S.A.

Outside the belt of former open fields the possibilities were different, and in-genious landowners and farmers of former times made a quite dissimilar impression. Ever since Roman times efforts to drain the eastern Fens have been in progress. Where a waterlogged area of some 750,000 acres was inhabited by a semi-amphi-bious race who lived on wild game and fish and who pastured a few cattle on the dry spots there is now an area of rich and productive farms intensively worked. The former inhabitants walked through the pools and sluggish rivers on stilts and their cattle often had to swim to their grazing grounds. The drainage, the work of centuries, has dried out the land so that it has shrunk, and roads and canals are now well above the surrounding cultivated land. It is a flat black landscape, divided into fairly large fields, where such crops as celery, potatoes and carrots are grown.

At the opposite side of the country there was the large area of marshy land, known as King's Sedgemoor, in Somerset, where the Monmouth Rebellion came to defeat at the end of the seventeenth century. Only a century ago this land was

Farm Waggon. Painting by Tristram Hillier, 1943

still not effectively drained, although an Act for draining it had been passed in 1791. The contours here, as in the Fens, were an obstacle, but the land has now been laid comparatively dry, and is intersected by wide deep drains called rhines. The marshland has become rich grazing land given over to cattle and dairy produce. The county, like Devon and Cornwall, is very varied in elevation. Taunton Vale, for example, is rich arable. Exmoor, formerly almost uninhabited, as Blackmore's *Lorna Doone* demonstrates, was reclaimed and made into productive enclosed farms by the efforts of the Knight family and its successors. This transformation has so far proved impossible on Dartmoor, still a wild waste, or on Bodmin Moor, though on both there are some tiny scattered holdings where life is painfully isolated.

It seems that neither Devon nor Cornwall passed through the open-field arrangement of farm lands, or, where they did, the change to individual enclosed fields was made at a very early date. Devon has always been famous for its breeds of cattle and sheep, the Red Devons being bred in the north of the county and a large less individual breed in the south. The main industry is mixed farming, with some early vegetables in south Cornwall. The high banks, with hedges growing on the tops enclosing the fields, and the narrow lanes of some parts of Cornwall, are familiar to modern travellers.

Dorset is famous for its breed of sheep. Defoe said that over 600,000 were kept within a few miles of Dorchester in the early eighteenth century. The large, now enclosed downland farms devoted to corn growing were formerly in open fields. The west of the county has always been devoted to dairy farming. The blue vinney cheese is renowned. Hampshire is divided into two parts, north and south, the former being largely downland, at one time in open fields, but now in large enclosed farms of big fields, still under a system of mixed farming combining grain growing with cattle and sheep. Here are to be seen some great and extensive enterprises run on the most modern lines. The New Forest in the south is an unenclosed area given up to deer and ponies, and on its fringes the homes of many retired people. From Chichester to the Kent coast runs the line of the South Downs.

The South Downs are open, mainly unfenced, and covered with short, springy grass of a most nutritious kind. The Southdown sheep still flourish, but not in their former numbers, and much of this land has now been cultivated. Heavy crops of grain are grown, using up the accumulated fertility of the centuries during which the lonely shepherd and his flock were the sole inhabitants. The coastal belt south of the Downs is shrinking before the onslaughts of modern town expansion. North of the Downs is the Sussex and Kentish Weald, an area of heavy land and small hedged fields that were gradually reclaimed from the extensive forest. Oxen were used for ploughing and transport in this area until recently. Here, too, settlement is increasing, and the farming area shrinking, as it is more rapidly on the North Downs though there are still pleasant rural places there.

Sheep seem to flourish everywhere, from the mountain to the marshes. The Romney Marsh breed is an example. The Romans began the draining of this Marsh, and the work has gone on continuously ever since until the whole area is divided into larger and smaller plots by ditches and waterways. The rest of Kent is renowned for its hops, orchards and productive land. It is an umbrageous countryside, since many hedgerow trees are left to grow and the hedges themselves are pretty well maintained. The agricultural heritage there has many components. In many parts an almost garden culture is given to remunerative crops.

Essex has some similarities to Kent. Many of its farms were made by felling the forest trees and opening up fields. Near London urban expansion is rubbing away at the farm land, and on the coast the same thing is happening; but much of the county remains under highly productive farming practice. There are still some smallish fields, mainly in the west. In the east and north the hedges, so carefully kept up in former times, are being eradicated, and large arable fields suited to modern farming machinery created – sometimes that is happening elsewhere in East Anglia.

Suffolk and Norfolk, and more particularly north-west Norfolk, were the site of the so-called agricultural revolution that slowly matured from the beginning of the seventeenth century, and was an example for the greater part of the kingdom. It formed the pattern for the productive mixed farming of the nineteenth century. This in turn was superseded as changes in equipment and science became possible and were adopted to meet the contingencies of the past half-century. There are, however, patches of unproductive land in both counties which are now being used for forestry.

William Cobbett in the 1820s remarked upon the fertile farms with large fields that had recently been made from the former wild waste of Lincoln Heath. In this huge county there are naturally differences in the way the land has been farmed. Some part of it was settled in long, rather narrow parishes, something like those on the north of the Berkshire Downs. There was grazing land on the saltings near the coast, arable on the slightly more elevated slopes, and grazing again on the upper hills.

The northern counties, from Yorkshire to Northumberland, and then west and south to Lancashire, have much in common, but also considerable differences. It is a countryside of wild hills and moors, but also productive farms. Some of it is thronged with the great populations of industrial cities and mining centres, but there are vast agricultural areas surrounding these centres. The Vale of York is a scene of enclosed fields and mixed farms. The Cleveland hills were the home of a famous breed of horses, the Cleveland Bay. The moorland of the East Riding, or at least a part of it, was enclosed and made into arable farms with large fields in the late eighteenth and early nineteenth century, largely by the efforts of the Legard family. There are still large areas of unreclaimed moorland in the West Riding, but there are also villages and farms, the latter necessarily small, with a trifle of cultivated land supported by hill grazing. There are also farms on some of the upland, which were made by enclosure; but most of the farms, and indeed villages, as elsewhere in these forbidding hills, are in the valleys. This is a county, too, where dry-stone walls, built of material from the fields themselves, take the place of hedges as boundaries. The same sort of walls confine the roads, many of them narrow and winding as the lie of the land makes necessary. Sheep graze the hills, and there are some dairy cows from whose milk famous cheeses, such as the Wensleydale, are made. Derbyshire hill farms and fields are enclosed in the same way, and so are those of Durham, the home of the famous Durham Shorthorn cattle. Northumberland, Westmorland, Cumberland and the hills of Lancashire present the same scene of dry-stone walled enclosures, and miles of these walls running across the slopes. Cobbett noticed the large grain and cattle farms about Hexham, and in the border country where the then most approved methods were practised. John Grey of Dilston had been one of the "improvers" here, and Ernle in his picturesque language described how Grey's father had "taken his axe (to cut the tall broom, etc.) and like a backwoodsman, cleared a space on which to begin his farming operations". Precisely a century ago his daughter, Josephine E. Butler, wrote a *Memoir of John Grey*, describing how some of these great farms had been made.

The farms of Cumberland and Westmorland were smaller, and were the homes of the owner-occupiers, the renowned "Statesmen". They were largely grazing farms. A large landowner, John Christian Curwen, made an example of his Schoose Farm to encourage improved farming about Whitehaven. The low-lying coastal land of Lancashire is used for dairy and arable. The southern borders of the county and across the river in Cheshire may be said to be the birthplace of potato culture on a large scale in England.

The flat Cheshire plain which stretches into Shropshire and parts of Stafford has been famous for dairy produce for a thousand years. It is a land of fields enclosed by hedges, many of them meadows where the cows find their pasture. These meadows have been carefully maintained through the centuries, first by treating them with marl, later with crushed bones to restore the phosphates extracted by the feeding animal, and today by combined fertilizers. The farmers were not slow to adopt the so-called artificial grasses to supplement the gifts of nature, and they also grow some arable crops. Southwards and eastward the hills rise again, and these are all used for cattle and sheep breeding. This is the part of the country where the "black neat" cattle were bred, the Longhorn breed to which Robert Bakewell mistakenly devoted his attempts to improve them.

Worcestershire and Herefordshire are both renowned for special crops. The former is fairly flat, the latter hilly in the west. The countryside of both is speckled with orchards containing all kinds of fruits. Soft fruits, too, are widely grown. Hop grounds flourish. It is a countryside with a flavour all its own. The hills towards Wales are the breeding ground of the renowned Hereford cattle.

This has been a brief tour of farming England, which could only be fully elaborated in much more space. Enough has perhaps been said to demonstrate the ever-changing character of rural England, where so many different facets of farming can be seen on the surface of a relatively small country. All these divergencies are indications, not only of the resourcefulness and industry of our forbears, but also of the adaptability and capacity of the present-day English farmer, who is doing his best to preserve England's agricultural heritage, whatever changes modern methods may force him to make in the superficial appearance of the rural scene.

Harvest in Suffolk – the classic farming scene. Detail from the background   London, National Gallery
of the portrait of Mr and Mrs Andrews by Thomas Gainsborough, c. 1749

Trees and Woodlands

MILES HADFIELD

In the remote future, when Macaulay's traveller from New Zealand stands on a broken arch of London Bridge to sketch the ruins of St Paul's, he will probably hear in the midst of the "vast solitude" the sounds of those birds we hear today in any woodland ride. Until man arrived, our islands were woodland; and to woodland they will at last return should man decide to retire and leave nature to wreak its will. Indeed, most of our natural wild life today is substantially the relic of a forest world. And the speed with which trees re-assert their domination could be seen during and after the last war on many a bombed site.

The astonishing permanence of minute pollen grains, preserved, for instance, in layers of peat – the species from which each one came being still identifiable and countable – has made possible a history of the types of woodland as they varied with the changes in the English climate.

About 18000 B.C., as the climate improved after the ice age or ages which had virtually obliterated vegetation, trees spread northward (we were not then an island) from Europe. The birch came, then Scots pine, hazel, oak and elm and alder. In the Boreal climate of 7000 B.C., which was warm and dry in summer, it is believed that hazel formed masses of pioneering scrub round dense pinewoods; the birch became very common. Oak and wych-elm increased.

Over the next 2,500 years the climate became moister and warmer; the alder spread, and the pine receded northwards. And then the land began to fall, and immigration slowed down. The oak dominated the dense forests, in which wych-elm and lime formed an important part.

The linking of the Atlantic and the North Sea to make Britain an island enables us to define the commonly used term "native". This is applied to the trees that had arrived here before that happening. Once we were separated from the European continent other kinds could come only if brought by man – who began this activity at least as early as the Iron Age. We can say with certainty that only the following qualify as true natives of England: the hawthorns (*Crataegus monogyna*, common, and *C. oxyacanthoides*, rather rare), the rowan, whitebeam and wild service (*Sorbus aucuparia*, *S. aria* and *S. torminalis*), crab-apple (*Malus sylvestris*), holly (*Ilex aquifolium*), beech (*Fagus sylvatica*), the pedunculate oak, with short-stalked leaves and long-stalked acorns (*Quercus robur*), and the sessile or durmast oak, with its long-stalked leaves and acorn cups sitting on the shoots (*Q. petraea*), the white and crack willows (*Salix alba* and *S. fragilis*) and various shrubby willows which sometimes reach tree size, the aspen (*Populus tremula*), possibly the black and grey poplars (*P. nigra* and *P. canescens*), a number of elms, particularly the wych-elm (*Ulmus glabra*) and the hedgerow elm (*U. procera*), which is believed to have originated in the Severn Valley, the two very common birches (*Betula pubescens*, with softly downy twigs, and *B. verrucosa*, with harsh rough twigs), the field maple (*Acer campestre*), the hornbeam (*Carpinus betulus*), the small- and large-leaved limes (*Tilia cordata* and *T. platyphyllos*), the alder (*Alnus glutinosa*),

In early Spring. Painting by John William Inchbold (1830–88)   Oxford, Ashmolean Museum

the wild cherry or gean (*Prunus avium*), the bird-cherry (*P. padus*), the yew (*Taxus baccata*), and the Scots pine (*Pinus sylvestris*).

No sweet or horse-chestnut, no sycamore, no larches, none of the "cedars" and "cypresses"; all of these, and indeed the vast majority of the 500 to 600 different kinds of tree which grow here now, had to be brought from overseas by man.

Probably the first tree introductions from the Continent were made in Neolithic times; but they were fruit trees, not affecting our forests except in so far as they would seed along their margins – much as we find them today. At that period, too, immigrants may well have introduced the elms we still see in East Anglia, not for their timber but for their foliage which was cut for winter fodder.

It is not difficult to imagine the landscape of England at the time of the Roman occupation. In places woodland was being gradually cleared, probably by burning, the wood ash adding fertility to the land. Since about 450 B.C. the Weald and Dean Forests had been producing iron; and this industry continued to use timber for fuel and for the charcoal required in the process until A.D. 1775, when coke came into use. In Roman times sheep grazing increased, and where sheep graze they destroy seedling trees. Yet these depredations still affected the forests but little; Roman Britain remained a country dominated by trees.

All the heavy, fertile, well-drained soils were covered with a dense growth of the English pedunculate oak, a hiding place for wild beasts and human enemies. On the lighter soils, and climbing up into the mountains (as it still does in Wales and the north), the durmast oak, able to thrive on a more meagre diet, was most conspicuous. There were ashes and limes on the limestone soils, and wych-elms in the north and west. Often, even in the dense shade, yews would be scattered. On the dry, heathy land oaks would again be scattered where the soil was thicker, but here would grow principally birches, thorns and hollies. In and around the many marshy places alders and willows would be found. The Scots pine had by then, by climatic changes, been driven from the south into Scotland. The beech was present only in southern England and South Wales, the hornbeam in an even more restricted area in south-east England. The Celts, like the Greeks, associated trees, particularly the oak, with gods, and had sacred groves in which their tribal deities were supposed to live.

Through this jungle, always on the firm, hard ground, the Romans ran their great roads. They successfully introduced the sweet chestnut (*Castanea sativa*) and the walnut (*Juglans regia*), both for their nuts (we only had the hazel) and the latter probably also for oil – we have no oil-bearing natives, such as the olive.

In the long Anglo-Saxon period that followed trees and forests played an important part in the making of the settlements. Trees abound in the Anglo-Saxon place names, and often marked boundaries. The more open areas of woodland in which deer lived were preserved for hunting, to become under the Normans royal forests, places under special laws, complex and severe, designed to preserve the deer and other sporting rights – the first woods preserved for "amenity".

The Normans produced the famous Domesday survey, which recorded the description and ownership of the land and, in a general way, its value. It is not concerned with boundary marks, and so, contrary to a popular belief, does not name a single tree. Nor is it much help in assessing the area or describing the type of woodland then existing. It gives no details of the royal forests (which contained much open land necessary for the health of the deer) as they were royal, not private, property, and it describes woodlands in terms of inconsistent measurements, more particularly the number of swine a wood could support on the acorns and beechmast – a figure that it is impossible to translate into any terms of area.

Norman and subsequent medieval agriculture, building, iron and glass production and ship-building made steady inroads on English trees, but there was still an over-abundance of timber. It is worth recalling that massive quantities were usually transported by water. Several of the great East Anglian ecclesiastical buildings were built of large timbers from the fertile soils of the Midlands taken eastwards down, for example, the River Trent. And it was the Church, not only by its great buildings, that made the first great assault on our trees. The Cistercians arrived in England during the reign of Henry I. By 1170 they had some forty houses. Unlike the other monastic orders they were entirely rural. Often settling in wild, woodland country besides a small river, as for example at Rievaulx, they farmed on a large scale, particularly with sheep. Nothing like this had been known before: Melrose Abbey eventually had about 12,000 breeding sheep. This phase lasted for some 200 years, devastating woodlands by the destruction of all young trees.

The next major assault on the forests was the increasing development of the iron industry, whose timber consumption leaped forward with the general introduction of the blast furnace at the time of Queen Elizabeth I. Ship-building, house-building, glass-making, leather-making (oak bark was used for tanning), brewing (for cask-making) – all expanded rapidly under the developing economy of Henry VIII. The lands owned by the monastic orders, with all their fine timber, came on to the market. Fortunes were made by the buyers. No replanting was done. For the first time, instead of having a superabundance of timber we were short.

The story of English woodlands subsequently is of devastation, with weak attempts to provide timbers for our ships, both naval and mercantile. With the use of iron and steel for these, and the removal of all import duty on imported timber in 1866, devastation turned to neglect. The rabbit had replaced the sheep as a devourer of young trees. Swine were no longer turned into the woods to fatten, and so, accidentally, to trample mast into the ground to assist its germination. At the beginning of the nineteenth century the introduced grey squirrel began to show a destructive fondness for trees. Generally, English woods produced little timber, though many were saved because of their sporting value. They became less healthy, if more picturesque. Only a handful of people realized that timber-producing forests might one day again be vital to the country.

While England's forests were, owing to neglect and reckless exploitation, losing their economic value as suppliers of timber, there was a growing interest in trees for other reasons, particularly in those kinds growing abroad which, it was found, would thrive when introduced into England.

The Romans, as I have said, had introduced the sweet chestnut and the walnut – unaware that the timber of the latter would in time be of great value for gun stocks and furniture. The sycamore (*Acer pseudoplatanus*) was brought to Scotland, where it is still called a plane, in medieval times. It has spread all over Britain, though it rarely grows to any extent in forests; it is a valuable tree for wind-swept situations, and the soft, white timber has long been valued for utensils and decorative work. In the sixteenth and early seventeenth centuries came the oriental plane (*Platanus orientalis*), still a rare tree and better known to us as a parent of the hybrid London plane (*P. hybrida* or *acerifolia*). The larch (*Larix decidua*) was brought over from the Continent at about that time, while the Scots pine (*Pinus sylvestris*), which had retreated to Scotland, was re-introduced to southern England and soon re-established itself. The common lime (*Tilia vulgaris* or *europaea*), a hybrid between our native large- and small-leaved limes, was an introduction also; we first read of it planted in avenues "both for shade and sweetness" in 1609. From Turkey, via France, came the horse-chestnut (*Aesculus hippocastanum*), first recorded in John Tradescant's garden in Lambeth in 1633.

The great nobles were largely responsible for the early collections for which these trees were acquired. Instances were the Lord Protector Somerset at Syon, whose adviser was William Turner (1515–68) the "father of English botany", the 1st Earl of Salisbury (1563–1612) at Theobalds, and Lord Burleigh (1520–98) at Hatfield.

In 1580 the shortage of oak was so serious that Burleigh ordered the sowing of acorns on thirteen acres of Windsor Park, the first recorded instance of forest planting. Little else was done until the Restoration. The brilliant court of Charles II, during their exile on the Continent, had seen something of the great gardens of Le Nôtre in which trees, planted to form dense bosquets or in long avenues, played a great part. Ornamental tree planting began here on a scale not hitherto known, and was to continue in formal style until the reign of Queen Anne. The Dutch are a nation of horticulturists, and the influence of William and Mary was considerable. Yet in spite of an increasing interest in trees, and their greatly increased use ornamentally, England's native woodlands continued to languish and our natural resources were exploited without any regard for the future.

After the return of Charles II the Royal Society was formed, and in September 1662 there was presented to it by the Commissioners for the Navy a paper on the desperate shortage of the rugged, angular, strong timber produced by the pedunculate oak, which was essential to build His Majesty's warships. The subject was referred to a committee, which body, as is not unusual, left it to one of its members, John Evelyn. On 15 October, 1662, Evelyn wrote in his diary: "I this day delivered my Discourse concerning Forest-trees to our Society upon the occasion of Certaine Queries sent us by the Commissioners of His Majesties Navy". This was the origin of his great work, *Sylva*, the first volume ever to be published by the Royal Society, and one of the most important. It was not only the first exhaustive study of our native trees and their uses, but the first to include introduced exotic trees that might be of value. It certainly resulted in many trees being planted. In the dedication to the King of his second edition in 1670 Evelyn claimed that his book had been the "sole occasion of furnishing your almost exhausted Dominions with more than two Millions of Timber Trees". Perhaps more important, his work may be said to mark the beginning of the remarkable British enthusiasm for arboriculture. A whole line of amateurs, from Henry Compton, Bishop of London, (1632–1713) down to the creators of such great collections as those at Dropmore and Westonbirt, on occasions supported by bodies such as the Royal Horticultural Society, have resulted in our small islands containing thriving specimens of more species from temperate climates than any comparable area in the world. The search for and experimental growing of exotic trees has had far-reaching effects on England's present forests and woodlands – indeed, upon the landscape as a whole.

The Norway spruce (*Picea abies*) has since ancient times been one of the most important timber trees in northern Europe, and in pre-glacial times it was present in England. When it was re-introduced is not known. Evelyn, however, describes it clearly and, except for the sweet chestnut, it was the first exotic to be grown for timber. Today, supplying when young the Christmas tree, it ranks as the fifth tree in numbers. The first use of an exotic on such a scale as to alter our forests entirely was in 1740. In that year the then Duke of Atholl began planting larches on high ground above Dunkeld, in Scotland. The trees succeeded. By 1826 he and his successors had planted over fourteen million; the first great change in Britain's treescape had begun.

Even more extensive changes were to follow. Between 1790 and 1795 Captain George Vancouver made his great voyage. Archibald Menzies was his surgeon and botanist. Menzies returned with an account of the great forests on the Pacific coast of North America. In 1824 David Douglas (1799–1834), a young Scot employed by what is now the Royal Horticultural Society, made his first visit to collect the trees Menzies had described. Between then and his early accidental death he introduced the Sitka spruce (*Picea sitchensis*), the Douglas fir (*Pseudotsuga menziesii*), the giant fir (*Abies grandis*) and the noble fir (*A. procera*). All these thrived in England. Two other exotic conifers have a similar power to produce good timber: the Corsican pine (*Pinus nigra maritima*), faster and taller growing than our native pine, introduced in 1795 from the Mediterranean, and the Japanese larch (*Larix leptolepis*) brought from Japan in 1861 (distinguished from the European kind by its red twigs in winter). These trees began to insinuate themselves into the woodlands of enterprising landowners during the latter part of Queen Victoria's reign; not until the present century did they begin to dominate them. They all produce valuable timber on poorer land than will support our native trees.

During the reigns of the Stuarts the planting of trees in formal designs had played an essential part in the development of the great estates. As I have said, the inspiration came from the huge French lay-outs which reached a climax in the reign of Louis XIV. The style was an international one. But as early as the late 1690s a reaction was developing among English men of letters against this rigidity of lay-out. It came into the open in Joseph Addison's *Remarks on Several Parts of Italy in the Years 1701, 1702, 1703*, in the writings of Alexander Pope and others, and later in the publications of philosophers such as Burke. Travellers on the Grand Tour returned in ecstasies not over the magnificent Renaissance gardens of Rome, but the irregular beauties of the Campagna, with its rough patches of woodland, its serpentine streams, and a scatter of classical remains.

The result was the creation of the English landscape garden, whose constituents were undulating grass, trees and water. A visit to Blenheim Palace will show what an important part trees played in its design. The exponents of this manner were Lancelot ("Capability") Brown (1716–83) and his successor, Humphry Repton (1752–1818). They were responsible for planting trees in immense numbers: 100,000 was not exceptional for a single Brown landscape. Even so, the impact that this school made on England's woodland is apt to be exaggerated. Brown and Repton between them landscaped only some 300 estates, most on land unsuited to agriculture, and largely in the Midlands and Home Counties. Though we may agree with the poet that their work

> . . . scoops in circling theatres the vale
> Calls in the country, catches opening glades,
> Joins willing woods, and varies shades from shades

we must not forget the less publicized but well-documented fact that the tree planting was frequently done eventually to increase the revenue from timber.

We cannot consider trees in the landscape without mentioning orchards. Though England grows some of the finest apples in the world the only native is a small, sour, inedible crab, which does not enter into the breeding of the kinds of apple we now grow. The gean is a native, and this does play a part in the breeding of "sweet" cherries. We cannot claim either pears or plums as native fruits, in the strict sense.

There is evidence that the Romans introduced some of the better kinds of fruit; but not until Tudor times did the English become serious fruit growers. The great period of development in fruit-cultivation began in the late eighteenth century. Immense progress in breeding was made by Thomas Andrew Knight (1759–1838) and others. Richard Cox (*c.* 1776–1845), a successful brewer who retired about 1820 to Colnbrook, near Slough, developed Cox's Orange Pippin sometime in the 1830s. Since then England has been in the forefront of fruit-growing. In the last two decades new methods have greatly altered the orchard scene – in Worcestershire, Herefordshire, Kent, Essex and Suffolk especially – by replacing spreading old trees with small, intensively grown bushes.

At the end of the nineteenth century many of England's woodlands were in a state of neglect, and of little economic significance. Much of the planting done in the early nineteenth century was of the type of oak suitable only for ship-building, of which the Napoleonic wars had shown we were desperately short. This was to be ready for use early in the twentieth century. But by that time, of course, steam, iron and steel had replaced our "wooden walls". The timber now required must be straight and strong for structural work or for producing veneer, not angular to provide crucks for ship-building.

A small number of landowners, however, had been experimenting with the new western American conifers, only too well aware that if there should be any interference with our huge imports of wood the economy of our islands would be badly hit. Governments ignored their warnings.

In 1914 came the dreaded climax of a century of neglect. Trees were felled indiscriminately. The need was for the moment: there was no time to consider the results. In 1919 the Forestry Commission was belatedly set up. It took over the few remaining royal forests, was given power to acquire land and plant trees – the larger areas they handled were called forests, now with a very different meaning from the old royal sporting reserves. Help was given to landowners.

The fact that the type of forestry practised was essential to twentieth-century needs aroused much hostility from a prejudiced public which still seemed to think on lines more applicable to the timber-framed houses of Shakespeare's day and the ships of Nelson's time. But by 1939 the gawky adolescence of our new forests was being outgrown, and a new type of forest, of great beauty, was being appreciated. Then war broke out again. Schemes of planting were calamitously disordered while improved methods of felling caused the destruction of old woodlands that had survived the First World War. Since 1945 the work has gone forward again. What was its purpose? Quite simply and brutally the key lies in the fact that we are now a debtor country and yet pay £500 million a year for wood and wood products that we could produce ourselves, if only on a limited scale.

What has to be recognized, when considering England's woodlands, is that since Tudor times the rate of destruction of trees has exceeded their natural power to replace themselves. As a result, virtually the whole of our treescape has become man-made, almost entirely for the provision of saleable, usable timber. There have been other very limited objectives, such as provision for sport. But seldom have our great woods been planted primarily for visual effect. Even the scenic ornamental planting of the eighteenth and nineteenth centuries did not ignore utilitarianism. Fortunately, good forestry results in good landscapes.

The English Village

PAUL JENNINGS

Let us imagine that in the twinkling dark cosiness of a village pub, among the regulars who have dropped in before lunch, there are two strangers. One is a young representative, who grew up in Manchester and is now buying a house in Croydon. He has spent almost all his life in an urban background, and neither he nor his wife have ever really had serious thoughts about living in the country. His company-provided new Cortina is parked outside.

Next to it is the fairly ancient Rover, smelling comfortably of old leather and wood, of the other visitor. He is one of those vague, scholarly men, with steel-rimmed glasses and some kind of old canvas shoulder-bag with many straps and buckles, who look as if they would be much happier walking than driving a car at all. He is in fact a leading authority on carved wooden screens, and has spent the morning examining the one in the church visible from the saloon-bar window (it is justly famous, although it is a matter of wonderful separate panels, the muntins as though carved of solid stone rather than wood, not fully integrated in an intricate whole design as in the full late Tudor glories, he is thinking).

For him this is a planned, prepared visit. For the other it is almost a casual stop. It is a matter of chance whether they fall into conversation; but the point is that the motives that made the first man stop are only a generalized and diffuse form of what appears in the other as a highly specialized enthusiasm. They are both attracted, in their different ways, by a village thing. The young representative may never have given two consecutive thoughts to "the English village" (although this would be unlikely – and foolish – in anyone with the opportunity of using a car intelligently); but even if he had only thought to himself, "Something attractive about this place; old church, grouping of buildings, air of peace, think I'll stop here for early lunch – besides, easier to park here," he would have been responding to an appeal which grows more and more irresistible as one's knowledge of the English village grows.

There are many now who dismiss the whole thing as Ford dismissed history; if they don't quite dare to go so far as to say it is bunk, they do say it is *sentimentalism*, an irrelevant attempt to opt out from the technological age into a vanished pastoral civilization. In actual fact, not only the quite substantial movement of settling-down young families to new estates in villages, and the new council housing, but even the disappearance of the ploughman from the old thatched cottages (sometimes to re-appear in a council house) and the modernization of those thatched cottages by the despised "sentimentalists", is part of a process which is still, after all these centuries, the distinguishing mark of the English village; the process of *organic growth*.

I do not think it is just one's natural chauvinism which makes one say that although everyone has a (doubtless romanticized) mental picture of "the English village", with thatched cottages and a church tower set among Rowland Hilder-type elms, our villages differ one from another much more than those on the

Village Scene. Charcoal drawing by Thomas Gainsborough (1727–88)

Continent. Of course a Provençal village looks different from those with one long street of varnished maroon bricks, mortar-lines picked out in white, and heavy stone lintels – more like Holland, really – which fill the first afternoon southwards from Calais; but neither France nor any other country offers, on the scale which England does, exploration in reverse, as it were. Exploration usually means a going outwards, a crossing of horizons; but here somehow the spiral goes the other way; one curls inwards, in a landscape where little low ridges, absent-minded lanes, spacious parks fitted into valleys or woods much too small for them by any rational arithmetic, culs-de-sac, glimpses of water, make one realize that over the centuries we have somehow created inner space.

It is the result of a national empiricism, a penchant for doing things by one and one, not according to any scheme, grafted on to a fortunate geological and geographical diversity. What a lot of sharply differentiated areas there are in England, each so definite in character that it gives the impression of being much bigger than it is. No Canadian prairie could give a greater impression of skyey immensity than the Fens. The Lake District, the Cotswolds, the Peak, the orcharded Severn valley, the bare Wiltshire downs – all these and many other countries-within-a-country each produce instantly recognizable types of village, absolutely in harmony with the landscape because built out of the material on which they stand. Incidentally, there is no need to say that modern transport has made such reliance on local materials another "sentimentalism" with no practical justification. But there is plenty of aesthetic justification, as may be seen when you drive out of the Peak National Park, where all new housing has to be of that beautiful sober stone; the first red-brick house on the road to Chesterfield hits you like an oath.

This is no place for trying to summarize Cox or Betjeman on churches (or Pevsner on everything, let alone the fantastically knowledgeable and entertaining authors of the Shell *County Guides*); but fundamentals are fundamentals, and a thousand years free from invasion have allowed our villages to develop in a uniquely local and individual way. And the church is indisputably the most obvious example in most villages.

Now and again you may find scars of old violence, such as the cannon-ball marks on the tower of St Mary the Virgin in Painswick, which was occupied by Parliamentary troops in 1644; and of course there were the image-breakers, like the man who pulled down some statues in Winchester Cathedral with ropes "and down came all ye golden godes with *heyho rumbelo*", or the appalling William Dowsing who went round East Anglia smashing things – at Southwold "we brake down 130 superstitious pictures . . . and 14 cherubims", and you can see angry mutilations scored on the delicious screen showing ARKEANGEL, SARAFYN (Seraphim), TRONEE (Thrones) and the rest. But the main impression is of peaceful continuity.

At Langford, hidden in Oxfordshire meadows, there is a Crucifixion and a Christ in Majesty that were there before William did his Conquering (and he might not have managed *that* if Harold had not had to rush down from beating Tostig and Harald Hardrada at Stamford Bridge). And every first-year art student draws (or used to draw) the great Anglo-Saxon church of Earls Barton in Northampton-shire, with its pilastered tower. Both these churches are in the central limestone belt that runs from Gloucester and Dorset to the Humber.

Whether built, like the houses surrounding them, of this stone, or of the flint which is all that was available in East Anglia or most of Sussex, or the Midland sandstone, or any other local material, many of the churches have, side by side, illustrations of succeeding styles. They may perhaps have started as aisleless build-ings; later a chapel will have been added, that will have been lengthened into a north aisle, followed perhaps by a south aisle in the fourteenth century, a tower in the fifteenth. At Southease in Sussex it is the other way round; in the fourteenth century it had a north and a south aisle; now it is aisleless. There are no *rules*.

Only development – in its proper sense, before it became a dirty word: develop-ment as organic growth, something uniquely local, never imposed – almost, you might say, the opposite of planning. Obviously there is an overall, general, wander-ing correspondence with the slow changes of time and style. The catastrophe of the Black Death in 1350 meant the end of Decorated Gothic, partly because there were no longer enough craftsmen, but also because the Perpendicular, the church as "a box of light" was invented, according to Dr Cox, at Gloucester; and it gave Gothic a new impetus which carried it to a last sophistication unknown on the Continent, where they were by that time on to Renaissance styles. Hence King's College, but also hence all those marvellous Perpendicular churches built well on in the fifteenth century, often with the endowment of a rich merchant or clothier – Thomas Spring at Lavenham, or Tame at Fairford with its unsurpassed glass. There is one in my own village of East Bergholt, where Cardinal Wolsey's seizure of monastic lands for his abortive college at Ipswich is traditionally connected with the abandonment of the church tower after only one stage; so our bells are rung on axles, in a wooden cage on the ground, to the endless delight of crowds of summer tourists.

That same Black Death loosened the tying of the villein to the land, and hastened the progress of consolidation from copyholder to yeoman farmer with hired labour; and of course the growth of the weaving-grazing complex into a big-money affair led to a hedging and boundary-making that reached its climax in the eigh-teenth century. But here again it happened in different ways in different villages. I used as a boy to walk from Coventry over fields, now built on, that still, as everywhere on the Midland clays, were ridged from medieval strip farming. Some villages still have huge commons, some have long since lost them. At Meriden one drives from Coventry to Birmingham past a little green on which the cross is said to mark the centre of England. At Eltisley, between Cambridge and Bedford, one drives across the hypotenuse of an enormous one; and not far away at Ickwell the green is half a mile across. In East Bergholt most of it was snapped up in the nineteenth century by what was later the house of Mr Randolph Churchill. At Aldborough, Yorkshire, the children dance round a maypole which turns out to date only from 1903.

And why not? Perhaps a real danger today is that of being self-conscious about self-consciousness. Granted that mechanized metropolitan audio-visual culture is everywhere, militating against the old "one and one" English variety, does it matter if old traditions are researched by historical-minded and sincere newcomers? Do not such discoveries enrich the lives of communities still evolving, round W.I.s where half the members were born in London, round pubs where the Saturday-night regulars may have come from twenty miles away? Where the smith not only welds farm equipment but shoes the ponies of little girls from suburban-looking estates and makes wrought-iron gates, weather-vanes and even ornamental tops for false wells?

In the face of the massive onslaught of the twentieth century the wonder is that so much *does* survive (and perhaps an awareness of the need for rural preservation, however self-conscious and, to your standard pragmatist, sentimental, has developed just in time). A friend of mine, a Londoner with one of the despised weekend cottages in Suffolk, demurred when the eighty-year-old man who looks after his garden suggested the garden tool shed were left unlocked, instead of the old man (who often went away) keeping the key. "We'll hang it up then," said the old man, "*in a shy place.*"

My friend will now certainly speak of "a shy place" for the rest of his life. But will the old man's grandsons? Sometimes I think we underestimate the immensely strong life of the rooted local past. Children whizz on their bicycles down the hill past my open window shouting almost impenetrable dialect to one another, although they may have watched three hours of dreary mid-Atlantic television last night. In the Norfolk village of Hickling the field names are Home Fanny, Middle Fanny, Top Fanny, Garbage, Shales, Pott's Pightle, The Spong, Rushy Bottoms, Honey Pots, Puttocks, Weasels, Pasture Aldermans, Pig's Pightle, Large Pictures, Little Pictures.

In Warwickshire a mole-hill is an *oonty-tump*. In Dorset they talk about an ant-hill as an *emmet-butt* – and *nish* or *nesh* is soft, to *plim* is to swell up, *linny* is a lean-to shed, a *tunnegar* is a funnel. In Willoughby, Lincs., *bluther* means to weep, *goosen* is to act silly, *gallibaulk* is a chimney, *kelter* is rubbish, and the extremely expressive way of saying "shut the door" is "*put wood i'th'wal*".

English villages, sited from the requirements of Anglo-Saxon agriculture on good soil by a stream ("the hill-top village, a frequent Continental feature, is here something of a rarity – there was never the same need for defence" says Charles Bradley Ford), have gradually replaced the forest, cleared or burnt (which is all *Brentwood* means), and in so doing they have all become as it were watertight pockets well able to maintain individuality.

Obviously there *is* a sense in which the village as an ideal place, a pastoral invented by metropolitan poets who do not know one end of a plough from the other, is something that has to be put in the past. But the not too remote past.

Probably most people, whether English or not, asked to write twenty words describing our countryside, would mention the hedges. Now it is true that some hedges are quite old. In fact, at a recent conference arranged by the Botanical Association and the Standing Conference of Local Historians, under the title "Hedges and Local History", Mr D. E. Allen of the Linnean Society read a paper called *Bramble Dating: A Promising Approach*, in which it appeared that since wild species take a definite number of years to die out, you can date a hedge simply by counting the number of species in it. (In the Isle of Man, where there are forty different species, he had found the oldest hedges to be the ones lining the road to the ancient Manx Parliament, the Tynwald.)

But of course there is nothing immemorial about our chessboard hedgerow landscape, most of which dates merely from the eighteenth century (and a lot of it resulted from enclosures which meant appalling dispossessions and hardships for agricultural labourers). And really it calls for a constantly intelligent and inquiring interest (and therefore increased joy) in the countryside not to have this merely "pastoral" interest in (for example) hedgerows. To preserve them as windbreaks, conservers of top-soil and wild life – good. To make prairies – bad. But to amalgamate two fields really too tiny for tractor working, on part of a rational well-run farm – good. And picturesque hedges on an all-meadow, stockbroker's tax-loss farm – bad. One can say this of abstract cases; perhaps only God or a computer could say it of actual ones.

So it is no use being romantically against big concrete barns or silos (quite nice shapes, actually, when you are used to them; they have tiny shiny domes, like little Baroque towers in Bavaria) or against any new housing being built anywhere in villages. With all its new inhabitants, the village is still the place that offers most chance of a sense of community. Possibly the period from the Elizabethan development of parish administration to the immediately pre-motor age was one of a now irrecoverable local identity. It is noticeable how many village histories tell of a much greater self-sufficiency fifty or a hundred years ago, with a cobbler, a baker, a watchmaker in places of any size. Kimcote, Leicestershire, in 1965 had only one shop; since 1846 the baker's, butcher's, tailor's and other shops had disappeared one by one.

You could almost say that the village went on becoming *more* itself during the railway age. Such "sentimental" newcomers as the railway brought, either to new Mr Franching-of-Peckham-style villas behind gloomy hedges or to genuine Georgian or earlier houses, in the Home Counties or the unspoilt bits of Cheshire, were indeed a separate element, the precursors of those in anyone-for-tennis plays who have a comic char from the village who comes in through the French window wearing a turban and smoking. (There is a ridiculous and highly convertible generalization. Village life is for *anyone* who loves it.) And it is curious how in many villages the post-Beeching railway line already looks as irrelevant, as archaeological, as a Roman road. Stations I myself have seen are used now (*a*) as a factory for making scientific glassware, (*b*) for painting Oxford Playhouse scenery, and (*c*) for rearing pigs.

Yet those grass-grown tracks, sprouting willow herb and marguerite daisies, represent the first stage on the road to what now amounts practically to the total accessibility of all villages. It is only necessary to get out of the car in any of them, and look at the church, or the pub, or the green, or to speak to someone, to count the species in the hedge, to see when the Methodist chapel or the station was built, to find the manor house or the stream, to know in what way it is still a unique place.

English Townscape

JOHN SUMMERSON

In every English town much conforms with the norm of modernity. All traffic signs are the same everywhere. The fascias and window-dressing of the chain stores are the same. Advertisements are the same. The brands in the shops are the same. The citizens are also very much the same. Most of them being strangers to each other, they are in no wise strange to the stranger. All this is very convenient; all urban life flows together into one continuous urban life and the approach to an unfamiliar town offers no problems. It might be added that all modern buildings are very nearly the same, or if they are not they very soon will be. What matters about them is not so much what form they take as where they are put.

No English town would be better worth visiting than any other English town were it not for the enormous, obstinate and overwhelming legacy of the past. There is so much of it that even the most affluent and rapidly developing town cannot entirely wipe its old self out. The buildings remain so long as there is no sharp economic incentive to replace them; or, more rarely, because the laws protecting historic buildings and urban amenities have come into action. It is this great hinterland of architectural lumber which gives each separate town its "character". The "character" of a town today is necessarily "historic character". But perhaps, after all, it is the same with people; "character" is a function of biography.

So, for the curious visitor, the town has to be unwrapped, layer by layer, horizontal and vertical, to reveal its true character: a complicated process because the layers interpenetrate; they never come away in continuous strips. Take the main shopping street of almost any town. What is it made of? One half of it (the lower half) is made of shops. The other (upper) half is made of semi- or demi-semi-houses. Their lower parts have been sheared away by the shop-keepers. But these scraps of houses themselves protrude from different layers of the town's growth. Some may still have fifteenth- or sixteenth-century timbering in them; this may have been exposed and fussed over (and spoilt) for prestige sake, or it may stay, suspect only, behind a coat of Georgian stucco. Other scraps may be substantial eighteenth-century work, the chamber floors of aldermen and attorneys, now riding on steel bressumers over plate glass. Others again may be the sometime residences of Victorian shop-keepers whose elaborate and demonstrative shop-windows were found inconvenient and ugly in the 'twenties and 'thirties of this century.

One can go further into the past life of a main street. What, for instance, happens behind the houses? What shapes are the sites and how far back do they go? We can probably discover this by slipping through a passage between buildings or into a tradesman's yard. The backs of buildings are sometimes less disturbed than the fronts. In scraps of forgotten garden, in a Georgian summer-house used for storing ironmongery or perhaps even in a Gothic gable or two which nobody has bothered either to destroy or restore we can see more strips of time fall away.

This is perhaps moving too far towards a specialized investigation of urban "character", but the point needs to be made that a town more than two centuries old (and most English towns go back, at least in name, five times as far) is a very complex sort of artifact: most complicated in the many-layered centre, less complicated in the fringes where the buildings, built not so long ago, have never been rebuilt or overlaid or, indeed, notably changed in their function.

In nearly all towns are three typical elements which may be sought and found even without the help of a guide-book. First there is the medieval centre, then the Georgian outgrowth, and lastly the Victorian perimeter. The relative positions of the first two are never quite the same, but half an hour's judicious driving round the town should discover them all. The Victorian perimeter is likely to be discovered first, and although perhaps it should be explored last it should not be dismissed. It subdivides. Somewhere there will be the favoured streets of Victorian success, with houses by *the* local architect (who probably lived in one of them). Some of the houses will be of stone or brown brick-and-stone in that curious mixture of Gothic and Italian Romanesque which a Victorian critic shrewdly labelled "latitudinarian"; others, after 1870, will have gone over to "Queen Anne", a brown-and-red brick style about which the first thing to be said is that it is almost everything which the architecture of Queen Anne's England was not. Elsewhere in the Victorian perimeter we shall find the inevitable rows of bay-windowed houses with cocky roofs and ferny panels, appropriate to the clerks and managers and piano teachers and widows with small means. And elsewhere again the stiff harsh regiments, in the commonest brick, of the houses suited to the workers on the railway or in whatever industry the railway brought to the town or fostered within it. In passing, it may be observed that the railway station is a key monument in any town.

Signs of affluence in the Victorian perimeter may well predict what we shall find in the medieval centre. Affluence will have produced an Italian Corn Exchange in the 1860s, an Anglo-Venetian town hall in the 1870s, some blocks of "business premises" in London style in the 'eighties, a school of art, perhaps, and a public library in the 'nineties. And affluence will certainly have restored the church.

The church is the great repository of the town's memories. An English town is inconceivable without a church – so much so that in designs for new towns, made in an age of galloping decline in church attendance, there is sometimes proposed some abstract "vertical feature", some object of superstitious non-worship to symbolize the steeple of the church which, were it built, would serve, but so much more expensively, the ancient inarticulate need.

Churches may be cathedrals, in being which they contract out of the rôle of being "the church". Even in cathedral cities there is always a principal parish church though it loses, in the cathedral aura, the dignity of the definite article. In middling towns "the church" is the object by which all distances and directions are estimated. Its silhouette, if it is at all striking, is accepted and cherished as the symbol of the town. It is impossible to utter such names as Grantham, Coventry, Newark or Boston without a silhouette crossing the mind; while to speak of Chesterfield is to allude, however obscurely, to the thing that happened there in the fourteenth century, when the newly built spire contorted itself irrevocably into a nameless and horrible shape.

Town churches have usually suffered from affluence. Rarely can one feel in them that deep penetration into the past which belongs to the poor country church. Often they have been rebuilt in whole or in part in the eighteenth century; or, if a medieval fabric has come through to the nineteenth, it will have been so expensively scraped and renewed as to have lost all the bloom of antiquity. The churchyard, too, will have been scraped and tidied, the head-stones laid flat to make a pavement or massed against the churchyard wall. Nothing will repay the visitor so well as the memorials within. They are a directory to what the town has been and who made it so.

The church will necessarily belong to the town's medieval pattern, its ancient self, and that pattern can sometimes be traced without more guidance than the sense of restriction and irregularity which the central streets afford. Not always, however. Sometimes the church stands apart, linked to the urban centre by a Church Street; sometimes the centre itself has shifted away from the church and the original centre been distorted or erased.

After the close of the Middle Ages towns grew ribbon-wise: new houses lengthened the main streets, they also grew in density; lesser houses were built behind and in the grounds of greater ones. But very rarely did any great increase or any formal novelty arrive before the eighteenth century. Under the Georges every town which had its share of agricultural and industrial prosperity acquired a suburb of mansions. In a small town this suburb may be simply one short street. In a larger town it may be a geometrical area of streets and squares. It is always there, and it is wonderful how often its integrity has survived. Its source is metropolitan; it is a piece of London attached, not without pride, to a country town.

These three elements – medieval centre, Georgian outgrowth and Victorian fringe – are constants in all towns with a deep past. Having said that, it may appear that there is something like a standard English town. There is not. There is perhaps a hypothetical standard which is useful. But if our three elements are constant in appearance their disposition and their ratio one to the other are not. Sometimes one, sometimes another of the elements dominates. It depends much on the geographical mould in which the town was cast and on which of the centuries saw its most energetic growth. The balance or imbalance of the three elements is what most notably gives towns their character.

Take first the cathedral cities. The presence of the cathedral, the space around it and its attendant buildings, at once dismiss the typical. The effects vary, however. At York, with its walls still standing, the medieval centre *is* the city; the Georgian outgrowth (the noble street called Bootham) is outside the walls. At Salisbury, on the other hand, the chosen Georgian area is around the cathedral and its close. At Exeter the city had before the war and still partly has a planned Georgian wing, like a piece of Bloomsbury. No two cathedral cities have developed alike, and their functions have, after all, not been wholly ecclesiastical. York, Norwich, Exeter, Salisbury, Chester and Bristol have always been regional capitals, a distinction independent of their rôle as the seat of a bishop.

The regional capital which is also the seat of a bishop is the grandest kind of English town. It can be seen as a miniature London. Bristol is still, despite the bombs, a wonderful likeness of what London was a century ago. The medieval centre is the "city" quarter with "city churches", a Guildhall and an Exchange. The Georgian outgrowth is the equivalent of London's "west end" and stretches into Clifton as London stretches into Bayswater but more gracefully and with continuously exciting contours. To compensate for having no "St Paul's" there is a stately if inconspicuous medieval cathedral and there is the spire of St Mary Redcliffe, a marvel which medieval London itself might have envied.

The regional capital has something of everything. In sharp contrast are those towns where the Georgian outgrowth has run away with the situation. They are towns which at a certain moment became irrevocably dedicated to health and pleasure. Bath is the queen of them. Bath is a medieval city, and the medieval pattern,

King's Parade, Cambridge. Painting by Thomas Malton (1748–1804)

the constriction of the long vanished walls, can still be felt in the streets around the cathedral. But beyond where the walls stood the Georgian outgrowth, begun under Queen Anne, gathered such momentum that by the end of the eighteenth century Bath was a very large Georgian city with a very small ancestral appendage. The hot springs were the cause of this. Elsewhere it was the sea. At Brighton the discovery that sea-bathing and sea-air were beneficial converted, within fifty years, a small fishing town with a small medieval church, and a few streets running down to the sea, into a metropolitan pleasure-centre. For two reasons Brighton is a special case. First, because of its early patronage by Royalty (and, consequently, the building of the Royal Pavilion). Second, because of its relative proximity to London. But the same elements are there, even if the "medieval centre" is almost nothing, the Georgian outgrowth regal, and the Victorian perimeter vast. This, incidentally, is a Victorian perimeter which contains, among other things, the finest collection of nineteenth-century Gothic churches of any town in the kingdom.

The health resorts mostly had Georgian seed-times and in some of them is a double Georgian harvest – first the formal pattern of streets, squares and crescents which Bath invented, and later the informal "picturesque", with villas disposed in calculated disorder. In Calverley Park at Tunbridge Wells, and at St Leonard's-on-Sea, the "picturesque" is most purposefully promoted by a single architect. Elsewhere, as at Cheltenham and Leamington, it grew more casually. Bournemouth started in this way as an early Victorian adventure in estate development, and became in effect one great Victorian perimeter with (how rare!) no medieval centre at all and not a solitary Georgian street.

Cathedral cities, regional capitals and health resorts are the English towns which by tradition and convention may be visited for the pure pleasure of visiting them. To them must be added that celebrated pair, Oxford and Cambridge. Of these it must be said that the only difference between them and dozens of other county towns, up and down the country, is that they have accidentally attached to themselves, in their very centres, institutions of world fame with buildings often venerable and sometimes sublime. But county towns they remain, as they go about their county business and their thriving industries. Oxford bus-conductors still do not know one college from another.

All these towns have "something to show". There remain the towns to which tradition and convention almost forbid a visit unless for a hard and positive reason. They are supposed to have nothing to show. This is sometimes but not always true. It cannot be said that Liverpool or Manchester or Birmingham have nothing to show. It is true that they are black. It is true that they have long ago ceased to be articulate and have merged with lesser towns into limitless "conurbations". But still if one seeks one finds the old elements as before – the ancient but dreadfully modernized church, the modest brick streets and stucco villas built before the industrial deluge and – one need hardly add – Victorian perimeters of the most tremendous proportions. But one finds also things special to these places. At Liverpool the proudest Classical building in Britain, after St Paul's Cathedral and the royal palaces, is the first thing the railway traveller sees as he emerges from Lime Street Station: St George's Hall. In the hinterland the greatest of modern Anglican cathedrals rises on one eminence, the most original of modern Catholic cathedrals on another. Down in the dock area is a miscellany of Georgian, Victorian and Edwardian architecture more extravagant than anything in London.

How can one or how should one evaluate towns? Each traveller must decide for himself. There is the hedonist evaluation on the score of sheer physical pleasure – the pleasure of walking through serene, quiet streets and in the shadow of ancient masterpieces whose performance seems, even in the late twentieth century, colossal. This experience is being shattered by modern traffic but where it is still to be had it is golden. A "beautiful" town is coming to mean a town in which it is a pleasure to walk. There is another, more rigorous, kind of evaluation which judges a town by the intricacy and strangeness of its growth and by the human invention to which its fabric bears witness, even if it is a grim fabric. The sense of curiosity rather than the sense of beauty is satisfied. Whoever favours the first kind of evaluation may find his goal in Ludlow or King's Lynn; whoever favours the second, in Halifax or Hull. But has the town ever been built which is of interest to nobody? If it has it is surely a very rare piece.

Some towns are more easily remembered than others and the main factor in the memory equation is wholeness. The town which can, today, be seen and felt as a whole is necessarily rare. Town walls, the best guarantee of wholeness, disappeared early in England. The walls of York and Chester are famous, but Berwick-upon-Tweed still has walls: walls built by Elizabeth I to keep the Scots at bay and still enclosing, uselessly but splendidly, a quietly beautiful market town. Intensity of function has been another effective promoter of wholeness. St Ives, in Cornwall, grew round its granite church as a granite settlement of fisher folk, hard and clustered against the sea. Today it is a holiday town, but the intensity is still visibly there. Of other towns it could be said that they have derived a certain wholeness from disaster. Warwick suffered a conflagration in the seventeenth century, the little Dorset town of Blandford in the eighteenth century. Both rebuilt themselves with a new sophistication and in the architecture of both it may still be felt. But when all is said and done it must be admitted that only a fairly small town – one that has not been particularly successful in the urban rat-race – is likely to have preserved this enviable and charming quality of being an imaginable whole. Towns grow and go on growing and not often do they unfold all their mysteries to the newcomer without some learning and perception on his part – some exercise of the rôle, humbly undertaken, of urban anatomist.

The English Country House

JAMES LEES-MILNE

At the turn of this century a traveller along the English lanes would observe from the saddle of his push-bicycle or the seat of his dog-cart one "big house" standing at an average interval of two miles from another. The "big house" might be a palace at the end of a long, impressive avenue. It might be a manor house little larger than a farmstead, and close to the dusty highway. Whatever its size and pretension the appurtenances, lawns and herbaceous borders would certainly present a trim and well-groomed air. It would not be a commuter's weekend retreat, for such places did not then exist. On the contrary, it was the nucleus of a large or small agricultural kingdom. It was a living, hierarchical community of indoor servants, outdoor coachmen, gardeners and labourers, revolving round an owner who "belonged" to the district.

Until 1888, when county and rural district councils were established, England was governed by the squires, regionally as well as nationally. After this date their authority waned; but until the outbreak of the last war their influence was still paramount. A glance at Burke's *Landed Gentry* confirms that their ranks were being recruited by new families throughout the 1930s. The ambition of the *nouveaux riches*, as the old families used to call them, was to acquire estates and country houses – occasionally to build new ones – in which to establish dynasties of their own. Since the last war this process has for obvious reasons slowed down, if not ceased altogether. Prosperous business men today prefer to live in the suburbs of industrial towns, known as "dormitories", in modest-looking villas equipped with every labour-saving device, to adorn their wives with mink, and cram their garages with smart cars. This change of social pattern has virtually doomed the squirearchy.

We must discriminate between the rôles played in past social history by the great and the lesser country houses, or rather by their inmates. Let us take the small squire first. Until a hundred years ago he was very much a countryman, spending most of his time on the hunting field and his own broad acres, active on the Bench, consequential in the church pew, and merry in the village taproom. His manor house, teeming with offspring, was no shrine of virtu, but a family home, architecturally robust or prim, and usually comely. The great lord, on the other hand, played little part in county politics, being too preoccupied by affairs of court or state at St James's or Westminster. Nonetheless, the land was very dear to him for ancestral, financial and prestige reasons. He sprang from it. It provided him with his wherewithal. He visited it as often as his metropolitan duties allowed. He returned to die upon it. Ever since the Reformation the great lord's interest had been to amass more and more acres. And the immense wealth of the sixteenth-century families like the Cecils, Russells and Cavendishes had derived from the expropriation of monastic lands. The great lord's wealth and station were commensurate with his acreage. His rent roll was assessable by the magnitude of his country seat. The two were interdependent. Even today a big house divorced from its estate seems anomalous, if not uneconomic.

From the sixteenth to the nineteenth century the great lord held himself conspicuously aloof from the common herd. His tenantry may have found him grasping and forbidding. His neighbours among the lesser gentry must have found him unapproachable. They were seldom, if ever, invited within his unwelcoming portals. Indeed, until 1945 some great houses like Woburn and Longleat had not for centuries been entered by anyone outside the family and a restricted circle of intimates. The public's extraordinary interest in them today may partly be explained by curiosity to see for themselves what sort of exclusive life was lived by dukes and marquesses until comparatively recent times.

It follows that the owners of large country houses in the past were not always popular. On the other hand they were often creative. By no means all were amateur architects of the calibre of Sir Roger Pratt (Coleshill), Lord Burlington (Chiswick) or Lord Sudeley (Toddington). Yet the majority had the taste to engage and the learning to direct the foremost architects and craftsmen of their day. Many, too, were remarkably discerning patrons of artists, like the 4th Earl of Pembroke (Wilton), the 1st Earl of Leicester (Holkham), the 3rd Earl of Egremont (Petworth), and – to descend the social scale – Sir Justinian Isham (Lamport), Sir Andrew Fountaine (Narford) and Sir George Beaumont (Coleorton). These earls and baronets filled their houses with paintings and rare manuscripts, sculpture, tapestry, furniture and porcelain, which they collected on the Continent, or commissioned from their contemporaries at home. Their halls and courts, which at one time were accessible to the few, are today open to the many. Not only in the country houses, but also in their contents, we can enjoy the greatest contribution which our nation has made to the visual arts.

Not satisfied with embellishing his house, a landowner endeavoured to fashion his estate into a concerted work of art. The whole domain became, as it were, an integral extension of the house. First the pleasure grounds, secondly the park, and thirdly the woods and fields beyond, were laid out with an expert's eye for picturesque grouping. It was as though the connoisseur owner had employed Claude Lorrain or Richard Wilson to transpose from canvas upon the smiling face of England idyllic and bucolic scenes of ancient Greece and Rome.

Between 1700 and 1800 the whole country was tamed into one gigantic parkscape. Rivers and streams were changed overnight into serpentine lakes. Unsightly villages were razed to the ground. Hillocks were moved from one horizon to another. By the early twentieth century, when our Edwardian traveller was bicycling or driving along the highways, the woods and hedgerows of the Georgian planters had reached their prime. England was the most picturesque, no, the most beautiful country in the world. Today we can enjoy the residue of this rapidly dwindling capital of natural beauty – but only just. We should make the most of it – since we are doing nothing to replenish it – for as long as it may last.

It is nowadays fashionable to deride the aristocrats of the past ages. Recent publications have made much play with their selfishness, exploitation of the oppressed, and their frivolity. One might just as well revile for their religious bigotry the bishops and abbots under the Plantagenets. These prelates sponsored the cathedrals and minsters which are now the lasting witness of their age. Likewise the patricians built the country houses which are the witness of theirs. We should not be deflected from admiring the visual sensibility of these men, however much we may choose to ignore some other virtues which, according to the standards of their day, they indubitably possessed. We should not, I suggest, withhold from them our profound gratitude. We should likewise feel beholden to the country houses for the numbers of great Englishmen they in their turn have given birth to and nurtured – statesmen, agriculturists, philanthropists, theologians, scientists and poets.

Until the Reformation English country houses, judged by cultural and social standards, were secondary to the monasteries, which were the seats of learning and healing, and the founts of charity. But like them they were, as dwellings, stark and uncomfortable. Oakham Castle (1180) consists of one vaulted, pillared hall like a church, in which a whole household and retinue of retainers dossed down on straw-strewn mud at nights, and lived and fed by day little better than beasts in a pen. At Boothby Pagnell, Lincs., the late-Norman manor house resembles a noncon-formist chapel in being approached from outside by stone steps, and having tiny twin-light windows in the thick walls, without glass but with rough, wooden shutters. The squat peel-tower residences, like Longthorpe in Northampton-shire (late thirteenth century) and Yanwath in Westmorland (fourteenth century) were unashamedly utilitarian. Fourteenth-century Bodiam and fifteenth-century Tattershall castles were still designed for defence, not delight. Gradually a con-geries of annexes would grow up round the nuclear peel. Compton Wynyates in Warwickshire is such a place. To a modest Henry VI core was added in the en-suing centuries a hotchpotch of towers, turrets, crenellated wings, black and white gables, twisted chimneystacks, and every variety of window, pointed, mullioned, arched, flat-headed, cusped, and even sashed. The result is the most lovable, picturesque jumble of a house imaginable. But it cannot be called conscious architecture. Its beauty is accidental, approximating to the beauty of the oaks and elms which have grown laboriously out of the English soil. Like these rugged, shaggy trees it becomes increasingly venerable with the passage of time.

After the Reformation the nobility, enriched by the spoils of the Church, were more sophisticated and art-loving than their predecessors, the uncouth barons who waged the Wars of the Roses. Patronage rapidly shifted from churchmen to laymen; and masons and craftsmen concentrated upon secular building. As the medieval churches had been raised for the glory of God the Renaissance houses were raised for – I was going to say, the sake of art – but I fear it was sometimes self-glorification. With the disintegration of Catholic England a crop of domestic palaces and manor houses sprang up in the shires. At first they were comparatively simple in plan and decoration. Sutton Place, Surrey (1520), is of this sort. Of modest dimensions, its plain brick surfaces are only enlivened by a few panels of terracotta. Within a decade country houses began to be ambitious and ornate. Hengrave Hall, Suffolk (finished 1538), and Dingley Hall, Northants (1558), indulged in polygonal turrets and finials, and jazzy skylines. By Queen Elizabeth I's reign country houses had ceased to be defensive, and became domestic. The largest were often ostentatious, even vulgar like Burghley and Wollaton, both of which conformed to the character of their newly risen owners. The Elizabethan and Jacobean raisers of palaces were as often as not unscrupulous adventurers. Yet, strangely enough, some of these wholly inestimable persons created the most alluring houses in existence. Among them may be included Hardwick Hall, Blickling Hall, Montacute House and Chastleton House. All these houses are distinguished by vertical lines, uncongested surfaces, and huge casement windows; and above all by extremely sympathetic materials. They are still Gothic, colourful and intensely romantic.

It goes without saying that the Tudor and Jacobean mansions have none of the pretensions to scholarship of the contemporary villas of the Brenta. Nevertheless, in variety of materials and inventiveness of patterns they have no equals. We have merely to consider some materials with which the different regions of England abundantly supplied the native builders: claret brick in the Home Counties, honey stone in the Cotswolds, silvery oak in the Midlands, icy blue flint in East Anglia, not to mention cob, clunch, thatch, parge and wattle and daub almost everywhere. Yet it is a fallacy to assume that the medieval, Tudor and Jacobean builders were deliberately "olde worlde". Nothing is further from the truth. They were undeviatingly functional. For example, the master carpenters of the half-timbered houses, who have been specially subjected to the charge of "quaintness", worked with hard-headed precision. They usually prefabricated the outer walls on the ground. Consequently they were obliged to measure and cut each beam and strut accurately to the fraction of an inch before they could raise and tenon the finished skeleton together. It is time and the seasons which have given the "black and white" buildings the weathered and warped look which the twentieth century finds appealing.

With the Caroline century came the recognition that what mattered in building was classical propriety. Adherence to Vitruvian rules assumed a vital importance. Inigo Jones was the first to introduce the rules from Italy. Wren, after profound study of French architecture, reaffirmed them. Meanwhile the native builders tried desperately to keep abreast with the foreign textbooks of Serlio, Fréart and Le Pautre. Often they failed signally to translate the new precepts into their work. Yet their first strivings towards classical regularity rendered houses like Ramsbury Manor (1675), Belton House (1694) and Hanbury Hall (1700) no less sympathetic to live in than the more correct achievements of their successors. For Caroline and Queen Anne houses, large or small, have the quality of homeliness and warmth.

Georgian houses, on the other hand, reach the ultimate excellence of art and craftsmanship. The golden age of enlightened patron and professional builder spanned the reigns of the four Georges. The partners, working together within strictly imposed limits and mastering the classical formulae, seldom put a foot wrong. The houses they created were as gracious and outwardly conforming as themselves. Their ostensible hallmark was manners. Architectural manners had to be as irreproachable as the expensive and elaborate clothes worn by the people who lived in these houses. The country-house way of life likewise became an art in itself. It persisted throughout the nineteenth and lasted even into the twentieth century. No one who did not experience it during its more relaxed years between the wars can conceive how civilizing were the amenities it offered.

The opening of the eighteenth century coincided with the building of vast country palaces in the Baroque style. The Chatsworths, Castle Howards and Blenheims were a triumphal expression of the aristocratic ascendancy over the monarchy, resulting from the Glorious Revolution of 1688. After the accession of George I the predominant architectural style was the Palladian. It was outwardly more staid, more glacial and less flamboyant than the Baroque, just as the Hanoverians were outwardly dull and respectable compared with the fabulous Stuarts. Holkham, Badminton and Wentworth Woodhouse come within the Palladian category. They are grandiose, not cosy houses. The Palladian style endured until the accession of George III in 1760. It was succeeded by the Adam-Wyatt style, which was more delicate, at times a trifle effeminate. Osterley, Syon and Shugborough are representative of this style. The rooms of these houses are so elegant that only the most refined furniture made by Chippendale, Sheraton or the *ébénistes* of Louis XVI looks well in them. Furniture of earlier or later date seems gross and out of place. Towards the end of George III's reign the Regency style was in the ascendant. Introduced by the Prince Regent, Holland and Nash, it has distinct Gallic and academic undertones. Regency decoration and furniture echo Napoleonic tastes and reflect Greek and Egyptian archaeological discoveries. Southill in Bedfordshire, Ickworth in Suffolk and Dodington in Gloucestershire attain an economy of line in architecture and furnishing which verges on the austere and pedantic. Inevitably the Regency gave way to the eclectic and often hectic over-ornamentation of the Victorian style.

The growth of our country houses has coincided with the evolution of the English race and language. It is impossible for anyone who professes to love the poetry of Shakespeare, Milton, Pope and Tennyson to be unmoved by them. Here we touch upon their peculiarly literary quality. By strict Italian standards they are sometimes amateurish, illogical and haphazard in design and composition. Yet they resemble rich pages of history which make compulsive reading. Their mellow walls, lichen-covered roofs, their family portraits, treasures and bric-à-brac, and their long continuity of ownership render them intrinsically poetic. You cannot tinker with poetry. The moment you start emending, correcting or bowdlerizing a Shakespearean sonnet or Tennysonian elegy you drive the magic out of it. Similarly, if you were to take a characteristic Cotswold manor house, cover the outside with fire escapes, rip out the panelling of the gallery, distemper the drawing-room a healthy hospital green, lino the oak floors, asphalt the garden paths and litter the lawns with classrooms, you might get a much needed reformatory for maladjusted teenagers. You would also have totally destroyed the ethos of the building. You would do better to raze it to the ground and cherish its memory.

Although taxation and the disappearance into thin air of the domestic servant have doomed the English country house as a single family unit, there are alternative ways of preserving some, if not most, of these national monuments. A few local authorities, the Ministry of Public Buildings, the National Trust and the Mutual Households Association provide praiseworthy compromises. Belgrave Hall, outside Leicester, has been filled with furniture and pictures that belonged to local families, and so beautifully arranged that the visitor may stroll through the rooms and garden under the happy illusion that he is the possessor of this medium-sized dwelling. Saltram in Devon, Dyrham in Gloucestershire, Danny in Sussex and Aynhoe in Northamptonshire still retain the splendid decoration and the principal contents which have always belonged to them. In these and in many other houses flats have been carved out of the bedroom floors and service wings, whereas the state rooms are regularly open to the public. Often the state rooms are used for concerts, exhibitions and various cultural activities. At Croft Castle, Herefordshire, different members of the Croft family live in separate corners of the house and share the ground-floor rooms with the public.

By these means historic country houses can still be kept alive; and, what is so important, their special character as homes is more or less maintained. After all, they were not built merely to be looked at and admired; they were meant to be lived in and loved as well.

Cathedrals and Churches

OLIVE COOK

For a large part of our population the symbolic meaning of our churches and cathedrals has become almost as remote as that of the Parthenon or the temples at Paestum. Already the fate of those pagan shrines threatens to overtake the sanctuaries of the Christian faith. Some have fallen into total disuse and have become derelict; others have even been pulled down in the interests of commerce; while many are in such bad repair that they could not endure without the splendid work of bodies such as the Historic Churches Preservation Trust and The Friends of Friendless Churches. But the vulnerability of these impressive monuments in a materialistic age heightens our appreciation of them as works of art and as the most eloquent of witnesses to the historic past. The visual scene in England is still dominated by our parish and greater churches. Their power simply as images, their magnificent variety, their enchanting detail, compel attention.

Cathedral and parish churches came into being for different purposes, and their design and evolution can only be understood if these differences are borne in mind. The cathedral was the focal point of a whole region while the parish church was the centre of both the religious and the social life of a local community. Its secular uses were varied: it became a place of refuge and defence in troubled times; the nave was the setting for miracle plays and for the feast of the patron saint; the porch (on the south side of the building) was used until the mid-sixteenth century for the rite of Holy Matrimony; and there tradesmen assembled to bargain and barter, lawyers interviewed their clients, and wool merchants stored their bales.

Churches which started their lives as the pivots of the parochial system (inaugurated in Anglo-Saxon times) were served originally by a single priest, whose sole concern was the spiritual care of the parishioners. The basic requirement was therefore no more than a two-celled structure, such as emerged in the north under Celtic influence, and the simplest form of which can still be seen at Escomb in Durham. Though a group of early churches in the south-east, inspired by the Augustinian and Roman missions, show a cruciform plan with an apsidal chancel, as at Worth in Sussex, these had little general effect on parish church design. The severe northern plan became the prototype of most parish churches, despite the fact that it was the Roman rite connected with the south-eastern foundations which eventually supplanted that of the Celtic church. The cruciform plan, on the other hand, was universally adopted for monastic and cathedral churches. And all cathedrals, except Exeter, were furnished with a central tower as well as two western towers, whereas the parish church normally had but a single western tower. Cathedral designers shared with the builders of parish churches a preference for the square-ended chancel. The apsidal terminations of Westminster Abbey, Tewkesbury, Canterbury and some Norman parish churches reflect Continental influence, and are exceptions.

The peculiarly English square end, like the strict adherence to an east–west orientation in both parish church and cathedral architecture (which significantly does not obtain in Italy), may perpetuate a pagan tradition which demanded that altar and celebrant should be bathed in the full light of the morning sun.

Parish church plans developed sporadically in accordance with ritual requirements and the growth, piety and wealth of the population; they were lengthened and they acquired aisles and chapels, built by trade guilds, or founded by wealthy merchants and nobles for the welfare of their souls. Thus the parish church embraces structures as touchingly small and plain as Strethall in Essex, and as complex and ornate as St Mary Redcliffe, Bristol. The plans of cathedrals and the greater non-cathedral churches were affected by different factors. In the Middle Ages there was no important distinction, except for the presence of the *cathedra* or bishop's throne, between a cathedral, a monastic church and a collegiate church (a church attached to a foundation prescribing a life in common for resident canons or chaplains). None was primarily directed to the requirements of a lay congregation, even though some Augustinian and Benedictine monasteries granted the laity the use of part of the abbey church. These great buildings were expressly designed to meet the doctrinal needs of the clergy, and to provide pathways for the Sunday processions.

The line of demarcation between the parish and the greater church has often been blurred by later developments. The present cathedrals of England include abbey churches like St Albans, converted to cathedral use in 1878, parochial churches such as those of Newcastle and Chelmsford, recently erected into cathedrals, and collegiate foundations like Ripon and Southwell. Westminster Abbey plays an exceptional rôle. Founded as a Benedictine monastery, perhaps as early as the seventh century, it became a cathedral for a decade only, from 1540 until 1550, and now, neither cathedral nor parish church, it owes its continued existence to its unique connection with the monarch and the state. It is the coronation as well as the burial church of England's kings and queens, and its chapter house was already referred to by Langland in the fourteenth century as the parliament.

Most abbey and collegiate churches, however, which were not reduced to ruins by the Dissolution became parochial. Among them were Binham and Wymondham in Norfolk, Blyth in Nottinghamshire, Romsey and Christchurch in Hampshire, Sherborne in Dorset, Tewkesbury in Gloucestershire, Abbey Dore in Herefordshire, and Malmesbury in Wiltshire. Unusual details in the plan of a parish church and unusually elaborate masonry such as the possession of a stone vault instead of the timber roof, which is among the most typical features of the normal parish church, can often be explained by its previous history as a monastic or collegiate building. Visitors to Fotheringhay in Northamptonshire, for example, will be struck by the fact that the spectacular tower, a massively square structure surmounted by an octagonal lantern, battlemented and pinnacled, rises at the east instead of at the west end of the church. The reason for this oddity is that the tower was formerly central, with beyond it a collegiate chancel which was demolished after the Act of Suppression of 1547. Again, anyone entering the church of Thorney, Cambridgeshire, for the first time must surely stand amazed at the aspect of the interior. Norman piers of giant girth protrude from the walls of the aisleless nave and soar to the low roof. The entire design, with its two stories of round-headed arches, is strangely cramped and altogether lacking in the sense of rhythm which informs most medieval churches. The mystery is solved when it is realized that the present parish church was once part of Thorney Abbey and that the arches represent the nave arcade and the triforium gallery of the huge monastic church.

Our cathedrals and parish churches are the highest expression of the art of architecture in the Middle Ages. They testify as much to the overriding enthusiasm for this art as to the piety of their founders and patrons. Their very size, the difficulties their builders confronted so boldly, problems such as that of supporting the central tower, and the inclusion of complicated and costly structures which were purely ornamental adjuncts, such as the cloisters attached to cathedrals like Salisbury and Wells, which were not originally monastic, are all eloquent of a passion for building for its own sake. The architects who so brilliantly sustained this passion, and of whose identities and activities more and more is being revealed by modern research, include Henry Yevele, Stephen Lote, John Wastell, Walter of Coventry, William Wynford, Thomas Witney, John Meppushal, John and William Ramsay, Nicholas of Ely and Christopher Scune.

The work of these and many other masters shows a progressive understanding of construction and materials, an advance from the massive, heavy compositions of the Normans, such as the naves of Peterborough, Selby or Waltham Abbey, towards ever lighter, airier and more harmonious organizations, culminating in the conception of the church body as a stone framework for long ranges of majestic windows filled with rectilinear tracery and, above all, as a unified design in which space is no longer divided longitudinally by bays and vertically by the three stages of arcade, triforium and clerestory, which are so emphatically differentiated in such works as the Early English nave of Wells or the late Norman nave of Malmesbury. In the most perfect examples of the last of the Gothic styles, the exquisitely clear-cut chapel of King's College, Cambridge, Bath Abbey and the stirring choir of Gloucester, these elements are all fused in an insistently vertical and totally coherent work of art. In each of these interiors the eye is led directly upwards to the fan vault, the feature which, although it cannot be separated from the constructional planning of the Perpendicular church, the shape of its arches and mouldings and the panelling of the walls, may be regarded as the apotheosis of our medieval period, an English development which owed nothing to foreign example.

Triumphant as was this last florescence of the Gothic spirit, there is not a stage in the whole architectural evolution which does not offer overwhelming experiences. Who that has seen them can ever forget the Norman nave of Durham, where the immense pillars, deeply channelled with spirals, flutes and zigzags, are as broad as the openings; the superb transepts of Hexham Priory, where a rippling band of Early English trefoil arcading is surmounted by two tiers of excessively tall, narrow arches; the enchanting stellar vault of the choir at Tewkesbury; the soaring spire of Salisbury – the tallest in England; the glorious western Norman tower of Ely crowned by its Gothic lantern; the famous central octagon of the same cathedral, designed to replace the Norman central tower which fell in 1322, a unique work, probably by John Ramsay, conceived in the shape of the popular octagonal chapter house of the period and raised up on high with incredible ingenuity and audacity; the chapter house at Wells where the vault ribs spring out from the central pier like jets from a fountain; the broad, bold angel choir of Lincoln; or the peerless nave of Canterbury, the great work of Yevele in his old age and of his successors, Lote and Mapilton?

English parish churches repeat this great progression in miniature; and whereas the cathedrals and greater churches are monuments of the best and most advanced art of their period, these humbler buildings are the memorials of local craftsmanship. In their case the interest of the development is enhanced by the existence of pre-Conquest work. For it is in our parish churches, and in them alone, that the

Salisbury Cathedral from the Bishop's garden.   *Private Collection, on loan to Birmingham Art Gallery*
Detail from an oil sketch by John Constable, c. 1822

building art of the Anglo-Saxons is displayed. The general impression made by such square, unbuttressed towers, delicately and flatly patterned with irregular arcading and pilaster strips, as that of Barton-on-Humber, and by such tall, narrow interiors as that of the nave at Bradford-on-Avon is of an architecture as distinctly linear and vertical as that of the Perpendicular period.

With very few exceptions, among them Salisbury Cathedral, built entirely in the Early English style, the cruciform church of Patrington in Yorkshire, a noble example of the Decorated mode, and a number of great Perpendicular churches including St Mary Redcliffe, Bristol, Salle in Norfolk, Lavenham in Suffolk and Saffron Walden in Essex, no English medieval church, either cathedral or parochial, exhibits a uniform style. Norman and Early English are juxtaposed at Chichester; Norman is combined with Decorated at Ely, Hereford, St Albans and Southwell; Perpendicular cloaks and joins with earlier styles at Worcester, Gloucester, Winchester and Ripon. At Cley in Norfolk a Perpendicular tower soars over a Decorated nave and chancel; at Edington in Wiltshire the wonderfully battle-mented, rambling exterior fuses the Decorated and the Perpendicular; at Eaton Bray, Bedfordshire, a fifteenth-century shell and a modern tower leave the visitor quite unprepared for the thirteenth-century door with its graceful, flowing iron-work and the pure Early English interior; at Monkwearmouth, Durham, a north aisle of 1874 dwarfs the Anglo-Saxon nave. This patchwork character, depending on economic factors as well as upon the desire to preserve the relics of earlier buildings, is typically English.

All medieval buildings are to some extent marked by regional characteristics. The individuality of the great arcaded front of Lincoln derives in part from the local yellow ironstone of which it is fashioned; the grey-green Purbeck piers of the nave of Exeter relate this cathedral to the south-west even if not to its immediate environment; and the chalky white clunch of the Ely Lady Chapel at once evokes the Cambridgeshire landscape. But the materials for such great churches were often brought from considerable distances. Thus King's College Chapel was built of stone from Weldon in Northamptonshire; the stone for Norwich came largely from Barnack, the quarry which also supplied material for Rochester Cathedral and for the Abbey at Bury St Edmunds; Clipsham limestone makes its appearance in cathedrals as far apart as Canterbury and York; and the stone for Beverley Minster was brought from the Thevesdale quarries near Tadcaster.

Parish churches are much more intimately connected with their local geological formation. In Norfolk and Suffolk, where there is little or no good building stone for quoins, rounds towers are common. In this same area flint is the conspicuous building material, and knapped flint appears as a wall-facing in conjunction with stone tracery. The intractable granite of which most Cornish churches are con-structed accounts for the simplicity of their window tracery and the severity of piers and capitals, while the high quality of Cotswold stone encouraged the designers of Norman doorways to fill the tympana with sculpture, and masons of all periods to excel in refined decorative work such as that which distinguishes the pinnacled, traceried porch of Northleach, with its ogee-framed door, canopied niches and statues. The former densely wooded character of Essex is expressed in the use of timber for towers which vary from simple bellcots to structures of several stages, like that at Blackmore. In Hertfordshire and south Cambridgeshire the lack of stone led to the invention of small, acutely pointed lead-sheathed spire-lets, as at Anstey, Knebworth and Duxford, which, known as "Hertfordshire spikes", rise from the centre of broad flint rubble towers. Splendid stone spires

Norman Ruins at Malmesbury Abbey. Watercolour
drawing by J. M. W. Turner (1775–1851)   Norwich, Castle Museum

occur in districts where good material lay close to hand. These spires are almost always octagonal, and are poised on a square tower by filling in the bases of the canted sides with semi-pyramids, called broaches. The home regions of the broach spire are Lincolnshire, Northamptonshire and Rutland.

The diversity of parish church architecture is not only the product of geology; it is also the expression of the preferences and particular skills of local masons and carpenters and of social conditions. Thus Devon towers are often furnished with a huge stair turret oddly placed along one of the tower walls instead of at an angle; and Somerset towers can be recognized by their tall pinnacles and elaborately worked open parapets, the pairs of buttresses each side of every angle, and especially by the windows in the belfry stage which are filled with perforated tracery. East Anglia is noted for the brilliant development of timber roof design, which ranges from the simple tie-beam type, as seen at Outwell in Norfolk, to magnificent and ingenious double hammer-beam structures like those at Needham Market, Suffolk, and Knapton, Norfolk, the latter adorned at the end of every hammer-beam and along the ridge-piece by angels, fluttering like giant moths against the dark woodwork. In Cornwall, Somerset and Devon, on the other hand, carpenters evolved a roof with a curved brace to every rafter, thus forming a series of closely set arches, which are usually boarded or plastered over to form a barrel or waggon vault. Cornwall and Devon are also remarkable for a distinctive local parish church plan. A strong wave of piety in the fifteenth century resulted in the re-building of many churches in the region, and in these churches the usual arrangement of a nave with aisles and clerestory was replaced by a structure with three aisles of equal length, height and breadth, each crowned with its own roof, so that the east end presented a range of three separate gables, as at Launceston, Bodmin, St Keverne and St Erth in Cornwall, and at Haberton, Berry Pomeroy and Staverton in Devon.

Local style is as much evident in the furnishings of medieval parish churches as in the fabric. The spreading fan vaults and bands of carved foliage in screens of the south-west, which usually run right across the church, contrast with the shorter, lighter screens of East Anglia, which are seldom vaulted. The square-headed bench-ends of West Country churches, carved with figure reliefs, differ from the trefoil-shaped finial terminations common elsewhere, and so inventively treated in the eastern counties. The latter region is further distinguished for a splendid series of fifteenth-century fonts whose octagonal sides are sculptured with figures illustrating the Seven Sacraments. There are sixteen examples in Norfolk and twelve in Suffolk.

Considering the terrible losses due to iconoclasm, and considering the wear and tear of the centuries, it is astonishing what immense quantities of woodwork, of sculpture in stone and even of painted glass survive in both parish church and cathedral. These arts are usually to be seen at their aristocratic best in the cathedrals. Canterbury and York are pre-eminent for their glass; St Albans and Chichester contain important wall paintings; while the canopied stalls of Winchester and Chichester, the 400 bosses in the nave and cloisters of Norwich, the thirteenth-century sculpture at Lincoln, Worcester and Westminster Abbey, all represent the highest flights of genius. Fine sepulchral sculpture, however, is just as likely to be found in the most obscure parish church as in the cathedral. It is only necessary to mention Rysbrack's half-reclining likeness of Sir Edward Ward at Stoke Doyle, Northamptonshire, J. F. Moore's monument to Earl Ferrers at Ettington, Warwickshire, or Nicholas Stone's memorial to Sir Thomas Lucy at Charlecote in the same county. All this imagery is as richly rewarding to the historian as to the connoisseur of art. Tombs and the heraldry decorating them reveal whole family stories. Furthermore, sepulchral effigies, including the flat brasses set in the floor of the church, mirror every change in fashion from the early Middle Ages to the end of the eighteenth century. And in buildings which were so closely connected with the lives of the people all the manifold activities of medieval man, of kings, nobles, knights and commoners, are vividly recorded in the sculptured and painted imagery. Misericords show tumblers, acrobats, itinerant musicians and clowns; hawking and hunting the stag, boar and hare with dogs; tournaments and ship-building. A boss at Ugborough pictures a blacksmith at work; sculpture at Lincoln and Malvern is concerned with seasonal work in the fields; a man on a capital at Winchester carries a chequerboard, and a capital at Manchester is carved with two men playing backgammon.

For the student of local history the parish church is an invaluable source. The registers of baptisms, marriages and deaths, dating, if they are complete, from 1538, provide essential information for the study of population changes, as well as of the state of public health over the last 400 years. The dedications and changes in dedication are also revealing. Unique dedications to rare saints probably represent actual foundations by the saints themselves. Such are St Gonand of the Rock and St Non, Altarnun, both in Cornwall. The richness or poverty of the church fabric will also furnish the historian with important clues. He will, for example, draw obvious conclusions about the state of the Fenland in the Middle Ages from the fact that a series of magnificent churches arose from the twelfth century onwards to the west and to the south of the Wash; and he will relate the fine Perpendicular churches of Wiltshire, such as those of Trowbridge, Calne, Lacock and Steeple Ashton, to a period of unusual prosperity in the fifteenth and sixteenth centuries.

A great gulf divides the churches of the Middle Ages from those of Renaissance and modern England. The events of the sixteenth century destroyed a living tradition of architecture by substituting Italianate, horizontal forms for the native Gothic, vertical mode; and the rejection of Catholicism meant that one of the chief incentives to building, the belief in the spiritual benefit of pious works, such as endowing a chantry or making a donation to the church fabric fund, no longer obtained. It is significant that although some of the most spectacular great houses were erected during the reign of Elizabeth probably less church building was carried out in that period than at any other time before the present century.

The break in tradition was, however, bridged for a brief moment by the genius of Wren, who created a brilliant synthesis between the Gothic and Classic styles in the churches he designed expressly for Protestant worship. Some of Wren's buildings were actually composed in the late Perpendicular manner, such as St Mary Aldermary; but it is in his original steeples that his great power of synthesis is most dazzlingly displayed. Infinitely versatile, they retain all the flickering, soaring character of Gothic architecture, even though they exhibit exclusively Classical motifs; and, like traditional Gothic towers, they all rise over a square plan. St Paul's, one of the supreme masterpieces of Classical art, unites Renaissance forms with a plan which, with its well-marked transepts, its long eastern and western arms and its twin-towered west front, continues the English medieval cathedral tradition, while the central feature – the eight great piers and the four counter-thrusts supporting the dome – alludes directly to the octagon at Ely.

Wren's followers, with but few exceptions, among them Nicholas Hawksmoor, author of the monumental and aspiring composition of Christchurch, Spitalfields, lacked his sense of tradition and became ever more "correctly" Classical. The west end of the church was transformed into the pillared portico of a latter-day Roman temple, behind which the tower degenerated into a superfluous accretion sitting on the nave roof, as at Mereworth in Kent and at James Gibbs's St Martin-in-the-Fields, London.

Victorian Gothic churches are interesting as attempts to revive the native tradition and as full-flavoured expressions of a discordant period. They were the work of men who believed that the vertical mode embodied the spirit of Christianity more fitly than the horizontal, Classical style, and who also were (mistakenly) convinced that good morals could produce good architecture and would enable them to foist the style of a truly religious age on to one that was eminently materialistic. But the church was no longer bound up with the lives of the people and the sharp dividing line between sacred and secular could not be erased. Architects of talent produced some original interpretations of medieval Gothic themes. The slate-hung lantern supported on tall, clustered cast-iron shafts at St James, Teignmouth, by Andrew Patey, repeats the Gothic idiom in a surprisingly new medium. Burges's weighty, ornate east end at Waltham Abbey is comparable in vitality and strength to the Norman work beside it, and Sedding's stone version of a Devon timber roof at St Peter's, Sheldon, is as arresting as his patterning of the arcades with giant rustications. But all too often Victorian interiors which were intended to inspire awe and devotion merely exude a crushing air of respectability, and this is as true of a meanly conceived building such as St Saviour, St George's Square, Westminster, as of the compellingly ugly but boldly planned red-and-black brick bulk of Street's St James the Less, in the same district.

Nevertheless, Gothic has persisted as the dominant style for church building until the present day. The gleaming, elegant church of St Mary, Wellingborough, by Sir Ninian Comper, completed in 1930, combines a late-Gothic framework and an elaborate plaster vault of fans, pendants and star patterns with a mixture of furnishing styles. And despite its grid walls of concrete and glass and its clear affinities with twentieth-century commercial building, Sir Basil Spence's Coventry Cathedral, consecrated in 1962, is basically Gothic. The proportions of the interior, the division of the space into nave and aisles, and the suggestion of a ribbed vault, all derive from medieval example even if they are utterly remote from any medieval church in feeling and execution.

Follies

BARBARA JONES

The English love to break down the natural scene. In the seventeenth and eighteenth centuries the areas of natural heath and scrub left untouched by medieval husbandry were vigorously taken in hand and built upon, gardened, afforested and landscaped; most of England was arranged by man. In the nineteenth century the whole country was netted over with railways, and the cities grew; but, in fact, the scene was not altered very much. In this century we have come to accept that scene as natural, as "the country". We in our turn are trying to break it down, with motorways, industrial sites and new cities.

At all times since the end of the Tudor wars there have been English landowners, with anything from a ducal estate to a suburban front garden, who have not been content with other people's ideas of breakdown, with the ordinary thing. Even if they have been able to commission idiosyncratic houses from great architects, they have still wanted something more, something wilder. The results of these impulses are scattered all over the country, and are called – by the other English – "follies".

Follies take many forms. We may discount at once the follies in name alone – houses of which neighbours disapproved, or houses built too far from water, or with too little money to finish them, and also various clumps and belts of trees (the word was corrupted from *feuillée*). And the ordinary garden house, temple or gazebo does not qualify either. The element of eccentricity is essential; follies are fantastic, a little crazy in desire or design. Architecture is building for shelter; follies are building for building, a purer art. Towers and obelisks build upwards; labyrinths and tunnels build down. Other follies are aggregates of unlikely materials, abstractions of shells and minerals, bark and branches, nearer sculpture than architecture, the desire to amass solids in space.

The earliest folly I have found is Freston Tower in Suffolk, built in the middle of the sixteenth century, a brick tower on the banks of the River Orwell, near Ipswich. At the end of the century Rushton Triangular Lodge was built in Northamptonshire by Sir Thomas Tresham. Everything is in threes: the plan is triangular; each wall three times three times three feet, three sets of three-by-three triangles on top of the walls; three floors; three windows each side on each floor; trefoils and triangular pinnacles. Ten miles away at Lyveden is the shell of Tresham's house, extending the arithmetic of three to five, seven and nine.

More follies and conceits, and some tunnels, were built in the next century, mostly surviving only in visitors' accounts of them, though there is a sinister temple of bark nailed over wood at Exton Park in Rutland, and there are fine grotto rooms of stone and shells at Skipton in Yorkshire and at Woburn Abbey in Bedfordshire.

In the eighteenth century follies became fashionable as well as eccentric; a nobleman's estate positively needed one. Towers, tunnels, and grottoes continued in production, and all sorts of new follies were invented – sham castles and ruins, hermitages, labyrinths, obelisks, and eye-catchers. In the nineteenth century fewer follies were built, and those more by the rich than the noble; but Druids' Circles were invented, and some superb folly gardens were laid out, with a curiosity round every corner. Late in the century fantastic gardening with broken china, slag, shells, flint, glass, coal, and coral became fashionable for the poor as well as for the rich. Only two or three dozen follies have been built in the twentieth century, but the little gardens continue, with gnomes added to the older materials.

The commonest sort of folly, and the easiest to find, is that which is built upwards. There are a great many ordinary little ones, but there are also some magnificent towers, built to commemorate great happenings or to command great prospects. There is a nice triangular one in London, in Castlewood Park at Shooters Hill, 64 feet high, built in 1784 to the memory of Sir William James and to "Record the Conquest of the CASTLE OF SEVERNDROGG on the COAST of MALABAR which fell to his Superior Valour and able Conduct on the 2nd Day of April MDCCLV". In the nineteenth century it was used for select parties, and now it is a teashop.

Another triangular folly is Haldon Belvedere, near Exeter, built by an ex-Governor of Madras, with a floor made of marble from Hyderabad, and really exquisite plaster work. At Wentworth Woodhouse in Yorkshire is Hoober Stand, 1748, a superb 100-foot soot-stained golden tower on a triangular plan, its sides tapering to a hexagonal lantern. It was built by Thomas, Marquis of Rockingham, in honour of George II. Nearby is Keppel's Pillar, built by the 2nd Marquis in 1782 to commemorate the British Fleet at Ushant. It soars up, supporting nothing, an amazing 150 feet. Also nearby is the Needle's Eye, a tall stone pyramid pierced by an ogival arch and crowned by a lovely urn, built, the story goes, for a crack whip to drive through after he had boasted that he could drive a coach and horses through the eye of a needle. At Wentworth Castle there are more conceits.

Many follies have good stories attached: you may be told that the builder is buried under the floor because he quarrelled with the parson, or is there standing on his head, or with his favourite horse under him. One man seems to have deserved all the stories: Mad Jack Fuller, who built a Needle, a Mausoleum, a Tower, a Rotunda, and an Observatory at Brightling in Sussex, and at Dallington a neat cone called the Sugar Loaf, to justify a night-time statement that he could see Dallington church spire from his dining-room window. In daylight this statement proved wrong, but he made a sham spire just over the skyline, to be right for his next dinner-party. Attached to his pyramid tomb is the most persistent of all the legends: that he is sitting at table inside, with a bottle and a bird before him.

At Tong in Shropshire are some pyramids with no legends at all, perhaps because the builder George Durant said exactly what everything was for – and imagination could invent nothing stranger. "Quaint buildings, monuments with hieroglyphs, and inscriptions alike to deceased friends, eternity, and favourite animals – were then to be found on every path of the demesne", says an old local guidebook. Pyramidal gate-piers are carved as though bound with heavy ropes, and such objects as lamps and snails are carved in panels on the walls. A gazebo called The Pulpit has animals and snakes. On a nearby farm there is also an Egyptian Aviary, a pyramidal hen-house labelled AB OVO. Durant was one of the few gentlemen of his time who not only longed to have a hermit in the grounds to show to visitors, but achieved a very contented one, for a gentleman who had fallen on hard times lived in a cave at Tong until he died in 1822.

The contemporary terms for the employment of hermits were usually much alike; a cave (or a rustic hermitage of roots, branches and knotty wood) was provided, and a hermit was advertised for, to serve a period of seven years, living secluded, with hair long, and nails unclipped, never speaking, with good food sent down from the house daily. But it seems that few people are even mock hermits by nature, or few people know how to employ one kindly. One gentleman was forced to use a wax image; and there are many records of early failure – the hermit went away, or he was found drinking in the village and dismissed. One known success, however, was the Hermit Finch, whose Sanctuary lies down in the woods of the park at Burley on the Hill in Rutland, preserved with most remarkable and imaginative rustic architecture and furniture, a pebble-and-knuckle-bone floor, and even the hermit's sacking bed.

The desire to dig downwards is rarer than the desire to build up. It is also much more expensive; so the tunnellers had to be very rich or very determined. The 5th Duke of Portland's underground rooms at Welbeck are the most famous mole-works. The Duke was said to speak willingly only to the men who dug the tunnels.

Most excavations have an air of sadness. Many have walls of bare earth, or lined with cement, or strung along with a handful of cockle shells. But they were highly esteemed in the last century, for the Catacombs at High Beech in Epping Forest were a pleasure resort. They are a wild descent into the dark earth of huge blocks of masonry said to have come from Chelmsford gaol, hidden under the garden.

As well as the plain tunnels of compulsive digging, there are excavations of great beauty in the form of grottoes, where the surface has been decorated with glittering minerals, exotic shells, fossils, tufa – all the natural objects that became commonly wonderful in the eighteenth century. I have referred to the shell rooms at Skipton and Woburn; in both of these there is contemporary architecture with an overlay of shells. In the eighteenth century this style continued in fashion, greatly refined, culminating in the exquisite Shell House made by the 2nd Duchess of Richmond at Goodwood in Sussex. True grottoes, though not always under-ground, look like caves under the sea, spar and shells arranged in waves and stalactites. We have the name of Josiah Lane as builder, with his son, of a series of superb grottoes – at St Giles House, Cranborne, in Dorset, Fonthill in Wiltshire, St Anne's Hill and Pain's Hill in Surrey, amongst others. The two-roomed grotto at Wimborne St Giles is in the park and is shown with the house; it has been restored and is probably the finest shellwork of this sort that we have, a wonderful composition of surfaces and colours, the insides of shells gleaming against the duller backs, small shells offsetting large.

At Stourhead in Wiltshire the National Trust owns a famous grotto, large and formal, built round one of the headwaters of the Stour, with fine statues of a nymph and a river-god. The walk round the lake runs through the grotto, a green, cool melancholy contrast to the splendid Capability Brown landscaping. Another remarkable grotto was built by Thomas Goldney in his garden on top of Clifton gorge at Bristol, with a cascade leaping from an urn held by Neptune, echoes from the wild water, a Lions' Den and fine shells.

All these grottoes are professional work, and look it, but by the beginning of the nineteenth century only amateur grotto-builders remained. The fashion spread wide; most towns, especially those by the seaside, have a bit of shellwork some-where. There is a big one at Margate, probably made by two brothers called Bowles in an existing excavation. It was lost to sight for about thirty years, and found again in 1834 or 1835 by a schoolmaster's son digging a duckpond. There is almost no fantastic origin that has not been claimed for it – Cretans, Druids, even

Tibetans, are supposed to have built it, and the simple amateur shellwork has been interpreted in a hundred gnostic symbols: we are a romantic-minded race. Druids were very fashionable in the first quarter of the century; there is a good sham Circle on the Yorkshire moors near Masham, a real prehistoric temple moved from Jersey to a back garden in Henley-on-Thames, and a Druids' Table among the bone grottoes and bone-lined caves at Banwell on Mendip in Somerset, elaborated during the years after 1824 by the Bishop of Bath and Wells over and down some mine-shafts and two natural caves with stalactites and stalagmites. Ancient animal bones were ready on the floor, and the Bishop made the most of them.

Back to the eighteenth century, and back above ground. The Middle Ages and the Barons' Wars became very modish, and Gothic architecture was admired again, not often for gentlemen's houses, in spite of Walpole at Strawberry Hill, but certainly for follies. Suddenly hundreds of gentlemen wanted to see the ruins of a Gothic castle crumbling at a suitable distance from the house. A few of them had real ones; the others plunged into the fun of building fakes. Some of the sham castles were ruinous in design, like that at Wimpole in Cambridgeshire; some rapidly became so through being knocked up in a hurry or on the cheap; and some were built very crisp and new like Sanderson Miller's Sham Castle outside Bath, a façade rising about forty feet on a hill-top, flat as a piece of scenery, which indeed it is, a wall without a room.

Some castles were in fact made of painted canvas on wooden frames, so great was the scramble to get them up. Some were rich with Gothic detail, trefoils and quatrefoils, and castellations and arrowslits, but often reproduced on an absurdly large scale as there was no need to consider the strength of the wall, and defence could become decoration. Others were so ungothic that they could not be called castles; they were curious spiky constructions, often of flint, that were given names used for no other architecture, like eye-catcher, terminal, conceit, or vista-closer. Many of them were undoubtedly designed by eager amateurs of the arts, and put up by the estate workers; but a timid amateur could find plenty of help in the dozens of books on the Picturesque or the Grotesque that were published, with illustrations, plans, elevations and dimensions of every variety of hut, retreat, cascade, bath-house, mosque and pagoda, from trifles made with Rude Branches to enormous Mauresque Pavilions beyond the Do-It-Yourself of all but the greatest estates.

Some people, having built one folly, went on. Hawkstone in Shropshire was an estate with many fine follies. The hermitage, with mock hermit, and an ornamental windmill have disappeared; but half a dozen survive, including a marvellous labyrinth that rises to the sunlight on top of a rocky bluff. Stourhead has a Rustic Convent, St Peter's Pump, and Alfred's Tower, as well as the grotto; and West Wycombe in Buckinghamshire has a Mausoleum, St Crispin's Cottages – built to look like a church from the house – a Sham Lodge, and caves, now with *son et lumière*.

Today, the folly impulse is concentrated in the small gardens, the miniature model villages that have succeeded the real ones of the rich, and a continuing tradition of topiary; we still have such gardens as the breath-taking solid geometry clipped from yew at Levens in Westmorland, that has been clipped since 1689. And there is a new one in Wolverhampton that has privet topiary of sixteen Scotch terriers, two cats and a rat.

The Industrial Heritage

L. T. C. ROLT

Other countries have their characteristic landscape beauties, their prehistoric and Roman antiquities, their great Gothic churches and splendid Renaissance architecture, but England's industrial monuments are unique. They are unique because it was here that the Industrial Revolution began. Because that Revolution, in a mere three hundred years, has changed man's way of life on this planet more profoundly than in the previous two millennia, even those who think life would have been better if it had never happened must agree that the physical traces of its beginnings have become monuments worthy of preservation and study. Yet, strangely enough, it is only in the last few years that we have become aware of the importance of England's industrial heritage. Only twenty years ago who would have thought that the National Trust could become responsible for such things as an early textile mill, a canal, or a Cornish beam engine? Or that government departments, hitherto preoccupied with prehistoric sites and medieval buildings, would be not only listing and scheduling such monuments but assisting both financially and practically in their preservation?

Today, when the bulldozer has become a symbol of our vastly enhanced power of rapid destruction, this belated recognition comes only just in time; it amounts to a last-minute rescue operation. This work of rescue is often peculiarly difficult. Pressure for demolition is particularly great because, by their very nature, industrial monuments often occupy valuable sites. Again, it is difficult to justify the preservation of an early industrial building which has ceased to serve its original purpose unless some alternative use for it can be found. However, the use of the Snape Maltings as a concert hall, the use as a theatre of the original London & Birmingham Railway locomotive round-house at Chalk Farm, or the recent proposal to convert Philip Hardwick's splendid range of warehouses at Telford's St Katherine's Dock into an Arts Centre are examples of what can, or might be, done in this direction.

One of the reasons why our industrial monuments have been so neglected until recently is that to most lovers of landscape or architecture "industrial" has become a loaded word, carrying a weight of ugliness. It has become so because we equate it with modern industrialism which, by its large scale and dreary uniformity, spells death to landscape beauty. In the eighteenth and early nineteenth centuries, however, industrial man had not acquired the power to ruin a landscape. His works were at best comely and at their worst dramatic or idiosyncratic. Only very seldom were they bleakly utilitarian or downright ugly. Consequently they are not only eloquent as evidence of bygone activity and aspiration, but often strangely beautiful. The artists of the Romantic Movement, with which the first momentous phase of the Industrial Revolution coincided, recognized this, whereas it is only just becoming evident to us. For this failure of vision the divorce of science and technology from the arts is mainly responsible.

That this divorce is a reality and not just an abstract theory was demonstrated when that fascinating exhibition "Art and the Industrial Revolution" opened at the Manchester City Art Gallery in 1968. At first it was poorly attended because the technologists felt it would be too "arty" to interest them while the artists thought it would be too technical. Eventually, however, the message got around that the exhibition was of equal interest to both sides, and for the last few weeks the gallery was crowded. What was true of this exhibition is also true of our industrial monuments; their appeal is to both sides, and we are belatedly becoming aware of this fact.

It was fortuitous that the beginnings of our Industrial Revolution coincided with a more conscious appreciation of natural beauty that enabled the artists of the Romantic Movement to record for us the landscape of a pre-industrial England whose unsullied loveliness now seems to us almost paradisial. It was in such an idyllic pastoral setting that the first manifestations of the new world appeared: a great steam-powered textile mill, an ironworks plumed with smoke and flame, a many-arched canal aqueduct or railway viaduct. Such striking contrasts appealed strongly to the imagination of the Romantic artist, who called them "sublime" or "awful" – using that word in its old sense. They regarded them with the same fascinated ambivalence that John Milton reveals in his attitude to Satan in *Paradise Lost*, an attitude that undoubtedly influenced William Blake and led him to coin the phrase "dark satanic mills". This is the vision we should try to recapture when we visit England's industrial monuments. It should not be too difficult because, whereas the contemporary artist could only grasp their significance intuitively through the exercise of his imagination, we, in the knowledge of all that has happened since, are only too well aware of it.

Most people regard the cotton industry of Lancashire as the precursor. It was certainly the first industry of modern type, organized on the factory system and producing for a world export market. But those textile mills of Lancashire and the Pennine Valleys to which Blake referred were already highly mechanized, with steam power driving their spinning frames, carding engines and looms. An industry organized on so intensive a scale could not have existed without three things: a plentiful supply of iron, mechanical power and an economical means of transporting goods in bulk.

It was Abraham Darby who provided a solution to the problem of England's iron industry by successfully smelting iron with coke in 1709, while Thomas Newcomen built the first successful steam engine in 1712, and the construction of England's canal system began in 1760 on the initiative of the Duke of Bridgewater and his engineer, James Brindley. These were the three key developments, and the Industrial Revolution rapidly gained momentum by the vigorous interaction between them. More coal produced more iron; more iron made possible larger and more powerful steam engines which enabled more coal to be won from deeper levels; canals were the essential arteries through which coal and iron flowed.

If any place in England deserves to be called the cradle of the Industrial Revolution it is that small industrial district of Shropshire in the vicinity of the Severn gorge where, at his Coalbrookdale Ironworks, Abraham Darby first smelted iron successfully with coke. Hitherto, English ironmasters had used charcoal in their furnaces and had to compete with other industries, notably ship-building, for the country's dwindling supplies of timber. So acute was the timber shortage that the ironmasters had to build their furnaces in remote and inaccessible parts of the country where timber was still plentiful – Wales, Cumberland and Scotland. Consequently the best preserved example of a charcoal blast furnace today is in the Scottish Highlands at Bonawe, near Taynuilt, Argyll. Slowly at first, but surely, Darby's discovery changed all this. For the fifty years before the coming of canals the Darby family in particular and the Shropshire ironmasters in general enjoyed a unique reputation which attracted enterprising men, civil and mechanical engineers and architects, from all over England. This success was due not only to their enterprise and skill but also to the fact that they had chosen one of the very few districts where natural supplies of coal and iron ore were situated conveniently close to a great navigable river – the Severn – which provided cheap bulk transport.

No wonder that this Shropshire district scored a succession of historic "firsts". In 1723 Coalbrookdale began producing the first large iron steam-engine cylinders, of which more anon. In 1767, to improve internal transport, the Coalbrookdale Company laid the first iron railways in the world, and in 1779 the ribs of the world's first iron bridge were cast at Coalbrookdale. This bridge, which has given a name to a place – Ironbridge, still spans the Severn with its single iron arch of 100 feet and is now England's finest industrial monument. It was within sight of this bridge that the famous ironmaster John Wilkinson, who owned the nearby New Willey Furnaces at Broseley, launched the first iron boat into the Severn in 1787. The assembled crowd fully expected it to sink, but were disappointed. It was this same John Wilkinson, incidentally, who perfected a machine which could bore a cylinder with sufficient accuracy to make James Watt's improved steam engine practicable. The cylinders for all Watt's early engines were cast and bored by him.

In 1797 the iron work for the world's first metal-framed building was cast at Coalbrookdale. This building, erected at Shrewsbury by Charles Bage, still stands, and is known today as Jones's Maltings. It was the first of many early iron-framed buildings in England, some of which still stand, most notably the Boat Shed at Sheerness. The latter building, although built in 1860, looks extraordinarily modern and is the true ancestor of every skyscraper.

Among the famous men associated with the Shropshire ironmasters were Thomas Telford, Richard Trevithick, and the Regency architect John Nash. Telford, when surveyor of Shropshire, was so inspired by their achievements that he became the first great master in the structural use of iron. He built his first iron bridge over the Severn at Buildwas. Although this bridge no longer exists, other Telford iron bridges survive, such as that over the Severn at the Mythe, Tewkesbury, which was cast by the Shropshire ironmaster William Hazledine. Telford was also responsible for the world's first iron trough aqueduct which carries the Shrewsbury Canal over the Severn's tributary, the Tern, at Longdon-upon-Tern, near Wellington. Its trough was cast at Ketley Ironworks by William Reynolds, who was closely associated with the Darby family. This aqueduct, too, survives. It was the prototype of Telford's famous aqueduct at Pont Cysyllte in the valley of the Dee just over the Welsh border.

Richard Trevithick was the great Cornish pioneer of the use of high-pressure steam who, by its aid, transformed the steam engine into a relatively small, light and compact power unit which, as he was the first to realize, possessed infinite possibilities in the field of mechanical transport, on rail, road and water. Recognizing the unique practical expertise of the Coalbrookdale Ironworks, Trevithick carried out many of his historic experiments there. One of the results was that the first steam locomotive in the world first ran on Coalbrookdale rails in 1802 before the more spectacular and better known trial on the Penydaren tramway in South Wales.

In a very different field John Nash recognized the possibilities of iron in architecture. In 1805 he designed for Lord Berwick at Attingham Park near Shrewsbury the oldest surviving roof-lit picture gallery. The slender, curving iron frames in which its glass rooflights are held were cast at Coalbrookdale.

The coming of canals enabled richer coal and iron districts, notably the Black Country of Staffordshire, to be tapped, and the Severn ceased to be a unique transport asset. Consequently the Black Country became the greatest iron-producing district in Europe, while the Coalbrookdale area declined. Although this was unfortunate for the Shropshire ironmasters it is fortunate for us because it meant that the scene of their activities became "frozen" at an early stage of industrial development, with the effect that this Shropshire birthplace of the new iron age has now become a vitally significant part of our industrial heritage. It retains an indefinable but strongly evocative atmosphere which few other places associated with early industry possess. Anyone with a spark of imagination who descends the steep hill from Madeley down into the Severn gorge at Ironbridge can hardly fail to be aware of this, particularly when dusk is falling, when lights are beginning to glimmer from the little brick cottages that spill down its steep slopes under the hanging woods but the graceful black arc of Darby's iron bridge is still visible against the sky-reflecting surface of the Severn.

Although this bridge is now the only substantial reminder of bygone achievement, at such a time it is easy to imagine the valley as it was when it was filled with the flare and fume of the iron furnaces and echoed with the thud of forge hammers. No wonder such dramatic activity, practised in an equally dramatic landscape setting, attracted contemporary artists like a magnet. Cotman, Turner and de Loutherbourg were three of the many who fell under its spell.

On the bank of the Severn downstream of the iron bridge stand some broken walls of blackened brickwork, heavily overgrown with wild creepers. This is all that remains of Bedlam Furnace, which Cotman painted in 1802 from the opposite bank of the river, its fierce glare – reflected in the night sky – lighting up the water and the landscape foreground. Turner used furnace light to similar effect in his *Lime Kiln at Coalbrookdale* (*c.* 1797) except that here stunted trees are sharply silhouetted as though against some unnatural sunset.

Thomas Newcomen, a blacksmith and ironmonger of Dartmouth, was responsible for building the world's first successful steam beam engine. It was the ancestor of the later Watt engine and the nineteenth-century Cornish beam engine, of which a number of good examples are now preserved in the Duchy by the National Trust in association with a local society. Until recently, magnificent beam engines of Cornish type were widely used throughout England for waterworks pumping. They are now disappearing fast, though efforts are being made to preserve a few of them. Of the earliest Newcomen type engines only a very few survive – two only outside museums. One of these is at a colliery at Elsecar near Sheffield, while the other stood near Coventry but was re-erected recently at Dartmouth as a permanent memorial to its inventor. The latter is almost certainly the oldest piston engine still in existence. Although it has been modified in later years its iron cylinder was most probably cast at Coalbrookdale in 1725. The cylinders of the earliest Newcomen engines were of brass, laboriously hand-finished. They were very costly, and necessarily of relatively small size. It was the ability of the Coalbrookdale Ironworks to cast and bore iron cylinders up to six feet in diameter that made possible the much larger and more powerful pumping engines that enabled deep coal seams to be exploited, particularly in the Tyneside area. It was James

Radio Times Hulton Picture Library

Coalbrookdale. Engraving by G. Perry and T. Smith, 1758

Watt who, by making a more economical, double-acting rotative engine, suitable for driving machinery, made possible a vast extension of the factory system. Hitherto the water-wheel had been the only practicable source of power. Many water-wheels, some of great size and power, still survive in England, but only in locations where a copious and unfailing source of water was assured.

The third of the essential prerequisites of the Industrial Revolution – cheap goods transport – was first provided by the canal system. Today this system represents our greatest single heritage of eighteenth- and early nineteenth-century civil engineering. Much of it is now disused commercially but has recently acquired a new lease of life as a pleasure-cruising ground. At many strategic points on the networks of canals covering the English Midlands it is now possible to hire a comfortable cruiser and set off on a voyage of exploration. There is no better way of appreciating just how rapidly English civil engineering developed during the great period of canal construction between 1760 and 1836. The best idea of its eighteenth-century beginnings can be obtained by travelling northwards from Banbury by the Oxford Canal, for this section of canal has remained virtually unchanged since it was built in 1778, when, to avoid earthworks as far as possible, engineers followed the natural contours. For this reason it is extremely tortuous, taking eleven miles to cover a point-to-point distance of only four miles.

To appreciate to the full the progress made, travel northwards from Wolverhampton towards Nantwich along the Shropshire Union Canal. Laid out under the direction of Thomas Telford, this was the last major line of canal to be built in England (completed 1836) and it cuts straight through the rolling countryside by a series of deep cuttings and lofty embankments. To experience the dramatic contrast between these two canals is to understand how the experience gained during the canal-building age paved the way for the railway builders.

Whereas we did not pioneer canals, steam railways were England's particular contribution to world communications. Completed by 1842 and still in use today, the first of our great main lines linking London with the north-west, with Bristol and Southampton, were engineered on a heroic scale by Robert Stephenson, I. K. Brunel and Joseph Locke, setting an example which the rest of the world soon copied but never surpassed.

Although the earlier builders of roads and canals made excellent pioneering use of cast-iron the railway builders found it too brittle and treacherous to serve their greater purposes. The only surviving example of a major railway bridge in which cast-iron was used is Stephenson's celebrated high-level bridge over the Tyne at Newcastle. It was opened in June 1849 and has been carrying increasingly heavy road and rail traffic on its two decks ever since.

An increasing output of wrought-iron from the nineteenth-century ironmasters enabled the railway engineers to perform feats of construction the like of which the world had never seen. Unfortunately, many early examples of wrought-iron railway bridges have been demolished in recent years, but happily two of the most outstanding historically are still in use. These are Stephenson's great Menai tubular bridge (1850), the first in the world, and Brunel's magnificent bridge over the Tamar at Saltash. In a different context Brunel's famous wrought-iron suspension bridge across the Avon Gorge at Clifton is the finest surviving example of its kind and makes an instructive contrast with the new Severn suspension bridge only a few miles away.

Just as the great Gothic cathedral epitomizes the Age of Faith, so, just as certainly, does the great Victorian railway station express the material aspirations of the Age of Steam. In such secular temples stone gives place to iron – cast-iron columns supporting huge vaults of wrought-iron and glass. Newcastle Central was the prototype. It was the work of a versatile local architect named John Dobson, who not only designed the station building but also the special machines with which the curving iron roof ribs were rolled. Some of his original work still survives in the present station. His work was the precursor of other great station roofs: York, Manchester Central, Bristol Temple Meads, Paddington and St Pancras. These were the most daring architectural adventures of their day, exploiting to the utmost the possibilities of what was then a novel structural material; yet how few of the hurrying crowds they shelter ever pause to give them a second glance.

England's Industrial Revolution was pre-eminently a new Iron Age, but it was not only in iron that a pioneer generation of engineers could express themselves. To study the classical grandeur and symmetry of Rennie's canal aqueduct at Limpley Stoke near Bath, or Brunel's towering tunnel portal at nearby Box, both in Bath stone, is to realize that these engineers, like the artists of the period, understood very well the significance of what they were doing. They were changing the world and they recorded that momentous fact in monumental masonry. So shameful an act of vandalism as the destruction of the Euston Arch must never occur again; for we owe it to posterity to cherish this eloquent heritage that the engineers of the past have bequeathed to us.

Mountain, Hill and Moorland

JACK LONGLAND

The English do not live in a land of great mountains. For those you must travel elsewhere, to the 2,000-mile belt of Himalaya, Karakoram and Hindu Kush which guards the Indian peninsula; or to the Andes, the high and lop-sided back-bone that runs the 5,000-mile length of South America. Look, nevertheless, at a small-scale physical map of England, and note how much of it is coloured brown. The high ground runs almost continuously, shaped like a capital L turned back to front, from the Cheviots on the Scottish border, down the long Pennine chain from Cross Fell to Kinder Scout, getting considerably less bumpy through Leicestershire and Warwickshire, at the turn of the L, and then picking up splendidly with the Cotswolds. Mendips, Quantocks and Salisbury Plain (which should be called Salisbury Plateau) then give on to the flatter parts of Somerset and Hampshire, but the hill-line is carried on, charmingly, through Dorset, and achieves a real wildness again, not seen since the tail-end of the Pennines, over Exmoor and Dartmoor. Beyond that, the eye of faith, or better still a pair of legs, can find some high ground all the way to the granite cliffs of Land's End. And east of this long line, the flatter half of England is delightfully variegated with hills and moors of a lesser kind, the North York moors, the Yorkshire and Lincolnshire Wolds, the Suffolk uplands. In the south-east corner come the long lines of the Downs, which Hilaire Belloc's forgivable patriotism elevated into "the great hills of the South Country".

England is so small that you are never very far from hill country. Indeed, you have to cross over into Scotland to find a mountain-top or patch of moor which is more than five miles away from a motorable road. Cross Fell, the highest point of the Pennines, can make you feel remote and lonely, as when my wife and I climbed it one Coronation night, to see the bonfire that wasn't there, because the men from two outlying villages couldn't agree which of them should carry up the fuel. Yet we steered our way down by compass to a car which a friend had driven on a moor-land track to within four miles of the summit. Or you could set out from Gilsland on the Roman Wall, and walk the hard way to Falstone on the North Tyne. Easy to start with, along the Roman road to Bewcastle with its fort and Saxon cross, but over Bewcastle Waste you would find only wild duck and wild goats, no sheep even, and it would be mostly stiff heather-hopping up to Sighty Crag and Black Knowe, before the long descent to Falstone. Here again, though you might feel splendidly cut off from the life of the towns, you are in fact never very far from a road, and nowadays, with the growth of the great Kielder Forest, there must be forestry roads all over the place.

This brings in another virtue of English hills and mountains. They are not only easy to reach by road, but nearly all of them can be walked over. This is true in the technical sense, that you can in theory climb any English peak with your hands in your pockets, though there are a few exceptions like Chrome Hill and Parkhouse Hill in upper Dovedale and two of the tops of Harter Fell in the Lakes, where you would have to be pretty expert to avoid using hands as well. It is true too that most of our hills can be walked over with fair ease, thanks to the efficiency of the grazing sheep in keeping thick vegetation down, and the past activities of man, in felling trees and clearing scrub.

Even if you are a climber and want to take your mountains the hard way, it is another fortunate accident of geology and weathering that so much of our English rock is sound and climbable. So we can climb at will on the volcanic ash of the Lake District, or the gritstone and dolerite and limestone of the Pennines, on the little sandstone edges in Kent, or on the good granite of Dartmoor and the cliffs of Cornwall. And technical improvements in climbing ability, in safeguarding devices and in the load of ironmongery that the modern climber carries round with him, have brought within his reach steep or overhanging cliffs which another generation thought impossible, and types of rock, such as limestone, which less well-equipped climbers had considered unsafely loose. But even the bravest young climber avoids the villainous chalk of Beachy Head, and, except when they are frosted into temporary firmness by a hard winter, the crumbling shales of Mam Tor in Derbyshire. Elsewhere, and leaving alone many of our less stable sea cliffs, it is becoming true that wherever rock is found, it can be, and is being, climbed.

It is again lucky for another reason that, in a small country without big mountains, there is so much rock that can be climbed. Mountaineering and rock-climbing began as a sport not much more than a hundred years ago. They were pursued by a very small number of enthusiasts, who were regarded as amiable lunatics. But since the last war climbing has undergone a population explosion, caused partly by giving a substantial fraction of young people some kind of mountain training to help them win the war – though the Mountain Division was in fact used on the island of Walcheren, which is mostly below sea-level – partly because climbing has come to share the popularity of those sports, such as sailing, canoeing, sub-aqua swimming, and horse-riding, which give the greatest possible contrast to the regimented life of cities, and indeed to the organized rules without which you cannot play team-games.

When I was at university, long years ago, to go and climb in the Lakes was a serious expedition, demanding the co-operation of the rare friend who owned a car, or a very difficult rail journey which could hardly be fitted into a term-time *exeat*. So we had to make do with college walls and roofs, or with the alarming chalk quarries at Cherry Hinton, just outside Cambridge. The current and growing demand for such an individual and adventurous sport as climbing could only have been satisfied by the concurrently enormous growth in the number of cars, to be owned, borrowed, sometimes stolen. It is not only Adventurous Man, but specifically Mobile Man (and of course Mobile Woman, as the opera sings) who crowds the cliff-faces and the climbing pubs. That is why it is today specially fortunate that we have so much rock around in England. The rocks must be accessible, and they are. There must also be enough unclimbed rock to challenge the skill of the young climbers who keep the sport in a state of continuous development.

There are obstacles, of course, to access to moor and mountain. For example, they are all owned by someone, private individual, shooting syndicate, the Crown, or such bodies as the National Trust. Even in the National Parks of England the land is not owned by the nation, as it is in America's national parks. Whole areas of Dartmoor are closed, because used as firing ranges by the Services. Afforestation has covered in trees open hills where once we walked freely. I found recently, over the Border in New Galloway, that it was almost impossible to get on to that fine range, the Rhinns of Kells, at any point, so close ringed was it with new plantations. But the Forestry Commission are beginning to open up many of their forests, with roads and picnic-sites, and in general access to our hill country is slowly being extended. In the Peak District it has been a fifty-year battle, sometimes literally fought out between walkers and gamekeepers, but after years of patient work by the Peak Park Planning Board, access agreements now cover most of the best and wildest moorland, and the most popular of the gritstone crags there. It took nearly as many years to open up the Pennine Way, which gives 250 miles of incomparably wild and rough walking from its starting point at Edale, in the High Peak, to the village of Kirk Yetholm across the Scottish Border. Bogey for the course is between 14 and 17 days, though it has been done in less. But the virtue of the Pennine Way for most walkers is that you can pick a section of it, mild or savage, long or short, genuine mountain or less arduous middleground, according to taste and the length of your legs.

Continued access to some of the hills where in the past we have been free to walk or climb, but which are privately owned, or which you must walk through farmland to reach, is beginning to be in doubt. The post-war flood of climbers is large, and contains many people who have never been disciplined in good mountain behaviour. Whether some mountains may be closed to us in future will largely depend on all of them learning to live, as well as to read, the Country Code.

I have so far dodged the question of when it is a hill, and when it is a mountain. There is no accepted formula based on height above sea-level, and I think it really depends on the *local* scale or scene. Scafell Pike, at 3,210 feet our highest English mountain, would be unnoticed if you dumped it in the middle of the Swiss Alps. But if you stand on top of Helvellyn, and look eastwards to the dark, long, menacing line of the Pennines, you have not the slightest doubt that these are real mountains, although there are few peaks, and those not spiky ones, and although that part of the Pennines is mainly high moorland, too. And the paradox about Derbyshire's High Peak is that there isn't one. If you walk across Kinder Scout or Bleaklow in winter, particularly when the cloud is down, you must navigate across a largely featureless tableland – with an excessively rumpled tablecloth on top of it. You scramble continuously down into and up out of deep twisting channels in the peat ("Groughs" is the local name), and you can lose your sense of direction completely in fifty yards, and wish instead you were on some nice sharp Lakeland ridge that *led* somewhere. So for all their unmountainy shape these are serious mountains. They are lonely in winter, blizzard or cloud can make it a fight to survive, and the walking is very rough indeed. Bleaklow lives up to its name, especially if you remember that the "low" part of it is the same as the Scottish "Law" and means hill.

Even smaller hills, in friendlier places, seem sometimes to deserve the title of mountain. There is of course no doubt that the humped whale-back of Bredon, patched with woodland and squares of arable, is just a hill, though my favourite hill in all England, as it was of the novelist John Moore. But the Malverns pose a more difficult question – certainly not mountainous in height, but the splendidly abrupt way in which they break out from the Worcestershire plain, the long chain of steepish peaks, and the bareness of sheep-cropped flank and top all help to make me see the Malverns as mountains, not hills. I do not think it is just a question of size. There is an old rhyme that goes:

The highest hills betwixt Tweed and Trent
Are Ingleborough, Whernside and Penyghent.

It's not true, of course, though early Yorkshire observers, unacquainted with trigonometry, gave them heights that varied between 4,000 and 6,000 feet, whereas Whernside, the highest, is only 2,415. But the instinct was right. Each of these, and particularly Ingleborough, is a distinctive peak, rising sharply and separately from the lower ground. And even if they're not, they *look* very high.

But I must not carry the upgrading of hill into mountain too far. If I did, I should put in a bid for the delightful little Gog Magog hills near Cambridge, where, they say, if you look towards a certain easterly point of the compass, you will find no ground higher than that on which you stand until you reach the Urals! Which goes to show that one reason why England has so many good hills and mountains is that she hasn't any wide plains or steppes.

What then are our English hills, to motorist, townsman, walker, climber? If you stand on the top, it is a simple and self-evident bit of achievement. But a hill is also earth set a little skew-wise, a glimpse of our geological history, a rapid passage through different zones of climate and of vegetation which it would take a thousand miles of journey northward on flatland to match. It is a perpetually surprising change of view, it is a reminder of the precariousness of our survival against wind, cold, snow or thunderstorm. Above all, a hill is *different* – non-human in scale, dwarfing even modern technological man, and telling him how small he is, and how short are his legs.

Ours is a lucky landscape, shaped by the lucky climate that surrounds us in this moment of geological time, 10,000 years away from the last Ice Age, and perhaps 10,000 on to the next one. It has given us hillscapes of infinitely varying charm and nature. You see how blest we are, in comparison, when you fly over Spain and those barren parallel ridges, looking like ribs which have come through the starved skin, or over the Persian rock desert, which really does look like the abomination of desolation.

I believe we have hills "in our bones" because our ancestors lived in an England where the valleys were choked with forest and swamp, and with rivers crossed only by hazardous fords. The trackways of primitive peoples ran along the high bare watersheds, and there you will find the remains of their settlements, like the great fortified camp of Maiden Castle, looking down on what is now Dorchester. And our new-found mobility is taking us back to those hills. I believe too that we need to go there, and that the more our population grows, and the bigger our cities become, the more we shall feel this need.

Let me take you back again, on a clear, rain-washed Cotswold day, to Bredon Hill, with the Herefords chewing a drowsy cud in the fields below. With luck you will see the little slate-blue triangle of the Wrekin to the far north-west, and the edge of the Brecon Beacons standing sharp over Wales, beyond the familiar Malvern Hills. South is the line of the Cotswold scarp, and you remember walking down the convex valley slopes there, and only at the last moment discovering the hidden limestone village, built alongside its quiet stream. Yes, we need valleys and villages, too, and towns, I suppose, but the poet who wrote, "There is much comfort in high hills" knew what he was talking about.

Seascape

JOHN LEWIS

The British Isles have over 7,000 miles of coastline. England must have something like 1,350 miles, excluding inlets. No wonder we have always been a maritime nation. Ours is a coast of much variety, offering disconcerting hazards to the yachtsman and often havens of peace to the motorist or the walker. However, the proper way to see a coastline is from the sea. Let us take a mythical cruise, starting at Berwick-on-Tweed.

The Northumbrian coast consists of low-lying sand dunes and limitless hard, sandy beaches. A few miles off this coast lie the Farne Islands, a string of bare rocks which are a nature reserve and the home of thousands of seabirds. On one of these rocks St Cuthbert established himself in a little cell in sight of his Abbey at Lindisfarne. Behind Lindisfarne (or Holy Island) there is a little natural harbour where a small vessel can lie protected from wind and sea. There could be no better introduction to seeing the coastline of England than to begin here, for much of English history starts at this point. The abbeys of Lindisfarne and of Jarrow and Wearmouth, some forty-five miles down the coast, provided one of the main spring-boards for the Carolingian renaissance. Today the abbey of Lindisfarne stands isolated and in ruins, brooding over the wastes of the North Sea, yet still retaining an atmosphere of peace and serenity. As the tide ebbs one can cross the causeway to the mainland and walk the few miles to Bamburgh – to see one of the greatest castles in England.

Sailing south from Lindisfarne one is soon in sight of the pit-heads of the Northumbrian coalfields. The coal port of Blyth offers protection for the night, and for entertainment the most important yacht club of the area. Few yachtsmen would be tempted into the industrial ports of the Tyne, and the twenty-five-mile coast of Durham has little of interest, with its low cliffs and even less protection. The Yorkshire coast is not much more hospitable, though Staithes is a fascinating little fishing village and Whitby has an abbey high on the cliffs and a harbour with a difficult entrance. Whitby is a seaside resort of some interest and is the birthplace of Captain James Cook, who trusted to Whitby workmanship to carry him round the world in the *Endeavour Bark*, a former Whitby collier. Robin Hood's Bay, another picturesque fishing port, is just south of Whitby. Sailing on down the coast, one passes the resorts of Scarborough and Filey. After rounding Flamborough Head one comes to Bridlington, where the coast is suffering constant erosion. The forty miles or so of coastline, from Flamborough Head to Spurn Head at the mouth of the Humber, are often spectacular but devoid of harbours and have nothing to offer the mariner. At Spurn, where there is a nature reserve, the shingle and sand that has been washed away from Bridlington Bay is helping to build up the spit that curves in opposite Grimsby, to provide most conveniently a safe anchorage for small craft. And they need it, for the Humber has fast tides, and a nasty sea can build up at the entrance to the estuary.

Hull and Grimsby are both important fishing ports, and are the main bases for the trawlers that fish the most distant fishing grounds. About half the fish netted by British fishermen is landed at these Humber ports. The Lincolnshire coast runs from the Humber to the Wash. It is a coastline without harbours and has only one important resort – Skegness, which is reputed to be "so bracing".

The Wash, a rectangular indentation about fourteen miles square, is an area of sandbanks and narrow channels. At low water, these banks rise up like miniature mountains. The common seal lies basking in the sun or swims lazily round one's boat. On the Long Sands fishing boats are stranded high and dry with their masts pointing in all directions. Between them there is a frieze of contorted figures. These are the fishermen digging for cockles. The Wash is reminiscent of the great Dutch estuaries, with the Lincolnshire coast revealed by a shimmering line of poplars and in the distance the tower of the great Boston church, the Boston Stump. It is possible to enter the inland navigable waterways at Boston and to travel by water all the way over the Pennines to Liverpool (providing your boat is shallow enough), or up the Welland to Stamford or the Nene to Wisbech and on to Birmingham (if your boat is narrow enough), or through King's Lynn, one of the most beautiful towns in England, to Cambridge and Bedford.

The coast of Norfolk is low-lying and there is no reputable harbour between the Wash and Great Yarmouth, a distance of seventy miles. However, there is Wells and there is Blakeney, whose harbours only those with much local knowledge would dream of entering. Once inside they are very rewarding. There is a bird sanctuary here, and Blakeney harbour is a large expanse of sandbanks and narrow channels that dry out at low water. Both villages and nearby Cley are all charming if wind-swept villages, where dinghy sailors and bird-watchers congregate. Sheringham and Cromer are both flourishing seaside resorts. Great Yarmouth is the Black-pool of the East Coast, and with Lowestoft is the main centre for the East Anglian trawling and drift-net fishing. The Scroby Sands lie off Yarmouth, forming the Yarmouth Roads and providing shelter for coasters in easterly winds, and also harbouring colonies of the grey seal, about which there has been so much con-troversy. Yarmouth and Lowestoft both provide access to the Norfolk Broads, and coasters can continue up the River Yare to Norwich. The Norfolk coast is a wreck-strewn coast; in the winter of 1865–6 a series of north-easterly gales sank over 500 collier brigs, billyboys and other vessels, many of them on these sands.

The next harbour southwards is Southwold, which with shifting shingle banks has an entrance that can change overnight. Once inside the jetties the harbour becomes the River Blyth. Across the marshes one can see Blythburgh church, and in a dinghy one can sail right up to it. As to whether Blythburgh or Southwold has the finer of these two magnificent knapped-flint churches, the traveller can decide for himself. Southwold lies on the north bank of the Blyth and is faced by Walbers-wick on the south. Wilson Steer used to paint his limpid watercolours here. A little further down the coast is what remains of Dunwich (most of it is under the sea) and then one comes to Minsmere. This is a great bird sanctuary, with rare visitors like the spoonbill and the avocet, which it shares with Havergate Island on the Orford River. There are bearded tits as well. The next landmark is the Sizewell Power Station, and then one comes to Aldeburgh, which has an R.N.L.I. lifeboat (it used to have two) and fishing boats drawn up on the beach. It has a music festival, a golf club and a yacht club, but to enter the Aldeburgh River one has to sail a dozen miles and round Orford Ness to reach Orford Haven (a miniature Spurn Head) for Aldeburgh once had a harbour with access to the sea. The Suffolk coastline is as low and featureless as Norfolk's, but to provide a little relief there is a succession of Martello towers erected against Napoleon's threatened invasion.

The Orford River is the northern limit of what is known as "East Coast sailing". The rivers southwards from here are the Deben, with an entrance as difficult as the Ore, the Orwell and the Stour at Harwich, the Walton backwaters behind the Naze, the Colne and the Blackwater, the Crouch and the Roach, and finally the Thames. For the East Coast sailor these are sailing grounds of infinite variety in spite of the featureless coastline. To reach the Thames one has to round the Maplin Sands, which may one day become a great airport. The Thames can at the moment hardly be called a yachtsman's paradise, though many sail out of Southend and Leigh-on-Sea, the home of the cocklers.

Over on the Kentish shore there is the Medway. In a suitable boat one can sail right up to Maidstone. The Medway towns of Rochester and Chatham still have a Dickensian flavour, and the marshes on the Isle of Grain are just as Dickens described them in *Great Expectations.* The Swale divides Sheppey from the main-land, and in the various creeks that run up to Faversham, Upnor and Sitting-bourne many small boats are kept. Sailing along the north coast of Kent, if the tide is high and there is an "R" in the month, one might drop anchor off Whitstable to buy some Whitstable natives. Continuing on one's way one passes the twin towers of Reculver's Anglo-Saxon church, once a Trinity House guide for shipping, and then, sailing inside the Goodwins, one makes for Margate with its fun-fairs and other jollifications before rounding the North Foreland. If the weather looks unpromising, one can lock into Ramsgate's Inner Harbour. The outer harbour is no place to lie in if a north-easterly wind is blowing, for the shallow shelf that extends out from Pegwell Bay can cause a sea that only Turner could paint.

Once past Deal and Walmer Castle and through the Downs, where sailing ships used to anchor waiting for a fair wind to take them down Channel, we can round the South Foreland, and the Channel opens up before us. Those vaunted but not so very white cliffs of Dover are surmounted by Dover Castle, one of the earliest (Norman) and least restored of English castles. As for Dover harbour, it is no place for a yacht. In fact it is no place for a harbour at all; but that is by the way. Harbours for small craft are once again far apart. Folkestone, which must be lovely for retired colonels, is no use for sailors, and there is nothing at Hythe. The still mysterious Romney Marsh lurks behind the low coastline, looking as if it ought to be somewhere in East Anglia. The Varne Light Vessel, in contrast to the plethora of lightships in the Thames Estuary, keeps solitary guard on the entrance to the Channel. One has to round Dungeness, featureless except for its power station, before coming to Rye Bay, where in fair weather and with some local knowledge one can make the entrance to the narrow cut that leads up to the old town of Rye. It is not much of a harbour and dangerous to enter, but Rye still has many charms, perched on a hill above the surrounding marshes. Hastings has a small fishing harbour; Bexhill and Eastbourne have plenty for the holidaymaker but nothing for the sailor, who will probably give them and Pevensey Bay a wide berth, sailing outside the Royal Sovereign Light Vessel to clear Beachy Head, a high cliff famous for the number of people who throw themselves off it each year. Newhaven not only has packet steamers but offers much better harbourage for yachtsmen than Dover. The coastline west from here is ribbon development all the way to Selsey Bill. This ranges from the shacks and bungalows of Peacehaven and Kemp Town to the Regency elegance of Brighton and Hove. At Brighton apple-bowed, clench-built fishing boats are drawn up on the beach, looking much the same as when John Constable painted them.

Rounding Selsey Bill, Chichester harbour is on the starboard hand, with a creek leading up to the old town of Bosham, where King Cnut's daughter is said to be buried in the little churchyard. The creeks are crowded with sailing craft. We have arrived at the heart of English yachting. Cowes, set at the mouth of the Medina River, is the yachting world's equivalent to Ascot or Longchamps. Osborne House, Queen Victoria's beloved "little home" is a mile from East Cowes. It is now a convalescent home for service officers and senior civil servants and is open to the public. In every creek and every river on both sides of the Solent and Spithead there are yachts. The River Hamble which runs off Southampton Water has a waiting list for moorings which won't be met in five years, and the other rivers are almost as crowded, though the pretty wooded shores of the Beaulieu River have at least been spared ribbon development. One leaves the Solent through the Hurst Narrows, with Hurst Castle on the starboard hand at the end of a long shingle spit. The Needles mark the westerly end of the Isle of Wight and the point where, as far as yachtsmen go, you can begin to separate the men from the boys. Behind the island lies relatively sheltered water, ahead the open channel, the Portland Race, the Chesil Bank and the wide spaces of Lyme Bay, which from Portland Bill to Start Point is nearly sixty miles across.

Lyme Bay has some spectacular coastal scenery, of great geological interest. It also has Lyme Regis and Sidmouth, both charming and unspoilt resorts – Sidmouth particularly, with its Regency architecture and gentle climate much loved by retired people – but they offer no protection to the yachtsman. The coastline is changing from shingle banks to rocky cliffs. The River Exe, however, is much like an East Anglian estuary, with low banks and shoal water. Halfway up the estuary on the west bank boats can lock into the canal that goes up to Exeter or they can sail up to Topsham with its strand of pretty Dutch-gabled houses.

From Exmouth to Land's End there is an abundance of seaside resorts, grand and expensive like Torquay, or minute like Mullion and Portloe. For sailors it provides a perfect sailing ground, with long Atlantic seas and clear green water. It is warmed by the Atlantic Drift and is the home of the lobster, the crab and prawns in their millions. Brixham and Newlyn are the main fishing ports, though there are plenty of inshore fishing boats, whose owners take time off in the summer to give tourists a taste for the water at places like Looe, Mevagissey and Polperro. The choice of rivers and estuaries for the yachtsmen seems unlimited. Whilst still on the red-cliffed Devon coast there is the Dart with high green banks; there is Salcombe, which is almost sub-tropical and is a good launching-off point for boats making a passage across West Bay; there is the Yealm, with Newton Ferrers just inside the entrance; and finally Plymouth Sound conjuring up memories of Frobisher and Drake, with one of the greatest natural harbours in the country. Plymouth is a large naval station and a commercial port. It is perhaps not ideal for yachtsmen, but with the Cornish rivers lying ahead who would want to linger in Plymouth? Fowey is only eighteen miles along the coast. It is a pretty river, and Fowey itself is an interesting old town with historical associations at least dating back to Edward III, when the town provided nearly fifty ships for the siege of Calais. Leaving Fowey, one can see the man-made mountains of white china clay behind St Austell. Mevagissey lies across St Austell Bay. It is a miniature Brixham, with, like Brixham, an inner harbour that dries out.

Falmouth Harbour and the Carrick Roads evoke memories of the last of the great square-rigged sailing ships, which would lie here awaiting orders to sail for Australia for their annual cargo of grain. These waters and the adjacent Helford

The Needles. Watercolour drawing by John Sell Cotman (1782–1842)

River provide perfect sailing grounds. There are miles of sheltered water and winding creeks. St Mawes in the pretty Roseland Peninsula is probably the warmest place in England. From Falmouth westwards it is advisable to get clear of the coast, for it is a coastline cluttered with reefs and rocks. The dreaded Manacles are the first obstacle. Hundreds of deep-sea ships, coasters and fishing vessels have been lost on this rock-bound peninsula. Rounding the Lizard, Mounts Bay lies between the point and Land's End. The sea floor shoals rapidly towards Marazion and the 250-feet-high St Michael's Mount, which is joined to the shore by a three-quarter-mile causeway, covered at high tide. This counterpart of Mont Saint Michel in Brittany has a castle and fourteenth-century chapel which are open to the public. Newlyn has fishing boats and artists. Penzance is the port for the Scilly Islands. The steamer sails the forty miles to St Mary's and passes the solitary Wolf Rock Light House on the way. There are over 100 islands in this archipelago, once thought to be part of the legendary Lyonesse of King Arthur. The Scillies enjoy the full benefit of the warm Atlantic Drift and have an even milder climate than Cornwall. They grow spring flowers, and on St Agnes there is a bird sanctuary. The only disadvantage these islands have for the yachtsman is that there is no anchorage that is protected from every direction. If the winds shift, the boats have to move also. Off the south-western end of the islands is Bishop's Rock, where Sir Cloudsley Shovell's flagship came to grief in 1707.

Land's End, with its ice-cream vendors and shacks selling rubbish to tourists, is better and more impressively seen from the sea. One has to pick one's weather, for the Longships are not something to trifle with in a strong south-westerly wind.

Once round Land's End, St Ives is the first possible harbour. It has, like Newlyn, both fishing boats and artists.

The north coasts of Devon and Cornwall are quite unlike the south of the peninsula. It is an unfriendly shore, with few harbours, and some of those little more than clefts in the rocks. However, its sandy beaches and roaring breakers provide magnificent surf-bathing at places like Newquay and Perranporth. Padstow, on the Camel estuary, has a harbour, and that is about the sum total of resting places for the yachtsman until he has sailed past Tintagel Head, across Bude Bay and rounded the fearsome cliffs of Hartland Point, to come to anchor in Bideford Bay or to cross the bar and to drop the hook off the little fishing village of Appledore, or even to sail up the Torridge to Bideford.

Lundy Island lies about twelve miles north of Hartland Point. It is an isolated pinnacle of granite, which provided the stone for the Victoria Embankment in London. The coast of Lundy is cliff bound, but there is a landing place at the south-east end behind Rat Island. Lundy is now a bird sanctuary and all through the summer nights one can hear the unearthly screams of the Manx shearwater. We are now in the Bristol Channel. Sailing eastwards, under the shadow of Exmoor, the Welsh mountains can be seen to the north. Steep Holme and Flat Holm lie ahead and the shallows of Bridgwater Bay are on the starboard hand. Weston-super-Mare has mud, jollity, a pier and steamers that cross to Cardiff. Tides are fierce and this is not an ideal place for small yachts. Our journey might well come to a stop at Avonmouth, or we might sail up the Avon Gorge under Brunel's Suspension Bridge past Clifton and come to rest in Bristol, a town still full of maritime history.

As this is a book about England we must miss the coasts of Wales and pick up the thread of our journey in the estuary of the Dee. The sands of the Dee are more suitable for "driving home the cattle" or for cockling than for sailing. Rounding the flat levels of the Wirral peninsula, one comes into Liverpool Bay and the mouth of the Mersey. Liverpool, that gutsy, brash place with its Liver Building and incomparable waterside, deserves a chapter to itself. However, we have no time to stop here and have to sail northward past Southport to the Ribble estuary. We might pick up a mooring off Lytham and St Annes, a resort famous for its championship golf course. But if the wind is blowing from the west, a vicious sea can be kicked up off Lytham so one would be well advised to sail up the river some five miles and lock into the Rufford Branch of the Leeds and Liverpool Canal. Travelling north past Blackpool, with its Golden Mile, Wakes' Week crowds and surprisingly expensive luxury hotels, the next port is Fleetwood. This is the north-west coast's equivalent of Grimsby or Hull, and is the main base for the deep-sea trawlers. The mountains of the Lake District, the Furness Fells and the Old Man of Coniston can be seen, if it is not raining, across the muddy wastes of Morecambe Bay. Morecambe Bay used to be a great centre for trawling. The fishing boats were pretty little counter-sterned cutters. The prawns are still to be found out in the Irish Sea, but cockling is the main activity of the Morecambe Bay fishermen now. There is a bird sanctuary at Leighton Moss and a Nature Reserve at Grange-over-Sands.

Our coastal tour is nearly over. Ahead lies the west coast of Scotland, which is indeed a yachtsman's paradise. All we can do is to round St Bees Head and take a northerly course for the Solway Firth, finally dropping anchor off the Roman fort at the western end of the Roman Wall at Bowness-on-Solway. We began our coastline tour with the seventh-century Northumbrian saints; we end with Hadrian's attempt to defend what is now England from the Picts in the second century A.D.

Yachts off Lytham St Anne's. Detail of painting by L. S. Lowry, 1955   Beaverbrook Art Gallery Foundation
Frederickton.

Rivers

MAURICE WIGGIN

To the river fancier, dry land is a necessary pre-condition which determines the direction, scope and gradient of streams. It guides them, separates them, and intermittently contains them. It modifies them and is itself modified by them. Though it would be an unpardonable licence to speak of symbiosis, yet it is true that they cannot leave one another alone. The river fancier, especially if he has some sense of history, sees the land almost wholly in terms of watersheds, which remain constant; valleys, which occasionally alter; and estuaries, which change continually. Rivers nourish his historical sense, delight his aesthetic sense, and, if he be an angler, ravish and enslave him – though not all equally.

Some of the best English rivers are of Welsh descent. The two noblest of them rise, not far apart, on the lonely wastes of Plynlimon – *Pumlumon Fawr*.

> Happy the eye
> 'Twixt Severn and Wye

sang the poet; and indeed it would be a baleful eye and a curmudgeonly heart which failed to respond to the enchantment of that gracious and haunted land, a land of creamy curd-cropping pastures, crooked little cwms and valleys, starspangled orchards, cottages clinging to hillsides and sending up blue smoke under pearly skies. I begin with Severn and Wye for the simple reason that I came to love them first, and most. I would not seriously try to erect some inflated structure of theory in defence of their "supremacy": the Severn can be really dull at times. It simply happens that to me, and to many, Severn and Wye are primely numinous.

The Severn, especially, has moved impressionable people to all sorts of extravagance. Belloc, of course, in his inimitable mixture of good fancy and good sense, dubious insight and indubitable observation, put it thus:

> The men that live in West England,
> They see the Severn strong
> A-rolling on rough water brown
> Light aspen leaves along.
> They have the secret of the Rocks,
> And the oldest kind of song.

"The secret of the Rocks . . .", "The oldest kind of song . . .", what rubbish it is, really. Yet Severnside does trick otherwise quite rational people into that sort of mysticism. The Romans came up short against Sabrina Fair; they stood a long time pondering its "rough water brown". Belloc had the essence of it, after all: rough water indeed, brown beyond question, and a-rolling, a-rolling ceaselessly, a very strong and formidable river. Not far from Newtown, and in other parts of its early or Montgomeryshire life, and again in its lower reaches, it is not very interesting; but between, say, Shrewsbury and Stourport, or even perhaps as far as Worcester and beyond to Upton, it is the very model of what a river may be. If you

On the River Greta. Watercolour drawing by John Sell Cotman, 1805   *Leeds, City Art Gallery*

observe the Severn upstream and downstream of the enchanting (now seriously threatened) eighteenth-century town of Bewdley, you see what a river may be when its gradient and width and flow are just right, and when they are complemented by exactly the right degree of steepness and woodedness in the banks or shoulders of the valley. A steep and deep-cut valley, suggesting the earlier immensity of the flood, and essentially green, embowered with trees – this suggests the antiquity of the river, occludes it from the casual vulgar eye, makes it an adventure. One does not want exactly a gorge, such as the Avon inhabits at Clifton: a gorge proper is too awesome. But neither does a river really come into its own when flowing through a valley so wide and gentle and flat that you are not conscious of the river until you practically fall into it. It may well be an extremely rewarding river – the Ouse and others of the East Anglian rivers are delightful in their own way, and the Hampshire rivers have their own perfection. But without the preparation and drama of the steep valley, somehow a river is robbed of some of its proper power.

There should, too, be a lot of *nature* left in a river. One that has been too assiduously tamed is too tame for full delight: I can never feel really at home in the Thames Valley. It is a pretty river, of course, and must once have been as numinous as the Severn. But people can rarely leave well alone. Anywhere downstream of Port Meadow the Thames is too well-regulated for my austere or anachronistic taste. Hardly an inch of the bank is original: the flow is directed, where it is not diverted, the locks come thick and fast, civilization is never far away, and the people on the banks and in the boats very nearly outnumber the fish within. I must concede that if you want to spend time *on* the river, there's none to match the Thames. It is the great beast of burden; it seems made to carry human traffic, and there are many less delightful ways of spending a holiday than in a punt on the Thames. There is no river from which it is more exhilarating to set sail for foreign parts; to set off in a trading steamer from Pool of London bound for Hamburg, say, used to be a bracing experience. Even to toddle jollily from Tower Bridge to Southend and back, on the *Golden Daffodil*, has been worth doing. One regrets nothing, not a minute, that was spent on or in or by the water. . . .

However, it is undeniable that the Thames is *used*, a bit too much used, over-modified: friendly though it is upstream of the Trout Inn at Godstow, pleasant then all the way to Lechlade, with its gentle tributaries, like Windrush and Evenlode, beloved of the fly fisher. But these do not, I think, bear comparison with Severn's splendid brood. Prime among those I name the Teme, also a river of Welsh descent, of course, which in stature and gradient is exactly what the fly fisher desires in his heart. Like the Usk above Abergavenny, a river unfortunately outside the scope of this essay, the Teme matches you blow for blow, it has the nature and the stature of a medium-sized man's medium-sized adventure river. It is virtually not navigable, in any serious sense, though one can, in imagination, quite see it strewn with coracles, like the incomparable Teify, princess of them all. No, it is the wader's dangerous river, rift with flaws, perilous to the unwary sliding in ever another yard for that unmanageable cast which will just cover the far fish's lie. . . . And it is embowered with trees, girt with greenery, suddenly come-upon. Anywhere from Tenbury Wells upstream, or almost anywhere, and even for a very few miles downstream, the Teme is the river of my dreams.

There is a clutch of Celtic rivers, some more or less mildly anglicized, which feed the Severn and the Wye, all beautiful, all seductive; they all have the Celtic grace. Clun, Arrow, Onny, Corve, Rea, Vyrnwy – even the thick Lugg which bears its load of Herefordshire loam. The rivers of the March drain a haunted land.

Different in character but similar in scope and magnitude is the veining of slower streams which drain the eastern parts of England. I hasten to acknowledge that these Anglian rivers also have an unearthly beauty, flowing as they do for the most part under wide pearly skies, through creamy loams that nourish an even richer greenery than the pastures of the March, which become attenuated when the rocks begin to rise. The Great Ouse is too mechanical and regulated for my wild taste, but it and its companion the Little Ouse have their own tranquillity. The rivers of the Broads, Bure and Waveney, are a float fisherman's delight, but prettier and comelier are streams like the Brett that feed the quiet Stour. I guess the quintessence of pastoral tranquillity is to be found, in the riparian sense, in Constable Country.

Further north the tranquillity is repeated, but less snugly, with an undertone of awe created by the greater range and vastness of the slightly harsher spaces, in the valleys of the Witham and the Ancholme. Lincolnshire has a curious quality: it is large and often louring, it is bracing but often dour. The river systems offer some consolation. Many the happy hour I have spent watching a float, by Ancholme and Witham: hours snatched from the ardours of airfields, always the most lowering environment created by man. Of course, one must never forget the two other river systems which drain into the Wash, filling the gap between the Ouse-Stour duality and the Lincolnshire rivers to the north: I mean the Welland and the Nene. Where else does the float fisherman's satisfaction find such perfect expression? Rivers of slow but perceptible flow, draining good land, peaceful and accessible . . . these are river valleys that induce peace. Whereas the rain-fed Celtic rivers which rise and fall, race and dwindle, in my heavenly March-land, go naturally with the fly fisher's energetic and optimistic pursuit, so these gentler and richer rivers of the east are perfectly suited to the float fisher's meditative and statuesque immobility.

It is odd to have written so many words about our rivers without even using the word which of all words means river, the British *avon* or *afon*. A lovely word it is. There are so many Avons it is hard to know where to begin. The Bard's Avon, that flows turgidly through Stratford? Yes, historically it must take precedence, and it can be a pretty little river, and certainly is a river rich in literary associations. But the fishing is very undistinguished, and it is vulgarized and put out of countenance by a multitude of pleasure boats and hemmed in by all too many caravans, right down from Stratford to Tewkesbury, where John Halifax, Gentleman, would wonder what had happened to his rural stream.

Little better is the equally turgid Avon that drains the Somerset marshes and debouches through Bristol into the affronted Severn. Its chief if not its only claim to fame is that gorge, that marvellous Clifton Suspension Bridge – and the fact that adventurers innumerable have started and ended their voyages upon its murky water.

Much the most distinguished Avon is that which enters the English Channel at Christchurch. It rises near Devizes and flows through Salisbury, Downton, Fordingbridge and Ringwood to that strange conclusion, an estuary almost without a peer in mystery. This Hampshire Avon, as it is naturally known, is the most celebrated coarse fishery in England – not necessarily the best, but the legendary one. It is also a river of great disappointment to many, for anglers coming to it from the slow streams of the Midlands and the east and north-east are sometimes cast down by its swift and remorseless flow, which imposes upon them stout tackle and heavy weights and methods wholly at variance with the "toothpick float" gossamer-web subtlety of their native waters. It is a river that yields up specimen roach, barbel and chub, excellent dace, some fine trout, and salmon which are infrequent but immense.

The keypoint about the Hampshire Avon, the quality which distinguishes it from other Avons and, indeed, from most other rivers, the component which allies it to a very rare and special group of streams, is that it is a chalk stream. What is a chalk stream? There are very few of them. They issue from underground reservoirs, vast storage reservoirs unseen by man, which lie below the chalk strata of downland country. The rain percolates through the chalk, the rivers run out from the points where the water-table is appropriate. It follows (a) that chalk streams are filtered, pure and clear, and (b) that they are not much affected by rainfall, in the short term. Whereas a rain-fed river, in the sense that most of the March-rising rivers and indeed all mountain-born streams are rain-fed, rises and falls in a direct and variably quick response to the rain falling in its upper valley, a chalk stream is little affected by either drought or flood. True, it has its ups and downs, but they are gentle and marginal – whereas a true "spate river", one that has a relatively short and relatively steep gradient and a bed mainly of rock or gravel, rises and falls almost like a lift. True, there are innumerable rivers that are neither spate rivers nor chalk streams – rivers which flow down a more or less gentle gradient, through rich alluvial land; these rise and fall in relation to rainfall, of course, but less suddenly than spate rivers, and vastly more abruptly than chalk streams, which to the casual eye seem not to vary at all.

Coming to a chalk stream is an experience which your Midland angler, for example, never quite gets over. I shall never forget my first sight of the Kennet. Leaning over a bridge and looking down, my favourite pursuit, I simply could not believe that water could be so pellucid. Rapid water I was familiar with, but even that had been dark and turbid in comparison. To see yards and yards away, the weeds and the fishes, as in a mirror – it was akin to the day when I walked out of the optician's wearing my first glasses, and really *saw*.

The Kennet, important only as a marvellous angling stream, rises on the north side of the chalk watershed of downland and flows, actually, into the old Thames – by a biscuit factory at Reading. But the great chalk streams of Hampshire flow south from this divide. The Avon, as aforementioned, empties itself into the sea at Christchurch. The Test and the Itchen flow into Southampton Water. The Bourne joins the Avon at that heavenly spot "where the bright waters meet". These are the pellucid and infinitely beguiling streams of the dry fly trout fisher, the real haven waters to which, in imagination, all dry fly fishermen retire. I have fished them rarely enough, in all conscience; they are fearfully expensive and exclusive. But no one who has cast a fly upon these waters ever forgets that experience.

Actually, the chalk stream is not confined to Hampshire. Chalk streams may rise elsewhere: the Driffield Beck and Foston Beck in Yorkshire – tributaries of the Hull! – are such; truly chalk streams, truly enchanting. Yet one thinks generally of the chalk stream as a glory of the south.

There is a whole group of related rivers of the West Country, not perhaps magnificent, but all with tremendous character, which one thinks of with affection undiminished throughout the years. The rivers of Devon take a hold of one's heart; they, like the Teme, are of just the right gradient and scope, they run through beautiful valleys, just steep enough and sufficiently well-wooded – oh, those endless stands of scrubby hanging oaks! – and they, too, offer treacherous wading, all sorts of chances of mishap, an infinite variety of pools and runs and glides – altogether the most beguiling, adventurous-on-a-small-scale, satisfying fishing. I suppose the Two Rivers, Taw and Torridge, the heavenly twins that enter the Bristol Channel via Barnstaple and Bideford at Appledore, are just about as attractive as smallish rivers can be. But the Dart has enormous charm and grace, the Teign is distinctive and delicious, the Tamar that divides Devon from Cornwall (and England from Abroad, some would say) is full of character if less strong on charm, the Exe and Axe and the Fowey all have their proper devotees. Yet another Avon, the Devonshire Avon, is most peculiar. It is for the most part of its inconsiderable length a mere bit of a bushed-over, tricky little trout stream; then suddenly and inexplicably, at Aveton Gifford, which is the head of the tide, it widens out into an immense lagoon – and the vast quantities of tidal water in this lake have to enter and drain away, twice daily, rushing through a tiny narrow mouth into the twisting estuary proper, which enters the sea near Thurlestone (Bantham Sands). Once fished, never forgotten. I love that river.

Rather strangely, the West Country group of westward-running rivers are counterparted north of the Mersey, where some quite Devonian rivers flow into the Irish Sea. The Eden and the Lune are for the most part both beautiful and productive; the Border Esk is celebrated, and the much smaller Esk that enters the sea near Ravenglass – name to conjure with! – is deeply attractive to those who have discovered it and return to fish Hugh Falkus's water year by year. I imagine that much the same was once true of the north-east coast rivers which feed the North Sea from the other side of the great divide; but industrial pollution, water abstractions, and sheer pressure of building and population have scarcely improved Tyne and Wear and Tees. The Aln and the Coquet remain to remind us what glories once were there.

The rivers of Surrey and Middlesex, which once were on a par with, say, the unsensational little rivers of Dorset and Somerset – Frome and Parret, Piddle and Brue – are now much reduced in value. One is thankful that the Mole and Wey are still there, on the grounds that any river is better than none; but they are poor things. The little rivers of Essex, almost all estuary, are the yachtsman's friend rather than the fisherman's; the rivers of Kent are inconsiderable; but the rivers of Sussex still wring a sort of rueful poetry out of sundry impressionable souls. Belloc raved about the Arun in his romantic way, and heaven knows I am indebted to Arun for many placid hours fishing for pike, and also for several colds and chills of unusual malignancy; it is a vaporous valley which can strike dankly chill to the unwary, its water is dark and glum. The Adur is a jolly little stream, and a funny one. The Sussex Ouse, which flows through Lewes and enters the Channel at the grim port of Newhaven, carries more sea trout than strangers are encouraged to think by the uncommunicative inhabitants of suspicious Sussex.

I have said too little about the heavenly streams of Yorkshire – Swale, Wharfe, Nidd, Aire, Greta, and the rest. They have their own sort of upland charm. They are in fact very good company. A river is the best of company for a man who can get his mind off money. If he can't, it will do the job for him.

The English Garden

ANNE SCOTT-JAMES

Of all forms of sightseeing, visiting gardens is the least historical. Churches, houses, pictures, furniture, tapestries, can often be seen in their original condition, or, if they have been altered, every step in their growth or restoration is probably on record. But a garden changes with time and with every new plantsman. A garden is a living, growing, progressing, backsliding thing, never the same for more than twenty or thirty years. However perfectly a garden is planned, later generations with new tastes, new knowledge and a wider range of plants to play with will seek to improve it. It may even go backwards, if it falls into the hands of a tactless plantsman or takes a knock from the weather.

So when one visits a historic garden one may speculate enjoyably on the men who planted it, and on the sort of life people lived in the Great House in the sixteenth, seventeenth, eighteenth or nineteenth centuries; but what one is seeing is an object of contemporary, not historic beauty. Every garden is alive.

There are almost no traces left of the earliest English gardens, though there are a few conscientious reconstructions. The medieval English garden was a utilitarian patch rather than a pleasure ground, with fruit trees, vegetables, vines, herbs, medicinal plants and a few flowers. Regrettably, we were poor gardeners compared with Continental countries, particularly Italy.

The first gardens with any aesthetic pretensions were Tudor. In 1520 Sir Thomas More, surely one of the most civilized men in English history, made a pleasure garden in Chelsea, with rosemary hedges, blossoming trees and flowers, and a view of the Thames. A few years earlier, Cardinal Wolsey had begun to lay out the gardens at Hampton Court in the formal Italianate manner which was to be the inspiration for the next two hundred years. After Wolsey's death these were extended and elaborated by Henry VIII in a complicated geometric arrangement of terraces, fountains, box hedges and alleys, embellished with topiary, mazes, carved heraldic animals and "knots" – elaborate patterns of clipped shrubs or herbs, filled in with coloured earth or flowers. It must all have looked very fussy.

Throughout the sixteenth century horticultural skill developed fast. Travellers brought home exotic plants; the first herbals were published; scented flowers were cultivated; waterworks and fountains were constructed (they didn't always work); and, as in the other arts, refugees from France and Flanders arrived and taught the inelegant English their more sophisticated Continental skills.

When great new houses were built, like Haddon Hall, Hardwick and Montacute, they were graced with spacious pleasure gardens, and, though no original plantings are left, some of these gardens (as at Haddon Hall and Montacute) still retain something of their Elizabethan shape and style. The formal style continued into the Jacobean period, the decorations becoming even more ornate. The garden of Hatfield House, built for the 1st Earl of Salisbury, had terraces, fountains, a crowd of statues and ornaments, an artificial stream, fish-ponds, trained fruit-trees and oranges (which were protected in winter) and a wide range of plants. Traces of the original garden are still to be seen, though there has been much restoration. The Restoration saw the climax of the formal garden, and English gardeners turned to a new master, the Frenchman, Le Nôtre, who was designing grandiose gardens for the palaces of Louis XIV. A Le Nôtre garden was an exercise in mathematics. Always a central vista stretched from the house to the horizon; on either side of it were elaborate parterres, formal lakes and canals, and groves of trees planted at exact intervals, the whole arranged on a geometric plan of axes, circles and squares.

Overlapping with the Le Nôtre period, the Dutch style was an influence in England, especially after the accession of William and Mary. This, too, was formal, but more intimate and inward-looking (a Le Nôtre garden, however vast, could be absorbed in one glance from the windows of the house), with many plantings of clipped evergreens and bulbs. But neither the French nor the Dutch style gardens laid out in England in the second half of the seventeenth century and during the reign of Queen Anne were ideally suited to the rounded contours of the English landscape, and most were later redesigned completely, but not all. At Chatsworth, the seventeenth-century cascade and the temple from which the waters flow (1703) are still to be seen in all their magnificence; and the gardens of Bramham Park, Yorkshire, and of Melbourne Hall, Derbyshire, retain their Queen Anne structure and the mood of Versailles.

Then the pendulum swung. It had to. Gardens had become so intellectual as to be absurd. The poet Pope was one of the first to laugh at man's distortion of nature and at the pretentiousness of all the topiary and statuary and parterres. In 1719 he designed a much simpler kind of garden for his own house at Twickenham. The landscape gardens which we admire so much today came into fashion; the first of a series of great exponents was William Kent, who was followed by Lancelot (Capability) Brown and Humphry Repton. In their hands, the garden ceased to be an enclosure; the house, its garden and the open country beyond were designed like a landscape painting; the whole picture was to be "natural", with a perfection which, of course, required consummate art.

In these growing, living landscapes, trees were gracefully grouped (many avenues fell to the axe), streams meandered, lakes were re-modelled in natural curves, there was often an artificial ruin or two, and the new device of the ha-ha, uniting the garden with the open country beyond, often replaced the old boundary hedge or fence. Flowers were not important – the scale of the landscapes was too large. Many of these eighteenth-century landscape plantings can be seen today; three notable examples are at Rousham House, a charming, cool, green garden with a classical arcade and perfectly placed statues by Kent; the park and lake of Blenheim Palace, by Capability Brown; and Sheringham Hall, by Repton.

The landscape style continued to be admired until the death of Repton in 1818, when a new style of garden came in with a new society. Industrialization, the rise of the middle class, the birth of many smaller estates, improved greenhouses, cheap labour and inventions like the lawn-mower, combined to produce à more mechanical style of garden which one can call neo-Italianate, or simply Victorian. The important elements were neat lawns, gravel paths, formal beds and carpet bedding. At the same time there was a wonderful increase in plant material, and exotics, like orchids, and strange trees, like the monkey puzzle, became Victorian status plants.

This return to formality was demolished for the second time towards the end of the nineteenth century when William Robinson and the redoubtable Miss

Jekyll introduced the "natural" or "wild" garden. Fiery characters both, they abominated bedding plants, topiary and Victorian knick-knackery, and extolled herbaceous plants, naturalized plantings, stream and woodland gardening, mixtures of exotics with simple native flowers, climbing and rambling plants, ground cover and a seemingly haphazard beauty. This is the style which is still dominant today.

But one does not visit a garden primarily to dig into history, although this can be a bonus pleasure. Most of us are not antiquarians, and we go partly for the visual delight and partly to learn something for our own gardens. There is nothing like a fine piece of planting to fire the humbler gardener to go home and do likewise – it is impossible to calculate the number of roses which are climbing up old apple trees as a result of visits to Sissinghurst.

There are something like two thousand gardens in England which are open to the public, either for charity or to earn money for the estate, and one can class them loosely in three categories: landscape gardens, country-house gardens, and cottage gardens.

The landscape gardens are those which surround the great houses of the eighteenth century, and they are not true gardens so much as pleasure grounds or parks; the important features are trees, lakes, vistas and small classical temples and follies. One visits these grand park-gardens, humbly, to admire rather than learn. Gardens like Stourhead, Blenheim, or Longleat are spectacularly beautiful, but as remote from one's own life as the court of Versailles.

If a foreign visitor had a single day for seeing one of the grand gardens, I think Stourhead, in Wiltshire, is the one he should choose. Stourhead is a landscape garden on the finest scale, designed in the middle of the eighteenth century by the owner of the house himself, Henry Hoare the younger, and developed and elaborated by his successors. The focus of the landscape is a serpentine lake which lies in a deep basin surrounded by hills which are richly planted with beeches and conifers. The visitor takes a long and winding walk round the lake, and at every turn his eyes fall upon some fresh and exquisite vista – there is a view to the bridge, the grotto, the rock arch, the Pantheon, the Temple of the Sun. The landscape at Stourhead is a masterpiece, but spoilt for some eyes, including mine, in the months of May and June, when modern plantings of rhododendrons come into fiery blossom and outrage the cool, classical landscape of water and trees and stone.

There are park-gardens on this splendid scale in nearly every region of England, from Heveningham Hall, Suffolk, which has a wooded landscape by Capability Brown and an orangery by James Wyatt, to Blenheim, Oxfordshire; from Castle Howard, Yorkshire, a Vanbrugh mansion with grounds and a Temple of the Four Winds by Vanbrugh, to Luton Hoo, Bedfordshire, with a park by Brown. These landscapes are perhaps the most important contribution to the visual arts that England has ever made – pay no attention to jealous mutterers who pretend that we cribbed them from the Chinese.

The second category is of country-house gardens, which are true gardens rather than landscapes, plantsmanship of flowers and shrubs being more important than trees. Though the site may be historic, the planting nearly always belongs to this century – I am thinking of such country-house gardens as Sissinghurst, Hidcote, Haseley Court, Great Dixter, Nymans, Sutton Courtenay, Charleston Manor, Bampton Manor and Highdown. However different the size and the site, there are characteristics common to nearly every modern garden, of which the first is an informality which descends from William Robinson, though judging, perhaps unfairly, from what is left of his own garden at Gravetye, many of the creators of these gardens were better artists than he.

Even if the garden near the house is formal (as at Haseley Court, with its pleached lime trees and topiary chessmen on the lawn) the newer plantings are nearly always in the cottage style; soft shrub roses are preferred to stiff hybrid teas; foliage plants carpet the ground; clumps of flowers spill over on to paths; planting is lavish and mixed, with climbers intertwining, roses spraying out between flowering shrubs, mixed herbaceous borders, bulbs naturalized in grass. The variety of plants is enormous, for the modern country-house gardener is increasingly a connoisseur. Rare, strange and species plants will be seen in these gardens, as will ferns, water plants, winter-flowering plants and green-flowered plants, like euphorbias and hellebores. The visitor to such gardens should take a notebook, for there are many mixtures, colour schemes and unfamiliar names he will want to remember.

The second principle which governs such gardens is the need for economy of labour. Therefore, shrubs and permanent planting have replaced in-and-out bedding schemes, and few gardeners, having seen the restful beauty of permanent gardening, regret the change. Unhappily, the vegetable garden, too, has had to go into decline; totting up the awful cost of home-grown vegetables, most garden owners limit themselves to a few choice varieties.

Of all country-house gardens, my personal favourite is Sissinghurst, in Kent, which was created largely since the last war by Sir Harold Nicolson and his wife, Vita Sackville-West, he designing and she planting in a supremely happy partnership.

The principle of the garden is "separate rooms" – a series of intimate enclosures leading one into another, each planted with a different theme: there is a rose garden, a herb garden, a spring garden, a white-and-grey garden, and so on. The plantsmanship is charming, so informal and free as to be almost cottagey, although the size of the garden, and the massing of plants in groups, make Sissinghurst an idealized rather than a literal cottage garden. The choice of highly scented climbing and old-fashioned shrub roses make it a paradise in June, while the white garden (conceived on a snowy day in January) is cool even in midsummer, with its white statue, white irises, white pansies, paeonies and lilies.

A perhaps even greater garden designed as "separate rooms" is Hidcote Manor, in the Cotswolds, which I put second only because I know it less well. It is an earlier garden than Sissinghurst – Miss Sackville-West drew much inspiration from it and wrote a graceful essay in tribute to its beauty – and was created at the beginning of this century from rough, untilled fields by an architect-botanist-plantsman, the late Major Lawrence Johnston.

Hidcote consists of a series of separate, secret gardens, enclosed by high hedges, opening (unlike Sissinghurst) off one long main vista. The gardens are of wondrous variety and delight – there are waterfalls, gazebos, pools, topiary, pleached avenues, winding steps, gateways of yew, a stream – but all have one common quality, that they are planted with extraordinary profusion. "What I should like to impress upon the reader is the luxuriance everywhere; a kind of haphazard luxuriance, which of course comes neither by hap nor hazard at all", wrote Miss Sackville-West. Trees, flowering shrubs, water plants, climbers, roses, tender plants, foliage plants, all are there in lavish masses, planted with a botanist's skill and an artist's eye.

Lastly, there are the cottage gardens; and, though the country-house gardens may claim to be "cottagey", they are not true cottage gardens. They are on too large a scale to be totally informal – there is always some group planting of trees, always some massed flowers or shrubs – and they need a gardening staff to work them. The true cottage garden is planted and worked by the owner, with a minimum of staff, is highly personal and informal throughout.

All over England there are old rectories, small manor houses, farms, mills and cottages with small, personal gardens which are opened to the public for one or two days every summer for charity.

The most interesting of all is the garden at East Lambrook Manor, Somerset, created by the late and much mourned Mrs Margery Fish. It is the paragon of cottage gardening. Mrs Fish was above all a plantswoman. She crammed her small garden with a spectacular variety of plants, trying form after form of each species because she thought it dull gardening to duplicate – she grew no less than seven forms of the lesser periwinkle.

Her garden is, therefore, a glorious jumble. Structurally it is a patchwork, with narrow beds and zigzag paths, and in the beds is the ultimate in cottage mixtures, the commonest lilies growing cheek by jowl with the rarest euphorbias. Some consider this garden too quaint, but to me it expresses such a love of flowers that it is pure joy to visit. It is a generous garden, with all the climbing, rambling things (there are wonderful clematis) spilling over the outer walls to give pleasure to passers-by.

There are many cottage gardens not unlike East Lambrook, of which notable features are always shrub roses, clematis, variegated plants, a great variety of ground-cover plants, winter-flowering plants, like hellebores, old-fashioned plants, like columbines and pansies. I confess that, since they are within my range, and I wouldn't want Blenheim even if I were offered it, I love these gardens best.

Finally, there are many gardens which do not fit neatly into any category, but are of interest to the specialist. The Royal Horticultural Society's 150-acre garden at Wisley, Surrey, has something exciting every month of the year, with exceptional wild and alpine sections. The Pleasure Garden at Westonbirt School, Gloucestershire, planted by a great arboriculturist exactly a hundred years ago, has one of the finest collections of trees and shrubs in the world. Highdown, Goring-on-Sea, Sussex, is a true country-house garden, of special interest because it was made in a chalkpit and shows what a wealth of plants can be grown on an alkaline soil. And Mr Roy Elliott's Alpine garden in Birmingham (seen by appointment only) has over four thousand alpine varieties growing in the heart of an industrial city.

Once you start visiting gardens, there is always another you feel compelled to see, and then another, and another. It becomes the most delightful of obsessions.

The "cottage" garden at Sissinghurst   *Edwin Smith*

London

London Postal Districts Middlesex

IVOR BROWN

London is a clay-saucer with a surrounding rim of hills which are promoted by estate agents to offer "most desirable properties on the Northern (or Southern) Heights". There is nothing mountainous to climb, but there are quite steep slopes once favoured by a few Georgians, then more thickly covered by the Victorians in search of an eminence, and now happily populated by families who value the nearby heaths and parks as well as the fresher air. In Hampstead or Highgate one can be housed 400 feet above the sea, and since the old nuisance of smoking chimneys has been drastically reduced the occupants of these ridges can look across the bowl on a clear day to the uplands of Kent and Surrey, to Greenwich Park or Epsom Downs.

Within the saucer rise the new, many-storied and many-windowed concrete piles of the new architecture. On a fine evening they catch the sunlight from the west, which makes these pallid monsters of day-time become surprisingly radiant and even roseate for an hour or so. If there is a clear sky or only a film of cloud one splendid antique, undefeated by the soaring office-blocks, can be seen standing staunchly for the old faith amid the clustered and domineering premises of the new commerce. From the steps of my front door in Hampstead I have the view which, when seen from the modest hummock of Primrose Hill near Regent's Park, moved an otherwise sad and sceptical minor poet John Davidson, to a memorable tribute:

> Dissolving, dimly reappearing,
> Afloat upon ethereal tides
> St Paul's above the city rides.

The German bombers failed to sink it. Still it floats. Below it Davidson felt "the heart of London beating warm". There is still that cardiac and cordial murmur, and still that majestic dome. Despite all its modern nuisances of noise, size and congestion, London has its pleasing prospects. The visitor who goes to a ridgeway suburb to meet friends or to see the local sites and pleasaunces should stop to gaze into and across the bowl.

London can be seen from the top in several places, from Wren's Monument in the City, from the far higher Post Office Tower near the Tottenham Court Road, or from the roof of a sky-scraping office block, most notably at the Millbank Tower on the Westminster riverside. To climb or to be lifted to any of them is useless unless the weather is fine. From the last of these I have looked out on a day which fortunately happened to be cloudless. Below me the devious and serpentine Thames was meandering on its way from Windsor Castle, just visible in the distant west, to the Port of London. It is the old, abiding lifeline, always in service since the Romans waded and then bridged it. A myriad merchants down the centuries throve on its banks, sometimes fouled the water, and sometimes beautified its shores. Viewed from a height the Thames cuts through the urban browns and greys which are pleasantly relieved by the green of many parks. Inevitably one gets the sense of an undisciplined sprawl, since London grew casually, first edging its way in a narrow strip along the ribbon of the river and later pushing backwards to the ridges as a container for the ever-multiplying population. Not even in the centre was it deliberately planned or grandly developed as a capital with broad avenues radiating from an imposing centre where palatial pomp was on display and there was august accommodation for the statesmen and the civil powers.

To enjoy the essence of the town it is necessary to nose one's way into it instead of peeping down from the sky. For that kind of penetration the river is the best of guides. One can traverse it by steam-boat from Hampton Court to Greenwich. One can follow it by car or on foot. That the Thames is "liquid history" is a statement so often quoted as to have become a cliché. But a cliché can be true. The familiar phrase sums up the chronicles of social change. The rich Elizabethans had their riparian mansions with their lawns leading to the water-gates. Royal, seigneurial, and ecclesiastical splendour was there established while the Commoners set their Houses of Parliament by the stream and crowded increasingly along the docks and factories.

It is a compliment to London that it should have been so magnetic, draining the country and the other towns of its talented and ambitious families. Now the attraction of being "with it" by being in it has become so powerful as to create a problem, the excessive overspill of population into South-East England. There are efforts to decant the flood but the eagerness to get in is stronger than the willingness to get out into the New Towns planned as a relief. London is people-jammed and traffic-jammed but the jam has not turned to vinegar and is sweet enough to defeat the designs for dispersion.

Those who wisely do their sight-seeing by or near the water should try to envisage the London of the Elizabethans. Their monarch was indeed a River Queen whose history was as liquid as illustrious. She was born at Greenwich, reigned at Whitehall, and died at Richmond. The Thames was then broader and shallower. The embankments are only a century old. But it was clean, even sweet and silvery to the poets, with salmon leaping among the swans and the stately, sumptuous barges of the great as they travelled about their business and their pleasures from Westminster to the City. That was the comfortable transport since La Straunde, which became the Strand, was then a rough and ill-kept road. On the southern shore of London Bridge is Southwark where there must be the most eminent of ghosts for those who can feel them in the air.

For a leisurely walk there can be few better than a stroll southward over Black-friars Bridge with a left turn past the eighteenth-century almshouses to take the waterside way to the east. Across the river the spires of Wren's City churches, gleaming round Tower Hill, are like stone set to music. The entry to Shakespeare's Bankside may evoke the protest that there is nothing of that now. Yet there is Southwark Cathedral, the old parish-church of the players, with its tombs of poets and playwrights. It contains a Harvard Chapel since the great John of American university fame was christened here in 1607. To this end of London Bridge came the travellers from the Channel, and there were many inns to receive them.

From one of them, the Tabard, Chaucer sent his pilgrims on the road to Canterbury. In another Dickens made Mr Pickwick meet Sam Weller. The novelist stayed as a boy in little-altered Lant Street while his father was imprisoned for debt in the neighbouring Marshalsea gaol. A notable survivor in the High Street is the

J. Allan Cash

The Vale of Health on Hampstead Heath

seventeenth-century George Inn, with its galleried courtyard. The coaches drew
in there and still do, with different traction. Horses will not be seen. London on the
Thames has become London on petrol. But, for me at least, the busy new Southwark is a place where the past unforgettably defies and so enriches the present.
Its Hop Market serves the brewers and the beer-drinkers where the Elizabethan
actors took their wine and the coach-and-four passengers in winter came off the
chilly roof for revival by steaming tots of spirits.

Since it was seldom deliberately planned London can be fairly described as a
"round-the-corner" city. The fine approach frequently misses the fine sight which
is round the corner. The view down Whitehall does not include the splendours of
Westminster. The Strand should have been a broad and notable conduit to the
majesty of St Paul's on Ludgate Hill. It has not happened thus. Dispersal of theatres
is convenient because it lessens the traffic-jam when audiences are coming and
going. But the concealment is excessive in the case of the two great "Royals",
Drury Lane and Covent Garden. They began their varied and intermittently lost
and renewed lives in 1662 and 1732, when entertainment was sought further east
than it is now. So they must be sought in narrow streets where there are market-
lorries instead of buses for passengers. The main road in Chelsea is now valuable
for the turnings off it. Make for the river and there is much of quality and history
to see. And so it is with Fleet Street. The lawyers' riverside Inns are to be found
by deviating into a narrow lane or down a passage. Legal, like political, power has
its corridors.

I thought that I knew the buried treasure of the London lanes and alleys fairly
well but the detailed guidance so well provided in this book has proved my ignor-
ance. There is much in the following pages about some nooks and niches which
deserve discreet penetration. In London the good pedestrian, like the good
motorist, must learn to take his corners.

The desire to live in a once neglected portion of the saucer or, better still, on one
of the rims has produced some odd migrations, especially of the professional

A. F. Kersting

The Nash Terraces on the edge of Regent's Park

classes and the followers of the arts. The high cost of central housing makes for dispersion. Camden Town was little thought of not long ago: it was a low-price, low-life area through which the bus carried me when I was a boy in Hampstead. I knew it only as the home of a famous murderer, Dr Crippen. Now the sad Victorian streets have their gloom dispelled by occupiers with stage, radio, television and gossip-column reputations. Mouldering façades have been brightened by new paint and colourful doorways. The same thing has happened on the slopes of Islington, where the Elizabethans went to shoot wild-fowl and the Georgians drank much more than water in the pleasure-ground of Sadler's Wells. There they took their coaches for the northward roads while Charles Lamb was happy with tongue, pen, and tobacco beside the canal. Then came decline. Now to be an Islingtonian is to be in the fashion. And so it is to live by a canal.

A home by the Thames is naturally prized where it looks over a great sweep of the river with its varied traffic of sail, steam, and racing oarsmen. That is the special attraction of Hammersmith and Chiswick. The vogue is less understandable when the view is of a static and murky "inland water-way". But the taste for such an outlook is strong and growing. In Maida Vale an old basin for barges has become known as "Little Venice", a title more complimentary than exact. It has culture in the air. Robert Browning was a Victorian resident and there are titled folk as well as authors and artists living round the pool. Out of it past Regent's Park and its Zoo, through Camden Town and under and into Islington wanders the old canal, sombre but alluring to those who prefer a liquid to a pavement view. To be on the bank is now to be fashionably in the swim. The promotion of once common-place suburbs has some excellent results. The new money coming in brings the ability to restore and re-decorate. A once grubby terrace begins to display a butterfly gaiety. There is a flutter of new tints, a pride in appearance, and life at a new tempo. There are many drab districts which are being taken over and given a face-lift. The London of tomorrow will be on the move upwards, and sensibly so.

Many strangers to London will bring memories of Charles Dickens whose

J. Allan Cash

Houseboats at Little Venice

reading public is so widespread and so constant. If they expect to find it as dark as he drew it their fears are groundless. He was haunted by the smelly suffocating fogs which were aggravated by the smoke from coal-fires in every house. "Give the people light, give them air" was one of his most urgent pleas. He would have rejoiced in today's multitude of windows and the spectacle of London floodlit. Among the many discomforts of noise and crowding imposed by recent conditions there has been one remarkable and insufficiently praised benefit. The compulsion to use smokeless fuel in many areas has effectively cleared the air and cleaned the surface of the town. The inevitable mists of winter are no longer loaded with soot and turned into the sticky mess which clogged the throat and menaced the lungs. Paint is not immediately smudged as soon as it is laid on. Not long ago it was impossible to see across the saucer from the ridges. Now there is no blanket of fumes over London. One can go about the streets without dreading the immediate smear of dirt on face, hands, and linen which our predecessors had to endure. With the diesel trains pouring in and out of the central railway termini there is an end to the nuisance caused by steam-engines belching thick smoke by day and night. If London strives to be colourful it is no longer frustrated by the winter "smog" and by the soot which even in summer blackened the grass in the gardens. London has washed its face.

What London has lost in civic calm it has gained in colour. In streets which not long ago were dingy one can see bright paint laid on to the previously scruffy doors and window-sills. These frontages are like a button-hole nosegay worn on a shabby coat. In the neighbourhood of the parks the mansions are kept in better trim. The stucco façades which make a sad spectacle if neglected and flaking away are now gleaming, most notably where Portland Place leads on to the Nash Terraces inspired by the Prince Regent. Overlooking the well-kept lawns and flower-beds of the pleasaunce which he ordered they have survived war-time disaster and their maintenance in splendour is a joy to the eye. Inside the parks there are more blossoming trees to make April earn the Shakespearian adjective, proud-pied. The flowering cherry showers its richness on the suburbs when the almond-trees are wilting. Front gardens are given a light golden gaiety with forsythia. Much more than in my boyhood does spring come "bursting out all over". It is the right time for a visit.

The skill of the gardeners, whether working for the Crown in the Royal Parks or for the Greater London Council in its numerous demesnes, deserves the public gratitude. They are not grudged money to spend and they have the craft to use it admirably. From the coming of the crocuses and the daffodils to the pomp of tulip-time and on to the autumn consolation of the chrysanthemums there is replacement and renewal in the flower-beds. "Never a dull moment" is the policy. Those who go in midsummer to the Open Air Theatre in Regent's Park pass the splendid array of roses in Queen Mary's Garden, a superb approach to the Shakespearian flowers of speech. The aeroplanes may sometimes drown the words first heard on Southwark's Bankside and lingering in the minds of men for ever. But many a traveller has been air-borne to London. He has had the advantage of speed before he finds amenity interrupted. He cannot have it both ways.

Britain has few opponents of the monarchy. If a stern Republican is using his freedom of speech to pour scorn on royalty from a dais at Speakers' Corner in Hyde Park he should remember that the Park was a royal gift to the people made by Charles I and that Cromwell wanted to hire it out for private exploitation.

The parklands and public gardens, of which Richmond and Kew are spacious examples, were not originally designed for public recreation. But to that good end these and others have come by gradual stages. Frequently there was royal initiative in their creation. St James's Park began as the site of a King's menagerie. Presented with camels, James I pastured them beside his palace. Now, gay with water-fowl, it is the perfect back-garden of Whitehall. The lawns of Kensington Palace became Kensington Gardens. Regent's Park would not be there unless the Prince had thought of saving its expanse from building and then of building magnificently on its rim. The monarchy has paid some handsome dividends in return for its inheritance of power and privilege. It helped to make London a landscape as well as a city.

Timber is plentiful and keenly guarded. If an elderly and ailing trunk is cut down there is immediate protest. There are vandals who misuse the common property, but there are also devotees who zealously resist any invasion or diminution of this legacy. They want their London to be as rural as may be. They proudly retain the name of Village for the oldest parts of their favourite suburbs. To be considered a Villager in Hampstead or Highgate, Dulwich or Wimbledon, delights the inhabitants.

The Dickensian demand for light and air is variously met. The street-lamps in some areas are criticized as inadequate, since the standards and methods change awkwardly from one district to another. Just before lighting-up time there are, especially in autumn, sunsets of rare beauty: to look west is to find in the sky that delicate texture of pink and grey which adorns the necks of the town's super-abundant pigeons. It is the hour of release for myriads and of plans for the evening's entertainment. The windows of the soaring offices begin to twinkle. Then comes the adroitly contrived floodlighting of the principal buildings, best seen along the river. It is a fascinating panorama with the contrast of the dark water and the brilliance overhead. The parks are London's paint-box by day. The city wears jewellery at night.

NOTE Car parks in London are scattered and often full by mid-morning; parking meters are operative almost everywhere except on Saturday afternoons and Sundays. We advise the motorized sightseer to leave his car on the outskirts of London and use public transport or taxis: the underground is fast and easy for strangers to use; the top of a bus provides the best view of the streets; and cruising taxis can be picked up at most times of the day.

London: Gazetteer

FRANCIS HOWELL

THE CITY, EAST END AND SOUTHWARK

This is where London began, and where visitors to London should also begin, but seldom do. When the Emperor Claudius and his elephants arrived here in A.D. 43 he recognized the military and commercial desirability of the site and 20 years later Tacitus was able to record that the city was already crowded with merchants.

The Romans called it Londinium, turned it into a port, built a bridge to the south bank – it remained the sole London crossing point of the Thames until 1750 – gave it style, opulence and order, and withdrew 367 years later, having suffered in the meantime a notable but soon avenged defeat at the hands of Queen Boadicea. For their future security they encircled the city with a stone wall with watch towers and six gates. This, for a long time, was the extent of London: 330 acres, with the whole of the south side a waterfront.

Between the departure of the Romans and the arrival of the Normans, London had capitulated to Christianity and variously endured or repulsed the Danes. ST PAUL'S CATHEDRAL, which had been built, twice destroyed and rebuilt, became a symbol of resistance and solidarity to the people, who in 1066 voluntarily acknowledged William the Conqueror instead of being defeated by him. Nevertheless, he founded the TOWER OF LONDON when he built the White Tower to keep the populace in their place as much as invaders out of it. He did, however, confirm the rights which the citizens had exercised under Edward the Confessor, which led eventually to the City acquiring the status and privileges of a county. In the Middle Ages the political and financial interdependence of the Crown and the City was established. Trades and crafts flourished, and the guilds which they formed founded such architectural riches as the GUILDHALL and several halls of liveried companies. Since members of the trades tended to congregate, we are left with descriptive street names such as Fish and Bread streets, Garlick Hill and Pudding Lane.

This 600-year consolidating period must have been one of great wealth, possibly of piety, certainly of manifold development, because by 1666 the City's tiny area boasted something over 100 churches, a bridge which outshone the Florentine Ponte Vecchio, and a mass of appalling slums. Then came the Great Fire. The plague had decimated the poorer population the previous year – the rich escaped to Westminster, Knights-bridge, HIGHGATE and other villages – but the fire knew no social barriers. During the four days of the conflagration it consumed 13,200 houses, 84 churches and St Paul's itself.

It is said that within a week Sir Christopher Wren submitted a plan for rebuilding, and John Evelyn and others later, but none was carried out. Wren eventually built 51 churches and spent the rest of his life fighting for "his" St Paul's. He also built the MONUMENT which still stands at the meeting of five streets, not far from London Bridge.

From then on London grew. The City boundaries crept outwards to embrace THE TEMPLE, FLEET STREET, HOLBORN and beyond Aldersgate and Moorgate, while suburbs engulfed the surrounding villages. But the City remains a commercial centre. When 164 of its 460 built-up acres were devastated during the war, it scarcely faltered. St Paul's was hit twice and everything around it was flattened. Once again there was a plan. It could be said that the new buildings have developed in spite of it rather than because of it, but they do, to some eyes, form an imposing background of anonymous planes against which the elegant spires and façades of remaining 17th-, 18th- and early-19th-cent. London are displayed.

While the City was stretching out greedily towards the W. and N., the area to the N. and E., the East End, was also developing. Its prosperity remains dependent on the DOCKS which are in Stepney, Poplar and Canning Town; except for the colourful Sunday street markets, the WHITECHAPEL ART GALLERY and the BETHNAL GREEN MUSEUM, there is little for the tourist. Architectural delights, like a terrace of Georgian houses in south Hackney, can be found only by the diligent walker.

Southwark, or more modernly the South Bank, is a faceless area, although it is nearly as old as the City; but such features as it has are of considerable note. Close to the south side of London Bridge stands SOUTHWARK CATHEDRAL built in the 13th cent.; nearby is the 17th-cent. GEORGE INN, the only galleried inn left in London. Near here, too, is the site of Shakespeare's Globe Theatre, now marked only by a plaque in the wall of a brewery. Further to the W. is the OLD VIC THEATRE, and then to the S. – the river curves right round here – are the FESTIVAL HALL and LAMBETH PALACE, London residence of the Archbishop of Canterbury, in continuous use since

Aerofilms

The City of London. St Paul's Cathedral stands at its heart, now encircled by modern office blocks

the 13th cent. A last landmark is THE OVAL, Surrey's cricket ground. For the rest, this is a district of railway stations, warehouses and rather dingy streets of identical houses, now giving way more and more to skyscraper blocks of flats. Here again are delightful examples of earlier domestic architecture, but, as in the East End, they must be sought out.

ALL HALLOWS BY THE TOWER, *Tower Hill* (16–32), also known as All Hallows Barking, was bombed twice in December 1940 which left some of its walls standing, most of the tower and little else. In the rebuilding more of its history was discovered. In the undercroft a piece of tessellated Roman pavement can be seen *in situ,* ashes of Boadicea's sacked London were found 7 ft below the building, an Anglo-Saxon archway was discovered, and pieces of two Anglo-Saxon crosses which had been used by later builders as hardcore. In the rebuilding of the church by Lord Mottistone concrete was cleverly used to produce galleries and a barrel roof, and the very big, clear east window makes the church exceptionally light, the better to see the interesting things it contains, many of which emphasize its connection with seafaring men. The pulpit, about 1670, comes from the Church of St Swithin, and outside the lovely spire of St Dunstan-in-the-East near BILLINGSGATE – all that survived the bombing of that church – can be seen some 100 yds to the W. All Hallows' own spire is a post-war addition, deliberately placed to fill a skyline gap.

A great deal can be learned about London in All Hallows, not least from its enthusiastic guardians. The register states that John Quincy Adams, 6th U.S. President, was married here, and William Penn was baptized here in 1644.

AMEN COURT (16–10). A very small and utterly delightful 17th-cent. oasis set quietly in the heart of London. Said to have been built by Wren, these flat-faced, dark-red-brick houses have plain iron lamps arched over the doorsteps, and an uncluttered elegance set off by the trees that shade the courtyard. They are residences of the enviable canons of ST PAUL'S. Amen Court is reached from Ave Maria Lane; the STATIONERS' HALL separates it from ST MARTIN LUDGATE. It stands on the line which the Roman wall took towards the river, and a remnant of it forms the base of a modern wall in the court. Another small section is in the basement of offices in Warwick Lane, just N. of Amen Court.

BANK OF ENGLAND, THE, *Threadneedle Street* (16–21), is an island surrounded on all four sides by streets. It stands very solidly indeed upon some three acres, and from the Lothbury side looks faintly oriental. After operating initially in Grocers' Hall, the Bank's first home was built by George Sampson, 1732–4. Only 50 years later Sir John Soane built the great, windowless structure with its clever columns and an interior which has been described as his masterpiece. Nevertheless, in 1921–37 it was rebuilt by Sir Herbert Baker, retaining only Soane's screen wall and adding seven stories above it and three below. Only the entrance hall is open to the public, a stolidly rich, rather complacent ante-room to power, upheld in one sense by 18-ft 6-in. high Belgian granite one-piece columns in pairs, in another by the dignified liveried gate-keepers in pink tails, scarlet waistcoats and top-hats.

The senior gate-keeper, during certain hours of the day and providing the inside temperature is below 70 °F., dons an upswept tricorne hat and red robe.

BARBICAN, THE (16–15). This huge scheme for building on the destruction wrought by the War in the N. of the City area, just W. of Moorgate, was conceived soon after the War and is as yet unfinished. The centre-piece is St Giles, Cripplegate, which has been there for 600 years. It received a direct hit in the very first air raid on the City, further damage by fire later, and was restored in 1960. Now its gravestones have been set in raised paving on its north side, which makes a promenade decorated with old street lamps for the inhabitants of one of the many blocks of flats; nearby will be a lake. Here are gravestones to John Milton, map-maker John Speed, and Frobisher.

All round the Barbican is a raised walkway. Sections of Roman wall found on the site have been imaginatively treated, one stretch being incorporated into St Alphage garden, beside the tiny, partly fenced-in remains of this ancient church. The Museum of London, incorporating the Guildhall Museum and the LONDON MUSEUM, will be established here, as will a London theatre for the use of the Royal Shakespeare Company.

BETHNAL GREEN MUSEUM, *Cambridge Heath Road* (16–2), is part of the VICTORIA AND ALBERT MUSEUM, and is known for its collection of early toys, dolls and dollshouses. There is also a good collection of ceramics and silver, and in the upper galleries a history of costume, with exquisite examples of work of the famous, once local, Spitalfields silk weavers.

BILLINGSGATE MARKET, *Lower Thames Street* (16–30). This market must be visited early in the morning to catch it in action. It was built in 1875 of yellow brick, with Britannia sitting more or less on the roof supported by dolphins standing on their heads. Fish has probably been sold here since Anglo-Saxon times, but now, although the market backs on to the river, the fish arrives by lorry. It is handled by men wearing special hats made of wood and leather. The market unofficially extends up the narrow lanes towards East Cheap – Lovat Lane, St Dunstan's Hill and St Mary At Hill, which goes past the church of that name. It is the fishermen's church, and cobbled lanes around make it seem like a small port. Pudding Lane, where the Great Fire started, and the MONUMENT, which perpetuates its memory, are to the W. Along Lower Thames Street is ST MAGNUS THE MARTYR, another Wren building.

DOCKS, THE (16–37). The London Docks proper, and St Katherine's, which was built by Telford in 1825, are immediately E. of Tower Bridge; hard by the Port of London Authority has its main office near THE TOWER and administers the docks from TOWER BRIDGE to Tilbury. These are grouped into five main systems – on

G. Douglas Bolton

The Docks: the stretch between London Bridge and Tower Bridge is called the Pool of London

the North bank London and St Katherine; India and Millwall; Royal Victoria & Albert and King George V; and TILBURY. On the south side there is just the Surrey Commercial, which handles for the most part timber. Each dock specializes in its own merchandise: spices, wines, quicksilver and dried fruits go to London; Millwall has pneumatic equipment to deal with grain. **St Katherine's Dock** is no longer used for commerce, and there are plans for converting the warehouses into an arts centre. In all, the Port of London handles nearly a third of the country's trade and more than 260,000 passengers a year use Tilbury for their travels.

GEFFRYE MUSEUM, TI E, *Kingsland Road* (16–1). With a bequest from Sir Robert Geffrye, master of the Ironmongers' Company and Lord Mayor of London in 1685, a group of one-story almshouses were built round a leafy courtyard in the country quiet of Shoreditch in 1715. It was then, and is, the centre of the cabinet-making industry. When London had overwhelmed this rural retreat the L.C.C. turned the property into a museum of furniture and domestic equipment arranged in a series of period rooms. Every detail is correct, and behind each window is painted a contemporary period view. Children are encouraged to come to the museum to draw and learn handicrafts, and even act historical scenes in appropriate costume in the rooms. There is a library, and students can get technical help from the staff.

GEORGE INN, *Borough High Street* (16–41), is the last galleried inn left in London; it used to be twice its present size. It is entered through an uninviting archway and overshadowed by a hideous chimney. You can still buy the landlord's "ordinary" and a pint such as Dr Johnson often

enjoyed, and from the gallery it is easier to ignore the inn's surroundings and imagine Shakespeare acting in his own play in the courtyard below. The inn now has a restaurant.

A little further S. down the street is the site of Chaucer's Tabard Inn, which survived as The Talbot until 1876. Across the road in Park Street a tablet on a brewery marks the supposed site of Shakespeare's famous Globe Theatre; at the bottom of Park Street is **Bankside,** a fascinating strip of no-man's-land with splendid views across the river to ST PAUL'S, and on the corner is a historic 17th-cent. inn, The Anchor, again with a restaurant.

GOLDSMITHS' HALL, *Gresham Street* (16–14). Tucked away in narrow Foster Lane which runs between Cheapside and Gresham Street is the imposing façade of the Goldsmiths' palatial hall, built for them by Philip Hardwick in 1835, with six great columns and four armorial shields in bold relief. From the street there is a glimpse of panelled interior opulence; admission will normally be granted on previous application. It contains a collection of plate and some portraits. It is the duty of the Goldsmiths' Company, incorporated in 1327, to assay and stamp silver and gold with the leopard's-head hallmark.

In this area, lying between ST PAUL'S and BANK OF ENGLAND, are to be found the guild halls of the Saddlers – whose guild is said to date back to the Anglo-Saxons – Wax Chandlers, Haberdashers, Coach-makers, Parish Clerks, Pewterers, Cordwainers, Coopers, Mercers, Grocers, Armourers, Brasiers, Brewers, Girdlers and the GUILDHALL itself.

GUILDHALL, *Gresham Street* (16–16). This building, destroyed by fire in 1666 and to some extent by bombs in 1940, remains the oldest lay

J. Allan Cash

Lambeth Palace is the London home of the Archbishop of Canterbury

building in the City and the centre of its civic life. The present façade, scrubbed clean, with four pinnacles and gay coats of arms, leads into a genuine 15th-cent. vaulted porch from which a dignified way leads on to the great hall. This is 15th-cent. but the famous wooden figures Gog and Magog were victims of the war, and have been replaced by new versions carved by David Evans. This hall is the setting for City ceremonial, the Lord Mayor's banquet, the election of the Sheriffs on Midsummer Day, the giving of freedoms and receiving of royalty. It was the setting for the trial of Lady Jane Grey and her husband; of Anne Askew, Protestant and martyr burned in 1546; of Henry Garnet, Jesuit, in 1606; and Henry Howard, Earl of Surrey. The hall contains memorials to national heroes, including Nelson, Wellington, the Younger Pitt, and Churchill by Oscar Newman.

There is an impressively vaulted crypt below, and to the E. are the gallery, displaying its own or loaned pictures, and the library, containing an ever growing collection of reference books dealing with the history of London, and the libraries of the Worshipful Companies of Gardeners and Clockmakers. Extensive restoration of the library and picture gallery was undertaken in 1969–70.

IMPERIAL WAR MUSEUM, THE, *Lambeth Road* (16–46), established 1920, is in the Geraldine Mary Harmsworth Park. It has a pair of huge naval guns in front of the porch. The building once formed part of Bethlehem Hospital

for the insane, better known as Bedlam, and many upstairs windows are still barred. It was severely damaged during the war, and again recently by fire. It is both a record and a memorial, displaying the devices of defence, guerilla and "home front" war, of both world wars and the Korean war. Apart from the large collection of model ships and instruments of war there is a library of war documents, books and photographs available for reference.

LAMBETH PALACE, *South Embankment* (16–47), is the London residence of the Archbishops of Canterbury, and has been for 700 years. It is medieval with Tudor brick and white stone facings, and a castellated gatehouse; the main entrance is by Morton's Tower. Its great hall has a 70-ft-high hammer-beam roof resembling that of WESTMINSTER HALL, and now houses the library which is based on books bequeathed by Archbishop Bancroft in 1610. Among nearly 1,500 manuscripts are some by Caxton, a letter of Francis Bacon, diaries of Gladstone, and Elizabeth I's prayer book. The guard chamber contains a collection of portraits of archbishops by many famous artists. There is a crypt, probably dating from 1200, and a chapel about 20 years younger. Here Wycliffe was tried for the second time in 1378, and the 15th-cent. Kentish ragstone Lollard's Tower was so named on account of having had Wycliffe's followers imprisoned in it. Near the gatehouse is St Mary's, the parish church of Lambeth. The palace garden has fig trees in it said to have been planted by Cardinal Pole. Originally the palace was nearer the water, and the archbishops made their way to WESTMINSTER by private barge; others crossed by the old horse ferry which was surplanted by Lambeth Bridge. Admission is only by previous arrangement and mostly on Saturdays.

LONDON BRIDGE (16–39), which has so long, according to the old song, been "falling down", has now been taken down and packed off to America. The new London Bridge, a beautiful flying design by the city engineer, Harold Knox King, will cost £3¼ million and take three years to complete. It will be 100 ft wide with six traffic lanes and two footways. The previous bridge, by John Rennie, took six years to build, from 1825, and cost £815,000.

No one quite knows when the first London Bridge was built, but it was probably early on in the Roman occupation of Britain. Certainly there was one in the time of Ethelred because it is known he extracted tolls from ships passing it. Thereafter it was frequently destroyed and rebuilt. In 1176 "old London Bridge" was begun, the first stone one, with 19 arches, but it was made into a street when houses and a chapel were added later. It became one of the sights of Europe, but began to sag and eventually the houses were demolished, though the bridge itself lasted until 1825.

LONDON STONE, *Cannon Street* (16–24). It is suggested that this stone was the *milliarium* of Roman London, the centre point of their great network of roads. Jack Cade struck it and proclaimed himself lord of London, according to Shakespeare. In 1188 Henry, son of Eylwin de Londenstane, was connected with it. It was moved from one side of Cannon Street to the other in 1742, and back again in 1798, when it was embedded in the wall of St Swithin's Church. When St Swithin's was bombed out of existence the stone was housed in the wall of the Bank of China, which arose on the site.

MANSION HOUSE, THE, *Mansion House Street* (16–22). The Lord Mayor's residence faces one corner of the Bank of England at the heart of the City, where eight important roads converge, where once a stream ran – the Walbrook – and where the streets bear such evocative names as Poultry, Cornhill, Lombard and Threadneedle. The Mansion House stands four square; its front door is on first-floor level approached by steps at either end of a balcony. It was erected by George Dance the Elder in 1739–53 in Palladian style with an imposing Corinthian portico. Inside – admission by written application to the Lord Mayor's secretary – are a series of sumptuous 18th-cent. state rooms, of which the 90-ft Egyptian hall is regarded as the greatest. Here banquets and balls are held in great pomp. This hall has no connection with Egypt; Dance modelled it on Vitruvius' Egyptian hall, also without Egyptian connections.

MERMAID THEATRE, THE, *Puddle Dock* (16–9). The City and public subscription supplied the money, Sir Bernard Miles and his wife the inspiration. The location was a blitzed warehouse between Blackfriar's Underground station and the river. This unlikely combination has resulted in the Mermaid Theatre, the first for 300 years to be built in the City.

A Statute of 1572 had stigmatized Common Players as "rogues and vagabonds". They could only perform under the protection of the Crown or a nobleman. The puritanical City fathers continued to keep them out but they could legally play in areas known as "liberties". Blackfriars provided one of these. Close to the historic site of the new Mermaid there was a theatre from 1576 until 1653. First it was occupied by the Children's Companies, whose popularity is mentioned in *Hamlet*. Later it was taken over by Shakespeare's company, the King's Men. Shakespeare was a shareholder in this venture, which prospered. Sir Bernard Miles built on traditional ground.

His theatre is a success. It is not decorative, but strictly functional. The stage has no proscenium or orchestra pit, but a 20-ft revolve and a splendid battery of floodlights. The sloping auditorium guarantees uninterrupted vision for its 498 seats. With its unadorned walls it is the prototype for many new theatres being built or modified throughout the country. There is also an 80-seat restaurant overlooking the Thames.

MONUMENT, THE, *Fish Street Hill* (16–27). This fluted Doric column of Portland stone was designed by Wren to commemorate the Great Fire of London. Its 202 ft are alleged to represent the distance from its site to the baker's shop in Pudding Lane where the fire originated. A spiral staircase of 311 steps leads to a caged-in public gallery, from which it was possible to get a splendid view of the City, but modern buildings have lessened its impact. There is an amusing view of the Monument down King William Street from beside the Bank, where the people at the top look curiously large.

OLD BAILEY, THE, *Newgate* (16–7). Officially the Central Criminal Court, it stands on the site of the old Newgate Prison, which was demolished in 1903. The 12-ft-high bronze figure of Justice by F. W. Pomeroy is a London landmark, standing on the roof with its 8-ft arm-span; figures over the entrance represent Truth, the Recording Angel and Patience. The exterior of the building is rugged Cornish granite and Portland stone; inside it is Edwardian baroque. There is often a long queue of spectators hoping to get into court. When executions were carried out in front of the prison, space was allowed for spectators, which is why Old Bailey, meaning the street of that name, is wider opposite the court.

OLD VIC THEATRE, THE, *Waterloo Road* (16–44). Many theatre-loving visitors to London will wish to see a performance here since it is, and probably till 1973 will remain, the headquarters of the excellent National Theatre Company headed by Sir Laurence Olivier. Originally called Royal Coburg Theatre because a prince and princess headed the subscription list, it was opened in 1818 with spectacular plays and ballets. It failed to draw a fashionable public because the district was then thought rough and a journey to it dangerous. Renamed the Victoria, it offered crude melodrama. Later on it became a music-hall with a bad reputation. In 1880 it was taken over for serious purposes by Miss Emma Cons and named the Royal Victoria Hall and Coffee Tavern. Music and lectures replaced comic songs and alcohol. Miss Lilian Baylis, niece of Emma Cons, expanded its work and in 1914 introduced Shakespeare's plays for which she found young stars in the making. John Gielgud was one of them. Badly bombed in the Second World War it was restored and offered the fine and now widely inclusive repertory, which has continued with increasing renown. A completely new National Theatre is planned for a site just E. of Waterloo Bridge on the South Bank.

OVAL, THE, *Kennington Oval* (16–48), is the Surrey County Cricket Club ground, and the final Test match every season is played there. It was opened in 1846. Kennington was a royal manor with a palace, given by Edward III to the Black Prince.

PATERNOSTER SQUARE (16–12) is part of the modern complex about ST PAUL'S which has given rise to such angry controversy. The public can use the viewing gallery on the seventh floor of Juxon House, level with the top gallery of St Paul's and with Justice on top of the OLD BAILEY; behind Wren's delicate lead spire of ST MARTIN is ST BRIDES, Fleet Street.

These large, glass-faced buildings form an irregular semi-circle about the cathedral, with steps leading up to Paternoster Square and thence to Cathedral Place, two flagged courts decorated with flowers, young trees, seats, all dominated by the bulk of Sudbury House, on stilts. The cathedral is beautifully framed at the top of the steps. The booksellers (breviaries and rosaries) and publishers, last remnants of Paternoster Row, devastated by fire in 1940, have now completely disappeared from this site.

ROYAL EXCHANGE, THE, *Cornhill* (16–26), stands in line with, but a few paces behind, the BANK OF ENGLAND. Their entrances are at right angles. The first Exchange, built at the behest of Sir Thomas Gresham, was burned down in 1666; likewise the second in 1838. The present building by Sir William Tite has a range of columns over which a tympanum depicts a series of city dignitaries, merchants of all races and Commerce. There is also a campanile with a grasshopper as vane and a carillon.

Inside is a large, glass-covered courtyard with wall arcades and a floor of Turkish honestone, in which the great merchants used to operate. Today the hard wooden benches beneath the

huge historical pictures, are occupied by recumbent figures and middle-aged couples, and the whole place echoes with whispers. The entrance to this arena is by the centre door. The flanking doors lead to insurance offices. In the entrance hall on the right is an 18th-cent., six-man, hand-operated fire engine, with its leather hose. There is also one of the oval wall plaques issued by the early insurance companies to make clear which houses were insured and therefore worth saving.

ROYAL FESTIVAL HALL, *South Bank* (16–42). This is one of only two buildings surviving from the 1951 Festival of Britain, the other being the National Film Theatre, which is actually beneath WATERLOO BRIDGE, but still a part of this South Bank cultural complex. The Festival Hall, designed by Robert Matthew and J. L. Martin, was completed in 1964–5 with an auditorium seating 3,000, claimed by some musicians to be acoustically the best in the world. It has two restaurants; linked to it are the Queen Elizabeth Hall, the Purcell Room and the Hayward Art Gallery, the whole interplay of grey planes supported on mushroom columns. There is an embankment walk in front of the group and a pier with summer steamer services to BATTERSEA PARK.

ROYAL MINT, *Tower Hill* (16–34). To visit this money factory it is necessary to write in for permission to the Deputy Master at least six weeks in advance – longer in summer. Most of the processes of coin-making are shown to the visitor. The Mint makes not only our coin of the realm, but also that of several other countries, besides medals and the state seals. There is a museum. The building was designed by Sir Robert Smirke in 1810, enlarged later, and bomb-damaged in 1941. From 1699 to 1727 the office of Master of the Mint was held by Sir Isaac Newton. When, in 1870, this office was absorbed by the Chancellor of the Exchequer, the Deputy Master became responsible for the actual running of the Mint.

In 1972 the Mint will move from London to amalgamate with its subsidiary in Wales.

ST BARTHOLOMEW-THE-GREAT, *Smithfield* (16–6), is the City's oldest church. The priory was founded in 1123 by Henry I's courtier, Rahere, who was ordered to do so in a vision, and became its first prior. The Order's concern was mostly for the poor and sick, which led to the founding of the adjacent hospital, best known as Barts.

This church has been greatly altered and misused; although shortened it is still big enough to be a cathedral; but it is dark and the initial impression is gloomy. The entrance from west Smithfield is through a 13th-cent. gate, to which the church once extended, with an Elizabethan half-timbered gatehouse above, and then across a small churchyard. Inside are huge Norman columns and arches, repeated on a smaller scale in the gallery. On the south side is an oriel window,

---

Woburn Walk this quiet row of houses preserves the atmosphere of the 18th cent. Picturepoint

spectacular valleys, Tavy Cleave (*see* Dartmoor). About 3½ m. NW. of Tavistock, **Collacombe Manor** is a fine Elizabethan house with exceptional transomed window, open by appointment.

At **Gunnislake**, 3¼ m. W., a medieval bridge spans the Tamar on the boundary between Devon and Cornwall.

TAWSTOCK, *Devon* (3–SS5529). In the 19th cent. it was said that here at one glance could be seen the most valuable manor, the best mansion, the finest church, and the richest rectory in the county. Now the mansion (used as a school), built in 1787 to replace one that was burnt, looks rather unkempt. For some 500 years from the 15th cent. either the Bouchier family (Earls of Bath) or the related Wreys lived here and there are many huge monuments to them in the church, which Nikolaus Pevsner found "one of the most architecturally interesting" in North Devon. Probably the biggest of these monuments is to the 5th Earl of Bath (d. 1680): four marble dogs crouching on one marble tomb carrying another on their shoulders. But it is closely rivalled by the 3rd Earl's: he and his wife recumbent with kneeling children in attendance, all red, black and blue. Perhaps the most attractive is the 14th-cent. wooden effigy of a woman in a recess in the north wall. Some of the inscriptions are quite witty.

TEIGNMOUTH and SHALDON, *Devon* (3–SX9473). Of South Devon's beautiful estuaries, the Teign is the most easily appreciated from the road, the least secluded by trees, and the only one, apart from the Tamar, crossed by a road bridge. Nor is it devious with creeks like the others, but broad and straightforward, brimming with boats when the tide is in, displaying mollusc-encrusted mud-banks at low tide. It looks particularly good from the bridge, and never better than from the club-house of the admirable Teignmouth golf course on the hill-top to the N., from near which the view is also splendid to the DARTMOOR peaks of Hound Tor and Haytor, especially in the evening. About 3 m. W. of Shaldon, **Coombe Cellars** is an attractive place with an inn formerly used by smugglers.

The two towns are very different: Shaldon, in its area E. from the end of the bridge, very daintily pretty with narrow streets of well-cared for late Georgian and Regency cottages; Teignmouth much bigger and busier, but less attractive. The nicest part of the latter is certainly The Den, which is on the sea-front. The Church of St James (dating from 1820 except for its tower) is curious. With Exmouth, Teignmouth is said to be Devon's oldest resort, popular since the mid-18th cent. It was a port that Frenchmen considered worth ravaging in 1340. In 1821 it shipped the Dartmoor granite for LONDON BRIDGE and nowadays the ball-clay of world-renowned quality found near **Kingsteignton** (4½ m. W.). It also builds good boats. E. of Shaldon, the Ness Headland is popular, council developed, with a "smugglers" tunnel leading to a beach. A little S. Labrador, of smuggling fame, is a pleasant cove.

THORVERTON, *Devon* (3–SS9202). Far from the holiday crowds yet within easy range of EXETER and in hilly and sheltered red-soil country, Thorverton is a genteel but extremely attractive large village with colonnaded butcher's shop (18th-cent.), much smart cob and thatch, the bridge over its stream draped with flowers in summer. It is also interesting for having an unusually well-recorded history, published by the local branch of the British Legion.

About 6 m. E., **Bradninch** is an example of an ancient and once important town, well sited on an orchard hillside, which never found adequate replacement for its medieval woollen industry.

Brampford Speke, 2½ m. S., was considered by a 1891 traveller "the most perfect [village] I have ever seen". He may have slightly overrated it, but it is still pretty.

TINTAGEL, *Cornwall* (2–SX0588). An undistinguished village usually full of tourists, but the ruin-strewn headland is wonderfully romantic and legend connects the site with King Arthur. The peninsula known as "the Island" is the best place from which to see the great black slate caverns on the north side of Tintagel Cove, the stream that from the vale forms a waterfall as it drops to the cove, and the cliffs with great slate peaks rising from them.

A monastery was founded on this peninsula in *c.* A.D. 500 and abandoned by 1086. It must have been in its setting a sort of Celtic Mount Athos. A Norman castle was built here in *c.* 1145 by Reginald, Earl of Cornwall, bastard son of Henry I. The ruins can be seen.

A Land Rover bus service runs from the café above the cove back to the village.

Beside one of the car parks is a museum of coins. The crinkly roofed old building on the south-west side of the village street, known as the Old Post Office, should be visited. Built in the 14th cent. as a minor manor house, it is one of the few fairly humble ancient residences open to the public. The National Trust preserves it. King Arthur's Hall on the other side of the street is the headquarters of the Fellowship of the Round Table.

Tintagel church, on the headland to the SW., is basically very old, most of its shell being Norman, parts even Anglo-Saxon. Inside it has several interesting things, including a curious five-legged Norman font.

Bossiney, ½ m. NE. of Tintagel village, has a good bathing beach. Sir Francis Drake was, in his later years, one of its two M.P.s.

There are beautiful walks in the richly wooded Rocky Valley about ¼ m. further NE., at right angles to the road to BOSCASTLE: either up it about 1 m. to St Nectan's (or St Knighton's) Kieve, a 40-ft waterfall, or down it to the sea. The "kieve" is the rock basin into which the water falls, and St Nectan, a Celtic hermit saint, is said to have had an oratory beside it.

At **Slaughter Bridge**, about 5 m. inland and 1 m. N. of Camelford, was fought in 823 a decisive battle between Celts and Anglo-Saxons and also a legendary combat between Arthur and Mordred.

Bedruthan Steps: a striking rock formation on the Cornish coast   *Noel Habgood*

TIVERTON, *Devon* (3–SS9512), is a prosperous industrial and agricultural town on the River Exe and its tributary, the Lowman, with a livestock market on Tuesdays. One of the first Anglo-Saxon settlements after their 7th-cent. conquest of the South-West, it was, during the heyday of the Devonian cloth industry in the 17th and 18th cents., the county's principal industrial centre, famous for its kersey. And then, just as the cloth industry was dying in the early 19th cent., John Heathcoat, a lace manufacturer, came from Leicestershire, where Luddites had smashed his machines, to try his luck and was rewarded. Today the Heathcoat organization is the town's dynamo, its products ranging from artificial fibres to agricultural machinery, embracing iron foundries and sawmills, employing about 2,000 people. Its main factory is on the west bank of the Exe just N. of the bridge. Viscount Amory, the former Chancellor of the Exchequer, is a member of the Heathcoat family, and was the local M.P. from 1945 to 1960. Lord Palmerston was the town's M.P. from 1835 to 1865.

Architecturally a fairly dignified medley of styles and materials, it has some good buildings bequeathed by its rich wool merchants, notably a big church, St Peter's, the old buildings of Blundells School and three sets of almshouses. The outstanding features of St Peter's Church, at the northern end of the town, are its sculptured south porch and chapel and its organ. It is said that on the latter, claimed to be one of the finest in England, Mendelssohn's "Midsummer Night's Dream" march was first played for a wedding (1847). Flanking the sanctuary are fine tombs of the merchants Waldron and Slee who were responsible for two of the sets of almshouses, in Wellbrook Street (E. of the Exe) and St Peter's Street respectively. The third set, in Gold Street, was endowed by another merchant, John Greenway, who also paid for the church's south porch and chapel. The Greenway and Waldron almshouses are both Tudor and have attractive chapels attached. Opposite the Slee ones (1610) is the pretty dark-red stone Chilcott School (1611). Gold Street leads from the town centre to the River Lowman, and just over this is "Old Blundell's" (1604). The new buildings of this famous school, whose pupils have included R. D. Blackmore, author of *Lorna Doone*, and Frederick Temple, Archbishop of Canterbury from 1896 to 1902, are beside the A373 on the eastern outskirts. Beside St Peter's are the remains of a 14th-cent. castle now incorporated in a private house but recognizable from the road.

A great fire in 1731 resulted in some good Georgian building in the town centre, and St George's – next to the fantastic, Victorian-Baroque Town Hall – is possibly the best Georgian church in Devon. St Andrew Street beside it leads to the museum in an old school which has a particularly good section on farm implements.

At the south-east edge of the town begins the Grand Western Canal, built 1811–14, 11 m. long, intended as a branch of the canal linking the Bristol and English channels which was, however, never built. Its tow-path is pleasant for walking.

The gardens of Knightshayes Court (1869), 2 m. N., the home of the Heathcoat Amorys, are sometimes open to the public.

Bickleigh, 4 m. S. on the main road to EXETER, is a much photographed riverside village, with thatched cottages by a five-arched bridge. Nearby stands Bickleigh Castle, for generations the home of the Carews, with a Norman chapel and an impressive gatehouse.

TOPSHAM; *Devon* (3–SX9788). From Roman times to the 19th cent. Topsham was EXETER's port. From 1282, when the spiteful Countess built her weir (*see* Exeter), till the Exeter ship canal was opened in 1567, it boomed. At other times some trade by-passed it. Although now part of Exeter, it has never become a suburb, always keeping its own character and life, in the past building ships, sending more ships than any other port to catch cod off Newfoundland, catching herring locally and salmon in the estuary. Its ports, like so many, died because it was too shallow for big steamships, but the remnants can be seen at the waterfront: derelict warehouses and shipyards; rotting hulls in the mud. The Strand is extraordinarily attractive with it row of "Dutch" houses built *c.* 1700–25 by merchants who sold cloth to Holland. It ends at a small slipway and a place where local children sail model yachts. Parking is generally difficult and there is no real tourist commercialization. There are, however, many pubs worth inspecting and, at No. 25 The Strand, a small museum.

Some 1½ m. NE., on what was then heath round **Clyst St Mary,** the 1549 Prayer Book rebels (*see* SAMPFORD COURTENAY) suffered their decisive defeat at the hands of Lord Russell, principal recipient of dissolved monastic lands in the West Country.

TORBRYAN, *Devon* (3–SX8266), has one of Devon's best village churches, *c.* 1440, spared both the Puritans and 19th-cent. restoration. It is beautifully light and simple, with box pews, a coloured screen with panel paintings and a coloured pulpit, very finely carved altar and fan-vaulted porch, and fragments (though these are less special) of medieval glass. It has an unusual gaunt grey tower. Apparently the vicar during the Civil War hid its treasures and white-washed the screen.

The tiny village is situated in a pastoral bowl sheltered by tree-bristled limestone tors from which, with the Norman de Bryan who owned the manor, it takes its name. The Church House (*c.* 1500) is now an attractive pub. Nearby (ask directions locally) are caves where the bones of prehistoric animals have been found.

TORQUAY, *Devon* (3–SX9164). In 1790 it was a fishing village "discovered" only by a select few. During the Napoleonic Wars it became the home of wives of officers from the warships anchored for long periods in Torbay. In 1815 Napoleon, a prisoner waiting to hear his fate, gazed at the site from the deck of the *Bellerophon* and pronounced it "*beau*". By 1850 it was calling itself "the Queen of Watering Places". Napoleon III came, as did Russian Royalty, and its fame gained a further boost from the discovery in Kent's Cavern of human bones with those of Ice Age beasts, proving that man had existed far earlier than had hitherto been thought. It grew fast – from a population of about 6,000 in 1840 to 54,000 in 1969 – and it is today the most glamorous, grandly sited and well planned of West Country resorts.

It has some ambitious modern buildings, if mainly blocks of flats, mingled with the great trees and sub-tropical shrubs to the SE. of the harbour on what is possibly England's most opulent headland. A drive round this – Marine Drive – is a good first move in order to taste the ethos and for the views over Thatcher Rock, with its clouds of sea-birds, and over Tor Bay to Berry Head (*see* BRIXHAM) and over **Babbacombe Bay** to the red cliffs of DAWLISH. Kent's Cavern, now a floodlit extravaganza of stalagmites and stalactites, with a few bones still to be seen, is at the east end of this drive close to Anstey's Cove, which is pretty when not too crowded. At the west end is the splendid cream façade of Hesketh Crescent (*c.* 1846), now the Osborne Hotel. Above it, Lincombe Drive is also worth following; then comes the harbour bright with boats on which – rather than on the long beach W. of it – the town converges. The sea-front continues excellent, past hillside gardens floodlit in many colours at night and the Princess Theatre (1961), to the now public grounds of the buildings collectively called Torre Abbey. These are the town's oldest buildings of consequence: a mainly 18th-cent. house containing the Corporation Art Gallery and Museum and, periodically, contemporary art exhibitions; a gatehouse (*c.* 1320); and a well-preserved tithe barn from the abbey founded for Premonstratensians in 1196. It is known as the Spanish Barn because prisoners from the Armada were locked up in it. Of the churches, the most notable is St John's (1861–71) by G. E. Street with Burne-Jones windows and murals. It is in Montpelier Terrace, off Union Street behind the harbour, and a little E. of it is the Natural History Museum specializing in finds from Kent's Cavern. The aquarium above the harbour's south pier has reptiles and tropical, as well as local, fish. In the suburb of Babbacombe, 1½ m. N. of the harbour, there is a model village, beautifully made and maintained; it even has wedding bells in its churches. Nearby is a cliff railway to Oddicombe beach which is also fun.

Paignton, about 3 m. SW., also has some splendid features. Oldway Mansion, the entrance to which is beside the A379, is the most sumptuous house in Devon; built *c.* 1874, with Versailles in mind, by Isaac Merritt Singer, American founder of the sewing-machine company; altered 1904–7, when the south colonnade was added by his son, Paris, among whose long-term guests was Isadora Duncan. It is now the Civic Centre, open at most times. The Zoo, off the A385 TOTNES road, is an outstanding one, said to have the largest collection of animals in England outside London, spread over 75 acres with peacocks, lake islands of gibbons, and a children's miniature railway through the "jungle". Kirkham House in Kirkham Street (about ⅓ m. NW. of Oldway) is a medieval house restored by the Ministry of Public Building and Works to show what life was like in the 16th cent. The red-sandstone St John's Church (about 200 yds W.) is mainly 15th-cent. and has a distinguished south transept chapel built by the Kirkham family with lavishly sculptured stone screen tombs, damaged by Puritans but still fine, and an excellent ceiling. The Festival Hall on the sea-front was built in 1967. The harbour is picturesque and there is an aquarium by it. Before it became a resort, Paignton was famed for its cabbages and cider.

From the Torquay sea-front you can ride 2 m. to **Cockington** by landau. It is a thatched village popular with tourists, with a pub (1934) by Sir Edward Lutyens. The grounds of Cockington Court, with a perfect village cricket square, are nice to wander through to see the pretty little 14th- and 15th-cent. church. The Court itself is basically Elizabethan with a 17th-cent. front. It was formerly the home of the Carys, then of the Mallocks, two of the three families (the Palks were the third) who guided Torquay's development.

About 1¾ m. W. of Cockington, near Marldon, is **Compton Castle**, the best surviving example of a medieval fortified manor house in Devon, home in the 16th cent. of Sir Humphrey Gilbert, the explorer. It dates from the 14th, 15th and 16th cents., with a restored great hall. It is all in excellent condition, cared for by the National Trust.

TOTNES, *Devon* (3–SX8060), has terrible suburbs even for South Devon which has, by and large, the dreariest in South-West England. But steep up its middle runs an attractive narrow old main street, which is spanned by a room marking its medieval East Gate and with one of Devon's finest churches. Moreover, well situated at the highest navigable point on the Dart, it is the starting point for steamer trips down that stretch of river whose beauty is almost completely denied the car-bound.

Ancient legend claimed that the town was founded by one Brutus, grandson of the Trojan Aeneas. More certainly it was an Anglo-Saxon town with a mint, and in the 15th and 16th cents., with a cloth industry and a port, was second in the county only to EXETER in merchant affluence. Slow, however, to respond to the fashion for the Flemish-originated "new draperies", it thereafter declined rapidly, till, in the 19th cent. retired *bourgeoisie* began to appreciate the charms of its hinterland. Manifestly recovered today it is a centre for rich farming (livestock market Tuesdays) and retirement country with some of the smartest antique shops and boutiques in Devon, and quite a colony of neo-craftsmen (potters, silversmiths, etc.). Its industries include bacon-curing, small-boat buildings, dairying and sweet-making, and its port still does some business.

Its great red church was built *c*. 1400–68, a great many people taking a hand, the local bishop having promised indulgence to all who helped. Its outstanding feature is a superb stone screen (1460), rivalled in the West County only by EXETER Cathedral's, but much else is splendid, notably its ceilings, pulpit, beautifully carved Corporation pew-fronts (16th-cent.) and monument to Christopher Blackhall (d. 1633). Immediately N. of the church, the 16th-cent. Guildhall has a court-room of 1553, council chambers of 1624 and various museum pieces. It is open when not in use. It stands on the site of the priory. Below the building spanning the High Street is an Elizabethan merchant's house which is now the museum.

At the top of the street is the arcaded Butterwalk, not comparable with DARTMOUTH'S but pleasant; and near it, in contrast, is the new Civic Hall, outside which there is a market on Fridays and in which, periodically, the local craftsmen exhibit. Some of the latter can be watched in their workshops (ask locally). About 50 yds N. of the Butterwalk are the ruins of a 12th-cent. castle, architecturally unexciting but good for views, and close to its entrance is the arch of the town's former North Gate and some pretty, well-restored cottages. A tree-shaded island just below the fine three-arched bridge (1826) over the river is a nice place to watch boats go by. And from the station a privately owned train carries passengers up the valley to Buckfastleigh (*see* ASHBURTON).

About 2 m. SW. of Totnes, **Hasberton** church has a finely carved rood-screen and stone pulpit.

TREVAUNANCE COVE, Cornwall (2–SW 7251), is one of the prettiest coves on the Cornish north coast. It has a safe (comparatively) beach, good for surfing. Like a fortress guarding a pass, a ruined tin-mining engine-house stands above the wooded combe by which you approach, and mineral ore stains its cliffs reddish brown. The area produced some of the best-quality Cornish tin and in 1794 a pier was built to make the cove a port. But the pier was washed away.

The buildings in the cove are modern and ugly, but fortunately few. There is a seal sanctuary, where sick or orphaned seals swim in a pool and sunbathe St Agnes Head, about 1 m. W., is a grand place to walk to. The off-shore rock islands are called the Man and his Man.

For hundreds of years till late in the 19th cent. the little town of **St Agnes** thrived on mining. Now it is a pleasant, unsophisticated place with cottages on steep slopes.

TRURO, Cornwall (2–SW8244). The county's cathedral city and in all but name its capital. On one of the many arms of the Fal estuary, it was in the Middle Ages an important port for the export of mineral ore, long before FALMOUTH was of any importance, and, from the early 13th cent. until 1752, a stannary town (*see* HELSTON). It is still a port but minor, mainly a market town and

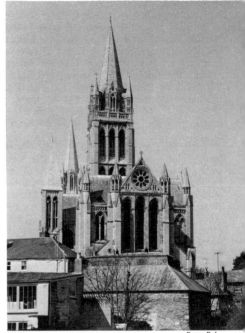

Peter Baker

Truro Cathedral

administrative centre with some light industry. In the 18th cent. it became fashionable with rich merchants who found Falmouth, though their place of business, a less wholesome residence, and, at about the same time, it was a hub of county society. As a result, it has some of the best Georgian terraces W. of BATH. From *c*. 1859 it became an important rail junction. In 1890 its cathedral was begun and in 1912 came the County Council. During the Civil War it stood strongly for the King; otherwise its history seems to have contained little public drama.

The main things to see are the cathedral, the museum, Lemon Street and Walsingham Place. The cathedral, incorporating the old Church of St Mary, was finished in 1910. Its architect was J. L. Pearson; the style he chose Early English. Though without the spacious precinct given to most provincial English cathedrals, it dominates the city, its spire 250 ft high. It is best entered via the south rather than the west door, because from the west the yellow stonework of its nave may seem dull; it is much more impressive looking back from the chancel entrance, and from there, too, the carved Bath stone reredos makes a splendid first impact. The attractive baptistry should not be missed. On the wall of the north choir aisle a terracotta relief of Christ, Romans and crowd on the way to Calvary, presented as a thanksgiving for two sons returned safe from the Boer War, is conventional yet fascinating. Close to it is a hefty restored Jacobean monument. Full architectural details are given in a leaflet available in the building. The chapter house extending into the small lawn to the N. was completed in 1967 and won a Civic Trust award.

Near the cathedral's west door, the old theatre and assembly rooms, which was a favoured rendezvous for 18th- and 19th-cent. Truro society, has a most excellent Georgian façade (1772). The museum, in River Street, is Cornwall's best. It contains a number of old masters, paintings and drawings and is notable particularly for its examples of Cornish minerals, but good on Cornish history, too, and all excellently laid out, diagrammed and captioned. Lemon Street, laid out *c.* 1795 and still mainly of that period, curves southwards from the city centre. Walsingham Place, about 20 years later, is an exquisite crescent, tucked away off Victoria Place, SW. of the cathedral. Strangeways Terrace, off Lemon Street, is fairly good Regency and from it you get one of the best views of the cathedral. The Victorian City Hall in Boscawen Street is worth a look: grand, dark-grey granite. About 50 yds N. in St Nicholas Street over a shoe-filled window is a remarkable florid Victorian facade. One of the city's most famed buildings, the former Red Lion Inn, which stood almost opposite the City Hall, had to be demolished after being lashed beyond repair by a lorry in 1967. In the 18th cent. it was the home of the parents of Samuel Foote, the actor. Near the top of Lemon Street is a monument to two other men of the city, Richard and John Lander, explorers of the River Niger 1825–30.

At Lake's Pottery in Chapel Street, one of Cornwall's oldest and most famous, visitors can see pots being made.

The launch-trip down the river to Falmouth is highly recommended, though the double journey takes the best part of a day.

The National-Trust-owned gardens of **Trelissick**, 4 m. S., contain many shrubs that cannot be grown in England outside South Cornwall. The house (not open to the public) has an elegant, porticoed façade of the 1820s.

At **Come-to-Good**, a little E. of Devoran, 4½ m. SW. of Truro, is one of the oldest Quaker meeting houses in England, *c.* 1710.

One m. SW. of Devoran, just off the A39, **Tullimaar House**, home of Princess Marthe Bibesco, contains a remarkable collection of Napoleonic relics, including a plaster head of him by David D'Angers and the cockade he wore at the Battle of Austerlitz. It is open to the public most summer afternoons.

VERYAN, *Cornwall* (2–SW9240). Veryan is made unique by five old round houses each with a cross on top, two at each end of the village, one in the centre.

The village marks the entrance to **Roseland**. The name seems appropriate to the soft, lush landscape, but in fact derives from the Cornish word *ros* meaning hill, spur or heath. A strange avenue of twisted elms leads into the village of **St Anthony-in-Roseland**. Behind a lawn and sheltered sandy cove is a Victorian mansion turned hotel incorporating in its kitchen part of the refectory of a monastery formerly on the site. And hidden behind and adjoining it (key from the hotel) is the Church of St Anthony, mainly 13th-cent. with a possibly Norman south doorway, heavily but pleasantly restored in *c.* 1850, unusual in having a central belfry.

The peninsula's tip is surrounded by pretty bays and woods and is mostly National Trust land. St Anthony Head is good for views, and the lighthouse below it can sometimes be visited.

WADEBRIDGE, *Cornwall* (2–SW9972), has one of the finest medieval bridges in Britain. It dates from *c.* 1485. The money to build it was raised by Thomas Lovibond, vicar of Egloshayle (½ m. E.), who considered the ferry too dangerous. It is said that packs of wool were used to make a firm base for the piers on the deeply-sanded river bed. Now just over 100 yds long, it has been widened twice and reduced from 17 to 14 arches, but most of the east side is original. A little riverside park just N. of its east end is an excellent place from which to look at it.

The Wadebridge–Bodmin railway was the first opened in Cornwall (1834) and in the 1960s was one of the first to be closed.

The Iron Age hill-camp of Kelly Rounds or Castle Killibury, 2 m. NE. then ½ m. down a track from a crossroads, has been suggested as a possible site for a fort of King Arthur: all you can see, however, is a couple of banks and ditches.

Two m. N., between Chapel Amble and Trewornan Bridge on an arm of the Camel Estuary, is the **Walmsley Bird Sanctuary** noted for geese and waders.

WATCHET, *Somerset* (3–ST0743), is a busy little commercial port with an attractive harbour. Wood pulp, timber, fertilizers, potatoes and tinned fruit are among its imports, paper its main export. Paper-making is its main industry, a local mill employing some 600 people. A port since Anglo-Saxon times and much raided by Vikings, it was made prosperous in the 19th cent. by iron mines in the Brendon Hills to the S. The closure of the mines and the wrecking of its harbour by a great storm in 1900 brought decline till the paper industry came. Coleridge is said to have thought of it as the port of departure for his Ancient Mariner. It has little architectural merit, yet is not unattractive. Its church, on the hill behind, contains good 16th- and 17th-cent. brasses.

Blue Anchor, 2½ m. W., has a good beach and, but for its caravan site, would be pretty, with various coloured cliffs and long views (painted by Turner) to MINEHEAD's north hill.

WEARE GIFFARD HALL, *Devon* (3–SS 4526). Built *c.* 1462 by the Fortescues (*see* SWIMBRIDGE) it contains a hammer-beam roof without rival in Devon, and is altogether one of the county's most fascinating houses, with whole rooms of beautiful panelling. In 1967 it was in sad repair when bought by two enterprising ladies who restored it at their own expense. It is now a private hotel. There is a fine panoramic view of the house and the church next door from the main BIDEFORD–Torrington road. The village is famous for its strawberry teas.

Beside the church at **Frithelstock**, about 2 m. SW., are the ruins of an Augustinian priory which was founded in 1220, dissolved in 1536. The west wall remains intact, though some of the masonry has been renewed in order to preserve it.

WELLOW, *Somerset* (4–ST7358). This attractive village, 6 m. from BATH, looks as if it should be in the Cotswolds. Its church (mainly *c.* 1372) is beautifully light, high and uncluttered, with fine undarkened carved-timber roofs, flagstone floor and some good bench-ends. Its original patron was Sir Thomas Hungerford, first Speaker of the House of Commons. The gabled 17th-cent. farmhouse opposite the school was formerly the Hungerford manor (*see also* FARLEIGH HUNGERFORD). Remains of a Roman villa were found near the village but there is now virtually nothing to see. There is a theory, encouraged by the church's dedication to St Julian, that Romans may have been converted to Christianity here. St Julian's Well, in the valley a little E. of the church, has a ghost story attached to it.

About 2 m. SW., Stoney Littleton Long Barrow is a prehistoric stone burial chamber. You can go inside. Apply at Long Barrow Farm for key and candle.

About 2½ m. E., and about ¾ m. NW. of Hinton Charterhouse village, are the ruins of the Carthusian **Hinton Priory**, founded in 1232. A three-story gabled building with vaulted rooms and stone staircase survives; also the refectory. They are privately owned and sometimes open.

WELLS, *Somerset* (3–ST5445), is a cathedral city and for centuries its contribution to history was purely architectural and ecclesiastical, national drama impinging on it only rarely, as when Monmouth's followers stabled their horses in the cathedral. In the 13th cent. its population was about 4,000, and has less than doubled since. Today it is important for its cheese and has other light industries. But the town still seems to hang humbly about the gates of what is the largest and best preserved medieval ecclesiastical precinct in the county. Taken as a whole the cathedral itself is one of the finest buildings (as well as the oldest of anything like its size) in Somerset. The best road approaches are from the E. and N.; the view of it from round **Dulcote**, 1 m. SE., probably the finest of all. The city's streets are one-way, and to save driving in circles it is wise to make at once for a car park: the nearest is in the Market Place just NW. of the cathedral.

Begun in *c.* 1180, the cathedral was built in stages: the east end of the nave is the earliest part, the astonishing west front and the nave west of the north porch *c.* 1235, and at roughly the same time the Lady Chapel was added and the choir reconstructed. The two western towers were the last additions, the south one *c.* 1384, the north *c.* 1424. Across the nave a brilliant swirl of arches was put up shortly after the central tower to stop it falling. Particularly beautiful are the 12th-cent. north porch, the nave, the Lady Chapel and its windows, and the choir's 14th-cent. east window. In the north transept is a remarkable 14th-cent. clock, across the face of which knights joust on the hour. Close to it a superb stone staircase leads to the Chapter House (*c.* 1300) which has a fine fan-vaulted ceiling emanating from a central column. The cathedral's south door leads to beautiful 15th- and 16-cent. cloisters.

Of the precinct's other buildings, the Vicar's Close, an outwardly little-altered street just N. of the Chapter House, has similar 14th-cent. houses. It houses the "vicars choral" – clerical assistants with special reference to singing. Above the entrance to it is their fine dining-hall with much of its original furniture. Just W. of this, beside the 15th-cent. Deanery, is the museum which has a collection of samplers and specializes in WOOKEY HOLE finds and local history. S. across the green, the moated Bishop's Palace (basically 13th-cent.) is not normally open, but the episcopal swans entertain by ringing a bell near the drawbridge when hungry.

The city's civic – as distinct from ecclesiastical – centre has traditionally been a few hundred yards to the W., beyond the shopping centre. Here is the 15th-cent. Church of St Cuthbert, which is tall and light inside with a tie-beam roof and, just to the N. 15th-cent. almshouses and the ancient Guildhall.

Almost all the numerous pubs between these two areas are in some respect ancient and attractive; in particular the City Arms, near St Cuthbert's Church, which was the city gaol till the 19th cent., and in the courtyard of the 17th-cent. Crown, William Penn, the Quaker, is said to have preached to an audience of 2,000 and been arrested. The new Public Library received a Civic Trust award.

WEMBURY, *Devon* (3–SX5148). The village has been developed as a seaside resort, but it has a medieval church which confronts the sea more boldly than any other in Devon, a landmark to shipping for some 600 years, superbly sited on a cliff above a rocky cove and a lush watermeadow. Moreover, it has a good 14th-cent. tower and several quaint monuments. From the field above its cemetery are fine views down the coast to the mouth of the Yealm to the E., to Rame Head to the W., and ahead to the Mew Stone.

Return through the village and turn E. and you pass a pretty row of houses dated 1682 and reach an attractive hamlet. Where, after a short distance, this road ends, National Trust land begins. Over it there are good walks to the Yealm estuary.

WESTON-SUPER-MARE, *Somerset* (3–ST 3261). Easily the county's largest seaside resort, it is also the biggest town on the West Country's north coast and the second biggest in Somerset. Though few resorts have grown so quickly – population under 100 in 1800, about 19,000 in 1900, today roughly 44,200 – it is to some extent planned, with splendidly wide sea-front roads,

A. F. Kersting

Wells Cathedral: the astronomical clock

Wells Cathedral: the Chapter House steps

A. F. Kersting

pavements and gardens. At low tide the sea retreats far, exposing mud, but this, it is said, gives off the ozone which is claimed to make its air so salubrious. It entertains lavishly: two theatres, two cinemas, a model village, aquarium, small zoo, ten-pin bowling, a dance-hall also used for concerts, variety shows and wrestling, three swimming-pools two of which are indoor and heated, two piers, donkey rides on the beach, marine lake where children can boat happily, motor-boat and yacht races, county cricket in early August, tennis courts, two golf courses nearby, and medicinal baths for a great variety of

ailments. Moreover, its public gardens, in particular the Winter Gardens, are excellent.

Though architecturally seldom distinguished, its Church of All Saints, just E. of Grove Park, is an outstanding example of its period. It was built 1898–1902 by G. F. Bodley, with later additions by F. C. Eden. The museum, in the Boulevard, includes finds from the Iron Age fort on Worlebury Hill, at the north end of the town, where there are earthworks and nice woodland walks. Immediately N. again, **Kewstoke** has a good Norman to 15th-cent. church and a long, very ancient flight of steps called Monks Steps which provide a good viewpoint.

About 3 m. NNE., is **Woodspring Priory** founded in 1210 by William Courtenay, grandson of one of Thomas à Becket's murderers. An extremely attractive group of 15th-cent. (or in some cases perhaps 14th-cent.) buildings remain – church, chantry, court-room and barn – recently acquired by the National Trust after long use as part of a farm.

Two m. S., **Uphill,** the ruined Norman Church of St Nicholas has been roofless since 1864, and was replaced because it was inconvenient to get to. It stands on the last western hillock of the MENDIPS, overlooking the mouth of the River Axe where, it is thought, Phoenicians traded, Romans had a port, and, if you like, that Joseph of Arimathea arrived from Palestine (*see* GLASTONBURY). It is worth the climb.

The tiny islands of **Flat Holm** and **Steep Holme** are, respectively, about 6 and 5 m. offshore. There are regular motor-boat trips to the former, which has a lighthouse and an occasionally occupied farm-house. The latter, more barren and rocky but growing rare plants, is privately owned, leased to naturalists and archaeological societies. Special permission is needed to visit it.

WESTON ZOYLAND, *Somerset* (3–ST35 34), was the headquarters of King James II's army before the Battle of Sedgemoor (6 July 1685) – England's last major ground battle – in which they defeated the untrained and primitively armed forces of Charles II's illegitimate son, the Duke of Monmouth, claimant to the throne. The battle took place about ½ m. NW of the church. It began between 1 and 2 am and was all over in one and a half hours. Sixteen of the King's men were killed, some 300 rebels. A number of prisoners were shot or hanged on the spot. About 500 were locked up in the church till daybreak, many of them wounded. Five died in the church. The survivors were then herded to BRIDG-WATER, some being hanged *en route*.

The church's superb yellow-grey tower is a landmark in a flat, fen landscape. The building is mainly 14th- and 15th-cent. Inside, it is high, light and uncluttered, with a tremendous tie-beam roof and great expanses of flagstone floor. The village is now a dormitory for Bridgwater's factories and has much new housing.

A memorial marking the battle site is down a track beside a rhine (ditch-canal) at the village's edge.

WIDECOMBE-IN-THE-MOOR, *Devon* (3–SX7176). Here headed Uncle Tom Cobbleigh and All in the well-known song. The village, as its name suggests, is situated high up on DARTMOOR. Its church has one of the finest towers (*c.* 1500) in Devon, 120 ft high and pinnacled, paid for by tin-miners keen to manifest their newly acquired wealth. It has a story attached to it: in 1638 in the middle of a Sunday service and during a thunderstorm, a "bolt of fire" hit the church, knocking down a tower pinnacle, killing four people, injuring 62, and generally causing great confusion. At once a survivor remembered seeing a mysterious traveller exposing, in an unguarded moment, a cloven hoof. You can read more about it inside the church. The Church House (National Trust) and Glebe House, both built *c.* 1600, are in a nice tiny square by the church gate. The fair takes place in early September.

About 3 m. NW., is **Grimspound**, probably the most impressive of the moor's numerous prehistoric settlements. It is Bronze Age; a village of at least 24 huts surrounded – for protection against wild animals rather than man – by a wall 10 ft thick and now about waist high. There is a magnificent granite-slabbed entrance on the south side and much else to see. It looks across a valley to good examples of old tin workings.

WOOKEY HOLE, *Somerset* (3–ST5347). Here, in the southern limestone slopes of the MENDIPS, is one of the major cave complexes in Britain. The floodlit Great Cave contains remarkable formations of stalagmites and stalactites. Through it, slow and blue-green, flows the cause of it, the River Axe. During the Iron Age and as late as the Roman occupation it was inhabited, and the implements found (serious excavation did not begin till 1912) have greatly increased knowledge of that period. Many of them can be seen in the local museum and that at WELLS. Its inner recesses are still being explored with the help of aqualungs. Of other nearby caves, one was a hyenas' den, probably towards the end of the Ice Age. Their bones and those of the animals they fed on, including mammoth and wild horse, were found in it, also traces of Stone Age human habitation. On the hillside above are ancient cultivation terraces. Visitors to the Great Cave should wear strong shoes and warm clothes, as the temperature is permanently low and it is damp.

Close to the path to it is one of the oldest paper mills in Britain (1610). It specializes in high-grade writing paper.

In a building beside the car park, Titania's Palace is probably the world's most intricate, lavish and fantastic dolls' house. It is a work of astonishing imagination, labour and ingenuity, begun in 1907 by Sir Nevile Wilkinson at his home in Ireland for his three-year-old daughter. It was finished in 1922 and has been exhibited all over the world.

Ebbor Gorge, ¾ m. NW., is a smaller, much more wooded version of CHEDDAR GORGE, with the advantages that no road goes through it and that it is a National Nature Reserve. It is most easily reached from the W., from the Priddy road where there is a car park, or you can walk from Wookey Hole.

WOOLACOMBE and MORTEHOE, *Devon* (3–SS4545). The former has, with SAUNTON, the finest sand and surf beach on this north-west coast N. of BUDE. The sea does not expose miles of mud at low tide as at many places on the Bristol Channel. It is enclosed by steep, moorland slopes rather than by cliffs, and its houses climb pleasantly up the gorse-covered hillsides behind. Beyond the houses are romantic bare combes, grand for walking or riding.

Mortehoe is older and has some pretty cottages. Its church, founded in Norman times, enlarged *c.* 1300 and subsequently, is small and quite interesting but not especially beautiful. From beside it a path leads to Morte Point where the slate cliffs are thrilling. The Morte Stone, the furthest point, claimed five ships in the winter of 1852. To the N. the lighthouse (1879) at Bull Point can be visited, but it is advisable to make an appointment.

YATTON, *Somerset* (3–ST4265). Within an old nucleus, thickly coated with modern housing for BRISTOL commuters, it has a grandly austere high-naved church, famous for its beautifully panelled and vaulted 15th-cent. porch and, displayed in a frame, an exceptional piece of 15th-cent. embroidery. The church also contains two unusually fine 15th-cent. effigy-tombs. With a population of over 4,000, factories making furniture and bird food and a large tannery, the village is well on the way to small township. It has a livestock market on Mondays.

Cadbury Hill (not the Camelot one), just to the E., is a good place for views and pictures. Excavations of an earthwork on it have produced interesting Iron-Age, Roman and Dark-Age finds.

Some 1¾ m. SE., **Congresbury**, too, has an attractive centre, an interesting basically 15th-cent. vicarage, and one of the best church spires in Somerset.

YEOVIL, *Somerset* (3–ST5515). An exceedingly busy town with more new glass-and-metal buildings springing up than in any other place within a wide radius. The headquarters of Westland Aircraft, Europe's largest helicopter company, it also has major, long-established glove, leather and dairying industries, numerous smaller ones, and two important livestock markets (Mondays and Fridays, the former specializing in pedigree cattle). With leather-working rather than wool traditionally its main living, it was spared the slump caused to many other Somerset small towns by the growth of the North's textile industries in the 18th and 19th cents. Since it became a borough in 1846, its population has nearly quadrupled. The Romans clearly liked its site in rolling fertile land beside the River Yeo.

Its older centre, which suffered greatly from fires in 1499, 1623 and 1640, and from Second

World War bombs, is congested but worth visiting mainly for its Ham-stone church. Scarcely beautiful, it is, however, big and ruggedly impressive. Moreover, built *c*. 1380–90, it is older than most of its size. It contains an outstanding 15th-cent. brass lectern, and the War Memorial window in the north aisle is intriguing.

About ¼ m. SW. of the church, the museum in Henford Manor has a good collection of firearms and local Roman finds; and the walk to it, via George Street past the municipal buildings (1926) and matching Post Office, shows quite a handsome bit of the town.

Other buildings worth seeing: Abbey Farm with medieval Ham-stone tithe barn, on the western edge of the town, beside the ILMINSTER road; Newton Surmaville, an early-17th-cent. manor house, just SE. of the main railway station; the Roman Catholic church in Higher Kingston (about ¼ m. N. of the parish church), which is pleasant neo-Gothic (1897–9). Babylon Hill, just E. of the town, is a good viewpoint and was the scene of a Civil War skirmish.

Two m. W., **Brympton d'Evercy**, now a school, is one of the most attractive places in Somerset: a fine mainly 16th- and 17th-cent. house claiming the longest straight staircase in England; beside it a good church, chiefly 14th-cent. The house is open one day a week.

YEOVILTON, *Somerset* (3–ST5422). Within the Royal Naval Air Station, which here straddles the A303, is the excellent Fleet Air Arm Museum. It includes most of the planes – Swordfish, Sea Fury, Sea Vampire and many others – used by the service since its formation in 1914, and scale models, many photographs, documents and equipment. There is also an enclosure where you can watch the planes of today taking off and landing.

Two m. SW., **Ilchester** was an important Roman military station on the Fosse Way. The main roads SW. and NE. follow for some way this great highway which they created between Lincolnshire and EXETER, and there are Roman bricks in the church tower walls. Roger Bacon, the remarkable monk-scientist, was born here in 1214.

ZENNOR, *Cornwall* (2–SW4538), is the most compact of the grey villages in the northern half of the gale-swept Penwith peninsula, its houses seeming to hug their church in a landscape of boulders, dry-stone-walled fields and almost no trees. On the side of a chair in the church's chancel is carved a mermaid. Legend says she came from the sea to hear the wonderful singing of the squire's son and lured him back there with her, never to be seen again.

The Wayside Museum has an excellent collection of relics of old Cornish crafts and industries.

The cliffs round Zennor Head, ½ m. N., are tremendous.

About ½ m. SE. is Zennor Quoit. A quoit was a chambered tomb formed by raising oblong boulders on end to support a vast slab for a roof and then walling it all in with small stones or turf. They date from *c*. 2500–1500 B.C. In all known cases the walls have long since gone. The slab of the Zennor one is the largest known in England, 18 ft by 9½ ft, fallen at one end. There are three others in the vicinity (*see* LANYON QUOIT).

Some 2¼ m. SW. – and about ⅓-m. walk from the road – is **Bosporthennis**, the site of an Iron Age "beehive" settlement, like those of western Ireland but much less well preserved.

Woolacombe sands

Jane J. Miller

East Anglia

Essex   Cambridgeshire   Suffolk   Norfolk

RONALD BLYTHE

In an age of new boundaries the old concise limits of East Anglia – Suffolk, Norfolk and the Isle of Ely – the South Folk, the North Folk and the Isle of Eels – have been stretched alarmingly in order to accommodate weather forecasts, regional develop- ment schemes and TV programme planning. While not allowing, as these authori- ties sometimes do, that the area reaches upwards to Hull and across to Birmingham, it is possible to see that Essex – the East Saxons – and Cambridgeshire do share an affinity with the chief characteristics of the region, though for the East Anglian proper his country begins in the Stour Valley, rides steadily out to the chilly North Sea in a fine parabola of heath, shingle and marsh, until it reaches the Wash, and concludes in the geometrical sluices and peat of the Fens. This was the kingdom ruled by the Wuffingas, whose burial ground at Sutton Hoo has thrown a very civilized light upon the Dark Ages. And before both the Roman and Anglo-Saxon conquests it was the highly populated kingdom of the Iceni.

Some logical as well as tribal instinct kept East Anglia's identity intact right up until the railway age. Its off-centre geography helped, too. Unless some specific business drew a man along the road to Norwich the entire plateau of little clay fields and huge forests was by-passed by centuries of travellers. The earliest travellers followed a low chalk ridge which sweeps up from the North Downs, crosses southern Cambridgeshire, and once joined the Lincolnshire wold. This was the track which became the Icknield Way. Marsh and forest dominated the eastern counties until comparatively modern times, and it is startling in the context of today's prairie-like conditions in many parts of the area that when Queen Elizabeth I made her extravagant progresses into Suffolk she rode through almost continuous woodland, and that the memory which the many emigrants from this part of England to the New World took with them was that of a still rather secluded place.

"Oaken" East Anglia disappeared because there was no forest law to protect the trees, and the wheat for which the "Whitelands", as the chalk-based farms of Cambridgeshire were called right up until the First World War, were so famous, spread across the Suffolk and Norfolk clays. In the eighteenth century Norfolk played a large part in the agricultural revolution, particularly in a respect to the famous sowing rotation called "Norfolk four-course" – wheat, roots, barley, seeds.

One of the most attractive features of East Anglia is the way in which intensively cultivated or inhabited districts alternate with patches of heath and solitude, so that history and prehistory have equal evidence. There is no better place to ex- perience the latter than Wandlebury, the Iron Age fort on the crest of the Gog Magog Hills at Cambridge. The approach to it is a pale stretch of unmetalled Roman road, part of the great Via Devana; and to stroll along it on a hot blue June day, with beech and wild mignonette filling the hollows from which the light earth was dug to make the camber of this classic country lane, is one of those rare travel experiences. From the height one can view the prototype East Anglian scene, the brilliant arable plain which was eventually to become the landscape of the eastern kingdom. A mile or two below lies Stourbridge Common, where for centuries was held the most important fair in Europe, and on which Bunyan based his Vanity Fair. Sir Isaac Newton bought his prisms here. West lies King's College Chapel. Thus, as in a compact airiness, can be seen from this modest hill those components which make up the character of the whole area: intense religion, leading to an equally intense questioning, and manufacturing giving way to farming.

The ancient Breckland further along on the chalk ridge shows a kind of East Anglian progress in reverse, for until the 1920s the moor here remained much as the prehistoric "dwellers of the field" had left it. Now its huge coniferous plantations have transformed it into a fragment of Schleswig-Holstein. A last-minute look at this unique region as it was before the forest hid it is described in that little masterpiece of naturalist writing, R. R. Clarke's *In Breckland Wilds*.

The celebrated architecture of East Anglia sprang from three more or less inexhaustible local materials, chalk, clay and wood. From the chalk came the flints used with such prodigious skill and fantasy to make decorative facings for the churches. It also supplied clunch for such exquisite ornaments as the Lady Chapel at Ely and the Gate of Honour for Caius College. The clays produced bricks of great colour variation. During the revival of brick-building in the fifteenth century and for centuries afterwards the glowing red bricks such as those found in Charsfield (Suffolk) church and the gatehouse at Layer Marney, Essex, were favoured, but Georgian architects later made elegant use of "Suffolk white-brick" in many a country house. Snape Maltings, one of the most beautiful industrial buildings in rural England, displays a whole spectrum of local clay hues in its walls. The glaring gault bricks with which so much of modern Cambridge is built are less attractive. Local clays, too, were used in and after the eighteenth century for the pantiles which, when they are not blue-glazed, as in Norfolk, give many an East Anglian village a faintly Tuscan look.

But *the* building material throughout the area is wood. For generations of forest-born carpenter-artists its uses were virtually limitless. There was wooden engineering (the whole oaks on which Ely's lantern is balanced), wooden visions of paradise (the church roofs at March, Blythburgh and in many other places), wooden lace to screen chancels, wooden houses and barns, and, all along the river estuaries, the unceasing construction of wooden ships. It seemed that the East Anglian, everywhere confronted by something so vitally enduring as oak, felt obliged to use it for his needs, to the limits of his strength and imagination. The most moving example of this forest art is not such a miracle of craftsmanship as the font cover at Ufford in Suffolk but the simple church at Greensted in Essex, made of split oaks which chemical tests have dated to A.D. 850. The Anglo-Saxon carpenters' adze marks are still plainly visible. Something of the sacredness of trees to a woodland community remains here. One thinks of the "gospel" oaks at Great Yeldham in Essex and Polstead in Suffolk, and then of the woodwoses – the old forest gods – which stand subjected by the weight of many an East Anglian font.

As might be expected, scientific farming is drastically altering the natural history of the area. Small farms are amalgamated into larger units as their tenancies lapse. Villages which fifty years ago had a dozen farms are now likely to have only three or four. Hedges fall and ditches are filled in to make big fields. The weedless crops present a bland gloriousness in the summer and there is something potent and splendid about a road sunk in tall unhedged wheat. But botanists and ornithologists must mourn the price paid for such efficiency, and the long-term effects of the new farming on the ecology of East Anglia remain unknown. Yet this is a country-side which is still full of wild patches and secret places, and one of the best corners of Britain for plant exploration and bird-watching. Pasch flowers and shimmering cotillions of Adonis Blue butterflies – as well as a silence which overwhelms – can be found on those gigantic defences near Newmarket known as Fleam and Devil's dykes, and at Framsden in Suffolk there are acres of fritillaries. Saltings, meres, marshes and estuaries all the way from the Blackwater to the Ouse make the East Anglian coast a thrilling bird territory, and avocets breed on Havergate Island. But those superb beasts the Percheron and Punch horses, which held monumental rank in the local animal kingdom almost up until the last war, have quite disappeared.

East Anglia has often in its long history accepted industrial change. The Little Domesday of 1086 shows it to have been the most densely populated part of Britain. During the late Middle Ages, after the manufacturing revolution created by the Flemish weavers, the whole region entered upon a period of wealthy trading. A handsome part of its profits went into the building of the great wool churches, the subsidizing of learning at Cambridge, and, incidentally, into creating conditions which bred a self-assurance and a dissenting frame of mind. Modern changes which have profoundly affected the area include North Sea gas, nuclear power stations at Sizewell and Bradwell – the latter poetically adjacent to the chapel built by St Cedd in the seventh century to generate "the true Light which lighteth every man" – the post-war foundation of the Universities of Essex and East Anglia, as well as Churchill College, Cambridge, the co-existence between groups of villages and the United States aerodromes which dominate them, the international standing of the Aldeburgh Festival, the revitalization of many a sleepy market town by emigrant London firms, and the drastic reorganization of the ancient parish-centred religious life. Yet visitors will, for a long time yet, find an open country with close secrets, a land where the peculiar extremes of the English character, a hard-headed rationality and great imagination, exist side by side.

Essex, the first part of the region, is grossly undervalued as a county to explore. At first glance this neat fifty or so miles stretching between the Thames and the Stour might appear to have been concreted out of existence. London surges into it, and over a million of its inhabitants – its growth-rate over the past century has been the fastest county population expansion in Britain – live in streets which seem a very long way from East Anglia. In the 1840s William Morris could stand in the fields of Walthamstow and see London far off with "the sun shining down in one flood of peaceful light over the long distance". Shortly after this the confines broke, and the towns and villages east of the Thames were overrun. During the inter-war years the more prosperous of these new Londoners extricated themselves from Victorian terraces and tried to get back into some kind of country life by building along the edges of the main roads. Ribbon-development, with its pebble-dash, appliquéd Tudor beams and sunburst gates, soon linked one piece of Essex–London with its neighbour. Specialists in urban sprawl will find much to interest them in this part of Greater London and may even find something touching in these diverse Jazz-age homes. Fill-in has, in most cases, destroyed their brief freedom. The fields behind them are now covered by estates. Tower blocks soar in the meadows. The roads in front which, not so long ago, were cheerful with Baby Austins and charabancs on the way to Southend, are now a solid welter of traffic. To many a motorist it must seem that this desert of supermarkets and garages strangely called Essex can never be crossed. Yet suddenly he finds himself in rich farmland or arriving at a remote clapboarded pub – which happens to be twenty miles from Marble Arch. So, far from being crushed out of existence by London, Essex is in fact attractively alive and flourishing.

It is a dipping, rolling, ambling kind of country, crossed by regularly spaced-out rivers and edged by undramatic but very individual islands: Canvey, Foulness, Wallasea, Havengore, Northey, Mersea, Horsey, etc., their very names carrying across the centuries a sense of the cries of the Viking invaders. The rivers themselves at first glance seem dull enough, yet if Britain had an Iliad its heroes might well have lived on their banks. This is the country of King Cunobelin (Shakespeare's Cymbeline or Old King Cole), Boadicea, Caractacus, and, above all, of Brithnoth, whose exploits are so superbly described in *The Battle of Maldon*.

The most Romanized part of Britain, because of the conquerors' decision to make Colchester their capital, Essex has had excellent roads from the very earliest times; and the traffic of today still uses great stretches of the ancient routes: Stane Street, Icknield Street and the Via Devana. For a road, like a river, divides and rules, bilaterally keeping the laws of the past and the present. And in Essex it is fair to say that all roads lead to Colchester, rather than to London. One cannot help feeling that if Colchester had been in southern Europe or Asia Minor it would have the literature and the draw of a Trebizond. When Tacitus described it in his *Annals* – the first time a British city had received a written record – it was already very old. Capital of the Icenic kingdom, sacked by Queen Boadicea at the time when St Paul was sending his Epistles to the new churches, possessing a complete second-century wall and the biggest Norman keep in Europe on foundations made by men who were contemporary with Christ, it is an enthralling place. There is no other town in the country in which the national myths and realities so overlay each other, making such an eloquent humus of over two thousand years of civilization.

To discover the best of Essex one should travel through the villages centred on Halstead, Dunmow and Thaxted. These range from Finchingfield (the most photographed) to Borley (the most haunted) and include the artistic Bardfields and the mysterious Belchamps. The Dunmow–Thaxted area has a special fascination, for it is here that a kind of Shavian version of art-cum-socialism took place under the direction of Lady Warwick. This is the country in which Holst composed "The Planets", Conrad Noel flew red flags from his church tower at Thaxted, and H. G. Wells wrote that best-seller of the First World War, *Mr Britling Sees It Through*.

The traditional products of Essex verge on the exotic – Colchester "natives" from the celebrated oyster beds at Brightlingsea, roses, Tiptree jam, Maldon salt and, not so very long ago, saffron from Saffron Walden, venison from the vast Waltham Forest – of which Epping is the remaining fragment – and candied eringo root. Its chief assets, however, still stem from its farms. The great industrial complexes, including Courtauld's, Crittall's, Ford's and the Thames docks, have so far not been able to obscure its essentially agricultural identity. Yet for the visitor the particular flavour of this county must always lie in the extraordinary contrasts it can present in so small an area. In Southend and Frinton one has the poles of the English seaside ideal. Everywhere one goes the suburban tide looks as if it must engulf all, yet "all" turns out to be astonishingly large and quite capable of looking after itself – *vide* the great Stansted victory. Essex, one feels, after its drab savaging by the developers, is now calling the tune.

Suffolk, the most eastern county in England, begins amidst pastoral scenes of overwhelming familiarity. Here, along the banks of the border river, John Constable painted his great series of Stour pictures – his "six-footers", as he called them, and here the churches, lanes, meadows, mills and farms, the originals of these paintings, remain in startling reality. At Sudbury, further along the same river, is the home of Thomas Gainsborough. Prospect Hill, the road along which he must have walked as a young man to paint his masterpiece *Cornard Wood*, after winding its way through a housing estate, slips back in time to produce the famous view. Constable's rich uncle owned this picture and it became an early influence on the Flatford miller's son. Two miles from Gainsborough's house in Sudbury is a country-house park in which the artist's school friend and his new wife sat for their likenesses, thus creating what has been described as the quintessence of the English portrait. *Mr and Mrs Andrews*, now in the National Gallery, reflects a moment in the East Anglian countryside which agricultural historians have called the golden age of English country life. A journey along the valley towns and hamlets from East Bergholt to Sudbury is thus one of the most remarkable that can be made, for it leads one to a great moment in art and a recognition of what is meant by "Englishness".

At Long Melford the West Suffolk parks become very grand, mounting in degrees of splendour until they reach the last word in Georgian rural magnificence – Ickworth. Nearby lies Bury St Edmunds which, twice in its history, has been the centre of a far greater world than it knows today. First when, as one of the most important shrines in Christendom, its semi-regal abbots inherited most of the remaining privileges of the ancient East Anglian kingdom, and again when, in Georgian times, the town became Suffolk's Bath. So the beginning of exploration on this side of the county is dramatic and extraordinary. Yet, take any lane east of the Stour and one is back on the high, lonely ground where the medieval clothiers lived and worked. Paced out over this central Suffolk cornland stand their churches, the towers still showing a kind of strategic munificence. Although one successful merchant's tomb shows a confident belief in heaven's not judging a man by his money – "This day a Sudbury camel passed through the eye of a needle" – the beautiful wool churches are saved from being merely great architectural displays by the deep and complex spiritual qualities still to be felt in them. The question they seem to ask is, profit – and lose? Lavenham church is the greatest surety paid by the Suffolk clothiers. Their names were Spring and Branch. The heart of the trade was in this corner of the county and hundreds of fine wood and plaster houses, some isolated in the fields, others lining the streets of Hadleigh, Bildeston, Boxford, Sudbury and Kersey, still contain the large rooms where the looms clicked, making what Shakespeare called "Lindsey-Kersey stuff".

Suffolk's wool empire collapsed in the seventeenth century, never to revive – though many of its skills were retained and have found an outlet in the silk-weaving industry at Sudbury and Braintree. The collapse coincided with an English traveller's thoughtful observation in Belgium of how the different fields on each farm were sown in a certain rotation. . . . Arable East Anglia as it is today took a long time in the making and endured agricultural disasters every bit as terrible as that of the wool trade. The latest – and worst – was movingly documented by that excellent Norfolk farmer (and novelist) Sir Henry Rider Haggard in his *Rural England*. The food needs of the nation, plus science, broke the curse in 1940. The prosperity visible today does not conceal the uncertainties of a farming society still in the full swing of a second agricultural revolution.

Ipswich, the county town, is prosaic but not negative. It takes its name from the upper reaches of the Orwell which are called the Gipping – Gipeswic. Thomas Tusser thought it "like Paradise", but this hasn't been the general opinion for quite a long time. There are many antiquities, but the most attractive sight is the docks at night, full of foreign ships, sentinelled by massive grain wharfs and profoundly silent.

The A12 runs up into Norfolk from here, dividing the claylands from the coastal heaths which are Edward FitzGerald's and George Crabbe's Suffolk. The rivers Deben, Butley, Alde and Blythe are tidal all along this coastal strip, the mysterious centre of which is Dunwich, once a splendid city, now scarcely a place at all; the sea has devoured it. The inland towns of East Suffolk maintain a great calm. Framlingham, for centuries the home of the different families who have possessed the dukedom of Norfolk, is pure Froissart. But it is Blythburgh church, which many people believe is the most wonderful building in a county full of fine architecture, that sums up the character of Suffolk. Its mixture of creative and destructive forces, its brightness and its darkness, are all unforgettably combined here.

Norfolk is the biggest and least populated county in the East Anglian group. Off-centre, and spread out before the best viewing-point in the county – Mousehold Heath – lies Norwich itself, a rare and extraordinary city. Norfolk is hard to know and has therefore been much generalized over. "Flat and cold" is the usual verdict. The first is more a hallucination than a libel because the scenery here carries undulation to the most subtle limits. Many of the loveliest villages are curiously reticent in their shallow valleys and behind artfully screening elms. The impression is often one of desertion, the little brick-and-flint cottages rigid with secrecy. Every church seems to contain the kind of treasure which would have made it famous were it in any other county, but which here is taken for granted. As for the climate, it is bracing – a word which means that one won't feel the chill if one keeps moving. Certainly, the notorious east wind is inexorable. But also the summers are really hot and the effect of the weather generally is one of Spartan well-being.

Almost a peninsular land, with a great semi-circle of variegated waters – marshes, broads, dykes, the Wash and the rivers Yare, Waveney and Little Ouse – isolating it, Norfolk has always been a place which men have visited for itself alone. One does not pass through Norfolk on the way to somewhere else. Norwich itself is not the usual cathedral city, but East Anglia's cultural and metropolitan centre. The controlling factor has been the calm and manageable growth of its population: 15,000 in the reign of Elizabeth I to only 120,000 in that of Elizabeth II. It has never allowed the short-term requirements of history either to deface it or to swamp it, and today it remains a lesson in urban expansion. Basically a medieval city based on Bishop Losinga's superb monastic cathedral, and crowded with churches, guilds, old inns and ancient squares which it calls "plains", it has never succumbed to the picturesque but has remained intellectually alive. London must have always been a second city for the Pastons, Nelson, Coke, Townshend, Sir Thomas Browne, the Frys and the Gurneys – even Sir Robert Walpole.

The religious life of the county, before the Reformation, was vivid and inimitable, its summit being the establishment of the *casa sancta* legend at Walsingham. Whether the angels carried the Virgin's house to Norfolk or to Loreto, Walsingham soon developed into one of the greatest pilgrimage centres in the Christian world. A twentieth-century Anglican revival of these devotions has given this interesting little town an extraordinary atmosphere.

But to most people Norfolk means the Broads, those wide expanses of water which have become obligingly trapped in centuries of peat workings. They lie between Oulton and Stalham on a flat, lush plateau across which the small, lethargic rivers Bure, Thurne and Ant creep towards them, creating a brack at the fringe of the lakes in which thrive the reeds for the famous local thatching. The Broads are a world of their own, a mixture of decoys, nature reserves and a nice kind of pottering indolence. They have a charming surrealism: sails glide through farms and apparently over fields. In the winter, the level monotonous sweep of land from Yarmouth and Blundeston has a violent and bitter feeling which is most impressive. It is the subject of one of Dickens's greatest descriptive passages as the coach carrying David Copperfield fights its way through a gale to the sea.

Broadland is complemented on the other side of the county by Marshland, through which the Fen waters drain to the coast. The names of the villages all around here – Walpole, Walsoken, West Walton – remind one of the endless preoccupation of the Marshland people with their flood walls. A flood board in West Walton church sums up the wasted effort:

> Surely our sins were tinctured in grain,
> May we not say the labour was in vain,
> So many washings, still the spots remain. . . .

In the seventeenth century the complex of dykes, cuts and sluices made by the Dutch engineer Vermuyden and the Lord Chief Justice Sir John Popham began a process of reclamation which has turned all the country between Burwell and Terrington into a district which seems to have become detached from the Zuyder Zee. This Dutch feeling also touches King's Lynn, a town which still emanates all the virtues of the old self-sufficiency in its handsome mixture of first-class religious, mercantile, public and private buildings.

North Norfolk includes the great hoop of the coast, along which lie the small and intimate seaside resorts of Hunstanton, Wells-next-the-Sea, Blakeney, Salthouse, Sheringham, Cromer (a Regency watering-place), Happisburgh (pronounced Hazeborough), Caister (with a fine castle) and Great Yarmouth itself, East Anglia's own favourite beach. Yarmouth is also, with Lowestoft, the major centre of the East Anglian fishing industry. This, and the fact that it is the focus of a thousand village outings, creates a cheerful confusion of riot and work.

Norfolk is a place which makes little or no effort to present or explain itself. It is a province full of slumbering parishes and containing one great wide-awake city.

Cambridgeshire, including the Isle of Ely, has a dual geographical atmosphere, that created by the Uplands, which is fresh and optimistic, and that ordained by the Fens, which carries with it many generations of prejudice, for this dramatic grid of dead-straight roads and water, inland wharfs, black soil and pale bleached windmills and churches is often very beautiful, and always intriguing. Cambridge itself stands at the point where Upland and Lowland meet, the University a jewel of the best English architecture of the last seven hundred years or so. The perfection of the grouping of the colleges cannot be exaggerated. The presence of nearby watermeadows, streams and pools, as at Ely, lightens the density of such great masses of stone.

A similar river-domination affects the whole county. Once the watery landscape provided conditions for famous local industries such as basket- and paper-making but, although the latter is still carried on at the famous mill at Sawston, it is modern drainage which decrees today's economy. Smallholdings on scraps of manageable

Jane J. Miller

The arable agriculture of East Anglia required many windmills to grind the corn: the post-mill at Saxstead Green in Suffolk

land have given way to broad acres of cereals on the upland and potatoes in the Fens. But the sparse villages of Cambridgeshire still have a quiet islanded quality, and for so small a county there is a surprising sense of distance. Nearly all the villages lie in the south-west, so that the north, with its flimsy farms and solitary causeways, wind-pumps and feeling of man-versus-the-elements, seems empty and strange. Ely itself is surrounded by some fourteen villages, each standing on its own island. It is curious how few miles separate this place, where men have found it difficult to exist because of the wet, and that part of the county in the south-east where men have never lived because it is an arid plain. Most evocative of all the Cambridgeshire river villages is, of course, Grantchester – Chaucer, Byron, Brooke – but a mixture of watermanship and ordinary farming, plus contacts with the University, have made many another village in this county unusually interesting.

The epithets generally applied to the 860 square miles of Cambridgeshire are "gentle" and "charming", which could be a kinder way of saying "dull". But a close investigation – particularly that part of it made on foot – will reveal an absorbing scene which is a mixture of the tough and the lyrical.

East Anglia: Gazeteer

MICHAEL WEBBER

ACRES, THE, *Norfolk* (11–TF8115). The most important of these villages is **Castle Acre** which has the remains of a Norman castle, the ruins of an 11th-cent. priory and an outstanding parish church. Of the great castle the main survivals are the earthworks, which have been described as "perhaps the finest castle earthworks in England". Of stone buildings little remains except the 13th-cent. gateway at the east end of the village. The castle was built for William de Warenne, 1st Earl of Surrey, on the line of the Peddars' Way, which was the work of the Romans. The road running N. from here to the coast still follows its line. Nearby is the River Nar and 4 m. to the S., on the A1065, is SWAFFHAM.

William de Warenne, the son of the founder of the castle, founded the priory *c.* 1090 for the Cluniac brethren. Though there was never a large number of monks the size of the building is remarkable, and the ruins are still extremely impressive. Once past the gatehouse the visitor will be struck by the beauty of the west front with its magnificent arcading of the 12th cent. Over the main Norman doorway is a large and, certainly at one time, beautiful window of later date. Attached to this west front are some of the priory buildings, notably the prior's house with its flushwork in chequer patterning. Within the area of the priory are the picturesque ruins of the old buildings.

Near the priory is the Church of St James, mainly Perpendicular. Inside are piers of earlier date which were used by the men who later added to the church. There is a noble font cover which is 26 ft high. There are traces of the original painting and gilding. Hardly less excellent is the hexagonal 15th-cent. pulpit with its painted panels, showing the four Latin Fathers of the Church.

One m. to the S. is **South Acre**, on the other side of the river. Here, in the Church of St George, are some important monuments: firstly some excellent brasses, one to Sir John Harsick and his wife, d. 1384, and another to Thomas Leman, d. 1534; then a strange wooden effigy, in a very poor state of preservation but almost certainly medieval, and another of a crusader of Norman times. A large alabaster monument in the Lady Chapel commemorates Sir Edward Barkham and his wife, d. *c.* 1623. Barkham was once a Lord Mayor of London. The screen under the tower arch is 14th cent.

To the W. is **West Acre**, once the site of an Augustinian priory founded *c.* 1100. It must have been a comparable institution to that at Castle Acre and the gatehouse is 14th-cent. and built of flint. The ruins which remain include parts of the church and the chapter house.

All Saints' Church next to the gatehouse is mainly Perpendicular with some parts of earlier date and has been restored. In the north porch is a small sculpture probably from the keystone of an arch and representing a seated figure (perhaps a Madonna), probably 13th-cent.

ALDEBURGH, *Suffolk* (11–TM4656), has become famous as the centre of the Aldeburgh Festival which was started by the great English composer Benjamin Britten in 1948, and which is held each year in June. The little town was, like its northern neighbours, DUNWICH, WALBERSWICK and SOUTHWOLD, at one time a prosperous port. This was in the 16th cent. Then came the sea and the storms which Britten captured so unforgettably in his opera, *Peter Grimes*. The quaint little Moot Hall, now almost on the seawall, was at one time in the centre of the town, which shows just how much has been eroded in the course of four centuries.

The Church of SS. Peter and Paul stands on a hill overlooking the town and the sea. Mostly of the 16th cent., it has a tower some 200 years older. There is an elaborate pulpit made in 1632 and several Elizabethan brasses. In the north aisle is a memorial by T. Thurlow to the Rev. George Crabbe (1847). Crabbe was born at Aldeburgh in 1754 and after leaving school became an errand-boy. He returned to his home town and studied medicine and in 1780 went to London to try to make a living by writing. He was ordained in Mayfair and became chaplain at BELVOIR CASTLE. He went back to East Anglia to GREAT GLEMHAM, in 1796, before finally settling in the West Country where he died in 1832 and was buried at Trowbridge. One of his most famous works is *The Borough*, published in 1810, which became the inspiration for Britten's opera.

The Moot Hall, *c.* 1520–40, is a timber-framed building, with end walls of brick, built over an arched ground floor which was at one time used as an open market. The tall chimneys to the S. date from the 16th cent., but most of the building was restored in 1855.

N. of the Moot Hall is the White Lion Hotel, and a terrace of typical 19th-cent. seafront houses ending with the Sundial House of the 1920s, a fanciful design by Oliver Hill.

S. of the Moot Hall, two roads run parallel:

Kenneth Scowen

Aldeburgh: the Moot Hall

Noel Habgood

Audley End, a magnificent Jacobean mansion

one is the High Street, the other runs nearer the seafront. The High Street contains a number of excellent shops and the Union Chapel of 1822. The seafront has many quaint cottages and several houses which date from around the time of the First World War. Above the High Street along the cliff top are a number of larger houses and lodges.

Along the seafront is a look-out tower, a tall square building with a spiral iron staircase running up the outside. The Martello Tower, Slaughden, is one of those built along the East Anglian coast in 1810–12 as a defence against Napoleonic invasion. The name comes from a "Torre della Martella" in Corsica seen by the British in 1794. Nearer to the Moot Hall is the site of the famous Aldeburgh lifeboat.

Alde House was the home of two famous sisters. Elizabeth Garrett Anderson, as she became by marriage, was born in 1836. She managed to enter the medical profession, at that time closed to women, and opened the hospital in London which still bears her name. She was at one time the Mayor of Aldeburgh, the first woman mayor in England. Her younger sister, Millicent, was a pioneer of women's suffrage and married the blind professor Henry Fawcett, who became Postmaster-General.

ASHINGDON, *Essex* (7–TQ8693). Near here Cnut defeated Edmund Ironside in October 1016, to succeed him as King of England when Edmund died just one month later. The Church of St Andrew has a long history, its first priest, Stigand, becoming the Bishop of Winchester in 1047. In 1052 he was uncanonically appointed Archbishop of Canterbury, an appointment which was finally ratified by Benedict X in 1058. In this capacity he crowned William the Conqueror. A few years later his fortunes changed yet again and he was deprived of his see, to die imprisoned two years later. In the church is a replica of a silver coin of Cnut found nearby.

AUDLEY END, *Essex* (11–TL5139). As splendid as this magnificent Jacobean mansion is today, it is but a part of the house built by the first Earl of Suffolk, Lord Howard de Walden. He inherited the estate of Audley End in 1603, on which site the Abbey of Walden had stood, given to Sir Thomas Audley by Henry VIII after the Dissolution. There is some resemblance to Hatfield House, but here the building is faced with stone, not brick. Sir John Vanbrugh was called in to work on the house early in the 18th cent. and demolished some of the building and more was destroyed later in the century, when it passed to the ninth Baron Howard de Walden, created Lord Braybrooke in 1788. The visitor is immediately impressed by the façade with its beautiful arrangement of windows, its many turrets with their delicate caps and the richly elaborate porches, making a striking composition as seen from across the park.

The Great Hall of the house features a massive screen carved with a Baroque profusion of detail. Facing it there is a stone screen of simple, classical design, in striking contrast to its partner. Behind is a dual staircase and above a flat ceiling enriched with timbering and panels of plaster.

East Barsham Manor is a fine example of Early Tudor architecture

One of the most interesting sections of the house is the chapel completed in 1786, an exquisite example of the Georgian Gothic style.

Apart from Vanbrugh some of the other great artists and architects who worked on the house were Robert Adam, Biagio Rebecca and Hobcraft. The grounds of Audley End were landscaped by Capability Brown and among the architectural fantasies they contain are the circular temple and bridge both by Adam, the Springwood Column (1774) and an icehouse lodge (1827). The house is owned by the Ministry of Public Building and Works and is open to the public. Audley End village lies outside the gates and the road leads to the College of St Mark (originally built as Elizabethan almshouses) and to the town of SAFFRON WALDEN.

AYLSHAM, *Norfolk* (11–TG1927). A small town on the River Bure with an attractive market place to the N. of which is the Church of St Michael, Decorated and Perpendicular. There is a two-story porch built in 1488, with good flush panelling. The font is 15th-cent. and has the arms of John of Gaunt on the shaft. The pulpit dates from 1637. There is a fine west gallery supported by posts and beams, some interesting stained glass and a number of monuments, including those to Humphry Repton, the famous landscape gardener and associate of Nash who died in 1818 and whose grave is in the churchyard, his body giving, as his own epitaph puts it, "form and colour to the Rose".

Around the market place are several good buildings among which is the Black Boy Inn of the Queen Anne period. Close to the market place are several fine houses, The Knoll, *c.* 1700, Aylsham Old Hall, 1689, The Manor House, 1608 and many others. Half a m. to the SW. are the remains of a windmill and not far away the former workhouse built in 1849 in Victorian Tudor style. Abbot's Hall, 1½ m. to the NE., is contemporary with the manor house and is on the site of the house which belonged to the abbots of BURY ST EDMUNDS. A similar distance to the NW. stands BLICKLING Hall (National Trust).

BARHAM, *Suffolk* (11–TM1451). St Mary's Church has parts dating from the early 14th cent. and a fine window in the vestry made early in the 16th cent. in the Early Renaissance style. Inside the church on the chancel floor is a brass to Robert Southwell and his wife (1514). In the chancel is a large 17th-cent. monument to Sir Richard Southwell and his wife.

Opposite the church is the gateway and wall of the former Barham Hall and ½ m. to the E. is Barham Manor, a good example of Tudor brickwork with octagonal chimneys.

A mile or so the the N. is **Shrubland Park** which contains the spectacular Shrubland Hall, now a health hydro. The original house, designed by James Paine in 1770–2, forms the centre-piece of the Italianate building designed by Sir Charles Barry in 1848–52. The gardens, also designed by

Barry, are terraced in the style of the Villa d'Este at Tivoli and fall in a remarkable display of steps, cascades and urns. The gardens were further developed by William Robinson in 1888.

The Old Hall in the grounds has two windows made of terracotta similar in style to that already noted in Barham church.

BARSHAMS, THE, *Norfolk* (11–TF9234). Changing the normal order of the compass you should first consider **East Barsham**, famous for the splendid Early Tudor manor house built by Sir Henry Fermor in 1520–30. Whether you first notice the battlemented top, the magnificent chimneys or the superb two-storied gatehouse, its warm brickwork is most attractive. The vertical buttresses and the bands of ornament in moulded brick, the patterning of the windows and the group of ten chimneys, each one carved differently from its neighbours, are all features which add richness to this architectural feast. Restorations done in the present century have not (as yet) affected the character of this enchanting building.

All Saints' Church, much affected by time, has a Norman south doorway and two pieces of sculpture worth noting: an alabaster group of St Anne teaching the Virgin to read and a splendid memorial to Mrs Calthorpe, whose family lived in the Manor House and who died in 1640. She is shown rising from her grave wrapped in her shroud in this monument made by John and Matthias Christmas, local sculptors whose work may also be seen in St Stephen's, IPSWICH.

North Barsham, by the River Stiffkey, has All Saints' Church with a 13th-cent. Purbeck marble font, a Stuart table and a Victorian pulpit.

West Barsham, making a triangle with its neighbours, has the restored Church of the Assumption of the Virgin. There is an early-13th-cent. doorway and the nave has pre-Conquest work, including two double-splayed windows.

BARTON BROAD, *Norfolk* (11–TG3421). This is one of the largest of the Broads and is now a broadening of the River Ant which flows directly through it. At one time the river was artificially led into and out of the broad, which like most of the others was once by-passed by the river. It is situated in the triangle of WROXHAM, Stalham and POTTER HEIGHAM. The basin reaches a depth of about 9 ft and reedswamp and alder fen may be seen growing at the ends of the peat ridges. Coypu have destroyed much of this plant growth in recent years, so much so that the character of the vegetation has changed considerably in the past decades. Mostly this has happened at the south end of the broad; the fen area at the north end has been allowed to grow more extensively and is more resistant to attack by these voracious rodents. The broad is freely open to boats.

BASILDON, *Essex* (7–TQ7189). The new town of Basildon is one of the eight planned after the last war which would encircle London and take over some of its surplus industry and population. It overlooks the estuary of the River Thames and is placed upon undulating country, containing seven parishes and an indigenous population of some 25,000. Placed as it was along the railway and the main A127 road from London to SOUTHEND it has been planned as a rectangle some 6 m. from W. to E., and 3 m. from N. to S. The number of people it will accommodate has increased from the original 50,000 and it seems likely that it will ultimately reach between 110,000 and 140,000.

Though the new buildings will attract immediate attention the visitor should not forget that the churches of the original seven parishes are worth noting. Holy Cross, Basildon, has a 14th-cent. nave, a brick chancel of 1597, and a weathervane dated 1702. At Laindon, St Nicholas has a timber belfry, weather-boarded and with a broach spire, with typical Essex timber framing inside. St Mary's at Langdon Hills is 16th- and 17th-cent., with a chapel rebuilt in the 19th. A feature is a royal coat of arms on the wall over the nave which is dated 1660. At Vange is All Saints, a church of Norman times, restored in 1837 when the west gallery was added. Nevendon has in St Peter's, a church showing work of the 13th, 14th and 15th cents., while there are two Victorian churches at Langdon Hills (St Mary's – 1876) and at Pitsea (St Michael's – 1871) with a tower dating back to the early 16th cent.

However, to see the buildings of the New Basildon you should start at the town centre, which really is right in the middle of the town. It lies just N. of the railway and over 1 m. S. of the A127 at the junction with the CHELMSFORD road. Sir Basil Spence was consultant to the architect of the Development Corporation, Mr A. B. Davis. The main feature is a traffic-free pedestrian concourse with the 14-story Brooke House which stands on eight reinforced concrete V-shaped supports, as its main vertical accent. The surrounding buildings are still in course of development.

Surrounding the town centre are a number of new areas which include much residential building of varying degrees of success and to the NE. major industrial areas.

BECCLES, *Suffolk* (11–TM4290). The town is nicely placed on the River Waveney. In Norman times the sea reached into the town which is now some 7 or 8 m. from the coast. Many of the Georgian houses have Dutch gables which remind the visitor of the many connections there once were between East Anglia and the Netherlands.

The 14th-cent. St Michael's Church has its tower standing separate from the main body of the church. Stone-faced and 97 ft tall it contains a peal of ten bells. The Old Town Hall, close by, was built in 1726. On the west side of the Old Market is St Peter's House built of brick in the 18th cent. and containing a remarkable Gothic fire-place of the same date. It is but one of a large number of attractive Georgian buildings.

Much earlier is Roos Hall, dated 1583, on the

Bungay road, its step gables again betraying Dutch influence.

The Church of St Benet (Roman Catholic) in St Mary's Road was built in 1889 in the Romanesque style for the Benedictine Order.

In the season the staithe (quay) by the river presents a busy picture with holiday vessels of all types at their moorings. There is an annual regatta which has often provided a subject for painters.

BELCHAMPS, THE, *Essex* (11–TL8041), is the name given to a group of three villages in the N. of the county near the border with Suffolk, and thus to the S. of the River Stour. **Belchamp Otton's** Church of St Ethelbert and All Saints was dedicated to the ancient king of East Anglia, and has a Norman nave, and a finely carved Norman south doorway. Each of the following centuries has added something to the church, one of the most attractive items being the belfry of the 19th. Just to the N. is **Belchamp St Paul**, so called because it was given to St Paul's Cathedral 1,000 years ago by Athelstan, King of England. The Church of St Andrew is mainly 15th-cent. with a fine west tower. It is especially famous for the carved misericords in the chancel stalls, which are among the very few in all Essex. Brasses to the Golding family (1587 and 1591) are reminders of Arthur Golding who was well known in the 16th cent. for his translations of Caesar, Ovid and Seneca, and whose work provided William Shakespeare with themes for many of his plays. A window in the church was given by one of his American descendants.

Belchamp Walter is the most southerly of the villages and above the stream which is a tributary of the Stour stands the Church of St Mary, mainly 14th- and 15th-cent. The nave is from the former, the tower, and the timbered porch from the latter. The interior features a number of paintings which include a *Wheel of Fortune*, and a 14th-cent. *Virgin suckling the Child*. The font is 12th-cent., the elaborate monument to Sir John Boutetort, d. *c.* 1324, is like *Hamlet* without the Prince, in that the tomb-chest and the effigy are missing. A later monument by Robert Taylor commemorates John Raymond, d. 1720, whose family built the very fine Hall in that same year. Additions were made in the 19th cent. and the Hall was restored in 1966.

BILDESTON, *Suffolk* (11–TL9949). At one time an important town for cloth. The 15th-cent. Church of St Mary is on a hill at the edge of the village. The south door is splendidly carved and the roof alternates tie-beams with hammer-beams. In the village are many timber-framed cottages with fine plastering and projecting upper stories. The market place has houses of the early 19th cent. and a Victorian clock tower. The King's Head and the Crown Inn are both of architectural interest. The Baptist chapel was founded in 1731, though rebuilt in the mid 19th-cent.

Garrod's Farmhouse S. of the market place dates from the 15th and 16th cents. and has many attractive and unusual features including much decorative carving.

BILLERICAY, *Essex* (7–TQ6794). Here in Mayflower Hall, opposite the church, the Pilgrim Fathers met before they set off on their voyage to America in 1620. Christopher Martin, the ship's purser, together with his wife Marie and her brother-in-law Solomon Prower were among the band who left England to seek freedom across the Atlantic. Not one of the group from Billericay survived the epidemic which accounted for so many of the *Mayflower's* passengers as she lay off Plymouth, Massachusetts.

Apart from the 16th-cent. Hall, there are many other buildings of note in this town, placed on the main SOUTHEND to BRENTWOOD road, the A129. Between it, and the neighbouring developing town of BASILDON, is the village of **Great Burstead**, with its Church of St Mary Magdalen. Billericay itself has its own church of the same name which stands at the junction of Chapel Street and High Street. Though the tower is early 16th-cent. and made of brick, the rest of the church is later, with three interior galleries supported on delicate cast-iron columns.

Close by are several attractive buildings: the Chequers Inn, the Nook and St Aubyns all 16th- or 17th-cent. From the 18th cent. come a number of houses in both Chapel and High Streets, while the early 19th cent. is represented by St Andrew's Hospital (1840), one of the earlier designs of G. G. Scott and originally the Poor Law institution. Quite apart from its importance as the meeting place of the Pilgrim Fathers, Billericay has its place in the history books as the scene of the peasants' revolt of 1381, when the followers of Jack Straw were captured during the many protests which followed the imposition of the poll tax in 1379.

BINHAM, *Norfolk* (11–TF9740). This small village was once a great Benedictine centre, and the priory founded *c.* 1100 by Peter de Valoines as an offshoot of ST ALBAN'S Abbey is still, even though no longer complete, an impressive sight. The Norman nave of this priory now forms part of St Mary's Church. However, the first thing to be seen is the west front which is one of the first examples of Early English architecture in the country, built before 1244. Even with its great window bricked up it is a noble composition of arches and columns whose refined proportions make a strong contrast with the sturdy Norman work of the nave. Three tiers of semi-circular arches line each side and of the original nine bays seven still stand.

The seven-sacrament font is built on steps. The ruins of the earlier priory may be seen around the church. In the village is the remains of an ancient cross.

BLAKENEY, *Norfolk* (11–TG0243), is a picturesque small town on the north coast of Norfolk on the estuary of the River Glaven. It is much favoured by yachtsmen and in the season its

A. F. Kersting

Blickling Hall, a surperb 17th-century house

has been said of Scolt applies to Blakeney but additional factors may be mentioned. One of these must be the hybrid grass *Spartina* which spreads so fast that it presents a great control problem. Another is the huge depth of shingle which is able to support a wide variety of vegetation, and a third the dunes which are formed beyond the reach of the normal high tides (though the exceptional conditions of 1953 are remembered by a mark which shows the abnormal level of water reached at that time).

Among the rarer plants here are some which are normally found far away. The *Limonium bellidifolium* is mainly Mediterranean, the *Suaeda fruticosa* is another which comes from the South and which has established itself in the unusual conditions prevailing here. Entomologists, too, have much to observe, as a wealth of insect life may be found at all seasons. Mammals such as rabbits, rats and shrews are numerous, and seals appear from time to time. The birds include those mentioned in the note on Scolt Island.

BLICKLING, *Norfolk* (11–TG1728). Here is one of the county's greatest show-pieces, a superb Jacobean house built between 1616 and 1627 for Sir Henry Hobart. The architect was Robert Lyminge and visitors who are familiar with Hatfield House will recognize his hand. Blickling Hall stands on land which is itself full of history. Once the property of King Harold, it was given by William the Conqueror to Herbert de Losinga, the Bishop of NORWICH and the builder of its great cathedral. Later it came into the possession of Sir John Fastolf, the builder of CAISTER Castle, and later still into the Boleyn family, though there is no evidence that Anne was born in the house. The present house was built within the existing moated area and it was altered in 1767–79 by Thomas, William, and John Ivory, a family of Norwich architects. As late as 1725 it was open to the N.

The façade, with gables, turrets with ogee tops and bay windows, is capped by a turret with an open-topped lantern. The interior is no less splendid with a great carved staircase, a magnificent dining-room, anteroom and drawing-room, and perhaps most beautiful of all, the gallery with its carved plaster ceiling. The gardens were attributed to Humphry Repton, buried nearby at AYLSHAM, and include a parterre designed in 1930 by Mrs Lindsay. One m. to the NW. of the house is the remarkable mausoleum designed by Joseph Bonomi in 1793 for the Earl and Countess of Buckinghamshire. It stands on a 45 ft square and is a perfect pyramid, a concept executed elsewhere in Europe at that time.

The Church of St Andrew must take second place, and though parts are Early English and Perpendicular, much was restored by Butterfield and Street in 1851 and 1876. The octagonal font (Perpendicular) is typically East Anglian and there are many monuments and brasses. One of the latter is to Anna Boleyne, d. 1479, and one of the former, to the 8th Marquess of Lothian, is by G. F. Watts, 1878.

quays present a lively scene. Though once a port of some importance it is now almost completely devoted to pleasure-boating. The other sport particularly associated with Blakeney and its near neighbour, CLEY, is wild-fowling. The Church of St Nicholas in Blakeney is curious in having two towers: the west tower is Perpendicular and over 120 ft high, the other tower at the north-east corner is only 8 ft wide and was used as a beacon to guide mariners. Another rather unusual feature is the low, finely arched chancel which has a chamber above it with its own window. The height of the nave is enhanced by this contrast. Inside is an Easter Sepulchre, stalls with good misericords and a Stuart table.

Contrasting with the many flint cottages is a red-brick house at the west end of the quay. The Guildhall stands on a brick vaulted undercroft and dates from the 15th cent., and just to the N. of the church is a house which includes some of the remains of the Carmelite friary founded in 1296.

Blakeney's chief feature is perhaps the great expanse of marshy creeks which extend towards Blakeney Point. From the Far Point to Cley is almost 4 m. and like Scolt Head (*see* BRANCASTER) is National Trust property and a paradise for naturalists. As at Scolt, barrier beaches enclose a vast area of marshy flats and the range of plant and bird life is immense. Much of what

BLUNDESTON, *Suffolk* (11–TM5197). The church has the tallest and thinnest round tower in East Anglia. The south door is 11th-cent. and the plate includes a chalice of the Civil War period. Blundeston House was one of Sir John Soane's earliest designs, 1785. A prison has been built in the grounds.

Readers of *David Copperfield* will remember that the hero of Dickens's novel was born at Blundeston and spent several holidays with Peggotty's family between here and GREAT YARMOUTH.

BLYTHBURGH, *Suffolk* (11–TM4575). Approached from the London to LOWESTOFT road the magnificent Church of the Holy Trinity rises from the marshy estuary of the River Blyth as majestically as does the Cathedral of ELY from its surrounding fens. There are few sights in Suffolk more splendid than this great church, whether standing out clearly in the crisp East Anglian light, or whether veiled in the mists that can hang over the marsh. It sails the horizon like some great liner, an impression enhanced should you see the church at night, when with windows alight it sparkles in the darkness.

Holy Trinity's size (it is 127 ft long and 54 ft wide), indicates the importance of Blythburgh in the 15th cent. when it had two annual fairs, its own mint and gaol and busy quays crowded with craft from home and overseas. Yet even before the century ended the town had begun the sad decline so typical of East Coast towns and due this time to the shallow channels which could no longer float the larger vessels. As the town decayed so did the church, described by Suckling in 1847 as "mouldering into ruin". In 1931, however, extensive restorations were begun which have continued to this day.

Now all is light and airy, the vast wooden roof no longer bearing the scars of the spire which crashed through it in the great storm of 1577, and decorated with carved angels and coloured patterns of painted flowers. Note the bookrests of the pews and the bench near the south porch door, made from the post of the old mill at **Westleton**, also the bench-ends showing the seven deadly sins: Greed with swollen stomach, Slander with protruding tongue and Avarice on his money chest. Apostles and saints may be seen in the carvings on the choir benches and a wooden "Jack-o'-the-Clock" is one of the few remaining in England.

Little remains of the busy town of long ago, which is now a through route for the holiday tourist, but still remains unsurpassed for the beauty of its site.

BOCKING, *Essex* (11–TL7623). A town which almost imperceptibly leads into BRAINTREE. It was to Bocking that George Courtauld came almost 100 years after his family had come from France as Huguenot refugees. Thus having been one of the great centres of the wool trade, East Anglia was to gain a new prosperity founded on another fabric – artificial silk. So the Paycockes

(*see* COGGESHALL) of one era were replaced by the Courtaulds of another. When George moved from **Pebmarsh** (to the NE. of HALSTEAD) to Bocking in 1809 he began an industry which was to bring not only trade to Essex but was, through the wisdom and generosity of his descendant Samuel Courtauld (1876–1947), to give England a wonderful collection of French paintings, the Courtauld Institute and his Robert Adam house in Portman Square. Through the famous Courtauld-Sargent concerts the musical life of the capital and the development of generations of young people was also enriched.

The 17th-cent. post-mill at Bocking is deservedly famous and with the Church of St Mary and the vast factories is among the more obvious architectural features. The church is 15th-cent., except for the chancel which is 14th-cent. The tower has buttresses and a corner stair-turret. Nearby are the factory buildings close to the river which played so important a part in the early days of the mill. In the town a number of buildings of great interest include Doreward's Hall, timber-framed, with a brick façade dated 1572, the Deanery and Bocking Hall, both timber-framed and, in Church Lane, Tabor House (16th-cent.), Wentworth House (17th) and Boleyns (18th). Leading to Braintree, Bocking End contains more buildings of note, including The White Hart, 17th-cent., with later alterations.

BOREHAM, *Essex* (11–TL7509). There are three buildings of great interest to be seen in this village just off the main CHELMSFORD to COLCHESTER road, the A12. Many motorists must have admired the beautiful façade of Boreham House set back from the main road, and now the training centre for Ford's Tractor Division. The house was built by James Gibbs for Benjamin Hoare in 1728 and its simple, yet impressive, façade is enhanced by the straight lake which calls to mind the Canal Pond at Chatsworth. The wings of the house were added in 1812 by Thomas Hopper. Inside are some superb rooms, notably the entrance hall and the salon which date from the building of the original part of the house.

New Hall is a splendid house, now a convent, which dates from the original Hall built by Henry VIII, *c.* 1520. The magnificent south façade which you see today gives some idea of the great richness of the original mansion. Seven superbly simple bay windows, the central one containing the entrance, are topped by a plain parapet. Since 1798 the house has been run by the canonesses of the Holy Sepulchre from Liège. In the chapel is a very fine carved coat of arms of Henry VIII, similar to that at CAMBRIDGE.

In the centre of the village is the Church of St Andrew, which has a central Norman tower topped by a pyramid roof. The nave and aisles are unusual in shape and the chancel is narrow, with the 16th-cent. Sussex Chapel which contains the triple monument to the three Earls of Sussex, d. 1542, 1567 and 1583. On the opposite side of the church is the Tufnell Chapel of *c.* 1800.

Salle: the Church of SS. Peter and Paul. Painting by Edward Bawden, 1968   *London, Fine Art Society*

BOTTISHAM, *Cambridgeshire* (11–TL5460). The Church of the Holy Trinity contains some interesting work of the 13th and 14th cents. The west or Galilee porch by the tower is perhaps derived from that at ELY. Inside there are two 14th-cent. parclose screens worth noting. Among the several monuments are those to Sir Roger Jenyns and his wife and to the two young Allington children, Lionel and Dorothe.

The village is also the site of one of the village colleges built in the 1930s.

Some 1½ m. to the NW is **Anglesey Abbey,** now in the care of the National Trust. Anglesey was an Augustinian priory founded in the 12th cent. Some time after 1591 the priory was converted into a house by the Fokes family. In the present century it was bought and altered by the late Lord Fairhaven and since that time the extensive gardens of over 100 acres have been created. Inside the house is an outstanding collection of paintings, sculpture and *objets d'art.*

BOURN, *Cambridgeshire* (10–TL3256). Bourn Hall, Jacobean but much restored, is on the site of an old Norman castle. St Mary's Church dates from Norman times with subsequent additions right up to the last century. The tower, probably dating from the middle of the 13th cent., is surmounted by a noteworthy spire.

The windmill at Bourn was recorded as far back as 1636 and has claim to being the oldest surviving windmill in the country. It is a post-mill, which means that the body of the mill which contained the machinery and carried the sails was kept turned to face the wind by being mounted on an upright central post.

BRADENHAMS, THE, *Norfolk* (11–TF 9308). **West Bradenham** is famous for its association with two men and two women. The men were Lord Nelson and Rider Haggard and the women were Nelson's sister and Lady Hamilton. Nelson's sister, Mrs Bolton, lived in the Hall which had been built *c.* 1760 and it was to this house that Lady Hamilton often came.

The Hall came into the possession of the Haggard family and it was here on 22 June 1856 that Sir Henry Rider Haggard was born. Before he was 20 he went to South Africa and at the age of 32 became Master of the High Court of the Transvaal. He returned to Norfolk to marry in 1880 and took a great interest in agricultural matters. *Dawn,* his first novel, was published in 1884, to be followed by *King Solomon's Mines,* 1886, and many other popular books.

St Andrew's Church, 13th- to 14th-cent., has an Easter Sepulchre and monuments to the Haggard family.

East Bradenham with its fine village green has the Church of St Mary (Decorated and Perpendicular). Some interesting monuments include those to John Greene, d. 1684, and Gibson Lucas, d. 1758, which are particularly attractive.

BRADWELL-JUXTA-COGGESHALL, *Essex* (11–TL8122), is situated on the A120 COL-CHESTER to BRAINTREE road some 2 m. W. of COGGESHALL, and should not be confused with the village of similar name on the estuary of the Blackwater. The Church of the Holy Trinity has many portions of Norman date with later additions in the Decorated and Perpendicular styles. It contains a series of wall paintings which date from *c.* 1320. Among the subjects are *Doubting Thomas, The Trinity,* and *Christ Rising from the Tomb.* There are almost certainly many other paintings underneath the plastering of the church but those that remain visible are distinguished by their artistic quality.

Beyond the traceried 15th-cent. screen, behind the altar, are particularly interesting monuments to Anthony Maxey, d. 1592 and his wife and to their son, Sir Henry Maxey, d. 1624, and his wife.

BRADWELL-ON-SEA, *Essex* (7–TM 0006), also known as Bradwell-juxta-Mare, lies near the Blackwater almost opposite MERSEA ISLAND. Its neighbour Bradwell Waterside is on the estuary. About 3 m. from the two villages, by the sea-wall and reached by a footpath, are the foundations of the Roman fort of Othona, similar in style to that at BURGH CASTLE, near GREAT YARMOUTH. Here also is one of the most ancient of all England's churches, St Peter's-on-the-Wall, which, as its name suggests, is built on the very walls of the Roman fort. It is almost certainly the church which was built by the priest St Cedd in about A.D. 654. All that remains is the nave, built mainly of Roman materials, and for many years this historic place of worship served as a humble barn, some 50 ft by 20 ft in area and with walls rather over 20 ft tall, until an observant visitor saw in it the outlines of the original Anglo-Saxon church.

Inland is the Parish Church of St Thomas which has a west tower added in 1706 to an earlier structure. Bradwell Lodge is a delightful Georgian house, which overlooks the river. Originally Tudor, it was rebuilt in 1781–6 for the Rev. Sir Henry Bate Dudley, friend of Thomas Gainsborough. The internal decorations are almost certainly by Robert Adam, and include paintings by Angelica Kauffmann, and beautiful fireplaces. On top is a belvedere of unusual size and charm, while within is a vaulted entrance hall and oval library.

Between the church and the Lodge is the village green surrounded by cottages. In striking contrast with the ancient Church of St Peter and indeed the district as a whole is the nuclear power station which was begun in 1957.

BRAINTREE, *Essex* (11–TL7622), grew up as a town placed at the junction of important Roman roads, Stane Street running E.–W. and, crossing it from SW. to NE. the CHELMSFORD to SUDBURY road, and also on the River Blackwater. Like its neighbour BOCKING, into which it gradually merges, it has derived its prosperity from the silk trade founded by the Courtaulds, which followed on the wool trade of an earlier age. Its other great industry is the making of metal

Sudbury: Cornard Wood, known as "Gainsborough's Forest".
Detail of painting by Thomas Gainsborough, 1748

windows which was established by Francis Crittal in 1884 and which has since developed into a very important international enterprise. Another famous Braintree character was Nicholas Udall (1505–56) who, after being dismissed from his post as headmaster of Eton, became vicar of Braintree in 1537. It was possibly at about the time he became headmastei of Westminster School (1554) that he wrote the first known English comedy, *Ralph Roister Doister*.

The Church of St Michael the Archangel has a good 13th-cent. tower with a shingled broach spire, but the rest of the exterior is mainly 19th-cent. Inside is a chapel built by Udall. Braintree itself has a town hall built 1926–8 and among several buildings of earlier date should be noticed the corn exchange of 1839, the 18th-cent. Horns Hotel, the Georgian Constitutional Club and the 16th-cent. Old Manor House. Near the White Hart (*see* Bocking) is another fine inn, The Swan, with good timbering.

BRANCASTER, *Norfolk* (11–TF7743). Almost 2,000 years ago this was the site of Branodunum, a Roman fort, of which little now remains. The village, which is close to the north coast on the A149, has a 14th-cent. church, St Mary's. There is a 14th-cent. font with a particularly remarkable cover, Perpendicular in style and telescopic in its action. Three Italian lanterns on poles are now operated by electricity.

One m. to the N. across the reeded, marshy flats is Brancaster Bay and 1 m. to the E. is Brancaster Staithe, a popular boating centre. From here you may go by boat to **Scolt Head Island.**

The island is about 4 m. long and one of the best known features of the coast. Bathing can be particularly dangerous due to the tidal currents. Scolt is a shingle ridge resting on sand flats, partly covered by dunes and enclosing marshes. (*See also* BLAKENEY.) Marram grass may be seen on the dunes, as well as many other types of vegetation. Behind the beaches the marshes support plant and insect life in abundance. The entire area is in the care of the National Trust and naturalists will find numerous things to interest them. Among the many birds to be seen are various species of gull (some rare), terns, even including an occasional arctic tern, gannets and arctic skuas. Cormorants, redshanks and greenshanks, oyster-catchers, ducks and geese in many varieties are only a few of the birds to be seen on this part of the coast which has one of the longest lists of birds in the British Isles.

BRANDON, *Suffolk* (11–TL7886). Brandon is situated in the NW. corner of the county almost on the Norfolk border and is part of the area known as Breckland. It is in that tiny portion of Suffolk which lies to the W. of the A11. Flints have provided its main industry for centuries. It is on the Little Ouse near the new State Forest of THETFORD Chase. St Peter's Church is some way from the town which grew up along the main road. The village displays the local building materials, flint of course, chalk, plaster and brick. The

school in the Gothic style dates from 1878. The old stone five-arched bridge links Suffolk with Norfolk.

Extensive Roman remains have been found here at Fenhouse Farm. Brandon Hall is 18th-cent. Simon Eyre, the shoemaker who became Lord Mayor of London in Thomas Dekker's *The Shoemaker's Holiday* (1600), was based on the Simon Eyre, native of Brandon, who became Lord Mayor of London in 1445.

BRECKLAND, *Norfolk* (11–TL8590). This is the name given to that part of East Anglia which surrounds THETFORD and through which runs the Little Ouse. For many years it was a barren region of heathland but now the work of the Forestry Commission and the immense tree-planting programme which they have undertaken has changed the character of a once empty area. Meres make for variety and provide the fisherman with sport and the bird-watcher with a chance to observe some of the many species which make Norfolk their home.

Breckland leads into the fens, and includes areas where cultivation has made agriculture a source of livelihood. There are still traces of the droves along which the nomadic tribes of ancient days travelled with their flocks across the width of England, and the flints which provided their tools were found at GRIME'S GRAVES and may be seen in many of the buildings of Thetford and in a number of the museums in the counties of Norfolk, Suffolk and Cambridgeshire.

BREDFIELD, *Suffolk* (11–TM2653). The birthplace of the famous writer Edward Fitz-Gerald who was born at Bredfield House on 31 March 1809. The building was damaged during the last war and has since been demolished. All that remains are the stables and some minor outbuildings. FitzGerald married Lucy, daughter of Bernard Barton, one of the WOODBRIDGE Wits and is best remembered for his translation of *The Rubaiyat of Omar Khayyam* and his letters, many of them written from the rectory in 1853–60, where he often stayed with the rector, George Crabbe, son of the poet. He died on 14 June 1883 and is buried at Boulge, 1 m. from Bredfield. A rose grown from a Persian seed, said to be from Omar's tomb, flowers on his grave.

The Church of St Andrew has Tudor brick battlements and flushwork decoration on the tower. Near the village is the village pump, with an elaborate wrought-iron crown dating from the 18th cent.

BRENT ELEIGH, *Suffolk* (11–TL9547). St Mary's Church contains much Jacobean woodwork (pulpit and box pews, etc.) and a south door (14th-cent.), also finely carved. There is a monument by Thomas Dunn to Edward Colman (1743), a Fellow of Trinity College, CAMBRIDGE, who built the library which once stood in the churchyard (since rebuilt). A series of wall paintings of the 14th cent. has recently been discovered in the church.

Brent Eleigh Hall is basically Elizabethan in plan but with additions from later centuries. The ceiling over the staircase has fine plastering surrounding a painted oval centre-piece. In the 1930s the Hall was added to by Sir Edwin Lutyens. Colman is commemorated again in the almshouses of 1731.

BRENTWOOD, *Essex* (7–TQ5993), lies off the main London to CHELMSFORD road, the A12, on the original roadway, the crossing point of the roads which run diagonally across the county. Its White Hart Hotel is a famous old coaching inn dating back to the late 15th cent. Also in the High Street are the ruins of the 14th-cent. St Thomas's Chapel. The present churches are modern, the new St Thomas's being built in the 1880s in the Gothic style, and the Roman Catholic cathedral dating from 1861. Rather earlier is the Congregational chapel of 1847.

Brentwood School was founded in 1557. Remains of old buildings in Ingrave Road include School House, a fine Georgian building dated 1773. Many additional buildings were added both here and in Shenfield Road in later centuries.

To the SW. Great Warley church (1904) should be seen for its elaborate display of Art Nouveau.

BRESSINGHAM, *Norfolk* (11–TM0780). Bressingham Hall, open to the public on certain days throughout the summer, contains an outstanding collection of steam locomotives, tractors and other engines, fairground roundabouts and a miniature railway. The owner, Mr Alan Bloom, is one of the country's leading horticulturists and the gardens, almost 6 acres in extent, will delight all lovers of hardy plants and Alpines. Among the collection of more than 20 different engines is the famous Britannia Class Pacific No. 70013 *Oliver Cromwell.*

The village is 2½ m. W. of DISS on the A1066 to THETFORD. The church of St John the Baptist was rebuilt in 1527 by Sir Roger Pilkington, though much of it was, of course, earlier in date. Its particular feature is its magnificently carved bench-ends, some of which show figures, while others have various combinations of grotesques and designs based on twining plant forms. There are also three collecting shoes dated 1631. These relics of the 17th cent. were used in churches to collect offerings before being replaced by bags and plates. They are not in fact shoes, but look rather like a modern dustpan.

BREYDON WATER, *Norfolk* (11–TG4907). This is not a broad in the true sense of the word. It is really an extension of the estuary of the River Yare which is almost closed off from the sea by the sandbanks upon which GREAT YARMOUTH is built. Along its banks may be found the yellow Flag Iris, *Iris pseudacorus.* Due to its proximity to the sea, river prawns, common to Holland as well as to Norfolk, may be found, and are locally known as Jack shrimps. Brown shrimps also abound but these only exist in salt water.

Breydon Water made an ideal natural harbour at the time of the Romans and it is on the high ground of its south-west end that the fortress of Gariannonum, now known as BURGH CASTLE, was built at the end of the 3rd cent.

Breydon is the site of a big electrically-powered water-pumping station opened in 1948 and capable of drawing 100 tons of water a minute.

BRIGHTLINGSEA, *Essex* (11–TM0816). Reached from the B1027 road from COLCHESTER to CLACTON-ON-SEA, Brightlingsea is almost an island on the River Colne. As such it is not only a centre for yachting and boat building but also for the cultivation of the oysters which are found at so many points along the Essex coast. Roman remains testify to its ancient origin, and Roman brickwork may be seen in the Church of All Saints which dates from Norman times, though it is now mainly in the Perpendicular style. The tower, the flint and flushwork are excellent examples of their kind. Inside the church is a rich collection of brasses and monuments. The former date from 1496 (to John Beryf and his wife) and the latter includes an important memorial to Nicholas Magens, d. 1764, made by N. Read.

In the High Street is an ancient timbered house, Jacobs, which was bought by the Beriffe family from the Jacobs in the early 15th cent. The house itself was mentioned as far back as 1315. There is an early 16th-cent. brick stair-turret and an interesting roof. Surrounding the house is an attractive pattern of narrow streets, Victorian cottages and Georgian houses.

BROADS, THE, *Norfolk* (around 11–TG4020). That unique combination of lakes, rivers and cuts which is to be found in the triangle bounded by NORWICH, LOWESTOFT and HAPPISBURGH. Famous for the magnificent boating they provide, they are also the home of a multitude of birds, flowers, insects and plants.

Largely man-made, the broads are the water-filled pits left by the turf cutters of long ago. Each is different and while some are fresh water, others are salt. If it were not for the coastal defence system, the entire region might well be flooded as it was in older times. While the main industry is now the tourist traffic, there is still evidence of the ancient crafts of thatching and basket-making, and many areas are managed as Nature Reserves.

It should be emphasized that while the area is excellent touring ground for the motorist, with its many picturesque villages, its fine churches and delightful countryside, it is not possible to gain a real idea of the true nature of the broads from the road. There are relatively few good viewpoints owing to the general flatness of the countryside, and to gain such a picture you must take to the water. Where good roadside views *are* obtainable they will be mentioned in the notes on individual broads. In this respect RANWORTH, ORMESBY and ROLLESBY are exceptional.

In recent years many of the broads have continued that silting up which began many years ago, and constant efforts have to be made to keep the waterways free for the traffic which is at its peak in the summer months. Boats may be bought or hired from the many yards and staithes. However, there are restrictions on entry to certain broads and a copy of the Navigation Map should be in the possession of anyone who intends to do any serious touring. Sailing requires much more skill and experience than the driving of a motor cruiser. Fishing, too, is a popular broadland sport with a wide range of fish including bream, perch, pike, roach, rudd and tench. Some areas are set aside for the use of anglers.

The main broads are as follows (notes on each will be found separately): Barton, Breydon, Hickling, Horsey, Hoveton, Ormesby, Ranworth, Rollesby, Salhouse, South Walsham and Wroxham. The Rivers Bure, Thurne, Ant, Yare and Waveney all flow into the North Sea at GORLESTON and GREAT YARMOUTH.

BUNGAY, *Suffolk* (11–TM3389). In the 12th cent. Bungay, which is now a market town and yachting centre on the River Waveney, saw the building of a great castle by Roger Bigod. Little now remains of the 70 ft square keep which includes in the south-west corner a mining gallery. This defensive feature was a tunnel supported by timbers which could be removed when attack threatened, thus causing the entire corner of the building to collapse on the invaders! The main headquarters of the Bigods was at FRAMLINGHAM though they retained a house in the town.

The Church of St Mary was once the church of the Benedictine nunnery founded in the 12th cent. by Gundreda. Like many other buildings in the town, it suffered considerable destruction in the Great Fire of 1688. Its tower, built at the end of the 15th cent., is one of the most remarkable in the county, with its polygonal buttresses and turrets. The Church of Holy Trinity contains a fine pulpit of 1558 and a monument to Thomas Wilson by Thomas Scheemakers.

In the market place stands the Butter Cross erected in 1689 after the fire. The statue of Justice which surmounts the dome was added in 1754. There are a number of Georgian houses in the market place and its immediate neighbourhood and that at No. 6 St Mary's Street should be noticed. Also note the oriel windows of Nos. 14–18 with the arms of the Drapers Company, the Maids Head of the Mercers Company, and a merchant's mark.

In the middle of the 18th cent. John King, a local chemist, established some baths here. As in so many East Anglian towns of similar size there was a theatre which at one time became a corn exchange and is now in commercial use. Bungay's chief activity since the 18th cent. has been printing.

BURGH CASTLE, *Suffolk* (11–TM2251). Situated in the north-east corner of the county, almost on the Norfolk borders, this was the Gariannonum of the Romans. By the end of the occupation it was one of a chain of fortresses guarding the East Coast. The massive walls and the round bastions still give the spectator some idea of the strength of the original building, probably erected *c.* A.D. 290. With the departure of the Romans the castle saw the coming in *c.* 640 of the Irish missionary St Fursey who founded a monastery within its walls. The pendulum of change saw the site used by the Normans as a castle once again and in later ages many of its stones were used to build houses for the villagers.

History again comes to life in the great beam in the Village Institute with its inscription carved in 1548. The Church of SS. Peter and Paul has a Norman round tower and has been much restored. The font (Perpendicular) is finely carved.

BURNHAM-ON-CROUCH, *Essex* (7–TQ 9496). Like so many of the Essex estuary towns Burnham-on-Crouch is noted as a yachting and boat-building centre and also for its oyster beds. Along the quay is a terrace of houses with, as its centre-piece, the White Hart Hotel. Nearer the sea is the headquarters of the Royal Corinthian Yacht Club built in 1931. The High Street has a mixture of buildings including weather-boarded cottages, Georgian houses and examples of the Victorian period. Among the latter is the Clock Tower of 1877. Where the High Street broadens out was doubtless the site of the old market.

One m. N. of the town itself is the Church of St Mary which overlooks the coast from its slightly elevated position. The exterior features battlements which may also be seen on the south porch, decorated with four stone coats of arms. The north porch is 16th-cent. and has a stepped gable. Inside the church the lack of divisions between the nave, chancel and aisles gives it an unusual appearance. The font is Norman and made of Purbeck marble, and a wall tablet reminds us of the Rev. Alexander Scott who was chaplain on H.M.S. *Victory* when Nelson was killed in battle.

BURNHAMS, THE, *Norfolk* (11–TF8243), are a group which once numbered seven parishes. It was at **Burnham Thorpe**, in the now demolished Parsonage House, that Horatio Nelson was born on 29 September 1758, the fifth son of the 11 children of the Rev. Edmund Nelson. As such it is one of our most historic sites. When he was nine his mother died and at the age of 12 the young Nelson was sent to sea. The puny-looking lad soon achieved rank and was a captain (on the frigate *Hinchingbroke*) at the age of 20. His marriage, his rapid promotions and his relationship with Lady Hamilton are part of our history, and his death on the *Victory* on 21 October 1805 is one of the unforgettable episodes in the chronicles of the British people. After lying in state in the Painted Hall of Greenwich Hospital, Nelson was buried in St Paul's Cathedral on 9 January 1806.

Though the house is no more, its site is marked by a plaque close to the road. The Church of All Saints (Decorated and Perpendicular) has a Purbeck marble font and many memorials of the great sailor, and a lectern made from the timbers of Nelson's ship *Victory*. There is hardly need to

The Broads: a typical scene on the River Bure

state the name of the village inn! **Burnham Market** is the central village of the group with a fine main street and at its west end St Mary's Church. On top of its tower is a battlemented parapet with unusual carvings of Biblical scenes from the Old and New Testaments. Behind the church is Westgate Hall, built to the design of Sir John Soane in 1783.

Just NE. of Burnham Market is **Burnham Overy**, and on the way is a fine windmill of 1814 (National Trust). Where the road crosses the River Burn stands a watermill and a charming group of cottages. St Clement's Church with its Norman central tower, which was later lowered to receive a cupola of the 17th cent., has a tiny painting of St Christopher, a Stuart table and tables of the Commandments. One m. to the N. is Overy Staithe with a small harbour for light craft.

Two other Burnhams include **Burnham Norton** where St Margaret's has a round Norman tower. Inside is a large square Norman font and a Jacobean pulpit of exquisitely delicate hexagonal design. The panels are painted and there is a backboard and canopy.

Burnham Norton was the site of a Carmelite Friary founded in 1241. The gatehouse is Decorated in style and has excellent flush panelling.

Burnham Deepdale, near the coast on the A149, has a tower dating from before the Conquest and a magnificent Norman font. Around it are 12 carved panels representing each of the months, all surmounted by a frieze of lions and foliage.

BURWELL, *Cambridgeshire* (11–TL5866). One of the largest villages in Cambridgeshire and the centre of barge-building, turf and other industries. The rebel Geoffrey de Mandeville was killed here in 1144. It is the site of a 12th-cent. castle, of which all that remains is the moat. The Church of St Mary is a fine example of the spaciousness and brightness of the Perpendicular style. The interior is mainly built of clunch, hard East Anglian chalk. Over the chancel arch may be seen some beautifully carved tracery enclosing a "wheel" window which is unusual in that the spokes are replaced by whirl-like arms known as mouchettes.

The village contains a number of very attractive buildings as well as two windmills, only one of which is in working order.

Two m. SW. is **Swaffham Prior** famous for having two churches in one churchyard. St Mary's, with its octagonal tower on a sturdy Norman base, will remind the visitor of the great octagon at ELY. St Cyriac's also has an octagonal tower, but the rest of the building has become derelict.

Swaffham Prior House was built in 1753 but even more interesting is Baldwin Manor, a beautiful half-timbered building from the first half of the 16th cent.

Two windmills, one preserved and one derelict, echo the two churches. Windmill Hill gives wonderful views of the chalk heights above the Icknield Way.

BURY ST EDMUNDS, Suffolk (11–TL8564). The cathedral town, and the county town of West Suffolk. Its motto, "Shrine of a King, Cradle of the Law" commemorates two of the outstanding episodes in its history. Edmund, last king of the East Angles, was killed in 869 by the Danes at "Haegelisdun" (possibly Hellesdon, near NORWICH). The English held his death to be a martyrdom; for many years he was patron saint of England. His remains were later taken to Beodricesworth and from the early 11th cent. this town was known as St Edmundsbury. In 1020 Cnut, having become king of England on the death of his rival, another Edmund, and no doubt glad to make a gesture that might help resolve discord between the English and Danish communities of his new kingdom, gave the monastery where the saint was buried the status of abbey.

At the time of the Conquest the abbot was Baldwin, a Frenchman and a Norman sympathizer, and town and abbey were spared disturbance.

The second historic episode took place on 20 November 1215 when the barons "Swore at St Edmund's altar that they would obtain from King John the ratification of Magna Carta".

Bury St Edmunds today still retains the complete rectangular plan set out by Abbot Baldwin in the 11th cent. It is essentially Georgian in appearance though many buildings and houses are of earlier date than their façades would suggest.

The famous abbey was over 500 ft long with a west front nearly 250 ft wide which made it one of the greatest churches in the country. What remains of it today, though but a small fragment of the original buildings, is sufficient to give some idea of its former splendour. The Norman Gate, c. 1120–50 stands squarely and firmly like some religious keep. It presents an interesting contrast to the Abbey Gate c. 1430–40 which, no less sturdy in appearance, has an altogether more refined pattern of decoration.

The remains of the abbey church are mostly those of the west front and into them have been built dwelling houses, a fact which still excites fierce controversy among those who would wish them to remain and those who press for their removal. Other parts of this once great abbey may be traced in the grounds which lead down towards the River Lark.

The cathedral church since 1914 has been St James's immediately S. of the Norman Gate. It is 16th-cent. with 19th-cent. additions by Gilbert Scott. There are plans to enlarge it to a size more in keeping with its status as the only cathedral in the county. St Mary's Church has a magnificent Perpendicular exterior and its interior is no less perfect. The stone pendant in the roof of the Notyngham Porch, the splendid roof of the nave as well as that of the chancel are among the finest examples of their kind.

Another outstanding religious building is the Unitarian (originally Presbyterian) chapel in Churchgate Street, 1711–12, comparable to that at IPSWICH. Its double-decker pulpit is noteworthy.

Bury, as it is locally known, abounds in fine examples of civic and domestic buildings. The Town Hall, originally designed in the 1770s by Robert Adam as a theatre, is a classically symmetrical composition of considerable charm.

Moyse's Hall, now an outstandingly interesting museum, dates from the 12th cent. (it may be East Anglia's oldest domestic building) and houses prehistoric, Roman and medieval exhibits. Only a little later in date is the famous Abbot's Bridge across the River Lark, near where Mustow Street meets Eastgate Street.

Bury is a town to walk in. Angel Hill, for example, with its spacious feeling of earlier days leads you into the central complex of the city with its many beautiful buildings of the 17th and 18th cents. Near the General Post Office is Cupola House built in 1693 and featuring above its steeply pitched roof the cupola or turret, from which pleasing views could be obtained.

Not far away is the Athenaeum with its ballroom, the work of Francis Sandys. At the far end of Crown Street is the Theatre Royal, built in 1819 by William Wilkins, architect of the National Gallery, and of Downing College, CAMBRIDGE. It has been restored as one of Britain's finest Regency theatres.

The Guildhall, built in the 13th cent., was remodelled in the 19th. Near St James's churchyard is the Provost's House, built in 1730, as an asylum at the bequest of Dr Clopton. Angel Corner (National Trust), a Queen Anne house, contains a memorable collection of clocks, watches and time-pieces of many kinds. Open on occasion is the Suffolk Regimental Museum, full of items connected with the famous regiment.

Among the famous literary figures associated with the town was "Ouida", Louise de la Ramée (1840–1908). Born at Bury, the daughter of a French teacher, for some years she lived in London but about 1874 went to Italy where she died after having written over 40 novels, including a book of stories for children, *Bimbi*. Edward Fitz-Gerald, the translator of *The Rubaiyat of Omar Khayyam* came here to school and Dickens wrote of the Angel Inn in his works. A tablet on a house in St Mary's Square commemorates Thomas Clarkson, the fighter against slavery (*see* WISBECH).

CAISTER-ON-SEA, Norfolk (11–TG5211), a seaside resort separated from GREAT YARMOUTH by the links of the Great Yarmouth and Caister Golf Club (18 holes) which are on the main A149 coast road. Excavations have shown the extent of the Roman town to the N. of the Caister–Acle road. In later centuries it was also an Anglo-Saxon town of some importance.

The Church of Holy Trinity dates from the 13th cent. though it has been much restored. Inside is a huge font almost 5 ft high and 3½ ft across. A

Commandment board has the familiar figures of Moses and Aaron and the Royal coat of arms shows some interesting changes to the dates which were originally painted on it.

Just over 1 m. inland is **Caister Castle**, one of the best of its period (15th-cent.) in the country. It was built in 1432–5 for the same Sir John Fastolf who appeared in Shakespeare's *Henry VI*. After his death in 1459 the castle came into the possession of the Paston family and it was here that many of the famous Paston Letters were written. Indeed it is a picturesque ruin, with one large tower at its north-west corner and its moat which indicates its original rectangular plan. At the opposite corner is the present Caister Hall with Georgian dressings to the original walls. A motor museum is open to the public.

CAISTOR ST EDMUND, *Norfolk* (11–TG 2303), which lies 4 m. S. of NORWICH by the River Tas, was the site of the Roman town of Venta Icenorum which suggests that it was probably here that the Iceni settled after Boadicea's revolt of A.D. 70. Some of the walls are still well preserved and excavations have revealed the porter's lodge at the south gate.

The Church of St Edmund is reached by crossing the moat of the old Roman city. It is a simple building with a chancel, *c.* 1300 and a later tower and nave. Its most remarkable feature is the font dating from *c.* 1410, octagonal in shape with many interesting carvings, among them angels, lions and the signs of the Evangelists. The nave has a large painting of St Christopher.

Caistor Old Hall, N. of the church, dates from 1647, but parts are earlier. The entrance, for example, is dated 1612.

CAMBRIDGE, *Cambridgeshire* (11–TL4658). Cambridge is one of the most important and beautiful towns not only in East Anglia, but also in Britain and even Europe. The quality of its buildings, in particular those belonging to the University, and the particular atmosphere caused by the felicitous combination of river and gardens have given the city a place in the itinerary of every visitor to this country.

The old phrase "Town and Gown" suggests the ancient division, culminating in riots in 1381 during Wat Tyler's revolt, between that part of the city which is devoted to the University and the remainder which is residential and commercial – the city of everyday life in fact. The University has influenced not only the architecture of the town but also its character: its bookshops are among the finest in the country, and the adventurous programmes of the two theatres and several cinemas, the frequency of excellent concerts and the wide range of restaurants reflect the tastes and interests of the academic population. The history of Cambridge began many hundreds of years before the first college, Peterhouse, was founded in 1284 by Hugh de Balsham, Bishop of ELY. In the century preceding the Roman Conquest a Celtic settlement had arisen on what is known as Castle Hill, lying between Castle Street and

Chesterton Road to the N. of the town. At the foot of the hill was a ford across the River Cam, and successive Roman developments probably included the building of a bridge at this point. This bridge became the only one to have given its name to an English county. Its location was of great importance as marking the place where the Roman roads, in particular the *Via Devana* from COLCHESTER to CHESTER, converged with the system of rivers and canals. As the northernmost point before reaching the fens such a site was of great strategic and commercial importance.

With the departure of the Romans the town continued to spread to its present position on the East Anglian side of the river. The Normans, however, rebuilt the castle and moved over to the opposite bank of the Cam. Nothing remains of the castle today but the mound. The 13th cent. saw the founding of the first Cambridge college and the consequent increase in the importance of the city as a seat of learning and a centre of communal life.

As the visitor will undoubtedly begin his tour with the University buildings, it is those which will be described first. A word on the possible origins of the University may not be out of place. In the 12th cent. students were still attached to the schools of the monasteries and cathedrals and the gradual development of universities in Italy and France was followed by the migration of scholars moving from one centre to another. Thus some went from Paris to OXFORD in 1167, and in 1209 further groups went from Oxford to Cambridge. Several religious orders settled in Cambridge in the 12th cent., and their houses attracted sufficient numbers of students for it to be recognized as a seat of learning by a writ for its governance made by Henry III in 1231.

In its early days the University used whatever accommodation was available, sometimes churches and on other occasions houses. The normal master's course was of seven years' duration and might sometimes be followed by a further ten years of study for a doctorate in theology. Students started earlier than now at the age of about 14 and generally completed their studies to become schoolmasters. The students at this time lived in lodgings in the town and due to the unsatisfactory conditions under which they had to exist, hostels in the care of one of the masters came into being. Such were the origins of the college system which prevails today.

Many of the colleges are on the main street (Trumpington Street, becoming King's Parade and then St John's Street) which runs parallel to the river between it and Market Hill. The "backs", peaceful green lawns running down to the river where it is crossed by bridges and shaded by willows, are in summer the essence of the Cambridge idyll of punting and May Balls.

Christ's College: Originally founded in 1439 as "God's House" and re-established under its present name in 1505 by Lady Margaret Beaufort. Imposing Gateway to St Andrew's Street. Fellows' Building added after 1640, important building of three stories plus dormers. 20th-cent.

Kenneth Scowen

Cambridge: the "Bridge of Sighs" links two of the buildings of St John's College

additions by Albert Richardson, P.R.A. Fine collection of plate, particularly Tudor, including Foundress's Cup pre-1440. Its most famous son was Milton.

Clare College: Founded as University Hall in 1326 by Richard de Baddow. Refounded by Elizabeth de Burgh of Clare, taking its present name since 1346. The court has, like Christ's, three stories plus dormers. The bridge, *c.* 1640, was built by Thomas Grumbold in the classical style, the first of its kind in Cambridge. New Court across the river was designed by Sir G. G. Scott and built 1924–35. Collection of candlesticks and foreign silver from Flanders, Germany, etc.

Corpus Christi: Founded by the town's merchants in 1352. Old Court still retains original appearance of the 14th cent. even though restored and added to. New Court built by W. Wilkins, 1823–7. The college has the best collection of silver plate in Cambridge. The Drinking Horn, *c.* 1347, may be the earliest piece of plate in Cambridge (*see* Trinity Hall). Christopher Marlowe studied here.

Downing College: A late addition, designed by William Wilkins in 1807, seven years after its foundation. Classic Grecian style and spacious grounds create admirable feeling of open-plan college. Additions in 1873, 1929, etc., and most imaginatively in 1969.

Emmanuel College: Founded 1584 by Sir Walter Mildmay on site of the Dominican or Black Friars house. In 1666 Sir Christopher Wren designed the chapel in the new classical style. Other additions in 18th and 19th cents., and in 20th cent. by Leonard Stokes. Fine collection of plate, both English and foreign. John Harvard, founder of the American college, was an alumnus.

Gonville and Caius College: Founded by Edmund Gonville 1348, re-established by Dr Caius 1557. Caius had studied at Gonville and determined to found a new college which would include his own. The three gateways, the Gate of Humility, the Gate of Virtue and Wisdom, 1567, a particularly impressive structure, and the Gate of Honour symbolize a student's progress. Monument in the chapel to Dr Caius by Theodore Haveus. Additions in 18th and 19th cents. and across Trinity Street in 20th. The plate includes two of the three "coco-nut cups" in Cambridge and the sceptre presented by Dr Caius first to the Royal College of Physicians and then to his own college.

Jesus College: Founded by Bishop Alcock of Ely in 1496. The number of students is not as great as in some of the colleges, and it is larger than many, which gives it a feeling of spaciousness. The chapel contains Norman portions dating from the nunnery which Bishop Alcock took over. It has decoration by Pugin, William Morris, Ford Madox Brown and Burne-Jones, and contains a memorial to Constable's son. Among its scholars were Coleridge, Laurence Sterne and Malthus.

King's College: Founded by Henry VI in 1441 at the same time as he established the school at ETON. Fellows' Building was designed by James Gibbs, 1723, in a simple classical style. A hundred

Cambridge: New Hall is a modern college for women

years later added to by William Wilkins, with further additions into the present century. The bridge, artfully sited, dates from 1818. The chief glory of King's College and of Cambridge itself is the chapel, considered by some the most outstanding building in Britain and the finest Gothic building in Europe. It was begun in 1446. Its unusual dimensions, almost 300 ft long, 80 ft high and 40 ft wide, prepare the spectator for its extraordinary system of spatial relationships. The effect of the interior is breathtaking. The shafts on either side of the chapel lead the eye up into the roof where the profusion of delicate fan-vaulting appears as if made of lace rather than stone. The placing of the organ case (1606) with its curves echoing those of the ceiling, and the superb quality of the woodwork of the screen and the choir stalls (1536) act as a perfect foil to the splendours above. No less important is the stained glass, dating from 1515, the year the chapel was completed. The windows tell stories from the Old and New Testaments. Note the *Adoration of the Magi* by Rubens, *c.* 1634, and the 20th-cent. bronze candlestick by Benno Elkan.

Magdalene College: Founded in 1542 incorporating the original monks' hostel which had been established in 1428 by the prior of the Benedictines at Cambridge, and which was the only early college on the west bank of the river. The first court and the chapel date from the mid-15th cent. and were named Buckingham College. After the Dissolution it came into the hands of Lord Audley

of AUDLEY END and was re-founded under its present name. Additions were gradually made to the original buildings including Pepys Building, which includes the Pepysian Library housed in his own bookcases together with his own desk. His diaries are on exhibition. A more recent building, Mallory Court, commemorates the famous mountaineer.

Pembroke College: Founded in 1347 by Mary, Countess of Pembroke. A notable addition was made by Sir Christopher Wren who designed the chapel, a gift to the college from his uncle, the Bishop of Ely. It was consecrated in 1664, the earliest classical building in the city. The famous Anathema Cup (1481-2) and the Foundress's Cup, perhaps even earlier, are among the fine collection of plate. Edmund Spenser, Archbishop Whitgift, Nicholas Ridley, William Pitt the Younger and the poet Gray were all Pembroke men.

Peterhouse College: This was the earliest of the colleges to be founded, established by the Bishop of Ely in 1281 and moving to its own hostels in 1284. The original hall is part of the south side of the Main Court but little remains due to the 19th-cent. restoration. The chapel, dating from 1632, seems to combine some of the features of the earlier chapel at King's, the corner turrets for example, with an awareness of some of the classical motifs which were to be fully realized by Wren in the next generation.

Queens' College: Whereas some of the colleges

were founded twice, Queens' was founded no less than three times. First in 1446, by Andrew Docket, under the name of St Bernard's College, then in 1448 by Margaret of Anjou, under the name of Queen's College, and finally about 1465 by Elizabeth Woodville, Queen of Edward IV. Thus it is not Queen's but Queens' College. Perhaps its most famous feature is the President's Lodge c. 1540, a picturesque timbered building over the north cloisters. Inside, the panelling, part carved and part linenfold, is particularly worthy of attention. The famous Mathematical Bridge was constructed in 1749 without the use of any nails. The chapel contains some interesting brasses, and a fine 15th-cent. painting. Erasmus resided here in 1510.

St Catharine's College: Founded in 1473 by Robert Wodelarke though none of its buildings of that time remain, most of them having been reconstructed at the end of the 17th cent.

St John's College: Founded by Lady Margaret Beaufort, mother of Henry VII, in 1511, again at the instigation of John Fisher. The First Court still manages to give a good idea of its original appearance. An elaborate gatehouse shows a fine display of heraldic carvings. The hall contains the original hammer-beam roof of the 16th cent. The Combination Room, with its patterned plaster ceiling and the library, c. 1623–4, are important additions, and the bridge built by Grumbold c. 1710 was based on designs by Wren. New Court, built on the other side of the Cam, 1825–31, was at the time the largest building of any college. The famous Bridge of Sighs which connects it with the old buildings was designed by Hutchinson in 1831. Later came the chapel by Scott and additional buildings in the present century. The Hercule's Cup is among its collection of plate. Roger Ascham, Herrick, Wordsworth and Palmerston were John's men.

Sidney Sussex College: Founded in 1596 by Lady Frances Sidney, Countess of Sussex, on the site of the Franciscan house. Much worked on by Sir Jeffry Wyatville early in the 19th cent. The chapel rebuilt in 1912 by T. H. Lyon is a fine building in the classic style. The painting over the altar is by Pittoni. The plate includes good examples from the 17th cent. to the present day. Oliver Cromwell entered as a fellow commoner in 1616.

Trinity College: King's Hall, founded 1336 by Edward III, was re-founded by Henry VIII as Trinity College, in 1546. At the same time another college, Michaelhouse, founded 1323, was also incorporated. A number of the original buildings including King Edward's Tower and King's Hall were utilized and considerable extensions commenced in the 16th cent. The Great Gate, 1519, was included in the Great Court, much of which was built under the direction of Dr Thomas Nevile, a court larger than any at Cambridge or Oxford. The Renaissance Fountain dates from 1602 and the magnificent library, the work of Sir Christopher Wren, was commenced in 1676. The carving is by Grinling Gibbons. Fine sculptures include busts of Newton, by Roubiliac, and of Byron, and there is also an exceptional

collection of plate from the 17th cent. onwards.

Trinity Hall: Founded in 1350 by the Bishop of NORWICH. The 16th-cent. library is the best remaining of its date. It is the only college still known as a Hall, to distinguish it from Trinity College, and is famous for the number of Chief Justices it has produced. An outstanding collection of plate includes a Founder's Cup, pre-1350, one of the two earliest pieces of plate in the whole of the University (*see* Corpus Christi).

1869 saw the founding of the first college for women, *Girton*, which moved from Hitchin to its present site in 1873. In 1871 Miss Anne Clough had founded *Newnham* which moved into its present buildings in 1875. *Selwyn College*, for men, was founded in 1881 to be followed by *Ridley Hall, Westcott House* and *Westminster College*, all theological institutions.

Though considerable building had taken place between the wars it was 1954 before another college was founded. This was *New Hall*, a third women's college. It is a striking modern design by Peter Chamberlin, with a remarkable dome as one of its central features. *Fitzwilliam Hall* (formerly House) is another completely new building by Denys Lasdum (1960). In the same year *Churchill College* was founded to designs by Richard Sheppard, again in an uncompromisingly modern idiom. The University buildings apart from the colleges include the *Old Schools*, commenced in 1350. Many additions were made in succeeding years including the Palladian part by Stephen Wright, 1754–8.

Senate House by James Gibbs, 1722–30, handsomely adapts the tradition of Wren to the Palladian style. Among the plate is the Essex Cup after the Earl of Essex, installed as Chancellor in 1598. The *Old Library* was built by Cockerell in 1836–42 and the *New Library* by Sir G. G. Scott in 1931–4. The many laboratories, etc., include the world-famous *Cavendish Laboratory* where Rutherford was Professor.

The *Botanic Gardens* in Bateman Street were opened in 1846, and the *Scott Polar Research Centre* in Lensfield Road dates from 1933–4.

The Fitzwilliam Museum was founded by the 7th Viscount in 1816 and was built to the design of George Basevi. It is an impressive classical building and contains a magnificent collection of works of art of all kinds. Antiquities from Egypt, Greece and Rome; works from medieval times, drawings, paintings and sculptures of all schools, and large collections of coins, ceramics, glass and armour make it one of the most important collections in the country. The city contains many churches of great interest, particularly *St Benet's*, the oldest church in the county. The tower is Anglo-Saxon, probably c. 1000, and the interior arch is exceptionally well preserved. *St Mary-the-Great*, the University Church, stands in the centre of town; basically 15th-cent., it has a 17th-cent. tower and 14th-cent. details. University sermons are given here. Other churches worth exploring are *St Andrew the Less*; *St Botolph's*; *St Edward's*; *St Mary the Less*; *St Mary Magdalene*, originally the chapel of the leper hospital at Stourbridge; *St*

Michael's and of course *Holy Sepulchre*, Bridge Street. This last is the oldest (*c.* 1130), of the four remaining round churches in England and though drastically restored in the 19th cent. it still conveys the strong character of early Norman architecture. There are no civic buildings of outstanding architectural importance.

Hobson's Conduit (1614), in Brookside, is a reminder of the one-time carrier who became Mayor of the city. It was from his insistence that customers took the first horse offered, that the expression "Hobson's choice" derives.

The Gog Magog (or Grogingog) "Hills" just outside the town are popular for walking and have a golf course; on the crest of the hills is Wandlebury, an Iron Age fort. Below it lies Stourbridge Common, where an important fair was held for many years.

CANEWDON, *Essex* (7–TQ8994). Here the Church of St Nicholas, with its large tower, stands in a fine position on a hill above the River Crouch. Like many an East Anglian tower, it may well have done duty as lighthouse and vantage point. The pulpit came from a City church (St Christopher's) and the font from the demolished church at Shopland. The vicarage was commenced in 1758, and has been much added to; Canewdon Hall, a simple but attractive building, dates from 1807.

Near the church is the lock-up of 1775, which contains the old stocks.

The village of the 1960s contrasts with the timber-framed Lambourne Hall, 1 m. to the E.

CANVEY ISLAND, *Essex* (7–TQ7783). Though mentioned as far back as Norman times the island, situated in the Thames estuary, to the W. of SOUTHEND-ON-SEA, was subject to flooding until it was walled by the Dutch engineer Joos Croppenburgh in 1622. Its associations with Holland are brought to mind by the two Dutch cottages, 1618 and 1621, one of which is now a little museum. Octagonal and thatched, they are reminiscent of the Round House near the village of FINCHINGFIELD, though they are, of course, earlier. Though the island is now almost one vast spread of bungalows and caravan sites, the Church of St Nicholas, 1960, is most interesting and there is a modern War Memorial Hall, opened in 1953.

That year is remembered in Canvey for the dreadful night when great storms whipped across the East Coast causing such terrible loss of life and property.

CASTLE HEDINGHAM, *Essex* (11–TL78 35). Built on a hill overlooking the River Colne is the great castle which gives the village its name. It was constructed by the de Vere family in about 1140 and remains one of the most impressive keeps in England. Reached by a bridge (*c.* 1500) over the protecting ditch the tower, almost 100 ft high, is dominated by the two corner turrets. The richness of the carved decoration and the strength of the heavy stone walls add to the effect

of grandeur. The Church of St Nicholas was begun some 50 years after the building of the castle, and the interior is a perfect example of the late Norman style, with fine arcades and a magnificent south door; in the churchyard is the War Memorial, a re-erected 12th-cent. cross. The tower was rebuilt in the 16th cent. and was renovated again in 1616 and this, together with the general impression of the exterior, makes the interior of the church rather a surprise. A particularly impressive monument is that to the 15th Earl of Oxford, d. 1539, and his wife, which was probably carved by Cornelius Harman (*see* SAFFRON WALDEN).

Apart from the castle and the church the town has a number of domestic buildings of charm and merit. Near the church is an old inn, and in Queen Street are two excellent houses of Georgian date: The Rectory and Trinity Hall. In 1191 a Benedictine nunnery was founded to the W. of the village, near the Colne, but nothing now remains of its buildings.

CASTLE RISING, *Norfolk* (11–TF6624), has the remains of the castle built in the middle of the 12th cent. by William de Albini, perhaps on the site of Roman earthworks. The great keep, one of the largest in England, reminds one of that at NORWICH. Its great breadth contrasts with its height of some 50 ft. The exterior walls are richly decorated with arcading. The castle is entered through a fore-building and a strong, dramatic staircase; there are only two stories, the upper containing the great hall. Kitchens, a gallery and a small domestic chapel were included in the structure.

The Church of St Lawrence is famous for its Norman west front with a fine Norman doorway on the lower level, and an even finer window above, on either side of which is a group of intersecting arcades. Above this is a round window flanked by further arcading. This latter window may have been added when the church was much restored in the 19th cent. The font, which has a richly carved square bowl standing on a short circular shaft, is especially noteworthy.

On the green to the W. of the church is a large 15th-cent. cross. On the other side of the church is the Howard Hospital founded by Henry Howard, d. 1614. It is now an almshouse for old ladies, and visitors may still see the rooms with their original Jacobean furniture. Its inhabitants attend church on Sundays wearing red cloaks bearing the badge of the Howard family.

CAVENDISH, *Suffolk* (11–TL8046). One of Suffolk's most attractive villages and former ancestral village of the Dukes of Devonshire. Around the village green are thatched cottages and the Church of St Mary – a typically English traditional scene. The church has flushwork panelling and a clerestory. The 14th-cent. tower contains a room with a fire-place and shuttered windows. There are two lecterns, one a brass eagle and the other of wood, and two interesting statues, one Flemish and the other Italian. Other buildings include the mill, part of a mainly 18th-cent. group; Cavendish Hall to the W., early 19th-cent. in classic style; and Nether Hall Farmhouse, near the church, a 16th-cent. timber-framed building of two stories.

The 16th-cent. Old Rectory is now owned by Sue Ryder, and is one of the many homes she has established for refugees from all parts of the world.

CAWSTON, *Norfolk* (11–TG1324). A village about 12 m. NW. of NORWICH on the B1149 which has one of the finest churches in the county. This Church of St Agnes in the Perpendicular style was much patronized by Michael de la Pole, Earl of Suffolk, d. 1414. The west tower, 120 ft high, is starkly impressive, its simplicity relieved by the combination of window and doorway. Inside the church, the nave of which was probably built after the tower, there is a magnificent roof with great hammer-beams and numerous carved angels. The screen still has its doors and the original paintings, while the 15th-cent. pulpit is delicately poised on a stone base. Some of the stalls and benches have carvings.

Off the AYLSHAM road S. of the Woodrow Inn is the Duel Stone which commemorates a duel fought between Sir Henry Hobart and Oliver Le Neve in 1698.

CHELMSFORD, *Essex* (7–TL7006). The county town of Essex, though in terms of historical, architectural and archaeological interest it cannot be compared with COLCHESTER more to the NE. corner of the county. However, its position on the main road from London to Colchester and IPSWICH and on the cross routes from the SE. to the NW. of the county as well as its placing on the River Chelmer and the River Can has made it an important thoroughfare town since Roman times.

The Parish Church of St Mary was raised to the status of a cathedral just before the First World War and with its fine 15th-cent. tower topped by an open lantern and spire added in 1749, is a prominent feature of the city. In particular the south porch with elaborate Perpendicular flush-work patterning demands attention. Restorations took place early in the 19th cent. and again early in the 20th. Many of the interior fitments such as the pulpit, the altar, the provost's stall and the bishop's throne are comparatively recent, but there are a number of interesting monuments from the 16th cent. and later.

The Shire Hall was built by John Johnson (who was later to work on the church) in 1789–91. Though not large it is finely proportioned and suited to the dignity of a small town. The County Hall was built in 1935. As an important market and thoroughfare town traffic came to Chelmsford by water and rail as well as by road and its continued development in the 18th and 19th cents. has left a number of good domestic buildings, inns and, in particular, mills of which those at Springfield, Barnes and Moulsham are the best examples.

Later industrial development came when Marconi developed his electronic industry here and at WRITTLE. Civic buildings of the 19th cent. include a number of chapels and meeting houses and the conduit of 1814. The main public library, municipal offices and civic theatre are at the top end of Duke Street, while the excellent Chelmsford and Essex Museum is in Oaklands Park near the junction of Moulsham Street and the Chelmsford bypass.

The town is well provided with sporting facilities, the County Cricket team play here and there is an excellent football team.

CHIPPING ONGAR, *Essex* (7–TL5502). A small town which derives its name from the old word "chipping" or market, which grew in the shadow of the castle built by the Normans in the 11th cent. and of which little remains but the mound some 50 ft high. The Church of St Martin of Tours is very much Norman with a belfry of the 15th cent. and dormer windows of the 18th. Inside is an attractive west gallery supported on columns. The pulpit is early 17th-cent. with strapwork decoration and there is a monument by the well-known sculptor, Nollekens.

Where the old market met, the High Street widens and close by are some interesting houses, one at the corner of the lane to the church is dated 1642, with opposite, the King's Head (1697). It was in the Congregational church (1833) that the famous missionary and explorer David Livingstone was trained. In the same church one of the pastors was Isaac Taylor, one of a famous family of writers, artists and craftsmen. It was the daughters of one of the Taylors who wrote *Twinkle, twinkle, little star* at LAVENHAM at the end of the 18th cent.

CLACTON-ON-SEA, *Essex* (11–TM1715), has for a long time been one of the most popular of holiday resorts, with behind it the two villages of **Great** and **Little Clacton**. The former has a much restored Norman church (St John the Baptist), the Mansion House (Georgian), the Ship Inn and the bow-windowed Queen's Head. The latter has St James's, another church of Norman origin with a Purbeck marble font.

Clacton-on-Sea developed in the 1870s and followed the pattern of the other resorts on the East Coast, such as FRINTON and WALTON. There are three Martello towers, a feature of much of the coast-line. The Royal Hotel was built in 1872, the Grand in 1897 and the other buildings associated with a resort soon followed. St James's Church in Tower Road was built in 1913, presenting an odd contrast in styles; the Roman Catholic church in Church Road was a little earlier (1902).

The pier has been rebuilt several times since it was first erected in 1873, to be followed in 1890 by the pavilion. The giant scenic railway, one of the most striking features of the front, was added in the 1930s at about the same time as the Town Hall.

Despite its name the Moot Hall is a private

Noel Habgood

Cley-next-the-Sea: the 18th-century windmill

house, built from timbers taken from an old barn at Hawstead, not far from BURY ST EDMUNDS. The rash of holiday camps which have spread along the coast provides excellent holiday facilities, if not adding anything to the visual appeal of the town. To the S. is **Jaywick Sands**, a caravan and chalet centre.

The beach is sandy, there is every possible holiday amenity and entertainment and there is golf at the Clacton-on-Sea Golf Course (18 holes) at West Road, on the A133.

CLARE, *Suffolk* (11–TL7645). It was here that William Dowsing, the infamous iconoclastic Parliamentary visitor of Suffolk churches, "brake down 1,000 superstitious pictures" and as a result there is little of the original stained glass left in the Church of SS. Peter and Paul. Though some parts, e.g. the tower, are earlier, the church is mainly 15th-cent. and contains some notable wood-carving, especially the delicate work of the chancel door.

The town was the site of a castle first mentioned in 1090, and on the mound stand some impressive remains. It was also the site chosen by the Austin Friars in 1248 for the first house of the order in the country. The prior's house, cellar and infirmary are still in use.

Clare is another of the beautiful towns along the LONG MELFORD–HAVERHILL road and many of the houses display that pargetry work (ornamental plaster coating) which is one of the specialities of the region. The Ancient House which has the date 1473 on some of its later parts, belonged at one time to the priest. The Grove is of similar date with additions from the 19th cent. The Swan Inn in the High Street has fine carving, and along Nethergate Street The Cliftons has

clustered chimneys of the 16th cent. On the Chilton road is Chapel Cottage with an original doorway of the 12th cent.

CLEY-NEXT-THE-SEA, *Norfolk* (11–TG 0444). Cley is situated on the North Coast Road (A149) some way inland from the sea and on the east bank of the River Glaven. At one time it was a busy and prosperous little port but embankments built in the 17th cent. led to its decline. The village itself has many small flint-built houses along narrow streets. The Church of St Margaret S. of the village is large and impressive with a remarkable clerestory composed of alternate circular and arched windows. The Perpendicular south porch is finely proportioned with a traceried parapet. The south transept which has been in ruins for centuries has a beautifully traceried window and inside the Galilee porch west of the tower is an equally beautiful doorway. Inside the church is some fine woodwork and brasses, while the churchyard contains, as at BLAKENEY, some carved 18th-cent. tombstones.

Perhaps the most picturesque sight in Cley is the windmill which dates from 1713 and stands like a sentinel over the great expanse of marshes which lie between it and the sea. The shingle beach is at the end of a long road across these flats. The front of the Post Office is apparently built with the ground-up bones of horses and cattle.

CODDENHAM, *Suffolk* (11–TM1354), was Combretonium in Roman times. The site was thought to be by the ford across the River Gipping, but modern research has located it more exactly in the Baylham House area, where many finds of archaeological interest have been yielded.

St Mary's Church was recorded in Norman

times and has many Perpendicular additions. There is a large Italianate painting of Christ and a rare 15th-cent. alabaster carving of the Crucifixion which escaped destruction by Dowsing (*see* CLARE), by being hidden in a village home. On the east gable of the nave is a stone sanctus bell turret. A double hammer-beam roof with angels and monuments to Captain Philip Bacon and the Puritan statesman Nathaniel Bacon are to be seen.

In the village street is the Post Office, once an inn, dating from *c*. 1500, and in a park is the 18th-cent. vicarage. One m. N. is an early 15th cent. building, Choppings Hill Farmhouse.

COGGESHALL, *Essex* (11–TL8522). The Roman road from COLCHESTER to the W., now the A120 passes through the village in which is one of the most famous Tudor houses in the country, Paycocke's House (National Trust), a superb example of a half-timbered building *c*. 1500. From the street the façade, even though restored, presents an ideal picture of the home of a wealthy Tudor merchant. Five bays composed of oriel windows above, and entrance door, windows and gateway below are divided vertically by timber studs and horizontally by an elaborate beam. On either side of the gateway are carved figures, and between the timbers are bricks.

Inside, there is a wealth of carving: on the beams of the hall, in the linenfold panelling of the dining-room and in the carved bressumer which supports the brickwork over the fireplace. There are equally fine ceilings in the upstairs rooms where some of the original Tudor flooring still remains. There is a handsome garden from which the house presents a very different appearance as it is completely plastered.

Next door, in what is now the Fleece Inn, lived some of the descendants of the Paycocke family.

The Church of St Peter has been carefully rebuilt after considerable destruction in 1940. Inside are a number of brasses to the Paycocke family and another to the remarkable Mary Honywood, d. 1620, who left 367 surviving descendants.

The village itself contains a large number of excellent houses, many displaying the traditional pargeting of the region, and in the Woolpack Inn one of the most picturesque hostelries in the country.

Not far from the village is Houchin's Farm, a beautiful timber-framed building dating from the early 17th cent.

Little Coggeshall just to the S. was the site of an abbey founded by King Stephen in the middle of the 12th cent. The foundations of the abbey have been traced and excavations have revealed many interesting features. Though the church itself has vanished, some of the ancillary buildings have survived, including a two-storied corridor and an early-13th-cent. gate chapel. The monastic priest-house contains possibly the earliest medieval brickwork in England. Not far from the chapel is an exceptionally interesting group of farm buildings with an early-16th-cent. barn.

COLCHESTER, *Essex* (11–TM0025). Colchester calls itself "Britain's oldest recorded town" and in fact, though in the 1st cent. B.C. it has been settled by the Trinovantes and named Camulo-dunum, the area has traces of settlements going back as far as the Bronze Age, *c*. 1000 B.C. In the early years of the Christian era it was the capital city of Cunobelin who reigned over South East England. In A.D. 43 the Romans invaded and it was here that Claudius received the surrender of the British kings. The first Roman city in this island was founded here, but it fell to Queen Boadicea despite its strengthened defences when she made her historic challenge to the might of the Romans. Though her armies had slain 70,000 people she was in the end defeated and the Roman city rose again to become a walled city and one of the most important Roman centres in Britain.

Parts of the walls of this ancient town still stand and within them have been found the remains of almost 100 buildings and relics. From this wall the Balkerne Gateway still survives as a ruined arch next door to an inn in Balkerne Lane where it was originally the main exit from the town to London and the west. When the Romans left, the town inevitably decayed and was the scene of invasions by the Anglo-Saxons, the Danes and finally the Normans.

The Normans found in Colchester a flourishing town of some 2,000 persons and its position made it an obvious site for a major fortress. Though the precise date of the commencement of building is not known for certain it is usually put at *c*. 1085. Though only the keep survives, its massive proportions convey an idea of the size of the original building. It was the largest keep built in Europe, almost 100 ft high and 150 ft in length by 110 ft in width. At the base the walls are more than 12 ft thick. Its great size is no doubt due to the fact that it was built upon the vaults of the great Roman Temple of Claudius. The castle is now a museum containing a fine collection of Roman and other antiquities.

Shortly after the castle was built St John's Abbey was founded just S. of the original Roman walls. All that remains now is the 15th-cent. gatehouse with its pinnacled towers on either side. Not far from St John's is St Botolph's Priory founded shortly after St John's as the first English Augustinian house. The remains of the priory are no less splendid than the castle itself. The great doorway with its rich carvings leads into the open nave bounded by the massive columns supporting tiers of Norman arches. Though the building itself is almost 900 years old the bricks with which it is made are more than twice that age, being made by the Romans themselves. Destroyed during the siege of 1648, until which time it was the principal church of the town, the priory has as neighbour a new church built in 1837.

Earlier than the priory is the tower of Holy Trinity Church with its Anglo-Saxon west door close by Trinity Street. It is in an unknown grave here that one of the greatest of Elizabethan composers lies buried. William Wilbye lived in a house close to the church for the last ten years of his life and was buried there in 1638. His madrigals have been sung for the past 300 years or more. Inside the church is the alabaster carving in memory of William Gilbert, Elizabeth I's physician, the first man to use the word electricity and who used to amuse her with his electrical experiments. Tymperleys, the house in which he lived, may be seen through the archway facing the church in Trinity Street.

Facing the castle is the Church of All Saints, now used as a Natural History museum. Almost opposite All Saints towards East Hill is Holly-trees, the best 18th-cent. house in the town, now a museum. Across the road is the Minories which dates from 1776 and which is now the town's art gallery holding frequently changing exhibitions of national as well as local interest.

Turning back to walk along the High Street, at the far end may be seen the red-brick water tower built in 1882 and locally known as "Jumbo". But before this extraordinary construction is reached you would pass the Red Lion Hotel, a timber-framed building of the late 15th cent. The earliest part, now the Grill Room, still has the moulded beams. On the right of the High Street is the Town Hall, built at the beginning of this century. The 162-ft-high tower supports the figure of St Helena and the façade contains a number of statues, including that of Boadicea.

During the Middle Ages the chief trade was that of making cloth, and the industry owed much to the help of the Flemish refugees who came in the 17th and 18th cents. Nowadays Colchester is famous principally for its oysters, which have been highly esteemed since Roman times, and for engineering and the growing of roses. The original Cant Nurseries were established in 1766 and the family is still one of the best-known growers in the country.

One of the sights of Colchester is undoubtedly Bourne Mill in Bourne Road in the south-east corner of the town. This was built in 1591, probably for use as a fishing lodge. At each end of the single-storied stone building are two gables which ascend in concave and convex curves. At some time the house was used as a water mill and the weather-boarded hoist-loft was added. A little further down the stream, Cannock Mill, another water mill, is still in working order.

On the outskirts of the town along the estuary of the River Colne is the University of Essex, one of the newest of the post-war universities. Set in Wivenhoe Park, made famous in a number of paintings by John Constable, the four huge residential towers, the library centre and the other university buildings are already becoming a familiar feature of the neighbourhood.

Before leaving Colchester the motorist can forge a link with ancient times by touring the area of the dykes. Leaving on the Lexden Road, there is near St Clare Road a tumulus, perhaps that of Cunobelin. First comes Triple Dyke then Grymes Dyke and once back at Lexden Straight Road leave the car near the Mormon Temple and walk up to Half Moon Dyke. These dykes formed

a huge fortified enclosure almost 12 square m. in area and have yielded many treasures, including that found in the Lexden Tumulus now on view in the Colchester and Essex Museum.

Colchester has one of the best small zoos in the country, at Stanway.

COLTISHALL, *Norfolk* (11–TG2619). Though nowadays known particularly for the R.A.F. Station 2 m. N. of the village, Coltishall, which is situated on the River Bure, is itself an attractive village with many pleasant 18th-cent. brick houses.

Rather earlier, and dated 1692, is The Limes, perhaps the best house in the village.

The Church of St John the Baptist, which is thatched, has two small Anglo-Saxon windows in the north wall and a Perpendicular west tower.

Between the village and the R.A.F. Station stands the church of Great Hautbois, now mostly in ruins but with a round Norman tower and a chancel which is still roofed.

A little to the SW. the village of **Horstead** has, in addition to the Church of All Saints with its 13th-cent. west tower, a famous mill by the River Bure which formerly stood on six arches, but has recently been partly destroyed by fire.

CONSTABLE COUNTRY, *Suffolk* (11–TM 0734). Constable, perhaps the most natural of all landscape painters, and one of the greatest English artists, was born in EAST BERGHOLT on 11 June 1776. His father was a well-to-do miller and though he hoped the boy would enter the Church, or at least take over the family mills, the call of art was to prove too strong. Such was the power of John Constable as a painter that through his eyes millions have been taught to see the countryside about which he himself cared so passionately.

Late in life he was on a coach journey from London when one of his travelling companions used the phrase "Constable country", a name which has ever since been used to describe the villages which the artist painted so many times. Each will be dealt with more fully but the places which, as Constable himself said "made me a painter", group themselves along the River Stour, whose reaches the artist loved to draw and paint. East Bergholt no longer boasts his place of birth which may be seen on some of his canvasses but the church still stands. It was at the rectory that Constable met Maria, the grand-daughter of the rector, Dr Rhudde, the girl he married. FLAT-FORD MILL, now a field studies centre, DEDHAM, Langham, Stratford St Mary, and the other villages of NAYLAND, STOKE-BY-NAYLAND, Brantham, Bures, POLSTEAD stretch towards COLCHESTER and form part of the country which time has caused to be given the name of the great painter.

COPFORD, *Essex* (11–TL9222). Just off the ever-busy A12 road from London to COLCHESTER, near the junction at Marks Tey, is the little village of Copford whose Church of St Mary the Virgin

Cromer: the old town and the beach

is one of the finest examples of Norman work in the county. Much of the original Norman work still remains: the nave, chancel and apse, though the barrel-vaulted roof was replaced with a wooden structure in the 15th cent. In this Norman work may be seen many Roman bricks and, in one of the arches of the south aisle, some of the earliest of English-made bricks. Though the architectural qualities of the church are so interesting, and though the font is solid Purbeck marble, the chief treasure is the marvellous series of wall paintings.

They date from the time of the construction of the church in the middle of the 12th cent. and although they have been restored they can still remind us of how the interior of this, and many other churches in East Anglia used to look. Over the altar Christ sits in glory, supported by angels, the arch which spans the apse shows the signs of the zodiac and among the other subjects to be seen are the Virtues.

Near the church is Copford Hall, a red-brick mansion of Georgian date, which is beautifully set in a fine wooded park. On this site, though not in this house, lived the bishops of London, and it is thought that Bishop Bonner, who died in 1569, may be buried in the church.

COVEHITHE, *Suffolk* (11–TM5281). Approached from WRENTHAM on the A12, Covehithe is a completely unspoilt village with a fine stretch of sandy beach. On the left stand the majestic remains of the church which was dismantled in 1672 when the town began to decline. Among many artists who have captured the spirit of these ruins was John Sell Cotman. The road continues past the church until a barrier prevents all but pedestrians passing through on to the cliff top. From the top of the cliff the coast sweeps N. towards LOWESTOFT and S. to SOUTHWOLD. The energetic can gain access to the beach by clambering down the face of the cliff, not as hazardous an adventure as it might sound. Those with a little more time can walk along the cliff top to the left where it gradually slopes down to the beach.

Those who prefer to bathe in almost complete isolation will find Covehithe much to their liking. They would be advised, however, to avoid weekends and Bank Holidays, the only times when any considerable number of people are to be seen.

CREAKES, THE, *Norfolk* (11–TF8538; North Creake), situated midway between **Burnham Market** and FAKENHAM these two villages have interesting churches and in the case of **North Creake**, the ruins of an abbey founded for the Augustinians in 1206. Though not extensive the ruins are impressive. St Mary's Church (14th- and 15th-cent.) has a good hammer-beam roof and a fine brass to Sir William Calthorpe, d. *c.* 1500, who did much for the church.

South Creake's church, St Mary's, is a mixture of the Decorated and Perpendicular styles, large in scale and with a hammer-beam roof over the lofty arcading of the nave. The 15th-cent. pulpit is another of those which tapers gently towards its base. The screen and font are also worthy of attention. Brasses include one to a priest, *c.* 1400, and another to John Norton, *d.* 1509.

Just to the S. of the village is the site of an ancient encampment of Iron Age origin.

CRESSING, *Essex* (11–TL7920). The Church of All Saints, though with much work of Norman date, must give way in interest to the two magnificent barns which are all that remains of the Temple of the Knights Templars and Hospitallers. There is a third barn, dated 1623, which is much later than the Wheat Barn and Barley Barn which stand near it. Tests have shown that the timbers f the Barley Barn date from the 11th cent. Those of the Wheat Barn are some two centuries younger, and with its length of 140 ft it is the largest of the three. The exteriors of the two barns differ: the Barley Barn is weather-boarded, the Wheat Barn has brick fillings in between the timbers.

CROMER, *Norfolk* (11–TG2142). A delightful seaside resort dominated by the splendid tower of SS. Peter and Paul, which, 160 ft high, is the tallest in the county. Originally a small fishing village, Cromer rose to popularity in the 19th cent. The cottages of the original village are picuresquely grouped around the church on top of the cliffs, and the later developments are along the terraces and cliffs.

The church is mainly Perpendicular and the tower with its decorated battlements and pinnacles very impressive. The interior with lofty arcades and chancel includes a chancel rebuilt in 1887–9 by Sir Arthur Blomfield.

From the cliff gardens pathways lead to the generally sandy beach which provides excellent bathing. The storm of 1953 damaged the pier, which has since been rebuilt. From the pier is launched the famous Cromer lifeboat, the *Henry Blogg*, named after the remarkable coxswain who saved so many lives in the period 1909–47. Before his death in 1954 he had been awarded 3 gold and 3 silver medals, the B.E.M. and the G.C.

Also to the E. is the lighthouse, open to the public on occasions. The rather grand Victorian hotels and the Town Hall typify the respect of the 19th cent. for wealth and solidity.

The cliffs are a favourite haunt of geologists and fossil hunters, and cliff top walks with fine views may be taken to N. and S.

Not far away is a zoo and an aviary, and the Royal Cromer Golf Club (18 holes and a six-hole practice course) is a famous seaside links at Overstrand Road, 1 m. E. of the town on the A149.

DAGENHAM, *Essex* (7–TQ5084). On the River Thames and the site of the Ford car factory, one of the largest in Europe. In consequence there is much utilitarian urban building of little distinction. However, the Church of SS. Peter and Paul is not only early but interesting, though its later additions such as the tower and the west porch are not really in keeping. The vicarage has parts dating from the 17th cent., and the Cross Keys Inn is even earlier.

The Civic Centre is at Becontree and was built in 1936 near the vast sprawl of the housing estates. The South East Essex Technical College in Longbridge Road was built at the same time.

DALHAM, *Suffolk* (11–TL7261). Dalham Hall belonged to the Rhodes family and though the more famous brother, Cecil, rests far from Suffolk, Francis is buried in the Church of St Mary where he was brought after his death in Capetown in 1905.

The village is by the River Kennet and contains many thatched cottages. The Hall was built

c. 1704–5 by the then Bishop of ELY, and has several tree-lined avenues including one which leads directly to the church.

St Mary's is remarkable for its monuments and for the great inscription which describes how the steeple was erected in 1625. Its spire was said to have fallen in the gale which swept England on the night that Oliver Cromwell died (1658). The monuments include those to Thomas Stutevyle (1571); Sir Martin Stutevyle, who voyaged with Sir Francis Drake (1631); and in the churchyard an obelisk to General Sir James Affleck (1833).

DANBURY, *Essex* (7–TL7805), set on a hill on the A414, CHELMSFORD to MALDON road, with some attractive houses, a green and a church set within an earthwork which may date back to Danish times. Inside the Church of St John the Baptist are the finely carved wooden figures of three knights, dating from *c*. 1300. Though the three figures all lie with legs crossed, each has a different attitude and expression, showing individual craftsmanship. The church is mainly 14th-cent. with a gallery of *c*. 1600 and a south chancel chapel rebuilt by Scott in 1866. On top of the battlemented tower is a spire which is a local landmark, rising as it does from the hill which is over 350 ft high.

Among the 16th-cent. buildings in the village are the Griffin Inn and Frettons. Hill House and Millington are 18th-cent. and Danbury Place, a large brick house in the Tudor style, was built by Hopper in 1832. Less than 1 m. NW. of the village are two interesting houses, Old Riffhams (early 18th-cent.) and New Riffhams (early 19th-cent.) while 2 m. to the SE. is Slough House, a timber-framed building of the early 16th cent.

DEBENHAM, *Suffolk* (11–TM1763), is at the source of the River Deben. The straggling village street, tree-lined and attractive, rises to the Church of St Mary with its superb west porch and 15th-cent. nave arcade with hammer-beam and tie-beam roof. Parts of the tower are pre-Norman and there are some interesting monuments. Many old buildings remain despite the fire of 1744.

Six m. SW. is Earl Stonham with its interesting church. Note the exceptionally fine hammer-beam roof and the 17th-cent. pulpit with its four hour-glasses.

At Mendlesham N. along the A140 there is in St Mary's Church a collection of armour of the 15th to 17th cents. This is kept in the chamber over the south porch which has been used as the parish armoury since 1593. Note, too, the pulpit, reading desk and font cover all made by John Turner in 1630, the fine west tower and the notable north porch with its perfectly preserved carving.

North again off the B1077 is **Bedingfield** where the family of this name lived at the magnificent Fleming's Hall from *c*. 1309. It was rebuilt *c*. 1586 with a moat, brick porch and timber-framed walls, clusters of chimneys and Dutch gables; it is one of Suffolk's most striking houses.

DEDHAM, *Essex* (11–TM0533). The village with its pinnacled church has been immortalized in the paintings of John Constable, who attended the local grammar school in the late 18th cent. The Church of St Mary, built about 1500, appears in so many of Constable's paintings that its silhouette has become familiar to many who have never set foot in the county, much less the village. There are some splendid timbers in the roof and a great many interestings monuments and furnishings. In the window above the Webbe tomb some fragments of old glass show the initials E.S. These refer to Edmund Sherman who was the direct ancestor of General Sherman, the hero of the American Civil War. Edmund's cousin, Samuel, left Dedham for Massachussetts in 1634 to settle in Contentment, 20 m. from Boston, a town which was later renamed Dedham. A modern addition is the Gallery Tower Door designed by the East Anglian architect, Raymond Erith, R.A.

Another famous East Anglian artist, Sir Alfred Munnings, lived at Castle House, Dedham. Munnings was born in 1878 and though he lost the sight of one eye early in his career he achieved remarkable success. In 1920 he moved to Castle House and married. The year before he had been elected an Associate of the Royal Academy and he became a full R.A. in 1925. In 1944 he received a knighthood and in the same year became President of the Royal Academy, the first East Anglian artist to be given that office, and one of its most outspoken and controversial holders. In 1949 Munnings retired from the presidency and he died on 17 July 1959. Castle House was opened to the public by Lady Munnings in 1961 as a tribute to her husband's memory. The building is partly Tudor and partly Georgian and contains the studios used by the artist and a collection of over 100 of his drawings and paintings.

Other buildings to note in the village include the Grammar School, part of it dating from 1732, Sherman's house with its elaborate Georgian façade, Southfields, a timber-framed house and the neo-Georgian Great House.

DENNINGTON, *Suffolk* (11–TM2866). Its chief attraction is the Church of St Mary, the resting place of Lord Bardolph who fought under Henry V at Agincourt and was probably the original of the Lord Bardolph in Shakespeare's *Henry IV, Part II*. He was buried here in the mid-15th cent. Especially noteworthy are the 15th-cent. parclose screens, complete with lofts and traceried parapets, and the fine 14th-cent. carved chancel windows, all creating an impression of lightness and elegance. The numerous benches contain some of the best carvings in Suffolk, representing birds and beasts both real and mythological. Note the sixth on the right in the central aisle with its "Sciapod", a fabulous creature said to live in the desert, shown lying on his back using his enormous foot as a shade against the sun. This is the only such representation in England.

In the north aisle is a sand-table used to teach sums to children in the mid-19th cent. Note, too, the tower clock in use from 1675 to 1948, and the very rare hanging pyx-canopy suspended in front of the altar.

DENVER, *Norfolk* (11–TF6101). A village just S. of DOWNHAM MARKET and on the edge of the FENS. St Mary's Church has a 13th-cent. tower made of carstone; the rest of the church is of flint. Denver Hall is 16th-cent. with a very fine stepped gable and a little gatehouse dated 1570. To the SW. is a fine windmill of the smock type (in which the cap only, and not the body, revolves), once used for grinding corn.

To the W. are the Sluices, with the road crossing them. Vermuyden, the Dutchman who had done much to drain the Fens, built the first sluice using mills as water-pumps in 1652. Later centuries saw a continuous programme of water control which has continued right up to the present time. The work of the Great Ouse Flood Protection Scheme was completed in 1964.

This is good sailing territory, and fishermen will find it much to their liking, too.

DEREHAM, *Norfolk* (11–TF9812). When people say Dereham, it is East Dereham that they mean rather than West, which can be confusing as the two places are very different in size and some two dozen miles apart. East Dereham is famous for its association with the poet William Cowper (1731–1800) whose unhappy life at last ended in this Norfolk town. Here also lived Bishop Bonner, 1500(?)–1569, chaplain to Cardinal Wolsey, and former Bishop of London. The cottages in which he lived are now the home of the Dereham Archaeological Society, and are dated 1502.

St Nicholas' Church, joined to the Market Place by Church Street, is noteworthy for having two towers, one central, the other, the bell-tower, detached, and both in the same sturdy, uncompromising style. The church itself shows a mixture of styles from Norman (south doorway) to Perpendicular (the south porch, etc.). The seven-sacrament font, which it is of interest to note cost £12 13s 9d in 1468, is one of the county's loveliest, with finely carved panels and vaulted top. The lectern is East Anglian brass, c. 1500 and there is a monument to Cowper by the great sculptor, Flaxman. A well in the churchyard reminds the visitor of St Withburga, who founded a nunnery here and died in A.D. 654.

Around the charming market place are many notable buildings, including the Assembly Rooms, 1756; the George and King's Arms Hotels; the Corn Hall of 1857 and the many Georgian red-brick houses. Near the Bishop's cottages is the Guildhall, late 18th-cent.

Spanning the road near the Market Place is an ornate gallows sign, erected to commemorate the town's 1,300th anniversary in 1954.

Less than 2 m. to the S. is the village of **Dumpling Green** where the writer George Borrow was born in 1803.

About 11 m. to the NW. is **Raynham Hall,**

built in the 17th cent. for Sir Roger Townshend, by William Edge. The interior was remodelled for the famous agricultural reformer "Turnip" Townshend, the second viscount, in the 18th cent. by William Kent.

DISS, *Norfolk* (11–TM1179). Right in the S. of the county almost on the Suffolk border, Diss is a small town built around a very large lake called The Mere. The market place is the centre of the town and contains a number of excellent buildings. The Shambles (Victorian shops), the King's Head and the former Dolphin Inn are all fine of their kind, especially the last with its half-timbering, over-sailing and impressive gable. At the head of the triangular market place is St Mary's Church with a tower built right up to the street and processional arches N. and S. The west doors are finely carved and inside are 14th-cent. arcades and a Commandment board with the figures of Moses and Aaron.

The streets which lead off the Market Place have many interesting buildings of Georgian and earlier date. On the right of Market Hill is the timber-framed Greyhound Inn, and opposite a house with a carved corner-post. A little further on is the Corn Exchange, 1854. The road leads to Lacon's Maltings, 1788, with its huge arches.

It was at Diss that John Skelton, the poet and tutor to Henry VIII, was rector. Skelton, b. 1460, took orders in 1498 and was given the living of Diss. He died in 1529.

DITCHINGHAM, *Norfolk* (11–TM3391). Rider Haggard (*see* THE BRADENHAMS) lived here in Ditchingham House, to the S. of St Mary's Church. This is a Perpendicular building with an elaborate tower, and containing, in the chancel, the Haggard family tomb. Ditchingham Hall dates from the first years of the 18th cent. and its grounds were landscaped by Capability Brown. S. of the church the gatehouse is dated 1613 and close by are a number of attractive mansions – Alma House, Waveney and Ditchingham Lodges, etc.

To the E. is the Community of All Hallows, 1858, which has been much added to in later years. The modern housing estate of Windmill Green is said to be the first in England (1947) to revert to terraced houses as opposed to the almost universal "semis" or "double-dwellers", as they are called in East Anglia.

DOWNHAM MARKET, *Norfolk* (11–TF 6003), stands above the surrounding fens, 12 m. S. of KING'S LYNN, on the River Ouse. Rich finds of Romano-British pottery show that the district was an important early centre, and the position of the crossroad at the junction of the A1122 and the A10 substantiates this.

The Church of St Edmund has a spire on top of its Early English tower; the rest of the building is Perpendicular. The west gallery is wooden and 18th-cent., and over the chancel door is an ancient Gothic crucifix.

Buildings worth seeking out include Howdale

Home, the former workhouse built in 1836 in the Elizabethan style; Mount Tabor Chapel in Bridge Street, 1809; and the cast-iron neo-Gothic Clock Tower of 1878.

DUNMOWS, THE, *Essex* (11–TL6221). **Great Dunmow** is on the main Roman road (Stane Street), now the A120 from Bishop's Stortford to BRAINTREE. **Little Dunmow** is 2½ m. to the E. on the side road which leads to FELSTED. The River Chelmer passes through the former and not far from the latter. It was at Great Dunmow that the fine amateur artist Sir George Beaumont was brought up. He became the first patron of John Constable and one of the two co-founders of the National Gallery. He lived at Clock House, a timber-framed house of the mid-16th cent., which owes its name to the clock turret dated *c.* 1651. The Church of St Mary, outside the town, has been much restored. Inside is a 15th-cent. wooden balcony and some stained glass of the same period. There are monuments to the Beaumont family.

In the town near the square is Doctor's Pond where the first lifeboat was tested in 1785 by Lionel Lukin. An early work of G. G. Scott was the Workhouse of 1840 on the CHELMSFORD road.

The famous flitch of bacon which the name of Dunmow brings to mind is presented at Little Dunmow to any couple able to swear, and prove, that they have never regretted their marriage for a "year and a day"! The ancient ceremony goes back to the time of Robert Fitzwalter, the marshal of the group which forced the Magna Carta on the King. One of his family, Walter (d. 1432), is commemorated in a beautiful tomb in the Church of St Mary.

The church is part of the priory of Augustinian canons founded in 1106 and long since destroyed except for its Lady Chapel, which forms the village church, and to which was added a turret in 1872. The present north wall was thus the south arcade of the original chapel and is notable for its superb piers, *c.* 1200. In the middle of the 14th cent. five windows were added, of which four have Decorated tracery, while the fifth is Perpendicular in style. In the chancel is the chair in which sits the winner of the flitch. The monument to Walter Fitzwalter, already mentioned, is one of the finest 15th-cent. English sculptures.

DUNWICH, *Suffolk* (11–TM4770). Lonely and desolate, apart from a few holidaymakers who appreciate the isolation of its shingle beach, Dunwich is one of the most evocative of East Anglia's villages. Little is left now of the once thriving town, apart from the ruins of the chapel of the leper hospital, the priory and its 19th-cent. church, and yet this is a historic site which has the power to move the traveller in a manner out of all proportion to its visible remains.

The Romans almost certainly were here, and were followed by Sigebert who came from Gaul to claim the throne of East Anglia and to convert the inhabitants to Christianity. Felix of Burgundy came here to become Bishop, and perhaps, too, the Irish monk, Furseus, who is said to have established the first recorded school in England. By the time of the Conquest the town was of considerable size, and at the beginning of the 13th cent. the town was granted its first charter by King John. No less than nine churches were needed to serve its population, many of whom earned their living from that same sea which was gradually to destroy their township.

Storms had already begun to eat their way into the town and the great storm of January 1326 caused such severe flooding that three more churches were washed away. The continuous erosion of the cliffs and the floodings of the storms have reduced one of the East Coast's busiest towns to a handful of cottages, an inn and a general store. The little museum tells the tragic tale and the fallen stones and the still-crumbling cliffs spell out the story of ruin and decline.

Dunwich has long been the haunt of artists and writers. Edward FitzGerald, the translator of *The Rubaiyat of Omar Khayyam*, one of the so-called "WOODBRIDGE Wits", a group which included the poet Bernard Barton and the artist Thomas Churchyard, stayed here; so did Henry James, Charles Keene, who drew it, Swinburne, whose poem "By the North Sea" it inspired, Jerome K. Jerome, and many others. During the Second World War the marshes were blockaded with squat cubes of concrete, the beach mined and the cliffs at Minsmere, now a bird sanctuary, became one of the first radar sites in England.

The houses with their lattice windows and Elizabethan chimneys were built by Frederick Barne, one of a line which had held the land since 1552 when Sir George Barne, Lord Mayor of London, came here; hence the three leopard's heads on the family crest, these being the assay mark for London. This long association ended when the estate was sold in 1947. The inn, the beach café and the fishermen's hut where you will be able to buy the freshest of fresh fish as soon as the local fishermen have berthed their vessels on the beach; the vast expanses of the heaths and the cliff-top walks, these are the pleasures of Dunwich today.

EARL SOHAM, *Suffolk* (11–TM2263). The long village street has a row of cottages and Georgian houses on one side and allotments on the other. St Mary's Church has a fine late-15th-cent. tower, and inscriptions on the buttresses of the church commemorate some of its builders. An octagonal font and a number of monuments to the Hindes family are interesting.

Earl Soham Lodge overlooks a moat and was at one time the home of the owner of FRAMLING-HAM.

A couple of miles to the NW. is **Monk Soham**, where the monks from BURY ST EDMUNDS came in earlier days. The Church of St Peter has a particularly wide five-light window in the chancel, a 15th-cent. seven-sacrament font which, though defaced, is full of admirable detail, and a 14th-cent.

iron-banded chest over 8 ft long. Among the excellent woodwork is a Stuart Holy Table.

In the last century Archdeacon Robert Hindes Groome, who became rector in 1845, did much to restore the church and four yews by its gates were given to him by his friend, the writer and poet Edward FitzGerald.

EAST BERGHOLT, *Suffolk* (11–TM0734). Here was born John Constable, one of the two greatest artists of East Anglia, on 11 June 1776. He was the son of a miller and his talent for painting was encouraged by the local amateur John Dunthorne whose son was a great friend of Constable. In 1799 he entered the Royal Academy Schools in London and exhibited there for the first time in 1802. Constable presents the greatest possible contrast to his great contemporary, J. M. W. Turner. Whereas the latter artist travelled continuously Constable loved his home landscape; "These scenes made me a painter", he said, and he never left England. Suffolk, SALISBURY, HAMPSTEAD, BRIGHTON, these are the places he loved to paint. A journey to the LAKE DISTRICT did not arouse his enthusiasm. Moving to London he lived in Charlotte Street and in Well Walk, Hampstead; both houses still stand. The death of his wife, to whom he was deeply attached, affected his life and work and did not compensate for his belated election to the Royal Academy in 1829. A perceptive lecturer on art as well as a superb painter of landscapes, he died suddenly on 31 March 1837.

His birthplace no longer stands but many of the scenes he loved to paint may still be seen (*see* FLATFORD MILL).

The Church of St Mary is remarkable for its unfinished tower which was begun in 1525. In the churchyard is the even more remarkable bell-house, a timber building of the 16th cent. which contains the bells which are hung upside down and are rung by hand. Inside the church is a 15th-cent. wall painting; a monument to Maria, the wife of the painter; and in the south window, a memorial glass to the artist by Constable of Cambridge (1897). The graves of his parents, of both the Dunthornes and of Willy Lott can be seen in the churchyard. North of the church is The Gables, a good timber-framed house of the 16th cent. There are also a number of good 18th- and 19th-cent. houses.

Until his death, Randolph Churchill, the son and biographer of Sir Winston, lived at Stour, his house in the village, where he created a famous garden.

EAST HARLING, *Norfolk* (11–TL9986), near the River Thet and some 10 m. to the E. of THETFORD. Though the village is attractive the great glory is the Church of SS. Peter and Paul, a magnificent building in the Perpendicular style. The tower is well buttressed and has a miniature spire which itself rises like a fountain out of a cascade of flying buttresses. The porch is flush-work and panelled and the interior is beautifully proportioned with an excellent hammer-beam roof. The base of the screen has very interesting carved panels which include a Crucifixion. The south aisle has an even finer screen, with doors, erected for Sir Robert Harling and his wife whose tomb (1435) is nearby. Another magnificent tomb is that to the Chamberlain family of 1462 with its richly carved canopy. Yet more treasures are to be seen in the stained glass in the east window. These panels are late 15th-cent. and their preservation today is due to their removal in earlier, more dangerous, times.

EASTONS, THE, *Essex* (11–TL6125). Two villages on either side of the River Chelmer close to the A130 road between THAXTED and GREAT DUNMOW. **Great Easton** has the remains of an ancient motte and bailey castle close to the church of SS. John and Giles with its Norman nave and 19th-cent. belfry. **Little Easton** has some spectacular treasures in the Church of St Mary. There are some outstanding paintings of a seated prophet, *c.* 1175, and a series of episodes from the Passion of Christ, early 15th-cent.; an 18th-cent. wrought-iron screen for the Maynard Chapel, at one time one of the gates for the now demolished Easton Lodge; and 17th-cent. stained glass from Germany in the south windows and a memorable group of brasses and monuments. These monuments are to various members of the Bourchier and Maynard families, and include those to Lord Maynard, elegantly posed leaning against an urn, surrounded by busts of his family and a portrait of his wife; to Sir William Maynard and his wife, a large wall-standing monument with figures in Roman costume; to Sir Henry Maynard and his wife shown as reclining figures; and tomb-chests to Lady Bourchier, *c.* 1400, and Viscount Bourchier and his wife, d. 1483.

ELVEDEN, *Suffolk* (11–TL8279). Elveden is another of those small Suffolk villages where you are suddenly reminded of the existence of famous men. In this village, surrounded by heathland and with its glorious park, lived Admiral Keppel and Maharajah Duleep Singh. The Admiral was a subject of one of the finest portraits painted by Sir Joshua Reynolds (Tate Gallery) and died at Elveden, after a remarkable career, in 1786. The house in which he had lived was purchased by the Maharajah in the 1860s and he was responsible for its conversion into a fantastic oriental palace. A profusion of marble carved on the spot by Italian workmen, eastern architectural devices and richly elaborate Indian detail were crowned with a vast dome of beaten copper. It appears that it took 150 men four years to complete the work and the house as it now stands surrounded by parkland, lakes and forests is one of the most striking sights in the county.

At the turn of the century the house was yet further enlarged by the 1st Lord Iveagh. In the neighbourhood are the estate houses and almshouses of red brick.

The Church of SS. Andrew and Patrick has been lavishly restored by both the Maharajah and, in the early years of the century, by Lord Iveagh. It is as elaborate in its Gothic fantasy as is the house in its oriental mannerisms.

ELY, *Cambridgeshire* (11–TL5380), stands above the River Ouse on a bluff which was formerly an island, accessible only by boat or causeways until THE FENS were drained in the 17th and 18th cents. It was the scene of Hereward's resistance to William the Conqueror. Just as the flat horizon of the fens is dominated by Ely's great cathedral so in its turn is the cathedral dominated by its magnificent west tower and the unique octagonal lantern. Ely itself contains, apart from its cathedral and two or three other buildings of merit, little of interest compared to some other East Anglian towns of similar size. Yet such is the splendour of the cathedral founded by St Etheldreda in A.D. 673 that the town cannot be omitted from any itinerary.

On entering the cathedral through the Galilee Porch you are passing through the first addition to the original Norman structure. At once the length of the nave is apparent; only those of CANTERBURY, ST ALBANS and WINCHESTER are longer than Ely's 537 ft. Passing the rows of Norman columns, you will see above you the painted wooden ceiling 72 ft from the ground followed at once by the octagon and lantern, a unique medieval inspiration. Conceived by Alan of Walsingham over 600 years ago, the extraordinary effect of its design with its beautiful fan vaulting and delicate tracery makes it one of the highlights of English architecture. A model on show in the transept illustrates the problem facing the medieval craftsmen who had not only to design a structure capable of supporting over 400 tons of wood and lead, but, with only simple equipment at their command, to get the great timbers into position.

Entering the choir with its admirably carved choir stalls you soon reach the point where the original Norman building was damaged when the central tower fell in 1322. The extension of the cathedral to the east is clearly seen in the line of delicately pointed arches leading up into the lierne vaulting of the roof. Here the relics of St Etheldreda were placed in their new resting place in 1252.

The chapels which surround this extension contain some of the most elaborate and extraordinary carvings to be seen in England, and the transepts on either side of the octagon are no less remarkable for their highly decorated roofs with angels as hammer bearers. At the north-east corner of the north transept is the Lady Chapel, the building of which was supervised by John of Wisbech and which was completed in 1349. Now the windows are plain and the whiteness of the walls gives the chapel a remarkable lightness. Once again the ceiling is important and each of the many bosses is a work of art in itself. Around the walls are stone stalls with fine carvings each of which has lost its head at the hands of some zealous reformer.

Around the precincts of the cathedral are the houses of the King's School founded by Henry

Ely cathedral with its commanding west tower and unique octagonal lantern

VIII. Nearby is the Bishop's Palace and St Mary's Church, in the vicarage of which lived Cromwell and his family from 1636 to 1647.

Looking back to the west front of the cathedral from the converted Fire Engine House at the end of the green you may speculate on the appearance of the cathedral had not the north-west transept disappeared in the 14th cent. Leaving Ely on the NEWMARKET Road to the SE. gives us perhaps the finest view with the east end, the lantern and the tower forming a noble composition. The village of **Stuntney** 1 m. to the SE. is where Cromwell once owned a farm; its hill commands a famous view of Ely.

EPPING, *Essex* (6–TL4602). What HAMP-STEAD Heath is to the North and West Londoner, Epping Forest is to those who live on its east side. Now some 6,000 acres, it was ten times this area 200 years ago. And 200 years before that it was probably as big again. In 1882 the forest was purchased for the public and it has inspired countless artists, among them the painter and sculptor, Sir Jacob Epstein. Its hornbeams are especially famous, and it was at **High Beach** that the poet Tennyson used to live in his early days. The Catacombs are an underground grotto built of huge blocks of stone in the 19th cent.

Despite its nearness to the ever outward sprawl of London, Epping retains its identity as a small market town. Its Church of St John the Baptist is Victorian, built in 1889 with the tower added 20 years later, by Bodley and Garner. The medieval Church of All Saints is at **Epping Upland**, to the NW. and is 13th-cent., with a 16th-cent. brick tower.

Not far from Epping are two houses designed by Kempe, Wood House, which is based on the marvellous Sparrowe's House at IPSWICH, and Copped Hall, both of the 1890s. Evidence of much earlier occupation may be found in the forest at Loughton Camp and Ambresbury Banks, Iron Age earthworks marking the site of encampments of long ago.

EYE, *Suffolk* (11–TM1473). On the mound overlooking this pleasant little town there stood the castle first built by the Malets, a leading Norman baronial family. It is the noble church of SS. Peter and Paul which attracts the visitor today. Its west tower, late 15th-cent., just over 100 ft high, is panelled in Suffolk flushwork from ground to parapet and the south porch has, like the tower, the arms of the de la Pole family incorporated in the structure. No less important is the elaborate rood-screen which has been finely restored in this century by Sir Ninian Comper, who was also responsible for the font-cover. The paintings in the lower panels portray the saints and some of our kings.

N. of the church is the Guildhall, a timber-framed building of the early 16th cent. On one of the angle-posts is a carving of the Archangel Gabriel. Further on, the Tudor House leads to the ruins of the castle and on the opposite side of Castle Street, Stayer House, with timber-framed back and a Georgian front, and Stanley House, with its Georgian doorway and some timber framing, are appealing examples of domestic architecture.

Linden House in Lambseth Street is *c.* 1750 and there are two cottages which have, like the

Guildhall, carved animals on the sills of some oriel windows.

The artist William Hoare was born in Eye, and was one of the first Members of the Royal Academy, being elected in their second year (1769) at the age of 63. Like his greater contemporary Gainsborough he left his native Suffolk for the fashionable town of BATH, where he died in 1792.

FELBRIGG, *Norfolk* (11–TG2038). A village 2 m. S. of CROMER, which must have moved from its former position near the Church of St Margaret (Perpendicular), 1 m. away in the grounds of Felbrigg Hall. Though difficult to reach, the church is worth discovering for its west tower and its brasses and monuments. The brasses commemorate Simon de Felbrigg and Roger Felbrigg and their wives, with inscriptions in Norman French, a great rarity. They date from 1351 and 1380. Other brasses are to the Windham family. Among the many monuments is a fine example of the work of that talented and eccentric sculptor, Joseph Nollekens (1813), and another carved by Grinling Gibbons.

Felbrigg Hall, through the grounds of which you may drive on Tuesdays and Fridays, is associated with two families – the Felbrigges and the Wymondhams, or Wyndhams. The present house was erected for the latter family in 1620, was enlarged in 1674-87 and then again in 1750. Though not a large mansion it is a most beautiful example of the Jacobean style, the south front being particularly attractive. On its parapet are traceried the words Gloria Deo in Excelsis. There are three sets of chimneys, each with three shafts. The later ranges have a similar charm, and inside are some outstanding examples of the art of stucco plastering, notably in the drawing-room of 1687. Other stucco work may be seen in the dining-room which also has a fine fire-place. James Paine designed the library and the staircase when he worked on the house in 1750. The grounds were laid out by Humphry Repton at the beginning of the 19th cent. and include an orangery (a century earlier), an octagonal dovecot and stables.

FELIXSTOWE, *Suffolk* (11–TM3034). One of the seaside resorts which developed at the end of the last century. As with some others it is also a port of some importance and in fact in recent years has handled an ever-increasing amount of freight and traffic.

Felixstowe was the site of a Roman fort which now lies in ruins beneath the sea. The Church of SS. Peter and Paul, much rebuilt, stands on what was possibly the site of the Benedictine priory of St Felix, founded in the late 11th cent.

The Landguard Fort which guards the entrance to the harbour at HARWICH, which is linked with Felixstowe by ferry, was first constructed in the middle of the 16th cent. and rebuilt in the 17th cent. and again in the 18th cent. It was painted by Thomas Gainsborough when he was a young unknown painter, at the request of his friend, Philip Thicknesse, at that time the fort's governor.

The Martello tower, S. of the Beach Station is comparable to that at ALDEBURGH and also dates from *c.* 1810–12. The pier which at one time was ½ m. in length was drastically shortened after the last war and some of the larger hotels have become offices, but the Amusement Park and 2 m. of concrete promenade as well as the shingle beach with its safe bathing ensure the popularity of Felixstowe as a holiday resort.

A number of boarding schools have developed in the town, which contains many large and typically Edwardian seaside houses. St Andrew's Church in St Andrews road is an interesting modern (1930s) design by Hilda Mason and the well-known East Anglian Member of the Royal Academy, Raymond Erith.

FELSTED, *Essex* (11–TL6720), sometimes spelt Felstead, lies to the S. of the Great DUNMOW to BRAINTREE road, the A120, not far from the River Chelmer. It is famous for its public school, founded in 1564 by Lord Rich. In fact you pass through part of the original school to reach the Church of the Holy Cross, with its Norman west tower topped by an 18th-cent. cupola. A 15th-cent south porch leads to the 12th-cent. doorway and inside the architecture shows a similar range of period. Its most splendid feature is the monument to Chancellor Lord Rich, d. 1568. This large wall tomb is probably by Epiphanius Evesham, one of the best known sculptors of his time (*see* the monument to John Troughton at INGATESTONE).

The Old School House through which you enter the church was part of the late medieval Guildhall; opposite stands a cottage with its beam proudly carved – "George Boote made this house 1596". Further along the main street to the E. are the Victorian buildings of the present school, dating from 1860 with additions at subsequent dates. From the days when Oliver Cromwell's sons were among its pupils it has had a fine record of academic and sporting success. It has a beautiful cricket ground nearby.

The unattractive factory used by the sugar-beet industry is something of a contrast, but its great expanse is to some extent relieved by the cottages and farm-houses to be found in and around the village.

FENS, THE, *Cambridgeshire* (11–TL5380). For thousands of years before the Roman occupation the area known as the fens had slowly evolved from ancient forests to a lonely expanse of marsh. The continual action of inundation by the sea and consequent flooding of land was followed by an emptying process caused by the rivers which found their way down to the sea along the East Coast.

The Romans, with their genius for civil and military engineering, set to work to drain many of the areas affected by tidal waters. They built great dykes to hold back the sea and causeways to enable them to travel from one part of the fen to another. With their departure the work of reclamation ceased and by the time of the Norman

Barnaby/Mustograph

Flatford: the bridge leading to Willy Lott's cottage and the mill

Conquest the fens were once again extensive areas of sea and marsh with occasional islands such as that at ELY rising above the surrounding level of the water.

The isolation of the fens made the district a natural area of resistance and also a refuge for holy men, robbers or anyone seeking isolation. The coming of the Norman Church and the re-establishment of religious communities at such places as Ely and THORNEY (where the original Anglo-Saxon foundations had been sacked by the Danes) led to renewed efforts to drain the region and reclaim the land. The local population tended their narrow strips of soil and caught the eels which gave Ely its Anglo-Saxon name. One of the first successful steps was the cutting of the 3-m. channel to Rebeck on the Ouse. Then in 1490 Bishop Morton cut the channel which still bears his name. Early in the 17th cent. an Act of Parliament was passed "For the recovering of many hundred thousand acres of marshes" and when the great Dutch engineer Cornelius Vermuyden was commissioned to tackle the problem the first real steps towards the reclamation of the fens had begun.

It is estimated that in the 17th and 18th cents. almost 700 windmills were at work draining the fens. The coming of the steam pump, first installed at BOTTISHAM in 1820, gradually led to the disappearance of the more picturesque windmill, and today diesel and electric power have in turn taken over from steam. A typical mill of the old type may be seen at WICKEN FEN where it still serves its original function.

This region of between 800 and 1,000 square m., covering an area extending from LINCOLN in the N. almost to CAMBRIDGE in the S., from HUNT-INGDON and SPALDING in the W. to Ely and WISBECH in the E. has, due to the accumulations of decayed vegetable matter, become the finest agricultural land in the country. The growing of fruit and flowers has been carried on for many years with much success on the rich, black, peaty soil.

FINCHINGFIELD, *Essex* (11–TL6832). There can be few more photographed scenes than Finchingfield's pond and green backed with its cottages and church in its perfect setting close by the River Pant. This great popularity has not at all affected its charm which owes a great deal to its irregularity and unplanned appearance.

The Church of St John stands on a hill where its Norman tower, surmounted by a pretty 18th-cent. cupola, dominates the village. The nave, aisles and chancel show the work of later centuries and the last-mentioned has a clerestory, an unusual feature. Inside are some exceptional screens, that for the rood being particularly complicated in its design. Among the monuments and brasses of interest is a sculpture by Westmacott (1811).

Near the church is the former Guildhall, a timber-framed building, *c.* 1500, and opposite the church on the other side of the green is Hill House whose five barge-boarded gables present a striking face to the general view of the village. To the N. is a fine windmill of the post variety and near it a hexagonal cottage, known as The Round House, built in the late 18th cent. by the owners of Spains Hall, the major mansion of the area situated about 1 m. to the NW.

This is an Elizabethan mansion of red brick whose irregularities of shape echo those of the village itself. At one time it was inhabited by William Kempe, d. 1628 (whose monument is in the church). It was he who made, and kept, a vow of seven years' silence, because he had wrongly accused his wife. While silent he apparently dug ponds in the vast grounds of his mansion; its present lake was made from two of the eight original ponds. Later the house passed to the Ruggles-Brise family, who still own it.

FINGRINGHOE, *Essex* (11–TM0220), is on the south banks of the River Colne, SW. of WIVENHOE. The Church of St Andrew is beautifully situated and has a Norman nave, the banded tower, south aisle and chancel being added in the 14th cent. The porch, too, is later, with fine flint flushwork and a lively carving of St Michael and the Dragon. Inside the church are some wall paintings depicting, among other subjects, St Christopher, St Michael and Christ. There is also a good brass and a monument to one George Frere, d. 1655.

The Hall has a brick front with three large gables, *c.* 1650, later rebuilt in the Georgian style. The Tide Mill, now no longer used, was one of the few in the county which were driven by the tidal waters of the river. From the quay there is a very pleasant view of Wivenhoe on the opposite bank.

FLATFORD MILL, *Suffolk* (11–TM0834). For ever associated with the great landscape painter John Constable and pictured in so many of his paintings, the mill now belongs to the National Trust. Standing beside the River Stour with its wooden bridge, timbered houses and Willy Lott's white cottage it presents a scene which has attracted innumerable artists since Constable first painted it at the beginning of the 19th cent. It was in this mill that Constable spent much of his boyhood, and the years that have passed have seen remarkably little change since his day. The mill itself is now used by the Council for the Promotion of Field Studies and though its students are not necessarily artists it is appropriate that they study those aspects of nature which Constable loved.

FOULNESS, *Essex* (7–TR0192). Foulness is the largest island in the Thames estuary and has recently come into prominence as the possible site of London's third airport in place of the original choice of STANSTED. Foulness is a tiny community with a church dating from 1850. It is reached from the mainland by way of **Great** and **Little Wakering,** both of which have interesting churches.

FRAMLINGHAM, *Suffolk* (11–TM2863). A pleasant old market town with some attractive domestic architecture around Market Hill. Its most interesting features are the Church of St Michael and in particular the castle, the site of which was given by Henry I to Roger Bigod in 1100 or 1101.

Beginning as a fortified dwelling-house and developed as a military castle by Hugh Bigod, the

A. F. Kersting

Framlingham: the monument to Sir Robert Hitcham

1st Earl of Norfolk, the existing walls and towers seem to have been reconstructed by the latter's son, Roger, before 1213 when he entertained King John within its walls. The vicissitudes of the Bigod family caused the castle to come under the direct control of the King who administered it through a constable. As king followed king so the castle changed hands, coming into the possession of the Mowbray family; in the last years of Elizabeth's reign the castle was used as a prison but it was restored to the Howards by James I in 1613. In 1655 it was sold to Sir Robert Hitcham who bequeathed it the following year to Pembroke Hall in CAMBRIDGE. The great hall was converted into a poorhouse and all except the walls, gatehouse and towers gradually demolished. The Ministry of Works took over the upkeep of the castle in 1913.

Around the massive walls are 13 towers, and a spiral stairway in the eleventh leads to the wall-walk along which, if you have a head for heights, you may walk at least part of the way round the castle before you have to retrace your steps at the ninth tower. Though Framlingham Castle is, in the words of the WOODBRIDGE poet Bernard Barton, "a fall'n dismantled pile" it is one of the most impressive of such remains. It was the site of the Proclamation in 1553 of Mary as Queen and the home of some of the great families of East Anglia.

The late Perpendicular Church of St Michael would be remarkable if it contained nothing else than the tombs of the Howard family, including that of the Duke of Richmond, brought to Framlingham from THETFORD Priory. He was the bastard of Henry VIII and son-in-law of the 3rd Duke, whose poet son, the Earl of Surrey, is also buried here. A hammer-beam roof enclosed in false wooden fan vaulting, the magnificent organ case (1674) by Thamar of Peterborough brought to Framlingham from Pembroke College in 1708, and the monument to Jane Kerridge by the great 18th-cent. sculptor Roubiliac are among its features.

Two sets of almshouses are worth noting as are a number of fine shop fronts on Market Hill and along Castle Street. Framlingham College in the Gothic Revival style is on the DENNINGTON road and was paid for out of the balance left after the building of the Royal Albert Hall.

FRESSINGFIELD, *Suffolk* (11–TM2677). The Church of SS. Peter and Paul has the best example of a stone sanctus bell turret in the county and a 15th-cent. south porch probably built by Catherine de la Pole. A magnificent hammer-beam roof and even finer woodwork may be found on the set of nave benches each beautifully carved with buttressed arm-rests and poppyheads. One bench-end has the initials A.P., possibly for Alice de la Pole, Duchess of Suffolk and grand-daughter of Chaucer. Outside the south wall of the church is the tomb of William Sancroft, Arch-bishop of Canterbury, who was forced to return to his boyhood home, **Ufford Hall** (2 m. SE.), as an old man of 72 when he refused to take the Oath of Allegiance to William and Mary.

S. of the church is the timber-framed Fox and Goose Inn, at one time the Guild House of the village. The figure of St Margaret is carved on one of its corner-posts.

FRINTON, *Essex* (11–TM2319). A select sea-side resort developed at the end of the last century by Sir Richard Cooker, and famous for its sand and its fishing. Its appearance has been changed recently by the construction of blocks of flats. Here may be seen one of the most famous ex-amples of English domestic architecture of this century, The Homestead, built in 1905 by C. F. Voysey at the corner of Second Avenue and Holland Road. It is an unusual building with subtle differentiation of levels and fenestration, which, though modern in concept, are in the main tradition of English country building.

In the Church of Old St Mary are some panels of Morris stained glass designed by Burne-Jones and only recently presented to the church.

Frinton Golf Course (18 and 9 holes) is a famous seaside course.

GESTINGTHORPE, *Essex* (11–TL8138). This village has a place in our history as the birth-place of Captain Lawrence Oates, who in 1912 walked out into the snow so that his comrades in the Scott Antarctic Expedition might have a better chance of survival. His home, Over Hall, dates from 1735 in its facing, though it was built a century earlier for a wealthy clothier. The high-light of the mansion is the drawing-room with its plaster ceiling and elaborate fire-place.

In the Church of St Mary is a plaque which commemorates Oates's selfless deed. The large tower was added at the end of the 15th cent., and the main body of the church has work of all three previous centuries. It is remarkable for its fine double hammer-beam roof, *c.* 1500, there not being many outstanding examples of roof tim-bering in Essex, in comparison with the numerous examples in the other three East Anglian counties. There is a good octagonal Perpendicular font and the screen, too, is worthy of note.

GLANDFORD, *Norfolk* (11–TG0441). A model village of flint and brick houses built like the church by Sir Alfred Jodrell of Bayfield Hall 1 m. to the S. The village is on the River Glaven 2 m. S. of BLAKENEY. In the village is the famous Shell Museum with its collection commenced by Sir Alfred, a collection which also includes pottery, jewellery, relics of Pompeii and a sugar bowl which once belonged to Queen Elizabeth I. The museum is open daily throughout the summer (except Sundays).

The Church of St Martin was in ruins until it was rebuilt in 1899–1906 in memory of Sir Alfred's mother, commemorated by a white marble angel of Florentine workmanship. The church is a Perpendicular restoration of the original and includes a copy of a typical East Anglian seven-sacrament font, stained glass by Kempe and his pupil Bryan, and a carillon.

GORLESTON, *Norfolk* (11–TG5204). The continuation of GREAT YARMOUTH, from which it is divided by the River Yare. It is a popular sea-side resort with a long, sandy beach backed by the cliffs which are a familiar part of the coast from here to the N. The pavilion built in 1898, the light-house built a little earlier and the swimming-pool are part of its more obvious seaside attractions.

Fishermen and sailors are both well catered for, and concert parties and other shows are part of the holiday scene.

The Church of St Andrew in Church Lane is chiefly remarkable for the interior with two aisles which run the complete length of the church. There is one of Britain's earliest brasses, *c.* 1320, representing a knight, one of the Bacon family. The 19th-cent. stained glass has been variously described as "terrible" and "dreadful". Not to be missed is the Roman Catholic Church of St Peter the Apostle by Eric Gill, 1938–9. All is based on the pointed arch, which is used without vertical members.

GOSFIELD, *Essex* (11–TL7829). A tidy village with some houses built by the Courtaulds in the last century (*see* HALSTEAD). The Hall (now belonging to the Mutual Households Associa-tion, but open to the public) is basically a Tudor building, though it has been much restored in later years. The west front preserves its original appearance, made of red bricks with some diaper patterns in blue. The Hall contains a very fine Tudor long gallery, and the almost inevitable secret room.

The Church of St Katherine dates from the 15th and 16th cents. An unusual addition, made in

1735–6 was the room to the W. of the north chapel for the local squire and his family. Here they might worship backed by a grand monument to John Knight, d. 1733, by the sculptor Rysbrack. The whole thing is very un-English and theatrical in concept.

GRANTCHESTER, *Cambridgeshire* (10–TL 4355). Two m. to the S. of CAMBRIDGE, Grantchester was immortalized in the famous poem by Rupert Brooke (1887–1915). Brooke settled at the Old Vicarage on leaving King's College, Cambridge. In 1911 he was made a Fellow of King's and published a small volume of poems. Extensive foreign travels were interrupted by the First World War. He served with the Royal Naval Division at Antwerp and in 1915 was sent to the Dardanelles and died in Scyros.

The Church of SS. Andrew and Mary is noted for its Decorated chancel, the design of which shows similarities to the Lady Chapel at ELY.

GREAT BARDFIELD, *Essex* (11–TL6730). Almost the Chelsea of Essex, so many famous artists having made their homes in this attractive little town. The Church of St Mary the Virgin is at the south-east end of the village and is mainly 14th-cent. with much fine tracery in both the windows and the stone screen which stands between nave and chancel. There is a brass to the wife of William Bendlowes, d. 1584, who built Place House, now the home of one of East Anglia's several Royal Academicians, John Aldridge. This is a timber-framed building with brick fillings, and has a bracket dated 1564.

Not far from the church, on a hill, above the River Pant, is the Hall, another timber-framed building of the 16th to 17th cents. On the green in the centre of the village and along the High Street stand the most important houses. The Town Hall built in 1859 is set back from it; the Friends' Meeting House of 1804 and the Cottage Museum are worth noting. The brick tower-mill is prominent from many parts of the village.

GREAT GLEMHAM, *Suffolk* (11–TM3562). The Church of All Saints is well worth a visit for it contains a fine seven-sacrament font with many interesting details in the carvings, all of which appear against a "rayed" background. Above is an arch-braced roof with carvings and bosses at the main intersections. Three of the bells have inscriptions in Latin (15th-cent.).

Glemham House was built in 1814 with gardens which were originally laid out by Humphry Repton. The stables and octagonal dovecot are on the west edge of the grounds.

Crabbe lived in Great Glemham from 1796 to 1801.

GREAT SAXHAM, *Suffolk* (11–TL8061). St Andrew's Church was rebuilt in the 18th cent. but contains a Perpendicular font, a Stuart pulpit and some Flemish and German stained glass in the east window. A monumental brass commemorates the merchant traveller, John Eldred, d. 1632,

the first man to bring nutmegs to this country. He built a great house named Nutmeg Hall which was burnt out in 1779.

Saxham Hall was commenced by its owner Hutchison Mure, abandoning earlier designs by Robert Adam, in 1779 and completed for his successor, Thomas Mills from Mansby, by Joseph Patience in 1798. In the centre is an octagonal room with a painted ceiling. The grounds were originally laid out by Capability Brown.

One m. to the NE. is **Little Saxham** where the Church of St Nicholas is famous for its circular Norman tower. Round the top of the tower runs a band of arches. Many other parts of the church date from Norman times. There is a monument to Thomas Fitzlucas and this was altered in the 17th cent. so that a grand memorial for William Crofts could be constructed. Crofts, the 1st and only Baron, entertained Charles II and Pepys, too; his tomb by Storey shows him with his wife, Ann. Note the Stuart bier with sliding handles – a rare example.

GREAT YARMOUTH, *Norfolk* (11–TG 5207). Yarmouth, or Yaremouth, owes its unique plan to its position where the three rivers, the Bure, the Waveney and the Yare converge to find their way into the North Sea. It lies on a spit of land which has the sea on the E. side and the river on the W. and this water-surrounded environment gives it a character which is very much reminiscent of some of the Dutch and Flemish cities. As a busy harbour, whose magnificent herring fleet is regrettably dwindling, a market town and a popular seaside resort it has a great deal to offer both the casual visitor and the long-term holidaymaker.

It was a town of some importance in Norman times and was granted its charter by King John in 1208. There are still remains of the walls of the medieval town which established a plan which has been rightly compared to a miniature Manhattan. Within its walls the various orders, Benedictines, Carmelites, Dominicans and Franciscans set up houses, and a complex pattern of narrow streets, The Rows, was created, which was preserved almost to this day. The 18th cent. saw the rise of Yarmouth as a seaside resort and the 19th saw its full development, which has made Yarmouth into one of the most popular resorts on the English coast, with 5 m. of sea front and every possible holiday amenity.

The River Yare divides Yarmouth from its neighbour, GORLESTON, which may be reached by passenger ferry. Cars and other vehicles have to cross the river by the bridge at the north end of the town. From this bridge just to the S. of BREYDON WATER, the two main quays extend N. and S. Just before South Quay is Hall Quay, with the Town Hall (1882), Barclay's Bank (by Salvin in 1854) and the Duke's Head Hotel (dating from 1609).

Its continuation, on the other side of Regent Street, is South Quay, which has been called the finest quay in England and provides a visual experience which may be compared with such famous Continental cities as Ghent. Here were the homes of the wealthy merchants of the town. The Elizabethan House (National Trust) is 16th-cent. with a façade dating from the early 19th. Inside is some splendid panelling and a remarkable plaster ceiling. Further along is the Customs House which was built about 1720 as the home of John Andrews, said to be the greatest herring merchant in Europe.

Behind the South Quay were The Rows. At one time there were 145 of these narrow alleys which were numbered as an aid to recognition. In some of the Rows lived the fisher-folk and other humble people of the town and in others lived some of those merchants who were not quite able to own properties fronting the Quay. The Old Merchant's House, now a museum, is a good example.

Returning to the bridge you reach North Quay which contains the north-west tower of the old walls of the town. It leads to Bure Bridge and the road to NORWICH.

The market place in the centre of the town is large and open and from it King Street, one of the main shopping centres of the town, leads down to the river. At the north-east corner of the market place is Church Plain with the Fishermen's Hospital, founded in 1702, one of the most attractive buildings in the town. Next to the hospital is Sewell House (1646), the birthplace in 1820 of Anna Sewell whose novel *Black Beauty* has remained a favourite. Close by is the vicarage which dates from 1718, with alterations made in 1781. The Church of St Nicholas, which was completely refashioned with a neo-Gothic interior, after its war-time destruction in 1942, is generally held to be the largest parish church in England. The original Norman church was successively enlarged so that at the present time the enormously wide aisles are broader than the nave which they enclose.

At the opposite end of St George's Plain is the Church of St George with its probably unique design by John Price. Built in 1714–16, it features a west tower enclosed within the body of the church by two quadrant bays on either side, with a lantern of two stages topping the tower.

Along the peninsula which separates the River Yare from the sea is the great Nelson Column designed by William Wilkins (*see* CAMBRIDGE), and built in 1817. At 144 ft high it is just 1 ft less than that in Trafalgar Square and was built, of course, much earlier. Though when it was erected it was in a lonely isolated position it is now surrounded by factories. It is particularly interesting that the figure of Britannia turns inland to the W. and not seawards to the E., a fact which shows that even at that date Yarmouth still centred itself on the river rather than on the North Sea.

As a seaside resort Yarmouth naturally turns towards its magnificent beaches. At the north end of the town the North Denes are the site of the famous race-course. Along the promenade which runs the full length of the town towards the S., there are many attractions for tourists: bowling greens, tennis courts, a boating lake, a swimming-pool and theatre, all of which at night during the holiday season are brilliantly illuminated to provide a gay spectacle. Britannia Pier with its theatre and Wellington Pier with its pavilion originally date from the 1850s, though with much rebuilding right up to recent times.

To the S. past the Royal Naval Hospital and the Nelson Column the factories give way to funfairs and caravan sites. During the season Yarmouth's many theatres and pavilions present a range of holiday entertainment which vies with that of its Lancashire rival.

GREENSTED-JUXTA-ONGAR, *Essex* (7–TL5404), contains one of England's architectural treasures, the Church of St Andrew. Here is the only surviving example of a wooden church made in Saxon times, with walls of solid oak. It has always been known to date from at least 1013, when the body of King Edmund rested here on its way to BURY ST EDMUNDS in Suffolk. Recent tests have shown that it may well be 150 years older. The nave is built of oak logs split into sections and fixed to a wooden sill. The present sill and plinth of brick dates from a restoration of 1848. The dormer windows, the porch and the chancel added in the 16th cent. make a charming composition. The wooden tower with its small, shingled spire was perhaps added at the same time. The lectern was made from a Greensted oak in our own time by a local craftsman.

GRIMES GRAVES, *Norfolk* (11–TL8290). These remarkable Stone Age flint workings are to be found $3\frac{1}{2}$ m. NE. of BRANDON in the neighbouring county of Suffolk. They were first excavated in 1870 and of the over 300 pits which have been discovered two are open to the public. The first is some 30 ft deep with seven radiating galleries which connect with five other pits. The second pit contains a mound of levers or pick-axes made from antlers which have seen 4,000 years of history. Over 200 such picks have been found in these two pits alone.

The site covers about 35 acres and it became the centre of an industry which still continues in the little town of Brandon where flints are still "knapped" (broken) as in ancient times. Then as now it provided a flourishing export trade, though the masses of trees planted by the Forestry Commission in recent years would have perhaps surprised the Neolithic men who once worked these darkly mysterious mines.

HADLEIGH, *Essex* (7–TQ8087), should not be confused with the town of the same name in Suffolk. It was here that the great landscape painter John Constable sketched the ruins of the medieval castle which he later made into one of his most powerful compositions. (One version is in the Tate Gallery, another, more finished, in the collection of Mr and Mrs Paul Mellon, U.S.A.) The ruins still remain after a landslide in earlier times, which destroyed much of what must have been a most impressive 13th- to 14th-cent. building. From it you can see the River Thames as it makes its way to the North Sea.

The tiny Church of St James the Less stands on

the busy SOUTHEND road. It is a remarkably unspoilt Norman building, with nave and chancel and, much rarer, a Norman apse. The little belfry was added in the 15th cent. Inside are some valuable remains of early glass paintings, including one of an angel and another of St Thomas of Canterbury, both late 13th-cent.

HADLEIGH, *Suffolk* (11–TM0242). Not to be confused with its namesake in the neighbouring county of Essex, Hadleigh, formerly a wool town, lies on a tributary of the Stour. The Church of St Mary stands among a remarkable cluster of medieval buildings. Here you first notice the lead-covered spire, 72 ft tall, on top of the 64-ft tower. The tower is 14th-cent., the rest of the church mainly 15th-cent. Outside the tower is a 13th-cent. clock bell, perhaps the oldest in the county. Inside the church is an octagonal 14th-cent. font, delicately carved with angels at each corner. A bench-end in the south chapel dates from the 14th cent. and depicts the legend which tells how a wolf found and guarded the head of St Edmund. There is an unusual brass engraved on both sides commemorating the martyr Rowland Taylor who was burnt at the stake in 1555 after the accession of Mary Tudor. An obelisk marks the spot where he was put to death. Legend has it that near a tomb in the south aisle lies the body of the Danish king, Guthrum, who was buried in A.D. 889.

W. of the church is the Deanery Tower, the red-brick gatehouse of which is the only surviving feature of the palace built by Archdeacon Pykenham in 1495. Multi-sided turrets stand either side of an arched centre section which is three stories in height in contrast to the towers which are six.

Nearby is the timber-framed 15th-cent. Guildhall, which has been at various times a school and an almshouse.

Hadleigh contains an unusually large number of excellent houses dating from the 17th to the 19th cents. Close to the market place is the former Town Hall of 1851, the Corn Exchange and the Congregational church. In the High Street, with its exceptional variety of fine buildings, is the White Lion Inn, and in George Street the Baptist chapel of 1830 and the Pykenham Almshouses of 1807. The station is early Victorian and there is a particularly good 17th-cent. house at Nos. 62–66 High Street. Toppesfield Bridge spans the river with its three arches of medieval date.

One of East Anglia's finest sculptors, Thomas Woolner R.A., was born at Hadleigh in 1825. He was for some time a member of the Pre-Raphaelite Brotherhood, and became a full member of the Royal Academy in 1874. Among his most famous monuments are those to Thomas Carlyle and Alfred Lord Tennyson in Westminster Abbey. He died in 1892.

Fr Hugh James Rose (1795–1838) was rector of Hadleigh from 1830 to 1833. A meeting held in the rectory in July 1833 was an important landmark in the beginning of the Oxford Movement.

HALESWORTH, *Suffolk* (11–TM3877). A small market town which expanded in the 18th cent. with navigation on the Blyth and in the 19th cent. with the coming of the railways.

The church is basically Perpendicular, with many Victorian additions, although it is on the site of the original Anglo-Saxon church. Beneath the piscina on the south wall are the famous "Danestones" discovered during the alterations of 1889. They have been dated as 9th-cent. and probably formed part of the original Anglo-Saxon building. On the wall by the north door a tablet commemorates the association with Halesworth of Sir William and Sir Joseph Hooker, Directors of KEW Gardens, and their Wedgwood portraits may be seen in the vestry.

Opposite the church you will find the Halesworth Gallery, open from May to September and set in a beautiful old 14th-cent. building. The house is mentioned in 15th-cent. archives and at one time housed the Flemish workers who were employed to drain the marshes in these parts. Later it was altered and was used as almshouses. Besides the gallery it also houses the public library.

Georgian and Victorian maltings and a number of interesting shop-fronts add to the charm of this unpretentious market town.

HALSTEAD, *Essex* (11–TL8130). A small town situated in the Colne valley, with the Church of St Andrew in the centre of the town. Mainly of flint, it has a tower built in 1850 and contains a number of monuments to the Bourchier family. Two churches by G. G. Scott are Holy Trinity (1843) and St James's (1845). An ecclesiastical remain of a very different kind is to be found in the chapel in Fremlin's Brewery, where may be seen the font cover, reredos and other items from All Hallows, London. In 1826 the Courtauld family set up a factory here (*see* BOCKING) and the magnificent weather-boarded mill is reflected in the water, reached by the causeway.

N. of St Andrew's is what is left of an old smock-mill, while 1 m. to the E. is Blue Bridge House. This was the home of England's most remarkable butcher, John Morley, known as "merchant Morley", born in 1655 and buried in the churchyard in 1732. The house came into his hands in 1700 and shortly after that the front was rebuilt, though the estate dates back to at least the reign of Edward III. Morley was the friend of lords, poets and men of letters, and a man of some consequence.

Great Yeldham, 6 m. NW., has a famous gospel oak.

HAPPISBURGH, *Norfolk* (11–TG3731), will never be found unless its correct pronunciation is used – Haysborough. A coastal village which extends from the red-and-white striped lighthouse to the Church of St Mary. The tower is over 100 ft high with a fine west window. Mostly Perpendicular in style, it has earlier features. Standing on three large steps is a very remarkable font, 15th-cent. octagonal, with a shaft which has carvings of seated lions and "Wild Men" known as "wood-woses" or "woodhouses".

G. Douglas Bolton

Harwich: fishing boats in the harbour

The lighthouse was built in 1791 and that its beam is vitally necessary is proved by the many graves of shipwrecked seamen in the churchyard, whose numbers would have no doubt been increased but for the sight of its striped tower and flashing light.

The village itself is rather a jumble of old buildings including Monastery Cottage in Church Lane, and more recent houses and cottages. Happisburgh Manor, built in 1900, of local materials, is an important house of its period.

HARLESTON, *Norfolk* (11–TM2483), which is on the River Waveney, is an attractive small town close to the Suffolk border, with two market places, of which the older has many good Georgian houses. Not far from the disused station (1855) is Candler's House, an outstanding example of an early Georgian town house with seven bays and two stories. The Swan Hotel has parts which pre-date the Georgian period and a very decorative scroll-work sign, which projects from the façade. In the new market place is a Victorian clock tower (1873) and not far away the Corn Exchange, built in 1849. The Church of St John the Baptist dates from 1872 and is of no great interest.

HARLOW, *Essex* (11–TL4711), like BASILDON, was one of the eight new towns planned to orbit London and relieve the capital of some of its excess population and industry. However, unlike Basildon it was planned so that it should develop alongside, rather than round, the existing old town. It lies therefore to the W. of the main road from London to NEWPORT, CAMBRIDGE and NEWMARKET roads, and just to the S. of the River Stort and the A414 road which links Hertford with CHELMSFORD.

The old town has the site of a Romano-Celtic temple and theatre, but now the principal building is the Church of St Mary the Virgin, with its central crossing tower, which was much restored towards the end of the 19th cent. The most interesting interior feature is the large number of brasses in the north transept (early 15th- to 17th-cent.). With the church on the east side of the main road are several good buildings: from the 18th cent. – many around Mulberry Green; from the 17th cent. – the Stafford almshouses; and from the 16th cent. – The Gables and The Chantry.

The new town was conceived in 1947, with Sir Frederick Gibberd as the chief planner. The aim is a population of some 80,000. The Town Centre was the first to have a pedestrian precinct, and its size makes it the dominant feature of the surroundings. To the N. is the market square, which, with its gay striped awnings, is reminiscent of that at NORWICH. To the S. is the main area of the civic buildings, all by Gibberd, and others including St Paul's, the College of Further Education, etc. A road to the N. leads to the railway station, one of the outstanding examples of railway architecture in the country – clean and sharp to match the feel of modern travel. Apart from the residential developments close to the town centre, known as The High, there are three main population areas.

The north-east cluster was the first to be built and is grouped round The Stow. Like the other clusters there are, in addition to the residential buildings, shopping precincts, community centres, sports facilities, schools and places of worship. The south-east cluster centres round Bush Fair, and the most recent to be built, the south-west, is grouped round Staple Tye and shows an increase in density of population compared with the earlier groupings. All these areas feature many novel and attractive schemes, which attempt to make the town a coherent whole.

HARWICH, *Essex* (11–TM2332), shares the fate of many ports of departure in that it is neglected by those who visit it only to leave. Dovercourt, its extension to the S., is the more popular resort, but it is Harwich which has more of interest and character. It is placed where the River Orwell (from IPSWICH) and the River Stour (from MANNINGTREE) join to enter the North Sea and is protected by the peninsula which stretches S. from FELIXSTOWE. On this small wedge of land old Harwich grew up, a tightly planned medieval town with one of the earliest lighthouses in Britain, and the Church of St Nicholas added in later centuries. The church, dating from 1821, is of yellow brick with a tall tower and spire visible from far at sea. Inside is a Purbeck marble font and a painting of Moses giving the Commandments (early 18th-cent.). The tall lighthouse, built of white brick, dates from 1818.

Another notable building is the Guildhall of 1769 built of red brick with a surprising Gothic doorway. The Low Lighthouse, painted on more than one occasion by John Constable, has the look of some Eastern pagoda, while there is an odd reminder of the discipline of earlier days in the Naval Treadmill Crane, S. of the church. The Town Hall was originally built as the Great Eastern Hotel in 1864; other hotels of note are the Pier, the Angel and the Three Cups.

Parkeston, where the Continental ferries tie up, lies round the bay on the north side of the peninsula; Dovercourt is on the south side facing out across Mill Bay, 106 m. from the Hook of Holland and 90 m. from Flushing. Like many of the East Anglian coastal resorts it was developed in the 1850s, when the local M.P., Mr John Bagshaw, decided to promote it as a seaside resort. Along the front with its sandy beach stretches the Marine Parade, and behind it the main road runs to Ipswich and COLCHESTER. There is an Undercliff Walk and all the usual amenities of a successful holiday resort. The two lighthouses by the pier date from 1862. The parish church is All Saints, with a Norman nave and a chancel of the 14th cent. The west tower is Perpendicular and battlemented.

From such seafaring places local men have set off on many expeditions. Christopher Newport sailed with Raleigh, Christopher Jones with the *Mayflower* of which he was the master, and here, too, in the Three Cups Lord Nelson stayed. Captain Fryatt, who operated out of Harwich during the First World War, is commemorated in an impressive memorial.

HAVERHILL, *Suffolk* (11–TL6745) – pronounced Hayverill – is a town which, as it forms part of the population overspill plans of the Greater London Council, will see considerable development in the coming decades. A fire in 1665 destroyed much of the Church of St Mary, which has been much restored in later centuries. There is an interesting Elizabethan monument to one John Ward.

The town is predominantly Victorian, exhibit-ing some of the worst, as well as some of the better, types of buildings of that era. The Gurteen coarse-clothing factory of the mid-19th cent. gave employment to large numbers, and a dozen houses in Weavers' Row should be noted. One of the major industrial buildings of the "new" Haverhill is the factory at Duddery Hill, 1956.

HEACHAM, *Norfolk* (11–TF6737). On the village sign appears the portrait of the Red Indian princess, Pocahontas, who married John Rolfe of Heacham Hall in 1614. (The hall no longer stands.) Though she died at the age of only 22, the princess left a son who settled in Virginia, U.S.A., and founded a line which was to include the wife of President Woodrow Wilson. St Mary's Church has a modern memorial to her, and a monument to Robert Redemayne, d. 1625, the step-father of John Rolfe.

Not far away is **Caley Mill,** the centre of the main local industry, lavender growing. It is Victorian, but may well stand on the site of a mill mentioned in the Domesday Book. Though inland, on the A149, a road leads to the Wash where there is a beach of pebbles, with sand at low tide.

HELMINGHAM, *Suffolk* (11–TM1857). Helmingham Hall, set within a moat, is owned by the Tollemache family who moved from Bentley at the beginning of the 16th cent., having acquired it by marriage. It is basically a square, half-timbered Tudor house, with Georgian and later additions, including crenellation by Nash. Standing on its moated platform with its stepped gables, tall chimneys and drawbridge, it presents a unique picture, almost as if a French château had to come to rest in the English countryside. Constable's great landscape *Helmingham Dell* was painted in the deer park.

The interior of the house, which the family has occupied again since 1953, is no less splendid. The boudoir, once the library, with Venetian woodwork and carvings, and the present library, once the drawing-room, are two of the best rooms. Above the library is the room in which Queen Elizabeth I is supposed to have stayed. There is a fine collection of family portraits and other paintings and treasures.

The Church of St Mary is also much associated with the Tollemache family, one of whom built the fine west tower *c.* 1543. Many monuments commemorate the family and there are statues to the Countess of Dysart and her husband, Lionel Tollemache, by Nollekens. The 15th-cent. font has lions supporting the shaft which stand on human heads.

HENGRAVE, *Suffolk* (11–TL8268). A minute church and a magnificent mansion make this little village well worthy of a visit. The 15th-cent. Church of St John Lateran has a tower less than 13 ft in internal diameter and possibly pre-Conquest in date. The remainder of the building is of later date. An astonishing collection of monuments includes the pillared and canopied memorial to Margaret, Countess of Bath, *c.* 1561;

her second husband, Sir Thomas Kitson, lies beneath, and her first and third husbands also rest here! There is another six-posted monument to a later Thomas Kitson and a very fine alabaster wall memorial to the 22-year-old Thomas Darcy. Another monument is that to Sir Edmund Gage, d. 1707, one of whose descendants introduced the greengage to this country.

The famous Hengrave Hall, next to the church, may be seen by appointment, and is now a Convent School for girls. Here the great madrigalist John Wilbye (1574–1638) lived for some 30 years and was in charge of the music in the great country house, which was visited by Queen Elizabeth and the entire court in 1578. Wilbye died in 1638 and is buried in COLCHESTER. The Hall itself is one of the show-pieces of the county. Commissioned by the merchant Kytson from John Eastawe, it was commenced in 1525 and took some 13 years to complete. Over the doorway is a wonderfully elaborate oriel window, triple-shafted and with superb detail in the carving; supporting the window are Italianate cherubs holding shields in the Renaissance style, the only exception to the predominantly late Gothic style of the house. The doorway leads to the courtyard with battlements and more oriel windows.

Inside, the Hall has been much restored but it still contains much fine workmanship, and in the chapel stained glass of the early 16th cent. shows scenes from the book of Genesis and the life of Christ.

HERRINGFLEET, *Suffolk* (11–TM4797). Right in the north-east corner of the county where the River Waveney winds on its way to the coast at GREAT YARMOUTH. The round tower of St Margaret's Church is early Norman and there are several other Norman features. Interesting stained glass assembled in the 19th cent. from pieces of English and foreign glass of the 15th cent. are in the thatched church.

There is an octagonal smock-mill which was used for drainage and which has been restored to working order. The Priory Mill which was built in the present century is also used for drainage.

Some 1½ m. NW. of Herringfleet is St Olave's Priory, founded in the early years of the 13th cent. for the Augustinians. At that time it was on an island site. The foundations and the space occupied by the cloisters are still visible and some rare early vaulting still survives.

Back in the village, Manor House Farm, dated 1655, has Dutch-influenced gables and one of the largest barns in Suffolk.

HEVENINGHAM HALL, *Suffolk* (11–TM 3372). One of the finest Georgian mansions in the county, the Hall was commissioned in 1777. Sir Gerard Vanneck, who had become the Member for DUNWICH, engaged Sir Robert Taylor, Court Architect to George III, to enlarge the family's Queen Anne house at Heveningham. Taylor screened the north front with Corinthian columns, added wings on either side and created an impressive building in the Palladian tradition.

The talented young architect James Wyatt took over from Taylor and became responsible for the interior design. The task of painting decorations was given to Biagio Rebecca, an Italian artist of the time.

Within the last few years the Hall, which has continuously belonged to the Vanneck family, has been open to the public. Highlights include a superb entrance hall, with a semi-circular vaulted ceiling, the large dining-room, the Etruscan room which may be compared with the Pompeian room at ICKWORTH and the gardens, laid out by Lancelot (Capability) Brown in 1781. The walled garden contains one of the finest serpentine or "crinkle-crankle" walls to be found in East Anglia. The beautifully proportioned Orangery is the work of Wyatt.

Among the rooms open to the public are those containing some of the Vanneck collection of paintings, and others with exhibitions of designs and plans by James Wyatt and Capability Brown.

HEYDON, *Norfolk* (11–TG1127), a small village of great charm centred around one of the county's prettiest village greens. Heydon Hall was commenced in 1581 and was subsequently enlarged. The façade is planned as a shallow E with gabled bays and, above the roof, fine groups of chimneys. Its three stories of brick give a delightful effect. In the grounds, to the N., is an ice-house and to the SE., a look-out tower.

The Church of SS. Peter and Paul is in the Decorated and Perpendicular styles and the tower, the west doors and south porch are all 15th-cent. The interior arcades belong to the previous century, however, and there are some good furnishings including a 13th-cent. font, a Perpendicular pulpit, a screen, family pews and iron railings.

HICKLING BROAD, *Norfolk* (11–TG4122). Situated between the coast and the A149 GREAT YARMOUTH to STALHAM road. Associated with this, one of the most large and popular of all the broads, are Whiteslea and Heigham Sounds. Though very large in area they are the shallowest of the broads; except where specially dredged for sailing, they are rarely more than 6 ft deep. A century ago the area was even larger, though the three sections were still separate. The complex is part of the Thurne Valley and there is free access to the usual river craft.

This is a region particularly noted for birds. In the summer spoonbills may be seen, diving ducks are especially characteristic and in the spring and autumn the many species of waders are evident. Due to its proximity to the sea Hickling sees the passage of many thousands of migrants on their way to or from our shores, and in the evenings of late summer flocks of starlings spend their nights in the reed beds.

The Pleasure Boat Inn at the staithe is a famous Broadland rendezvous.

HINGHAM, *Norfolk* (11–TG0202). It was from this Hingham that Robert Peck set off in the early

A. F. Kersting

Holkham Hall: the entrance hall

17th cent. to found Hingham in Massachusetts, there to find the religious freedom denied to him and his associates at home. Connections are still maintained between the two towns. Peck was joined by Samuel Lincoln (*see* SWANTON MORLEY) in 1637, and it was from this Samuel that the great Abraham Lincoln was descended. (*See also* HEACHAM for other American associations.)

The town is most attractive, with Georgian houses grouped around an irregularly shaped market place to the W. of which is the green. St Andrew's Church has a fine 14th-cent. tower with a west doorway and window above. It is unusually consistent in its Decorated style. The interior has fine arcades with clustered columns and the east window (seven-light) is large and was considerably altered to fit the early-16th-cent. German stained glass purchased for the church in 1813. However, pride of place must go to the great monument to Lord Morley against the north wall of the chancel, described as one of the most impressive of its date (mid-15th-cent.) in the country. Standing the full height of the chancel wall, it has at its base the tomb-chest with shields and in the deep recess elaborate tracery which includes ten kneeling figures. The main arch of the tomb is enclosed within a magnificent framework which rises up to a veritable crescendo of fine carving.

HINTLESHAM, *Suffolk* (11–TM0843), is the scene of yet another festival which takes place each July. Hintlesham Hall, based like so many others on an Elizabethan house, built by Thomas Timperley, has an early Georgian façade and forms the centre of the annual festival. A filigreed plaster ceiling in the drawing-room is one of the finest in the county, and probably dates from the end of the 17th cent. The Hall is open during festival times and on other occasions by appointment.

The Church of St Nicholas has associations with the Timperley family and contains monuments to Thomas Timperley, d. 1593 and to Captain John Timperley, d. 1629 – a fine armoured figure engraved on a large slate. A fragment of a St Christopher wall painting remains opposite the south entrance in the nave.

Here in 1939 died Henry Havelock Ellis, the writer on sex and psychology who was born at Croydon in 1859. He was also the editor of a series on the English dramatists and published several volumes of art criticism.

HOLKHAM HALL, *Norfolk* (11–TF8944). A magnificent mansion in the Palladian style and one of the architectural show-pieces of the county. The Hall is the seat of the Earl of Leicester and on the return of the 1st Earl from the customary Grand Tour in 1718 he decided to rebuild the family home, the foundation stone being laid in 1734. The design was entrusted to William Kent who also designed much of the furniture. The basic plan is an H – a centre section with four wings, an arrangement which gives Holkham an extraordinarily elaborate interior. The entrance by way of the ground floor into the wonderful stone hall shows Kent's genius at its peak, and its effectiveness is intensified by contrast with the severe classical portico which is at the centre of the south side.

The hall is of alabaster, used not only on the walls but also on the columns which support a coffered ceiling of rich and splendid design. Around the gallery is an outstanding collection of sculptured panels. To mention all the rooms is impossible but the Saloon cannot be omitted. Beneath another coffered ceiling of great splendour is the original Kent furniture. The state bedrooms with their fascinating use of ceiling panelling and the lavish use of tapestries, fabrics and furniture show a masterly hand. There is a magnificent collection of pictures, and the long library has a fine collection of 18th-cent. books.

The grounds were laid out by Capability Brown in 1762, and contain a large lake W. of the Hall. To the N. is a monument to the son of the 1st Earl, Thomas Coke, who is better known as Coke of Norfolk. His work as an agricultural reformer is commemorated in a column 120 ft high designed by Donthorne and commissioned by his tenants at a cost of £4,000 in 1845. The gardens also contain an obelisk (1729), a temple of the same date and statuary by Boehm and Charles Smith. The south gates and the triumphal arch and the north gates are *c.* 1850.

In the park is the Church of St Withburga which was commenced in Anglo-Saxon times and was much restored in 1870. It is well placed on a slight rise and contains monuments by Nicholas Stone and Boehm. The Hall and park are open to the public in summer.

HOLLESLEY, *Suffolk* (11–TM3544), pronounced Hozely, is a tiny village close to what is perhaps the quietest of all Suffolk's quiet seaside places, **Shingle Street**. The Church of All Saints has been much restored, though its west tower is mid-15th-cent. This tower, like so many others built along the coast, served sailors as well as parishioners. From the sea it provided a welcome landmark which must have guided home many fishermen.

Here, too, is one of the Martello towers (*see* ALDEBURGH and LOWESTOFT) which were built at the beginning of the 19th cent. as part of our defence system. The Hollesley Bay Labour Colony was established in 1905 and became a Borstal institution for delinquents.

HOLT, *Norfolk* (11–TG0738), the site of the famous Gresham's School founded by Sir Thomas Gresham who was born here in 1519, and who also founded the Royal Exchange in London. The school was founded in 1555 and one of its former buildings stands on the site of his manor house in the market place, where it was built in 1858 in Tudor style. The school moved out to Cromer Road in 1900 and the "Big School", the chapel and the various houses form an interesting group.

The town itself has some pleasant buildings and a milestone recording the distances to many of the famous halls and houses of Norfolk. Attention should be drawn to the large and elaborate Home Place (1903–5) on the CROMER road, one of the most extraordinary private buildings in the county, now a convalescent home.

St Andrew's Church was destroyed by the fire which also destroyed much of the town centre in 1708. It was much restored by the Victorian architect Butterfield in 1864.

HOLTON, *Suffolk* (11–TM4077). An attractive village not far from HALESWORTH. You may just as easily see first the great mill as the Church of St Peter. The church has a round Norman tower and a Norman doorway, also a 15th-cent. octagonal font and a 16th-cent linenfold pulpit.

The post-mill dates from 1752 and has been carefully restored. It is beautifully situated on a hill among pine trees. The house close by has interesting pargeting of recent date.

Gavelcroft Farm has gables of Dutch design and there are Norman ruins at St Margaret's Chapel ¾ m. to the S.

HONINGTON, *Suffolk* (11–TL9174). Here was born one of East Anglia's most famous literary sons, the writer and poet, Robert Bloomfield. The cottage in which he was born in 1766 still stands close to the church. His father died when he was

one year old and he was brought up by his mother who kept the village school. He worked as a shoemaker in London, living in great poverty, and composed his first major poem *The Farmer's Boy* while he worked at the bench. It was published, with illustrations by Bewick, with the help of a local squire, Capel Lofft, in 1800. No less than 26,000 copies were sold within three years. Other works followed but Bloomfield died in poverty in 1823 at SHEFFORD in Bedfordshire.

The Church of All Saints has a good Norman doorway with typical decoration. The font is 14th-cent. with delicate tracery and a carved Crucifixion which shows the sun and the moon above the arms of the cross. Remains of wall paintings showing St Nicholas and St Thomas of Canterbury are above the south door of the nave.

HORNING, *Norfolk* (11–TG3517). A well known Broadland centre on the River Bure, with many picturesque cottages and occasional attractive glimpses of the river from the main street. The Church of St Benedict has pinnacles representing the four Evangelists, and is mainly 13th- and 14th-cent. It has some carved bench-ends, with fantastic imagery. The Priest's Doorway is 13th-cent. and has carved dogtooth ornament.

One m. E. of the church on the road to St Benet's Abbey (*see* LUDHAM) was St James's Hospital. All that remains is the chapel which is now a barn in Horning Hall.

HORSEY MERE, *Norfolk* (11–TG4523). Only a barrier of sand dunes separates this broad from the North Sea. The seepage of sea water makes this the most brackish of all the broads and the water level stands 2 or 3 ft above the general level of the surrounding land. The basin is shallow, being only some 6 ft deep, and in comparison with many of the broads its size has changed little in the past century due to regular clearing of the vegetation which would otherwise have covered its surface. Due to the brackish water the plant, bird and insect life is rather special. A grey shrimp known as the opossum may often be found and some of the copepods are only to be found here and at nearby HICKLING. Bitterns also tend to favour the saline waters of the broad.

HOUGHTON HALL, *Norfolk* (11–TF7828). This was the mansion built by Sir Robert Walpole in 1721. The architect was Colin Campbell, assisted by Thomas Ripley, and much of the interior was the work of William Kent (*see* HOLKHAM). One of the most striking modifications to the original plan is the idea of the domes on the four corners – a conceit of James Gibbs. The façade has a classical portico and the vaulted entrance hall sets the tone of the building. Above it are the stone hall and the saloon, the first being a perfect cube of 40 ft dimensions. The effect of the carving is almost overwhelming, from the bustle of the ceiling to the fire-place carved by Rysbrack, whose work again appears over the fire-place in the dining-room.

Ickworth House has an impressive domed rotunda and a landscaped park

In a house noted for the brilliance of its ceilings and carvings the overmantels in the parlour should be noted as the work of the great Grinling Gibbons. The house at one time contained a collection of paintings which matched in magnificence the Hall itself, but unfortunately these had to be sold to the Empress of Russia in 1779 for the then high price of £40,000. The grounds of the house contain the stables and a water house, and S. of the gates is the village commenced shortly after the Hall itself. The house may only be seen by private arrangement. Among those who declined it when it was offered to them were the Duke of Wellington, who preferred Strathfieldsaye in Hampshire and Edward VII, who, when Prince of Wales, preferred the more intimate charms of SANDRINGHAM.

HOVETON BROADS, *Norfolk* (11–TG3118), comprises two broads known as Great and Little. The larger broad has changed considerably in size in the past 100 years, due to the continued encroachment of vegetation which has not only reduced its size but has also overgrown the various channels which linked it to the main curve of the River Bure. Only one such channel now remains, at the E. of the broad.

Whereas the large broad is inside the curve of the river, the Little Broad is on the outside of a curve further downstream. It tends to divide into two sections, an inner and an outer, linked by a channel cut through the peat and clay. In 1840 both sections were linked with the river, but now only the east section is linked by a channel by a dyke. This outer broad is open to the public but the inner one is private.

HOXNE, *Suffolk* (11–TM1877). Pronounced Hoxen, the village has for centuries been held to be where St Edmund was martyred, although Hellesdon agrees better with the "Haegelisdun" of the Anglo-Saxon Chronicle. This was in 869 after he had attempted to repel the invading Danes.

His body was taken to BURY ST EDMUNDS. Here, too, was one of East Anglia's two cathedrals until 1078 when the bishop moved to THETFORD.

The church of SS. Peter and Paul has a fine west tower and, inside, some very interesting wall paintings showing St Christopher, the Seven Deadly Sins and the Seven Works of Mercy, all dating from the 15th cent.

HUNSTANTON, *Norfolk* (11–TF6842). A resort, or almost two resorts, on the west coast of Norfolk, facing into the Wash. One of its features is the vast beach, shingle and sand, backed by cliffs. Old Hunstanton was the home of the le Strange family for 900 years and their hall was a moated mansion which has suffered in two severe fires, one in 1853 and the other in recent times. The Church of St Mary was extensively restored in the 19th cent. but has an interesting porch, traceried as if it were a window, and an east window of five lights with unusual tracery. There is a simple Norman font and a 16th-cent. screen. Among the good collection of brasses is that to Sir Henry le Strange, d. 1506, and the even earlier one to Edmund Greene and his wife, *c.* 1480.

Just to the S. is Hunstanton proper, sometimes known as St Edmund's after the church of that name, built in 1865. A window shows the saint landing on the coast, a site supposedly marked by a chapel near the lighthouse. On the green is the shaft of the village cross which once stood in the old village. Much of the town is, like the church, Victorian as it was built at the same time as the extension of the railway line from KING'S LYNN. Perhaps the most famous feature is natural, the striped cliffs to the N. of the pier.

ICKWORTH, *Suffolk* (11–TL8161). Near the church in the village of Horringer are the gates of Ickworth House which was conceived by Frederick Hervey, 4th Earl of Bristol and Bishop of Derry, in 1792. His family had owned the land since the

15th cent. and the bishop, whose income was considerable, was able to indulge his interest in architecture. One of the several houses he had had built in Ireland had a domed rotunda inspired by that on the mansion on Belle Isle on Lake Windermere. This domed rotunda became the central feature of his new fancy at Ickworth. The architect was Francis Sandys, who based his design on plans by Asprucci, the Italian architect. The bishop liked tall rooms and his original idea was that the elliptical rotunda would contain the living accommodation, with one wing to house his collection of pictures and the other for his sculpture. The collection was confiscated, however, when Napoleon invaded Italy, and the earl bishop died in 1803 before the building was complete.

Work on the house was finally resumed in 1826 by the 5th Earl. In 1907 further changes were made on the accession of the 4th Marquess who ordered the reconstruction of the main staircase. In 1956, after his death, the house and almost 2,000 acres of the estate, together with many of the works of art it contained, were handed over to the National Trust.

The park, landscaped by Capability Brown, effectively screens the house behind magnificent oaks and cedars, even though the building is over 600 ft in length and the dome 104 ft high. The entrance hall contains a noble marble group by Flaxman, whose illustrations to Homer formed the basis of the designs for the frieze in terracotta relief round the cupola. The library contains important pictures by Hogarth and Gravelot, the teacher of Thomas Gainsborough, three of whose finest portraits hang in the great drawing-room. A superb collection of silver, partly Bristol, *objets d'art* and miniatures are among the treasures to be seen by the visitor.

INGATESTONE, *Essex* (7–TQ6499), now bypassed by the A12, lies on the Roman road between BRENTWOOD and CHELMSFORD, and is closely linked with **Fryerning**. The tall west tower of the Church of SS. Edmund and Mary (an unusual combination of saints) is built of red brick with typical diaper patterning in black bricks. The west window has Perpendicular tracery and in the nave the north wall, built by the Normans, makes use of Roman bricks. The south chapel was added by the Petre family in 1556 and the church has a number of monuments to them, that to Sir William (d. 1572) and his wife being of especially high quality. They are seen resting, hands clasped in prayer, on rolled mats. Robert Petre, who died 21 years later, rests in the south chapel and John and his wife lie beneath a major wall monument in the north chapel. There is a elegant portrait bust set in an oval recess of John Troughton, d. 1621.

The Petre family lived at Ingatestone Hall, the former manor of the Barking nunnery. The house is of brick and dates from the mid-16th cent. The gateway was rebuilt at the end of the 18th cent. at which time the bell turret was added. The big stepped gables are echoed by those of the nearby barn. The house is now shared between the Essex County Council, whose admirable Record Office use it for exhibitions of local interest, and the Petre family, who occupy the south wing. It is open only at exhibition times.

The pleasant High Street has a number of 18th-cent and earlier buildings. Larger buildings include the Spread Eagle, the almshouses of 1840 and the Congregational church of the same date. Towards the end of the last century a development of Victorian-Tudor houses was built by the local architect, George Sherrin. A more recent development features a number of houses of adventurous design.

The owner of the Hyde, now destroyed, was the Rev. John Disney, whose collection of classical marbles now forms part of the Fitzwilliam Museum, CAMBRIDGE. Nearby Fryerning has a church (St Mary's) with a Perpendicular tower, again diapered in brick, and a Norman nave which again makes use of Roman bricks. The font is early (*c.* 1200) and there is a brass with figures on both sides. Not far N. is a post-mill which has been carefully restored.

IPSWICH, *Suffolk* (11–TM1744). The county town of East Suffolk, Ipswich is less immediately glamorous than its rival NORWICH. For one thing it has no castle and for another, no cathedral. Yet there is something about its cluster of narrow streets, its open parks and the dockland area by the River Orwell which makes Ipswich, though an unspectacular town, by no means unmemorable.

In its upper reaches the Orwell is called the Gipping. From the Anglo-Saxon name Gipeswic (the "g" being pronounced as a "y") comes the present name of the town. It is a place with a long history, a borough even before the Norman Conquest and with a charter granted by King John in 1199. Its fortunes fluctuated after it had reached a peak of importance in the 16th cent. but then in the 19th it began to rise again and is now not only a major port and market town but also the county town of East Suffolk, with a population of over 100,000 people.

Ipswich was the birthplace of Cardinal Wolsey and the home for some years of the rising star of English painting, Thomas Gainsborough. Many more will perhaps remember it for its association with Mr Pickwick, and with Margaret Catchpole, the adventuress who was deported to Australia for horse-stealing in 1801.

Northgate Street, Westgate Street and Tower Rampart help establish the medieval walls of old Ipswich, and Priory Street reminds us that the Augustinians, Franciscans, Dominicans and the Carmelites all set up houses in the town. In 1527 Wolsey founded the Cardinal College of St Mary. It was to remain unfinished, all that is left is the red-brick gateway, with its royal coat of arms, in College Street close to St Peter's Church.

Perhaps the most spectacular of all the buildings of Ipswich is the Ancient House in Butter Market. The house was built in 1567 and is also known as Sparrowe's House after the family who lived in it for a long period. The main front of the

Ipswich: pargeting on the Ancient House in Butter Market

house is an outstanding example of the East Anglian art of pargeting, the carving of plasterwork into decorative features and patterns. Underneath its oriel windows are panels representing the then known continents of the world. Inside there is magnificent oak panelling and ceilings with heavy carved beams. The house is now one of East Anglia's most important bookshops.

Not far away at the corner of Tavern Street and Northgate Street is the Great White Horse Hotel where Mr Pickwick had his adventures, commemorated in the murals which line the diningroom.

In Christchurch Park on the other side of Crown Street is Christchurch Mansion which stands on the site of the Priory of the Holy Trinity founded by the Augustinians. It was in 1548 that Edmund Withipoll began building his new house which was twice visited by Queen Elizabeth I, most appropriately as it had been designed on the Elizabethan E plan. In the 17th cent. it was apparently damaged by fire, and much rebuilding took place. At the end of the last century it was proposed that the house and land be cleared to make a housing estate, but this scheme was thwarted by the generosity of the Cobbold family who presented the house to the town on condition that the grounds were purchased and made into a park. Thus came into existence what has been called the finest park in any provincial town and a museum which contains a fine collection of furniture and pictures as well as an art gallery, a memorial to Wolsey, with works by Gainsborough, Constable, Munnings and many other famous Suffolk artists.

The Ipswich Museum of Archaeology and Natural History is in the High Street and contains an impressive collection of birds and animals, geological specimens and many other things which would delight adults as well as children. Among many exhibits which relate to Suffolk are some from the Anglo-Saxon cemetery at Ipswich and replicas of the treasures, now in the BRITISH MUSEUM, which were found at SUTTON HOO and MILDENHALL.

On the quayside is the Old Custom House built in the Palladian style in 1844, an otherwise symmetrical composition except for the Clock Tower at the north-west corner.

The civic church is St Mary-le-Tower, in Tower Street, rebuilt in the 19th cent. but with many interesting brasses. Among the other churches in the town must be mentioned St Margaret's close to Christchurch Mansion; St Matthew's with its outstanding 15th-cent. font; and St Peter's with its Tournai font, one of seven similar fonts in England made of black marble imported from Belgium at the end of the 12th cent. In contrast is the Congregational church in Dryden Road built in 1957–8 in contemporary style. Again not to be missed is the Unitarian Meeting House in Friars Street, 1699–1700, a building of simple dignity with a fine pulpit and brass chandelier.

The developments which made Ipswich essentially a town of the 19th cent. have in recent years been accelerated, so that a new Ipswich is rising, particularly on the west side of the town round Civic Drive where the tall blocks of modern flats and offices present a skyline very different from the medieval city which is at the heart of the town.

Just off the A45 to the SE. is Ipswich Airport adding a further dimension to the network of roads, railway and river which have served Ipswich for so long. Two m. to the S. of the town is Freston Tower, a red brick mid-16th-cent. folly containing six rooms one above another, in a park beside the River Orwell.

IXWORTH, *Suffolk* (11–TL9370). Not far from the village, in Stow Lane, are the remains of a Roman building, part of what might have been a large settlement near the camp of the Iceni.

Then in 1170 an Augustinian priory was founded here. The remains form part of **Ixworth Abbey**, on the site of the old priory.

The Church of St Mary has an elaborate canopied tomb to the memory of Richard Coddington, d. 1567, and his wife. They may be seen, with their children, in portrait brasses.

A couple of m. NW. is **Ixworth Thorpe**. The little Church of All Saints is thatched with a weather-boarded bell turret. The Norman doorway is less than 3 ft wide and only 5 ft high to the springing of the arch. Inside are a number of bench-ends showing more than two dozen animals, birds, humans and even a mermaid. A copy of a "Degree of Marriage", printed in 1771, is believed to be the best preserved in Suffolk.

KEDINGTON, *Suffolk* (11–TL7046). This small village contains one of Suffolk's most interesting churches. SS. Peter and Paul has been built over Roman remains, has an Anglo-Saxon cross and was recorded in Norman times. Inside, the number of important monuments has caused the church to be known as "The Westminster Abbey of Suffolk" (Cautley). Though there are no early clerestory lights the interior is bright due to the skylights added in the 19th cent. in the 16th-cent. roof.

Most of the monuments are to members of the Barnardiston family. The earliest seems to be that to Thomas Barnardiston who died in 1503; one dated *c.* 1610 shows another Sir Thomas with his two wives, the lid of the coffin protruding below. Next to it is another to his daughter Grissell, shown kneeling on a cushion.

The woodwork is exceptionally fine with many rare features: an alms-box made from a hollow tree trunk, a three-decker pulpit of Jacobean period, and special pews for children with seats for their school-teachers so that they might supervise their charges.

KELVEDON, *Essex* (11–TL8618), like its neighbour, Witham, has recently been bypassed by the main A12 road from London to Colchester. As a result, its 18th-cent. character may well be preserved. There is much of earlier date, timber-framed cottages and the 17th-cent. Ormonde House, for example. The village runs along the old Roman road and is crossed by the River Blackwater and it was here that the famous preacher Charles Spurgeon was born in 1834. Joining the Baptists in 1850 he soon went to London where his sermons were so popular that the congregation invariably overflowed his church. His own church, the Tabernacle, was opened in 1861 and his sermons were printed and sold by the thousand. He died in 1892 and is buried at Norwood.

The Church of St Mary the Virgin has arcading of the 13th cent. and a 14th-cent. tower. It was restored in the 1870s. It contains an unusual carving of Esther and Ahasuerus which came from a local house and was probably originally brought from Flanders where it had been carved in the 17th cent.

Tourist Photo Library

Kersey village

King's Lynn: Customs House

A. F. Kersting

There is much to see in the High Street, good houses and shop-fronts of the 18th and 19th cents., the chapel of 1853 and the Friends' Evangelistic House, a century earlier. Just under 1 m. N. of the church is Felix Hall which was built *c.* 1760 and much altered later. There is a large and impressive classical portico, added *c.* 1830 by Lord Western and based on the Temple of Fortuna Virilis in Rome.

Nearby there is evidence of the Roman settlement of Canonium, and near the Freemasons' Hall excavations have resulted in important discoveries of Belgic and Roman material.

KERSEY, *Suffolk* (11–TM0044). Perhaps the most photographed of all Suffolk's villages and certainly one of the most picturesque. Set in a V-shaped valley, the centre-piece is the watersplash across the stream which runs through the village. On one side the road up the hill leads to the Church of St Mary and the vista is one of unforgettable loveliness. The church is mentioned in the Domesday Book but was much added to in the 14th and 15th cents. The roof of the south porch, though small, is of great beauty, being divided into 16 panels, filled with, and surrounded by, elaborate tracery. Look at the carving in the arcade of the north aisle and you are reminded of the Black Death which caused the cessation of the work in 1348. An unusual lectern has delicate buttresses attached to its hexagonal shaft.

The village was famous in earlier days for cloth. "Kersey" in fact was mentioned by Shakespeare in *Measure for Measure* and *Love's Labour's Lost* where a character speaks of "honest Kersey noes", and it is not difficult, even in the present century to imagine oneself back in the late Middle Ages while walking among the half-timbered cottages with their projecting upper stories and little steps which jut out on to the pavements.

Priory Farm has the remains of an Augustinian priory founded in the late 12th cent.

KESSINGLAND, *Suffolk* (11–TM5286). Another seaside village whose church tower has served as a landmark to generations of sailors. There are too many caravans and the holiday-maker seeking peace would be advised to go on to DUNWICH or COVEHITHE. However, it is not without some charm. The tower of the Church of St Edmund was built by Richard Russell of Dunwich who had also designed that at WALBERS-WICK. Inside, there is a 14th-cent. font, one of Suffolk's finest, with excellent carvings on both the shaft and the bowl (both octagonal).

The heroes of Kessingland have been its life-boatmen who saved 144 lives in the period 1869–1936.

Close by there is the Suffolk Wild Life and Country Park with several acres of woods and parkland and a large collection of animals, birds and children's pets.

KETTERINGHAM, *Norfolk* (11–TG1503), is a small village some 6 m. from NORWICH. The Church of St Peter, though it has a good west tower rebuilt in 1609, is mostly of interest for its monuments and brasses. It also has an octagonal font and a three-decker pulpit. The earliest brass appears to be dated *c.* 1470; there is another to Sir Thomas Hevenyngham and his wife, *c.* 1499; and one to a baby who died in 1530. Among the monuments are those to Sir William and Lady Heveningham, d. 1678 and Edward Atkyns, d. 1750. Others are by the well-known sculptors Westmacott (Edward Atkyns, 1807) and Flaxman (Harriet Peach, 1825).

The church and the adjacent thatched and timbered cottages stand in the grounds of Ketteringham Hall, now a school, but originally built in Tudor times. It was much altered in 1840–50 in the Victorian Gothic style.

KING'S LYNN, *Norfolk* (11–TF6220), before it became Royal property was called Bishop's Lynn. Nowadays the town is usually known simply as Lynn. It combines the attractions of a busy town, seaport and agricultural centre. Once it was a walled city of considerable importance; traces of the walls still remain. Its two great churches, two market places and two Guildhalls tell of its former size and there are many reminders of the Grey, Black, Austin and White Friars, all of whom had houses in the town. It had long been a port handling large quantities of wool, cloth and agricultural products and its position 2 m. S. of the mouth of the Great Ouse made it a natural site for a harbour. Most of the development is on the east bank. **West Lynn,** connected by ferry, is famous for the views it provides of Lynn proper.

The town centred round the Saturday Market and Tuesday Market, the former with its Church of St Margaret and the latter with that of St Nicholas. Its first charter was received from King John in 1204. Soon after the Conquest Bishop Losinga of NORWICH founded a priory here and commenced St Margaret's, a huge church, 235 ft long, made of white limestone. In keeping with its size it has two towers at the west end, a very rare feature for any parish church. There are many impressive features including the chancel with multiple columns and finely carved caps, the west window of the nave (between the towers) which has seven lights, and the Perpendicular shafts of the chapel attached to the north-west tower. The early Georgian pulpit, the brass lectern and above all two brasses, perhaps the largest, and certainly among the most famous, in the country, are immensely fine pieces.

St Nicholas' in St Anne's Street, is almost as long, and its west front has an even more magnificent window. There is a superb Perpendicular south porch *c.* 1410, not dissimilar to those at WALPOLE ST PETER and PULHAM ST MARY. The font was given to the church in 1627, but an earlier one is still in the church. One of the bench-ends has a medallion with a remarkable carving of a bishop.

Saturday Market and Tuesday Market both have interesting houses. Greyfriars in St James's

Street was founded in the mid-13th cent. and enlarged at the beginning of the 14th cent. Its tall octagonal tower survives. All Saints' has the remains of a Norman chapel. The most remarkable ecclesiastical building is probably Red Mount Chapel, built on a mound, octagonal in shape and dated *c.* 1485. It served as a wayside chapel on the Pilgrim's Way to WALSINGHAM, and is situated in a park called The Walks. Slightly later in date, *c.* 1520, is the South Gate, the last surviving gate of the town walls, through which traffic still passes on the main London Road.

The Guildhall and Town Hall in Queen Street are both built in a striking chequer design in flint. The Guildhall was built in 1421 for the Guild of Holy Trinity and the façade features a tall Perpendicular window of seven lights. Next to the Guildhall is a decorative porch, patterned in flint to match its neighbour and added in Elizabethan times. Inside the Guildhall is a remarkable collection of regalia including King John's Cup, a beautiful piece of medieval plate, gilded and decorated with translucent enamels showing hawking and hunting scenes, and the King John Sword, another medieval piece. The Town Hall close by dates from 1895.

One of the most photographed and famous of King's Lynn's many outstanding buildings is the Customs House built in 1683 by Henry Bell. Bell was a local architect who achieved far more than local reputation. The roof is surmounted by a lantern tower, and a niche contains a statue of Charles II.

Facing the Guildhall is Thoresby College, founded in 1500. Mostly 17th-cent. it includes a Perpendicular archway. Nearby in Nelson Street is Hampton Court, timber-framed and now converted into flats. Opposite is the Hanseatic Warehouse (1428) which served as both home and warehouse for Hansa merchants. Other merchant buildings of great interest include Clifton House, restored and rebuilt in 1708, and the Greenland Fishery House in Bridge Street (1605), again timber-framed and now a museum. St George's Guildhall in King Street dates from 1406 and was adapted as a theatre in the 1950s. The Museum and Art Gallery in Market Street contains items of natural history and archaeology, displays concerned with domestic life and the sea and a collection of paintings, glass and pottery.

The King's Lynn Festival of Music and the Arts takes place in July and features some of the world's leading orchestras and soloists. The Sailing Club has its headquarters in Ferry Lane, and the King's Lynn Golf Club (18 holes) is at Leziate, 4½ m. from the town on the B1145.

KNAPTON, *Norfolk* (11–TG3034). This is a church which is visited for the beauty of its roof, one of the finest in the county, and its font, not that the rest of the church, which is Decorated and Perpendicular, is of poor quality. The lover of the artists of the Norwich School will want to see the weathervane which is said to have been designed by the great John Sell Cotman, when he was giving drawing lessons in the neighbouring

house. But the roof is its most remarkable feature – a grand affair spanning a width of over 30 ft. It can be dated with reasonable accuracy to 1504 and, like so many East Anglian roofs, boasts a host of angels who perch like pigeons on every conceivable vantage point.

The font itself is 13th-cent. Purbeck marble, and now stands on three steps. Its cover, dated 1704, is a decorative piece of work with a palindrome (in Greek) which reads "Wash my sins and not my face only". The pulpit is said to be Victorian but all authorities agree that it looks much earlier.

LAKENHEATH, *Suffolk* (11–TL7182). Situated in the north-west tip of Suffolk and one of its few villages W. of the A11. It overlooks the fens and is the site of one of the largest United States Air Force bases in this country. No doubt due to its position away from the centre of the county its magnificent Church of St Mary is less well known than it should be. Its great number of interesting features make it one of the finest in a county famed for its churches.

The chancel arch is Norman and above is a splendid wooden roof carved with angels. More fine carving is to be seen on the benches in the nave and in the 15th-cent. octagonal pulpit. Every authority agrees that the font is the best 13th-cent. example in the county. Octagonal in shape it has deeply moulded arches and is supported by slender columns clustered around the main shaft. The many wall paintings include St Edmund, St John and scenes from the life of Christ. Brasses and monuments add to the interest of the interior.

Not far to the E. of the village there is evidence of Neolithic and Iron Age settlements and of later Roman occupation.

LAVENHAM, *Suffolk* (11–TL9149). This beautiful small town developed through the rise of the cloth trade before and after the 15th cent.

The Church of SS. Peter and Paul is, if not quite as remarkable as that of LONG MELFORD a splendid building. The great square-buttressed tower of flint, 141 ft high, tends to dwarf the main body of the church, but details compensate for any lack of proportion, for example, the superb porch, with its carvings and fan vaulting, the gift of John de Vere, 13th Earl of Oxford.

On entering the church the visitor is impressed by the air of spaciousness. Note the parclose screen round the tomb of Thomas Spring, a wealthy Lavenham clothier who endowed the steeple, and his wife, Alice. This is a fine piece of carving, possibly by Flemish craftsmen early in the 16th cent. More good woodwork may be studied in the chancel, which has misericords decorated with fantastic medieval imagery. The Spring and Branch Chapels are surrounded by beautiful screenwork.

The bells of Lavenham are so famous that they were broadcast on the death of H.M. Queen Mary and each year on 21 June a special peal is rung to celebrate the "birthday" of the tenor

A. F. Kersting

Layer Marney: the gatehouse

bell, made in 1625 by Miles Graye of COLCHESTER, reputed to be the finest toned bell in England, if not the world.

The domestic architecture of Lavenham includes a Guildhall, erected shortly after the founding of the Guild of Corpus Christi in 1529. A superb timber-framed building, one of its corner posts carries a full-length figure of the founder of the Guild, the 15th Lord de Vere. The Old Wool Hall, Tudor Shops, the de Vere House and several of the houses in Church Street, in particular Nos. 11, 12, 13 and 15 are all worthy of note. The pargeting on the façades, the timbering, the whole atmosphere of Lavenham is unique.

LAXFIELD, *Suffolk* (11–TM2972). Here was born the man whose name has become hated by all who love our heritage of church ornament. William Dowsing was appointed by the Puritans to destroy all manner of "superstitious things" in the country's churches, and guide-book after guide-book tells just how well he carried out his task. Like a man possessed he travelled the county smashing the stained-glass windows which formed an irreplaceable part of our cultural heritage. He once destroyed 1,000 pictures in a day, not to mention carvings; when the Restoration came he returned to his native village, where, by a master-stroke of irony, a tablet in the Church of All Saints commemorates his name!

All Saints has an excellent flint panelled tower. Inside is a tremendous seven-sacrament font standing on steps, the upper one of which is in the shape of a Maltese cross. The Stuart reading desk with its grotesque supporters, the pulpit and the benches of similar date are all well worth noting.

Opposite the church is the Guildhall, a small timbered building, and there is also a restored smock-mill, now power-driven.

LAYER MARNEY, *Essex* (11–TL9217). The most westerly of three villages, and without doubt the most rewarding. Some 7 m. SW. of COLCHESTER it may be found off the B1022 road. In the reign of Henry II the Marney family settled here and it was Sir Henry, in the reign of Henry VIII, who decided to build a grand hall in keeping with the family's position. His death in 1523, shortly after inheriting the title, followed two years later by that of his son, forestalled his plans and only the gatehouse and west wing were finished. The gatehouse was, however, one of the great buildings of its age. Larger than that at OXBURGH, and those of the CAMBRIDGE colleges, it was grander even than those of the Royal Palaces.

The magnificent towers flank an archway surmounted by two stories, each with an elaborate window. The exterior pair of towers have eight stories, the interior pair, seven, with a much flatter gateway in between. The red brickwork is diaper-patterned in blue, and there is much use of terracotta.

Close to the Hall (in private hands but open on Sunday afternoons in the summer or by arrangement) is the Church of St Mary the Virgin, again of brick, with diaper patterns in blue bricks. Its battlemented appearance and many-faceted tower owes much to the rebuildings of the Marney family in the 16th cent. Inside are many items of interest. A wall painting of St Christopher of the 15th to 16th cents., an iron-bound chest, bequeathed by Lord Marney in 1524, but almost certainly much older, and some stained glass must all give place to the tombs of the Marney family. These, in the Marney Chapel, remind the visitor of the line that ended as far back as 1525, with the death of John, Lord Marney.

Layer Breton, to the E., has a church of recent date (1923) with some interesting old sculptures – Italian, and English. Most easterly is **Layer-de-la-Haye** where the church now overlooks the reservoir. Mostly 14th-cent., there are parts dating from Norman times.

LEISTON, *Suffolk* (11–TM4462). There can hardly be a greater contrast than that between the monastic discipline which prevailed in the abbey, now the principal monastic monument to be seen in Suffolk, and Summerhill the experimental school founded close at hand by the educationalist A. S. Neill. The abbey, originally established on the Minsmere Marshes in 1182, was moved to its present site by Robert de Ufford in 1363. As one of the smaller religious houses it was bestowed by the King on his brother-in-law, the Duke of Suffolk, in 1537. For hundreds of years the church was used as a barn and the abbey precincts as a farm, until in 1918 it was restored as a House of Prayer by Ellen Wrightson. The Ministry of Public Building and Works assumed custody of the ruins in 1964. Built into the nave and north side of the cloister is a dwelling used as a retreat for the local diocese.

Leiston itself is a busy industrial town which stands near the coast. One of the Garretts who ran the Iron Works produced a famous portable steam engine and threshing machine. His bust may be seen in the church (fine 13th-cent. font), and three of his stove-pipe hats in the council chamber.

Nearby is **Sizewell**, a small seaside village chosen in 1958 as the site of a new atomic power station.

LITTLE GLEMHAM, *Suffolk* (11–TM3459). On the main road from SAXMUNDHAM to WICKHAM MARKET. The Church of St Andrew has a Norman door to the nave and a white marble statue made by John Gibson in 1833 to the memory of Dudley North. Little Glemham Hall is a large brick mansion of the early 18th cent. which was built on the site of a still earlier house. Two projecting wings are, like the central section, three stories in height and the house contains a fine staircase, panelled rooms and Queen Anne furniture. There is a notable walled garden which, like the house, is open on occasions to the public.

LITTLE WENHAM, *Suffolk* (11–TM0738). Here is Little Wenham Hall, the oldest house in Suffolk, a miniature castle built *c.* 1270–80. Not only was it built as a house and not, despite its battlemented appearance, as a keep, it also represents a very early post-Roman use of brick for domestic building. The tiny chapel is rib-vaulted with a boss representing St Petronilla, a reminder that the house was inherited by Petronilla of Nerford in 1287.

The Church of All Saints is largely of the same date as the Hall, though the tower is later and the south porch 15th-cent. There are a number of wall paintings and a fine double-canopied brass with the figures of Thomas Brewse and his wife, d. 1514.

One m. SW. is **Great Wenham**. The Church of St John has a Perpendicular west tower and in the chancel unglazed patterned tiles, probably 15th-cent. The East family arms, complete with sword and helmet, are inside the church, and one of the 15th-cent. bench-ends is now in the collection of the VICTORIA AND ALBERT MUSEUM, London.

LODDON, *Norfolk* (11–TM3698), is a small town on the BECCLES to NORWICH road and divided by the River Chet from its sister village of **Chedgrave**. The village is built around a square on one side of which is the large Church of the Holy Trinity, late 15th-cent. Over the west door is a group representing the Holy Trinity. The interior is spacious and lit by 15 clerestory windows. Among the very interesting contents is the seven-sacrament font, on three traceried steps, the top one of which is shaped like a Maltese cross. There is a fine screen painted with scenes from the life of Christ, and less usual, the martyrdom of William of Norwich, and in the south aisle a painting of Sir James Hobart and his wife. Hobart was Attorney General to Henry VII and the background of the painting shows the church and a bridge. The Jacobean pulpit and large poor-box are worthy of note. Some excellent brasses (to the Hobarts) and an outstanding marble sarcophagus to Lady Williamson, d. 1684, who gave so much to the building of City churches after the Fire of London.

The square has some good buildings and close by is Loddon House, *c.* 1711, the best in the town. Around Loddon are several successfully planned modern estates by the local architects Tayler and Green.

Across the river, Chedgrave should be seen for its Church of All Saints, with a tower north of the chancel and a richly decorated Norman doorway.

LONG MELFORD, *Suffolk* (11–TL8646). One of Suffolk's loveliest villages, remarkable for the length of its main street, hence the epithet. To walk along the High Street, passing its fine houses and hotel, then progressing by way of the green to the magnificent church is a memorable experience.

Though the Church of Holy Trinity, considered the finest in Suffolk, comes almost last in the walk along the High Street, such is its size and splendour that it dominates the view and forms an almost symphonic climax to the progression. It was almost entirely rebuilt towards the end of the 15th cent., and its great length and enormous area of glass and flushwork are immediately striking. The well-proportioned tower is more recent, being built in 1903 around the earlier brick tower of the 18th cent. Its pinnacles emphasize the vertical lines of the Perpendicular style of the rest of the church.

From inside the church, the nave and chancel, over 150 ft in length, almost disappear in perspective and the arches of the arcade contrast with the timbering of the roof. The Lady Chapel built at the end of the 15th cent. is surrounded by its own ambulatory. In the Clopton Chantry is the carved monument to John Clopton, d. 1497, a tomb without an effigy. Many brasses of the greatest interest show the styles in clothing and hair-dressing of the early and late 15th cent. In the chancel is the noble monument to Sir William Cordell, d. 1580, the builder of Melford Hall, Speaker of Parliament and the Master of the Rolls to Queen Elizabeth.

The stained glass is late 15th-cent., and the church still contains a great deal that has either escaped destruction or has been carefully restored and replaced.

By the church, Melford Green is large and triangular and slopes down towards the village. At the upper end is the Hospital and Melford Hall. The former building dates from 1573 but was much restored in 1847. The Hall is one of the best early Elizabethan houses left to us and is now owned by the National Trust. A superb brick house of three sides surrounding a courtyard and facing a garden, it is open to the public and contains a collection of pictures, furniture and porcelain.

A little to the N. of the village is Kentwell Hall, built *c.* 1563 by the Cloptons, also in brick and approached through a long avenue of lime trees. Returning to the high street on the right is Mill House, on the left the timber-framed Bull Inn and Brooke House. Georgian brick and timbered houses follow and finally Melford Place, the old home of the Martyn family, where the chapel has been made into the entrance hall.

LOPHAMS, THE, Norfolk (11–TM0381; South Lopham).

Two villages near DISS, **South Lopham** on the main A1066 and **North Lopham** on the B1113. South Lopham should be seen first for its Church of St Andrew which has a marvellous central Norman tower. The arcading is simple but effective, and the parapet is Perpendicular. In the tower is an Anglo-Saxon window and later styles may be seen in the Decorated chancel and Perpendicular clerestory. The octagonal font has sensitive tracery and there is a great dug-out chest in the tower which is 8 ft long and may be of similar age.

Just to the S. of the village is the border with Suffolk and, on either side of the B1113, the sources of the Ouse and the Waveney.

North Lopham's Church of St Nicholas (Decorated and Perpendicular) is passed as you enter the village from the S. The west tower is Perpendicular, and the font has the same delicate tracery as that at South Lopham.

LOWESTOFT, Suffolk (11–TM5493).

A seaside town of some character which pivots around the Swing Bridge, an area of, at times, intense traffic congestion. The Ness is the most easterly point in England. The area around the bridge across the estuary of the Lothing contains the harbour which makes the town into one of our most important fishing ports. This was where Joseph Conrad served when he arrived in England in 1878 to go to sea on the *Skimmer of the Seas.* The trawlers and other vessels, and the constant bustle of traffic, make Lowestoft a place of fascinating activity, with its still picturesque fishing quarter.

The site of the first recorded lighthouse in England, the town's North Light, is open to the public on weekdays. This north side of the town is noted for the Scores, narrow lanes which connected the road to the beach below. The area is now monopolized by a huge frozen-food factory, though one or two of the old houses for smoking the herrings remain. Just past the Light is the Royal Memorial in Belle Vue Park and the Sparrow's Nest close to the park in which summer concert parties perform. Further still, the road leads to Corton or GREAT YARMOUTH and GORLESTON.

South of the bridge lies the bathing and holiday section of the town with several hotels of note and Claremont Pier. Kensington Gardens, a little further on, is pleasantly laid out, with electric boats in addition to the usual amenities. Should the bridge be out of action, the road would follow the west limits of the town to OULTON Broad, the scene of more holiday activities and a busy boating centre.

St Margaret's Church is on the Oulton Road on the north side of the town, and is a fine 15th-cent. building which contains glazing in the south window of the chancel, by Robert Allen (1819) of the famous Lowestoft china factory. While you may well try to find pieces of Lowestoft ware while in Suffolk, do not be surprised if the prices they fetch are at least as high as those obtained in the capital. The wares of this small, but appreciated factory, which functioned from 1756 to 1803, are now much sought after.

Perhaps Lowestoft's most famous son is the composer Benjamin Britten, born here in 1913 on the anniversary of St Cecilia, the patron saint of musicians. Thomas Nashe, 1567–1601, the satirist, critic and playwright, was also born in Lowestoft.

Places of interest near Lowestoft must include **Pakefield** to the S., with two churches sharing not merely the same churchyard, but even the same building. Nowadays Pakefield is very much a residential and holiday suburb of Lowestoft. To the N. of the town lies **Gunton** with its ancient church, **Corton** and **Hopton**, now given over to holiday camps, BLUNDESTON and SOMERLEYTON.

Fritton with its small church and long wooded decoy for trapping wildfowl is some 6 m. to the NW. of the town on the A143 and is well worth an afternoon's drive.

LUDHAM, Norfolk (11–TG3818).

A pleasant Broadland village on the B1354 which links WROXHAM with POTTER HEIGHAM. South of the village the Rivers Bure and Thurne wend their quiet ways and to the W. the River Ant runs into BARTON BROAD. Womack Broad is just by the village and the Staithe is at the end of a lane to the SE. The village centre has some very attractive Georgian houses and the Church of St Catherine, mainly 15th-cent., is outstanding. The wheel which is the emblem of that saint may be seen in the spandrels of the nave roof and the interior is impressive with the painted tympanum as one of the main features. This is a 15th-cent. painting of the Crucifixion, with, on the reverse, the Royal coat of arms of Queen Elizabeth I.

More important still as an example of early painting is the beautiful screen dated 1493. The tracery is most delicate and the paintings are of rare quality, showing saints and kings. Between the panels, are detached buttresses, another rare feature. Also to be noticed is a large iron-bound poor-box and the octagonal font.

Ludham Hall has a Georgian front covering an earlier Jacobean building. The brick chapel is 17th-cent. and the house at one time belonged to the bishops of NORWICH. The Bishop of Norwich is still Abbot of **St Benet's**, the ruins of which are almost 2 m. SW. near the junction of the Bure and the Ant. The first Sunday in August sees a visitation by the Abbot, made by water. Around the village are several ruined windmills.

MALDON, *Essex* (7–TL8506). A picturesque town set above the River Blackwater (and also the River Chelmer), it possesses a feature unique in England – the triangular tower of All Saints' Church. The town's commanding position made it the site of a fortress built early in the 10th cent. The Old English poem *The Battle of Maldon* tells of the fearsome struggle between a Danish and an English army in 991. All Saints' dates from the 13th cent. and apart from the tower is particularly renowned for the elaborate decoration of the south aisle built early in the 14th cent.

Of the Church of St Peter, only the tower remains, the building having been converted into a library by Dr Plume in 1704, rather than rebuilt as a church. St Mary the Virgin's Church has a shingled spire on top of a heavy tower, and though much restored still reveals traces of its Norman origin.

The 15th cent. saw a number of interesting buildings, of which the Moot Hall, once known as D'Arcy's Tower after its builder, the Blue Boar Hotel, with additions from the early 19th cent., the Swan Hotel and the vicarage are the best examples. Even earlier are the remains of the St Giles Hospital, founded for lepers in the 12th cent. Georgian buildings of some distinction are numerous and a stroll along the High Street, Silver Street and Market Hill will reveal much of interest.

Once down by the river the atmosphere of a fishing harbour and small resort is strengthened by riverside inns, the marine parade and the marine lake leading to the estuary and the marshes as the river makes its way slowly to the sea. About 1 m. to the N. is **Heybridge**, with a Norman church – St Andrew's – and the 17th-cent. Heybridge Hall and 19th-cent. The Towers. There is an attractive mill, W. of the church, and impressive ironworks, 1863.

Just over 1 m. to the W. are the remains of the 12th-cent. **Beeleigh Abbey**, which were incorporated in a picturesque house of the 16th cent.

MANNINGTREE, *Essex* (11–TM1031), stands, like MISTLEY, on the estuary of the River Stour, and has many Georgian and Victorian buildings of character. The Strand attracts swans in great numbers. The Roman Catholic church was converted from the old Corn Exchange.

The village centre is at the crossing of High Street and South Street; there are some pleasant buildings here, and in South Hill. Prominent is the Methodist church, 1807, with its cupola.

MAPLESTEADS, THE, *Essex* (11–TL8034; Great Maplestead). Of the five round churches built by the Knights Templars and Hospitallers, St John the Baptist in **Little Maplestead**, was the last to be built, *c.* 1335. The others at London,

LUDLOW, NORTHAMPTON and CAMBRIDGE were all Norman. Though the church was drastically restored after 1851 it is still possible to appreciate its design where, as in the Church of the Holy Sepulchre in Jerusalem, the nave is in the form of a circular rotunda. Here, though, there is a chancel complete with apse. The font is quite possibly older than the church itself.

The Church of St Giles at **Great Maplestead** has a strong Norman tower at one end and a Norman apse at the other. In between is an Early English chancel. The Perpendicular font was at one time brightly painted. Now, the most striking features are the monuments, especially that by William Wright of Charing Cross to Lady Deane, built in 1634 by her son behind whom she stands enshrouded, a very spectral concept. That to her husband, Sir John Deane, d. 1625, shows him resting on his arm, with the figures of his sorrowing wife and children kneeling above.

The Deane family lived at Dynes Hall, 1 m. to the S., which is mainly late 17th-cent. but with parts dating back to the previous century.

MARCH, *Cambridgeshire* (10–TL4197). At the centre of the network of railways linking the FENS to the surrounding counties, the town is particularly famous for its church, St Wendreda's, at the south end of the town in Church Street. The most spectacular feature of the church is the roof, one of the most quoted and photographed of all East Anglian church interiors. It is of double hammer-beam construction with, on every conceivable vantage point, finely carved angels spreading their wings.

There are few other buildings of interest in the town but a small, former Guild Hall, rebuilt as a school in 1827, now a store, should be noted.

MARGARETTING, *Essex* (7–TL6601). The tower of St Margaret's should not be missed, for it is built, like that of St Lawrence's, **Blackmore**, on ten wooden posts of immense dignity and strength, which are braced with additional beams. More timber-work of the same period, 15th-cent., may be seen in the north porch. Inside the church the east window boasts a complete "Stem of Jesse" window of 15th-cent. glass. The tree winds its way round medallions showing Abraham, Jacob, Joseph, King David and King Solomon, and finally the Madonna and Child. A brass of a knight and his lady reminds us of their connection with Killigrews, a moated house of Tudor date, but with additions from the 18th cent. (the east front) and later.

MELTON CONSTABLE, *Norfolk* (11–TG 0433). Melton Hall, built 300 years ago, is a perfect example of the country mansion in the Wren style, impressive yet not oppressive. It was built by Sir Jacob Astley in the second half of the 17th cent., and the minor additions do not affect the beauty of the house. The interior boasts some superb plastering on the ceiling of the Red Drawing Room, which is dated 1687 and which may well be by the same master craftsman who worked at

FELBRIGG and at HINTLESHAM at about the same time.

The small Church of St Peter is in the grounds of the Hall, at the north-east edge. It is basically Norman, with a central tower, but the visitor is warned that the doorway in the west wall is a 19th-cent. imitation. Most unusual is the opening above the west tower arch with a sturdy Norman pier dividing the opening into two sections. There are, of course, many monuments to the Astley family in the same modest taste as the house.

MERSEA ISLAND, *Essex* (11–TM0314), lies between the estuaries of the River Colne and the River Blackwater, separated from the mainland by the Pyefleet and linked to COLCHESTER by the B1025, known as the "Strood". **East Mersea's** Church of St Edmund, King and Martyr, commands attention because of its large Perpendicular west tower complete with buttresses and battlements. Inside is an octagonal 15th-cent. font. Sabine Baring-Gould's novel *Mehalah* is set here.

West Mersea was a settlement in Roman times and when the burial mound, a mile or so to the NE. of the church, was excavated, the remains of a cremated body were found in a tiled burial chamber of the 1st cent. Now there are caravans and a large summer holiday population, but still the village retains much of its old charm. Weatherboarded and Georgian brick cottages tell of its earlier days as a small fishing, oyster and sailing centre.

SS. Peter and Paul's is in the old village and dates from Norman times. The tower has 14th-cent. additions and the nave was raised in the 19th cent. The font is 13th-cent. Purbeck marble and there is a sculptured lunette by, or in the style of, della Robbia.

MILDENHALL, *Suffolk* (11–TL7074). Lying just off the A11 at the Barton Mills junction, Mildenhall is in the north-west corner of the county. It has one of the finest churches for miles around, large in scale and with many superb features. Of all these perhaps the most famous is the roof, elaborately carved with biblical scenes, fantastic beasts and other designs and with a host of the angels for which so many Suffolk churches are renowned. This wonderful roof was peppered with shot by the zealous iconoclasts of the 17th cent. Fortunately, however, their action had little effect.

Over 160 ft in length with a tower over 110 ft in height this Church of St Mary has a particularly lovely north porch, over which is a Lady Chapel. The east window is of rare design with seven lights and like the chapel to the north of the aisle is of ELY design.

Pleasantly situated on the River Lark, Mildenhall was the site of the Mildenhall Treasure found in 1946. Now on display in the British Museum, this splendid hoard of more than 30 pieces of silver table-ware included the great dish showing Bacchus and Hercules. Some of this 4th-cent. Roman ware may well have originated in Rome itself.

The Royal Worlington and Newmarket Golf Club close to the town has been described as the best nine-hole course in the world.

MISTLEY, *Essex* (11–TM1231). On the estuary of the River Stour and noted for the swans which frequent its banks in large numbers, Mistley was drastically altered when Richard Rigby decided to turn it into a spa in the 18th cent. The original Church of St Mary survives only in its flushwork porch on Mistley Heath. When the village was given its "face-lift" a new church was built by Robert Adam. He had been called in by Digby, who had made extensive alterations to the Hall and its grounds, in about 1774. His first project, which came to nothing, was to design a bathing station by the river. Next came the church. Adam made use of the earlier church of 1735 and added to it two square classic towers, topped with drums and domes, and supported by free-standing columns. All that remains of Adam's part in these schemes are the two towers and the lodges built in 1782 for the Hall. The nave of the church was pulled down when yet another church was built in 1870, and the Hall itself no longer stands. The final St Mary's is Victorian Gothic.

Much of the village survives, however. Near the square stands the fountain, with its swan, which was to have symbolized the spa. The maltings and the quays remind us of the town's grander days.

MUNDESLEY, *Norfolk* (11–TG3136). A small seaside resort with a superb sandy beach and excellent bathing. Though at one time it was planned to develop the resort it has fortunately remained unspoilt. The larger hotels, the Continental (1892) and the Manor (1900) rival those at CROMER, 7 m. to the NW. In the village is Rookery House of the Queen Anne period, but rebuilt in the present century, and Cowper House, at which the poet stayed.

All Saints' Church was almost completely rebuilt just before the First World War. Just S. of the village is a smock windmill complete with cap and sails.

NAYLAND, *Suffolk* (11–TL9734). A village set in beautiful country by the River Stour, and at one time a busy cloth town. The bridge over the Stour into Essex was erected by William Abell who also made considerable additions to the Church of St James in the early 16th cent. Perhaps one of the most interesting features of the church is the altar-piece painted by John Constable, who was born nearby in EAST BERGHOLT. The subject is *Christ blessing the bread and wine* and it was painted early in his career in 1809. It may be compared with his still earlier painting of *Christ and the Children* painted in 1804, and now in the Church of St Michael at Brantham.

At the south end of Church Street is Alston Court, which dates from the 15th cent. and has magnificently carved timbering, especially the barge-boards. Various additions were made to the building in the following centuries. Inside, the finest rooms are the hall, dining-room and solar, all of which have fine beams and notable carving.

In the market place may be seen an obelisk milestone and a number of attractive cottages and inns.

NEEDHAM MARKET, *Suffolk* (11–TM 0855). A thoroughfare town on the IPSWICH to BURY ST EDMUNDS road (A45). There is much of interest, including Georgian houses in the High Street, the Bull Hotel with carved corner-post, the Friends' Meeting House and Graveyard and the 17th-cent. timber-framed Grammar School. The Church of St John the Baptist, while not especially remarkable outside, contains a unique timber roof. It is remarkably complex in structure and dates originally from the latter half of the 15th cent., although much of it had to be restored in the 1880s.

One of the Ministers of the Congregational Church was Joseph Priestley (1733–1804), famous as a chemist and for "discovering" oxygen when he settled in Pennsylvania in 1794.

NEWPORT, *Essex* (11–TL5234), stands by the River Cam on the main CAMBRIDGE to BISHOP'S STORTFORD road, the A11, at the junction with the B1038. The village is one of the county's most attractive and has a number of timbered houses, two of which are of particular interest and beauty. These are Crown House, which was faced with magnificent pargeting (decorative moulded plasterwork) in 1692, and Monks Barn, 15th-cent., timbered and with brick nogging. The Church of St Mary the Virgin is a big flint building with parts dating from the 13th cent., with many later additions, including the tower of 1858. While the 13th-cent. octagonal font is a good example, the great rarity is the 13th-cent. chest, which contains early paintings and must have been used as a portable altar-piece.

Less than 1 m. NE. is Shortgrove, a 17th-cent. H-shaped house, which was rebuilt in the 18th cent. and burnt down in the 20th.

NEWMARKET, *Suffolk* (11–TL6463). Though it contains little of overt architectural or archaeological interest Newmarket is a memorable town, due to its magnificent situation on the downs and heaths which straddle the main road from London to NORWICH, and for its historical associations as the centre of the English horse-racing world.

It is perhaps seen at its finest approached from the A11 across the Devil's Dyke (Anglo-Saxon earthworks), when against a background of blue sky the heath stretches as far as the eye can see. On the left as you enter the town is the racecourse, the scene of so many great classic meetings since the first recorded race in 1619, and the headquarters of the turf. Signs warn the driver of the dangers of meeting the string of horses which are taken for exercise on the heath and should it be the day of a race meeting you may well find yourself in a queue of traffic extending for 2 m. from one end of the town to the other. Just before the town proper is the Cooper Memorial Fountain of

1909 and then you pass the first of many fine houses and hotels which line the main road as it continues to the N.

On the right may be seen the Headquarters of the Jockey Club built in 1772 and restored and enlarged by the late P.R.A., Sir Albert Richardson. Further on is the Rutland Arms Hotel, a historic building with Georgian red-brick front, and even older interior walls. Next is the Jubilee clock tower, now a traffic roundabout, and, as you leave the town, many fine houses, the homes of trainers, owners and leading jockeys. Shortly afterwards the road divides, the Norwich and THETFORD roads straight ahead and, branching to the right, the road to BURY ST EDMUNDS and IPSWICH.

Newmarket is the home of more studs than any other town in England, among them the National Stud, which moved to its especially built home in 1964. The stud is open to visitors on Sunday afternoons and on the mornings of race days, and its fine design, by Peter Burrell, C.B.E., and its magnificent collection of stallions make it a must for all those interested in horses.

Horse-racing has taken place here for over three centuries and the heath has been the subject of innumerable paintings by the masters of English sporting pictures – Stubbs, Marshall and many others. Horse sales take place here every year.

NORTH ELMHAM, *Norfolk* (11–TF9821). Before the Normans came to Britain this was the site of an Anglo-Saxon cathedral, the centre of the See of Norfolk until it was moved to HOXNE, finally transferring to NORWICH itself in 1095. The ruins which remain are dated by the Ministry of Works as early 11th-cent. After the See moved to Norwich the cathedral was turned into a house by Bishop Henry le Despencer in 1370, who began the task of moating the dwelling. What remains is, though small, of much interest.

The present Church of St Mary has an imposing tower containing a west porch. The north doorway is also surprising, as it has a hood of leaved capitals, perhaps part of some other section of the church. Inside are tall 13th-cent. arcades which must have been added to an earlier, Norman, building. The pulpit dates from 1626, and was made by the parish clerk, who received £5 3s 4d for his labours! The rood-screen has painted figures of the saints and there is an altar-table of 1622.

NORWICH, *Norfolk* (11–TG2308). "Norwich has everything", says Sir Nikolaus Pevsner, and what greater compliment could be paid to this beautiful city, the capital of Norfolk? Norwich developed by a large double bend in the River Wensum, and within its medieval walls it was second only to London. By the time of the Conquest it was already a town of importance and the castle which was built, together with the cathedral which soon followed, gave the city the two focal points that remain to this day.

The great stone keep of the castle dates from *c.* 1160, and is perhaps the most splendid of all

A. F. Kersting

Norwich cathedral

surviving examples of Norman military architecture apart from the TOWER OF LONDON. However, in its external decorative scheme it yields to none, only CASTLE RISING approaching it in style. It is approximately 90 ft square by 70 ft high and the elaborate patterns of blank arcading which cover the walls were carefully refaced in 1833–9. After serving as the city prison it was adapted as a museum in 1894 and contains an outstanding collection of works by the artists of the Norwich School, headed by John Crome and John Sell Cotman. In addition, there are displays of archaeological interest and a fascinating collection of natural history, with many tableaux of birds in their natural surroundings. Important touring exhibitions are shown here at various times during the year. A new central rotunda has been added.

Norwich Cathedral, the Church of the Holy and Undivided Trinity, is one of the country's finest examples of Norman cathedral architecture, and lying in a depression, it is its superb spire which at first commands attention. The See of East Anglia set up at DUNWICH in A.D. 630, moved to NORTH ELMHAM, HOXNE, and on to

THETFORD. In accordance with the Normans' policy of having their cathedral in the largest town, the See moved to Norwich in 1095 under the great Bishop de Losinga, as by that time Norwich with its original castle and market place had already established itself as the foremost town in East Anglia. Losinga commenced his new cathedral a year later and when he died in 1119, to be buried in the chancel, the work continued under his successors. The cathedral was finally consecrated in 1278, but was substantially complete well before that date.

The Norman plan, the only one to survive in this country, featured a bishop's throne at the east end, in an apse behind the altar. The throne may be 1,000 years old, which would make it the oldest bishop's throne in any English cathedral.

The arcading of the nave is covered with a magnificent roof which contains many of the 800 roof-bosses in the cathedral. Those in the nave tell the story of the Old and New Testaments, and "read" from E. to W. The chancel is taller than the nave, with a clerestory added *c.* 1360 and the roof is, if anything, even more splendid than that of the nave. From outside the cathedral you will be able to see the astonishing array of flying buttresses which enabled the Norman walls to support this huge additional burden. Within the church, the stalls feature some of the finest English carving; Bishop Goldwell, who added the chancel roof in 1490, is buried beneath his masterpiece.

The spire which dominates the close and the city was added in the late 15th cent. by Goldwell, and at 315 ft high it is second only to SALISBURY. The cloisters are the largest in Britain, and though originally Norman were rebuilt in the 13th to 15th cents. Here again are many roof-bosses, easier to study because of the lower height of the vault.

Within the precincts is Norwich School, once Carnary College, founded in 1316. Its most famous pupil was Horatio Nelson, another was the writer George Borrow. Two gates lead from the town into the close. One is Ethelbert Gate which was built in 1316 by the townspeople to make amends for the riots of the previous century. It was restored by Wilkins (*see* CAMBRIDGE and GREAT YARMOUTH) on the basis of the original designs. Erpingham Gate, built in 1420 by Sir Thomas Erpingham, is exceptionally fine and contains a statue of its builder. By the river is the 15th-cent. Water Gate, now forming part of Pull's Ferry. It is one of the most picturesque and often painted Norwich scenes.

Inner Norwich may be traced in the city walls which follow a route encompassing an area N. of the river as well as the major portion to the S. of it. Carrow Hill, Queen's Road, Chapelfield Road, Station Road, Bakers Road and Bullclose Road surround an ear-shaped area as big as the City of London. In this congested centre are no less than 32 surviving churches, though 400 years ago there were many more. All the churches are medieval and many are of exceptional interest. Close by the great market place is the beautiful St Peter Mancroft, commenced in 1430, with a great west tower and a length of 180 ft, and entirely Perpendicular in style. Facing the church is the Guildhall built 1407–13, with a gable end of gaily patterned flint flushwork completed in 1535. It was in use as the seat of the City Council until the new City Hall, on the west side of the market place, was completed in 1938. This has been called the most impressive public building in England of its period. Its 200-ft tower makes a strong vertical accent, a foil to that of the cathedral.

Other notable buildings include St Andrew's Hall by St Andrew's Plain. Here it may be remarked that the term "plain" is in common use in Norwich and Norfolk and echoes the Dutch *plein* used of squares in Holland and Flanders. St Andrew's was the Black or Dominican Friary of the city and has been converted for use as a public hall. The Assembly House in Theatre Street dates from 1754 and has now been restored to its former function. Strangers' Hall is mid-15th-cent., with a façade of 1621 and is now a museum with rooms representing various periods. The Bridewell Museum in Bridewell Alley was first built about 1370 and became the gaol 213 years later. In 1925 it became a museum which specializes in local industries. Another museum not to be missed is that in the Church of St Peter Hungate, in Elm Hill. The church was built by the Paston family (*see* PASTON) in the 15th cent. and now houses a collection of ecclesiastical art, mostly East Anglian.

Elm Hill itself is one of the most attractive and frequently photographed and painted of all Norwich's streets. Its cobbled road and its irregularly placed houses gives it a medieval feeling, yet a century ago it was derelict and its present charm is due to the Corporation who restored it. It is the centre of the Norwich antique trade and as such it is irresistible to lovers of art and antiques. At the bottom of Elm Hill is Wensum Street, leading to the cathedral and Tombland. This name has nothing to do with tombs, but comes from an ancient word for market. Here is commemorated Nurse Edith Cavell, who was executed in the Great War and is buried in the cathedral precincts. Nearby is the Samson and Hercules House, now a ballroom, with the two figures who act as supporters for its porch. Across the river we are reminded of two famous women and the founder of the Norwich School. Elizabeth Fry, the famous prison reformer, was born in 1780, in Gurney Court and in the same house in 1802 was born the writer: Harriet Martineau. St Michael's Church in Coslany boasts a wonderful façade, which shows the East Anglian art of flushwork at its best. Of interest to art lovers is the fact that the tracery of the west door was drawn by Cotman, whose house at Palace Plain may still be seen. Cotman's great contemporary John Crome is buried in St George's Church nearby, the only one of East Anglia's four greatest artists to rest in his home county. Crome was born in 1768 in a Norwich ale-house, and after a brief education the young boy became errand boy to a local doctor. Two

years later he was apprenticed to a sign painter and thus developed his taste for painting. Helped by Thomas Harvey of Catton, a local collector and banker, Crome was able to study the Dutch painters and also the work of Wilson and Gainsborough (*see* SUDBURY). He thus developed his style of landscape painting in oils and watercolour. Only once did he go abroad, to France in 1814 – the results may be seen in some paintings of Paris and Boulogne. He died in April 1821.

Medieval Norwich had one of the largest Jewish communities in England and like similar cities, traces remain in cemeteries and in the houses which were built for the wealthier Jewish merchants and money-lenders. The Old Music House in King Street was built for such a man in the 12th cent. and was much added to in subsequent centuries. It is now a club. The monument of another faith is seen in the remarkable Roman Catholic Church of St John the Baptist, built in the Early English style in 1884–1910 by Sir George Gilbert Scott and J. O. Scott. It is a huge building 275 ft long and over 80 ft high inside the chancel. The tower is yet higher. As an exercise in architectural scholarship and unity of style it is an astonishing performance.

Modern entertainment takes place in the Maddermarket Theatre, rebuilt in the Elizabethan style, and in the television studios in the old Agricultural Hall (1882) in Prince of Wales Road, near the old G.P.O., converted from a bank of 1866. The municipal Theatre Royal has a coherent programme of music and drama and there are orchestral concerts in the St Andrew's Hall. There are many facilities for sport – the football fan is catered for by the Norwich City F.C. who play at Carrow Road. There are several golf courses, including the Royal Norwich at Drayton Road, Hellesdon, on the A1067 to FAKENHAM which has 18 holes.

Earlham Hall on the western edge of the city is now the home of the University of East Anglia, one of our most architecturally adventurous universities, whose unusual buildings are now an accepted part of the Norwich scene. The architect was Denys Lasdun.

The new buildings of the University typify the forward-looking attitude of the city which, famous for so many different things, from mustard to insurance, is at once a great treasury of medieval Britain and an expanding industrial centre.

ORFORD, *Suffolk* (11–TM4250). Once a populous small town, Orford, like so many similar places along the Suffolk coast, fell into a decline from which it only recovers during the holiday season. It is famous for its castle, the earliest in the kingdom for which documentary evidence survives in the form of the pipe rolls of the medieval exchequer. Its great tower or keep, which is now all that survives above ground level, was in earlier days the final strongpoint of a considerable military complex. The keep dates from 1165 when Henry II attempted to re-establish the royal power in East Anglia. Of unique design, the tower is cylindrical within but multi-sided on the exterior, and is buttressed by three rectangular projecting turrets whose tops with their battlements rise above the main body of the keep. It stands 90 ft high and the walls of the central tower are almost 10 ft thick – little wonder that it has withstood the buffetings of the past 800 years. Legend tells us of a merman who was caught by the local fishermen shortly after the building of the castle, but escaping from his captors he returned to the sea and has never been seen since.

Orford Church saw the first performance of some of Benjamin Britten's compositions, including *Noye's Fludde* in 1958 and *Curlew River* in 1964. There has been a light on the ness for over 300 years and radar experiments were carried out on the spit in the mid-1930s.

Famous today for its "Orford Butleys", a variety of smoked herring, and for other smoked fish, the village also boasts an amusing shop-sign, that of one Edward Pipe licensed to sell tobacco.

There is an Atomic Weapons Research Establishment on Orford Ness.

ORMESBY BROAD, *Norfolk* (11–TG4615), forms part of a complex of no less than five broads, of which the others are ROLLESBY (to the S.), Lily (to the SE.), and to the S., **Filby** and **Little Broads**. Due to the main road (the A149) which cuts across between Ormesby and Rollesby and also to the A1064 which crosses to the S. at Filby Bridge, the motorist can obtain superb views of the broads from the seat of his car, (rarely possible in this region). To diminish the risk of flooding, this group of broads has had its once-navigable dykes closed by sluices; this affects not only their use by pleasure craft but also the ecology of the area.

These are deep broads, and this factor also affects the nature of insect, plant and bird life which they can support. Thus in summer the water is often thick and green with algae, and all three known species of mud-dwelling water-fleas can be found on the bottom.

OULTON, *Suffolk* (11–TM5292). Oulton, the village to the W. of LOWESTOFT, is also the most southerly of the BROADS. It is the centre of a very lively boating industry and in the holiday season presents a colourful scene.

The church overlooks the River Waveney into neighbouring Norfolk. George Borrow once lived here in a house beside the broad, but no trace now remains. The North Landing of the Broad is one of the imaginative pieces of modern architecture to be found in this part of East Suffolk and East Norfolk.

The broad presents a remarkable sight at the time of the carnival which usually terminates with a grand firework display, the water reflecting the myriad colours of the set pieces and rockets.

OXBURGH, *Norfolk* (11–TF7401). The Hall, one of the most romantic and picturesque buildings of its period in the country, was begun in 1482 by Sir Edward Bedingfeld. It was built to a square plan and surrounded by a moat, crossed by a drawbridge and entered by a magnificent gatehouse. Though the drawbridge was replaced by a stone bridge in 1710 the great gatehouse remains, one of the most outstanding brick examples in the country and similar to those in such other East Anglian places as LAYER MARNEY. Through its mighty archway passed Henry VII when he came to visit the Bedingfeld family in 1497. Its octagonal turrets rise 80 ft from the surface of the moat, and though it cannot have been designed as a pure fortress, the effect is splendid.

The square plan was wrecked when Sir Richard decided to pull down the south side in 1776–8, but sensible rebuilding by another Bedingfeld, Sir Henry, at the beginning of the Victorian era, made amends with a fine south-east tower and careful restoration of the windows, etc. Inside the house, which is now owned by the National Trust, are excellent rooms containing many relics of the Bedingfeld family and tapestries worked by Mary Queen of Scots and Bess of Hardwick.

The chapel was built for the family in 1835 by Pugin and contains a number of items of Flemish origin, such as the Antwerp Altar of 1525, the communion rails, *c.* 1700 and some 16th-cent. stained glass. The Chapel of Our Lady and St Margaret is Roman Catholic, the faith of the Bedingfeld family.

The Parish Church of St John the Evangelist had at one time one of the tallest (150 ft) steeples in Norfolk, but in 1948 it collapsed, destroying much of the nave and south aisle. The chancel and the Bedingfeld Chapel were fortunately spared and the terracotta monuments to the family survive. They are extraordinarily vivacious, in the Italian Early Renaissance style.

PARHAM, *Suffolk* (11–TM3060), is set in the valley of the upper Alde. Parham Hall is a picturesque 16th-cent. moated house, timber-framed brick with much diaper patterning.

The Church of St Mary is mainly Decorated in style, with bells still hanging in their 14th-cent. frame. Little remains of Parham House, built at the beginning of the 17th cent. It was at Parham that Crabbe lived after he married Sarah Elmy, though his house, Ducking Hall, no longer stands.

A number of the buildings in the village display carvings representing animals as well as human beings.

PASTON, *Norfolk* (11–TG3234), is a village famous for its associations with the Paston family who lived here from the 15th cent. Letters written by John Paston and other members of the family cover the period 1422–1509 and are one of the most important surviving sources of our knowledge of life and manners in the 15th cent. In addition they give much information on the Wars of the Roses and on the members of this remarkable family. A very complete collection was published in 1904 by James Gairdner, and in 1956 a fictional study by Barbara Jefferis appeared entitled *Beloved Lady*.

The mansion of the Pastons has long vanished but a great barn, 163 ft long, constructed of flint is one of the county's finest. The title, too, is no more, the line having died out in 1732. The Church of St Margaret is 14th-cent. and is thatched. Some interesting wall paintings and memorials to the family include two by Nicholas Stone, dated 1628 and 1632.

POLSTEAD, *Suffolk* (11–TL9938). Near the Church of St Mary, Maria Marten met her doom in 1827 in the famous Red Barn which was to provide the Victorian stage with one of its most famous melodramas. The church itself still retains a considerable amount of Norman work and may indeed contain some of the earliest bricks made in England. The tower is 14th-cent. and is the only one in Suffolk which still has its original spire.

Polstead Hall was rebuilt in the Georgian style *c.* 1819, but still has some timbering from the 16th cent. More old woodwork is to be found in Pond Farm House which was re-fronted in 1760. The gospel oak, between the church and the hall, is said to be over 1,000 years old.

POTTER HEIGHAM, *Norfolk* (11–TG4119). One of the most popular of the Broadland centres and well known on account of its bridge and its boatyard. Situated on the River Thurne the old village is close to the 13th-cent. bridge with its three arches. The Church of St Nicholas has a thatched nave and chancel, and a round tower of Norman date with an octagonal top added in the 14th cent. A great rarity is the octagonal font made of brick. There are a number of paintings in the church, including in the south aisle, *The Works of Mercy*, and the screen has painted panels of many of the saints.

Also over the river is the railway bridge – a structure about which it is possible to have mixed feelings. Around the boatyard a new village has developed to cater for the large numbers of holidaymakers, who visit this busy little yachting centre both by road and water.

PULHAMS, THE, *Norfolk* (11–TM2185). The first thing to see here is the south porch of the Church of St Mary the Virgin in **Pulham St Mary**. This is a wonderful piece of 15th-cent. architecture, full of beautifully carved detail on the façade and with flushwork panelling at the sides. In the spandrels of the arch the Annunciation is depicted, and above this are the figures of some music-making angels. The west tower is also fine, but the second most interesting feature is the 13th-cent. piscina which is elegantly designed with three delicate columns within a square frame and surmounted by interleaved arches of considerable refinement. There are some well-carved bench-ends and some stained glass of the 14th and 15th cents.

The village school incorporates the schoolroom built by William Pennoyer in 1670, which in turn included the remains of a Guild Chapel of 1401.

Pulham Market, about 1 m. to the NW. is a very attractive village whose colour-washed cottages surround the village green. The Church of St Mary Magdalen is mainly Perpendicular with a large west tower in four stages. Across the disused railway tracks is the hangar in which were built the great airships R.33 and R.34. Almost 2 m. NE. is the Manor Farm, originally 16th-cent., but which has been restored leaving many of the interior features intact.

RANWORTH, *Norfolk* (11–TG3514), lies between two broads, with a church containing some of the country's finest treasures. St Helen's is mainly Perpendicular; its west tower may be climbed (quite safely) to yield some wonderful views over the surrounding Broads. The first thing to see is the 15th-cent. painted screen which has been described as "probably the finest coloured screen in the country". The central portion has eight "windows" and below them are panels with paintings of the 12 Apostles. Projecting wings with delicately carved buttresses show St George and St Michael and are flanked by small chapels on either side. These also have paintings of the saints.

Next you should see the lectern, *c.* 1500, just a little later in date than the screen. On one face is an eagle and part of the Gospel of St John and on the other, a medieval versicle in plain-song. This is not all that Ranworth has to offer, however, for locked away, but shown on request, is the Sarum Antiphoner containing verses of the Psalms arranged for part singing. It dates from *c.* 1400 and is beautifully illuminated.

Ranworth Broad is the largest in the Bure Valley even though now much smaller than it was a century ago. The dyke which leads from the River Bure links the smaller, inner broad with the outer section, sometimes known as Malthouse Broad. This latter is open to pleasure craft but the smaller section is a Nature Reserve and is only available to rowing boats and then only in summer and with permission. Some of the derelict marshes in the area have been flooded to provide shallow reedswamps for breeding duck. Archaeologists have discovered traces of iron-workers who worked in the area in the first century A.D. Now this tree-surrounded broad provides the motorist with some attractive views as the road descends almost to the level of the water.

REDENHALL, *Norfolk* (11–TM2684). A mile or so to the E. of HARLESTON on the main A143 road is the village of Redenhall, where the Church of St Mary has one of the finest Perpendicular church towers in the country. Superb flushwork panelling is contained between the impressive polygonal buttressing. The north porch is no less beautiful. Inside is an octagonal font and an unusual double-headed brass lectern. Of East Anglian manufacture, it dates from *c.* 1500. There is another eagle lectern in wood and later in date, and also a wooden chest from Gawdy Hall (now demolished), carved outside and with paintings inside the lid.

REDGRAVE, *Suffolk* (11–TM0478). Situated near the River Waveney close to the Suffolk/Norfolk border. It was here that the young Wolsey was rector of the Church of St Mary. Among its many interesting features is a 14th-cent. font, and 18th-cent. paintings of Moses and Aaron with the Commandments, and a particularly fine brass of 1609 to the memory of Anne Butts, who, with her husband Sir Nicholas Bacon, older brother of Francis, is seen in the outstanding monument by Nicholas Stone. Another work by Stone is the tablet to Lady Gawdy, d. 1621. The elaborate memorial to Sir John Holt, the Chief Justice, d. 1710, was made by Thomas Green of Camberwell.

Of the Bacon family home, only the ruined Tudor kitchen survives.

REEDHAM, *Norfolk* (11–TG4201). Situated on the River Yare, crossed by a chain ferry, which takes cars as well as passengers and makes a vast difference to the length of journeys around the county. Its gentle clanking, together with the sounds of the birds and cattle, are pleasant on a hot summer's day.

The Church of St John Baptist has a large Perpendicular west tower, and is thatched. It is unusual in that the nave and aisle have been made into one, with the two arches still remaining. The Berney Chapel contains monuments to the family and some interesting brasses. It has some stained glass worth noting, probably from the Netherlands.

Several windmills in various states of decay have been replaced by pumps driven by oil or electricity. But the famous **Berney Arms Mill**, 3 m. to the NE., is in full working order and at 70 ft high is the most splendid in the county, if not in East Anglia. It is open to visitors (Ministry of Public Building and Works).

REEPHAM, *Norfolk* (11–TG1023). There have been many towns in East Anglia where two churches have shared a common churchyard, but Reepham goes one better, for though only one ruined wall now remains of Hackford Church (1543) the other two churches still stand. The parish church is St Mary's and contains the fine tomb of Sir Roger de Kerdiston, d. 1337. The knight lies on a bed of stones or pebbles and the side of the tomb-chest is carved with the figures of eight mourners in various attitudes. Over the chest rises a canopy of two arches arranged so that a delicate pendant hangs between.

Close by is St Michael's, the parish church of Whitwell. It has a tall Perpendicular west tower and inside is a Jacobean pulpit with sounding-board.

Facing St Michael's is the attractive market place, with on the north side Dial House *c.* 1700, a good town house of some size. Hackford Hall, 1½ m. away to the W., is a further reminder of the now ruined church.

RODINGS, THE, *Essex* (11–TL5813), is the name given to a group of villages which lie between GREAT DUNMOW and CHIPPING ONGAR along or near the B184 in the valley of the River Roding. There are eight altogether and the name is often pronounced Roothings. Alphabetically they are:

Abbess – with St Edmund's Church, rebuilt 1867 and with some attractive monuments;

Aythorpe – with St Mary's Church and a fine post-mill, ½ m. to the SE.;

Beauchamp – with the tall tower of St Edmund's Church;

Berners – (pronounced Barnish) where the church, a simple structure with a weather-boarded belfry, is in the grounds of the Hall;

High – with a large barn at New Hall (the house no longer exists) and All Saints' Church, with a 19th-cent. bellcot and a north door with 13th-cent. ironwork;

Leaden – St Michael's Church has a weather-boarded belfry and a Norman nave and chancel;

Margaret – has a church of the same name, with a Norman doorway, Norman windows and a 19th-cent. bellcot. The doors here also have ironwork of the 13th cent.;

White – where St Martin's Church has a Norman nave, using Roman bricks, a south door with more 13th-cent. ironwork and a square Norman font of Purbeck marble, with incised decoration. About ½ m. to the W. of the church is Colville Hall, basically 15th-cent. with later additions. There is a Tudor gateway and a large barn with timber and brick nogging.

ROLLESBY BROAD, *Norfolk* (11–TG4415). Part of the ORMESBY BROAD complex (*q.v.*) and well seen from the A149 which runs between the two broads to give some of the best views in Broadland. As both share similar conditions much of what has been said concerning the one concerns the other. Archaeological excavations have shown the existence here of communities of the men known as Beaker Folk after the wares which they made in the period about 2000 B.C.

SAFFRON WALDEN, *Essex* (11–TL5438). Though it lies just to the E. of the main A11 LONDON to CAMBRIDGE and NEWMARKET roads, the town, which is one of the most delightful in the county, has a long history. There are remains of an Iron Age fort at Ring Hill, 1½ m. W. of the town; evidence of Roman occupation and the remains of a 12th-cent. castle. Most impressive of all is the great Church of St Mary the Virgin, perhaps the only rival to that at THAXTED, 7 m. to the S. Almost 200 ft long, the church has a spire which reaches to not far short of the same height. Its style reflects the traditions of neighbouring Cambridgeshire and Suffolk as well as those of its native Essex. Apart from a crypt and some of the arcades the church was rebuilt in the Perpendicular style between 1450 and 1550. The splendid stone spire was added in 1831. Windows, battlements and buttresses make the exterior full of interest and beauty. Inside the church are superb carvings and roofs magnificent in their variety and quality. The brasses date from the

15th to the 17th cents. and there is a black marble tomb-chest to Thomas, Lord Audley, the Lord Chancellor, d. 1544 (by Cornelius Harman).

Near the church are numerous buildings of merit. The former Sun Inn is famous for its pargeting, nowhere better to be seen than on the façade of this building. Close by is the Cross Keys and the Rose and Crown. While these buildings are 15th- and 16th-cent., those nearer to the Market Place are from the 19th – the corn exchange and the altered Town Hall (originally 18th-cent.).

Like all the towns in this region, Saffron Walden derived its prosperity from the cloth trade, but as its name indicates its other great trade came from the growing of saffron, formerly used as a dye and as a medicine. The Youth Hostel in Bridge Street with its timbering and courtyard survives from this period. Even older in its origins is the maze which is on the common at the E. of the town, one of the few surviving town mazes in the country. Close to the castle is the town museum, which is one of the most interesting in the county, especially for local material.

Much could be said of the surroundings of the town. Some 5 m. to the E., on the B1053, is **Hempstead.** Here was born the infamous Dick Turpin, a butcher's apprentice who became a robber and a murderer. The newly rebuilt tower of the church commemorates William Harvey (1578–1657), the discoverer of the circulation of the blood who lies buried here and whose image may be seen in the Church of St Andrew, a fine sculpture by Edward Marshall. Three m. to the NE. on the Ashdon road is **Hales Wood**, now a nature reserve, and most important of all, 1 m. to the W. is the great mansion of AUDLEY END.

ST OSYTH, *Essex* (11–TM1215). Here off the B1027, by one of the little creeks which run into the River Colne, are the remains of the 12th-cent. abbey which includes a gatehouse with beautiful flint and stone flushwork. St Osyth was the daughter of the first Christian king of East Anglia and near the site of the priory she established a nunnery before she met her death as a martyr in A.D. 653. A priory was established for the Augustinian canons by the Bishop of London, *c.* 1127. Later it became an abbey, which was eventually dissolved in 1539, to come into private hands. The gardens are open to the public throughout the summer, and the gatehouse during August (afternoons only).

While some of the early parts of the priory, to use the name by which it is generally known, may still be seen, it is the splendid gatehouse which is the most significant and impressive feature. In the richness and intricacy of its patterning it reminds the visitor of the gatehouse of St John's Abbey at COLCHESTER, built at about the same time in the 15th cent. Though lacking the latter's turrets and pinnacles, its battlemented top makes a satisfying conclusion to its façade. In the 16th cent. Abbot Vintoner added a mansion of brick with its own imposing gateway. When the building came into the possession of Lord Darcy in 1558 he made further additions to the structure, including the surviving south gable and clock tower, now with an 18th-cent. lantern. At the outbreak of the Civil War in 1642 the mansion was sacked.

The Church of SS. Peter and Paul is just to the SE. of the priory church. Though the mainly Perpendicular exterior with its 14th-cent. west tower is not without interest, it is the interior with its brick-built piers and arches which is most memorable. The Darcys are commemorated in two large wall monuments, *c.* 1580.

About ½ m. to the SE. is St Clair's Hall, a 14th-cent. H-shaped house with a central hall of unusual timbered construction. There are three Martello towers, a feature of the East Anglian coast, on the beach and on Beacon Hill.

St Osyth's priory gatehouse

A. F. Kersting

SALHOUSE BROAD, *Norfolk* (11–TG2714). Situated on the opposite (south) side of the River Bure to HOVETON BROADS, and therefore not far from WROXHAM. Discoveries in recent years have indicated that the nomadic settlers of the Middle Stone Age rested here. At the present time the area of reed-swamps provide the materials for the thatching of houses and ricks and a small local industry has developed.

Situated above the tree-fringed broad is the village of Salhouse; All Saints Church has a thatched roof and a 14th-cent. arcade. Salhouse Hall (1860–70) is a brick-built castellated mansion, symmetrical in design.

SALLE, *Norfolk* (11–TG1024), should be pronounced Saul and is famous for the Church of SS. Peter and Paul, considered by some the finest in the county. Its great size is out of all proportion to the size of the village as it now is, and it was built in the 15th cent., mainly by three local families, the Briggs, the Fountaynes and the Boleyns, though there is no proof that the body of Anne, wife of Henry VIII, is buried here. One wonders whether such a magnificent building would ever have been built to the glory of God in such a place at any other time.

The tower is 126 ft high and this sets the pattern of the church which is 171 ft long, with nave, aisles and transepts in proportion. The entire building dates from the 15th cent. and is in the Perpendicular style. There are two porches, of which the north is perhaps the finer with its intricate detailing. The interior is lofty and impressive. The chancel roofing is embellished with bosses, and the font is unique in having below the panels of the seven sacraments emblems of each of them. The font cover is a 12-ft tall canopy with 16 radial buttresses.

Another remarkable feature is the 15th-cent. pulpit complete with backboard and Jacobean canopy. More fine woodwork is to be seen in the carvings of the stalls and benches, with poppyheads and misericords. There are many brasses and monuments to the families chiefly associated with the church.

SANDRINGHAM, *Norfolk* (11–TF6928). Famous above all for Sandringham House, the residence of the Royal Family. The Royal Estate includes the 19th-cent. house, the park and the church, and the park is open to visitors when the Royal Family is not in residence. The house was purchased by Edward, Prince of Wales in 1861, in preference to HOUGHTON HALL, no doubt due to its more intimate atmosphere. It was much added to in the 1870s and again later in the century. The Norwich Gates, so called because they were made in NORWICH as a wedding present to the Prince from the County of Norfolk, were shown at the Great Exhibition of 1862.

The estates are extensive and include several parishes and farms, woodlands and other agricultural activities which are managed on behalf of the Royal Family. By tradition it is to this quiet spot the family comes each Christmas. It was here that King George V and King George VI died, the former in 1936 and the latter in 1952. King George VI was also born and baptized at Sandringham.

The Church of St Mary Magdalene is, of course, as the Royal Parish Church, of exceptional interest and attracts large numbers of visitors. The church was extensively restored in 1857 and has since been greatly enriched with many gifts, many from the Royal family themselves and others from their admirers. The organ was the last gift of King Edward VII and the roof of the nave, of English oak, was the gift of King George V. The unusual folding lectern was given by King George VI.

One of its most generous benefactors was the American Mr Rodman Wanamaker, among whose many gifts were the solid silver altar and reredos, presented to Queen Alexandra in 1911; the jewelled bible in the Sanctuary, presented in 1915; the silver processional cross, given in 1920 to commemorate the men from the estate who had died in the First World War; and the solid gold and richly jewelled set of communion plate presented to King George V in 1927.

The church contains many other items of exceptional interest. There are medallions in memory of King Edward VII, Queen Alexandra, King George V and Queen Mary, a richly panelled pulpit built of oak and covered in solid silver, a great deal of stained glass depicting many of the saints and at the foot of the tower a small baptistry which contains an exquisite Florentine marble font, presented by King Edward VII.

The chancel is richly decorated, both walls and ceiling being painted. It thus presents a striking contrast to the nave where the treatment is restrained and plain. Set into the floor of the chancel is a brass cross above which the coffins of members of the Royal Family have rested before being taken to WINDSOR. There is a tradition that no one may walk on this cross and even members of the choir divide as they pass it.

Outside the tower at the west end of the church is a remarkable Greek font over 1,000 years old and made from one solid block of marble.

SAWSTON, *Cambridgeshire* (11–TL4849). Among Sawston's claims to fame is the first village college built in 1930. The colleges were the idea of Mr Henry Morris and were intended to be regional centres serving a wide range of educational, social and cultural needs.

St Mary's Church is partly Norman and contains several interesting brasses.

Sawston Hall is the only Elizabethan mansion in the country to be built of clunch, the hard chalk which underlies the whole of the East Anglian outcrop at various places along its western edge. It was the material used in the Lady Chapel at ELY as well as in many of the cottages and farmbuildings along the Cambridgeshire and Norfolk borders. The Hall was probably built between 1557 and 1584. Queen Mary had spent a night in the original house in 1553 before it was burnt by a mob. The Hall, which has been occupied by the same family, the Huddlestones, for the past 400 years, is open to the public at various times during the year.

SAXMUNDHAM, *Suffolk* (11–TM3863). The town straddles the main IPSWICH to LOWESTOFT road and is some 6 m. from the coast. Its main street begins at the south end with cottages and Georgian houses and ends with the Post Office built in the 1950s. Along the way you will pass the Angel, the Bell Inn (1842) with Tuscan porch, and the former Town Hall of 1846. Just off the main road is the station and a level-crossing.

The Church of St John the Baptist, at the south end of the town, has been much restored, and under its hammer-beam roof are a number of good monuments by Nollekens, Westmacott and Thurlow who was himself buried in the churchyard. Near the church is Hurts Hall, built in 1893 in the Elizabethan style to replace an earlier mansion by Wyatt. The grounds contain the largest dovecot in Suffolk.

SAXTEAD GREEN, *Suffolk* (11–TM2664). Now an ancient Monument and in the care of the Ministry of Public Building and Works since 1951, Saxtead Green Mill is one of the finest examples of a traditional Suffolk post-mill. A windmill was recorded at Saxtead as long ago as 1309 and the present mill was certainly in existence in 1796, the miller at that time being one Amos Webber. Since that date the mill changed hands many times and was altered or rebuilt on a number of occasions.

The "buck" or body of the mill is set on a painted brick "roundhouse" and is rotated to face the sails into the wind by the "fantail" at the rear. Those who can climb the steep staircase into the buck will find the millstones and other machinery in perfect order and the entire mill is so well balanced that it may be revolved on its trackway at a touch.

The total height of the mill is 46 ft and the span of the sails almost 55 ft. Until the First World War the mill produced flour but then was given over to grinding foodstuffs for animals. It continued to work until 1947.

SCOLE, *Norfolk* (11–TM1579). As befits its position halfway between IPSWICH and NORWICH (on the A140), the village boasts a magnificent coaching inn, The White Hart, which dates from 1655. Built of brick with five Dutch gables along the facade and additional gables at the ends, the inn unfortunately lost its gallows sign which at one time stretched right across the main road. Despite modern traffic it is not too difficult to imagine yourself back in the great coaching days captured by Pollard and some of the other sporting painters of the times.

St Andrew's Church was damaged by fire in 1963 but has since been reconstructed with a modern interior and glass by Patrick Reyntiens, of COVENTRY and LIVERPOOL Cathedral fame.

SHELTON, *Norfolk* (11–TM2192). In this small village is one of the finest Perpendicular churches in Norfolk. It was built by the order of Sir Ralph Shelton who died in 1487 leaving instructions that it be completed as it had been begun. Thus the west tower is of flint in the Decorated style and the rest of red brick with stone dressings. The resulting effect is both novel and highly decorative, the magnificent windows of the aisles contrasting with those in the clerestory. Inside the church the tall arcading and the Perpendicular design of the panelling create an effect of airy spaciousness. A beautiful set of the the Royal Arms of William III may be seen above the tower arch, and monuments to the Shelton family are worth noting. There is an interesting memorial with a number of seated figures to Sir Robert Houghton, d. 1623, in the south aisle. The aisle windows have 15th-cent. stained glass.

SHERINGHAM, *Norfolk* (11–TG1543). Another in the chain of pleasant seaside resorts around the Norfolk coast. It faces N. and has a shingly beach with sand at low tide. Really there are two Sheringhams: Lower Sheringham is the resort and Upper Sheringham is the village built on the hillside above the coastal strip. As with CROMER and the other resorts Lower Sheringham developed at the end of the last century and the beginning of this. The hotels are typical of their time, but much newer is the cliff-top terrace dating from 1936, by which time the Roman Catholic Church of St Joseph was completed. This was an early work of Sir Giles Gilbert Scott and was commenced in 1910. St Peter's is a Victorian church, built in 1895 in the Early English style.

At the west end of the beach is the lifeboat, another in the series which ring the North Sea coast. One of the old boats is still on view close by.

Upper Sheringham's All Saints Church is mainly Perpendicular in style and has a fine 15th-cent. screen with an interesting overhang. Among the carved bench-ends is one representing a woman in a shroud. There are good brasses and a fine wall monument to Abbot Upcher by Bacon and Manning.

Sheringham Hall was built to the design of Humphry Repton, 1812–17. The grounds are certainly planned by him, although authorities think the house is more likely to be by his son. It may be seen by appointment on application in writing.

SHOTLEY, *Suffolk* (11–TM2533). On the peninsula formed by the Orwell and the Stour as they meet the sea between HARWICH and FELIXSTOWE. Such a place has always attracted mariners and it is appropriate that it is the site of H.M.S. *Ganges*, the Naval Training Centre where boys are prepared for a life at sea. The spectacular ceremony at which one lone cadet climbs to the top of the highest mast as "button-boy" is a famous occasion.

St Mary's Church, the nave of which is 14th-cent., was given a new chancel in 1745, elegantly

Georgian. From this time dates the panelling which includes paintings of Moses and Aaron, as well as the communion table. The churchyard has a cenotaph to those who fell in the World Wars with an inscription by Rudyard Kipling.

SIBLE HEDINGHAM, *Essex* (11–TL7734). The Black Prince, Paolo Uccello and the city of Florence are all brought to mind in this most unlikely place. Here was born Sir John Hawkwood, one of the most famous mercenaries of his time. He fought with the Black Prince at Poitiers, then moved on to Italy where he formed his own army which became so sought after that he was almost constantly fighting for one or other of the city states. Eventually Hawkwood became commander of the Florentine armies and when he died in 1394 he received a triumphant burial in that city's cathedral, where a fresco by Uccello shows Hawkwood mounted proudly in a great procession. Legend tells that his body was returned to England and he is commemorated by the monument in the south aisle of the village church (St Peter's, 14th-cent.)

Near the church is the White Horse Inn, 15th-cent., and the rectory, 18th-cent. Further along the main (Roman) road is Hawkwoods, the home of the Hawkwood family.

SNAPE, *Suffolk* (11–TM3959). Whoever has been delighted by Britten's *The Little Sweep* will have sung of Snape, up-river from ALDEBURGH and one of the homes of the June Festival. The magnificent concert hall built on the site of the old Maltings was the pride of Suffolk until the first night of the 1969 Festival when it was cruelly destroyed by fire. However, that it will rise again is certain. The Maltings themselves are a group of early industrial buildings whose appeal lies in their diversity. On the banks of the Alde, they were for many years the centre of a thriving trade and vessels from these quays plied the North Sea routes loaded with their cargoes of barley.

The Benedictines founded a priory here in 1155 and the village grew in importance even though it was some way from the sea. The decline of the Maltings Quay came with the development of road transport and the consequent lack of trade for the barges which were for many years a feature of the East Anglian coastal run. In 1966 the Aldeburgh Festival directors signed a 50-year lease to enable them to build the concert hall inside the shell of one of the great brick buildings.

As well as the June Festival the hall is used for concerts at other times and is the scene of a major Antiques Fair each September, one of the many which have proliferated in Suffolk's towns in recent years.

The Church of St John the Baptist contains a richly carved 15th-cent font. It was at the barrow on the S. of the road to Aldeburgh that Anglo-Saxon remains were found in the 19th cent. These were of similar date to those at SUTTON HOO, not far away to the SW. Some of these items are now in the BRITISH MUSEUM.

SNETTISHAM, *Norfolk* (11–TF6834). On the KING'S LYNN to HUNSTANTON road, the A149, the village has a superb Decorated church, St Mary's. Originally cruciform, the demolition of the chancel has left the once central tower at the east end. The west end is very fine with a six-light window of exquisitely ornate design. At the corners are huge octagonal buttresses complete with miniature spires which are echoed in the pinnacles standing at each corner of the tower and supported by lighter flying buttresses.

Just to the W. of the church is the Old Hall made of carrstone and brick in the 17th cent. This is a distinguished-looking house with Dutch gables over the two bays. The village itself has an attractive sign, and there is another in the neighbouring village of **Shernborne**, 2 m. to the E., which commemorates the Coronation of King George V.

SNORINGS, THE, *Norfolk* (11–TF9533). The two villages of **Great** and **Little Snoring** share one of the most delightful of the many quaint names in which East Anglia abounds. They are on the by-road which joins the A1067 and the A148 to Little WALSINGHAM. Great Snoring's Church of St Mary shows a mixture of styles from Early English to Perpendicular. The entrance door (15th-cent.) has good tracery and inside the church is a large 17th-cent. Commandment Board with representations of Death, Heaven, Hell and Judgment, and a good set of Royal Arms dated 1688 but probably earlier.

The Rectory is rather remarkable: an elaborate building of 1525 which at one time belonged to the Sheltons, and was used as their manor house.

Little Snoring has in the Church of St Andrew an architectural curiosity. The present church must have replaced an earlier one, and made use of some of its fabric. The builders left the pre-Norman tower and commenced the new church several feet from it, re-assembling the south doorway of the old church in the newer "pointed" style. Inside is a circular Norman font with carved medallions, of a sturdy nobility.

SOHAM, *Cambridgeshire* (11–TL5973). Here in the early 7th cent. St Felix of Burgundy established an abbey a few years before Etheldreda founded ELY 5 m. to the NW. across the causeway.

Soham Abbey, however, unlike Ely, was not rebuilt after it had been destroyed by the Danes. St Andrew's, a great cruciform church of unusual interest, has some Norman work but also much from the succeeding centuries. The fine tower is Perpendicular, *c.* 1500, and the roof of the nave is interestingly constructed of hammer-beams alternating with tie-beams and queen posts.

SOMERLEYTON HALL, *Suffolk* (11–TM 4897). Somerleyton Hall was reconstructed in 1844 on the basis of an Elizabethan house owned by the Jernyngham family. It had been purchased by Sir Samuel Peto who created not only the Hall but an entire village with school, chapel and *cottages ornés*. The result was a building in the

Anglo-Italian style designed by John Thomas, a pupil of Barry whose work may be seen at **Shrubland.**

The Oak Parlour contains carvings by Grinling Gibbons and the beautiful dining-room has pictures by Wright of Derby, Ferdinand Bol (one of Rembrandt's pupils) and Clarkson Stanfield. In the house there are many big-game trophies testifying to the sporting interests of the Somerleyton family who have lived in the house since Sir Francis Crossley, Bt came there in 1861.

The gardens contain a large number of magnificent trees and shrubs, a number of walks and a maze of clipped yews.

SOUTHEND-ON-SEA, *Essex* (7–TQ8885). Though the great days of Southend as *the* holiday resort for Londoners have perhaps receded into the past with the coming of cheap Continental holidays, it still retains a unique place as the nearest resort to the capital. To this is due its popularity with the armies of day-trippers who invade the town in their coaches and trains, as well as with those who are able to sample its almost limitless tourist attractions for rather longer. Faster travel has also made it into a London "dormitory" for the thousands of commuters who make the journey each day.

Southend's history as a holiday resort dates from the early years of the last century when the villages of **Leigh** and **Prittlewell** commenced that expansion which now stretches along the mouth of the Thames estuary for some 7 m. The mention of the name Southend evokes an almost automatic response – "The Pier", and with its length of almost 1¼ m. it is in fact the longest in the world – a far cry from the small wooden jetty erected in the 1830s. The pier with its railway, its amusements and its arcades caters for the fun-seeking tripper as well as serving as a port of call for the ships which make the voyage to London and the French ports. Excitement may be found, too, at the famous Kursaal, where every possible fairground device makes the season one long Bank Holiday fair.

The quieter side of life may be found at the resorts along the coast – at **Westcliff**, with its Edwardian bandstand, and at **Thorpe Bay** on the other side of the pier. As it has grown, so Southend has swallowed the villages which were once its neighbours. **Eastwood**, Leigh, Prittlewell, **Shoebury** and **Southchurch** once had separate identities, and each still retains something of its old character. Of the old churches and buildings which remain, the oldest are the ruins of Prittlewell Priory, founded *c.* 1110 in Priory Park by the Benedictines. The churches of Prittlewell, Southchurch, Eastwood and South Shoebury have Norman work and those of North Shoebury and Leigh are interesting though later.

Porters in Southchurch Road, Southend, is the Mayor's Parlour and is early 17th-cent. Southchurch Hall, now a library, was a moated manor house of the 14th cent., while Thorpe Hall along the boulevard is dated 1668. As might be expected in a town that is still growing, there are a number

of recent buildings, some worth noting: the bowling centre by the pier, the new Keddie's store in Warrior Square and some of the 20th-cent. churches in the various parishes for example.

All sports are catered for, angling and yachting, of course, and the Essex County cricket team plays in the town, as does the Southend soccer team. There is an airport of ever-increasing importance as a cross-Channel take-off point.

SOUTH WALSHAM BROAD, *Norfolk* (11–TG3813). An elongated broad which like that at RANWORTH now consists of an inner and outer section joined by a narrow channel. The outer broad is open to the public but the inner one is private. South Walsham is one of the likely centres of the Norfolk salt-making industry. Before the Norman Conquest salt helped the inhabitants preserve meat for the winter and in medieval times was used to preserve the herrings caught in the North Sea.

South Walsham village, not to be confused with the town of North Walsham, some 15 m. to the N., is famous for having two churches in adjoining churchyards. The Church of St Mary, Decorated, has an unusual font and a screen with an inscription commemorating John Gate, a serf who had been freed in 1437. A stained-glass window in the south aisle represents Astronomy and was made by R. O. Pearson in 1907.

There is an engraved slab to Richard de South Walsham, d. 1439, Abbot of St Benet's Abbey, which has a strange history. The slab has been used as the doorstep of a house in NORWICH and when the house was demolished it eventually found its way to its present position. The adjoining Church of St Lawrence is partly in ruins as a result of a fire in 1827.

SOUTHWOLD, *Suffolk* (11–TM5076). Southwold is a pleasant and dignified seaside town built on the cliffs overlooking the North Sea. With its triangular market square, its contrast between narrow streets and spacious greens around which are set cottages in flint, brick and colour wash, and the lighthouse which stands gleaming white in the very heart of the town in Stradbroke Road, Southwold presents vistas of quaint attractiveness. The greens came as the result of the fire of 1659 which caused the almost complete destruction of the town and led to more spacious planning when rebuilding was commenced, and the influence of the Dutch on the architecture may still be seen in the gables of the museum and in some of the cottages along Church Street.

From Norman times Southwold was a busy fishing port and the town developed in competition with its neighbours, WALBERSWICK and DUNWICH. With its beach of sand and shingle and its harbour, the town is now a lively little seaside resort with a small pier, competent local theatre company and the atmosphere of a rather more refined gaiety than may be found in its larger competitors.

Perhaps the chief pride of the town is the Parish Church of St Edmund built between 1430 and

Kenneth Scowen

Stansted Mountfitchet: a corner of the village

1460. With that of BLYTHBURGH this is the greatest of the churches of East Suffolk. It has a beautiful south porch, built of flint and stone arranged in the decorative patterns typical of the region, now empty of the statues which once stood there, and impressive carved entrance doors. The tower is 100 ft in height and on the roof should be noticed the *flèche*, a reproduction of the original Sanctus bell turret.

Careful restoration has given the interior of the church an unforgettable appearance of light and colour created by the large windows and the painted and gilded woodwork. The painted screen, dating from about 1500, is one of the most beautiful to be found in England. It runs across the full width of the church with magnificent figure paintings on the panels representing the Angels, Apostles and Prophets. The faces of Isaiah and David, were repainted by George Richmond, R.A. who often stayed in the town. More fine painting and carving is to be seen in the pre-Reformation pulpit of the 15th cent. It was repainted in 1930 with money provided by the people of Southwold, Long Island, U.S.A., the settlement founded by travellers from Southwold in the 17th cent. The stalls and return stalls in the choir are finely carved with many grotesque heads including a jester, a monkey and strange bearded and winged figures. High above them all, are a lofty clerestory and a hammer-beam roof.

The museum which was founded in 1932, has a good collection of local interest, and the Sailors'

Reading Room on the cliff-top has a further collection of relics and models. From the cliffs there is an extensive view N. to KESSINGLAND and LOWESTOFT and S. to DUNWICH and ALDEBURGH and beyond to ORFORD Ness.

STANSTED MOUNTFITCHET, *Essex* (11–TL5124), will remain famous as the proposed site of London's third airport, but which launched a campaign so vigorous that the plan was abandoned (*see* FOULNESS). Nine hundred years ago it was the home of the Norman family from whom it derives its unusual full name. The origins of St Mary the Virgin's Church may be seen in the Norman arch of the chancel, and in the north and south doorways. The brick tower is 17th-cent. and carries a small spire. There are many monuments, including those to Hester Salusbury, d. 1614 and Sir Thomas Middleton, d. 1631, late Lord Mayor of London.

Traces of the Norman castle may be found near the 19th-cent. Church of St John the Evangelist. The tower mill is in exceptional condition. Stansted Hall (1871) is now a college and at Norman House is a popular wildlife park.

STEEPLE BUMPSTEAD, *Essex* (11–TL 6741). Another of the many East Anglian villages with delightful names. St Mary's Church has a Norman west tower with a brick top added later. There was a major restoration in 1880. The wall monument to Sir Henry Bendyshe, d. 1717, shows the knight in an elegant pose, framed by "barley-sugar" columns and an elaborate pediment. In the village which runs past the church is the restored Guildhall – an attractive half-timbered building dating from *c.* 1592. Moyns Park, to the SE., is a moated Elizabethan house with the remains of the Tudor south-west wing, half-timbered with three gables. To the SE. of the village is another house with Tudor remains – Latchleys.

STIFFKEY, *Norfolk* (11–TF9743). Whether it is pronounced as it is spelt, or as is often said, "Stewkey", is still a subject for argument. Famous for its cockles, it is a brick and flint village on the edge of the marshes between WELLS and BLAKENEY, and follows the course of the river of the same name. St John the Baptist's Church is mainly Perpendicular with a 13th-cent. chancel which was restored in 1848. A monument to Nathaniel Bacon, who owned the Hall, was erected before his death in 1615, and consequently does not include the date.

Stiffkey Hall was built by the Bacons and work commenced by 1578. Of the original large flint building only the west wing remains, together with some of the ruins of earlier sections destroyed by fire in the 18th cent., and a gatehouse dated 1604.

STOKE-BY-NAYLAND, *Suffolk* (11–TL 9836). A picturesque village with a fine group of half-timbered cottages near the Church of St Mary, the tower of which was one of Constable's favourite subjects. It is 120 ft high, built largely of brick with stone dressings, with four pinnacles that dominate the local landscape. The magnificently carved south doors, over 10 ft high, still have their figures intact. Many outstanding brasses include those to an anonymous lady of *c.* 1400; Sir William Tendring, 1408; Dame Katherine Howard, 1452; and some of the Mannock family of the 17th cent.

The Mannock home was Giffords Hall, a Tudor brick-built mansion with brick towers and a gateway bearing the family crest.

Nearer the church in School Street are the Guildhall and the Maltings, timber-framed buildings of the 16th cent. All that survives of Tendring Hall, designed by Sir John Soane in 1784, is a fishing lodge overlooking the lake.

STONDON MASSEY, *Essex* (7–TL5800). It was here that the great Elizabethan composer William Byrd (1543–1623) spent the last 30 years of his life. His home, Stondon Place, has been rebuilt at least twice since he settled here in about 1590. It is of interest to music lovers that two Elizabethan composers lived in Essex, the other being William Wilbye (*see* COLCHESTER). Though it is not known for certain where Byrd is buried he almost certainly rests in Stondon in accordance with his wish to be buried next to his wife.

The Church of SS. Peter and Paul has a Norman nave and chancel and a belfry, near the west end of the church. The pulpit is dated 1630 and has strapwork decoration.

STOW BARDOLPH, *Norfolk* (11–TF6205). A village associated with the Hare family whose home, Stow Hall was built in Tudor style in 1873. Holy Trinity Church contains an odd curiosity in the wax figure of Sarah Hare who died in 1744, like the Sleeping Beauty, from the prick of a needle. She is seen dressed in the clothes which she herself desired to wear, and being life-size she presents an almost horrific appearance. Other monuments in the church which has Norman work in the mainly Perpendicular tower, and was much rebuilt in 1848–9, include those to other members of the Hare family: Sir Ralph, d. 1623; Sir Thomas, d. 1693; and also to Susanna and Mary Hare.

STOWMARKET, *Suffolk* (11–TM0458), is a small market town with some light industry almost halfway between IPSWICH and BURY ST EDMUNDS on the A45 road, at the junction with the east–west road from FRAMLINGHAM to SUDBURY. The Church of SS. Peter and Paul contains a number of monuments to the Tyrell family, some grotesque carvings on the bench-ends and a rare wrought-iron wig stand dated 1675.

The railway station, built in 1849, is in the Victorian mock-Elizabethan style. The area around the market place has many buildings of the early 19th cent. and late Georgian periods while Stow Lodge Hospital in Onehouse Road was built as a workhouse *c.* 1777.

It was to Stowmarket that John Milton came to visit his tutor Thomas Young, who lived in the vicarage and is buried in the church near the lectern; here, too, George Crabbe spent some of his schooldays. The Tyrell family lived at Lynton House between the church and the site of the railway station.

The Abbot's Hall Museum of Rural Life in East Anglia is an admirable and essential collection, a visit to which will take you back to the days when farming was a simple family affair and when individual craftsmanship was of a high order.

STRADBROKE, *Suffolk* (11–TM2373). Possibly the birthplace of Robert Grosseteste. Though of humble family he was educated at OXFORD and Paris and in 1235 became the Bishop of Lincoln. Before this he had been rector of the Franciscans at Oxford where his beliefs led him into conflict with the Pope, the King and the monks of CANTERBURY and of LINCOLN itself. A prodigious writer of books on theology, philosophy, mathematics, agriculture and other subjects, he was a Greek and Latin scholar whose influence was felt for many years after his death in 1253.

The Church of All Saints has been much restored but its west tower is 15th-cent. and its turret stairs are higher than the main part of the tower itself. A screen with paintings of two kings is of excellent quality.

Hepwood Lodge Farm has features of Gothic Revival style and there is a well-designed modern school.

SUDBURY, *Suffolk* (11–TL8741). Sudbury on the River Stour is a very ancient borough, mentioned in the Anglo-Saxon Chronicle, and formerly an important cloth and market town. The "Eatanswill" of *Pickwick Papers*, the town is also famous as the birthplace of Thomas Gainsborough (1727–88). On Market Hill stands a bronze statue to the great painter, whose house nearby has been adapted to serve partly as a memorial and partly as a local art centre. The house was originally Tudor but the fine Georgian front was added by the painter's father, a local cloth merchant, shortly before Thomas was born. After studying in London the artist married and returned to Sudbury, shortly afterwards settling at IPSWICH. Success as a portrait painter led him to move to BATH where he very soon established himself in the first rank. In 1768 he was invited to become one of the founder members of the new Royal Academy in London, the President of which was his great rival Sir Joshua Reynolds. Though a portrait painter by profession, Gainsborough was by inclination a painter of landscapes and also a musician of considerable talent. His nephew, Gainsborough Dupont, was his only recorded pupil, some of whose best works have been attributed to the master himself. Gainsborough House contains a number of pictures by the artist, and many relics of his period. He died in 1788 and is buried in KEW Churchyard.

St Gregory's, at the west end of the town, was rebuilt *c.* 1365 on a very ancient foundation by

Archbishop Simon of Sudbury, the Archbishop of Canterbury who was murdered in 1381 at the time of the Peasants' Revolt. His head is preserved in the vestry. The telescopic font-cover is one of the finest in the country.

The Parish Church of St Peter, mainly late 15th-cent., on Market Hill was the chapel of ease of St Gregory's and an important wool church; it contains an interesting painting of Moses and Aaron *c.* 1730 by Robert Cardinall, a local painter; and a 15th-cent. embroidered velvet funeral pall. All Saints', another 15th-cent. wool church, has a painting showing the family tree of the Eden and Waldegrave families.

The Corn Exchange on Market Hill is an excellent example of early Victorian civic building.

Past Gainsborough House at No. 46 Gainsborough Street, you come to Stour Street with The Chantry and Salter's Hall, a merchant's house, both 15th-cent. Note the half-timbering and corner posts of the former and the fine carving on the latter.

SUTTON, *Suffolk* (11–TM3046). High on the heathland, this was the site of the Sutton Hoo ship burial, the great archaeological discovery made in 1939. Eleven mounds had stood on this spot for 1,300 years and the fourth mound to be opened revealed the impression in the sand of a ship and a priceless collection of relics of the Wuffinga dynasty of East Anglian kings. The ship was a rowing boat 89 ft long, the cenotaph to a great king, and the treasures it contained may now be seen in the BRITISH MUSEUM, London, including magnificent golden jewellery, Merovingian coins, Swedish armour and Byzantine silverware. Together they form what has been described by Norman Scarfe as "probably the most momentous single revelation of the Dark Ages ever made".

All Saints' Church once had a tower, but it fell in 1642. The early-15th-cent. font is octagonal, with an unusual narrow top.

Not far away is the American air base, R.A.F. Bentwaters, whose powerful jets contrast violently with the peace in which the Anglo-Saxon vessel lay for centuries beneath the earth.

SWAFFHAM, *Norfolk* (11–TF8109), a busy market town situated at the junction of the A47 and A1065 roads. Legend tells of the "Pedlar of Swaffham" who dreamed that if he travelled to London he would find treasure. Travel he did, and met a man who told him that he, in his turn, had had a dream that if he went to a village called Swaffham he would find treasure beneath a certain tree. The pedlar returned home, dug away and found riches which enabled him to build the north aisle of the great Church of SS. Peter and Paul. The pedlar is to be seen in the village sign, in a monument in the market place and in several carvings in the church.

The little town has a triangular market place with a "market cross" – in this case not a cross but a domed rotunda built in 1783 by the Earl of Oxford. A number of good Georgian houses may

be seen, including School House and the neighbouring Headmaster's House, the Assembly Room and several others. The Methodist Church dates from the early 19th-cent., the Shire Hall from 1839.

The Church of SS. Peter and Paul is 15th-cent. with a grand tower completed in 1510. On the roof is a graceful *flèche*. The west doorway is deeply recessed with a great window above and the south porch has its own hammer-beam roof. Inside the church the eye is held by the fine arcading and in particular by the great double hammer-beam roof with angels, open-winged, at the ends of the brackets. The Swaffham Pedlar, together with his dog, may be seen at the end of the prayer desk, a reminder of the north aisle which he had caused to be built at about the same time that the tower was completed (1510). The church possesses a large library of ancient books which may be seen on application.

SWANTON MORLEY, *Norfolk* 11–TG 0117). Beside the East DEREHAM road (the B1147) is a plot of land (National Trust) with the remains of the cottage in which lived the ancestors of Abraham Lincoln (*see* HINGHAM). The house belonging to Richard Lincoln, one of the family, has been converted into the Angel Inn. All Saints Church was begun sometime before 1378 and appears to have been completed about 50 years later. At once the attention is taken by the west tower, which has large bell-openings at the top and small rectangular sound holes below. Beneath is a fine doorway and at the sides the aisles of the church extend from the base, each having tall west windows with delicate tracery.

THAXTED, *Essex* (11–TL6131). The lofty spire of the church and the tower windmill are perhaps the first things the visitor notices as he arrives at this small town on the A130 between GREAT DUNMOW and SAFFRON WALDEN. The Church of St John the Baptist is one of the largest and grandest of all the Essex churches and its great size (183 ft long with a spire of almost exactly the same height), indicates the importance of the town in earlier days. It was in fact one of the centres of the cloth trade, and before that an important centre for cutlery.

St John's is an uncommonly fine example of a church which later restoration has dealt with kindly. The exterior is full of interesting detail: architectural, as in the battlements, buttresses and pinnacles; and sculptural, as in the carvings on the north porch and the north transept, etc. The interior of the church, due to the clear glass and use of white paint, is full of light and air. The tall arcades (*c.* 1340) were followed by various additions made in the following centuries and it may be noted that all the roofs are original. The font is unusual in that it is completely encased. The pulpit dates from the late 17th cent., the same period as the screens of the north and south chapels. Though the greater part of the glass in the church is clear there are some notable pieces of 14th- to 16th-cent. stained glass.

Though Thaxted has many attractive smaller houses and cottages, most of them traditionally timber-framed with plaster covering and pargeting, the most memorable building apart from the church itself is the 15th-cent. Guildhall. This is a three-storied building, each story overhanging the one below, the ground floor being open on three sides. Its restoration in the present century has hardly affected its medieval appearance. Near the Guildhall are some of the town's most picturesque houses, notably the Recorder's House.

S. of the church is a tower windmill built in 1805, on a site occupied by mills for centuries past.

Horham Hall, to the SW., is a Tudor brick mansion with a remarkable large bay window in its great hall.

THETFORD, *Norfolk* (11–TL8783). It hardly seems possible that this small market town on the River Thet and centrally placed at the junctions of no less than eight main roads was at one time the cathedral city of East Anglia. In the 11th cent. there were already 13 churches; by the time of Edward III there were 20. In addition there were at least four monastic houses and other buildings of some importance. Yet of all this splendour only three churches remain today and any number of attractive and worthwhile buildings of later date.

With the Dissolution Thetford seemed to come to a halt. The seat of the early Kings of East Anglia, it was the site of important Anglo-Saxon settlements. The castle Mound, still prominent, was the site of the Castle, demolished in 1173. Just 100 years before, the See of East Anglia had moved to Thetford from NORTH ELMHAM before it finally settled at NORWICH in 1095. Suddenly expansion stopped and Thetford lay dormant until around 1820 an attempt was made to make it a spa. But it soon slipped back into obscurity, and Thetford has remained a quiet little town, though recent years have seen an expansion of industrial and shopping facilities.

Perhaps its most famous citizen was Thomas Paine, the author of the *Rights of Man*. Paine was born in White Hart Street in 1737, son of a Quaker farmer. He left his wife in 1774 to settle in America where in 1776 he published *Common Sense*, a plea for American Independence. It was shortly after his return to England that he published the *Rights of Man* (1790–2), his most famous work, which sold 1½ million copies in England alone. Its notoriety made it necessary for him to flee to France where he wrote *The Age of Reason*. 1802 saw his return to America where seven years later he died in New York.

Thetford's churches are St Cuthbert's, St Mary-the-Less and St Peter's, all of which have been much restored and rebuilt. The Roman Catholic Church of St Mary and the Congregational church both date from the early 19th cent. Though the churches are not of great architectural interest the monastic remains are, and include those of the Cluniac Priory of Our Lady, founded in 1103, where at one time the Howard tombs were, later to be transferred to FRAMLINGHAM in Suffolk. Among the other scattered but impressive ruins are those of the Augustinian Priory of St Sepulchre and the Nunnery of St George. The Grammar School in London Road occupies the first site of the Cluniac priory.

In a town full of interesting streets and buildings space should be found for the timber-framed Ancient House, now a museum. Its main room has a fine ceiling of moulded and decorated Tudor beams. The early-16th-cent. Bell Hotel is also half-timbered and shows the early wattle and daub construction in a section which has been allowed to remain on view. The Dolphin Inn is dated 1694 and is of brick and flint. Behind the Guildhall, rebuilt in 1900, is the former lock-up and in Old Market Street stands the Old Gaol, a flint building dated 1816. King's House in King Street carries the Royal Arms as a token of the fact that an earlier house on the same site was used by King James I.

A statue to Thomas Paine stands opposite the Bell.

THEYDONS, THE, *Essex* (7–TQ4598; Theydon Bois). **Theydon Bois**, once a Norman forest, is now being eroded by the spread of the capital city. To the NE. **Theydon Garnon** has a church of particular interest. The tower is dated 1520 and the aisle 1644. The interior is attractive and contains a fine pulpit, some good brasses and monuments to the various members of the Archer family. The third village, to the E. of Garnon, is **Theydon Mount**, with a brick church of 1611–14 built on the hill by the Smith family, who are commemorated in a series of monuments and who owned the local mansion. Hill Hall has been described as one of the most important earlier Elizabethan houses in England. It was built by Sir Thomas Smith, a lecturer at CAMBRIDGE, who died in 1578. Inside the house, which is now run as an open prison for women, is a series of wall paintings of exceptional interest on the theme of Cupid and Psyche.

THORNEY, *Cambridgeshire* (10–TF2804). The most northerly of the Fenland islands, it was the site of a monastery founded at the end of the 7th cent. and destroyed by the Danes. Here Hereward the Wake made one of his last stands against William the Conqueror whose victory saw the rebuilding of the abbey. Much of it was removed at the Dissolution to provide building material for Corpus Christi College, CAMBRIDGE. All that remains is the tall west front and the nave incorporated in the Parish Church of SS. Mary and Botolph which was restored by Inigo Jones.

Many of the buildings in the village as well as the terraced houses were built to the order of the Dukes of Bedford, who owned the village and the abbey lands and were also responsible for much of the drainage of the surrounding fens.

THORNHAM MAGNA, *Suffolk* (11–TM 1072). Charles II stayed in this village with the Killigrews, subject of one of Van Dyck's portraits. Later it came into the hands of Lord Henniker (d. 1821), whose magnificent tomb by Kendrick may be seen in the Church of St Mary. The church itself was much restored in the last century.

About 1 m. away is the village of **Thornham Parva** with a small thatched church dating from Norman times. Its most interesting feature is the painted retable of *c.* 1300. The painting is in its original frame and contains a Crucifixion and eight saints, four to the left and four to the right. The figures are elegant in design and have a gesso background worked in various patterns. The painting was discovered in Lord Henniker's stables in 1927.

THORPENESS, *Suffolk* (11–TM4759). Thorpeness was planned as a seaside resort, a kind of garden city of the coast, by Stuart Ogilvie at the beginning of the present century. In 1910 a 65-acre lake known as the Mere was made, to be followed by the country club and the various houses which make up the estate. An inn and a small shopping centre are, like all the other buildings, built in a mock-Tudor style. One of its most fantastic creations is "The House in the Clouds", a water tower disguised as a house. Close to the tower is a fine early-19th-cent. windmill which was brought from **Aldringham**. Aldringham itself has in the Church of St Andrew an excellent 15th-cent. font and a Stuart Holy Table.

TILBURY, *Essex* (7–TQ6376), is an important port opposite GRAVESEND, the first of the Port of London docks on the Thames estuary. It was here that the first mission to the East Saxons was arranged by Bishop Cedd, and it was at Tilbury that Queen Elizabeth I came to address her troops as they prepared to face the Spaniards. Tilbury Fort, with its classically columned gateway, was built *c.* 1670 as a defence against other attackers, the Dutch and French, and ironically was designed by a Dutchman in 17th-cent. French style. It was in fact built *after* the Dutch had landed at **East Tilbury** in 1667. The huge docks have been steadily developed since the first installations were built in the 1880s.

At East Tilbury is St Catherine's Church, situated above the Coal House Fort of 1866. The church dates from Norman times; the fort was built by Gordon of Khartoum. The Bata shoe factory (1932) is in the style of the company's factories in Czechoslovakia. Recent additions include its recreation centre (1957) and near the docks a very advanced British Rail signal box.

TOLLESBURY, *Essex* (11–TL9510). On the estuary of the River Blackwater, Tollesbury is a fishing village popular with wildfowlers. It is also a centre of the Essex oyster trade. There is a charming square with old houses and a lock-up, placed in the corner of the churchyard. St Mary's has a tower and nave of Norman date, though the tower was buttressed in *c.* 1600. The 18th-cent. octagonal font has a strange carved inscription to

remind visitors of a fine imposed on its builder. Kempe stained glass, a good brass and a cartouche monument add to its interest.

Tollesbury Hall is timber-framed and dates from the 15th cent. One m. away is Bourchier's Hall, the home of the holders of the manor for over 240 years (1329–1570). The house is beautifully plastered and has a particularly interesting interior. To its W. is Guisnes Court, now a country club, which contains a fireplace taken from Bourchiers.

TOLLESHUNTS, THE, *Essex* (11–TL9011; Tolleshunt Major). A group of three villages around the B1026, MALDON to COLCHESTER road. **Tolleshunt Knights** is now associated with the Orthodox church which uses the old parish church of All Saints, which does in fact contain a much damaged figure of a knight holding his heart in his hands.

Tolleshunt Major is so in name but not in size. The name comes from the tenant at the time of Domesday. The Church of St Nicholas is remarkable for the large brick west tower added in the middle of the 16th cent. by the owner of nearby Beckingham Hall. It shows that beautiful diaper patterning typical of the county. The Hall itself is not especially important, but to its 16th-cent. structure was added a brick wall to the N. which contains an interesting gatehouse. It can be dated because there is a piece of the panelling of the house in the VICTORIA AND ALBERT MUSEUM, London, and is marked 1546, shortly after Stephen Beckingham obtained the manor from Henry VIII.

Tolleshunt D'Arcy is the largest of the three villages and its Hall dates from 1500, with additions from the following centuries. The Hall is surrounded by a moat crossed by an Elizabethan bridge dated 1585. D'Arcy House has a fine Georgian front. The Church of St Nicholas is Perpendicular in style with a battlemented west tower. Once inside, the visitor will not fail to admire the coved ceiling of the nave painted in 1897 by the Rev. E. Geldart, and also the excellent collection of brasses dating from the late 14th cent. The owners of the manor, Sir Thomas D'Arcy (d. 1593) and his wife may be seen as kneeling figures in a monument.

TRIMLEY, *Suffolk* (11–TM2736). Another case of two churches sharing the same churchyard. The church of Trimley St Martin is now mostly 19th-cent. That of St Mary has a ruined 14th-cent. west tower with a fine medieval doorway. Inside is a cartoon by an Italian artist showing the Madonna with the Infant Christ and John the Baptist.

The villages themselves are on the main road from IPSWICH to FELIXSTOWE and subject to ever-increasing traffic between the two towns, both of which are ports dealing with heavy freight.

Not far away is Grimston Hall, a farm-house where was once the home of Thomas Cavendish (1560–92), the second Englishman to circumnavigate the globe. Cavendish sailed with Raleigh,

Grenville and then set off from PLYMOUTH in July 1586 and returned two years and two months later with a ship full of treasures. Three years later he set out again but died off Ascension Island, leaving his ship to return home in 1593.

TRUMPINGTON, *Cambridgeshire* (10–TL 4455). The Church of SS. Mary and Michael contains a memorial brass to Sir Roger de Trumpington dated 1289 which is thus the second oldest brass in the country. The earliest recorded brass is that to Sir John Daubernoun in the Church of Stoke d'Abernon, Surrey, which is dated 1277. The church itself is elaborate and was much restored by Butterfield in 1876. Another monument of importance, though much more recent, is an inscribed tablet, an early work by Eric Gill dated 1914. Four reliefs by the same artist may be seen at the foot of the village cross, erected to commemorate the First World War.

Anstey Hall, built *c.* 1700, and Trumpington Hall slightly later in date, are among other attractions in the village which also boasts a 16th-cent. inn, The Green Man.

TRUNCH, *Norfolk* (11–TG2834). The Church of St Botolph is Perpendicular and is famous for one thing above all, its hexagonal font canopy. However, it is but one remarkable feature in a very interesting church. The nave roof has hammer-beams with spandrels filled with elaborately carved tracery, the priest's door porch is remarkable for having a buttress right in the middle of its roof and the beautiful carving of the screen, even though the paintings are rather faded, is a delight.

But it is to the font that the visitor will return, for here is one of the only four font canopies in England. Norfolk has another, at St Peter Mancroft, NORWICH. It may best be described as a crown set upon a hexagonal shaft which is in turn supported by six columns. The columns are full of intricately woven carvings which twine up to the second stage; this has six panels which were at one time probably painted. Finally comes the canopied top, richly crocketed (i.e. with a repeating pattern of twisting leaves), and with a finial on the top. The font which is enclosed by this astonishing construction is itself quite unremarkable.

The Manor House is $\frac{1}{2}$ m. to the E. – a farm of Elizabethan or Jacobean date with interesting chimneys.

UFFORD, *Suffolk* (11–TM2953). A village by the ford of Uffa, an Anglo-Saxon chieftain. Its greatest treasure is the spectacular font-cover in the Church of St Mary. Incredibly elaborate, with a profusion of intricately carved detail it is 18 ft high above the font. Even Dowsing, whose sorry record of destruction has often been mentioned, remarked in 1643: "There is a glorious cover over the font . . . all gilt over with gold." Little now remains of the original gilding and coloured gesso-work. The roof of the church has alternate hammer-beams and tie-beams and many finely carved bench-ends.

A. F. Kersting

Waltham Abbey

Contrasting with the almshouses built in 1690 and some houses of similar and slightly later date is an estate of well-designed modern houses on the site of Ufford Place.

WALBERSWICK, *Suffolk* (11–TM4974). You may come to Walberswick by road from BLYTH-BURGH or on the ferry which plies across the estuary of the Blyth from SOUTHWOLD. Once one of the prosperous towns of the East Coast, its decline followed an all too familiar pattern. The ruins of St Andrew's, of which the west tower and the south aisle remain, are an indication of its former importance. Now it is a select resort, famous for sailing, with fine walks across the heaths and along the coast.

It was much painted by Wilson Steer early in this century. The estuary is untidy, but the sight of the ferry, a simple rowing boat, as it crosses to and fro takes you right back to the paintings of the great Dutchmen, van Goyen and van der Velde.

WALPOLE ST PETER, *Norfolk* (11–TF 5016), a marshland village which lies between the A17 and A47 roads, near the county boundary and the River Nene. The great Church of St Peter has been known as the "Queen of the Marshes" and in this respect it is worthy to be compared with those of ELY and BLYTHBURGH. Its quality is at once apparent in the lovely south porch with its fine doorway surrounded by panelling, buttresses, niches and window. The church is battlemented throughout and it is evident that the chancel was added to make the church over 160 ft long and even grander in design. It is in the Early Perpendicular style throughout, and though the west tower is less elaborate than the rest of the church it is none the less impressive. Elsewhere there is a profusion of sensitive detail, even in the pinnacles at the east end of the nave.

Under the east end of the chancel is a passage used for church processions as the chancel extends right to the church boundaries. The inside of the church is noted for the screen, c. 1610, which extends the full width of the church. It contains a rare example of a "hudd" or "hood". This was a movable shelter, like a sentry box, which was used for funerals held in inclement weather. In a church full of interest the chandelier (1701), the octagonal font (16th-cent.), the tall Jacobean font cover, the Jacobean pulpit, the brass eagle lectern and the carvings on the stalls are all of high quality.

WALSINGHAM, *Norfolk* (11–TF9336). Of the two Walsinghams it is Little Walsingham which is the more important because of its long history as a centre of pilgrimage. It was in 1061 that the Lady Richeld saw a vision which commanded her to build a replica of the House of Nazareth in which Gabriel appeared to the Virgin Mary. Accordingly a simple hut was built which contained a wooden statue of the Virgin and Child and to this shrine came pilgrims in their thousands, from simple people to the kings and noblemen of the land. On their journey they would stop at wayside shrines and the last of these to be reached before Walsingham itself was at **Houghton St Giles** where the Slipper Chapel (now Roman Catholic) was the spot where many of the more devout pilgrims would remove their shoes, to walk the final mile barefoot. During the next century a priory of Augustinian (or Black) Canons was founded and incorporated the shrine in its church. Henry III and Edward I were among the visitors and by the 15th cent. the priory had become the richest in the county, except for that at NORWICH itself. At the time of the Reformation the shrine, the priory and an additional friary founded by the Franciscans were all destroyed.

In 1897 the cult was revived and the New Shrine was built between 1931 and 1937. The remains of earlier buildings include the east wall of the church, which now is a very handsome archway with elaborate buttresses and turrets, and the south wall of the refectory. One room of the priory, which is open to visitors, is intact. The gatehouse led from the church into the town.

The friary ruins are by the FAKENHAM road and are now private property. Some of its buildings still remain. Of the shrine itself nothing, of course, remains today. It is almost certain that it stood to the N. of the north aisle of the priory church.

The village itself is charming, with many picturesque buildings of the 16th cent. and later. The High Street runs N.–S. and at its foot is the market place, or Friday Market with St Hugh's House, a prominent red-brick Georgian building. N. of the gatehouse is the square or Common Place containing a 16th-cent. conduit, or pumphouse, made of brick and octagonal.

The Church of St Mary, restored after damage by fire in 1961, is in the Decorated and Perpendicular styles. The font is deservedly famous as one of the most perfect in the entire county. It stands on three steps, the topmost of which is in the shape of a Maltese cross, a not uncommon feature. The stem is finely carved and the bowl of the font shows the seven sacraments and the Crucifixion. There is a second font in the church, which is less fine and lacks the Jacobean cover of the other. There are some good brasses and monuments, including a famous modern sculpture, *The Risen Christ* by Sir Jacob Epstein.

Great Walsingham, 1 m. to the N. contains St Peter's, a fine church with a set of magnificently carved benches. To the N. of the church is Berry Hall, an Early Tudor house, and other domestic buildings of merit.

WALTHAM ABBEY, *Essex* (6–TL3800). Here, only 16 m. from London, is one of the finest surviving examples of Norman architecture in the country, worthy to be ranked with DURHAM and NORWICH, even though on a smaller scale. In fact, though the great nave, or rather what remains of it, is 12th-cent., the abbey was actually begun before the Conquest, by Earl Harold, an admirer of the Norman manner. It had been founded as a collegiate church in 1030 and was consecrated by Harold on 3 May 1060, some years earlier than the great abbey at Westminster, built by his brother-in-law, Edward the Confessor.

The present church of The Holy Cross and St Lawrence is less than one half of the original buildings much of which were destroyed after the Dissolution. What has survived is a magnificent Norman nave, whose sturdy columns support a gallery and a clerestory. The circular piers are, like those in the cathedrals mentioned earlier, patterned with deeply cut spiral or zigzag grooves while the arches above the heavy Norman caps all have zigzag ornaments.

The present tower was added c. 1556–68 to replace the original crossing tower which had collapsed. It features chequer-work in flint and stone and strong diagonal buttresses. The present church ends with the east wall which was rebuilt in 1859 by W. Burges. The windows have stained glass by Sir Edward Burne-Jones while the reredos was sculpted by T. Nicholls after 1876. Like the altar which is carved from American black walnut it was presented by Mrs Edenborough.

In the Lady Chapel may be seen the remains of a 14th-cent. painting on the east wall over the altar. The brilliantly designed ceiling of the nave was painted by Sir Edward Poynter in 1860.

Among the tombs contained in the church is that to Sir Edward Denny (d. 1600) and his wife and an elaborately carved alabaster monument to Captain Sir Robert Smith, d. 1697. One of the two slabs of Purbeck marble in the north aisle is from a tomb of an abbot, and the other has been held to be from the tomb of King Harold himself.

Little remains of the abbey buildings which were to the north of the nave. Some say that Harold was buried in what would have been the chancel and the spot is marked on the grass. A small section of the vaulted cloister is all that remains of the convent buildings.

Until 1540 the church organist was the great composer, Thomas Tallis (1505–85). In addition to Tallis, Essex was the home of two other of our greatest English composers, William Byrd (*see* STONDON MASSEY) and John Wilbye (*see* COLCHESTER).

WALTON-ON-THE-NAZE, *Essex* (11–TM2421). A seaside resort with fine sands and excellent sea-bathing due in part to its situation on the Ness which stretches into the North Sea. The red crag cliffs contain many fossils of interest to the geologist.

The resort itself was developed at the beginning of the 19th cent., and Marine Parade, then the Crescent, was built in 1832. Hotels, villas and cottages soon followed. There is a pier, the Naze Tower, originally built as a beacon in 1720, and a Martello tower.

WELLS-NEXT-THE-SEA, *Norfolk* (11–TF9143), is a village, a small port and a seaside resort, on the North Coast road, the A149. There are three focal points, the church, the Buttlands and the quay. St Nicholas' Church is the Victorian (1880s) rebuilding of the original church destroyed by fire in 1879, and stands just S. of the large green known as the Buttlands, an attractive green lined by trees and surrounded by Georgian houses. The upper end of the green leads to the quay through narrow streets like the "rows" at GREAT YARMOUTH and the "scores" at LOWESTOFT.

The quay still sees activity with local boats as well as some pleasure craft, but the beach to its N. is perhaps more popular nowadays. The little bathing area is about 1 m. from the village and is locally known as Abraham's Bosom, a name which may owe something to its earlier use as a harbour. Only 2 m. to the W. is HOLKHAM HALL with the National Trust reserves at Scolt Head and BLAKENEY some 6 to 8 m. on either side of the village.

WENDENS AMBO, *Essex* (11–TL5136). Its unusual name is only part of its charm, and comes from the joining of the two parishes of Great and Little Wenden in the 17th cent. It lies almost on the western boundary of the county, not far from AUDLEY END and SAFFRON WALDEN. St Mary the Virgin's Church is finely placed, and its sturdy Norman tower, surmounted by a later spire, has a Norman doorway made with Roman bricks

which shows how the conquerors of one era made use of the material left by the conquerors of another. There is a 15th-cent. pulpit and a 16th-cent. domed font-cover. Perhaps the most interesting feature is the cycle of medieval paintings discovered in 1934 on the theme of the life of St Margaret.

WESTHALL, *Suffolk* (11–TM4280). A small village off the HALESWORTH to BECCLES road which has a church of more than usual interest. It is that of St Andrew and it shows continuous development from Norman times through to later centuries. The present south aisle was once the Norman nave, and until the 13th cent. when the west tower was added there was a fine Norman west façade. Similar discoveries may be made in many other parts of this fascinating church. There is a fine seven-sacrament font, which still retains traces of its original colouring and gesso decoration. An elaborately carved screen shows paintings of a number of saints and biblical characters. A tomb in the south-east corner of the south aisle commemorates the late Nicholas Bohun, d. 1602, and over it is an unusual brass with a genealogical table of the Bohun family.

Westhall Hall, which was rebuilt in the 1870s, has typical Dutch/Flemish gables.

WESTHORPE, *Suffolk* (11–TM0469). The Church of St Margaret has a long history, but what survives is mainly in 14th- and 15th-cent. styles. There is a 14th-cent. parclose screen with intriguing patterns in the arches. The Barrow Chapel contains a white marble monument to Maurice Barrow who left £500 to be spent on a tomb in 1666.

Westhorpe Hall, a Georgian farm-house, still has a Tudor bridge over the moat. It was the residence of Henry VII's daughter, Mary Tudor. Her early marriage to Louis XII of France was short-lived and she then became the wife of Charles Brandon, the Duke of Suffolk. She is buried in St Mary's Church, BURY ST EDMUNDS.

WEST STOW, *Suffolk* (11–TL8170). Though there is nothing particularly special about the Church of St Mary, some of the panels which formed part of its painted screen are now in London's VICTORIA AND ALBERT MUSEUM.

West Stow Hall, between the A1101 and B1106, is remarkable for its red-brick gatehouse dating from the 1520s and reminiscent of others in Suffolk, Essex and Cambridgeshire. Rather severe turrets flank a centre section with a stepped gable, which includes the arms of Mary Tudor, sister of Henry VIII, who died in 1533 (*see* WESTHORPE and BURY ST EDMUNDS). Little survives of the original house but in the room above the gateway there are some famous Elizabethan wall paintings representing the four ages of man, together with a hunting scene.

WICKEN FEN, *Cambridgeshire* (11–TL5770). Wicken Fen is a Nature Reserve which belongs to the National Trust. It consists of three main areas:

Sedge Fen, Adventurers' Fen and St Edmund's Fen. Sedge Fen is open to the public and the visitor, having left his car in the car park, is advised to obtain the excellent guide book from the Keeper's Cottage. Once you cross the foot-bridge over Wicken Lode and start to follow the recommended route round the fen you enter another world in which only the cries of birds and busyings of insect life disturb the silence. The "lodes", or waterways are the ancient canals which served not only to irrigate the land but also acted as the highways through the flat fenland landscape. The fens themselves were crossed on foot through the "droves" and in ancient times the inhabitants cut the sedge for thatching and animal litter and dug into the ground for the abundant supplies of peat. Changing ways of life altered the original pattern of vegetation and in recent years the National Trust has tried to re-establish the old sedge fields without at the same time losing the rich variety of flora and fauna which had grown up.

There is thus a great variety of vegetation not only on the banks but also in the water of the lodes. A tower hide enables the visitor to study the rich bird life of the fen and the brick pits dug deep into the clay sub-soil have become pools containing numerous plants, insects and animals. A once derelict windmill has been restored and once again is used to pump water into the dykes. It stands as a symbol of the hundreds of mills which were once used to drain the fens. The complete walk of a little over 2 m. is full of scenes of strange

natural beauty and interest and the visitor cannot fail to be captivated by the spell of this unique Nature Reserve with its echoes of the past and its peaceful balance of the elements of land, water and sky.

WIMPOLE, *Cambridgeshire* (10–TL3350). Placed at the end of a 2 m. long avenue of elms is Wimpole Hall, almost certainly the finest mansion in the county. The original central block was built *c.* 1640 for Sir Thomas Chicheley. Later owners added to the property and when the house was taken over by the Earl of Hardwick, the Lord Chancellor, in 1740 major alterations were made, giving the building much as we see it today.

Perhaps the most impressive room is the chapel with its outstanding painted decorations in the Italian style by Sir James Thornhill, the father-in-law of William Hogarth. The wrought-iron altar rails *c.* 1730–5 and the pulpit are also worthy of attention. The library and gallery precede the Yellow Drawing Room, the work of Sir John Soane, *c.* 1793, an ingenious design with its dome, lantern and semicircular apses.

Originally formal in design, the gardens contain an important reminder of the English vogue for the Picturesque in the form of an artificial ruin built by Sanderson Miller. Shortly after the 1st Earl died the garden was landscaped by Capability Brown and then again in 1801 by Humphry Repton.

To the E. of the house is St Andrew's Church, much changed in the rebuilding of 1887. It

Wicken Fen Nature Reserve

G. Douglas Bolton

contains an outstanding collection of monuments by some of the most notable sculptors working in England – Scheemakers, Westmacott and Flaxman among others.

WINGFIELD, *Suffolk* 11–TM2276). Here is the only inhabited castle in the county and an unusually impressive church. The castle is picturesque and romantic, a four-sided moated building with gatehouse and angle-towers. A drawbridge remains over the moat and on the west side part of the original structure was replaced by a Tudor house. It was built by Michael de la Pole, in and after 1384. The original door still stands.

St Andrew's Church is connected with the founding of a medieval college here by Sir John Wingfield on his death in 1360. The tower is 14th-cent. and the north chancel contains a monument in memory of Sir John. Between the chancel and the south chapel is the monument to Michael de la Pole who died in 1415, a rare example of the use of wooden figures. The chapel itself is exceptionally elaborate. A further monument to John and Elizabeth de la Pole, *c.* 1491, has their effigies in alabaster under a canopied altar tomb. Elizabeth was the sister of Edward IV and Richard III.

WISBECH, *Cambridgeshire* (11–TF4609). Wisbech stands on the River Nene almost 12 m. from the sea. At one time it was only 4 m. away but changes in the river patterns have altered its position in relation to the Wash. Unlike MARCH whose church is perhaps the main reason for a visit to the town, the architectural beauties of Wisbech lie in its domestic buildings.

As you stand on the bridge over the Nene North Brink extends to the W. The impression is of an anglicized Delft with the terrace of mainly Georgian houses providing variety without sacrificing unity. The most famous of the buildings on the bank of the river is Peckover House, built in the 1720s and an important example of domestic architecture of the period. It is now in the care of the National Trust and you may see inside fine examples of decorative work in plaster and wood. The garden contains a number of rare trees, including one of the largest Maidenhair trees in the country and a glasshouse containing orange trees.

After the Friends Meeting House and a group of gabled houses a number of smaller houses lead to the buildings of the North Brink Brewery. Though North Brink is the more photographed and famous side, South Brink on the opposite bank is hardly less charming. Close to the bridge stands the monument designed by Sir George Gilbert Scott to Thomas Clarkson, one of the fighters for the abolition of the slave trade.

Still active as a port Wisbech is the centre of the agricultural and flower-growing industries of fenland. In the late spring of each year, usually at the end of May, the town is the centre of various routes through surrounding orchards. These routes, which are usually signposted, enable the motorist to see as much as possible of the beauties of the spring blossoms and at the same time avoid the heavy traffic on the main roads.

The large Church of SS. Peter and Paul has the unusual feature of twin naves and aisles. The tower built in the 16th cent. contains a host of sculptural detail and within the church is the monumental brass to Sir Thomas de Braunstone, an armoured figure some 7 ft long.

WISSINGTON, *Suffolk* (11–TL9534). On the Stour close to NAYLAND and one of the southernmost villages in the county. The Church of St Mary is Norman with several well-preserved original features. The south doorway to the nave is richly decorated with Norman carving and the two shafts have different patterns, alternate spirals on the left and horizontal zigzags on the right. The nave arch also has fine carving, with three recessions, two of which are patterned. The famous series of wall paintings dating from the 13th cent. give some idea as to the appearance of country churches at that time. On the south wall of the nave are representations which include the Magi asleep in bed, the presentation in the temple and the Nativity and on the end wall women gossiping encouraged by devils, and St Francis preaching to the birds.

Considerable restoration was undertaken in the 1850s when many additional features in a Victorian-Norman style were incorporated.

Wiston Hall stands close to the church and was built for the Admiral of the Fleet, Sir George Creasey, and enlarged by Sir John Soane in 1791 for Samuel Beechcroft of the Bank of England.

WITHAM, *Essex* (11–TL8114). It was only recently that the by-pass took the traffic away from this delightful town placed on the main A12 CHELMSFORD to COLCHESTER road, just where the River Brain crosses it. The town still retains its Georgian character, though its actual history goes back to the days when King Alfred's son, Edward, built the huge mound as a defence against the Danes, a mound later cut through by very different invaders, the railway engineers of the early Victorian age. Near the site of the mound, at Chippinghill, is the Church of St Nicholas, 14th-cent. Decorated style in flint, with a Norman south doorway and excellent carved mouldings and columns.

The High Street follows the ancient Roman road and is continued at either end by Bridge Street, and Newland Street, the three sections containing many pleasing houses of the 16th cent. and later. Prominent is the Spread Eagle, timber-framed and bow-windowed, a famous Essex inn. Two others are the White Hart and the Red Lion. Near the church, once the site of an old market place, are more attractive houses, many timber-framed, with a little distance away, Powers Hall, 16th-cent. with a large barn, and Howbridge Hall, also 16th-cent. On the River Blackwater is the weather-boarded Blue Mills, part of a picturesque group which includes Mathyns, a Georgian house of red brick.

Plans to expand the town have resulted in an

increase in industrial development, but the by-pass will deflect heavy traffic.

Tiptree, 4½ m. E., is famous for its fruit-preserving and jam-making industries.

WIVENHOE, *Essex* (11–TM0321), is on the River Colne, 5 m. from COLCHESTER. On the other side of the river once linked by a ferry, is **Rowhedge**. Wivenhoe park was painted by Constable and is now the site of the University of Essex (*see* Colchester) whose tall tower blocks are already a prominent feature of the landscape. The original house was built in 1758–61 but was much altered and enlarged in the 1850s. The University has been planned by Kenneth Capon and it is expected that it will ultimately accept some 3,000 students.

The attractive quay is still as it was long ago, a centre for boat building. The Church of St Mary the Virgin is mainly 19th-cent., though the west tower dates from 1500 and is surmounted by a wooden cupola of later date. Inside is a majestic brass to William, Viscount Beaumont, d. 1507. In East Street, S. of the church, is a house with one of the finest displays of pargeting in East Anglia.

Gourmets will appreciate the local oysters, an important industry.

WOODBRIDGE, *Suffolk* (11–TM2749). The River Deben which flows through Woodbridge to the North Sea made the town a busy seaport. Now it is mainly a sailing centre with a winding channel which finally emerges on the coast between Bawdsey and FELIXSTOWE. It is a most attractive small town, with its shire hall dominating the market square, its quays and river frontage and its many fine houses and cottages.

The high gables in the Dutch style were added to the shire hall about 1700, and the lower floor was at one time a covered market. Around the square are houses and shops dating from the 16th cent., many with Georgian fronts. The town has always been associated with the arts, and two art galleries continue this interest today. The artist Thomas Churchyard lived here; so, too, did Fitz-Gerald, and Tennyson was among those who stayed in the town. He stayed in the Bull, in the stable of which is the resting place of one George Carlow, who desired to be buried there rather than in the church in 1738.

SW. of Market Hill is the Church of St Mary, a stately building with an imposing tower, standing apart from, and above, the town. To the N., Theatre Street is so called after the Georgian building which is now a sale-room. Seckford Street leads to the library, a rich source of local information, housed in a 16th-cent. grammar school and then the red-brick almshouses, 1835–40, and the site of the old cattle market. New Street brings us to St John's Church (1842) with its *flèche* on the roof and also to the thoroughfare with fine houses and good shopping.

Thomas Seckford, a well-known Elizabethan public benefactor, did much to mould the character of the town and his name is commemorated in Seckford Hall, a Tudor mansion of distinctive character, now a country-house hotel. The list of local buildings of architectural merit is lengthy; it must include the Bell, Angel and King's Head Inns, the Georgian houses of Thoroughfare and Cumberland Street and as an industrial curiosity, the old steelyard, or lever weighing machine, which may be seen at the Bell, used for weighing wool, hay and hides. The tide mills along the estuary, the barns and Kyson Hill, parkland owned by the National Trust, are other unique features which the visitor may enjoy.

The nearby air bases give the town a character which in some way echoes its days as a busy maritime port, when strange accents and foreign tongues must have been commonplace. The ships have been replaced by modern jets, and the carriages and horses of the past by American cars so huge that you wonder how their drivers can navigate them through the narrow streets and country lanes which surround this remarkably unspoilt little town.

Five m. N. of Woodbridge is **Charsfield**, whose church is worth visiting to see its glowing red bricks.

WOOLPIT, *Suffolk* (11–TL9762). One's expectations on entering the Church of St Mary through its magnificent stone south porch are fulfilled by the sight of the interior of this beautiful church. The elaborately carved porch dates from the mid-15th cent. and is big enough to contain the chamber above and the lierne vaulted roof. The nave has a superb double hammer-beam roof, renowned for the carved angels that grace it, and a beautiful screen high up over the chancel arch below the east window of the nave. The tiny aisles are less than 9 ft wide and again have beautifully timbered roofs. The brass eagle lectern is 16th-cent. and is said to have been the gift of Queen Elizabeth I. The tower and spire were rebuilt in the middle of the last century to replace the original tower which had collapsed after a storm.

In the village are some attractive timber-framed Tudor and Georgian houses as well as the Swan Inn, some parts of which are dated 1759 and others 1826.

WRENTHAM, *Suffolk* (11–TM4982). A large village which has grown up along the main A12, with side roads leading to COVEHITHE and SOUTHWOLD. The local garage has a display of carriage and vehicle lights and you might be fortunate enough to see the beautifully restored traction engine should there be a fête or rally in the neighbourhood.

The Brewster family built a Hall here in the 16th cent., demolished in the 19th. They were prominent as propagators of Puritanism. The Old Meeting House Farm is on the site of a chapel built in 1710. The brass effigy of Humphrye Brewster, 1593, may be seen in the church.

WRITTLE, *Essex* (7–TL6706). Now almost part of CHELMSFORD; it was from the village of

Writtle that Marconi sent out his first broadcasts. He had come to England from Bologna, and his radio factory, the first in the world, led to the subsequent developments in telegraphic and broadcasting techniques. Here, too, is one of the most famous village greens in the county, framed by some fine houses and to the S., the Church of All Saints. The west tower was rebuilt in 1802 and the 13th-cent. body of the church in 1879. Among the monuments is one by Nicholas Stone to Sir Edward Pinchon (1629) – a remarkable work, with harvest symbols crowned by an angel standing on a rock. There are brasses in plenty, many of them 16th-cent., and fine carving on stalls and benches.

On either side of the church stand beautiful houses: Aubyns, a half-timbered house dating from the early 16th cent., and Mundays, a plastered 17th-cent. house. Excavations at King John's Castle brought to light traces of buildings of the 13th to 15th cents., perhaps a link with the fabled palace of King John, and Robert Bruce of Scotland, who, legend has it, was born in these parts.

WROXHAM, *Norfolk* (11–TG2917). A yachting centre which has grown up on either side of the River Bure, which is spanned by a bridge first built in 1614 and later widened in 1897. It carries the A1151 from NORWICH, 6 m. to the SW.

Wroxham itself is a busy place which even out of season has the atmosphere of a yachting centre. All seems to converge on one crossroads with one general store which caters for every possible need. Wroxham Broad itself, while not large, is very popular for sailing, and the headquarters of the Norfolk Broads Yacht Club is on its west bank.

The Church of St Mary has a famous north doorway, with seven orders and three shafts. The churchyard contains the Trafford Mausoleum built in 1831 although medieval in appearance. Just to the SE. of the church is the manor house, in which is a panel dated 1623. The stepped gables betray Dutch influence.

In addition to boat-building, local light industry includes the canning of soft fruits.

WYMONDHAM, *Norfolk* (11–TG1101), lies on the main LONDON to NORWICH road, the A11, at the junction with the B1135. It is consequently a busy market town subject to heavy traffic. Its name is pronounced Windham, and its centre is still the market place with the market cross, a charming octagonal building dating from 1617 and raised on wooden arcading. Nearby are some timbered houses, including the Bridewell with the goal attached (1787). Among the many fascinating local inns are the King's Head, the Crossed Keys, and especially the Green Dragon, half-timbered and most attractive. However, the pre-eminent building is, of course, the great Abbey Church of St Mary and St Thomas of Canterbury.

The priory was founded in 1107 by William de Albini for the Benedictine order. In 1448 it became an abbey and its remains are dominated by the two fine towers, unusually placed one at either end of the church. The octagonal one was originally a central crossing tower, for at one time the church continued well beyond its present position. Differences of opinion between monks and villagers caused the church to be not only spiritually but physically divided and when the abbey section was destroyed it was the part belonging to the parishioners which was saved. Even so it is incomplete, for the west tower never received its parapet and battlements.

From the outside the church appears to be Perpendicular in style, as are its windows and panelling. Within is a magnificent Norman nave; this, however, has a superb 15th-cent. hammer-beam roof, decorated with angels and huge star bosses. The east end is still shut off by the wall built as the result of the disputes centuries ago and is now faced with an elaborate reredos made in 1935 by Sir Ninian Comper. Near the altar is a terracotta monument to Abbott Ferrers, similar to that at OXBURGH, and therefore probably of the same date, *c.* 1525.

There are the remains of the 13th-cent. font of Purbeck marble, and another typical East Anglian font complete with the Four Lions and Four Wild Men. The association of the church with the St Thomas whose name it bears is brought to mind in the Chapel of St Thomas à Becket, in Church Street. It was begun shortly after his murder and rebuilt in the 14th cent. It is 84 ft by 40 ft and is now a library.

The fire of 1615 caused considerable rebuilding in the town and as a result there are some fine houses; among later Georgian houses is Caius House, and others near it in Middleton Street.

The dissolution of the abbey in the 16th cent. resulted indirectly in the conflict between Robert Kett and John Flowerdew which led to the famous Kett Revolt of 1549. Kett's Oak associated with this is some 3 m. NE. of the town on the A11. Kett himself was put to death shortly after his short-lived success.

YOXFORD, *Suffolk* (11–TM3968). A deceptive village, because unlike so many on the main London to GREAT YARMOUTH route it developed not parallel to what has become an increasingly busy highway, but at right angles to it along the river. The result has been a community which has kept much of its original character.

The Church of St Peter contains some interesting brasses but more interesting is Cockfield Hall, originally built by Sir Arthur Hopton during the reign of Henry VIII. Catherine, a sister of Lady Jane Grey, was kept here at the orders of Queen Elizabeth I. The central block was rebuilt early in the 17th cent. and other alterations have taken place since, including, in 1896, the building of the "Stuart" great hall. The village is surrounded in addition to the parklands of Cockfield Hall by those of Grove Park and Rookery Park and this, together with the main street with its timbered, bow-windowed and balconied houses, gives the village its unique character.

Wymondham Abbey   Edwin Smith

The South-East Midlands

Hertfordshire   Buckinghamshire   Bedfordshire
Huntingdonshire   Northamptonshire

LAURENCE W. MEYNELL

"South-East Midlands" is a somewhat arbitrary grouping, a portmanteau word; and a portmanteau may be full of treasures, or it may be disappointingly empty. Happily there is no question of emptiness where the five English counties which are the subject of this section of the book are concerned. Buckinghamshire, Hertfordshire, Bedfordshire, Huntingdonshire and Northamptonshire make a compact block stretching from the urbanity of the Thames valley on its south-west to the comparative wildness of the still mysterious Fens on the north-east.

Scenery and structure are inescapably connected, and nowhere is this more evident than in the territory we are considering. The water which once covered the whole of Britain left on its recession a belt of limestone and clay which, starting at Portland Bill on the south coast, runs north-eastwards all through the Cotswold country, takes in the high parts of Northamptonshire and so eventually leaves our area towards the Wash. There is no better building material than limestone, and where iron has added a warm touch of colour to the coldness of the stone the effect is wholly pleasing.

Higham Ferrers, Oundle with its lofty spire, and Apethorpe are – at least as far as the old parts of them are concerned – splendid examples of how "right" local architecture using local materials can be. Turvey, on the Bedfordshire Ouse, was almost entirely rebuilt of native stone in the mid-nineteenth century; its long street of substantial houses dotted with good trees is most effective. The wide High Street of Brackley, lined with buildings of local stone, remains dignified despite the traffic.

All along this limestone belt you get churches with splendid spires – "a country of spires and squires" the old saying goes. Oundle's lofty crocheted one is notable; and, although off the limestone belt, the lofty broach spires of Huntingdonshire – Warboys and Alconbury particularly – are impressive.

Such an abundance of magnificent building material called into being a number of individual quarries which have been famous for centuries. We know that the Romans won stone from the quarries at Barnack, which continued to supply material all through medieval times. The church at Boston, the cathedral at Peterborough, and many churches in the Fen district (where water transport was easy) were hewed out of Barnack; and at one period the Abbot of Ramsey in Huntingdonshire paid the Abbot of Peterborough a fee of 4,000 eels for the right of quarrying Barnack stone. The Totternhoe (Beds) quarry was one of the gifts which Henry I bestowed on the Priory of Dunstable at its foundation in 1130, and a good deal of Windsor Castle and the interior of Westminster Abbey came from there. In contrast, the stones for old Saint Paul's were almost entirely quarried at Weldon (Northants).

Many of these good stone buildings are roofed with "Collyweston slates", thin layers of stone which weather to a delightful greeny-brown.

Parallel to the limestone ridge, and immediately to the south-east of it, there runs a belt of chalk and flint, and if, in Hertfordshire and Bedfordshire for instance, this does not give us lovely stone buildings harmonious with their surroundings it makes itself felt in other ways.

In Hertfordshire the underlying structure of things is more apparent in agriculture than in architecture. It has always been a great area for wheat and barley. As far back as 1586 Camden commented on "the incredible number of corn merchants, maltsters and dealers in grain". In the valley of the River Lea the fertile soil has given rise to the existence of the vast "glass-house" activities of Waltham, Cheshunt and Broxbourne. Not only is the valley soil naturally fertile, but the district was near enough to the Great Wen to get the benefit both of an insatiable market on the doorstep and of soil from earth closets, manure from stables and soot from innumerable Cockney chimneys to help keep that market supplied.

It is the clay – a deep stratum of Oxford clay near the surface, and thus easily workable – which gives rise to one of Bedfordshire's most interesting industrial features – the great brick works at Stewartby, where a single kiln holds more than nine million bricks. Stewartby works and the adjacent model village are a striking testimony to the imagination and energy of the late Sir Malcolm Stewart.

Where the Oxford clay mingles with the Lower Greensand belt a soil of great fertility results, and so we get what is sometimes rather unkindly referred to as the "brussels-sprouts" country of Sandy, Potton, Shefford and Biggleswade. Market gardening repeats itself in the Ramsey area of Huntingdonshire; and at Fletton close to Peterborough we have clay and therefore bricks again.

The third great structural influence literally underlying the area is the chalk of the Chiltern massif which, running in a fifty-mile curve from the Thames to the north-east, is strikingly displayed on Luton and Dunstable downs. The chalk gives us beautiful things. Blue flowers, blue butterflies, the hornbeam and the oak all flourish on it; but its greatest glory is the beech.

Hornbeam and oak you will see in plenty in the woods near Ashridge (the house has long since ceased to be in private occupation and is now a political college); indeed this whole south-east area was once very extensively wooded. Rockingham Forest (Northants) was once vast, and, although ruthlessly despoiled by Charles I in order to raise ready cash, and eroded by all sorts of changes since, it still remains pretty substantial, and the flat and fenny lands of Huntingdonshire still show round Kimbolton and north of Alconbury substantial remains of what were originally huge forests.

There are some notable and historic individual oak trees in the area, including what remains of that one at Hatfield House under which on 17 November, 1558, Elizabeth was told of the death of her half-sister Mary and so of her own accession to the throne. Better preserved is Waller's Oak at Coleshill (Bucks) under which Edmund Waller wrote some of his poems, and which is probably a thousand years old. But it is the beech which is the peculiar glory of the chalk, the beech which is lovely and colourful in all weathers. The very name Buckinghamshire proclaims this fact if the derivation from buccan (beech) is correct. "Leafy Bucks" it is indeed, and nowhere more gloriously so than at Burnham Beeches.

If geology has determined how things look it has also largely determined the way – literally – that they have gone: the lines of communication of the area. The first primitive footpaths were almost invariably on the hills; height meant safety and good going since you avoided the denser undergrowth and the swamps of the low-lying land. Tentative footpaths hardened into recognized trackways, and so the Icknield Way came into being.

In prehistoric England the most important inhabited region was Salisbury

Plain, and there was always the need of a highway from that religious and civic centre to the great cornlands of East Anglia. The Icknield Way was ancient when the Romans came, but they adapted very little of it; by their time the centre of gravity of the island had shifted from Salisbury Plain to the south-east, and the need was for a south-east to north-west link. Hence the Watling Street, of which the modern equivalent, running roughly parallel to it, is the M1.

Even today, notwithstanding traffic lights, chromium shop fronts and other belittling modernities, I always feel the authentic thrill of history in the very middle of Dunstable, at Dunstable Cross, where that primitive track, the Icknield Way, crosses the majestic authentic artery of Rome, the Watling Street. This nodal point was always important, especially when the adjacent scrub and woodland was infested with bandits; so much so that the town of Dunstable was founded by Henry I for the express purpose of guarding the safety of the ways. There used to be an Eleanor Cross here, one of a sequence built to mark the nightly resting places of Queen Eleanor's body on its journey from Leicestershire to London.

Of the Watling Street it may be interesting to recall that the legions normally reckoned to march eleven Roman miles (the equivalent roughly of twelve modern miles) in a day, so the Watling Street itinerary hereabouts reads Verulamium (St Albans) to Durocobrivae (Dunstable) 12 miles; Durocobrivae to Magisvinium (Little Brickhill, Bucks) 12 miles. The need for a London link with the north-east (to connect with the highly important Colonia at Lincoln) was met by the Ermine Street on which Godmanchester (Hunts) was one of the principal stations.

Man had to make roads; nature made rivers for him. Perhaps it was out of gratitude for this bounty that he gave them such delightful names – the Ivel, the Flitt, the Hiz, the Ouse and the Ousel in Bedfordshire; in Hertfordshire the Mimram, the Bean, the Rib, the Stort and the Lea; Northamptonshire's Nene; in Huntingdonshire the Nene again and the little Kym; then Buckinghamshire's Ray, Thame, Chess (with its watercress beds), Wye, Lovat, Lyde, and the disappearing Misbourne. The Thames – "Liquid History", the term is surely justified – only skirts our territory; the Ouse is central to it, the Ouse of quiet meadows, of straight-backed cattle lifting dripping muzzles, and of wind-bent willows with silver undersides. Chaucer knew the Lea, the "sedgy Lea" he called it; Izaak Walton loved and immortalized it.

Perhaps the most publicized river in the area is in fact really a canal; this is the New River constructed in 1609 by Sir Hugh Myddleton for the vital necessity of giving London a water supply. It is interesting to note that Royalty took a hand in trade with this enterprise, for James I shrewdly paid half the cost of the undertaking in exchange for half the profit. Starting at Amwell – where the church has a delightful Norman apse – the New River has brought water to London for three hundred years. When it first did so the water mains of the capital were hollowed-out elm trunks, and within the last five years I have seen specimens of these hollowed elm boles brought to light by road excavations and lying on the ground in Lincolns Inn.

Of canals proper the area has a splendid example in the Grand Junction, built in 1793 to connect London (via the Thames) with the Midlands. It was the natural successor to the highly successful canals built slightly earlier in the North by Brindley and his patron, the Duke of Bridgewater. Since canals must be fed it brought into being the great Tring reservoirs, now famous for black tern, crested grebe and many other wildfowl.

Along the roads and the rivers ran history. There are few parts of England where the story of man has been more continuously and intensively made than in the South-East Midlands. In the flat marsh-lands of Huntingdonshire the bones of wolf, hippopotamus and earlier mammals tell us of the very earliest things. Henlow (Beds) is now as modern as possible, with its R.A.F. flying establishment, but Stone Age implements discovered there speak of more primitive matters. At Maiden Bower near Sewell (Beds) you may see the great earthworks, ten acres in extent, thrown up in the Late Stone Age and occupied later by men of the Bronze Age. Dunstable Downs, hard by, are now much used for gliding; so does the past merge into the present and the present into the future.

Grim's Dyke, which is in some ways the most impressive prehistoric survival in the area, can be traced at many spots: near Berkhamsted and Wheathamp-stead in Hertfordshire, and in Buckinghamshire near Monks Risborough, in the woods of Lacey Green and at Bradenham, where later Isaac Disraeli was to live in the Great House (his better known, but not better read, son Benjamin came ultimately to Hughenden in the same county). The exact origin and purpose of the Dyke are both uncertain; but it seems more likely to have been a boundary mark than a defence. High above Hitchin (Herts) is Ravensburgh Castle, a prehistoric hill-fort of which now only the site remains.

Roman remains have been found at a score of places in the region. Biggleswade and Welwyn come to mind for coins and toilet articles; Shefford has the remains of a Roman cemetery; and farther north three important Roman roads met at Godmanchester. Roman pottery made at Castor (Northants) was famous all over Europe. Nowhere was the hand of Rome more clearly seen than at St Albans. Here, or hereabouts, was the headquarters of Cassivelaunus, the strongest chieftain in the island at the time of the first Roman invasion, and it was here 116 years later, in A.D. 61, that Boadicea, rebelling against the Roman establishment, attacked, captured and sacked Verulamium. Having dealt, after considerable difficulty, with Boadicea, Imperial Rome rebuilt the town on an imposing scale, giving it the enormous amphitheatre which has lately been excavated.

On the whole the Roman influence on the region was constructive; those great colonizers were by preference builders, not demolition contractors. The Vikings, to whose raids this part of England was particularly liable, were another matter. They brought their boats as far inland as Hertford, and at Willington (Beds) you can see the nausts or docks they used. Huntingdonshire shows us many villages – one thinks of the Sawtry and Woodwalton area – built a little away from the road so as to avoid if possible attracting the attention of the marauding Danes. They were beaten at Luton in 817, and again at Tempsford; but it was not until Alfred's peace of Wedmore in 878 that the Danish trouble was finally contained, and then only by granting them a very considerable slice of England – the Danelaw – which included the whole of Huntingdonshire, although oddly enough Huntingdon-shire place-names show very little trace of Danish influence.

The Saxons left a fine 80-foot high tower at Clapham (Beds), and the Mass Dial on St Mary's church at Stevington in the same county may well be Saxon, too. Certainly a great deal of Wing church in Buckinghamshire is Saxon work and if there are few or no Saxon remains in Hertfordshire this is probably because there was no local stone available there. At Kimbolton (Hunts) the present castle, put up by Sir John Vanbrugh, is but the parvenu successor to the Saxon one which at one time stood on the same site and which belonged to Earl Harold.

The ever-increasing predominance of London inevitably affected the five counties of the South-East Midlands. They were always near enough to the capital to provide hunting grounds for Royalty; and Ampthill, where Queen Catherine of Aragon was imprisoned, Hatfield and Enfield Chase were the favourite spots. Northamptonshire, that "county of squires", is still great hunting country: Fitzwilliam, Grafton and Pytchley are bugle calls to many stout hearts.

Castles will be looked for almost in vain. Only the mound exists at Huntingdon, the building itself having been destroyed in the time of Henry II. Fotheringhay, which saw the execution of Mary Queen of Scots in 1587, has vanished. Of Bletsoe, where Margaret Beaufort, great-grand-daughter of John of Gaunt and grand-mother of Henry VIII, was born, only some slight remnants can be traced in a farm-house.

Civil Wars luckily touched this area but little; the opening engagement was fought at St Albans in 1455, there was a second battle half-way between that town and Harpenden six years later, and almost the last encounter of the war took place at Barnet in 1471. Perhaps the attitude of the district in the matter could be summed up by the action of William, 5th Earl of Bedford, who fought with deter-mination for Cromwell at Edgehill and later with equal gallantry for the King at Newbury.

Of the great houses Hatfield must surely be put first. It is the most impressive Jacobean house in England; even if one ignored the amount of English history which has been forged here there would still be the superb gardens, with their hornbeams and their great mulberry trees so loved by John Evelyn. Woburn is ducal, has been great, and is now a sort of superior fun fair. Althorp, with its gallery of fine pictures, is a splendid example of successful late-eighteenth-century remodelling, and some two miles south-east of Stamford stands the splendid Elizabethan mansion of Burghley House, where Grinling Gibbons's "heavenly room" is to be seen. In opulent Edwardian days the Rothschilds invaded Bucking-hamshire and at one time owned seven large establishments within an eight-mile radius of Aylesbury. Of these Halton is now an R.A.F. training centre, but Waddesdon may still be seen in its fullness of French Baroque, so unexpected in that homely setting. The manor house at Mackery End (Herts) has been immortal-ized in one of Elia's best known essays, and probably no one needs to be reminded that George Washington's forebears came from Sulgrave (Northants).

But there are more homely things than castles and great houses to be seen. The inns of England are magnificently represented here: the Roebuck at Knebworth, the George & Dragon at Buntingford, Much Hadham's Red Lion, Disraeli's famous Red Lion at High Wycombe, the Saracen's Head at Ware, which used to house the Great Bed, and the other Saracen's Head at Towcester, where Sam Weller ate "a very good dinner" though perhaps no better than the meal which Nicholas Nickleby and Mr Squeers ate at the White Horse at Eaton Socon (Beds) while "five little boys were put to thaw by the fire". St Albans claims that its Fighting Cocks is the oldest inn in England; and no less an authority than Professor Sir Albert Richardson of Ampthill stated categorically that the Swan at Bedford was "architecturally the finest in the country".

Nonconformity has always been a prominent thread in the tapestry of local history. John Bunyan was born at Elstow in 1628, and, as all the world knows, was imprisoned in a Bedford gaol. Jordans among the Chiltern Hills has long been a stronghold of the Quakers. Nearly every village in the area can show its little chapel, sometimes admittedly quite hideous, but occasionally splendidly satisfying in its whitewashed simplicity.

So, with the necessities of geology underneath and the accidents of history on the surface, we see the five counties of the South-East Midlands as they are today. Fast electric train services (Amersham, remember, is on the London underground system), arterial roads and motorways have inevitably made their impression. Once sleepy little towns with a marked individual flavour, like Bedford or High Wycombe, have felt in full the impact of immigration and the levelling effect of over-easy transport. At one time straw-plaiting, with its delightful terms – maiden's choice, fire strand, lovely lady and speckled – was a widespread cottage industry essential to the rural economy, as was shoemaking with leather tanned by the oak bark from Rockingham Forest. There is no cottage lace-making now, and boots and shoes are machine-made by the hundreds of thousands in the factories of Northampton. The blast furnaces and steelworks at Corby, the huge brickworks at Stewartby and Fletton, the industries of Luton and Northampton, are the marks of modernity.

Even so, the area still remains largely rural; a great deal of it, as in the north of Bedfordshire and much of Huntingdonshire, is still homely and pastoral. Standing on the bridge over the Ouse by the Woolpack Inn between Huntingdon and Godmanchester Cobbett called what he saw "the most beautiful scene and by far the most beautiful meadows that I ever saw in my life". The outspoken old Radical would not have to alter his opinion much today.

Delightfully improbable English names are still scattered through the countryside – Puddephats, Gubblecote, Potters Crouch, Raisins End, Hinton in the Hedges, Christmas Common, Lacey Green, Maids Moreton. The peculiar English sense of humour still declares itself from the signboards of inns: the Cold Bath at Hertford, the Labour In Vain at Much Hadham, the Tom in Bedlam at Redbourn, the Rats Castle at St Albans, the Three Cranes at Turvey, the Jumps at Marston Moreteyn. The old sayings and the homely expressions of wisdom have not entirely vanished: your Hertfordshire man "stolches" through the mud; the harassed housewife of Bedfordshire claims she is "urged"; but she is "aggled" in Bucks. On the Chiltern Hills they talk of the "bud and the brown" meaning spring and autumn.

Aldbury, Little Missenden, the toy-like Old Warden, and Aynho with the peaches trained against the cottage walls, remind us that many of the old ways and things were beautiful; but the area can show imaginative modern development too, it boasts those two bold idealistic efforts, the garden cities of Welwyn and Letchworth, and much more recently the new towns of Hemel Hempstead and Stevenage.

Buckinghamshire, Bedfordshire, Huntingdonshire, Hertfordshire and Northamptonshire – in these five counties the traveller will look in vain for startling and dramatic scenic effects; but if he is looking for a quiet and gentle countryside, with a great deal of natural and man-made beauty in it, and impregnated with the continuous story of English history, he will be amply rewarded.

The South-East Midlands: Gazetteer

THERESE APPLEBY

ABBOTS LANGLEY, *Hertfordshire* (10–TL 0902). It was in this village that the only English pope was born, 800 years ago. Nicholas Breakspear by name, he became Hadrian IV. He was the son of a poor man who entered ST ALBANS monastery and left him to his own resources.

Langley House, now Breakspear Roman Catholic College, was built in commemoration of him in 1770.

The large, square vicarage, also Georgian, lies behind the church, and the manor house, gabled and cemented, is to the SW. of it.

St Lawrence's Church is of great architectural interest, with Norman arcades and a low west tower with diagonal buttresses which are of the 13th cent. as can be seen from the small lancet windows. The nave, of two bays, is short and the chancel lower than the nave. There are Perpendicular windows and the south chancel is very fine, its exterior of flint and stone mixed with brick, whereas the rest of the church is of flint with stone dressings. The chancel has interesting frescoes and the octagonal font is Perpendicular with quatrefoil embodying shields. There are many monuments of note, one in the south chapel to Dame Anne Raymond, a dignified and elegant figure; against one of the aisle walls is the semi-reclining figure of Lord Raymond, dated 1732.

Between the village and the Victorian Leavesden Mental Hospital are the Model Cottages, erected in 1896 at Prince Albert's request, in his efforts to improve the conditions of the working classes. They were first seen at the Great Exhibition in 1851 and were meant to be models for improved flats.

ALCONBURY, *Huntingdonshire* (10–TL1875). This small village has a brook on either side of it, Ellington and Alconbury, which flow into the River Ouse. Its hump-backed bridge with four arches is medieval and beside one brook is the long village green and old cottages. Manor Farm, of the 17th cent., has a handsome chimney stack with a barn standing beside it, built a century later. The manor house still retains much of its original Elizabethan timber-frame construction.

The Church of SS. Peter and Paul is Early English. The tower has a good 13th-cent. broach spire and the chancel is of the same period, with rich shafting and, on the north and south walls, high blank arcading on shafts. The clerestory has plain Y-tracery and the nave buttresses are chamfered.

To the NE. is Monks Wood, 375 acres of wood-land acquired by the Nature Conservancy in 1953. It is notable for its rare plants and insects.

ALDBURY, *Hertfordshire* (10–SP9612). This village on the edge of the Chilterns is one of the most attractive in the county. Standing on the brow of Moneybury Hill in a ridge of beeches is a massive monument to the 3rd Duke of Bridgewater, in commemoration of his pioneering of English canals. The views and scenery are of outstanding beauty.

Life in the valley below centres around the large triangular village green with a pond overlooked by the church. On the green are the old stocks and the whipping post, and, surrounding it, many thatched cottages, with the tiny 300-year-old black-beamed, yellow almshouses a little further on. The timbered manor house is of the same period, its lattice windows looking on to the pond, and there are other lovely houses to be seen.

St John the Baptist's Church has a tall, slender tower, a long, low nave and a low chancel. The oldest part of the church is the masonry in which there is a tiny 13th-cent. lancet window. The arcades of the nave have octagonal piers with moulded capitals typical of the 14th cent. The timber lectern is of the 16th cent. and the church's most impressive feature, the Pendley Chapel, is divided from the aisle and chancel by a medieval stone screen in which is a monument to Sir Robert Whittington, 1471, showing him with his wife on a tomb-chest on which are carved family shields. There are other monuments and brasses in this beautiful church.

ALDENHAM, *Hertfordshire* (6–TQ1198). This little village centres around its green and ancient church, and from the hillside are magnificent views across the Colne Valley to ST ALBANS.

Aldenham House, 2 m. SE., is a brick building of the early 18th cent., with magnificent gardens of rare trees and flowering shrubs planned by the Hon. Vicary Gibbs in the latter part of the last century. He was a banker who specialized in horticulture and did little to disturb the beauty of the house he inherited. The house is now the home of Haberdashers' Aske's public school. Another public school which originated here is Aldenham School, on a hilltop, founded in 1597 by Richard Platt, a London brewer, for "children of poore people inhabitinge the parish of Aldenham and for children of the freemen of the company of Brewers London". Its original articles laid down that neither the Master nor Usher should take

Noel Habgood

Aldbury: the manor house

part in games or visit alehouses or taverns. It has been greatly enlarged in recent years and has extensive modern buildings. On the hillside is the little pond of Hill Slough, which is said to be the place where the body of William Weare, the victim of a brutal murder, was discovered.

St John the Baptist's Church, in the village, is full of beauty and interest. It is of flint with stone dressings and is long and well-proportioned. It has a complex history, with a Norman window in the south aisle, a 14th- and 15th-cent. nave, a Tudor vestry and a 13th-cent. font. The screen between the south aisle and south chancel chapel has been much renewed. There are many brasses of interest, for they show the changes in custom throughout the centuries. The most important one is in the south chancel chapel of two ladies of the Crowmer family with identical tomb-chests, forming one composition, with canopies above the four-centred arches. In the churchyard is a pedestal with a large urn to Lt-Gen. R. Burne, showing the places where he fought all over the world.

Edge Grove, a late-18th-cent. house with a four-column Ionic porch, is N. of the church, and further N. is Wall Hall, a cemented house, castellated and turreted, with a large Gothic conservatory and in the grounds an ice house. A short distance further on is Bricket Wood Common, reached by a narrow lane in richly wooded countryside, with rare flowers and trees of many types.

ALWALTON, *Huntingdonshire* (10–TL1395), is just off the A1 with the River Nene to the N. of it. It is a pretty, peaceful village with a cottage with mullioned windows dated 1645 and, NE. of the

church, the rebuilt porch of a house originally in CHESTERTON where Dryden lived. This has a round-arched doorway, two storied Tuscan columns and a patterned gable. It dates from about 1625. Manor House, nearby, is of the same period with wooden casements and a Venetian window. Alwalton was the birthplace of H. Royce of Rolls Royce cars and his ashes are buried in the parish church.

St Andrew's is a cruciform church with a late 13th-cent. tower and a chancel of the same period which was originally vaulted in two bays. Its oldest feature externally is the south doorway which has a Norman motif. The nave has three arches on one side and four on the other, all Norman. The font has been here since the 15th cent., and the altar table, in post-Reformation style, from the 17th cent.

Lynch Farm, which is 1 m. NE. of the village, is an L-shaped building with mullioned windows, a small gable and a round corner turret.

AMERSHAM, *Buckinghamshire* (6–SU9597). This old town stretches along the A413 in the valley of the River Misbourne. At the foot of the steep Gore's Hill is Bury Farm, once the home of Guilielma Springett who became the wife of William Penn. The broad High Street is a mixture of fine old buildings of many periods with timbered and gabled cottages and inns opening on to the road.

In the middle of the road stands the Market Hall, built by Sir William Drake in 1682. It is supported by arches above an open piazza with an old twin lock-up. Nearby is the old timbered grammar school and, behind four lime trees, a group of almshouses with a cobbled courtyard.

The Martyrs' Memorial, a monument to the many religious persecutions which took place in Amersham, lies just off the main road up a short hill.

The Crown Hotel is named in records of 1620 but wall paintings are judged to be Elizabethan and in the lounge a Tudor coat of arms, with the quarterings of England and France and the lion and dragon supporters, is thought to commemorate a visit by Queen Elizabeth to Shardeloes, the 16th-cent. mansion standing in parkland about ¾ m. from the town.

The King's Arms Hotel is 16th-cent. and the old gables are still in evidence at the back of the building. The Swan Inn has gable wings with the date 1671 on a chimney. The Elephant and Castle has an interesting sign, a gabled front and an old brick chimney. In 61 High Street, believed to have been once part of an inn, are wall paintings of great antiquarian interest. One depicts Julius Caesar wearing a scarlet cloak and blue helmet, another Duke Joshua in 16th-cent. armour. King David, shown with a harp, Hector of Troy, Charlemagne and Godfrey de Bouillon adorn the walls in panels.

The village church is 14th- to 15th-cent. The roof of the nave is supported on stone corbels of angels and grotesque figures. A spacious building, it was externally renewed in 1890. The vaulted porch, north chapel and tower are all 15th-cent. and the east window has 17th-cent. painted glass of foreign provenance, with Apostles and Evangelists, added in 1760. There are many large, heavy monuments to the Drakes. John Knox preached in this church.

In the 18th-cent. rectory garden is a timbered well-house with a well which was worked, within living memory, by a horse, and watermills stand at each end of the old street.

Amersham is a growing town with an extensive parish and several newer, residential areas. The traditional furniture, bricks, and craft wood products are still manufactured but many other industries have grown up, including that at the Radio-Chemical Centre which supplies radioactive materials for hospitals and research stations.

AMPTHILL, *Bedfordshire* (10–TL0337), is slightly on a hill with fine, wooded views below and is reached by winding roads in attractive countryside. It is a well-preserved little town of historical interest, for which Henry VIII had a great love and where Catherine of Aragon stayed during the period of her divorce.

It was originally a coaching town and at its crossroads is an obelisk pump, dated 1784, with distances and directions engraved on it. Nearby is the Victorian brick Moot Hall, with shaped gables and a cupola. There are many picturesque cottages and gracious Georgian houses and in Dunstable Street is the 18th-cent. White Hart Hotel, three stories high with seven bays and a doorway with an open pediment. A little further along is the large, red-brick Victorian workhouse with an octagonal centre. The modern offices of

the Rural District Council are neo-Georgian with a cupola. Two Victorian Nonconformist chapels are in the same street, one Baptist and the other Methodist.

Avenue House, in Church Street, is probably the town's finest building and was built about 1780 for the brewer John Morris.

The Church of St Andrew's is in a small square, surrounded by pretty and gracious buildings. The Feoffee Almshouses, with a timbered front, were founded in 1690. Dynevor House, dated 1725, of chequer brick, with seven bays and a parapet, has a doorway with fluted pilasters and in the upper windows are frilly lintel bricks. Brandreth House is opposite, with curious corbels on its door-hood, and at the end of the square is the church.

It is of ironstone, rather small, with 14th-cent. arcades and chancel. Angels decorate the Perpendicular nave roof, and in the east of the south aisle is the sculptured head of a lantern cross. In the roof of the west tower is a wooden angel. On the west wall of the nave are interesting brasses and in the north aisle a fine standing monument to Richard Nicholls, 1672, with the cannon ball which killed him at Sole Bay. He became the first Governor of Long Island after fighting the Dutch in America.

In Woburn Street are thickly thatched cottages and the new Court House, a piece of simple, pleasant, modern architecture. Behind the parking space is Catherine's Cross, erected in 1773 in memory of Catherine of Aragon and bearing the arms of Castile and Aragon with verses on its base by Horace Walpole. A little further out are the Oxford Hospital Almshouses, erected by Wren and founded by John Cross of the university for old servants of OXFORD colleges. It is a handsome building of chequer brick, with three bay wings and a hipped roof. Below the pediment in the middle is a small chapel. Along a footpath off Park Hill is a very unusual pavilion added to Russett's Lodge, a 17th-cent. cottage.

Ampthill Park is now a Cheshire Home, but it originally belonged to the first Lord Ashburnham who built it in 1694 on land given to his family by Charles II. It has a hipped roof and is of blue brick with red dressings.

The remains of Houghton Conquest House – the "House Beautiful" of *The Pilgrim's Progress* – are nearby. The house is believed to have been built about 1615 by Inigo Jones, or a pupil, for Mary, Countess of Pembroke.

ASHWELL, *Hertfordshire* (10–TL2639), is a large attractive village with the River Rhee below it. There are many trees of interest but the ash is predominant.

The buildings of the village are well-preserved, mainly timber-framed or gable-bricked. Halfway along the High Street is St John's Guild Hall, a long building of the 17th cent. with closely spaced timber uprights and adjoining cottages, dated 1681, with bold rustic pargeting. Near the end of the High Street is Chantry House, opposite which is Westbury Farm, a plastered building with symmetrical gables. The Town House, which is the village museum, shows the history of Ashwell from prehistoric days to the present time, with Roman coins, straw-plaiting tools, a metal harvest horn, implements of the Stone and Bronze Ages and tools used by farmers, shepherds, blacksmiths, coach-builders and wheelwrights. It is now an Ancient Monument.

St Mary's Church is a magnificent 14th-cent. building, very light inside, with a high tower crowned by a lantern with leaded spike, in which clunch has been used as a facing material as well as elegant timber. The chancel is without aisles but has large windows; there is a screen in the Lady Chapel with 15th-cent. tracery, and the pulpit, dated 1627, has panels of diamond-cut pieces. The tower has two interesting *graffiti*, one inscription in Latin saying "Miserable, wild and distracted, the dregs of the people alone survive to witness . . .", a reference to the Black Death in England which killed one man in three. The lych-gate at the entrance to the church is of the 15th cent.

ASPLEY GUISE, *Bedfordshire* (10–SP9337), is an old village lying below pine woods which cover the sandy hills. It centres around the cross-roads and has holly hedges 30 ft high and bracken growing out of the sand.

Aspley House is of chequer brick, two stories high with seven bays. It is dated 1695 and its door-way has an open pediment with cherubs' heads on corbels. The garden side of the house, added 50 years later, has two doorways with Doric pilasters and, in the middle bay, Venetian windows.

Guise House is early 18th-cent. with five-bayed front, and its doorway has a hood on carved brackets. The oldest house in the village is Old House, about 1575, a timber-framed building with good panelling.

St Botolph's Church, which is of ironstone, is externally almost completely Victorian, but the tower is Perpendicular and the north aisle and nave are also old. The font is drum-shaped and the screen Perpendicular. There is a brass to a priest, *c.* 1410, showing him kneeling with John the Baptist, and one to a knight, *c.* 1500.

AYLESBURY, *Buckinghamshire* (10–SP8213). Built on a hill in the heart of Buckinghamshire, at the junction of six main roads, this ancient town gives its name to the broad vale which it overlooks, stretching from the borders of Bed-fordshire to those of Oxfordshire, a rich pasture-land with many dairy farms.

Despite the modern industries and new build-ings which it now contains – the County Council offices are a fine symbol of modern architecture – this busy county town with its narrow meandering streets is still a place of great historic interest.

In the cobbled Market Square, once the cattle market and now a car park, stands a Victorian clock-tower and three massive monuments: to John Hampden, at the top of the slope; Disraeli; and at the end of the square, Lord Chesham. John Hampden, the great parliamentarian whose home was nearby, is renowned for his stand against King Charles I in 1635 when he refused to pay Ship Money, since he believed the tax was for the King's own pocket and not for the Navy. Al-though he lost the suit against him, the judgment was eventually cancelled and his protest in the name of freedom had been made.

Reached through arches under the Victorian Town Hall at the foot of the square is the Cattle Market which is still in use today and where farmers from miles around hold sales of cattle, sheep and pigs.

A noteworthy inn stands in the square, the King's Head which has been given to the National Trust. Dating from the 15th cent. and once a monastery guesthouse, it is entered through a medieval gateway to a cobbled courtyard. The lounge has a magnificent leaded window with the arms of Henry VI and his Queen, Margaret of Anjou, and those of Prince Edward who died at the Battle of TEWKESBURY. "Cromwell's Chair" rests in a corner of the lounge for it is here he is believed to have stayed on his journey back to Worcester. In the Civil War the town was a base for both the King and Parliament, according to the way the battle went. Holman's Bridge, on the BUCKINGHAM road, was the site of a crushing defeat for Prince Rupert and his Royalists. In one of the little alleys on the west side of the square will be found the Dark Lantern Inn.

The County Museum in Church Street, housed in a delightful Georgian building, has much of interest and is open to the public. One section of it tells the history of the county from prehistoric times. There is a splendid art gallery. Louis XVIII dwelt at Hartwell House, near Aylesbury, for five years of his exile and in the museum are many things used by him including a bed and confes-sional chair. The 15th-cent. roof of the museum was only discovered a few years ago.

Down Parson's Fee, a cobbled lane, will be found Prebendal House, an 18th-cent. building, now a girls' school, which was formerly the house of John Wilkes, the satirist and Member of Parlia-ment for Aylesbury until he was expelled for insolence and libel. There are many 17th-cent. houses as well as old almshouses to be found.

Away from the bustle of the town is St Mary's Square, old terraced houses lining three of its sides, with the Parish Church of St Mary beyond the churchyard on the fourth side. Substantially 13th-cent., it is a large, handsome, cruciform building. Considerably restored by Sir Gilbert Scott in 1848, it still holds many of its former features. The 13th-cent. tower, on which rests a lead clock-tower and spire added in the 17th cent., is impressive. The font, late 12th-cent., is bor-dered with foliage and fluting, its cup-shaped bowl resting on a square base. From this font came the style known as the "Aylesbury Font" of which other examples are to be seen in the county.

An exquisite alabaster monument to Lady Lee of Quarrendon is of the Elizabethan period, show-ing Lady Lee with her three children and an inscription pleading that red flowers should always be left by her tomb, a request that is still observed.

F. Jewell-Harrison

Aylesbury: the County Council Offices and Library

With the Grand Union Canal adjoining it, Aylesbury is becoming a cruising centre and at the canal basin cabin cruisers may be hired to explore the beautiful, unspoilt scenery.

One of the town's great claims to fame was its ducks which were exported all over the world. Although they are still bred, the output has considerably declined since the war.

A house which can sometimes be visited is **Nether Winchenden House**, 6 m. SW. of Aylesbury. A Tudor manor with 18th-cent. additions, it was once the home of Sir Francis Bernard, the last Governor of New Jersey and Massachusetts in 1761. Formerly the property of Notley Abbey it then housed the monks who served in the churches and worked on the farms. The riverside grounds of the house are attractive.

Also for public viewing is **Wotton House** in Wotton Underwood, built in 1704 on the same plan as Buckingham House, which later became Buckingham Palace. Its park contains a lake and was laid out by Capability Brown.

AYNHO, *Northamptonshire* (10–SP5133). This is the county's southernmost village and one of its most attractive. It stands on the top of a hill from which can be seen the beautiful countryside of

Northamptonshire and Oxfordshire. The wide road running through it twists and turns on its way to London or BANBURY.

On the Banbury side is **Aynhoe Park**, a 17th-cent. mansion open to the public, which was the residence of the Cartwright family for nearly 350 years. It now belongs to the National Trust.

During the Civil War the house was burned by the Royalists, for the family were Cromwellians, but it was rebuilt shortly afterwards.

On many of the ancient stone cottages, which line the roadside with their pretty unfenced gardens, are climbing apricot trees, which provided the fruit with which the cottagers used to pay the Lord of the Manor's toll.

The Church of St Michael is reached by a no-through road leading to the village square, where stand its few shops and a row of thatched cottages. The church has a rich 15th-cent. tower but the body of it was altered in 1723. The simple interior has a gallery, box-pews and a Georgian pulpit, as well as an old carved wooden chair showing the Baptism. The majority of the monuments are to the Cartwrights, the best of them being a Victorian marble cross to Lady Elizabeth of Newbottle Manor.

The Rectory is 17th-cent., as is the Old Grammar School, now a private house. Although some new buildings have been added to the village, they are all in keeping with its character and are of light stone, similar to the older buildings.

AYOT ST LAWRENCE, *Hertfordshire* (10–TL1916). This is a picturesque, rural village with black-and-white timbered cottages and buildings of several centuries. It is reached through Priors Wood and a wooded dell.

George Bernard Shaw, the playwright, lived here for 44 years until his death in 1950, and his house, Shaw's Corner, a late Victorian building now National Trust property, is open to the public. His ashes were scattered in the garden.

In the village are the ruins of the old church, partly demolished by Sir Lionel Lyte until the bishop prevented further destruction. The new St Lawrence's Church, designed in 1778–9 by Nicholas Revett, is externally of Grecian style, while internally it has the classicism of Rome. It has a Greek temple portico with fluted columns. A columned screen separates the rectangular nave from the vestibule. The nave, flanked by two arched recesses, has a coffered ceiling.

Ayot House, of Georgian origin, was the seat of Sir Lionel Lyte. Its main front has three stories with the middle of the five bays slightly projected. Bride Hall, 1 m. S. of the church, is a Jacobean manor house, still retaining, in the hall, its original fireplace and ceiling beams.

Silk for royal vestments is produced at Lady Hart Dyke's Lullington Silk Farm, open to the public in the summer months.

BALDOCK, *Hertfordshire* (10–TL2434). is centred on four main streets which meet and form a cross, and was probably a coaching town in former days. Its architecture is mainly Georgian with little of earlier periods. Its main street is lined with trees and grass banks. At Quickswood Farm is a clock which has told the time since the reign of Charles I. The Wynne's Almshouses, dated 1621, are one-storied brick buildings, with a raised gateway in the wall which separates them from the street.

Simpson's Brewery, in the same street, is Georgian with a chequer-brick house. The brewery has seven bays and a centre of yellow brick. The Bull's Head, at the far end of Church Street, has close vertical timbers.

By the crossroads are the late Victorian Fire Station Buildings, of red brick with a tower on one corner.

St Mary's Church is spacious. Most of the interior is early 14th-cent. with 15th-cent. screens and roofs. It is mostly of flint, although the lower part of the chancel is in stone. There is a double piscina, part of which is 13th-cent., and a turret in the north-west section. The octagonal font, on nine shafts, is 13th-cent. and there are many early monuments.

BARLEY, *Hertfordshire* (10–TL4038). At the entrance to this village are pretty overhanging cottages and, at the top of the hill, a 300-year-old inn, the Fox and Hounds; its sign spans the road.

Town House, an original Tudor building with great oak beams, has a jutting-out porch at each end with an exterior staircase to the upper floor, which is one long room, once used "for the keeping of maides' marriages". The rooms on the ground floor were originally almshouses.

At Shaftenhoe End is the Big House, the doorways of which have hoods on carved brackets. The upper story projects on the south porch, dated 1624, and there is a large outer chimney and diagonal chimney stacks.

The foundations of St Margaret's Church were laid in Norman times but only the tower, a deep splayed ground-floor window and the round-headed upper windows are original. Most of the rest of the church is Victorian, although the screen is 15th-cent. The date of the pulpit, with its fine back and tester, is 1626. A brass of Andrew Willett, rector here for 23 years, shows him praying. Two other vicars of Barley became archbishops of Canterbury and one of them crowned Henry VIII.

BARNACK, *Huntingdonshire* (10–TF0705), is a village famous for its stone from which PETERBOROUGH Cathedral, and many other abbeys, churches and houses, were built. The quarries were used from Roman times until the 18th cent. when they were exhausted and large mounds and hollows, known as the Hills and the Holes, mark their site.

There are many interesting houses in the village. Kingsley House, the former rectory, incorporates the remains of a medieval house, and Littlefield has a canted bay window, a small arched Anglo-Saxon window and a 13th-cent. fragment. In Millstone Lane are the 15th-cent. Feoffee Cottages with arched doorways, cross-

slit windows and a traceried gable-end. There are several other attractive cottages and a derelict windmill.

St John the Baptist Church is of several periods. It has an Anglo-Saxon tower of two stages with long-and-short Saxon work and narrow stone pilaster strips. An octagonal belfry and spire were added in the 13th cent., and there are two large bell openings. The large, beautifully moulded nave arcades date from 1180 and 1220. The chancel is about 1300 and its east window has fine tracery. The Walcot Chapel is Perpendicular with richly decorated battlements and parapets. There is a late Anglo-Saxon sculpture of Christ in Majesty, and many interesting monuments.

Walcot Hall, ¾ m. SE. of the village, is a fine 17th-cent. house with a hipped roof and four square chimneys. It has a delightful garden with large trees, and in it are two temples and a rotunda.

BARNWELL, *Northamptonshire* (10–TL0485), was originally two villages with separate churches. Now the two villages have grown into one; joined by an old bridge and three fords that cross the stream running through it.

The original Barnwell Castle was built by Berengar le Moine in 1266. Its remains consist of a quadrangular court with towers at each corner and a large gateway flanked by two towers. It stands in the grounds of what is now called Barnwell Castle, an Elizabethan manor, the home of the Duke of Gloucester, and is open to the public once a year.

There are pretty stone cottages on either side of the stream, and almshouses founded by Nicholas Latham, a Jacobean benefactor who was for 51 years parson of the Church of St Andrew's which contains a bust of him. This church has a lovely spire rising from the 13th-cent. tower with its west doorway, circular window and belfry lights. Although the chancel is the oldest part of the church it has a large 15th-cent. east window. Both the altars in the east walls are ancient and the oak pulpit is Jacobean.

All that remains of the other church, All Saints, which is some distance along the stream, is the chancel with its large 15th-cent. windows. The church is filled with the memorials of the Montagus, who originally owned the present Barnwell Castle; one of special interest is a rather sad figure of a little boy who was drowned aged three, in 1625. He stands under a canopy in a gown of red and gold with ten painted shields above him and a shield and eagle beneath. Part of the inscription describes him as "a witty and hopeful child".

BEACONSFIELD, *Buckinghamshire* (6–SU 9490). The old town of Beaconsfield is separated from the new by over a quarter of a mile of wooded country. It is developed around what must have been two main highways, from London to OXFORD and from WINDSOR to AYLESBURY. There are coaching inns on opposite corners of the cross-roads.

Along the roads centred by a green are houses of the Queen Anne and Georgian periods. The main inns where the coaches halted in the 18th cent. are the Royal Saracen's Head, a large building of half-timbered construction, and the Royal White Hart at which Queen Elizabeth I stayed and where Oliver Cromwell stationed his troops in the grounds.

The old town retains much of the charm of former days with the buildings standing back from the roadside, allowing ample parking space.

The Old Rectory, overlooking the churchyard, is of the 16th cent., half-timbered with a panelled room and spiral staircase, and is now the parish meeting place. Edmund Burke, the great parliamentarian, lived in this village and was buried here in 1797, and G. K. Chesterton was resident here for many years.

Hall Barn House, a 17th-cent. brick mansion, is S. of the main road. It is ornately decorated and has stone pilasters and a garden filled with obelisks and temples.

St Mary's Church, on the corner of the crossroads, is of medieval origin, although mainly rebuilt in the last century. It has a fine flint tower rising above the trees, and between the chapel and the chancel is a section of a 15th-cent. screen. There are many monuments of interest and an exquisite tapestry. Of note is an iron-bound chest covered in paintings of ships by a quayside. Opposite the church is a Victorian building in which the police station is housed.

The new town of Beaconsfield, which began to form in 1909, is a pleasant residential area. Of particular interest is Bekonscot Miniature Village in Warwick Road, laid out with tiny cottages, farms and meadows, churches, a railway, a lake, streams and an airport. The village is modelled on the scale of 1 in. to 1 ft, and is a children's paradise.

Close by are the Chiltern beechwoods at **Coleshill** and just E. of the town is the golf course, adjacent to **Wilton Park**, a historic estate, from which can be seen the beauty of the countryside around.

BEDFORD, *Bedfordshire* (10–TL0449). This is the county town and, although a centre of industry, it has a great deal of interest both in its buildings and in the history connected with it. It has been a trading place for nearly 1,000 years and its position on the River Ouse, which divides the town in two, has added to its prosperity, as many of its manufactured agricultural implements are transported by barges. Its main industries now, however, are engineering and metallics.

The River Ouse has also given the town much of beauty, for around it has grown the Embankment, a fine street with public gardens on either side of the river. There are two bridges of note: one is Georgian, designed by Wing, with five segmental arches and stone balustrades; and the other, a suspension bridge for pedestrians only, is late Victorian.

Among the many old inns, the most notable is the Swan Hotel, at the northern end of the stone bridge. Built in 1794 for the Duke of Bedford, it is a gracious building, with a staircase believed to have been designed by Wren, with twisted balusters and a string, and taken from the dismantled Houghton Conquest House at AMPTHILL. Opposite the Swan Hotel on the south bank of the Ouse stands the tower block of the County Hotel.

The town's centre is St Paul's Square and the High Street, with the massive Church of St Paul, considerably restored in the last two centuries. The doorway of the church is Early English, but much of the rest seems to be 14th- and 15th-cent. with embattled clerestory and aisles and, on the upper floor, statue niches. Most of the interior was also restored in Victorian days but its most interesting feature is that the aisles are the same height as the nave with clerestory windows. The font has a decorated base and the ornate pulpit is 16th-cent. The rood-screen is by Bodley. Monuments of particular interest include one to the S. of the altar to Simon de Beauchamp, 1208, and to Sir William Harpur and his wife.

Bedford has always been one of the foremost centres for education, due mainly to Sir William Harpur, who eventually became Lord Mayor of London. Born in Bedford in 1496, he purchased land in London for a nominal sum and from the profits which accrued built the Bedford Grammar School. Just over 200 years later the value of the property had increased to £30,000 and the trust which administered it founded other schools, until, in 1866, 1,860 children were being educated from it. Part of a school house, built in 1756, is now the Town Hall, with Sir William's statue in the doorway. It is ashlar-faced and part of it was added in 1859. Behind the Town Hall are the new municipal offices, seven floors high.

The present Bedford School in De Parys Avenue is late Victorian, Gothic-styled with a turret, and in Harpur Street is Bedford Modern School. The 19th-cent. Public Library has a Greek Doric temple front. Bedford High School for Girls, of the same period, is one of the finest of the school buildings. In Tudor style, with giant pilasters in the centre, its corners have attractive half-domed bow-windows.

In Dame Alice Street is a long range of late Georgian, dark red-bricked almshouses (one range was demolished in 1968) and in the High Street is the Lion Hotel, of about the same time, stuccoed with large pilasters and first-floor balconies.

In Mill Street are buildings commemorating two of the town's most famous people, John Howard and John Bunyan. The stuccoed Congregational chapel is in memory of John Howard, born 1726, who spent his youth at CARDINGTON, travelled the world widely and became High Sheriff of Bedfordshire. He learnt of the appalling conditions in Bedford prisons, which were due mainly to the fact that the gaoler was not paid a fixed wage but extorted money from prisoners before allowing them to go free. Howard's discoveries and complaints led to two bills being passed in the House of Commons reforming goals. A statue of John Howard stands in St Paul's Square.

Bunyan Meeting House with its fine bronze doors commemorates the man who, born a tinker, was a Cromwellian soldier and eventually acquired deep religious convictions, preaching all over the country. At the time of the Restoration, this was illegal for one not ordained, and as a result he spent many years in prison, where it is believed he wrote *Pilgrim's Progress* and other notable works. The Bunyan Museum, adjoining the Meeting House, is filled with articles of interest, including his iron fiddle and other musical instruments, and the Public Library has a valuable Bunyan collection. A statue of him stands on St Peter's Green and the town has several plaques to his memory, including one on the County Gaol. In the surrounding countryside people still refer proudly to the fact that it is "Bunyan country".

In Kempston Road are the Victorian Britannia Ironworks, fine buildings with an interesting gateway.

Facing the river, close by Market Square, which has open markets twice a week, is Shire Hall, a late Victorian building of red brick and terracotta, with a Gothic porch and Elizabethan windows. Across the river is the new County Hall complex with council chamber, library and record office. Nearby is the Corn Exchange with an attic upon which are four massive chimneys. The mid-Georgian prison, with three pavilions and an archway in the middle, was designed by Wing and has been twice extended. The north wing of the Bedford General Hospital, in Kimbolton Road, incorporates the former 18th-cent. workhouse and has a hipped roof and an 11-bay brick front.

There are numerous medieval, Victorian and modern churches, St Peter's being the largest. St Merton de Merton shows evidence of Anglo-Saxon workmanship. It has a central Norman tower with twin bell-openings, and a Norman south doorway. The present chancel was the nave of the Anglo-Saxon church. The octagonal font is large with quatrefoils and motifs. St Mary's Church, in St Mary's Square, is also partly Norman, with a crossing tower containing large twin bell-openings. It has a simple but charming plaster and whitewash interior with plain Georgian benches and a sculptured Norman head.

The Cecil Higgins Art Gallery has a superb collection of paintings and prints, sculpture, including works by Epstein and Henry Moore, 18th-cent. furniture and old lace and embroidery. There is also a fine collection of English and Continental porcelain.

Bedford Museum tells the county's history, with Iron Age and Roman archaeological finds, works from Anglo-Saxon times, local animals and birds, and specimens of lace-making and straw-plaiting.

BENINGTON, *Hertfordshire* (10–TL3023). This enchanting village, slightly modernized on the outskirts, is reached through a wooded country lane winding upwards to the village green, with a pond overhung by willows. By the green are picturesque 16th-cent. cottages of timber and plaster and the old Bell Inn.

St Peter's Church, a simple village church of the 13th to 15th cents., has a lovely north chancel chapel, with flowing tracery in the windows and under one of its two arches a monument with two fine portraits of a knight and his lady. The workmanship is early 14th-cent. The chancel has much-restored sedilia decorated with crocket capitals. The octagonal font is 15th-cent. and the benches are of the same period.

The 17th-cent. Old Rectory has altered during the years but of particular interest are the windows in the gables. The Lordship is a Georgian house, converted to match the remains of the keep of Benington Castle, hiding behind the church. The kings of Mercia lived in the castle, and on the hill Berthulf is said to have held a council in A.D. 850.

BERKHAMSTED, *Hertfordshire* (10–SP 9907). This small town, of ancient origin, was the birthplace of William Cowper the hymn-writer and has much to interest the visitor, with its old churches, inns and other buildings. The rolling countryside adjoining it is attractive and the 1,200-acre common, with its beech and birch trees, gorse and bracken, is pleasant to walk and picnic in.

The town is set on a hill-top and although little remains today of its castle, except the motte and bailey and a unique double moat, it was once one of the most important castles in the country. William the Conqueror made a gift of it to his half-brother, Robert of Mortain, and Thomas à Becket spent 10 years there during his period as Chancellor. Besieged by King Louis of France in 1216, it eventually became an appendage of the Dukes of Cornwall. In 1376 the Black Prince spent the last days of his life there. Earthworks in the grounds are impressive and it is open to the public.

St Peter's Church is a large, handsome, cruciform building of flint with the outstanding feature of a blue and gold clock on a timber belfry. Five periods can be distinguished in the building, although it was heavily restored in 1871. Of 13th-cent. origin, it retains its original chancel, nave, transepts and central tower. It was added to during the centuries, and of particular interest are St Catherine's Chapel, of the 14th cent., its porch which was added later, St John the Baptist's Chapel and the 15th-cent. clerestory in the nave. The top story of the 13th-cent. tower was added 400 years ago. The screen in the west tower arch is of the 15th cent. and is adorned with many figures of importance. A carved chest is 300 years old and the pulpit, decorated with angels, is of 19th-cent. origin. The church contains many fine monuments and a medieval coffin with a floral cross. There are numerous brasses of interest.

The High Street, centred around the church, runs parallel with the River Bulbourne. Court House, a 16th-cent. timbered building with a projecting upper story, is SW. of the church and nearby, S. of the church, is Berkhamsted's finest building, Incent's House, also of the 16th cent. Half-timbered, with an overhanging upper story, it has been carefully restored in recent years. It is believed to have been the residence of John Incent, Dean of St Paul's, who founded Berkhamsted Grammar School in the 17th cent. The school, to the N. of the churchyard, its red brickwork mellowed with the years, has stone mullioned windows and a fine timber entrance. Its chapel has an altar reached from the nave by 19 steps.

The town has four inns of importance. There is the red-bricked King's Arms, with three bay windows on the first floor, and, by the War Memorial in the narrow part of the High Street, is the plastered and gabled Bell Inn. Swan Inn, of the 17th cent., has two gables, and near it are 18th-cent. houses with quoins and dressings. The Red House Hotel, also of the 18th cent., is ornate; its handsome porch of seven bays and Ionic columns and pediments has a large Venetian window above.

Also in the High Street are the Friends' Meeting House, dated 1818, and the Victorian Baptist church, a building of red and yellow brick, typical of its period.

The gabled Elizabethan house, Berkhamsted Place, the remains of a courtyard house built about 1580 and twice altered in the following century, has a central hall and entrance, an original oriel window and large fireplace, the latter altered in the 17th cent. On the first floor is an interesting ceiling. On the north-west side of the building the stone and flint chequer design is of the 16th cent.

The Sayer Almshouses, 1684, a row of six brick houses of one story centred by a large pediment, are close by Boxwell House, which was built in the early 18th cent. with three wide bays and a cemented front decorated with quoins.

One m. S. of Berkhamsted is Ashlyns, a large house built on the top of a slope in about 1800, with a charming bow-front centre and an iron veranda.

BIGGLESWADE, *Bedfordshire* (10–TL1944), is on the River Ivel and it is the river which gave the town its past prosperity, for within the memory of some of its oldest inhabitants the Ivel was navigable from the sea to just W. of the town. When the Romans built a major road, they made a ford over the river here and this ford formed the basis of what is now the town itself. The bridge which spans the river has three pointed arches and is of the 14th cent. Two great flour mills stand on the river's bank.

It has for long been a busy market-gardening area and recently light engineering has become its second largest industry. Market Place is the centre of the town, where a general market is held each week. The Old Market House is timber-framed with a timber roof, and the former Victorian Town Hall has a five-bayed stuccoed front with massive Roman Doric columns. The White Hart Inn is also timber-framed and the late-18th-cent. Crown Hotel has pleasant Art Nouveau lettering.

In London Road is the Limes, the former workhouse, of yellow brick with an octagonal centre and wings, dated 1835.

Berkhamsted is situated on the Grand Union Canal on its route from London to Birmingham

Raymond Lea/Spectrum

St Andrew's Church is large and, although externally renewed, is mainly Perpendicular. The tower is 18th-cent. and has round-arched bell-openings. Towards the nave is a high tower arch of the 14th cent. The font has a Perpendicular shaft, and the 15th-cent. south door a full traceried head. There is a brass to William Halsted and his wife dated 1449.

In St John's Street is the church of the same name, a yellow-brick, Victorian building with red-brick decoration. On the east gable of the nave is a big bellcot and there are several long lancets.

To the S. of the town, on the HITCHIN road, is a windmill, and to the N., Shorthand House, of yellow brick with a large Tuscan porch, built in the 18th cent.

BISHOP'S STORTFORD, Hertfordshire
(11–TL4821). This hilly town, although greatly modernized, is of medieval origin with numerous old buildings and many of the Victorian era.

The George Hotel, at the corner of High Street and North Street, is two-storied and pargeted in the old part, with an early Victorian addition of three stories. In Bridge Street is the 16th-cent. Black Lion, a picturesque building, with exposed timbers, gables and an overhanging upper story. Nearby is the equally attractive Boar's Head, and across the bridge over the River Stort are the ruins of Waytemore Castle, with a narrow 40-ft-high mount. At the top of a hill is the 17th-cent. Cock Inn and in the same street are handsome 17th-cent. houses and one which is late Georgian. Hockerill Training College, of red brick, is Victorian with diaper work with stone edgings.

The Corn Exchange, in the Victorian part of the town, was built in 1828 in a neo-Grecian style. The ground floor has Tuscan piers and in its upper floors is a giant Ionic portico. Bishop's Stortford College is in the Gothic style with a memorial hall of the present century which is elegantly neo-Georgian.

The Congregational church in Water Lane is an elongated building of stock-brick with two towers and Italian-style edgings.

Windmill Hill has houses and cottages of several centuries with a 17th-cent. malthouse and granary attached to one group of cottages. Down Northgate End, amid large suburban houses and old cottages, is Brooke House, a fine building of white brick in three stories with lower wings and a Roman Doric doorcase.

Bishop's Stortford was the birthplace of Cecil Rhodes in the Old Vicarage, which is now a museum, are preserved many of his possessions. These include the bed in which he was born, his bible, a watercolour he painted and his ceremonial uniforms.

There are two churches of interest. All Saints in Hockerill is of modern origin and overlooks the town, its large square tower supported by a hipped roof and with long, lancet windows. St Michael's is a large 15th-cent. church with a tall, prominent spire added to the tower in 1812. The only other later additions are the tall south

vestry and the north chancel chapel, both 19th-cent. The chancel stalls have poppy heads in the front seats and misericords in the back. The large screen is richly carved with two tall four-light sections on each side of the entrance. The square 12th-cent. font is of Purbeck marble.

Wickham Hall, 1¾ m. NW. of the town, and Stortford Park, 1½ m. W., are particularly handsome farm-houses.

BLEDLOW RIDGE, Buckinghamshire
(6–SU 7898). One of the finest beauty-spots in the county, Bledlow Ridge is reached by a steep hill with a road running across it. It is part of the Chilterns, with the village of its name deep in the valley below. The historic **Icknield Way** runs at its foot and the woods are thick with trees of many varieties: beeches and cherries, yellow limes and bronzed hornbeams. The green fields below have indents of white showing the chalk beneath the soil. To the W. of the ridge top lie the long, uneven lines of the hedgerows. Down the curving road, lined with yew trees and elms, is Wain Hill, on which, with the turf cut away and the white chalk beneath revealing the shape, is a great Greek cross, one of the only two turf-cut crosses in the county.

BLETSOE, Bedfordshire
(10–TL0258). Set back from the main road, this little village has the remains of what was once a castle. It is now a farm-house, with à long Elizabethan front and a Jacobean staircase. Henry VII's mother, the Lady Margaret, was born here and it was visited by Queen Elizabeth I.

St Mary's Church, down a small turning off the main road, is mostly 14th-cent. with a 13th-cent. doorway and some Victorian restoration. The nave has traceried windows and the Perpendicular font is of octagonal shape with arched panels. In the north transept is a large alabaster monument to Sir John St John, 1559, with his family. That to Frances, Countess Bolingbroke, 1678, is a fine tablet with two urns.

The old Falcon Inn, by the river, was a favourite haunt of Edward FitzGerald, the translator of *The Rubaiyat of Omar Khayyam*, and his friend Thackeray.

BOUGHTON, Northamptonshire
(10–SP7565), is a tiny, attractive village, on the outskirts of which are some prosperous houses. It has picturesque cottages, some of ironstone and some thatched. For 500 years a village fair was held on the green, which lies beside the ruins of the old church. In the village is the Church of St John, with a battlemented 15th-cent. tower. It has a simple interior, without aisles, and its nave and chancel have been rebuilt.

Boughton Park, nearby, with falconry towers which were used when hawking was fashionable, was rebuilt in Tudor style in 1844. The lodges and follies surrounding it, however, are Georgian.

BRACKLEY, Northamptonshire
(10–SP5837). Negotiations on the Magna Carta took place at

Brackley Castle (no longer in existence) in 1215. It is a charming, residential town which was once a large wool centre. Its wide main street, over a mile long, is flanked by trees and there are good parking facilities. It is dominated by the 18th-cent. Town Hall which was built by the Duke of Bridgewater and has high roofs and a cupola. The streets running off the main one are very narrow, with old cottages. The oldest building is the Hospital of St James and St John, a monastery that became a school at the time of the Dissolution and it is still used for the same purpose. It is known as Magdalen College School, because in the 15th cent. the OXFORD college of that name purchased it and when the Plague raged its Fellows took refuge there. It has one of the oldest school chapels in the country, for although greatly restored it still retains many original features, with a Norman doorway and Norman font and a 13th-cent. tower.

Nearby is the manor house, also a school, with the old manor cottage adjoining it. There are several old inns, one of interest being the Plough, with its circular brick wall and large archway leading to what were once the stables. The Fire Station is Victorian and the long row of old almshouses has recently been modernized. On the outskirts are modern buildings and industries as well as the Brackley Saw Mills.

St Peter's Church is behind the main street. It has a 13th-cent. tower, the west front of which is enriched by arcades and corbels and a tiny lancet window. It has a Norman south doorway and has been much restored, but the spacious crypt has 700-year-old vaulting and over the west door are worn statues of St Peter and St Hugh. The windows are very fine and there are several monuments.

The National Trust Park covers three acres, a public park as well as a children's playground. From it can be seen fine views of the Ouse Valley.

BRADENHAM, *Buckinghamshire* (6–SU8297). This village, among wooded hillsides NW. of HIGH WYCOMBE, was the home of one of Britain's most renowned prime ministers, Benjamin Disraeli. He lived at Bradenham Manor with his father, Isaac Disraeli, who was a writer of repute and whose works include *Curiosities of Literature*.

Queen Elizabeth I was entertained at the manor during one of her many travels. The churchyard in which Isaac Disraeli is buried lies on one side of the house and the other side overlooks the large green which is now the village cricket ground. Around the green stand old cottages.

St Botolph's Church, by the side of the manor, has a 15th-cent. tower with a pyramid roof holding two of England's oldest bells. The nave and the doorway were both built about 1100; the latter has a modern porch. The richly carved lintel and pillars hold a simple tympanum within which is the figure of St Botolph adorned with flying swans and a model of a church. Almost overpowering the small building is a massive wall monument to Charles West, with life-sized 17th-cent. figures and a cherub's head at each

corner of the tomb. The modern rood-loft, with its attractive screen, stretches from wall to wall.

BRAMPTON, *Huntingdonshire* (10–TL2170), is on the loop of the River Ouse, with Alconbury Brook on its north side, over which stretches Nuns Bridge. New houses have been built here recently, but it still retains its village green, on which stands an 18th-cent. obelisk, a signpost for HUNTINGDON and London.

There are many picturesque old cottages and an ancient watermill, as well as the Black Bull Inn which is 300 years old. Samuel Pepys spent much of his time in Pepys House, a farm-house on the Huntingdon road. Brampton Park and the manor house have both been rebuilt.

St Mary's Church is mostly Perpendicular, but the chancel and the piscina are both late 13th-cent. The tower, with the date 1635 over the door, appears to be Decorated. The octagonal font has pointed quatrefoils and the Decorated rood-screen, with its one-light divisions, has doors with ogee arches. Three medieval stalls have finely carved *misereres* and the altar rails are 17th-cent. There are several monuments, one of particular interest, dated 1689, is to Mrs Jackson, sister of Pepys and the last member of the family to live in the parish.

BRILL, *Buckinghamshire* (10–SP6513), is one of the county's loveliest villages, reached by a climb of 600 ft. It commands magnificent views both of the Vale of Aylesbury and into Oxfordshire. The 17th-cent. red-brick windmill on the hill has been restored by the National Trust. One of its beams is carved with figures and letters.

The cottages and almshouses of this interesting village are set around two delightful greens. A royal palace existed here in Anglo-Saxon and Norman times. In 1664 it was the winter quarters for Oliver Cromwell's troops. There is a timber-framed Tudor manor house with red-brick gateposts.

The 12th-cent. parish church has been added to in later years. The low 15th-cent. tower has a small lead spire. Entered by two narrow Norman doorways, it has a Norman window above the pointed tower arch. The Jacobean chancel roof with its ornamental arches resting on a tie-beam and its five-pierced central arch is of special interest. The chancel and the font are both 14th-cent.

A short distance away, reached through a wooded valley down a steep hill, is Boarstall Tower belonging to the National Trust. The gateway to Boarstall House, it is now all that remains of this once massive building. It has a moat spanned by an 18th-cent. bridge.

During the Civil War this area formed the dividing line between the King at OXFORD and Cromwell at AYLESBURY and was held first by one side and then by the other until after two years the King surrendered.

BRIXWORTH, *Northamptonshire* (10–SP74 70), is situated about 6 m. N. of NORTHAMPTON and has one of the most remarkable structures in the county: the Church of All Saints, which was built about the 7th cent. by the monks of PETER-BOROUGH, when the district had only just been converted to Christianity. Most of the exterior is of stone rubble but the abaci and the arches have Roman tiles. In the 10th or early 11th cent. part of the present sanctuary and the circular staircase turret were added and the two-storied porch transformed into a tower, the top of which together with the spire, is medieval. In the tower is an upper chamber, reached by the staircase, with a window looking into the nave. The apse was restored on its old foundation in the mid-19th cent. Built into the side of the south doorway is an Anglo-Saxon carving of an eagle. The 17th-cent. south chapel is separated from the choir by 13th-cent. arches, in one of which is a 15th-cent. screen. The font is medieval, with a small bowl on a tall round shaft. In a recess in the south chapel is the 13th-cent. tomb of Sir John de Verdun, on which he lies in chain mail and a surcoat. Around the church, outside the apse, is the ambulatory or sunken passage, entered from the inside, for pilgrims viewing relics housed in recesses in the outer walls.

The church stands back from the village, in which there are old stone houses and an early 19th-cent. Methodist chapel. There is also part of the 14th-cent. market cross. Brixworth and the surrounding district have been a centre for hunting for as long as can be recalled and the Pytchley Hunt kennels are good neo-Georgian buildings.

BROMHAM, *Bedfordshire* (10–TL0051). One of the features of this residential village is its bridge with 26 archways which crosses the River Ouse. Although restored in the last century, it dates back to the 13th cent.

Charles I stayed at Bromham Hall, which was the home of Sir Lewis Dyve, a Royalist, who escaped during the Civil War by swimming the River Ouse. The house has a large 14th-cent. doorway.

St Owen's Church, set high in parklands with views of the valley below, appears to be originally 13th-cent. The interior of the church is of varying periods and has a high stair-turret attached to the tower, an octagonal Perpendicular font with tracery, a lectern with poppyheads and an hour-glass stand. Interesting monuments include a brass with 4-ft-long figures of Thomas Wideville and his two wives, 1435, and an alabaster five-poster with the reclining figure of Sir Lewis Dyve on a half-rolled-up mat, dated 1603. An early Victorian monument to twelve-year-old Eva Trevor shows her floating to heaven.

BROUGHTON, *Huntingdonshire* (10–TL 2878), nestles in a deep, secluded valley among delightful scenery, with only the top of the church spire indicating its existence. It was originally the chief administrative headquarters of the Abbots of RAMSEY, but only a moat marks the site of the mansion.

On the village green is an oblong-shaped brick lock-up of the 19th cent., and there are several

outstanding Jacobean and Georgian farm-houses and a 17th-cent. house, SW. of the church, with a square porch, shaped end-gables and a frill cut into the bricks of the doorway.

Most of the Church of All Saints is Perpendicular, with its stone tower and broach spire. The chancel, with its double piscina, however, is Early English and the south doorways of the nave about 1300. The square font is Norman and has blank arcading, and the communion rail is 18th-cent. There are several paintings, including Doom, over the chancel arch, which is 15th-cent., and Expulsion, with Adam delving and Eve spinning. Only part of a brass to Laurence Marton and his wife, about 1490, is preserved.

BUCKDEN, *Huntingdonshire* (10–TL1967. This pretty village, once a posting station, was originally the site of the palace of the Bishops of LINCOLN. Only a little remains of what was, in the 13th cent., a very large building. There are still the outer gateway and walling, the inner gatehouse and the Great Tower, which is three stories high and oblong in shape, of red brick with dark blue bricks in the diapers. There is a basement entrance and a ground-floor entrance. The inner gatehouse is also three-storied. Buckden Palace, which incorporates the remains, has been restored and is now a Roman Catholic school. It is open to the public on Sundays.

In the High Street are several attractive brick houses, the best of which is Jessamine House, N. of the palace. The timber-framed Lion Hotel was built about 1500 and its entrance hall has moulded beams and a large boss with the Agnus Dei. The George Hotel, opposite, part 17th- and part 18th-cent. is a long, three-story brick building. The vicarage is in Church Street, as is the timber-framed Manor House, of the 16th and 17th cents. Bridge House is Georgian, and opposite it are yellow-brick Victorian almshouses.

St Mary's Church has a Perpendicular tower with a graceful steeple. The nave, dated 1436-9, is divided from the aisles by five-bay arcades. There are 16th-cent. Flemish Passion scenes on the readers' desks. The many interesting monuments include a lovely large white Gothic triptych to Robert Whitworth, dated 1831. The octagonal font is Perpendicular and the pulpit Jacobean.

BUCKINGHAM, *Buckinghamshire* (10–SP69 33). In the north of the county, reached through unspoilt countryside, is this town with its many historical associations. Situated on a hill-top and once the county town, made so by King Alfred in 886, it is now a place of great antiquity and is delightful to wander through with its steep narrow streets.

A typical market town, its main street is lined with old buildings which, although mostly converted into shops, have not been changed in structure from the times in which they were built.

In former days Buckingham was an important area for wool but because of its inaccessibility this industry declined and was lost. Perhaps

Burnham Beeches

because of its lack of any main industry, the town retains much of its original character.

Catherine of Aragon rested in Buckingham in 1513 and Charles I held a council of war in the old banqueting rooms of Castle House, still in existence, the fireplace and carved mantelpiece bearing the date of 1619.

The red-brick Georgian Town Hall holds much of historical interest, its clock-tower surmounted by the gilded swan of Buckingham. In the plain 14th-cent. Manor House Queen Elizabeth I dined in 1578; its fascinating twisted chimney is Tudor. The Old Gaol in the centre of the Market Square is 18th-cent. and was built on the assumption that the assizes would again be held there. The Old Latin School, of 16th-cent. origin and a National Trust property, is built on the site of a 13th-cent. chantry chapel and has a carved Norman doorway. Edward VI and Dame Isabel Denton gave monies to support the school.

The town has many old almshouses and inns, two of the most notable being the Swan and Castle Inn and the White Hart Hotel, the latter built in the 18th cent. after an earlier inn on the same site had been destroyed in a disastrous fire which swept the town in 1725. The portico and sign were added in Victorian times.

The Parish Church of SS. Peter and Paul, twice rebuilt in 1777 and 1862, and prominent on a hill-top, is believed to be on the site of an Anglo-Saxon fortification. The chancel is Victorian but the carved bench-ends, with shields and quarterings, bear the date 1619. A great shield, carved with a swan, rests over the west door. The Buckingham Needle and Thread Society have donated many things which give the church its lovely interior. In 1890 its east window, representing the *Te Deum*, was given by the Society, as well as the delightful altar cloth and the reredos depicting the Nativity. Presented in 1471 by John Rudying, a Latin manuscript Bible is preserved under glass now as it was once stolen and only recovered in the 18th cent.

BURNHAM, *Buckinghamshire* (6–SU9382). This fairly large residential village is of ancient origin, its greatest claim to fame being the forest of Burnham Beeches with huge pollarded beeches, glades and winding lanes. It stretches for nearly 600 acres. Centuries ago it was part of the Chiltern forests and is bordered by Dorneywood, a National Trust property. It is one of the country's finest beauty-spots.

On the slopes by an orchard still exists a fair that was famous in medieval days.

Although the village has modern shops and residential roads the old charm remains and there are many 15th- and 16th-cent. houses and a fine 13th-cent. church. The church has a tower with an oak-shingled spire. The great altar rails dated 1663 have five beautifully carved oak panels. At the end of the nave are many interesting brasses and by the south door a white marble wall monument sculptured by John Bacon.

To the S. of the centre of the village can be seen the remains of Burnham Abbey, founded in 1266, and although much rebuilt, still retaining segments from Norman times.

BUSHEY, *Hertfordshire* (6–TQ1395). This once small village has extended greatly in the past two decades, turning into a rambling commuter centre for London, but still retaining much of interest for the visitor, mainly around the old church.

St James's Church, in the High Street, enlarged in the last century, has a high 15th-cent. nave and west tower with a stair-turret. Built of flint, its chancel is of the 13th cent. and the windows to the N. and S. are original. An unusual feature, a tympanum with the royal arms of Queen Anne, rests on a large beam and divides the nave from the chancel. The Jacobean pulpit has strapwork motifs and the original sounding board above.

The Rectory, E. of the church, although altered in the 19th cent., still has many of its original 17th-cent. features, including two interesting fireplaces.

Around the church is a pretty group of cottages and, higher up the street, Bushey House, with a Greek-Doric portico built at the beginning of the 19th cent. Bourne Hall, opposite, is Georgian, three stories high with eight bays. There are a number of pleasant 19th-cent. Gothic villas but the Cloisters is mid-Victorian. Both the Congregational and the Methodist churches were built in 1904, the former in a style typical of the period.

In Aldenham Road, a little further out, is Bushey Hall, a large Victorian brick and stone mansion, its tower on the left standing away from the main structure.

There is an interesting 18th-cent. house, once known as Sly's Castle and now called Hilfield, in Hilfield Lane. It is a cemented building, castellated and turreted and has a gatehouse with porticullis.

CARDINGTON, *Bedfordshire* (10–TL0847). This attractive village, with much history attached to it, has an R.A.F. station, and has long been connected with aviation, as will be seen by the large sheds rebuilt for the two airships R100 and R101. The latter crashed on its maiden flight in 1930, killing all but eight of the people on board and the ensign that survived the disaster is now in Cardington church; there is a monument in the churchyard.

John Howard, the philanthropist, spent most of his life here and his house, Howard Villa, an 18th-cent. building with three bays, is by the village green. Many pleasant old houses surround the green, as well as several estate cottages built by John Howard, dated 1763, 1764.

Cardington Bridge, with its five brick arches, was built for Samuel Whitbread, the brewer, by John Smeaton in 1778. Samuel Whitbread also built the mill.

St Mary's Church is large and mainly of 1900, but the chancel, south doorways of the nave and south chapel are Perpendicular. The rare font, a gift of Harriet Whitbread in 1783, is of black Wedgwood basalt. The carved lectern dates from 1955. There are many splendid monuments, several of which are to the Whitbread family. Two tomb-chest brasses of special note are of Sir William Gascoigne, and his two wives, 1540, who was comptroller of Cardinal Wolsey's household, and of Sir Jarrate Harvye and his wife, 1638.

CASTLE ASHBY, *Northamptonshire* (10–SP8659). There are two places of interest here: Castle Ashby House and its church. The house is set in grounds covering over a square mile, which were landscaped by Capability Brown, although its avenues were planted after a visit of William III. There are seven ornamental lakes and lovely views. The house was started by the 1st Lord Compton, who eventually was created Earl of Northampton, in 1574, and is still owned by the same family. It was originally built in the shape of an E, but in the 17th cent. the openings were joined by a screen by Inigo Jones. It has numerous windows and two octagonal towers. In the parapet of the east wing is a carved Latin inscription. The great hall has a timber roof of 1770, as well as an organ and a minstrels' gallery, and the 17th-cent. wooden staircase is carved with animals, snakes, trees and cherubs as well as hunting scenes. There is a valuable collection of paintings and furniture, a collection of Greek vases and a pair of bellows by Benvenuto Cellini. House and gardens are open to the public.

The church, in the grounds, has a large yew standing by the gate and the building is much restored. It is 14th- and 15th-cent., with an attractive tower topped by a pyramid roof. A screen with Jacobean panels is at the end of the south aisle and the 17th-cent. pulpit has an ornate sounding-board. There are many monuments to the Comptons, but of particular interest is a brass in the chancel floor of the rector William Ermyn, 1401, his cope elaborately decorated with 10 saints all standing under traceried canopies.

CASTOR, *Huntingdonshire* (10–TL1298), is of Roman origin, standing on the banks of the River Nene, in beautiful countryside with grey stone farms and thatched cottages. At the west end of the village is Village Farmhouse, which has an Anglo-Saxon window in the side entrance. Castor House, at the east end, is a Georgian building of two stories with five bays. A mile further on, opposite PETERBOROUGH golf course, are two standing stones named Robin Hood and Little John, believed to date from the Bronze Age.

Milton Hall, the seat of the Fitzwilliam family, is in a vast park. The north front is Elizabethan and the south side 18th-cent. Sir William Fitzwilliam was the custodian of Mary Queen of Scots during the period of her imprisonment at FOTHERINGHAY. Nearby is Milton Ferry with its three-arched bridge, built in 1716.

The cruciform Church of St Kyneburgha is the only one in the country dedicated to this saint, who was the daughter of the pagan King Peada of Mercia, who eventually became a Christian and founded Peterborough Abbey. It has a fine Norman tower with a richly decorated steeple with an inscription 1124 recording the consecration of the church. The tower is in four stages, its walls panelled in Romanesque detail. There are fragments of older carvings and additions of the 14th cent. The pretty transept was once used as a village school. Three wall paintings depict the life of St Catherine, and a small stone statue of a man stands in the chancel and is believed to be 9th-cent.

Near the church are Roman remains excavated in 1822. Pavements, temples, villas and baths were found and covered up again.

A half m. SE. of the village at **Mill Hill** is the site of a Roman villa. It was a two-winged house with a small building nearby which was possibly the bath house.

CHALFONT ST GILES, *Buckinghamshire* (6–SU9993). A pretty village, lying in the valley of the Misbourne on the A413 to AYLESBURY, is renowned for its connections with John Milton the poet.

Milton came here during the plague year of 1665 to find peace and write. Growing old in loneliness and blindness it was here he wrote *Paradise Lost* and it was from here that his friend Ellwood the Quaker suggested he should write *Paradise Regained. Paradise Lost* brought him the princely sum of £5. Milton's cottage is now a museum open to the public.

The Church of St Giles is very much a family church. Built of flint, part of it is 12th-cent. Reached by a gateway, the doorway of the medieval church is decorated with 600-year-old ball-flowers, and the interior is a rich array of 14th-cent. paintings and 15th-cent. angels displayed on the roof. The tower was built in the 15th cent. when the church was refashioned.

In the churchyard lies a man of modern times, Bertram Mills, who will ever be remembered for his circuses. He was greatly beloved for his widespread charity.

The old Chalfont mill is on the River Misbourne, which is but a trickle now, and nearby is The Vache, the handsome 16th-cent. manor house often visited by Captain Cook who gave its name to a South Sea Island. A monument to him is in the grounds.

CHEQUERS, *Buckinghamshire* (10–SP8506). Near to Kimble, with ELLESBOROUGH as its parish church, stands the country home of the Prime Minister, hidden away from the road in hundreds of acres of parkland.

Chequers Court was given to the nation for the benefit of the prime ministers of Britain in perpetuity as a thank-offering for the ending of the First World War.

The 13th-cent. manor house was rebuilt by Sir William Hawtrey in the 15th cent. and in one of the great fireplaces are entwined the initials A.H. and W.H. The sister of Lady Jane Grey,

Lady Mary, was confined there in disgrace by Elizabeth I after her secret marriage to Thomas Keys who died in prison.

CHESHUNT, *Hertfordshire* (10–TL3502), is an old rambling village with its High Street stretching for over a mile. Much of this thoroughfare and the surrounding streets has been drastically modernized.

In Turner's Hill is a group of old houses with, of particular interest, the yellow-brick early-19th-cent. Grange and the 18th-cent. Manor House, three stories high with two-bay lower wings and a doorcase with rusticated pilasters. The Dewhurst Almshouses, 10 one-storied brick cottages in a line, were founded in 1642. The 18th-cent. red-brick Clock House, with seven bays and two stories is in Blind Man's Lane, and in College Road will be found the large houses of Cheshunt Cottage, early 19th-cent. with hood-moulds over the windows and bargeboard gables, and Brookside House, of the same period.

Cheshunt Great House, ½ m. NW. of the church, was originally a large moated house. All that remains is one wing of a courtyard house, and this is impressive with its late-15th-cent. great hall, 40 ft long with an original timber roof. The house was converted at the beginning of the 18th cent. and added to in the following century.

Near to the church in Churchgate and Churchfield can be seen some of the old character of the village, of particular note the brick-built Dewhurst Charity School, dated 1640, with three gables and mullioned brick windows.

St Mary's Church, built in the 15th cent., has an embattled west tower of ashlar stone and a south-east stair-turret. There are a number of brasses of interest.

CHESTERTON, *Huntingdonshire* (10–TL12 95), is not really a village, for there are no shops or main centre, but it has two features of interest, the church and the Roman ruins on the outskirts.

The entrance to the Church of St Michael is down a narrow path off a road running past spacious, modern houses. The church is of the 18th cent., a period of which there are few examples in the county, but it has a fine Early English tower with long lancets and twin bell-openings under a pointed arch. There is much Georgian work in the interior, including the chancel, a wooden screen in Roman Doric style and a broad reredos. The altar table, communion rail and font are also of this period. There is a monument to William Beville, 1483, and a Jacobean one to Sir Robert Beville and his family, showing two kneeling couples with their children facing them. There is also a memorial to John Dryden, cousin of the poet.

On the A1, a mile or so past Chesterton, are the extensive earthworks of **Durobrivae,** a Roman town enclosed in 40 acres, scheduled as an Ancient Monument.

CHILTON, *Buckinghamshire* (10–SP6811), stands on a hill with magnificent views all around it. It is a simple, unspoilt village with many old cottages, some timbered, others of wattle and daub. Roofs are both thatched and tiled.

St Mary's Church is sited on a rise and its foundations are Norman. The 14th-cent. tower has grotesquely carved gargoyles; the 16th-cent. roof of the nave is supported by corbels adorned with angels; and between the 13th-cent. chancel and the chapel is an oak screen with carved balusters. Within the chapel is the elaborate Jacobean tomb of the Croke family, with Sir John, his wife and 11 children. One of the red-robed sons was Speaker of the House of Commons during the reign of Elizabeth I.

Adjoining the church is Chilton House, the home of the Croke family for many generations. It is a handsome 18th-cent. building, said to be modelled on Buckingham Palace.

Claydon House: a door in the Chinese Room

Edwin Smith

CHORLEY WOOD, *Hertfordshire* (6–TQ 0396), is a pleasant little Victorian village surrounded by extensive gorse commons and magnificent views over the Chess valley.

C. F. A. Voysey was the architect of some of the houses of interest. His own, The Orchard, in Shire Lane, has identical gables and well-balanced centre. The hall of the house, together with its staircase and fireplace, are some of Voysey's best work, and the metalwork is typical of his direct style. Hill Cottage, further along the lane, has an addition on the right-hand side by Voysey, and Hollybank, which is most attractive, is also his work.

Christ Church, situated by the great common, was built in 1870 by George Street. It is of flint with a low-shingled spire. Inside there is a triple traceried opening connecting the chancel with the south chapel and in the churchyard are massive cedars.

CLAPHAM, *Bedfordshire* (10–TL0252). This residential village has attractive old buildings as well as many modern ones, for it is so near to BEDFORD that it is almost a dormitory. A picturesque thatched cottage stands on a ford of the Ouse on the outskirts of the town.

Two features are of interest here, the most important being St Thomas of Canterbury Church with its enormous Anglo-Saxon look-out tower, added to in Norman times, and over 80 ft high. There is a triangle-headed doorway to the simple Norman tower arch, Jacobean balusters on the ladder of the tower's ringing floor and a monument to Thomas Taylor, 1689, with an inscription with drapery and an urn at the top.

Clapham Park was built in 1872 for James Howard, founder of the Bedford Britannia Ironworks. In Tudor Gothic style, it is red-bricked and gabled, and in 1965 was added a chapel, designed by Desmond Williams, circular in shape with an octagonal roof and abstract stained glass, for the Society of Daughters of the Holy Ghost.

CLAYDON VILLAGES, *Buckinghamshire* (10–SP7126). The four villages of **Botolph Claydon, East Claydon, Middle Claydon** and **Steeple Claydon** are set apart from the rest of the county in wooded countryside, a few miles from each other, down lonely, winding lanes reached by the main road from AYLESBURY to BUCKINGHAM. Very small, they are dominated by the thatched roofs of timbered houses with gleaming-white stonework.

Claydon House, a National Trust property, was transformed in 1752 by the 2nd Earl of Verney to further his political ambitions and outdo the great house of Stowe, the home of one of his rivals. The foundations of the house, however, are several hundred years older. Situated in the village of **Middle Claydon**, the house is reached through lodge gates and the immediate impression is one of simplicity, with cattle grazing in the park. Although the transformation was never completed, through lack of money, the building contains magnificent state rooms with rococo decoration carved by Lightfoot, reputed to be the only known work by this craftsman.

On the walls of the house are many portraits of the Verney family, who still occupy it. The doorways and ceilings, long-shuttered windows and fine fireplaces in the hall, the drawing-room and the picture gallery are all delightful. The grand stairway inlaid with ebony and ivory has balusters with scrolls, ribbons and cornstalks of iron. In the Chinese Room, with its rococo alcove carved in wood, is a carving of a Chinese family at a picnic table complete with crockery and fringed tablecloth.

A suite of rooms once occupied by Florence Nightingale, sister of Parthenope, Lady Verney, and editor of the Verney papers, is now a museum to her. The tall cedar and cypress trees in the park are said to have been grown from seeds Florence Nightingale brought back from the Crimea.

Reached across a small lawn is Middle Claydon church, with its 15th-cent. tower. Inside the church door is a tomb to Margaret Giffard, a Verney ancestor who died in 1539. The chancel is 16th-cent. and the oak pulpit 17th-cent. Four of the windows and the south doorway of the nave have been here for 700 years. The church was restored by Sir Harry Verney, brother-in-law of Florence Nightingale and an M.P. for some 50 years. It was due to his interest that the 16th-cent. chancel screen, with panels of delicate tracery and a wide doorway with leaves in the spandrels, is in existence. One of the newest memorials in the church is a bronze relief of Sir Harry by Harry Pegram. The church holds many other memorials to the Verneys, the most important having been erected after Sir Ralph's wife, Mary, died at Blois. It was designed and made in Rome in 1652. Made of many-coloured marbles, with the Verney arms portrayed on it and the phoenix at the top, it has portrait busts of the family.

Despite the domination of Claydon House, the other villages are worth a visit. **East Claydon**, in agricultural country, has pretty black-and-white cottages near the church with its demon-faced angels on the chancel arch and, high up on the inside of the tower, a woman's head craning forward.

Steeple Claydon, a village of wayside cottages, has a church with one of the few steeples in the county. The manor was given to a great scholar, Sir Thomas Chaloner, by Mary Tudor; he is mentioned in Hakluyt's *Voyages*. His son was tutor to Prince Henry, the brother of Charles I. Thomas Chaloner built the school and created a trust for the schoolmaster. He was one of Charles I's judges and signed the death-warrant. The old school was restored by Sir Harry Verney in the last century and his son Edward opened the red-brick building which is the Chaloner library. A cheque for £50 from Florence Nightingale towards the cost of the books is still exhibited in the library.

The house of the Verneys can be seen from the churchyard and by the roadside is the Camp Barn where Cromwell's soldiers once stayed.

Botolph Claydon, with its old manor house now a farm-house, is attractive for its rural atmosphere, its black-and-white thatched cottages and its delightful scenery.

CLIVEDEN, *Buckinghamshire* (6–SU9185). Standing in magnificent wooded countryside is the great house of Cliveden. To discover it you turn off the A4 from London to MAIDENHEAD. On the left is Taplow Court, now the offices of British Telecommunications Research, with a Victorian lodge house at its gates. Along the Cliveden road is a superb avenue of Lombardy populars and on the left is the Canadian Red Cross Hospital.

Cliveden is now the property of the National Trust and is open to the public. The wooded area surrounding the house includes one of the most beautiful reaches of the River Thames. Built in 1851 this was the former home of the Astor family and was the third house of its name of this site. Standing above terraces, the impressive building contains many treasures, with fine tapestry and period furniture. In the large grounds are temples designed by Giacomo Leoni and among the trees and avenues of shrubs are sculptures and statues set in niches.

The road from the house winds steeply down in beautiful countryside as it follows the bends of the Thames.

COLLYWESTON, *Northamptonshire* (10–SK 9903), is a charming stone-built village, the home of the famous Collyweston tiles that cover the roofs of the houses here and in many other parts of the county. The tiles are still manufactured in the traditional way in the village. There is a manor dated 1696 and, W. of the church, an Elizabethan dovecot.

The church was built by Ralph Cromwell, who fought at Agincourt. It has a fine pinnacled tower and a 15th-cent. south doorway, the arch of which has a pinnacle on each side and moulding with carved flowers. The pews are carved with open tracery and the bench-ends have poppy-heads of fruit and foliage. The choir stalls are decorated with carvings of pelicans, the Christian symbol of sacrifice.

CONINGTON, *Huntingdonshire* (10–TL1785), is on the edge of the Fens, from which can be seen the Isle of Ely. It has moated enclosures, including those at Bruce's Castle Farm and at Round Hill, the latter being five-sided and covering $17\frac{1}{2}$ acres. Holme Fen, just to the N., is a reserve of the Nature Conservancy.

Conington Castle, which was owned by the Cotton family from 1460, one of whose members started draining the fens in 1639, has recently been demolished.

All Saints Church is large and mainly Perpendicular. The massive tower is ashlar-faced, in four stages, with panelled polygonal buttresses, a recessed doorway with a pointed tunnel vault, bell-openings under four-centred arches and large pinnacles. The remainder of the church,

Daventry lies in typical rolling Northamptonshire country

with its embattled nave and aisles, is of cobbles, as is its higher rood stair turret. The chancel chapels are of only one bay, and the sedilia in the chancel have three small hanging vaults. There is a shelf in the piscina and the octagonal Norman font has intersecting pointed arches. Several screens are of interest. The stately wooden chair, resembling a throne, its armrests adorned with angels, swans and doves, is said to have been used by Mary Queen of Scots at FOTHERINGHAY while she was awaiting execution.

DAVENTRY, *Northamptonshire* (10–SP5762). This ancient town, whose major industry in the 18th cent. was whip-making, has expanded greatly in recent years, with large car factories and light engineering works, modern houses and new schools.

It still retains some of its past, however, with pleasant Georgian houses, the Roman Catholic church which was once the old grammar school of 1600, two inns of note, the Saracen's Head and the Wheatsheaf, and the tall, ironstone 18th-cent. Moot Hall, now council offices.

Daventry was an important coaching town in the 18th cent., for it lies on four main roads. It has been a market town since 1255 and dates back to the Iron Age, as is evidenced by the camp on Borough Hill, N. of the town. Borough Hill is 650 ft above sea-level and from its highest point may be seen seven counties. Nearby are the giant masts of the B.B.C.'s overseas transmitting station, near the spot where Charles I's army camped during the Civil War, before the Battle of NASEBY. The King spent several nights at the Wheatsheaf Inn, which has barely changed since those days.

The Church of the Holy Cross is mid-18th-cent., made of ironstone with a bulky tower and a solid steeple. In each of its aisles is a gallery, hidden behind Tuscan columns. The roof is groined, and the richly-coloured Resurrection reredos shows the Archangels Raphael and Gabriel.

DEENE, *Northamptonshire* (10–SP9492). In this tiny, unspoilt, limestone village, hiding among trees on the edge of Willow Brook, is Deene Park, the home of the Brudenells since 1514. It is imposing, with some of its original structure and additions and alterations made in the Elizabethan, Jacobean and Georgian periods. Built of pale Weldon stone, it has a large battlemented tower and the Georgian rooms overlook lakes formed from the Willow Brook. The ballroom has superb stained glass and a heavy marble fireplace built in memory of the 7th Earl of Cardigan who commanded the Light Brigade in their famous charge in the Crimea in 1854. His uniforms are still there. The house has many features of architectural and historical interest and in the spacious well-wooded grounds are rare trees and shrubs. It is open to the public.

DENHAM, *Buckinghamshire* (6–TQ0487). This picturesque village in wooded countryside off the A40 has many houses and brick and timbered cottages of interest. One of these, Old Cottage, a half-timbered Tudor building, has a fascinating unevenly-shaped front. There are several old inns and a tiny 1820 Wesleyan chapel.

The River Colne flows through the grounds of Denham Place which is at the end of the street, behind a high brick wall. It was built in Restoration times and beneath its high-pitched roof can be seen dormer windows. Captain Cook stayed here, as did Lucien and Joseph Bonaparte.

The Parish Church of St Mary, surrounded by limes, beeches and cypress trees, is of the 15th cent. A 500-year-old wall painting of Judgment Day adorns the walls in which can be seen the figure of an archangel sounding the Last Trump. Mounted on slender round pillars is the 13th-cent. font, the church's oldest possession. On each of the eight sides of the bowl are two pointed arches. There are many brasses of interest on the floor before the altar. The table tomb shows the figures of Sir Edmund Peckham and his wife. Sir Edmund was Master of the Mint to Henry VIII.

Set apart from the village, N. of the railway, are the famous film studios.

DINTON, *Buckinghamshire* (10–SP7610). This pleasant, unspoilt village, in rural countryside, was once the scene of a great historical occasion, for it was to Dinton Hall that Cromwell rode triumphantly after the Battle of NASEBY. His sword is still preserved in the Hall, a large light red-brick manor with an imposing porch and a large number of Tudor chimneys towering above the trees. One side of the house has eight gables, and there are lovely dormer windows and a 600-year-old cellar. It was once the home of Simon Mayne who fought with Cromwell in the Civil War and who was one of the signatories of the king's death-warrant. Although sentenced to death at the Restoration, he died in the Tower before the execution could take place and his body was brought to Dinton for burial.

In a field by the roadside stand the ruins of Dinton Castle, an 18th-cent. folly containing many ammonites embedded in its walls.

The varied farm buildings are gabled and timbered with lichened roofs and on the lawn by the church are the village stocks and the whipping post.

Next to the manor house is the Church of SS. Peter and Paul with its Norman door bearing an inscribed lintel. The great turreted tower is of the 15th cent., the font is 600 years old and in front of the 13th-cent. chancel is a finely carved Jacobean pulpit. In the churchyard is the shaft of an old cross.

DORNEY, *Buckinghamshire* (6–SU9379). The Palmer Arms, though modernized at the front, is an old coaching inn and was at one time the public house for the estate workers who were employed by the lords of the manor, the Palmer family, who have occupied this position for several hundred years.

The village itself is mentioned in the Domesday Book. Among the many historical buildings is an attractive flintstone cottage by Dorney Reach.

On the outskirts of Dorney is ancient BURNHAM Abbey, some distance from the road and completely hidden away by old outbuildings.

Down the High Street are many brick and timbered cottages with beech trees overhanging the road, and on the right is a dilapidated Victorian schoolhouse.

The little Church of St James is of Norman origin, and is reached down a tree-lined lane close to Dorney Court, which dates from the 15th cent. The red-bricked roof of the church is Tudor and the box-pews of the 17th and 18th cents. The nave and the font are Norman and at the west end reached by a short flight of stairs, is the music gallery with its oak seats and oak balusters, built in 1634. An unusual feature is a Jacobean monument to Sir William Gerrard and his wife, with their 15 children below them, some holding skulls to show that they died in infancy.

The first pineapple to be grown in England was produced at Dorney and given to King Charles II.

DUNSTABLE, *Bedfordshire* (10–TL0221), is a modern town, still retaining a few ancient and some Victorian buildings. It was originally a royal market town established by Henry I when he founded the Augustinian priory here in 1131. Until the Dissolution it was of some consequence and at the priory the annulment of Henry VIII's marriage to Catherine of Aragon was pronounced. Between 1742 and the coming of the railway it was a coaching town but is now mainly manufacturing, with the motor-vehicle industry as one of its largest trades.

There is a Victorian town hall, with three bays and a turret, and the white Municipal Offices in the High Street are early-19th-cent. with two pairs of Tuscan columns to the porch. Dunstable School, late Victorian, is of plum brick with a slender spire above it. Composed of two parts, it is linked with a square tower.

Most of the older buildings of interest are centred round the crossroads which are part of the ancient **Icknield Way** and **Watling Street**. Several have been preserved in West Street, the most important of which is the Windmill. In the High Street is the Sugar Loaf Hotel, dated 1717, of blue brick with red dressings, two and a half stories high with nine bays. The priory house has a fine early Georgian exterior with arched windows, a pedimented doorway and quoins and, on the ground floor, a long rib-vaulted room. The gardens are open to the public. Further S. are the Cart Almshouses of 1723, a row of blue and red brick houses; and Chew Grammar School, 1719, founded by Jane Cart, has two attractive figures of schoolboys over the doorway. It has a fine front with an unusual turret cupola.

Also near the crossroads are the new civic centre and shopping precinct.

A modern building of note is the Fire Station at the northern end of the town.

St Peter's has substantial parts of the old priory church. The original nave, which is very wide, still remains. Massive wall-shafts separate the bays, and the interior, richly decorated, has been restored through the centuries. The font is large, circular and Norman, and the rood-screen has five bays and is elaborately carved. The square pulpit, of red marble, is Victorian, but the pulpit cloth was donated in 1732. The Fayrey Pall was a gift of Henry Fayrey, a wealthy

A. F. Kersting

Earls Barton: the Anglo-Saxon tower

merchant, for use as a coffin covering at funerals. It is of red brocade with figures embroidered on the borders and is believed to be Flemish. There are many interesting monuments dating from the 13th cent. One, by Thomas Green of Camberwell, is of William Chew with two figures of naked boys and a death's head between them. The arch at the centre is draped and garlands decorate the top.

On the road towards IVINGHOE and Tring are fine views of Dunstable Downs.

Five Knolls is the finest prehistoric burial ground in the county, with eight sites consisting of two pond, three bell and three bowl barrows. It dates from the Early Bronze Age, but has earlier traces. In the largest and smallest mounds were found fragments of Neolithic and Beaker pottery when they were opened up. Two thousand years later pagan Anglo-Saxons were buried here.

EARITH, *Huntingdonshire* (10–TL3875), is a large riverside village to which, at one time, barges brought wood from Scandinavia. It is on the border of Cambridgeshire and was of vital importance at the beginning of the 17th cent. when the draining of the Fens began and impressive artificial waterways, 20 m. long, were constructed. These formed the Old Bedford River and the New Bedford River or Hundred Foots River, and they run to Salter's Lode Sluice and DENVER Sluice in Norfolk. The Ouse flows slowly past the village on its way to the great sluices.

Woodlands stands in the main street, of yellow brick with red-brick dressings, Doric pilasters, a pediment to its doorway and a Venetian window.

Near the bridge, which is comparatively new, is a field of 4¾ acres with earthworks probably

from the Civil War, in which are four arrow-shaped angle bastions. It is known as the Bulwark.

EARLS BARTON, *Northamptonshire* (10–SP8563). There is one feature of this large, overgrown village which justifies a visit, for its Church of All Saints has an outstanding Anglo-Saxon tower, one of the finest in England. Built of plaster, it is in four stages with pilaster strips from the ground to the belfry, round arches in the second stage, pointed arches in the third, and narrow window openings in the belfry. On the first floor are doorways which are inaccessible. There is a Norman entrance door on which are carved animal faces, and almost every century up to the 19th is represented. The clock is dated 1655. The chancel screen, of the 15th cent., is striking, and by it stands the Jacobean pulpit.

To the N., beyond the churchyard wall, is a mound which marks the site of the old castle.

EATON SOCON, *Bedfordshire* (10–TL1658), on the A1, borders on Huntingdonshire. It has a green with a Victorian lock-up in which there are two cells. The White Horse is a red-brick Georgian building with a panelled parapet. Charles Dickens is said to have stayed at the low, timber-framed Old Plough Inn. The Methodist chapel and the workhouse are both Victorian, the latter of yellow brick with an octagonal centre.

In Duloe Hill, 1 m. N., is a tower windmill without sails, with a cottage attached.

St Mary's Church, which borders on the River Ouse, was almost completely gutted by fire in 1930 and only the south arcades of five bays, the south clerestory and the west tower remain. The tower is high, with transomed two-light bell openings. The square font, of Purbeck marble, is Norman, and there is a large Flemish tapestry of the 17th cent. and a brass of a civilian and his wife, about 1450.

Close to the river bank and E. of the church are the Hillings, earthworks of a castle built in the 11th and 12th cents. Bushmead Priory, 4 m. NW., has some remains of the former conventual buildings.

EDLESBOROUGH, *Buckinghamshire* (10–SP9719). This tiny village, set on the edge of the Chilterns, has as its landmark the Church of St Mary the Virgin. At its foot, in a 16th-cent. barn stands a dovecot, and WHIPSNADE ZOO is on the outskirts of the village.

The tower of the church, with its high turret, is 14th-cent. The low 15th-cent. roof is supported by corbels, decorated with picturesque carvings. The fine woodwork justifies the church's claim to fame. The exquisite oak screen, in red, blue and gold, was carved to resemble a fine lace canopy in 1450. The pulpit is graced with a three-tiered carved canopy of great beauty. The *misereres* are adorned with fine, intricate carvings, a mermaid suckling a beast, dragons, frogs, owls and eagles.

Many brasses decorate the aisles and a small 15th-cent. stained-glass window shows a pilgrim in a red cloak and bright yellow hat carrying his bible and staff. In an iron bracket, near the pulpit, is an hour-glass, which the priest once used to time his sermon.

ELLESBOROUGH, *Buckinghamshire* (10–SP8306). The undulating road from WENDOVER to Ellesborough follows the tracks of the Icknield Way. From the high ground can be seen Wellwick Farm, down in the valley, a building of rose brick and flint, which is reputed to have been the house of the notorious Judge Jeffreys. The chimneys bear the date 1616 and the 17th-cent. barns have open timber roofs. Further along the road stands the old thatched Rose and Crown Inn.

The Church of SS. Peter and Paul, reached by a steep hill, is the parish church for CHEQUERS, the Prime Minister's country residence. This 15th-cent. building has a Norman tower and from the churchyard, which contains a sculpture of the Crucifixion, can be seen in the distance the vast expanse of the Vale of Aylesbury. Fragments of old stained glass cover the vestry windows, one showing the head of Christ crowned with thorns. The piscina in the 15th-cent. chancel is carved with flowers. The reredos with its charming triptych was designed by Sir Ninian Comper. On an imposing tomb lies a statue of Bridget Croke who was a member of the Hawtrey family, the original owners of Chequers. Four black pillars support the roof of her resting-place, under which she lies in Stuart dress, one hand holding a book.

Near the church are small 18th-cent. alms-houses, the gift of Dame Dodd in 1746.

Towards Kimble, on the hillside, is **Cymbeline's Mount**, its Roman ramparts having commanding views of the valley below.

ELSTOW, *Bedfordshire* (10–TL0547). This attractive village, with many thatched cottages and houses, was the birthplace of John Bunyan, and the Moot Hall, *c.* 1500, a medieval market hall which is open to the public, houses a collection illustrating his life and times. The hall is of timber and has an overhanging upper floor which contains the main room.

The sister of William the Conqueror founded a nunnery here which had its own gallows, pillory and ducking pond. Remains of the nunnery's church are incorporated in the Church of SS. Mary and Helen. This was begun as a 13th-cent. building and, although much restored, still has fine Norman work. The vestry was once a small vaulted room, and its most unusual feature is a detached bell-tower of the 15th cent., with a spike on top and on each side transomed bell-openings. The octagonal font, Perpendicular and large, is decorated with quatrefoils on the bowl and figures on the base. The wooden pulpit is of the same period, with tracery panels. There are several interesting monuments.

Behind the church are the remains of Hillersdon Hall, built in 1616 from stone from the old abbey.

ELTON, *Huntingdonshire* (10–TL0893). This well-preserved, attractive and rather sprawling village is situated on the border with Northamp-tonshire, with the River Nene flowing past it. It has two main streets of stone-built houses and cottages with finely thatched roofs.

Cooper's Hospital is an almshouse founded in 1663 by the Rev. John Cooper, and the Methodist church, dated 1864, has arched windows. The 16th-cent. parsonage is gabled and there are many old houses around the green, some of the 17th cent., some Georgian. The Black Horse Inn is also Georgian with five bays on one side and a battlemented one on the other.

All Saints Church has no spire but an ashlar-faced lofty tower, which is Perpendicular, with a doorway with traceried spandrels. Much of the interior dates from around 1300. There are many windows of interest and an arch in the chancel appears to be pre-1300, with triple shafts and a nailhead. The simple octagonal font is about the same period. There are many monuments, including some to the Sapcote family who were owners of Elton Hall in the 15th cent. Two wheel-head crosses in the churchyard are Anglo-Danish.

Elton Hall, on the road towards OUNDLE, is set in a park of 200 acres. Parts of it are 15th-cent., including the gatehouse with a four-centred arch and a vaulted crypt. The house was mainly ruined during the Commonwealth, then rebuilt by Sir Thomas Proby later in the 17th cent., with altera-tions continuing for 200 years. It has been the seat of the Proby family for 300 years. It is open to the public and has fine pictures, 18th-cent. furni-ture and valuable books, including Caxton volumes, Henry VIII's bible with his signature, prayer books and early manuscripts.

ETON, *Buckinghamshire* (6–SU9678). This little town, known the world over because of its association with the famous school of this name, is of ancient origin. During the 11th cent. it was the residence of Queen Edith, wife of Edward the Confessor.

Eton College, the second oldest public school in the country, was founded by royal charter by King Henry VI in 1440. Originally it had 70 scholars who were fed and educated free of charge. Today, among its 1,100 pupils, there are still 70 who pay very low, or sometimes no, fees.

In the narrow streets of Eton, life focuses round the college, and the small shops have catered for the school for decades.

The school itself occupies a large part of the town and its extensive buildings are all of dif-ferent architectural periods. The Lower School, dating from 1443 and still in use, was for 200 years the only schoolroom. The Upper School was built in 1694 and on the desks and panelling will be found the carved names of Walpole, Shelley, Gladstone, Macmillan and Eden. The chapel nearby is the finest Perpendicular building in the county, noted for its exquisite fan-vaulted roof of Clipsham stone. There are many features of interest in the college, including Lupton's tower, built in 1571, the beautiful cloisters and the 18th-cent. college library. Both the Natural History Museum – a modern building – and the college are open to the public.

A short stroll will bring you to the 15th-cent. Cockpit, once used for cock-fighting, and beside it are the parish stock and whipping post. If you visit the town during term-time everywhere will be seen the boys of the school, distinguishable by their coats and stiff Eton collars.

By the river, where there have been common lands since the 7th cent., there is a fine view of WINDSOR Castle. The famous boathouses by the bridge are a popular summer meeting place.

EYE, *Huntingdonshire* (10–TF2202), was built on an island before the Fens were drained and is now one of the largest villages in the north of the county, with brick-making as its major industry.

It has a straight village street of yellow-brick houses, with a tower windmill 80 ft high and of eight stories dominating the flat countryside. It is now power driven and used for producing animal foods. Eyebury Farm, of the late 17th cent., has a hipped roof, a Classical doorway and windows with mullions and transoms.

St Matthew's Church is early Victorian, a cruciform building with a broach spire on the tower and lancet windows. The octagonal font with eight supports is 14th-cent. and came from the church which previously stood on the site.

Three Bronze Age barrows lie on the S. of the parish, in one of which a food vessel was found.

FINEDON, *Northamptonshire* (10–SP9272), is a fairly large village with most of the newer buildings on one side and the older ones on the other. Scattered around are curiously decorated ironstone Victorian houses and cottages, built by the last squire of the village, Mr Mackworth Dolben, whose three sons all died tragically.

The Bell Inn is claimed to be the oldest licensed house in England, for it is on a site where an inn has been since 1042. On the road to Thrapston is the Round Tower, commemorating the Battle of Waterloo.

Near the church, which is at the far end of the village on a steep slope, is Thingdon Cottage, a curious building of several different heights. The Hall, the stone Vicarage and the schools are all of the same period. Finedon Hall has a courtyard with embattled walls, and the house has fine ornamental gables, on the walls of which are the two shields of the families of Mackworth and Dolben.

Reached through a lych-gate is the Church of St Mary, standing in a churchyard with hollies and yews. It is of dark ironstone, built in the 14th cent., with a large tower and a graceful spire rising to about 133 ft. There are lancets in the belfry, which has gargoyles at each corner, and inside, across the nave in front of the chancel, is an unusual strainer arch. The font is Norman and the 18th-cent. organ-case is by Shrider. The pews, which are original, have traceried panelling. In a room over the porch is an 18th-cent. theological library.

FINGEST, *Buckinghamshire* (6–SU7791). Along a narrow byway, lying in a deep hollow

of the Chilterns, is this lonely village, set among beechwoods, with one of the country's finest churches, the Church of St Bartholomew. It has a rare Norman tower, topped by twin gables. A high ancient roof covers the long narrow nave, the low seats giving height to the church. It is said that the nave was once the chancel, in which case the Norman arch spanning the width of the tower must have been the chancel arch. The four-ft thick walls have narrow slit windows and in the chancel are two slim lancets. The 15th-cent. font still has the staples which locked the cover to prevent water being stolen.

In the large churchyard are two 17th-cent. wishing gates which are part of the boundary wall, guarded by an avenue of limes.

Ruins of the palace of the bishops of LINCOLN are nearby and The Chequers inn is 300 years old.

FLAMSTEAD, *Hertfordshire* (10–TL0814). This little village lies above the River Ver and has many old cottages. Saunders Almshouses, dated 1669, are one-storied brick buildings with round-headed entrances and two-light windows. To the E. of them is Vine Cottage, an elegant, timber-framed house with brick infilling.

The Church of St Leonard, surrounded by giant sycamores, lilacs and red and white chestnuts, has the best wall paintings in the county after those in ST ALBANS Cathedral. Its low west tower is of flint, random stone, brick and Roman brick with a thin spike. Most of the structure is of the 14th cent., although there are traces of Norman work. The nave roof, on carved stone corbels, is a century later, and the pulpit later still. The screen is particularly interesting with tall arcades, the central mullion running to the apex of the arch and Perpendicular tracery. The wall paintings, not revealed until 1930, are between the spandrels of the nave arches and show, among others, St Christopher, Christ in Glory, and the Last Supper. Two monuments of note include one by Stanton of Saunders children, 1670, which is a large altar tomb with the figures of five young children praying, with the sixth kneeling on the floor. It is said to have cost £1,500. The other by Flaxman, 1762, is of Sir Edward Sedbright, with Hope and Faith, reclining on a slender fluted urn.

There are particularly fine views around the village.

FLETTON, *Huntingdonshire* (10–TL1997), is an industrialized town with only one building of note but that, St Margaret's Church, is of national interest.

The town itself is the centre of the largest brick-manufacturing area in the country and Fletton bricks have a world-wide reputation. Tall round brickyard chimneys dotted all over the horizon have replaced the trees that were here less than a century ago.

The church has Anglo-Saxon remains in the east buttresses dating from the first half of the 9th cent., before Alfred's time. They came from PETERBOROUGH Abbey after it was burned down in 1116 and are discoloured pink from the fire. They probably belonged to a frieze: one has human figures and the others are decorated with little birds and quadrupeds. The chancel arch, north chapel arcade and north arcade date from about 1160. Two panels of saints are also of the same period. The Norman chancel has a corbel table and buttressing. The tower has Y-traceried bell-openings, a broach spire and two tiers of lucarnes. The octagonal font, with plan panels, is about 1661.

In the churchyard is an Anglo-Saxon cross with a shaft of two handles and a wheel-type cross-head. It has an inscription in Norman lettering.

FLITWICK, *Bedfordshire* (10–TL0335), is a growing residential village with thatched cottages round its green and the River Flitt running through it. By the river lies the boggy Flitwick Moor in which can be found rare plants.

The Manor House, much modernized, is of three periods, 17th-cent., 1736 and mid-Georgian. It is of brick with a panelled parapet and in the garden is a grotto.

SS. Peter and Paul Church, though mainly Victorian, has an Early English south doorway and in the north wall a massive moulding from a Norman doorway with beakhead-like faces. The chancel arch is original and the west tower Perpendicular. The font has a fluted trough and is 12th-cent.

NW. of the church is the Mount, the remains of a small motte and bailey castle.

FLORE, *Northamptonshire* (10–SP6460), is on a gentle slope above the Nene valley, with modern buildings added to the old village, which appears in the Domesday Book as Flora.

In a small thatched house named Adams' Cottage are said to have lived the ancestors of John Adams, President of the United States after George Washington. The 17th-cent. Old Manor, standing next to the church on the edge of the village, is gabled with pinnacles and is surrounded by fine trees. Nearby is the village school which has the names of May Queens since 1890, for the festival it holds on May Day is the important local event.

The church, amid sycamores, cypresses, cedars, limes and yews, is partly 13th-cent. All the doors are medieval and richly carved. The massive tower is 14th-cent. The interior is graceful, its tower opening on to the nave through three arches, and the screen, with open tracery, is 15th-cent. There are Tudor panels on the priest's desk and the choir stalls. The font, which is 16th-cent. and is barrel-shaped, was for a time used as a cattle trough. There are several interesting brasses.

Brockhall, reached by a road N. of Flore, is an Elizabethan manor house with an Adam wing and a fine staircase of the same period. It can be viewed at any time, by appointment.

FOTHERINGHAY, *Northamptonshire* (10–TL0593). The road to this village runs through beautiful countryside and crosses the 18th-cent. bridge spanning the River Nene, over which hang tall willows.

There are many old cottages with small doors in the historic village, where Mary Queen of Scots was beheaded in 1587, and parts of the old inns still remain. The site of the old castle is down a narrow lane on the bend of the road opposite a row of thatched cottages, and it is necessary to park the car and walk to the site. The castle is now only a mound, but it was built by Simon de St Liz in the 12th cent. and enlarged

Fotheringhay: the view from the site of the castle where Mary Queen of Scots was beheaded

in the reign of Edward III. Richard III was born in the castle, in the hall in which Mary was executed. In the grounds are Scotch thistles which the Queen is said to have planted during her imprisonment.

The tower of the Church of St Mary and All Saints rises in stages and the whole building has a profusion of windows. On the corners of the first stage are four small turrets and crowning them, in place of a spire, is a superb octagonal lantern with two sets of lancet windows in each side adorned with tracery. Above are eight pinnacles surmounted by the badge of the House of York, a falcon and a fetterlock. The lower part of the tower opens three ways into the body of the church and is fan-vaulted. Behind the altar is an 18th-cent. reredos with three arches in which are set, in fine gold letters, the Lord's Prayer, the Commandments and the Creed. The pulpit, a gift from Edward IV, is one of the church's most attractive features, with its double canopy and much fine carving. The stone font, with heads of lions and foliage on its base, is 15th-cent. In the sanctuary are stone monuments in memory of Richard of York, Cecily Neville and their son Edmund, which were put there on the instructions of Queen Elizabeth I when she visited the village.

FURNEAUX PELHAM, *Hertfordshire* (10–TL4327), is a little village, its main street lying in a hollow, at the end of which stands the Hall, a 16th-cent. brick manor house with shaped gables covered in creeper and a delightful garden.

St Mary's Church, mid-13th-cent., has an inscription painted round the clock on the tower: "Time Flies – mind your business". In the low-pitched nave roof are figures of angels with bright yellow hair and leopards with lolling red tongues. The windows are Late Perpendicular and the chapel was built in the early 16th cent. There is an octagonal font of Purbeck marble, and a splendid monument in the south aisle, a tomb-chest with quatrefoils and shields. Under a cusped canopy lie the exquisite brass figures of a man and woman.

GAYHURST, *Buckinghamshire* (10–SP8446). A small hamlet on the River Ouse, Gayhurst is renowned for its part in the Guy Fawkes Gunpowder Plot. Its Elizabethan manor was given to Sir Francis Drake by Queen Elizabeth I as a reward for his travels round the world. But Drake did not want it and sold it the next day to William Mulsho, who refashioned it and turned it into the beautiful building that exists today. Mary Mulsho married Everard Digby who became involved in the Gunpowder Plot and it was from here that he was taken to the Tower.

The house is now partly a school. It has mullioned and transomed windows and pinnacles, and old stone stables and coach-houses.

The church, built in 1728, has a low square tower with a cupola and the chancel has carved wooden coping. There is a three-decker pulpit with a magnificent canopy and a monument to Sir Nathan Wrighte with a dragon's head crest. The Royal arms are at the east end of the church.

GEDDINGTON, *Northamptonshire* (10–SP 8983). This is a lovely, sprawling village, in wooded countryside, with many old cottages, most of them thatched. It is centred round the Eleanor Cross in the square, believed to be the finest of the remaining crosses erected by Edward I to mark the places where the coffin of his queen had lain for the night on its long journey to WESTMINSTER ABBEY in 1290. Square-shaped, of stone, it is finely and intricately worked, the small statues of the Queen showing her veiled.

The Church of St Mary Magdalene is medieval with some Anglo-Saxon and Norman work. The tower has an octagonal spire and gargoyles similar to those on the nave and chancel walls. The entrance is by a narrow 13th-cent. doorway and the nave is filled with light. The chancel has a double clerestory and a large window with five lancets. There are several lovely screens: one of the 14th cent. between the chancel and the south aisle is in richly carved woodwork.

Around the church are old cottages and nearby is a Victorian infants' school with a weather-vane.

Leading out of the square is the medieval bridge over the River Ise, beyond which are more thatched cottages and a larger thatched house, now the Post Office. The Congregational church is Victorian.

GODMANCHESTER, *Huntingdonshire* (10–TL2470), is an ancient Roman town, pentagonal in shape, with charters dating back to 1214, when it became a self-governing manor, a form of government which made the inhabitants free tenants, for which the town paid King John £120 a year. It became a borough in 1604.

Godmanchester adjoins HUNTINGDON by the ancient bridge crossing the River Ouse. It is said that the bridge, described in Huntingdon, was partly built by Godmanchester and partly by Huntingdon, that the two ends were started at the same time, without any co-ordinated plan and that by luck the workmen met in the middle, which accounts for the awkward curve in the bridge.

The town has many old thatched brick and timber cottages, ancient farm-houses on the outskirts and a wide common. In the centre is the Victorian town hall. Queen Elizabeth's Grammar School was founded in 1560 and parts of the original building are still in use. Near these two buildings is the delightful Chinese Bridge, constructed in 1827, which leads to the islands in the River Ouse.

The Causeway, which opens on to the river, is medieval, and on its east side is a timber-framed house dated 1597 and a yellow-brick late-Georgian building. In Earning Street is a two-gabled house dated 1625. Plantagenet House has gables and an oriel window with bargeboards, and Tudor House, built 1600–3, is timber-framed with gabled wings and overhanging upper stories. In London Road is Porch Farm and the former Shepherd and Dog Inn, and in Post Street is the 17th-cent. Island Cottage with overhanging stories and, lying back from the street, Island Hall, a large, red-brick building, two and a half stories high with lower two-bay wings. Farm Hall, in West Street, was built in 1746 of red and rubbed brick with a Tuscan porch and cast-iron railings. There is an avenue of limes in the garden and another leading towards the river.

The Parish Church of St Mary, one of the largest in the county, is mainly 13th- to 15th-cent., with a tower added in 1623. The church is of brown cobbles and the tower ashlar-faced. The chancel is Early English and has a rare 13th-cent. mass-dial on one of the buttresses. The rood-screen is 1901, but the misericords on the stalls are late 15th-cent. and show a variety of finely carved animals. There is a 16th-cent. brass with a figure of a civilian.

The Roman town can be defined by the present roads which encircle it and recent discoveries are the south and west gates and a suite of baths, near Pinfold Lane, which were built about the 2nd cent. Traces of another building of the same date have been uncovered.

GOLDINGTON, *Bedfordshire* (10–TL0750), is now a suburb of BEDFORD, with one of the largest village greens in the county.

It possesses a modern power station with a cooling tower 165 ft high and a church which is over 500 years old. St Mary's has a Perpendicular tower and chancel. The round font is early 14th-cent., decorated on the underside. In the porch is an upright effigy of a lady, also of the early 14th cent., and there is a detailed black-and-white marble tablet to Benjamin Haselden, 1676.

Two m. E. are the 700-year-old ruins of Newnham Priory, known as **Risinghoe Castle**, with a 20-ft-high motte. Nearby is a small bridge known as "Bloody Battle Bridge" which is believed to have been an outpost for the Danes.

GRAFHAM, *Huntingdonshire* (10–TL1669), is a small village with a tiny, whitewashed church and an old rectory, part of a 16th-cent. house, adjoining it. All Saints Church has a west tower and three ancient bells. The chancel and double piscina are 13th-cent. The octagonal font is Decorated and there is a 14th-cent. effigy of a priest in the south porch.

Recently a new reservoir has been constructed which is said to be the largest man-made sheet of inland water in the country, 1,570 acres. It has become a favourite spot for fishing and sailing and there is also a bird sanctuary. Grafham Water Sailing Club is a three-story building of outstanding sculptural quality and won an award from the Civic Trust for a building which paid particular respect to the character of its surroundings. The reservoir also won an award as a landscaping project making an outstanding contribution to the surrounding scene.

GREAT GRANSDEN, *Huntingdonshire* (10–TL2755). This is a charming village, quite large yet unspoilt. It has many thatched cottages with pink or white plaster walls and two particularly pretty ones opposite the church, timber-framed,

one with russet tiles and one thatched. The alms-houses, still in use, were built in 1679 by the Rev. Barnabas Oley, an ardent Royalist, who was vicar here for 53 years except during the Civil War when he went into hiding.

Although Rippington Manor House is Eliza-bethan, built on an H-shaped plan with a vast stone chimneybreast, the first Lord of the Manor was Alfar, brother of Hereward the Wake. A church is named here in the Domesday Book, but it was rebuilt in the 14th cent. Great Gransden Hall, a moated mansion, stands in a large park. It is 17th-cent, part early and part middle. In the centre is a panelled parapet curving to a higher centre part and the side-pieces of the front are two-bayed with massive Dutch gables. The College Farmhouse was also built at separate times in the same period. The vicarage, with its hipped roof, is Jacobean and was built by Barnabas Oley.

Half a m. E. of the village is a wooden postmill.

St Bartholomew's Church is of brown cobbles and completely Perpendicular, embattled throughout. Its tower, in four stages, has two-light bell openings and a spike. The fine roof is decorated with figures and in the chancel is a crocketed piscina. The screen has 15th-cent. tracery and the pulpit, with carvings of fruit and foliage, was a gift of Barnabas Oley. The carillon and chimes of the church clock were added to celebrate the jubilee of the Rev. Barnabas Oley. There is a large stone slab monument to Thomas de Museum, parish priest, 1350.

GREAT LINFORD, *Buckinghamshire* (10–SP 8542). This small town on the Grand Union Canal was once a place of great commercial interest.

Its Church of St Andrew is a pleasant blend of 18th-cent. workmanship and Decorated Gothic. The 12th-cent. building has a 13th-cent. tower, a beautiful arcade and many fine windows. There are two porches, one with a winged figure of pre-Tudor period and the other with a vaulted roof. A brass of Roger Hunt and his wife relates how he paved the church during the years of the Wars of the Roses. The aisle has a 16th-cent. brass to Thomas Malyn, with his wife and child, and the chancel contains 17th-cent. brass portraits of John Uvedall, his wife and their eight children. There are box pews and a monument to Sir William Pritchard who lived in the manor and was at one time Lord Mayor of London.

It was Sir William who built the delightful red-roofed almshouses. The village has a Tudor rectory, a barn of the same period and a dovecot which houses 400 pairs of nesting birds.

GREAT MISSENDEN, *Buckinghamshire* (10–SP8901). Lying in the valley of the Chilterns with woods around it, this roadside town has many old houses and inns in the narrow High Street. The George Inn is 15th-cent. and the gate-way has original timbers and a room over it.

On a plateau standing back from the village is the 14th-cent. Church of SS. Peter and Paul. This spacious church is filled with light from windows added 500 years ago. Stone angels with shields support the nave roof and the chancel wall has an exquisite arcade of seven bays with finials and pinnacles ending in small carved heads. The Norman font is an octagonal basin, the sides of which were re-cut in the 15th cent. Its stem has chevrons and its base is finely carved. In the transept pews are many 15th-cent. traceried panels. An interesting monument over the south doorway is that to William Blois, a scholar who lived in Stuart times.

Incorporated in the Abbey Mansion are the ruins of the Augustinian abbey which was founded in 1133 for the Black Canons. In earlier times it was used as a stopping place for English sovereigns travelling from their palace at BRILL to that at ST ALBANS. The abbey grounds are on steep slopes, covered by beechwoods.

Prehistoric flints and Roman coins have been discovered in the neighbourhood, and the moated earthworks at Redding Wick and Grim's Ditch near Woodlands Park have been scheduled for preservation as Ancient Monuments. In Rook Wood is a prehistoric earthwork.

GREAT PAXTON, *Huntingdonshire* (10–TL 2164), has large thatched cottages and the views from Paxton Hill are probably the most beautiful in the county. On one side are rolling downs and on the other thick woods. The River Ouse is clearly visible from the road with boats passing by.

Holy Trinity Church is Anglo-Saxon, very grandiose, a true cruciform church with its crossing as wide as the nave, chancel and transepts. Although the stubby steeple at the west end is 14th-cent., most of the cemented interior is original. The nave is striking, with proper compound piers, and the sedilia in the chancel are original. The responds are of long and short stones and under the tower arch is a Perpendicular screen. The south door has 13th-cent. ironwork.

GRENDON UNDERWOOD, *Buckinghamshire* (10–SP6720). This is a long straggling village, with many 17th-cent. cottages and Shakespeare Farm, of 16th-cent. origin, where, according to tradition, Shakespeare gained his inspiration for *A Midsummer Night's Dream*. In his time this farm was an inn, the sign of which – the Ship Inn – hangs in AYLESBURY Museum. The farm-house, with its lovely timbered and brick framework, is gabled and has windows containing the original lattice and leaded glass.

The River Ray runs through the village and in the Church of St Leonard Shakespeare is reputed to have lain in his drunken slumbers. The carved doorway is very beautiful and just inside it is a 15th-cent. stoup. The thick walls of the nave are evidence of their Norman origin but the tower is of the 15th cent., the hexagonal pulpit Jacobean. In the stair turret is a 15th-cent. door. The three bells in the church were made by Robert Atton and Richard Chandler in the 17th cent.

GRETTON, *Northamptonshire* (10–SP8994), is an old country village, standing on a hill-top, reached by a winding street. Magnificent views of the Welland valley are visible from the village green, on which still remain the old stocks and the whipping post.

The houses are all of stone, some spacious, others thatched cottages. On one old chimney is a sundial, and the inn sign is of oak leaves wrought in iron.

The Church of St James the Great is a medieval building with a brown stone 15th-cent. tower contrasting with the grey of the chancel and nave. There are Norman pillars in the nave which has Decorated aisles and fine carving. In the 17th cent. the chancel was raised to incorporate the Hatton family vault. The panelling and altar rails are of Queen Anne period, as is the pulpit, and the font is 15th-cent.

Two m. SE. of Gretton is **Kirby Hall,** which is open to the public and is now an Ancient Monument. It was begun in 1570 by Humphrey Stafford who owned the estate, in which there was then a village and church. Christopher Hatton, a favourite of Queen Elizabeth, bought it shortly afterwards but it was his descendants who lived there, entertained James I and his queen there, and commissioned the architect Inigo Jones to transform it into the beautiful house it became in the 17th cent. The long west front is Elizabethan, of Weldon stone with many gables, obelisks and chimneys. The north front is the work of Inigo Jones and resembles a Renaissance palace. The outer courtyard has three gateways, and across a large open space is the inner court, in which is a range of two-storied rooms, with a magnificent loggia by Inigo Jones at one end and the great hall at the other, 30 ft high with its original roof and a minstrels' gallery. The gardens, which have been restored, are also lovely.

HAMBLEDEN, *Buckinghamshire* (6–SU7886). This attractive village in the valley of the Chilterns is approached by a narrow road sheltered by beeches.

In the centre of the square under tall chestnut trees is the village pump, still in use. There are Georgian houses, including the Rectory surrounding it, and old cottages have been transformed into village shops. The Manor House was built in 1604.

On the River Thames, reached by a road used by the Romans, is the white-timbered Hambleden Mill, named in 1338, with a weathervane resting on its turret. Nearby is a lock and the river can be crossed by a narrow bridge from Hambleden to the Berkshire bank.

The archaeological museum houses a model of a Roman farm, discovered in the fields behind Yewden, complete with implements in use in Roman times.

St Mary the Virgin Church dates from the 14th cent., although much of it has been restored. Its size and beauty dominate its surroundings. In the tower, which was rebuilt in 1721, is a fascinating 16th-cent. panel, believed to have been the bed-head of Cardinal Wolsey and bearing the cardinal's hat and the Wolsey arms. The Norman font, simply carved, is believed to be that in which

Noel Habgood

Hambleden Mill on the River Thames

Thomas Cantelupe, who was canonized, was baptized.

The chancel contains beautiful carving and a decorated sedilia and piscina. On the walls are many interesting brasses and in the north transept the lovely monument showing Sir Cope Doyley with his wife Martha and their 10 children. The epitaph on the tomb was written by Lady Doyley's brother, Francis Quarles, the poet.

HARROLD, *Bedfordshire* (10–SP9456). This old village, in pleasant countryside, with its narrow bridge and causeway with 11 pointed and rounded arches dating back to the 14th cent., has now added modern houses which do not in any way spoil its character or its older buildings.

On the small village green, with its handsome trees, remain the old circular stone lock-up with a conical roof and the graceful octagonal Market House. Nearby are pretty thatched cottages and in the High Street is the Old Manor, *c.* 1600, in which is a fine wooden mantelpiece.

St Peter's Church was originally of the early 13th cent. and still retains one lancet window indicating, by its position, that the chancel has since been shortened. Some 50 years later the south arcade, with its octagonal pier, was built. In the Decorated north chapel is a tall arch and the west tower, of the same period, has a Perpendicular spire. The Jacobean screen has original woodwork. A monument in the church to Dame Anne Jolliffe, who lies buried in the chancel, is of

interest. In 1732 she founded almshouses and later married Dr Richard Mead, physician to Queen Anne and other members of the royal family, who established the practice of inoculation and spent much time and vast sums of money in seeking remedies to eradicate the plague.

HARTWELL, *Buckinghamshire* (10–SP8012). This quiet village two m. W. of AYLESBURY, with its now ruined 18th-cent. church, built to resemble YORK Minster, is famous for the house that bears its name.

It was in Hartwell House that Louis XVIII stayed with his court during the Napoleonic wars. The Queen of France died here during their exile and her coffin was taken from here to Sardinia. Standing in a walled park, it is a splendid Jacobean building with an 18th-cent. front and decorations. The entrance to the house is by a porch, flanked by carved pillars of stone, and a carved doorway. Above is a magnificent round oriel window sitting on embroidered stone corbels. The splendid staircase has carved newels supporting historical and mythical figures. The stone of the house and of the walls surrounding the garden came from a nearby quarry. Superb trees abound in the park, some of them bearing carvings by the Frenchmen who spent nearly a decade here. One of the park's splendours is its long lake fed from the springs nearby, with a stone bridge decorated by an ornamental parapet and containing an arch brought from Kew Bridge, Surrey. The house is now a school. In the old rectory is a moulded beam bearing the date 1552.

Hartwell has many charming cottages and its walls contain ammonites discovered in the local clay pits.

By Weir Lane are to be found the Egyptian springs which run into the lake at Hartwell House. Among the thickly overhanging trees and the clear spring water is a stone seat built in the Egyptian style and bearing an Egyptian inscription.

HATFIELD, *Hertfordshire* (10–TL2309). This is a town divided into the old and the new, the latter being an industrialized area of pleasant modern construction, the former retaining many of its characteristics of earlier times.

Its most famous and prized possession is the illustrious Hatfield House, built by Robert Cecil, the 1st Earl of Salisbury, between 1608 and 1612. The Cecil family still live there. It is exceptionally large, about 300 ft by 150 ft, with domes and towers and magnificent windows. A clock tower rises from the roof of the great hall, surmounted by an octagonal dome. The hall extends over two floors of the building and contains a spectacular screen of Jacobean carving. On the first floor is the long gallery, and the great staircase, with its elaborate tapering banisters and carved decorations, is a superb piece of workmanship. The house has its own chapel and every room holds much of beauty and interest. In the gardens, re-fashioned in the 19th cent., are original fountains, a large relief of Queen Elizabeth I and a maze. The park is the largest in the county and the remains of the oak tree, under which Princess Elizabeth was sitting when news was brought of her accession to the throne after the death of Mary Tudor, are still preserved. At the entrance to the park, opposite the railway station, is a large monument to the 3rd Marquis of Salisbury, Prime Minister in the last century. The house and grounds are open to the public.

Near Hatfield House is the Old Palace, which was built in 1480–90 and was the residence of Cardinal Morton. Over the archway of the gate-house are ancient beams and a mullioned window. The west front of the palace is heavily buttressed with a square tower, and at the end a stepped gable is surmounted by a twisted chimney. The great hall is still there, with a few other rooms. It was in this palace that Queen Elizabeth I and Mary Tudor spent many years of their childhood, in virtual imprisonment.

Old Hatfield has many houses of interest, some half-timbered of the 16th cent., others Georgian. On the corner of Fore Street and Park Street is the low-roofed, timber-framed and gabled Eight Bells Inn which has barely altered since it was built in the 17th cent. Dickens referred to this inn as having been visited by Bill Sykes in *Oliver Twist*.

Fore Street, a fairly steep hill with some fine Georgian houses, leads to the churchyard with its ironwork gates made about 1710 and taken from ST PAUL'S CATHEDRAL.

The Parish Church of St Etheldreda dates from the 13th cent., but the exterior of the broad nave was rebuilt in 1872. The Salisbury Chapel holds the tomb of the 1st Earl of Salisbury: entirely in the Dutch tradition, it is ornate with figures surrounding that of the earl. There is a lovely 18th-cent. screen which was brought from Amiens by the 3rd Marquis and many other monuments of interest.

HELPSTON, *Huntingdonshire* (10–TF1205), is a large, pleasant, stone-built village, once the site of a Roman settlement, and ¾ m. S. of the village will be found Roman remains that were excavated in 1827.

The peasant poet, John Clare, was born here in 1793 and was buried in the parish church 70 years later. A rather odd memorial to him stands at the crossroads on the village green. The attractive village cross, which dates from about 1300, has a tall polygonal base with gables and battlements and four circular steps.

There are several fine houses, including College House, which is S. of the church, with two buttresses, a slit window and a four-centred archway, and Helpston House, up the hill from the village green, which has a canted bay window, gables and dormers.

St Botolph's Church has a Norman tower which was partly rebuilt in 1865. The tower becomes octagonal when it reaches the level of the clerestory and has 14th-cent. bell openings and a short spire of the same period with a tier of lucarnes. The chancel, with its arch of filleted shafts, is about 1300 and the sedilia and piscina are original. The porch entrance is early 14th-cent. On one wall is a large painting of the Royal Arms of James I.

Woodhall Manor, which dates back to 1146 and is one of the oldest houses in the county, has recently been remodelled and it received a commendation under the Civic Trust Awards as a work of restoration which paid particular respect to the character of its surroundings.

HEMEL HEMPSTEAD, *Hertfordshire* (10–TL0506). The Domesday Book mentions the mills of this attractive market town stretching along the River Gade. Like other towns in the county it has its old and new sections, with many recently developed industries as well as paper mills which were of importance in the 19th cent.

The High Street is delightful, rising in a gentle curve towards the church and churchyard. The 18th-cent. houses are of purple brick and red dressings and the Sun Inn is dated 1726. There are rambling cottages and the half-timbered King's Arms which retreats into a side alley, one of several alleys off the High Street. The neo-Jacobean town hall is of red brick with dressings and was added to in the 19th cent.

Off the High Street is the Friends' Meeting House in St Mary's Road, an early 19th-cent. building of purple and red brick with a burial ground at its side.

Lockers House, on Bury Hill, has an Elizabethan wing and elaborately decorated ceilings, and Lockers Cottage is an attractive timber-framed brick and plaster building. In the Marlowes, a street running parallel to Bury Road, are Little Marlowes House and Old Marlowes House, two-story cottages of the late 18th cent. with some early Georgian workmanship. Corner House, near the end of the street, is of the 15th or 16th cent., timber-framed with overhanging stories.

Near the church is Henry's Banqueting Hall, two brick and timber cottages built 300 years ago, their overmantels a mixture of Tudor roses, crowns and fleurs-de-lis.

The Church of St Mary's, a large 12th-cent. church standing at the far end of the town, is reputed to be one of the finest in the country. It has a 14th-cent. timber spire nearly 200 ft high. Most of its workmanship is Norman, with a nave of six bays, a clerestory, a crossing tower on the lower stage and a circular staircase turret in the upper. The roofs of the transepts are 15th-cent. with arched braces decorated with traceried spandrels. There is a fine brass to Robert Albyn and his wife.

On the road to **Piccotts End** is Marchmont House, an early 19th-cent. building with a Greek Doric doorway, and off Gadebridge Lane is Gadebridge, standing in its own grounds, the front 11 bays wide with a portico of massive Ionic pilasters.

Half a m. N. of Hemel Hempstead, on the B486, is Piccotts End, with a remarkable house with 14th-cent. wall paintings only discovered in 1953.

HEMINGFORD GREY, *Huntingdonshire* (10–TL2970), was the home of Dendy Sadler, the artist, and although a new housing estate has risen on its outskirts it still retains its old-world charm, with thatched cottages and timbered houses. The views from the banks of the River Ouse, on which it stands, are delightful.

N. of the church is Hemingford Grey House, built of red brick in 1697. It has a hipped roof, segment-headed windows and two stories. By the river's edge is one of the biggest plane trees in England, planted in 1702. River House, in the High Street, is late 18th-cent., of yellow brick with a handsome doorway, and Broom Lodge, at the corner of Braggs Lane, is another five-bay house with shaped end-gables. Further E. is the timber-framed Glebe Cottage, with thatched roof and closely set studs, dated 1583.

But of major interest is the manor house with its garden stretching to the river and a moat surrounding the house on the other three sides. Built of stone, it is one of the oldest inhabited houses in England, for much of it is 12th-cent. It is two stories high, with a first-floor entrance door, now a window, and its hall is on the first floor. There are Norman two-light windows in the west, south and east walls. Inside, the splendid Norman chimneypiece has two columns with scalloped capitals. The central chimney stack was added in the 16th cent.

St James's Church, on the river bank, has a Perpendicular tower with ball finials of the 18th cent. on the buttresses, and a truncated spire with eight ball finials. The remainder of the spire was destroyed by a hurricane in 1741. Of the north arcade, part is about 1180, with the east bay 13th-cent. and the west bay 14th-cent. The chancel is 13th-cent. with a lovely double piscina, its intersecting arches standing on Purbeck shafts. There are two inscribed panels, dated 1682 and 1715, one inside and the other outside the church.

HERTFORD, *Hertfordshire* (10–TL3212). This rural town is the county town of Hertfordshire. It centres around Parliament Square, which was formed as an open space in 1821, and is filled with many features of interest. In its picturesque streets stand houses and cottages of varying periods, with three rivers, the Lea, Beane and Rib, meeting at its centre.

Only a little remains of the ancient castle, built by the second son of King Alfred – Prince Edward – to protect London against the Danes. Today it is a modernized 15th-cent. gatehouse, now used as offices by the council, with walls 22 ft high. It stands in a charming park stretching down to the river and has four towers. The Gothic-style windows and one wing were added at the beginning of the 19th cent., and over the doorway is the coat of arms of England and France, for many kings stayed here, and Elizabeth I lived in the castle during her childhood. In the grounds, which are open to the public, is a boundary mark, a monument in the form of a pebble stone dated 1621. Near to the pebble stone is a beautiful tulip tree, one of the finest in England.

In Fore Street, leading off Parliament Square, will be found Christ's Hospital School for Girls, founded in 1683 for younger children by the governors of Christ's Hospital in London, the famous Bluecoat School. In the gateway and on the walls are figures of the Bluecoat boys and girls. The building has been enlarged in the last two centuries and in 1935 a new library was added.

The Victorian Corn Exchange and Public Hall has a stone-faced front, three bays with large Corinthian pilasters and a Cinquecento-style window. The Salisbury Arms, at the corner of Church Street and Fore Street, although much restored since the early 17th cent., still retains its Jacobean staircase and projecting upper floor.

Shire Hall, in the middle of the town, is of the 18th cent. and, although designed by the Adam brothers, it is not as graceful as might be expected. It is a simple yellow-brick building and its rear arcades originally gave access to a covered market. In the centre of its upper floor is a splendid rotunda and in the hall are portraits of famous personalities including a painting by Sir Joshua Reynolds of Charles James Fox.

The old Hale's Grammar School, by the churchyard, is a 17th-cent. building of red brick with an interesting chimney and small dome. It is gabled and under its hood moulds are brick windows. The new Richard Hale Grammar School still retains the door from the old school.

Near Salisbury Square, on Bull Plain, is Lombard House, facing the River Lea, with its original 17th-cent. brick, timber and plasterwork intact. This was the home of the Hertfordshire historian and judge, Sir Henry Chauncy, who conducted one of the last witchcraft trials to be held in England, on Jane Wenham. Queen Anne reprieved her after she was sentenced to death and the case led to the abolition of the witchcraft laws.

Of modern interest, but fitting well in this ancient town, is County Hall, built in 1939, a large group of buildings fashioned in Scandinavian style with a slim cupola, fluted portico and ornamental motifs.

At Hertford Heath, 2½ m. to the SE., is **Hailey-bury College**, the boys' public school. Originally founded in 1806 as the East India College for the sons of Englishmen serving with the East India Company, it took its present status in 1862. The older school buildings are grouped round a spacious quadrangle.

HEXTON, *Hertfordshire* (10–TL1030), is set in beautiful countryside surrounded by the Barton Hills, part of the Chilterns, with an avenue of laburnam trees in the street and large yews surrounding the church.

St Faith's Church is early 19th-cent., except for parts of the nave and tower which seem to be 15th-cent. The piers of the nave on the south side are circular and on the north side quatrefoil. The south chancel chapel has a vault and Command-ment Boards. There is a plain monument, 1601, to Peter Taverner and his wife.

One m. SW. on the Barton Hills is **Ravensburgh Castle**, an Iron Age hill-fort. It is oval-shaped, 22 acres in size, and has a large ditch surrounding it and high banks. The west side has a double ditch and there is an entrance in the north-west corner.

HIGHAM FERRERS, *Northamptonshire* (10–SP9669). On the outskirts of this delightful town, which is a borough and appears in the Domesday Book, are many new buildings, but once you turn into the High Street you will be greeted by much that is ancient and beautiful. The High Street is a long main road with many of the houses, of local limestone with Collyweston tiles, raised above street level.

In the Market Square in the centre is a 13th-cent. cross carved with oak leaves and ballflowers, with a Crucifixion on one side and a Madonna on the other. All around are buildings of interest, including the Regency Town Hall, the Elizabethan manor house, the Ivy House (1633) and the Green Dragon which has a dovecot. On one corner of the street is an old thatched cottage which is the local barber's shop.

67 High Street is on the site of the birthplace of Henry Chichele, who eventually became Arch-bishop of Canterbury. Beside the church, reached by a short lane (no cars allowed), is the striped stone Bede House which he built for 12 poor old men, with an open hall with an oak roof, a chapel and a vaulted crypt. He was also responsible for the Chantry Chapel, a lovely piece of architecture, which is separate from the church and was used for some time as a school until it was reconse-crated.

The beautiful spire of St Mary's Church, 170 ft high, dominates the skyline for miles around. The richly crocketed steeple has a pierced parapet, flying buttresses and Early English mouldings. The 13th-cent. tower has a carved doorway similar to the style of WESTMINSTER ABBEY. The interior is a double building with two naves, the south being 13th-cent. and the north 14th-cent. The carved woodwork, both old and modern, is very good. The stalls with misericords carved with animals, birds, kings, angels and grotesque figures, were given by Henry Chichele, as was the choir screen. In all, the church has seven screens. There are many interesting and elaborate brasses.

HIGH WYCOMBE, *Buckinghamshire* (6–SU 8593), stretches along the Wye Valley from WEST WYCOMBE in the W. to Loudwater and Wooburn in the E. It is the county's second largest town and has been a place of importance since Roman times. It has been notable throughout its history for its dissenters – Anabaptists, Independents and Quakers – and Cromwell also had a strong follow-ing here during the Civil War, although he treated the town so harshly during his rule that on the restoration of Charles II it became strongly Royalist.

At that time it was an important wool centre, having its own guild of craftsmen, but in time that trade gave way to lace-making and straw-plaiting which were its main industries until the 19th cent. In the 17th cent. the furniture industry, for which High Wycombe is now world-renowned, started in the simple form of chair-making. Among its other important modern industries are paper manufacture and engineering.

On the hills of the town are prehistoric buildings and ancient earthworks.

Standing in the Market Place, scheduled as an Ancient Monument, is the Guildhall, dating from 1757. In the upper story, supported on stone columns, is the large Council Chamber and ante-room, and beneath it, on market days, are gaily decked stalls. Facing the Guildhall is the Little Market House, or Shambles as it is called, also scheduled as an Ancient Monument. It was built in 1761 by the Adam brothers and is of a curious octagonal shape. On a wall above one of the stalls is a panel giving the toll prices for the privilege of holding a stall there.

The Museum, at Castle Hill, which is open to the public, shows many examples of craftsman-ship of the 17th and 18th cents. Chairs made through the reigns of James I to Queen Anne are exhibited and there are examples of Chippendale, Hepplewhite, Sheraton and Windsor furniture.

The imposing Town Hall, in Queen Victoria Road, was erected in 1904 and is in the late Renais-sance style. Its main hall, with a fine organ, seats over 1,000 people. The Oak Room, with its lovely windows, was panelled by local craftsmen.

Adjoining the Town Hall and of modern con-struction are the public library and the Art Gallery, which is open to the public.

Wycombe Abbey, now a girls' public school, stands in 250 acres of grounds. Built in 1795, it was

originally the house of Loakes Manor, designed
by James Wyatt for the first Lord Carrington.

Still standing in the High Street are two old
inns, the White Lion and the Red Lion. It was from
the balcony of the latter that Disraeli made his
first speech and he is said to have had a special
affection for the town.

Although the town is greatly modernized there
are still many old buildings of interest, including
the Elizabethan almshouses in Easton Street and
others in Bowerdean Road.

The Parish Church of All Saints is a large town
church, the biggest in the county, with a 13th-cent.
exterior and a 15th-cent. interior. In its tower,
rising 100 ft above the street, is a peal of 12 bells.
There is much fine woodwork to be seen on
screens and stalls. In the south chancel is a screen
erected by Richard Redehole and dated 1468.
Through the centuries much has been added to
give the church its present beauty. A reredos,
designed as a screen and stretching across the
chancel behind the high altar, was erected as a war
memorial in 1922. A large stained-glass window is
particularly noteworthy. This was a gift of Dame
Francis Dove in 1933 in memory of famous
women, and depicts 17 of them, including Queen
Victoria, St Hilda, St Bridget, Emily Brontë,
Elizabeth Fry and Florence Nightingale. In the
north chancel aisle is a monument by Peter
Scheemakers to the Earl of Sherburne.

The town has many good examples of modern
architecture, including the General Hospital and
the College of Technology, and surrounding it are
large areas of natural beauty.

HITCHIN, *Hertfordshire* (10–TL1829), is one
of the most interesting of the county's towns.

Down by the River Hiz, which flows through
the town, are the early-17th-cent. Biggin Almshouses, built round a narrow courtyard with a
Tuscan colonnade. In Sun Street, off Market
Square, are many buildings of quality. The Sun
Inn, a well-preserved building of blue brick with
rubbed-brick dressings and a central carriageway,
has a low, half-timbered range in the courtyard
and an assembly room which was added in 1770.

In Tilehurst Street is the Victorian Baptist
church with giant angle pilasters and Tuscan
columns. In the church is a chair given by John
Bunyan. No. 35 Tilehurst Street is a late Georgian
house of brick; on this site stood the house
of George Chapman, the Elizabethan poet and
playwright. Other houses in the street range from
the 15th to the 19th cent.

On the west side of Market Square is the Victorian Corn Exchange, fashioned in the Italian
style with a large Venetian window and a lantern
turret. Around the square are ancient and interesting buildings interspersed with modern ones, and
on its east side is Queen Street, mostly of Victorian
buildings, with the Lister House Hotel at the end,
a Victorian house in Georgian tradition.

Bancroft, a continuation of the High Street
with houses of several centuries, is very fine and at
its end range the Skynner Almshouses, dated 1670
and 1698.

In Brand Street off the High Street is the early
Victorian old town hall by Bellamy, adjoining the
library of the same period with a closed Tuscan
porch and a temple front. The new town hall is
opposite.

A house of particular interest is the Priory,
built in 1770. Surrounded by a moat, it is in stone
with a Palladian south front incorporating a semi-
circular porch and two projecting wings with
Venetian windows. The County Council owns it.

St Mary's Church, in the Market Place, has
woodwork that is without equal in the county.
It is representative of a wealthy late medieval
town, for when the church was built the town had
a thriving wool industry. It is embattled all around
and its most outstanding feature is the south
porch with a staircase turret, window openings, a
lierne-vault and the arms of the Staple of Calais on
the wall. The nave is of flint, the chancel of stone.
There is a fine series of roofs with cusped panels
and principals on stone angels.

The 15th-cent. screens, of which there are
several, are rich and beautiful. Of the same period,
the stone font has mutilated figures under arched
canopies, and the pulpit has angle buttresses and
restored panels. The painting of the Adoration of
the Magi is Flemish. There are many interesting
monuments but none of outstanding importance.

HOUGHTON, *Huntingdonshire* (10–TL2871),
is a delightful riverside village with many picturesque cottages. There are pleasant walks along
the tree-shaded paths and it is a popular yachting
and boating centre.

On the village green is an elaborate Gothic-
style pump in cast-iron, the only one of its kind in
the county. Nearby is a bust of Potto Brown, a
wealthy miller who worked the mill which still
remains here. He was the village philanthropist
and a devout Nonconformist. The watermill, believed to be the oldest remaining one on the River
Ouse, is a massive timbered building of the 17th
cent. It is the property of the National Trust and is
used as a Youth Hostel.

The yellow-brick Union Chapel is early Victorian with an arched doorway and windows.
Houghton House, late Victorian, is fashioned in
the Elizabethan style with a large segmental pediment above the porch and a square bay window
of 11 lights.

St Mary's Church, partly Decorated and partly
Perpendicular, is of brown cobbles. The double
piscina appears to be earlier, however, and the
tower is an unusual shape, with buttresses
finishing beneath the bell-openings, above which
the tower becomes octagonal and has a stone
spire with two tiers of lucarnes. The pulpit was
made from a tree from Houghton Park.

HUGHENDEN, *Buckinghamshire* (6–SU8695).
N. of HIGH WYCOMBE is Hughenden Manor, a
large mansion modernized in Victorian times by
Benjamin Disraeli, Earl of Beaconsfield and Prime
Minister of Britain. He lived here with his wife
from 1847 until his death in 1881 and the house
holds many relics of his youth. It stands on the

Barnaby/Mustograph

Houghton watermill is believed to be the oldest one remaining on the River Ouse

slope of a hill with woods at its rear running down to a lovely stream in the valley below, and a parkland, with great trees, in front of it.

Disraeli's study is still as it was at the time of his death and there are manuscripts of his novels and letters from Queen Victoria.

The church on the estate, where Disraeli is buried, shows the work of Sir Arthur Blomfield; it still contains a medieval chancel and chapel and a bell of the pre-Reformation period. Outside the church and cut square is a yew, planted in 1690.

The house and gardens, which are National Trust property, are open to the public.

HUNTINGDON, *Huntingdonshire* (10–TL 2371). This is the county town, attractive with much of interest. The official name of the county is now Huntingdon and Peterborough. The town's narrow main street stretches for nearly 1½ m., but many of the places to visit are off this thoroughfare.

It has ancient origins, for Roman coins and pottery have been found here. The Anglo-Saxons created it a burgh, the Danes invaded it from the river and in 921 Edward the Elder repaired the damage they had made. At the end of that century a market and a mint were established, both indications of prosperity. In the 13th cent. there were 16 churches, of which only two remain, for the Black Death in 1348 caused devastation and the town lost its prosperity and became a backwater, except for the short period during the Civil War when first Cromwell and then Charles I made their headquarters here. Agriculture has always been its main industry.

Oliver Cromwell was born in the town; the grammar school which he, and Pepys, attended, founded about 1565, is now a museum of Cromwelliana. This building was originally the Hospital of St John the Baptist, founded about 1160, and considerable parts of the old structure remain. Cromwell House, in the High Street, is on the site of the Austin Friary.

All Saints' Church, in Market Place, is part of a previous building and is mainly 15th-cent. The upper stages of the tower were rebuilt after the Civil War and the top is Victorian. The organ chamber is attractive and the Perpendicular chancel roof has carved bosses. The bowl of the font is 13th-cent.

Nearby is the stately town hall, built in 1745 of red brick with three stories. Around the walls of the ballroom are interesting paintings, one by Gainsborough.

There are two interesting inns, the George, which still has two sides of its 17th-cent. courtyard, in one of which is an open gallery and external staircase, and the Falcon, with oriel windows and a massive door, which is believed to have been the headquarters of Cromwell during the Civil War.

At the end of the town, separating it from GOD-MANCHESTER, is the early-14th-cent. bridge, with cutwaters on both sides. It is said to be one of the finest medieval bridges in the country. Nearby, in a public open space, are the extensive earthworks of a castle founded by William the Conqueror.

The town is composed mainly of Georgian buildings, but there are a number of the 16th and 17th cents. Walden House, now council offices, is of red brick with a hipped roof and giant Ionic pilasters. The County Hospital in Brampton Road is of yellow brick and Victorian, as is Petersfield Hospital, a former workhouse, in St Peter's Road. In the same road is the former county gaol, built in 1828 of yellow brick. Cowper House, where the poet lived in 1765, has a steep three-bay pediment and window lintels with brick frills on the first floor. In George Street are rather humble yellow-brick almshouses of the Victorian period and in the High Street is Whitwell House, 1727, with three stories, segment-headed first-floor windows and pretty garden railings. Montague House, also Georgian, has an attractive doorway below its Venetian window. In Hartford Road is the Roman Catholic Church of St Michael, of brick and stone with a round arch.

St Mary's Church, in the High Street, has the remains of Norman buttresses in the corners of the nave and south aisle, the chancel is early 13th-cent. with a priest's doorway, and the solid ornate tower is Perpendicular. The arches have fine mouldings and there are several 17th-cent. inscriptions. Under the tower are a number of tablets, the largest to the Carcassonnett family, dated 1749.

About ½ m. away, on the road to BRAMPTON, is **Hinchingbrooke**, the seat of the Cromwell family, now a school, where Queen Elizabeth I was entertained in 1564. It has a gatehouse which is thought to have come from RAMSEY Abbey.

Along the river banks are pleasant walks, good fishing and yachting, and nearby is Portholme, a large meadow where rare wild flowers can be found.

HUSBORNE CRAWLEY, *Bedfordshire* (10–SP9535). This tiny village, with many old cottages, stands on the road to AMPTHILL, on the edge of Woburn Park.

Its Manor House, in front of the church, is a timber-framed building of the late 16th cent., and nearby is Crawley Park, a late-18th-cent. building of red brick.

St Mary's Church has a tower built of rare green sandstone and is in a wooded, hilly setting. The Perpendicular west tower has a higher stair-turret, and near the south doorway is a large stoup. The tower arch is pleasantly decorated with capitals and there is a large alabaster monument to John Thompson, 1597, with five columns and a studded ceiling. Another monument is to Talbot Williamson, 1765, with an urn before an obelisk.

ICKFORD, *Buckinghamshire* (10–SP6407), is a tiny village lying in some of England's best grazing land. The River Thames flows past it and is crossed by a 17th-cent. bridge with three attractive arches.

The Rectory, which is partly 16th-cent., was occupied by Archbishop Sheldon who was rector here for many years. He was imprisoned as a Royalist during Cromwell's rule and, after he became Archbishop of Canterbury, helped to rebuild St Paul's Cathedral.

The Church of St Nicholas was built in the 13th cent. and its saddleback tower, gabled walls and font are all of this period. The sanctuary has a modern window showing striking figures of Edward the Martyr and Edward I, but it still contains some 14th-cent. glass.

A strange Tudor tomb, the oldest monument in the church, is of Thomas Tippin with his wife and nine children. It is said that he had the tomb built in his lifetime.

ICKWELL, *Bedfordshire* (10–TL1445), is one of the county's most beautiful villages, its vast green surrounded by low thatched houses with dormer windows. On the green stand a gaily striped maypole and the smithy where Thomas Tompion, the clock-maker, once worked. At the northern end is a more formal house of the 18th cent.

Ickwell Bury, once a priory, was rebuilt after a fire in 1937. The new building, of a free neo-Georgian style, stands in a richly wooded park, and near a long avenue of limes and chestnuts is the octagonal dovecot of the 17th cent., with a revolving post and projecting beam. The stables adjoining the house are original, built in 1683 with 10 bays and a square cupola.

IVER, *Buckinghamshire* (6–TQ0381), is a delightful village in a scattered parish with shady lanes and Iver Heath nearby. There are modern film studios close by, but it has many 16th- and 17th-cent. houses, mostly built around the church, which is a mixture of styles. The 500-year-old tower has an ancient bell-chamber and the nave is Anglo-Saxon. The church's most beautiful feature is the 12th-cent. chancel with a wide pointed arch and a double piscina and triple sedilia. The pulpit, carved with cherubs, is 200 years old and the Norman font is a square marble bowl standing on round pillars. A brass inscription on the floor is to Ralph Aubrey, Clerk of the Kitchen to Prince Arthur, the first husband of Catherine of Aragon. There are many brasses and monuments of interest.

A house of particular note is the 18th-cent. Bridgefoot House, a clever blending of brick and glass.

In this village the family of the Dukes of Kent have resided for many years.

IVINGHOE, *Buckinghamshire* (10–SP9416). Ivinghoe Beacon belongs to the National Trust and is reached by a narrow road just outside the village. From the top of this hill, nearly 800 ft high, can be surveyed the extensive line of the Chilterns, the Quainton Hills and the Dunstable Downs. Only walking will take you to the summit but the scenery well justifies the climb.

This agricultural village, from which Sir Walter Scott took the name of his novel *Ivanhoe*, holds much of interest. An ancient windmill still remains in a field. The King's Head, a 15th-cent. inn rebuilt 200 years later, retains its oak beams and broad fireplaces.

The Church of St Mary the Virgin is very beautiful. Of 13th-cent. origin, it was greatly altered in the following two centuries. The roof is of great grandeur, with the outspread wings of angels reaching to the timbers, on which rest heads of people and animals, carved in stone corbels. The timbers are adorned with flowers. The chancel is graced with roses and leaves as well as angels. The pulpit is Jacobean and the lectern Elizabethan. Of amusing interest are the ends of the 38 pews, for within the poppyheads are distorted faces, typical of the work of medieval craftsmen.

JORDANS, *Buckinghamshire* (6–SU9791). Down a quiet country road, about 2 m. W. of CHALFONT ST GILES, lies this secluded village built around its green. A few minutes' walk will take you to some of the most enchanting scenery in the county, among the Chiltern beechwoods.

History has made Jordans famous, for it is the burial place of William Penn, the Quaker, founder of Pennsylvania, U.S.A. The little brick Friends' Meeting House, just outside the village, was built in 1687, and the unvarnished deal benches standing on a plain brick floor still remain. Erected immediately after James II issued the Declaration of Indulgence, the building is a constant reminder of the days when men were beginning to want to think freely, since, although William Penn was the friend of kings, he was many times imprisoned for his outspoken Quaker beliefs. The walls of the Meeting House are decorated with portraits, autographs and other reminders of the pioneers of the period.

In the graveyard nearby are simple headstones recording the names of the Friends buried there. These include William Penn and his two wives, Mary and Isaac Penington, who supplied money for the Meeting House, and Joseph Rule, known as the White Quaker, a Thames waterman who wore undyed clothing.

Old Jordans Farm, the home of a yeoman in the days of Charles II, was where the Friends met and is now a hostel. The Mayflower Barn, set on walls of brick, has timbers which are reputed to have been taken from a ship, and one of the beams has on it the letters R HAR I, believed to stand for Mayflower, Harwich.

KETTERING, *Northamptonshire* (10–SP8778), is an industrial town set in pleasant countryside, with footwear as its main industry, for which it has its own Boot and Shoe College. It is an ancient town, dating back to 956, and in 1227 Henry III granted it market rights.

Its places of architectural interest are mostly near the church, which is reached by a narrow twisting High Street, round the bend of which is the large market place where open markets are held three times a week. There are many Victorian and Edwardian public buildings, including the Alfred East Gallery which has a good collection of paintings, with many by the artist who gave his name to the gallery, himself a native of the town. The Museum has local Roman and Anglo-Saxon remains, and the Corn Exchange and public library are typically Victorian. In Sheep Street are the 17th-cent. Sawyer's Almshouses

and beside the church is the old Georgian manor, now the Town Health Department. There are two earlier buildings: one in Gold Street is the Toller Chapel, which has records of early persecuted Nonconformists, and in Lower Street is the Mission House, where the Baptist Missionary Society was founded in 1792.

The steeple of the Church of SS. Peter and Paul, behind the market place, soars above the busy town. It is of Barnack limestone with lead roofs. Although much restored, it was originally Perpendicular and parts still remain of this period. The body is long and low.

About 1 m. from the town, towards Barton Seagrave, is Wicksteed Park which covers 100 acres of ground and was purchased by Charles Wicksteed at the turn of the century to create a pleasure park for the people of Kettering. It has many amenities, including a lake, miniature railway, ponies, and pools for model yachting, bathing and paddling.

Three m. N. on the road to Corby, set in flat, lush countryside, is **Boughton House**, resembling a miniature Versailles, for the Duke of Montagu, who lived there, had been Ambassador to the Court of Louis XIV. He brought back with him a fine collection of French furniture and china, which the house still contains. Many royal visitors have stayed there, for it is one of the seats of the Duke and Duchess of Buccleuch. The superb avenues of elm which surround the house were planted by the 2nd Duke of Montagu with the idea of linking the house with his London residence, 70 m. away. It can be viewed by appointment.

KIMBOLTON, *Huntingdonshire* (10–TL0967), is a small, beautiful town in a valley, with the River Kim running through it. It has a wide High Street, with several interesting houses, and this runs parallel with East Street, in which the buildings are also attractive. Narrow lanes connect the main streets.

There is a Moravian church, the only one in the county, erected in 1823.

The town is historically important because Kimbolton Castle, now a school and open to the public, was the last home of Catherine of Aragon, who died there. The castle stands in a large park. It was bought and remodelled in 1620 by the 1st Earl of Manchester, whose successor again remodelled it from a design by Sir John Vanbrugh. The portico in the north front is the largest feature of the house, with two giant Tuscan columns. Inside are many superb paintings on walls and ceilings by the Venetian Giovanni Pellegrini. The square gatehouse was designed by Robert Adam.

St Andrew's Church has a 14th-cent. tower with a broach spire, and at the top of the tower are carvings of small heads. The arcades of the church are early 13th-cent. The nave roof is original and the large, rather ugly font is about 12th-cent. In the south chapel is a fine screen of *c*. 1500 with paintings of kings and angels on four of the panels of the dado. There are several interesting monuments to the Manchester family.

KNEBWORTH, *Hertfordshire* (10–TL2520). Old and New Knebworth are separated from each other by about a mile of delightful countryside. Deard's End, at the top of a hill near the railway station, is a large farm with fine brick and timber barns.

In New Knebworth, on a hillside, is St Martin's Church, built by Lutyens. It is of red brick with stone dressings, without a tower but with extensively projecting roof eaves. Arches on Tuscan columns separate the aisle from the nave, and dividing the crossing from the transepts are two massive Tuscan columns.

Two buildings by Lutyens in the old village are the Golf Club House and Homewood, with its cottage windows on the low ground floor and its five weather-boarded gables.

The Church of SS. Mary and Thomas, surrounded by acres of green fields, is entered by a lych-gate covered with wild roses. The nave, chancel and tower are of the 15th cent. as are the plain benches. In the low Norman chancel is a blocked Norman window. The 18th-cent. pulpit has carved Flemish panels. The font is of the 15th cent. and a fine iron screen of a later period crosses the tower arch.

The Lytton Chapel was added at the beginning of the 18th cent. to contain lavish monuments to the family who have lived at Knebworth for over four centuries. There are three marble tombs as well as other memorials and brasses. The names of Strode and Robinson appearing in the chapel are all part of the Lytton family name.

From the church can be seen Knebworth House which, with its vast park, is open to the public. It started as a Tudor mansion in 1492 and the body of the house still remains. The plastered ceiling in the great hall and the detailed screen are both Jacobean, and the superb panelling in the hall, ending in the reredos which stretches the width of the room, is 17th-cent. The house was largely rebuilt in 1843 by Sir Edward Bulwer-Lytton, the 1st Lord Lytton, statesman and author of *The Last Days of Pompeii*. It contains some of his manuscripts, and has fine furnishings, relics and portraits. Many people of literary note stayed here, including Dickens and Disraeli. The grounds are lovely to wander in.

Not far away is the Victorian Lytton Arms built for employees of the big house.

LEIGHTON BUZZARD AND LINS-LADE, *Bedfordshire* (10–SP9125). The two towns, divided by the River Ouse, were only recently made into one. On the Linslade side, which is more industrialized, is the Grand Union Canal.

Leighton Buzzard, a fairly large, pleasant market town with narrow streets, is mentioned in the Domesday Book. There are still thatched brick and timber cottages, and the pentagonal Market Cross, dating from about 1400, is very fine, rising in two tiers of arches and topped by a pinnacle 20 ft high. In the upper story are five statues: of Christ, the Madonna and Child, a bishop, a king and St John the Baptist. In 1650,

during the Commonwealth period, it was repaired and a fourpenny rate was levied on the townspeople to pay for it.

By the Post Office is the Golden Bells Inn of the 14th cent., originally built as two cottages and still retaining its old oak fireplace and oak beams.

The majority of buildings of interest are near the Market Place. Opposite the cross is the Swan Hotel, an early Victorian white building, in a Classical style. In North Street is the town's most impressive house, Holly Lodge, built in the late 17th cent. of blue and red brick with two cross gables. Just past it is the Friends' Meeting House, 1789, with wooden cross-windows and a simple exterior. Nearby are the Wilkes Almshouses, of yellow brick with gables, to which an interesting ceremony is attached, for on Rogation Monday parts of the founder's will are read aloud while a choir boy stands on his head.

In Lake Street is a 17th-cent. inn, the Unicorn, three stories high and nine bays long. The County Branch Library, a Grecian-style building with four unfluted Ionic columns, is Victorian.

The Church of All Saints, a large, ironstone building, dates from the 13th cent. It has a crossing steeple and a high spire with large broaches on which are tiny pinnacles. Additions were made to the church two centuries later and it has a complete collegiate chancel with its original seating and screens still intact. The ironwork on the west door is that of Thomas of Leighton and the Kempe windows are very fine. There are medieval *graffiti* on piers and walls, the Early English font is cauldron shaped, and on the lectern is a finely carved wooden eagle of the 14th cent.

In Linslade, close to the canal, will be found St Mary's Church, of yellow limestone and ironstone, with its early-12th-cent. nave masonry and its unmoulded chancel arch. The west tower is 15th-cent. and the chancel 16th cent. The nave is embattled and there are no aisles. The circular font of the 12th cent. has a band of scrolls and beasts and there are the remains of a 15th-cent. screen.

E. of the church is Manor Farmhouse, an interesting 18th-cent. building of vitreous and red brick, its centre bay flanked by giant pilasters.

LITTLE GADDESDEN, *Hertfordshire* (10–SP9913). This is an ancient village verging on superb scenery of magnificent beechwoods, commons covered with bracken, massive oaks and wild cherry trees, all part of the National Trust and a sanctuary for wildlife.

The house of John of Gaddesden, near the Post Office, is a large timber-framed 15th-cent. building with an overhanging upper floor and a timber roof, and was named after the famous royal physician. The manor house, a century older, is of stone, with stepped gables to its two turrets and mullioned and transomed windows. It has interesting Elizabethan wall paintings and a collection of early keyboard instruments. Its beautiful gardens which, together with the house, are open to the public, have unusual ornamental yew hedges.

Ashridge House was built in 1276 and stands in a vast park on the ridge of the Chilterns. It was originally erected as a College of Bonshommes in Norman days and is now the Bonar Law College. During Mary's reign, Princess Elizabeth stayed here. The house of Totternhoe stone was restored by James Wyatt in 1808, but it still retains its former beauty. Its chapel has a twice stepped back tower and a tall slender spire. The main building has a three-arched loggia, tall entrance-hall windows and a staircase tower. In the grounds, facing the rose garden, is the barn which has much of the original monastic work.

The Church of SS. Peter and Paul is outside the village. The tower is of flint with diagonal buttresses and the remainder cement-rendered. The 15th-cent. screen is much renewed and some of the benches have poppyheads. Its main interest is its monuments. The kneeling figure of Elizabeth Dutton was removed from ST MARTIN'S-IN-THE FIELDS, London. There is a large Classical monument to Elizabeth, Viscountess Brackley, with an epitaph in script; one to Elizabeth, Countess of Bridgewater; and one to Francis Henry, 8th Earl of Bridgewater, with an inscription saying he bequeathed £8,000 to literary men who wrote religious essays.

LITTLE HADHAM, *Hertfordshire* (10–TL44 22). On the outskirts of this little village are many timber-framed cottages and farm-houses and on the ground rising above it stands a delightful windmill.

Hadham Hall was built for the Capel family in the 16th cent. Although parts of the building were destroyed by fire, it still retains much of its Elizabethan structure with entrance turrets, octagonal chimneys and a gallery nearly 140 ft long. Its brick outbuildings, with a gatehouse and a large brick barn, appear to be older than the house itself.

The small Church of St Cecilia lies N. of the village street. Its 14th-cent. tower with diagonal buttresses has a fine arch and the nave has Perpendicular windows. There is an interesting timbered south porch, the sides of which are trefoil-cusped along the tops. The transept opens in a four-centred arch and the three-decker pulpit, decorated with a big tester, is dated 1633. The screen is of the 15th cent. and there are two brasses of the same period.

LITTLE MARLOW, *Buckinghamshire* (6–SU8788). This tiny village lies on the Thames at the end of a no through road. It still holds the fragments of a 14th-cent. Benedictine nunnery and in its centre is a gabled Jacobean manor house with its original staircase.

Adjoining the manor is the Church of St John the Baptist, of Norman origin with a fine 14th-cent. tower. The chancel is divided from a chapel by a Norman arch; the font is of the same period and a Norman piscina can be found on a window-sill. The double-swinging lych-gate is worked by a pulley and the attractive churchyard was the burial place of Edgar Wallace.

LITTLE MISSENDEN, *Buckinghamshire* (6–SU9298). This is an unspoilt village containing many old houses and cottages centred round an Elizabethan manor house and a grey church, that of St John Baptist. The River Misbourne flows through the fields nearby and the Chiltern Hills which flank the village are thick with beechwoods. The manor house, with its numerous windows, has an interesting collection of outhouses and stables. The garden and terrace were designed by Angelica Kaufmann.

The church, which dates back to Norman times, is principally renowned for its series of wall paintings discovered in the 1930s. Those of St Christopher, St Catherine and the Crucifixion are all 14th-cent., and there are numerous fragments dating from the 12th to the 18th cent. A Norman font still remains and a key 15 in. long hangs on the wall. There is an interesting series of modern stained-glass windows.

LITTLE WYMONDLEY, *Hertfordshire* (10–TL2127). This little country village, with its attractive main street, has several buildings of interest.

S. of the church is the 16th-cent. Wymondley Bury, a gabled brick building with a moat surrounding it and a gabled dovecot in its grounds. Wymondley Hall is a handsome, early-17th-cent. timber-framed house with a six-gabled front and an interesting group of chimneys. It has a large attractive barn with elaborate medieval timbers supporting the tiled roof. The late Georgian Wymondley House is near the west end of the village. It is two and a half stories high, with five bays, and has a cemented front and a porch with Ionic columns.

Half a m. N. of the village is Wymondley Priory, originally a 13th-cent. Augustinian house and now a farm-house with a few remains of the original arches.

St Mary's Church, set on a small hill, has a 15th-cent. nave and small tower with an Elizabethan bell, but the rest of the church was added in 1875.

LONDON COLNEY, *Hertfordshire* (10–TL 1603). This little village stands on the River Colne and has several interesting old houses and inns.

Of particular note is All Saints Convent, an attractive late-Victorian building of red and purple brick and stone with a neo-Tudor front with a turret. The lower refectory has a big dais window and the gatehouse has a figure frieze above its door.

St Peter's Church is slim with a cemented façade and is in the Norman Revival style dated 1825. The interior is without aisles and the columns of the west gallery have Norman capitals. The stained glass, representing the Ascension, is in a slightly Raphaelesque style.

One m. E. of the village is Tyttenhanger, a large brick house built in the middle of the 17th cent., with brick quoins and window frames, a hipped roof and a squat cupola. It has a magnificent staircase and rather unusual doorcases in the staircase hall. There is a chapel on the second

Barnaby/Mustograph

Long Crendon: the Court House was given to Queen Catherine of Aragon by Henry VIII

floor with a two-decker pulpit and the Ten Commandments over the fireplace. A long gallery runs the length of the house and there is a great deal of Elizabethan panelling.

LONG CRENDON. *Buckinghamshire* (10–SP6908). This attractive village, with its many 16th- and 17th-cent. thatched cottages, was once an important lace-making centre.

The 15th-cent. Court House, now a National Trust property, was given to Catherine of Aragon by Henry VIII. Long and low with timber frames, the upper story overhangs the lower in five bays, four of which form one large room with a timbered roof. At the end of the house is a massive fireplace, with a 16th-cent. wood lintel, as well as a round brick oven.

There are two other interesting houses in the village, the 15th-cent. manor house, with tall Tudor chimneys and a dovecot, and the lovely Long Crendon Manor.

St Mary's Church is of medieval origin. The roof to the nave is of 16th-cent. oak and the three porches are each of different centuries. The 14th-cent. font is surrounded by lions, with angels with outstretched wings adorning its brim. The Dormer tomb is a richly decorated monument with Sir John Dormer in complete armour and his wife in a long dress of blue and white, her head resting on a cushion. The lace for the altar and communion cloth was made by village lace-makers.

One m. E. of the village is **Notley Abbey**,

founded in 1162 by Augustinian monks and now a private residence.

LUTON, *Bedfordshire* (10–TL0821), is the largest town in the county. It is very prosperous, famed for its straw-plaiting and straw-hat-making which began in the 17th cent. Other industries have, to a great extent, replaced this trade, although 5 per cent of the town's industry is still hat-making. There is light engineering and a large motor-vehicle trade. It has its own airport.

In the centre of the town is Wardown Park with many amenities, including a large boating lake and a county cricket ground. The Victorian mansion, Wardown, is an art gallery and museum, housing many exhibits of local interest from the Stone Age to the present day.

The Town Hall, built in 1934 of Portland stone, with a clock tower rising to 144 ft, is a fine building. Water Tower, in West Hill Road, is one of the most pleasing buildings in Luton. In Moat Lane at Biscot is Moat House, the one remaining medieval house in the town, with a fine roof of *c.* 1500 and embattled collars and purlins. By way of Copt Hall will be found the ruins of Someries Castle, built by Lord Wenlock in the 15th cent. It still has a brick gatehouse, a brick chapel and other features of interest.

Dray's Ditches, near the South Bedfordshire golf course, have a linear dyke about half a mile long. In the excavations have been discovered Bronze Age urns and Iron Age pottery and ditches. Half a m. N. of Leagrave station is

Marlow: the River Thames is here the scene of lively activity

Waulud's Bank, an earthwork abutting on the River Lea. Inside a broad flat-bottomed ditch have been found Neolithic Rinyo-Clacton pottery fragments. Long Barrow is in the recreation ground of Sundown Park and stands over 7 ft high.

The town has many Victorian and modern churches. The chapels include the Union Chapel in Castle Street, early Victorian and one of the best buildings in Luton, with three bays and giant Greek Doric columns at the entrance.

St Mary's Church is the town's link with the past and one of the largest churches in England. It is a magnificent building begun in the 13th cent. and enlarged in the 14th and 15th cents. The exterior is of flint and stone chequer-work. The tower has a stair-turret. The elaborate Wenlock Chapel is very high and in two tiers, and opposite is the little chantry chapel of Richard Barnard, vicar in 1477, with an ornate vault. The octagonal font is of Purbeck marble *c.* 1330–40 with a majestic font canopy which contains a vault. There are several fine screens and the stalls in the chancel have carved heads on the arm-rests. There is a wealth of monuments, all of interest.

LUTON HOO, *Bedfordshire* (10–TL1018). In richly wooded countryside on the A6 to LUTON is the magnificent house of Luton Hoo, open to the public and situated in a park of 1,500 acres, landscaped by Capability Brown a year after Robert Adam started plans for the house itself. It has been the home of the Wernher family since 1903 when it was remodelled for Sir Julius, a diamond magnate. It originally belonged to the Earl of Bute, then Prime Minister.

The building is of ashlar stone, mainly of three stories, and has its own chapel. In the grounds are two lovely lakes, and the stables are by Adam. About 1¾ m. S. of the house is Lady Bute's Lodge, mid-Victorian but with a Norman doorway.

The house contains the Wernher collection, with paintings by Titian and Rembrandt, a fine collection of porcelain and china, magnificent tapestries and furniture, 16th- and 17th-cent. jewels and, in the Russian Room, robes worn at the court of the Tsars and mementoes of the Russian Imperial Family.

MARLOW, *Buckinghamshire* (6–SU8587). This fascinating little town, which has much to interest the traveller in its mixture of the old and the new, is planned in such a way that none of the new buildings in any way detract from the charm of the older ones.

In the High Street are many old houses, but its most famous feature is the suspension bridge, built in 1831 to the design of William Tierney Clark who constructed several similar bridges, including one linking Buda and Pest in Hungary. The one in Marlow, however, is the only remaining example of his work. From its centre are panoramic views of the river where swans are often to be seen and pretty gardens and handsome beech trees reach down to the water's edge. It is the dividing line of Berkshire and Buckinghamshire and on the opposite side, adjacent to the bridge, is the "Compleat Angler" Inn with its reminders of Izaak Walton's book. Adjoining the bridge, in the town itself, is All Saints Church, which contains a monument to Sir Miles Hobart, set up by Parliament to commemorate the parliamentary rebel, who in 1628 locked the door of the House of Commons until certain taxation resolutions were passed.

A short distance from the church is the obelisk milestone in the Market Place, erected in 1822, an indication that in the early 19th cent. the town was an important stopping-place for travellers. It is closely connected with the Cecil family of HATFIELD House, Hertfordshire, who were great sufferers from gout and used Marlow as a short cut to take the waters at BATH.

The Crown Hotel, originally called Remnantz, was reputedly a place where the famous highwayman Dick Turpin took hospitality and, probably, purses.

In West Street is Albion House which was once the home of Shelley, where he lived in 1817 with Mary Godwin whom he married. The 17th-cent. grammar school, which Shelley frequently visited, is nearby. West Street is familiarly known as Poets Row.

The Parsonage, in St Peter's Street, is believed to be the oldest house in the town, dating from the 14th cent.

MEDMENHAM, *Buckinghamshire* (6–SU80 84). The road from MARLOW to Medmenham is lovely with its woods, hills, green verges, farmhouses and views of the river. It lies in a hollow of the Thames Valley under chalk cliffs, with flowers and brambles.

An inn of great interest is the Dog and Badger, built about 1390. This area was strongly Royalist during the Civil War and it is interesting to note that a cannon-ball was dug out of the wall of the Dog and Badger when the only reconstruction that has taken place in the inn since it was built was being carried out.

Nine Lombardy poplars line the roadside in this rambling village with its flint-stone cottages and its yew topiary. Down by the bottom of the village road, by the church, is the River Thames and the motorist should take care here for the tarmac road ends abruptly at the water's edge. It is a place to sit for a while with the water, overhung by willow trees, flowing by.

The Normans built an abbey here which fell into disuse and was later rebuilt by Sir Francis Dashwood to become a home for the Hell Fire Club.

The little church with its Norman doorways and 15th-cent. tower is flanked by chestnuts. The chancel of the same period is of oak with king-post tie-beams.

On a steep hill, above the crossroads, is Lodge Farm, a gabled property now belonging to the National Trust. A short walk to reach it will give good views of the countryside below.

MELCHBOURNE, *Bedfordshire* (10–TL 0365), has a street of 18th-cent. thatched cottages which leads to St Mary Magdalene Church and Melchbourne Park. It was once the home of the Knights Hospitallers who used to hold a weekly market here.

The church is a Georgian building with a medieval tower and medieval masonry included in the Georgian chancel. The nave is wide with large arched windows, and there is a family pew with an unusual open fireplace.

Melchbourne Park, built of red brick about 1610, was previously the family seat of Lord St John of Bletsoe. It was fashioned in an H-plan with a big chimneybreast and was remodelled in 1741 when the two projecting wings and low parapet were added. The porch has two pairs of Tuscan columns and, inside, the staircase hall has a dainty plasterwork ceiling and a fine gallery.

MEPPERSHALL, *Bedfordshire* (10–TL1336), was originally in two counties but in 1888 it lost its association with Hertfordshire. Outside the village, SW. of the church, are the Hills, the remains of a motte and bailey castle, probably a stronghold in the 12th cent.

The Manor House, standing just by the church, is early 17th-cent. and one of the most outstanding timber-framed buildings in the county. It has two big gables with timber decorations, between which are smaller gables. On the front of the middle one is a single pargeted thistle and crown.

St Mary's Church has a Norman crossing tower and is of ironstone. The crossing arches have all been restored at different times. In the south transept is a Perpendicular reredos with tracery and panels. The nave and north aisle, dated 1875, are by Sir Arthur Blomfield, but the chancel is 13th-cent. The aisle has a steep lean-to roof. There is an ancient parish chest and monuments to John Meptyshall and his wife, 1440, and to John Boteler and his wife, 1441.

St Thomas's Chapel, Chapel Farm, has a late Norman north doorway, lozenges in the arches and decorated capitals. It was probably built in the early 12th cent.

MONKEN HADLEY, *Hertfordshire* (6–TQ 2497). This rare village combining Hadley Common and Hadley Green has a centre of Georgian buildings, the green and the triangular common separated by the church.

The common, with Hadley Wood in the background, has on the north side the 17th-cent. brick Church House and Mount House, probably the best house in the village, a red-bricked, five-bayed building with a pediment and a pedimented doorcase. On the south side it has Gladsmuir House, of red brick with a Victorian front, Hurst Cottage, of two stories and five bays, and Hadley House, a large 18th-cent. building with stables and a fine cedar tree in the front.

Hadley Green has on its west side Old Ford Manor House and Old Ford Manor Golf Club House. The latter, which was originally two cottages, has a 19th-cent. gateway, its parapet bearing on engraved ornament in the Sloane style. On the south-east side of the green are

Ossulton House, with a Gibbs-style surround to the arched doors, Hadley House, the biggest on the green with a Roman Doric porch and large stables, Fairholt, Monkenhold and the six Wilbraham Almshouses, dated 1612, of red brick with one story and interesting windows. On the edge of the green is Battle Obelisk, of Portland stone, recording the Battle of Barnet in 1471. In Drury Road to the S., is a ·Victorian brewery, which is rather out of keeping with its surroundings.

St Mary's Church has a date on the tower of 1494. The tower has diagonal buttresses and a higher turret. It is of flint and ironstone with white stone dressings and a rare copper beacon surmounting it. There are squints in the chancel chapels. The plate is old and very fine. The church has many brasses. In front of the altar is one of a lady, and another, of Sir Roger Wilbraham, 1616, is by Nicholas Stone.

N. of the church is the Priory, mainly early 19th-cent., but with some 16th-cent. remains, and just by the church is White Lodge with an early Georgian doorcase.

MONKS RISBOROUGH, *Buckinghamshire* (10–SP8104). Rising above this village on the slopes of the Chilterns can be seen the Cross of Whiteleaf cut out of the turf. The white chalk of the cross is visible many miles away for it is 80 ft in length and a similar distance in width.

In the village itself, hidden away amid glorious countryside thick with trees, are many thatched and timbered cottages and houses of distinction. It is said to have belonged to the monks of Christ Church, CANTERBURY until the Dissolution of the Monasteries.

St Dunstan's Church stands in a pleasant churchyard with high hedges and many trees, with the rectory close by. Its main structure is 15th-cent. but much of the interior is of earlier periods. The 12th-cent. font is fluted and exquisitely carved with foliage. The 14th-cent. tower has six inscribed bells, and the attractive rood-screen, of the 16th cent., is carved with flowers and has six brightly painted pictures of the Apostles.

MUCH HADHAM, *Hertfordshire* (10–TL 4319). This well-preserved village is perhaps the most attractive in the county. Its long main street is filled with buildings of fine quality.

There are gabled 17th-cent. houses such as North Leys, built in chequered brick, its canopy above the straight door supported by carved brackets. From the windows of the old Red Lion Inn can be seen meadows edged with lime trees. The Lordship, mid-18th-cent., is a large country gentleman's house with its own stables. It has two stories with nine bays, a Tuscan porch and, at the rear, a wing of what was probably part of a Tudor mansion.

The New Manor House is a Victorian building, picturesque but architecturally rather dull. Overhanging cottages adjoin Woodham House, of the 17th cent., with its fine exposed timbers, sym-

metrical gables and doorcase of a later period. Old House and Green Shutters also have fine timbers.

Much Hadham Hall is the most splendid mansion in the village. Standing beside a massive tree, the house, built in 1735, has a central Venetian window, a sloping roof and, beside the stables, an arched carriageway with four windows on each side. Camden Cottage and Castle House are both delightful, the latter in white with a 19th-cent. front and Gothic porch. Morris Cottage, also with exposed timbers, is probably of the 16th cent., and nearby is the 18th-cent. Moor Place, set in large grounds. It has blank arches on the entrance side of the ground floor and a fine interior with good fireplaces. The south wing was added in 1907.

St Andrew's Church is large with a complicated history. Although originally a 12th-cent. church, apparently nothing remains of that period. Rebuilding began with the chancel *c.* 1220, with its blocked north lancet window, then the south aisle, *c.* 1250, and the north aisle, *c.* 1300. The tower was added in 1382–1404 and has three stages and a tall spire. The clerestory, roofs and south porch were added in the 15th cent., when many windows were renewed. The screen has panel tracery and is also of the 15th cent., as are the stalls with poppyheads. There are two large rare *c.* 1400 chairs. Several brasses are interesting, in particular one of Judith Aylmer, wife of the Bishop of London.

Standing near the church is the Palace, for 800 years the country residence of the Bishops of London, and the birthplace of Edmund Tudor, father of Henry VII. It is a long brick house in which the old tie-beams are visible. The magnificent staircase and panelling are Jacobean.

The Rectory, S. of the churchyard, is early-17th-cent.

NASEBY, *Northamptonshire* (10–SP6878), is famous for the battle which decided the outcome of the Civil War. In June 1645 the opposing sides met in the fields outside the village. Cromwell defeated the Royalists, and King Charles I lost most of his army but managed to escape. Naseby Field has been enclosed since the battle and in it can be seen a dip in the ground where most of the fighting took place. There are two monuments: an obelisk dated 1823, which does not actually mark the site of the battle, and a more recent memorial on the field itself.

NEWPORT PAGNELL, *Buckinghamshire* (10–SP8743). An ancient town referred to in the Domesday Book as Newport, Pagnell being the name of the owners of the manor; it is situated on two rivers, the Ouse and the Lovat, the latter dividing the town. Once the greatest of all lace-making towns, it is now a busy industrial centre.

Built of iron in *c.* 1810, now an Ancient Monument, Tickford Bridge crosses the Lovat; the stone North Bridge crosses the Ouse. Near to the Ouse and close to the church is Tickford Abbey, now modernized but still on the site of the priory founded in Norman times and in use until Cardinal Wolsey appropriated its funds for the construction of a college at Oxford. Remains of the old building are preserved within the newer version.

The 14th-cent. church oversees the whole town from the centre where it stands. It has two fine porches, one with a vaulted roof and a priest's room over it, the other with a 15th-cent. roof, beneath which are decorated corbels. The interior has many arcades typical of the period and a 14th-cent. piscina. A brass monument of a man in the dress of the times is on the turret doorway, next to the chancel porch. The finely carved screens are worth closer inspection.

Despite the numerous modern buildings, the town still has many Georgian houses and the late Victorian building of Queen Anne's Hospital, on the site of an earlier one built for the poor of the town by Queen Anne of Denmark, wife of James I, which has a 17th-cent. beam bearing the words of an appeal for money for those less fortunate who were treated in the hospital.

NORMAN CROSS, *Huntingdonshire* (10–TL1691). About ¾ m. N. of this little village is a monument of a bronze eagle on a column, erected in memory of the 1,800 French soldiers and sailors who died here as prisoners during the Napoleonic Wars.

On the road to YAXLEY is a three-storied house with parapet walls and three bays, which is believed to be the house of the commandant of the former prison built for French prisoners-of-war in 1796.

NORTHAMPTON, *Northamptonshire* (10–SP7561). This is the county town and a county borough in its own right. Its entrance from the S. is unprepossessing and slightly confusing, but leaving it on the other side, past large modern houses on the road to WELLINGBOROUGH, it slowly merges into the countryside.

It is an ancient Anglo-Saxon town, and during the Wars of the Roses the Yorkists captured Henry VI here at the Battle of Northampton in 1460. The Lancastrians were defeated through treachery, and as a result Edward IV seized the throne. During the Civil War the trade for which it is now famous, boot and shoe making, became important, since Northampton shod most of Cromwell's army.

In the centre of the town is All Saints' Church, occupying a whole square. Most of the building was destroyed in a fire, but the medieval tower survives. Charles II gave 1,000 tons of timber for the rebuilding and his gift is commemorated by a statue of the king on the wide portico. The west doors of the nave are richly carved and the nave is handsome, with timber and plaster ceilings. The font and pulpit are about 1680, and the crossing dome stands on Ionic columns. The medieval crypt is below the chancel.

By the church, in George Row, is the Sessions House, built in 1676, a small attractive building with cherubs perched on its balustrade and a hipped roof. Opposite is the Victorian Town Hall, an ornate building in the Venetian Gothic style, with a gable flanked by two turrets and a clock tower.

St John's Church, in Bridge Street, was a hostel for travellers in the 12th cent. and an almshouse at the time of the Reformation. It is now a Roman Catholic church with medieval windows and parts of the original roof. Opposite is the old Charity School. Hazlerigg Mansion, in Marefair which leads from Gold Street, was built just prior to the fire and survived it. Its original owner was Sir Arthur Hesilrigg, a Cromwellian who died in the TOWER. Further along is another church which also survived the fire: St Peter's, one of the county's most impressive churches. It is large and predominantly Norman in style, with massive buttresses on the exterior and a 17th-cent. squat tower. Inside there is no chancel arch but an array of Norman carvings which run from east to west. There are many varied capitals and a 14th-cent. font with tracery and pinnacles.

Only 5,000 people inhabited this town in the 18th cent. During the Napoleonic wars they poured in to make army boots, increasing the numbers to 15,000, and now the population is over 120,000, which is more than a third of the whole county. It is surprising, for what was once a small town, how many churches of note there are in Northampton

In Sheep Street, which has several Georgian houses, is the interesting and unusual Church of the Holy Sepulchre, one of the four surviving round churches in England, built from the time of the Crusaders. It is of ironstone with a tall tower and spire. The original nave, dating from the 12th cent., is round, and 50 years later another nave was added to form the choir. The clerestory is 15th-cent., with old Norman columns supporting it, and the chancel, which is rich in design, is mid-Victorian. In Campbell Square, on the far side of the church, is one of the town's earliest industrial buildings, Manfield Warehouse, in ornate Italian style with a tall tower and many windows. It was built in the 1850s.

St Giles' Church, in St Giles Street, is a big, golden, ironstone medieval church with a central tower and the only peal of 10 bells in the county. Inside, where the clerestory is of paler stone than the rest of the building, there is a 17th-cent. pulpit and finely carved oak chair, a 15th-cent. Gobion tomb, chained books and Victorian glass of note in the east window.

The museum has many interesting exhibits, including a cobbler's shop and Queen Victoria's wedding shoes, as well as the ballet shoes of Fonteyn, Ulanova and Nijinsky. There are also archaeological finds dating from the Iron Age, medieval pottery, and paintings and furniture. Opposite stands the Victorian Repertory Theatre with an ornate painted ceiling and a gilt and red-plush auditorium.

The Market Square, believed to be the largest in England, is reached by a narrow street off Mercer's Row, which is on one side of All Saints' Church. It still has many Georgian and Victorian buildings and in one corner is Welsh House, which also survived the fire and dates back to 1595, with obelisks and heraldic shields on the front. It belongs to the days when the Welsh brought their cattle to the market. There is a large car park in the square and at the far end is a vast ornamented Victorian building called the Emporium Arcade, a covered market with little shops leading off the street inside. On the second floor, with a wooden balcony, are shops and offices, and in the ends and centre is an additional floor.

The railway station is on the site of the old medieval castle. It has a water garden, a statue of St Christopher and a wall decorated with features describing the history of the town's footwear industry.

Along the KETTERING road is a large recreation ground, the former race-course, and on the far side, in St George's Avenue, is the College of Technology, a pleasant modern building specializing in the theory and practice of leather and footwear. The county cricket ground is on the Wellingborough Road and just past it is Abingdon Park Museum, set in large grounds. The house dates from the 15th to the 18th cent. and contains a collection of English and Chinese porcelain, Northamptonshire lace, children's toys and agricultural and domestic exhibits of former days. In the beautiful grounds, now a public park, is a mulberry tree planted by David Garrick, and nearby is the old village church, originally Norman but rebuilt in the last century after damage by a storm. On the Billing road, to the SE., is Billing Aquadrome with five lakes, including one with exotic birds, and outdoor amusements of every description, as well as a folk museum in Billing Mill.

About 1½ m. S. of Northampton on the A508 at Hardingstone, is one of the Eleanor Crosses, now an Ancient Monument, which Edward I had erected to mark the resting place of the coffin containing his queen as it made its way from HARBY in Nottinghamshire to London.

To the S. of the town on the A43 is another Ancient Monument, Danes Camp on Hunsbury Hill, really an Iron Age earthwork. Six m. to the NW. is Althorp, the residence of the Earl Spencer, a 16th-cent. house much altered in later restorations, with a magnificent collection of portraits, furniture and china.

NORTH MIMMS, *Hertfordshire* (10–TL2304) is a tiny village in glorious wooded countryside.

North Mimms House, standing in 1,000 acres of parkland, is a magnificent building surpassed in the county only by HATFIELD House. It is fashioned on the H-plan in the late Elizabethan style, and is two stories high, with large windows, projecting gabled wings and a central porch behind which is a small cupola. The doorway is flanked by Tuscan columns with a triglyph frieze. The entrance hall has a French chimneypiece dated 1515. There are many outstanding paintings in the house, and in the grounds a renowned rose garden.

The Church of St Mary standing in the park is still almost all 14th-cent., although the panelled pulpit is Elizabethan. There are many fine monuments of interest including a brass to a priest, *c.* 1360, showing God the Father holding the soul of the priest in a cloth and the head of the priest in the canopy above. In the chancel is a large upright wall monument of John Somers, lawyer and parliamentarian, who framed the Declaration of Rights and became Lord Chancellor. Near the church is the late-17th-cent. vicarage.

SE. of the village is the park of **Gobions**, where the ancestral home of Sir Thomas More once stood. An 18th-cent. "folly" arch survives from the former mansion.

OAKLEY, *Bedfordshire* (10–TL0153). Wide views of the Ouse valley can be had from the hills surrounding this residential village, which is of ancient origin, its bridge still having arches of medieval stonework.

Oakley House, for long a seat of the Dukes of Bedford, is 17th-cent. although remodelled, and has a hipped roof and verandas on three sides. The Bedford Arms is a modernized but unspoilt old inn.

St Mary's Church has small slit-windows in its 12th-cent. tower, and the rest of the battlemented exterior is of the same time or a little later. The screen in the north chapel has paintings on the coving of Christ seated on a rainbow and that in the south chapel has rib-vaulted coving. The Perpendicular octagonal font has tracery motifs. Of the monuments, one has a coffin lid with a foliated cross growing from an animal, and another, early-14th-cent., is an effigy of a lady in a low tomb recess.

ODELL, *Bedfordshire* (10–SP9658). This winding, attractive country village, on a bend of the River Ouse, has many pretty thatched cottages of stone and a thatched pub. Odell Great Wood is a fascinating place for rare flowers, butterflies and birds.

There was formerly a castle here in Norman days and the mound of it still remains. The outbuildings of a 17th-cent. house can still be seen.

All Saints Church, set on the slopes of a hill, is a fine example of a 15th-cent. church built all at one time. The massive west tower is in four stages with clasping buttresses. The lovely interior has tall arcades, an original rood-screen under the tower arch and attractive diamond-pattern flooring in the nave and aisles. In the east window of the south aisle is a remnant of stained glass of rare and simple beauty showing a group of seraphs. A richly adorned monument of the 17th cent. is to the Alston family.

OLD WARDEN, *Bedfordshire* (10–TL1343). This little country village on a steep-banked lane is a pretty place with honey-coloured thatched cottages. The Church of St Leonard is late-12th-cent., its tower a little older, and is of brown cobbles. It has much good woodwork and was restored and renewed by Lord Ongley in 1841,

with a strong Continental influence. The large font originally had 12 shafts and is of the 14th cent. There is stained glass from Warden Abbey, and there are several monuments, including one, of particular interest, to Sir Samuel Ongley, dated 1726 and signed by Scheemakers, and Delvaux.

Old Warden Park was built for Joseph Shuttleworth in Jacobean style in 1872. It is of yellow brick with a large tower and a clock surrounded by an unusual openwork stone grille.

One m. WSW. is Warden Abbey, originally founded by Walter Espec in 1135. All that remains now is part of the early Tudor brick house of the Gostwicks, which was probably built about 1537. It has a chimney breast and a decorated stack and in the rear is a stair-turret.

N. of the church are the earthworks of Quint's Hill which are probably early Iron Age, although the site is unexcavated.

Of more modern interest is the aerodrome of the **Shuttleworth Trust**, with a unique collection of aircraft ranging from Blériot to the Spitfire. It is open to the public and there are regular flying displays.

OLNEY, *Buckinghamshire* (10–SP8851). Famous for its long-standing connections with William Cowper, Olney is the main town of north Buckinghamshire. It was once a lace-making centre but since the decline of that industry other trades have taken its place.

Its buildings are a mixture of new and old and in the market square is the red-bricked Cowper Memorial Museum, where William Cowper lived with his friend Mary Unwin, who cared for him during his bouts of insanity. It was here he wrote his poems and hymns. In glass cases round the walls are editions and illustrations of his work, and Mary Unwin's room holds her workbox and lace bobbins.

The broach spire of the Church of SS. Peter and Paul dominates the countryside, for it rises to 185 ft. Dating from the 14th cent., it is one of the county's finest churches. The tower is in four tiers, each containing a gabled window. Grotesque heads decorate the pinnacles and others peep out beneath the parapet of the chancel. John Newton was curate here during the time Cowper resided in Olney and became his close friend, writing together with him many of the Olney Hymns, such as "Hark my soul it is the Lord", "God moves in a mysterious way His wonders to perform", "How sweet the name of Jesus sounds" and "Glorious things of thee are spoken".

The splendour of this magnificent church can be seen from the small bridge which passes over the narrow strip of the River Ouse adjacent to the church at the end of the long main street of the town.

Olney's claim to world renown is its pancake race, which takes place every Shrove Tuesday and has survived since the middle of the 15th cent. In the town of Liberal in the United States a similar race is held annually. In Olney it is run between the market place and the church and the first housewife to complete the course is rewarded by a kiss from the bellringer and a silver cup.

OUNDLE, *Northamptonshire* (10–TL0488), is an old country town, dating back at least to 972 when its markets and tolls were confirmed by King Edgar. Although its narrow main street carries heavy traffic, very little has changed in recent years.

The buildings, of stone and Collyweston tiles, are of three centuries, some tall and dignified with steeply pitched roofs, others gabled with oriels. There are fascinating alleyways and narrow yards; old almshouses in North Street, Church Lane and West Street; many ancient inns, the most notable being Talbot Inn, a gabled 17th-cent. building with a fine oak staircase; and numerous tiny old cottages with minute windows. The Town Hall is Victorian, as is the large Police Station.

The famous Oundle Public School and Laxton Grammar School were founded by the same man, William Laxton, a grocer who was born here in the 16th cent. and eventually became Lord Mayor of London. The two schools were separated in the last century, but Oundle is still owned by the Grocers' Company. Many of its buildings date from the 30 years during which Frederick Sanderson, who became headmaster in 1892, transformed it into the type of school it is today. It covers a large part of the town and houses over 600 boys. Both schools still remain under one headmaster and the boys of Laxton School join those of Oundle when they reach fifth-form level.

There are several churches in the town, with two of some note. Jesus Church was built in 1879 by Arthur Blomfield, who was also responsible for the improvements in the school. It is in the form of a cross, in Gothic style, with lancet windows in the nave, transept and chancel. It has an unusual central lantern, a turret which starts as a square and finishes as an octagon, with a dome-shaped ceiling. The other interesting church is St Peter's, large and opulent with a magnificent steeple and large surfaces of the tower panelled vertically towards the spire. The 15th-cent. south porch is richly decorated with battlements, pinnacles and gargoyles. The pulpit, painted with stars, dates from before the Reformation. There are two fonts, one of the 18th cent. and one dated 1909, several Perpendicular screens and a great many memorials and brasses.

Around the town flows the River Nene, making it a great sailing centre, and the views from the river are delightful, as is the countryside which greets you as you leave the town.

Cotterstock Hall is 1½ m. N. of Oundle and open to the public. It is a 17th-cent. grey stone manor house, built in an E-shape with good stone chimneypieces and Dutch gables. In the attic room Dryden wrote his *Fables*. It stands in a large garden with an avenue of elms leading down to the River Nene. Five m. to the N. lies the pretty village of **Apethorpe**, built in the local stone, with a Perpendicular church.

Olney: the spire of the 14th-cent. church dominates the countryside   Noel Habgood

PEAKIRK, *Huntingdonshire* (10–TF1606), is an ancient stone village on the edge of the Fens, completely unspoilt. Close by are the Waterfowl Gardens, property of the Wildfowl Trust, with a variety of aquatic birds in the various waterways. The gardens are open to the public and there are good parking facilities.

In 716 St Pega, sister of St Guthlac, founded a cell here. On the site of the original cell is the Hermitage, E. of the church. After being in ruins for many years it was drastically restored, but the chancel dates from about 1280, its east window of three lights. There is also a fragment of an Anglo-Saxon cross-shaft with foliage.

St Pega's Church is the only one dedicated to her in the country. The west wall is part of a Norman building and the bellcot is also Norman. In the south doorway is an elaborate Norman tympanum and most of the interior is also Norman. The 14th-cent. lectern, with its wooden stem and slender attached shafts, is a rarity. The octagonal font is medieval. There are many wall paintings, mostly of the 14th cent., including Christ washing St Peter's feet, the Last Supper, the Crucifixion and the Resurrection, and also one of St Christopher of a later date. The north aisle has a rather unpleasant painting of the Three Quick and the Three Dead and another of two women whispering to each other with a devil pressing their heads together.

PENN, *Buckinghamshire* (6–SU9193). This is a long straggling village, on the remote edge of the Chilterns, rather typical of other villages in the county with 17th-cent. cottages of wood and brick and of wood and flintstone.

The Crown Inn and the village church are adjacent to each other by the village green, around which there are many Georgian houses. On the top of the hill is the Knoll, which was for a time the home of Princess Anne during the reign of William of Orange. A small belvedere in the roof of the house is called Princess Anne's window.

Holy Trinity Church has a medieval structure, the roof – one of the finest in the county – being 15th-cent. It was greatly altered by the Penns and the Curzons during the 18th cent. when many of its treasures were installed. Discovered in 1938 is the magnificent wall painting of "The Doom" of the Last Judgment. It was painted in the 15th cent. and hangs on the south wall. There are many brasses to the Penn family and although William Penn of Pennsylvania is buried at JORDANS, many of his descendants rest here under the floor of the south chapel.

From the churchyard, on this high ridge, can be seen about a dozen different counties and Penn Woods, nearby, is one of Buckinghamshire's many beauty-spots.

PETERBOROUGH, *Huntingdonshire* (10–TL 1999), is a prosperous city with an outstanding cathedral and is the biggest town in the county. As well as being a market town, it has many industries, including the processing of sugar beet grown in the surrounding countryside, and engineering.

In its centre is the Market Place where the old guildhall, built in 1671, predominates. This was once used as a butter market and above its open ground floor on Tuscan columns is the chamber, reached by a tiny spiral staircase. It was built to commemorate the Restoration of Charles II, and has a hipped roof and a steep gable. Nearby is St John the Baptist's Church, built in 1402 and containing the nave of a church that was in the precincts of the cathedral. In its tower, of rubble and ashlar, are 16th-cent. embroidered pictures of the Crucifixion. The octagonal font is large with quatrefoil panels, of about the same period as the church. Of the many monuments, an interesting one is by Flaxman, 1826, showing a mourning Grecian beside a tall pedestal and a medallion with the heads of Mr and Mrs Squire.

In Cumbergate are the Feoffee Almshouses, dated 1903, and the 17th-cent. old workhouse, of rubble on the ground floor with an overhanging timber-framed upper floor. Through a passage in the Causeway is Peterscourt, formerly St Peter's Training College, built in 1856 in Gothic style, and in St Mary's Street are new council flats which received a commendation in the Civic Trust Awards for the high-density development scheme of 139 flats with an underground garage on a site of $3\frac{1}{4}$ acres, one of the objectives being to secure minimum interference with views of the cathedral. In Westgate is the Bull Hotel, an early-18th-cent. low two-storied building. The Georgian Royal Hotel is plain and handsome and the Wortley's Almshouses are early Victorian in a Tudor style, with an inscription above the entrance from a previous building of 1744. In Lincoln Road are Victorian cottages.

The best Georgian houses are in Priestgate, on the corner of which is the three-storied Angel Hotel with its original staircase.

The town hall, in Bridge Street, built in the 1930s in a neo-Georgian style, has an imposing façade with Corinthian columns, a turret and cupola. The entrance hall and staircase are spacious and the whole building is in keeping with the architecture of the city. The gaol, in Thorpe Road, is Victorian but of Norman style with a gatehouse in the middle, and the Victorian St John's Close, formerly a workhouse, is now a hospital.

In Priestgate is the museum and art gallery, which was built in 1816 and has served as a private house, an infirmary and now a museum. It contains a fine collection of local exhibits, including the carved bone and marquetry work made by prisoners-of-war who were detained at Norman Cross Camp during the Napoleonic wars. There are archaeological finds from Romano-British and Anglo-Saxon times, and the natural history section has fossils from the local clay. The Mary Queen of Scots Room contains her own needle-work and tiles and fragments from the castle at FOTHERINGHAY where she was executed. The art gallery has interesting paintings.

The bridge which crosses the River Nene was built in 1934 to replace a Victorian iron structure. By its side stands the former customs house, built

---

Hemingford Grey church: the spire was partly destroyed in the 18th cent.

about 1700, of rubble with a hipped roof and cupola. From here can be seen delightful views of the river which has good fishing and boating.

Peterborough Cathedral is a breathtaking sight. It was founded as a monastery in 655 by King Peada of Mercia, soon after he was converted to Christianity. It was destroyed by the Danes in 870 and refounded 100 years later by King Edgar. Hereward the Wake attacked and plundered it in about 1070 and 46 years later it was destroyed by fire. In 1118 the rebuilding of the present church started. After 80 years the nave was completed, and in 1238 the church was dedicated. Apart from restoration work, the only new building which has taken place since that date is the Retrochoir or New Building at the east end, about 1500.

The cathedral is of Barnack stone, and is 481 ft long, 206 ft wide and 81 ft high. Its tower reaches to 143 ft. It stands in a garden and the precincts are entered by a large gateway with the King's Lodging and Abbott's Prison on one side and St Thomas's Chapel on the other. A few yards past the chapel on the left-hand side is a large detailed map showing places of interest in both the interior of the cathedral and its surrounding buildings. The interior of the west doorway is of finely carved woodwork. The wooden nave ceiling is superbly decorated with saints, kings and grotesque monsters, and in the south aisle is heavy quadripartite ribbed vaulting. The carved wooden choir stalls, pulpit and bishop's throne are all Victorian, but the brass eagle lectern is 14th-cent. In the Retrochoir beyond the apse the ceiling has magnificent fan vaulting, and the Hedda Stone, an important piece of Anglo-Saxon sculpture, dates from about 800. The font, a decorated marble bowl, is 13th-cent. with modern pillars.

Just in front of the Retrochoir are two important burial places. On the left is that of Catherine of Aragon, whose ex-husband Henry VIII established the church as a cathedral in 1541, two years after the Dissolution, and on the right is that of Mary Queen of Scots. Her son, James I, instructed that the body should be removed to WESTMINSTER ABBEY, where it now rests. During the Civil War and Commonwealth the contents of the cathedral as well as carved stonework were savagely destroyed by soldiers, but after King Charles II came to the throne services were resumed in the building, which has been gradually restored through the centuries.

The city has been incorporated in the new county of Huntingdon and Peterborough.

PRINCES RISBOROUGH, *Buckinghamshire* (10–SP8003). This old-world town, with its growing residential population, has many 16th-cent. cottages and delightful houses.

In its centre is its brick Market House with open arcades where in former days a weekly market was held. Crowning the roof is a turret with a clock and bell. Vine House, a Tudor building very close to Market House, is gabled with herringbone brickwork and has a vine tree growing up it.

The Manor House, with its pilastered front, is of 18th-cent. origin. It has a beautiful Jacobean oak staircase and 18th-cent. wainscoting.

The Norman Church of St Mary's, which was heavily restored in the 13th and 14th cents., has a modern spire. It still possesses a Norman window and in the south aisle is a lovely triple lancet window. The pulpit was carved in the time of the Restoration.

RAMSEY, *Huntingdonshire* (10–TL2885), lies in cultivated fenland and is the agricultural centre for the large district surrounding it. Its long, wide street, the Great Whyte, was constructed in 1852 and covers the culverted Bury Brook which ran through the centre of the town.

Ramsey Abbey was founded in 969 and was one of the most important monastic houses until the Dissolution. Only the 13th-cent. Lady Chapel, the porter's lodge and a fragment of the 15th-cent. gatehouse remain. The new house, built about 1660, is now a school and has been greatly added to. The gatehouse, which is now National Trust property and open to the public, is ornate. It has a small doorway and panelled buttresses. Inside, on the ground floor, is a marble monument to Ethelwine, or Ailwin, the founder of the abbey.

Beside the gatehouse is Abbey Green, on which stands a former Victorian school and gabled stone almshouses of the same period. In the middle of Great Whyte is a Victorian clock on a cast-iron column, and there are several yellow-brick houses of the early 19th cent. The Methodist chapel and the Baptist chapel are both late Victorian.

St Thomas of Canterbury Church was originally built as a guest house for visitors to the abbey, in about 1180. The chancel is Norman, distinguished by a heavy rib-vault. The west doorway is in the ashlar-faced tower of 1672. The plain hexagonal font is of dark marble, probably 13th-cent. There is a faded painting of a man and an angel above the north arcade of the nave and there are several monuments.

Bodsey House, 1½ m. to the N., is moated and was originally a hermitage of the abbey. It was converted into a house after the Dissolution and has a fine 17th-cent. chimney stack and an unusual coved and panelled ceiling.

Not far from Ramsey is **Woodwalton Fen**, scheduled as a National Nature Reserve and occupying 514 acres. The large copper butterfly has been introduced here, and there are many rare birds, insects and aquatic plants.

RENHOLD, *Bedfordshire* (10–TL0953), is a straggling village, stretching down to the River Ouse, in attractive countryside reached by narrow twisting roads. The Danes occupied this part of the county at one period.

The Church of All Saints has brown cobbled walls and a Perpendicular tower with a lead spire. The Norman font, which is drum-shaped, has unfinished carvings on an ornamental band. The pulpit, with detailed panels, is of the 17th cent., but of special interest is the high altar tomb-chest, richly carved, with the figures in brass on the lid of Edmund Wayte and his wife, dated 1518.

Beechwoods in Ashridge Park, near Little Gaddesden   *Picturepoint*

Howbury Hall, 1¾ m. SE., although built in 1849, is in a pre-Victorian style with a five-bayed front and angle bay windows with cast-iron balconies. There is a top balustrade and a staircase with rustic columns.

One m. through the village, at Salph End, is Abbey Farmhouse, a large and delightful 17th-cent. house of brick and timber, with projecting gables either side of the centre and a small baking oven protruding unexpectedly from the wall.

RICKMANSWORTH, *Hertfordshire* (6–TQ 0594). This lovely old town, where three rivers meet, has lakes and water-meadows and one of the finest bathing lakes near to London, the Aquadrome.

In the long, winding High Street is the seven-bayed Basing House, where William Penn lived with his wife after their marriage. Close by is St Joan of Arc's Convent School, a red-brick Georgian house with a central pedimented door. The 18th-cent. stables of a brewery are now used as offices, and further along is the Swan Hotel with its original Jacobean panelling, fireplaces and staircase. The Victorian Baptist church is simply designed with lancet windows.

In Rectory Road, set in rural surroundings, is Parsonage Farm, and in Uxbridge Road is York House School, a two-storied red-brick Georgian building with five bays. Further along still is Longland Farm, of yellow-washed brick with timber-framing and weather-boarded barns.

St Mary's Church, originally built in 1630, was twice almost completely rebuilt in the last century. The tower and the yellow-brick aisles and early Gothic windows are all that remain of the old church. There is a brass monument to Thomas Day and wives, and a tomb-chest of Henry Cary, Earl of Monmouth.

Near the church in Church Street is the Vicarage, a half-timbered medieval building with later alterations. It has enchanting gables, a bay window on the ground floor, and an overhanging oriel on the first floor. Around the church are two buildings of interest: the Bury, with brick and timber framework, an original staircase and carved overmantels; and the Priory of brick and timber.

Moor Park Mansion House is 1 m. SE. of Rickmansworth. Reconstructed in 1727 by Sir James Thornhill and Giacomo Leoni, it is a baroque house with superb interior decorations. Originally built in the 15th cent. for the Archbishop of York, it eventually became Cardinal Wolsey's country seat. The gardens were the work of Capability Brown. Both house and grounds are open to the public.

ROCKINGHAM, *Northamptonshire* (10–SP 8691). This pleasant village, with the River Welland below, is on a steep hill lined with many old thatched cottages, as well as new buildings of flint-stone, which harmonize with the surroundings.

On the summit of a hill, from which can be seen five counties, stands Rockingham Castle. The original castle was built on the instructions of William the Conqueror, and although the site of the keep is now a rose garden surrounded by yew hedges, the moat remains, as well as foundations of the Norman hall and the twin towers of the old gatehouse. King John used it as a hunting lodge for Rockingham Forest, which once covered a vast area of the northern section of the county. The present building is mainly Elizabethan.

Rockingham is a pleasant village in which old and new buildings blend harmoniously

J. Allan Cash

James I was entertained there in 1603, and Dickens spent much time at the house and dedicated *David Copperfield* to the owners, Mr and Mrs Watson, whose descendants still reside there. In the house is an interesting collection of pictures as well as fine furniture and it is open to the public.

St Leonard's Church, by the castle, was rebuilt in the 19th cent. from the 13th-cent. building which was severely damaged during the Civil War. It has a Jacobean pulpit and many 17th- and 18th-cent. monuments to the Watson family.

ROTHWELL, *Northamptonshire* (10–SP8181). This small and interesting old industrial town makes footwear and has engineering works. It is reached by a slight hill and on the outskirts is a large thatched cottage with steep stone steps leading to an old door dated 1660. In the centre of the town is an Ancient Monument: Rothwell Market House, an elegant square building built in 1577 by Thomas Tresham, father of the betrayer of the Gunpowder Plot. Around its cornice are 90 coats of arms of county families. Nearby is a little old Sunday school, and further on is another small building, Rothwell Free Grammar School for boys and girls, founded in 1538. There are many Victorian buildings mixed with some more modern and some older ones, indicating Rothwell's continued importance through the centuries.

There is an annual Charter Fair which, started in 1204, lasts a week and is officially declared open by the reading of the Charter on Trinity Sunday. It was formerly an important trade fair.

The almshouses, known as Jesus Hospital, were built by Owen Ragsdale, who endowed the grammar school. They are grouped round a courtyard and were originally for old men who were allowed a room each and a hall for every four. They have recently been modernized and now house four married couples and six single people. In 1655 the county's first Nonconformist church was established here, in a barn, and the present Congregational church is dated 1735.

Holy Trinity Church is a large cruciform building, mainly 13th-cent. It is reached by a path past the Queen Anne manor house, now council offices, and is said to be the longest parish church in the county. The spire collapsed in the 17th cent., but its top was saved and reset on the turret beside the tower. The interior of the church is very light. Above the nave arcades are 14 clerestory windows and there are larger ones in the aisles of the chancel, all 15th-cent. The stalls have carved misereres. There are four old brasses, one of Owen Ragsdale which hangs above his altar tomb in the south chapel. The elaborate font is 13th-cent. Beneath the south aisle is the charnel, a vaulted crypt containing thousands of old bones, which were discovered in the 18th cent. by a sexton while digging a grave.

Leaving the town on the road to RUSHTON, there are magnificent views of the surrounding countryside.

ROXTON, *Bedfordshire* (10–TL1554), lies between the main road and the River Ouse, with thatched cottages and barns dotted about.

Of special interest is Roxton Chapel, a Congregational church of a most attractive and unusual design with a thatched roof and a tree-trunk veranda. It was founded in 1808 by Charles Metcalfe, the lord of the manor, who converted it from a barn into a chapel and later added two wings.

St Mary's Church, lying behind a row of pines, has brown cobble walls and a short west tower. A doorway in the south aisle is *c.* 1300, as are the three-bay arcade and the nave. There is a Perpendicular screen with painted saints on the dado, an early-15th-cent. Italian rood painting and, in the chancel, a tomb-chest to Roger Hunt, 1438, who was Speaker of the House of Commons and Baron of the Exchequer.

Earthworks will be found in Yarwood in a solitary mound 40 ft in diameter.

ROYSTON, *Hertfordshire* (10–TL3541). This small town, with its narrow streets and old inns and houses, lies at the crossing of Ermine Street and the old Icknield Way.

Below this crossroads is a strange monument, the bottle-shaped Royston Cave, discovered in 1742. Cut out of chalk, it is about 28 ft deep and 17 ft across. On the walls are crude carvings of, among others, St Christopher and the Crucifixion, but the date of their origin is in dispute. The cave, reached by a winding passage, is below the ground.

The remains of James I's palace are in Kneesworth Street, with two large original chimneys, the rest of the building having been rebuilt in the 18th cent. In the same street are Georgian houses, the white-bricked Rookery and the red-bricked Yew Tree House, with segment-headed windows.

W. of the crossroads is a large Victorian workhouse and in Melbourne Street are several interesting red- and purple-brick houses, and the white-brick Banyers Hotel, part 17th- and part 18th-cent. with massive Ionic pilasters and mullioned windows in two gables. Then comes the Victorian Town Hall in yellow brick.

In the High Street are many buildings of character including the early Victorian Bull Hotel of yellow brick, and in John Street a small Victorian Court House in Italian style. Next is the Priory, an enlarged Georgian building, on a site which was probably originally part of the monastery.

SS. John's and Thomas's Church, which lies on the corner of the old and new roads of the town, was originally 13th-cent. and later, but was greatly changed in the Victorian era. The west wall is of the old monastic church. There is oak panelling of the 14th cent., a 13th-cent. font bowl on a base of a later period, and the piscina is genuine 13th-cent. The exact dates of much of the rest of the church seem to be in dispute. Of the monuments, an effigy of a knight with angels at the head is 14th-cent. and a thin brass cross in the chancel is 15th-cent.

To the W. of the town is Therfield Heath on which are five round barrows and one long one, the only one of its kind in the county.

Sandon Mount at Notley Green is covered by a clump of trees. It is 87 ft in diameter, surrounded by a wide ditch in which there is an entrance. It was probably used as a look-out in the 13th cent.

RUSHTON, *Northamptonshire* (10–SP8483), is set amid lovely countryside and is reached by a narrow humped bridge. The buildings are old and of golden ironstone. Rushton Urban District Board School, 1892, is of red brick with iron railings and tiny windows high up.

Rushton Hall, now a school for the Royal Institute for the Blind, was built about 1500 and is open to the public. It was the home of the Tresham family, and Sir Thomas, who built many unusual structures expressing religious themes in the surrounding districts, was a Roman Catholic convert and was many times imprisoned for his beliefs. His son Francis was the betrayer of the Gunpowder Plot. The house has 17th-cent. plaster ceilings, a hammer-beam in the roof of the great hall, and a painted relief of the Crucifixion dated 1577. Screened by cedars, in a remote corner of the grounds of the house, is one of Sir Thomas's curiosities, Triangular Lodge, now an Ancient Monument. It has three sides, three floors, trefoil windows and three gables on each side; in fact everything plays on the number three, as an emblem of the Trinity.

The River Ise runs by the churchyard, separated only by a row of chestnuts. The church has a 13th-cent. tower, with a weather-vane on each of its four corners rising from the 15th-cent. battlements. The Norman nave is divided from the north aisle by three 13th-cent. arches. In the north chapel is a monument to William de Goldingham, a knight, 1296, and between the chapel and the chancel is the altar tomb of Sir Thomas Tresham, grandfather of the recusant Sir Thomas, showing him in the robes of a Grand Prior of the Knights Hospitallers, of which he was the last.

ST ALBANS, *Hertfordshire* (10–TL1507). This ancient city, with its narrow, twisting, hilly streets, was once one of the largest and most important Roman towns ever established in the country. The abbey is visible from miles around, and the town is a fascinating place to visit, with a wealth of features dating from Roman times to the present day.

The remains of Verulamium, open to the public, were only excavated in the present century. When the Romans occupied this part of the country a British settlement already existed here, according to Julius Caesar, since he refers to it in his *De Bello Gallico*, when he tells of his invasions in 54 B.C. By the middle of the 1st cent. A.D. it had become so important that it was elevated to the status of a *municipium*, the only British city to attain such an honour, which accorded the inhabitants the right of Roman citizenship. In A.D. 61 the town was sacked by Boadicea, but after her defeat and death it was rebuilt and re-covered its prominence. Remains of the walls, some reaching to 12 ft, can still be seen. The theatre, the only Roman one in Britain, has been excavated and restored. Semi-circular in shape, it is 180 ft across and provided for 1,600 spectators. Among the other remains to be seen are a temple, to the S. of the theatre, and a mosaic floor, with the Roman form of central heating still intact.

In the museum are displayed jewellery, pottery, a Mithraic token, household implements and many other exhibits discovered during the excavations.

The cathedral, St Albans Abbey, was built on the site where the first British martyr, Alban, was beheaded in the 4th cent., after being converted to Christianity and assisting a persecuted priest to escape. Constructed largely from brick and flint taken from Roman remains, its nave is nearly 300 ft long. The crossing tower, of great breadth, appears squat because of its massive size. The abbey dates from the 11th cent., but every century has seen additions and alterations to it. The Lady Chapel, completed in the 14th cent., was made into a grammar school at the Dissolution, the nave was lengthened in the 13th cent., and the reredos erected in the 15th cent. The rood-screen, separating the monastic choir from the nave, is of stone. The large circular stone pulpit in the nave has 13th-cent. diaper patterning and was given by Lord Grimthorpe, who in 1879 personally paid for the restoration of the cathedral, which had deteriorated greatly in the 19th cent. The restoration is believed to have cost £130,000. The choir stalls were added in 1905, the font and cover in 1933. The watching loft of timber with a narrow staircase opens on to the Shrine of St Alban which was erected in the 14th cent., later destroyed and rebuilt in the 19th cent. after its several thousand pieces were found. Because the construction was of Purbeck marble it was possible to identify the pieces and they were pieced together by Sir Gilbert Scott. On the south side, the upper part shows the figure of King Offa. A scene of the martyrdom is at the west end and in the base are several holes, supposed to be healing holes, since miraculous cures are said to have occurred at the shrine. The medieval paintings are said to be unique in England, and there are many monuments of importance, three of particular interest being the chantry chapels to the Duke of Gloucester, 1447, Abbot Wheathamstead, 1465, and Abbot Ramryge, 1519. There is also a large collection of brasses.

The early-15th-cent. clock tower, facing the High Street, has a bell which still strikes on the hour and is older than the tower itself. From the tower, which is open to the public, can be seen a splendid view of the abbey and the surrounding countryside. Nearby, the Victorian fountain replaced a market cross which was erected after the famous Eleanor Cross, commemorating Queen Eleanor's brief resting place as her coffin was conveyed to its burial, was pulled down.

Beside the clock tower is the narrow Market Place, in which stands the 19th-cent. Town Hall,

G. Douglas Bolton

St Albans Abbey

facing St Peter's Street, its pillared front with a massive portico resting on fluted Ionic columns. It was here that two fierce battles took place during the Wars of the Roses. French Row, W. of the tower, is a reminder of French occupation in the early 13th cent. In the Fleur de Lys Inn, considerably restored but with much of its original timber framework, King John of France was imprisoned after the battle of Poitiers in 1356. Several of the buildings in this street date back to the 14th cent.

A few of the houses in the High Street are of medieval construction, although partially modernized. From the crossroads runs Holywell Hill, with the River Ver at its end. In the upper part of the street are Georgian buildings, several with massive angled pilasters and attic stories. The White Hart is a 15th-cent. restored building, and just off Holywell Hill, by Sumpter Yard, is the 18th-cent. Old Rectory, two stories high with five bays and Venetian windows.

Further down the hill, Sopwell Lane, with interesting small houses, runs parallel to the river. The ruins of Sopwell Nunnery are covered in ivy.

St Stephen's Hill crosses the river and leads to the 17th-cent. Vicarage, two and a half stories high with five bays and quoins. St Stephen's Church has many facets of Norman times: a window, chancel masonry and a blocked arch. There are other features of varying centuries: a 15th-cent. font heavily carved, an eagle lectern in brass of the early 16th cent; and stained glass mainly of the 19th cent. A brass monument to William Robbins and his wife is dated 1482, and in the churchyard is a Roman milestone.

In St Peter's Street is St Peter's Church, restored by Lord Grimthorpe into a Victorian building. Inside is a monument to Edward Strong, chief master mason of ST PAUL'S CATHEDRAL. He built Ivy House, further up the street, a three-storied building with four bays, giant pilasters and an interesting doorcase. Opposite the church is the Grange, a Georgian country-style house.

Nearby are the 16th-cent. Pemberton Almshouses and in Hatfield Road the Marlborough Almshouses, erected by the Duchess of Marlborough in 1736, with an open courtyard in which stands a large cedar tree.

George Street, which begins at the clock tower, has a number of medieval buildings with protruding upper stories, and off it is Romeland, with a green fronting the cathedral. By the side of the green, in Abbey Mill Lane, is one of the oldest inns in England, Fighting Cocks Inn, an octagonal, timber-framed building. Opposite it is an 18th-cent. silk mill, three stories high and nine bays long.

Romeland House, in Romeland Hill, a continuation of George Street, is of purple and red brick with seven bays, a large pedimented doorcase on Tuscan columns and a Venetian window.

Before crossing the river, in Fishpool Street is St Michael's Manor House with nine bays and an impressive entrance. Over the river in St Michael's Street are timber-framed houses. St Michael's Church, within the boundary of the Roman city, has an Anglo-Saxon nave, chancel walls of the 10th cent. and aisles of the 12th cent. The nave roof, on carved stone corbels, and the octagonal Perpendicular font are 15th-cent., and the pulpit with finely carved bookrests is 17th-cent. There are many monuments, but the most famous is that of Sir Francis Bacon showing him sleeping comfortably in a chair.

Gorhambury House and Park, 2½ m. N. of St Albans near the A5, is open to the public and was the home of Sir Nicholas Bacon, father of Sir Francis. Built in 1568, the original masonry of the hall, the porch and a projecting wing still survive. The porch has Tuscan attached columns on the ground floor and Ionic columns on either side of the two-light upper windows. The house was rebuilt in 1777 and the interior has magnificent fireplaces, many portraits of value and 16th-cent. enamelled glass. Numerous famous oaks, including one associated with Queen Elizabeth I, are in Gorhambury Park.

ST IVES, *Huntingdonshire* (10–TL3171). The town, which is a borough, presumably because of its important cattle market, traces its origin back to a village called Slepe, which was on the north bank of the River Ouse and meant slippery landing place. It was a manor of RAMSEY Abbey in 969 and eventually became a priory of the abbey, dedicated to St Ivo, a Persian bishop, and has been called St Ives ever since.

Henry I granted it the rights of an annual fair in 1110 and the town grew up around the fairground, to which people came from all over the country and abroad. The Black Death of 1349 caused its temporary closure and the town declined in importance.

St Ives is picturesque, with delightful riverside views. It has a narrow six-arched bridge built about 1415 with a bridge chapel, one of only three of its kind in England. There is single-line traffic across the bridge, controlled by traffic lights. On the far side is Bridge House, of the 18th cent., with a round arched window overlooking the river. Oliver Cromwell had a farm here and his statue stands in the Market Place.

Only a ruined wall remains of the priory, by the side of the modern council offices. There are many Georgian and Victorian houses in the Broadway, where a monument commemorates Queen Victoria's Jubilee, and in Bridge Street, including the manor house dated about 1600 with three gables on the river side and four on the street and ornamental bargeboards.

The Corn Exchange and the Post Office are both Victorian and the Cattle Market was opened in 1886. The Free Church in Market Hill is dated 1642 and has a steeple 156 ft tall. In the twisting roads are many brick and timber houses.

All Saints Church, reached by a footpath through the Waits, overlooks the River Ouse. Built about 1450 it is large with an exceptionally fine steeple. The west door is ornate, with two niches, and in the south aisle is a double piscina which is early 13th-cent. The octagonal font is Norman and the pulpit, with elongated blank arches, is Elizabethan. The richly painted rood-screen, which fills the chancel arch, is modern, as is the loft and organ-case. Both are by Comper.

In Ramsey Road is Clare Court, a new housing development which received a Civic Trust Award for its outstanding contribution to the surrounding scene.

ST NEOTS, *Huntingdonshire* (10–TL1860). This pleasant, ancient market town on the River Ouse owes its origin to a priory founded in the 10th cent. by Benedictine monks. The Danes invaded it, and after the Conquest it was refounded and given to the Abbey of Bec in Normandy in 1081. The monastery was dissolved in 1539 and disappeared, but excavations have recently taken place and some of the foundations have been uncovered.

The town centres around Market Place, which is long and spacious. The Bridge Hotel, beside the modern bridge, dates from 1685 and has wall panelling that is even earlier. The Cross Keys Inn, of the same period, is low with two-bay windows, and the King's Head in South Street has a curious doorway. In Church Street is the Victorian vicarage with ivy-covered walls and gabled Tudor enlargements. To the left of it are walls and gate-piers with fine wrought-iron gates of the 18th

St Ives: the 15th-cent. bridge with its bridge chapel

Noel Habgood

cent. W. of the church is Brook House, built about 1700, with a hipped roof, seven bays and three stories. The Sun Inn was built about 1680 and apart from the fact that its thatched roof has been replaced by tiles, little has changed since that date. The oak beams still remain in the low ceilings and so do the open fires and many brasses.

St Mary's Church is one of the largest medieval churches in the county and very beautiful. It is tucked away from the town centre in a large churchyard. Of ironstone and pebbles with ashlar dressings, it has a fine tower, and the roof is almost completely flat. The tower is 130 ft high with high solid pinnacles. The windows are all large. The nave is separated from the aisles by high-bay arches. The nave, aisles and chapels have ornately decorated roofs. The pulpit and stalls are Victorian but a few of the latter are late 15th-cent. There are several Perpendicular screens. In the chancel is an unusual monument to Mr Rowley and his wife, which rises almost to the roof, with a gilded iron screen in the lower part.

Five m. to the E., the little village of **Eltisley** has an exceptionally large village green.

ST PAUL'S WALDEN, *Hertfordshire* (10–TL 1922), is a small, rural village, of particular interest because it was the birthplace of Queen Elizabeth, the Queen Mother. Her home was the Bury, a grand red-brick house, partly by Robert Adam, with polygonal bay windows, a hall with a vault and apses at each end screened by columns. On three sides of the drawing-room are bay windows, and in the grounds is Garden House, with Gothic-pointed windows.

Reached through the park of Walden Bury, with its avenue of fine trees, is the Church of All Saints. It is a low, flint church, its tower giving a majestic effect. It has a south-east stair-turret and the thickness of the nave wall suggests that it is older than the 14th-cent. windows. Other windows are Perpendicular, as is the nave clerestory. The chancel was remodelled in 1727 and is separated from the nave by a beautiful screen. The Queen Mother was baptized in the 15th-cent. font. In the tower window is a lovely 14th-cent. figure of the Virgin, clad in brown and olive green, with the Child in red. There are six bells in the tower, one subscribed by the villagers at the time of the coronation.

Stagenhoe, which was rebuilt after 1737, has an 11-bay front, its outer wings two-storied, the others three-storied. It stands in a magnificent park with avenues of limes and chestnuts and a great lake.

The Strathmore Arms, deep in the valley, is a delightful old country pub, its name a reminder of the close connection of the village with the Earls of Strathmore.

SANDY, *Bedfordshire* (10–TL1649). This is a small, but growing town, in pleasant countryside. It is mentioned in the Domesday Book and lay on a Roman road between GODMANCHESTER and Verulamium. The River Ivel runs through it and joins the River Ouse at the north boundary.

Although some light industries have recently developed, it is basically a market-gardening town.

St Swithun's Church, built in the 14th cent., was considerably restored in the 19th cent. It is a large, cruciform building of ironstone. Both the octagonal south piers and the west tower are medieval. The font is believed to be older than the original church. There is a fragment of a 15th-cent. alabaster panel in the chancel and several monuments. Of particular interest is a statue in white marble of the son of Prime Minister Sir Robert Peel, Captain William Peel, who was one of the first recipients of the Victoria Cross.

S. of the church is Sandy Place, once the home of the industrialist Sir Malcolm Stewart who built the model village at STEWARTBY. It is 18th-cent., of red brick with five bays.

Just outside the town on the Cambridge road is the Victorian Sandy Lodge rebuilt in a Tudor style of yellow brick with an unusual cupola over the stables. It is now the headquarters of the Royal Society for the Protection of Birds. There is a nature trail to the bird sanctuary, which is open to the public, and it is one of the most beautiful areas in the county.

NE. of the railway station, on a hill-top overlooking the Ivel, is Hillfort, enclosing 7 acres, where Roman remains have been found.

On Sandy Heath stands the ITV aerial.

SARRATT, *Hertfordshire* (6–TQ0499), is a tiny village in wooded countryside with a long village green and 17th-cent. farm-houses.

The small Church of the Holy Cross is of flint, with a short nave, and of particular interest are the arches in the chancel which are 12th-cent. The tower, of a later period, has a brick top with an unusual saddleback roof, its ridge at right angles to the line of the nave. On the wall of the south transept are some faded paintings and there is a monument to William Kingsley and his wife, dated 1611, with five sons and a daughter, all wearing ruffs.

Opposite the church are the pre-Victorian almshouses, with pointed windows and doors, and nearby is the tiny Cock Inn.

SAWTRY, *Huntingdonshire* (10–TL1683), is a large village near the A1 and overlooking the Fens. It has a triangular village green, on which stands the old lock-up. There are 17th-cent. cottages; the Manor Farm of the same period, with a flat framework of pilaster strips and large shaped end-gables; the moated Grange Farm and Abbey Farm with some monastic stonework.

William Sawtry was born in this village in the 13th cent. He became a priest and a follower of Wycliffe, was unfrocked because of his attitude to the faith, and was burnt in chains at Smithfield in 1401. He was the first Christian martyr to be burnt in England after the Conquest.

SE. of Sawtrey is the village college, a structure of progressive modern design and a cultural centre for the district.

There were two ancient parish churches here

until the last century when they were destroyed. All Saints Church, built in 1880 by Sir Arthur Blomfield, incorporates some material of older workmanship, including the north chapel with its two-bay arcade. The west window of the north aisle is 13th-cent., with bar tracery and a straight-headed window. One bell is believed to be 14th-cent. and there are tiles of the 13th and 14th cents. A 15th-cent. brass shows the figures of Sir William le Moyne in armour, with a lion at his feet, and his wife in a veiled head-dress, with a dog at her feet.

About 2½ m. SSE. of Sawtry is the excavated site of Sawtry Abbey, founded in 1147 for Cistercians. The foundations of the building can still be traced and the four fish ponds remain.

SHARNBROOK, *Bedfordshire* (10–SP9959). Amid lovely countryside is this attractive village with many old cottages, one of which, in the High Street, is now a bank. The Post Office is Victorian.

There is a Victorian Baptist chapel, its yellow-brick front trimmed with red, arched windows with Venetian tracery in the bays and a low gable stretching the length of the front.

Part of the 1613 structure of Tofte Manor, which originally belonged to Newnham Priory in BEDFORD, still remains, but an additional higher castellated section was added this century. The Grange is 17th-cent. and Colworth House, now the property of a commercial firm, is early Georgian, built of ashlar by Mark Antonie for the Magniac family.

St Peter's Church is an elegant building, the Perpendicular spire connected by thin flying buttresses. The south doorway is 13th-cent. but the remainder of the exterior is Perpendicular. The arcades of the interior are Early English, as is the chancel arch. The octagonal font is Perpendicular with fleurons on the underside. There are two interesting screens and several monuments of note, including one in French style to Hollingworth Magniac, dated 1867. The Magniac Mausoleum in the churchyard is also unusual and has wrought-iron gates dating from the 18th cent.

A short distance away, to the S., is an Iron Age settlement. Pieces of pottery of the 1st cent. A.D. were found in the floor of an hut, which was probably the home of a Belgic craftsman.

SHENLEY, *Hertfordshire* (10–TL1900), is a long, rambling village, reached through wooded countryside.

A small round hut on the village green with a beehive roof was once the lock-up. Of 18th-cent. origin, with an inscription: "Do well, be vigilant and fear not", it is of brick and plaster with a pointed door and small barred windows.

St Botolph's Church, 1 m. N. of the village, has only the remains of its former building, built from monies left by Maud, Countess of Salisbury, in 1424. The walls are of squared flint with brick dressings, and the windows, with two-centred arches, have simple Perpendicular tracery. There are the remains of a Georgian gallery with Tuscan

columns, and under the yews in the churchyard lies Nicholas Hawksmoor, the great architect and friend of Christopher Wren.

The most interesting house in the village is Salisbury Hall, 1 m. NE. of the church. It is a brick building, surrounded by a moat, with splendid fireplaces, fine staircase and panelling. It was built by the treasurer of Henry VIII and partially modernized in the 17th cent. In the interior its most important features are the medallions, purported to have come from Sopwell Nunnery, ST ALBANS.

One m. SE. of the village is High Canons, built in 1773, a five-bayed, two-story house in large grounds.

SHILLINGTON, *Bedfordshire* (10–TL1234), is on the borders of Hertfordshire, a sloping village street on the edge of a chalk-pit. The ancient Church of All Saints dominates the scenery. It is of ironstone, very long, with two square east turrets. Built about 1300, it has hardly been altered since. The chancel is divided from the nave by three fine arches and a screen of exceptional wealth, very high with one-light divisions. There are several other attractive screens in the church. Under the chancel is a fine vaulted crypt, part of which is built into the slope of a hill.

In nearby **Pegsdon,** 3 m. S., is a round barrow, 4 ft high and 20 ft in diameter. Knocking Knoll Long Barrow, 1 m. SSW. of Pirton, is 100 ft long and 10 ft high. The site was excavated in the 19th cent. and the mound now resembles two round barrows.

SIBSON CUM STIBBINGTON, *Huntingdonshire* (10–TL0997), is a double village on the banks of the River Nene and just off the A1. It is small, attractive and prosperous, with 17th-cent. buildings mostly of stone and a few thatched cottages. Its Hall has a fine façade, E-shaped with gables and mullioned and transomed windows and a long gallery. The gateway into the garden has strapwork with ogee curves on top. On either side of the church are the rectory, with a mulberry tree and sycamore in the garden, and Stibbington Lodge Farm House, with flat fronts and mullioned windows. Sibson Manor House, ¾ m. SSE. on the A1, is also of the 17th cent.

The Church of St John the Baptist is mainly Victorian, although the chancel is medieval and a little of the west doorway is Norman. The chancel arch, however, is 12th-cent. and inside are several structures of the same period. The octagonal font is also of the same time. In the chancel is a defaced, 14th-cent. effigy of a priest.

Just outside the village, on the A1 towards STAMFORD is an old inn, the Haycock, built as a posting house about the middle of the 17th cent. with the bedrooms centring round the courtyard and many outhouses. The exterior appears to be original and the interior is pleasantly and simply decorated with many old oak beams still remaining. A plaque in the courtyard states that Queen Victoria spent the night there in the early part of her reign.

Wansford Bridge, which is just past the hotel, dates from three periods, 1577, 1672 and 1795, and has 10 fine arches of varying shapes.

SLOUGH, *Buckinghamshire* (6–SU9779). This is the largest town and industrial centre in the county. It is a place of multiple trades with 800 factories on the Slough Trading Estate employing over 28,000 people. The estate was one of the first of its kind and has been copied in other parts of the country.

The town has many amenities for its large population, including a greyhound track, a golf course, cricket and football grounds and over 400 acres of parks and open spaces.

But despite its modernity the town still has links with the past. Its ancient roots are in the outskirts of Upton, around which the life of the village once evolved. Sir William Herschel the astronomer lived here and from the giant telescope in his garden he discovered the planet Uranus.

The Norman Church of St Lawrence can be reached by way of the Windsor road in the Upton section of the town. Although restored in 1850 the church still retains much Norman work. It is entered through a Norman doorway, adorned by chevron moulding and with carved capitals. The nave and the tower are 12th-cent., as is the chancel. The roof, in four bays, is 15th-cent. and the font was created by Norman craftsmen, who probably carved the pillar piscina. One of the church's treasures is a fascinating 16th-cent. almsbox with three locks. In the churchyard, reputed to be the inspiration of Gray's *Elegy*, are many ancient yews. Next to the church is the park of the 15th-cent. Upton Court, the property of Merton Abbey before the Reformation.

A short distance from the centre of Slough, on the same road as St Lawrence's Church, is Montem Mound, near Salt Hill. At this ancient spot an unusual ceremony was held by pupils from Eton College for the collection of "salt". A procession from the collage to the mound was led by twelve resplendent "salt-bearers", followed by the rest of the school. On reaching the mound the leader ascended it and waved a royal standard. After a short ceremony came the collection of "salt", which was, in fact, money, and Queen Victoria, who rarely missed the ceremony, was always stopped by the words, "Salt, Your Majesty, salt." The money so collected was given to the head boy of the school for payment of his expenses at King's College, Cambridge.

SPALDWICK, *Huntingdonshire* (10–TL1272), is a delightful country village beside Ellington Brook, with a 15th-cent. bridge of three arches. On the village green, shaded by chestnuts, is a fragment of a medieval cross.

The large Victorian Free Church has three arched windows, and the George Inn, dating from the 17th cent., has wall paintings on its upper floor. Manor Farm, Beech House and the Limes are Georgian, and Ivy House, with its flat bay front and giant angle pilasters, is dated 1688.

St James's Church has a fascinating 14th-cent. tower which is 152 ft high, and the stair-turret has a stone vault. The Norman north doorway is the oldest part of the church, and the chancery, with fine tracery windows, is 13th-cent. There is a Perpendicular screen in the south aisle and an Early English font.

STAGSDEN, *Bedfordshire* (10–SP9849). This is a tiny village, with thatched cottages and an old church, St Leonard's, standing on high ground with a 13th-cent. tower and a short lead spire. In the old Stacheden Chapel, named after the church's first vicar in 1220, is a lovely piscina and sedilia and the remains of a stone altar. The font is richly decorated with carvings of two praying figures, and the screen, with its four-light divisions, is Perpendicular. The tower has six bells.

Stagsden Bird Gardens are a breeding establishment for rare species of wild life. There are over 1,500 specimens, with a collection of shrub roses. The gardens are open to the public and are reached by turning N. at the church.

STAMFORD BARON, *Northamptonshire* (10–TF0305). Otherwise known as Stamford St Martin Without, this is part of STAMFORD, in Lincolnshire, which lies S. of the River Welland.

Apart from an almshouse near the bridge, built and endowed by Lord Burghley in 1597, it has but one building of interest which more than justifies a visit.

Burghley House is one of the largest Elizabethan mansions in the country. It is oblong, 240 ft by 125 ft, with short square towers, turrets, frilled balustrades and tall chimney-shafts. Built mainly of Barnack stone, the style is uniform throughout. William Cecil, who spent his childhood in an earlier house on the same site, built this mansion, which took nearly 30 years to complete, during the time that he was Secretary of State, Chancellor of the Gate and, during Elizabeth I's reign, Chief Secretary of State, when he became Lord Burghley. The house has belonged to the Cecil family since that time. It is built round a courtyard and the lofty kitchen was completed first. Then came the great hall with its steep, double hammer-beam roof and its huge fireplace. Next Scagliola Hall, the Marble Hall and the Andromeda Hall were built. The house has many beautiful rooms with painted ceilings, silver fireplaces and over 700 works of art, tapestries and furniture. The grounds were landscaped by Capability Brown, with an orangery, stables with a hipped roof, a bath-house overlooking the lake, a boathouse and a superb rose garden. Both house and grounds are open to the public.

STANDON, *Hertfordshire* (10–TL3922). To this tiny village came the first traveller from the skies, Vincenza Lunardi, a young Italian, who arrived by balloon in autumn 1784. A stone commemorates his landing 2 m. NE. of the village.

Half a m. away is the Lordship, now modernized but still including the remains of an early Tudor house, the home of Sir Ralph Sadler who looked after Mary Queen of Scots in Edinburgh. It retains its old carriageway with a four-centred arch and flanking turrets.

St Mary's Church has two features which are unique in the county: a big west porch and a detached tower. The church is on a hill so that the chancel is reached by raised steps. It is early 13th-cent. The arch of the chancel is rich with carving and from it can be seen three lancets over the altar. There is a tomb in the chancel to Sir Ralph Sadler, with his seven children and a pole that once bore the Royal Standard of Scotland.

S. of the church is the Endowed School, a long, two-storied, timber-framed building of the 16th cent.

Nearby is Upp Hall, a 17th-cent. manor house, and a spectacular barn, 140 ft long with original pointed-arched openings.

STANSTEAD ABBOTS, *Hertfordshire* (10–TL3811). This old village lies on the slopes of the Stort Valley, amidst cedar and pine trees.

The six Elizabethan Baesche Almshouses are two-storied brick buildings with three gables. In the village street will be found the 17th-cent. old Clockhouse School with quoins and a tiny cupola, a Victorian mill, now a factory, with a Greek temple roof, and the Red Lion Inn of the early 17th cent. with overhanging stories and gables. One house in the street is dated 1752 and is an unusual red-brick building, its circular stair-turret bearing an embattled top.

The centre block of Briggen was built in the early 18th cent., the bow windows added a century later, and extensions made in 1908.

Near to the church is Stanstead Bury, a picturesque manor built in the 15th cent. and altered during each successive century. It has a half-timbered stair-turret and seven bays in the garden front and is reminiscent of a large villa.

St James Church has a completely unspoilt interior with 18th-cent. box-pews and a three-decked pulpit. It is mainly of the 15th cent. with an open timber porch and Perpendicular windows. The tall, solid tower screen is of the 17th cent., but the nave is 12th-cent and the chancel 13th-cent. There are a number of monuments, including two of particular interest by Manning in the 19th cent. of Mrs Booth and Sir Felix Booth.

STEVENAGE, *Hertfordshire* (10–TL2325), is a fascinating place to visit for it has achieved the unexpected: a completely new town, spacious, well-planned and attractively modern, yet retaining in Old Stevenage its ancient charm and much of historical interest.

The new town has a number of varied industries as well as large office blocks and two modern buildings of particular interest. Barclay Co-educational Secondary Modern School in Walk-ern Road, has a variety of blocks and materials, good details and fixtures, and its main staircase is on a concrete spine not attached to the wall. There is a curved screen in the front entrance by Henry Moore. The new church is an unusual building with a semi-circular roof and the upper half of the structure almost completely of glass.

In the old town, which is centred round the broad main street with its avenues of horse chestnuts and limes and good parking facilities, are old cottages and houses, mostly used as shops, but still retaining their original features. At the end of the street is the grammar school, greatly extended now but with one room built in 1562 as Alleyn's Grammar School still with its original brickwork and open timber roof. The Grange, an early Georgian house, with a broad 12-bay front and large carriageway was formerly a coaching inn. Nearby is the Yorkshire Grey, another old inn with its original exterior of widely spread windows and the Tuscan pilasters of the door, but its interior is greatly modernized. Running off the High Street are narrow little streets with 17th-cent. cottages.

About ¾ m. S. are the Barrows of Six Hills, believed to have been built in Roman times for burial purposes.

Standing nearly a mile from the centre of the town is the Church of St Nicholas, dating from the 12th cent. It is of flint and its low Norman tower has a leaded spire. The roof, screens and stalls are 15th-cent., but the font is 13th-cent. There are screens between the aisles and chapels, chancel and chapels, and nave and chancel. The choir seats are decorated with misericords. There are two monuments of note: a brass to a 15th-cent. priest, Stephen Hillard, and an effigy of a woman with a wimple, accompanied by an angel and a priest, c. 1300.

The Roebuck Inn, 1 m. along the A1, is 400 years old and although the original building is still there, it has been extended greatly and is now called the Roebuck Motor Hotel.

STEVINGTON, *Bedfordshire* (10–SP9853). This village, with its rather grey buildings typical of old Bedfordshire, is on a narrow crossroads centred by the village cross, which is decorated with capitals and a large finial.

The Church of St Mary, on a terrace above the River Ouse, is reached by a cul-de-sac off the crossroads, down Church Road. It is a place of ancient pilgrimage for it is said that in medieval days people visited its holy well, which springs out of a rock on which the church stands and the waters of which are reputed never to have dried up. The church has a pre-Conquest tower and windows and a high screen under the tower. The arcade, with high quatrefoil piers, has deep hollows in the diagonals. Much of the workmanship is Decorated and Perpendicular. There are interesting poppyheads on the benches and a brass to Thomas Salle, 1422.

At either end of the street are old drinking fountains, Opposite one, in Church Road, are the church rooms, dated 1897.

On the other side of the crossroads, leading from the church, are ancient almshouses amidst many old cottages.

The windmill, built in the 18th cent., can be seen from the main road to BROMHAM, but to reach it turn up a narrow country lane. The keys for it may be obtained from a thatched cottage nearby. A wooden post-mill, it has recently had new sails attached, putting it back in working order.

STEWARTBY, *Bedfordshire* (10–TL0241), is believed to have the largest brickworks in the world, turning out about 650 million bricks a year. The kiln, which took a year to re-heat after the Second World War, holds 9 million bricks. The peculiarity of the clay from which the bricks are made is its high oil content.`

The model village, built for the employees, is attractive and well laid out, with its own village hall, club, secondary modern school and old people's homes, as well as an open-air swimming-pool.

Sir Malcolm Stewart built the village and named it after his father.

STOKENCHURCH, *Buckinghamshire* (6–SU 7596). On the top of the Chilterns is this little chair-making village with its magnificent beech-woods. The small factory was once a Sunday school, established in 1769 by Hannah Ball, one of the original founders of these schools. She was a close friend of John Wesley and prepared the plans of the Wesleyan chapel, which still holds her writing table and her diary, as well as the clock which timed the services.

In the village is a 17th-cent. coaching inn and an attractive 12th-cent. church with Norman columns and a Norman nave. The five-bayed roof has tie-beams and carved spandrels. In the rebuilt transept is a canopied piscina. There is an ancient font and there are brass monuments to Robert Morle, dated 1410 and 1415, and to Bartholomew Tipping and his lady.

STOKE POGES, *Buckinghamshire* (6–SU 9882). In the heart of the countryside, N. of SLOUGH, this out-of-the-way village is of interest for its connections with Thomas Gray, for it is here that he is said to have written his famous *Elegy.* St Giles Church, built about the 13th cent., stands back from the roadside and is reached by a short lane. In the large field at the side of the church is a simple 18th-cent. monument which is a National Trust property.

An altar tomb in the church, close to the walls, is the grave of Thomas Gray and his mother. The church is entered by two lych-gates and a long pathway edged with rose-trees. There is a fine timber porch and a massive nave roof, both of which are 14th-cent. An unusual feature in a stained-glass window is a kind of medieval "bicycle".

The Garden of Remembrance, close to the church, covers 30 acres. It is a garden graveyard, without stones, set in an avenue of trees and wild flowers leading to a delightful lake with a fountain and rose garden. Here one can, indeed, feel oneself "Far from the madding crowd's ignoble strife".

Behind the church is the Elizabethan manor house where Queen Elizabeth I was entertained and where Charles I was held prisoner. It is now the residence of Lord Grantley. Stoke Park, one of the great houses of the district, is now a golf club-house, while Stoke Court, once known as West End Cottage, the home of Thomas Gray and his mother, now forms the offices of a nationally famous research concern.

To the E. are Black Park and Langley Park comprising 1,060 acres, which are preserved as part of the green belt around London. Delightful walks can be taken in Black Park, which has a lake, and in Langley Park are the famous rhododendron gardens.

Stoke Poges: the unusual "bicycle window" in the famous church

Jane J. Miller

STOWE, *Buckinghamshire* (10–SP6736). Three m. N. of BUCKINGHAM, reached by an avenue of elms and beeches, is the historic house of Stowe, which was formerly the seat of the dukes of Buckingham and Chandos. The noble Corinthian Arch spans the road leading to the 800 acres of parkland which are dotted with Classical buildings.

The grounds and garden buildings are open to the public, but the magnificent house, the front of which is 900 ft long, is now one of the youngest of England's great public schools. Robert Adam, Vanbrugh, William Kent and Grinling Gibbons all took part in the construction of the buildings and the grounds in the 17th and 18th cents.

In the extensive grounds, laid out by Kent and Capability Brown, are many ornamental temples. In the Temple of Worthies can be seen busts of Drake, King Alfred, Inigo Jones and Shakespeare. The Congreve Monument was built by Kent in 1736. There is a temple containing armoury, and another, for music, has a Roman pavement. Across one of the delightful lakes is an ornamental bridge.

In the corner of the grounds can be seen the remains of Stowe Castle, built in the early 19th cent.

Also in the grounds of Stowe is the humble little medieval Church of the Assumption of the Blessed Mary. Notable for its general atmosphere rather than the building, it has interesting 17th-cent. monuments. The tower and a crucifix over the doorway are both 14th-cent. Nearby is an obelisk to the memory of General Wolfe.

SULGRAVE, *Northamptonshire* (10–SP5545). This tiny village, 7 m. from BRACKLEY, is dominated by its associations with the ancestors of George Washington who lived here for a century, over 300 years ago. The north wing of the house where they lived, Sulgrave Manor, is of the Queen Anne period but the other part was added in this century when the building regained its former glory after having been a farm for some considerable time. The house, a popular place of pilgrimage for Americans, contains many George Washington relics, including his black velvet coat and a fragment of the wedding dress of his bride Martha. The interior of the house, which has been restored, has great fireplaces complete with medieval implements, and there is a child's tea-set of 63 pieces. In the parlour is a spinet, and the great bed chamber, with its original oak mullioned windows, has a four-poster bed with a carved cradle at its foot, all hung with Elizabethan needlework. Over the porch is carved the original of the American flag, three stars and two stripes, and also Queen Elizabeth I's arms. A relief on the lid of a snuff-box, dated 1777, shows the President in uniform.

The 14th-cent Church of St James has three doorways of different periods, the west door in the tower suggesting that it was the site of an Anglo-Saxon church. On the chancel are heads of Edward III and Queen Philippa. The south porch bears the date 1564 with the initials E.R. and the

fleur-de-lis. There are monuments to the Washingtons, including a pew and a chest in their name.

SUTTON, *Bedfordshire* (10–TL2247), has an unusual feature, a packhorse bridge, with two pointed 14th-cent. arches, which carries foot and horse traffic over the tributary of the Ivel. It is in the centre of the village.

In Sutton Park, with avenues of great limes, is a broad, deep moat marking the site of John of Gaunt's Hall, a mansion given to the Burgoyne family in perpetuity by John of Gaunt.

In the 13th-cent. All Saints Church are many monuments to the Burgoynes. In the south aisle is a Decorated piscina, and the ironstone tower is Perpendicular. There is a tall arch to the nave and, except for the chancel, all the church is castellated. The pulpit, 1628, has a sounding board, and the communion rail is 17th-cent., as are some of the box pews. A stone monument to John Burgoyne, 1608, is large and ornate, with a reclining effigy. A curiosity of the church is its barrel organ, which is still in use.

TAPLOW, *Buckinghamshire* (6–SU9182). This is a riverside resort with smooth grassy slopes leading down to the Thames where yachts are moored and fishing is a favourite sport.

CLIVEDEN can be seen in the distance from the cliffs high above the river, and in the woods near the water is Taplow Court, a Victorian mansion fashioned in Norman style, the residence of Lord and Lady Desborough. On the lawns of the house is an Anglo-Saxon tumulus.

There are many old cottages in the village as well as an Elizabethan farm-house and a modern 20th-cent. church with a copper spire reaching above the trees. In the chancel is a stone screen with a rood incorporated and the Norman font came from the old church which stood on the site. Many fine brasses of the 15th and 16th cents. are among its attractions.

TEMPSFORD, *Bedfordshire* (10–TL1653), is on the A1 where the Ouse and the Ivel meet. It is historically important for in 921 the Danes fortified it as a base against the Saxons, until it was captured by the son of King Alfred, Edward the Elder, who slew every man, woman and child there. Ninety years later the Danish army burnt down the town.

The bridge crossing the river has three round arches, and near the river is Gannock's Castle, earthworks 115 ft by 85 ft, probably of the 12th cent.

Across the A1 is Tempsford Hall, a large Victorian gabled building of red brick, built in the Elizabethan style, to which a new section has recently been added.

St Peter's Church, originally 12th-cent., has been much restored, but the tower is Decorated as are the windows of the aisle. The rest is mainly Perpendicular, but the nave is Victorian. The wooden pulpit, with traceried panels, is Perpendicular and old parts of the screen are in the dado.

N. of the church is Gannock House, a well-preserved, timber-framed house of the 15th cent. with large bracing and ogee members.

TEWIN, *Hertfordshire* (10–TL2714). This tiny scattered village, only an hour from London, is attractively situated above the River Mimram in wooded countryside with narrow lanes, sloping fields and winding paths.

The small Church of St Peter is still partly of the 11th cent. Its chancel was remodelled in the 13th cent. and the south aisle with lancet windows is of the same period. Changes have been made in the intervening centuries and a monument to the Governor of Gibraltar, General Joseph Sabine, is of *c.* 1739. The font is a fluted 18th-cent. bowl.

Close to the church is the Rectory, a Georgian house of two stories with five bays and timber-framed barn and stable.

There is a superb lake at Tewin Water, 1 m. WNW. of the village, which has a house built in 1819 in the neo-Grecian style, with seven bays, a recessed centre adorned by giant Ionic columns, shallow box windows and a tiny curved balcony.

About ¾ m. SW. of Tewin is Marden Hill, a house built in the 18th cent. of yellow brick. Later additions have turned it into a beautiful building with its Ionic porch, entrance hall and dining-room. The staircase is of special interest.

Queen Hoo Hall, beyond the upper green of Tewin, is a tiny, well-preserved, early Elizabethan house of brick. It has an unusual half-E plan, the projections having corbelled gables with honeycomb decorated finials. The brick windows are mullioned and there are Tudor arches and, in an upper room, Elizabethan mural paintings.

THORNHAUGH, *Huntingdonshire* (10–TF 0600), is a tiny, secluded village in a deep valley just off the A1. The rectory, although enlarged dates from about 1680, and the nearby manor house is also of the 17th cent. The large area of plantations between the UPPINGHAM and Kings-cliffe roads is known as the Bedford Purlieus. In Sibberton Lodge are the remains of a 14th-cent. building with a vaulted undercroft of two bays.

The 13th-cent. church was damaged when the spire fell at the beginning of the 16th cent. Its tower and chancel are original but the nave and chancel roof timbers are 15th-cent. In the south chapel, which is Perpendicular, is the tomb of William, Lord Russell of Thornhaugh, the 1st Duke of Bedford.

TODDINGTON, *Bedfordshire* (10–TL0129). The village is on a hill above the River Flitt and around the spacious village green are attractive houses and cottages, many of them Georgian. The best is Old Wentworth House, of chequer brick and built about 1700. Of its seven bays the three centre ones lie slightly back. Its doorway has fluted pilasters and there is a top parapet.

There is an old town hall and a village pond, as well as a new school of pleasant modern architecture.

The manor house was originally built about 1570, a quadrangular building with a large inner court. All that remains today, however, is a small oblong building with a hipped roof, believed to have been the Elizabethan kitchen, and a round tower.

St George's Church is a superb cruciform building of Totternhoe stone, built in the 13th and 15th cents., with the unique feature of a separate three-storied priest's house. The church has a central tower and is embattled. Beneath the battlements is a frieze of animals, a fish and a mermaid. The tower has bell-openings. In the transept is a double piscina. The crossing arches are low and the roof of the nave is decorated with angels and bosses. In the aisle are fascinating paintings and there are many monuments of interest.

E. of the church is Conger Hill with a motte and the remains of earthworks. One m. NW. of the village is Toddington Park.

TOSELAND, *Huntingdonshire* (10–TL2362), is mentioned in the Domesday Book. It was a meeting place of one of the four hundreds of the county and has a Moot stone in the churchyard where the Toseland Hundred met. It still gives its name to the Petty Sessional Division. An old Roman road passes near the village and in a wood to the N. are remains of an ancient camp.

Of great interest is its manor house, Toseland Hall, built towards the end of Queen Elizabeth's reign, with the original thatched barn, with tie-beams on braces and collar-beams, farm buildings and stabling. The house is of two stories with attics in the gables. In the main front are mullioned windows, a central porch and three gables. The clustered chimney stacks are octagonal. Its exterior is of mellow red brick.

The little pebble-built St Michael's Church, almost hidden in a field, with the Blue Ball Inn in front of it, was considerably restored in the latter part of the last cent. It was originally Norman and the masonry is mostly of that time, as is the south doorway. The chancel arch is also Norman and the capitals have volutes. The chalice is Elizabethan and a 17th-cent. oak table has twisted legs.

TOTTERNHOE, *Bedfordshire* (10–SP9921), has famous stone quarries, tunnelled into the Chilterns, which have supplied the stone for many of the county's churches. The stone is a soft limestone called clunch.

The ancient castle was once one of the strongest in the county, and its oldest building is NW. of the motte.

About ¾ m. E. of the castle remains is a site of chalk quarrying in which traces of Bronze and Iron Age settlements have been found, including fragments of vessels and an enclosure ditch in which was discovered a bronze, vase-headed pin dated back to the 6th cent. B.C.

The Cross Keys Inn, which is a thatched, half-timbered building, has a fireplace dated 1433.

St Giles Church is built from the quarries in the village and has a fine exterior. The gable of the nave has rich flint flushwork decoration. The building was begun in the 14th cent. and

Turvey: most of the houses in this village were rebuilt of local stone in the last century

completed in the 16th. The church is embattled and the north vestry pretty. Under the low tower arch is a screen in single-light divisions. There is a brass in the chancel floor to John Warwekhyll, vicar, 1524.

N. of the church is Lancotbury, a fine manor house with timber frames and closely set studs. It is probably 16th-cent.

TOWCESTER, *Northamptonshire* (10–SP69 48). This ancient town, once a coaching stop, stands on the site of the Roman settlement Lactodorum, with Watling Street running through it. The Anglo-Saxons fortified it and the Danes attacked it. Benedetto Gaetano, who eventually became Pope, held the living here in the 13th cent., and the Archdeacon Sponne, who was rector here in the 15th cent., founded the school and chantry and left a sum of money to pave the town.

The Town Hall, like many other buildings here, is Victorian. There are a number of Georgian houses including the Post Office dated 1799, and many old cottages. A number of old inns remain, including the Talbot, 1440, and the Saracen's Head which Dickens made famous in his *Pickwick Papers*.

By the side of the Town Hall is Chantry House and gateway, built of stone in the 15th cent., with an oak doorway and oak beams.

St Laurence's Church, reached by a narrow lane by the side of the Town Hall, has a tall, ironstone, Perpendicular tower. There are two ancient mass dials, one outside and one inside. In the modern chancel arch are two Norman pillars, and traces of Norman carving can be seen above the south arcade. The crypt is 13th-cent., and on the south chapel arch a jester's head is carved. The clerestory and font are 500 years old.

The chancel roof bears the date 1640 and other beams are of the 17th and 18th cents. In a long stall, with carved panels, are valuable black-letter books attached by chains. One of these is the Treacle Bible: "Is there not triacle [balm] in Giliad?" The exotic organ came from FONTHILL Abbey. There are wall paintings of interest and a sculptured head of William Sponne, the bene-factor, with a skeleton beneath it.

Dame Edith Sitwell is buried in the churchyard at **Weedon Lois,** about 6 m. W., and on her grave is a monument by Henry Moore.

Gayton Manor, about $2\frac{1}{2}$ m. E. on the A5, is an Elizabethan house, of cruciform shape with unusual gables, and is open to the public. On the outskirts of the town is Easton Neston House, late 17th-cent., and in the park is Towcester race-course. Stoke Park Pavilions, 3 m. off the A508, with pavilions by Inigo Jones, a linking colonnade and beautiful gardens, are open to the public.

Although the centre of the town maintains its old atmosphere, there are new buildings on the outskirts and its industries include the manu-facture of electrical engineering components and compound cattle food. There are also wool warehouses which serve the surrounding districts. On the road to NORTHAMPTON is a hump-backed bridge and lovely countryside.

TURVEY, *Bedfordshire* (10–SP9452). Although historically ancient, the village was mainly rebuilt of local stone in the 19th cent. It is on the border of two counties, Buckinghamshire being reached by the long bridge and causeway with 16 arches, some of which are believed to be 13th-cent. On a tiny island, midway across the River Ouse, are two statues, one of recent origin, the other of Jonah, which was originally in the monastery of Bonshommes at Ashridge.

There are old cottages here, an old inn and ancient almshouses, as well as two stately houses.

Turvey Abbey is a gabled, irregular Jacobean house, made interesting by balustrades and pinnacles brought from Easton Maudit in Northamptonshire. The chimney-pieces are of particular interest and there is a medieval oblong dovecot and Georgian stables.

Turvey House, built nearly 200 years later, has giant Corinthian pilasters, the exterior much decorated. There is a cast-iron staircase in the house which came from the Crystal Palace.

The Church of All Saints tells the history of the countryside, for it is of Anglo-Saxon origin, although much restored. The 12th-cent. font has carved capitals at the corners, and the nave and tower are Anglo-Danish. The sedilia and piscina have 13th-cent. carvings and the fine ironwork is by Thomas of Leighton, a Bedfordshire man. Of special interest is the 14th-cent. painting of the Crucifixion in the south aisle. There are many monuments of interest, including several of the family of Mordaunts who lived for many centuries at the Old Hall.

UPWOOD, *Huntingdonshire* (10–TL2582), is a tiny village of old cottages and haystacks, with Cross Keys Inn and Carlton House both dating from the 17th cent.

Upwood House, W. of the church, is also 17th-cent., with two projecting wings on its red-brick front and two large flat chimney breasts which are probably older than the house. The beautiful grounds are open to the public under the National Gardens Scheme.

St Peter's Church has much Norman workmanship, including the font. In the nave is a Norman north arcade and a Norman chancel arch. There are simple screens of one-light divisions in the chancel and north chapel. A tablet to Peter Phesaunt dated 1649 has a Latin inscription, and one to Sir Richard and Lady Bickerton, 1811, has an urn with an inscription above.

WADDESDON, *Buckinghamshire* (10–SP74 16). W. of AYLESBURY on the road to BICESTER, this large village is famed to art lovers. There are many charming houses and an old inn with whimsically shaped yews.

The church, part Norman, part Perpendicular, is reached by an avenue of chestnuts. The tower is 15th-cent. and above the Norman doorway is a porch with a 14th-cent. recess holding a little statue of St Michael. The splendid nave, dominating the church, is in three arches renewed 600 years ago from the original materials of the old church. There are pretty heads between two of the arches. An oak screen decorates the Lady Chapel in which is a 14th-cent. piscina. The font is 600 years old. At the entrance to the chancel lies a statue, nearly 7 ft long, of a knight in armour with his hands on a sword and lion at his feet. It is believed to be Sir Roger Dynham.

Waddesdon Manor, resembling a French *château*, was built in the years 1880–9 by the architect Hippolyte Destailleur for Baron Ferdinand de Rothschild and is now National Trust property. It stands on a hill encircled by woods and parkland and is reached from the west end of the village. Its great state rooms contain exquisite oak panelling in rococo style brought from 18th-cent. Parisian houses. Important English, Dutch, Flemish and Italian paintings adorn the walls, and there are fine collections of French furniture, Savonnerie carpets and Sèvres porcelain. The Bachelor's Wing also contains a display of small-arms. A magnificently painted ceiling by De Witt is in the Red Room. The manor is open to the public.

WADENHOE, *Northamptonshire* (10–TL 0083), is a delightful agricultural village with picturesque scenery. At the end of the village, with its stone cottages and thatched and tiled roofs, the River Nene broadens and ripples over the ford beside the old mill, and the farms have limestone barns. To the W. is an enclosure called Castle Close in which are earthwork foundations, and on the Pilton road is a farm with a dovecot.

George Ward Hunt, a member of the notable Wadenhoe family, lived here. He was Chancellor of the Exchequer under Disraeli and it is said that the village had the first rural telegraph office in Britain installed so that he could keep in touch with Whitehall.

Above the river, up a steep, winding footpath, is the church. It has a rare saddleback tower, little Norman windows and dates back to the 13th cent. Large, amusing heads support the chancel arch. The bench-ends of the pews are 14th-cent., but the font is crudely carved with a medieval head. There are several monuments, including one to Joan Bridges Genersh showing two weeping cherubs and dated 1792. The keys for the church should be obtained before mounting the hill.

WALTHAM CROSS, *Hertfordshire* (10–TL 3600), lies on the New River on the borders with Middlesex. Not far from London, it is now mainly suburban.

About ¼ m. from the border stands one of the few remaining Eleanor Cross monuments erected by Edward I to commemorate the resting-places of the coffin of his queen, Eleanor of Castile, on its way to WESTMINSTER ABBEY. The cross was begun in 1291 and has been heavily restored. It is hexagonal, an unusual shape, and has three figures standing in niches under canopies. It is profusely decorated.

In the High Street, S. of the cross, is Harold House, a yellow-brick building with Ionic doorcase and a decorated pediment.

Nearby is **Theobalds Park**, built by William Cecil, Queen Elizabeth's leading statesman. James I found the palace so attractive that he persuaded Robert Cecil, the Prime Minister, to exchange it with HATFIELD. It was dismantled shortly afterwards and four small houses were built in its place. Of these one remains, Old Palace House. Of the original palace only a high brick wall remains, which is part of the gardener's cottage.

At the entrance to Theobald's Park is a massive construction which was Temple Bar, erected in 1672 in FLEET STREET, London, by Sir Christopher Wren and removed to its present site in 1887. Below the house is an ornamental lake formed from New River.

WARBOYS, *Huntingdonshire* (10–TL3080), is a large, fenland village with, in its centre, a Victorian clock tower of yellow and red brick with a pyramid roof.

The Old Rectory, also of yellow brick, is early 19th-cent., and in its garden is a section of a large pier believed to have come from RAMSEY ABBEY.

A strange tale is attached to the village, where the trial of the Witches of Warboys took place in 1593. An old lady in her eighties by the name of Samuel visited the sick child of her next-door neighbour with a black cap on her head. The child called her a witch, and when she became worse the doctor said witchcraft was responsible. The child's sisters also became ill and Mother Samuel's reputation as a witch grew. Eventually she, her husband and her child were all tried and executed.

In Ramsey Road is a Georgian house named the Chestnuts, with gates of Grecian design in cast-iron. The brick manor house, N. of the church, with Dutch-shaped gables, is mid-17th-cent., and an inn in the High Street is of the same period.

St Mary Magdelene Church is of brown cobbles with a 13th-cent. steeple and a broach spire. It is a stately building with a high tower and broad flat buttresses, lancet windows, bell-openings and three tiers of lucarnes. The chancel arch is Norman with scalloped capitals, the two arcades each with four bays are different, one having round and octagonal piers and arches, and the other with round piers, round capitals and round arches. The north doorway is of about 1300 and in the chancel is a 12th-cent. door knocker with a lion's head, the ring showing two dragons fighting.

WARE, *Hertfordshire* (10–TL3614), is where Lady Jane Grey was proclaimed Queen in 1553, and where John Gilpin ended his famous ride in Cowper's poem.

Two rivers cross the town, the Lea and New River. Along the Lea towpath, which is lined with trees, are houses with picturesque gazebos. Running parallel with the river is the High Street, with a mixture of gabled and straight-fronted houses dating from the 16th cent. In West Street is the old town hall, a simple Regency building with a heavy unfluted Ionic column. In Bluecoat Yard is Bluecoat House, the town's former manor house, a 15th-cent. timber-framed building which for nearly a century was the home of the famous Bluecoat School until it moved to HERTFORD in 1761. Opposite the house is a terrace of timber-framed cottages built in 1968 for nurses and children. The Corn Stores in Star Street include a 17th-cent. quadrangle of store-houses, with open-timber lean-to roofs. Outer ladders give access to the upper floor.

Baldock Street has many timber-framed and gabled as well as red-brick houses, the best one of the earlier period being the Bull Inn with overhanging stories and first-floor oriel windows. At the north end of the street is Thunder Hall, a tall red-brick Jacobean house, with a central porch and gable. A gatehouse and cloisters were added in the 19th cent. Canons Hotel, opposite, is of yellow brick and has a Greek Doric porch. Nearby are Canons Maltings, red-brick malt-houses of *c.* 1600, with a row of buttresses on one side and a three-light brick window on the other.

The famous Great Bed of Ware, mentioned in the plays of Shakespeare and others, came from the Saracen's Head Inn, but is now in The VICTORIA AND ALBERT MUSEUM, London. The inn is now demolished.

The Priory, now council offices, has the remains of a house of Franciscan monks built in the 14th cent. It was refashioned after the Dissolution but still contains the old cloisters with three lancet lights and a four-centre arch.

Facing the bridges, across the river, is Amwell House, once the home of John Scott, the Quaker poet. It is a noble red-bricked building dating from about 1730. The Grotto, which was formerly in the gardens of the house, is now in Scott's Road. It is a delightful building with a confusion of passages and chambers lined with quartz, flint, bits of glass and shells. The biggest rooms are only about 12 ft by 6 ft.

The Church of St Mary is large and handsome although externally considerably restored. It lies in the centre of the town and is of flint, all embattled. The unusual feature of the church is the transepts which are carried to full nave height, with clerestories. The 14th-cent. octagonal font is probably the most elaborate in the county, with quatrefoil panels on the stem and figures of the Virgin and saints on the large bowl. The pulpit, with raised panels, is 17th-cent. There are several attractive monuments, one with a row of books at the foot of the obelisk.

About $1\frac{1}{4}$ m. NE. of the town is Fanhams Hall, a Queen Anne building with an interesting staircase and gallery 107 ft long.

WATFORD, *Hertfordshire* (6–TQ1196), is the county's biggest town, much modernized, with many industries including brewing and printing. It is, however, an ancient town, and there are still many buildings of interest to be seen.

The long narrow High Street leads down to the River Colne, which skirts the hill on which the town stands. A 16th-cent. half-timbered house, with an overhanging upper story, is on the corner of Church Street and High Street and to the S. are several houses of character. Lower down is the imposing 18th-cent. dwelling house of Benskin's Brewery, two and a half stories high with five bays and a lower outer wing, and behind it are the tall, yellow-brick Victorian brewing premises with 1836 maltings on the opposite side of the road. At the end of High Street is Frogmore House, three stories high, built about 1700. Its rusticated doorcase has Roman Doric columns topped by carved metopes.

In Church Road will be found the Victorian Salter's Company Almshouses, a long central line of houses of red-brick Tudor style with a tower and a stepped gable. Around the buildings are fine cedar trees and the gates to the street are of ornate iron.

About 1½ m. NW. of the centre of the town are two first-class farm-houses, Grove Mill House and Heath Farm House, and also the Grove, a red-brick house with stone quoins, which was built in 1756 and twice enlarged. It has two principal fronts accentuated by angle pilasters. The lodges, towards the Hemel Hempstead road, are late 18th-cent. stuccoed.

There is a modern town hall in the centre of the town with a "Scandinavian" lantern but it is generally fashioned in neo-Georgian style. It forms the nucleus of Watford's civic centre.

Cassiobury Park, once the home of the Earls of Essex, is now a golf course and part of it forms an attractive public park running down to the River Gade, where the banks are overhung by lovely willows.

There are several churches in the town but two are of particular interest, Holy Rood and St Mary's.

Holy Rood, a Roman Catholic church in Market Street, is Victorian with fine examples of the Gothic Revival style. The exterior, with its vestries and outer rooms encompassed in a square plan, is of flint, and its main feature is a square north-west tower and two turrets with copper spires.

St Mary's Church, standing in the large churchyard, is basically 13th-cent. with additions of the the 15th cent. It is long, broad and low, made of flint with a large tower which has diagonal buttresses, a stair-turret and a spike. In the chancel is a beautiful double piscina. The Essex Chapel (1595) is its most important feature. It is separated from the chancel by a Tuscan arcade and holds the tombs of the Morrisons of Cassiobury, both showing reclining life-sized figures under rich canopies with kneeling mourners. Many other lesser monuments are of interest.

Around St Mary's churchyard are pleasant low cottages and Mrs Elizabeth Fuller Free School, a charming brick building dated 1704, with a central cupola, a door with segmental pediment and arched windows. The Bedford Almshouses of 1580 have a five-gabled plastered front with outer gables.

WATTON-AT-STONE, Hertfordshire (10–TL3019).

The River Beane flows through this straggling little village and becomes a wide lake in Woodhall Park nearby. Near the little bridge crossing the river is a slate-roofed mill, a successor to that mentioned in the Domesday Book.

Watton Hall is a plastered house with timber frames, three overhanging gables and three trefoil brick arches, and picturesque twisted chimneys. Inside is a beam dated 1636 on which are inscribed the words Watton Hall alias Watkins Hall. Nearby is a fascinating cast-iron 19th-cent. pump of baluster shape.

SS. Andrew and Mary Church is 15th-cent., of flint and embattled. It has a castellated porch, stair-turrets and a tower. Although most of the windows have been renewed, the east window is original. In the interior is a four-bay arcade with Perpendicular piers. A north chapel, added in 1851, has a tunnel-vault. There are many early monuments and brasses of interest, including one to John Botelier of Woodhall on a 15th-cent. slab with the inscription upside down.

About ¾ m. W. of the village is Broom Hall, a 16th-cent. brick house with a central chimney and porch and brick mullioned windows in the upper floor.

Two m. NE. is Aston Bury, a fine house with particularly good chimneys.

WELLINGBOROUGH, Northamptonshire (10–SP8968),

is a residential as well as a manufacturing town, standing at the junction of the Rivers Ise and Nene. It is mentioned in the Domesday Book, was granted market rights by King John in 1201, and for a short while became a spa when it was visited by Charles I and Queen Henrietta in 1628. Its industries include footwear and clothing.

In Sheep Street and High Street are many old buildings and a 15th-cent. stone-built tithe barn. There are two old inns: the Hind and the Golden Lion, which has a minstrels' gallery. Cromwell stayed at the Hind on his way to NASEBY during the Civil War.

The Georgian Swanspool House, in Swanspool Gardens, now council offices, has gardens of 10 acres which are used by the public, and the Swanspool brook flows through the town. There is a private zoo, which is open to the public, in the grounds of Croyland House in Croyland Road.

The newly built Technical College is a fine piece of modern architecture with numerous windows.

At the end of High Street, by Broad Green, are the Manor and Hatton House, and fine avenues of trees line the roads.

Wellingborough has a public school, founded in the reign of Richard II as a grammar school. Some of its old buildings remain near the church, and the present one is built in Queen Anne style of brick and stone.

There are two churches of note: All Hallows and St Mary's. All Hallows stands back from the street in a tree-shaded churchyard. Parts of it are 600 years old and it has a tower and a broach spire. The chancel, with its outstanding east window, is Decorated. The roof, screens and stalls with misericords, are all 15th-cent. There are good, modern stained-glass windows by Piper, Home and Reyntiens.

The Victorian St Mary's Church was built by Sir Ninian Comper. It is very large and plain outside, but the interior is brilliantly coloured with a fine screen and, suspended above the nave, a large blue and gold painting of Christ in Majesty. The north chapel is attractive and the general impression is of light and spaciousness.

Sywell Aerodrome, off the main road to NORTHAMPTON, is the county Aero Club.

WELWYN, *Hertfordshire* (10–TL2316). This little old town still retains its charm, despite its proximity to WELWYN GARDEN CITY.

Most of the houses are Georgian, including Lockleys, ½ m. W. of the village, a nine-bay brick house now a school, which was built early in the period. The pediment of the doorway is on Roman Doric pillars and the windows are segment-headed. The dressings are of rubbed brick. A Roman villa has been excavated in the grounds and a plan of it is shown in turf and brick, indicating a rectangular five-roomed house of timber and mud, built in the 1st cent. A.D. The house and grounds are open to the public.

The village has two inns, the White Hart and the White Horse in Mill Lane. In School Lane is New Place, a Victorian building built by Philip Webb for his brother. It is L-shaped, of brick, with a steep-pitched roof, buttresses and sash-windows.

The River Mimram runs through the village and across the bridge, towards the church, is Bridge Cottage, with an iron veranda and a monkey puzzle in the garden, then Bridge House, and W. of the church the Wellington Hotel which, although Georgian, has some old half-timbering.

St Mary's Church is greatly restored externally so that it has lost its original character. Much of the interior was built in 1910 but the double piscina, with trefoil heads, is 700 years old and there is a long lancet window in the chancel. Edward Young, author of *Night Thoughts* and *On Original Composition*, was vicar of Welwyn from 1730 to 1765 and there is a monument to him in the church.

WELWYN GARDEN CITY, *Hertfordshire* (10–TL2412), was begun in 1919 as an artificially planned town in accordance with the ideas of Ebenezer Howard. Although the planning was wasteful of ground space by later standards, this "garden city" marked a significant development in 20th-cent. town planning. Originally developed by a private company with idealistic rather than commercial aims, the town was taken over in 1948 by the Ministry of Town and Country Planning as a "new town" to be linked with HATFIELD.

WENDOVER, *Buckinghamshire* (10–SP8708), is an old town on the edge of the Chilterns with many claims to history. The Icknield Way meets the main London to AYLESBURY road. There are many timbered cottages with dormer windows and at the junction stands a little Victorian building with a clock tower and a drinking fountain. It has a small, ivy-covered, red-brick room which was once the lock-up, and above the steep four-sided roof, green with moss, are a clock, an open lantern and a weathervane.

Among Wendover's many interests are its old inns. Of particular note is the Red Lion Hotel, a half-timbered building with brick nogging. Its old fireplace with chimney corners in the lounge still remains and the sturdy stairway leads to the room where Oliver Cromwell slept in 1642 while his soldiers packed the street below. Robert Louis Stevenson also visited the house on his walk through the Chilterns and wrote about it.

17th-cent. Bosworth House, in the village street, is an old timbered building now divided into three: a post office with panelled walls and doors, a cottage with a room over the open gateway, and a house. In the wall of the gateway is a 15th-cent. pillar piscina. When alterations were made to the building, many 16th- and 17th-cent. wall paintings were discovered of which two remain in the house, the others having been transferred to the Aylesbury Museum and the VICTORIA AND ALBERT MUSEUM in London.

There is a windmill, now a house, and a watermill by the side of the stream running through Wendover has been transformed into a white-and-green timbered dwelling.

The church and manor house, lying side by side, are reached by a short walk down a pretty lane beside the stream, just outside the town.

The manor house was owned by John Hampden and his family. Hampden represented Wendover in five Parliaments and was the cousin of Oliver Cromwell.

Wendover church is mainly 14th-cent., although much restored. A tall 14th-cent. tower rises over the church and the manor and the churchyard path is flanked with limes, sycamores, chestnuts and two great yews. There are amusing carved heads on the arches of the chancel. The capitals of the pillars are beautifully carved with fruit, flowers and animals.

Along the village street and the **Icknield Way** is found some of the most breathtaking scenery in the county. Boddington Hill is on one side, Backham Hill on another and, crowning them both, Coombe Hill, one of the highest points in the Chilterns, over 850 ft. At the summit is a monument dedicated to the men of Buckinghamshire who fought and died in the South African War. On fine days it is claimed that from this viewpoint can be seen ST PAUL'S CATHEDRAL.

WEST WYCOMBE, *Buckinghamshire* (6–SU 8394). W. of HIGH WYCOMBE is this fascinating village where every house is National Trust property. The main street has been carefully repaired to retain the architecture of buildings ranging from the 15th to the 19th cent. which are of half-timbered construction and have mellowed tiles with red brick and stucco overhanging gables.

Of particular interest is Church Loft House, its upper story projecting over the pavement and forming a long room with a roof of 15th-cent. beams. In a corner of the roof is a 17th-cent. bell-turret and an unusual clock overhangs the pavement.

Adjoining the village is West Wycombe Park, its great house built by Repton in the Adam style with fine collections of paintings, tapestries and antique furniture. In its wooded park is a pillared Temple of Music. It was built for Sir Francis Dashwood, Chancellor of the Exchequer in 1762 and founder of the Hell Fire Club, and the family are still closely connected with the village.

On the hill opposite West Wycombe Park, over 600 ft above sea-level, can be seen the great golden ball on top of the tower of St Lawrence's Church which was also built for Sir Francis Dashwood.

In the church tower is a room seating ten people where the members of the Hell Fire Club, who also met at MEDMENHAM Abbey, are said to have foregathered to practise black magic. In the caves beneath are many curiosities of interest and these are open to the public.

The church is placed within an Iron Age flint earthwork. There are fine oak carvings behind the altar and cherubs by Grinling Gibbons on the east windows. The font, of silver gilt, is adorned with four doves, the stand encircled by a serpent gripping an escaping dove. It is a strange, but interesting, church.

The mausoleum, of flint with plastered columns, adjoins the church. It is a massive building open to the skies and contains the tomb of Lady Despencer, an ancestor of the Dashwoods.

WHEATHAMPSTEAD, *Hertfordshire* (10–TL1713), has grown in recent years and developed some modern industries, but it still retains its picturesque charm, and although the little cottages are now mainly shops they are interesting

and pleasing to look at. On a corner near the church is an unusual building, octagonal in shape, which houses a chemist's shop.

Hills look down on the village and the River Lea flows through it. The path by the river is overhung with trees.

On the north side of the road from ST ALBANS, are Roman remains, and two stretches of earthworks can be found on the heath of the slopes above the river: the Devil's Dyke and the Slad, both National Trust property. The Dyke is 1,400 ft long and the Slad is almost the same length but narrower and not so deep.

St Helen's Church was begun in the 13th cent. It is a large flint building with the nave the same length as the chancel and a crossing tower with a lead spire dominating the scenery. Both the north window in the north transept and the south window in the south transept have ogee tracery. The church is richly designed and contains a fine reredos and, in the chancel, a canopied piscina. The octagonal font is early 14th-cent., its carved leaves bearing quatrefoil circles. The pulpit is Jacobean and, like two benches in the north transept, was taken from a chapel at Lamer House. In the same transept is a Jacobean screen. There are many monuments showing the history of the village. One in the north transept, dating from about 1436, shows the figures of Hugh Bostok and his wife, parents of Abbot Wheat-

Wheathampstead: the ford over the River Lea at Water End

Barnaby/Mustograph

hampstead of ST ALBANS. Also in the north transept is the Garrard Monument, the largest in the church, probably early 17th-cent., with big surrounds and columns and semi-reclining alabaster figures. There are many Garrard tablets here, for the Garrard family came from Lamer Park. One of particular interest shows Sir John, who was one of the earliest baronets, dressed in armour, with his wife and six sons and eight daughters. In the north transept is a rare stone reredos with seven canopied niches.

Water End Farm, 1¾ m. E. of the village, is a charming house by a ford. It was originally the manor of the Jennings family and was built of brick in about 1610; it has large decorated chimney stacks.

Mackery End, 1½ m. NE. of the village, is where Charles Lamb often visited and about which he wrote some delightful essays. He describes it as a gentle walk from Wheathampstead. It is a brick-fronted building with Dutch gables and a brick-plastered central porch.

The mill in the village is mentioned in the Domesday Book, and close by is Bricket Hill, a fine mansion of c. 1790.

WHIPSNADE, *Bedfordshire* (10–TL0117), famous for its zoo, is a small village on the edge of the Dunstable Downs and the Chilterns.

It has a delightful church, St Mary Magdalene's, with a 16th-cent. tower and an 18th-cent. nave, with arched windows and a Jacobean pulpit. The communion rail, with its slim twisted balusters, dates from about 1700. Green Cathedral, although not laid out as such, is a plantation of trees with 25 different species and services are held there.

The zoo, high on the Chilterns, is set in lovely countryside with the animals kept in natural and spacious enclosures. It has over 2,000 animals and is famous for its breeding record. It is open to the public and you may walk or drive round it.

WHISTON, *Northamptonshire* (10–SP8560), is a tiny limestone village, behind which is the lovely 16th-cent. Church of St Mary the Virgin, on a wooded hillside. Its tower, in two stages, is of ironstone and ashlar with delightful gargoyles and four pinnacles, and it is decorated with many separate stone carvings of humans, angels and animals. Richly carved wall-plates are in the roofs of the nave and aisles, and there is no chancel arch. In the reredos, carved in oak, is a copy of Leonardo's *Last Supper*. There are several monuments, including two sculptures by Nollekens, one showing a figure of a woman leaning on a torch and the other of a cherub wiping away a tear with his little hand.

WILLINGTON, *Bedfordshire* (10–TL1150), is of interest for its dovecot, an oblong structure with two nesting chambers and several stepped gables, and its stables, both of which are National Trust property and open to the public. They form part of the Manor House, of which only two minor buildings survive, where Sir John Gostwick,

Master of the Horse to Cardinal Wolsey, entertained Henry VII in 1541.

St Lawrence's Church is mainly late Perpendicular. It is of bluff stone with a fine north chapel of the early 16th cent. It was built by Sir John Gostwick and there is a large plain monument to him in the form of a tomb-chest dated 1541, as well as two other monuments to the Gostwicks which are also of interest. A bell bears the inscription: "Thomas Tompion fecit".

WING, *Buckinghamshire* (10–SP8822). To the NE. of AYLESBURY, reached through delightful rolling countryside, this growing village, with its many modern buildings, contains the Anglo-Saxon Church of All Saints, the most important of that period in the county. The walls of the nave are Anglo-Saxon, as is the crypt, surrounded by a gallery, and one of only eight crypts surviving from this period in England. Seen from the churchyard, the apse, on narrow pilasters, is unusual; only four of these Anglo-Saxon apses remain in the country.

There is much of interest of later date. The roof of the large nave reached through a 14th-cent. doorway, is decorated with carved bosses, angels, kings and saints. The screen, beautifully decorated, is 16th-cent. and the pulpit 17th-cent. Brass memorials are from the time of the Wars of the Roses and the series of Dormer monuments are splendid in design.

The village itself, the centre of a hundred in Norman times, still has many 17th- and 18th-cent. cottages, as well as the Dormer hospital built in 1569.

Half a m. E. of Wing is the house of **Ascott**, now a National Trust property and open to the public. Once the home of the de Rothschilds, it houses a fine collection of pictures, French and Chippendale furniture and outstanding Oriental porcelain with examples of Ming, K'ang Hsi, and Chun pieces of the Sung dynasty. The house, incorporating medieval timberwork and Jacobean work, is surrounded by 12 acres of grounds, and unusual trees grow in the gardens.

WOBURN, *Bedfordshire* (10–SP9433), is an old village, situated in picturesque, wooded countryside, with thatched red and white brick cottages. The yellow-brick almshouses have fine Jacobean stepped gables and are mid-Victorian. The village is attractive with several old inns. The Bedford Arms was formerly a famous posting-house and has extensive stabling at the back.

In the centre of the village is the Market House, red-bricked with an oriel, dated 1830. The mid-18th-cent. Old Rectory is a stately building with several columns, an attic over the centrepiece and the side of the house overlooking the cemetery.

The chapel is Victorian and beside it are the remains of the tower of Woburn's medieval church. It has an open octagonal stage and a crocketed spirelet. In it is a monument to Sir Francis Staunton and his wife, dated 1630.

Next to the chapel is the old school, of ironstone with mullioned windows.

Of major interest is Woburn Abbey, the residence of the Duke of Bedford. It is open to the public. There are paintings by Canaletto, Rembrandt, Van Dyck, Gainsborough and many others of renown, and a collection of 18th-cent. French and English furniture. There are 14 state apartments. Its 3,000-acre park contains 11 varieties of deer and many rare animals, as well as a bird sanctuary. The Antique Market is a great attraction.

St Mary's Church, in the village, is a large, solidly built, Victorian building, an estate church in late-12th-cent. style.

YAXLEY, *Huntingdonshire* (10–TL1892). On first appearance from the main road, this large and highly productive village has little to offer, but on turning down a side street you reach its centre and discover many buildings of interest. There are several 17th- and 18th-cent. houses, many attractive black-and-white thatched cottages, a thatched inn, a village green and an old pump. The village school is dated 1812 and has large trees in its playground. The Congregational church and the Methodist church are both early Victorian, as are a number of the houses.

St Peter's Church is on the top of a hill. It is large, cruciformed and its elegant steeple has flying buttresses. It is mostly 13th-cent. with some Perpendicular workmanship, and the chancel and transepts are of different roof levels. The font is original and the fine oak chancel screen is of the 15th cent. Above the screen is a large organ gallery and case by Temple Moore, 1904, who restored the church. The Perpendicular stalls are kneeling-desks with poppyheads on the ends and panels in front. The pulpit with a sounding board is dated 1631. In the north transept is a monument showing two arms holding a heart, representing a heart burial and attributed to William de Yaxley, Abbot of Thorney.

On the outskirts of the village are several old farms.

YELDEN, *Bedfordshire* (10–TL0366), has some of the most interesting earthworks in the county. On the mounds above the River Till are the remains of a castle mentioned in the Domesday Book. The oblong motte is about 130 ft by 90 ft, and there are two large baileys and stone foundations, including the bases of two round towers in a corner of the principal bailey. On a smaller mound nearby is also a round tower base. It is reputed that there was battle on the site between the Romans and the Iceni.

St Mary the Virgin Church was built in the 14th cent., but has certain features which are Early English, such as south aisle and chancel doorways and the south arcade. The Decorated tower has bell-openings with flowing tracery and a corbel-frieze with flowers, animals and heads. Old timbers still remain in the roof of the nave, on one of which are carved the arms of Trailly. From the wooden Perpendicular pulpit John Bunyan preached one Christmas Day, but for permitting this the vicar William Dell was ejected from his living. On the walls are interesting paintings, one of St Christopher. In a carved recess in the north wall of the nave is a figure holding his heart, and in the south aisle a large and splendid tomb recess with spandrels and crockets on the gable.

Woburn Abbey: this 18th-cent. mansion was remodelled by Henry Holland in 1802

Camera Press

The West Midlands

Oxfordshire Gloucestershire Warwickshire
Worcestershire Herefordshire

H. L. V. FLETCHER

If you approach the West Midlands from the east the change in the countryside is so gradual as to be imperceptible. It is undramatic, and you can cross from Buckinghamshire into Oxfordshire or from Northamptonshire into Warwickshire with nothing more than a roadside label to tell you where you are. Coming from the west it is a different story. The actual transition from Wales to England is not noticeable at first because when you leave the central plateau of Brecon, Radnor and Montgomery there are further lines of low hills; but once you cross the foothills the world opens out to reveal as wonderful a view as you are likely to see anywhere in England.

The best time to see it is in the evening, with the sun in the west, and it is never so striking as when rain is due. Before rain everything will be crystal clear and you can view the land plainly as far as the eye can see.

There are many places from which to look over this incomparable bit of England. One of my own favourite spots is Kingswood Common on the little ridge beyond Kington. The valley of the Wye lies below, and the level part of the central plain stretches for mile after mile after mile. It looks flat. After the crumpled hills of Brecon and Radnor it is bound to appear so. But it is not flat, not level at all; the portions of hard rock stick up like knuckles on a hand and if you have to walk up them, or even motor up such places as the ridge between the Wye and the Golden Valley, you will find there are some notable hills.

But the view seems to stretch without interruption from this last outpost of the Welsh mountains, and a man could stare at all this a long, long time and not have his fill. I was told once that from here one could see a fifth of England. These local legends grow and are repeated and sometimes are believed. Yet they do not have to be wholly true to hold the essence of truth. I have heard the same story about the Malverns, and from them it could be that the view is even finer than the one you see coming out of Radnorshire.

If you dawdle at Kingswood or on the Malverns you are looking on what was once part of the kingdom of Mercia. When boundaries swung to and fro as they often did in those days strange things could happen, and they left their effects. For instance, in Herefordshire long ago the Welsh got pushed away from the Wye up to their cold hills and they left a whole area full of their own people, like an island in a turbulent sea. And what did these castaways do but make peace with their neighbours and stay where they were? In return for being allowed to live in their own Welsh ways and keep their own Welsh laws and customs they allied themselves to the Anglo-Saxons and even fought with them in their wars. It was no forced service. This was an alliance of friends, and to the Men of Archenfield – that was the name of the colony – belonged the posts of honour in war. Camden, the historian, who wrote in Latin, left an account of them: *Viri de Archenfield, cum exercitus in hostem pergit, per consuetudinem faciunt Avantward, et in reversione Rereward.* "They marched in front of the army as it advanced, and held the rear as it retreated." An old story; all gone now except the name – yet not gone either, for the effects are in names and ways of people still part of the countryside.

All over this land there were, often still are, strange and individual customs and laws. There is the Forest of Dean, that almost unvisited tract between the Wye and the Severn, where coal and iron have been mined since pre-Roman times under almost rural conditions. There are a few small industrial towns, like Coleford, yet you could wander right across the Forest without a sight of industry. The Forest of Dean has so many private laws that they demand a volume of their own to do them justice. At Speech House (now a hotel) near Cinderford the Verderers' Court still meets to adminster them. High above the Wye at St Briavels there is the Castle that was once the headquarters of the Warden of the Forest, and if you visit it, remember those early English kings, from despised John downwards, who loved this spot.

The Forest of Dean is a fairy-tale forest, a forest in the Grimm tradition, where witches live and poor foresters purposely lose their children, and where robbers share out their gains under spreading oaks. What of other forests in the area? Well, Hereford no longer has any forest worthy the name, only sylvan woods where the wild daffodils bloom in their tens of thousands in spring. But in Warwickshire there is still something left of the Forest of Arden, and this you can learn of in *A Midsummer Night's Dream*. A wood near Athens, forsooth! Shakespeare discovered that wood in his native county, and he peopled it with village labourers from Bidford and Aston Cantlow and Snitterfield. I met a descendant of Bottom the Weaver myself in a pub not a hundred miles from Stratford, a nice, harmless, bragging, ignorant fellow who could set you right on everything, and knew everything, and could do everything: "Let me play the lion too: I will roar, that I will do any man's heart good to hear me."

Warwickshire is haunted by Shakespeare. How he loved this part of England! At every turn quotations come crowding into the memory. "Sweet lovers love the spring." It was a Warwickshire spring. Nowhere does it come more happily than in the Warwick lanes. "A day in April never came so sweet to show how costly summer was at hand." *Costly* summer: what could it be but an English one. Such richness the poet found nowhere as fully as he had at home in his youth. In the tragedies his powers towered to their greatest height, but in the early plays his country upbringing brought out the full, youthful, singing joyousness of life.

Warwick itself has one of the finest castles of England, second only to Windsor, yet the place it dominates still has some of the atmosphere of a country town. But the county is not all fields and woods. North is industry and the cities, absorbed in manufactures, noisy, dirty, crowded – everything the quiet villages in the south are not. Coventry, rebuilt after the bombing, has its notable cathedral that seems to set it apart, but Birmingham is typical and representative of the group. It is not the place you would choose for your summer holidays. Yet in Domesday Survey the place was as rural as Barton-on-the-Heath. "Richard holds of William four hides in Bremingeham. The arable employs six ploughs; one is in the demesne. There are five villeins and four bordars with two ploughs. Wood half a mile long and four furlongs broad. It was and is worth 20 s." I know it is sentimental and quite unrealistic, but stuck on a Birmingham pavement edge waiting for the mechanical flood to halt so that I can dart across a street I remember "wood half a mile long and four furlongs broad." It really *was* like that where we dodge and scurry, and somehow I like Birmingham the better for it.

From Bristol to Bromwich, from Henley to Hereford, this is a region for which the word peaceful seems specially coined. There are the few cities: Hereford and Gloucester, Worcester, Warwick and Oxford; but they have, especially to those who have known them for a long period of time, still something of the atmosphere of market towns. Over the region as a whole quietness reigns. It was not always so. This, especially in pre-Conquest days, was a cockpit for the whole country. On the whole the Romans avoided trouble. Not that there was never fighting or bloodshed, but generally the natives and colonists managed amicably, whether it was iron-working near Ross, or holding an outpost against the unruly Welsh at Kentchester outside Hereford. But after the Romans left successive waves of invaders passed through. The Danes came, burning what they could not take with them. Other Scandinavians appeared, ravishing and destroying. Some wanted to settle, and if you are going to settle you must, sooner or later, come to some sort of terms with your neighbours. It was those who came seeking what they could devour who despoiled the country; those who wanted to get back to their long ships, and get their long ships back in their home waters.

Not all raiders were from the east. Over the Severn and the Wye the Welshmen waited and watched.

> The mountain sheep are sweeter,
> But the valley sheep are fatter;
> We therefore deemed it meeter
> To carry off the latter.

When the time was ripe they swooped, stole flocks, killed and destroyed. Leominster went up in flames more than once, while Hereford was practically wiped off the map for a time. An uneasy truce must have existed some of the time on the border, but the Welsh did not stay. They took what they could; then went back to their cold hillsides.

Much has been made of the sufferings along the Marches under the Norman barons, but it is possible that it was not as bad a time as many have believed. The Marcher lords had power of life and death, so at times there was oppression. But the Normans came to settle. They were land-hungry, and they wanted rich acres, a prosperous countryside, land cropped and harvested, valleys thick with corn. You don't get valleys thick with corn if you bully the men who grow the corn, or burn their houses. The Marcher Barons used their brains, and after some inevitable tyranny the West Midlands developed into as rich an agricultural area as you could find in most of Europe. On the foundations laid then Cotswold wool became one of the richest commodities in the world and the six "W"s of Herefordshire – Wool, Water, Wood, Wheat, Wine and Women – became the envy of the rest of England.

Occasionally the fighting was resumed, chiefly during the Wars of the Roses. The battle of Mortimer's Cross was as disastrous to the western counties as any battle could be. The final but less cruel conflicts came with the Civil War. Naseby is just outside our area, but the stupid mix-up of Edgehill was inside. So is Worcester, while Hereford and Gloucester as well as many other places were besieged, some more than once. The great castle at Kenilworth was taken and left in ruins by Cromwell. Minor skirmishes, like the one in Ledbury streets, went on everywhere, and there is difficulty in remembering who was chasing whom. But often battles were mainly for the gentry and the layabouts; sensible folk kept out of the way, and when the warriors had chased each other off the map they came out and got on with carrying in the corn.

There are differences between our five counties, but it is difficult to say exactly

Kenilworth Castle. Detail from a watercolour drawing by David Cox, 1804–6

Birmingham, City Art Gallery

what the differences are. They are so subtle as to defy accurate description. Not every visitor could say whether he was in Oxfordshire or Worcestershire, but there is a variety in the roll of the land, the gradients of the hills, the wild flowers, the trees and the crops.

If I were pressed to differentiate my five counties I suppose I would point to the Wye and the orchards and hops of Herefordshire; the Severn, the Forest of Dean and the Cotswolds in Gloucestershire; the mixture of Shakespearean rurality and intense industrialism of Warwickshire; the Malvern-dominated fruit and market gardens of Worcestershire; and the willowy banks of the upper Thames in Oxfordshire, pointing out that relics of Roman and pre-Roman remains lie everywhere, while Dorchester-on-Thames might well have become the capital of England.

In this portion of what was Mercia there are half a dozen lovely, quiet country towns like Cheltenham and Cirencester, Stratford and Ross, Fairford and Faringdon, and the multi-syllabled Stow-on-the-Wold, Moreton-in-Marsh and Bourton-on-the-Water. The names trip off the tongue like a poem. The villages between stand as thick as stooks in a cornfield. On the wide rolling Cotswolds there is one in every valley. You can find churches within a few miles of each other as different as Norman Kilpeck is from cathedral-like Abbey Dore. In the Cotswolds the medieval wool merchants erected some of the finest churches in the country, great buildings like Northleach or gems like Fairford. Cirencester has the oldest parish church in the kingdom. From Stratford town you can pay a visit to the house of Mary Arden, Shakespeare's mother, in Wilmcote village, and there you will find one of the best museums of farm implements in the country.

The churches of Oxfordshire are noted for their spires, and, in spite of industrial envelopment, the best are in Oxford itself. There, too, is concentrated in a few square miles some of the best-preserved architectural treasures of England – the colleges.

The domestic building varies enormously. There are country houses of great charm and centuries of historical association. You find an Oxfordshire house such as Chastleton with its memories of the Gunpowder Plot (many of the conspirators met there) and its great treasure, the Bible Charles I at his execution gave to Bishop Juxon. Chastleton is stately, while Minster Lovell has its legends and its ghosts. What are we to say of Blenheim? Either you like it very much or you dislike it very much. Vanbrugh, its builder, was blamed for the load he laid on Mother Earth, but Sarah, Duchess of Marlborough, was probably to blame – or to be praised – for that weight. At quiet Bladon, nearby, Sir Winston Churchill is buried.

The houses of humbler folk vary as widely. There are timbered houses everywhere. Besford Court and Salwarpe Court are notable Worcestershire favourites. I do not know of a finer example than The Ley at Weobley, though Staick House at Eardisland in a different style runs it close. But then Weobley itself is notable for its black-and-white buildings. Perhaps it was because John Abel, the Hereford builder, King's Carpenter and restorer of churches, came from neighbouring Sarnesfield. To see the style of the period (though John Abel did not build it) there is the Old House in the centre of Hereford. It was natural to build timber-framed houses in a district so rich in sturdy oak and elm. There are fine trees on the Cotswolds, too, but stone is abundant and stone was used for the typical dry walls as well as for building. The old grey houses, with their heavy stone tile roofs, are beautiful, as everyone knows. But that is beside the point. They were built by local men in local methods and from local materials for local men to live in. The beauty evolved from the good taste and proportions that are a part of good craftsmanship.

Oxford: Merton College Gateway. Watercolour and black chalk drawing by Sir William Nicholson, 1904   Collection, A. W. Bacon Esq.

The West Midlands: Gazetteer

GERALD BARRY

ADDERBURY, *Oxfordshire* (5–SP4635), is a hilly village of ancient sun-soaked stone houses, some Georgian, some much earlier, 3 m. S. of BANBURY off the A423 OXFORD road. The 17th-cent. gabled Adderbury House was once the home of the profligate Earl of Rochester who was nevertheless a splendid Stuart poet. It is now a home for the elderly. The sturdy church with its unusually good Decorated and Perpendicular features is set off by a superb spire which no doubt inspired the local tag "BLOXHAM for length, Adderbury for strength and Kings Sutton for beauty". The interior of the church was mostly restored in the 19th cent. The 15th-cent. screen, however, retains much of its original beauty.

ALCESTER, *Warwickshire* (9–SP0857). This small town lies 8 m. W. of STRATFORD-UPON-AVON at the confluence of the Rivers Arrow and Alne and the junction of the A422, originally a Roman road, and Ryknild Street (the A435). These routes and the town's name (pronounced Olster) suggest Roman occupation and excavations have confirmed this.

Particularly attractive is the narrow Butter Street, off the High Street, with its jumble of ancient roofs. Just at the top is the 17th-cent., three-bayed, brick Churchill House with some fascinating carved friezes. Henley Street has among its features a timber-framed house with an overhang on carved supports. Church Street has remarkably unspoilt Georgian houses. Two of them at one time formed a single coaching inn which lost its clientele with the coming of the railways. Lovers of Victoriana will like The Priory, once the site of a Benedictine Abbey, where there is a house with a perfectly proportioned Doric porch, to which has been added a fantastic Victorian neo-Gothic folly. The oldest Alcester house stands in Malt Hill Lane off Church Street. This is a two-gabled, half-timbered building called the Old Malt House, built in 1500. The Classical Town Hall was built in 1618, a gift of Sir Fulke Greville.

Only the late 13th-cent. tower and 15th-cent. door witness to the early foundation of the Church of St Nicholas. The exterior is mostly restored Victorian Gothic, though the simple Classical interior designed by Thomas and Edward Woodward in 1729 is relieved by the rather grand altar-tomb of Sir Fulke Greville.

ALDERMINSTER, *Warwickshire* (9–SP 2248), just 3 m. S. of STRATFORD-UPON-AVON on the A34 to OXFORD is a delightful village with an unusual row of old cottages spaced out along the main road. Its parish church has a good 13th-cent. tower with lancet windows looking across the Stour valley to Meon Hill and the Cotswolds. It has a Norman nave, with the rest of the church unfortunately much restored. Records show that the church was for some reason reconsecrated in 1286. Note the curious carved faces between the arches and the altar table standing on an altar stone with the original consecration crosses still showing. On the west bank of the Stour stands the little church of Whitchurch: also Norman and enlarged in the 15th cent. when a good east light was built. Just over the door inside is a medieval Agnus Dei carved in bas relief. It means leaving your car and walking across fields to see this mostly 11th-cent. gem.

Also just off the A34, ½ m. NE. of **Preston-on-Stour**, is a good Gothic Revival building, Alscot House. Started in 1750, it was built by James West, a secretary to the Treasury. Most of the present house was completed in 1764. The porch was added in 1825 by Thomas Hopper. The house is well planned and there is much good Victorian wrought-iron work inside. The river flows through a fine deer park to complete a typically late 18th-cent. ensemble. James West lies buried in the nearby parish church of Preston-on-Stour. It contains an unusual amount of 16th-cent. Continental stained glass which West presented to the church. The village of Preston is worth strolling through. It differs from the usual Cotswold villages but remains astonishingly unspoilt.

ALFRICK, *Worcestershire* (8–SO7453), is a pleasant little village, deep in the countryside towards the Herefordshire border. It is most easily reached by turning W. off the A4103 about 3 m. from WORCESTER and following an unclassified road through Leigh. Set in the shelter of the Suckley Hills among cherry orchards, it has an unchanging air. There is an old inn called the Wobbly Wheel, scattered cottages and a long low church with good 17th-cent. stained glass. There is a 15th-cent. panel portraying St Bernard of Clairvaux. It has two Norman windows and a wood-shingled bell-turret. Lewis Carroll was a frequent visitor to the nearby tall red-brick Georgian house, where his brother lived when he was the curate here.

ARBURY HALL, *Warwickshire* (9–SP3389), lies 3 m. SW. of NUNEATON, off the B4012. Its

Arbury Hall is a fine example of Gothic Revival

claim to fame lies in the fact that most experts consider it the finest example of the Gothic Revival in England. It was originally a Tudor house which had been built on the ruins of an Augustinian monastery suppressed under Henry VIII and demolished in the reign of Queen Elizabeth I. Lord Chief Justice Anderson bought it and later exchanged houses with the Newdegate family who have owned it ever since. Sir Roger Newdigate (who spelt his name with an "i") set about Gothicizing the house at the same time that Horace Walpole began at Strawberry Hill, which in turn gave its name to this peculiarly English 18th-cent. revival.

Set in 300 acres of parkland with lakes and streams, the Hall remains a tribute to Sanderson Miller, Henry Keene and Henry Couchman of WARWICK who all had a hand in the exterior work and the unrivalled period décor within.

The plasterwork and fan vaultings seem to lighten the rather heavy Gothic chimney-pieces. The house is open at advertised times and the visitor has an opportunity of seeing much of the family collection of furniture, china and glass, and fascinating documents of the Newdegate history.

About ½ m. S. of the Hall is South Farm, where Mary Ann Evans was born in 1819. She was known to posterity as George Eliot the great novelist. *Adam Bede, The Mill on the Floss* and *Silas Marner* are all impregnated with this Warwickshire countryside where her father was agent for the estate.

A little W. of Arbury Hall lies the village of **Astley**. This was once the home of the family of Lady Jane Grey. Not a great deal remains of the 16th-cent. Astley Castle, though the outer walls and moat date from before the 12th cent. In 1343 Sir Thomas Astley built a great collegiate church of which the former chancel is now the nave. Most unusual are the choir stalls with their painted backs of Apostles and Prophets. There are remains of what must have been very fine stained glass. Still discernible are a bear, human faces and birds and animals. The triptych over the altar is a 16th-cent. painting of the Flemish School of The Descent from the Cross.

ATHERSTONE, *Warwickshire* (9–SP3097), is a small market town on the A5 and owes its relative importance to its position on the Roman Watling Street. It has several attractive 18th-cent. houses. Its Grammar School boasts a 16th-cent. charter. Outside the gabled coaching inn, the Red Lion, with its unusual Gothic windows stands an old milestone incised "100 MILES LONDON". Though much of the parish church is modern restoration, it was originally the church of an Augustinian friary. Here Henry of Lancaster took the sacrament on the morning of the Battle of Bosworth. It has a good 15th-cent. stained-glass east window. The Old Swan is a fine timber-framed house with an overhang supported by diagonal braces. It was once the centre of the felt hat industry. A curious game of football is still played on the streets on Shrove Tuesday, a custom dating back to the 13th cent.

The ruins of **Merevale Abbey** are a little way W. of the town, near a minor turning off the A5. They are worth the short, signposted walk across a field.

BAGINTON, *Warwickshire* (9–SP3474), lies S. of the A45 near COVENTRY Airport. This village has the ruins of the 14th-cent. castle built by Sir William Bagot, characterized in Shakespeare's *Richard II*. In 1398 Henry Bolingbroke rode out from here to challenge the Duke of Norfolk in the lists before Richard II, both noblemen being banished for their pains. Although little remains of the castle, excavations have made a visit worthwhile.

The Church of St John the Baptist is Early English and tiny. It has a particularly fine brass of Sir William Bagot above the Priests' Door which brings the visitor straight into the chancel with its unusually good triple arch in Early English style. Sconces of candles and oil lamps still light the church. It possesses some good examples of late 17th- and early 18th-cent. silver plate.

The Old Mill, now a restaurant, was mentioned in Domesday Book and valued at ten shillings and eightpence per annum plus ninepence for the two ploughs. For 900 years the mill throve and then became a private residence for a few years before the Second World War. Gardens and willows make a pleasant setting for it by the River Sowe.

A Roman fort overlooking the river is being

excavated and restored to its original condition, with reconstructed defences and barrack blocks.

BAMPTON, *Oxfordshire* (5–SP3103). This quiet little market town was once known as Bampton-in-the-Bush owing to its difficulty of access in the 17th cent. Although it is on the busy A4095 S. of WITNEY towards FARINGDON, it lies in flat sleepy country, on the upper reaches of the Thames Valley. It comes to life at least twice a year. The Horse Fair on 26 August dates from Edward I's time and though there is little horse dealing done today, the merriment is maintained. At the Whit Monday Fête the spectator may see genuine English Morris dancing at its best and in its most classical form. There is a traditional fool known as "The Squire", and a "Sword-bearer" who holds a cake on his sword and distributes it to bystanders. A piece of cake is considered lucky, and recipients are expected to contribute to the "Squire's treasury". The little town hall stands in the centre of the market place surrounded by some good Georgian-fronted shops. The parish church is surmounted by a 13th-cent. buttressed spire rising 170 ft from its massive part-Norman tower. Each buttress is pinnacled at its base by an apostle in flowing drapery. The remarkable steeple was once the only way the traveller could find his way into Bampton. In the early Middle Ages it must have had quite an importance. The Empress Matilda built a fortress here and Aymer de Valence, Earl of Pembroke, erected an impressive castle of which only a doorway remains, now incorporated into an old farm-house, Ham Court. Just W. of the church is a fine Tudor manor considerably re-stored in Georgian times, known as the Deanery, which was once the summer residence of the Deans of EXETER, who still hold the living. The Grammar School is one of the oldest in the county. This Bampton should not be confused with its namesake in Devon, which also has a famous horse fair.

BANBURY, *Oxfordshire* (5–SP4540), at once evokes the well-known nursery rhyme. The origi-nal cross was destroyed by the Puritans in 1602 and the present one is a Victorian replacement. It is believed that the "fine lady" of the rhyme, was a member of the Fiennes (pronounced Fines) family who still live at and own BROUGHTON Castle. Its other distinction is the making of Banbury cakes to a 300-year-old recipe for flaky pastry lined with currants. Although many fine old houses remain, as well as twisted little medieval streets which retain their atmosphere, Banbury appears to have had a flair for destroying its own history. The citizens blew up with gunpowder their beautiful part-Norman, part-Decorated and Perpendicular parish church in 1792. They then commissioned S. P. Cockerell to build a neo-Classical church in 1793. The somewhat cold exterior is remedied by the use of bright colour in its inside. At least the old gabled and mullioned vicarage of 1649 was saved. The town once possessed a fine collection of municipal silver, but nearly all of this was sold in the early 19th cent. Two fine maces have come back into the town's possession, however. Banbury has two splendid old inns, richly timbered, gabled and mullioned. The most famous, the Reindeer Inn in Parsons Street, was responsible for another loss to the town: in 1912 it pulled out, dismantled and sold its priceless Globe Room with a superb plaster ceiling, panelled walls and 16th-cent. mullioned windows. It is now in Banbury Museum.

Yet it remains a flourishing progressive com-munity with an aluminium works contributing to its growing wealth as an important Midland industrial centre.

Chacombe Priory, in the little village of Chacombe, is just 5 m. NE. from Banbury off the A422. Its Caroline façade belies its antiquity. The first priory was built before 1066 and was occupied by the Anglo-Saxon, Lord Bardi, until William the Conqueror bestowed it on a Norman knight. It has been lived in ever since. A disas-trous fire destroyed the old priory in 1600 and the restorations date from this period. Eleven of the many rooms of this historic house are open to the public except during the winter. The fine early furniture, the paintings in the picture gallery and the Silver Room all form an impressive collection. The restored chapel is also on view. The owner of the house keeps rare ornamental fowl in the grounds.

BARFORD, *Warwickshire* (9–SP2660). On a loop of the River Avon with a splendid three-arched bridge across it, Barford lies 3 m. from WARWICK and 7 m. from STRATFORD-UPON-AVON. The village has many mellow brick cot-tages and Barford House, a white Regency house of nine bays with monumental Ionic columns, stands just to the SW. But it owes its fame to being the birthplace of Joseph Arch who revolutionized attitudes to the working conditions of farm labourers. From their ranks, he succeeded in getting into Parliament and became a friend of the Prince of Wales; he lived in the tiny cottage by the church and died there in 1919.

The Church of St Peter was entirely restored in 1844. Ancient yews line the path to the porch. The street leading to the church has some remarkably good early 18th-cent. houses.

BARNSLEY, *Gloucestershire* (5–SP0705), 3 m. SW. from BIBURY on the A433 is a perfect Cotswold village. Apart from the fine stone cottages, there is also the Palladian Barnsley Park with its magnificent plaster ceilings. It was here that Sir Isaac Newton's library of nearly 1,000 volumes was discovered after it had been moved from Thame Park. It is now in the posses-sion of the Royal Society. The church has some good Norman arches, carvings and a corbel table with grotesque heads. The tower was built at the beginning of the 17th cent. and the church suffered some over-enthusiastic restoration in the mid-19th cent. There is Victorian glass by Wailes.

BERKELEY, *Gloucestershire* (4–ST6899), in a pleasant valley of the Severn Estuary is about halfway between BRISTOL and GLOUCESTER, just W. of the main road. The little Georgian town is dominated by its formidable castle, surrounded by 14-ft-thick buttressed walls. Most of what can be seen from the fields dates from the 14th cent., including the great hall, 60 ft long. Within the courtyard, however, still stands the solid Norman keep built in the reign of Henry II for the Fitzhardinges, whose family became Earls of Berkeley and still own and live in the castle. In its early history it had more than its share of gruesomeness. This was the scene of the frightful murder in 1327 of Edward II, instigated by his wife and the Earl Mortimer. The castle is open at certain advertised times to the public.

The fine Early English parish church with some original Norman features has a tranquil setting and some excellent Berkeley family monuments. By the chancel is the grave of Edward Jenner, discoverer of vaccination, who was born here in 1749 and came back to his home where he died in 1823. Today the town is famous for its manufacture of Double Gloucester cheese and for the great nuclear power station near the Severn.

BERKSWELL, *Warwickshire* (9–SP2479). Six m. W. of COVENTRY and S. of MERIDEN lies one of the most attractive villages in the county. It has red-roofed white cottages with weathered timbers and a most curious set of stocks. Legend says that their holes were to hold a recalcitrant villager with a peg leg and his two inseparable companions. One of the most delightful buildings in the village is the 16th-cent. Bear Inn, formerly the Bear and Ragged Staff. It has Cromwellian associations. Its great open fire-place is original.

The Church of St John the Baptist is one of the best of many good Norman churches extant in Warwickshire. The earliest part of the present church dates from 1150. The east end of the chancel is Norman. There is an unusual two-storied gabled and timbered porch dating from the 16th cent. The doorway is pure Norman but was moved to its present position in the 14th cent. The church's remarkable feature is, however, its Norman crypt, early enough to have given rise to a belief that part of it is Anglo-Saxon. It has a magnificent arch spanning the centre with vaulting on each side and lit from seven lancet windows.

A few steps away outside the churchyard gate is a 16-ft-sq. tank walled with stone with clear water running inside. This is the well of the village name. The two-gabled Old Rectory is 17th-cent. with some interesting moulded window surrounds. Berkswell Hall is notable for its rhododendrons. It is well worth the short walk, so too is Ram Hall about ½ m. SSE., built in the early 1600s.

BEWDLEY, *Worcestershire* (8–SO7875), is one of the pleasantest towns in Worcestershire and can best be appreciated by coming into it from the W., on the A456 which skirts the once mighty **Wyre Forest** and crosses Telford's beautiful three-arched stone bridge. This was completed in 1801; its unique approach is fenced by elegant cast-iron pillars. This leads on to the main thoroughfare, the wide and elegant Load Street. The Town Hall built in 1808 has a Classical self-assurance derived from its massive Doric pilasters. The Post Office is housed in a timber-framed, 16th-cent. building with a delightful recessed centre gable. The Angel Inn sheltered Charles I in 1645. In the Assembly Rooms, the famous actress Mrs Siddons laid the foundations of her successful career. The George Hotel, an old posting house with bay windows has authentic charm. The 17th and 18th cents. determined the whole character of the town. Its main church, St Anne's (1746), situated at the upper end of Load Street, has a pleasing exterior.

Bewdley was the birthplace of Stanley Baldwin, three times Prime Minister between 1923 and 1937. His family home was at Astley Hall 5 m. S. of the town. Nearby on a hillside to the W. is **Tickenhill Manor**, first given to that Roger Mortimer whose descendant became King Edward IV. It was a privileged royal palace and it was here in 1499 that Prince Arthur, Henry VIII's elder brother, was married by proxy to Catherine of Aragon. The house, now fronted with Georgian brickwork, has much of the earlier building surviving. The great hall has considerable Tudor work left and many of the beams date from the 13th cent. The Folk Museum formerly here has been removed to **Hartlebury Castle** just SE. of STOURPORT.

One m. S. of Bewdley on the banks of the Severn is the little village of **Ribbesford**, latterly much spoiled. Turreted and gabled Ribbesford House, once the home of the Beauchamps and the Actons, became the training centre for officers in General de Gaulle's Free French Forces between 1942 and 1944. The little village church was much restored in late Victorian times. It has, however, a trenchant Norman tympanum with a carving of a knight transfixing a fish with his sword. Members of the Quaker family of William Penn are buried near the east window. Although Ribbesford has been so suburbanized there are still lovely river and forest walks all around.

BIBURY, *Gloucestershire* (5–SP1106). This Cotswold village attracts many visitors and stands on the busy A433, so it is perhaps best seen late on a summer evening. William Morris described it as "the most beautiful village in England". The houses are of golden stone. Many cottage gardens face the little River Coln. The early 17th-cent. cottages of Arlington Row fronting the river are now owned by the National Trust. The old coaching inn the Swan at the end of the river-fronted street, opposite the bridge, leads on to a water garden where the Bibury Spring gushes 2½ million gallons of water every 24 hours. Over the bridge is one of the best known trout farms in England.

Bibury church has considerable remains of its Anglo-Saxon original, with Norman and Early English work harmoniously added. Splendid tombs in the churchyard are an indication of

J. Allan Cash

Bibury is built throughout of the local stone

Bibury's former wool-based wealth. Just behind the churchyard is the Jacobean Bibury Court with a 1639 wing reputed to be by Inigo Jones.

A little NW. of Bibury, and also on the River Coln, is the hamlet of **Ablington**. The old Manor House dates from 1590 and has a curiously inscribed gabled porch. The manor farm possesses a fine barn. Nearby is a prehistoric long barrow with a beehive chamber.

BICESTER, *Oxfordshire* (5–SP5822). Although there are no Roman remains to justify the "castra" ending of its name, the fact that it is only 1 m. N. of the site of the Roman town of Alchester on the present A421, itself following a Roman road, would suggest that there had been a military settlement here. Today it has one of the largest army depots in the country, in spite of which it is a curiously unspoilt little market town. The three-cornered Square has an interesting building once the Town Hall. There are several old gabled houses, mostly 16th-cent., in Sheep Street, where, from the many sadlers' shops you will smell the tang of good leather and saddle soap. Bicester is the centre of the Bicester Hunt, established in the late 18th cent. The roads surrounding and coming into the town have broad green verges on both sides and the hedges and ditches are trimmed, dug and maintained by a community proud of its hunting tradition.

The street going towards the church has some old stone houses. St Edburg's, the parish church, has some interesting 12th- and 13th-cent. features. One of the arches with a triangular head may well be Anglo-Saxon. It is joined by three Norman arches, one of which is now the chancel arch, the others having once formed part of a central tower. It possesses many fine monuments and some exceptional roof beams as well as some curious medieval carvings placed in unexpected parts of the church.

BIDFORD-ON-AVON, *Warwickshire* (9–SP 1051), lies 7 m. SW. of STRATFORD-UPON-AVON on the A439 and has Shakespearean connections. Accredited to the Bard is the famous doggerel

Piping Pebworth, dancing Marston
Haunted Hillborough, hungry Grafton
Dodging Exhall, Papist Wixford
Beggarly Broom and drunken Bidford

composed after a drinking bout at the Falcon Inn. This house has not been a tavern for generations. It has mullioned windows in a good 16th-cent. Cotswold exterior, but there are unfortunate signs of dereliction. The red telephone box outside the house obtrudes.

Bidford has a fine ancient bridge. It is mostly 15th-cent., but some of its eight irregular arches are of a much earlier period.

The Church of St Laurence has a fine medieval tower but was completely and badly restored about 1835 and again in 1889 when the chancel was rebuilt.

The Roman road crossed the river by the ford near to the church and here in 1922 an Anglo-Saxon burial ground was discovered with the graves of some 200 fully accoutred warriors and their women.

The main street has some good 15th- and 16th-cent. houses and is worthy rather of a market town than a small village.

BIRMINGHAM, *Warwickshire* (9–SP0787). With a population of well over one million, Birmingham is Britain's second largest city. The municipal boundaries enclose an area of 80 sq. m. Although mentioned in the Domesday Book, it developed slowly until the middle of the 16th cent., when it had already established its reputation as a small industrial town. Even then the Bull Ring was the centre of its many activities. Birmingham's metal industry had already advanced to such a state that it tempered over 16,000 sword blades for Cromwell's forces during the Civil War. Its Roundhead allegiance led in 1643 to a clash of arms in the Bull Ring area with Prince Rupert's forces. He had been ordered to clear a communications route for the Royalists between OXFORD and YORK after the citizens of Birmingham had seized King Charles I's plate and coin while the king was *en route* to relieve the besieged

BANBURY Castle. Some 90 houses were destroyed and 400 people made homeless. The town was fined £30,000, about £1 million in terms of today's values.

There is a great concentration of industry in the city, with factories, workshops, and head offices of international concerns. While metals remain a high priority, jewelry, toys, chemicals, brass, plastics and rubber products are manufactured. The chocolate and cocoa capital at Bourneville is within a few minutes of the city centre. The motor industry has a place to itself. Although some of the largest factories in Europe are established here, the individualistic character of Birmingham is maintained: the city still has over 1,500 separate firms of all types and sizes in production.

It was the Industrial Revolution that produced Birmingham's expansion – so rapid that in 1889 Queen Victoria declared it a city. Eleven years later it had its own university and in 1909 gave England its first official Town Planning Act.

Birmingham's new Bull Ring Centre is dominated by wide roads, banked by large buildings of concrete and glass with the shopping centre, terraced underneath the flyovers. This area is completely traffic free and is linked by subways with the older shopping streets where many of the department stores are. There are most kinds of retail shop, an open and a covered market, banks, restaurants and offices moulded into a whole that is dominated by the multi-storied Rotunda on its highest rise.

Among Birmingham's remarkable buildings is the Town Hall which is modelled on the Jupiter Stator in Rome. Here some of the world's leading orchestras may be heard. The City Museum and Art Gallery with its magnificent staircase and Joseph Southall's frescoes, are striking. Here can be found some of the best examples of the pre-Raphaelite period of painting, including important works by Burne-Jones (who was a native of the city) and William Morris. The Science Museum houses the earliest English locomotive actually built (1784) among its vast collection of mechanical apparatus which placed England in the forefront of 19th-cent. technical development.

The city's most famous church is St Martin's. This forms a counterpoint to the architectural patterns of the new Bull Ring. The most ancient part of the present church dates from the 13th cent. Restoration has left only the interior of the lower part of its tower intact.

The fine 18th-cent. Cathedral Church of St Philip with its Baroque tower is notable for its inspired Burne-Jones windows.

A. W. N. Pugin designed the red-brick Roman Catholic cathedral in 14th-cent. Gothic style. It contains some fine works of art, mostly gifts of local industrialists.

The Reference Library in Ratcliff Place is one of the most comprehensive in the country and contains the Shakespeare Memorial Library with 40,000 books in some 90 different languages.

The Birmingham Repertory Theatre in Station Street has, through the energy and drive of its founder, the late Sir Barry Jackson, created a tradition of forward-looking theatre second to none.

In the new planning for Birmingham, it has not been forgotten that this is one of the few great cities in the world not built upon the banks of a river. So, incorporated in the plans is a decision to retain some of the attractive, yet mostly hidden, canals that criss-cross the city. In 1769 Samuel Simcock under the direction of James Brindley built a waterway from the coalfields of WEDNESBURY right into Birmingham's Paradise Street. With the intersections of the Birmingham Canal, the WORCESTER–Birmingham Canal and the Birmingham–Fazeley Canal being tidied up to form the eastern gateway to the Birmingham Canal Navigation system, Birmingham was left with more miles of waterway than Venice. There are pleasant walks along the canal right in the City Centre, and there are good vistas from Summer Row to Kingston Row where 18th-cent. cottages have been restored. Gas Street Basin will have moorings for the traditional narrow painted boats which have preserved their true folk-craft colourings as well as for modern pleasure cruisers. Restaurants and pleasant cafés all form part of this exciting experiment in the city's development.

BIRMINGHAM (SUBURBS) (9–SP0787). Most famous of the Birmingham suburbs is **Edgbaston**, about a six-minute car drive from the city centre. Here in hidden places are wedded good late Georgian, Regency and Victorian houses. In busy Hagley Road is Cardinal Newman's Classical church, the Oratory, with its typical Roman narthex and wealth of marble. Edgbaston boasts a fine Botanical Garden. Laid out by Loudon in 1831, it has the greatest varieties of trees and shrubs, Alpine plants, a rock garden, a rose garden and abundant cacti. Besides the plants there are cockatoos, bush babies and monkeys.

Edgbaston produced the Chamberlain family who made an indelible mark on England's political history.

Most remarkable, in a city of industrial expansion and change, is the fact that a great Jacobean House, **Aston Hall**, still stands among it all. Its building was begun in 1618 by Sir Thomas Holt, who took up residence in a house of truly palatial proportions 13 years later. The house seen today is in all major respects exactly as it was in 1635 when it was finished.

Its balustraded staircase sweeps right up to a second story of the house. The panelled long gallery is one of the best in the country. A treasure house of paintings, marbles and valuable furniture, it is set in fine parkland. It is open to the public at advertised times throughout the year.

Bournville is an unusually agreeable suburb just 4 m. SW. of the city centre. Inspired by Quaker idealism, the chocolate manufacturers George and Richard Cadbury started a new housing estate around their factory, to provide pleasant and hygienic surroundings for their workers. This grew rapidly into the Bournville Estate which was

Birmingham: the garden city estate at Bournville incorporates factories and houses in a model setting

to provide a model for many garden cities of England and today numbers some 4,000 houses. They are set in tree-shaded avenues with enviable amenities.

In the parish church of **Handsworth** is a fine statue of James Watt, who produced his steam engine at the Soho works in partnership with Matthew Boulton, the silversmith.

Longbridge is the centre of the Austin Morris Division of British Leyland Motor Corporation. The first factory rose on a small site here in 1905 and grew rapidly into one of the biggest automobile works in Europe. It is possible to watch the whole assembly line at work from the arrival of the steel to the finished motorcar. Particularly impressive is the Car Assembly Hangar designed by one of America's foremost industrial architects, C. Howard Crane. It should be mentioned that it is also possible to arrange to see over the Standard Car Works and those of the Rootes Industries.

Perry Barr, about $3\frac{3}{4}$ m. N. of the city, contains within its boundaries Oscott Roman Catholic Theological College, set in parkland. Permission can be obtained to visit this treasure-store of ecclesiastical art which is contained within the buildings built mostly by Pugin and Joseph Potter between 1835 and 1838.

Selly Oak, 3 m. SW. of the city, is chiefly renowned for its Quaker Woodbrooke College which possesses one of the most famous glass chalices in the world. It was originally found in the Crimea and is believed to be a 1st-cent. liturgical cup, with a Greek inscription. Here, too, is a priceless collection of ancient manuscripts.

Solihull, home of the Rover car works, is a county borough and not strictly a suburb of Birmingham. It has its own modern shopping centre – but also Tudor houses, some of them in the High Street. Its parish church has a 168-ft tower and a splendid peal of bells. From here came John Peckenham to be chaplain to Mary Tudor and finally to be the last Benedictine Abbot of Westminster. Just S. of Solihull stands the late 16th-cent. Malvern Park Farm, an excellent example of Warwickshire domestic architecture, which is now a school.

Just $1\frac{1}{4}$ m. E. of Solihull is another finely moated 16th-cent. house, Berry Hall, well worth seeing, since it has not suffered in any way from ill-conceived restoration.

BLENHEIM PALACE, *Oxfordshire* (5–SP 4416). John Churchill, 1st Duke of Marlborough (1650–1722), was responsible, both as soldier and as statesman, more than any other one man, for checking Louis XIV's imperialist ambition in Europe. He inflicted a crushing defeat on the French at Blenheim on 13 August 1704 and though he followed this up with many other victories, Queen Anne decided that his reward must match the importance of his achievements. In gratitude she conferred the Royal Manor of Woodstock with the hundred of Wootton on the Duke of Marlborough and his heirs forever, and a sum of £500,000 was voted by Parliament for the building of Blenheim Palace. Sarah Jennings who married John Churchill at the age of 18 was Anne's favourite companion before she became Queen in 1702. She had great influence over her and enjoyed royal patronage for many years until eventually it was dissolved with bitter recriminations. During the first period she obtained a dukedom for her husband. She was the real architect not only of her husband's fortunes but also of the great palace, whose foundation stone was laid in 1705. It was she who rejected Sir Christopher Wren's plans and chose those of Sir John Vanbrugh. He built this vast edifice covering 3 acres of ground (which can compare in magnitude with the largest palaces in Europe) between 1705 and 1722. Its park was first laid out by Henry Wise, gardener to Queen Anne, and his formal designs were later modified by Capability Brown in conformity with the task for the "natural" which was then popular. It covers some 2,500 acres and it is said that Brown planned the avenues and trees on a sketch of the actual campaign of the Battle of Blenheim. The vast lake was achieved by damming the River Glyme; it is spanned with a 390-ft-long bridge from which beautiful vistas may be seen in all seasons. In the distance is the enormous Column of Victory surmounted by the Duke swathed in a Roman toga. Everywhere are

A. F. Kersting

Blenheim Palace was built for the 1st Duke of Marlborough; it covers 3 acres of ground

charming walks through beechwoods, while winding paths skirt the shore-line of the lake. The late Duke had the terraced gardens on the south side redesigned, to follow Wise's original lay-out. The tremendous Triumphal Way, designed by Sir William Chambers and flooded by Brown, is one of the finest examples of landscape gardening in Europe. The sunken Italian Garden merits similar praise. The Water Gardens were designed by Duchêne in the early part of this century and are reminiscent of Versailles. The house's vastness defies description; perhaps it is best summed up by Pope's epigram:

"Thanks, sir" cried I, "'tis very fine,
But where d'ye sleep or where d'ye dine?
I find by all you have been telling
That 'tis a house and not a dwelling."

There is too much to appreciate in one visit: the magnificent tapestries, for which Queen Anne's ambassadors combed Europe; the splendid State Rooms; the Long Library with its statue of Queen Anne and its great organ; the priceless paintings and *objets d'art*; the doorcases carved by Grinling Gibbons and the flamboyant ceiling painted by Sir James Thornhill in 1716 depicting the Battle of Blenheim; the chapel with its marble tombs. In complete contrast is the small room on the ground floor where Sir Winston Churchill was born. It is simply furnished with a plain brass bed, some framed cartoons on the wall, a chest of drawers and a small marble fire-place and is somehow in keeping with the unassuming side of the great leader's character. Blenheim Palace and gardens are generally open to the public in spring, summer and autumn, though arrangements can sometimes be made for parties during the winter.

BLOXHAM, *Oxfordshire* (5–SP4235), is a largish village 3 m. SW. of BANBURY on the A361. Its stone houses rise on each side of a valley, one hill surmounted by a mid-Victorian public school and the other by a 14th-cent. church with a 190-ft-tall spire which is an outstanding landmark. While the building, originally Norman, is mostly 13th-cent., it was considerably enlarged

and improved in the 14th and 15th cents., and Street carried out restorations in the 19th cent. The circular arched west door has rich moulding and carvings of flowers and birds, and canopied steps, each set with an apostle before Christ in Judgment at the apex, are an unusual feature. The Milcombe Chapel has a much restored 14th-cent. reredos, as well as some 15th-cent. murals. The chancel screen is 15th-cent., again restored, but with some of the original colouring still showing. The glass in the great east windows is by William Morris and Burne-Jones. When the school is in residence, the choir music can be quite outstanding.

BODENHAM, *Herefordshire* (8–SO5251), is an attractive village with old timbered cottages, good stone houses and an interesting church. It can be reached by turning E. off the A49 HEREFORD–LEOMINSTER road on either side of Dinmore Hill. The River Lugg makes a loop and flows under an old bridge at the end of the village, where stand an octagonal 18th-cent. dovecot and close by a mid-Georgian brick house of considerable architectural originality. The black-and-white cottages are sheltered by a well-wooded hill. The parish church, set among riverside orchards, is remarkable for its lofty 14th-cent. arcades and its massive and impressive tower surmounted by a curiously small spire. Restrained restoration work was carried out in the last century when the church acquired a new chancel arch; this did not detract from its atmosphere, derived from good light and a sense of spaciousness. On the north wall is an interesting 14th-cent. monument of a wimpled mother with her baby.

There are some good medieval houses in the area. Outstanding is the 14th-cent. stone and timber building of Maund Farm, which has a fine 15th-cent. ceiling of moulded beams and an appearance that was somewhat radically changed by an extra wing added in the 17th cent. Bodenham's most impressive house is Broadfield Court, dating originally from the 14th cent. but much enlarged in the 16th. It has all the appearance of a Cotswold manor: gabled, with a good stone porch arched with ball-flower decoration. It seems to have every type of window from traceried Gothic and mullioned Tudor to Victorian bays, and gives the impression of a much loved and lived-in home. The stone-walled terrace and garden are well cared for.

BOURTON-ON-THE-HILL, *Gloucester-shire* (5–SP1831), is built at the top of a steep hill W. of MORETON-IN-MARSH. St Lawrence's Church at the summit of the hill has a fine Norman south arcade with good scalloped capitals. At the bottom of the hill is the splendid 18th-cent. Bourton House. It has one of the most remarkable 16th-cent. tithe barns in the county, strongly buttressed and with a tall gabled porch. The cottages in the village with terraced gardens have attractive bow windows. A little to the S. of Bourton-on-the-Hill lies **Sezincote** at the head of the River Evenlode. In pleasant parkland is an extraordinary house built in the opening years of the 19th cent. for Sir Charles Cockerell. This was the early period of British ascendancy in India and Samuel Pepys Cockerell, Charles's brother, and Thomas Daniell collaborated in building a house that was English in plan but included such features as Oriental arches and onion domes. Humphry Repton landscaped the gardens in Indian terms. The total result was the inspiration for the Prince Regent's Pavilion at BRIGHTON. The house is extremely effective and gains much from the pinnacled north wing and greenhouse pavilion. The water garden, with lotus pools and stepped shrines to Indian gods, was completed by about 1803. There is a snake-headed fountain and the whole garden abounds with fine trees and rare plants. It is occasionally open to the public and is worth seeing.

BOURTON-ON-THE-WATER, *Glouces-tershire* (5–SP1620), lies 4 m. SW. of STOW-ON-THE-WOLD. The Windrush flows beside the lawn-bordered main street under low-arched bridges and good Cotswold stone houses abound. Behind the New Inn there is a stone model of the village which is a popular attraction for tourists. At the other end of the village is an old mill. The chancel of the parish church dates from 1328 but the church suffered badly from restoration at the end of the last century. The roof, however, has some good modern heraldic painting. W. of the A429 unclassified roads lead to two pretty villages, **Lower Slaughter** and **Upper Slaughter**. The first village has a stream flowing under little stone bridges, a much painted scene. Both church and manor have charm; the former retains its 12th-cent. arcade but was much restored in the 1860s. The second village also has a tributary of the Windrush running through it. There are the usual picturesque Cotswold stone cottages and a good 17th-cent. parsonage. On a rise above the village is an Elizabethan manor house, perhaps one of the most visually satisfying in the Cotswold countryside. The church has many good Norman features and an unusual 14th-cent. sanctus bellcot. This church, too, suffered from

19th-cent. restoration, though the 15th-cent. chancel was left intact.

A short distance N. along the same unclassified road are two more famous villages, **Lower Swell** and **Upper Swell**. Sheltered in the green hills the little River Dikler flows through both villages. When restoration work was being done on Lower Swell church during the last century considerable finds of Roman jewels and coins were made. The church has some of the finest Norman carving in this part of the county. Upper Swell is particularly appealing, partly because of the fine trees which line the course of the Dikler. By the bridge it still turns a great millwheel and the pool beyond has many waterfowl. The small manor house above the little river has a fine Renaissance doorway. The church has something of all periods to offer with a good Norman doorway and an untouched 15th-cent. porch. All these villages can best be enjoyed by leaving the car and strolling by the riverside.

BRAMPTON BRYAN, *Herefordshire* (8–SO 3672). The story of this little village, to the W. of Leintwardine on the A4113 KNIGHTON–LUDLOW road, is really the story of a famous family, the Harleys. It derives its name from Bryan de Brampton who built a fortress here in the 13th cent. His daughter married Robert Harley who commenced building the castle, the substantial ruins of which can be appreciated in the massive two round towers leading to the inner gatehouse and the hall. All this is set in the great park of the Georgian brick mansion to the W. of the castle. The castle was irretrievably destroyed in spite of Sir Robert Harley's wife Brilliana, who, while her husband was away fighting for Parliament, bravely withstood a siege by the Royalists. After a short respite the Royalists again attacked and burnt down the castle, and only what is described above remained. The church was destroyed but rebuilt after the Civil War in its charming village setting of black-and-white cottages. It has a fine original hammer-beam roof and a 14th-cent. monument which survived the war and may be that of Margaret Harley who founded the line of this redoubtable family. In spite of continuing political and religious change they survived in power throughout the centuries. Harley Street in London is named after perhaps the most famous of them all: Robert, Earl of Oxford. Just to the N. of Brampton is **Coxwall Knoll**, some 400 ft up in the hills, a prehistoric camp half of which lies in Herefordshire and half in Shropshire. It is claimed locally to have been the site of the last battle between Caractacus and the Romans when the defiant Celt was finally taken prisoner and led to Rome.

BREDON, *Worcestershire* (8–SO9236), one of the loveliest river villages in the county, at the foot of the 991-ft Bredon Hill. Beside the Avon are well-weathered old cottages, timbered houses and a 14th-cent. tithe barn which is 132-ft long, with five porches, one with unusual stone cowling. The National Trust owns it. The village street is

enhanced by the one-storied stone Reed Alms-houses built in 1696. St Giles's is a cruciform Norman church with a graceful 14th-cent. spire, 160 ft high. One doorway is sheltered by a two-storied Norman porch, sturdily vaulted. Two other Norman doorways have chevron-mould heads. The Mitton Chapel is Early English, with an array of trefoiled lancets. There is a vast alabaster and stone canopied monument to Giles Reed, whose grandchildren built the Alms-houses. In the 14th-cent. chancel are some in-comparably rare heraldic tiles on the altar steps. The four chancel windows are filled with good 14th-cent. stained glass. There is a modest memorial to the much loved Bishop Prideaux, of WORCESTER, who died during the Common-wealth; he had to sell all his possessions during the Civil War and was left with only a few shillings to eke out his last days. On the top of Bredon Hill is a notable south Worcestershire landmark: a re-markable Iron Age camp. The inner rampart covers 11 acres and was built at the end of the last century B.C. Since the encampment was excavated, more than 50 bodies have been dis-covered, all brutally hacked to pieces, near the entrance, apparently massacred when the fort was breached. Just inside the fort is a curious 18th-cent. tower known as Parson's Folly.

Great Comberton lies at the northern foot of Bredon Hill and has half-timbered farm-houses and thatched cottages. The walls of the extra-ordinary round dovecot in the village are over 3 ft thick and have more than 500 holes. Another dovecot, square, red-bricked and four-gabled, has no less than 1,425 nesting holes and is reputed to be one of the biggest in England. The church, which has a squat, square tower, appears to be early Norman. Nearby **Little Comberton** has Nash's Farm, a 17th-cent. black-and-white farm-house with circular stone dovecot, believed to be medieval. The church is Norman with many alterations over the centuries. The north doorway has its fine oak waggon roof over both the nave and chancel.

Off the road between EVESHAM and PERSHORE is a pretty village of black-and-white cottages facing the Avon called **Cropthorne**, and well worth visiting. In the old Norman church was discovered one of the finest Anglo-Saxon crosses in the country. Its intricate carving portrays birds and beasts in starkly bold trails and the sides are decorated with a Greek-key design. Local lore says that the cedar growing in the village was planted before the Conquest. On the opposite side of the river, past Charlton Hall, is another delightful village, **Fladbury**. Grouped behind its landing stage is an old inn, a watermill and a Norman church with much later addition and a chancel completely and unfortunately restored by the Victorians. The fine brasses on the large tomb-chest under the tower where John Throck-morton and his wife are buried are dated 1445.

BREDWARDINE, *Herefordshire* (8–SO3344), lies just off the B4352 road between HEREFORD and 7-m. distant Hay-on-Wye. It is one of the most beautiful spots on the banks of the Wye, sheltered by wooded hills. The 1,045-ft **Merbach Hill**, with its famous Neolithic long barrow called Arthur's Stone, rises behind and the summit can be reached as easily from here as from **Dorstone**. A mellow 18th-cent. brick bridge crosses the river and encourages the visitor to enjoy the view. The village also has an early 18th-cent. red-brick inn called the Red Lion and a long, curiously shaped Norman church, partly built of tufa. The west end is completely Norman but the elongation work curving slightly to the N. was completed in the 14th cent. The tower is 18th-cent. The plain interior is relieved by the effigies of two medieval knights, the later one carved in alabaster and almost certainly the figure of Sir Roger Vaughan, who was with Henry V at Agincourt. The Vaughans then lived at the castle, of which only the earthworks remain on a spur of land overlooking the river to the SE. of the church-yard. The diarist Francis Kilvert was the vicar here in the 1870s.

BRINSOP, *Herefordshire* (8–SO4344), lies 5½ m. NW from HEREFORD just N. of the A480 Hereford–KINGTON road on an unclassified road and near the woods of Credenhill and Merry-hill. In a valley stands a famous old 14th-cent. moated manor house, Brinsop Court, once the home of the Tirrels and the Danseys. It is a lovely rambling old house with its original great hall. Much of the house is Tudor in style with Jacobean and Georgian additions. A new wing was built early in this century, but all periods seem to have blended harmoniously into a whole. Wordsworth was a frequent visitor when his brother-in-law lived in the house and understandably had a deep feeling for a building so rooted in the soil of the county. The little St George's Church set in orchard land allows its unprepossessing exterior to hide a gem of a church inside. The 12th-cent. tympanum has flowing lines. The church itself is mostly early 14th-cent. In the chancel is a much defaced wall painting of the Annunciation. There are two beautiful pieces of 14th-cent. glass and some modern glass portraying the Nativity, in memory of Wordsworth and his family. The gilded oak chancel screen with gilded angels holding tapers dates from the 14th cent., as does the magnificent Christ in Majesty reigning from the Cross. Even the modern additions like the alabaster reredos or the windows portraying St Francis and St Hubert, erected to the memory of Hubert Astley, have all been achieved with a sensitive taste that has never allowed old and new to clash. Near the church are some earth-works believed to be Roman as some years ago a Roman well was discovered. Brinsop lies just off Stone Street and not far from Roman Kenchester, so this seems quite likely.

BRISTOL (4–ST5872). This thriving ancient city-port with its growing population of nearly half a million inhabitants has long been impor-tant to English trade and commerce. Three years before the death of Edward III in 1376, it was separated from neighbouring Gloucestershire and Somerset and made a county with its own sheriff. One hundred and fifty years previously the city installed its own mayor, and its first known royal charter was granted 28 years before this. The earliest proof of its commercial activity goes back to the time of Ethelred II in the 10th cent. when silver coins were minted here. All this was due to the fact that the Rivers Avon and Severn were navigable and to the natural basin, once fed by the little River Frome, which is now known as the Floating Harbour. Today this is dominated by the statue of Neptune. Bristol has several focal points; the Floating Harbour is the pivot of the city's life. From here Edward I's writ was sent up to the Constable of the already 100-year-old Bristol Castle, demanding the king's due: a considerable quantity of eels, hake, haddock, plaice and skate from every Bristol fishing-boat coming into port. From here, too, during the Hundred Years War, Bristol sent 22 ships and 600 men to France. A tablet nearby records that from this port John Cabot of Genoa and his Bristol-born son Sebastian set sail in 1497 in the 100-ton *Matthew* and with 18 sailors reached the mainland of North America, in Newfoundland.

The year A.D. 1552 saw the incorporation of the Merchant Venturers and from then on the fame of Bristol-based ships reached every port of the known world. They gave the English language the expression "all ship-shape and Bristol fashion". Wines and particularly tobaccos and chocolate gradually replaced wool as the main cargoes and the wealth of the city grew – not least on the slave trade – making it one of the most important towns of Britain. Over the last two centuries with the increased size of ships the docks, too, have increased in size. From Prince Street Bridge can be seen Prince's Wharf and Wapping Wharf where Baltic timber and Dutch merchandise are discharged. On Prince's Wharf is a tablet recording the launching in 1838 of Brunel's first steamship, *The Great Western*. Edging Wapping Road is the New Cut made in the last century channelling the Avon. From Mardyke Wharf opposite, the dockside bustle is seen to advantage. From nearby Hotwells Road can be seen the Albion Dockyards and Cumberland Basin where ocean-going vessels come in from the Avon. It is possible to visit the Avonmouth Docks by application to the Port of Bristol Authority in Queen Square.

For convenience, Bristol may be divided into seven main centres of interest. The old city is the area from Bristol Bridge, across Corn Street, up Broad Street to St John's Church. The first Bristol Bridge was built in the 13th cent. It was the entry to the walled town of the period. Over the bridge are the remains of the Church of St Nicholas and its Norman crypt. A traditional curfew is still rung every night at nine o'clock from its re-hung bells. The tower of St Mary-le-Port adjoining is the oldest part of the city. All Saints is a Norman foundation, much restored in the 18th cent. when the present cupola was added.

In nearby Corn Street is the splendid Classical building designed by BATH's famous John Wood, the Exchange. The four bronze pillars outside are known as "The Bristol Nails" where the city merchants completed their financial dealings – "paying on the nail". The Old Council House, rebuilt in 1828 by Sir Robert Smirke (who designed the BRITISH MUSEUM façade) on the site of a 16th-cent. building, has an unusual enamel and brass staircase. Beyond the recently restored Guildhall is the tranquil little 17th-cent. Taylors Court; its buildings once housed the Merchant Taylors' Guild. In the angle of Broad Street and Wine Street stands Christ Church where the poet Southey was baptized. The remarkable figures (the Quarter Jacks) striking the old bells on either side of the galleried and canopied clock are leased to the church by the Bristol Corporation for half a crown a year. St John's Church is built over an original (and the last) of the city's gates. There is some fine Jacobean woodwork inside this originally 14th-cent. church. The two famous figures niched in the arch outside are Brennus and Belinus, the reputed founders of Bristol.

King Street, which has many good 17th- and 18th-cent. buildings, leads off from the Centre, another area of interest, and has the renowned Theatre Royal, first opened to the public in 1766 and therefore even older than the 18th-cent. theatre at RICHMOND, Yorkshire. It preserves its Georgian lay-out and original décor. The Victorians gave this delightful theatre a pleasing façade. In 1943, when its future was in doubt, an Old Vic company took over the theatre; since 1962 it has been administered by a Civic Theatre Trust, and a high standard of performance is maintained. Nearby is the 18th-cent. Coopers Hall and the earlier St Nicholas Almshouses on the corner. Llandoger Trow, built in 1664, is one of the city's oldest inns. Nearby is a beautiful example of very early 18th-cent. town planning in Queen Square, built to commemorate the visit of Queen Anne in 1702. Parts were destroyed in riots in 1831 and later rebuilt. The first American Consulate in Europe opened in 1792 at No. 37.

Although a whole rebuilding scheme has been completed in the Redcliffe area since the Second World War, it has done no more than give an added vitality to one of the most historically rewarding parts of Bristol. It is dominated by a graceful 19th-cent. spire rising 285 ft from street level, resting on the fine 13th-cent. tower of St Mary Redcliffe. This is the church described by Queen Elizabeth I on her visit to Bristol as "the fairest, goodliest and most famous parish church in the kingdom". It has the breadth, width and height of a cathedral and has been cherished by the city these 600 years. The hexagonal north porch is exquisitely beautiful and all its carvings of men and beasts have survived every restoration or extension to the building. The church, with its 240-ft-long nave, its open parapets, immense areas of glass and superb flying buttresses, owes its first reconstruction to William Canynge in the 14th cent. His son, also William and one of the greatest of all Bristol's merchant princes, con-

Bristol Cathedral: bosses in the roof

A. F. Kersting

Bristol: the Clifton Suspension Bridge

Noel Habgood

The Temple Mead area, around the main railway station, has two interesting churches. One with a leaning tower is the old Temple Church which was much damaged during Bristol's air raids but is now preserved by the Ministry of Public Building and Works. The other is the fine 18th-cent. Classical Church of St Thomas built on Norman foundations. The Organ Gallery built in 1728 is one of the finest in the country.

The Broadmead area stretches from Old Market Street up to St James's. The modern shops and supermarkets which have sprung up since the Second World War, skirting the edge of St James's Park, are in the main a dull tale of missed opportunities. Among them are a number of historical buildings which survived both blitz and development. Just off Horsefair is the New Room, the first Methodist chapel in the world. John Wesley preached his first sermon here in 1739. On the other side of the Broadmead Circle are the cloisters of a Dominican friary which, having passed through various vicissitudes after the Dissolution, were acquired by the Society of Friends: hence their strange name of Quaker Friars. Further up, just off Haymarket, is St James's Church, reputed to be the oldest building in Bristol. Built by Robert, Earl of Gloucester, in the early part of the 12th cent., it is said that every tenth stone acquired for the building of the great keep, was set aside to build this church. The Romanesque wheel window surmounting the interlaced arcades of the west front was described in a manuscript of A.D. 1150. The Stag and Hounds in Old Market Street is one of the most ancient inns and centre of a medieval fair where the Court of Pie Poudre (the dusty feet) is still ceremoniously opened every 30 September.

The University of Bristol is growing rapidly and marks another of the city's areas of interest. This was the first British university to offer a faculty in drama. Its high tower is in a carefully reproduced Perpendicular style and was opened in 1925. The Great George bell which strikes the hour commemorates the visit of George V. Nearby in Park Row is the Red Lodge built for the Elizabethan merchant Sir John Young. Now a museum and cultural centre, it was once a girls' reformatory financed by Lord Byron's widow. The richly carved oak room is a particularly splendid example of period panelling. The City Museum and Art Gallery has one of the most interesting geological and archaeological collections in the provinces. In the Art Gallery is a fine Hogarth triptych from St Mary Redcliffe and some good early Lawrences. Sir Thomas Lawrence was born in Bristol. The nearby 16th-cent. Grammar School, though founded on the present site, was entirely rebuilt in late Victorian times. More interesting is the neighbouring Royal Fort, a house built by a rich Bristolian merchant in 1761. The interior plasterwork and sweeping staircase are elegant.

The last of the areas lies around College Green. Across the way from Cabot Tower on Brandon Hill is the 12th-cent. Augustinian abbey, now Bristol Cathedral. Commenced in 1142, it retains much of its Norman solidity, particularly its

siderably enlarged and enriched his father's work on the church, all of which can be seen in the stone, timber and glass of its interior. This younger Canynge, who was twice member of parliament and mayor five times, renounced his wealth in 1467 and became a collegiate priest of the church he had so generously endowed. He sang his first Mass in the church on Whit-Sunday 1467. This is still commemorated every Whit-Sunday when the chancel is strewn with fresh rushes and the Lord Mayor and Corporation of Bristol attend the service. Admiral Penn, father of Pennsylvania's founder, is commemorated here. Nearby is the house where Thomas Chatterton, the tragic poet, was born in 1752. It is now a Chatterton Museum. In Colston Parade on the other side of the church is Plimsoll House where the inventor of the safety loading line, Samuel Plimsoll, was born in 1824. Across Redcliffe Hill is the famous Shot Tower where in the 18th cent. William Watts experimented by dropping tiny quantities of molten lead into water from the top of the tower to make perfectly spherical shot. He thus made his fortune and his tower is still used for this same purpose.

fine chapter house. From the 13th to the 15th cent. new chapels, transepts, choir and aisles were built. In the 16th-cent. choir stalls can. be seen some of the most imaginative of carving. In a later age, Grinling Gibbons created his superb organ case for this not too well known cathedral. The east Jesse window has 14th-cent. glass. The fine bosses in the roof of the north transept can now be seen to advantage since all the dirt has been removed by modern processes. Further up, in a turning off Park Street, stands a perfectly preserved house of the late 18th cent., built by John Pinney, who made a fortune in the West Indies. Called the Georgian House, this, too, is now a museum. All its décor, furniture and fittings are Georgian. The New Council House is neo-Georgian; not everybody likes it, but it sweeps in a graceful curve about College Green. Queen Elizabeth II opened in 1956. On the other side of the Cabot Tower is the Queen Elizabeth Hospital School, founded in 1590. As at Christ's Hospital, boarders wear the ceremonial blue cassocked coat with yellow stockings and buckled shoes.

Two other places of interest deserve mention. The first is St Stephen's Church in the centre with its hundreds of gilded bosses in the roof of the nave and its monument to Martin Pring, a sea captain who sailed with Sir Walter Raleigh and discovered Plymouth Harbour, where the *Mayflower* docked. The other is the famous Christmas Steps at the top of Colston Street, which is named after one of Bristol's many 17th-cent. benefactors, Edward Colston. The Steps lie just behind Quay Street and were built about 1669. Good antiques, old books and silver can still be discovered. At the top of the steps is the Chapel of the Three Kings of Cologne, a curious and ancient connection with the Rhineland city.

About 4 m. N. of the city, out over Durdham Downs, going out by Westbury Road, is Henbury. Here are 400 acres of woodlands, now owned by Bristol Corporation. This is **Blaise Castle Estate**. The castle is a folly with four castellated towers, built by Thomas Farr, Master of the Society of Merchant Venturers, in 1771. There are foundations of an ancient chapel to St Blaise nearby and caves. The Folk Museum is contained in a Georgian house by Nash and Paty. The reconstructed farm-house kitchen gives an idea of the old rural way of living. An 18th-cent. corn-mill and John Nash's early 19th-cent. thatched dairy have been preserved. The Blaise hamlet comprises nine thatched cottages on Hallen Road, also designed by John Nash for estate pensioners and grouped round a contrived village green, complete with a pillared sundial on a stone village pump.

Bristol Airport Terminal lies S. on the A38 at Lulsgate and is important and busy. It has a 6,600-ft runway and has been extensively modernized to handle the new large freight and passenger aircraft and continues Bristol's traditional rôle.

As the prosperity of Bristol increased in the late 18th cent. the wealthy began to move out to

Clifton. The elegant Windsor Terrace and Cornwallis Crescent date from this time: Royal York Crescent and the Paragon were built a few years later. Many famous civic houses and institutions have their setting in this pleasant area. It also has a famous Victorian public school. Clifton is best known for its Suspension Bridge, built by Brunel in 1864. It spans the Avon Gorge, separating Gloucestershire from Somerset, at a height of 245 ft above the river's high-water level. **Leigh Woods** at the Somerset end are National Trust property and open to the public. Above the Suspension Bridge is the Observatory with its camera obscura. It is open to the public in the summer months. Bristol Zoo also has its home in Clifton; it has a fine collection of animals, well displayed.

The Avon Gorge has some of the finest panoramic views any city can offer. The famous Scarlet Lychnis, known as the Flower of Bristowe (this was an earlier form of the name; the present "l" is a quirk of Bristol speech that also turns ideas into ideals and bananas into bananals), almost indigenous to this city, grows on the rocky slopes of the Bristol side of the Gorge.

About 4 m. NE. of the city centre on the A38 is **Filton**, once a village. Now it is a huge centre of a giant aircraft industry. The British Concorde prototype was built here. Hidden away is the parish church, mostly modern but still possessing its fine medieval tower with its 12 curious gargoyles.

BROADWAY, *Worcestershire* (9–SP0937), lies 6 m. SE. of EVESHAM where the A46 crosses the A44. The view of its long and broad Main Street, grass-verged, climbing up towards **Fish Hill**, epitomizes the perfect Cotswold village. In spite of its popularity with tourists from all over the world (it is said to be the most publicized "show village" in England) it has retained its character and nothing has been allowed to impair its beauty. On both sides are lovely old cottages and fine gabled houses, nearly all built of golden Cotswold stone. Notable is the Abbot's Grange, which once belonged to the Abbots of Evesham and dates from the 14th cent. It has Elizabethan additions and two well-planned wings built in this century. It has its original chapel, hall, solar and abbot's study. The next house facing the green is the late 17th-cent. Farnham House. The Broadway Hotel in contrast is mostly timber-framed, with only one wing built of stone. Perhaps the best known building is an inn now called the Lygon Arms but originally known as the White Hart. At an even earlier date it was probably an important manor house. The Torrington Diaries of 1742–1813 record that the walls were very thick, "door oaken and wide, with a profusion of timber and remains of much tapistery for carpetting". The writer went on to record that he was lodged in "the grand bedchamber of an old family seat". All of which, in spite of the additions of 20th-cent. plumbing and heating, is true today. During the troubled years of 1645–51 the house sheltered at different times both Charles I and Cromwell. With its recessed centre and projecting wings, its gables and dormer windows, its mullions and transoms and the beautiful preservation of its stone, it is still the most exciting of the many beautiful houses in the village. The Tudor House is often considered a rival, but its very formal symmetry may relegate it to second place for some people. Another beautiful old gabled house restored with care is now St Patrick's Tea Room.

There is another delightful little manor house called Hunters Lodge, built during the Commonwealth towards the top of the hill. This is now a hotel. Fish Inn was once a summer-house or gazebo on Sir John Cotterell's estate and has a curious rusticated Venetian window and frieze. A little to the S. of the inn is the Beacon Tower (sometimes called Fish Hill Tower) built by Lady Coventry and completed as a folly at the end of the 18th cent. It stands over 1,000 ft up and commands a view over several counties. On a fine day TEWKESBURY Abbey, WORCESTER Cathedral and WARWICK Castle can all be made out.

The old Parish Church of St Eadbury is hidden away at the other end of the village. A cruciform church with a central tower, it contains much of architectural merit from the 12th to the 17th cents. It is little used now. The present parish church was built in the 19th cent. Spring Hill House, 3 m. to the SE., was Lord Coventry's mansion. He commissioned Capability Brown to build it in 1763. Some 70 years later it was sold to General Lygon who added to it. Much of the landscaping has been altered over the years.

BROMSGROVE, *Worcestershire* (8–SO9570), is an ancient and sizeable market town, still famed for its manufacture of nails. Although an industrial town, its situation on the Lickey Hills is surrounded by lush orchard country. On the summit of a hill stands the fine red sandstone Church of St John the Baptist. It is reached by a long flight of easy steps. The lime trees surrounding the church were planted in 1790. The 14th-cent. tower and spire soar 200 ft into the sky. Little remains of the original Norman church. The 13th-cent. chancel has a restored priests' doorway but the old chancel arch with its nail-head capitals is original. Chained to a 17th-cent. lectern is a copy of Jewel's *Apology*, once an obligatory accessory in all Anglican churches. There are two monuments, in alabaster, one with the effigies of Sir Humphrey and Lady Stafford dated 1450, the other of Sir John Talbot dated 1550. The churchyard has some fascinating early 18th-cent. tombstones but none more interesting than two commemorating a railway accident which befell two engine drivers on 11 November 1840. The inscription on each reads:

My engine now is cold and still,
No water does my boiler fill:
My coke affords its flames no more;
My days of usefulness are o'er!

Not far from the church is an old timbered house with a floodmark 4 ft up the wall com-

memorating a disastrous rise in the water in 1792. The Golden Lion at No. 7 Worcester Road is an enchanting 18th-cent. house with Gothic Venetian windows. The old Hop Pole Inn was previously in the High Street and was taken down, removed and rebuilt with some considerable restoration, in New Road. However, most of the 1572 decoration has been left unimpaired. Bromsgrove School, also on the Worcester Road, is an excellent late 17th-cent., two-storied, five-bayed house with a splendid doorway, pedimented on carved brackets. The school was considerably enlarged in Victorian times, but these buildings are not visible from the road. Sir Giles Scott built the New Chapel during the 1930s and completed his work in 1958. The poet A. E. Housman was at school here. The views from the 1,000-ft Beacon Hill, the highest point of the Lickey Hills, rewards the climb. Just outside Bromsgrove is the little village of **Barnt Green** with a gabled, timber-framed mansion, Barnt Green House, of early 17th-cent. date and considerable charm.

BROMYARD, *Herefordshire* (8–SO6554), stands on a plateau 400 ft above sea-level, surrounded by orchards and hopfields that rise to gorse-covered hills with splendid views in every direction. The Frome flows through this smallest of Hereford's market towns, about halfway between WORCESTER and LEOMINSTER on the A44. It has a solid Norman church with a low central tower and flanking aisles. On the south side is a Norman doorway with a curious figure of St Peter carrying huge keys above some rich carvings. The interior has some high arcades of five bays. The slenderness of the piers is accentuated by their having been further heightened at the beginning of the 19th cent. There is an interesting tub-shaped Norman font with interlaced and zigzag decoration. The church has an extraordinary number of tomb recesses both inside and outside, all dating from the 14th cent. There are a number of interesting black-and-white houses in the town. Outstanding is the Tower Hill House built in 1630, where Charles I sheltered on the night of 3 September 1644. Just behind the little Market Place in Rowberry Street is a 16th-cent. house. It is a timber-framed building with good diagonal bracing and well worth visiting. At the other end was the Elizabethan Grammar School now part of the modern secondary school.

Lower Brockhampton, 2 m. E., has a timber-framed manor house of about 1400, owned by the National Trust and open at advertised times.

BROUGHTON, *Oxfordshire* (5–SP4238), lies 2½ m. SW. of BANBURY on the B4035 road to SHIPSTON-ON-STOUR. The village is an ingress for its historic church and castle. To reach the church, turn left before the Saye and Sele Arms, an inn on the left-hand side of the village. From the church, the mass of Broughton Castle can best be seen for the first time.

The castle is a splendid example of English 14th-, 15th- and 16th-cent. imaginative yet utilitarian building. It was first erected by Sir John de Broughton above Sor Brook as a fortified stone manor house in 1306. Some 70 years later on the death of his sister, it passed into the possession of William de Wykeham, founder of WINCHESTER School and New College, OXFORD. In 1405 Thomas Wykeham converted the manor house into a castle, adding the battlements and gatehouse, the latter as it stands today across the moat. The grand-daughter of Sir William's sister married Sir William Fiennes, 2nd Lord Saye and Sele, in 1451. The castle, which is open to the public in the summer and by arrangement at other times of the year, is still owned and lived in by the Fiennes (pronounced Fines) family.

By the end of the 1500s, the Fiennes were enjoying a period of affluence and built on two stories, inserted huge mullioned and leaded windows, removed the battlements and gabled and re-roofed the house, to complete the pleasant Tudor building seen today. No less ambitious were the interior decorations carried out at the same time, adding a beautiful plaster ceiling with hanging bosses to the Great Hall. The house is filled with romantic vaulted passages and curious stairways. One of these is very ancient and leads to the private chapel with adjoining priest's room, one of the oldest rooms in the castle. It contains many historical treasures, paintings, and carved chimney-pieces. Celia Fiennes, the 17th-cent. traveller and diarist, was a member of the family.

During and after the Civil War the family showed considerable political astuteness and in this period William Fiennes, Lord Saye and Sele, promoted with Lord Brook a Puritan settlement in Connecticut. The name remains in Saybrook and Saybrook Point on the Connecticut River.

The nearby church has a fine stone screen of the Decorated period and the tower, spire and tracery are of the same date. The coloured tomb of the original Sir Thomas Broughton is in a good state of preservation and so are the monuments of the Wykehams and the 1st Viscount Saye and Sele who died in 1662. There are traces of early wall paintings on the north wall of the chancel and interesting, ancient glass roundels with heraldic devices. At the right time of year, the water lilies in the moat surrounding the mellowed brickwork of Broughton Castle are particularly beautiful.

BURFORD, *Oxfordshire* (5–SP2512), is situated 20 m. W. of OXFORD on the A40 road to NORTH-LEACH. It can rightfully claim to be one of the most beautiful of the Cotswold towns. Its wide High Street slopes not too steeply down to the sparkling little River Windrush crossed by a narrow three-arched bridge, and on the way down every variety of golden Cotswold stone house can be seen. Some remain unaltered in appearance since the 15th cent. The Bear Inn, the Grammar School and the Crown Inn all date from this period. So, too, does the Bull, but like many Burford houses it was later given a Georgian façade. The Great House in Witney Street is a typical example of this practice. Halfway down is the twin-gabled 15th-cent. Tolsey where once the wealthy wool merchants of Burford held their meetings. It now houses a museum which contains among its many interesting collections some ancient maces and charters as well as a perfect dolls' house with 18th-cent. rooms and costumes. Down by the river is the four-gabled 16th-cent. house built by Symon Wysdom and which he gave to the Grammar School. The ancient alms-houses nearby were rebuilt in 1828. The Priory was another famous Elizabethan house, which was rebuilt in the early 1800s. It still has its Tudor gables, and the heraldic arms over the doorway are a reminder that the famous William Lenthall, Speaker to the Long Parliament, once owned the house.

The fine church with its slender steeple is one of the largest churches in Oxfordshire. It lies at the bottom of the High Street on the east side in pleasant meadows with the River Windrush beyond it. The west doorway is pure Norman and so is the central part of the tower, to which another stage was added in the 15th cent. as a base for the spire. Most of what is seen in the church today dates from this period. The fine south porch has dual stories above the doorway, with pinnacled niches enshrining its ancient saints. The ceiling is fan vaulted and there are no less than five medieval screens dividing various chapels. The North Chapel houses the ornate tomb of the religiously divided Tanfield family. By contrast Speaker Lenthall at his own request has no monument, though he is buried in the church. Considering that Cromwell suppressed the Levellers' Rising in the churchyard in 1649, surprisingly little damage was done.

In A.D. 752 the Anglo-Saxons defeated the Mercians at Battle Edge, now a playing field near to the church. Even earlier a council was convened at Burford in A.D. 683 attended by the King of Mercia at which the date of Easter was fixed for the English Church, to conform with the rest of Western Christendom.

The sheep country which was the source of Burford's great wealth in the Middle Ages rises beyond the church fields to a plateau separating the Windrush and Evenlode Valleys; a rural scene of ever-changing beauty.

CASSINGTON, *Oxfordshire* (5–SP4510), is a short distance out of OXFORD between **Yarnton** and **Eynsham** just off the B4449. A pretty village with stone-built thatch-roofed cottages surrounding the green, it has a fine Norman church with a splendid Decorated spire visible to boaters on the upper reaches of the river a mile away. Norman doorways, arches and font are set in a Norman tripartite building, whose peaceful atmosphere is partly derived from the muted colour from roundels of old foreign glass set in the windows. The oak pews or benches are among the oldest in use in the country. The Jacobean canopied stalls came from Oxford Cathedral. The coloured screen and wall paintings are also of interest. The shroud brass on the walls is of a

16th-cent. Hebrew scholar, Thomas Nele.

Just beyond the village, turn right for Yarnton which is 4 m. NNW. of Oxford. Another old village with stone cottages, its early 17th-cent. Manor House was built by Sir Thomas Spencer. After much Civil War damage it declined into a farm-house but was restored towards the end of the 19th cent. and gardens, walks and terraced lawns were laid out.

The 13th-cent. church was considerably restored by Sir Thomas Spencer who built on a chapel which has two excellent English Baroque family tombs; the latter was erected in 1684 and shows the development of this style from the earlier font of 1609. It has a good Jacobean screen which contrasts favourably with the 15th-cent. alabaster reredos behind the high altar. This was found in extraordinary circumstances as part of the floor of a house. The glass is mostly old English and Flemish and was presented by an antiquarian benefactor at the end of the 18th cent.

South of the Yarnton–Cassington road at a junction of the A4141 is Eynsham, a typical Oxfordshire village or very small market town. Approached from the attractive Swinford Bridge, an 18th-cent. parapeted construction, a toll must be paid at the stone-shingled toll-house. The village square surrounded by stone houses has an old arcaded Market Hall which has served in turn as prison, Roman Catholic chapel and public library. The 14th-cent. church with its two-storied porch has been spoilt by much restoration.

CHALFORD, *Gloucestershire* (4–SO8902). In the Golden Valley SE. of STROUD where the Frome offers good fishing is the steep village of Chalford. On wooded slopes stand the handsome houses of the master-weavers whose broadcloth brought fortune to Stroud. On Chalford Hill is a 17th-cent. cottage where Huguenot weavers once lived. There are still some of the original mills dating from the 18th-cent. heyday of prosperity. The church was built in 1724 but was refashioned in the mid-19th cent. The sculpture over the south door was executed by John Thomas who also worked on Sir Charles Barry's HOUSES OF PARLIAMENT. There is some good modern carving inside. One of the most impressive houses in the area is the sternly Classical St Mary's Mill House with its balustraded roof line hiding a quaint dormer window. Skaiteshill House, which was built at the beginning of the 19th cent., has considerable charm; so, too, has Springfield House with its unusual Regency staircase. Most of the streets on this hillside are too steep and too narrow to admit cars. Grand views down the valley reward those who explore the little streets on foot.

CHALGROVE, *Oxfordshire* (5–SU6695), has a stream flowing each side of its charming village street in which the front doors of thatched cottages are reached by little bridges. Its Transitional parish church with unusually good 14th-cent. wall frescoes is found in the middle of a modern estate housing an overflow from OXFORD.

The Battle of Chalgrove Field saw the mortal wounding of John Hampden, whose opposition to Charles I's Ship Tax was one of the original factors which sparked off the Civil War. Prince Rupert coming from nearby **Chislehampton** led his troops to victory over the Parliamentary forces in June 1643. An obelisk ½ m. from the village marks the site of the battle, which covered a wide flat area that was easily converted into an airfield during the Second World War.

CHASTLETON, *Oxfordshire* (5–SP2429). On a wooded sloping ridge of the Cotswolds, protruding into Warwickshire, is the little village of Chastleton about 4 m. SE. of MORETON-IN-MARSH and 5 m. NW. of CHIPPING NORTON. It possesses a superb Jacobean house (open to the public) and a small church of considerable interest, much of it Norman. A hill-fort once stood here, strategically situated on the meeting point of the Gloucester, Worcester, Warwick and Oxford shires. An older house on the site was owned by Robert Catesby who had been obliged to sell his property to pay the colossal fine imposed by Queen Elizabeth for his adherence to the cause of the Earl of Essex. It was bought by an affluent Cotswold wool merchant, Walter Jones, who built the present lovely symmetric house with its five gables and two towers. The house, still in possession of the descendants of Walter Jones, contains most of the original furniture. The secret room where one of King Charles's supporters, Arthur Jones, hid after WORCESTER and escaped due to the ingenuity of his wife in drugging the wine drunk by his pursuers, can still be seen. The Long Gallery on the top floor and the state rooms are perfectly preserved, avoiding a museum atmosphere. There are many historical treasures to be seen, among them a Bible given by Charles I to Bishop Juxon, who ministered to the King on the day of his execution. There are also some interesting miniatures of the King's head made specially for Queen Henrietta Maria.

Much of the 17th-cent. garden still remains with some excellent examples of imaginative topiary. The dovecot built on arches dates from 1751.

CHEDWORTH, *Gloucestershire* (5–SP0511), is a stone village W. of the Fosse Way (A429) in the hills around the little stream that flows down to the River Coln. The countryside is breathtakingly beautiful. It has a handsome church; the five splendid windows lighting the tall nave give it a mainly Perpendicular aspect, but the north side has a good Norman arcade and aisle. The tower is Norman with a 13th-cent. belfry added. Inside, the church has a wealth of good carving and a 15th-cent. wine-glass pulpit as well as a Norman interlaced font. A little to the N. is Chedworth Roman Villa near **Yanworth**; the remains are perhaps the most comprehensive of their type in England. Set in 6½ acres of woodland owned by the National Trust, it is open to the public. Here you can learn something of life as it was lived between the years A.D. 180 and 350 during the

Cheltenham: the Promenade

Roman occupation of Britain. It was first discovered in 1864. The mosaic pavements and bath-house are remarkable. There is a museum housing the smaller finds from almost continuous excavations. In the hamlet of Yanworth, standing in a field among farm buildings, is a small Norman church with fine zigzag carving almost untouched by time or weather.

CHELTENHAM, *Gloucestershire* (4–SO9422), 10 m. from GLOUCESTER is intersected by the A40 and five radiating major routes, making it easily accessible from all major towns within a radius of a hundred miles or so. Set on a sheltered ridge between the high Cotswolds and the Severn Vale the town enjoys a pleasant and equable climate. Cheltenham is one of the finest spa towns in Europe, with a wealth of Regency houses bordering elegant squares, crescents, terraces and open spaces. Two hundred and fifty years ago it was a typical Cotswold stone village, but its fortune was made when a mineral spring was discovered in 1715 by means of watching the habits of some extremely healthy pigeons, according to tradition. Today the pigeon is incorporated in the city's crest standing on a roundel with bars of silver and blue symbolizing the waters. In 1738 the first pump room was built and 50 years later the spa was founded. George III, an inveterate frequenter of spas, visited the town in that year and set his seal of approval by staying at Bayshill Lodge. In this period of imperial expansion it was rapidly discovered that the mineral waters were extremely beneficial to the military officers and colonial administrators returning from the tropics with liver complaints. The medicinal reputation of the spa grew so rapidly that a small number of brilliant architects were entrusted with plans to lay out an entirely

new town. Here elegance and good taste were to provide a setting in which people steeped in classical culture and with ample means for enjoying their period of retirement could live in comfort. Cheltenham was thus rebuilt as a residential town with wide streets and tree-shaded open spaces between 1800 and 1840 in the Grecian idiom, with occasional Gothic or Italianate variations. In spite of war damage and certain modern desecrations it has, on the whole, retained its unique character.

J. B. Papworth was responsible for much of the best architecture: Lansdown Place and Montpellier Parade, among similar thoroughfares, and the Rotunda, the design for its dome being based on the Pantheon in Rome. Montpellier Walk with its shops separated by caryatids must be one of the most unusual shopping precincts in the world. Many of the houses and villas still have their splendid Regency ironwork balconies and verandas. All this careful planning culminated in the Promenade which was finished about 1825. The Municipal Offices dating from this period are probably best seen floodlit at night when their detail shows to advantage. The Promenade is dominated at the far end by the Queens Hotel built in 1838 with Classical colonnades by another renowned Cheltenham architect, W. Jearrad. The Imperial Gardens opposite have colourful flower displays all the year round. Outstanding in a town with so many fine examples of Regency architecture is the Pittville Pump Room built in 1825 by J. B. Forbes in a parkland setting as an assembly hall suited to the growing social life of the spa. The interior of the dome, which has been restored since the Second World War, is particularly beautiful. Out on the BATH road are two of Cheltenham's famous schools. Cheltenham College for Boys was originally built between 1841 and 1843 by J. Wilson in early Gothic Revival style. As the college grew in importance, particularly as a public school for sons of Indian Army officers, considerable extensions to the building were made. Nearby is Cheltenham Ladies' College, founded by Miss Beale, the ardent Victorian champion of good education for girls.

Although rightly concerned with preserving its invaluable heritage, the town is none the less a lively modern community. Its industries include the design and assembly of jet aircraft; the manufacture of watches and clocks and small high-precision instruments. It manufactures air-venting equipment and houses the world's largest makers of thermostatic mixing valves. On the cultural side it has established the Cheltenham Festival of Music as one of the most important in the country. While providing a platform for modern British composers is one of the Festival's main concerns, it is equally possible to hear a superb Bach choir, listen to jazz or enjoy folk-singing in the Shaftsbury Hall. The Festival, with many "fringe" attractions, begins in the first half of July. In October there is a Festival of Literature which each year grows in popularity. Racing and cricket are the predominant sports. The Cheltenham Gold Cup is one of the main features of the English racing year. The attractive race-course is out at Prestbury Park to the N. of the town.

CHINNOR, *Oxfordshire* (5–SP7500), lies under the shelter of the Chiltern woods, just off the A40, a few minutes' drive out of THAME. It would be easy to be put off by the unsightly cement works, yet it possesses a moated manor house and a Decorated church which contains two beautiful 14th-cent. stained-glass windows, their greens, yellows and browns still brilliant, superbly leaded and depicting among other subjects St Lawrence and the proto-martyr St Alban. The early brasses are among the best in the country. Particularly fine is that of Reginald de Malyns, 1385, and some depicting vested priests are among the earliest extant. The carvings on the mouldings are also outstanding.

CHIPPING CAMPDEN, *Gloucestershire* (5–SP1539), near the Worcestershire border is 4 m. E. of BROADWAY. It is one of the most typical towns of the affluent wool merchants of the 14th and 15th cents. There are many gabled stone houses with oriel, dormer and mullioned windows with medieval monastic-looking doorways giving a good impression of how many of the richer market towns looked during the late Middle Ages, for instance the arched and timber-roofed Market Hall and the house in the main street of William Grevel, ancestor of the Warwick family, which has a beautiful upthrusting two-storied gabled bay window built about 1380. Many of the houses date from the 17th cent., among them the attractive group of almshouses built in 1624, raised above street level. At the end of the town stands a magnificent Perpendicular church, with an elegant 15th-cent. pinnacled tower. There are some Norman traces and 13th-cent. stone work; the porch with scratch dials and north aisle and chancel all date from the 14th cent. The tall nave arcades with their soaring columns, the clerestory and chancel arch, were all built at the peak of Chipping Campden's prosperity in the 15th cent. The unusual window above the chancel arch portraying the Last Judgment was inserted during the 19th cent. with commendable care so as not to disturb the superb proportions. Among the excellent brasses are those of William Grevel and his wife set into the chancel floor before the high altar. One side chapel is leased perpetually to the Noel family who were linked in marriage with Sir Baptist Hicks, a philanthropist of considerable standing with Charles I, who did not hesitate to borrow very considerable funds from his friend. Sir Baptist Hicks built Campden House, a beautiful country residence, but ordered it to be burnt to the ground rather than let it fall into the hands of the Parliamentarians. The ruins, comprising a habitable lodge, two pavilions and an almonry, can be seen a stone's throw from the church. In the Noel Chapel is a fine 17th-cent. bust of his daughter Penelope and her sister-in-law Anne Noel, and an imposing monument to Sir Baptist, who became 1st Viscount Campden, and his wife. There is a rare collection of fine English embroidery, some dating back to the time of Richard II. Altar frontals, dorsals (one with angels' wings lined with peacock feathers), orphreys and a beautifully preserved medieval cope are displayed under glass on the west wall of the church.

A little way out of the town on the top of Broadway Hill is Broadway Tower, a gazebo built in 1797; a Gothic Revival fantasy, it has machicolations and three circular towers.

CHIPPING NORTON, *Oxfordshire* (5–SP 3127), is the highest Cotswold town in the county. One of the old wool towns, its prefix "Chipping" comes from an Old English word for market, and it was prosperous as early as the 13th cent. The typical Victorian pinnacled and turreted tweed mill built in the 19th cent. brought much-needed employment to the town which was gradually decaying. Once a great Norman castle stood on the mounds above the beautiful wool church which still dominates the town. The usual wide Cotswold market place contains many good examples of the 16th- and 17th-cent. stone-masons' craft. Outstanding are Henry Cornishe's Almshouses built in 1640. There are several well-built inns, particularly the 17th-cent. White Hart.

The Parish Church of St Mary is mainly of 14th- to 15th-cent. construction, though it incorporates much earlier features. The polygonal porch with a room above it has fascinating bosses of strange creatures tying the ribs of the vaulting. The Perpendicular clerestory fills the church with light from its vast expanse of glass. A lot of the medieval stonework has been restored. The font is 15th-cent. and its intricate tracery has a pleasing delicacy.

The Market Hall was built in 1842 to blend with the Cotswold atmosphere of the town and is an outstanding example of the work of the architect George Stanley Repton.

A brewery and a glove factory continue to ensure prosperity to the town.

CHIPPING SODBURY, *Gloucestershire* (4–ST7282), is an attractive little market town on the A432 just off the A46 from Old Sodbury. It has a typical wide Cotswold main street, with several good Georgian brick as well as some rather severe Cotswold stone houses. At the top of the street stands a 16th-cent. market-cross. Although its Town Hall is 15th-cent., it is masked by a Victorian Tudor façade built on to it in 1858. The fine 15th-cent. Church of St John the Baptist with its lofty pinnacled tower was considerably restored in 1869 by Street who built London's LAW COURTS. There is a 14th-cent. doorway with an enthroned Christus and a 13th-cent. chancel arch with a curious carving of a master clothworker and his wife. The unusual pulpit with its pinnacled canopy is reached through a hole in one of the nave pillars supporting the barrelled roof of the church. It had been completely lost and was rediscovered by Street when he was restoring the church.

Two m. SE. of Chipping Sodbury lies **Dodington Park**, landscaped by Capability Brown. Many generations of Codringtons have lived in the splendid early Regency Dodington House built by James Wyatt in 1796–1817. He gave the beautifully proportioned house a façade of six Corinthian columns surmounted by an imposing pediment. Inside is one of Wyatt's most elegant staircases, which must have been seen at its best during balls given to celebrate the victory of Trafalgar where one of the Codringtons fought with Lord Nelson. The imposing stables are well worth a visit. Wyatt built the little Classical church about six years after the house. The lakes and lodges in the park make for an interesting drive. Dodington is open to the public during the summer months.

CHURCHILL, *Oxfordshire* (5–SP2824). Two m. SW. of CHIPPING NORTON is the little hill village of Churchill. It is of historical interest as the birthplace in 1732 of Warren Hastings, the first Governor-General of India. He was impeached on charges of corruption and cruelty during one of the longest trials in English history, which ended with his acquittal and a handsome annuity from the East India Company. The house where he was born still stands in the village. So does the house of William Smith, born here in 1769, who first mapped the rock structure of England and was the founder of modern geological science. The Georgian Gothic church was copied from various OXFORD sources, its tower being a ⅔ scale reproduction of Magdalen Tower.

CIRENCESTER, *Gloucestershire* (5–SP0201), claims with some justification the title of Capital of the Cotswolds. It was certainly the capital of the Dobuni when as Corinium Dobunorum in A.D. 43 it became one of the chief Roman administrative centres for South-West England. By the 4th cent. its situation at the hub of a network of Roman roads, the Icknield Way, Ermine Street and Fosse Way, made it the second most important town in Britain. With the withdrawal of the legions, it went into a complete decline until a later Anglo-Saxon town was built. It slowly regained its prosperity with the development of sheep rearing on the rich Cotswold meadowlands surrounding the town. This was due to the industry of the monks who completed a great abbey church in the reign of Henry II. Dissolved by Henry VIII, nothing remains of this vast abbey other than the Spital Gateway, a late Norman construction which stands on the site of the northern end of the abbey precincts. Such was the tremendous wealth of the wool merchants in the 15th cent. that they were able to build one of the greatest "wool churches" in the kingdom. The Parish Church of St John the Baptist with its superb tower and three-storied fan-vaulted porch which faces the market place has been judged one of the most beautiful Perpendicular churches in England. The lofty nave is supported by six great arches on either side, and above these a tall clerestory with fine glass reaches to the richly bossed and panelled roof, sending down a flood of light. Both the east and west windows have rich medieval glass which reflects glowing colours on to the stone and woodwork below. The painted and gilded wine-glass pulpit is a very rare pre-Reformation example of this unusual design. There are many fine brasses of wool and wine merchants to be seen, particularly in the Lady Chapel. It is worth walking some distance from the church to appreciate the parapeting, embattlements and crocketed pinnacles which distinguish the skyline of Cirencester. The church possesses some priceless silver plate which is occasionally on view to the public.

Apart from some old houses in Coxwell Street, most of the interesting buildings date from the 18th cent. The Palladian building housing Lloyds Bank in Castle Street is a particularly good example. The Corinium Museum in Park Street is a treasure-house of Roman finds. Excavations have established the complete lay-out of the Roman town, and some well-preserved and vivid mosaic pavements can be seen in the museum, together with other Roman relics. The Roman amphitheatre is just outside the town at the Querns earthworks.

Cirencester House, seat of the Earl of Bathurst, has a 3,000-acre park, complete with a charming folly built in 1721 by the 1st Earl of Bathurst aided by Alexander Pope. It is called Alfred's Hall, a buttressed, castellated false ruin satirizing every possible quirk of medieval building. Pope stayed here to recover from the ardours of translating the Iliad. A roofed rusticated stone seat on the edge of the avenues called the Seven Rides is named after him. Although the house is not open to the public, the park, with its superb 5-m.-long avenue of chestnut trees can be enjoyed freely by everyone. It is an important centre for polo and matches take place from May to September on most Sundays, in which some of the country's best players participate.

The Royal Agricultural College to the SW. of the town is housed in a huge mansion designed in Gothic style by Daukes.

At **Daglingworth**, to the NW. of Cirencester, the Church of the Holy Rood retains features of its Anglo-Saxon predecessor. On the walls of the nave and aisle are three Anglo-Saxon carvings discovered on the site of the priory nearby. They are a Christ in Majesty, a Crucifixion, and a burly St Peter, brandishing a key.

CLENT HILLS, THE, *Worcestershire* (8–SO 9380), lie 3 m. SE. of STOURBRIDGE and are largely in the care of the National Trust. They rise N. and E. of the village of Clent to a height of 1,035 ft. The area covers the two main heights of the Clent and Walton Hills and all the common-land, farmland and woods of the Clatterbach Valley. On the east side of Clent Hill is St Kenelm's Chapel, said to mark the site where this Anglo-Saxon saint was buried; according to legend, he was murdered while still a boy. The chapel has a Norman doorway. Nothing remains of a town which once stood on the hillside. These lovely hills draw hikers from all over the industrial Midlands. The village church has a well-restored late 12th-cent. arcade and a good waggon roof. Much restoration took place in the 1860s. **Walton Hall** is a red-brick Georgian mansion. Of Clent House only the stables with a fine cupola, dated 1709, remain.

CLIFTON HAMPDEN, *Oxfordshire* (5–SU 5495), is a Thameside village 7 m. S. of OXFORD on the A415 from ABINGDON to DORCHESTER. The river is crossed by Sir Gilbert Scott's six-ribbed arched brick bridge, which takes the traveller into Berkshire. This popular weekend spot was chosen by Jerome K. Jerome as a setting for one of the riotous incidents in his *Three Men in a Boat*. There are several attractive Elizabethan cottages. The Plough Inn has an ancient crutched foundation and the church, situated on a cliff along the river, has some very early features remaining in Scott's almost complete restoration of the building in 1844.

COLWALL, *Herefordshire* (8–SO7542), on the west side of the Malvern Hills has two major claims on the visitor's attention. It was where Elizabeth Barrett Browning spent her youth, at a house called Hope End which no longer exists. It is only 3 m. NW. of the famous **Hereford Beacon**, one of the most dramatic of the summits of the Malvern range. Situated on the Herefordshire-Worcestershire border at 1,114 ft above sea-level, it is the site of a remarkable Iron Age camp covering 44 acres and with a citadel formed of a thick stone wall, and some 50 yds in circumference, 60 ft above the fosse. The intricate network of ditches and earthworks cut into the hillside must have made it a formidable stronghold to attack. Besides

the ramparts an earthwork extends to N. and S., 1½ m. in circumference and enclosing 20 acres. Very early pottery has identified the Celtic people who first fortified the camp; it seems probable that the Normans also took advantage of its strategic position and strengthened the citadel. As late as 1405 Owen Glendower is said to have rallied forces here in the struggle between England and Wales. On the south side below the camp is a rock with a cave cut into it, known as Hermits or Clutters Cave. Nearby is a spring called Walm's Well for which medicinal claims are made. The 13th-cent. Colwall church has a good south arcade and entrancing carvings of medieval men and women peering from behind the leaves of the capitals. A good walk along the crest of the hills leads 4 m. N. to the **Worcestershire Beacon**.

Not far away to the W., about 5 m. NNW. of LEDBURY on the A4154, is **Bosbury**, one of the county's most important hop-growing centres. Its grand late Norman red-stone church contains two splendid Elizabethan tombs of 1573. There are attractive black-and-white houses in its short street and the hop kilns characteristic of this borderland. The Crown Inn has a fine panelled room of 1571. N. of Colwall and also on the A4145 is **Cradley**, a sizable village sprawled out on the plain at the foot of the Malvern Hills with good groups of black-and-white houses. The most remarkable of these is the 15th-cent. parish hall with an overhanging story on brackets with exceptionally attractive timberwork. The church with its sturdy Norman tower has been much restored. It is believed by some that the 20-ft timbers supporting the interior of the tower were taken from an earlier Anglo-Saxon church. It has an amusing panel dated 1795 of admonitions to bell-ringers.

Ye Gentlemen Ringers both far and near,
That are disposed for to Ring here;
Observe this law and mark it well.
The Man that Overthrow his Bell;
Six-pence he to the Clerk must pay,
Before that he go hence away,
If he Ring with Glove, Spur or Hat,
Six-pence he must pay for that.
If he either Curse or Swear,
Six-pence must pay while you are here,
This is not a place to Quarrel in,
To Curse and Swear it is a Sin.

COMPTON VERNEY, *Warwickshire* (9–SP 3052), is a fine Classical mansion with its West Range built in 1714 (reputedly by Vanbrugh) in a sternly Palladian style. It was created for George Verney, 12th Lord Willoughby de Broke, who was Dean of WINDSOR. The Verneys lived in this wooded valley from 1440 to 1921. Before then Alice Perrers, Edward III's mistress, had owned the estate, and before her the Norman Murdaks. The house lies just off the Fosse Way on the B4086 between Kineton and Wellesbourne Hastings on the WARWICK to Kineton road. By 1780 Robert Adam began his work at Compton Verney. He gave the windows more importance and spaced them more widely. On the ground floor he put in a splendid Venetian window of a type he often used. Although the interior work is not particularly notable, the setting of the house is beautifully landscaped. Its cedar-bordered lake is crossed by a three-arched bridge, also attributed to Robert Adam. The grounds are reputed to have been laid out by Capability Brown, who certainly designed the chapel in 1772. This has some interesting 16th-cent. brasses of Verney forebears as well as alabaster tombs and sarcophagi. The 16th-cent. stained-glass windows for which the chapel was famed were sold and removed to America.

COMPTON WYNYATES, *Warwickshire* (9– SP3341), is one of the most visually satisfying houses in England. It lies in a hollow of hills stretching from Brailes to Tysoe and Edge Hill, just 8 m. W. of BANBURY and 11 m. SE. of STRAT-FORD-UPON-AVON. It is a composition of early Tudor pink brick, weathered wood and mellow stone. It was built from 1480 over a period of about 40 years. The earliest records show that in 1204 Philip de Compton, direct ancestor of the present owner, the Marquess of Northampton, was in possession of the late Norman manor house. The present house was begun when Edmund de Compton pulled down the old Norman house and built four diapered brick wings enclosing the courtyard, exactly as they stand today. The house passed to Edmund's son William who in 1493 was a young page to Prince Henry, afterwards Henry VIII. Some 19 years later, William distinguished himself at the Battle of Tournai and was knighted. Among his other royal rewards was the vast but ruined Fulbrook Castle near WARWICK. From here, he brought much of the material to build his battlemented towers and the great porch which still stands and has the arms of Henry VIII and Catherine of Aragon above the original door with its curiously contrived locks. From Fulbrook, too, came material to build the great hall; its four-bayed timbered roof was brought over intact and re-erected. The elegant oriel window likewise came from that castle. The minstrel gallery and carved panels depicting the Battle of Tournai all date from this period. The carved friezes in the hall are of later date. The two fine Early English portraits painted on wood are of John Talbot, 1st Earl of Shrewsbury who led the English against Joan of Arc, and Margaret his wife who was a daughter of Richard Beauchamp, Earl of Warwick. The 16th-cent. tapestry of Cupid picking grapes is believed to have been designed by Raphael's pupil Giulio Romano. The dining-room, hung with portraits of Compton ancestors, has a fine Elizabethan or perhaps early Jacobean ceiling. So, too, has the drawing-room, with its Giorgione painting. The house is filled with secret passages, stairways, sliding panels and hidden rooms. It is said that there are nearly 100 rooms and about 300 windows. Henry VIII did sleep here, in a room that has an unusual ceiling with curious bands and squares in its design.

In 1644, during the Civil War, the house was besieged and finally captured. Four hundred Parliamentary troops were billeted here in what are still called the barracks. The church was completely demolished at this time. The house was finally returned to the Comptons on condition that the moat was filled in and a fine of £20,000 paid. The gardens are remarkable for the imaginatively sculptured yews.

Compton Pike, a spire not quite ½ m. SW. of the house, is a beacon believed to have been built at the time of the Armada; it is also said to have indicated the position of Compton-in-the-Hole, a one-time alternative name to Compton Wynyates.

The church constructed from materials salvaged from its predecessor wrecked in the Civil War period is a perfect Restoration example of its kind. There is no chancel, just a central arcade which still has its original box pews. The plaster ceiling has two paintings of the firmaments, one by day and one by night. There are 17 hatchments or family arms hung on its walls. Many of the Compton effigies which were thrown into the moat by the Parliamentary forces were recovered and can be seen at the east end of the chapel. A bronze plaque to John Berrill reminds posterity that it was a good steward who saved Compton Wynyates from destruction. Reckless gambling and a disastrously costly election made the Lord Northampton of the time decide to pull the house down. The contents were sold in 1774 but Berrill merely bricked up the windows. Sixty years later the 2nd Marquess and his son were thus able to restore the house to its full Tudor glory, without any material alterations to the original 15th- and 16th-cent. buildings.

CORNWELL, *Oxfordshire* (5–SP2727). Within easy walking distance of CHIPPING NORTON on the A44 to MORETON-IN-MARSH, the first lane to the left is signposted to Cornwell. A sharp turn leads to one of the prettiest villages in this area, nestling in a fold of hills with a stream running through it. It has a fine Georgian house with formal gardens, which, like the rest of the village, has had restoration work done by Clough Williams-Ellis of Portmeirion fame. The little Norman church has two good doorways and a round 12th-cent. font set on four lions. The church, which suffered poor Victorian restoration, is somewhat dark and the little chancel arch with beautifully scalloped corbels might well be missed.

COVENTRY, *Warwickshire* (9–SP3379), is a thriving city, with a growing population of 350,000. It probably owes its origin to the erection in the 7th cent. of an Anglo-Saxon convent. However, it was the later Benedictine abbey founded by Leofric, Earl of Mercia in the 11th cent. that gave the town its first impetus to growth. No account of Coventry can ignore the legend of Godiva, who, it is said, in order to obtain relief for the town from the taxes levied by her husband Leofric, rode naked through the city, modesty

Compton Wynyates in its beautiful setting in a fold of the Warwickshire hills

Kenneth Scowen

Coventry Cathedral: the Graham Sutherland tapestry

British Travel Association

preserved only by the length of her hair. The first recorded instance of the story only dates back to 1235; with the embellishment of a "Peeping Tom" not added until a century later. In A.D. 1553 it was granted its first charter.

Coventry, centrally situated, has always owed much to its communications but never more than today, when it is well-served by the motorway network and an electrified and modernized railway. From the Middle Ages, wool, needles and leather all contributed to its prosperity. The mechanization of the 19th cent. brought the manufacture of sewing-machines and bicycles right into the city. The Daimler Company produced the first English motorcar in 1898 and the car industry increased rapidly, giving rise in its turn to aircraft production. Workers not only from every part of Britain but from all over the world have been drawn here. The city has multiplied its population six times since the turn of the century.

In November 1940, much of the city was wiped out by a devastating air raid which almost completely destroyed the Cathedral Church of St Michael (it had only been raised to this dignity in 1918, the church previously being within the diocese of LICHFIELD), leaving only the magnificent medieval tower and spire standing.

In 1951 an open architectural competition for a new cathedral was won by Basil Spence, since knighted. The new cathedral, which draws thousands of visitors from all over the world, has been acclaimed as one of the most striking examples of modern architecture. The first impression of a long cliff of rosy sandstone with vertical lines suggesting Gothic buttresses is unforgettable, especially

for visitors who have not seen this delicately coloured stone before; the canopied link between the entrance to the new church and the charred walls of the old is a gesture of genius. Going in through John Hutton's engraved glass doors, the eye is at once held by a suggestion of great length. Yet the nave is only 270 ft long and 80 ft wide. The interior is coloured by deep greens, golden yellows, rose and vivid reds, blues and sombre purples from the splendid glass, mostly stretching from floor to ceiling. These glass windows, conceived and executed by Laurance Lee, Geoffrey Clarke and Keith New, with the Great Baptistry window by John Piper, have done much to give back to England her medieval fame for stained glass. Everything seems to culminate, as Sir Basil Spence intended it should, on the massive block of the altar stone surmounted by Geoffrey Clarke's metal abstraction of Cross and Crucified. The final focal point is the 75-ft-high tapestry designed by Graham Sutherland and woven in France, representing in almost Byzantine terms the Redeeming Saviour of the World. The green background sets off the muted whites, reds and purples woven into Christ's robes and the four medallions of Evangelists. Between the feet of Christ stands Man, diminutive, yet thrust against the background with dynamic force. The chapels are all designed to have the same sense of immediacy and involvement in modern life. Notable is the Chapel of Christ the Servant, with its maps giving the names and positions of all the industrial plants of Coventry. The Chapel of Unity has for its theme understanding among all races and religions. Finally, the visitor is likely to be impressed by the rugged Epstein bronzes of St

Michael and the force of Evil, two separate figures, outside the cathedral, against the walls immediately to the right of the flight of steps leading up to the entrance to the cathedral.

Few buildings remain from the medieval city. Most important of these is the Church of Holy Trinity, facing the new Precinct and thus immediately behind the cathedral. The proximity of two such important churches as the old destroyed St Michael's and Holy Trinity is a reflection of a medieval feud when the townspeople were roughly divided between the prior and the earl and were continually at loggerheads. Particularly splendid are the timbered ceilings, the 15th-cent. brass eagle lectern and pulpit of the same period. The other historic place of worship deserving mention is the Collegiate Church of St John the Baptist first built by the wife of Edward II. Nearby stand two black-and-white gabled houses. Bond's Hospital is the more important, facing the north side of St John's. Founded by a Coventry draper, Thomas Bond, in 1506 for the care of 12 elderly poor men, it still possesses some excellent period furniture. The other house is Bablake School alongside Hill Street and has a history much antedating its conversion to a school for boys. The only other medieval buildings of consequence, apart from two well-preserved city gates, is St Mary's Hall in Bayley Lane. It was built in 1340 as the hall of the Merchant's Guild. It possesses, as well as some fine early stained glass, a superb tapestry of the late 15th cent. depicting the Assumption of the Blessed Virgin with the kneeling figure of Henry VII and his wife. There is also a minstrel gallery.

The city has been in the throes of rebuilding ever since the Second World War. All this springs from forward-looking post-war planning. The Precinct in the city centre was the first stage. It started with what is now the Leofric Hotel facing Holy Trinity. The traffic-free shopping area has provided a prototype for all the new town centres of Britain. The architecture is undistinguished in the main, but the scale is more human and the place easier to use than some more pretentious centres.

The University of Warwick, whose first building took shape in 1964, has perhaps the finest campus in the country, covering an area of about 400 acres. Its white-tiled residential, tutorial and laboratory blocks are attractive against the foliaged green background. It houses 800 of its present 1,600 roll of students but is to cater for more than 15,000 in the foreseeable future. A £300,000 Arts and Sports Centre is planned. The university is situated 4 m. out of Coventry on the A46 WARWICK road at Gibbet Hill.

Arrangements can always be made to visit the great Coventry motorcar factories by prior application.

CRASWALL, *Herefordshire* (8–SO2836), is in wild, beautifully wooded country on the Herefordshire side of the Black Mountains, some 1,000 ft up with splendid views down the valley. It can be best reached by taking the road W. out of Vow-

church in the GOLDEN VALLEY to the upland village of **Michaelchurch Escley** with its stream rushing down to meet the River Monnow and the secluded 17th-cent. Michaelchurch Court. The village church has on its north wall a very rare painting of Christ of the Trades surrounded by shears, axes, ploughs and flails. The road crosses the Monnow by an inn and follows the west bank of the river until it crosses back again into Craswall. The scenery is as impressive as any in the Black Mountain country and the search for the ancient Craswall Priory is now made easy by the new road into Hay. It was once a small Benedictine priory founded in 1222 by Roger de Lacy as an affiliation of the Norman Grandmont congregation which had only three houses in England. It was suppressed in the reign of Edward VI and its revenues diverted to Christ College, CAMBRIDGE. It is in the care of the Royal Commission for Historic Monuments. Many interesting fragments of painted glass, excellent encaustic tiles and a leaden altar casket for relics have been discovered. It is said that the present chancel window in the little parish church a mile away was originally brought from the priory. Many of the secluded farm-houses hereabouts are Tudor and in default of roads can only be reached on horseback; this is a paradise for romantics and escapists.

CROFT CASTLE, *Herefordshire* (8–SO4565), is 5 m. from LEOMINSTER and 9 m. from LUDLOW, and reached by turning right at Cock Gate just past the hamlet of Bircher on the B4362. The 1,363-acre parkland of Croft Castle is a remarkable property, now owned by the National Trust, which has been in the Croft family since the time of the Conquest, with one break of some 170 years from about 1750 when it was sold. The Crofts bought it back in 1923 and it passed to the National Trust in 1957. The castle as seen today retains its 14th- and 15th-cent. walls and pink-stone round towers. Its castellated front and interior was much modified during the 16th and 17th cents. The Gothicized bays on each side of the gabled front and the fine Gothic staircase and ceilings were added by the family of Thomas Johnes of Hafod between 1750 and 1760. The Blue and Gold Room with a splendid chimney is impressive. The porch was added as late as 1914. The park has some of the finest Spanish chestnut, oak and beech avenues in the county. It is open at advertised times in the summer months. The attractive little church nestled right up to the house contains the splendid tomb of Sir Richard Croft and his wife, who was a widow of one of the Mortimers. The effigy of Sir Richard is resplendent in finely carved armour copied from that he wore at the Battle of TEWKESBURY. Also on the estate N. of the park is the nearly 1,000-ft-high edge of Leinthall Common with an Iron Age camp. The fortification covered an area of about 24 acres and was occupied from 400 B.C. to A.D. 50. It is worth the climb as apart from its antiquarian interest it is said that more than a dozen counties can be seen from the summit.

CROOME D'ABITOT, *Worcestershire* (8–SO8944), lies mid-way between PERSHORE and GREAT MALVERN, with the M5 motorway actually intersecting the estate. Although now a school, Croome Court is one of the most impressive mansions in the county. It was built in 1751 by Capability Brown for the 6th Earl of Coventry. Some 10 years later Robert Adam was commissioned to complete the interior decorating. Much of this has been dismantled and sold; one of the ceilings was shipped intact to the United States. The house retains its correct Palladian exterior, built of Bath stone, and the library its fine Venetian window and the elegant bookcase specially designed by Adam. The gate piers with the Coade stone urn can still be seen as well as the rotunda, but many of the 18th-cent. structures in the park are becoming derelict. Quite outstanding is the Panorama Tower built by Adam in 1766, looking towards Severn Stoke. Beyond the lawn is a fine temple façade also by Adam. Still further away towards **Earls Croome** is a magnificent "eye-catcher" called **Dunstall Castle**. It stands on the western edge of Dunstall Common. The church, one of the earliest examples of the Gothic Revival, was intended principally as a mausoleum for the Coventry family and its interior elegance is typified by the black-and-white marble late Renaissance tomb of Thomas, 1st Lord Coventry. The wooden font is exquisite.

CROPREDY, *Oxfordshire* (5–SP4646). Six m. N. of BANBURY at Cropredy Bridge was fought one of the fiercest battles of the Civil War in 1644. The Royalists under the leadership of Charles I were encamped on the east bank of the Cherwell. The Parliamentary forces led by Waller believed they could pierce the defences of their opponents and Waller gave orders for the attack across the bridge. During the mêlée the villagers, fearing for their church and its treasures, withdrew a beautiful eagle lectern from the building and dropped it in the river. However, the fighting reached such a pitch that much of the artillery of the Parliamentarians was lost and the Royalists, seizing their advantage, pushed back Waller's troops. After his victory the King spent the night at nearby Williamscote, a fine house built by Walter Calcolt in 1568 and still standing. In the ensuing confusion the villagers forgot the spot where they had dropped their precious lectern and it was not until many years later that it was recovered from the mud and restored to the parish church. This 14th-cent. building with part of its "Doom" fresco over the chancel arch still discernible, possesses many relics of the battle.

The walks along the river and canal with their many locks and bridges are rewarding for connoisseurs of canal engineering.

CUDDESDON, *Oxfordshire* (5–SP5902), is one of the many lovely little villages just outside OXFORD. Only 5 m. out of the city, it is within walking distance of Cowley. Two other villages, **Denton** and **Garsington**, are almost linked together in the pleasant undulating countryside

which rises to 400 ft in places. This village saw much of the terror of the Civil War in 1644 and the Manor House and old palace of the Bishops of Oxford were burnt down to prevent them falling into the hands of the Parliamentarians. The palace was rebuilt by Dr Fell. The Theological College founded by Bishop Wilberforce was designed by G. E. Street who built London's LAW COURTS.

The cruciform parish church is set on a green slope and is partly Norman, with a particularly good door of this period. The late Transitional builders achieved an effect of lightness in the tower arches springing from the massive 13th-cent. piers. The village slopes down to the river which is crossed by a bridge. Nearby is an 18th-cent. watermill still in working order.

DITCHLEY PARK, *Oxfordshire* (5–SP3821), 5 m. SE. of CHIPPING NORTON, 1½ m. off the A34 beyond **Kiddington**, is one of the greatest 18th-cent. classical houses in the county. Designed by Gibbs (who built the Radcliffe Camera in OXFORD) for the 2nd Earl of Lichfield, it stands on the site of an earlier building owned by the Lee family, ancestors of the famous Confederate general of the American Civil War, Robert E. Lee. Here James I made his headquarters when hunting in WYCHWOOD FOREST. The Lees were ennobled by Charles II when Edward, the 1st Earl, married the king's daughter by the Duchess of Cleveland. Capability Brown laid out the lovely gardens and William Kent was responsible for most of the elegant interiors, including the splendid Great Hall. It is open to the public for three months during the summer. It is of recent historical interest as the weekend headquarters of Sir Winston Churchill, who directed operations here during the Second World War. The house is now used mainly as an Anglo-American Conference Centre under the Ditchley Foundation.

DORCHESTER, *Oxfordshire* (5–SU5794), is an ancient settlement of great importance, its history going back to the Bronze Age. It is a village of great charm easily reached from OXFORD, 8 m. away, and ½ m. above the meeting of the waters of the Rivers Thame and Thames. Its earliest communities built ditches, some as much as 36 ft wide, discovered by aerial photographs taken over the Dyke Hills. The Romans founded the town of Dorocina between the present village and the River Thames. An altar to Jupiter and Augustus has been discovered here, as well as tessellated pavements, Roman coins and other remains. The town was at this time well situated on the road linking Silchester with Alchester. In A.D. 634, the Milanese missionary Birinus came to preach to the West Saxons and here he baptized Cynegils, King of Wessex, and founded a bishopric whose territory reached up to the borders of Northumbria. Some years later, the see was transferred to WINCHESTER. The Venerable Bede tells the story at some length. Nothing remains of the old Anglo-Saxon cathedral, but the remarkable abbey built by the late Norman

Augustinian canons remains. It was enlarged in the 13th and 14th cents. Although much restored by Butterfield and Scott in the 19th cent., nothing could diminish the beauty of this 200-ft-long church. Its three outstanding treasures are the superb Norman lead font, arched and foliated with graceful sitting figures; its Jesse window with tree branches of stone enshrining the original carved figures and richly coloured glass telling the story of Mary's genealogy; and its beautiful 14th-cent. three-seated sedilia under the south window with its piscina. The finely traceried canopies have curious triangular windows with very old glass depicting the life of St Birinus.

To see the village to the best advantage the motorist should leave his car and go on foot. There is a variety of interesting old houses, particularly the gabled George Hotel, which stands almost opposite the abbey gates. The old School House contains some remains of the priory which was pulled down at the Dissolution. The bridge was constructed in 1815. A short way beyond the bridge is the fascinating hamlet of Overy with old thatched cottages, one of them with the intriguing name of Mollymops.

DOWN AMPNEY, *Gloucestershire* (5–SU 1097), 5½ m. SSE. on the A419 from CIREN-CESTER going towards SWINDON the fourth un-classified road to the left leads to Down Ampney, the most charming of all the many Cotswold Ampneys in the Upper Thames countryside. Surrounded by pleasant old cottages is an ancient village cross which was restored with a canopied Calvary in the 19th cent. by the owners of the beautiful gabled Tudor manor house. The manor is separated from the mostly Early English parish church by a large yew hedge. The fine church tower is surmounted by its original spire with a gilded weathercock. The buttressed porch is 15th-cent., while the north arcade is early 13th-cent. The pointed arches rest on late Norman pillars with varied capitals. There is a painted Jacobean oak screen which embodies parts of a gallery from the great church at Cirencester. In the panelled transept is the tomb of Sir Anthony Hungerford, dated 1653. The chapel in the south transept has two 14th-cent. recumbent effigies of Sir Nicholas Villiers, who fought in the Last Crusade, and his daughter Margaret. The chancel has been much restored, but with taste and sensitivity.

DROITWICH, *Worcestershire* (8–SO9063), is an old town. The Romans called it Salinae as its natural brine springs were already known. The Anglo-Saxons called it Wic (pronounced with a "ch") and to this first element of the name, meaning customary right or perquisite, was added in Norman times. The radioactive springs rising from beneath the town are said to be 10 times saltier than ordinary sea-water and even saltier than the waters of the Dead Sea. Droitwich was perfectly sited for its development as a spa in the early part of the 19th cent. because of its position in an undulating plain, sheltered by the Malvern and Lickey Hills. This development

Edwin Smith

Dorchester Abbey: the Jesse window

was due to a far-seeing businessman, John Corbett, who by 1828 realized its tremendous possibilities, taking the waters being then fashionable. He not only built St Andrew's Brine Baths, which were rebuilt twice during the present century, but he remodelled the ancient timbered Raven Hotel, then a 16th-cent. house, and established other luxurious hotels. He may have been influenced in all this by his French wife. For her, just outside the town at Dodderhill, he built an imposing French château in the style of Francis I. Set in a well-wooded, 70-acre estate, it is now transformed into a hotel.

Droitwich is not large and a tour on foot is the best way of discovering its 16th-, 17th- and 18th-cent. houses. St Andrew's Church, in St Andrew's Street, has some good 13th-cent. features. St Peter's, 1 m. S. of the town, has a good Norman chancel and chancel arch with a Perpendicular timber-framed clerestory. In the south transept is some early 14th-cent. stained glass in the typical yellows and dark greens of the period. Nearby is St Peter's Manor, a 300-year-old timbered building which has been considerably restored. It has an old dovecot with 750 holes. The Roman Catholic church on the Worcester Road attracts a large number of visitors by its splendid series of mosaics depicting the life of Droitwich-born St Richard, who became a much-loved Bishop of Chichester in the reign of Henry III. The mosaics by Gabriel Pippet are in the manner of Ravenna but are inclined to harshness, perhaps because of their newness. The town has a number of fine parks, one of which has a swimming-pool filled with natural brine and water to reproduce the salinity of the Mediterranean. Droitwich still functions as a spa.

Just a little way S. of the town the Droitwich-Worcester Canal is cut through the little village of Salwarpe between the 16th-cent. half-timbered Salwarpe Court and the sandstone Norman church. It is a tranquil place, its valley watered by both the canal and the River Salwarpe. The gabled court with tall chimneys was once the home of the famous Talbot family. There are a number of memorials to this family in the church, which has a fine Transitional arcade but was much spoilt in the mid-Victorian restoration. However, there is some good 15th-cent. stone carving in the screens, and the richly chasubled effigy of a priest in the sanctuary marks the tomb of William Richepot, rector here between 1367 and 1401. The rectory is a good Georgian building. The Old Mill House reflected in the canal completes the peaceful scene.

DUDLEY, *Worcestershire* (8–SO9390), is called the "Capital of the Black Country", with some justification, as it was here in the 17th cent. that coal was first used for smelting iron, and its vast ironworks have prospered ever since. It lies 9 m. W. of BIRMINGHAM and is almost surrounded by Staffordshire, in which county its newer districts lie. From the keep of its Norman castle, the only important ruin of its kind in Worcestershire, the panorama extends over seven counties, often

smoke-hazed. There is an interesting 14th-cent. barbican to be seen and two drum towers. Its courtyard is surrounded by a 14th-cent. wall, over 8 ft thick in places, which has defied time and attack. Within the grounds is an excellent zoo with over 450 species, including rare fish. A chairlift brings visitors up the 200-ft slopes on which the castle stands. Below the castle are great limestone caverns which have not been quarried since the early 1920s. **Wren's Nest** is in fact sited in both Worcestershire and Staffordshire and is the only geological nature reserve in the country. It is the classical source of fossils from the Upper Silurian Dudley limestone. Over 300 species of fossil fauna are represented and they are at least 330 million years old. They were first studied here in 1686. Just across the county line is the excellent early 19th-cent. Church of St Thomas dominating the town from the heights and well worth visiting.

DURSLEY, *Gloucestershire* (4–ST7597). Some good Georgian houses remain among much new building in Dursley, a reminder of the town's 18th-cent. prosperity. The 18th-cent. Market Hall stands elegantly on 12 arches, enhanced by the fine statue of Queen Anne. The parish church has a good 15th-cent. chapel raised by one of the town's wool merchants and a Gothic tower which was built by Thomas Sumsion in the early 1700s. Although modern industry is bringing back a new surge of life to the town, nearby **Woodmancote** seems to escape suburbanization and has an interesting main street with good houses, among which Ferney Hill House and the Georgian Gothic Rangers are typical. A little further along the B4066 to the E. in wooded hills is the long village of **Uley**. It is a weaving village of great antiquity with some of the best 17th- and 18th-cent. houses in the county. At Wresdon Farm lived John Eyles who built the house in 1687. He won renown in Uley as being the first inhabitant to weave Spanish cloth. The house has some of the original furniture, including his four-poster bed. About 1 m. outside the village is a 14th-cent. house called Owlpen Manor which used to be famous for its yews. N. of Uley is the famous Stone Age barrow known as Hetty Pegler's Tump. It is one of the best preserved of these Cotswold barrows and is some 120 ft long and 90 ft wide with burial chambers enclosed within its stone walls. The views from the heights of the Tump extend right across the Severn to the Welsh mountains. On nearby Uley Bury about 800 ft above sea-level was a huge Iron Age camp later used by the Romans, whose hoards of coin and pottery have been discovered here.

EARDISLAND, *Herefordshire* (8–SO4158), lies 5 m. W. of LEOMINSTER on the A44. It is a lovely village, with a wealth of timber-framed cottages set on the banks of the River Arrow. A fisherman's paradise, it always attracts anglers in the mayfly season. The river widens just beyond the bridge and the tree-lined banks focus the eye on the beautiful Staick House, built about 1300 as a comfortable yeoman's hall. Although excellently restored in the early part of this century, it retains most of its original timberwork, doorways, windows and very early fire-places. An east wing was added in the 17th cent. The gabled outlines of the house are most satisfying and the low line of the roof of the recessed hall range is practically all the work of the original builder.

By the bridge stands the old village whipping post. On the south side is the old Schoolhouse and opposite is a 17th-cent. manor house with Queen Anne additions. It has a rare type of tall brick four-gabled dovecot which always arouses admiration. The church, which has a few interesting features, was mostly restored about 1864. One m. S. of Eardisland is an 18th-cent. house, Burton Court, with an excellent example of architect Clough Williams-Ellis's concept of the picturesque in the neo-Tudor frontage he gave the house some little time before the First World War.

ELKSTONE, *Gloucestershire* (5–SO9612). This small high windswept Cotswold village possesses one of the most rewarding Norman churches in a county in which so many are preserved. It lies less than 1 m. E. of the A417 which follows the Roman Ermine Street linking CIRENCESTER with GLOUCESTER. On the other side of the road is Syde, a little village which also has an old Norman church and an ancient stone-buttressed barn well worth visiting. Elkstone is first mentioned in the Domesday Book, deriving its name from Ealac's Stone which many believe is the curious pagan stone against the wall of the vestry. The church dates from about 1160 and has a sturdy Perpendicular tower at the west end with thick stone walls. This replaced the old central Norman tower which collapsed when Gloucester Cathedral was being built. The arches which supported the Norman tower separate the little choir and sanctuary from the tall nave. Although the porch is 14th-cent., the south door has preserved its beautiful romanesque tympanum with Christ in Majesty on a cushioned judgment seat with the symbols of the four Evangelists below. Above the finger of God points down and the surrounds have remarkable ornamentation deserving of close study, as the zigzags of the 12th-cent. arches and the little east window. The solid oak roof of the nave dates from the 15th cent., as do the font and the windows in the nave and the chancel. An almost unique dovecot above the chancel is reached by a stairway near the pulpit. There are a number of interesting monuments to various local yeoman families on the north side of the nave as well as two 17th-cent. table tombs which are both fine examples of their kind.

In the south-east corner of the churchyard, the little stone house with 15th-cent. windows was once the Priest's House and is now divided into two cottages. The Rectory, which has been well restored, has Stuart foundations, a Queen Anne façade and Georgian additions at the back. An interesting walk of about 2 m. is to the neighbouring villages of Syde and Winstone, through the Frome Valley.

ETTINGTON, *Warwickshire* (9–SP2447), is a village 5 m. SE. of STRATFORD-UPON-AVON on the A422 BANBURY road. Its chief claim to fame lies 1½ m. SW. of the village, towards Newbold-on-Stour where in Ettington Park stands one of the most impressive High Victorian houses in Warwickshire. It was the seat of the Shirley family, whose lineage went back to earliest Norman times. They tore down the old house in 1858 and commissioned two architects, John Prichard and J. P. Seddon, to remodel it completely in 13th-cent. Gothic style. The house, now a hotel, has an interior incapable of matching the skill shown in its exterior. However, the staircase hall is a good piece of Victorian inventiveness, producing an Henri IV atmosphere which catches some semblance of authenticity from the Elizabethan chimney-piece in the entrance hall. The Shirley motto "*Loyal je suis*" is much displayed.

Just behind the house stands a 17th-cent. summer-house or loggia, its perfectly proportioned double arches separated by a fluted pillar. Here, as a child, William Croft may well have gained inspiration for his later works of church music. He was born in 1677 and brought up in the Shirley household. Near the house is the old church with a partly Norman tower. The bell openings date from about 1200. The south wall of the chancel still stands and the ruins are dramatically continued by a splendid avenue of tall trees. In 1825 a south transept was built to contain the mortuary monuments of the Shirley family. There is a very good example of the work of the Irish stained-glass artist, Evie Hone, set into the east light between 1948 and 1949.

A short walk leads to one of the earliest Friends meeting houses in the county. Stone built in severe Quaker style, it is only 18 ft by 24 ft in area and has a typical Warwickshire mullioned window. It is one of the few meeting houses to possess all its original furniture.

EVESHAM, *Worcestershire* (8–SP0344), is an important market town and the centre of the fruit-growing area of the VALE OF EVESHAM. Its tree-lined walks and lawns along the Avon give it both distinction and charm. The precincts of its ancient ruined Benedictine abbey founded in 714 run right down to the river bank. Its two splendid churches share the same churchyard with Clement Lichfield's beautiful 110-ft-high bell-tower built in 1539 between them. Abbot Lichfield was the last of a succession of 55 abbots; for the Dissolution occurred in the same year that work was completed on his tower. Its superb panelled faces, ogee arches and elaborate decoration of its buttresses, together with its delicate pierced parapet and finely ornamental pinnacles, place it among the treasures of English architecture. The oldest part of All Saints' Church dates from the 12th cent., although it gives a general impression of being Perpendicular. It has an embattled tower with an octagonal spire. The porch has some intricate heraldic carving made up of the Tudor rose, the fleur de lis, the three ostrich feathers of the Prince of Wales, a rose

Eardisland: Staick House, a 14th-cent. yeoman's hall on the River Arrow

Evesham: the bell tower is a superb example of Perpendicular architecture

halved with a pomegranate and a crowned rose. The most rewarding part of this church is the Lady Chapel, built when Clement Lichfield was still Prior and therefore dating from before 1513. Coming through the panelled four-centred arch, the visitor can only be amazed at the richly carved fan vaulting of the roof, springing from shafts at four angles and from the centre of the south wall. The band of quatrefoils beneath the windows is particularly handsome. The Abbot is buried in a marble tomb which lost its brass inscriptions during the Puritan regime. The church has suffered much from Victorian restoration.

On the other side of the bell-tower is the Church of St Laurence, rebuilt on the site of an ancient chapel in the 16th cent. It has suffered badly over the centuries from both neglect and poor restoration work. However, the east end of the chancel has some good Perpendicular panelling and the chantry chapel of Abbot Lichfield has a fan tracery roof with a pendant boss. There is some good modern glass by the late Geoffrey Webb. The very fine exterior of the east end is worth close examination.

Evesham has many fine houses and old inns, notably the late 15th-cent. Booth Hall or Round House. It has been dramatically but beautifully restored with all its close timberwork seen to good advantage. On the south side of Bridge Street is the old Crown Hotel built round a courtyard. At the end of this street is part of the town's original medieval wall. Dresden House is perhaps the

finest building in the town. Of mellowed brickwork, it has a richly carved cornice and a doorway with enormous iron brackets dated 1692. About 1 m. NW. on the Worcester Road is the Abbey Manor, probably built around 1840. It stands in pleasantly wooded gardens where an obelisk commemorates the terrible Battle of Evesham. Here on 4 August 1265 in the fury of a thunderstorm Henry III's son, Edward, by cunning strategy, defeated Simon de Montfort who was slain while leading the forces of the rebel barons. De Montfort's son Henry, some 18 barons, 160 knights and 4,000 men-at-arms perished in a battle lasting three hours.

FAIRFORD, *Gloucestershire* (5–SP1501), on the A417 from LECHLADE to CIRENCESTER is best seen from the parapet of the little bridge crossing over to Fairford Mill and looking across the stone roofs and curving grey walls to the Perpendicular Parish Church of St Mary. This wool church is one of the best surviving examples. Built in the latter part of the 15th cent. by John Tame, a wealthy cloth merchant, it has notable uniformity of design and construction. The parapeted central tower with well-proportioned pinnacles and quatrefoil piercing, the clerestoried nave, porch and the chancel with the original priest's door into the sacristy are all well-preserved. The carvings in wood and stone, particularly the amusing carved misericords, are worth close examination. The Founder's Tomb lies under the screen separating the church from the Lady Chapel where there is a good 16th-cent. tomb of a member of the Lygon family. There are stone angels supporting the timber roof and the remains of the original wall paintings. The church is most famous, however, for the 15th- to 16th-cent. painted glass windows, the finest in such quantity in England. There are in all 28, telling the Christian story from the Creation, with the stories of Moses, David, Solomon and the Queen of Sheba all vividly portrayed, right up to the Crucifixion and the early development of the Church. Finally, in the west window the Last Judgment is depicted in horrifying detail.

In a house in the tree-lined square John Keble, the poet and cleric, was born in 1792. His classic work *The Christian Year* did much to revive a liturgical renaissance in the Church of England, and Keble College, OXFORD, was founded in his memory. In and around the square are several old inns.

FOREST OF DEAN, *Gloucestershire* (4–SO 6209). Gloucestershire has within its borders one of the greatest primeval forests in the kingdom. It is said that over 20 million trees go to make up the Royal Forest of Dean: oaks, ash-trees, hollies, birches and conifers. Forest wild life abounds and wild flowers, rare kinds among them, thrive. It is said that there are over 2,000 m. of woodland paths. The people who live in and around the Forest of Dean are known as Foresters. They preserve their ancient privileges and customs. Below the woodlands is a 22,000-acre coalfield and now abandoned iron-workings.

The Romans mined here and traces of these so-called scowles can often be discovered under small green mounds. Forest of Dean ironworks provided the material for most of the weapons used by the English soldiery during the later Crusading centuries. Part of the open land within the forest is used for grazing the Foresters' sheep and feeding the pigs when the acorns fall. A few charcoal-burners still practise their craft.

The forest is bounded on the E. and S. by the Severn, on the W. by the Wye and on the N. by the Herefordshire border. **Newnham** on the A48 makes an excellent gateway into the forest. This is a very pleasant little town right on the banks of the Severn. It was from here that Henry II set sail for Ireland to consolidate and control the conquests of his vassal Strongbow, Earl of Pembroke. It has some good 18th- and 19th-cent. houses. The good view from the churchyard can be best appreciated on a fine day. NW. of Newnham is the village of **Littledean** on the edge of the forest. Besides having one of the most splendid views of the Severn valley, there are many traces of Roman road pavings leading to their well-worked mines; the best are to the E. of the village. It has an interesting 13th-cent. church with some earlier Norman pillars with shamrock carving.

To the W. of the main road going S. are **Upper** and **Lower Soudley** with the magnificent Soudley Valley between. Little roads and criss-cross paths make this ideal forest country for the walker, but it is a good idea to have a compass handy. The A48 continues S. towards **Blakeney**, another natural gateway to the forest. It rises steeply from the distant Severn shore ½ m. away, its hillside is wooded and many of the stone houses are colour-washed. Thomas Sternhold, who with John Hopkins wrote the first vernacular metrical version of the Psalms, was born in a Blakeney house called Hawfield in the 16th cent. A walk out to nearby **Gatcombe** can be rewarding for the dedicated fisherman. The main road now follows the original Roman route a short distance to the rather uninspiring little town of **Lydney**. The park known as Camp Hill has the remains of a Roman temple dedicated to a Celtic god called Nodens. Several other considerable finds have been made, including a hoard of Roman coins. The market cross is 14th-cent. A visit to the little dock may be a reminder that many Elizabethan ships were built of timber hewn in the nearby forest.

Hewelsfield is a high village between two stretches of forest and between the Severn and Wye. It is a good centre for walks northwards into the forest and another road dips dramatically westwards to the Wye and Tintern Abbey. In the 17th cent. members of the famous Throgmorton family were buried in the mostly Norman village church. The B4234 running directly N. from Lydney leads to the heart of the forest. The first village reached on this road is **Bream's Eaves** adjoining the lower village of **Bream**. Here can be seen the Roman scowles. The huge caverns are mysterious and masked in the depth of a wood. The colliery village has the usual colour-washed stone houses. Unclassified roads to the W. are signposted to **St Briavels**, an understandably favourite halting place for visitors to the forest. It stands high above a wooded valley which drops steeply down to the Wye. There are remains of a fortified stronghold covering more than an acre, built in the 13th cent. as protection against Welsh marauders. The gatehouse has two round towers still standing. The Norman church with 13th-cent. additions has been much restored.

Continuing northwards from Bream's Eaves, **Parkend**, a colliery village, is reached. The miners are independent and their workings unnationalized. The village has a good Gothic Revival church built in 1822. A forestry school has also been established here. The mysterious Cannop Ponds on the road N. are well worth stopping at for a short halt.

Coleford, a scattered miners' village, claims the title of capital of the Forest of Dean. Its 17th-cent. Market Hall was restored in the 19th cent. Its charter derives from Charles II, since the manor had sheltered Charles I after the Battle of Edgehill. The B4226 runs diagonally across the heart of the forest through **West Dean**, a mining village of red-stone houses in the depth of the oak forest. In an old inn called the Speech House, the Foresters' Court is held 10 times a year. The ancient rights and privileges of the forest are upheld in the galleried court room with its open hearth and court officer's rostrum. Some of the hollies in Speech House Wood are said to be over 300 years old. Walks in the area are particularly good. The road continues to the north-east edge of the forest at **Cinderford**; its mining connections are as obvious as its name suggests, but it is edged by superb oak woodlands. It is a useful departure point for **Mitcheldean**, the northernmost tip of the forest. It has an interesting parish church with a tapering spire and a good Market Hall. Easily reached from here is the orchard village of **Blaisdon**, famous for its plums. So, too, is **Brierley** and not far distant **English Bicknor**, high up above the Wye with panoramic views across the forest. It has all the reticent attractiveness of the forest towns and villages. Its Norman Church of St Mary has some interesting early 14th-cent stone figures.

FOWNHOPE, *Herefordshire* (8–SO5734), lies 7 m. SE. of HEREFORD on the B4224 on the banks of the Wye. It has black-and-white cottages and an imposing Transitional parish church with a tall Norman tower carrying a 14th-cent. broach spire. The remarkably good Norman tympanum has been shifted from its doorway to the interior of the west wall for the sake of preservation. The Virgin is seated, raising her hand in blessing. The hand of the Infant Jesus catches the rhythm of the gesture. The flowing design is continued in the rich foliage work which enfolds a lion with extended claws and a bird, perhaps an eagle symbolizing St John the Evangelist. Some good and interesting houses to see, within walking distance of the village, are the Jacobean Fown-hope Court, the Georgian Nash Farmhouse, and Capler Farm which has a good barn. A short distance NW. is **Holme Lacy**, another Wye village as rich in beauty as in history. It has a little church set in meadowland about 1 m. from the village. Dedicated to St Cuthbert, it has a low roof and a six-bayed 14th-cent. arcade of great merit. The Scudamore monuments, particularly those of the 16th and 17th cents., are noteworthy for Classical elegance. This was the family which built the Palladian Holme Lacy House towards the end of the 1670s. The house still contains much beautiful carving, though some of the best is now in the Metropolitan Museum, New York. The house was much modernized in 1910 when a new ballroom and an impressive main staircase were added. This is the house where Alexander Pope is reputed to have written his eulogy to the "Man of Ross". The park has some fine trees and the little orangery is attractive. The house is now used as a mental hospital.

GLOUCESTER, *Gloucestershire* (4–SO8318). Gloucester began with Glevum, a Roman fort which guarded the lowest Severn crossing and the legions' routes into Wales; it became one of the four *coloniae* of Roman Britain. Anglo-Saxon Gleawcester was a royal *burh* or fortified town in Alfred the Great's time and had its own mint. The Norman and Angevin kings often made it their residence and it was here that William the Conqueror decided on the Domesday survey.

The city has long been an inland port. It has its own harbour master and now stretches for miles along waterways handling an ever-growing out-flow from local engineering industries. Industrial and commercial developments have kept the bulldozers busy in Gloucester. Much has been demolished but the opportunity has been taken for archaeological excavation. This has revealed the site of a complete Roman forum, which must have covered about 2 acres. The site of the basilica or administrative building has been discovered as well as the flanking colonnades on the east and south sides. Fragments of an equestrian statue of an emperor have been collected and identified, and also the bronze tassels of his saddle and the plinth of the statue. The excavation has apparently confirmed the hypothesis that there were two Roman occupations. The principal finds are in the City Museum.

The city's main thoroughfares still follow the Roman roads and meet at the Cross. In Eastgate Street stands the Guildhall. Nearby in Brunswick Street is a memorial to Robert Raikes, who founded the Sunday school movement in St Catherine Street. New Inn in Northgate Street was a timbered 15th-cent. pilgrims' hostelry; the interior has been modernized but it preserves its courtyard with surrounding balconies. Another ancient inn, the Raven Tavern in Hare Lane, has been saved from demolition by private subscription. It was once the home of the Hoares, who sailed in the *Mayflower* to New England. At the bottom of Westgate Street is an old 16th-cent. gabled house built by Thomas Payne, a mayor of Gloucester, and nearby are the 15th-cent. St Bartholomew's Almshouses much Gothicized in the 18th cent. Also in Westgate Street is a 16th-cent. timber-framed house reputed to have sheltered Bishop John Hooper on that February night before he was burnt at the stake in 1555 in the reign of Mary Tudor. It now houses one of the best folk museums in the country with comprehensive collections of everything to do with early trades, crafts and industry as well as exhibits of historical interest. Among these is a whole gallery entirely devoted to the story of the Civil War siege of Gloucester in 1643. Another section has the Port Book records showing Gloucester's maritime importance from 1580 onwards. The medieval Church of St Mary de Crypt in Southgate Street has been much restored. It has a peal of eight bells cast by Rudhall, the famous Gloucester bell founder. Inside the church is the font where George Whitefield, the preacher, was baptised. He was born in the city and attended the St Mary de Crypt Grammar School next to the church.

The cathedral is still the chief glory of Glou-cester. Its Norman plan and structure were preserved as the body of this magnificent church, to which the work of later periods was added. It therefore affords an illustration of architectural development which can hardly be bettered anywhere in Europe. The Norman pillars of the 174-ft-long nave up to the stone screen remain as they were during the first building period of 1089 to 1100. Here the merging of Norman into

Transitional style can be seen. The vaulting above the nave dates from 1242. The south transept has the earliest Benedictine essays in Perpendicular style, following hard on the splendid Decorated work. The choir was built for the abbey (it did not become a cathedral until the reign of Henry VIII) in 40 years of fervour between 1337 and 1377. Even this fine choir really only masks the original Norman one with the Norman crypt beneath it. The beautiful Lady Chapel was built nearly a century later. The east window has some glass whose colour is unrivalled even at YORK; many of the heraldic devices are those of families who fought at Crécy in 1346. It is 78 ft high and has over 2,700 sq. ft of traceried stone and glass. Its theme culminates gloriously in the Coronation of the Virgin amid a host of saints, apostles, popes and kings. The 225-ft pinnacled tower, with its open parapets and flying buttresses at the corners of the church, is built of beautiful Painswick stone and took nearly 100 years to achieve, being completed during the troubled times of the Wars of the Roses. The Great Peter weighing 3 tons is reputed to be the oldest medieval bell of this size in the country. The cloisters have the earliest and most exquisite fan vaulting achieved by the abbot's stonemasons between 1351 and 1412. It was the inspiration for the roof of Henry VII's Chapel in WESTMINSTER ABBEY and the equally superb fan vaulting of St George's Chapel, WINDSOR. The cloister still encloses the monastic garden with its 14th-cent. well in the centre. On the south side of the cloisters are the arched recesses of the scriptorium; at the other end is the vaulted lavatorium with the original washing basins on recesses for holding towels. The glass is mostly modern, though there are roundels with 16th-cent. glass from Prinknash, country home of the later abbots of Gloucester. The Chapter House has the original Norman barrel roof. The change to cathedral at the Dissolution fortunately caused little iconoclastic damage, though some of the monuments suffered defacement. One of the loveliest examples of medieval funerary art remained unscathed: it portrays Edward II, whose remains were brought here by the monks after his brutal murder and interred in 1337. The library is well worth a visit and has some priceless 10th-cent. manuscripts. Gloucester, with HEREFORD and WORCESTER Cathedrals, is one of the centres of the Three Choirs Festival – the oldest festival of its kind in Europe, founded in the first years of the 18th cent.

GOLDEN VALLEY, *Herefordshire* (8–SO 3537), extends from **Pontrilas** in a WNW. direction to **Dorstone** and offers some of the most tranquil and beautiful scenery in this part of England. It is backed to the W. by an undulation of hills rising to the 2,300-ft ridges of the Black Mountains and to the E. by gentle hills extending from the 376-ft Forty Acre Pitch to Green Hill rising to the 824-ft summit that looks down on MOCCAS COURT. Down this valley flows the Dore from its source in the hills above Dorstone.

Pontrilas is a convenient point to start a tour of the Golden Valley, but has little to interest the visitor other than the 17th-cent. stone mansion Pontrilas Court, from which it is believed the village took its present name: its original name seems to have been Elwistone. The next village along the B4347, **Ewyas Harold** has a great deal of charm and an interesting history. Osborn Pentecost was one of the early "Trojan Horse" Normans who infiltrated the country in the reign of Edward the Confessor and built a castle, at the same time ruthlessly terrorizing the countryside. The castle was destroyed by Earl Harold, claimant to the Confessor's throne, in 1052. Between then and 1066 another Norman, William FitzOsborn, built and fitted out some 60 ships in Normandy for the Conqueror's invasion. He was rewarded in part by the lands and castle of Ewyas. After a short period as joint regent of England in the king's absence, he returned to Normandy and was killed at Cassel. His eldest son Harold inherited his castle and it is from the village derives its name. Only the conical mound and earthworks remain. The view is entrancing across the Dulas Brook which flows round the much-restored Early English church with its squat 13th-cent. tower. On the north side, recessed into the interior chancel wall, is a curious 14th-cent. effigy of a woman clasping a heart casket. She wears an unusual headdress which shows she had taken a vow of chastity. From here the valley becomes rich and green, with scattered orchards as the road follows the river upstream. On the east side stands **Abbey Dore.** Cistercians founded the church in 1147 – six years before the death of St Bernard, who revolted against the architectural extravagances of Cluny and restored simplicity to all his subsequent churches. The rebuilding of Dore Abbey between 1175 and 1220 reflects the dynamics of this discipline. Later, when the house had become wealthy, a more splendid retro-choir was built which throws the simplicity of the earlier building into greater relief. The way the red sandstone of the fabric contrasts with the rich green surroundings makes the interesting proportions of this unusual church vividly apparent. However, the 17th-cent. tower set between choir and transept rather disturbs the rhythm of line. It must be remembered that though the monastery was destroyed at the Dissolution, it is thanks to the good offices of Lord Scudamore, who in 1633 called in the gifted John Abel, later known as the "King's Carpenter", to restore the abbey as a parish church, that one of the finest examples of Cistercian-inspired Early English architecture in the country has been preserved. The cathedral-like grandeur of the presbytery with its 13th-cent. ambulatory and the three-bayed choir, lit by a clerestory pierced by lancets, never fail to impress. The choir has its original stone altar of remarkable size, rediscovered many years ago in a local dairy. The 17th-cent. glass floods the interior with colour. John Abel carved the oak screen and surmounted it with three armorial bearings: those of the Stuarts, Viscount Scudamore and Archbishop

Laud. He also did the ceiling. Besides two mutilated and worn effigies, one in each of the choir aisles, there is an interesting collection of fragments of sculpture left behind after the Dissolution. The 13th-cent. tiles in the chancel with heraldic devices are interesting. Those around the font are undecorated but of the same period.

The timber-framed 14th-cent. Grange Farm just outside the village makes a worthwhile short walk from the abbey church. It has a porch with good plasterwork and a ceiling dated 1603.

Bacton is one of the prettiest villages in the valley and has a 13th-cent. church on a hill with a 16th-cent. battlemented tower. It possesses an ancient rood-beam and staircase which connected with the rood-loft. This must have been demolished after the Reformation. Its main treasure consists of some exquisite embroidery worked on an early altar frontal with large formalized flowers, beasts and birds, tiny insects and a boat with two passengers. It is popularly believed to have been the work of Elizabeth Parry, maid of honour to Queen Elizabeth I. Her alabaster monument showing her curtseying to her queen has a lengthy inscription ending with the line "wythe maeden quene a maede dyd ende my lyffe." It is worth leaving the B4348 that runs through the upper half of the valley to visit the little village of **Vowchurch**, where a bridge crosses the Dore by the 16th-cent. Old Vicarage. The church, rebuilt in the 14th cent. and with 15th-cent. additions, has a profusion of woodwork and carving in its roof, screen and communion rails. All this makes an interior of splendid richness which stands out well against the plaster and scraped walls of the nave and chancel. The church owns a most unusual wooden chalice carved from beechwood and dating from the first years of the 17th cent. Poston Lodge, an Adamesque shooting box somewhat spoiled by later Victorian additions, lies about 1 m. N. in wooded country, high enough to give lovely views of the valley. Nearby is a prehistoric hill-fort later used by the Romans. At **Peterchurch** the valley opens out into meadowland and cornfields. A little to the E. of the not particularly attractive village is Wellbrook Manor. Stone built, with its original interior timber-framing and its solar wing preserved, it is one of the best examples of a 14th-cent. hall in the county. The stone chimney-piece and shaft have withstood 600 years of use. Another heritage from feudal days is Urishay Castle, 1½ m. SW., once a medieval fortress house later domesticated into a Jacobean manor and now a ruin. However, the chapel, which had long served as a barn and was later restored to its original use, is almost certainly a Norman building. The village church is Norman and has a notable double chancel. On the south side is a door with excellently preserved zigzag moulding. Of the three round-headed archways spanning the church, the centre one also has fine zigzag ornamentation. Not least of its features are the good modern hand-beaten ironwork fittings for the electric lighting of the church.

From Peterchurch the more interesting route runs W. of the river through the hamlets of Hinton and Fine Street. One m. before Dorstone are the remains of **Snodhill Castle**, high on a mound whose earthworks cover about 10 acres. It existed when the Domesday Book was compiled and was rebuilt in the reign of King Stephen. There are remains of round towers and considerable parts of the 14th-cent. bailey. It was of importance to the defence of the border and was at one time a fief of Warwick the Kingmaker. The 17th-cent. stone-built Snodhill Court lies just S. of the castle; a farm-house now, it has a fine hall with an oak ceiling and a good Jacobean oak staircase. The road into Dorstone passes the ruins on the castle tump standing nearly 30 ft above the surrounding fosse. In the 13th and 14th cents. it belonged to the Sollers family who gave their name to a village on the outskirts of HEREFORD called Bridge Sollers. Hills rise all round the village, the highest being the 1,045-ft Merbach Hill. Climb to the Arthur's Stone long barrow for good views down the valley. Dorstone was the last refuge of Richard de Brito, one of the four knights who slew Thomas à Becket. The church, which has some 13th-cent. features left intact, was almost entirely restored in 1889. It possesses a 13th-cent. pewter chalice and paten, discovered in a tomb built into the wall beneath a recess on the south side. The church bells are very ancient.

GOODRICH, *Herefordshire* (8–SO5719), lies between the A40 and **Kerne Bridge**, 5 m. SSW. of ROSS. It is dominated by the splendid ruins of Goodrich Castle built high on a spur above the Wye. The name derives from Godric's Castle and is mentioned as such in an early 12th-cent. document. The lands and castle were bestowed on William Marshall by King John in the early 13th cent. Marshall considerably enlarged the castle and added many amenities. It was approached by a vast barbican which led to a bridge supported by arches crossing the exceptionally deep moat cut into solid red rock. The gatehouse has an enormous semi-circular tower which housed a chapel. It is vaulted and had portcullises on both sides. The most ancient part of the castle is the grey stone keep, a typical four-square Norman tower, three stories high. The castle is rectangular with angle towers in each corner of the courtyard. The great hall in the west range was 65 ft long with its trefoil-headed windows in good repair. In the west wall, the fire-place still stands with its corbelled hood. Beyond the hall is the huge south-west tower which housed the buttery and pantry.

In the 14th cent. Goodrich Castle passed to the Talbots, and in the 17th cent. by marriage to the de Grey family. It was the last Herefordshire defence to hold out for Charles I, under the leadership of Sir Henry Lingen. It finally fell under the assault of a locally-made cannon called Roaring Meg, the walls being breached on the south side by Parliamentarians under the command of Colonel Birch. Roaring Meg has been preserved and stands on Castle Green by HEREFORD Cathedral. Some of the cannon-balls weighing 200 lb can be seen in the castle grounds.

Kenneth Scowen

Great Malvern: the Malvern Hills provide fine walking country close to the town

The Parish Church of St Giles with its unusual unbuttressed tower carrying a 14th-cent. broach spire is closely associated with the Swift family. Dean Swift's grandfather, Thomas, was vicar here and his tombstone is under the high altar. The vicarage was attacked several times by Parliamentarians as Thomas Swift was known for his Royalist sympathies. He was to give proof of these by swimming the moat of Raglan Castle and handing to the Governor the remains of his fortune in gold sewn into his waistcoat pocket. St Giles's still possesses the chalice which had been looted from him. Dean Swift recovered the silver vessel and gave it back to the church in 1726.

Wordsworth loved all the Wye valley and was a frequent visitor to Goodrich, where he met the little girl who was the inspiration of the poem, "We are Seven". About ½ m. away from the castle, Blore built a fantastic mock castellated house in 1828 called Goodrich Court. It so infuriated Wordsworth by what he called its "impertinence" that he wished it could be blown up. The house has recently been demolished and shipped stone by stone to the United States. An inn called Ye Old Hostelrie built in 1830 has, however, survived. With all its pinnacles and Gothic windows it may well be true that it was copied from an ancient illumination. About ½ m. NE. of Goodrich is **Flanesford Priory**, the mellow ruin of an Augustinian priory built in 1346 and well worth the short walk. Some of the 14th-cent. windows remain in a barn belonging to the farm now built on the site.

GREAT BADMINTON, *Gloucestershire* (4–ST8082), 5 m. E. of CHIPPING SODBURY, owes its tidy stone cottages, its church and most of its living to the 52,000-acre estate of the Dukes of Beaufort. Badminton House was originally built for the 1st Duke of Beaufort in 1682. The present magnificent façade, seen in dramatic perspective

at the end of a 3-m. avenue of beech trees, was the result of a remodelling of the house undertaken by William Kent about 1740 for the 3rd Duke. Kent was also responsible for the superb Worcester Lodge which provides a grand approach. His whole Palladian concept was achieved with absolute integrity. He surrounded the spacious grounds with a wooded belt extending for 12 m. He preserved much of the early lay-out of the grounds, but his was an age of inventive variety and any possibility of monotony was broken by additional lodges and castellated follies, of which the keeper's lodge is perhaps most typical. Here is a small square "castle", with round tower and turreted stairway with window slits. These whimsical structures set off the natural grandeur of the deer park and the ancient oaks and elms. The house contains a wealth of Grinling Gibbons carving and is filled with priceless paintings, *objets d'art* and worthy ducal furnishings. It is open to the public for most of the summer months. The church, built in 1783 and reached through a rose arbour, within the precincts of the garden, is very much a mausoleum for the Beaufort family. It contains many fine tombs, notably that of Henry Somerset, the 1st Duke, his effigy robed in his Garter mantle. It was brought from the Beaufort chapel in WINDSOR. There are several Rysbrack monuments of interest and some impressive Italian paintings.

The present renown of Badminton derives from the most important annual equestrian event in the kingdom, the Three Day Horse Trials, usually attended by the Queen. The kennels of the famous Beaufort hounds can also be visited at certain times.

On the far edge of the park is the hamlet of **Little Badminton** with its Early English church, roofed with ancient Cotswold tiles, set in a peaceful meadow. Its turreted dovecot is very old, and local lore says it has as many nesting holes as days of the year. The cottages probably antedate the great mansion by at least two centuries. Out on the BATH road is an old inn, the Beaufort Arms, which readers of Jane Austen will remember from a description in her novel *Northanger Abbey*.

GREAT MALVERN, *Worcestershire* (8–SO 7845). Set in the 9 m. range of the Malvern Hills, Great Malvern has a Continental flavour, partly because of the way it is terraced on its hillside site. Its history as a settlement probably begins in the 11th cent. with the foundation of the Benedictine priory. Its modern history possibly owes its beginnings to a treatise by Dr Wall published in 1756 extolling the medicinal virtues of the waters of the **Malvern Wells**, which had in fact been discovered 100 years earlier. Within 30 years of Dr Wall's death, a pump room, baths, and residential terraces of houses and hotels were built on ground above the priory. One of these early hotels, the Foley Arms, has survived with its splendid cast-iron verandas intact and much of its original furnishings. From the time of Princess Victoria's visit here eight years before she became Queen to Princess Mary of Teck's visit with members of the German court in 1891, the town expanded continually. Malvern College for boys was founded in 1862 and Gothic Revival churches sprang up everywhere. Malvern could compete with BATH, BUXTON and CHELTENHAM and like them attracted the same element of retired colonial administrators and army officers. Few spas can match the beauty of its surroundings. Today, the spa no longer exerts its importance as such. It has become much more a popular resort and even a dormitory town for WORCESTER and BIRMINGHAM.

The Norman Priory Church of SS. Mary and Michael is still Malvern's most dominant feature and its most cherished possession. Built less than 20 years after the Conquest, it became almost immediately a dependency of WESTMINSTER ABBEY. Originally a great cruciform building with a central tower, considerable additions were made in the 13th and 14th cents. including a Lady Chapel in Decorated style which was destroyed after the Dissolution. It was mainly in the 15th cent. that a tremendous reconstruction of the Norman church was undertaken. The piers and arches of the early building were enclosed in the new style of architecture then prevailing. A lofty clerestory and roof were added filled with jewelled lights. A new tower rose on the foundations of the old. Its massive lines were decorated in the same manner as the tower of GLOUCESTER Cathedral, which it resembles. It seems likely that the same masons worked on both. Everything E. of the tower was rebuilt at the same time. The famous tiles were all handmade in the monastery, mostly between 1453 and 1456. About 1,000 were used in the decoration of the church, and over 100 different designs. Some can be seen in the outer wall of the apse. Occasionally it took four tiles to complete a small design. At the time of the reconstruction 40 vast windows were filled with

stained glass, in colour and design rivalling even that at YORK Minster. The east window is filled with jewelled fragments, some almost pictorially complete. The later clerestory glass should be seen from the aisles of the choir. During the First World War, all the medieval glass was removed and stored in a place of safety. The releading and restoration after the war left the glass probably in better condition than it had been over two centuries. The other remarkable furnishings which have survived the years since the Dissolution are the two rows of original dark oak monastic choir stalls with finely carved misericords. They date mostly from the 15th cent., though some may be earlier. The carvings portray the seasons with vividness and often humour. St Anne's Chapel in the south choir aisle, much restored, has a stairway to the tower and belfry which has a bell dating from the 14th cent. Two of the early priors are buried here. In 1860 the whole church underwent a restoration by Sir Gilbert Scott. Thirty-four years later the north-west porch was rebuilt and a year after this the tower was repaired and strengthened. Of the monastery, only the gatehouse survives.

The town owns Priory Park with its fine trees and abundant flowers and, in keeping with Malvern's importance as an inland resort, an open-air heated swimming-pool. The fish pond, with huge golden carp, is the same pool used by the Benedictines more than 400 years ago. There is good walking to be had on the hills behind the town; the ascent of the **Worcestershire Beacon**, where William Langland is supposed to have composed *Piers Plowman*, is recommended.

Little Malvern, the smallest of the Malverns, has a wooded setting against a rising hill and St Giles's, a gem of a church which is all that remains of another great priory, founded in 1171. The tower and chancel survive from this period. Bishop Alcock of Worcester rebuilt the rest in the late 15th cent. He inserted a fine west window, now fragmented, that portrays Edward IV and Elizabeth Woodville, his queen. There is a 14th-cent. altar tomb with four figures carved in the panels. The floor has encaustic tiles from the priory kiln at Great Malvern. Almost adjoining is Little Malvern Court which incorporates part of the priory buildings. It is mostly 15th-cent., but the round tower is probably part of the original 12th-cent. edifice. It has been in the possession of the Roman Catholic Berrington family since the 17th cent. and can claim that through all the religious struggles the Mass has been said here during the last 800 years. Through a window in the roof can still be seen the priests' hiding hole used in the days of persecution. One treasured possession is a travelling trunk and a quilt owned by Catherine of Aragon. Two m. NE. is the moated **Madresfield Court**, owned by the Earls of Beauchamp since 1260. It is set in a magnificent park, with a mile-long avenue of trees making a majestic approach. Five m. SE., in fine pasture-land sheltered by the Malverns, is a timbered grange called **Birtsmorton Court**. It is still completely encircled by a watered moat. One of the bridges leads to a 14th-cent. embattled stone gateway with two round bastions. Four wings surround the courtyard built between the 13th and 20th cents. The earliest south wing contains the great hall. Here is a secret hiding place where Sir John Oldcastle, the Lollard leader, sheltered after his first escape from the TOWER OF LONDON. Here, too, during the Wars of the Roses, Queen Margaret of Anjou fled with her son Edward, Prince of Wales. The chamber in which they hid is still there. Thomas Wolsey, who was to become cardinal under Henry VIII, was once a simple house chaplain to Sir Richard Nanfan, who probably introduced him to the Court. The Queen Anne plaster ceiling in the great hall is most handsome and the earlier Elizabethan panelling is perfectly preserved. Originally built by the Birt family, it was bought back by one of their descendants in this century but has now passed out of the family again. It is open to the public at advertised times, particularly in the summer season; it can be reached most easily from the A438, midway between TEWKESBURY and LEDBURY. The little 14th-cent. church has a good marble tomb of Sir Richard Nanfan, who died in 1504.

GREAT MILTON, *Oxfordshire* (5–SP6302), lies just off the A40, 4 m. W. of Tetsworth, beyond flat cornfields in a wooded hollow. A largish stone-built village, it is renowned for the fine tomb with relief carving of Sir Ambrose Dormer who fought at Calais in 1347 and is buried in the church. The entrance to the Early English church is opposite the Red Lion Inn. The 14th-cent. tracery and windows are outstanding. The four-poster Dormer tombs of Sir Michael Dormer, who died in 1618, has rich allegorical sculpting, depicting Youth, Age and Immortality. Nothing remains of the original Dormer mansion other than a fine Renaissance gateway, set into a wall near the church, which frames a charming timbered country house. **Little Milton** nearby is the more beautiful village, with weathered and thatched stone cottages and a Manor House.

GREAT WITLEY, *Worcestershire* (8–SO75 66), lies 5 m. SW. of STOURPORT at the junction of the A451 and the A433. Woodbury Hill rises to the S. At this main junction is a pleasant red-brick Georgian inn called the Hundred House. From the road on the hillside the Classical lines of the Parish Church of St Michael with its burnished dome can be seen through the trees of the parkland of the once great estate of the Foley family. Witley Court at the bottom of the hill was practically burnt to the ground in 1937. It was originally built by the 1st Lord Foley in the early part of the 18th cent. and sold to the Earl of Dudley in 1838 to house Queen Adelaide in suitable state. It is, however, the church built by Lady Foley in 1735 which excites most interest and admiration. It was considerably embellished by the Earl of Dudley and presents a riot of colour and plasterwork in its interior. The superb ceiling and painted windows were brought from the Duke of Chandos' demolished palace in Canons, Middlesex. They were re-erected in 1747. The white and gold plasterwork and scrolls by Pergotti show to great advantage the magnificent ceiling paintings by Laguerre from the original designs of Verrio. The elegant organ casing above the balustraded organ-loft once housed the instrument on which Handel played and composed at Canons. Even the 19th-cent. Gothic woodwork and carving fits into this glorious display of 18th-cent. elegance. The south transept is dominated by the massive monument of figures, draperies and Grecian urn set against a pyramidic background, which Rysbrack carved to the memory of the 1st Lord Foley. The motorist should not be deterred by the bad state of repair of the private yew-lined road leading to the church, for its rococo work can hardly be matched in England. It is sad that the magnificent Italian gardens are now overgrown and the fountains which jetted more than 90 ft into the air no longer play.

Little Witley to the SE. of the park has a Gothic chapel built very much as a labour of love in 1867 by A. E. Perkins at the inspiration of the rector, the Rev. C. Sale and his wife, who were both accomplished carvers. While the rector built the chancel of his church, Mrs Sale carved both the pulpit and font. To the N. of Great Witley rise the Abberley Hills with views across into Herefordshire. On the northern side of the hills is the village of **Abberley** with an attractive old country church which is partly in ruins and a somewhat grand Victorian church just outside the village, built in the mid-19th cent. in late 13th-cent. style. The rectory is pre-Reformation and mostly ruined, though its solar still has its timber-framing intact and the roof over the original hall. The mid-19th-cent. Abberley Hall, just outside the village, came into the Jones family from the Moilliets, who employed Dawkes to build the house in an Italianate style. It is now a school. Joseph Jones's son John built a fantastic Gothic clock tower in 1883 between the Abberley and Woodbury Hills to the memory of his father and, according to gossip, to impress his noble neighbour at Witley Court. It is very high and visible for miles around. Its 20 bells are so tuned that 42 different melodies can be rung out over the countryside. It was soon known as Jones's Folly.

GUY'S CLIFFE, *Warwickshire* (9–SP2866). Just outside WARWICK, on the main Warwick-KENILWORTH road, is a place of history and legend by the River Avon. Tall cliffs, caves, a ruined house, great cedars, oaks and fir trees all tend to give the legend the greater prominence. It is said that here in the 10th cent. Earl Guy, having slain the Danish giant Colbrand, strangled a wild boar and killed dragons, retired to live the life of a hermit in the cave that bears his name. There are many caves cut into the great cliff where later hermits sought shelter and escape from the world, and in due course it became a place of pilgrimage. Between 1422 and 1423 Richard Beauchamp rebuilt the chapel and endowed a chantry. One of the first of these chantry priests was the renowned antiquary John Rous who compiled the famous Rous Roll, chronicling the lives and events of the Earls of Warwick from the time of Guy to the holder of the title in his day. This can be seen in the BRITISH MUSEUM. Beside the cave in 1751 a beautiful Palladian house was built by Samuel Greatheed and much added to in 1818 by his son. An earlier Elizabethan mansion had stood on the site. That so splendid a house should in this century have been allowed to fall into ruin is a sad commentary on the age. The actress Sarah Siddons was once a ladies' maid in the house.

The chapel is cut into the rock and has an interesting doorway and good fan vaulting. On the right of the chapel is the 8-ft statue of Guy carved out of the rock some time in the late 14th cent.

Down at river level is the old Saxon Mill. A building with great charm, it belies its claim to a greater antiquity than the record which states that a mill, probably on this site, was given in the 12th cent. to Gilbert of Warwick and became the property of Kenilworth Priory. The present building with its 100-ft timbered balcony is now a restaurant and dates principally from 1822. An earlier part, however, is 17th-cent. It was much painted by David Cox and greatly admired by Ruskin.

HAGLEY HALL, *Worcestershire* (8–SO9181). This is one of the stateliest houses in the county, at the foot of the CLENT HILLS. The entrance to the park lies a little outside the village of Hagley, 2 m. S. of STOURBRIDGE. The great Palladian mansion was built by the 1st Lord Lyttelton between 1754 and 1760. The Lyttelton family still owns it. Sanderson Miller, who designed the building, built on the site of a much earlier Lyttelton home. Its rich brown stone contrasts well with the raised lawns with their low stone walls. Pedimented in pure Classical style, its roof balustrades run the length of the four square-towered wings in the tradition of Inigo Jones. A bad fire in the 1920s damaged part of the interior; it was skilfully restored. The entrance hall has charming stucco decoration. The dining-room has a magnificent rococo ceiling; this, too, was damaged but restored. The fine gallery also has a rococo ceiling and is rich in tapestries and pictures. The park is imaginatively landscaped with an Ionic temple, a rotunda, now rather weathered, and a folly in the form of a Gothic ruin. The house has entertained many great poets, architects, scientists and politicians; Gladstone was one of them. Hagley Hall has a fine collection of Chippendale furniture. It is open to the public in the summer season.

One m. NE. is Wychbury Hill Camp, a prehistoric fortification with splendid views over the Stour Valley.

HALESOWEN, *Worcestershire* (8–SO9683), lies 4½ m. E. of STOURBRIDGE and 9 m. from BIRMINGHAM. It is an industrial town: its products include electrical apparatus, agricultural implements and weldless tubing. It is undergoing a considerable rebuilding and modernization. The early 13th-cent. remains of its Premonstratensian abbey, founded in 1218, are incorporated into the 19th-cent. Manor Farm to the S. of Manor Lane. The long wall surrounding the farm-house originally enclosed the cloister garth and has a 13th-cent. coffin lid carved in relief with a Calvary. In a recess barely a foot and a half high is a 14th-cent. effigy of a knight with crossed legs, holding the hilt of his sword. The large and impressive Norman Church of St John the Baptist is masked by later Perpendicular work and has an outer aisle built in the 1880s. The 15th-cent. tower rises with its spire and three tiers of gabled lights from the centre of the nave, rather more to the west than the original Norman tower which collapsed. It rests on arches with huge piers, one of which contains a stairway. William Shenstone the poet is buried in the churchyard and has a monument dated 1763 in the north aisle of the church. The Leasowes was the home of the poet. He spent long years here and much money on beautifying the house. It is now pebble-dashed and serves as the club house of a golf course, where part of the old landscaping remains.

HALFORD, *Warwickshire* (9–SP2545), is set in wooded country 7 m. SE. of STRATFORD-UPON-AVON on the Roman Fosse Way. The name of the village is pronounced Hah-ford. Below the new bridge crossing the River Stour is a much older bridge considerably damaged in the Civil War. There are views of the weir and the old mill from here. The small Church of St Mary possesses what is perhaps one of the best preserved pieces of Romanesque sculpture in England in its Norman tympanum over the north door. A seated angel holds aloft a scroll; the wings are spread and delicate drapery flows over the protruded knees. Inside is a good Norman chancel arch with carved capitals in the restrained Transitional associated with early French Cistercian influence. A Norman niche was discovered high above the arch in 1960 with a much defaced seated figure, probably that of the Virgin Mary. Another empty niche on the opposite side seems likely to have held a statue of St John. A plain Norman doorway is set into the south wall. The rest of the church, other than its 13th-cent. tower, was badly restored towards the end of the 19th cent. The octagonal 16th-cent. font has a carved oak crocketed cover with five mitred heads upon it. The curious fire-hooks to be seen to one side were kept to draw off burning thatch from the nearby cottages. Outside the west end is a gargoyle in the form of a monkey, its arms clutched round its head. Just N. of the church is the Old Manor House with ancient woodwork and 16th-cent. Cotswold stone. It is well restored and blends perfectly with its setting.

HAMPTON-IN-ARDEN, *Warwickshire* (9–SP2081). An attractive village with steep streets and several 15th-, 16th- and 17th-cent. houses, many of the earlier ones with overhangs, stands in what remains of the Forest of Arden. This is said to have been Shakespeare's setting for his *As You Like It*, although claims have also been made for the Belgian Ardennes. The most interesting feature of all is Moat House, built in the 16th cent. It stands W. of the church. The uncommonly good 15th-cent. timbers are in perfect condition. The best can be seen at the rear of the house. The Church of SS. Mary and Bartholomew suffered somewhat from late 19th-cent. restoration, but it has a late Norman nave. In the south wall is a recess with a curious 13th-cent. column. The blue and white Calvary tiles are extremely rare and probably date back to the time of the Wars of the Roses.

About 1 m. SE. of the church flows the River Blythe, and near Bradnocks Marsh is one of the few packhorse bridges left in the county. This is 15th-cent. work. Five stone arches support the narrow parapet-less bridge. On one of its piers is the base of its original wayside cross.

HANBURY, *Worcestershire* (8–SO9663), is a long scattered village 2½ m. E. of DROITWICH. From its hill-top church, the landscape rises and falls with wooded hills stretching away to the Malvern Hills and Bredon Hill. The Church of St Mary's has a late 18th-cent. exterior and west tower. The piers of the nave are late Norman. The chancel was rebuilt by Street in 1860. It has some splendid monuments to the powerful Vernon family. Hanbury has three impressive country houses. **Hanbury Hall**, set in 13 acres of parkland, was built for Thomas Vernon in 1701. Red-brick and in the style of Wren, it has suffered little change with the passing of time. The staircase and hall were painted by Sir James Thornhill, illustrating the story of Achilles, in 1710. The Long Room had remarkably good plaster decoration. There is a distinctive Queen Anne orangery in the gardens. Acquired by the National Trust, it is open to the public. Some 1½ m. S. of the village is **Mere Hall**, the home of the Bearcroft family since the 14th cent. and one of the largest timbered houses in the county. It has an unusual ball-topped lantern above its four recessed gables and the windows in the supporting wings of the house are filled with delightful Gothic glazing bars making a pleasant curved contrast to the vertical, horizontal and diagonal beams. The Georgian forecourt has two pretty Queen Anne gazebos built of brick. Most of the present house dates from 1560; the date 1337 on a bracket refers to the earlier structure. Also nearby is the late 16th-cent. twin-gabled timber-framed Broughton Court, once the dower house to Mere Hall.

HENLEY-IN-ARDEN, *Warwickshire* (9–SP 1465), is a delightful old market town consisting of a High Street almost 1 m. long with nearly every type of English domestic architecture. It is situated where the WARWICK–Redditch road crosses the A34 9 m. NW. of STRATFORD-UPON-AVON. Once a stronghold of Plantagenet power, Henley belonged to the influential de Montfort family and after the death, at the Battle of EVESHAM, of Simon de Montfort it was pillaged

and burnt to the ground. Having risen from its ashes, it obtained a charter from Henry VI in 1449 and still has its High Bailiff elected annually by the Court Leet. Its 15th-cent. Guildhall was built by Sir Ralph Boteler. Henley has many ancient inns, among them the White Swan dating from the early 1600s. The most interesting buildings are on the north side of the main street, notably the Old George and the Blue Bell Inn, part of which is 15th-cent. The White House, now a restaurant, is a good example of a 16th-cent. dwelling.

Where the wide High Street narrows, rises the tower of the Church of St John the Baptist. It is purely 15th-cent. The roof has fine stone corbels, tie-beams and unusual queen-posts.

Just outside of Henley-in-Arden in **Beaudesert** is a good example of a Warwickshire Norman church built in the 11th cent. A little to the N. of the church lie earthworks protected by a deep entrenchment. The Mount, as it is called, is all that remains of the castle of the de Montforts.

HENLEY-ON-THAMES, *Oxfordshire* (5–SU7682), is a picturesque Thamesside town separated from the neighbouring county of Buckinghamshire by an elegant bridge spanning a wide stretch of the river. The bridge was designed by Salopian William Hayward in 1786 and he was aided by a remarkable woman sculptor, Anne Damer; she was a cousin of Horace Walpole and her friendship with the Emperor Napoleon caused much gossip. The bridge is decorated with keystone masks of Father Thames and the goddess Isis. The town, approached from OXFORD by the famous Fair Mile, has a great variety of buildings to offer the sightseer. The red-brick Red Lion Inn on the banks of the river, the Catherine Wheel in Regency white stucco and at least 20 other old inns indicate a town hospitable to visitors. It was at the Red Lion that Shenstone scratched a well-known quatrain on a pane of glass in the mid-18th cent.:

Whoe'er has travelled life's dull round
Where'er his stages may have been,
May sigh to think he still has found
The warmest welcome at an inn.

Among the many interesting houses is that of William Lenthall, who was Speaker of the House of Commons during the Long Parliament. The Victorian Town Hall tends to obstruct the pleasant vista of Market Street. In New Street are some bow-windowed houses, among them the Henley Brewery Office, a reminder of the days when Henley boasted a number of "gentlemen brewers". Chantrey House is a good timber-framed house with an overhang, built by a zealous priest in 1420 as a school for poor boys. It is now the Church House. In 1805 the people of Henley, who were very theatre conscious, built their own Kenton Theatre, with a charming curved gallery. Its round leaded windows still look out on to the street below. The flint- and chequer-work parish church, with its tall Perpendicular tower serving as a landmark, has some 14th-cent. features but is

Henley-on-Thames is linked to Buckinghamshire by an elegant 18th-cent. bridge

mostly 15th-cent. with later additions. It is rich in monuments to wealthy benefactors to the town. In the churchyard is the tomb of Richard Jennings, master builder of St Paul's under Christopher Wren.

The Henley Regatta has brought more fame to the town than any other of its many activities. The first inter-university boat race was held here in 1829, and by 1839 it had become a recognized event and its reputation established by splendid prizes offered by patrons. Not least was the patronage afforded by the Prince Consort who bestowed the title of Royal Henley Regatta. By late Victorian and Edwardian days it had become one of the highlights of the English Season, with fashionable and pretty girls vying for attention with the athletic prowess on the river. It is held at the beginning of July and lasts for four days, usually ending with a splendid fireworks display on the Saturday.

Stonor Park is a beautiful old manor house of splendid proportions which lies 5 m. N. of Henley on the B480. It is open to the public for a considerable part of the year. Set in richly timbered parkland beneath a wood-crested hill, its mellow Tudor brickwork is unimpaired by time and weather. The Stonors have worshipped in the private chapel of the house for over 600 years. The original medieval buildings were made into one house in Tudor times, and the library and Great Hall date from this period. In 1760 a new roof and additional windows were incorporated, giving Stonor Park the appearance it has today.

In the Elizabethan religious unrest Edmund Campion was a constant visitor and had a secret printing press in a concealed room. The park is one of the most beautiful in southern England with paths winding under the shade of spreading nut trees. It is worth asking the way to the little hamlet of Maidensgrove and going on foot, since directions are too complicated to write down.

HEREFORD, *Herefordshire* (8–SO5040), is situated on a level plain bounded in the distance by low-lying hills. The southern area of the town is edged by the River Wye which flows under a medieval bridge, to the W. of which is a modern span of concrete and steel carrying the new ring road over the river from its route along the line of the medieval city wall. Hereford is a cathedral city, albeit of modest size, and also an important agricultural centre. It has a bustling cattle market where farmers from either side of the border mingle. Hereford's history is closely bound up with Wales. Great changes are taking place in the city at present, with much modern development.

The Cathedral Church dedicated in honour of SS. Mary and Ethelbert is likely to be the first monument to arouse the visitor's interest as he comes down Broad Street. That there was an ancient Celtic bishopric here before the arrival of St Augustine in England seems very likely. The cathedral owes its foundation to King Offa of Mercia, who built the famous dyke that runs 6 m. to the W. of the city and defined and defended English territory. Offa was responsible for the beheading of Ethelbert, King of East Anglia. In expiation he built a costly shrine to receive the body of the martyred king. In 825 a new stone church was built over the shrine and in 1030 this was replaced by a still larger church which was destroyed by Welsh marauders in 1056. The cathedral was probably begun by the Norman Bishop Robert Losinga in 1079, although documentary evidence credits Bishop Reynelm with founding the present church.

Besides the massive red sandstone tower built between 1300 and 1310 (the pinnacles were only added in the last century), the cathedral is notable for the superb Norman work which has survived in the great pillars of the nave arcade. What is seen today, however, is only a part of what the Norman builders achieved. In 1786 their lofty west tower collapsed and destroyed two bays of the nave and the greater part of the original triforium and clerestory. The efforts of famous architects throughout the last 200 years to try to restore the balance of the building have not always been successful. To the rest of the varied architecture, every age has added something of value. The beautiful Lady Chapel is Early English in style. It possesses some of the oldest

Hereford: a distant view of the cathedral across the River Wye

stained glass in the cathedral. To the south is a screen dividing it from Bishop Audley's magnificent two-storied chantry, with its stair-turret. The three original chantry chapel doors are particularly fine. The north transept is perhaps the most rewarding part of the cathedral. It was planned by Bishop Aquablanca in the reign of Henry III. He was the friend of Peter of Savoy who built the palace of that name in London. The bishop is buried here in a tomb which is a worthy tribute to his sensitivity and taste. The work is Early English at its purest, with tall slender windows rising to the full height of the transept. It was probably built about the mid-13th cent. as Aquablanca died in 1268. The work was completed by St Thomas Cantilupe who died in 1282 and was canonized in 1320. The rich pedestal of his shrine is still here, arcaded with Purbeck shafts and guarded by 15 carved effigies of Knights Templar, of whose order Bishop Cantilupe was Grand Master. In the south transept is a fine German 16th-cent. triptych of the Adoration of the Magi. Most unusual here is the ancient fire-place; one of only two of its kind to survive in England. Another rare treasure is the ancient Mappa Mundi; a map of a flat world, drawn and painted by a prebendary of Hereford, Richard of Haldingham, probably at LINCOLN in 1275. Measuring 65 in. by 53 in. it includes considerable, if curious detail. Jerusalem is shown as the centre of the world and England and Ireland on the very outside edge. Above the east aisle is the biggest chained library in the world. It consists of some 1,500 books, both printed and handwritten. Its most ancient treasure is a 7th-cent. commentary on the Gospel of St Matthew; the early centuries are spanned by a most unusual collection. Seventy printed books date from before 1500, including two by Caxton.

Much of the exterior of Hereford Cathedral has suffered from the ravages of time, battle and restorers. In the mid-19th cent. there was a general restoration by Sir G. Gilbert Scott whose work generally replaced the rebuilding undertaken by James Wyatt after the disaster of 1786. Wyatt's west front was rebuilt to Oldrid Scott's plans between 1904 and 1908.

The Bishop's Palace stands on the south side of the cathedral overlooking the river. It presents a fine Georgian façade which conceals a Norman hall with wooden columns and arcades. It was well restored in 1954. The Vicars College can be reached through a door in the south-east transept. It is connected to the cathedral by an oak-roofed gallery dating from the 15th cent.

Hereford Cathedral shares the Three Choirs Festival with WORCESTER and GLOUCESTER and this major musical event is held here every third year.

Hardly less important in Hereford's history is the 14th-cent. Church of All Saints. Most of the present church was built in the early 14th cent. and by the beginning of the 16th cent. it was more or less as it is seen today. An earlier church had close connections with Vienne, near Lyons. It was a *Commanderie* hospice of the Order of St Anthony the Hermit which was absorbed into the Order of St John of Jerusalem during the Crusades. In the south chapel is yet another chained library of considerable importance. It possesses a copy of a book on the seven Deadly Sins by an Englishman, Alexander Carpenter, but printed in Paris by Pierre Levet in 1497. The choir stalls are 14th-cent. and have misericords that include two mermaids, two mice and two bears. David Garrick was baptized here in 1717.

In the centre of the town stands an attractive timber-framed house which was built in 1621 and is known as the Old House. It houses an excellent collection of 17th-cent. furniture. Down a narrow passage near the Old House is the ancient Booth Hall, now a hotel. Its main restaurant is in the 14th-cent. panelled and timber-roofed hall on the first floor. It seems likely that this was the original Merchants' Guild Hall. The City Museum and Art Gallery in Broad Street, apart from contemporary watercolours, has a fine collection of Roman remains, including two tessellated pavements dug up from the nearby garrison centre of Kenchester (Magnis). The nearby Green Dragon Hotel has on its first floor a Jacobean room with some lovely plasterwork and a wooden frieze of dolphins. On the other side of the road what is now the City Arms Hotel was once the 18th-cent. residence of the Dukes of Norfolk.

In Gwynne Street, earlier known as Pipe Lane, down towards the river, is a tablet recording the site of the house where Nell Gwynn was born. Charles II made her son Duke of St Albans and his son became Bishop of Hereford. N. of the junction of High Street and High Town is Widemarsh Street, at the end of which stands the Coningsby Hospital founded in 1614. It retains parts of the 13th- and 14th-cent. Templar house of the Knights of St John. Just behind is the only surviving friars' preaching cross in England, a reminder that adjoining was a "Blackfriars" built in 1322 in spite of the opposition of the cathedral chapter to the coming of the Dominicans. One of the most pleasant places to stroll is Castle Green with its almost 30-ft-high ramparts, once the bailey of the castle. The Castle Pool Hotel stands approximately where the moat was. The Nelson Column on the Green reminds the visitor that Lord Nelson was a freeman of the City of Hereford.

A major contribution to modern Hereford's prosperity is its cider industry and it claims the world's biggest cider-making plant. The special bitter-sweet varieties of cider apples are grown all over the county and gathered towards the end of the autumn season. They are then delivered to the Hereford factory where the process of fermenting, filtering and blending can be viewed on a guided tour of the factory. Some $2\frac{1}{2}$ m. SE. of the city is Dinedor Hill with splendid views across the FOREST OF DEAN. Its summit, sheltered by beeches, is said to have been the camp of the Roman general Ostorius Scapula when attacking the forces of Caractacus.

Much Dewchurch, 6 m. SSW. of the city on the B4348 linking the A465 and A49, is a charming old village with a timbered inn. The church, which has a Norman chancel arch, contains memorials to the Pye family who defended KILPECK Castle during the Civil War. **Lugwardine** is another typical little Herefordshire village just 2 m. E. of Hereford on the A438. The ending -wardine is also typical of the county. In Anglo-Saxon days it referred to an enclosed farmstead, like the names ending in -worth, of which it is a variant. Just above the banks of the River Lugg, which is crossed by two ancient bridges, one of them 14th-cent. or older, it has the usual trim black-and-white cottages far removed from the rather drab newer building at the other end of the village. The red-sandstone church appears to have had Norman origins though the tower is good 14th-cent. Its 17th-cent. monuments and brasses are interesting. There are two good country houses in the area. Longworth House about $1\frac{1}{4}$ m. to the SE. was built in 1788 by Anthony Keck. Almost opposite is New Court, an interesting Georgian house, much Gothicized with castellations and turrets at the beginning of the 19th cent. Its Georgian integrity is preserved inside where there is a fine rococo plaster ceiling completed in the early 1750s.

HOARWITHY, *Herefordshire* (8–SO5429), is a pleasant village about 6 m. NW. of ROSS, crossed by a loop in the Wye, where the salmon fishing (privately owned) is particularly good. It can be reached by an unclassified road turning off the A49 about halfway between ROSS and HEREFORD. It possesses an extraordinary Italianate church, built in the 19th cent. complete with a good campanile. William Poole, a prebendary of Hereford and vicar here for nearly 50 years, spent a fortune on building and embellishing the church. A large team of Italian workmen was brought over to work with local craftsmen and a number settled in Herefordshire. The chancel is enriched with marbles brought from Ireland and the Continent, and the choir dome is supported by columns of pink-grey marble from Devon. Everywhere the glitter of gold mosaic and the lavish use of lapis lazuli catch the eye. Mosaic pavements and cosmati work such as may be seen in early Roman basilicas complete the Italian effect.

Little lanes lead through a countryside of great charm to **Kings Caple**, past the Aramstone estate where unhappily the 18th-cent. red-brick mansion has been torn down, though left with fine outhouses and stables. The village has a red-sandstone church with a good 14th-cent. tower and spire. It contains interesting monuments to the Scottish Ferguson family, who were connected by marriage with many of the neighbouring county families. Also a short drive away through unspoilt country is the little village of **Fawley** with its tiny Norman church and Fawley Court, a splendid timber-framed farm-house that stands by a pond and has beautiful black-and-white barns. The staircase with turned balusters points to a prosperous 18th-cent. period, as does much of the unimpaired panelling in the house.

HONINGTON, *Warwickshire* (9–SP2642), just off the A34 N. of SHIPSTON-ON-STOUR, is an agreeable parkland village set round a green with its main street tucked discreetly away. It seems to have come into being because a London merchant Sir Henry Parker built Honington Hall in 1682 as an expression of his prosperity. The Church of All Saints has only a 15th-cent. tower to justify its claim to antiquity; the rest of the building is purely late 17th-cent. Classical with some excellent English rococo work. The Stour flows close by and is crossed by a five-arched bridge with 22 stone balls on the parapet. Just by the gate piers stands a timber-framed building known as Magpie House, well worth the short walk to see it.

KELMSCOTT, *Oxfordshire* (5–SU2499), is a place of pilgrimage for devotees of the Pre-Raphaelite movement, founded by William Morris (who is buried with his wife in the churchyard) and his friend Burne-Jones. They were joined in a community venture by Rossetti, Ford Madox Brown and the architect George Edward Street, and revolutionized design in English interior decoration. Kelmscott enshrines their conception of beauty and their attempts to uphold the individuality and dignity of hand work against the uniformity of mass production. Morris moved here from Kent in 1871 and bought the

Elizabethan manor house, now owned by the Society of Antiquaries. He died in 1896. His grave is under the shade of an evergreen with a simple stone carved by Philip Webb with oak and vine leaves. The little 12th-cent. church has some wall paintings in the north transept and original scroll paintings in reds and golds on the inside of the rounded arches. The village with gabled stone houses remains well cared for. Its name gave Morris the imprint for his private printing press.

KENCOT, *Oxfordshire* (5–SP2504). About 2½ m. S. from BURFORD, on the A361, an unclassified road off to the left leads through meadows and orchards to the village of Kencot, with its ancient elm islanded on a small green. An interesting small Norman church makes the detour well worth while. The tower base was begun in the 13th cent. and completed 200 years later. The south door has an unusual Norman tympanum with a centaur shooting an arrow into the throat of a fearsome beast. The sculptor inscribed it with the word Sagittarius to show its astrological significance. Inside are good Norman pillars and a painted Jacobean pulpit.

The little by-road winds on to an adjoining village called **Broadwell** which has some fine weathered stone cottages. The tall Early English spire was built on to a late Norman church with good chevron and dogtooth carving.

Just beyond these two last villages on the same winding lane is another attractive stone village, **Langford,** which is set in the meadows of the upper reaches of the Thames. How such a splendid very early Norman church came to be built in this little backwater is something of a mystery. There was certainly an Anglo-Saxon church on which the Normans built. Carvings and grotesques round the gabled roof date from the time of King Stephen. The 12th-cent. doorway is set between two flying buttresses. The most interesting features are the Norman rood with later 14th-cent. carvings of SS. Mary and John; their heads turned away from the cross. On the other side on the east wall is a carving of Christ which may well be Anglo-Saxon. The chancel and west end are Early English and have unusual distinguishing features which add to the interest of this most unusual church. Within walking distance are two other villages with delightful English names, Filkins and Broughton Poggs.

KENILWORTH, *Warwickshire* (9–SP2872), lies between COVENTRY and WARWICK on the A46. It is rapidly becoming a dormitory for Coventry. Its rather pretentious Victorian residential area was given some of its impetus by the fame of Sir Walter Scott's historical novel. On the north side of the town several old houses of considerable charm survive from an earlier phase of building from the 15th cent. Kenilworth Castle remains the chief glory. This has been called the grandest fortress ruin in England. Norman, Plantagenet and finally Tudor monarchs all played a part in its development.

Starting as a wooden fortress built in A.D. 1112 by Geoffrey de Clinton, who was chamberlain and treasurer to Henry I, it rapidly gained in importance. The keep that still stands was built in 1162 by a son of the first de Clinton, with money provided by Henry II. King John paid several visits to Kenilworth and provided £2,000, a lot in those days, to be spent on its defences. In 1199 another de Clinton surrendered all his rights to the king. Henry III gave it to his sister who had married Simon de Montfort. By 1361 Kenilworth Castle came into the possession of Blanche, of the Lancastrian house, who married John of Gaunt. He was the first owner to transform it from a fortress into a grand castle.

He built the great hall and the long wing of private apartments. Much of this is still recognizable in the ruins. From John of Gaunt the castle went to his son Henry IV and remained a royal residence, until in 1563 Queen Elizabeth gave the castle to her favourite Robert Dudley. The queen conferred on Dudley the title of Earl of Leicester. Then began a new and magnificent period for Kenilworth. Costly entertainments such as had rarely been seen in England were provided for the pleasure of the queen. Leicester converted all the old apartments and erected a great range of new buildings to adjoin the chapel built by Henry VIII. Nothing remains of this chapel other than the foundations. The Long Barn and Great Gatehouse were all built by him at this period. It was only after his death that Kenilworth began its slow decline.

The end came with the Civil War when Cromwell ordered the castle to be dismantled. After the Restoration it passed into the hands of the Clarendon family, whose successors passed it over to the state shortly before the Second World War. The ruins are now in the care of the Ministry of Public Building and Works.

The Church of St Nicholas, though mainly Perpendicular in style, has a good Norman doorway. It is believed that it may have been an entrance to the old priory church of the Augustinians which like Kenilworth Castle was founded by Geoffrey de Clinton. It is situated in Abbey Fields where intelligent excavation has revealed practically the whole lay-out of this great abbey, dissolved by Henry VIII.

KIDDERMINSTER, *Worcestershire* (8–SO 8376). This great carpet-manufacturing centre on the River Stour lies on the north-west fringe of the county, 17 m. from BIRMINGHAM and 15 m. from WORCESTER. Flemish weavers gave Kidderminster a certain prosperity between the 13th and 14th cents. and in the 18th cent. the foundations of its carpet industry were laid. John Broom speculated three fortunes on improving his hand-loom and by 1735 Pearsall had built the first factory. There is a good museum in Exchange Street with a working model of the old carpet loom, complete with specimen carpet. It also has some fine examples of Japanese silk embroideries. There is little in the town to excite interest except its late medieval, red-sandstone church. The building is rich in fine monuments with an excep-

British Travel Association

Kilpeck church: the south doorway

tional brass dated 1415 to the memory of two warriors, the richer armour and scabbard denoting the knight, Sir John Phelip, and the plainer armour his wife's first husband, Walter Cookesey. The lady is in early 15th-cent. dress and stands between them with a little dog looking up at her. Tombs of Lady Joyce Beauchamp and Thomas Blount, the latter dated 1569, are worthy of note. A famous son of Kidderminster was Sir Rowland Hill who established the penny post. There is a statue of him in the centre of the town. Nearby is also a statue of Richard Baxter, the 17th-cent. Presbyterian divine, who attracted such vast crowds to the church to hear him preach that five galleries had to be built to hold them. He was imprisoned for nonconformism. He made the town his principal centre of evangelism.

One m. NW. of the city in pleasant wooded countryside is **Harvington Hall**, a 16th-cent. gabled brick house with stone and mullioned windows masking a late medieval building. It is surrounded by a moat crossed by two bridges and was the home of another man persecuted for his faith, John Wall, a Roman Catholic priest and one of the last men in England to be martyred for his faith, in 1679. The house originally belonged to the Pakington family and passed from them by marriage to the Throckmortons. That the house had long been used as a shelter for hunted priests is evidenced by the honeycomb of secret passages, trapdoors, sliding panels and the hidden rooms called priests' holes; one of them is secreted under a false stairway. The house now belongs to the Archdiocese of Birmingham. This house is open to the public at advertised times. There is a portrait of John Wall in the Roman Catholic church and a crucifix to his memory in the churchyard.

KILPECK, *Herefordshire* (8–SO4430), owes its fame to its small Norman church, the most perfectly preserved and architecturally the richest example of its kind in the British Isles. Kilpeck lies about 9 m. from HEREFORD, just S. of the A465. It had a long military and monastic history. Little remains of the castle other than the ruins of what must have been an important motte and bailey: the walled enclosure was of impressive size and included the church. Nothing remains of the priory. It seems that Hugh FitzNorman gave the land to the Benedictines of St Peter at GLOUCESTER, who founded the priory in 1135 and built the church within the next five years on the site of an earlier Anglo-Saxon structure, of which some stones remain in the north-east corner of the nave. The south doorway is sumptuously carved. In the tympanum is a formalized Tree of Life bearing thick grapes. The outer arch is rich in linked medallions of birds, mythical monsters, fish, a lion with a very human face, a phoenix in flames and dragons swallowing each other with such abandon that the final dragon is swallowing itself. A flying angel with a palm restores a sense of the triumph of order. The shafts are equally decorated with snake-like monsters entwining other figures. Two men wearing Phrygian caps and tight trews are intriguing. The stone to build this church must have been well chosen for it has weathered nearly 900 years, and the detail remains clear. The interior of the church, consisting of nave, chancel and apse diminishing in both height and width, gives a great sense of length. The two chancel arches demand particularly close attention as the carving is obviously by a different hand. The draping of the haloed apostles is most graceful. On the piers of one of the arches are three groups of male figures, one on top of the other. The top one carries a book and cross, the middle one, a book and key, and the lowest, a book and water sprinkler. On the exterior a corbel table embraces the whole church with such a wealth of carving that the visitor could spend hours on a summer afternoon and still not exhaust the humour of the figures. There are at least 80 figures left (when very careful Victorian restoration work was carried out, some of the figures were considered too erotic in detail and removed). The west window is quite unusual, nook-shafted with good interlacing. A holy-water stoup standing by a curious carved figure has an enormous bowl clasped by elongated arms and resting on a base carved with snakes' heads. Under the Jacobean gallery (which does not seem out of place) at the west end, is a huge Norman font carved out of breccia standing on five shafts, one of which has been restored. Coming out into the light of day the visitor may be surprised at the wealth of late Georgian tombstones in the churchyard.

Dippersmoor Manor nearby is 15th-cent.; its owners breed pedigree Jersey cattle.

KING'S PYON, *Herefordshire* (8–SO4350), lies 8 m. NW. of HEREFORD just W. of the A4110 in a beautifully wooded part of the countryside with views of the Malverns on one side and the distant Welsh hills on the other. The church in a lovely setting overlooking the village has a Norman south doorway with a Transitional chancel arch. Its chief glory, however, is its superb early 14th-cent. black-and-white roofs over the nave and over the south transept. In this transept under a Decorated canopy are two 14th-cent. alabaster effigies of a somewhat mutilated hip-belted knight and his lady wearing a curious square-topped headdress. One m. S. of the village is the Butthouse (pronounced Buttus locally), an unusual early 17th-cent. timber-framed house with an even more interesting ornamented gate-house dated 1632 incorporating a dovecot. The ancient Augustinian priory of Wormsley was near this site. A little to the SW. is a farm called Black Hall which has a medieval barn with cruck trusses. This is yet another Herefordshire village which invites the motorist to leave his car and wander off in almost any direction to enjoy an infinitely varied and tranquil countryside.

KINGTON, *Herefordshire* (8–SO2956), is a small and ancient market town sheltered by the 1,389-ft Hergest (pronounced Hargest, the "g" hard) Ridge. It is situated near the Welsh border on the A44, 14 m. W. of LEOMINSTER. The River Arrow flows through. It remains important for its sheep and cattle market. Its Norman church can be seen at the top of a steep hill from an old stone bridge crossing the river. Although it retains its Norman tower and doorway as well as an exqui-site 13th-cent. chancel, most of the church was unfortunately restored in 1874. It has a fine tomb with the alabaster figures of Thomas Vaughan and his wife. He was killed at the Battle of BANBURY in 1469. Many of the more interesting buildings were either swept away or restored out of recog-nition in the mid-Victorian period. However, some good Georgian houses escaped. Just outside Kington is the Vaughans' mostly 15th-cent. Hergest Court, a farm-house since they departed. It was reputed to be haunted by the ghost of a black bloodhound and by Black Vaughan. On nearby Rushock Hill and Kennel Wood is a good stretch of **Offa's Dyke**. Like CHURCH STRETTON in Shropshire, Kington claims England's highest golf course.

KNOWLE, *Warwickshire* (9–SP1876). This vil-lage, where much new housing has been built, lies almost on the perimeter of **Solihull** on the main WARWICK road. The village centre remains remarkably unspoiled. Knowle has perhaps the best Perpendicular church in Warwickshire, built by Walter Cook and completed in 1402. Fourteen years later it became a collegiate church with 10 priests attached to it. This was due to the rapid rise of the guild which Cook had founded. The church has a handsome screen and carved choir-stalls all dating from the 15th cent. On the pulpit may be seen a curious 17th-cent. hourglass for timing sermons. Cook's beautiful guild house, with a timbered hall, stands just W. of the church-yard.

Chester House in the High Street is a fine twin-gabled, timber-framed house of the 15th cent.

A worthwhile ½-m. walk northwards out of Knowle leads to Grimshaw Hall, built about 1560. Its lovely leaded upper windows are set into overhanging gables with varied herringbone and lozenge timber designs. The house with its fine projecting porch has undergone little restoration and the oriel windows on brackets are just as they were when it was built.

The new shopping centre fits quite well into its village setting.

LAPWORTH, *Warwickshire* (9–SP1671). Just SSE. of Hockley Heath, on the WARWICK road, this scattered village has great charm and an interesting church. There is a small Norman north window, but most of the church dates from the 13th or 14th cent. An unusual feature is the partly detached tower which is connected by a passage with the north aisle. There is some good modern glass in the north window and a sensitive carving by Eric Gill of the *Mater Amabilis* on the west wall. It is well worth visiting the porch with an unusual room above it which was possibly used for the exposition of relics. A good walk 1½ m. E. to Kingswood leads to a cast-iron bridge at a junction of the Grand Union and STRATFORD-UPON-AVON Canals, with good views over the basin.

LEAMINGTON SPA, *Warwickshire* (9–SP 3166). This town of about 50,000 inhabitants owes its being to the passion for taking the waters which was at its fashionable height in the late 18th and early 19th cent. It followed in the wake of BATH and was contemporaneous with MAT-LOCK and BUXTON. Camden had in fact dis-covered the curative qualities of its waters in 1586 but it was only in 1786 that William Abbots built the first Spa Bath.

Dr Henry Jephson, a brilliant physician who received Queen Victoria in 1838, was really responsible for the planning of the town as it is today, and gained it its royal prefix. The Pump Room dates from 1814 but was rebuilt in 1925. All the lovely Georgian, Regency and early Vic-torian terraced houses are to be found on the north side of the River Leam crossed by the Victoria Bridge. Lansdowne Crescent, where Nathaniel Hawthorne lived at No. 10, and New-bold Terrace can compare with the Bath streets and crescents. Napoleon III lived at No. 4 Clarendon Square for a while after the débâcle of 1870. The Jephson Gardens were laid out as a memorial to the town's great benefactor, whose foresight had drawn to Leamington Spa not only the Queen but the Duke of Wellington, Long-fellow and Sarah Bernhardt, and many more of the famous and the great, to take its waters. These gardens along the River Leam remain a popular place of promenade. The Church of All Saints was built in rather pretentious French Gothic style between 1843 and 1869, though it possesses, through benefactors, some good Tudor and 17th-cent. plate.

LECHLADE, *Gloucestershire* (5–SU2199). Almost on the borders of Oxfordshire, Berkshire and Wiltshire, where the tributaries Leach and Coln flow into the Thames, here called the Isis, is the unspoilt village of Lechlade. It has a good number of small brick and stone Georgian houses. The elegant spire of the 15th-cent. Perpendicular church dedicated to St Lawrence dominates the village. The panelled chancel roof is ornamented by some 40 exquisitely carved bosses and stone corbels, and the exterior is parapeted with two rich tiers of quatrefoils. Pinnacled buttresses bear the weight. Lechlade is naturally a favourite place for boating. It is interesting to remember that stone for Sir Christopher Wren's dome of ST PAUL's was loaded into barges here.

LEDBURY, *Herefordshire* (8–SO7037). Almost on the borders of Herefordshire, Gloucestershire and Worcestershire, Ledbury stands on the lower slopes of a ridge running parallel to the nearby Malvern Hills which lie to the E. of the ancient town. It is situated on the A438, roughly midway between TEWKESBURY and HEREFORD and is a good centre for exploring an exceptionally beautiful part of England. Ledbury is traversed by a long street with its angled Market Place dominated by a delightful black-and-white Market House, timbered in herringbone pattern, raised on 16 columns of oak timber. The windows have leaded panes. It was built between 1617 and 1655. Cobbled Church Lane connects the Market Place and the church and epitomizes Tudor and Stuart streets. It has half-timbered houses with overhanging upper stories and a well-used and lived-in air that enhances its beauty. Almost opposite the Market House is St Katharine's Hospital founded in the 14th cent. by Bishop ffolliott. Only the red-stone chapel, with some stained glass and some tiles, belongs to this period; of the remainder some was rebuilt by Smirke in 1822 and the rest in 1866. The famous Feathers Hotel nearby is one of the best of the many good half-timbered buildings of which Ledbury is justly proud. First place of honour must, however, be given to the five-gabled Ledbury Park built by Lord Biddulph in 1590. Along the WORCESTER road is an early 19th-cent. extension and the garden wall skirts along Southend. From this house Prince Rupert directed a successful engagement with the Parliamentarians in 1646.

By New Street is another old inn, The Talbot, which possesses a beautiful panelled room with an overmantle, all of which dates from 1596. On the opposite side is The Steppes, equally old but partly restored. The mostly 14th-cent. Church of St Michael claims pre-eminence among all the parish churches of Herefordshire. It has an unusually wide nave and side aisles. The nucleus of the original church is Norman, as can be seen from the chancel arcade with its round pillars supported on sturdy square bases. The west door has a round arch and late Norman zigzag work. The north porch is Early English and a jamb of the door still bears the incision of a consecration cross. The upper story of the porch seems to have been added in the 14th cent. The detached early 13th-cent. tower of the church has an 18th-cent. recessed spire 202 ft high built by Wilkinson of Worcester to replace an earlier timber spire. A great deal of the glass in the church is Victorian, by Kempe, though there are some very early fragments, particularly in the north chapel which also possesses a fine effigy of a 13th-cent. priest in full eucharistic vestments. The church is rich in monuments, especially of the Biddulph family. The Renaissance Skynner Tomb is a particularly interesting piece of humanized funerary sculpture. The five slightly bearded sons and five Stuart-capped daughters kneel beneath the canopied slab with the two beruffed parents kneeling with a plump baby in long clothes between them. At the east end of the north aisle is a monument to Edward Moulton Barrett who is buried here. He was the unbending father of Elizabeth Barrett Browning who was brought up at nearby Hope End, where at 15 she had the accident which was to aggravate her long illness. Three nearby houses are of considerable interest. The 15th-cent. Woodhouse Farm, gabled with tall chimneys, has a great hall and buttery. The five-bayed Dingwood Park, approximately 1¾ m. SSE. from the town centre, was built about 1700 and has elegant stucco ceilings with flower and vine designs. Poet Laureate John Masefield was born in a Ledbury house called the Knapp in 1878.

Eastnor, a village in lovely countryside, is just 2 m. E. of Ledbury on the A438 and has black-and-white cottages set against a tree-lined green. There is a pyramid-roofed well with interesting terracotta panels. In 1812 the 1st Earl Somers built a romantic baronial castle reminiscent of the Marcher days of Edward I. It was completed by the architect Smirke in 1814. He built a great hall 60 ft long and 65 ft high in the centre of the castle. The drawing-room was both designed and furnished by A. W. N. Pugin. The castle, which is open at advertised times to the public, is set in a fine deer park. This is beautifully wooded and has many rare trees. The collection of armour, paintings, tapestries and *objets d'art* is quite outstanding. The parish church, though a Norman foundation, is practically entirely the work of Sir G. Gilbert Scott who rebuilt the church and rectory between 1849 and 1852. The 14th-cent. tower was rebuilt but a late Norman south doorway was left intact. One of the church's acquired treasures is a superb embroidered Venetian red-velvet altar-frontal. A pleasant walk may be made 1 m. eastwards to Bronsil Castle which is a genuine but romantic ruin of the crenellated fortress of Richard Beauchamp, treasurer to King Henry VI. Little remains but the inner moat, which is still filled with water, and part of the gatehouse. The tall obelisk nearby was raised by Earl Somers to the memory of his son, who died in battle at Burgos the year building commenced on Eastnor Castle. Two m. to the E. lies the greater part of an Iron Age hill-fort marked by the twin summits of Midsummer Hill and Hollybush.

LEOMINSTER, *Herefordshire* (8–SO4959), pronounced "Lemster", was for 500 years one of the great wool markets of England and is now the centre of a thriving agricultural area. It is set among pastureland, hopfields and orchards in a countryside watered by three streams, the Lugg, the Pinsley and the Arrow. The narrow High Street runs N. and S. and is fronted by medieval timber-framed houses with overhanging gables. Drapers Row, behind High Street, and even narrower, has some good Tudor houses. Broad Street and Etnam Street by contrast are wide thoroughfares with Georgian brick houses telling of Leominster's 18th-cent. prosperity, when the fine wool known as Lemster Ore was renowned in all England. In Bridge Street is a house, No. 29, dating from 1400. The mid-Victorian Italianate Town Hall leaves something to be desired, the more so as comparison with the old Town Hall is inevitable. The latter, near the ancient priory church and now known as Grange Court, was built in 1633 by the remarkable John Abel, and originally stood at the crossroads in the town centre. Up to the time of its removal in 1855, its ground floor with its colonnade of oaken Ionic columns was used as the butter market. It was sold for the derisory sum (even for Victorian days) of £95. It was re-erected on its present site and the ground floor filled in with masonry. It is one of the loveliest timber-framed houses in the county, two-storied with fine bays and adorned with elegant carvings. The windows of the upper-story project and have unusual carvings of male and female busts. John Abel's original inscription can still be read on the frieze in which he says his columns support the fabric as "noble gentry . . . support the honour of a Kingdom".

Although Leominster is so rich in early English domestic architecture it is its reddish stone Priory Church set on open swards of green which can never fail to delight and impress the visitor. Its foundation is generally attributed to Earl Leofric, husband of Lady Godiva, who established a nunnery here. Nothing survives of the Anglo-Saxon church and in Norman times a Benedictine priory was founded from READING Abbey, which was already wealthy in the time of Henry I. The north aisle with its massive Norman columns gives a majestic sense of spaciousness while the triforium with interlaced arches and the rounded windows of the clerestory give an impression of height unequalled in any other Norman church in the country. This is the earliest part of the priory church which has no less than three naves. The central nave is enriched with a traceried 15th-cent. west window. The 14th-cent. aisle has superb Decorated windows. The west tower was built in the following century with fine Perpendicular panelling. In 1699 a disastrous fire destroyed the original chancel and damaged the arcade, necessitating the rebuilding of the columns supporting it. The more recent restoration work has been carried out with restraint and such skill that the church has probably not looked more beautiful during the last 250 years than it does today. It possesses one of the finest 15th-cent. chalices in

England. A ducking stool is preserved in good working order in the church. Silver birches, limes and yews grow in the churchyard.

Leominster Out Parish, the area S. and W. of the town, has a number of interesting houses. There are timber-framed farm-houses, barns and hop-kilns as well as some fine Georgian brick mansions. Outstanding among these is Broadward Hall, 1½ m. S. of the town, a two-storied building with a good Venetian window and an earlier square dovecot bearing the date 1652. Wharton Court, a rather severe Jacobean house, should also be seen. It has not suffered from undue restoration. It is famous for its elaborate staircase, dating from the first year of James I's reign, which sweeps upwards to the third story of the house. About ½ m. beyond Wharton on Brierley Hill is an Iron Age hill-fort, one of the most interesting prehistoric camps in the county.

About 3 m. N. of Leominster, just W. of the A49, is **Berrington Hall**, a handsome red sandstone 18th-cent. house built by the younger Henry Holland between 1778 and 1781 for Thomas Harley. The house, owned now by the National Trust and open at advertised times during the summer season, is practically as Holland built and decorated it. The hall, library and drawing-room all have remarkable plaster ceilings and are splendidly furnished. The Classical staircase is most impressive. The house stands in 455 acres of parkland, with rare trees, shrubs and plants. This includes the famous pool of 14 acres laid out by Capability Brown in 1780. About 1¼ m. W. of the A49 Leominster–LUDLOW road, reached by an unclassified road, is **Eye Manor**, also open to the public at advertised times. The house, set in fine grounds, was built by a Barbados slave-trader Ferdinando Gorges in 1680. The beautiful interior, with splendid plasterwork and rich in furniture and paintings, is an abiding testimony to the profitability of that inhuman commerce. There is a collection of books and period costumes. The church has a fine porch of carved oak.

Some 7 m. WSW. of the town on the A4112 road to Brecon is the village of **Dilwyn**, with a number of half-timbered houses and a fine parish church, wide, with lofty 13th-cent. arcades and clerestory. It has its original medieval roof. It has three finely traceried screens, dating from the 15th cent.; that of the chancel is elegant, with fan vaulting springing from fluted columns. The massive tower belonged to an older church and dates from the late 12th and early 13th cent. The little spire was added 200 years ago. About 1½ m. WNW. of the church is a timber-framed manor house called Luntley Court. Not least of its charms are to be found in its outhouses and gabled dovecot with 500 nesting holes. Two m. in the opposite direction lies Swanston Court which had major additions in the 18th cent. but retains its 14th-cent. hall range in its cross-wings. One m. to the N. is yet another uncommon house, Bidney Farm with an early 17th-cent. black-and-white dovecot. All around is pleasant walking country.

MAPLEDURHAM, *Oxfordshire* (5–SU6776), is one of the villages in South Oxfordshire which lie on the banks of the River Thames. It is a short distance from PANGBOURNE and Caversham on a by-lane off the main Goring to READING road. Sheltered by wooded hills, it slopes down to the river, dotted with picturesque cottages, and boasts an ivy-clad mill and a row of early 17th-cent. almshouses. They were built by John Lister, a member of the ancient Blount family. Sir Michael Blount built the impressive pink-brick Tudor manor house, Mapledurham Court, where he entertained Queen Elizabeth I. Two of his descendants were the somewhat eccentric Martha and Teresa Blount, friends of the poet Alexander Pope. The lovely manor houses many art treasures and is still privately owned. It is open to the public at weekends during the summer and on weekdays by arrangement.

The church built between 1381 and 1397 has some fine monuments to the Bardolphs and the Blounts. At one time, the living of the church, which is still in the possession of ETON College, was regarded as one of the plum benefices of the Church of England and a stepping stone to a bishopric. The south aisle remains a Roman Catholic chapel owned by the Blounts, who adhered to this faith. The oak-timbered arcaded ceiling is particularly rare.

MARSHFIELD, *Gloucestershire* (4–ST7773), just off the A420 road into BRISTOL, is almost on the borders of Wiltshire and Somerset. It was once the last staging post for the coaches carrying nobility and gentry into the fashionable BATH of the late 18th cent. Most of the houses date from this period and the inns of the village still carry the stamp of their coaching past. Long before LUTON, Marshfield's fame for making sun bonnets was unrivalled. The long grey-stone street is dominated by the church tower with a graceful gold cock weathervane. The height of the village makes this a landmark for miles around. The church is spacious but not conspicuously interesting. Nicholas Crispe's Almshouses at the other end of the street were built in 1625 and are well worth visiting. So, too, is the great 15th-cent. tithe barn nearby with its 15 splendid bays. Just by the Three Shire Stone outside the village is the entrance to an imposing mansion called the Rock with its avenue of beeches; it was built on to a late Norman castle. There are good views down the valley.

MAXSTOKE CASTLE, *Warwickshire* (9–SP2386). Just off the A47, 1½ m. E. of Coleshill, and reached by a twisting road, stands a square red sandstone fortress, looking rather like a Crusaders' castle of Asia Minor, with turreted polygonal towers and battlemented curtain walls. Maxstoke Castle was built in about 1345 by William de Clinton, Earl of Huntingdon, and has been lived in continuously ever since. It was partially remodelled by Humphrey Stafford, 1st Duke of Buckingham, in 1440 and came into the Dilke family in the late 16th cent. Many of the alterations which have remained to modern times were accomplished by Sir Thomas Dilke. A fine avenue of trees leads to great oak gates where a portcullis once hung. A stone bridge now crosses the perfect moat which is exceedingly deep in places. The great hall of 1345 survives and much history has been enacted within its walls. Many treasures from the time of Richard III to the late Stuarts are preserved here.

From the castle, country roads lead through an area of dairy farms to the village of Maxstoke, where to the W. of the Church of St Michael are the ruins of an Augustinian priory founded in 1336 by that same William de Clinton. The principal items of interest are the two sides of the central tower, the outer gatehouse (the inner gatehouse became an Elizabethan dwelling) and the west wall of the infirmary. The priory originally housed the prior and 12 canons.

MINSTER LOVELL, *Oxfordshire* (5–SP81 11), is one of the most attractive of all the Windrush villages and is famed in history and romantic verse as the home of the ill-fated Lovells. It is situated just off the A40 between WITNEY and BURFORD (5 m. away) across the ancient bridge and sheltered by a hillside. The home of the Lovells, now in ruins, is under the care of the Ministry of Public Building and Works. Francis Lovell, "Lovell the Dog", in the old rhyme, was implicated in the schemes of Richard III and fled after the defeat at Bosworth in 1485, returning in 1487 to champion the Pretender Lambert Simnel. After the débâcle of the Battle of Stoke it is said he returned to Minster Lovell and hid in a secret room. He was looked after by a single servant who died, and Lovell, locked in his concealed room, is said to have perished by starvation. When repairs to the house were being effected in 1718 a vaulted room was discovered with a skeleton seated at a table and the skeleton of a dog at its feet – whether it was Francis Lovell will never be known. The other well-known story connected with the house is that known as "The Mistletoe Bough": a bride of one of the Lovells playing hide-and-seek on her wedding night hid in an ancient chest which locked itself under the weight of its heavy lid. A skeleton was found in a chest many years later. The ruins of the house are open to the public.

The church is Perpendicular and has fine vaulting under the central tower. The church suffered from 19th-cent. restoration but still possesses some 15th-cent. glass.

MOCCAS COURT, *Hereford* (8–SO3542). On a curve of the River Wye, just S. of the little village of **Monnington-on-Wye** off the A438 HEREFORD to Hay road, a lane called Monnington Walk leads to an elegant lodge designed by G. S. Repton, who was working for John Nash at that time. The road leads through the park to Robert Adam's severely Classical brick house, Moccas Court, built between 1775 and 1780 by Anthony Keckby for the Cornewall family. The interior is extraordinarily rich. The Circular Room is exquisite with panelled Etruscan or Pompeian designs. The furnishings are all in keeping with the grand scale of this country house. The grounds were landscaped by Capability Brown. In the park stands a beautiful Norman church which has been carefully restored. It was built of tufa about 1130 and possesses some fine 14th-cent. stained glass with two tiny but interesting figures. The proportions of the round chancel arches are perhaps only second in the county to those at KILPECK.

MORETON-IN-MARSH, *Gloucestershire* (5–SP2032), is a pleasant, prosperous-looking small town with a wide grass-verged main street. The word marsh is a corruption of march, meaning a boundary. The broad street is actually built on the Roman Fosse Way and was originally the crossroads of four counties. It is only 8 m. from CHIPPING NORTON on the A44 Evesham road and 4 m. N. from STOW-ON-THE-WOLD. The old curfew bell still hangs in its tower overlooking the Fosse Way which has a 17th-cent. clock. The church is new but possesses some good Elizabethan plate. Most unusually in this part of the country, it is dedicated to St David. The town has some good 17th- and 18th-cent. houses and has had long connections with the Redesdale family. The Redesdale Arms is a famous old coaching inn and one of several interesting inns in the town. The railway station has long been popular with children for the topiary on its platform.

MORTIMER'S CROSS, *Herefordshire* (8–SO4263). Some 6 m. WNW. of LEOMINSTER on the A4110 is the approximate scene of one of the bloody battles of the Wars of the Roses. An obelisk was erected in 1799 to perpetuate "the memory of an obstinate, bloody and decisive battle fought near this spot in the civil wars between the ambitious houses of York and Lancaster on the second day of February 1460". All this part of Herefordshire was the feudal domain of the powerful Mortimer family. The leader of the Yorkist force on this occasion was Edward Mortimer, Earl of March. The Lancastrians supporting Henry VI were under the command of the Earl of Pembroke and the Earl of Wiltshire. Some 4,000 men were slain in that one day, one of the almost unknown warriors who was taken prisoner and who was later executed in HEREFORD was the Welshman Owen Tudor, whose grandson was to turn the tables and found the Tudor dynasty. With an army of 30,000 men, Edward Mortimer was on his way to London to avenge the murder of his father the Duke of York by Queen Margaret, when he received word of the Lancastrian force barring his way. His victory won him the crown of England to which he laid claim, through his descent from Philippa Plantagenet, grand-daughter of Edward III. One month later the 19-year-old Herefordshire warrior was crowned in London as Edward IV.

All around are delightful villages, many with black-and-white cottages. **Lucton** is nearby with its schoolhouse built by the London merchant John Pierrepont in 1708 and still a public school. **Aymestrey** is set in countryside which invites even the sluggard visitor to walk. Its church has an impressive tall rood-screen. Nearby Yatton Court is a Georgian country house with a very fine Venetian window.

MUCH MARCLE, *Herefordshire* (8–SO6533), is almost on the Gloucestershire border on the A449 ROSS–LEDBURY road and set among cider orchards. It has a beautiful 13th-cent. church, its spacious nave arcades lit by lofty clerestory lights. Its unusually long chancel holds an exquisite 14th-cent. effigy of Blanche, Lady Grandison, her splendidly fitted gown flowing away gracefully and her beautiful hands seeming barely to touch her rosary. The wooden effigy of a man on the window-sill, carved in oak with slender folds, is of one of the rarest types of effigy found in England. Sir John Kyrle is buried in the north chapel in an alabaster tomb. His feet rest on the hedgehog crest of the Kyrles while those of his wife rest on bear's paws, signifying that she was one of the great Scudamore family.

The Kyrles still own Homme House. The early part of the house dates to the beginning of the 16th cent. and the east front is purely Georgian. Above and behind the house is a delightful gazebo dated 1670. The other famous mansion in the neighbourhood is Hellens, a fine Jacobean brick house and once the seat of the Walwyns. There are several superb period rooms, some with very early plaster ceilings. The monogrammed dovecot in the grounds bears the date 1641.

About 1½ m. W. of the Much Marcle church, by the television mast, is an Iron Age hill-fort. Part of the original enclosure exists but the south side has been almost obliterated by cultivation.

NORTH CERNEY, *Gloucestershire* (5–SP 0208). A little to the E. of the CHELTENHAM–CIRENCESTER road, in the Churn valley, is the lovely village of North Cerney. It has some unusually good 18th-cent. houses, Cerney House and the Queen Anne rectory among them. No less attractive are the old farm-house, the mill and the weathered inn. The church is an example of Anglican liturgical taste at its best. The way in which colour has been used enlivens this Norman and Early English church and the whole suggests a continuing sturdy faith. The saddleback west tower was started by the Normans and completed a century later. The south door has five rows of good zigzag Norman ornament. The door and the ironwork on it are at least 600 years old. The rood-loft is modern with an early 17th-cent. Italian Christus. The woodwork of the rood-screen is Jacobean. The church possesses its pre-Reformation altar stone, some good candelabra and altar candlesticks, as well as a 15th-cent. carved wooden statue of the Virgin. Three of the windows at least have 15th-cent. glass. Both pulpit and font are superb examples of the 15th-cent. stonemasons' art. There is a 14th-cent. cross in the churchyard.

Worcestershire: springtime in an orchard in the Teme valley　　　Kenneth Scowen

NORTHLEACH, *Gloucestershire* (5–SP1114), was one of the very prosperous wool towns of the Cotswolds, and its rich, lofty Perpendicular church is a worthy memorial of those days. There is a certain faded beauty about the twisting streets and green-swarded market place and a tranquil imperturbability that ignores the arterial traffic on the A40. There are some pleasant old houses which have also ignored the passing of time: 16th-cent. almshouses, timber-framed houses with overhangs, and a 17th-cent. manor house as well as a tall gabled grammar school.

Its main feature to encourage the motorist to stop is certainly its 15th-cent. parish church with its beautiful south porch. Here canopied niches shelter their ancient saints, centred by the Blessed Virgin Mary, while the upward thrust of the buttressed arch finds its apex in the carving of the Trinity. The vaulted roof rests on six rounded shafts with flowered capitals. The irrepressible humour of this robust period is caught in a grotesque of a cat fiddling to three rats. The nave with its tall clerestory was built by John Fortey. Near the chancel under the north arcade is a brass recording his death in 1458 showing him with his feet on a wool sack and sheep. There are many fine brasses worth close inspection. Nearly all show, by the richness of their clothing, the wealth of the burgher class of Northleach in the Middle Ages. To see the beauty of the battlemented tower and line of parapets and pinnacles at its best, the church should be seen from just outside the eastern boundaries of the town.

OTMOOR, *Oxfordshire* (5–SP5614). This curious area of almost wild fen-like desolation has been described by various writers as "bewitched Otmoor", the "forgotten land", and "sleeping Otmoor cast under a spell of ancient magic". Yet its mysterious centre is only about 5 m. from Headington. The B4207 leaves OXFORD by Magdalen Bridge and leads via Headington to **Stanton St John**, with its fine thatched farms, its stone mullioned houses, its ancient Manor House and lovely church. John White, chief founder of the State of Massachusetts, was born here. From this village it is possible to make a ring tour of the little villages that surround Otmoor. From nearby **Beckley** a sweeping vista of these 4,000 acres of almost roadless moors meets the eye. There are green tracks, however, one of which follows an ancient Roman road between DORCHESTER and Alchester near BICESTER. There are some interesting though much eroded wall paintings in the church. From Beckley the road runs to Studley, with timbered and thatched cottages and an Elizabethan house, Studley Priory, built on the site of an ancient Benedictine nunnery. From here the road winds up to wooded **Boarstall**, with its tower owned by the National Trust, once the gateway to a moated castle. The next village is **Murcott,** right on the edge of the moor, crisscrossed by tributaries of the Ray, once the scene of bloody disturbance during the riots following the 18th-cent. Enclosure Acts. Although very liable to flooding, all this forgotten territory is

still good grazing land. From Murcott the little road crosses humped stone bridges across the Ray and its many streams and comes into **Charlton-on-Otmoor**. The Perpendicular parish church has a fine rood-screen. Its high Early English tower can be seen for miles around. May Day is celebrated by the garlanding of the church by the village children and May Day dances. This area is a paradise of wild-fowl and rare wild flowers and in spring the blackthorn blossom and later the deep pink of the wild roses have to be seen to be believed. Here is the tiny village of **Oddington**, with an unusual if somewhat horrifying brass of a 16th-cent. parson in a state of decomposition. From Oddington the road twists down to the most important of the villages surrounding Otmoor. **Islip** once had the palace of the most important Anglo-Saxon kings and in 1004 St Edward the Confessor was born here. Nothing remains of this building. Three major battles were fought here during the Civil War. Swift once tried to get the living of this church but instead became Dean of Christ Church in Dublin. The little main street has picturesque cottages. A short drive on the B4027 leads you to another little lane, signposted **Noke**, the remotest village on Otmoor. On the other side of the road is perhaps the prettiest of all its villages, **Woodeaton**, with its woods, charming village green and Early English church which has an enormous 14th-cent. mural of St Christopher. The translation of the Norman-French scroll emerging from the Saint's mouth reads: "Whoever will see this image today will not die a violent death".

The country lane now leaves Otmoor to lead to **Marston**, headquarters of the Cromwellian troops during the siege of Oxford. This is all good walking country, but you should only attempt crossmoorland walks in dry weather. Providing attention is paid to this, the nature lover will find much satisfaction both here and in the distant WYCH-WOOD FOREST country in the west of the county.

OXFORD, *Oxfordshire* (5–SP5305). This great university town is, for its history and associations and for its architecture, one of the most rewarding in England. In spite of recent industrialization, its beauty and dignity have emerged relatively unscathed. "That sweet city with her dreaming spires", as Arnold called Oxford, seen from the top of Boar's Hill 3 m. away is an evocative and unforgettable sight.

The university is the second oldest in Europe, acknowledging only the Sorbonne in Paris as its senior. One theory as to its origins attributes its foundation to the expulsion of foreign students from Paris in the 13th cent., but in fact evidence of organized teaching there can be traced to the 12th cent. A chancellor was appointed in 1214 and the collegiate system began in the latter part of the 13th cent. with the establishment in Oxford of various religious orders. There was much conflict between "town and gown" in the Middle Ages as charters from successive monarchs conveyed privileges upon the university which caused hardship to the city merchants. During the Civil War

Chedworth: a mosaic from the Roman villa   *Picturepoint*

Oxford was important as the Royalist headquarters and the seat of Charles I's parliament.

The centre of the town is Carfax, where the main E. to W. and N. to S. roads converge. The four streets leading from it are the High Street (E.), Queen Street (W.), Cornmarket Street (N.) and St Aldate's (S.). The best way for a visitor with limited time to spend in Oxford to see the city is to obtain a guide and map from the information centre in St Aldate's, giving recommended walking tours of different lengths.

All Souls College was founded in 1437 by Henry Chichele to commemorate Henry V and those who fell at Agincourt. It has no undergraduate members, only graduate fellows elected for their academic distinction. Its architecture is among the finest in Oxford. The frontage on the High Street with the gateway over which a carving depicts souls in purgatory and the front quadrangle remain virtually unaltered since their foundation. The north quadrangle and the twin towers are by Hawksmoor, also the architect of the Italianate Codrington library. The chapel is remarkable for its reredos, which was uncovered and restored by Scott in the 19th cent., its oak stalls and misericords and the 15th-cent. glass in the ante-chapel.

Balliol College, originally founded in the 13th cent. by John de Baliol, has always enjoyed a high academic reputation, associated with Benjamin Jowett, the famous Master in the 19th cent. Most of the buildings, by Salvin and Butterfield, are 19th-cent. and two modern blocks have just been completed.

Brasenose College was founded in 1509 on the site of an earlier community. Its name is thought to be derived from an ancient brass knocker in the form of a nose brought to the college from a house in STAMFORD called Brasenose Hall to which some students retired in the 14th cent. from the unrest rife in Oxford. The front of the college, the first quadrangle and the gateway tower date from the foundation; the hall and chapel are attributed to Wren (1663 and 1666).

Christ Church occupies one of the finest positions in Oxford overlooking the beautiful meadows leading down to the Thames and the Cherwell. It was founded by Cardinal Wolsey and licensed by King Henry VIII under the name of Cardinal College in 1525, several religious foundations having been suppressed to make way for Wolsey's grandiose design. A new see was created in 1542 and the Church of St Frideswide became the college chapel and the cathedral of the diocese. The front quadrangle, known as Tom squad, from the great bell in the tower over the gateway which is dedicated to St Thomas of Canterbury, is the largest in Oxford. There is a magnificent hall, notable for its fine timbered roof and its collection of portraits, among them those of Henry VIII and Wolsey, traditionally by Holbein. The cathedral, the smallest in England, has many beautiful features from many centuries: Norman vaulted aisles, Perpendicular fan-tracery in the roof of the choir, the Decorated Latin Chapel and window in St Lucy's Chapel, a 15th-cent. shrine of St Frideswide and the fine Early English

chapter house, adjoining the cloisters on the south side.

Corpus Christi College, though small, has much rich, Perpendicular architecture dating from its foundation in 1516. Among its treasures are the altar-piece in the chapel, which has been ascribed to Rubens, its library of rare books and its fine collection of old plate.

Exeter College was founded by a Bishop of EXETER in 1314, but most of its buildings have been restored or rebuilt. The Victorian chapel is by Sir Gilbert Scott and contains tapestries by Burne-Jones and William Morris.

Hertford College occupies the site of several earlier halls but in its present form was incorporated in 1874. Its buildings are all 18th-, 19th- and 20th-cent.

Jesus College has always been associated with Wales since its foundation by Queen Elizabeth I in 1571 at the request of Hugh ap Rice who endowed it and provided scholarships for Welsh students. Its chapel and library date from the 17th cent.

Keble College was erected by subscription as a memorial to John Keble and aimed originally at providing an education based on the precepts of the Anglican Church. Its red-brick buildings designed by Butterfield can be regarded as hideous or as a fine example of high Victorian architecture, according to one's taste. The chapel is well worth visiting for its rich mosaic decoration and Holman Hunt's famous picture *The Light of the World*.

Lincoln College, founded in 1427 by Richard Flemyng, Bishop of LINCOLN, has an interesting chapel built in 1630, an example of very late Perpendicular architecture.

Magdalen College, founded by William of Waynflete in 1458, is one of the largest and most beautiful of all the Oxford colleges. Its most striking feature is the Perpendicular bell-tower, begun in 1492 and completed in 1509. Here the choristers sing their traditional Latin hymn at five o'clock on May-day morning. The main quadrangle is surrounded by cloisters and above the west walk is the library, which contains an exceptionally valuable collection. To the N. of the cloisters are the New Buildings, an 18th-cent. Classical range, overlooking the Grove, a deer-park where open-air plays are performed every summer.

Merton College, founded in 1264, is one of the three oldest colleges. Among its fine buildings the library and chapel are outstanding. The library, lying on two sides of the so-called mob quad, dates from the 14th cent.; the choir of the chapel is of pure Decorated workmanship and has exquisitely traceried windows. There is also a beautiful garden.

New College was founded by William of Wykeham, the founder of WINCHESTER School, in 1379, and the connection between the college and the school still survives today in the form of a number of closed scholarships. Many of the original buildings, in the Perpendicular style, survive as evidence of Wykeham's magnificent design. The cloisters and the chapel, the latter restored by

Oxford: New College chapel

Oxford: the Radcliffe Camera

James Wyatt and Sir Gilbert Scott, should be seen, as well as the pleasant garden enclosed by the remains of the ancient city walls.

Oriel College, though endowed by Edward II in 1326, has no buildings of this age, the oldest being 17th-cent. In the 19th cent. it became associated with the Oxford Movement, Keble, Thomas Arnold, Newman, Pusey and Froude all being elected fellows.

Queen's College is named in honour of Queen Philippa, wife of Edward III, and was founded in the 14th cent. by Robert de Eglesfield. The statue overlooking the High Street depicts Queen Caroline, wife of George II. The splendid Classical buildings are by Wren and Hawksmoor, and the library is of particular interest for its valuable collection and its carvings by Grinling Gibbons. There is some medieval stained glass in the chapel, preserved from the earlier chapel on the site.

St John's College, founded in 1555, has particularly fine gardens and an interesting back quadrangle with a south wing attributed to Inigo Jones in Classical style and cloisters of the same period on the north and west sides.

Trinity College, the traditional rival of Balliol next door, was founded in 1555. Its most interesting feature is the chapel, with a rich alabaster tomb of Sir Thomas Pope, the founder, and a carved screen and altar-piece by Grinling Gibbons.

University College is the oldest of all the colleges, although the exact date of its foundation is difficult to determine. Whether or not claims that Alfred the Great established it in the 9th cent. are justified, it is certain that a college in something like its present form was in existence in the mid-13th cent. The oldest part of the present buildings was begun in 1634 and the chapel, though redesigned by Sir Gilbert Scott, contains woodwork and windows of this period. There is a romantic statue in white marble of Shelley lying in the building to the right of the lodge.

Wadham College has some fine Classical buildings coeval with its foundation in 1612. In the quadrangle is a clock by Wren, an undergraduate of the college.

Worcester College also has a frontage in the Classical style dating from its foundation in its present form in 1714, but the buildings surrounding the quadrangle are of much earlier date. The beautiful gardens and lake are well worth visiting.

Among the colleges of comparatively recent foundation are the five women's colleges: Lady Margaret Hall, Somerville, St Hilda's, St Anne's and St Hugh's. Women account for about one-seventh of the undergraduate population. The newest male undergraduate college is St Catherine's, which should be seen as an example of how modern architectural design copes with the problems of providing residential quarters for students.

Among the graduate colleges are that of Lord Nuffield's foundation (1937) and St Antony's, which accepts both men and women students.

The widest street in Oxford is St Giles, with

colleges, ecclesiastical study houses and old inns on either side. Sir Gilbert Scott's Martyrs' Memorial, commemorating Ridley, Latimer and Cranmer, stands on an island with the Church of St Mary Magdalen. In St Giles Street on the first Monday and Tuesday following the Sunday after St Giles's Day the colourful St Giles Fair takes place.

The Ashmolean Museum built in the mid-19th cent. by C. R. Cockerell houses one of the oldest museum collections in the world, with fine displays of Greek, Roman, Egyptian and British antiquities, Chinese porcelain, Indian and Persian miniatures and a large and valuable collection of Old Master paintings and drawings, as well as a good collection of Pre-Raphaelite pictures. The Radcliffe Camera is one of the reading rooms for the Bodleian Library, its dome a landmark in Oxford's centre. The Bodleian Library is one of the oldest in the world, second only in importance to the Vatican Library in Rome; possessing as it does many of the rarest manuscripts extant. The visitors should see Duke Humphrey's Library and the old Divinity School with its exquisite groyned and traceried ceiling.

The Sheldonian Theatre at the west end of Broad Street was designed by Christopher Wren. Started in 1664, it was completed in 1669 and it is here, at the end of the summer term, that Commemorations or Encaenia are held and degrees are conferred. The busts of emperors, much eroded by time, are held in considerable affection. The interior with its gallery and tiered seats holds the chair of the Vice-Chancellor of the University and its Classical decoration is enhanced by a splendidly painted ceiling. From Wren's cupola can be seen practically all the colleges and important buildings of Oxford.

Just off the Cornmarket, through Frewin Court, is the building which houses the Oxford Union, the famous University Debating Society, founded in 1823.

The walks in little back streets, strolls along the banks of Christ Church Meadows where the River Isis becomes the Thames, or further down the Cherwell, all help to capture the atmosphere of Oxford, which is perhaps seen at its best during Eights Week, when everyone goes down to the river to watch the races. One of the most rewarding walks is to go through Port Meadow along the footpaths to the old Trout Inn at Godstow. In a meadow nearby are the ruins of the convent where Fair Rosamond, rival to Queen Eleanor of Aquitaine for the affection of Henry II, died in 1176.

Just opposite Magdalen College and close to the High Street are the earliest surviving Botanic Gardens in Britain. Laid out in 1621 on the instructions of Henry, Earl of Danby, as a Physic Garden, it retains something of the agreeable formality of that period. You enter through the beautiful Italianate Gateway designed by Nicholas Stone, to find open beds of flowers, trees and greenhouses full of rare plants which have been collected over the centuries from every part of the world.

The industrial centre of **Cowley** is 2½ m. SE. of the city, off the ring road. It was here that William Morris, later Lord Nuffield, took over a building in 1912 to make bicycles and ended up as the Henry Ford of Britain. From the modest beginnings of Morris Garages has sprung one of the biggest motorcar industries in the world. The factories of what is now the British Leyland Motor Corporation employing vast numbers of workers has brought great prosperity to this little Oxford suburb and great philanthropic benefits to the university city itself. There is little left to suggest Cowley's great antiquity, but it was important even when the Domesday Book was compiled. Its parish church, though enlarged and restored, still possesses two Norman doorways and a Norman chancel with Early English developments.

About 2 m. away on the B480 is the village of **Littlemore**. It was in this village, where an important 12th-cent. nunnery was founded by Roger de Sandford, that Newman and his fellow Tractarians, particularly Dr Pusey, formed a community in a farm-house, from which the "Tracts for the Times" were issued. Newman was vicar in the Gothic Revival church in the village, until his secession from the Church of England.

Another suburb of the city 2 m. SE. of Oxford and on the banks of the river is the village of **Iffley**, with one of the richest Norman churches in the country. Built in 1170 on an earlier Anglo-Saxon church, its west front has one of the finest examples of beakhead and zigzag carving. Its splendidly proportioned tower has perfect Norman arcades. A later window was inserted into the base of the tower in the 15th cent. Inside the north door, a 12th-cent. black slate font is set on a central pillar supported by four corner columns. The Norman chancel has an excellent vaulted roof with a curious central boss of grotesque faces.

Just N. of the London Road out of Oxford is the suburb of **Headington** which also boasts a 12th-cent. church with a perfect Norman chancel arch. It was much restored in Victorian times. Headington was once famous for its stone quarries which supplied most of the stone for the colleges of Oxford from the 14th to the 18th cent.

PACKINGTON HALL, *Warwickshire* (9–SP2284). Just off the A45 about 7 m. W. of Meriden, set in 700 acres of woodland and reached only by lanes, are Great and Little Packington. Packington Hall, not open to the public, is one of the most remarkable Italianate houses in Warwickshire. It was built in 1693 but considerably enlarged in 1766 by the 3rd Earl of Aylesford. About 16 years later the 4th Earl employed Bonomi who produced a Pompeian scheme of décor unmatched in England.

The Old Hall, a much smaller brick house incorporating an even earlier timbered building, was where Charles I stayed on his way to Edge Hill. Later Charles II stayed in the house with Jane Lane who rescued him dramatically after the Battle of WORCESTER. She lies buried in the church which Bonomi built between the two

Halls in 1790 to look as if it had been lifted bodily from Italy. The interior has fine paintings by Rigaud. Capability Brown laid out the park.

PACKWOOD HOUSE, Warwickshire (9–SP1872), is a rewarding example of domestic Tudor architecture with later additions. It is situated 1¼ m. E. of Hockley Heath, 11 m. SE. of BIRMINGHAM. The National Trust owns it and it is open to the public. From a side road, coming through an old gateway, this mellowed timber-framed house with its later 17th-cent. brickwork makes an almost theatrical impact. The restorations were undertaken with care for authenticity, how successful they were can be seen by the excellence of the renewed gabling. The National Trust has put much valuable and interesting period furniture into the house. The beautiful Jacobean panellings are original but only that in the Ireton Room, which also has a splendid overmantel, is in its original position. Lovers of needlework and tapestry will find here much to interest them. There is some unusual lead work which can be seen on the exterior of the house. The groupings of chimneys are visually most satisfying.

The stables, built before 1666 by John Fetherstone in his enlargement of the house, are perfectly proportioned. Fetherstone's greatest achievement is his celebrated Yew Garden, the glory of Packwood House. Clipped yews of a symmetry unexcelled in their period, they are generally held to represent the Sermon on the Mount. The garden leads to an avenue called Multitude Walk. There are twelve large Apostles; four even higher Evangelists and finally a huge yew, which represents Christ. The whole garden was planted about 1650 and has weathered walls with a particularly decorative gateway: 30 unusual bee boles are niched on either side of it.

The nearby Church of St Giles is 13th-cent. though it has been much, and badly, restored. Its register contains the record of the marriage of Michael Johnson of LICHFIELD to Sara Ford "of these parts". They were the parents of Samuel Johnson.

PAINSWICK, Gloucestershire (4–SO8609), high up on the Cotswolds, edged by a woodland valley sweeping down to GLOUCESTER, is one of the most interesting of all the many wool towns. Parking is something of a problem and the motorist is advised to pass the churchyard in the direction of STROUD for a few hundred yards to where the town has opened a "trust the motorist" parking area. Painswick has many houses and inns dating from the 14th to the 18th cents. Among these, the most important is Painswick House, built in 1737 with some later work by Basevi, who designed the Fitzwilliam Museum in CAMBRIDGE. It is open to the public on Sundays during the summer. Castle Godwyn; the Court House, gabled with tall chimneys and a fine terraced garden; Tocknells Court; Lovedays; the Yew Tree House and the ancient Little Fleece, owned by the National Trust, are a few of the buildings worth seeing. The Beacon opposite the churchyard has splendid interior stucco décor and may well have been the work of the younger Wood who designed many of the Georgian streets and houses in BATH.

The churchyard of St Mary's is famed for its 99 clipped yews, planted in 1792. The church with its high spire built in 1632 on to the square early 15th-cent. tower became a dangerous ranging mark during the Civil War when Charles I stayed in Painswick after a defeat inflicted on the Parliamentarians in 1643. The church has been much restored, though the nave dates from 1480. The 19th-cent. work was in no little measure due to a terrible thunderstorm in 1883 when lightning struck the spire, causing 40 ft of it to crash on to the nave roof and also to damage many of the tombstones. There are many good monuments within the church and an excellent example of modern glass, in a memorial window designed and executed by Payne, a local Minchinhampton artist.

The Painswick Feast Sunday with its Clipping Ceremony dates back to the early 14th cent. It is held on or near 19 September, the Feast of the Blessed Virgin according to the old calendar. "Clipping" in this case comes from an early English word meaning to enclose and has nothing to do with the clipping of yews.

A little to the N. of Painswick is delightful undulating country centred around the hamlet of **Sheepscombe**, rich in Cotswold stone cottages. Cranham Woods is a lovely beech forest. There is little of interest in the village itself. The 14th-cent. church was much restored in the last century but the Tudor rood-screen was left intact. The nearby hamlet of **Paradise** has appropriately an inn called the Adam and Eve. On the other side of the main CHELTENHAM road is the principal entry to the Benedictine abbey of **Prinknash** (pronounced Prinnage). The drive curves down the hillside to the 250 acres of Prinknash Park in the valley. Here in 1520 on a terraced shelf William Parker, the last Abbot of Gloucester, rebuilt the ancient hunting lodge, derived from a privilege granted by Edward III in 1355. The lovely Cotswold manor house was to see many changes. Shortly after being entertained here by the abbot, Henry VIII dissolved all the monasteries. By 1540 Prinknash ceased to be Benedictine property and passed through the centuries into the possession of many distinguished families. It is believed on good authority that Prince Rupert directed the siege of Gloucester from here. In the late 19th cent. it was sold to Thomas Dyer-Edwards who desired that if possible the property should return to Benedictine use. By a curious sequence of events, a remarkable man of vision, Abbot Aelred Carlyle, had attempted to restore Benedictine life within the Anglican communion by establishing a community on Caldy Island in Pembrokeshire. Its eventual reception into the Roman obedience left the community homeless in the second decade of this century. An offer by Dyer-Edwards was accepted and after many difficulties the Benedictines returned to Prinknash, where by diligent application they have made the name of this monastery world-famous. The pottery, which can be visited by the public, sells its wares right across the globe. Down in the valley a new monastery of concrete, steel and glass is fast rising as the modern designs of John Broadbent take shape. When this great new abbey and church are completed the old manor house will continue to dispense Benedictine hospitality in accordance with the Benedictine rule.

PAUNTLEY, *Gloucestershire* (4–SO7328). In a rather remote part of the beautiful valley of the Leadon, about 9 m. NW. of GLOUCESTER, and reached by unclassified roads, is the village of Pauntley. It is situated between Upleadon and Redmarley D'Abitot. Its renown derives from its having been the birthplace in the late 1350s of one of England's greatest merchant princes, Dick Whittington. Alas for the pantomime myth, he was born of a knightly family and married a woman of considerable estate. He was, however, four times Lord Mayor of London and he did achieve his great wealth by his own endeavours and left many great benefactions to the City of London. He died in 1423. Almost certainly he added the fine tower to Pauntley's 12th-cent. Norman church with its huge rounded chancel arch and splendid zigzagged doorway. Dick Whittington's coat of arms can be seen in the west window of the tower. The ancient moated Pauntley Court was long associated with the Whittingtons until they moved to Notgrove in the mid-16th cent.

PEMBRIDGE, *Herefordshire* (8–SO3858). This large village lies a short distance from EARDIS- LAND on the A44 to KINGTON. It has many lovely half-timbered houses, a number of them dating from the 14th cent. The 16th-cent. Market Place, diminished in importance now, is screened behind the main street. On the north side is an interesting hostelry called the New Inn, built in the early 1600s. Pembridge has a fine early Decorated church with a detached, 14th-cent. belfry that looks more Essex than Herefordshire. It is sup- ported inside by a host of great timbers. There are two interesting almshouses in the town: one founded by Bryan Duppa, Bishop of Winchester, in 1661; the other by Dr Thomas Trafford in 1686.

PERSHORE, *Worcestershire* (8–SO9446), lies 9 m. from WORCESTER on the west side of the VALE OF EVESHAM. The River Avon flows to the S. of the town and from the modern bridge can be seen its six-arched, mostly medieval, bridge with its central larger arch restored after Civil War damage. It is a delightful, prosperous, Georgian town, situated in the heart of the fruit-growing country, in an area particularly renowned for its plums. It remains a country town with many impressive houses lining Bridge Street. Of these Barclays Bank and particularly Perrott House, built in 1760, still have their large gardens backing on to the Avon. This is equally true of the High

Street, where the Angel Hotel, restored in 1920, has some fascinating rooms; in one of them there is an inlaid overmantle with a painted figure and the date 1575. At the end of Broad Street known as the Square is an old house with beautifully pro- portioned bay windows. The Three Tuns Inn has a most elaborate ironwork veranda.

The history of the town seems to have begun with St Oswald's religious foundation in 689. With the coming of the Normans, the Benedic- tines built what was probably one of the greatest pre-Reformation abbeys in the country. It was certainly much larger than Worcester Cathedral and its destruction at the Dissolution must rank as one of the major disasters of that period. The beautiful surviving remnant was preserved be- cause the people of Pershore bought the monastic part of the church for their own worship. This section has a splendid Transitional to Early English lantern tower of remarkable proportions, enhancing the strength of the curves of the Norman arches supporting it. The beautiful arcading of the presbytery is all 13th-cent. Inside the lantern is fine trefoiled arcading which screens a passage. From the exterior the corner turrets with spirelet pinnacles present a perfection matched perhaps only by those of LINCOLN Cathedral. The Church of St Andrew opposite came into being when Edward the Confessor seized the revenues of Pershore Abbey for the benefit of his royal foundation at WESTMINSTER. The church is mostly 15th-cent. and has little to attract attention other than a tympanum carved with a cross and shell-like bosses. Roman pottery has been discovered in this area as well as early Roman coins.

Overbury is an exceedingly pretty little village with BREDON Hill for a background. The church, greatly restored, has an Early English chancel with a much earlier Norman nave. All around are attractive timber-framed stone or brick houses of considerable merit. Overbury Court is early 18th-cent. with interesting upper window heads. The garden and park with many rare trees are beautifully kept.

RAGLEY HALL, *Warwickshire* (9–SP0755). Two m. SW. of ALCESTER on the A435 large, simple iron gates between two well-proportioned lodges open on to a driveway to Ragley Hall. This 15-bayed house is full of treasures and one of the stateliest homes of England, owned and occupied by the Marquess of Hertford. Built between 1680 and 1690 by Robert Hooke, it is one of the out- standing Warwickshire country houses. Many great artists and decorators have contributed to its magnificence over the centuries, yet it retains the atmosphere of a house lived in and loved by its owners.

James Gibbs designed the great hall for the 2nd Lord Conway, who became Earl of Hertford in 1750. The Baroque ceiling medallion is an arresting feature of this grand room, 70 ft long, 40 ft wide and 40 ft high, and is attributed to Vassali, who was working at Ragley about this time. From the library, with Reynolds's painting

A. F. Kersting

Ragley Hall: a fireplace in the great hall

of Horace Walpole, is a sweeping view of the lake, with the horizon bounded by the Cotswolds. The china room has a wonderful Worcester dessert set displayed to perfection. The Blue drawing-room has a much envied portrait of Marie Antoinette, and pale blue Sèvres china. The Red saloon has rich hangings, an Angelica Kauffmann ceiling and the Rubens painting of the Holy Family. In the Green drawing-room are some fine examples of chinoiserie. The fire-place came from an old family home in Lisburn in Ireland. The Prince Regent's bedroom is a perfect period piece. There is a portrait of Queen Victoria, and one of the Prince Consort by Winterhalter. Thirty guests can sit at table in the dining-room.

The original park was laid out by Capability Brown in the 1750s though the gardens were much altered towards the latter part of the 19th cent.

Ragley is by no means the largest stately home in England, but it comes near to epitomizing all the rest.

The house is open at advertised times in the summer months.

REDDITCH, *Worcestershire* (8–SP0467), 13 m. S. of BIRMINGHAM, is the centre of the needle-making industry. It was established here by the monks of the now-vanished Cistercian abbey of Bordesley. This abbey was built in the 12th cent. From the needle industry was developed the manufacture of kindred fish-hooks and tackle. Whole new industries have been set up in and around the town, which is undergoing a long-term modernization plan.

RICHARD'S CASTLE, *Herefordshire* (8–SO4969), is right on the Shropshire border, 3½ m. S. of LUDLOW on the B4361, with only the earthworks left of a Norman castle. A steep path has to be climbed to reach them on the flank of Vinnall's Hill. The castle was built by a Norman knight in the reign of Edward the Confessor and is one of the two pre-Conquest fortresses in the county. The old Parish Church of St Bartholomew retains its 17th-cent. bow pews. The tower is 14th-cent. and there remains some good stained glass of the same period. The hatchments on the walls are mostly memorials to the Salweys, one of the most ancient families listed in Debrett. The 17th-cent. Court House to the SE. of the village has an old cider mill in the grounds and a much earlier dovecot.

ROLLRIGHT STONES, *Oxfordshire* (5–SP3030). Third in importance only to STONEHENGE and AVEBURY, these Bronze Age monolithic circles are about 3 m. N. of CHIPPING NORTON just off the A34 and right on the Oxfordshire-Warwickshire boundaries on the edge of the Cotswolds. There is a circle, popularly called the King's Men, and a group of stones called the Whispering Knights. A third menhir enclosed by iron railings is called the King's Stone and actually stands in Warwickshire. Archaeologists agree that the stones pre-date 1500 B.C. and were probably used for funerary ceremonial purposes but certainly had nothing to do with the later Druids. The main circle is about 100 ft across and consists of stone varying from a few inches to some 7 ft in height.

Nearby is the village of **Great Rollright** with grey stone cottages overgrown with climbing roses, set on undulating breezy heights. It has a Norman church with a good Perpendicular tower and a 12th-cent. carving on the tympanum of a crocodile swallowing a man. It also has a 15th-cent. painted rood-screen.

Little Rollright seems almost forgotten, set down in meadow land and reached by a rough lane. As a result it is quite unspoilt, with little cottages supporting a once important manor farm-house. The old church has a narrow nave with two disproportionately large 17th-cent. monuments to the Blower and Dixon families in the chancel.

ROSS-ON-WYE, *Herefordshire* (8–SO6024), is a modest market town set on a red sandstone cliff above a lovely sweep of the River Wye, and a magnet for summer tourists. Although its origins may well go back to Roman times, the essential character of the town as it is seen today is due to the extraordinary efforts of one man, John Kyrle. He was born in Dymock, Gloucestershire, in 1637, studied at OXFORD and the Middle Temple and then resided in Ross until his death in 1724. He was wealthy yet his own tastes were simple, enabling him to become a great benefactor of the town he loved. Such was his modesty and unassuming nature that had it not been for Alexander Pope who, staying frequently at nearby

G. L. Ward

Ross-on-Wye owes much of its charm to the generosity of John Kyrle, a 17th-cent. resident

Holme Lacy, wrote his praises as the "Man of Ross" in his *Moral Essays*, posterity might have known little about John Kyrle. His house can still be seen at No. 34 in the triangular Market Place. It is possible to visit the little garden at the back; this must have been laid out some time before the end of the 17th cent., which makes its Gothic summer-house and grotesque ornamental arches all the more remarkable. The Market Place is dominated by the 14-arched, double-gabled, 17th-cent. Market Hall, of sandstone with medallioned upper windows and arched lights. Between the two gables is a carved medallion of Charles II. Parts of the timber balcony and balustrade of the older Booth Hall which stood on the same site are incorporated into the building.

Among the many aspects of early town planning initiated and financed by John Kyrle is the Prospect, a walled public garden, SW. and E. of the church. There are good views of the town, and not least of the elegant new bridge carrying the rebuilt A449 across the river. Kyrle's gates survive on the E. and S. with their Classical elegance unimpaired. They bear the cipher of his name and the date A.D. 1700. He also planted the famous elms in the churchyard and raised the causeway leading to the splendid 16th-cent. Wilton Bridge which was reinforced during the First World War and has since been considerably widened. It is a bridge to lean upon and watch the eddying river below; although an 18th-cent. sundial on the parapet has a moral verse inscribed against the vice of wasting time. Kyrle also gave the town its first water supply and repaired the upper part of the 208-ft, 14th-cent. spire of St Mary's and added pinnacles. From the early 13th cent., when it was begun, until the 15th cent. the church acquired much good stained glass (that in the east window is notable and dates from 1430) and new windows were inserted in the north aisle. The arcades were considerably raised in the mid-18th cent., greatly changing the

aspect of the church. Although still lofty and light, St Mary's suffered from the work of restorers between 1862 and 1878.

The church is rich in monuments, particularly those to the right of the chancel arch in the south aisle belonging to the Rudhall family. The alabaster tomb of William Rudhall, who was Attorney General to Arthur, the elder brother of Henry VIII, was carved by one of the last of the great medieval guilds in NOTTINGHAM and was brought to Ross by packhorses. Among the saints carved on the tomb is the unusual St Zita of Lucia, the patron saint of domestic servants. In the north wall of the sanctuary is the monument to the "Man of Ross". He is buried under the sanctuary floor. The churchyard contains a rare plague cross, restored, but its base still bears the inscription "Plague, Ano. Dom. 1637. Burials 315. Libera nos Domine." The picturesque almshouses with their gables and diamond-leaded dormer windows in Church Street were built by a member of the Rudhall family in the early 17th cent. Some good Georgian houses still stand on the north-west side of the Market Place. Walks N. and S. of the town along the river banks will give as much enjoyment today as they did to the young Victoria, who stayed at the Royal Hotel overlooking the river before her accession to the throne.

To the S. of the town are the lovely **Penyard Woods** and nearby is the site of the Roman settlement of Ariconium, then a great forge for the arms of the Roman legionaries stationed in Britain. Bearing a little to the W. through leafy lanes, the walker can reach **Kerne Bridge** with its fine vistas up and down stream. Nearby devoted anglers can be rewarded by visiting the site of the home of Robert Pashley, one of the most remarkable salmon fishermen who ever lived. The fame of the "Wizard of the Wye" extends across the English-speaking world. He died in 1956.

Brockhampton-by-Ross lies 5 m. to the N. of

Ross and just off the B4224. It has a remarkable concrete and stone church built by W. R. Lethaby in 1901–2. It has honest craftsmanship – Lethaby was a disciple of William Morris – and an integrity of structure which, although medieval in inspiration, looks forward to modern architecture. Burne-Jones designed the tapestry and Morris & Co. made it. Lethaby's design is in perfect harmony with its rural surroundings and is approached by a thatched lych-gate on massive semi-circular supports. The ruins of the old church stand in the grounds of what is now the Brockhampton Court Hotel which incorporates a gracious rectory of the late 18th cent.

ROUSHAM HOUSE, *Oxfordshire* (5–SP47 24). Twelve m. N. of OXFORD off the BANBURY road (A423) is the grey-stone walled village of **Steeple Aston** above the valley of the Cherwell. They say its ancient inn, the Hopcroft's Holt, still rings with the ghostly sounds of horse's hooves as Claude Duval rides by. He was a French highwayman who found the village well situated for his exploits, which led him eventually to Tyburn gallows.

The Early English church owns one of the finest examples of the *Opus Anglicanum* embroidery in the world. Originally a magnificent cope, it was cut up after the Reformation and framed as an altar-frontal and is often on loan to the VICTORIA AND ALBERT MUSEUM. Nearby is one of the great Jacobean mansions of England, Rousham House, built by Sir Robert Dormer in 1635. It was considerably improved in the following century by William Kent. Many of the rooms remain exactly as he left them with all their original furniture. One of these has a beautiful painted ceiling and remarkable plasterwork. The fire-places and door-cases are examples of the graceful proportions this English master of 18th-cent. domestic interiors invariably achieved. In 1764 Thomas Roberts, who had done the plasterwork of Christ Church library in Oxford, was called in to redesign the library at Rousham as a salon. This was accomplished with undeniable aesthetic success. There are over 150 magnificent portraits and other paintings to be seen. The house is open to the public through most of the spring and summer. Nowhere can William Kent's genius as a landscape gardener be better than here, where his work has remained completely unspoilt. It extends over 30 acres of ground with the River Cherwell flowing through, crossed by an ancient bridge. Kent used all the natural advantages he found, to achieve a visual effect epitomizing the civilized horticultural conceptions of his age. If he borrowed from Italy, he did so with an economy that could be adapted to the aristocratic taste of his English patrons. These were the Cotterell-Dormers, whose family still own the property. He used the Cherwell to provide attractive waterfalls. One of the many lovely vistas he created was the view from the statue of Hercules to the Praeneste which aroused the admiration of Horace Walpole. The sturdy walker should walk northwards up to an extra-

ordinary structure (now a farm-house) with a pinnacled Gothic gable and supported by flying buttresses on each side. It was known as the Temple of the Mill. Above this on the hill, Kent built one of the outstanding follies in the county, appropriately called the Eye Catcher. It resembles a castle gateway with three narrow, round-topped arches and surmounted by small pinnacles like jagged teeth. The manner in which it is buttressed gives a different appearance from every angle of vision. It is hard to reach, but rewarding for the student or connoisseur of English follies.

RUGBY, *Warwickshire* (9–SP5075). The town of Rugby developed during the later stages of England's industrialization. There are railway engineering works and heavy electrical equipment and, more recently, radio components are manufactured. Its main claim to fame, however, lies in its public school. Rugby School is known all over the English-speaking world through Thomas Hughes' *Tom Brown's Schooldays*. Equally famous is the football game that bears its name. The school was founded in 1567 by a local grocer, Lawrence Sheriff who, having made his fortune in London, endowed a free grammar school for boys. The buildings were moved to the present site in the mid-18th cent. It was under Dr Thomas Arnold, headmaster from 1828 to 1842, that the school grew tremendously in importance and established the pattern of education followed by the greater number of public schools in the mid-Victorian era.

It was Dr William Temple, later Archbishop of Canterbury, who during his headmastership from 1857 to 1869 did most to expand the material resources of the school. He was responsible for a great deal of building, for which he commissioned the architect Butterfield. Victorian Gothic and Tudor can often be inventive and exciting but the general impression of the exterior of Rugby School is somewhat dismal. It boasts many great names on its rolls, among them Walter Savage Landor (expelled); Matthew Arnold, the poet son of the headmaster; C. L. Dodgson, better known as Lewis Carroll, who came here from RICHMOND in Yorkshire; Rupert Brooke, the poet; and Wyndham Lewis, writer and artist.

A granite tablet on Doctors' Wall tells briefly the origin of Rugby Football, "the exploit of William Webb Ellis, who with a fine disregard for the rules of football as played in his time, first took the ball in his arms and ran with it, thus originating the distinctive feature of this Rugby game A.D. 1823". It should be remembered that players at this time often numbered as many as 50 a side and by 1871 laws regarding the number of players and rules of play became necessary. The Rugby Union was thus formed.

SHIPSTON-ON-STOUR, *Warwickshire* (9–SP2540), is an old sheep-market town on the A34, 10 m. SSE. of STRATFORD-UPON-AVON. Its former wool-based wealth is expressed in its many Georgian houses. It has a number of interesting old inns, among them the Horseshoes in Church Street and the George Hotel in the High Street. Shipston's situation in the Vale of the Red Horse makes it an excellent base for exploring the northern spurs of the Cotswolds. Ilmington Down, at 854 ft the highest point in Warwickshire, can be reached by unclassified roads and Meon Hill gives a good view. **Upper Brailes**, reached by way of Fant Hill, stands 757 ft up with lovely views over the Stour and Avon valleys. **Lower Brailes** on the opposite side of the valley has a fine 14th-cent. church known locally as the "Cathedral of the Feldon". Another unclassified roads leads to Edgehill, an L-shaped ridge 4 m. long rimming the Civil War battlefield at **Radway**. On 23 October 1642, 14,000 men of the Royalist army under the command of Prince Rupert confronted 14,000 Parliamentary troops, led by the Earl of Essex. It was a confused, disorderly battle. King Charles claimed the victory and marched to London. However, a young captain called Oliver Cromwell from Huntingdon had been present among the Parliamentarians and he learnt several stern lessons to the advantage of his side.

At the time of the battle, Radway Grange in the village was owned by a John Washington, of the Washington family from Sulgrave, and an ancestral connection of the first President of the United States. In 1712 the house was acquired by Sanderson Miller, whose son was one of the great protagonists of the Gothic Revival in England. He was responsible for the delightful folly, a yellow freestone sham castle known as Radway Castle or Radway Tower.

SLIMBRIDGE, *Gloucestershire* (4–SO7303), 4 m. E. of Sharpness just off the A38 in the Vale of BERKELEY, has the biggest and most varied collection of waterfowl existing in the world, under the direction of the Severn Wildfowl Trust founded by artist and ornithologist Peter Scott in 1946. Here swans, flamingoes, geese and ducks can be seen in natural surroundings: as many as 5,000 wild geese winter in the Severn Estuary and visitors can observe them from towers. Slimbridge is open to the public and enjoys a deserved popularity.

The village Church of St John has late 12th-cent. nave arcades with particularly beautiful capitals, some of which have been described as exemplifying the best traditions of the medieval stone-carvers in England. The rest of the church suffered from poor restoration work in the mid-19th cent.

STANTON HARCOURT, *Oxfordshire* (5– SP4105), is set in gentle stream-crossed meadowlands and lies to the W. of OXFORD about 3 m. S. of Eynsham on the B4449. The square tower of the Early English cruciform church with its Norman windows, its pinnacled buttresses and late Norman doorways is mirrored perfectly in one of the nearby ponds. The partly painted screen is very old, at least 13th-cent. Among the many baronial tombs of the ancient Harcourt family is a particularly fine 17th-cent. example of

the Baroque. The Harcourt family lived here from the 12th to the 18th cent. when they moved to **Nuneham Courtenay**. The Manor was where Alexander Pope lived while translating Homer's *Iliad*. He left a record on a pane of glass, "In the year 1718 Alexander Pope finished here the fifth volume of Homer." The curious kitchen with its ingeniously conceived chimney with a pyramidal roof giving fool-proof ventilation and crowned with a griffin weathercock still stands in the private garden. The splendid three-storied tower where Pope had his study can also be seen reflected in the pools. Aerial photography has proved the existence of a Bronze Age settlement here and three prehistoric stones which are known locally as "The Devil's Quoits" can be easily seen in a nearby meadow.

STONELEIGH, *Warwickshire* (9–SP3272), is an interesting village situated near the confluence of the Rivers Sowe and Avon on the A444, 6½ m. S. of COVENTRY. There is a nine-arched bridge of considerable antiquity as well as a later 18th-cent. one. Some of the old houses are of brick and timber, others are in the local red sandstone. A chestnut tree actually shades a smithy by the village green. It is best, if possible, to drive to Stoneleigh Abbey from LEAMINGTON SPA, through Stoneleigh Park. Here, the River Avon flows by the original sandstone gatehouse of the abbey dating from the 14th cent. Stoneleigh Abbey has been described as the grandest, most dramatic Georgian mansion of Warwickshire. Originally a Cistercian abbey founded by Henry II in 1155, it was one of the smaller abbeys, having only 12 monks and an abbot at the Dissolution. Although the king's commissioners reported favourably, nothing could save it and it passed into the hands of the Duke of Suffolk. It was later sold in 1651 to Sir Thomas Leigh whose family have owned it ever since. Part of the original monastery still survives. The gabled Elizabethan part of the house, which is seen from the Park Drive, dates from this period. In 1710 Francis Smith created the present grand west range for the 3rd Lord Leigh. It might be described as a brilliant piece of Italian Baroque expressed with English understatement. It was completed in 1726. It remained almost unchanged until the Elizabethan long gallery was removed to make way for the fine north porch built in 1836 by C. S. Smith, who was responsible for much of the building in Leamington Spa. He also built the present long gallery into which he incorporated some good Elizabethan glass. There is a good description of the house before Smith made his alterations given in a letter of 1806 written by Jane Austen, whose mother was a Leigh.

The house has been closed to the public since a disastrous fire on the upper floors in 1960. It contains some of the finest furniture attributed to Grinling Gibbons and Chippendale, and superb paintings, tapestries and carvings as well as other great historical treasures.

The Parish Church of St Mary has a fine chancel arch with its Norman carvings still clearly defined. There are many other Norman features, particularly a north door with a weathered tympanum, sculpted with serpents and dragons. The tall sandstone Old Almshouses in the village with their strikingly beautiful chimney stacks date from 1594. They were built by Alice Leigh, whose father was Lord Mayor of London at the time of Queen Elizabeth I's coronation.

Stoneleigh Park is the permanent site of the Royal Agricultural Society's show.

STOURBRIDGE, *Worcestershire* (8–SO8984), is an industrial town on the south bank of the Stour, situated on the edge of the Black Country. This makes for a striking contrast between the conglomerate of industries on one side of the town with pleasant Midland scenery on the other. The town does not have a great deal to interest the tourist. Its early importance was due to its glass-making industry, introduced by refugees fleeing from 16th-cent. religious persecution in Hungary. Its modern rebuilt Edward VI Grammar School stands on the site of a stipendiary priests' school established in 1430. In the High Street is an old 17th-cent. inn, the Talbot, with some 18th-cent. additions. From Old Swinford, the oldest part of the town, a belt of fireclay runs generally north-eastwards. It is reputed to be the best fireclay in the world. The countryside around Stourbridge has much to recommend it. One m. SSW. of the town, **Kinver Edge** is easily reached by a winding uphill lane from Whittington. There are splendid views from the top and the site of a Danish camp. The Norman village church has a good late 16th-cent. tomb and brasses. About 1½ m. S. through Old Swinford is the little village of **Pedmore**, sheltered under Wychbury Hill, crowned with its pre-historic camp. The Norman Church of St Peter has a primitive tympanum with Christ in Glory, wearing a drooping moustache and with an over-emphasized hand raised in blessing. He is surrounded by symbols of the Evangelists. The church was much restored in the late 19th cent. Nearby Pedmore Hall is 17th-cent. with later additions that included huge pilasters.

Two m. WNW. of Stourbridge on the BRIDG-NORTH road is **Stourton Castle,** where in 1500 Reginald, Cardinal Pole and Archbishop of Canterbury was born. Further along the same road is Enville with its Tudor Hall which was much altered in 1760 by the poet Shenstone. It has a fine park with the splendid Shenstone Cascade, a water ornament in best Classical Italian style.

STOURPORT-ON-SEVERN, *Worcester-shire* (8–SO8171). This town owes its prosperity to a number of industries, among them carpet manufacture and the largest chain-works in Europe, and it is overshadowed by a huge power station. Nevertheless, it remains a place of pilgrimage for those who love canals. It stands where the River Stour meets the Severn, 4 m. SSW. of KIDDER-MINSTER. The town took on its importance from the realization of what seemed to be a dream of an illiterate farmer's son. Derbyshire-born James Brindley came to Worcestershire in 1756 with the idea of cutting a canal which would link up the navigable Rivers Trent and Severn. He proposed to end his canal at BEWDLEY. To their later regret, the people of Bewdley refused to cooperate. Brindley then explored this junction of the Severn and Stour. From that moment a new town came into being around the basin that linked the river with his canal. Today much of the Georgian charm of this waterway remains, with the original long red-brick warehouse with its spark-ling white wooden clock tower, and at its south end the Tontine Inn opened in 1788 by the canal company. The renewed interest in canals has led to an even greater interest in Stourport. The basin is always gay with every type of inland water craft taking advantage of the 46-m. stretch of the Staffordshire and Worcestershire Canal up to its junction with the Trent and Mersey Canal at Great Haywood.

Across the Severn is the scattered village of **Areley Kings,** reached by a fine cast-iron bridge. It is famous for having been the home of Layamon, the priest who in *c.* 1200 wrote *Brut,* a poem based on a Norman-French work but written in English, giving a somewhat mythical history of Britain.

At Hartlebury, 2 m. E., the heavily restored church has parts of its medieval chancel and a 16th-cent. tower. **Hartlebury Castle** is a red sand-stone 17th-cent. mansion on the site of a medieval castle, from which the moat remains. For cen-turies it has been the palace of the Bishops of WORCESTER; part of it is still used. The north wing houses the Worcestershire County Museum. Its collection includes items illustrating the social and industrial history of the county.

S. of Stourport, towards **Astley,** are the Hermit-age or Redstone Caves. They are made up of a whole series of chambers and cells dug into the rock and are believed to have been used by hermit monks. Bishop Latimer said of them that they could house 500 men.

STOW-ON-THE-WOLD, *Gloucestershire* (5–SP1925). At an altitude of 800 ft, this is the highest town in the Cotswolds and is situated where eight roads meet. It is easy to understand that this was once the most thriving wool market in the kingdom. Daniel Defoe, long before he wrote *Robinson Crusoe,* records that the year he came to Stow Fair 20,000 sheep were sold. The large Market Place has an old Market Cross with a restored lantern head and some fine old gabled houses clustered around the square. Particularly notable is what was once the little Elizabethan Grammar School. The gabled and spired Town Hall has some good, and some not so good, paint-ings of outstanding figures of the Civil War and the Restoration. In a central niche is a statue of King Edward the Confessor looking across to another fine old house appropriately called St Edward's. Behind this stands the parish church, which is dedicated to St Edward. Each age from Norman times down to the present has added something of interest to this building. Norman walls were buttressed by the work of 13th-cent.

masons and 13th-cent. quatrefoil tracery and good windows grace the north porch. The canopied sedilia in the moderately restored 14th-cent. chancel are interesting. The south aisle has a 17th-cent. Flemish painting of the Crucifixion by de Craeyer, a pupil of Rubens. There is some good early glass, and some by the mid-19th-cent. stained-glass revivalist, William Wailes, whose output seems to have been enormous. The church has a sturdy 15th-cent. tower. Cromwell imprisoned 1,000 captured Royalists in the church after one of his victories.

STRATFORD-UPON-AVON, *Warwick-shire* (9–SP2055), on the west bank of the River Avon, stands at the hub of many radiating trunk roads, the A34, A46, A422 and A439 among them. It is perhaps the least spoilt "cult town" in the world. It has kept its essential character of a thriving Midland market town. Not only does it possess fine 15th- and 16th-cent. timber-framed houses but has a good Georgian overlay. However, it cannot be denied that its later prosperity has derived considerably from the fact that on or about 23 April 1564 William Shakespeare was born here and a few days later baptized in the Parish Church of Holy Trinity. Yet it was through the enthusiasm of the actor David Garrick some 200 years later that a Shakespeare Festival was first held. The idea slowly began to attract visitors to the town over the next 100 years and that attraction has now grown and raised Stratford to become England's prime tourist centre outside London.

There was a Bronze Age settlement here and a Romano-British village. A monastery was founded in Anglo-Saxon days and by 1196 the Bishop of WORCESTER granted the town the right to hold a weekly market. Its growing prosperity led to independence and by the 13th cent. the great Church of Holy Trinity was being built, and at the same time the prosperous and powerful Guild of the Holy Cross built its chapel. The guild generally assumed the powers of municipal government. Henry VIII suppressed it in 1547. The guild was replaced by a bailiff, 14 aldermen and 14 burgesses. In 1568 the office of bailiff was held by John Shakespeare, William's father. Little is known of Shakespeare's boyhood other than that he went to school in Stratford. In 1582 he married Anne Hathaway, a women eight years his senior. In 1590 he had met William Alleyn, the actor who was to found DULWICH College. About this time Christopher Marlowe made a marked impression on him. By 1592 Queen Elizabeth, her court and the citizens of London had shown their approval of the playwright and in 1597 he was able to buy New Place, regarded as the finest house in Stratford. By 1603 he had been summoned to the court of James I as a member of the King's Players. Between 1610 and 1612 he often spoke of retiring permanently to his native town and possibly did so in the latter year. Four years later on 23 April 1616, his 52nd birthday, Shakespeare died. His tomb in Holy Trinity Church is incised with the following lines:

Kenneth Scowen

Stratford-upon-Avon: Halls Croft

Good frend for Jesus sake forebeare
To digg the dust encloased heare!
Bleste be the man that spares the stones
And curst be he that moves my bones.

Among the many buildings in Stratford that have direct association with Shakespeare are the reputed and likely birthplace in Henley Street; a glorious Tudor gabled house, Halls Croft, in the Old Town, where John Hall who married Shakespeare's daughter Susanna lived; Anne Hathaway's cottage at Shottery; New Place, the playwright's own home; and just outside of the town Clopton House which is well signposted. Much useful information may be had from the Shakespeare Birthplace Trust, which has its new centre comprising museum, library and records collection in a wholly modern building in Henley Street, opened in 1964. This was designed by Laurance Williams and has some fine engravings on the glass doors by John Hutton, who did similar work for COVENTRY Cathedral. The statue of Shakespeare inside the building was the work of Douglas Wain Hobson.

The existence of the Royal Shakespeare

Theatre was due to the enthusiasm and liberality of Charles Edward Flower, the brewer. He first established the Shakespeare Memorial Association. The first theatre was opened in 1879 and over the years demand rapidly outgrew availability of seats. In 1932 the present theatre, by Elizabeth Scott, a cousin of the architect Sir Giles Scott, was opened – fire destroyed the old one in 1926.

There is much to see in Stratford-upon-Avon quite apart from the Shakespearean connections. The 14-arched Clopton Bridge is most visitors' gateway into the town. It was built by Sir Hugh Clopton between 1480 and 1490. The Town Hall at the top of Sheep Street is a fine Palladian building erected in 1767 by Robert Newman. Harvard House on the High Street, between Ely Street and Wood Street, dates from 1596. Thomas Rogers built the house, and his initials and those of his wife, Anne, are carved on the front of the house. Their daughter Katherine married Robert Harvard of Southwark and it was their son, John, who founded Harvard University in the United States. The Falcon Hotel has some of the most attractive timberwork in the town and has not been marred by the modernization achieved at the rear of the building. Opposite the Falcon the Guild Chapel on the corner of Church Street and Chapel Lane has some remains of a remarkable medieval fresco of the Last Judgment. Next to it stands the ancient Guildhall and next to that the almshouses founded by the guild in the 15th cent. They still house 24 elderly townsfolk.

The Bancroft Gardens and walks are well laid out and by the Avon can be seen Holy Trinity with its Georgian pastiche steeple, which was erected in 1763.

The Canal Wharf on the BIRMINGHAM Canal is most attractive and the southern section of the Stratford-upon-Avon Canal has been completely restored by the National Trust. This canal was first opened in 1816 and has unusual interest because its sections were constructed at different periods with different engineers. Each stamped his own individuality in the bridges and lockhouses which were built.

Stratford-upon-Avon in its original rôle as a Warwickshire market town is best seen on market day. Around and in the town, brewing, fruit-canning and light metalwork are carried on. It is perhaps as well that Stratford's own unique celebration, the annual Mop Fair, is held out of the tourist season on 12 October. This was the day in pre-Tudor times when farmworkers and apprentices offered themselves for hire. The mayor, aldermen and macebearers preside at the Roasting of the Ox. Country-dancers compete with pop-singers. The scene cannot be much different from the days when wandering players and jugglers from Coventry set up their carts on this day to entertain the townsfolk.

Four m. E. of Stratford-upon-Avon is **Charlecote Hall**, home of the Lucy family since the 12th cent. A turning N. off the B4086 runs alongside Charlecote Park with views of an Elizabethan house, rebuilt in 1558. The octagonal towered gatehouse is completely unaltered since that time. The house, expanded in the 19th cent., is now owned by the National Trust, although the family still live here. It is open to the public at advertised times. It has much fine furniture and paintings acquired by the Lucys over the ages. It was in the Deer Park, with two rivers flowing through it which meet near the house, that Shakespeare is alleged to have been arrested for deer poaching. The fallow deer seen today have been bred from the same stock for the last 200 years.

STROUD, *Gloucestershire* (4–SO8504). A steep old town once famous as the country's most important centre for the manufacture of broadcloth. It still supplies most of the world's requirements for billiard-table cloth and has a flourishing dye trade. Its scarlet dyes are world renowned. Some of the 18th-cent. woollen mills witness to this important past. Piano manufacture is now included in the activities here. The museum at Lansdown under the Cowle Trust is one of the most interesting in the county. It illustrates old methods of cloth-weaving, local crafts and industries, and there is even a detailed collection of pin-makers' tools. The Archaeology Room has finds from prehistoric barrows at nearby Nymphsfield and Rodborough. There is a good geological section and a collection of local costumes.

All round Stroud is the most beautiful hill country. Four m. SE. is **Minchinhampton** with panoramic views. The village has ancient ties with Normandy. Matilda, wife of William the Conqueror, asked her husband to present the Manor of Hampton to the newly founded Abbaye-aux-Dames in Caen. It is well worth a ¼-m. walk to see the old church with its curious corona and pinnacled tower.

Amberley, S. of Stroud, is some 630 ft above sea-level with glorious scenery all round. Take a short walk across National Trust common land to Tom Long's Post. The view from here is breath-taking. Rose Cottage in the village was described in the Victorian novel *John Halifax, Gentleman*. A short distance from Amberley, still overlooking the valley across to Stroud, is Rodborough Hill, surmounted by an 18th-cent. castellated house called Rodborough Fort. It is a landmark for miles around. Between Stroud and Amberley is **Woodchester**, which has the foundations of one of the largest Roman villas ever excavated in England. The site is generally covered and only rarely can the magnificent mosaic paving depicting Orpheus be seen. The monastery and Dominican convent were designed by Hansom, who invented the cab of that name.

Further S. lies the Cotswold village of **Nymphsfield** at the top of the Stroudwater Hills. The poorly restored church retains its good 15th-cent. tower. It has a pleasant old inn with tall chimneys. The prehistoric Buckholt Barrow is nearby.

STUDLEY, *Warwickshire* (9–SP0763). This small town is probably the largest needle-manufacturing centre in Europe. It is set in pleasant Warwickshire countryside, just 5 m. N. of

ALCESTER. It has been making needles for more than 300 years, though it was in 1800 that Pardow first applied steam power to mass produce them in a factory. The town has old houses and inns dating from its handcraft days. The Barley Mow is a good example of the latter. A little way E. of the main road are the gabled Castle Cottages, near the church. In Elizabethan days it was one complete, rather grand house. The church, dedicated to the Nativity of Our Lady, has a Norman nave, a Jacobean pulpit and some good medieval roodstairs. The 13th-cent. coffin lid brought from the ruins of Studley Castle is a particularly beautiful example of the stonemason's art. The manor house on the main street is a good 17th-cent. domestic building with a fine doorway. The Old Castle just N. of the church dates from the early 1500s and was built on the site of the original Studley Castle.

The present Studley Castle, until recently an agricultural college, was built in 1834 by Beazeley who showed considerable inventiveness in its design. Three m. N. of Studley, walled in on a hill and a little off the A435, is Gorcott Hall. It seems to have been hodge-podged together since the 15th cent. and has recently been extremely well restored. Its timberwork, high gables, diamond-paned windows and high chimneys all make for a wonderful variety of line and texture. It is now privately owned.

SUTTON COLDFIELD, *Warwickshire* (9–SP1296). Although a municipal borough with a population of over 80,000, Sutton Coldfield is only 7 m. from BIRMINGHAM and has become mainly a residential area for that city. Its nucleus is the old market town, important in the Middle Ages, and it has its own modern shopping centre. The Parade reflects a continuity of spirit from its early days. The town owes much to a native son, John Veysey, who became Bishop of EXETER in 1519. He lived at Moor Hall, now in the park adjoining the golf links. Many of the buildings he erected still stand, notably Veysey Grange in Weeford Road, New Hall Mill, High Heath Cottage, and the Old Stone House. He not only founded the school here, but built the Moot Hall and completely paved the streets of Sutton. He is buried in the large Parish Church of Holy Trinity, with his brilliantly painted effigy lying upon his tomb.

Sutton Park is one of the largest and finest pleasure gardens in the county. Its 2,400 acres of woodlands and lakes has the ancient Roman Ryknild Street running through it. Presented to the Warden of the Royal Town by a Charter of Henry VIII, it is still administered by the Corporation of Sutton Coldfield. Just N. of the park is one of the main television transmitting stations with its 750-ft mast.

SWINBROOK, *Oxfordshire* (5–SP2812). Halfway between WITNEY and BURFORD, a signpost points northwards to **Asthall** and following this provides a pleasant country drive to Burford through the valley of the Windrush away from diesel fumes and traffic on the A40. Asthall is a charming village with little picture-calendar cottages, a manor house and an attractive Transitional church. Following the river, the road turns right across a new stone bridge into Swinbrook. It has the usual attractive stone cottages of the Windrush valley backed by meadows and little brooks sparkling their way into the river. The village is famous for the storied tombs in the Church of St Mary the Virgin of the Fettiplace family who flourished with great wealth and influence in Tudor and Stuart days. One of them married a Portuguese princess and brought her to the chillier climate of Oxfordshire. The family are reputed to have owned land in 15 counties. Nothing now remains of their great mansion except the terraced fields beyond the church. The number and size of their tombs make this little Oxfordshire church a rather crowded mausoleum. The best tomb is that designed by Annis of London in 1743 commemorating the 5th and last baronet – a delicate Italianate work.

SYMOND'S YAT, *Herefordshire* (8–SO5516). This famous beauty-spot lies 5½ m. SW. of ROSS-ON-WYE on the Gloucestershire border. The Wye in its narrow gorge flows in a 5-m. loop around Huntsham Hill to make a near-island only a few hundred yards across at the neck. "Yat" is an old form of the word gate and also meant "gap" or "pass".

Relics of cave-dwellers of 20,000 years ago were found in King Arthur's Cave in the Doward Hills some 3 m. downstream.

TEMPLE BALSALL, *Warwickshire* (9–SP 2076), was, as its name suggests, an important centre and Preceptory of the Knights Templars. Simon de Mowbray gave it to the Templars in the reign of Stephen. After the papal suppression in 1248 it passed to the order's successors, the Knights Hospitallers, who were finally established throughout Europe as the Knights of St John of Malta. The Hospitallers at Temple Balsall were suppressed by the Act of Dissolution under Henry VIII. The chapel fortunately remains and as it was not a parish church it has no division between nave and chancel; only gradations of floor levels to meet the knights' liturgical needs. That it all has the appearance of being too new is due to the fact that it was almost geometrically restored by Sir Gilbert Scott in 1849. Even so it remains an awe-inspiring building with a superb east light. After the Dissolution and several owners, Lady Katherine Leveson and her sister bequeathed part of the property as an almshouse for 20 impoverished women. This almshouse survives; its tenants still wear the grey gowns, shawls and headgear prescribed by Lady Katherine. There are many walks around Balsall; one leads nearly 3 m. to the Moat Farmhouse, built about 1500, which has all its original timbering.

TENBURY WELLS, *Worcestershire* (8–SO 5968), is a friendly little market town on the banks of the Teme in a countryside of orchards and hop-

Tewkesbury: the mill and the Abbey tower

fields, where Worcestershire, Herefordshire and Shropshire meet. In 1839 saline springs were discovered, a pump room was erected and for a time it enjoyed some popularity as a spa, particularly as the London to North Wales coaches stopped here. In Market Street the black-and-white Royal Oak is a reminder of these days; so, too, is the King's Head, which is a timber-framed building with an overhang on brackets. The bridge over the Teme takes the traveller into Shropshire. Its three arches are medieval. Almost any of the inns in the town will supply information about the excellent trout-fishing to be had. The chancel of the parish church is probably 14th-cent., but almost the entire fabric was rebuilt in 1865. The square tower is late Norman.

TETBURY, *Gloucestershire* (4–ST8993), lies almost on the Wiltshire borders between STROUD and MALMESBURY. A quiet little market town, it gains distinction from its mid-17th-cent. Town Hall, built up on three rows of pillars. It has a heritage of good 18th-cent. houses with its earlier Chipping Square reached by well-worn steps. In 1781 Francis Hiorne completed one of the best early Gothic Revival churches in the country. The interior is singular and rather Nonconformist in aspect with its typically 18th-cent. gallery and wooden supporting columns; box-pews, however, strike an Anglican note. The pinnacled tower with its lofty spire was rebuilt at the end of the last century. There are a number of interesting monuments from an earlier church.

Tetbury Upton, a village just to the N. of the town, has an elegant 18th-cent. house set in parkland and some good stone houses.

To the SW. on the A433 is **Westonbirt** with its 19th-cent. Italianate house built by Lewis Vulliamy, now a girls' school, but still set in its splendid park with beautiful gardens, terraces and fountains and an unrivalled collection of rare plants and shrubs. Beyond this on the west side of the road, partly in Wiltshire, is the Westonbirt

Arboretum covering 116 acres, managed by the Forestry Commission and open to the public. Started by Robert Slayner Holford in 1829, it is generally regarded as one of the finest collections of trees in the world. The seasonal colourings can be breathtaking, and azaleas, camellias and rhododendrons thrive.

TEWKESBURY, *Gloucestershire* (4–SO8933), is an attractive old town with a wealth of ancient houses and timbered inns. The Bell Inn, one of the best examples, was once a monastery guest-house and has some 13th-cent. wall paintings dating from that time. Like so many places in Tewkesbury, it has associations with Mrs Craik's *John Halifax, Gentleman*. The Hop Pole is yet another ancient inn with a good 14th-cent. fire-place before which, in Dickens's book, Mr Pickwick warmed his coat tails. The house of the Nodding Gables next to the rebuilt Swan Inn has an appearance consonant with its name. Warwick House is 16th-cent. The Cross House on Tolzey Lane has splendid Elizabethan panelled rooms and is believed to have been the Court House of the Lords of Tewkesbury. The Baptist Chapel is one of the oldest in England; the present building was put up in 1690 and has some good 17th- and 18th-cent. furnishings. The Tudor House, a hotel, dates from 1540 and has a priests' hiding hole in the chimney of what used to be the mayor's parlour and is now a coffee room. The Classical Town Hall has some fine portraits in the mayor's parlour. Among them is a good half-length portrait of James Martin, a late 18th-cent. M.P., painted by George Romney. The oldest inn of all claims to date from 1308. This is the Black Bear, a half-timbered building at the top of the High Street near King John's Bridge which crosses the River Avon and has incorporated into it part of the bridge built in 1200. The town stands by the confluence of the Severn and Avon and from the heights of Mythe Tute, between the two rivers, there is a view of the riverside country around, dominated by Thomas Telford's graceful iron bridge with its 176-ft span over the Severn.

Tewkesbury was the scene of one of the bloodiest last battles of the Wars of the Roses. After the death of Warwick the Kingmaker at Barnet, Margaret of Anjou, wife of Henry VI, determined to make a final desperate bid for the Lancastrian cause. On 4 May 1417 the Queen's forces took up their positions on what is now known as Queen Margaret's Camp, Gunhill Manor and Lincoln Green. The Yorkists led by Edward IV took advantage of the poor tactics of the Lancastrians under the Duke of Somerset and destroyed them. The site is still known as the Bloody Meadow and can be seen from Lincoln Lane off the A38.

There is evidence that monks were settled in Tewkesbury by 715 and built a church in these meadows by the river. The Norman nave and tower of the present Tewkesbury Abbey are comparable to the best found anywhere in southern England. The tower is 132 ft high and 46 ft square. The pinnacles added in the 17th cent. might be regretted, but even these cannot detract from this majestic tower. The top affords a panoramic view of the Avon and Severn valleys, the Malvern Hills and, on a fine day, the Welsh mountains. The west front has a recessed sixfold Norman arch, 65 ft high, the largest of its kind in the kingdom. The great window was inserted in 1686. The 14 Norman columns supporting the 14th-cent. vaulting of the roof are some 19 ft round and over 30 ft high. Six chapels radiate from the 14th-cent. apsidal choir. Monuments to the historic families of the De Clares and Despencers abound. The beautiful Warwick Chantry was endowed by the Beauchamps (the family to which Warwick the Kingmaker belonged) and many of them lie buried in the abbey. The choir windows have some of the best English 14th-cent. glass. The south transept has its original Norman apse built before 1178. It now serves as a side chapel and has a Raphael painting which once hung at Versailles. The abbey possesses three organs. One is known as the Milton Organ and was in fact built for Magdalen College, OXFORD. The organ case is a great deal older. Cromwell had it removed to HAMPTON COURT and it is from this time it derives its name, as it is believed that Milton played upon it while he was secretary to the Protector.

Some of the loveliest stretches of the Lower Avon can be navigated for some 32 m. from Tewkesbury to Offenham, 2 m. above EVESHAM.

THAME, *Oxfordshire* (5–SP7006), is an ancient, broad-streeted market town whose charter goes back to the days of Wulfhere, King of Mercia. Only 14 m. from OXFORD and less than 50 m. from London, its enormously wide High Street is packed once a year with all the colour of a medieval fairground at the time of the Thame Show.

The High Street is lined with every style of architecture, weathered and blended from the 15th cent. to the present day. It has many famous inns but none more famous than the Spread Eagle. This was due to John Fothergill, who between the two World Wars was responsible for the vast improvement in country-inn catering throughout Britain. Beyond the 16th-cent. almshouses at the north end of the High Street is a gabled stone building of 1569. This was the famous Thame Grammar School which numbered Milton, Speaker Lenthall and John Hampden among its pupils. In 1878 the school moved to less distinguished quarters. Nearby is the house where John Hampden died in 1643 after being wounded at the Battle of Chalgrove.

The cruciform Church of the Blessed Virgin stands down by the bridge which crosses the Thame on the north side of the town. The present church, possibly built on early Anglo-Saxon foundations, is mostly 13th-cent. This part comprises the chancel, the nave arcades and the lower part of the central tower which was raised nearly 100 ft in the 15th cent. There was considerable and intelligent restoration work carried out at the end of the last century. Particularly notable are the altar tombs of the Quatremain family, all 14th- and 15th-cent. work. The most magnificent is the tomb of Lord Williams who died in 1559 and who had acted as host to Princess Elizabeth as a prisoner and entertained her twice as Queen. Later adapting himself to the changes wrought by Mary Tudor, he supervised the burning of Archbishop Cranmer and his companions at Oxford.

Thame Park, just about 1½ m. S. of the town, stands on the site of Thame Abbey, listed as the third richest Cistercian house in England at the Dissolution of the Monasteries. Many features of the abbey are incorporated into the house, which is now a private residence.

THORNBURY, *Gloucestershire* (4–ST6590), is a quiet little town with good views across the Severn. It has many interesting houses which witness to its earlier importance and a broad street sweeping down to an early 16th-cent. church with an earlier buttressed and parapeted tower. This is a landmark for miles around. There has been a manor here since 925, in the reign of King Athelstan. At the time of the Norman Conquest William I bestowed the manor and all the lands on his wife Matilda. It later passed into the hands of 28 generations of the Stafford family, until it was sold to the Duke of Norfolk in the early 18th cent. and it remained in the Howard family until 1959. In 1508 Edward Stafford, 3rd Duke of Buckingham, started to rebuild the present castle on the site of the old manor. An indiscretion treated by Cardinal Wolsey as an insult led to the duke's impeachment and execution in 1521, before his castle was completed. Henry VIII and Anne Boleyn spent some time here, as did Mary Tudor. The castle had a long period of disuse though the south side of the gatehouse was re-roofed in 1720. A certain amount of restoration work was done by Salvin in 1850. The inner court has perhaps best preserved the atmosphere of the original castle. There is a huge double chimney even larger and more elaborate than those of HAMPTON COURT. Below the heraldic arms of the Staffords is the date "Anno Christi 1514". The castle now houses a restaurant. It is worth trying to see some of the extracts from the Duke of Buckingham's household book, when he fed 589 persons on Christmas Day, 1507.

TYSOE, *Warwickshire* (9–SP3344), lies on the Warwickshire-Oxfordshire border, 7 m. WNW. of BANBURY. It is divided into Lower Tysoe, somewhat sparsely populated; Middle Tysoe, with its splendid late 11th-cent. Church of the Assumption and charming cottages with Venetian windows and doors, and Upper Tysoe, which has a manor house dating from the 16th cent. The great house of COMPTON WYNYATES lies within the parish boundaries.

The district has long been famous for the enigmatic Great Red Horse of Tysoe cut into Sun Rising Hill (where the A422 rises in a 1 in 6 up-grade). It seems that there have been in all five Red Horses of Tysoe. Aerial photography in 1964 revealed that three horses had been cut on the hill called the Hangings between Lower and Middle Tysoe. One was nearly 300 ft long and 210 ft high and was probably the horse which gave its name to the Red Horse Vale – and to the stories of a horse of vast size that had been current for centuries. In 1965 the Institute of Archaeology officially undertook scientific investigation of the site.

Hill-walking in this area can be rewarding since much can still be learnt from the friendly people living hereabouts or in the inns about the ancient festivals of the Red Horse, including the famous Scouring of the Horse every year on Palm Sunday.

UPTON HOUSE, *Warwickshire* (9–SP3545), is an impressive late 17th-cent. mansion 1½ m. from Radway and 8 m. NW. of BANBURY on the A422. It stands high up to the S. of Edge Hill with fine views. It is owned by the National Trust, conveyed to them by the 2nd Viscount Bearsted, together with one of the finest collections of pictures and *objets d'art* in the country. It is open to the public at advertised times. Its interior setting is modern and adapted to its use as a museum. Practically every European school of art from Early Flemish onwards is represented. Rare Brussels tapestries, 18th-cent. furniture, porcelain and a collection of exquisite Chelsea figurines can all be seen under conditions it would be hard to better. The gardens also are open to the public and at the south end is Temple Pool, a charming Tuscan-columned edifice, believed to have been built by Sanderson Miller.

UPTON-ON-SEVERN, *Worcestershire* (8–SO8540), is a pleasing country town on the banks of the Severn 10 m. from WORCESTER and 7 m. from GREAT MALVERN. It is full of delightful houses from early Tudor to early Victorian. Two superb Georgian houses are Waterside House and the Malt House near the river. In the High Street is a very early 17th-cent. timber-framed hostelry, the Anchor Inn. This street also has the famous

three-storied stuccoed White Lion with its huge pilasters and porch surmounted by a lion. This was a setting used by Henry Fielding in his novel *Tom Jones*. All that remains of the old church is its red sandstone tower. The new church was built in 1879 by Blomfield. It does, however, possess a 14th-cent. effigy of a cross-legged knight grasping his sword, presumably saved from the earlier church. The graceful modern single-span bridge crossing the river was completed in 1940. Upton is ideal as a centre for some of the best river cruising in the county. It is possible to sail from here right into the centre of EVESHAM.

VALE OF EVESHAM, THE, *Worcestershire* (9–SP0943), is comprised of most of the county immediately to the S., the SE. and E. of EVESHAM. Like Kent, this lovely countryside is called the Garden of England, a title based on orchard blossoms, and massed fields of daffodils and narcissi. Market-gardening, too, has brought considerable prosperity; asparagus beds are particularly fine. **Wickhamford** lies 2 m. SE., off the A44. There is a modern highway growth of bungalows and market-gardeners' sheds but the heart of the old village is set among trees by Badsey Brook, with its waters rushing over a weir. Here are age-old cottages, a fine timber-framed farm-house, the gabled and timbered 16th-cent. manor house, shadowing with its authority, a perfect little village church. Built on the site of an earlier grange belonging to Evesham Abbey, it was owned by the Sandys family who were connected by marriage to George Washington's family. There are two particularly fine Sandys tombs, canopied and carved in alabaster, in the church. This has a good 13th-cent. chancel with a Decorated arch and east window. Its tower is 16th-cent. It still has the box-pews built for the gentry with linenfold embellishment and under the pulpit the lower tiers of the original three-decker. On the east wall is an ancient wall painting of the Virgin and Child.

E. of Evesham is **Badsey**, another village with a new and not particularly attractive fringe around its original core. The manor house, once an infirmary for the monks of Evesham, is of mellowed stonework and timber-framing. Much of this work was the result of the rebuilding when the property passed to Sir Philip Hoby in 1545. Since 1946 it has been much overgrown with its old carriageway blocked. Just by the church is the late 17th-cent. Stone House with twin gables, looking like a typical Cotswold manor. The church in its yew-shaded churchyard is mostly Norman and early 14th-cent., but suffered a rather ruthless restoration in 1885. The canopied wall monument to Richard Hoby (who died in 1617) and his wife Margaret is interesting because the sculptured children are made to kneel facing W. instead of E. to show that they were Margaret's children by a previous marriage.

A short distance away on the B4035 is the village of **Bretforton** watered by three tributaries of the Avon. The 600-year-old Fleece Inn is timbered and has a Cotswold stone roof. It houses a

The Vale of Evesham: the old Fleece Inn in the village of Bretforton

priceless collection of Stuart pewterware. The most interesting feature of St Leonard's Church is the fine range of 12th- and early 13th-cent. arcades. Carvings on the capitals include a terrifying dragon swallowing a saint who is obviously rescued at the last moment by the hand of God. The tower is 15th-cent. Perpendicular. The three-gabled manor house by the church was built in the early part of the 17th cent. and restored with additions in late Victorian times. Bretforton Hall is a perfect example of early 19th-cent. Gothic with its porch supported by pillars carrying narrow ogee arches which in turn support a semi-circular balcony with elegant ironwork. The Grange Farm is medieval, much rebuilt during Tudor and Jacobean days. Prince Rupert sheltered here in 1645. It has a beautiful 15th-cent. tithe barn. The village has what is probably the largest village collection of dovecots in the country; one at least was built by the monks of Evesham and at least two are early 17th- and 18th-cent. respectively.

N. of Bretforton are three villages, **South Littleton**, **Middle Littleton** and **North Littleton**. The first village consists of a red-brick manor house built on to a Tudor building in 1721; it has dormer windows, a splendid weathercock and a fine yew hedge in the gardens. The church has a 14th-cent. tower but much earlier Norman doors. Its chief treasure is a finely carved Norman bowl, on its font. It also has some of the oldest Decorated pews in the county. The chancel was over-restored in the last century. Middle Littleton has a pleasing group consisting of a three-gabled Elizabethan manor house, a tithe barn built by an Abbot of Evesham in 1376 of beautiful blue lias and Cotswold stone dressing. It looks like a largish church, being some 140 ft long and 40 ft wide

and is in fact not only the biggest but one of the finest in the county. This is followed by an impressive dovecot with some 750 holes. The parish church has good early lancet windows, some well-preserved medieval tiles and an excellent Norman font. The embattled chapel built over the porch was added by Thomas Smith in 1532. The last village has little to recommend it other than one Hans Andersen sort of cottage with a very early medieval window.

The road continues N. to nearby **Cleeve Prior** with its broad streets, its air of prosperity and its stone cottages set on rich green verges looking on to a triangular village green, dominated by an old elm. It derives its name from the priors of WORCESTER who were the lords of the manor. The tall-chimneyed manor house is seen through an avenue of 12 clipped yews leading up to its Jacobean doorway. There is a priests' hole in the house which secreted Thomas Bushell, who acted as banker to Charles I during the Civil War. The churchyard boasts a 600-year-old yew and some intriguing headstones. The Church of St Andrew has a Norman nave and doorway, Early English lancet windows and a 14th-cent. tower. The King's Arms probably dates from the 15th cent. The motorist with a little time to spare should ask the way to the footbridge across the river, where a beautiful stretch of the River Avon is enhanced by a weir and an old mill.

WARWICK, *Warwickshire* (9–SP2865). This is one of the least spoilt county towns in England, set at the hub of radiating roads: the A41, A46, A425 and A445. The town stands on a north rise from the River Avon which is crossed by two bridges, the Castle Bridge and the Old Bridge in the castle grounds. It was this dominant situation that accounted for its early importance. One of the daughters of Alfred the Great, Ethelfleda, raised a fortress on the mound here to ward off attacks from the Danelaw. By the time of the Norman Conquest, it became a royal borough, increasing considerably in size and importance. Shortly after the Conqueror's death it was given to Henry de Newburgh, who began the present castle and became the 1st Earl of Warwick. He was the predecessor of the Beauchamp family who held the title for the following 400 years. After this line became extinct, Queen Elizabeth revived the earldom, conferring it upon the Dudley family who still hold the title.

A small remainder of the medieval town encircles the present centre, the result of a terrible fire which broke out in the centre of old Warwick in 1694, burning down more than 250 dwellings and a very considerable part of the cathedral-like St Mary's Church. The damage was such that practically the entire town had to be rebuilt.

Some of the most delightful pre-1694 houses are to be found in Castle Street. Outstanding is the isolated timbered house of Thomas Oken which, carefully restored, is now a Doll Museum, with an interesting collection assembled by Mrs Joy Robinson.

Most famous of all the remaining medieval houses is Lord Leycester's Hospital by Warwick's West Gate. Originally the Guild House of St George, by the end of the 14th cent. it had become the home of the united and powerful Guilds of the Holy Trinity and Our Lady. Their powers were such that the affairs of Warwick were virtually governed from here. After Henry VIII's dissolution of the guilds, the buildings, considerably rebuilt, became the beautiful timbered, gabled, and terraced structure seen fronting the street today. It was transformed in 1571 by Robert Dudley, Earl of Leicester, into almshouses or a hospice for old and disabled "brethren", usually soldiers who had served with the fighting earls. Today 12 brethren and a master still occupy the building. Their quarters have been modernized in keeping with the structure. On special occasions they still wear their traditional Elizabethan dress. The chapel, somewhat restored, the courtyard with its oriel windows, the kitchen and the banqueting hall are perfectly preserved and used. Other famed houses of the period are Tinker's Hatch at No. 105 High Street and Tudor House in West Street. Out at Bridge End is Brome Place built in the mid-15th cent.

Of the post-conflagration period, the Court House in Jury Street shows that rebuilt Warwick reflected the power of the wealthy burgesses as well as the earls. Francis Smith built it between 1725 and 1728 with an Italianate Doric colonnaded façade of rusticated stone. The eye is held by a statue of Justice by Thomas Staynor. Among its treasures are the Great Mace of 1672 and Thomas Oken's painted chest. The one-storied, pedimented Shire Hall in Northgate Street built in 1753 has fine coffered and stucco ceilings and an original octagonal lantern. The Town Hall in the Market Place is now a museum. Landor House (1692) has a doorway with a pediment on brackets. It is now part of a girls' school. Walter Savage Landor, poet and essayist, is one of Warwick's most distinguished sons. Other examples of this remarkable period are Eastgate House in Jury Street and the Pageant House which is late Georgian.

Apart from the castle, the dominant architectural feature of Warwick is the lovely Church of St Mary with its 174-ft tower and pinnacle. Situated on one of the highest points of Warwick, it is on the site of an early Norman church. The great fire destroyed the nave and aisles of the Norman and 14th-cent. building; only the crypt, the chancel and the south transept can really give a true idea of its collegiate splendour. The crypt has enormous Norman circular piers with four diagonal shafts and scalloped capitals. An impression of tremendous strength is gained, suggesting it must even then have supported an enormous building. The chancel's soaring roof is a perfect example of the vision of Perpendicular architecture. In the centre is the tomb of Richard Beauchamp, the Earl of Warwick who figures in the story of the burning of Joan of Arc. One of the great figures of the Middle Ages, he commanded Calais for Henry V. The tomb constructed by John Borde in Purbeck marble with the effigy cast by William Austen, a Londoner, is one of the most beautiful in Europe. The Beauchamp Chapel is incomparable. Other tombs of interest are built to the memory of the later Dudleys. Ambrose, who died in 1590, was given the vacant title by Queen Elizabeth. The tomb of Robert, his brother, is exuberantly heraldic. The Chapter House, which has been restored, contains a monument to Fulke Greville, the poet who was counsellor to Queen Elizabeth and James I, and yet another famous son of this city.

Another Warwick place of worship of contrasting interest is the old Friends' Meeting House built in 1695 with its original simple furnishings.

Warwick Castle must compare favourably with any of the great fortress houses of Europe, not even excluding WINDSOR. The outlines of the original motte or keep with its bailey which contained the domestic buildings are still visible. None of the present buildings date back before the 13th cent. It is still the home of the Earls of Warwick. The outstanding buildings are Caesar's Tower, the Gatehouse or Clock Tower, Guy's Tower, which is 128 ft high, and the south range housing the living quarters of the present earl, dramatically set above the winding river. The guides in Warwick Castle are expert and well worth listening to. The great hall must be seen, so, too, the state dining-room. The fine library was carefully restored after the fire in 1871.

In the conservatory is the famous Warwick Vase found by Sir William Hamilton in the grounds of Hadrian's villa at Tivoli. It is attributed by scholars to Lysippus.

The castle contains a fine collection of Classical paintings from all over Europe.

The magnificent gardens were laid out by

Capability Brown, who began his work here in 1753.

The Old Bridge across the Avon was built in the late 14th cent. and has romantically overgrown arches.

WATLINGTON, *Oxfordshire* (5–SU6994), is 7 m. S. of THAME and once owed its importance to its position on the **Icknield Way** following the foot of the main Chiltern Hills. Its narrow streets have many old half-timbered houses, some of stone and some in chequered brickwork. They are mostly 17th-cent. The gabled Town Hall built in 1664 on open arcaded work of brick stands prominently on the triangular market place. As late as the 19th cent. the "County" gave balls in an Assembly Room in the Hare and Hounds Hotel which was connected with the first floor of the Town Hall by a bridge.

The Church of St Leonard stands nearly a mile from the market place and is reached through tree-lined meadows. It was completely rebuilt in 1877 and only the tower is original, though it stands on the site of an ancient castle. It has a good painting by one of the pupils of Annibale Carracci who decorated the Farnese Palace in Rome, given by a benefactor.

WELFORD-ON-AVON, *Warwickshire* (9–SP1552). This is a pretty village with old timber-framed houses. It lies 4 m. SSW. from STRATFORD-UPON-AVON and has become a dormitory area for that town, but remains unspoilt. On the village green stands a tall striped maypole surmounted by a golden ball and a fox weathervane. On May Day there are genuine traditional revels on the green with all the fluttering ribbons, the clatter and red-streamered straw hats of Morris dancing in its most authentic form.

The lych-gate leading to the church is said to be one of the oldest in Warwickshire. Part of the church is Norman, and it has an interesting 15th-cent. sanctus bellcot. Just NE. of the church is a good Georgian brick house called Cleavers, well worth looking at. The village is situated on a loop of the Avon where there is an inn with a painted sign showing a king, a parson, a soldier and a farmer, with a quaint verse indicating that it is always the countryman who pays for all. The inn is called The Four Alls. Some say this is a corruption of Four Ales.

WELSH BICKNOR, *Herefordshire* (8–SO 5917), an isolated parish on the Gloucestershire border near the Wye, reached by a minor road from GOODRICH. Welsh Bicknor is where the boy grew into young manhood who became Henry V, hero of Agincourt. Courtfield Park became the country seat of the Herefordshire Vaughans, one of whose sons was the 3rd Cardinal Archbishop of Westminster. The house is now a home of retirement for Roman Catholic priests. The church, rebuilt in the mid-19th cent., retains the 14th-cent. tomb of Margaret Montacute with her recessed effigy above a 12th-cent. coffin lid.

WEOBLEY, *Herefordshire* (8–SO4051), pronounced without the "o", has a wealth of early timber-framed houses and lies to the E. of the A4112, about 9 m. NW. of HEREFORD. Mentioned in the Domesday Book, its later importance was such that before the 1832 Reform Bill it was a borough returning two Members of Parliament. After the Battle of NASEBY in 1645, King Charles stayed at a long, low timbered building then called the Crown Inn, later the Throne, and now a private house. The old Red Lion Inn was built in the 14th cent. but many additions were made in the 17th and 19th cents. The little cottage at the back is said to be the oldest house in the county.

In local lore Weobley has always been famed for its witches. Once there were said to be more than 50 sorceresses within a 2-m. radius of the village. Its early prosperity was based on the manufacture of gloves and ale. The church has a fine buttressed spire and some good monuments. In the sanctuary is a marble figure of Colonel John Birch who took Hereford for Parliament. He later quarrelled with Oliver Cromwell and is reported to have been imprisoned no less than 20 times. He afterwards played a leading part in the Restoration. He was Member of Parliament for Weobley from 1678 to his death in 1691. In the churchyard is a preaching cross on its original medieval base; local legend associates it with conjuring up the Devil. The house called the Ley, situated about ½ m. to the SW., is dated 1589 and has an attractive line of uneven gables.

WHICHFORD, *Warwickshire* (9–SP3135), is a charming village just far enough off the A34 OXFORD to STRATFORD-UPON-AVON road to have preserved its serenity. The old schoolhouse built 100 years ago stands at the top of the wide green which is flanked by some substantial, mullioned stone houses built by yeoman farmers. Some have been excellently restored to their original beauty, making amends for a Victorian phase of too much money and too little taste. All have thatched or stone roofs. The village pumps are 19th-cent. The old Church of St Michael, and a castle of which there are few traces, was built by a Norman knight De Mohun. The earliest part of the church is the south doorway which has a good Norman dogtoothed arch supported by two single piers, with one capital carved with a beast, the other an empearled pattern having a suspended cord, Byzantine in feeling. The tympanum is plain with a rim of geometric ornament. The north-west tower is well-proportioned and dates from the early 13th cent. The clerestory with five good square-headed windows was a 15th-cent. addition to give more light. The church contains two remarkable tombs and a south chantry chapel with the recessed 14th-cent. heraldic coffin lid of Sir John Mohun, the last male heir of the family, who died in battle. From the female side of this family were descended the Earls of Derby. The fine table tomb on the north side of the chancel has a superb alabaster slab incised with the effigy of John Merton, rector and chaplain to the Earl of Derby who died in 1537. On the south side of the chancel is the tomb of Nicholas Asheton, an early post-Reformation rector whose brass inlay shows him in Geneva gown and broad-scarf. At each corner of the tomb is a shield of lead portraying his arms.

Whichford House next to the church was once the rectory. Records at WORCESTER seem to suggest that the present house was built on to a much earlier rectory and the contrasting and unusual roof lines seen from the back of the house would seem to confirm this. The early 18th-cent. part of the building was planned ambitiously to have seven bays but the two left-hand ones were never built, giving a charming variety to a dignified pedimented façade with one dormer window high up in the roof looking like an afterthought. The house has been thoroughly restored by the present owners who have laid out a pleasant English country garden with loving care, to achieve variety of line with a blaze of colour. The clematis on one wing of the house sets off the weathered stonework. The gardens are occasionally open to the public. Beyond the grounds the wooded countryside rises to Great Rollright.

WIGMORE, *Herefordshire* (8–SO4169), is a village of history and beauty to the SE. of Leintwardine on the A4110. Wigmore Hall at the south end of the village is notable with its gabled two-storied porch. The church, at the top of the village street with its clustered half-timbered houses, has some good Norman herring-bone masonry. To the W. of the church is the mound of Wigmore Castle built by the Norman William Fitz Osborn on the site of a fortress erected by the daughter of Alfred the Great. It passed into the hands of the great Mortimer family and it was from here Edward Mortimer set out on his journey which was to give him his victory at MORTIMER'S CROSS. Wigmore Abbey, about 2 m. to the N. of the village, was founded in 1179 by the Augustinian Canons of St Victor of Paris and became the last resting place of generations of Mortimers. The weathered stonework and ancient timbers are lovely in decay. Part of the western range of the abbey is preserved in Wigmore Grange in **Adforton**. The remains of the outer gatehouse, and the inner gatehouse with its stone arch surmounted by black-and-white work with braced timbered building on either side, are striking and open to the public.

A good walk is from Wigmore to **Lingen** through the ancient **Forest of Deerfold**. This wood was a sanctuary of the Lollards during their persecution period and Sir John Oldcastle hid in nearby Chapel Farm for four years before his capture and execution. A fine mistletoe oak still flourishes in the forest. From Lingen, a lane leads down to the banks of the River Lugg. Here may be discovered the ruins of the Augustinian nunnery, **Limebrook Abbey**, founded by Robert de Lingen in 1189. The woods above have ancient trees and wild flowers abound: the *Assarabacca*, purple iris, the cuckoo flower, the little alchemilla, columbines, the brilliant veronica and a particularly beautiful species of lungwort all thrive. The total walk is about 3 m.

WINCHCOMBE, *Gloucestershire* (5–SP0228), lies 7 m. NE. of CHELTENHAM in beautiful hill country by the River Isbourne. In Anglo-Saxon times this little town was the capital of the kingdom of Mercia and boasted a remarkable abbey founded in 797 which housed the shrine of the young King Kenelm, said to have been martyred. Destroyed by Henry VIII, its ruins are still being excavated. The Parish Church of St Peter was begun in Perpendicular style in the mid-15th cent. It has an embattled and pinnacled tower with a brilliant gilt weathercock. It has almost 40 remarkable grotesques carved on its walls. The 700-year-old pilgrims' inn, the George, with its galleried coachyard, still bears on the lintels of its lion-headed doorway the monogram of Richard Kidderminster, the last but one Abbot of Winchcombe.

On the heights above Winchcombe is a 178-ft-long Neolithic barrow called Belas Knap in which many prehistoric objects have been found. Just to the S. of the town is **Sudeley Park** with Sudeley Castle, once the home of Catherine Parr, the last wife of Henry VIII. Little remains of the old medieval castle, but parts of the 15th-cent. structure are incorporated into Sir Gilbert Scott's reconstruction of 1858. There are some fine pictures, priceless tapestries and good furniture to be seen. The castle is open to the public at advertised times in the summer season. Catherine Parr's tomb in the chapel was destroyed in the Civil War; the present ornate canopied tomb was designed by Sir Gilbert Scott. The formal gardens with trimmed yews screening the pinnacled chapel are particularly beautiful.

WITNEY, *Oxfordshire* (5–SP3509). Just 10 m. W. of OXFORD on the A40 is the prosperous little town of Witney. Its fame for blanket-making has made its name known all over the world. The Domesday Book mentions the existence of two mills established here in 1085 and it has derived its wealth from weaving for centuries, being situated on the Windrush, on the very edge of the rich Cotswold sheep-rearing area. It is a mellowed stone-built town with a wide street gradually narrowing and continuing for nearly a mile. This leads to a green, bordered by cool lime trees and interspersed with the Cotswold merchants' houses. Its Butter Cross was built in 1683 and is surmounted by a clock-turret and sundial. It rests on 13 stone pillars; the central one is thought to have been the column of the original Market Cross. The nearby arched Town Hall is almost Provençal in its appearance. The Grammar School, set in an avenue of elms, was built and endowed by a wealthy grocer, Henry Box, in 1663, and the Old Blanket Hall with its one-handed clock dates from about 1720. The library possesses an edition of Homer with an imprimatur of 1542. The architectural outlines of the church show various styles from Early English onwards. There is good evidence of all this having been built on to an even earlier Norman church. It has a good Transitional doorway and porch with a cornice above which are curious carvings of animals. All this, however, is dwarfed by the splendour of the 156-ft-high Early English spire which is visible for miles around the countryside. The soaring arches of the tower supporting the steeples are no less impressive. The church has some good 15th-cent. monuments to the Wenham family, who were making blankets in Witney 300 years ago.

Even the blanket factories do not spoil the beauty of the town. The most modern blanket factory blends serenely into the warm stone buildings adjoining. It is sited on the foundations of an earlier weaving mill founded by the present Early family some 300 years ago. In 1669 Thomas Early started making blankets, some of which he shipped out to the North American colonies. This connection with Canada and the United States has been maintained to the present day.

Just outside of Witney, towards Oxford, turning right at the Griffin Inn, a short walk leads to a little hamlet called **Cogges**. The fine Decorated church was built and owned by the Benedictine monks of Fécamp in Normandy, who also built and maintained the Manor House. The chantry chapel to the north of the chancel is particularly fine. The hamlet is full of strange little twists and turns and has some good old stone houses which partly obscure the church.

Another walk 1 m. NE. of Witney leads to the little village of **North Leigh** with a romantic disused windmill on its hill-top. The church has an Anglo-Saxon tower and Norman and later work. The Wilcoate Chapel has a Perpendicular fan tracery roof, while the north aisle is in 18th-cent. Classical style. It also possesses an unusual collection of coffin plates.

A short walk to the NE. leads to the remains of a Roman villa, with a tessellated pavement and a hypocaust or central-heating system. It is unwise to try to drive a car to the villa as it is at the bottom of a steep and narrow lane with no turning space.

WOODSTOCK, *Oxfordshire* (5–SP4416), is a fascinating old country town 8 m. N. of OXFORD, bisected by the handsome bridge over the River Glyme. It shares with WINCHESTER and WINDSOR the title of royal demesne, since from Anglo-Saxon to late Tudor days it saw a succession of monarchs in residence. The Black Prince, son of Edward III, was born here in 1331. His ancestor Henry I had not only a deer-park in Woodstock but, most unusually, a zoological collection of wild beasts. Another ancestor, Henry II, set up his mistress "The Fair Rosamund" in some state here. The royal country house was known as Woodstock Manor. Its site is roughly N. of the bridge which crosses the lake in the Duke of Marlborough's park. It was probably rebuilt several times and here as well as at HATFIELD the Princess Elizabeth was held as a prisoner by her sister Mary. The house was practically destroyed in the Civil War, but enough remained to shelter Vanbrugh when he was building BLENHEIM PALACE. A square well still fed by a spring is about all that remains of the old manor enclosure. Even Woodstock's market owes its

origin to King John. By the time Elizabeth I came to the throne, and she returned in state to the scene of her imprisonment, the town had become one of the greatest glove-making centres in the country; the industry is still carried on today. There are many lovely old stone houses, and the famous Bear Inn was already old when the palace was being built. According to local lore it dates back to 1237. Much of the present structure is 16th-cent. The Town Hall was built by Sir William Chambers in Classical style in 1766 with funds provided by the Duke of Marlborough. Particularly fascinating are the shapes and sizes of some of the ancient chimney pots, one of which, a soaring medieval construction, was climbed by Sir Winston Churchill at the age of 12. The church has a Norman south door with arched bands of chevrons going right to the ground, dispensing with the usual Norman capitals, and in contrast to the Classical 18th-cent. tower. The 600-year-old octagonal font with its unusual traceried panels is noteworthy, and so is the 15th-cent. screen. The bosses on the roof are particularly fine. The church bells have a different chime for every day of the week. The pleasant streets lead inevitably to the great palace, since this is the magnet that brings thousands of visitors from all over the world.

Just outside Woodstock on the south side of Blenheim Park, is the little village of **Bladon**. The village pump, the Old Malthouse with its tall 15th-cent. chimneys and mullioned windows, and its quaint cottages all testify to its claim to be the mother parish of Woodstock. The present church is a dull Victorian reconstruction of 1894 on the site of an earlier church, itself rebuilt in 1801. In January 1965 Sir Winston Churchill was buried very simply in the churchyard at the head of the grave of Lady Randolph Churchill, his mother. She was the beautiful Jenny Jerome, daughter of an American newspaper magnate of the last century. His father, Lord Randolph Churchill, is buried alongside. The plain slab tomb bears the simple inscription "WINSTON LEONARD SPENCER CHURCHILL 1874–1965". Cars should be left in the official village car park and the short, steep climb to the church made on foot.

WOOLHOPE, *Herefordshire* (8–SO6135), on high ground between FOWNHOPE and LEDBURY and reached by twisting lanes, is of major interest to geologists all over the kingdom as the place of origin of the Woolhope Society of Naturalists and Archaeologists. A phenomenon here is the Silurian limestone protruding through the red sandstone of the hills. Woolhope is associated with Lady Godiva and her sister Wulviva who gave the manor to HEREFORD Cathedral in the 11th cent. The Norman church was much restored by the Victorians, some of it well done, some of it regrettable. A modern window portrays the traditional Lady Godiva.

WOOTTON WAWEN, *Warwickshire* (9–SP 1563), a village on the busy A34, 6 m. NW. of

Worcester: the Guildhall was designed by a pupil of Sir Christopher Wren

STRATFORD-UPON-AVON, has the most ancient church in the county. Although no Anglo-Saxon traces are evident from the outside, the church, in fact, embodies work of this period, particularly the lower parts of the tower, resting on four arches, which date from about 1042. There was, however, a much earlier church dating back to 723 when an Anglo-Saxon nobleman named Ethelric received the land from Ethelbald, King of Mercia.

During the 13th cent. the church grew in importance and size and the three distinct periods of building give almost the impression of three churches joined together. There are some good brasses and monuments; particularly fine is the tomb of John Harewell who died in 1428. Wootton Hall just E. of the church is a dignified late 17th-cent. house with good Classical pediments, triangular and segmental in the accepted Italian tradition.

WORCESTER, *Worcestershire* (8–SO8555). The ancient cathedral city of Worcester lies in the centre of its county. Although built on both sides of the Severn the principal part of the city has grown over the centuries on the steeper eastern bank. This was in order to avoid the flooding which frequently was a greater menace

than the many marauding armies the district has known: Romans, Anglo-Saxons, Danes and the Welsh all contributed to a turbulent history. The fertility of the surrounding Severn valley was always sufficient to make Worcester a coveted prize. The Civil War inflicted terrible damage. Worcester was the first city to declare for the King and the last to surrender in 1646. In 1651 Cromwell's "crowning mercy" was the final battle at Worcester when Charles II was completely defeated and had to flee for his life. Modern Worcester is at the hub of radiating main roads and the M5 skirts it. Road-building has meant the loss of much that was old, beautiful and even great,

The first cathedral church at Worcester was built by St Oswald who later became Archbishop of York and a friend of St Dunstan, who considerably influenced him. He attached a community of Benedictine monks to the church in about 961. Some 80 years later the church was almost destroyed by the Danes. In 1062 Wulfstan, Prior of Worcester, was made bishop. This English prelate submitted to William after Harold's death and was not therefore replaced by a Norman. He started work on the present cathedral in the year 1084. The crypt, one of the most inspiring parts of this very beautiful cathedral, is to all practical purposes exactly as St Wulfstan (or

Wulstan) built it. The interior of the cathedral blends different styles harmoniously. The two west bays of the nave are fine Transitional work with both round and pointed arches. In the early part of the 13th cent. the master mason engaged on the building of LINCOLN Cathedral started work on his design for the choir. Building went on unabated for more than 100 years in the Early English style. The visitor today sees a forest of slender pillars supporting a high vaulted roof. In the centre of the exquisite chancel, in front of the high altar, is the tomb of King John. He was buried here in the cathedral between the shrines of St Wulfstan and St Oswald by his own wish, expressed in his will which has been preserved. On the south side of the chancel is the tomb of Henry VII's eldest son, Prince Arthur, who died at the age of 15 in 1502. The tomb is contained in a Perpendicular chantry chapel of delicate stone-work. The arches of the Lady Chapel behind the high altar are perhaps among the most beautifully proportioned 13th-cent. work to be found in the country. The cathedral library above the south aisle of the nave contains some leaves of a copy of a Mercian Gospel written in the 8th cent.

The cathedral has suffered a great deal from restorers. Between 1857 and 1874 practically the whole of the surface of the exterior was completely restored including a number of windows.

A 13th-cent. gateway opens out on to College Green, virtually all that the cathedral has in the way of a precinct. It leads on to the cloisters, the King's School and the chapter house as well as the ruins of the old Guesten Hall – the guest-house the monks built in 1320. The cloisters are mostly 14th-cent. but have Norman outer walls. East of the cloisters is a very early Norman passageway known as the Slype in which are a number of stones reputed to have formed part of Oswald's original Anglo-Saxon church. They are certainly the oldest stones in the cathedral. The Norman chapter house was built probably about the year 1120. It was the first to be built in this country with a single central pillar supporting a vaulted roof. More than any other, the view from College Green of the monastery ruins, the magnificent cathedral, the watergate and the ferryways all conveys an impression of monastic Worcester. Just to the W. of the gateway, which is also called the Edgar Tower, is the deanery, an early 18th-cent. house with a particularly beautiful pedimented doorway. Just outside St Peter's Gate is the 15th-cent. Commandery (now owned by the National Trust), on the site of the Hospital of St Wulfstan founded in 1085. It is timber-framed with a most impressive great hall which has a lofty open roof and is divided into five bays. It has some good 15th-cent. stained glass. The magnificent Elizabethan staircase leads to upper rooms, one of which has fine 16th-cent. wall paintings of various religious subjects.

The river below the cathedral is crossed by a fine stone bridge built by John Gwynn between 1771 and 1780. It was later enlarged.

Worcester's other great claim to fame is the Royal Worcester Porcelain Works, whose ware ranks with some of the world's greatest. It all started with a Worcester citizen, Dr Wall, anxious to restore the prosperity of the city after the decline of the cloth trade. He worked on a substitute for china clay which, up to that time, had not been found anywhere in these islands. By 1751 he was able to open a porcelain factory in the city which not only copied Chinese and Japanese porcelains, and Sèvres, Dresden and Meissen ware, but attracted gifted designers who achieved originality and attracted the patronage of the great. Dr Wall died in 1766 but the royal seal of approval was given by King George III some 12 years later. There were difficult days ahead but in the early 1860s the Worcester Royal Porcelain Co. was formed to maintain the exquisite craftsmanship which had been the hallmark of the 18th cent. The Works and Dyson Perrins Museum in Severn Street may be visited by appointment.

Worcester's other still flourishing industry is that of glove-making. Worcester Sauce really is made in Worcester, from the receipe of an early Governor of Bengal, Sir Marcus Sandys, who lived in the county.

Worcester retains a number of interesting old houses. The Guildhall is one of the most gracious Queen Anne buildings in the county. Of brick with stone dressing, it has a great pediment carved by its probable architect, Thomas White, who was a pupil of Sir Christopher Wren. Two niches each contain statues of Charles I and Charles II; Queen Anne looks down from a central niche over the doorway. On the top floor is the splendid Assembly Room in which hangs a Reynolds portrait of George III presented to the town by that monarch. The painted ceiling has a light-heartedness in keeping with its period. The old timbered Queen Elizabeth House has been moved back a few yards to Trinity and is now called Trinity House. King Charles's House in New Street is now a shop but has an interesting inscription over its 1577 doorway. Next to No. 32 Friar Street is what was once the guest-house of the Franciscan friary established in 1239. The present building dates from about 1480 and is now owned by the National Trust. It is one of the most beautiful timber-framed and tiled houses in Worcestershire. Additions were made in the 17th and 18th cents. The National Trust also owns Nos 14, 16 and 18 in the same street. These are also timber-framed and tiled and were built between the 15th and 16th cents. Some are now partially converted to shops, but with no diminishment of their beauty. Other fascinating old houses can still be discovered in Fish Street and New Street where Nos 5 to 7 form Nash's House, a typical important town house of the 16th cent. It has unfortunately had to be considerably restored with the loss of buildings at the rear. Opposite is an ancient inn, the Old Pheasant. The Berkeley Hospital on the corner of Shaw Street is one of the best early 18th-cent. buildings in the city. It was actually founded six years before its completion in 1703. Nearby Foregate Street has a wealth of Georgian houses, significant of that period of prosperity.

Bromyard: the 15th-cent. manor house at Lower Brockhampton　　　　　　　*Picturepoint*

Further on in Upper Tything is St Oswald's Hospital, founded in 990 and rebuilt in 1873 to house 37 elderly people. Also close by is the remains of White Ladies, a convent founded in 1250. The east wall of their chapel is still preserved. Near to this is Britannia Square with a spacious green, setting off to advantage Britannia House which dates from the Queen Anne period. It was probably the work of the same architect as the Guildhall.

Outstanding among the many important parish churches of the city is St Helen's, built on the site of an early church in honour of the mother of Constantine and considered the mother church of the city. It is now used as the County Record Office. The 245-ft spire of St Andrew's still stands, though the church has been demolished. Across the river is St John's in Bedwardine with a beautiful late 12th-cent. north arcade. Built of red sandstone and set among trees, it is one of the most attractive churches in the city.

The Roman Catholic church in Sansome Place was built in 1829 on the site of an earlier chapel used by James II. It was much embellished in the 1880s and is a place of musical pilgrimage: Sir Edward Elgar was organist here like his father before him. Elgar's birthplace at **Lower Broadheath** is open to the public. Every three years in late summer the city is packed for the famous Three Choirs Festival.

The terminus of the Worcester and Birmingham Canal is a reminder that in the 18th cent. the junction at Diglis Lock led to a network of canals linking every part of the country.

WROXTON ABBEY, *Oxfordshire* (5–SP41 41), 3 m. NW. of BANBURY on the A422 is Wroxton Abbey, a fine early 17th-cent. gabled house which was built on the site of an Augustinian priory founded in 1207. There are traces of this original building built into the basement foundations. There are three Holbeins to be seen and a superb Zucchero. Among its other many treasures and mementoes of the numerous royal personages entertained in the house is a quilt embroidered by Mary Queen of Scots, and the bedroom where George IV as Prince Regent slept can be seen. Sir William Pope built the house and was host to King James I. It later passed to the North family, one of whose ancestors was Lord North, who as Prime Minister was responsible for losing those North American Colonies which became the United States. His tomb lies in the 14th-cent. parish church and is remarkable for its sculpture of Britannia by Flaxman. There are many other important tombs and memorials in the church, including that of Thomas Coutts, the Edinburgh merchant's son, who founded the banking house. The church has a good example of a Georgian Gothic tower built by Sanderson Miller. The village is attractive with mullioned cottages of brown stone, many of them still thatched.

WYCHWOOD FOREST, *Oxfordshire* (5–SP3418). An entry to some of the loveliest scenery

in Oxfordshire lies about 4 m. N. of BURFORD in what remains of the ancient Forest of Wychwood. Passing through **Fulbrook**, which has an interesting Transitional church with sturdy Norman pillars and grotesque roof bosses, the CHIPPING NORTON road climbs Fulbrook Hill from the Windrush valley to a high plateau, descending to the Evenlode valley. The bright little Evenlode river winds its way through the valley against the dark woodlands of Wychwood. This was once a favourite hunting ground of the Plantagenet kings.

The village names are delightful: **Milton-under-Wychwood** follows **Shipton-under-Wychwood** to nearby **Ascott-under-Wychwood**. A little to the NW. of this region and reached by twisting by-lanes is the long ridge of Daylesford leading to the village of **Kingham**. The whole of this area with streams and watermeadows banked by the woods is a delight to ornithologists because of the many varieties of rare birds which seem to flock to this completely unspoilt beauty spot. Perhaps no one expressed the quiet beauty of the Evenlode River better than Belloc, who wrote "A lovely river, all alone . . . Forgotten in the western wolds."

Shipton-under-Wychwood has many fine old houses, among them the 1603 Shipton Court. An old inn called the Shaven Crown was originally a hospice run by the monks from Bruern Abbey, which is now a private house. The Great Hall, now the lounge of the hotel, was the monks' refectory, while a bedroom (number 11), was the original hospice chapel. The parish church is a fine example of the Early English style. Particularly interesting is the font with a panel carved with the Bear and Ragged Staff, device of the Earls of Warwick. Note the 18th-cent. double tomb in the churchyard. In a wooded setting nearby is the ancient Prebendal House with its 15th-cent. chapel, reminder of the days when the church was a prebend of SALISBURY Cathedral. Turning right in the centre of the village, a road leads to Ascott-under-Wychwood which has an interesting partly Norman church surrounded by weathered stone houses. Continuing on the road to the right of the village green, following a signpost to Leafield a turning to the left leads to the larger **Charlbury** which lacks the character of the smaller villages. Just beyond Charlbury the road opens up views of some of the loveliest vistas of the Evenlode valley and leads to the boundary of Wychwood Forest.

Nearby is **Shorthampton**, whose basically Norman church contains box-pews, a three-decker 18th-cent. pulpit and some good medieval frescoes. Almost every winding lane will take the traveller to surprisingly little-known places like Hawkstone, a prehistoric monolith, or Knoll Bury on Chadlington Downs, an encampment whose origin is unknown. Nearby is Cornbury Park which gives some idea of the former density of the ancient forest. Further to the E. lie the little hamlets of **Finstock** and **Fawler**, originally built by the Romans. This area and that surrounding OTMOOR is the most unspoilt in the whole county.

Symond's Yat is a famous beauty spot on the River Wye Kenneth Scowen

The North Midlands

*Shropshire   Staffordshire   Derbyshire   Nottinghamshire
Leicestershire   Rutland   Lincolnshire*

PHIL DRABBLE

The region here described as the North Midlands includes Rutland, the smallest county in England, and Lincolnshire, the largest but one. Industries range from the mass production of cigarettes in Nottinghamshire, manufactured by sophisticated methods of automation, to fishing off the Lincolnshire coast, which is among mān's most primitive trades. You can enjoy timeless solitude on the barren Derbyshire Pennines, or watch rare birds on Shropshire meres. If you appreciate the individual qualities of real craftsmanship you will find glass being made today, in Staffordshire, as good as the best on show in antique shops. The chains forged for ships' anchors are still so much better than any in the land that it is worth transporting them all the way from the heart of the Midlands to the sea. Whatever your tastes you will find something to admire – and probably something to dislike – in the North Midlands.

On the western borders of Shropshire it is impossible to tell without the map where England ends and Wales begins. Old battle scars have healed along Offa's Dyke, yet there is still an indefinable air of strife, so that neither Welsh nor English appreciate being confused with the other.

At the top of Hope Valley, on the way from Shrewsbury to Bishop's Castle, are the scars of industry instead of battle. Large areas of sterile grey waste still obtrude where vegetation refuses to cloak the dross left by old-time lead miners. Beneath your feet are shafts and crumbling buildings, but if you look backwards to Wales from the hilltops, or forward to England, the views are superb and the air crystal clear and free from industrial haze.

Gliders find the Long Mynd, at Church Stretton, the perfect place to soar upwards on the eddies, as the west wind buffets skyward from the steep escarpment; and they can spiral like buzzards on the thermals. The wind hums round them so that, at close quarters, they are not nearly as silent as they seem. The whole midland plain rolls out below Ketley, stretching eastwards, apparently flat and featureless. But when you climb down it isn't flat at all. It is richly wooded, with unexpected hills and delightful tree-strewn parks, like Aqualate, near Newport, which has a herd of fallow deer that can wander down to the mere to drink.

Staffordshire is not really one county but two, with little in common between the north and south. Both have industry, of course, and it is so famous that strangers believe that the Black Country, in the south, stretches unbroken to the Potteries in the north. But there is wonderful country between. Cannock Chase covers some sixteen square miles, about half of which is still indigenous heather and birch and oak, though the other half has been planted with softwoods by the Forestry Commission. There is a large motorless zone, where the public can wander, with nothing to distract them but a sweet wilderness, which seems as remote as the centre of Dartmoor. There are grouse in the heather and green woodpeckers in the trees. In the centre is a hut built on stilts from which it is possible to watch foxes and wild deer and badgers and red squirrels and rare birds. This hut can be hired by the day from the Forestry Commission offices at Lady Hill, near Rugeley. It is an unexpectedly wild spot for central England, but further east the landscape mellows into fertile farms, with some of the best dairying land in the country around Uttoxeter. The water meadows of the Dove are unsurpassable for beef, and a local saying proclaims that "in April, Dove's flood is worth a King's good [ransom]".

The north of the county, past the Potteries, merges into the moorlands of Derbyshire and the craggy hills of the Pennine chain. It is bleak, stone-wall country, with rocks so near the surface that the soil has never been defiled by ploughs or other tools of man. This is a sparsely populated area for the reason that the land here is miserly with her gifts. Cattle drink from ancient dew ponds, and the milk churns are returned to isolated farms filled with drinking water, because pure water is so scarce on these wild hills. The air is fresh and you hear the limpid cries of curlew and sighing winds in bended trees, which were planted in clumps as some protection for the lonely farmsteads. The primitive vigour of these Derbyshire hills was once emphasized for me by the unexpected music of a pack of blood-hounds in full cry. They were streaming over the stone walls, hot on the scent of their quarry, which was not deer or fox but an athletic man.

Nothing could contrast more with this than the neighbouring county of Notting-ham. It is well wooded, with scores of small villages but few big towns. Its coal-fields still thrive, when others are spent; but do not run away with the idea that it is a county of dereliction, for it is not. There is gypsum in the Newark area, a central clay plateau, round Ollerton, and limestone east of Trent.

But the charm and individuality of Nottingham are in Sherwood Forest and the Dukeries. Neither are what they were. Once the great monastic houses of Welbeck and Newstead and Rufford Abbey stood proudly on the sandy soil. When the monasteries were dissolved, the nobles built great houses there instead. There were Welbeck and Thoresby and Clumber and Worksop Manor. The Dukes of Portland and Newcastle and Norfolk and Earl Manvers had their seats here. Sherwood Forest has few of the fine oaks and beeches left, which made it once so famous. The Forestry Commission has planted part with firs and pines. As compensation, large tracts are now free for the public to roam in and dream of Robin Hood and other robbers like him who made sport with the purses and the wenches of the rich from here to Needwood Forest in Staffordshire.

To the east of Nottingham, Lincolnshire is one county by name but three by nature. Almost a million acres of the northern part is Lindsey, which was once a Saxon kingdom on its own. Kesteven is about half the size, and Holland a little over a quarter of a million acres. They are separate administrative areas and of different character.

The chalk uplands, running towards the Humber, were once rounded tree-clad hills, but now have been tamed into superb farmland. The marshes between the wolds and the sea are famous for their Lincoln red cattle, but the most famous part of all is the Fens. Drainage was started here by the Romans, who cut dykes which were continued by the monks. Land left by the waters dried out into rich, black peat, the most fertile soil in England. Now it is a wasting asset, shrinking year by year, some carried on crops and some being lost by windblow. Gigantic farm machines need huge fields, with room to gambol and cavort about. But the ferocious east wind whips up the dry dust from these great fields into a vortex which drops out on another farm. We may live to see this rich ground wither into infertility.

Such flat land reveals enormous skies. Views are spacious and enlivened by

Sport and General

Hunting country. The Quorn Hunt moves off from a meet in Leicestershire

photogenic windmills. The bulb-fields and Lincoln red cattle paint kaleidoscopic
mosaics, and it always comes as a delightful surprise to find sea-going trawlers
moored in the heart of towns like Boston, apparently land-locked and marooned.

Turning back to the west, little Rutland, only sixty square miles in area, lies
uneasily between Lincolnshire and Leicester. Opencast iron workings tear at her
vitals, water undertakings covet her rich farmlands for reservoirs, and neighbours
have tried to carve her up to make Big Brother administrations even bigger. But
Rutland still remains prosperous, still independent, and still beautiful. Along the
Welland valley, which divides her from Northamptonshire, cattle graze on pastures
as lush as the Dove valley in Staffordshire or the marshes of Lincolnshire. Apart
from the belt of ironstone, the rest is predominantly fertile plough, with no major
industries to clog the roads with commuters or lorries. The limestone belt running
through the county has produced villages of dignity and charm, with two major
schools, at Uppingham and Oakham, a generous allowance for a county of less
than twenty thousand souls.

Leicestershire, between Staffordshire and Rutland, has extremes of scenery.
Charnwood Forest, a tumbling mass of crags and boulders, is as untamed now as

Noel Habgood

Tulip fields near Spalding in Lincolnshire

in prehistoric times. In summer, when green leaves clothe its vigour, it might be any lovely wooded spot in England. But when leaves are off, in winter, it has a strangely rugged grandeur of its own. At the other extreme, Leicestershire can be unutterably drab and depressing. Anyone who is unmoved by the murk of Coalville or the dull brick-and-slate hosiery villages must be immune to squalor.

The most typical scenery of Leicestershire, however, is neither industrial villages nor untamed woods. Much of the county is gently rolling clay, with villages widely dispersed. It is well-clothed clay, with sweet green grazing, shadowed by noble trees. By no means all are hedgerow or parkland trees. Many have been set in clumps or little woods, which give a delightful variety to the landscape. Although the views they give are so superb, they were not put there by aesthetes; they were planted strategically as fox coverts designed to give the finest hunting in the land as hounds pushed their fox from one covert to the next. The fields are divided by thorn hedges which, as well as keeping cattle in their place, test the courage of the highest jumping horse and the most unimaginative rider. Even the roads seem to have been made with one eye on the hunting field. The hedges are so wide that foxes lie hid in their immensely thick bottoms, and horses have a soft green verge to tread. The Quorn and the Belvoir are among the fox-hound packs which have made Leicestershire famous throughout the sporting world.

Windblow from the rich peat in the Lincolnshire fens is but one of the factors which are changing the industries in this region more, perhaps, than in any other generation. The face of the land has been lined by more roads since the last war than at any time since the Romans came. And modern roads have an insatiable appetite for concrete. In consequence, machines are gulping gravel, undisturbed since the Ice Age, from the whole valley of the Trent. Land there is being replaced by huge lagoons which flood the worked-out gravel pits outside Nottingham. Sails now appear by the sides of Midland roads as dramatically as along the lanes near Norfolk broads.

Easy transport and modern industry are depopulating the wilder parts of western Shropshire, and there is a real danger that numbers will shrink until there are not enough ratepayers to pay for essential services. Yet a century and a half ago the Ironbridge gorge throbbed with trade. When the raw materials petered out the whole area was discarded as a derelict memorial. Even the churchyard at Jackfield was not immune from subsidence, and the graves split open to gape at man's misdeeds. Now efforts are being made to reintroduce more industry, to encourage folk to stay in the remoter areas. The most ambitious scheme is Telford New Town which, if it is successful, will breathe new life into bones which have rotted since the last Industrial Revolution.

The whole region provides raw materials to ensure our industrial future. The coalfields of Nottingham and Derbyshire and Staffordshire are still productive. There is ironstone at Scunthorpe, gravel in the basin of the Trent. These may well mar the beauty of the North Midlands, but you couldn't have some of the pleasanter things without them. There would be no sweet-toned bells from Loughborough, chiming their message across quiet countrysides, without the coal to cast them. There would be no delicate glass from the Black Country, nor fragile china from Stoke-on-Trent, nor motor-cars nor kitchen goods, if we didn't tear the heart from the earth for raw materials. And sheep on the Shropshire hills, cattle by the Dove, and the seas of waving corn in Lincolnshire far outweigh the industrial eyesores.

The famous people of the region are as varied as the scenery. You can take your choice from men of letters, like Dr Johnson, from Lichfield, or Byron and D. H. Lawrence, who added immortality to the county of Nottingham. Or you may prefer to remember the engineers, like Boulton and Watt, who worked at Smethwick and laid the foundation stone for the civilization we are accustomed to. Charles II played hide-and-seek with the soldiers of Cromwell in the oak at Boscobel, and those who are tired of oppression by bureaucracy may have a sneaking regard for Hereward the Wake, Robin Hood or Guy Fawkes, whose gunpowder plot was hatched at Holbeach House, in Staffordshire.

I think my own choice of North Midland people falls on Bess of Hardwick. Not that she was comely or had an attractive personality. I admire Bess because of the great houses she left as the result of her scheming.

The whole of the North Midlands is architecturally rich. This richness ranges from the restrained delicacy of little Lichfield Cathedral to the magnificence of Lincoln. Crowland Abbey in the same county, or Chartley Castle in Staffordshire, or Ludlow Castle in Shropshire are comforting links with the past, and the Derbyshire villages, in the Peak district, are surely as unspoilt as villages can be. But Bess of Hardwick at various times owned or built some of the most remarkable houses in England. She had a flair for marrying people who left her their estates. When fourteen years old and almost penniless she married Robert Barlow, who died and left her his Derbyshire estate next year. She didn't remarry until she was over thirty, when she became the wife of Sir William Cavendish. Later she married Sir William St Loe, who left her his West Country estates, and lastly she married the Earl of Shrewsbury. During this time, she built Hardwick Hall, in Derbyshire, and was connected with fine houses at Rufford Abbey and Bolsover Hall and Welbeck Abbey. Her most magnificent memorial is Chatsworth.

Quite the most bizarre building associated with Bess, though she did not make it so, is Welbeck Abbey. She started the house, which went to her grandson and, by marriage, to the Duke of Portland. Bess was said to have been such a compulsive builder because she was told by a gypsy that she would only escape death as long as she was building. Similar blood must have coursed through the veins of the 5th Duke of Portland. Ancient aristocracy was traditionally addicted to follies, and the life-sized weeping willow in the garden of Chatsworth, which deluges visitors with sprays of water from its hollow branches, would win awards for practical jokes in almost any age. But the 5th Duke of Portland had a horror of ostentation. So he built a tunnel at Welbeck, a mile and a quarter long, big enough to take a horse and carriage, simply so that he could enter or leave his estate unseen. For eighteen years he employed around fifteen thousand men, mainly building underground. He built a riding school, and a complete suite of subterranean rooms, including a ballroom and three libraries. These were prodigious feats for unmechanized days, when every ton of soil had to be shifted by a shovel and barrow and sweat.

We take our pleasures now more simply. Whether we ride or walk, there are wild deer to watch on Cannock Chase in Staffordshire or in Bradgate Park, now owned jointly by the town and county of Leicester. On every reservoir there are sailing boats or birds to be seen; there are seals in the Wash. Local authorities are wisely siphoning off hordes of people with no specialized tastes to organized amusement parks, like Alton Towers or Trentham Gardens, in Staffordshire.

The most outstanding area of unspoilt natural beauty in the North Midlands is the Peak District National Park. It was the first of our national parks so to be designated, in 1951. The southern part, known as the White Peak, is rolling lime-stone uplands and wooded dales. The Dark Peak, north of Hope Valley, is equally beautiful, though more exposed, moorland. To the south-west, over the border of Staffordshire, a few wallabies, whose ancestors escaped years ago, still roam wild on the moors above Leek, and the Roaches there are cascading crags which seem to threaten the road below.

The Peak Planning Board, based at Bakewell in Derbyshire, issues a whole range of excellent leaflets; and of interest to motorists and walkers alike will be *The Shell Guide to the Pennine Way*. You can start from the park, along the Pennine Way, which is the first and longest national footpath. If you are stout enough, you can walk two hundred and fifty miles along the Pennines and over the Cheviots to the Scottish border. There is pony trekking and youth hostelling, rock climbing above ground or pot-holing below. There is skiing and gliding for the adventurous, and motoring through the finest scenery in the land for the less energetic. You can watch sheepdog trials on the hillsides, or the ancient folk customs of well-dressing in villages like Eyam or Tissington or Wormhill. You can eat roast venison from a deer on the spit at Whitworth Show, and if it is the climax to a hard day's walking on the hills, it will taste as sweet as any shot by Robin Hood in Sherwood Forest in days gone by.

The North Midlands: Gazetteer

NIGEL BATLEY AND BETTY JAMES

ABBOTS BROMLEY, *Staffordshire* (9–SK 0824). Five inns, a cluster of old black-and-white cottages, a church with 14th-cent. arcades and an old butter cross make this one of the most charming villages in the county. But Abbots Bromley, 5 m. S. of UTTOXETER, owes its fame not to its buildings but to its annual Horn Dance, normally performed on the Monday after the Sunday following 4 September. The dance, which is believed to have religious, or at least ritualistic connections – the dancers' gear is stored in the church – probably dates from before the Normans came to England. Twelve people take part in the dance: a man on a hobby horse, a maid, a jester, a boy with a bow and arrow, six men wearing reindeer antlers and two musicians on accordion and triangle.

Abbots Bromley once had strong connections with the Bagot family. They lived at a moated manor house at Bagots Bromley, 1 m. NW., from the time of the Conquest until the 14th cent., when they moved to nearby BLITHFIELD. The old house was used as a farm until it was demolished in 1811. A stone in Monument Field marks the site.

ABDON, *Shropshire* (8–SO5786). A small, scattered village, 8 m. NE. of LUDLOW. It lies in the lee of Shropshire's highest hill, the 1,792-ft Brown Clee. There are three Iron Age forts on Brown Clee, the most important being Abdon Burf. The others are Clee Burf and Nordy Bank – but little remains of any of them. However, those who tackle the climb are rewarded by magnificent views of the Shropshire countryside.

ACTON BURNELL, *Shropshire* (8–SJ5301). Tucked away in a corner of this pretty village, so that it has to be looked for, stands the ruin of one of the oldest fortified houses in England. Acton Burnell Castle was built for Robert Burnell, chaplain and secretary to Edward Longshanks, later Edward I, between 1284 and 1293 at the time that Burnell was Lord Chancellor and Bishop of Bath and Wells. Built of warm red sandstone, the castle is more like a small country house with a fortified tower at each corner and, apart from its roof, is almost intact. The setting in smooth lawns, and the giant cedar which overtops one of the 40-ft towers, emphasize the manor house aspect. Today the castle is in the care of the Ministry of Public Building and Works and can be viewed.

The beautiful Church of St Mary is the same age as the castle. Built of grey stone, with a squat tower added in the 19th cent., the church is plain

from the outside but inside offers much to please the eye. The font is 13th-cent., the pulpit Jacobean. There are medieval tiles on the floor of the north transept and strangely carved heads everywhere. Among the monuments is the tomb of Sir Nicholas Burnell (1382) bearing a fine brass likeness of him; and in a recess the full-length figures, in alabaster, of Sir Richard Lee and his wife, dated 1591.

Looking E. from the castle stand the remains – two large, near-triangular stone gables – of what was believed to have been the castle barn, a building more than 150 ft long. Some say that it was in this barn that England's first properly constituted parliament, including commoners, was held here during a visit of Edward I to Bishop Burnell.

The village of Acton Burnell is an English blend of black-and-white cottages and larger Georgian houses. One of the roads approaching it from the S. is arrow-straight, part of the Roman Watling Street; and near it, excavations have revealed part of a Roman bridge.

ALBERBURY, *Shropshire* (8–SJ3514). Situated about 8 m. W. of SHREWSBURY on the B4393, Alberbury once had a castle, part of the stone curtain built to keep back the marauding Welsh; all that remains is an ivy-clad tower, which is almost linked to the Church of St Michael by a flying buttress. The church, surprisingly large for such a village, has a massive, 14th-cent. saddleback tower and contains interesting memorials, including seven embossed brasses, to the local landowning family, the Leightons. About 1 m. NE. of the village are the remains of Alberbury Priory, founded about 1225 and now part of a farm-house. **Loton Park**, still in the ownership of the Leightons, is now used for motor sport: the Severn Valley Motor Club promote National Hill Climb meetings there on the last Sunday in April, and in the autumn, when ancient Alberbury resounds to 20th-cent. noise.

ALDRIDGE, *Staffordshire* (9–SK0500), is chiefly famous for Barr Beacon, about 2 m. SW. of the town, which, with the adjoining 150 acres, is preserved as a natural park. The land was bought by a Colonel Wilkinson as a memorial to the Warwickshire and Staffordshire men who died in the First World War. Rising to about 750 ft, the Beacon offers wide views over the surrounding countryside which can be viewed through a mounted telescope.

The town of Aldridge was mentioned in the Domesday Book but the only remaining bits of its

Express & Star, Wolverhampton

Abbots Bromley: the traditional Horn Dance is held annually

early history are in the square-towered medieval church. There are two 14th-cent. effigies: in a recess in the south wall of the chancel is one of a priest, and at the eastern side of the south aisle is Sir Robert Stapleton (d. 1333) in full armour.

ALFRETON, *Derbyshire* (13–SK4155). Although this was originally a mining area, Alfreton is more attractive than many such small industrial towns and boasts a fine church, a pleasing main street, several attractive old houses and one of the most modern lidos in the county. The latter is its most recent acquisition, built for £85,000 in the grounds of the park. It was opened by the Duke of Edinburgh in 1964, contains a championship-size swimming-pool, a separate diving pool and a children's pool, and is open daily throughout the summer.

Alfreton Hall, built in 1730 but added to during the 19th cent., is an imposing mansion which is now an Adult Education Centre. St Martin's, standing at the entrance to the Hall grounds, is a large church founded in the 13th cent. and added to and altered over the following 200 years.

ALKBOROUGH, *Lincolnshire* (13–SE8721). The village is bleak, but views from the 11th-cent. church are splendid, since it stands on a high ridge overlooking the Falls where the Trent and the Ouse join to form the Humber. From the tower can be seen LINCOLN Cathedral, BEVERLEY Minster and YORK Minster. Nearby are the remains of a Roman camp now known as

Countess Close, named after the Countess Lucy, wife of Ivo Tailbois, who owned the Manor in Norman times. At Julian Bower, through a five-barred gate, is a maze cut in the ground, believed to have been made by monks in the 12th cent. A replica of the maze is cut into the floor of the church porch and a picture of it is incorporated in the rebuilt Victorian triple-lancet east window of the chancel. A pretty cliff walk leads southwards from here above the Trent to **Burton-upon-Stather.** In this parish is Normanby Park, former home of the Sheffields.

ALREWAS, *Staffordshire* (8–SK1715), is one of the prettiest black-and-white villages in the county; the wide main street contains many Tudor thatched cottages. A settlement already existed when the Romans came and for many centuries the village was famous for its eel fishery and for the basket-weaving of its inhabitants, who used the osiers which then grew thickly along the banks of the River Trent. There was probably a church here in the 9th cent.; the present building is mainly 13th- and 14th-cent. It contains much that is worth a second look, especially the 14th-cent. font, embellished with four grotesque heads.

Alrewas keeps its ancient tranquillity and there are pleasant walks by the winding Trent and the Trent and Mersey canal. At Wychnor, close by, the fine gardens of the park, containing a remarkable yew hedge, are occasionally open to the public. The Wychnor Flitch, still hanging in the Hall, performed a similar function to that of

DUNMOW, in Essex, which is presented to any couple who can prove that they have never regretted their marriage.

ALTON, *Staffordshire* (9–SK0742), is one half of "The Rhineland of Staffordshire"; the other half is ALTON TOWERS. The stone-built village of Alton lies E. of CHEADLE, on the rocky, wooded slopes of the Churnet valley, all towers, turrets and spires. Every road and lane is a hill; every bend or gap in the trees or houses offers the kind of view more usually associated with central Europe than with the English Midlands. Above the village, on the edge of a sheer cliff high above the river, are Alton Castle, now a Roman Catholic boys' preparatory school, and Alton Hospital: impressive and picturesque buildings designed by A. W. N. Pugin for the 16th Earl of Shrewsbury and built between 1840 and 1852. In the gardens of the school stand the remains of the medieval castle – a ruined round tower and a part of the wall – the last link with Alton's Norman beginnings. The castle was built about 1175 by Bertram de Verdun, a Crusader with Richard Lionheart, and an arcade in the nearby church dates from about the same time. Alton itself contains some interesting old houses but the most unusual building is the sinister-looking tower in the centre of the village. Circular, built of heavy, dark-grey stone, with a small door and no windows, this was the village lock-up.

ALTON TOWERS, *Staffordshire* (9–SK0742), is the other, and more exciting half of Staffordshire's "Rhineland". Once the home of the Talbot family, the Earls of Shrewsbury, Alton Towers, about 1 m. from ALTON along the CHEADLE road, is now one of North Staffordshire's two famous playgrounds and pleasure gardens. The other is TRENTHAM.

The mansion, an array of towers, battlements, turrets and spires, is now virtually a shell. During the Second World War, it was requisitioned and used by an officer-cadet training unit. For six years afterwards it stood untouched and the combined effects of neglect and rough treatment made restoration impossible. Now only a small part of it is in use, housing a model railway, gift shops, a bar and a cafeteria. But, shell though it may be, Alton Towers is still a magnificent if slightly incredible sight, especially appealing to the romantic imagination in misty or lowering weather.

Nowadays it is the grounds, and especially the gardens, of Alton Towers which are the focus of attention: justifiably, because, to a large extent, the grounds pre-date the house. Hundreds of acres of North Staffordshire came into the hands of the Talbots in the mid-15th cent., but it was not until early in the 19th cent. that Charles, the 15th Earl, visited Alton, then known as Alveton, and dreamt of creating a heaven on earth from the 600 acres of wild countryside in the Churnet valley. On the site where the Towers now stands was Alveton Lodge, the house of the earl's bailiff; all around, where the woods now shelter the gardens

and grounds, was farmland, and an enormous rabbit warren in the slope of the valley.

Charles, nearing 60, had no intention of building a great mansion; his aim was to give rein to his considerable talent for landscape design. In 1812, the hill and parks were planted with their sheltering screen of trees and two years later the earl moved into Alveton Lodge to supervise the transformation of the wilderness. Money was not spared. Builders, masons, carpenters and other skilled craftsmen, and a multitude of labourers, began the work of laying out the gardens and terraces which are there now. Thousands of tons of soil were excavated to make the lakes and pools; water was channelled from a spring 2 m. away in the hills to the N. Walls and staircases were built. Paths were laid out apparently at random, but in fact the line of each was meticulously worked out so that at each twist and turn a new view could be obtained. The buildings were put up which are still features of the gardens today: the various fountains, the most impressive of which is the Chinese pagoda fountain at the bottom of the gardens; the Gothic-style Chinese temple; the conservatories; and the Swiss cottage, built as a home for a blind Welsh harpist so that he could play, often unseen, for strollers in the gardens. Finally came the trees and plants themselves which, saplings and seedlings then, can now be seen in their mature beauty: thousands of rhododendrons; azaleas; roses; heathers; Japanese maples; dwarf conifers; giant Wellingtonias; gracious cedars; Judas and tulip trees; hemlocks; and many other rarities.

During the 12 years he was creating his garden, Charles also took over Alveton Lodge as his summer residence and enlarged it in Gothic style, renaming it Alton Abbey – despite its lack of any religious connection. The only other person who played a major part was John, the 16th Earl, who succeeded to the title on the death of Charles, his uncle, in 1827. John inherited not only the Talbot title and lands but also his Uncle Charles's determination to make Alton one of the wonders of England. In 1831 he made Alton his permanent home and it was he who enlarged Alton Abbey with towers, turrets and galleries and called it Alton Towers.

He also completed the gardens with the classically beautiful "Her Ladyship's garden" beside the chapel, the terraced gardens near the conservatory, and the Dutch gardens. He also erected in memory of his uncle the copy of the Choragic monument to Lysicrates in Athens, which bears the inscription "He made the desert smile" and has pride of place at the head of the gardens.

In 1924 the Shrewsbury family sold the estate to a private company who opened it to the public. Today Alton Towers can accommodate both the lover of beauty and the seeker of fun. The visitor can row on the large lake, take an aerial cable car at tree-top height over the gardens, marvel at the £5,000 model railway, travel on the miniature railway, watch the trio of sea-lions disporting in their pool, or enjoy all the fun of the fair. Alton

Towers can now boast truly of offering something for every taste – which was possibly not quite the 15th Earl's intention.

ALVELEY, *Shropshire* (8–SO7584), is a pleasing stone-built village with a part-Norman church whose most treasured possession is an altar frontal first used 500 years ago. The original colours, vertical stripes in what might have been cream or yellow and green or red, are now much faded but the embroidered figures of Abraham and the cherubs can still be easily made out. At a crossroads about 1 m. NNW. stands an old butter cross with a solid circular head which probably marked the site of a medieval open-air market.

ANCASTER, *Lincolnshire* (13–SK9843). Lying in a natural break in the limestone hills of Lincoln Edge, Ancaster is famous for its local stone, which hardens rapidly after quarrying. The 9-acre site of Causennae, a Roman camp and posting station, is situated on Ermine Street. Coins, pottery, an altar, a milestone, kilns and mosaic flooring of the 3rd cent. found here are in GRANTHAM Museum. The Romans are supposed to have raced chariots in the long valley nearby. The church is built of local stone and retains some Norman work. Two massive coffins in the churchyard are reputed to be Roman.

Ashbourne church, "the cathedral of the Peak"
Kenneth Scowen

ANNESLEY, *Nottinghamshire* (13–SK5052). Near this vanished village with its forest background is Annesley Hall, once the home of Mary Chaworth, the subject of Byron's first unrequited boyhood love – his "bright morning star of Annesley". They used to meet in the home park, on Diadem Hill, 578 ft above sea-level and a landmark for miles. In the ruined church lies William Chaworth, Mary's father, who was killed in a duel with his cousin, Byron's great-uncle, the 5th Lord Byron. Up the hill is the new village of Annesley where the church, built in 1874, houses a beautiful Norman font and the alabaster figure of a man.

ARBOR LOW, *Derbyshire* (12–SK1662), is Derbyshire's most ancient monument, a prehistoric "henge" ranking in importance with STONEHENGE and AVEBURY. Situated just off the A515 about 8 m. SE. of BUXTON, Arbor Low is open to the public. At a height of more than 1,200 ft above sea-level on Middleton Moor, the monument consists of a plateau about 50 yds across on which more than 40 huge slabs of limestone lie in a circle. None of the stones is still standing and all are irregular in size, shape and thickness. There are also several similar slabs lying in the centre of the circle, one of them 14 ft long and another more than 8 ft wide. Outside the plateau is a circular bank, 15 ft high in places; and inside that a ditch about 5 ft deep. Close by Arbor Low is the largest round barrow in the county, Gibb Hill.

Arbor Low was constructed during the Late Stone Age or Early Bronze Age (2000–1600 B.C.) but the significance of its name, which is Anglo-Saxon, is unknown. Certainly the monument must have been there about 2,500 years when the Anglo-Saxons first came to Derbyshire.

ASHBOURNE, *Derbyshire* (12–SK1846), is the gateway to the Izaak Walton country of DOVEDALE. It lies at the southern end of the Peak District. A small market town, its main street, Church Street, still looks much as it did when Charles I attended a service in St Oswald's Church after his defeat at NASEBY in 1645.

The church, with its 215-ft spire, has been called "The Cathedral of the Peak". George Eliot, who set her novel *Adam Bede* in Ellastone, 4 m. SW. of Ashbourne on the Staffordshire bank of the Dove, described Ashbourne church as "the finest mere parish church in the kingdom". Consecrated in 1241, it has been weathered and scarred: marks made by the Parliamentary artillery in 1644 can still be seen on the outside west wall of the nave, near the figure of St Oswald. That the damage was so slight was due to the courage and indignation of the townspeople of Ashbourne who sent out a deputation to remonstrate with the Parliamentary forces – and made their point.

The pillars of the main wrought-iron gates bear an unusual decoration of skulls and flames. The inside of the church is impressive, with its 176-ft nave and chancel and spectacular crossing-tower. There is some of the original glazing in the great 14th-cent. east window; the font is 13th-cent.;

and both pulpit and lectern are ornamented with Derbyshire's famous Blue John stone. Monuments abound. That to Sir Thomas Cockayne bears what is believed to be the earliest rhyming epitaph in existence ("And did his house and name restore, Which others had decayed before"). His son's tomb has a good brass of 1538. But the most famous monument is that to five-year-old Penelope Boothby, a life-size figure in white Carrara marble, carved by Thomas Banks in 1791. Penelope, who lies asleep, is said to have been able to speak in the four languages inscribed on her tomb: Italian, French, Latin and English. The English inscription reads: "She was in form and intellect most exquisite. The unfortunate Parents ventured their all on this frail Bark, And the wreck was total."

If spring is early, the churchyard will be full of daffodils when one of Ashbourne's major annual events takes place on Shrove Tuesday and Ash Wednesday. This is the ancient and robust football game between the inhabitants of two banks of the Henmore Brook. The goals are 3 m. apart, at Sturston Mill and Clifton Mill, the rules are few, and any number can play.

Ashbourne, like BAKEWELL, can claim fame for a foodstuff. Ashbourne Gingerbread, a ginger shortbread biscuit with an unusual flavour, came to the town from France with the 300 French prisoners from the Napoleonic Wars who were billeted here. The recipe has been passed from baker to baker down the years.

Many reckon Church Street the finest street in Derbyshire. Its varied parts have mellowed into a harmonious whole. A number of the buildings are worth more than a casual glance: the Elizabethan Grammar School; two sets of almshouses, Owlfield and Pegg's; the Mansion House where Dr Samuel Johnson was once a regular visitor; and the curiously named Green Man & Black's Head with its inn sign right across the street and a tiny courtyard.

Within easy reach of Ashbourne are some of the prettiest villages in Derbyshire: HARTINGTON, 9 m. N., just off the BUXTON road, in a beautiful setting; **Osmaston**, 2 m. S. off the DERBY road, with its thatched cottages; **Parwich**, 5 m. N., with ancient earthworks nearby; and **Fenny Bentley**, 3 m. N., where there is a most curious monument in St Edward's Church, the shrouded figures of Thomas Beresford, his wife and 21 children, carved in alabaster.

ASHBY-DE-LA-ZOUCH, *Leicestershire* (10–SK3516). One of the few towns in Leicestershire, Ashby (deriving from the Old English *æsc* for ash and the Scandinavian *byr* for a habitation) received its distinguishing nomenclature from the Breton nobleman, Alain de Parrhoet la Souche, who acquired the manor by marriage in about 1160. The town is pleasant. Market Street is long and wide and often perfumed by the soap factory nearby. This specialized industry supplies the most expensive brands. S. of the west end of the street is the Grecian, or Spa, quarter which contains Gilbert Scott's 70-ft cross to the memory of

Lady Loudoun, who died in 1879 gratefully remembered by the people of Ashby for her goodness. Her house, built in the 19th cent., is now part of the Boys' Grammar School.

Lady Loudoun was a member of the famous Hastings family so closely associated with the impressive ruin, Ashby-de-la-Zouch Castle, which stands to the E. of the town. Originally a Norman manor house, it was granted to the first Baron Hastings by a grateful Edward IV in 1461. Towards the end of the Wars of the Roses in which Lord Hastings and his private army played a leading part on the Yorkist side, the magnificent tower was added, designed as a self-contained fortress. In 1569 and 1586 Mary Queen of Scots stayed in Ashby Castle as the prisoner of Lord Hastings's grandson, who had been created 1st Earl of Huntingdon by Henry VIII. She occupied the mainly 15th-cent. solar, a long, narrow room with a beautiful fireplace and great twelve-light mullioned windows. James I visited the castle with his entire following in 1617, almost impoverishing the earl. Charles I and Henrietta Maria stayed in 1634, but when Charles returned 11 years later it was only to rest for a few days before and after the Battle of NASEBY. By then Henry Hastings, Lord Loughborough, brother of the earl, was holding the castle for the king. He held out against the Commonwealth troops for more than a year. After his final surrender the castle was slighted – disarmed and demolished – by Lord Grey. The remains comprise the tower, parts of the walls and solar, and various domestic buildings including the huge kitchen dating from about 1350. Sir Walter Scott laid the scene of the famous pageant and tournament in *Ivanhoe* in the fields nearby.

Not far from the castle is St Helen's Parish Church where the east window contains some ancient heraldic glass taken from the ruined castle chapel. There are various Hastings monuments, including one to Lady Selina, who joined Wesley and formed Lady Huntingdon's Connexion of Nonconformist chapels. There is also the only known survival of a finger pillory, consisting of two beams with 13 grooves each, which were fastened with a lock on the hands of those who were absent from, or misbehaved in church.

ASHFORD-IN-THE-WATER, *Derbyshire* (12–SK1969). There are three bridges across the River Wye in this small village 2 m. NW. of BAKEWELL. The oldest is the Sheepwash bridge, as narrow today as it was the day it was built, and one of the others dates from 1664. Close by the village are the quarries from which the famous Ashford marble came. The Church of the Holy Trinity was rebuilt about 100 years ago but the fine Norman tympanum, showing a tree of life, was incorporated over the south doorway. Inside hang four paper garlands, rare and ancient, of the kind which were carried at funerals. At Fin Cop, 1½ m. NW. of the village, are the remains of an Iron Age fort.

ASHOVER, *Derbyshire* (13–SK3463). One of the few Norman lead fonts remaining in England is in the church of this unspoilt village in the valley of the Amber, about 3 m. NE. of MAT-LOCK. The church, 600 years old, has a slender spire 128 ft high, a landmark for miles around, and contains an early 16th-cent. rood-screen and an alabaster tomb of the same date. It still uses a bell which cracked while ringing out the news of Napoleon's fall in 1814. Not far from the village stand the ruins of the Elizabethan Eastwood Hall, a once-fortified manor house destroyed by the Parliamentarians in 1646.

ASLOCKTON, *Nottinghamshire* (13–SK7440). In this tiny village just E. of BINGHAM Thomas Cranmer, first Protestant archbishop, was born and lived for 14 years in an old manor house which no longer exists. It is thought to have been in the fields by the path now called Cranmer's Walk. On this path towards Orston, past the ugly 19th-cent. church, there is a castle of motte and bailey type with a moated mound about 16 ft high, said to be part of an ancient earthwork. This is Cranmer's Mound, where he sat as a boy and "surveyed the face of the country and listened to the tunable bells of Whatton", the church across the River Smite. He returned infrequently for short periods only after going to CAMBRIDGE. In the village mission room are the remains of the walls of an ancient chapel he must have known before it was desecrated in the Reformation, in which he was martyred.

The village also contains the only three mud cottages in the county.

ASTON-ON-CLUN, *Shropshire* (8–SO3981). A huge oak tree draped with flags of all nations is the first sight which has greeted visitors to this tiny village, about 2½ m. W. of Craven Arms on the B4368 to CLUN, for almost 200 years. Tradition has it that the flags were first hung on the Arbor Tree on 29 May 1786, to celebrate the marriage of local landowner John Marston to Mary Carter, and the custom has continued ever since. If you want the full story you will almost certainly get it from one of the customers at the village's oddly named Kangaroo Inn. The village has a third curiosity: a tiny round stone house, one of the few remaining in the country.

ATCHAM, *Shropshire* (8–SJ5409), is a place whose name can confuse the visitor because here is **Attingham Park** which some people refer to as Atcham Park. The explanation is that Atcham is a corruption of Attingham, the village having settled for the shorter form while the park, with its fine Hall, retains the longer name. The village lies beside the wide, fast-flowing Severn, and is distinguished by having two bridges, side by side, over it. The original bridge, with its seven graceful arches, was built by John Gwynne of SHREWS-BURY, a founder-member of the Royal Academy, 200 years ago; the new concrete one was erected in 1929.

Near the river are two of Atcham's three most important buildings: the church, with its unique dedication to St Eata; and the imposing red-

brick Georgian hotel, curiously named the Mytton and Mermaid. The red sandstone church, a little of it Norman, but mainly 13th- and 16th-cent. contains what are probably Roman stones brought from nearby WROXETER. There is some interesting 15th-cent. glass in the windows. Opposite the Mytton and Mermaid stands the classically-simple lodge to Attingham Park. The Hall, now a National Trust property, is used as Shropshire's Adult Education College. Designed by George Steuart in 1785 for Lord Berwick, the Hall is famous for its interior decoration; the drawing-room is especially worth seeing, and the Picture Gallery is interesting as the earliest roof-lit picture gallery to have survived.

ATTENBOROUGH, *Nottinghamshire* (13–SK5134). Oliver Cromwell once stabled his horses in the nave of the lovely church lying in broad Trent fields between the main road and the river. A farm-house with its garden adjoining the churchyard still bears traces of the Ireton brothers, who were born there and whose names appear in the register in 1611 and 1615. Henry, the eldest, married Cromwell's daughter, Bridget, and became Cromwell's right-hand man. He signed the death-warrant of Charles I, died of overwork and the plague, lay in state at SOMERSET HOUSE and was buried in WESTMINSTER ABBEY. At the Restoration he was taken from his grave and hanged from Tyburn Tree for a day. He was then buried again, under what is now MARBLE ARCH. His younger brother, John, also a loyal Cromwellian, became Lord Mayor of London, was imprisoned and then released and transported to the Scilly Isles.

The Church of St Mary Magdalene has a tower 500 years old and the interior is also much as the Iretons must have known it. The doorway is 14th-cent. and the door itself is said to be one of the oldest in the country, possibly 13th-cent. Under the tower are two 700-year-old arcades which were each halved when it was built. The altar table is Jacobean but the font is 13th-cent. There is some lovely stained glass, and four Jacobean panels preserved in the modern choir stalls are carved with mermaids, mermen, a sea-monster and a dragon. A 14th-cent. craftsman has carved the capitals around a mitred bishop's head with grotesques, some pig-faced others puny-headed, with wings, huge hands, claws and limbs but no bodies.

AXE EDGE, *Derbyshire* (12–SK0370), is one of the county's finest viewpoints. Standing about 1,600 ft above sea-level, Axe Edge is crossed by the A53 some 2 m. S. of BUXTON. There are good walks around here and panoramic views in all directions, especially W. into Cheshire. Just over the border stands the Cat and Fiddle Inn, the second highest inn in the country. Here at the southern end of the Edge is the source of the River Dove.

AYSTON, *Rutland* (10–SK8601). This is one of the prettiest villages in this loveliest of English counties, with cottages built of the ubiquitous local ironstone and roofed with thatch or Colly-weston slates. In a small, well-timbered park and beautiful garden stands Ayston Hall, a handsome late-Georgian mansion. Neatly adjoining is the Church of St Mary, with work of all centuries from the 12th to the 16th. The windows contain some glass 500 years old showing the crucifixion, and there is a curious fragment of ancient sculpture in which the figures of two sisters, one-armed twins, are just recognizable. In spite of their affliction they made enough money by spinning to buy a field, which they left as a legacy to the poor of UPPINGHAM. The craftsman carving the memorial was moved to give one of the cripples two hands, that they might be represented clasped in prayer.

Well kept and on high ground about a mile from Uppingham, Ayston is worth a small detour.

Take the secondary road due N. and then E. at the T-junction from here to **Preston** on the A6003 to visit this attractive village of stone-built houses, constructed for the most part in the Stuart period; it includes a particularly fine gabled manor house of about 1600. Although there was almost certainly a church here in Anglo-Saxon times, as is suggested by the name "priest's village" in translation, the present building is basically Norman. The chancel, the south arcade and the font are all 14th-cent. and the handsome, canopied sedilia have been in place for 600 years. It is interesting to see that much of the church furniture is of eastern origin. Two pieces of marble

floor mosaic on either side of the chancel step were brought from Constantinople after its destruction by the Turks; an almsbox comes from a church in Asia Minor; and some of the lamps and candlesticks once officiated in Damascus. The yew trees in the churchyard, traditionally planted to make supple bows for England's defence, were brought from the Garden of Gethsemane.

BAKEWELL, *Derbyshire* (12–SK2168), has a beautiful setting and contains much of interest. The small market town is built almost entirely in warm, brownish stone and lies in a sheltered valley of the Derbyshire Wye with rolling wooded hills to the N., W., and E. which make fine walking country. Bakewell's most impressive building is the large Parish Church of All Saints, standing halfway up the hill on the west side of the town, its spire a landmark. Parts of the present buildings date from the 12th cent. but there is evidence of a church here in Anglo-Saxon times; and in the churchyard stands an 8th-cent. sculptured cross, much worn but with many of the symbols carved on it still recognizable. Many other stone fragments dating from Anglo-Saxon times are on view in the church porch. Among the monuments in the church is an imposing table tomb to Sir George Vernon, the last of his line, known as the "King of the Peak" because of the lavish hospitality he provided at nearby HADDON HALL.

Bakewell's name has nothing to do with baking or its renowned pudding. The first part comes

Bakewell: the medieval bridge was originally built for packhorses

Kenneth Scowen

from an Anglo-Saxon personal name and "well" refers to the warm springs which come to the surface here – you can swim today at the 17th-cent. Bath House in water which remains at a natural 15 °C. winter and summer. Other buildings of interest are the 13th-cent. bridge over the Wye, one of the oldest in England; the old Town Hall, dating from 1709; the Old House, just above the church, the oldest house in the town and now a museum; and the Rutland Arms Hotel where the Jane Austen Room is still preserved. It was here that the famous novelist stayed in the early 19th cent. while working on *Pride and Prejudice* and it is believed that the Lambton in the novel is, in fact, Bakewell, and that two of the novel's romantic scenes are set in the room at the hotel.

The hotel is also connected with the "discovery" of the famous pudding, the result of a misunderstanding between a Mrs Greaves, then mistress of the hotel, and her cook. Instead of stirring the egg mixture into the pastry and then filling the tart with jam, the cook put the jam into the tart and then poured the egg mixture over it. So successful was the outcome that the recipe was preserved and Bakewell puddings have been made to the original formula ever since 1859 at the pudding shop in The Square.

Bakewell is a convenient centre from which to explore much of central and western Derbyshire. DOVEDALE, DARLEY DALE, **Monsal Dale** and **Lathkill Dale** are within easy distance; HADDON HALL and CHATSWORTH are not far away; ARBOR LOW, a prehistoric monument, is only 7 m. SW.; and EYAM, the plague village, only 6 m. N. At **Flagg**, about 6 m. W., are held each April the exciting High Peak point-to-point races; near BIRCHOVER, 4 m. S., are strange rock formations; and a number of the local villages engage in the Derbyshire custom of well-dressing.

BAMFORD, *Derbyshire* (12–SK2083). Set in the hills about 11 m. NE. of BUXTON, this small village boasts a church tower as tall and slim as any in the county, surmounted by a sharp spire. The countryside around adds to Bamford's attraction. To the N. lies the chain of three huge reservoirs, Ladybower, Derwent and Howden, separated by massive dams, under whose waters lie two villages. An exciting scenic drive is along the shore of the Ladybower and on over the famous Snake Pass to Glossop. Each year sheepdog trials are held at Bamford.

BARDNEY, *Lincolnshire* (13–TF1169). A rather plain little Fen town with a long high street leading down to the River Witham where a large sugar-beet factory stands next to the bridge. Bardney was once famed for the great Benedictine abbey traditionally founded in the 7th cent. by Ethelred, king of Mercia, and his queen, Ostryth, niece of Oswald, king of Northumbria. Many years after Oswald was slain in battle in A.D. 642, Queen Ostryth brought his remains to Bardney Abbey and buried them within the walls; these still remain, covering 25 acres and mostly overgrown. Pilgrims flocked to the shrine until the

abbey was destroyed by the Danes in 870. In Norman times it was sumptuously rebuilt by the Earl of Lincoln, and its abbots sat in Parliament as Lords of Lindsey. In the Domesday Book it was valued at £429 a year.

In 1912 the abbey ruins were excavated and many relics and interesting bits of stonework are now preserved in the Parish Church of St Lawrence. The church is mainly 15th-cent. with a later medieval brick chancel, and one of the finest of the monuments unearthed from the abbey is that of Abbot Richard Hornastel, who died in 1508. The high altar is said to be the body-stone of King Oswald. Many of the other relics discovered, including a Roman lock 2,000 years old, are in LINCOLN Museum.

BARDON HILL, *Leicestershire* (10–SK4513), just beyond the west edge of CHARNWOOD FOREST, is the highest point in Leicestershire, rising 912 ft above sea-level. One can certainly imagine it as an ancient stronghold hidden in moor and primeval forest, through which it is said a man could walk to Beaumanor without once seeing the sky. A Bronze Age axe, 3,000 years old, was found here when the present huge granite scars were being quarried from the sides of the hill.

Though it is necessary to leave the car and climb on foot, the glorious views over the hills of Derbyshire and Shropshire are worth the effort. On a clear day can be seen the Malvern Hills, the Wrekin, the Sugar Loaf and Black Mountains of Wales, Dunstable Downs, and the Wash. LINCOLN Cathedral rises gracefully amid factory and colliery chimneys 60 m. away.

BASWICH, *Staffordshire* (8–SJ9422). N. of this village about 3 m. ESE. of STAFFORD are the ruins of an Augustinian priory dedicated to St Thomas of Canterbury. It was founded about 1174 by Gerard Fitz Brien of Stafford; his work was completed by Bishop Richard Peche, who was buried there in 1182. In the village is a church with a medieval tower and chancel arch, a three-decker pulpit and a large galleried pew.

BEESTON, *Nottinghamshire* (13–SK5336), is mainly remarkable as a monument to the 1st Lord Trent, who started work in his mother's herbal shop in Nottingham at the age of 14 and opened Jesse Boot's in Goosegate as his own business when he was 27 in 1877. His drug factories now cover over 1¼ million square feet and into them have gone 20 acres of glass, enough cement in bags to reach from Beeston to Paris, and steel bars from Beeston to Constantinople.

The Trent is pretty at Beeston Weir.

BELTON PARK, *Lincolnshire* (13–SK9239). Three m. from GRANTHAM is Belton House, the ancestral William and Mary period home of Lord Brownlow. The house and main drive of the park are open to the public. It was built in 1689 from designs by Christopher Wren, altered about 80 years later by James Wyatt, and has some superb

Belvoir Castle has been rebuilt many times; the present building is largely 19th-cent.

Grinling Gibbons's wood-carvings, especially in the cedar-wood chapel. There is also a fine collection of paintings and porcelain, tapestries and antique silver, and the fabulous "blue bed" of William III. Of more recent interest are some personal souvenirs of King Edward VIII (now the Duke of Windsor), to whom Lord Brownlow was Lord-in-Waiting. The car park is free and refreshments are available in the Camellia Café in the gardens.

The Church of SS. Peter and Paul contains a Norman font, and the villages of **Belton** and neighbouring **Manthorpe** are two of the loveliest in Lincolnshire.

BELVOIR CASTLE, *Leicestershire* (10–SK 8133). When William the Conqueror gave the Mound and all the land visible therefrom to his standard-bearer, Robert de Todeni, he built a castle there and named it Belvedere (now pronounced "Beever").

Most of the imposing, castellated pile dominating the valley is now a mixture of medieval and 19th-cent. It has passed in almost direct descent to the present incumbent, the 19th Earl and 10th Duke of Rutland. In the years between the castle has been destroyed, rebuilt, and improved countless times. In 1461 Thomas Lord de Ros, who had inherited the property via the de Todeni female line and fought on the wrong side in the Wars of

the Roses, was beheaded. The castle was given to Lord Hastings, who removed part of it to build ASHBY and let the rest fall into decay. Twenty-four years later Henry VIII restored the castle to a de Ros, who died childless. Belvoir passed to his sister, who married Sir Robert de Manners, thus introducing the Manners's ownership. The first Earl of Rutland was created in 1525 and he rebuilt a great portion of the castle.

In 1603 James I visited the castle and it is recorded that "before he went to break his fast, he made forty-six knights; among them were Sir George and Sir Oliver Manners".

By the second marriage of the 6th Earl there were two boys, who both died young of "wicked practice and sorcery". The accounts of the trial and confessions of the alleged witches are hair-raising, culminating in one of them calling for bread and wishing it might choke her if she lied. Taking a piece in her mouth, she immediately fell dead.

Belvoir was again destroyed during the Civil War and rebuilt in 1668, with gardens and plantations added. In 1703 the 9th Earl was created Marquis of Granby. It is his great-grandson – a very extravagant fellow, who was moved at one time to write to his wife: "It is impossible we can continue our present mode of living long . . . you must not purchase everything your eye is attached to. . . ." – whose bald-headed likeness is suspended from so many public houses. His son, the 5th Duke, decided to re-model his home into a semblance of a medieval castle and obtained the services of James Wyatt, much of whose work was destroyed by fire in 1816. The Duchess, who fancied herself as an architect, then decided to take over, aided by the Duke's cousin the Rev. Sir John Thoroton. The results of many of their efforts are unfortunate.

The interior, much of which is by Wyatt's sons, Benjamin and Matthew, contains magnificent Gobelin tapestries, paintings by Van Dyck, Reynolds, Hogarth, Murillo, and one of the finest portraits of Henry VIII by Holbein. The gardens, particularly the azaleas and rhododen-drons in the Water Garden, are splendid. Outside the Mausoleum is a monument to the first Vis-count Norwich (Duff Cooper), husband of Lady Diana Manners, daughter of the 8th Duke. The altar within the mausoleum consists of a white marble memorial to the 5th Duchess, whose rise to heaven amid eerie lighting is welcomed by her four dead children offering her a crown of glory.

Belvoir is open to the public and refreshments are served inside.

For those who are wondering about the famous Belvoir Hunt, which sports the best-looking pack in the country, it should be added that, though Leicestershire is a huntsman's paradise, the Belvoir actually meets in Lincolnshire. The Fernie alone hunts in Leicestershire exclusively.

BERESFORD DALE, *Derbyshire* (12–SK 1359). Although the scenery is not as dramatic as that in DOVEDALE, Beresford Dale is the genuine Izaak Walton stretch of the River Dove. It was here that he and his friend Charles Cotton spent many hours fishing. Beresford Hall, Cotton's birthplace which looked down on the Dale, is now in ruins; but the famous Fishing Temple still stands, a stone-built, single-roomed structure with a pyramid roof, erected by Cotton in 1674. It is now in private hands but can be seen from the footpath on the other bank. Halfway along the dale is the Pike Pool, so named by Cotton because of the "pike", a tall, narrow grey rock which sticks up out of the waters like a giant fish.

BETLEY, *Staffordshire* (8–SJ7548), is a serene village about 5 m. W. of NEWCASTLE-UNDER-LYME, with a wide street and half-timbered houses. There is a 13th-cent. church, which was restored during the 17th cent. and contains a remarkable amount of timber; the splendid roof, nave arcades and clerestory are all of oak and the eight nave pillars have been carved from fully grown oaks. In the late summer a flower show with a high local reputation is held at Betley Court.

BIDDULPH, *Staffordshire* (8–SJ8857). Not far from this small town, which almost touches the Cheshire border, rises the River Trent, one of England's longest rivers, which then flows for 170 m. through the Midlands. The river rises on Biddulph Moor, 1,100 ft above sea-level. Not far

away are the BRIDESTONES, a Neolithic burial chamber to which a later legend became attached: a Viking and his English bride were said to be buried here. There is a Norman-based font in the church, and some glowing Flemish glass. Of the two big houses here one, the 16th-cent. Old Hall, is a ruin. It was destroyed by Cromwell's men during the Civil War, for the Biddulphs were Royalists; the other, the Grange, is now a chil-dren's hospital and is set among magnificent gardens laid out by the famous 19th-cent. horticulturist, James Bateman.

BINGHAM, *Nottinghamshire* (13–SK7039), is a rapidly growing village, with a sports centre which is a prototype for the whole country.

Its other main interest is the Early English Perpendicular-style steeple of All Saints'. It has one of the finest broach spires in the country, broad and strong with corner buttresses and an additional buttress in the middle of each side. Notable lancet windows set into the thickness of the wall support two-light lancets higher up.

A wooden floorstone commemorates one of the most famous of Nottinghamshire warriors. Sir Thomas Rempstone – rechristened by Shakes-peare, probably for reasons of metre, John Ramston – appears in *Richard II* as of the company listening to John of Gaunt declaiming: "This royal throne of Kings, this sceptred Isle". Sir Thomas helped Henry defeat Richard and claim the crown.

At the west end of the church there is a carving of the Seven Deadly Sins, and a sequence of memorials culminates in the figure of Ann Har-rison, who worshipped at this place for all of her 99 years. A fish-seller, she put every other half-crown she earned into the collection. Her photo-graph is displayed at the beginning of the Book of Honour to the Fallen for which she paid with her contributions. It is laid on a splendid lectern given to the church by the men who came back.

BIRCHOVER, *Derbyshire* (12–SK2462), is a small village 5 m. S. of BAKEWELL. Many of the strange rocks in the area are believed to have connections with the Druids, a belief reflected in the name of the village pub – Druid Inn. Behind the inn are the Row Tor Rocks, a pile of gritstone about 80 yds long by 50 ft high which includes two "rocking stones", one estimated to weigh 60 tons. The Rev. Thomas Eyre, vicar here in the late 17th cent., had seats carved in some of the rocks and he also built the Church of the Holy Name of Jesus to which the chancel was added in the mid-19th cent. Along the road to Winster can be seen Robin Hood's Stride, two pinnacles of rock which are occasionally tackled by climbers.

On nearby Stanton Moor, which reaches more than 900 ft in parts, are many Bronze Age remains including numerous barrows and several stone circles, the largest of which is known as the Nine Ladies. Many of the finds made in excavations on the moor can be seen in the Heathcote Museum in the village. The old stocks have been restored to their original position at Upper Town.

BISHOP'S CASTLE, *Shropshire* (8–SO3288). Bishop's Castle was the smallest borough in England until 1967, when it lost that distinction, but none of its quaintness. Situated off the A488 from SHREWSBURY to Knighton, it clings to a steep little hillside, 500 ft up – yet overtopped by the hills which surround it. Its Town Hall, one of the smallest in England, stands at the top of the High Street, forcing the road to bend to pass it, with a clock-tower above and an old stone lock-up in its basement. Included in the town's insignia are two fine silver maces, hallmarked 1697.

Administratively linked with CLUN, 5 m. to the S., Bishop's Castle is in the centre of sheep country. There are several fine Tudor houses: the Old Hall, believed to be the birthplace of Edmund Plowden, the builder of Plowden Hall (*see* LYD-BURY NORTH); the Old Porch House; and the aptly named House on Crutches. There are also several Georgian houses. Of the original castle, now only part of a wall remains, flanking a bowling green which is the highest point in the town.

The little town had an unusual origin. An Anglo-Saxon landowner, Egwin Shakehead, was cured of his palsy at the shrine of St Ethelbert in HEREFORD and in gratitude bequeathed his manor of Lydbury North to the Bishops of Hereford. They built a castle on the land and in the 13th cent. the little settlement which had sprung up around it became a separate parish, with its own church. Of that first church, very little remains for it was fired and ruined during the Civil War when Bishop's Castle was loyal to the King.

The oldest inn in the town is probably The Three Tuns whose history has been traced back to 1642, but may well go beyond that. The inn is distinguished today by being one of the few left where the landlord still brews his own ale. The brewhouse stands beside the inn.

BLEAKLOW, *Derbyshire* (12–SK1096), is one of the largest areas of England still uncrossed by a road. It is an almost completely unpopulated area of the High Peak in the NW. of the county running up to the Yorkshire border. It lies between the A628 and the A57 and is, as its name suggests, a grim, bleak stretch of high, bare country best avoided in winter; but in summer it is a place for those with an eye for wide skies and an ear for silence, a strange but beautiful area. Bleaklow Hill is over 2,000 ft and to the S. Alport Moor is only a little lower. Several rivers rise in Bleaklow, including the Derwent and the Alport.

BLIDWORTH, *Nottinghamshire* (13–SK5855). In what remains of SHERWOOD FOREST, with good views, is the Church of St Mary where, so it is said, Will Scarlet is buried. It is also said that Maid Marian left her home at Blidworth to marry Robin, and that on the hill on which this picturesque colliery village stands is a cave where the outlaws stored their food. Even if the stories are apocryphal they are nevertheless charming.

It is possibly the same ability for telling a fine tale with conviction which accounts for local assurances that a natural boulder at the foot of the hill – 90 ft in circumference, 15 ft high and with a passage through the middle – is part of Druid remains.

BLITHFIELD HALL, *Staffordshire* (8–SK 0423), has been the home of the Bagot family and their ancestors, the de Blithfields, for almost 900 years. N. of RUGELEY on the UTTOXETER road, the present Hall, mainly Elizabethan with Georgian and Regency additions, is open to the public. The wooded parkland of the Blythe valley makes a gracious setting for the house which is built round a central courtyard and contains much fine woodwork, notably the magnificent carved oak staircase. There is a unique collection of relics from the Stuart period, a children's toy museum, and an exhibition of needlework figures. Georgian costumes are displayed on life-size figures and the old family coaches can be seen in the stables. Outside, views of Blithfield Reservoir can be obtained from the landscaped gardens which contain an 18th-cent. orangery. The Bagot family's link with ABBOTS BROMLEY is maintained by a performance of the ancient Abbots Bromley Horn Dance at the Hall each September.

BLYTH, *Nottinghamshire* (13–SK6287). An old village of great architectural merit on the ancient highway from London to YORK. In the centre of the wide main street there is a long, elm-shaded island on which stands a building with mullioned windows, stone walls, and a 700-year-old doorway still preserved. This building, now serving as a school, was once the property of the Hospital of St John, founded for the care of lepers in the 12th cent. The parish church is developed from the original nave and aisles of a priory built by Roger de Busli in 1088 as a cell of the Abbey of St Catherine at Rouen, and contains the oldest example of Norman architecture in England in its style, if not in date. The south aisle was enlarged to its present size in 1290, with five windows and seven grotesque gargoyles, and the beautiful west tower, 100 ft high, was added in the 14th cent.

BOLSOVER, *Derbyshire* (13–SK4770). This small industrial town, 5 m. E. of CHESTERFIELD, offers a striking visual contrast between what was and what is: down in the valley is all the evidence of the mining industry and its offshoots which make the town important today, while perched on a wooded eminence above the town stands the castle. The original castle was built in Norman times by William Peveril, but the building which occupies the site today, in the care of the Ministry of Public Building and Works and open to the public, was built in the early 17th cent. by Sir Charles Cavendish. The date of its building makes this one of England's most curious castles, for this was not a time when men felt the need, as they had done 500 years earlier, to build fortresses for themselves. It is thought, indeed, that Sir Charles's main intention must have been to re-create the atmosphere of times gone by. That he succeeded is there for all to see today, for although his

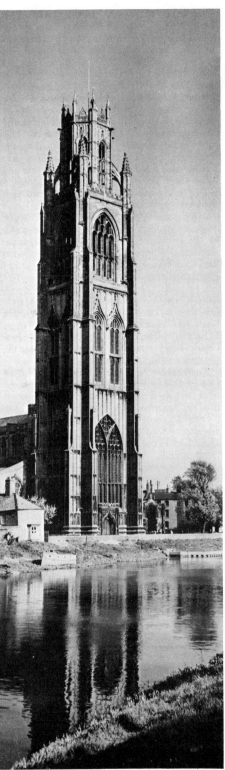

G. Douglas Bolton

Boston Stump

castle has battlements and turrets, it also has two pretty cupolas, picturesque riding stables and rooms with names like the Star Chamber and the Heaven Room.

Also worth a visit in Bolsover is the Parish Church of St Mary. It was gutted by fire towards the end of the last century and much reconstruction work had to be done, but the 13th-cent. greystone tower escaped the flames, and inside is a large relief sculpture of the Nativity, also 13th-cent.

BOSCOBEL, *Shropshire* (8–SJ8308). Here, among leafy lanes about 5 m. E. of SHIFNAL, stands the house where Charles II hid from the Parliamentary troops seeking him, after his defeat at WORCESTER on 3 September 1651. Boscobel House was put up about 1600 by John Giffard, a Catholic, and therefore included a number of built-in hiding places. In one of these, which is shown to visitors, the king spent one night. And nearby stands a majestic oak tree, successor of the one in which Charles remained concealed during the day while Cromwell's men searched Boscobel House and its grounds – but never, apparently, lifting their eyes.

About 1 m. away stands another building which has associations with Charles II and which, like Boscobel House, is now in the care of the Ministry of Public Building and Works and can be viewed. This is **Whiteladies** where the king was also briefly sheltered in a house near the ruins of the 12th-cent. nunnery.

BOSTON, *Lincolnshire* (13–TF3244). The name Boston is thought to be a corruption of "St Botolph's Town" and its earliest associations are with this Anglo-Saxon monk whose history is shadowy but whose relics are spread as far as Denmark and Norway. There are 80 churches dedicated to him in England, but Boston is the most famous with its Boston Stump rising to 272½ ft, said to be the second highest church tower in Great Britain.

By 1204, when King John granted a charter to Boston, its fame as a port was second only to that of London, and by the end of the 13th cent. it was paying more than London in customs duties. The great church, whose beacon-light shining from the octagon guided travellers over land and sea for centuries, was rebuilt on the foundations of the St Botolph's mentioned in the Domesday Book. The merchants, growing rich in the wooltrade with Flanders, fashioned it somewhat in the manner of Antwerp or Bruges. It was started in 1309, though the tower was not added until 1460, and for those with energy enough to climb 365 steps there is a splendid view of ships going down the River Witham to the sea. The interior, the oldest part, is magnificent with its high embossed roof. The elaborately carved and brightly coloured stalls with hinged *miserere* seats, all but two of the original 14th-cent. ones surviving, are among the finest in the land.

Plagues, floods, and the turning of trade towards new lands across the Atlantic with the subsequent super-importance of western ports like BRISTOL, turned Boston into a distressed area by the end of the 16th cent. But in the years between, the nucleus of the first Pilgrim Fathers was arrested while trying to escape religious persecution and imprisoned in the Guildhall, where their cells can still be seen. In the following year, 1608, they finally sailed to Holland, reaching the shores of New England some 12 years later, 10 years after others had landed in Plymouth, Massachusetts, and founding the town of Boston. In 1633 John Cotton, Boston's famous Puritan vicar, sailed to America with Richard Bellingham, who became the first of five subsequent Lincoln-Boston Governors of Massachusetts. To this day the whole town flies the Stars and Stripes on 4 July, and Fydell House, built in 1726 and now housing the Pilgrim College, still keeps one room dedicated to the use of visiting American Bostonians.

Other famous Boston men are remembered by the Australians: Sir Joseph Banks, who sailed with Captain Cook in the *Endeavour*, and George Bass, who sailed right round Tasmania and discovered the Strait which still bears his name. The town is proud of Jean Ingelow whose poem, "High Tide on the Coast of Lincolnshire", written in the 19th cent., describes the devastation of the floods of 1571 when the water reached halfway up the church. A remnant of her house still stands opposite the Guildhall, and the tune played on the church chimes was composed in honour of her poem. In the Market Place is a statue of Herbert Ingram, who founded the *Illustrated London News*, the first publication of its kind, in 1842.

There are many fascinating streets, ancient houses and old warehouses in Boston. Those who drive through too fast might later be sorry to have missed a significant part of our history.

BOTHAMSALL, *Nottinghamshire* (13–SK67 73). A neat, quiet village on the slopes of the valley where the Meden and the Maun flow together to become the River Idle. At the join of the rivers is Conjure Alders. Ash and alder trees grow here by the place the Anglo-Saxons used as a ford called Coningswath.

Bothamsall Castle, W. of the village, is probably the earthwork of a Norman castle. A climb up through the sycamores, beeches and elms growing over it to the old oak rising from the top of the hill is well worth the effort for the fine views over SHERWOOD FOREST.

BOTTESFORD, *Leicestershire* (10–SK8038). Here again we pick up the history of BELVOIR CASTLE, for this village church with a lovely spire is where the lords of Rutland have brought eight of their earls to lie in great splendour, together with the monuments of ancestors originally buried in the priory at Belvoir. The first to be buried in the Church of St Mary was Sir Thomas Manners, Lord de Ros, and 1st Earl of Rutland, favourite of Henry VIII. His tomb cost £20 and is surrounded by mourners in the shape of his nine daughters and six sons, one of whom, John, made

a romantic match with Dorothy Vernon of HADDON HALL. The 5th Earl, who endowed the white almshouse opposite the church in 1612, has the richest tomb, with a peacock at his feet. His wife's effigy is also on the tomb though she, the only child of Sir Philip Sidney, was buried at Shoreditch. Francis, the 6th Earl, lies between his first and second wives – the second one, Cecilia, being the mother of the "two sonnes, both of which died in their infancy by wicked Practice and Sorcerye" as is recorded on the monument. This tomb reaches up to the chancel ceiling and was the cause of shocked consternation when it was erected since it hides the altar from the nave and leaves very little room for the choir and clergy to pass. The Marquis of Granby is also buried here, but has no monument.

All these memorials afford a splendid study in changing aristocratic tastes. In the market place, by the stump of the ancient cross, stand the stocks and whipping post to remind us of what happened occasionally to those who could not afford monuments.

BOURNE, *Lincolnshire* (13–TF0920). Mainly famous now for the B.R.M. works, this market town was certainly the birthplace of Robert Mannyng in about 1264 and is reputed, since Charles Kingsley made it so, also to have been the birthplace of Hereward the Wake.

An abbey for Augustinian canons was founded here in 1138 in which Robert Mannyng, whose work was so important to the development of English, inscribed his translations from the French. The only Norman remains of the abbey are incorporated in the nave of the church, four round arches on massive piers supporting scalloped capitals.

The four main streets converge on the Market Place where in 1520 Lord Burghley, statesman and founder of the Cecil fortunes, was born in which is now the Burghley Arms Hotel. Near the disused railway station is Red Hall, an Elizabethan brick building, the home of the Digby family in the 18th cent.

One of the best sports grounds in Lincolnshire, with a splendid swimming-pool, is endowed by an ancient charity at Abbey Lawn. Ever since 1770 another charity has bought bread for the poor after a race by schoolboys over a measured distance at White Bread Meadow. Bidding for the field continues until the boys finish the race and the highest bidder holds the land for a year, giving his rent to the charity.

BRADGATE PARK, *Leicestershire* (10–SK 5908). One of the earliest of the fine Leicestershire houses built for pleasure rather than fortification, Bradgate in its 1,000-acre park 6 m. from the centre of LEICESTER was started by Thomas Grey, Earl of Huntingdon and 1st Marquis of Dorset, in about 1490 and finished by his son, grandfather of Lady Jane Grey. Born in 1537, she spent the only happy part of her life here with her tutor, Aylmer, later Bishop of London, before her scheming father married her at the age of 16 to

Lord Dudley with whom she was beheaded in the Tower not long afterwards.

The house is now a ruin, but the park, which is open only on Thursdays during the summer to motorists, incorporates much of CHARNWOOD FOREST where the woods, bracken-covered hills, striking granite outcrops and charming by-ways make delightful walks. Bradgate Park is also a reserve for Leicestershire Trust for Nature Conservation. Take the path from the main gate, turning left uphill past the war memorial to Old John, the highest point. There is a folly tower there with an adjoining arch and a direction indicator from which to choose a number of walks, all of them equally lovely.

BRADWELL, *Derbyshire* (12–SK1781). Situated in the beautiful Hope Valley about 2 m. S. of HOPE, this small village has not only a rocky dale of its own, but also its own cave. The well-known Bagshawe's Cavern, approached by more than 100 descending steps, contains some weirdly beautiful stalactites and other crystallized formations. This is also another of Derbyshire's well-dressing villages, two being dressed each August.

BRAMCOTE, *Nottinghamshire* (13–SK5037), is worth finding for its beautiful views over five counties and the Trent valley, and because it is one of the prettiest villages hereabouts. The Manor House, one of the finest brick buildings in Nottinghamshire, was in existence in 1564 and has been turned into charming dwellings set about a rockery with pools.

The famous Hemlock Stone, 30 ft high, of red sandstone, which has resisted the action of the elements longer than man can tell, also belongs to Bramcote. It is about 70 ft in circumference and probably weighs over 200 tons. It is popularly connected with Druid rituals and has been declared an Area of Special Scientific Interest.

BRAUNSTON, *Rutland* (10–SK8306). Amid beautiful hilly country, Braunston lies on the side of a hill rising from the valley of the little River Gwash. The farm-houses, cottages and church are built of the charming, dark-brown local ironstone. The church is externally 15th-cent. Perpendicular but there is evidence inside of an originally Norman building of the 12th and 13th cents. in the responds of the chancel arch and the doorway from chancel to vestry. There are also still some traces of medieval wall paintings.

The name was Danish, meaning "Brand's village". About one mile NW. of the village are sunken roads and ancient earthworks where pottery has been found.

Leave by the road to Tilton and LEICESTER which affords fine views over the wooded hills. One m. SE. of Braunston is **Brooke**, only 2 m. from OAKHAM, yet pleasingly remote. In particular, Brooke's charming little Church of St Peter is worth a detour to visit. The tower is 13th-cent. and there are traces of Norman work, but it is the Elizabethan craftsmanship which is the most interesting. In 1577 the "archdeacon's visitations" described the church as ruinous and the curate often "marvellously overcome with drink". But it was rebuilt in 1579, a most unusual time for church building, and retains an impression of the worshippers of the time still being there, surrounded by the screen, benches, box pews, family pews, pulpit, reading desk and communion rail of the period.

Stones on the chancel floor record the depressing life of one Henry Rawlins, and his four wives, who all died within 13 years. His fifth wife, however, managed to break the curse, and buried *him* in 1742. There is also a lovely Renaissance alabaster monument to Charles Noel, which was erected in 1619 and still retains its original colours. In 1549 the Noels bought the site of Brooke Priory, founded before 1153, the only monastic house in Rutland. They built a large mansion on it of which only the ruined gateway and porter's lodge are left. The present house, called The Priory, is late 17th-cent. and the porter's lodge became an 18th-cent. dovecot.

BREEDON-ON-THE-HILL, *Leicestershire* (10–SK4022). The village is uninteresting, but people who climb the rocky road up to the Iron Age encampment still known as "The Bulwarks" on the top of the hill find the place weird and uncanny.

As early as the 8th cent. there was an Anglo-Saxon monastery here of which some sculpture still survives in the present church. There are 30 fragments built into the structure, Mercian work which, fitted together, would cover 60 ft. The strips of frieze are about 9 in. high, the longest one is behind the altar and the most beautiful one, an angel, is 3 ft long. The Danes obliterated this monastery and only ruins were left until the early 12th cent., when the foundations were used to build an Augustinian priory, traces of which still remain in the west end of the tower. In the 13th cent. a new chancel was added, constituting the present building.

BRIDGNORTH, *Shropshire* (8–SO7193), is really two towns, High Town and Low Town, connected by many flights of steps and a railway with the steepest gradient in Britain. The setting, part spread across the red sandstone ridge, part at its foot, is unique in England; and the buildings in the town live up to it. The oddest is undoubtedly the remains of the 12th-cent. castle which was destroyed by the Parliamentarians in 1646. They left about 30 ft of the tower of the keep and this still stands – or leans – unbelievably at 17 degrees from the perpendicular, more than three times the lean of the tower at Pisa. The castle grounds are now a public park and a fascinating view of the Low Town can be had from Castle Walk, a promenade running 100 ft above the River Severn.

The next most conspicuous building is the Town Hall; half-timbered and set on arches, it straddles the High Street, traffic passing beneath it. There are many half-timbered and 18th-cent. houses in the High Street, which is one of the most pleasing thoroughfares in the county, straight, wide and gracious.

One of the best vistas in the town is to be had in East Castle Street which vies with High Street with its many fine, well-proportioned houses. The street is a cul-de-sac, sealed off by Bridgnorth's most striking church, St Mary Magdalene's. Built in white stone with Tuscan columns, a square, pillared tower surmounted by a lead dome, the church looks as if it would be more at home in a Mediterranean town than in its English setting. Its designer was the engineer Thomas Telford.

The Parish Church of St Leonard, badly damaged during the Civil War, was almost entirely rebuilt about 100 years ago in its 15th-cent. style. In red sandstone, the church is remarkably wide. It has an impressive tower and a stair turret topped with a miniature spire.

Climbing up steeply from Low Town to High Town is the Cartway. Here are caves, hewn out of the sandstone, where people lived until little more than 100 years ago. Here, too, is the town's oldest house, a near-perfect example of Elizabethan black-and-white building which was the birthplace of Bishop Thomas Percy. The bishop is mainly remembered for his collection of old English poetry, *Reliques of Ancient English Poetry* (1765).

There are some interesting houses in Low Town: Cann Hall where Prince Rupert lodged in 1642; Diamond Hall, built by Colonel Roger Pope in the late 17th cent. with the winnings of his horse, Diamond; and the 17th-cent. Vine Inn by the river.

BRIERLEY HILL, *Staffordshire* (8–SO9187). Fine glass has been made here since French glassmakers came to the town at the beginning of the 17th cent. and many examples, including historical pieces, can be seen in a collection at the Central Library in Moor Street. On Ashwood Heath are the remains of a 1st-cent. Roman camp.

BROCKLESBY, *Lincolnshire* (13–TA1311). The 1,000-acre park of this, the still almost feudal family seat of the Earls of Yarborough, was laid out by Capability Brown. The house is of red brick, set amid lily-ponds and dating originally from 1730. It contains beautiful works of art, magnificent furniture, and paintings by Lely, Romney and Reynolds. The family, who are descended from Elizabeth I's eminent military commander, Sir William Pelham, are famous for the trees they have planted in the park. They began with 40,000 saplings two years before the French Revolution and the 1st Baron is recorded as having planted 12,552,700 trees between 1787 and 1823. His wife, Sophia, is buried at Limber Magna in the Brocklesby Mausoleum, built by James Wyatt, with a statue by Nollekens, amongst cedars on what was once a tumulus. Roman combs, rings, urns, beads, bones and ashes have been found there.

Some of the Pelham ancestors are buried in the

Bridgnorth: a view from the High Town

13th-cent. church in the Park in tombs ornamented with the Buckle badge which can also be seen in many Sussex churches. This badge was granted to Sir John Pelham for his courtesy on the field of battle at Poitiers, where he captured King John of France.

BROWNHILLS, *Staffordshire* (8–SK0405). Close to this town on the edge of the Black Country is one of the country's largest watersports centres, Chasewater. The 260-acre lake is used by the Cannock Sailing Club, and the South Staffordshire Hydroplane and Speedboat Club and in summer there is always something for the visitor to see. There are also gardens, an amusement park and a paddling pool. In Brownhills, at a junction on Watling Street (A5) near the railway station, stands what is believed to be one of the oldest signposts in England, dated 1777. Three m. to the E. is the ancient Roman site of WALL; and at Ogley Hay is a relic of Roman earthworks.

BUILDWAS ABBEY, *Shropshire* (8–SJ6304), is reckoned one of the three finest ruined abbeys in England. In a meadow beside the Severn on the road from MUCH WENLOCK to IRONBRIDGE, its Norman ruins contrast with a six-chimneyed modern power station. More surprising than its location, perhaps, is the fact that after 800 years so much of the abbey should still be standing; this is largely due to the rescue operation carried out by the Ministry of Public Building and Works.

The abbey was founded in 1135 by Roger de Clinton, Bishop of Coventry and Lichfield, and the present buildings are believed to date from about 15 years later. Impressive but not over-poweringly so, the abbey is about 180 ft long. The nave, with its huge round pillars and Norman arches, is almost intact save for the roof: and parts of the chapter house, the sacristy, the crypt and tower still stand. The piscina, the stone seats for the priests and other pieces of carved stone from the time of Henry II and Becket also remain for the visitor to see.

BUNNY, *Nottinghamshire* (13–SK5829). Much of this pretty village was designed by the eccentric but kindly "Wrestling Baron", Thomas Parkyns. Encouraged by his mother in ideas which were then almost revolutionary, Sir Thomas did all he could to improve the lot of his tenants, rebuilding farm-houses and dwellings, many of which still bear his initials, and designing four charming 17th-cent. almshouses and a school (now used as a village room) near the church gate. They still have mullioned windows and on the division between the first and second floors Sir Thomas, who had compiled a Latin Grammar and displayed tags wherever he could, has had inscribed: *Scientia non habet inimicum nisi ignorantem* – "Learning has no enemy except the ignorant man".

In designing his own home, Bunny Hall, Sir Thomas showed his eccentricities to the full. His greatest interest, however, was in wrestling and he wrote a book about it called *The Cornish Hugg* which he dedicated to George I. When he died in 1741 he was buried in the 14th-cent. church in one of the stone coffins he used to collect and give away to anybody who asked for one. He designed his own monument which depicts him standing aggressively, waiting to start a wrestling bout. By his side is a tiny little figure lying flat on a pallet with Father Time by his side. Part of the epitaph reads: "That Time at length did throw him it is plain".

BURFORD, *Shropshire* (8–SO5868), is a small village, 1 m. from Tenbury Wells and separated from Worcestershire by the River Teme. Tucked away down a quiet lane off the A465, the red sandstone Church of St Mary bears traces of its Norman origins but much of the present building, including its imposing tower and battlements, dates from the late 19th cent. The most striking of the many church monuments for which Burford is famed is a triptych, 11 ft tall, signed by the Italian painter Melchior Salaboss and dated 1588. The two panelled doors are painted with the figures of the Twelve Apostles and these open to reveal life-size paintings of three of the Cornwalls, lords of Burford for 400 years until the family sold their lands in 1721.

A more recent source of fame are the Burford House clematis. Burford House, which stands on the site of the original Cornwall castle, is a typical early Georgian (1726) mansion, part of which can be looked over. In 1954 the gardens round the house were completely re-designed and re-claimed from nature, and were opened to the public for the summer months four years later. Many unusual shrubs and plants from all over the world are on show and scattered among them, mostly informally, are more than 120 species of clematis. But it is the clematis in the glasshouses, with flowers the size of plates, which remain most strongly in the memory.

BURLEY, *Rutland* (10–SK8710). The village is chiefly famed for the most beautiful country house in the county. Burley-on-the-Hill. It is best admired from the S. on the OAKHAM–STAMFORD road, looking up the great avenue of trees to the top of what must once have been an ancient earth-work 500 ft above sea-level, the highest point in Rutland, overlooking the Vale of Catmose.

The first house was built in the 16th cent. by Sir John Harington, who entertained James I there on his way to be crowned. By the time he revisited it in 1620 it had been bought and rebuilt by his favourite, the Duke of Buckingham. Before that building was destroyed by Cromwell's armies, Charles I and Henrietta Maria had also paid it a visit, and it was on this occasion that the famous Oakham Dwarf, Jeffery Hudson, jumped out of a pie as it was cut at the dinner-table. Henrietta Maria was so enchanted with the dwarf that the Duchess gave him to her, and Van Dyck painted the two together in a picture now hanging at PETWORTH in Sussex.

The present house, with its beautifully re-strained detail, was designed by John Lumley for David Finch, Earl of Nottingham, in 1694–1705. In 1815 the Duke of Wellington thought of buying and rebuilding it, but was most fortunately directed elsewhere. The church, almost ruined by the Victorian "restorer" Pearson, still bears Norman and 13th-cent. traces inside. There is a lovely, very pathetic, marble monument to Lady Charlotte Finch, governess to the children of George III, but, oddly enough, no other mem-orials to the family.

In the woods behind the house is a circular hermit's sanctuary, built of rustic-work in 1807.

BURTON-UPON-TRENT, *Staffordshire* (9–SK2423). On a warm day the rich, "home-cook-ing" smell of beer being brewed hangs in every street of this important brewing town. Here, too, are the huge buildings bearing the names familiar to everyone who takes a glass of ale. Yet Burton was not always a brewing town; once its pros-perity was geared to the clothing industry, although story has it that a 13th-cent. abbot of Burton used the water from the local wells for brewing. Of his abbey only fragments remain and the man most remembered here in stone and brick is Michael Bass, a member of the famous brewing firm who became Lord Burton during Mr Gladstone's premiership. To Lord Burton the town owes its fine Town Hall, the beautiful St Paul's Church, St Margaret's Church and a number of other public buildings.

The parish church is St Modwen's, dedicated to the founder of the first Christian settlement at Burton in the 7th cent. The church, standing near

Burton-upon-Trent: a bridge across the river

the Trent, was built in the early 18th cent. and contains a 15th-cent. font, probably a relic from an earlier church.

Fine views of the river can be had from the three bridges – the main Burton bridge, the iron Anglesey Bridge, and the long footbridge, known as the Stapenhill Viaduct.

BUXTON, *Derbyshire* (12–SK0673). Buxton's fame rests on both its air and its water. This is the highest town in England – just over 1,000 ft above sea-level; it is also one of the oldest spas in the country. The Romans were the first to appreciate the value of the waters which come to the surface here but it was the efforts of the 5th Duke of Devonshire from 1780 onwards – and those of his two successors to the title – which established Buxton as a second BATH. The 5th Duke had the sweeping Crescent, still the finest sight in the town, built close to the original St Ann's Well which is open daily throughout the season. In the Crescent, too, are the Natural Baths which stand upon the site of a Roman Bath. Today the nine springs, which are estimated to be between 3,500 and 5,000 ft below ground, produce about a quarter of a million gallons of warm water each

day. It gushes into a beautiful white Italian marble basin which emphasizes the colour of the pale blue water. It is also Buxton's claim that this natural mineral water is without the unpleasant smell and taste usually associated with spa waters.

Buxton sets out with firm purpose to entertain the visitor and nowhere more so than in the Pavilion Gardens, 23 acres of lovely grounds surrounding the Pavilion itself, which contains a large concert hall and a ballroom. In the grounds are putting and bowling greens and tennis courts; there is boating on the lake; and there is a children's play area which includes both model and miniature railways. There are other pleasing open spaces, such as the Serpentine Walks by the Wye and the walk to Grinlow Woods and the strange tower known as Solomon's Temple on the south side of the town. Corbar Woods are another worthwhile goal for the walker and there are paths to the top of Corbar Crags with their fine views.

In Buxton Museum in Terrace Road can be seen collections of local rocks and fossils, and ornaments made of Blue John stone and Ashford marble. There is another museum at Poole's

Cavern housing ancient British, Roman and animal remains found in the Cavern; the cave itself is also open to the public.

Derbyshire play county cricket at the charming ground just off the town centre; and there are two 18-hole golf courses, one high above the town on the road to Glossop which is reckoned one of the driest courses in the country.

Buxton is in the heart of impressive scenery, some of the best being seen by taking the minor road to the small villages of **Peak Dale** and **Peak Forest** to the NE. Here you cross the roof of England, a wide, almost prehistoric landscape, criss-crossed with grey, drystone walls, here and there a hill rearing up, and the bareness relieved only by the occasional cluster of trees in a sheltered hollow, rarely enough to make a wood.

CAISTOR, *Lincolnshire* (13–TA1101). High on a western spur of the Wolds, with views of LINCOLN Cathedral, Caistor, in the county division of Lindsey, is now a quiet little market town serving the rich farming country surrounding it.

It was once a walled Roman camp, succeeding a British hill-fort called Caer-Egarry, and the Roman Ermine Street passed near it. Fragments of the Roman wall can be seen in the garden of the headmaster of the Grammar School, a 17th-cent. building carefully restored in 1930, where once the poet, Sir Henry Newbolt, was a pupil.

The Venerable Bede mentions Caistor as an Anglo-Saxon place of importance called Tunne-Ceaster and some mounds just outside the town are supposed to mark the site of the battle in A.D. 828 in which King Egbert of Wessex defeated the Mercians.

The Church of SS. Peter and Paul has early Anglo-Saxon and late Norman work in the lower part of the tower and there is a Roman well still in use nearby. At the east end of the north aisle is the Crusader tomb of Sir William de Hundon and the vestry contains an alabaster monument to Sir Edward Maddison, who died in 1553, aged 100. A "gad whip" – one of four still in existence – is preserved in the church.

The village of **Cabourne**, 1½ m. E. on the A46, has a church tower dating from before the Norman Conquest, and Pelham Column, 128 ft high, erected in 1840 to commemorate the planting of 12 million trees by Lord Yarborough of BROCKLESBY.

CALVERTON, *Nottinghamshire* (13–SK6149). Famous as the probable birthplace of the inventor of the stocking-frame, an Elizabethan parson called William Lee. It was due to Lee's invention that the hosiery industry flourishes today, though he made no money out of it and it was eventually developed in France. This frame, the most amazingly complete invention ever to be devised in a single operation, was the first machine to produce a looped or knitted fabric and was the beginning of the great hosiery and lace-making factories which abound in Nottinghamshire to-day. The more romantic story about the invention was that Lee nearly 400 years ago was

courting a lady who infuriated him by continuing to knit while he paid his addresses. In exasperation he gave up the care of his parish to invent the knitting machine, taking it to Queen Elizabeth, who refused to grant him a patent because it only made wool stockings. Lee then made another frame to produce silk stockings, but the Queen again refused a patent in case it threw the hand-knitters out of work. There are still hand-knitters in the cottages of Calverton today, recognizable by the wide windows where globes of water hang to catch the light.

The Church of St Wilfrid has seven Norman stones carved into the belfry illustrating the "occupations of months".

CANNOCK, *Staffordshire* (8–SJ9710), now a thriving industrial town, owed its existence originally to CANNOCK CHASE, lying to the N. It is more than likely that there was a small settlement of some kind 1,000 years and more ago; and to the NE. of the town is an area of about 18 acres known as Castle Ring which was an Iron Age encampment.

There was a church on the site of the present St Luke's Parish Church in the 12th cent., and a few traces of that original building remain. The church was rebuilt in the 14th cent., and has several times been altered and restored since. A more curious and unusual building is the Tank House. Built of brick, hexagonal and with a pyramid roof, this was where the pipe bringing Cannock's first secure water supply, in 1736, came out.

One of the most attractive buildings is the white 18th-cent. former mansion which houses the Council offices – and next to it is one of the most perfect bowling greens in the Midlands, which has been in constant use for more than 170 years. Within easy reach of the town, on the edge of Cannock Chase, is the famous Beaudesert Golf Club; and the nearby Hednesford Hills are good for walks.

CANNOCK CHASE, *Staffordshire* (8–SJ 9816). Once, 1,000 years and more ago, there were so many trees, many of them giant oaks, on Cannock Chase that a stranger could lose himself in half an hour. Today, crossed by one good road, bordered by others and networked with tracks and forest rides, the Chase consists of some of the most beautiful country in the Midlands, easily accessible to motorist, rambler and walker. Where once the kings and nobles of England hunted for sport, keeping the Chase as their own private preserve, the visitor today can wander freely in countryside that looks well in all seasons, but is perhaps loveliest in spring and autumn.

Today there are fewer trees but the Forestry Commission have established many plantations. Some of the majestic oaks remain in Brocton Coppice; this is where, with luck, wild deer may be glimpsed.

The forest rides between South Street and Abraham's Valley offer pleasant walks through the orderly pine and spruce plantations. Many areas in high summer are seas of waist-high bracken; but to the W. of Sherbrook Valley heather and gorse take over the hillside. There is a large variety of bog-plants to be seen in Sherbrook Valley or down Oldacre, including the rare fly-catching sundew – and the even rarer long-leaved sundew. Beetles abound near the streams. Birch trees grow on the Black Hills and from any of the hilltops near Seven Springs can be had magnificent views over large areas of the Chase. Besides trees, gorse and heather there is the Trent flowing beneath the fine bridge at Colwich. Low, narrow and with 14 grey-stone arches – once it had 43 – the Essex Bridge, as it is now called, was perhaps built by the Elizabethan Earls of Essex as a short cut to the Chase.

CANWICK, *Lincolnshire* (13–SK9869). One m. SE. of LINCOLN, off the B1188, Canwick offers such world-famous views of the cathedral that it is worth visiting if for nothing else. It can also be reached on foot by taking the charming path down the cliff by the edge of South Common and up the tree-lined ridge.

But the church is also interesting, built by the Normans on the tessellated floors of a Roman villa. No Roman traces remain, but there is a Norman chancel still standing amid the many alterations which continued until the 19th cent.

Canwick is in the North Kesteven district of Lincolnshire and the Hall is the ancestral home of the Sibthorps. John Sibthorp was a famous 18th-cent. botanist; the Rev. Richard scandalized the early Victorians by dithering for years between the Church of England and the Roman Catholic faiths, finally dying a Catholic and insisting on being buried with the English rites; and politician Charles sold his land to the railway for the GRANTHAM–Lincoln line on the condition that it never ran on a Sunday; this it never did. The line is now closed to passengers.

CASTLE BYTHAM, *Lincolnshire* (13–SK 9818). Cottages cluster up the hill towards the church in this very charming village in the South Kesteven district of Lincolnshire. On the other side of the stream flowing down to the River Glen are the great earthworks mentioned in the Domesday Book as held by Earl Morcar, brother of King Harold. Morkery Wood, W. of the village, still bears his name.

Finished by the Conqueror's half-brother, Odo, the castle stood here until it was besieged and razed to the ground by Henry III in 1221. A second castle was built by William de Colville which was burned in the Wars of the Roses.

The Church of St James is 12th-cent. though it has a Norman nave. It is cruciform and on the south of the tower is an 18th-cent. sundial inscribed with the pun, "Bee in Thyme". The brass candelabra was made just after Waterloo. In a corner of the nave stands a ladder inscribed, "This ware the May Poul 1660" – the village maypole later used as steps to the belfry.

CASTLE DONINGTON, *Leicestershire* (10–SK4427). Castle Donington is the administrative centre of a rural district covering 37 sq. m. and including East Midlands Airport. It was once the site of the first Norman castle, built by Henry de Lacy, Earl of Lincoln, whose London home was LINCOLN'S INN. In 1595 Sir George Hastings, 4th Earl of Huntingdon, "ruined the castle" and built a house in the park 2 m. away. The Hall, designed by Wilkins, architect of the NATIONAL GALLERY, is now a hotel. A castellated building close by called the Kings' Mill overlooks the Trent at a popular boating and picnic spot with a weir, many small islands, and a row of white cottages.

The town itself still has some lovely houses, in particular the Old Key House, a timber-framed building halfway up the hill to the SW. of the church. Houses and cottages incorporating the original stone now stand on the site of the castle with their gardens in part of the old moat.

The Church of St Edward is essentially 13th- and 14th-cent. Brass-rubbing enthusiasts should visit the fine memorial to Robert de Staunton and his wife. The oldest tomb is that of a tonsured monk sculptured in about 1320. The inside of the pulpit is constructed of memorial slabs to children, taken from the floor.

Castle Donington has a fine power station, a lesson to those who think these must always be monstrosities.

CASTLETON, *Derbyshire* (12–SK1582). This is the country of the caverns. Four of the most famous in the country are to be found in and around this large village in the northern Peak District, about 8 m. NE. of BUXTON. But the first thing the visitor sees are not the caverns but the ruined Norman Peveril Castle, immortalized in Sir Walter Scott's *Peveril of the Peak*, which stands high above the village. Now in the care of the Ministry of Public Building and Works, much of the castle has been fittingly restored to its former grandeur. It is well worth the climb to see it.

William Peveril was given the land for the castle by William the Conqueror and immediately set about the building. The site was well chosen: terrain offered natural protection on three sides and only the N. called for serious fortification. It was here that Peveril threw up the curtain wall which survives almost in its entirety – although much repaired over the years. The typical Norman herringbone masonry can easily be detected. Traces of other Norman parts of the castle can also be seen. The imposing keep came almost 100 years later, erected by Henry II in 1176.

The nearest cavern to the village and the castle is the Peak Cavern and indeed a passage has been discovered connecting one of the branches of the Peak, Devil's Cavern, to the castle. Peak Cavern always comes as a surprise to the first-time visitor to Castleton: there is a little street with a stream running beside it, and there in this rural and domestic scene the huge mouth of the cavern gapes. Centuries ago, in dangerous times when raiders from the north swept down into Derbyshire, the whole population of the village used to seek refuge in this cave, living here for considerable periods. The smoke from their fires produced the blackened ceiling seen today. From the Peak Cavern, passages lead into others with names like Roger's Rain House, where water trickles continuously down the walls; the Bell House; Devil's Cavern; and the Orchestral Chamber where, from time to time, choral concerts are held.

W. of Castleton, just off the A625 to CHAPEL-EN-LE-FRITH, is a spectacular ravine called The Winnats, and Speedwell Cavern lies beneath it. The approach to this cavern has to be made by boat along an old channel, about 750 yds long, made by 18th-cent. lead-miners. The guide propels the boat along by pushing against the walls of the passage leading to the cavern. Here the visitor can look down into the Bottomless Pit and watch – and hear – the water disappearing into the darkness.

The other two sets of caverns are both in Treak Cliff, the Treak Cliff Caverns at its foot, the Blue John Caverns at its summit. These are beautiful. Flood-lighting has been installed in the Treak Cliff Caverns to illuminate the strange rock formations, the stalagmites, stalactites and anemolites and the arch of Blue John stone. Easy paths lead to a grotto.

Similar underground scenery characterizes the Blue John Caverns, where spacious chambers and connecting passages are believed to run for two miles into the hills. Here the unusual Blue John stone, found nowhere else in the world, can be seen in its natural setting. Some of the finest specimens of it are at CHATSWORTH, KEDLESTON HALL and in ASHBOURNE parish church, all in Derbyshire, and in the Vatican Library in Rome. Trinkets and other articles made from the stone are sold at the caverns and in the villages. Many interesting finds from the caverns can be inspected in the Douglas Museum.

St Edmund's Church in Castleton was of Norman foundation, but only the fine chancel arch remained after rebuilding in 1837. The church possesses an unusually large library, including works on divinity, biography and history, and a rare "breeches Bible" of 1611. It is also the scene of the climax of an unusual custom that commemorates the restoration of Charles II. On 29 May each year, known locally as Garland Day, a group of Morris Dancers, led by the "King" and his "Consort" and accompanied by a band, goes in procession through the village to the Market Place, when the maypole is plaited and a garland of flowers from the shoulders of the "King" is hoisted to the top of the church tower.

CHAPEL-EN-LE-FRITH, *Derbyshire* (12–SK0580). The church here has an unusual dedication – to St Thomas à Becket – which points to the age of the place and explains its puzzling name. It is known that the first church here was a chapel built in the early 13th cent. – not many years after Becket's murder – by the men who worked in the Peak Forest; and the little settlement at that time would quite likely have been in the edges of the forest – "en le frith". Today's church dates

from the early 14th cent. and the tower was brought up to date about 1733. The small market town, itself set on a high ridge in the north-west corner of the Peak District – the market place is 776 ft above sea-level – is ringed by even loftier hills and is one of the gateways to the famous walking and climbing country in this part of Derbyshire, and to the caverns at CASTLETON. Chapel-en-le-Frith is sturdy rather than picturesque but several of its old inns are still in business. It has a 17th-cent. market cross and the old town stocks are still there.

CHARNWOOD FOREST, *Leicestershire* (10–SK4914). The Forest covers an area of about 15,000 acres NW. of LEICESTER but many of the large private estates have been sold for building, quarrying, or coal-mining, and the trees have been felled. It can be motored through on the A50 to ASHBY-DE-LA-ZOUCH in 10 minutes but it is a pity to rush through this Triassic landscape, which had a large active volcano in one corner when mammals were beginning to appear on the face of the earth. There are still some 212 acres of forest and moorland (with Nature Reserves at BRADGATE PARK and **Swithland Wood**) preserved around **Beacon Hill**, the **Hangingstone Rocks**, and **Windmill Hill** at **Woodhouse Eaves**.

Leicestershire footpaths are not often very clearly defined but a lovely, quiet walk through the Forest starts from **Groby**, leaving the A50 just N. of the church and going down to Groby Pool. Walk back between Groby and **Newtown Linford** to the footpath on the far side of the quarry which leads into Newtown Linford and the entrance to Bradgate Park. Walk past the ruins of Lady Jane Grey's home to the top of Old John, where there is a direction indicator and extensive views. Continue in the same direction to the park boundary, turn left and follow the wall back to the village. An alternative route starts almost opposite the main entrance to the park, crosses the Newtown–Groby road and leads by the edge of Old Wood and Lady Hay Wood to the A50 a third of a mile NW. of the starting point. This is a walk of approximately 7 m.

CHATSWORTH, *Derbyshire* (12–SK2670). Everything about Chatsworth – house, furnishings, pictures and gardens – invites the superlative. Here, in a lovely park about 2½ m. E. of BAKEWELL, is one of England's great houses, the Derbyshire home of the Dukes of Devonshire, open to the public for the summer months.

The first house at Chatsworth was set, like the present one, on ground overlooking the River Derwent, and its designers were Sir William Cavendish and his wife, the famous Bess of Hardwick. Bess, who later became the Countess of Shrewsbury, was said to be "building-mad" and although nothing of her building at Chatsworth, except the Hunting Tower, among the woods above the present house, remains, she was to leave a more durable memorial in HARDWICK HALL. The present Chatsworth was begun by her great-great-grandson, the 1st Duke of Devon-

A. F. Kersting

Chatsworth House: the chapel

shire, and continued at intervals by his successors, notably the 4th and 6th Dukes. In the course of all this work the aspect of the house was changed from E. to W., a big bend in the Derwent was straightened, the gardens were created much in their present form, and the entire village of EDENSOR was moved to its present position out of sight of the house.

Chatsworth is a harmonious complex of stone buildings of palatial appearance, set against a wooded slope and with the drive curving over an old bridge across the Derwent. But if the house is imposing from the outside, inside there is beauty, elegance and splendour.

The architects involved were William Talman, Thomas Archer and Sir Jeffry Wyatville, all renowned in their day; three French masters are generously represented – Tijou, the smith, whose wrought-ironwork can be seen in the Painted Hall, and Laguerre and Verrio, responsible for much of the painting on ceilings and walls. There are several works by Van Dyck, notably the full-length portraits of Arthur Goodwin and Jeanne de Blois in the Dining Room, a Tintoretto (*Samson and Delilah*) and a Landseer (*Bolton Abbey*). Much of the fine carving both in wood and stone is the work of Samuel Watson of Heanor and there are a number of William Kent chairs. In the Entrance

Hall stands a 1st-cent. Roman sculpture of a mother and child. There are Mortlake tapestries and a fine collection of blue and white Delft tulip-vases. In face of the richness of all this workmanship and colour and texture it is easy to overlook the house itself, a perfect casket for the treasures it contains.

Outside there is a beauty of a different order. Little remains of Bess of Hardwick's Elizabethan garden apart from Queen Mary's Bower (where Mary Queen of Scots spent some time during her periods of imprisonment); there is evidence of the "loose landscape" style incorporated during the period about 1760 when Capability Brown was brought in as adviser; but today's gardens owe most to the ideas and skill of the 6th Duke's employee and friend, Joseph Paxton, later to design the Crystal Palace. Outstanding are the many waterworks: the Sea Horse and Cascade Fountains, the large Canal Pond and the spectacular Emperor Fountain which can throw its jet to a height of 290 ft and is operated solely by the natural pressure of the head of water from the large pond which Paxton constructed on top of the hill to the E. Recent additions include a yew maze planted in 1962 and the serpentine beech hedge near the Ring Pond. Paxton's "Conservative Wall" has been restored.

CHEADLE, *Staffordshire* (8–SK0043). The outstanding building in this old market town is the red stone Roman Catholic church with its 200-ft spire, a landmark for miles. The church, built in 1846, was designed by A. W. N. Pugin, and is regarded as one of his masterpieces. Brass lions rampant guard the west door and inside all is rich colour. Cheadle's parish church, only eight years older, retains the communion rails and an oak chest from an earlier church.

About 3 m. E. of Cheadle lies the village of Oakamoor and between the two are the 250 acres of the **Hawksmoor Nature Reserve** which is also a bird sanctuary. Hawksmoor was bought by public subscription and presented to the National Trust by its founder, Mr J. R. B. Masefield, a well-known Staffordshire naturalist. The Reserve was opened to the public in 1927 and six years later the gates at the entrance were erected and opened by the founder's cousin, the late John Masefield. There are nature trails through the Reserve, which rises to 750 ft in one part. Birds of all kinds, including curlew and pheasant, can be seen; and unusual trees such as lodge pole pine and red oak have been planted.

CHECKLEY, *Staffordshire* (8–SK0237). Much that is ancient can be seen in and around this small village in the Tean valley about 5 m. NW. of UTTOXETER. There are ancient earthworks at Toothill; in the churchyard are the shafts of three Anglo-Saxon crosses, 1,000 years old; and there is the church itself built 900 years ago, with an old sundial on its outside wall and a Norman font inside. The lofty chancel dates from the 14th cent. and some of the traceried windows are filled with glass of the same date.

Kenneth Scowen

Church Stretton: the view towards Caer Caradoc

CHESTERFIELD, *Derbyshire* (13–SK 3871). Well known for its strange landmark, the crooked spire of its parish church, Chesterfield is also worth a visit for some of its fine, modern buildings. The new courthouse, circular and with a many-gabled roof, is a striking building in the modern idiom, while a new but more conventional structure is the glass and concrete block which houses the Accountant General's Department of the Post Office. The Town Hall, a gracious, long-fronted building with an impressive pillared entrance, built just before the Second World War, is set among wide lawns. The new College of Technology is another building which catches the eye. The footbridge linking Queen's Park and the piazza of the Accountant General's Department building, a graceful arch of pre-stressed concrete, is a beautiful design.

Although its spire is what has made the Church of St Mary and All Saints famous, the building itself is a fine example of 14th-cent. church architecture. Cruciform and 173 ft long by 110 ft wide, the church is beautifully proportioned. The font is Anglo-Saxon, there is an unusual hagioscope and three medieval screens, and a collection of perfectly preserved monuments to the Foljambe family, covering the latter half of the 16th cent. The octagonal spire, 228 ft high, leans 7 ft 6 in. to the S., 7 ft 10 in. to the SW., and 3 ft 2 in. to the W. and its odd twist is believed to have been caused by the changing temperatures reacting on the lead covering of the wooden frame. Although it appears in imminent danger of toppling over, it has a very low centre of gravity and is quite stable.

The Anglo-Saxons called the place Cestrefeld, the first part of the name showing that the Romans had preceded them on the site. Some of the street-names are ancient: The Shambles, Glumangate, Packer's Row and Knifesmithgate among others. In The Shambles stands the only remaining Tudor building in the town, the attractive Royal Oak. At Old Whittington is the Revolution House, then known as the Cock and Pynot (magpie) Inn, where the Earl of Devonshire and his fellow-conspirators in 1688 plotted to overthrow James II and put William of Orange on the throne. The house is now a museum.

Chesterfield has strong links with George Stephenson. He supervised the building of the railway through the town and spent the last years of his life at Tapton House. He is buried in Holy Trinity Church. The glorious window in the church, and the Stephenson Hall which now houses the Civic Theatre, the Library and Information Centre, are memorials to him.

The town has a growing reputation in the sporting world. The main soccer club plays in the Football League; Derbyshire County Cricket Club play matches on the pleasant Queen's Park; and, in an annexe to the Park, in May 1962, was opened a sports stadium with a running track of championship standard, to which a new indoor swimming-pool has been added.

CHURCH STRETTON, *Shropshire* (8–SO 4593). It is the surrounding hills and the famous golf course, rather than the little town itself, which draw visitors to Church Stretton, 13 m. S. of SHREWSBURY. This is Mary Webb country: she spent her honeymoon here and the Shepwardine of her novels is Church Stretton.

The bleak, heathery Long Mynd to the W. is 10 m. long, from 2 to 4 m. wide, and reaches almost 1,700 ft. Some of it is accessible to cars, but most of it demands that the visitor walks. The views reward the effort. One of the most noted beauty-spots is the **Carding Mill valley**. Further S. are the less well-known valleys of Ashes Hollow and Callow Hollow, each with its stream, and the latter with a small waterfall, too.

The 18-hole golf course, set among some of the Long Mynd hills, contests with KINGTON, in Herefordshire, the claim to be England's highest. Much of it is around or above 1,200 ft and few courses can offer such views: from the 3rd tee the town itself; from the 11th the steep-sided Carding Mill valley that leads up to Robin Hood's Butts; and on the 14th green, on Bodbury Hill near the site of a clearly marked Iron Age camp, the golfer reaches the highest point of the course. Besides the Bodbury Ring camp, there are many ancient barrows hereabouts and along the whole length of the Long Mynd runs the Portway, a track which must be centuries old. All of this makes good walking across sheep pasture, sometimes with sailplanes from the Midland Gliding Club overhead.

Fine walks are also to be had among the seven hills of the Caradoc range. Caer Caradoc, the highest, rises to 1,500 ft. Some say Caractacus (an earlier form of Caradoc Latinized) fortified this hill and the cave below bears his name.

Church Stretton became a fashionable resort towards the end of the 19th cent. and much of its architecture, including the half-timbered buildings, dates from then. The Parish Church of St Lawrence is the outstanding exception, a fine building with much of its Norman work remaining. The nave is pure Norman, with the carving peculiar to that period, and the crossing-tower dates from the 12th cent. There is a Sheila-na-gig, a fertility figure, over the north doorway and the raftered roof of the nave is believed to be 700 years old.

N. and S. of the town lie the adjoining villages of **All Stretton** and **Little Stretton**. The latter boasts one of the few thatched churches in England, but the black-and-white building, though pretty, is not old, dating from 1903. About 2 m. SW. of Church Stretton, still in the lee of the Mynd, is the tiny village of Minton: cottages clustered round a small green, with a manor house beside a large Anglo-Saxon mound.

CLEETHORPES, *Lincolnshire* (13–TA3008). A hundred years ago Cleethorpes was a little fishing village. Now it has a permanent population of 33,970 and a million visitors a year during its short season. Its attractions include some 3 m. of sands, a boating-lake in half a mile of beautiful park, a scenic railway, the largest open-air swimming-pool on any part of the coast and a magnificent zoo complete with its Marineland full of performing dolphins. There are also a winter garden, paddling pools, children's entertainments and an 18-hole golf course.

The view of the Yorkshire coast with Spurn Head's light revolving 6 m. away is attractive. And it is interesting to park on Marine Walk and watch the ships bound for HULL or GRIMSBY at the mouth of the Humber.

CLEOBURY MORTIMER, *Shropshire* (8–SO6775), is 12 m. from LUDLOW on the A4117, the other side of the Clee Hills. Although some have doubts about it, the inhabitants claim it as the birthplace of William Langland, author of the 14th-cent. *Piers Plowman*. A beautiful east window in the green sandstone Parish Church of St Mary is dedicated to the poet, showing Piers "dreaming his dreams". The church is also notable for its wooden spire which, despite efforts to straighten it, still has a distinct twist. The main street has a quiet charm with its pavements at different heights, its row of pollarded trees and its mixture of mellowed timbered and Georgian houses. The most striking building, apart from the church, is the Talbot Hotel, built about 1560, once a coaching inn, with an old stone mounting block on its forecourt.

CLIFTON CAMPVILLE, *Staffordshire* (9–SK2510), is renowned for the beautiful, slender, 189-ft spire of the 14th-cent. Church of St Andrew. The church itself is regarded as the best example of medieval church architecture in the county. It contains much fine carving, some unusual monuments and an ancient chest carved from a solid tree-trunk. The unspoilt village, clustered round a hill, takes its name from the family of Camville, lords of the manor from 1200, one of whom married an heiress to the manor of Clifton.

CLIPSTONE, *Nottinghamshire* (13–SK6064). One of the gateways into the Dukeries – the land taken back by the dukes when the monasteries disappeared in 1536–40. Roads through SHERWOOD FOREST became private drives entered by impressive gateways. Streams were dammed to make lakes, forests replanted for hunting. Now most of the peers have gone.

In Clipstone are the remains of what is now known as King John's Palace, built before the time of King John and the favourite Royal Hunting Lodge until the end of the Tudor reign.

Two m. away on the EDWINSTOWE road is a Gothic arch built by the eccentric 4th Duke of Portland in 1844. It has buttressed walls and it is known as Archway Lodge, or Duke's Folly. On its north and south sides are niched figures of Richard Lionheart, who is supposed to have stayed hereabouts on his return from the Crusades in 1194, Robin Hood, Friar Tuck, Maid Marian, Little John and Allan-a-Dale.

CLUMBER PARK, *Nottinghamshire* (13–SK 6274). Until 1938, when the land was sold and the house pulled down, this was one of the only three remaining rich estates of the old Dukeries. In 1707 a licence was given to John Holles, Duke of Newcastle, who lived at WELBECK ABBEY, to enclose a park "for the Queen's use". Nothing was done until 1770, when a house was built, followed in 1774–89 by the enclosing of the still beautiful lake. In Victorian days the house was grandly rebuilt and improved with princely gardens for the incumbent Duke of Newcastle by Sir Charles Barry, architect of the House of Commons. After a fire in 1879 it was refurbished by his son, another Charles, who designed BURLINGTON HOUSE. The lovely church which still stands was built at a cost of £30,000 in 1886 of red Runcorn sandstone and white Steetley stone. It is 107 ft long with a spire 180 ft tall and contains Belgian wood-carvings and stained glass by Kempe. It belongs to the National Trust and services are held there during the summer. It stands reflected in the lake, a lovely memorial to the passing of an age.

The park of over 3,400 acres is open to the public and offers many lovely walks amid SHERWOOD FOREST country. Some of the grounds were ruined during the war when they were used as an ammunition dump, which caught fire. Roads are excellent, particularly Duke's Drive, a famous avenue 3 m. long bordered with limes.

CLUN, *Shropshire* (8–SO3081), is one of A. E. Housman's "four quietest places under the sun" (see *A Shropshire Lad*); the others are the nearby Clun valley villages of **Clunton**, **Clunbury** and **Clungunford**. This small town was not always peaceful and evidence of its stormy history is all around. Caractacus, the Ancient British chief, resisted the Romans hereabouts: Gaer Ditches is thought to have been one of his camps. A few miles W. is **Offa's Dyke**, the 8th-cent. earthwork which runs 81 m. through the border country and was part boundary mark, part Mercian fortification against the Welsh. It was around Clun that Edric the Wild, the English earl, harried the Normans whose castle keep stands high in a bend of the River Clun. For centuries, Clun was disputed between the English and the Welsh: four times between 1195 and 1400 the Welsh attacked the castle and burned the town.

Clun was a settlement before recorded time. In the museum – once the town gaol – in the Georgian Town Hall are flint and stone tools, weapons and the partial cremation of a Bronze Age inhabitant. At Pen y Wern, a little to the SW., stand the ruins of a stone circle.

CODNOR, *Derbyshire* (13–SK4149). The ruins of what was once one of Derbyshire's most important castles are to be found near this village, about 2 m. N. of Heanor. Preservation work is now being carried out to prevent further deterioration, but parts of the high outer wall and of the circular towers, an unusual stone dovecot, and other fragments can be seen. The castle, built on the site of an original Peveril fortress, dates from the early 13th cent.

CONDOVER, *Shropshire* (8–SJ4906). The Hall in this quiet village in Mary Webb country is one of the most handsome 16th-cent. houses in the county. Built of creamy-pink stone, the wide-fronted house, with its gables and chimney-stacks, makes an impressive picture at the end of its short, yew-lined drive, especially when seen framed in the arch of the entrance gates. For some years the Hall has been a school for deaf and blind children but it is open for viewing in August each year.

Nearby, again built in creamy sandstone, is the Parish Church of St Mary and St Andrew. Little remains today of the original Norman building, the church having been substantially rebuilt in the mid-1600s. More remarkable than the building itself are the monuments inside it which include, most unusually, two babies and their mothers. There is a bust of Martha Owen, with her baby lying in front of her, dated 1641; and the even more touching sculpture of Alice Cholmondeley, carved by her husband Reginald in the mid-19th cent. She lies asleep, a wife for only a year, her baby in her arm, its empty cradle at her feet. The inscription on the white marble reads: "Reginald, always standing by, carved me with his own hand".

Less moving but even more striking is the life-size sculpture of another Cholmondeley, Sir Thomas, who died in 1864. The kneeling, bearded figure in the uniform of a soldier of the Crimean War, looking heavenwards, his hands clasped on his sword, was carved by the famous Victorian artist, George Frederick Watts.

CONINGSBY, *Lincolnshire* (13–TF2258). A Fenland village near TATTERSHALL, notable for its church of St Michael and All Angels which has a handsome 15th-cent. tower with a pathway through it. Its unique feature is a one-handed clock, 16½ ft in diameter, the largest in the world.

Laurence Eusdon, an 18th-cent. rector of Coningsby, was said to have been made Poet Laureate because he flattered the Lord Chamberlain. According to Thomas Gray, Eusdon was "a drunken parson" and certainly his lines dedicated to George II on his coronation have nothing to recommend them. "They virtues shine peculiarly nice," he carolled, "Ungloomed with a confinity to vice".

About a mile N. up the A153 is the pretty village of **Tumby**, E. of which is a 100-acre wood full of oak and larch and wild lilies of the valley in season.

CORBY, *Lincolnshire* (13–SK9925), is remarkable mainly for the lovely medieval wall paintings discovered under nearly 1,200 sq. ft of plaster when the church was being restored in 1939. These paintings are among the most significant medieval remains in the country.

There is an ancient market cross, erected in the reign of Edward III, and an annual October Sheep Fair to which sheep are brought from England, Scotland and Wales.

COTTESMORE, *Rutland* (10–SK9013). About 4 m. NE. of OAKHAM on the B668, Cottesmore was made famous by the hunt, one of the most famous in this pre-eminently fox-hunting part of England. The Cottesmore Hounds were established in **Exton** in 1732 but moved here in 1788. They are now kennelled about halfway along the road from Oakham to Ashwell.

The airfield and quarries spoil the village but there are some charming stone-built and thatched houses and good trees. The Church of St Nicholas has a complicated history, with a font probably of *c*. 1200, a 14th-cent. spire and 17th-cent. pulpit. Anglo-Saxon finds have been excavated in the neighbourhood.

Up a small lane 1½ m. to the NW. **Barrow** stands high and commands fine views to Leicestershire.

From here take the road due E. crossing the A1 past **Stretton** to **Clipsham**, a journey of about 4 m. to see this pretty show village on the borders of one of our loveliest yet most unsung counties. There are many fine 16th- to 19th-cent. buildings of the famous honey-coloured Clipsham limestone, particularly Clipsham Hall, which is 18th-cent. and has a splendid yew hedge and a bird and fish topiary avenue.

The Church of St Mary has a 14th-cent. broach spire of unusual design and an originally Norman interior. In the north chapel is some heraldic glass, once part of the ancient church at Pickworth, which was shattered in the Wars of the Roses.

Try to visit the quarries, which have been worked since the mid-13th cent. and have supplied stone to PETERBOROUGH and ELY cathedrals, many OXFORD colleges and the house at BURLEY. It was also chosen for the rebuilding of the bombed House of Commons. There is no blasting. The stone is excavated with drills and wedges.

At **Greetham**, 3 m. away on the B668 to Oakham, is the well-known Ram Jam Inn.

CRESWELL CRAGS, *Derbyshire* (13–SK 5274). Here, in a narrow gorge between cliffs of grey limestone are the caves where men of the Early Stone Age lived and rested between their hunting forays. In these caves, situated almost on the Nottinghamshire border about 9 m. E. of CHESTERFIELD, and given such names as Mother Grundy's Parlour, Robin Hood's Cave and the Pinhole, have been found remains from this prehistoric culture, including bones of the mammoth and primitive tools and weapons, some of which are now in the BRITISH MUSEUM.

CRICH, *Derbyshire* (13–SK3554). One of the most unusual museums in the country is situated in this hill village 5 m. SE. of MATLOCK. It is devoted entirely to tramcars. The unique collection of trams of all kinds – there are 40 in all – has been gathered from all parts of the country, and abroad, by the Tramway Museum Society. Visitors are welcome at weekends and Bank Holidays and no charge is made except during the annual Grand Transport Extravaganza each September. The museum is a "live" one for it is housed in the disused Cliff Quarry, and a number of lines have been laid so that the trams can still run.

The visitor can ride in Sheffield 15, a single-deck horse-car built in 1874, drawn by Bonny, the museum's resident mare; or in Blackpool 59, one of the two-deck, open-top trams which used to carry holidaymakers along the promenade at the Lancashire resort; or in Glasgow 1297, a sleek modern tram, built as recently as 1948 and in service until the 1950s; or in a number of other trams. One of the museum's prized possessions is a steam tram, built for the New South Wales government in 1885.

Standing on the edge of Cliff Quarry, on a site known locally as Crich Stand, is another of Crich's sights – the tower with a beacon light, standing 950 ft above sea-level, which is the war memorial of the Sherwood Foresters. The regiment's annual pilgrimage is made here every July.

Crich is also known for the views from the surrounding hills; and for its Norman church, in which can be seen one of the rare stone Bible rests.

CROMFORD, *Derbyshire* (12–SK2956), is where the first rumblings of the Industrial Revolution were heard. In this sturdy-looking, stone-built village S. of THE MATLOCKS, in 1771, Sir Richard Arkwright built the first mechanized textile factory in the world, equipping it with the cotton-spinning machinery he had recently invented. The original mill still stands by the road, dour, forbidding, intended to be stout enough to withstand any attacks by the frightened weavers, bent on smashing Arkwright's machines. Two more of Arkwright's important buildings still stand in Cromford: the Church of St Mary and Willersley Castle. Many of the old cottages are those he built for his workpeople.

Not far from Cromford are the famous **Black Rocks**, a rugged mass of gritstone on the hills on the WIRKSWORTH road. The rocks are about 80 ft high and erosion has left them with a face which makes particular appeal to rock-climbers from all parts of the country. They also offer a fine viewing point, the panorama stretching across the valley in which The Matlocks lie to Riber Castle on its peak.

Also from Cromford runs a beautiful stretch of road with a Latin name. But the **Via Gellia** owes nothing to the Romans; it was constructed during the 19th cent. by Philip Gell of Hopton Hall, Wirksworth, along a wooded ravine between Cromford and Grangemill. It is particularly colourful in bluebell time and is famous for its lilies of the valley.

CROWLAND, *Lincolnshire* (13–TF2310). Three-quarters of a mile from the ruins of the Benedictine abbey raised by his relative, King Ethelbald of Mercia, to his memory, St Guthlac landed his boat in the swamps at a place still called Anchor Church Field. Born in A.D. 673, he had had a wild youth until he decided to become a hermit, building a cell to which people came for help and advice. He died in 714 and the abbey, partly destroyed and rebuilt many times, was at one time the wealthiest mitred abbey in the county. The ruins still have great magnificence, the north aisle now being used as the Parish Church of St Mary with SS. Guthlac and Bartholomew. A tower at the west end survives, and the west front with five tiers of sculptures representing personages associated with the history of the abbey, and saints and apostles.

A fascinating triangular bridge of three semicircles meeting at an apex, built in the 13th cent. when the streets were waterways, still stands in the village. Henry VI and Edward IV landed here – Edward on his way to FOTHERINGHAY Castle. For about 200 years a seated figure of Our Lord holding the world has adorned the bridge.

CROXDEN ABBEY, *Staffordshire* (9–SK 0639), is where it was thought for many years that the heart of the little-loved King John was buried. But this has now been disproved: the mistake arose because of confusion with Croxton Abbey in Leicestershire. Croxden was founded by the man responsible for ALTON Castle, Bertram de Verdun. Enough of it still stands to show how noble it must have been: the remains of the west front, the south transept and parts of the sacristy, chapter-house, parlour and abbot's house. The ruins are now partly incorporated into a farm-house.

DALE ABBEY, *Derbyshire* (13–SK4338). There is an interesting legend concerning the foundation of this abbey. A DERBY baker saw a vision of the Virgin Mary which led him to renounce the world and live as a hermit. He crossed the River Derwent and made himself a hermitage in the sandstone cliffs of Deepdale. Later the abbey was raised on the same site. Today the hermitage in the rocks can still be seen but all that remains of the once splendid abbey is the superb arch of the east window. It gives a clear indication of the fine proportions of the abbey – and emphasizes strongly the difference between that building and the present village church, surely one of the smallest and most curious churches in England. The chancel and nave measure a mere 25 ft by 25 ft – and the whole church is under the same roof as a farm-house. It has Norman masonry in the walls, and wall paintings dating from the 13th cent. The building is full of box-pews and there is a gallery; the raised altar has drawers and cupboards underneath it.

DARLEY DALE, *Derbyshire* (12–SK2762), is part of the lovely valley of the Derwent running N. from THE MATLOCKS and offers pleasant walking country for the visitor. Here is a fine 13th-cent. church with part of the shaft of a carved Anglo-Saxon cross, two fonts – one Norman, one Jacobean – some fine stained glass believed to be by Burne-Jones and, in the church-yard, perhaps the oldest tree in Britain, a yew reputed to be 2,000 years old.

Sir Joseph Whitworth, the engineer and inventor, lived part of his life in Darley Dale and the extensive park is a memorial to him. There is an annual show at **Whitworth**. Wild rhododendrons grow profusely in Darley Dale. There is a fine walk along a footpath known as Lady Grove which offers a view across the valley to Knab Rocks, the dramatic, sheer gritstone cliffs on the other side. On another wooded hill can be seen the square stone tower commemorating the passing of the Reform Bill in 1832.

DERBY, *Derbyshire* (12–SK3435). Despite its rapid expansion over the last 100 years to a thriving industrial town of more than 200,000 people, Derby, county town and cathedral city, has retained much from its past. It has Roman roots; the legions had a camp near the east bank of the Derwent. The town was named by the Danes, who made it one of their Five Boroughs, the key points of the Danelaw. By the time the Domesday Book was published in 1086, Derby was a town of 2,000 inhabitants with six churches and 14 mills. It received its first market charter from Henry II in 1154 but by the time, 600 years later, that it gave a cool reception to Bonnie Prince Charlie, the town had grown but little. Not until the Industrial Revolution and the eventful establishment of the Midland Railway's

Crowland: the triangular bridge; the carved figure is believed to have come from the abbey

Kenneth Scowen

great works in the town, did it begin to grow apace.

The links with the Midland Railway are underlined by a scale working lay-out in the museum in the Strand, which also includes a large technical and industrial section; archaeological exhibits; local porcelain; and paintings by Derby's own Joseph Wright.

The most striking building is the cathedral with its pinnacled, 178-ft tower, built during the reign of Henry VIII and second only to BOSTON Stump as the tallest parish church tower in England. Apart from the tower, the Parish Church of All Saints as it then was – it was elevated to cathedral rank in 1927 – was rebuilt by James Gibbs in the early 18th cent. It contains the large, carved alabaster tomb of the much-married, "building-mad" Bess of Hardwick, Countess of Shrewsbury. There are other interesting tombs and a bishop's chair which came from Asia Minor. But the cathedral's great treasure is the superbly fashioned wrought-iron screen, the work of Robert Bakewell. More of Bakewell's brilliant craftsmanship can be seen in the entrance gates to the cathedral which once stood in front of a private house, but were given to the cathedral and dedicated in 1958.

Derby's oldest church is St Peter's, largely 14th-cent. but with some Norman work. There are also several other interesting churches, notably St Werburgh's, which has a wrought-iron font-cover by Bakewell and parish registers dating back to 1583 – they contain the entry of Dr Samuel Johnson's marriage to Tetty Porter; St Mary's Roman Catholic church with its 117-ft tower topped by a figure of the Virgin Mary, designed by Pugin; and St Mary's Chapel, Bridge Gate, one of the few surviving chapels built on bridges.

There are also a considerable number of interesting old houses, some Georgian, some earlier: among these the oldest are the black-and-white Dolphin Inn in Queen Street, and the 17th-cent. gabled building in Wardwick. Modern developments include a well-designed bus station, a huge modern hotel, and an open-air market.

Derby is well-blessed with open spaces. There are almost a score of parks, the oldest of which, the Arboretum, was given to the town by Joseph Strutt and contains a monument to the eminent car-maker, Sir Henry Royce; the firm of Rolls-Royce has been associated with Derby since 1908.

DONINGTON, *Lincolnshire* (13–TF2135). An ancient little town, once the most important flax and hemp centre, and still a flourishing twice-yearly venue for horse and cattle fairs. The earliest attempts at reclamation were made here in the Fenland by the Romans at Carr Dyke and the Roman Bank. Traces remain of Salters Way, built by them from the Midlands to the coast. Subsequent silting up of the Wash has recovered a 10-m. stretch for cultivation.

The market place is still cobbled and has Georgian and earlier houses and a delightful grammar school founded in the 18th cent. by Thomas Cowley "for twenty poor children to be taught to read English and write". Over the old portico is a sundial dated 1719.

The church has a fine Decorated tower and spire rising to 200 ft, built in the 14th cent. and surmounted by a golden ball and weathercock.

Donington was the birthplace of Matthew Flinders in 1774. He went to sea after reading *Robinson Crusoe*, and travelled with Bligh, after the *Bounty* mutiny, and with Bass of BOSTON. He was the first to discover the error of compasses due to iron in ships, and he died in Donington on the day of the publication of a book on his voyages, in 1814.

DOVEDALE, *Derbyshire/Staffordshire* (12–SK 1452). This famous dale forms the boundary between Staffordshire and Derbyshire. It has connections with Izaak Walton and his companion angler Charles Cotton, and other literary figures, and its magnificent scenery has earned it the name of "Little Switzerland". The first-time visitor may be surprised how short it seems on a map – it stretches little more than 2 m. But he will be delighted by the constantly changing views and many unusual features it has to offer. Some of the dale can be seen by car, but to explore its beauty in full the visitor needs to walk.

Dovedale is part of the Peak District National Park and its southern entrance is near the village of ILAM, guarded by two hills, Thorpe Cloud (900 ft) and Bunster Hill (1,000 ft). It is here that the narrow, twisting limestone gorge begins, its steep wooded banks rising high above the river. Many of its rocks and rock formations have been weathered into strange shapes and colourfully named: Dovedale Castle, the Twelve Apostles, Lover's Leap, the Tissington Spires, the Lion's Head and the Ilam Rock, slightly on the tilt. There are, too, the caves like the Dove Holes and Reynard's Cavern with its arched entrance 30 ft high and 15 ft wide.

The Dove, of course, is not just a river to look at but also one to fish – for the descendants of the trout which old Izaak and his friend cast for and caught there. Many of the hotels in the area offer angling facilities in the Dove to their guests. Dovedale, too, is famous for its sheepdog trials held near the Izaak Walton Hotel at the southern end of the dale each August. And it offers access to other dales including **Milldale**, **Wolfscote Dale**, **Hall Dale**, **Narrowdale** and BERESFORD DALE; and to the beautiful MANIFOLD VALLEY.

DRAYTON BASSETT, *Staffordshire* (9–SK 1900). This village, 4 m. S. of TAMWORTH, was where Sir Robert Peel, Prime Minister, father of our police force and Corn Law repealer, was born. His house, Drayton Manor, is no more – but in the park which was once part of the grounds is now a golf course and the Drayton Manor Park and Zoo. The zoo occupies 15 acres of the 160-acre park and contains a wide selection of animals. There is a large amusement park and a lake. Aerial cars run above it all at 60 ft for a distance of $\frac{1}{3}$ m.

Kenneth Scowen

Dovedale: stepping-stones over the River Dove

DUNSTON, *Lincolnshire* (13–TF0663). Still a lonely village on the enormous Heath, Dunston used to be lit by the famous "Dunston Pillar", a "land lighthouse" 92 ft high, with a lantern 15 ft high, placed there by the otherwise infamous Sir Francis Dashwood of the Hellfire Club to guide travellers to LINCOLN and protect them from highwaymen. Sir Francis lived at Nocton Hall, which came to him through his wife. Twenty years later, in 1810, his successor removed the light and raised in its stead a huge statue of George III to celebrate his jubilee. This statue proved a danger to aircraft during the last war, and so was removed and the pillar shortened.

EAST STOKE, *Nottinghamshire* (13–SK7549). Half a mile N. of the village is the site of Ad Pontem, a Roman fort built on a crossroads at Fosse Way, which led to a crossing close by over the River Trent. Round the small, mainly 17th-cent. church amid the trees of the park of Stoke Hall are mounds marking the site of a medieval village.

East Stoke was the scene of a spectacular and bloody battle in 1487. In 1486 Henry VII had tried to end the Wars of the Roses by marrying Elizabeth of York, but there was still unrest, particularly in the breast of the one-time heir apparent, the Earl of Lincoln. With the help of a priest named Richard Simon, the earl found Lambert Simnel, the son of an OXFORD joiner, who resembled the Earl of Warwick (also a claimant to the throne) and took him to Dublin

where he was "crowned" king of England. Then he crossed with an army of some 6,000 and landed on the Lancashire coast to march against the king. On 16 June the armies met at East Stoke and Lincoln's force was cut to pieces. The Yorkists were driven from Fosse Way down to the road to Fiskerton Ferry, which is still called Red Gutter, and their dead were buried in what are known as Dead Man's Fields. Lambert Simnel was contemptuously pardoned and allowed to work as a scullion in the royal kitchens.

Lord Pauncefote, the first British ambassador to the United States, had his home at Stoke Hall and is buried in the churchyard.

EASTWOOD, *Nottinghamshire* (13–SK4646). "The scene of my Nottinghamshire-Derby novels all centres round Eastwood, where I was born: and whoever stands on Walker Street will see the whole landscape of *Sons and Lovers* before him." Admirers of D. H. Lawrence should visit this place, still peaceful and rural in the midst of the colliery area. Here he lived with his parents, described in the first section of *Sons and Lovers* – his mother, whose maiden name was Lydia Beardsall, feeling so superior to her miner husband. Yet it was from his father who "loved the countryside, just the indiscriminating feel of it", that Lawrence inherited his imagination.

ECCLESHALL, *Staffordshire* (8–SJ8329). This typical small market town, 6 m. SW. of STONE, has long associations with the bishops of

Lichfield: six of them are buried in the large, 12th-cent. parish church and its churchyard. For 700 years the bishops of Lichfield lived at Eccleshall Castle, of which one of the towers, the moat and the bridge over it are preserved. The square, pinnacled tower of the church, which is almost 100 ft high, contains some carved Anglo-Saxon stones, a rare possession.

EDALE, *Derbyshire* (12–SK 1285). Immediately S. of the Peak District's highest area, the Kinder Hills, the village and dale which give their name to this area are quiet and unspoilt. The valley offers delightful walking country with the rugged hills all around. Crowden Head at 2,070 ft is the highest point visible, but Win Hill, with its Roman road, Lose Hill, **Mam Tor**, Mount Famine and Rushup Edge are almost as high. Mam Tor, more than 1,700 ft high, is known as the "Shivering Mountain" because of the landslides which regularly occur, caused by the unusual composition of alternate layers of grit and shale. Near the top is an Iron Age camp covering 16 acres within a circumference of 1,200 yds. The Kinder Hills can be reached by the path called Jacob's Ladder which climbs over a shoulder in the hills, past a cross dated 1610. During the winter months the famous white, or mountain hares of Kinder can be seen zig-zagging across the faces of the slopes. The village of Edale has a gentler appearance than many of the Derbyshire hill villages. In the church, the third on the site, is a Bible in English printed in 1541 by Edward Whitchurch. The parish registers date from 1633.

EDENHAM, *Lincolnshire* (13–TF 0621). The whole village is extremely impressive, as befits the setting for **Grimsthorpe Castle**, the home of the Earls of Ancaster and the grandest house in Lincolnshire. The cottages are of stone and the church is large, shaded by 100-year-old cedars and containing the shaft of a medieval cross in the churchyard. Nearby is the vicarage where Charles Kingsley is supposed to have written *Hereward the Wake*.

Vestiges of architecture from Anglo-Saxon times remain inside the church and it is full of valuable possessions. But it is the grandiose monuments to the Willoughby de Eresby family, Dukes and Earls of Ancaster, which catch the eye: the one to the 12th Baron, who died at Edgehill in the arms of his son; another to that son, Montague, who fought at NASEBY and was one of the few people courageous enough to attend Charles I's funeral at WINDSOR. The huge monument to Robert Bertie, 4th Earl of Lindsey and 1st Duke of Ancaster, was sculptured by Scheemakers, and the pretentious tomb opposite for the 3rd and 4th Dukes is by Charles Harris. This noble structure informs us that the 3rd Duke lived "with Magnificence and Liberality" but died of a "lingering bilious disorder". A charming bust of Lord Gwydyr, who married the sister of the 4th Duke, is by Nollekens.

Grimsthorpe Castle stands palatially in its 2,000-acre park, some 16 m. round, easily seen just over a mile from the road. It has a magnificent chestnut avenue and is famed for its herds of fallow and red deer. Most of the original quadrangular building was erected by Charles Brandon, Duke of Suffolk, in Tudor times, but a bastion in the south-east corner dates from the 13th cent.

The 1st Duke of Ancaster commissioned Vanbrugh to rebuild the north side in 1722 in stone quarried from the park. Vanbrugh died four years after finishing this, the last of his castles. His magnificent 110-ft hall houses paintings of seven kings to whom the Willoughby de Eresby family owe a great deal of their wealth, they having been successive Lord Great Chamberlains of England.

The castle contains Brussels tapestries, paintings by famous masters such as Lawrence and Reynolds, a Van Dyck of Charles I and his family, and the actual dress worn by Charles when he sat for the portrait. There are coronation chairs, and robes worn by sovereigns since James II. There is the House of Lords clock, which stopped the minute George III died, and the table on which Queen Victoria signed her oath of accession.

EDENSOR, *Derbyshire* (12–SK 2469), must be one of the few villages in England set in what was a private park, and still to be entered through a white gate. It is probably the only one which was moved from its original site to satisfy the aesthetic whim of an aristocrat. Originally Edensor could be seen from the great mansion of CHATSWORTH, on the further bank of the Derwent. The 6th Duke of Devonshire, deciding that it spoiled the view, had it demolished in 1839 and the present model village built about a mile away. The result, to a large extent, reflects the eccentricity that was present at its birth. Only the fact that all the houses, many of them detached, are built in the same local stone gives the village any unity. Otherwise everything is a jumble of gables, porches and odd windows. The entrance lodge looks like a small fort; in another corner stands a mock Swiss chalet in brown stone; one house has Tudor chimneys, another Italian-style windows. The setting is charming with the road winding round the church and up a small hill which is a cul-de-sac. It is worth the short climb to the top of the hill not so much to see the octagonal-shaped house there as to obtain the view over the village, across the wide Derwent valley to the Hunting Tower of Chatsworth high in the woods on the far bank. And from here, too, the large village church with its tall slender spire does not seem as out of place as it does from the entrance gate. The church was built in 1867 to the design of Sir Gilbert Scott, but a few fragments of the original Norman building can still be seen.

EDWINSTOWE, *Nottinghamshire* (13–SK 6266). Near Warsop on the River Maun, Edwinstowe lies at the edge of the spacious common leading to Birklands and Bilhagh, two of the most beautiful parts of SHERWOOD FOREST, with a good road between them. Bilhagh has the grandest remains of the old forest and Birklands has a wealth of beech and silver birch and – within a mile of the Church of St Mary – the Major Oak, reputed to be over 1,000 years old, probably the biggest oak in Britain. It has a hollow trunk 30 ft round, inside which it is reported that seven people once ate breakfast. A mile and a half W. of here is another oak called Robin Hood's Larder in which Robin is said to have hung his game. Those who believe in Robin Hood will believe that he married Maid Marian in the 12th- to 13th-cent. church at Edwinstowe.

ELFORD, *Staffordshire* (9–SK1810). The church in this village about 5 m. ENE. of LICHFIELD is well known to heraldry enthusiasts for it contains a remarkable collection of shields, all in excellent condition. Here, too, is a monument commemorating the death of a child at play: the grandson of Sir John Stanley holds the tennis ball which is reputed to have struck him on the temple and caused his death in 1460. Nearby are two Anglo-Saxon barrows which are said to have been used as shooting butts by Robin Hood. The paper mill by the bridge was owned for about 50 years until his death in 1801 by Robert Bage who wrote the novel *Hermsprong, or Man as he is Not.*

ELLESMERE, *Shropshire* (8–SJ3934), is 30 m. from the sea, but has many boats. This small market town, set among nine meres, is the capital of Shropshire's Lake District. The scenery, pretty rather than impressive, is in marked contrast to that in the S. of the county. All the meres are accessible to the visitor: Blake Mere and tiny Kettle Mere, joined to it, are set in woodland, as is Cole Mere; White Mere is the headquarters of the Shropshire Sailing Club; Hanmer Mere is 5 m. away but is usually included in the group; Crose Mere and Sweat (Sweet) Mere are haunts for birds; while The Mere, the largest and covering 116 acres, has been developed as a pleasure resort. Fishing and boating are available on some of the meres.

The town itself has strong nautical associations, and an arm of the Shropshire Union Canal ran into it. Although nothing now remains of the castle, and little of the Norman church, Ellesmere still has attractive old streets and houses, and the roof of the chancel chapel in St Mary's Church is reckoned one of the finest in Shropshire.

EMPINGHAM, *Rutland* (10–SK9408). Rutland is at its loveliest in this large, attractive village with a splendid church on the road from OAKHAM to STAMFORD. The three churches of Empingham, **Exton** and KETTON, which all lie near to one another, would be hard to match for beauty and interest.

It is worth stopping at Empingham to study St Peter's: well proportioned, with a handsome tower, spire and west front, largely 13th-cent. with 14th- and 15th-cent. alterations. Considerable

traces of medieval colour remain, and some fragments of ancient glass. The chancel has such a beautiful double piscina and triple sedilia that even those who usually look away at the mention of such details should try to find somebody knowledgeable enough to point them out.

Nobody should leave Rutland without making time to stay at Exton, about 3 m. NW., since this thatch and limestone village and the fascinating monuments in the Church of SS. Peter and Paul cannot be appreciated in a hurry. The best approach, particularly lovely when the may blossom is out, is N. from Empingham along a small secondary road, which gives a splendid view from the S. of Burley-on-the-Hill, and thence along Barnsdale Avenue, thickly lined with chestnuts, limes, ash, birch, beeches and sycamores, to 1,000-acre Exton Park. The Old Hall, now in ruins, was probably built by Sir James Harington in the time of Elizabeth I, and was destroyed by fire in 1810. It was the home of the Noels, Viscounts Campden, Earls of Gainsborough. The New Hall was completed in 1852. The church, accessible to the public, was struck by lightning in 1843 and was somewhat drastically rebuilt in 1850.

It is not, however, the building, but the monuments inside which will attract the visitor – marvellous English sculpture from the 14th to the 18th cents.: Nicholas Grene, *c.* 1379, John and Alice Harington, 1524; the splendid tomb of Robert Kelway, 1580, erected by his daughter and her husband, the first Lord Harington, who are depicted kneeling with their daughter, Lucy; the tomb of their son, Kelway Harington, aged 21 weeks; the appealing epitaph to Sir James and Lady Lucy Harington, 1591; the exceptionally beautiful tomb of Anne, grand-daughter of the first Lady Harington, 1627; the monument to 18-year-old James Noel, "grave, discreet, and wise" and his two baby brothers; Grinling Gibbons's colossal statue to the 3rd Viscount Campden, for which he charged £1,000, 1683; the Nollekens to the Countess of Gainsborough, 1771, and Lt-Gen. Bennett Noel, 1766.

Do not miss the angel seated at the organ on the tower screen and the helmets, sword, gauntlets and spurs in the nave arcade.

You should also walk round the village on the east side of the park to see the excellent buildings dating from the 16th cent., beautifully grouped on all sides, the well with its stone roof and eight brick pillars, the 14 sycamore trees on the green, and the glimpses of old-world gardens and green hills behind.

EPWORTH, *Lincolnshire* (13–SE7803). Now the administrative centre for the Isle of Axholme, Epworth was the birthplace in 1703 of John Wesley. His brother Charles, who wrote over 6,000 hymns, was born four years later. John was the fifteenth of the nineteen children of Samuel Wesley, who arrived here as rector in 1696 and is buried in the churchyard of St Andrews – the tomb on which John stood to preach night after night in 1742 when he was denied access to the church itself.

The old rectory belongs to the Methodist church and is open to the public, but it is not the famous one which was burned down in 1709 by a furious mob who objected to Samuel Wesley's political sympathies, and from which John was only rescued a moment before the roof fell in.

In the district there survive remnants of the open-field system of medieval agriculture.

EYAM, *Derbyshire* (12–SK2176). A chair in the 13th-cent. church in this small village 6 m. N. of BAKEWELL and a gravestone in the churchyard tell the story of tragedy and courage which put Eyam into the history books. The chair is inscribed MON 1665 EYAM and it commemorates William Mompesson, the rector of Eyam at the time the Great Plague of 1665–6 descended on the village. The infection was brought to the village in a box of clothes and within a matter of months had claimed more than 80 per cent of the inhabitants as victims. By example and character the rector persuaded the people not to flee from the stricken village – and thus the plague was prevented from spreading into Derbyshire and further afield. Among the victims was Mompesson's wife and it is her grave you can see in the churchyard. During the plague the rector preached in the open air, from a rock in a dell which has since become known as Cucklet Church. It is here that an annual commemoration service is held on the last Sunday in August. The Sunday before, a well-dressing festival is held. Mompesson's Well can also be seen. It was there that the villagers dropped the money for goods which were delivered to them during their grim siege.

In the churchyard is an Anglo-Saxon cross, dating from early in the 9th cent., which is remarkable because the cross-head is still there, and an unusual 18th-cent. sundial which tells the time throughout the world by a curved graph. Near the village are several spots worth a visit: Sir William's Road, a hill-track almost 1,200 ft up from which much of the Peak District can be seen; the so-called Rock Garden with its strange echo; and Wet Withens, on Eyam Moor, a Bronze Age circle of 16 stones.

FOREMARK, *Derbyshire* (12–SK3326). Not far from this small village which lies near the River Trent about 5 m. S. of DERBY is what is known as an "anchor church" – caves in a cliff once occupied by an anchorite. Nearby, too, at **Ingleby**, is an unusually large collection of Danish burial mounds. There are 60 in all, the biggest 15 yds across and several feet high; they are believed to date from the late 9th cent. In the church dedicated to St Saviour in Foremark itself are wrought-iron communion rails thought to be work of Robert Bakewell – one of whose major pieces, the "Birdcage", can be seen at nearby MELBOURNE Hall. There are also a three-decker pulpit and original box-pews in the church, which was entirely built in 1662.

GAINSBOROUGH, *Lincolnshire* (13–SK81 89). King Alfred married Ealswith here in 868,

E. Preston

Eyam: the sundial telling world-time

and Cnut's father, Sweyn, King of the Danes, died at his camp at Thonock Park in 1014. Gainsborough was a frequent battleground between Royalist and Parliamentarian troops. George Eliot used it as the prototype of St Ogg's in *The Mill on the Floss*, describing the curious tidal wave known as the Bore, or the Aegir, which rushes up the Trent to a height of several feet during the spring tides. There are some interesting 18th-cent. warehouses on the quayside, but otherwise Gainsborough only retains one outstanding example of its past history, the Old Hall in Parnell Street, one of the largest and most important of the surviving late medieval houses in the country open to the public.

It was built by Lord de Burgh in 1484 after the Lancastrians had wrecked his former home, and here he received Richard III. Henry VIII visited the house in 1509, and in 1540 was introduced there to his last wife, Katharine Parr, widow of Lord de Burgh's eldest son. Thomas, the last de Burgh to live here, was Queen Elizabeth's ambassador in Scotland and Lord Deputy in Ireland, but so extravagant that the year before he died in 1597 he had to sell his property in Gainsborough to William Hickman of London. Several generations of Hickmans lived here until 1720 when they moved their family seat out to the "sylvan pleasaunces" of Thonock. Thereafter the Old Hall became in turn a parish church, a linen factory, a corn exchange, a mechanics' institute, a Congregational church, a selection of tenements and shops, a theatre, a soup kitchen after the Napoleonic Wars, a 19th-cent. public house, an auction sale-room, a public ballroom, and a Masonic temple. Perhaps this is something to be grateful for. The resulting lack of desire to improve and modernize, as in the case of most private dwellings, has left it with the best surviving example of a medieval kitchen in the country, a magnificent timbered great hall containing the finest remaining single-arch braced roof, and a very lovely stone oriel window.

GOTHAM, *Nottinghamshire* (13–SK5330), is a very ordinary village of mines and plaster works, but who has not heard of the 16th-cent. *Merrie Tales of the Mad Men of Gotham*? The men who sent cheeses rolling downhill to NOTTINGHAM, dragged a cart to the top of a barn to shade the roof from the sun, burned a forge to get rid of a wasps' nest, tried to drown an eel in a pond, and built a hedge round a cuckoo so that it might stay and sing for them all the year round. Cuckoo Bush Hill, Cuckoo Bush Mound, and the Cuckoo Bush Inn are here still to remind us; though many think that the men of Gotham only pretended to be mad in order to deter King John, who was threatening to build a hunting lodge in the middle of their village.

If Gotham does not please you, drive to the wooded hills behind it, where there are masses of bluebells in the spring.

GRANTHAM, *Lincolnshire* (13–SK9335). The best preliminary view of the 281-ft spire of St Wulfram's Church, a landmark for miles around, is obtained by leaving LINCOLN along The Cliff to the A607, passing two other notable spires on the way: the impressive one at **Leadenham**, and the apparently crooked one at **Caythorpe**.

Grantham, centre of fine coaching inns serving the old road to the North, once belonged to Edith, queen of Edward the Confessor. It was the second place in which an Eleanor Cross was erected, as Edward I directed they should be wherever his wife's body rested on its way back to London from HARBY, where she died. The cross

was destroyed in the Civil War and now a statue of Sir Isaac Newton, unveiled in 1858, stands in its place opposite the Victorian guildhall.

St Wulfram's magnificent, cathedral-like church is in Swinegate. There are six pillars left of the Norman church which it replaced, but its greatest beauties are its 14th-cent. additions: the lady chapel with a lovely six-light traceried window, the north porch, the double-vaulted crypt, and the splendid steeple. Above the south porch, in what was once a priests' recess and washroom, is the chained library left to the church in 1598. The oldest book was printed in Venice in 1472, and 83 of the 150 are still attached to their original chains.

Immediately E. of the church is Grantham House in 25 acres of land, making an open space in the middle of the town. It is now the property of the National Trust, open to the public at certain times. The central hall is late 14th-cent. and once housed Princess Margaret Tudor, daughter of Henry VII, on her way to marry James IV of Scotland.

Separated from the churchyard by a narrow lane is the 15th-cent. grammar school, now known as King's School. The building with its high-pitched stone roof and mullioned windows is little changed. Among the hundreds of signatures on the sills are those of Isaac Newton, who arrived here in 1654, aged 12, Colley Cibber, and Queen Elizabeth's great treasurer, Lord Burghley.

In the Market Place is the stone conduit built in 1597 to protect the water brought by the Grey Friars from the springs at Gonerby. The two most important coaching inns are the 18th-cent. George Hotel, and the Angel & Royal Trust House Hotel, one of the very few medieval hostelries left in the country, established by the Knights Templar. The gatehouse dates from the 15th cent. and King John held court in 1213 in a room still known as the King's Chamber.

The fine 20th-cent. museum and library is interesting for, among other things, some charming valentines and other bygones. And, in spite of the 40 shillings left by Michael Solomon, the 18th-cent. landlord of the Angel & Royal, for a sermon to be preached against drunkenness in the parish church, nobody should leave without visiting the Beehive Inn in Castlegate. It has a living sign – a real beehive perched in a lime-tree outside.

GREAT CASTERTON, *Rutland* (10–SK99 09). The town was named after the *castrum*, or Roman fort, always known to have lain NE. of the church where Ermine Street crossed the River Gwash into Rutland. However after the abnormally dry summer of 1959 cropmarks appeared and the remains of a 2nd- to 5th-cent. town and a late-4th-cent. villa were discovered. With the 1st-cent. fort and defences, best seen from the little secondary road to RYHALL, this epitomizes the history of Roman Britain. In 1966 a road-widening scheme revealed a Romano-Saxon burial site, a stone coffin from which is now in the County Museum at OAKHAM. Other relics have also been excavated, among them some Romano-Saxon pottery and a hoard of coins from the 4th and 5th cents. buried under a joist beneath the floor of the villa.

Those who like beautifully plain, white-washed, and almost completely unrestored churches should visit that of SS. Peter and Paul to admire especially the early-13th-cent. foliated capitals. The square Norman font is also exceptional. The tower is 15th-cent. and the pulpit Georgian, and the churchyard contains some good examples of carved and winged Ketton headstones.

The poet John Clare, peasant son of an inarticulate labourer, worked on a farm in Great Casterton and met there his wife – "Sweet Patty of the Vale".

GRIMSBY, *Lincolnshire* (13–TA2810). This old, world-famous fishing port is operated as a twin to **Immingham** about 5 m. N. up the coast (though by road it may only be approached on the tortuous A1136 skirting both towns). Whereas Immingham owes its fame to the 20th cent., when modern, deep-water docks were constructed to accommodate ocean-going vessels from Oslo, Lisbon, Istanbul and Africa, the history of Grimsby was written during the Danish invasions of Britain, even though it comes down to us only in the 14th-cent. *Lay of Havelock the Dane*. This tells how Havlok, son of a Danish king, was pushed out to sea in a boat after his father was murdered. He was rescued and brought up by a Lincolnshire fisherman named Grim. When Havlok grew up he regained his kingdom and richly rewarded his rescuer, who used this wealth to found the port of Grimsby.

Little ships from the North Sea ports sail into Grimsby, the oldest chartered town in England (1202), and 56 per cent of all plaice and 40 per cent of all turbot for England and Wales are landed here. The Fish Dock is the largest fish market in the world, and is in the biggest town of Lincolnshire.

The Pilgrim Fathers sailed from Immingham Creek to Holland in 1608 before crossing the Atlantic in 1620. Street names, and a monument at South Killingholms Haven tipped with a fragment of Plymouth Rock, celebrate this historic occasion.

Four miles N. of Grimsby, where the Humber meets the North Sea, is the seaside resort of **Humberston Fitties**. Those tiring of too much industry might like to drive S. of Grimsby down the B1431, W. of which they will find **Hatcliffe**, tiny, loftily sited above the wooded Ravendale valley, and one of the show-pieces of Lincolnshire. Almost opposite, on the other side of the same road, is **Ashby-cum-Fenby**, where the church has a particularly beautiful medieval oak screen, and almshouses built by Lady Wray during the reign of Elizabeth I. A little further S., down a secondary road off the B1203 is **Wold Newton**, which is noted for the modern figures of the saints in its church.

HADDON HALL, *Derbyshire* (12–SK2366), embodies many of the romantic writer's ideas of an English castle: grey-stone walls and battlemented towers and turrets, a heavily wooded slope as its backdrop, an ancient bridge over the River Wye at its feet and the general air not of a grim fortress but of a gracious, rambling house.

The fine, stone-built Hall, regularly open to the public, has changed little over the past 300 or more years. There are traces of the original building which William Peveril, illegitimate son of William the Conqueror, built in the 11th cent., notably parts of the Peveril Tower and the chapel. The house then was probably no more than a modest hall of its period, but under the later Peverils and the three families who succeeded them as owners – the Avenels, the Vernons, here from 1170 to 1567, and the Manners, from 1567 to the present day – Haddon Hall grew to its present delightful form.

Visitors can look over most of the house, much of it still furnished as it was. In the huge kitchens are the ancient water storage troughs and a dresser worn through with long use; and the bench, salting trough and chopping block can be seen in the butcher's shop. In the fine banqueting hall is a tapestry from the 15th cent. and the antlers on the wall have been there since Charles II's day. There is much heraldic panelling and carving in the dining-room, and a magnificent ceiling; on the staircase landing are three of the set of five Mortlake "Senses" tapestries, probably made originally for Charles I.

There is a small museum at the hall containing many items recovered from behind wainscoting and from under floors during restoration work – coins, dice, knives, pipes, keys, rings etc.; and there is also a rare type of short-pendulum clock, dating from about 1670, and the death-mask of Lady Grace Manners.

The gardens at Haddon are also open to the public. Lying mainly on the south side, they are laid out in a series of stone-walled terraces, with lawns, clipped yews and flower-beds. The rose is the flower of Haddon; there are masses of them everywhere, in formal beds and climbing against the stone walls. These serene gardens make an altogether English setting for this great house.

HAMBLETON, *Rutland* (10–SK9008). Start at Upper Hambleton on its sharp 417-ft hill with fine views over the Vale of Catmose. Upper Hambleton also has a church with a 13th-cent. tower and stumpy spire so characteristic of Rutland. It is essentially 12th-cent., particularly in the south doorway and north and south arcades, but much Victorian rebuilding and decoration has been added. Near the church is the 16th-cent. Priest's House, and there is a 17th-cent. manor house near the modern Hall.

Middle Hambleton is of little account, but tucked below is Nether Hambleton with a delightful Jacobean house of 1610, now a farmhouse but still retaining its gables, colonnades and balustraded balconies.

Leaving Hambleton due S. along the village street brings you to **Egleton** where there is an exceptionally interesting church with rich Norman work, dating from about 1160, in the chancel arch, font and south doorway. Leaving E. along the hilltop you will find the little white Church of St Matthew standing lonely in the now denuded park of the old estate of **Normanton**, which once belonged to the vastly rich Sir Gilbert Heathcote, one of the original founders of the Bank of England in 1694, and Lord Mayor of London in 1711. The village which once stood near the church was pulled down in 1764 by Sir Gilbert in order to enlarge the park. The villagers were transferred to EMPINGHAM.

HARBY, *Nottinghamshire* (13–SK8770). An unremarkable village but historically interesting because the gentle Queen Eleanor of Castile died here on 27 November 1290 in the manor home of Richard de Weston. She had come with Edward I to spend some weeks in SHERWOOD FOREST. He wrote of her: "I loved her tenderly in her lifetime, and I do not cease to love her now she is dead". She was embalmed at LINCOLN and taken to be buried in WESTMINSTER ABBEY, each resting place on the way being marked by a cross – the last and most famous at CHARING CROSS in London. The only original crosses remaining, however, are at GEDDINGTON in Northampton-shire and at WALTHAM CROSS in Hertfordshire.

The old manor house has gone, apart from a small section of its moat next to the churchyard. The chapel Edward I built to her memory has also gone but two relics are preserved in the rather ugly Victorian St Helen's Church built in 1882: the plain Norman doorway to the vestry and the 14th-cent. font. A brass plate on the altar step records her death, and a statuette in a niche above the tower doorway is flanked by shields of Castile and Leon, England and Ponthieu, as on her tomb in the Abbey.

HARDWICK HALL, *Derbyshire* (13–SK46 63). It is impossible not to be impressed, even if not wholly favourably, by Hardwick Hall, one of the trio of great Derbyshire houses – the others being HADDON HALL and CHATSWORTH. Hard-wick, 6 m. SE. of CHESTERFIELD, is the monu-ment to Bess of Hardwick who, to make sure no one forgot that this house was her creation, indeed her *chef d'œuvre*, had her initials, writ large, set on top of the four massive, square towers of the west front.

The present building, now in the keeping of the National Trust and open to visitors, is in fact the new hall. The ruined shell of Hardwick Old Hall, where Bess was born in 1520, stands a little distance away. Bess was married four times, the last time to the Earl of Shrewsbury, and with each marriage she became richer, more powerful and more of a character. She became a widow for the fourth time in 1590, at the age of 70, and the following year began her most ambitious under-taking, the creation of a new Hardwick Hall. The building took six years to complete and is distin-guished for its symmetry – a rare architectural attribute in Tudor England – and for the fact that there is more glass than stone in the walls. There

are no fewer than 50 windows, some of them enormous, in the imposing west front.

The exterior of the Hall is plain, not to say severe; but inside much of the furnishing and decoration is lavish. To a large degree the interior is much as it must have been in Bess's day and some of the elaborate plasterwork, the exquisite needlework and tapestry is as fine as any in the country. Of the latter, some of the most valuable are the pieces of needlework representing the Virtues; the Mortlake tapestries telling the story of Hero and Leander, on the main stairs; and the 13 pieces of Flemish tapestry hanging in the gallery telling the story of Gideon and which Bess herself bought in 1592 for £326, a prince's ransom then.

HARTINGTON, *Derbyshire* (12–SK1360), is unusual for the county in that the small town is built round a very large, spacious square of a kind more often found much further S. in the country. This, together with the mellow, fawn stone buildings, lends Hartington a Georgian grace not often seen in Derbyshire's hill country. On the River Dove equidistant from BUXTON and ASHBOURNE, some 2 m. W. of the A515, Hartington is famous for its scenery. The road to the A515 winds its way through a narrow valley with limestone crags often rising sheer on either side. BERESFORD DALE can be reached by a footpath from the village. Overlooking the town stands the Church of St Giles, built in red sandstone and with a sturdy tower, battlements and a curious collection of gargoyles. Just off the square stands the old Town Hall, a pretty, arched building dating from 1836 which is now a shop.

HATHERSAGE, *Derbyshire* (12–SK2381). There is a fine open-air swimming-pool in this small hill town, about 8 m. N. of BAKEWELL. It is said that Little John, Robin Hood's henchman, was born here; and that from a cottage here he shot the arrow to mark the spot where he wished to be buried. The Church of St Michael occupies a commanding position on the highest point of the town, and accentuates it by its spire. Built towards the end of the 14th cent., but restored by Butterfield in 1862, it is highly thought of by authorities on church architecture; and is re-nowned for its wealth of good brasses, memorials to the Eyre family dating back to 1459.

HAUGHMOND ABBEY, *Shropshire* (8–SJ 5415). Built in the lee of a hill, about 5 m. NE. of SHREWSBURY, the abbey was founded about 1135 by William Fitzalan as a house for Augustinian canons. It was rebuilt about 50 years later when the church was considerably enlarged, and had an uneventful history until the Dissolution. Then it passed into private hands and at times was used as a dwelling house.

Apart from the church, much of the abbey still stands substantially as it has done for 800 years. The first impression of the grey-stone front of the abbot's lodging, with its large bay window and oriel window, is of a gracious country house.

The impression is heightened by the spacious hall, the kitchen with its large chimneys, and the doorways which led into the buttery and pantry. Perhaps the most impressive building in the abbey is the 12th-cent. chapter house with its finely carved Norman doorway. Here a small museum of architectural fragments has been established, including an ancient font and a 13th-cent. sculpture of the Virgin and Child. At the north end of the abbey the foundations indicate that a noble church once stood there; in front of the high altar are two Fitzalan gravestones.

HAYFIELD, *Derbyshire* (12–SK0386), is a village in the highest ground of the Peak District and offers the best approach to **Kinder Scout** which reaches 2,088 ft. On the journey there can be seen the Kinder Waterfall with the Mermaid's Pool at its foot. Much of the high plateau is a private grouse moor, but large areas are open for walkers, climbers and ramblers by access agreements which have been made with the landowners. Further E. is the area known as Derbyshire's Lake District, the string of three reservoirs, Howden, Derwent and Ladybower, which run through **Derwent Dale.** The scenery of the whole area is never less than magnificent and occasionally awe-inspiring.

HECKINGTON, *Lincolnshire* (13–TF1444). The village is not exciting and the landscape is flat. Nevertheless there are two things which make Heckington worth visiting: its well-preserved eight-sail windmill, the only one in England still operating, and one of the finest Decorated cruciform churches in the country.

The church, St Andrew's, was built in the 14th cent. by the rich abbots of BARDNEY, and is an enduring and unaltered monument to English architecture at its best. It is the third church on the site but embodies none of the features of the others. The outside is richly carved, buttressed, canopied, turreted, and pinnacled. The inside is disappointing apart from a wonderful Easter sepulchre built by Richard de Potesgrave, vicar of the church and chaplain to Edward III. His tomb and stone effigy are in the chancel next to the sepulchre. Two other features of note are the beautifully carved sedilia and the tracery in the east window.

HOAR CROSS, *Staffordshire* (9–SK1223). Many aver that the church in this small, pretty village about 8 m. W. of BURTON-UPON-TRENT is the most beautiful built in England during the 19th cent. – and some would include the 20th. The architect was George Frederick Bodley, and he chose red sandstone which comes wonderfully alive in evening sunlight. He gave it a strong, embattled central tower more than 100 ft tall to catch those slanting rays. The church, built in 1876, was the inspiration of a young widow, Emily Meynell Ingram, daughter of Viscount Halifax. In 1863 she came to the village as the bride of Hugo Meynell Ingram, of Hoar Cross Hall, and it was his early death, eight years

later, which prompted his widow to build the church.

The desire to make this a beautiful building is reflected inside as well as out: in the magnificent stained glass, again the work of Bodley; in the lofty pillars and soaring arcades; in the black-and-white marble floor with the Meynell Ingram arms set at the foot of the altar steps; in the exquisitely carved woodwork, especially the spire-shaped oak canopy to the font. Here, too, are the monuments to the widow and her husband, both recumbent figures in alabaster: he, in the uniform of the Staffordshire Yeomanry with a favourite hound at his feet; she, head on a cushion, hands raised in prayer with her pet dog at her feet. Some of the painting is so close to the medieval style that a couple of genuine old Italian paintings were for a long time thought to be 19th-cent. work.

HODNET, *Shropshire* (8–SJ6128). The beautiful Hall gardens, which are open to the public, and an old church are the chief attractions of this predominantly black-and-white town about 5 m. SW. of MARKET DRAYTON. Hodnet Hall, a large attractive red-brick house, Elizabethan-looking but built only about 100 years ago on the site of an older house, is not open to the public but good views of it can be obtained from the gardens. Thoughtfully landscaped and covering more than 60 acres, the gardens were created from a wilderness of shrubs covering a narrow, marshy valley by the late Brigadier A. G. W. Heber-Percy, whose son and family still live at the Hall. The work was begun in 1922 and took 30 years and today the gardens, which contain many unusual plants and shrubs, offer interest and beauty at all seasons. The gardens are laid out to incorporate a necklace of pools of various shapes and sizes and these, together with the forest trees and sweeping lawns, form a perfect setting for the great splashes of daffodils, rhododendrons, azaleas and lilacs, the peonies, roses and primulas of summer and the foliage and berries of the autumn shrubs. There is a fine cedar tree planted in memory of the founder and a garden built round a glacial boulder of granite. The visitor can take tea in a pretty half-timbered building which contains an unusual collection of big-game trophies; and a little way from the house stands a timber-framed barn dating from 1619.

The Church of St Luke crowns the hill round which the small town clusters and has a christening gate in the churchyard and wedding steps leading to the drive to the Hall. There is Norman work in the church, the octagonal tower of which is unique in Shropshire. One of its treasures is a small chained library which contains a Latin Bible printed in Nuremberg in 1479, only 10 years after the first printed book. The church's most famous rector, from 1807 to 1823, was Reginald Heber who later became Bishop of Calcutta. The coloured tile paving in the chancel is in memory of this man who wrote many famous hymns, among them "From Greenland's icy mountains" and "Brightest and best of the sons of the morning"

HOLBEACH, *Lincolnshire* (13–TF3925). Holbeach, in the midst of the aptly named "Parts of Holland" bulb-growing district of Lincolnshire, was mentioned in the Domesday Book. The Church of All Saints is a little later than the one at HECKINGTON and a good example of the transition from Decorated to Perpendicular. The tower and spire are magnificent and there is typical flamboyant tracery in some of the windows. On a large tomb inside, the effigy head of Sir Humphrey Littlebury, killed during the Wars of the Roses, rests mysteriously on the head of another man, caught in a net.

William Stukeley, one of the founders of the Society of Antiquaries in 1718, was born in Holbeach in 1687. Another native of this market town was Susannah Centlivre, born about 1667. Six years before her marriage at 29 to Joseph Centlivre, chef to Queen Anne and George I, she had written her first play. Until she died in 1723 she wrote one play a year, all full of rich comedy and invention and in one of them David Garrick played the lead.

HOLME, *Nottinghamshire* (13–SK8059). Rather inaccessible between the Trent, Slough Dike and the Fleet, Holme once stood on the west bank of the Trent, but is now on the east due to one of the river's medieval changes of course.

Small St Giles' Church is one of the most remarkable in the county, for nearly everything about it is early Tudor. It was rebuilt in the late 15th cent. by John Barton, who made a fortune out of the wool trade with Calais and had, so it is said, an inscription in the window of his house which read: "I thanke God, and ever shall. It is the shepe hath payed for all." His monument in two tiers, with a rotting corpse in the lower one, lies between the chancel and the chapel. It is thanks to the sensitive restoration begun in 1932 by Mr Nevil Truman that this little church is still so attractive with its leaning walls, original screens, and benches carved with poppy-heads. Also due to Mr Truman is the east window, a medieval medley of pieces including John Barton's memorial glass. A room above the porch is known as Nanny Scott's Chamber, after an old woman who took refuge here with plenty of food when the plague struck Holme in 1666. From the small window she watched the funeral cortèges of her friends until, forced down to get more food, she found only one person still left alive. Horror-stricken, she returned to her chamber to die; the coffin-shaped chest in which she kept all her possessions is still there.

You will be told that Dick Turpin stopped at a cottage here to give Black Bess a drink on his famous ride to YORK.

HOPE, *Derbyshire* (12–SK 1783). Two m. E. of CASTLETON and in the centre of the Hope Valley, this rather plain village is known for the fishing and rough shooting available here. On the nearest Saturday to St Peter's Day (29 June), a well is dressed in the village; and in late summer, the Hope Valley Agricultural Show with its well-known sheepdog trials is a major attraction. The parish church has a 14th-cent. tower with a broach spire, and a number of remarkable gargoyles, large and crude. In the churchyard is a 9th-cent. Anglo-Saxon cross shaft. Near the village – and looking rather like a miniature Cape Kennedy – are the works of a famous cement company.

HOPTON CASTLE, *Shropshire* (8–SO3678). The most striking thing about Hopton Castle is the unexpectedness with which the traveller comes upon it. There are several approaches, but the easiest to find is the turning off the B4367 at Hopton Heath. About 1 m. down this country lane you turn a corner and there in a field stand the ruins of the castle. The lovely setting makes it seem incredible that this was the scene of one of the most brutal minor encounters of the Civil War. Colonel Samuel More held the castle for three weeks for the Parliamentarians against the Royalists; 31 defenders against 500 besiegers the records say. When the garrison eventually was forced into surrender, the Royalists shot everyone except the colonel and threw the bodies into a nearby pool. The castle can be viewed.

HORNCASTLE, *Lincolnshire* (13–TF2669). Situated at the south-west foot of the Wolds where they come down to the Fens, at the confluence of the Rivers Bain and Waring, was the Roman fort of Banovallum – the walled place on the River Bain – which forms the central part of this little market town. The walls of the fort are still visible, though the town was largely rebuilt in the middle of the 19th cent. A well-preserved portion of the Roman wall was incorporated in the structure of a library built in 1969.

Horncastle's ten-day August Horse Fair was once famed throughout Europe and is described by George Borrow in *The Romany Rye*. The frequently restored Church of St Mary has many relics of the Battle of **Winceby**, which was fought nearby in 1643 with Cromwell and his Roundheads. Cromwell's horse was shot dead beneath him and as he scrambled to his feet he was charged by Sir Ingram Hopton. Seizing another horse, Cromwell charged again and won the battle which sealed his fame; Sir Ingram Hopton was killed in the second charge. Next day Cromwell rode into Horncastle and arranged for Sir Ingram to be buried in the church, so it seems ungrateful that Cromwell should be described on Sir Ingram's elaborately painted canvas memorial as an "arch-rebel". In the church are also pikes from the battle and 13 scythes, used either at Winceby or in the Lincolnshire Rising in defence of the monasteries. On the north wall is a brass of Sir Lionel Dymoke of SCRIVELSBY wearing the armour of the King's Champion, and on the floor below a worn brass depicting him in his shroud, 1519.

In a corner of the market place once stood Sellwood House from which Louisa and Emily, daughters of Henry Sellwood, a Horncastle solicitor, married Charles and Alfred Tennyson.

E. Preston

Ironbridge is the site of the first cast-iron bridge ever erected

HUCKNALL, *Nottinghamshire* (13–SK 5349). The village of Hucknall is remarkable only for its church, and the Church of St Mary Magdalen is remarkable only for two things. It was here that Lord Byron's body was brought to be buried with his ancestors when his family discovered that permission for him to be interred in WESTMINSTER ABBEY was unlikely to be granted. It is a place of pilgrimage for Greeks into whose War of Independence Byron had thrown himself too wholeheartedly for his already weakened constitution, and for whose cause he died. His bust is on the chancel wall with a lamp of brass burning continually, and in the floor is set a stone sent by the King of Greece and decorated with a brass laurel wreath. His mother had been brought to be buried here from the family home at NEWSTEAD ABBEY 13 years before. His one child, Augusta Ada, was buried by his side in 1852. It was only in 1968 that a memorial of Lord Byron – "mad, bad, and dangerous to know" – was allowed in Poets' Corner at the Abbey. The other remarkable thing about the church is the set of 25 stained-glass windows by Kempe. This is Victorian stained glass at its best. It begins with the east window of 1883; the others are mainly 1888 to 1890.

At Broomhill Park is Sherwood Zoo, covering 17 acres. It has polar bears and parrots, falconry displays and large picnic areas.

ILAM, *Staffordshire* (8–SK 1351), is where the empirical Dr Samuel Johnson carried out his experiment with marked corks to satisfy himself that the stream which emerges from the cliffs in the grounds of Ilam Hall was indeed the River Manifold which disappears underground about 4 m. N. Ilam village is another of the model villages which were rebuilt during the last century, this one by Jesse Watts-Russell, who also built the stately Hall on the site of an earlier house. The Hall and its 50 acres of wooded grounds are now owned by the National Trust and are always open to the public; the Hall itself is, in part, a youth hostel. Watts-Russell's wife is also remembered in Ilam in an unusual monument. Close by the bridge over the Manifold he had erected to her memory a Gothic cross as tall as a house.

The village church, in the Hall grounds, dates from the 13th cent. but it was much restored in 1856. The oldest relics are three Anglo-Saxon crosses: two in the churchyard and one in the grounds of the Hall. The church has a Norman font; and a 13th-cent. shrine to St Bertram who is believed to have been the man who brought Christianity to the area. There are a number of fine monuments in the church, the most impressive of which is that depicting the deathbed scene of David Watts, the work of Sir Francis Chantrey (1781–1842), sculptor of the "Sleeping Children" tomb in LICHFIELD Cathedral. The sculpture shows the dying man raising himself from his couch to lay his hand on the head of his daughter (the woman commemorated by the cross in the village) with her three tiny children clustered around.

Ilam has a link with the English stage; it was here in 1693 that William Congreve, the Restoration dramatist, wrote his comedy, *The Old Bachelor*, while recovering from an illness. Here also is the spot which Dr Johnson is said to have used as his model for the Happy Valley in *Rasselas*.

Ilam is the gateway to the MANIFOLD VALLEY and gives access to DOVEDALE. Here, too, the Dovedale Sheepdog Trials are held each August.

ILKESTON, *Derbyshire* (13–SK 4642), on high ground above the Erewash Valley, is the third largest town in the county and is only just inside the county boundary. There was an Anglo-Saxon settlement here before the Danes came in the 9th cent., but not until the late 19th cent. did the small village begin to develop into today's industrial town. The oldest building in the town is the Parish Church of St Mary. Although much restored about 100 years ago, parts of the original Norman building can still be seen and there is an unusual 14th-cent. stone screen and a Crusader's tomb. The county cricket club play a number of matches each season in the Rutland Recreation Ground; and Ilkeston retains its links with its past in the annual three-day fair held in the Market Place in October.

INGESTRE, *Staffordshire* (8–SJ9724), on the River Trent about 4 m. NE. of STAFFORD, has a rare possession – a Wren church. St Mary's was built in 1676 by Walter Chetwynd to the designs of Sir Christopher. The documents relating to its building have been lost but architectural authorities are convinced from its style that it is indeed one of the master's works. Fruit and flowers are the dominant motifs inside – on the plasterwork ceiling, the oak panelling in the chancel, the oak chancel screen and the pulpit. The Hall, a Jacobean building and home first of the Chetwynd family and then of the Earls of Shrewsbury, was burnt down in 1882 and the present building, now an Arts Centre, is a skilful reconstruction of the first Hall. Part of Capability Brown's landscaping for Ingestre – his first Staffordshire commission – survives.

On the road from Stafford stands the shell of Tixall gatehouse, one of the most important remaining examples of early Elizabethan architecture, and all that remains of a large mansion.

NW. of Ingestre lies **Hopton Heath**, where in 1643 a Parliamentary army defeated the Royalists under the Earl of Northampton.

IRONBRIDGE, *Shropshire* (8–SJ6703), must have been an attractive spot before the Industrial Revolution, for the little town is set on steep limestone slopes above a narrow gorge through which the River Severn flows. Ironbridge has become famous because the world's first iron bridge was built here. It was designed by Abraham Darby II and cast, in 1778, at his foundry in nearby Coalbrookdale. Today the bridge is restricted to foot traffic but it is well worth walking across it, and along the bank to get a distant view of it. Then, for all its size (it is 196 ft long, with one major span of 100 ft and two smaller ones at one end, and weighs 380 tons) the bridge looks insubstantial.

KEDLESTON HALL, *Derbyshire* (12–SK 3140), is reckoned by many to be the finest Robert Adam house in England. Kedleston, 4½ m. NW. of DERBY, has been the Derbyshire home of the Curzon family for 850 years, but of the original house nothing remains. It was pulled down in the last years of the 17th cent. and then began a period of building, alteration and rebuilding which went on until late in the 18th cent. The first architect employed was Matthew Brettingham, and his basic plan for a main block with two projecting wings linked to it by corridors is what gives the house its present-day form. At a later stage, another architect, James Paine, at that time more famous than Robert Adam, was called in and to him goes the credit for the imposing north front with its giant columns and triumphal arch. Adam came on the scene in 1760 and he was the designer of the more unusual south front and of much of the interior, his masterpiece being the Marble Hall with its 20 huge columns of pink, veined alabaster, its floor of Derbyshire stone and Italian marble, its alcoves containing statues and its monochrome panels round the walls depicting scenes from Homer. This is considered one of the most splendid rooms in Europe.

Many of the other rooms in the Hall are of a piece with this famous room. In the Music Room is a gilded organ designed by Adam and the chimney-piece is inlaid with Derbyshire's own stone, the Blue John. The outstanding feature of the State Drawing Room is a beautifully proportioned Venetian window. The Saloon is a rotunda with a dome 62 ft high, and the State Dining Room, a symphony of browns, buffs and whites, is distinguished by a semi-domed alcove for the better display of the table silver. Pictures by such artists as Reynolds, Reni, Van Dyck and Veronese adorn the walls; there are magnificent marble fireplaces, furniture designed by Chippendale and Adam, a plaque made by Josiah Wedgwood, and much early Crown Derby china dating from 1760. Visitors may also see Adam's original drawings for the work, outside and in, which he did at Kedleston; and the Indian Museum containing the collection of silver, ivories, ancient weapons, including poisoned arrows, and Oriental

A. F. Kersting

Kedleston Hall: the Marble Hall was designed by Robert Adam

works of art made by Lord Curzon while he was Viceroy of India from 1898 to 1905.

In the grounds can be seen the Boathouse and graceful bridge, both designed by Adam; and the 13th- and 14th-cent. Church of All Saints which contains a remarkable collection of Curzon monuments.

KEGWORTH, *Leicestershire* (10–SK4826). Kegworth is saved from being commonplace by its Church of St Andrew, which stands on a hill above the water-meadows of the Soar, stately and cohesive in its architecture. It is late Decorated with an extra aisle on each side taking the place of transepts, and every window, with the exception of the large east window, is of the same size and pattern. The nave roof has a medieval choir of men and women playing musical instruments, and the chantry roof is supported by ten stone angels.

Thomas Moore brought his young wife, Bessie, to live in Kegworth in 1812 where, he wrote, "she runs wild about the large garden". His house, The Cedars, stands on the LOUGHBOROUGH road. Here he composed some of his *Irish Melodies* and here his favourite daughter, Anastasia, who died of consumption when she was 16, was born.

There are some houses worth noting in the main street running S. from the church. The first, dated 1698, is the best. Behind the Britannia Inn is an old stockinger's cottage which was used for the purpose until 1956.

KELHAM, *Nottinghamshire* (13–SK7755). Kelham Hall casts its spiky reflection on the waters of the River Trent. It was built by Sir Gilbert Scott after the first Kelham Hall, said to be the house in which Charles I finally surrendered to the Scots, was destroyed by fire in 1857. Now a theological college, Kelham Hall was once described by the Archbishop of Canterbury as "extraordinarily like St Pancras station". The chapel, built in 1928, has a plain but inspiring interior with a beautiful modern crucifixion scene by Charles Sargeant Jagger. The Church of St Wilfrid contains a monument to Lord and Lady Lexington and their son who died aged 15. The inscription telling of Lord Lexington's career is long, ponderous and not very pious. There is also a monument to a daughter of the 7th Earl of Scarborough by the then very fashionable Gaffin of REGENT STREET.

Leave the village by Kelham Bridge, which was snapped in two by a small iceberg in the terrible winter of 1854–5, and stop in **Averham** to look at the Robin Hood Theatre. It was built in 1914 by a rector of St Michael, a smaller replica of a West End theatre. The late Sir Donald Wolfit made his first stage appearance there in 1917. Later rectors found it embarrassing to have a theatre in their garden, and it was bought by a private enthusiast who puts on all types of amateur and professional shows.

KETTON, *Rutland* (10–SK9704). A large and most attractive village full of excellent building in the famous butter-coloured local stone, which has been quarried from here since the Roman era. The Parish Church of St Mary, with its exquisite tower and spire, rises amid trees above the sepia' Collyweston slate roofs of the village. This church is one of the finest in the North Midlands, large for a village. The west front is an excellent example of 12th-cent. work and the rest of the church is almost entirely 13th-cent. apart from the chancel rebuilt by Sir Gilbert Scott, but good nevertheless. The east window and altar are by Sir Ninian Comper (1907). The church is of stone from BARNACK, a village SE. of STAMFORD, but there are some beautiful Ketton headstones in the churchyard, in particular one near the lychgate depicting masons' tools. It was carved by William Hibbins (1717), whose family still flourish in Ketton as stone masons. Some of their tools can be seen at the County Museum at OAKHAM, along with a fine specimen of their work.

From Ketton drive due W. past Normanton Park about 3 m. to **Edith Weston**, charming, like nearly all Rutland villages. Edward the Confessor gave his wife, Queen Edith, this western part of the county, hence the name. It remained a royal manor until Henry I gave it to his chamberlain, William de Tankerville, who in turn gave it to the Norman abbey of St George de Boscherville. The abbey established a cell at Edith Weston where there were never more than two or three monks, and only one in 1357.

The village is built round a green, surrounded by thatched cottages, and it stands on a limestone plateau between the valleys of the Chater and the Gwash. The old rectory, W. of the church, is dated 1626 and the hall is 1830-Tudor.

The church has an original late-Norman nave, with a north aisle added around 1190, and a south aisle added immediately afterwards. Changes were made in the 14th cent. and the tower was added in 1380. The chancel was rebuilt in 1865. The church possesses one of the oldest positively dated timepieces in England, known as the Commonwealth Clock. It is 300 years old and has recently been restored.

KINGERBY, *Lincolnshire* (13–TF0392). The 19th-cent. Hall stands on the elevated site of a Roman camp, but the mound itself was occupied by Ancient Britons, whose skeletons have been found buried in sawdust with mosaic bracelets on their arms. The Church of St Peter, opposite a wood full of flowers in spring, is especially interesting. The Young family, who owned the Hall for many years, were Catholics and so this Anglican church escaped too much restoration. The tower and south door are both 12th-cent. and there are a lead roof and Georgian lead windows. Two stone effigies of knights rest on the floor and against the chancel wall is a 600-year-old coffin-shaped monument to a member of the Disney family. It shows the bust of a man under a canopy, his feet in another niche below resting on a dog. The space between is occupied by a cross and two shields.

KINGSTON-ON-SOAR, *Nottinghamshire* (13–SK5127). Kingston Hall, built by the first Lord Belper, the son of Jedediah Strutt of hosiery fame, is not particularly exciting except for the lovely fir, pine and cedar panelling lining its walls.

The church is ugly, but contains one of the most important and fascinating church monuments in the county – the Babington ·chantry. When the church was rebuilt in 1900 the monument, dating from about 1550, was moved to its present position intact. The columns are covered in tracery, shields, small figures and trailing vines; there are coffins giving up their dead with some climbing to heaven and others falling into the jaws of a monster. The main capitals are carved with what is a pun on the Babington name – about 200 babes in tuns. A Sir Anthony Babington is said to have erected the chantry. Another Anthony Babington, a Roman Catholic, is said to have hidden on its canopy after his share in the conspiracy to put Mary Queen of Scots on the throne. He was beheaded in 1586, aged only 25, for his part in the plot.

As you move S. out of the village notice the fine buildings of the NOTTINGHAM University School of Agriculture. These were used as German prison camps during the War.

KINOULTON, *Nottinghamshire* (13–SK6730). Stop here, if only for the glorious view over the Vale of Belvoir with the cattle on the horizon, and the woodlands known as the Borders. The Grantham Canal runs under the road. Opposite the forge is the bright red brick church built by the Earl of Gainsborough in 1793. Close to Fosse Way is the site of the old church with slate headstones including one of the finest in the county. Kinoulton has one of the best village cricket grounds in Nottinghamshire, and the Neville Arms is the rendezvous of the Nottingham Old Crocks Car Club.

KINVER, *Staffordshire* (8–SO8483). One of the finest Staffordshire views is to be had from the famous Kinver Edge, below which this small town clusters, in the south-west corner of the county. On top of the Edge, National Trust property, is an early Iron Age hill-fort; and there are also the strange "rock houses" at Holy Austin Rock, rooms carved out of the solid sandstone, their "chimneys" holes in the hillside. Two m. away stand the remains of Stourton Castle, birthplace of Reginald Pole, Archbishop of Canterbury during the reign of Mary Tudor.

KIRKSTEAD, *Lincolnshire* (13–TF1762). Here by the Witham in 1139, Hugo Brito, son of a Lord of TATTERSHALL, founded the Cistercian abbey of which all that remains is a corner of the transept and the now solitary little Church of St Leonard – the Cistercians' "church outside the gates" for lay worshippers. Standing on bumpy pastoral land described in a charter of the time as, "a horrible and vaste solitude surrounded by swamp and bramble bushes on all sides", this church should not be left out of the sightseers' itinerary since it is an unspoilt example of 13th-cent. architecture and contains what is thought to be the second-oldest timber screenwork in England. It has a charming arcade of three arches with a window in the centre and is still lit by candles in two fine candelabra. The triple lancets in the east wall are enriched with dogtooth carving, foliage, and clustered and banded shafts. The altar stone from the abbey is now on the floor. A figure of a knight in a flat-topped helmet with a long slit for the eyes is thought to be the 2nd Lord Tattershall, who died in 1212. The abbey was dissolved in 1537 on the "confession" of the abbot that his monks had "vainly, detestably, and ungodly devoured their yearly revenues in continual ingurgitations of their carrion bodies, with vain and unholy expenses, enormities and abuses".

The Abbey Lodge Inn near the ruins is 18th-cent. There is good fishing in the River Witham at this point.

LAMBLEY, *Nottinghamshire* (13–SK6245), has beautiful scenery in a deep sheltered vale with the Lambley Dumble running through the village. The excellently proportioned Perpendicular Church of the Holy Trinity was built for Ralph de Cromwell, Lord High Treasurer of about 1450, who is credited with having produced the first budget. One of the wealthiest nobles of his time, he was born at Lambley in 1394 and though his body lies at the church in TATTERSHALL, his badge of office, a purse, is carved on the outside of the east window here. Originally there was a two-storied chantry on the north wall built by the sixth Ralph Cromwell. The "squint" from its upper room is still visible in the stones of the wall.

LANGAR, *Nottinghamshire* (13–SK7235). The large church with a tower over the central crossing is often called the Cathedral of the Vale of Belvoir. It is badly restored outside but is nevertheless mentioned in a number of reference books because of its monuments. The one of Lord Thomas Scroope (1609) and his wife, Philadelphia, is a splendid, free-standing alabaster, which has been described as "almost the finest effigy in England". Details of the robes are worth close study, though this is not easy since the doors of the chapel are locked and the visitor has to look down from a stone balcony. This monument was erected by their son, Emanuel, who is represented as a curious, small bearded figure kneeling at their feet and holding a book. In the north transept the Chaworths of whom Mary of ANNESLEY, Byron's first love, was the last of the line, dying at Langar in 1832. Admiral Earl Howe (of the Glorious 1st of June) – whose family lived in the Hall before it was rebuilt – is buried in the south transept, though his main monument is at WESTMINSTER ABBEY. The 16th-cent. altar cloth is made from Italian material he brought back to England from one of the seven ships he captured on the day of his famous battle. You will note that the other two Howe monuments have the Christian name Scroope, the Scroopes and Howes having been linked by marriage in the early 18th cent.

Just near the church is the Georgian rectory where Samuel Butler was born. He used Langar as the prototype for Battersby in *The Way of all Flesh* after his harsh and embittering childhood behind those too-narrow windows.

LAXTON, *Nottinghamshire* (13–SK7266). This village is famous for preserving the old agricultural system of open-field farming. This was Saxon in origin, consisting of hedgeless, one-acre, co-operatively farmed strips; after the Norman Conquest the method was adapted to the manorial system, with one field for the bread crop, one for the drink crop, and one fallow. The strips were a furlong (furrow-long) in length and a chain (the length of a cricket pitch) in width; an individual's holding was scattered to ensure a fair share of good and bad land. The open-field system at Laxton is registered as an Ancient Monument.

LEEK, *Staffordshire* (8–SJ9856). Leek stands at the southern end of some of the most impressive scenery in the county. N. of the town, the road to BUXTON climbs over a stretch of wild moorland, patterned by black, drystone walls and dominated by the fortress-like hills known as The Roaches. The highest is Five Clouds, 1,500 ft high; but perhaps the best-known is the solitary, grim-looking Hen Cloud. Here occurs at midsummer a remarkable phenomenon, the so-called double sunset: the sun, having dipped behind one of the hills, re-appears and then slowly slips out of sight again.

Leek was settled before the Romans came. Roman remains have been found at Abbey Green, and at Cock Low, a mound which stood near the present Spring Gardens, was found a funeral urn believed to be pre-Saxon. This can now be seen at the town's Arts Centre in the Nicholson Institute. In the churchyard of St Edward's, the parish church, is the shaft of a cross which may be Danish, and another which may be Anglo-Saxon.

Of the Abbey of Dieulacres, founded in 1214 by Ranulph, 7th Earl of Chester, only traces remain, but there are a number of interesting old buildings in the town. The church, with its eight-pinnacled tower, dates mainly from the 14th cent. although the chancel was almost wholly rebuilt about 100 years ago. Prince Charlie's House commemorates the fact that the Pretender stayed in Leek in 1745 on his way to DERBY. There are a number of old inns, notably the Red Lion, dating from 1626, the 17th-cent. Swan, and the Bowling Green and the George which were built in the 18th cent. That part of the town near the church known as Petty France is a reminder that French prisoners-of-war were brought to Leek during the Napoleonic Wars.

Leek has long been known as a silk and textile town and it was a group of women from the town who in 1885–6 spent 12 months making a copy of the famous Bayeux Tapestry. The copy was purchased in 1895 and presented to READING Museum.

LEICESTER, *Leicestershire* (10–SK5904). The history of this thriving and largely modern city, the centre of the Heart of England, goes back over 2,000 years. Long before the first wave of Romans established their township of Ratae in the lush meadows beside the River Soar the Celtic peoples were here. Traces of roads they built are still to be found, but the Romans, in their 400 years of more or less benign occupation, constructed the highways that inspired the building of today's fine network across the county.

The most impressive surviving memorial of these ancient times is the Jewry Wall, believed to date from A.D. 130, a massive fragment 73 ft long and 20 ft high, in alternate courses of brick and stone. Until recently the deep arched recesses, edged with tiles, on the east face of the wall were thought to be openings in the western gateway of the city. Excavation has now shown them to be windows of a vast basilica. Behind the wall a courtyard 175 ft wide has been opened up, revealing porticos leading into shops, the whole area having once been the forum from which the governor administered justice and laws were passed on to the British people. It is here that the largest Roman bath in England was found. Nearby are tessellated pavements with intricate designs in colour, and coins, pottery and other relics are housed in the new museum.

The hub of the city is the clock tower, a Gothic structure erected in 1868 to commemorate four benefactors of Leicester since the Norman Conquest. The most famous of these was Simon de Montfort, Earl of Leicester, the powerful baron whose hatred of tyranny eventually forced Henry III, his brother-in-law, to grant the first English parliament in 1275. The other three were William Wyggleston, Sir Thomas White and Gabriel Newton, all of them founders of schools or charitable institutions.

Leicester Castle in its original form dates from 1088, but the red-brick frontage added in about 1690 has sadly diminished the grandeur of the earlier concept. Behind it is the great hall which was once part of John of Gaunt's country residence and is now the assize court. The architecture of the stone hall places it almost certainly between 1140 and 1160. The roof of braced beams which span the whole of the building is particularly imposing. An outside flight of steps leads down to what may have been cellars or dungeons. A few yards away is the new work, or Newarke as it is known today, a walled enclosure of about four acres, outside the castle boundaries, in which stood the noble Collegiate Church of St Mary, founded by Henry, Earl of Leicester and Lancaster in the 14th cent. The finest monument of the Newarke is the high stone gateway at the east side, with three arches, a vaulted canopy and ornamented square-topped windows.

The beautiful Church of St Mary de Castro, the church of the castle, is a direct link with the Norman ascendancy. From having been completely Anglo-Saxon it was rebuilt by succeeding Earls of Leicester. The pinnacled tower and the belfry were begun in the 13th cent. and the slender spire was added a hundred or so years later. Of especial antiquarian interest are the five sedilia, or priests' seats, and the magnificent 700-year-old font.

Older still is the Church of St Nicholas, whose history goes back through Saxon times to obscurity in the Roman basilica; but the natural choice for the cathedral of the diocese of Leicester on its re-establishment in 1926 was the civic church of St Martin. Although this noble edifice has been much restored in recent times, not always in harmonious accord with the styles of earlier reconstructions, the graceful old arches and rich decoration of the interior remain unchanged. The bishop's throne is unsurpassed in splendour, standing about 16 ft high and reaching almost to the roof in declining tiers adorned with tracery. Adjacent to the cathedral is the 14th-cent. guildhall, now a repository for books and other exhibits connected with the past. Two m. from the city centre, Belgrave Hall, a small Queen Anne house and garden, is worth a visit.

Leicester today combines the charm of its ancient foundations with the forward march of industry. Two hundred years ago only hosiery was produced here. The bulk manufacture of boots and shoes emerged in the 1850s. In the present century the majority of its people are employed in engineering.

LICHFIELD, *Staffordshire* (9–SK1209). Although Lichfield is a thriving centre of light engineering, it is not industrial installations but the "Ladies of the Vale", the three spires of the cathedral, that the visitor first sees, from whatever direction he approaches the city.

The present red sandstone cathedral, begun in the 1190s and completed about 150 years later, shows splendid Early English and Decorated work. Although this is one of the smallest and most heavily restored cathedrals in the country, the west front has an indisputable grandeur. The twin spires flanking the doorway are almost 200 ft high; the central tower is 60 ft taller. Within the arcades and panels of the front are 113 statues: figures from the Old Testament, the Holy Family, the Apostles, saints, bishops, 24 kings of England, including William the Conqueror and Edward the Confessor, and two genealogies of Christ. Much of this carving dates from the 19th cent.

The most prized treasure is the early 7th-cent. manuscript book known as the St Chad Gospels – the complete gospels of St Matthew and St Mark, and part of the gospel of St Luke – which can be seen after application in writing to the Cathedral Librarian. The name of the manuscript commemorates the first bishop to have his cathedral at Lichfield, in 669, though the gospels themselves did not come to Lichfield until many years after his death. (Lichfield was made an archbishopric in about 787, in mighty Offa's reign, but was a bishopric again by 803.) Another priceless possession are the Herckenrode Windows in the Lady Chapel, among the most beautiful glass in England. The glass was originally in a Cistercian abbey at Herckenrode, near Liège in Belgium, and was brought to

England by Sir Brooke Boothby in 1802. He presented it to the cathedral for just £200, the price he had paid for it. At the east end of the south aisle is the famous "Sleeping Children" monument by Sir Francis Chantrey.

Lichfield has a pleasant cathedral close, a cobbled market square, narrow streets, and many links with Dr Johnson. A statue of the great man sits at one end of the Market Square, facing – but not looking at – his birthplace on the corner of Breadmarket Street. This house, where Samuel's father Michael had his bookshop, is now a museum of Johnsonian relics: it has his favourite armchair, his walking stick, his silver teapot, and many of his manuscripts and letters. Johnson's birthday, 18 September, is celebrated on the Saturday nearest to it with an official gathering round his statue and a candle-lit supper in the Guildhall.

At the other end of the Market Square, looking in the direction of the cathedral, is a statue of Johnson's biographer, James Boswell. At this end, too, is a memorial to Edward Wightman of BURTON-UPON-TRENT, who was burnt at the stake there for heresy on 11 April 1612, the last person so to die in England.

Further along Breadmarket Street is the birthplace of the antiquary and herald Elias Ashmole, who presented his unique collection of antiquities and documents to OXFORD University. In Beacon Street is the house where Dr Erasmus Darwin, grandfather of Charles, lived and the site of one where David Garrick, the actor, often stayed.

Lichfield also has long military associations. At Whittington Barracks, home of the Staffordshire Regiment, a little way out on the TAMWORTH road, the Regimental Museum is open to visitors.

Masons, carvers and joiners can be seen working in wood and stone on the premises of a local firm in Dam Street – appropriately near the cathedral, that treasure-house of their forerunners' skills.

LILLESHALL, *Shropshire* (8–SJ7315). This village is now famous because of the national athletics centre which has been established in the Hall. This is not open to the public, but Lilleshall Abbey, in the grounds of the Hall, is. The ruins are among the most impressive in Shropshire, a group of roofless walls in a lovely setting. The abbey is Norman, founded in 1148. The high west front is particularly grand and through it you can look down the whole length of the 228-ft abbey and through the graceful arch of the empty east window to the trees beyond.

The Church of St Michael is also Norman in part, with a simple Norman font and an unusual monument to two members of the Leveson family, who were given Lilleshall by Henry VIII on the Dissolution of the Monasteries. Sir Richard Leveson and his wife rest on shelves, he above in robes, she below in a shroud. He died in 1661 and she lived on for another 13 years.

The village also has a 70-ft obelisk, commemorating George Greville, Duke of Sutherland – for whom the Hall was built – who died in 1833.

Kenneth Scowen

Lichfield Cathedral with its three spires

LINBY, *Nottinghamshire* (13–SK5350). This is one of the prettiest villages in Nottinghamshire: stone cottages, red roofs, two village crosses, and a little stream flowing on each side of the road.

There is Norman masonry in the north wall and the south side of the chancel in the Church of St Michael, which was mentioned in the Domesday Book. The door is also Norman. But it is Castle Mill, E. of the village and halfway to **Papplewick**, which is of the greatest interest. It was rebuilt and castellated by the Hon. Frederick Montague, 18th-cent. Lord Treasurer, as part of his Papplewick Improvements. Here in 1785 James Watt put up his first steam-engine for cotton-spinning and the 163 graves in the churchyard tell of the pitiful little children who were imported from London to work in it and died under the forced labour conditions of the Industrial Revolution. Castle Mill is now converted into flats but the water wheel, 100 ft round and one of the biggest in England, is still there.

At Papplewick, E. along the B6011, is Papplewick Hall, built in 1787 for the Hon. Frederick Montague by the Adam brothers. In the grounds are an urn to the memory of his friend, Thomas Gray, the poet, and a little temple to William Mason, who wrote part of his *English Garden* here. Frederick Montague also rebuilt the little church in 1795 and his grave is in the churchyard under a sort of stone table on six legs. Part of the legend of Robin Hood still exists here in a cave cut in the rock and guarded by an old oak, where the outlaw is said to have stabled his horses.

LINCOLN, *Lincolnshire* (13–SK9771). The ancient part of this historic city occupies a rugged hill-top rising 200 ft above the River Witham. In earliest times the Celtic tribesmen called their settlement Lindon, "the hill-fort by a pool", until with the coming of the Roman IXth Legion in A.D. 47 the name was latinized to Lindum and later Lindum Colonia, from which the name Lincoln was derived. The subsequent history of this turbulent place was always determined by its geographical position. The elevated limestone plateau provided a natural strategic command of the valley below, and the river served as an extra wall to slow the advance of the enemy. Excavations show that the first Romans maintained a garrison here from which to pivot their forces for the control of eastern England. The river also functioned as a main artery through which flowed the trade that brought prosperity to the whole community.

Roman Lincoln had fine colonnaded streets, and elaborate public baths which are only slowly being revealed through careful archaeological digging. It has been found that drinking water was supplied in earthenware pipes, under pressure, from a source a mile and a half away from the hill. The dominant industry of this important region was agriculture, the successful development of which resulted in a major extension of the town walls to encompass a well-planned suburb. The present Stonebow stands on the site of the Roman south gate here, and beyond this, where Newport Arch still bestrides the ancient Ermine Street, the advanced settlements of the 3rd cent. A.D. started a trend towards civilized living that was to continue in later periods of Lincoln's history.

With the ending of the Roman occupation the Middle Ages inherited road and canal systems, a labyrinth of sewers, working farms, and a wealth of tile and stone. In Anglo-Saxon times Lincoln became part of the kingdom of Mercia, and after Paulinus had introduced the Christian faith a stone church is said to have been built within the old Roman walls. The Danes made Lincoln the chief of the Five Boroughs of their Danelaw, as street names like Saltergate, Danesgate and Hungate bear witness, but it was to be the Norman invaders whose influence made Lincoln one of the most important cities in the realm.

Lincoln Castle was founded by William the Conqueror in 1068. His purpose, like that of his predecessors, was to create an invulnerable stronghold. Even today the battlemented castle walls inspire awe in the beholder. The building encloses a roughly quadrangular area of more than six acres, with lawns and trees. The walls vary from 8 to 10 ft in thickness and double this in height. At the north-east corner there is a low tower known as Cobb Hall and on two great detached mounds on the south side are the Observatory Tower and the uprights of the Norman keep.

Cobb Hall was added in the 14th cent., to be used as a place of punishment. The iron rings to which prisoners were fastened are still to be seen in the walls, and the roof of the tower remained a place of public execution until 1868. Within the passage of the castle gateway is all that is left of the Eleanor Cross, which was set up close to the Gilbertine priory of St Catherine, where the body of Eleanor of Castile, the wife of Edward I, was embalmed. This was the first of the famous crosses erected to mark the halting places of the queen's funeral procession from HARBY in Nottinghamshire to WESTMINSTER ABBEY.

The domestic architecture of the period is splendidly represented by a building put up in about 1170 and known as the Jew's House. This fine example of Norman house construction, serving today as an antique dealer's shop, is at 15 The Strait and is notable for its superb decorated doorway and chimney above. Close by on the east side of Steep Hill is Aaron's House, a well-preserved building dating from the period when Lincoln was at the height of its wool-based prosperity. It is said to be the oldest inhabited house in England.

In Castle Square there is a faithfully restored timbered building of the 16th cent. which is now the premises of the Westminster and National Provincial Bank.

The Cardinal's Hat, probably named in compliment to Cardinal Wolsey, who was Bishop of Lincoln in 1514, is another attractive, timber-framed building leading off The Strait in company with others similarly restored. Some 300 yds from here stands the imposing 15th- and 16th-cent. Stonebow Gateway of which the upper story accommodates the city Guildhall. The wide central archway in massive stonework carries on the south face canopied statues of St Mary and the Archangel Gabriel. Over the arch are the arms of James I. On the battlemented roof the mote bell, dated 1387, is still rung to summon council meetings. It is believed to be the oldest mote bell in Britain. In the Guildhall itself is Lincoln's magnificent collection of civic insignia, which includes the sword given by Richard II in 1387, Henry VII's sword, believed to have been presented after a victory over the Earl of Lincoln in 1487, and the blade of a sword presented by Charles I in 1642.

Other monuments to Lincoln's ancient story include Greyfriars, a fine medieval building now altered for use as the City and County Museum. This was originally a two-story church, dating from the 13th cent., which in 1574, some 40 years after the suppression of the monasteries, became a free school. The building is the earliest church of the Franciscan order now surviving in England. A further continuous link across the years is provided by the Newport Arch, already mentioned here, which exists as the only Roman gateway in Britain still used by traffic. There is also evidence in the prison chapel of the castle that man's inhumanity to man persisted well into the 19th cent. This is part of the debtors' prison built by John Carr of YORK, where the worshippers were ordered in one at a time and compelled to occupy narrow enclosed pews, which prevented them from seeing their companions, made standing impossible, and afforded only a view of the preacher in his pulpit high above the floor. A more pleasing reminder of the last century is the great bronze statue of the Lincolnshire poet, Alfred, Lord Tennyson, sculptured by his friend G. F. Watts and set in the lawns of Minster Green in 1905.

The most modern repository for Lincoln's treasures is the Usher Art Gallery, on the Lindum Road, which was given to the city by James Ward Usher in the fulfilment of his promise, made in 1916, that a gallery to house his gift of precious jewels, watches and miniatures would belong to his birthplace for ever.

Lincoln Cathedral is the third largest in England, exceeded only by York Minster and St Paul's. Its area is about 57,000 sq. ft. In 1072 William the Conqueror appointed Bishop Remigius to the vast diocese sweeping from the Humber in the north to the Thames, and directed him to build a new cathedral commensurate with the importance of the area. By 1092 the work was done, and a great church some 325 ft long dominated the crown of Lincoln hill. A disastrous fire in 1141 resulted in major restorations being carried out by the third bishop, Alexander the Magnificent, who greatly enriched the stonework and added to the height of the existing west towers. More changes were to follow, for in 1185 an earthquake devastated the structural bulk of the cathedral. A year later a Carthusian monk, Hugh of Avalon, became bishop and it was he who in 1192 began the immense task of rebuilding in Early English style the noble edifice which has endured to this day as the glorious, triple-towered Cathedral Church of St Mary.

The nave, choir and retro-choir are all aisled, each having a triforium and clerestory. The nave belongs to the first half of the 13th cent. and contains a rare black mid-12th-cent. font in Tournai marble. St Hugh's Choir, named after the founder, is remarkable for the profusion of pinnacles and wealth of carved misericords in its 14th-cent. choir stalls. The shrine of St Hugh is housed in the retro-choir, or Angel Choir, which is a supremely beautiful monument of English Geometrical Decorated work. The splendid east window, judged the finest of its period, is filled now with 19th-cent. glass, but the windows east of the aisles delight with a medley of brilliant 13th-cent. figure glass. Shining into the great transept are the two Eyes of the cathedral, the Dean's Eye at the north end, a rose window containing vividly coloured glass made for it between 1200 and 1220, and the Bishop's Eye at the south end, containing a mosaic of ancient fragments assembled in the 18th cent. Another important feature of Lincoln Cathedral is the arcade designed by Sir Christopher Wren in 1674, the year in which he began the rebuilding of St Paul's in London. Above this is Wren's library, in which are kept first editions of *Paradise Lost, Don Quixote* and part of Spenser's *Faerie Queene*. Two more valuable possessions, now removed from the library to one of the cathedral chapels in the north choir aisle, are William of Normandy's charter for the transfer of the see from Dorchester in Oxfordshire to Lincoln and the finest of four contemporary copies of the Magna Carta still extant. This is the only part of the cathedral for which an admission charge is made.

Modern Lincoln owes its prosperity to the many technological advancements of the engineering industry. A consequence of the great agricultural wealth of the countryside was the mechanization of farm implements in the middle of the last century. This was followed by a diversification into engineering manufacture for general use. Today the city of Lincoln provides employment for some thousands of people in heavy industry while still retaining the character and tone of a long and noble past.

LITTLEBOROUGH, *Nottinghamshire* (13–SK8282). In this tiny village looking across the Trent to Lincolnshire is one of the smallest Norman churches in the county. It is aisleless, with large areas of herringbone masonry, a nave 24 ft long and a chancel barely 13 ft. A few Roman tiles appear in the stonework, and in the drought of 1933 when the river was very low the stone-paved ford made in Hadrian's time was revealed. Harold crossed here with his army on their way to HASTINGS. The ford is said to be the oldest in England, used since Roman days without a break, now almost abandoned. Roman finds have been made at various times, including the perfectly preserved body of a young woman wearing a garment fastened with a Roman brooch. It was dug up in the graveyard and crumbled to dust immediately. It is assumed from these finds that this was the site of the Roman station known as Segelocum, through which ran their road, still known as Tillbridge Lane.

LLANYBLODWEL, *Shropshire* (8–SJ2322). This tiny village, with a Welsh name and within hailing distance of Wales, is wholly English in appearance: a handful of old cottages scattered on the hillside above a swift-running river, a hump-backed stone bridge, a 16th-cent. black-and-white inn and, among the trees, one of the strangest churches in the country.

The early history of the Church of St Michael the Archangel is obscure, although there are traces of its Norman origins. But the present building, inside and out, is largely the work of one of its vicars, the remarkable Rev. John Parker, incumbent from 1845 to 1860, who, had he not gone into the Church, would undoubtedly have made his name as architect, church furnisher or artist. During his years at Llanyblodwel he transformed the church, drawing up the plans, carrying out some of the work himself, and footing a substantial part of the bill. His great work may appal some and amuse others. Certainly his church is unique, especially its strange tower and spire, looking like a moon-rocket ready on its pad. Almost detached from the rest of the church, the structure is 104 ft high with a slightly swelling outline to midway and no break at all between tower and spire. Octagonal in shape, it cost £1,529 13s. 10d. – and much anxiety to the masons – to build.

There is plenty of evidence inside the church of the vicar's eccentric approach to his self-imposed task: the most obvious are the meticulously painted texts which cover almost every available blank piece of wall. One thing he left was the battered south door dated 1713; and another is the portion of a 14th-cent. tombstone, in the porch, on which is carved the figure of a running hare being chased by a greyhound (only the head of the latter is there).

LLANYMYNECH, *Shropshire* (8–SJ2620). Half in England, half in Wales – the border runs through the Lion Hotel – this large village, 6 m. S. of OSWESTRY, lies beneath the cliffs of Llanymynech Hill. The hill is honeycombed with the shafts and galleries of the Roman mine workings which once produced copper, silver, zinc, lead and limestone. In 1965 a party of schoolboys exploring one of the shafts known as Ogof's Hole found a hoard of 33 silver Roman denarii which are now on display in Oswestry Library.

From the top of the cliffs, which from a distance look like castle walls, there are magnificent views in all directions. The 8th-cent **Offa's Dyke** and the subsidiary and less well-known **Wat's Dyke** can be seen, and to the S. a wide view across the lovely Vyrnwy valley to the Breidden Hills where Caractacus is said to have gathered his tribesmen for the last stand against the Romans. On the hills, too, can be seen the monument the farmers of Shropshire and Montgomeryshire erected to Admiral Rodney, said to be a tribute to the famous admiral for buying timber from the area.

LONGDON-UPON-TERN, *Shropshire* (8–SJ6215). It was in this small village in 1794 that Thomas Telford built the first cast-iron aqueduct, to carry the Shropshire Union Canal over the River Tern. Like a long, narrow, straight-sided iron bath, raised on four arches, the aqueduct is still in use today.

LOPPINGTON, *Shropshire* (8–SJ4629). This small village 3 m. W. of WEM has one most unusual claim to fame: in front of the Dickin Arms is preserved the only bull ring still in existence in Shropshire.

LOUGHBOROUGH, *Leicestershire* (10–SK 5319). The second largest town in the county, which became the only borough in 1888, Loughborough was an ancient hamlet long before the Romans came, or the Danes sailed up the River Soar to plunder, burn, and then to settle. A tour should start in the Market Place, the centre of the town's life and of its street system. The Thursday market has been in existence since the right was granted in 1206 by Hugh Despenser, who had inherited the hamlet by marriage from Hugh Lopes, Earl of Chester, who in turn had been given it by William I. The town hall is the only building of interest here, built in 1855, with a kind of double bellcot.

From the Market Place go by Church Gate, past the Baptist Chapel, to the large and prosperous Parish Church of All Saints. Very much restored by Scott in a manner almost obliterating its 14th-cent. origins, the church contains in its 100-ft, 500-year-old bell-tower some of the bells the famous John Taylor came from OXFORD to recast. He liked Loughborough so much that he stayed to set up in 1840 the foundry in Cherry Orchard now renowned all over the world. This foundry also cast Great Paul of ST PAUL'S CATHEDRAL, the biggest bell that rings in England. The Taylor memorials are in the lower chamber of All Saints', and the *Book of the Taylor Foundry* is preserved in a glass case on the south wall. On Easter morning in 1909 ten ringers took part in a feat of pealing, starting at 8 a.m. and, not stopping to eat, ringing 18,027 "Stedman Caters" in just over 12 hours.

The organ case was carved by a Belgian refugee who received hospitality in Loughborough during the First World War, and in the outer south aisle is the Burton Chapel, the memorial to Thomas Burton, the town's most notable benefactor. In this chapel is also a splendid alabaster altar table with early-18th-cent. wrought-iron legs. Thomas Burton, a prosperous wool-merchant, died in 1496, the money he left being used to found a grammar school. A new school has risen on the foundations of the old one just W. of the Leicester Road but the leafy Burton Walks are still there.

From All Saints' return to the Market Place and take the stretch called Devonshire Square to little Queen's Park where the war memorial contains one of the finest carillons in the country, set up in a tower 151 ft high, from which was made the first broadcast of bell music. The climb to the top is by 138 steps, past a small museum. Forty-seven bells hang in the chamber, the heaviest weighing over 4 tons and the smallest 20 lb., all made at the Taylor foundry.

Along the Ashby Road S. out of Loughborough are the colleges that arose over the last generation: the University of Technology, given its charter in 1966; the largest training colleges in the country; a college of art and a technical college; a students' village; a campus with an all-weather recreation area; and the modern Loughborough College Grammar School.

From 1400 to 1600 the town was an important centre of the wool trade. In the 1700s it was famous for its maltings. 1800 introduced the worsted hosiery trade with some 6,000 persons clattering away on their stocking frames and, the legs of both sexes being worthy of adornment, seldom working (according to a writer of the time) less than three days a week and earning the princely sum of 15s. doing it. In 1809 Mr John Heathcote brought the lace bobbin here but the Luddites, led by the half-witted Ned Lud, stormed and burned his factory in 1816, destroying 53 bobbin-net machines worth £6,000 in half an hour. So disgusted was Mr Heathcote that he moved his works to TIVERTON in Devon. Now Loughborough is a thriving industrial town full of young and enterprising firms with famous names.

We must not leave without mentioning one of the sons of which it is most proud, the Cavalier poet, John Cleveland, son of a Loughborough schoolmaster, scholarly, witty, one of the most ardent and outspoken supporters of the Royalist cause. In those days his name would sell almost anything, but his writings are too topical to be appreciated nowadays except by keen students of his time. He died in 1658 almost on the eve of the Restoration.

LOUTH, *Lincolnshire* (13–TF3287). Louth is an old market town, deriving its name from the River Lud, near the wooded gorge of Hubbards Hill. Although Roman and Anglo-Saxon remains have been found in the area the main interest concentrates on the spacious Perpendicular Church of St James, a splendid example of late Gothic design, rising to the height of 300 ft. The building was completed in 1441 and the spire added between 1501 and 1515. Twenty-one years later the sermon which incited the Pilgrimage of Grace, in which 20,000 Lincolnshire men took up arms in defence of the monasteries, was preached from the pulpit. Henry VIII was quick to suppress this well-meaning rebellion, describing the townsfolk in his reply to their petitions as the "rude commons of one shire, and that, one of the most brutal and beestlie of the whole realm". The vicar and more than 60 other men from Louth, and as many more from surrounding parts of the country were hanged at Tyburn. The fine Cistercian abbey which inspired the Lincolnshire rising was built by the monks at the instigation of Bishop Alexander of Lincoln in 1139. It flourished until the Black Death almost wiped out the inmates, and was finally destroyed shortly after the Dissolution. All that may be seen today are two gaunt fragments of chancel wall and a maze of mounds and dykes.

The exterior of St James's Church is impressive for its lofty windows, its brave array of battlements, and the east gable with a pierced parapet surmounted by a cross. The tower and crocketed spire are almost equal in height and completely in harmony. Inside there is an interesting modern font in alabaster, and in the north aisle an early-15th-cent. font with a buttressed stem enriched with traceried panels.

Louth is and has been for centuries the busiest cattle market in Lincolnshire, but now in addition to local industries, which include the manufacture of farm implements, plastic sheeting, and packaging materials, a huge malt-silo has been constructed at Newbridge Hill.

LUDLOW, *Shropshire* (8–SO5175). Few towns in England have more to show for their history than Ludlow. The most spectacular approach to the town is from the W., along the small road from Wigmore, over Mary Knoll which rises to about 900 ft. For the last mile or so the road drops sharply to show Ludlow spread over its own hill below, a view that is beautiful in clear weather and magical in the mist.

Anglo-Saxon coins unearthed here indicate that the defensive assets of the rising ground partly circled by the Rivers Teme and Corve had been recognized long before Roger Montgomery, Earl of Shrewsbury and Arundel, arrived here in 1085 and built his massive castle. Some authorities attribute its building to Roger de Lacy, one of Montgomery's chief henchmen, but whoever occupied it during its early years was as likely to have had to contend with fellow-Normans as with the marauding Welsh against whom it was built. Today much of it still stands and the visitor tours a fortress seen by Edward IV; the so-called Princes in the Tower; Catherine of Aragon, when a young bride; Henry VIII's brother, Prince Arthur, who died here; Sir Philip Sidney; John Milton, whose *Comus* was first performed here in 1634; and a host of other great figures.

The castle is impressively large. The outer bailey is as big as a cricket ground. The inner bailey is large enough to house actors and audience for the performance of a Shakespeare play during the annual Ludlow Summer Festival.

Ludlow: a misericord in the church choir

A. F. Kersting

Within the inner bailey is the most unusual part of the castle: the circular nave of the Norman chapel.

The tower of the Parish Church of St Laurence at 135 ft stands higher than the castle. This is one of the largest parish churches in England with almost cathedral-like proportions. There are earlier fragments but substantially the church is 15th-cent. Interesting and historic features abound, notably the misericords in the choir. The east window in the chancel, 30 ft high by 18 ft wide, depicts the life, history and miracles of the patron saint in 27 separate scenes containing about 300 figures.

The finest thoroughfare in Ludlow is Broad Street where every building dates from the 14th or 15th cents. It climbs from the sturdy, hump-backed stone Ludford Bridge, through Broad Gate, the only remaining gateway in the original town walls, past the black-and-white timbered front of the Angel Hotel, where Nelson was once a guest, to end at the Butter Cross.

Near the church are two buildings of unusual interest. In the churchyard itself is the Reader's House – formerly the Church House. It is part-medieval, part-Tudor and has a very fine three-story Jacobean porch. It is believed that Mary Tudor was imprisoned here for some time. The plaster ceilings are adorned with floral emblems.

Tucked into a courtyard off Church Street is the Rose and Crown, first licensed in the 16th cent. Another hostelry, known to travellers from many parts of the world, is the Feathers Hotel in the Bull Ring, one of the best examples of 17th-cent. half-timbered work in England – and standing now firmly, but far from straight and true. It is believed the entrance door is the original one – more than 300 years old; in the centre of the dining-room ceiling is an embossed copy of the arms of James I, surrounded by thistles, acorns and grapes.

Ludlow is an admirable centre from which to explore south Shropshire: the Clee Hills are only a short journey to the E., Wenlock Edge and the Corve valley to the N., and the Long Mynd country to the NW.

LUTTERWORTH, *Leicestershire* (10–SP54 84). This large village rises steeply from the foot of its pretty 18th-cent. bridge. On the horizon is the church made famous by Canon John Wycliffe, the 14th-cent. religious reformer.

Here Wycliffe lived in semi-retirement for 20 years while he was translating the Bible from Latin into English. Thirty years after his death his writings were condemned and his body was disinterred, burned, and thrown into the River Swift.

The Parish Church of St Mary, towering over grazing land, was ancient even before Wycliffe arrived. There are traces of 13th-cent. work in the chancel and tower; the clerestory and nave roof festooned with coloured, shield-bearing figures are 500 years old. In 1712 the tower crashed down in a storm and one of the stones which fell is preserved in the church; a rather insipid Wycliffe memorial in white marble dated 1837 hangs under the east window of the south aisle; some brasses to John Fielding, 1403, and his wife, 1418, are in the north-east corner, and, due to the fame John Wycliffe finally achieved many years after his death, St Mary's also contains a number of alleged but spurious "relics", which one feels are hardly in keeping with his teachings against the usury of monies from pilgrims. Amid Gilbert Scott's ubiquitous restorations two other things of interest have also been left. Above the chancel arch is a 14th-cent. doom-painting of agitated white figures rising from their tombs and trying to make their way up to Christ, who is seated on a rainbow resting on the sun and moon, and attended by trumpet-blowing angels. In the north aisle is another painting of the same period which, it is suggested, represents Richard II with his queen and John of Gaunt. It is more likely, according to experts, to picture a favourite 14th-cent. subject of three dead and three living kings – a representation of a royal hunting party faced with three crowned skeletons urging them to repent.

There are some pretty, timber-framed, thatched cottages, in particular a 17th-cent. one in Bell Street, and The Terrace contains a dignified building, c. 1840, which marks the end of good construction in Leicestershire for some considerable time thereafter.

LYDBURY NORTH, *Shropshire* (8–SO3486), lies almost in the centre of a wide, flat-bottomed valley 4 m. SE. of BISHOP'S CASTLE. The square tower of the Norman church, large for a village of this size, dominates the village. The heavy door, in an impressive porch, swings on strap hinges 500 years old, and is bullet-scarred. Inside, there is much rich wood-carving: the pulpit is dated 1624; the screen to the north chapel, the Plowden Chapel, is a century older; the altar rails are 17th-cent.; and the rare wooden, baluster-shaped candlesticks are dated 1640. Above the rood-screen are painted the Creed and the Commandments and the date, 1615.

Lydbury North has long connections with its two famous houses, Walcot 1 m. to the S. and Plowden Hall 2 m. to the E. A fine view of the timber-framed Plowden Hall, built in the days of Elizabeth I for the notable lawyer, Edmund Plowden, and still in the same family, can be had from the road to Plowden village. Walcot, occasionally open to view, is a large brick mansion, built for Clive of India in the latter half of the 18th cent. It looks down over fine grounds to a large lake where Canada geese can sometimes be seen.

Snowdrops grow thickly around Lydbury North, especially in the lane which climbs N. out of the village to join the curiously named Stank Lane, more than 900 ft up. From here the view stretches W. to the Welsh hills, S. to Clunton Hill and SW. to Bury Ditches, an ancient British camp.

LYDDINGTON, *Rutland* (10–SP8797), lying entirely along one street, is a place to be explored in leisurely fashion on foot if one wants to see what English builders at their best could do in the days from Elizabeth I onwards. Several cottages carry date-stones and it is possible to study the change from Jacobean mullioned windows and straight hoods to the classical style.

The bishops of Lincoln had a stopping-place here in the time of King John, since it lay on the lines of travel over their vast diocese which stretched from the Humber to the Thames. The present Bede House was built by Bishop Russell as an episcopal residence in the late 15th cent. and is a good example of its period. The great hall, with its carved cornice, oriel window, and open fireplace, is particularly worth seeing. In 1547 the bishop was forced to surrender the manor to Henry VIII. It then passed in Elizabeth's time to Lord Burleigh. In 1602 Thomas Cecil, Earl of Exeter, converted it into an almshouse. Hence its name, since Bede derives from "biddan" – to pray; for people receiving charity were bound to pray for those who advanced it to them. At the southwest angle of the precinct is a watch-tower built over the village street, known as The Bishop's Eye, and in a field NE. of the church are trenches which were once the bishops' fish-ponds.

The parish church is mainly Perpendicular of the late 15th cent., though the tower and chancel are part of an older building erected about 1320–40. Particularly interesting are the earthenware jars built into the walls, with their openings towards the chancel – a primitive type of acoustic.

MABLETHORPE, *Lincolnshire* (13–TF5085). The principal attraction of this small holiday resort a few miles N. of SKEGNESS is the invigorating sea air sweeping in from the E. For this reason, and because the new groynes costing nearly £2 million have provided a splendid beach of firm, golden sand, the combined watering-places of Mablethorpe and **Sutton on Sea** are especially good for children throughout the season. In addition the 11-acre Queens Park offers facilities for bowling, tennis, putting, a second boating lake, a children's pool and an adequate car park.

Like many other little townships of Lincolnshire its roots go back to medieval times. The only church surviving the onslaught of the sea is St Mary's, a rather squat building with a steep pitched roof which is higher than the tower. The south doorway and the nave arcades are 13th-cent., but the main fabric dates chiefly from 1714. Among other medieval relics is a 14th-cent. tomb with a broken helmet hanging above it, said to be that of a knight slain in a duel at Earl's Bridge 2 m. away. His opponent also died in the encounter and is similarly represented by a stone figure in the church at **Maltby-le-Marsh** nearby.

MANIFOLD VALLEY, THE, *Staffordshire* (12–SK1154). This valley, which starts near ILAM, is for its first few miles an area of gentle countryside with sloping fields on either bank. But from about halfway up the valley its scenery becomes almost as impressive and dramatic as that of its neighbour the Dove. Beeston Tor, a forbidding precipice, is the equal of any rock formation in DOVEDALE; the caves in the Tor have yielded interesting Roman pottery and Anglo-Saxon coins. Animal remains found there, including the teeth of a brown bear and of a hyena, are now in BUXTON museum. Further up the Manifold is Thor's Cave which is entered through an arch almost 40 ft high. The River Manifold, and the River Hamps which flows into it a little below Thor's Cave, disappear underground in dry weather. Their waters fall away through a stretch where the bed is porous to flow underground before re-appearing on the surface in the grounds of Ilam Hall – a phenomenon which the ever-sceptical Dr Samuel Johnson refused to believe until he had tested it with marked corks.

MANSFIELD, *Nottinghamshire* (13–SK5361). Now one of the most important industrial centres in the North Midlands, Mansfield was once a place of only a few thousand inhabitants in the heart of SHERWOOD FOREST. It was the home of a community from earliest times, however, as is proved by the number of remarkable cliff dwellings hewn out of the sandstone in Southwell Road. These are known as the Rock Houses and were fully inhabited in the 1860s, the last tenant leaving in the early years of the present century. Coins found dating from the times of Vespasian, Constantine, Marcus Aurelius and later emperors and the remains of a villa in the adjoining mining village of **Mansfield Woodhouse**, pinpoint the area as a Roman settlement. During the Anglo-Saxon heptarchy the city was a temporary residence for the Mercian kings. In the time of Edward the Confessor it was a royal manor, and remained one until Stephen de Blois granted it to the Earl of Chester. Henry VIII gave it to the Duke of Norfolk as a reward for his gallantry at Flodden Field. It then reverted to the crown until the reign of Elizabeth, when it was held by the Earl of Shrewsbury. In 1631 it was owned by William Cavendish, Earl of Newcastle, from whose family it passed to the Dukes of Portland.

One of the earliest of Mansfield notables was John Cockle, known as the Miller of Mansfield, who entertained Henry II after finding him lost in the woods, and, not realizing who his guest was, served him a great pasty stuffed with venison poached from the king's own forests. Mansfield was also the birthplace of Archbishop Sterne, who was present at the scaffold when William Laud was executed and was the grandfather of Laurence Sterne, author of *Tristram Shandy*. Another famous man born in Mansfield, in 1704, was Robert Dodsley, who ran away to London to become a footman. In 1732 he produced a book of poems called *A Muse In Livery*, which brought him to the notice of Alexander Pope. Pope helped him to produce a play, *The Toy Shop*, a great success at COVENT GARDEN. With his profits Dodsley opened a bookshop, and in 1738 he published *London*, which he had bought for

£10 from an unknown author called Samuel Johnson. The two became great friends and it was Dodsley who suggested to Johnson the scheme of the English Dictionary. Finally Dodsley became one of the greatest of the 18th-cent. publishers, bringing out works by Pope, Goldsmith, Horace Walpole, and Sterne.

The prosperity of modern Mansfield, standing amid the remains of the Dukeries, rests principally on the coal lying under its surface. No collieries are in the town itself, but many of the 55,000 inhabitants are employed in the ones nearby. Mansfield is famous, too, for its hosiery manufacture, footwear and "cotton doubling" – a twisting together of several threads of cotton yarn to make lace, net and quality cloths.

In the middle of the town rise the high arches of the railway viaduct, cutting off the market place from the Parish Church of St Peter. This church has an exceptional Norman steeple but the main impression is 14th-cent. The Church of St Mark in Nottingham Road is worth a visit, since it is one of the best Victorian churches, built in 1897 by Temple Moore. The market place Moot Hall was given to Mansfield by the lady of the manor, the Countess of Oxford of WELBECK ABBEY, in 1752. In 1836 a neo-Classical town hall was added and later still a huge memorial was erected to Lord George Frederick Cavendish Bentinck, son of the 4th Duke of Portland, whose biography was written by Disraeli.

About 1 m. away, on the secondary road to SOUTHWELL, is the enclosure containing the grave of Charles Thompson, who endowed Brunt's School in Mansfield. He became rich in Europe and the East, but after the shock of seeing Lisbon destroyed in the earthquake of 1755 he returned and settled in his home town. He was buried in 1784 in the grave he had chosen because the place reminded him of the spot where he had been standing when he witnessed the appalling spectacle in Portugal.

MARKET BOSWORTH, *Leicestershire* (10–SK4003), was an important market town in the Middle Ages but is now a quiet place, more village than town. It is well worth exploring since it has some pretty thatched cottages and a famous Hall and school. For about 300 years Market Bosworth was associated with the Dixie family, the first of whom, Sir Wolstan Dixie, bought the Hall with the fortune he had inherited from his namesake who was Lord Mayor of London in the time of Elizabeth I. In 1601 he refounded the Tudor grammar school in the market place. There young Samuel Johnson – uncouth, shabby and sullen – taught as second master, or usher, and officiated as a kind of domestic chaplain to Sir Wolstan and said grace at his table. Boswell says of him at this time: "the dull sameness of his existance . . . was as unvaried as the note of a cuckow: and he did not know whether it was more disagreeable for him to teach, or the boys to learn, the grammar rules." The Hall is a fine piece of English Renaissance of the time of Queen Anne, very much like HAMPTON

COURT, in red brick and white stone. The mainly 14th- and 15th-cent. Church of St Peter is set amid trees and has many memorials to the Dixie family and a lovely peal of bells.

Market Bosworth is associated with the Battle of Bosworth, which ended the Wars of the Roses on 22 August 1485, but the battle actually took place on Redmoor Plain between **Shenton,** SUTTON CHENEY and STOKE GOLDING. Alongside Shenton station is a farm-house, behind which is King Dick's Well on Ambien Hill protected by a little wall. Here it is said King Richard took his last drink before going into battle with his crown over his visor, crying "I live a king: if I die, I die a king." At the Sutton Cheney end of Bosworth Park is a spinney called King Dick's Clump where Richard is supposed to have raised his standard for the last time. Near it is the site of the Duke of Norfolk's camp, still known as Dickon's Nook after the note the duke found affixed to his tent, warning him: "Jack of Norfolk, be not too bold! For Dickon, thy master, is bought and sold!" And near Stoke Golding is Crown Hill, the traditional site of the "coronation" of Henry Tudor, when Sir Reginald Bray is said to have found the crown fallen from the dead Richard's head in a thorn bush and to have placed it over the helmet of the new king.

About 2 m. S. on the A447 is the little village of **Cadeby,** once considered to be the perfect village and easily passed unseen amid its trees. On the secondary road N. from the centre of Market Bosworth is the oddly named **Barton-in-the-Beans,** a reminder of Roman times when the land was cultivated exclusively for beans, a staple food. And about 8 m. E. on the B582 is the castle of **Kirby Muxloe,** which was built by Lord Hastings, who obtained "licence to crenellate" in 1472. The building of the moated "fortified home" was begun in 1480 but was brought rapidly to a close in 1484 following the execution of Lord Hastings in London the previous summer. It is open to the public all the year round.

MARKET DRAYTON, *Shropshire* (8–SJ67 34), is an attractive old town, famous as the birthplace of Robert Clive – Clive of India. He was a pupil at the Grammar School, founded in 1558, and his desk bearing the carved initials R.C. is still preserved. Clive, so the story goes, also has a connection with the fine parish church, St Mary's: he is reputed to have climbed the lofty tower and perched on one of the gargoyles. The church is mainly of 14th-cent. origin but has a Norman doorway.

A market has been held in the High Street every Wednesday since Edward I granted the charter to hold one almost 700 years ago. There are many black-and-white buildings and others dating from the 17th and 18th cents., including the Butter Market, the Crown Hotel, Sandbrook's Vaults, the Red House and the Star Hotel.

Market Drayton also possesses a fine modern amenity, the Shropshire Lido which contains a swimming-bath 165 ft long and 50 ft wide.

MARKET HARBOROUGH, *Leicestershire* (10–SP7387). Market Harborough was first mentioned as a place of commerce in 1203, but was created by Henry II long before especially to be a market. Visitors should make straight for the Square, a most pleasing triangular piece of townscape with the steeple of the fine church – a rare dedication to St Dionysius – forming the focal point. This church started as a "chapel of ease" to **Great Bowden**, about 4 m. N., which originally owned Market Harborough, so it has no protecting churchyard and looks almost Continental. The steeple is one of the finest in England, Decorated, with a tower of singular beauty covered with a broach spire and in contrast the building and interior are a little disappointing. Local tradition ascribes St Dionysius, of early-13th-cent. origin, to John of Gaunt, but the Decorated work is earlier and the Perpendicular later than his time. The church bells are rung every November to commemorate the rescue of a merchant lost on the Welland marshes in 1500 and the ringers receive "one shilling for beer".

Just S. of the church is the charming half-timbered and gabled old grammar school founded by Robert Smythe in 1613, which is supported on wooden pillars with a freeway beneath. Under these cool arches was once the butter market, but now both the school-children and the market women have gone. Many of the lovely old houses around the market and the High Street are now shops, but none the worse for that.

Market Harborough is famous now for its Fernie Hunt and owes much of its present prosperity to the Symington family and their red-brick Victorian factory behind the church – where liberty bodices were founded, but now concentrating on soups and groceries. It was historically important, however, as the headquarters of the Royalist army on the eve of their defeat at the Battle of NASEBY in 1645. Charles I returned here twice, once in disguise to join the Scots, and again when they had failed and he was a prisoner on his way back to London.

The largest inn here, the Three Swans, was immortalized in Whyte-Melville's great Victorian hunting novel, *Market Harborough*, and it still has one of the most beautiful and famous wrought-iron signs in England, dating from the 18th cent.

About 4 m. N. of Market Harborough on the A6 and 1 m. W. up the secondary road is tiny **Foxton** where an impressive system of ten locks conveys gaily-painted narrow boats, small barges and motor craft uphill from the Grand Junction Canal to the Market Harborough Basin. At weekends in the summer these locks are crowded with spectators helping to man the gates or just watching other people at work.

MARKET OVERTON, *Rutland* (10–SK8816). Situated high on a limestone plateau and commanding extensive views, Overton is a place of great antiquity, which had a market as early as 1200. The Church of SS. Peter and Paul stands within the remains of Roman earthworks, and

some remarkable finds of the early Anglo-Saxon period have also been made since the beginning of ironstone working here in 1906. Gold, bronze and silver ornaments from A.D. 600 are now in the County Museum at OAKHAM, proving that there was a flourishing community here in the late pagan period maintaining contacts, probably along Ermine Street, with the rest of England and thence with the Continent, mainly south Germany.

The church is mainly 14th-cent. but the tower-arch is pre-Conquest – 10th-cent., the only work in Rutland of this date. A stile in the churchyard is set between two Anglo-Saxon baluster shafts, once part of the ancient belfry. Under a group of trees on the village green are the stocks and whipping post still in use when Sir Isaac Newton, whose mother came from Market Overton, was a little boy living in the village with his grandmother, after his mother had married again.

On a corner of the church tower is a sundial said to have been presented by the family of Sir Isaac, who was born six months after his father died and was so small his mother used to say that she could have cradled him in a quart mug.

Market Overton Hall is Early Georgian and there are many attractive houses and cottages surrounding it.

There is a delightful rural walk SW. to **Ashwell**, which takes its name from the ash-lined stream nearby, and then W. to WHISSENDINE.

MATLOCKS, THE, *Derbyshire* (12–SK3060). The Matlocks are usually taken to include Matlock Bath and Matlock itself, which consist of the chain of small towns running N. to S. down the lovely, wooded Derwent valley. Known as the area of a thousand views, and one of the gateways to the Derbyshire Dales, the Matlocks typify Derbyshire scenery at its best: a combination of river valley, steep-sided, wooded hills, and the occasional dramatic limestone crag and peak. Happily, there is a network of paths which enable the visitor to explore this countryside and to find his own favourite views.

Matlock Bath became renowned during the 19th cent. for its thermal waters which maintain a constant temperature all the year round. At the Grand Pavilion a music festival is held each year in June; motor-boat trips start from the landing-stage alongside it, and rowing boats can be hired. Between the Pavilion and the river lie the charming Derwent Gardens and opposite them, on the other bank, the so-called Lovers' Walks. Coloured lights illuminate the gardens and the walks during September. The thermal waters here are the cause of several unusual features: in the Fish Pond adjoining the Grand Pavilion can be seen rare and many-coloured fish; the growth in the pools and grottoes in Derwent Gardens contain particularly lush vegetation; there are the famous Petrifying Wells, one of Nature's curiosities; and the thermal springs also produce a material known as tufa which looks like a rocky sponge.

Opposite the Pavilion are the famous Heights

of Abraham, given their name by an officer who fought with General Wolfe at Quebec and likened Matlock Bath's eminence to the plateau on which the battle took place. On the Heights stands the Victoria Prospect Tower, right on the crest, offering views over the whole area. In the grounds, too, are two caverns, Rutland and Masson, which can be explored; both were once worked by the Romans for lead and offer the newcomer an easy initiation into caving. In Matlock Dale, just N. of Matlock Bath, rises the impressive peak of High Tor. Paths provide an easy climb to the top of the Tor which gives views of the 1,100 ft Masson Hill and the gorge below.

Further up the valley, Matlock Dale gives way to Matlock town itself and here are the Hall Leys, pleasure gardens where there are facilities for many outdoor sports and a recreation ground for children. Here, too, is Riber Castle, the most famous landmark in the Matlocks. This, despite its battlements and turrets, is not truly a castle. It was built in the mid-19th cent. for Mr John Smedley, a local textile manufacturer who was the man who developed Matlock as a spa. For a number of years the castle, perched 800 ft up, was a school but between 1930 and 1950 it fell into ruins. In 1962, however, a group of zoologists acquired the ruin and its grounds and established there a zoo for British and European animals which is open to the public. Smedley's former Hydro now houses the County Council offices.

In the northern end of Matlock is the Lido with two pools, one covered and one open-air, and only a walk away is the famous Wishing Stone in Lumsdale. You may not get your wish granted but you will have the pleasure of one of the best of Matlock's thousand views.

MAYFIELD, *Staffordshire* (9–SK 1545). This old village hugs the western bank of the Dove and is linked to Derbyshire by the Hanging Bridge. It is said that on this bridge, in 1745, a number of Scottish rebels were hanged after the Jacobite rebellion of that year, but the name of the bridge is known to 'date from much earlier times. Charles Edward Stuart, the Young Pretender, had reached DERBY by December 1745 when he was turned back by the superior forces of the Duke of Cumberland. Evidence of the skirmish that must have taken place in Mayfield in that winter of 1745 can still be seen in the bullet-scarred door of the parish church.

Moore Cottage, now a farm-house, at Upper Mayfield is where Thomas Moore lived for four years in the early part of the 19th cent. and wrote his most famous work, *Lalla Rookh*. Buried in Mayfield churchyard is Moore's baby daughter, Olivia. It is believed that her tragic death was in his mind when he wrote the second verse of his famous poem, "Those Evening Bells":

> Those joyous hours are passed away
> And many a heart that then was gay
> Within the tomb now darkly dwells
> And hears no more those evening bells.

The bells are undoubtedly those of St Oswald's Church, ASHBOURNE, only a mile or so across the river.

The Hanging Bridge itself is a bridge within a bridge: the original 14th-cent. arches, grey stone and pointed, can still be seen inset into the wider bridge which was rebuilt in 1936.

MELANDRA CASTLE, *Derbyshire* (12–SK 0394). This was the most northerly of the three Roman forts in Derbyshire – and lying as it does about 1 m. WNW. of Glossop, it is only just inside the county boundary. The fort measures 130 yds long by 120 yds wide and covers an area of 2 acres. Excavations by members of the Derbyshire Archaeological Society have revealed the foundations of the corner towers and the guardrooms. Some finds, including Roman bricks and sherds, can be seen in BUXTON Museum.

MELBOURNE, *Derbyshire* (13–SK 3825), which takes its name from the mill stream running through it, is a small town about 8 m. S. of DERBY with a direct link with its Australian namesake: Lord Melbourne, Queen Victoria's famous Prime Minister, was born at the Hall in this Derbyshire townlet and the Australian city, then a small settlement, was named after him.

Melbourne Hall, the most charming and homely-looking of Derbyshire's great houses, is as famous for its large, formal gardens as for the house itself. These were thought for some years to have been the work of André Lenôtre, who laid out the gardens at Versailles, but it is now known that they were designed by Henry Wise who was much influenced by Lenôtre. The terraced, sweeping lawns, the lake, the yew hedges and the avenues of limes form a gracious

Melbourne Hall: the "Birdcage" of wrought iron

Country Life

setting for the occasional discreetly placed feature such as the two embracing cherubs, the little lead cupids and the Four Seasons monument. Perhaps the two features which most readily catch the eye are the long yew tunnel, and the so-called Birdcage, a masterpiece in wrought iron, as delicate as a piece of jewellery, made by Robert Bakewell.

The house itself, which is still lived in, can be visited, as can the gardens, during the summer months. There are many delightful rooms, charmingly furnished, and a particularly fine collection of portraits by such artists as Cornelius Janssens, John Hoppner, Sir Peter Lely and Michael Dahl.

St Michael's Church is one of the most impressive Norman churches in the country, with a fine crossing tower and two unusual pyramid-roofed towers at the west end. The inside is dominated by the huge Norman pillars of the nave.

There was an important castle here in the 14th cent., but now only a part of one wall remains.

Melbourne was the birthplace of another well-known Englishman, Thomas Cook of travel-agency fame.

MELTON MOWBRAY, *Leicestershire* (10–SK7518). This world-famous home of pork pies, Stilton cheeses and the Quorn Hunt, where once to be rated a "Tip Top Meltonian" was to rank as a buck of the first water, has the stateliest and most impressive church in all Leicestershire. It is 154 ft long with a tower 100 ft high and is one of only four English parish churches with transepts flanked by aisles. It represents Early English, Decorated and Perpendicular, the last outstandingly evidenced by an amazing clerestory with 48 windows, the tower and bell-story, pinnacles, battlements and quatrefoil frieze. It is cruciform · with eight pinnacles, the bulk of it built between *c.* 1280 and *c.* 1330. There is a beautiful Early English door leading into the nave, with canopied niches on either side. The best view is from the south-west Galilee porch at the west end; very white and clean, it rises over the market town whose buildings are not generally of great consequence.

The one house of distinction is Egerton Lodge, 1829, once the hunting lodge of the Earl of Wilton with lawns sloping down to the river by the bridge, and now the offices of the Urban District Council. There is also a house *c.* 1700 in the Market Place with the upper floor supported and projected over the pavement. Next to the church is the house which it is said Henry VIII gave to Anne of Cleves, together with the manor and parsonage, for as long as she lived in England; but there is no evidence that she ever occupied it. It has a lovely old roof and a three-light window overlooking the churchyard. In the street opposite is the charming Bede House, or Maison Dieu, founded in 1640 by Robert Hudson, who was later created a baronet by Charles II. He endowed it for six old men to whom he left 1*s.* 6*d.* a week. A hundred years ago this was increased to 4*s.* by the Rev. H. Storer, who also provided for six old women.

Those who want to know what Melton was like in its 19th-cent. heyday of "larking", "ragging" and midnight steeplechases, when to be "in the swim" meant at least £1,000 a year spent on hunters alone, and the Quality came from all over the world for the hunting season, should search diligently for the paintings of John Ferneley. A poor Leicester lad born in **Thrussington** nearby, he was charging, and getting, at least £2,000 for his pictures around 1823.

MELVERLEY, *Shropshire* (8–SJ3316), is only just in England, almost where the Rivers Vyrnwy and Severn join, and is chiefly remarkable for its black-and-white church. This is one of only two timber-framed churches in the county: the other is at Halston but has a brick tower. Melverley's church is wood throughout and black and white inside as well as out.

MEOLE BRACE, *Shropshire* (8–SJ4811). The big, sandstone Church of Holy Trinity, with its bold square tower, is imposing enough to catch the eye from the outside. But its real glory is inside. Here is what is reckoned to be some of the finest stained glass in the county, if not further afield, almost all of it made by William Morris and his friend Burne-Jones. Dating from the year after the church itself was built in 1868, many rate it the best example of Morris glass. The three windows glow like jewels and depict the Crucifixion and other biblical scenes including the Garden of Eden, the building of the Temple, the wedding at Cana, the miracle of the loaves and fishes, and the raising of Jairus's daughter.

MORETON CORBET, *Shropshire* (8–SJ5523), is a quiet village now, about 5 m. SW. of Hodnet; but when the famous Shropshire family, the Corbets, lived here, it must have throbbed with life. The village's history is that of the family. In the Church of St Bartholomew, with its Norman chancel, are many memorials to past Corbets including the fine, coloured tomb of Sir Robert and his wife (1513) and, in contrast, a graceful monument to four young Corbet boys, all in different-coloured marbles. Outside, in the churchyard, is a bronze sculpture in memory of 13-year-old Vincent Corbet who died at Eton in 1904.

But perhaps the most striking memorial to the Corbets is the shell of their 17th-cent. castellated mansion which stands near the church, gaunt but still impressive. Begun in 1606 but never finished, it is open to view.

MORLEY, *Derbyshire* (13–SK3941). There is some excellent stained glass in the parish church of this small village about 5 m. NE. of Derby. Much of it came from Darley Abbey at the time of the Dissolution and can now be seen in the north windows in the chancel of St Matthew's Church, a rich reminder of the skill of the medieval craftsmen. The church possesses Norman arcades, a 13th-cent. tower and spire, and much 14th-cent. work.

MOSELEY OLD HALL, *Staffordshire* (8–SJ9304), is where Charles II lay in hiding for two days after his defeat at the Battle of WORCESTER on 3 September 1651, while Parliamentary troops scoured the countryside seeking him. Now in the care of the National Trust, the house, on the edge of CANNOCK CHASE about 4 m. N. of WOLVERHAMPTON, is open to the public.

The king, who had spent the previous night in hiding at BOSCOBEL, came to Moseley Old Hall in the early hours of 8 September. The house was then owned by the Whitgreave family – and it continued in their possession until 1925. Today the visitor can enter the house through the "orchard door" which the king used that night, and retrace his steps up the twisting back staircase to his room. There can still be seen the four-poster bed in which he slept and, leading from this room, the secret hiding place – a cramped recess beside the chimney, only 5 ft long – where the king crouched during the following day when Cromwell's men visited the Hall. The soldiers came to accuse, without justification and, as it turned out, unsuccessfully, the son of the house, Thomas Whitgreave, of fighting with the king at Worcester. They were unaware that the man they really sought lay only yards from them.

At a casual glance the Hall does not appear old enough to have been the scene of this dramatic piece of English history. Originally it was a typical black-and-white, half-timbered Elizabethan building – it was built in 1600. But in 1870, because of its poor state of repair, the whole house was encased in brick and, from the outside, only the gables and the heavy chimneys declare its age. Inside all is still much as it must have been during the king's stay and the garden, too, has been laid out in the style of the 17th cent., using only those plants which were then in cultivation.

MUCH WENLOCK, *Shropshire* (8–SO6199). The changes of the last few centuries have been superficial in this small market town, so it has kept a great deal of its medieval character. The two most scenic approaches are the roads running either side of Wenlock Edge: the B4371 from CHURCH STRETTON along the northern escarpment of the Edge, and the B4368 from Craven Arms up through the lovely Corvedale. There are splendid views from the B4371 where the ground falls away sharply from Wenlock Edge; and a few miles short of Much Wenlock are a string of sizable limestone quarries, still being worked.

Much Wenlock's most famous attraction is its ruined priory. Originally founded as a convent by St Mildburga in the 7th cent., the Danes destroyed it in the late 9th cent. It was rebuilt about 100 years later at the instigation of Lady Godiva, but was razed again by the Normans. The final restoration was begun in 1080 by Roger de Montgomery when it became a Cluniac priory, and it is the remains of this, with subsequent additions, which the visitor can see today. There remain considerable parts of the west front; the walls of the chapter house, one of them with a

Edwin Smith

Much Wenlock: a carving in the priory

remarkable pattern of interlaced Norman arches; the 13th-cent. south transept; parts of the broken columns; a fragment of the monks' lavatory; and pieces of sculpture.

Not far from the priory stands the old Guildhall, black and white, built on the sturdy oak arches of the butter market. It is still in use as a court and also houses the Council Chamber. In the courtroom, over the presiding magistrate's chair, is a curious inscription, dated 1589, in which the nouns in the top line have to be associated with the verbs immediately below them in the bottom line to make sense. The old stocks, on wheels, are preserved.

Parts of the Parish Church of Holy Trinity are Norman but the best of this work is hidden: the Normans added a tower to the west front after the church had been built. There is a 14th-cent. porch with a room built over it which is kept as it was in the days when it served as the deacon's living quarters.

Picturesque houses abound in Much Wenlock. Those in the Bull Ring are notable; also the 15th-cent. house near St Owen's Well which has an archway made of three pairs of oak boughs.

Within striking distance of the town are two more historic houses which are open to the public: the romantic-looking, 16th-cent. stone house, **Benthall Hall,** 4 m. NE., with its fine, original plaster ceiling and unusual carved oak staircase; and **Shipton Hall,** 6 m. SW., an Elizabethan manor house with a beautiful garden. In the district is **Coalbrookdale,** the site of the ironworks where iron was first successfully smelted with coke and a place of great importance in the Industrial Revolution of the late 18th cent.

MUGGINTON, *Derbyshire* (12–SK2843). Here, 7 m. NNW. of DERBY, is a village with a Norman church – and a tiny chapel founded in a manner which must be unique. The story has it that one Francis Brown, a farmer, decided on a moonless night early in the 18th cent. to ride into Derby. He had been drinking and when he finally tracked down his horse in a field and tried to halter it he discovered it had horns. Brown thought that he was trying to halter the Devil and fainted with shock. On recovering – and sobering up – Brown was convinced that the only way he could send the Devil finally packing was to build a chapel – and the present building, enlarged in 1890 and now attached to a farm-house, was the result. It is known as the Halter Devil Chapel. The Parish Church of All Saints had a more orthodox foundation in the early 13th cent. and contains much interesting work from the two following centuries.

NEWARK, *Nottinghamshire* (13–SK7953). The name "The Key to the North" was given in late Anglo-Saxon times, for Newark, or New Work, lay between the River Trent and the River Devon and was also a point of vantage on the Roman Fosse Way. There is no evidence that the Romans built fortifications here; the first recorded owner of the town was Lady Godiva, the famous wife of Earl Leofric, ruler of Mercia. In 1055 Lady Godiva presented the small township as her gift to the monastery of STOW, further down the Trent. In Stephen's reign it was held by Bishop Alexander of LINCOLN, who in 1125 entirely reconstructed the existing timber castle in stone. The north gateway, the largest and most elaborate of the sort in the country, and the chapel on the first floor, still surviving, date from the brief period after 1139 during which it was surrendered to the Crown. Other 12th-cent. remains are the tower at the south-west corner of the building and the eight-bayed crypt, which lies below ground level under part of the west wing. King John frequently stayed at the castle both before and after he came to the throne. During the struggle which ended with the granting of Magna Carta the castle was seized by the barons. It became the king's again in the following year, and here he died in 1216 from overeating, but some say from poison.

The greatest days in the history of Newark Castle came with the Civil War. The people of Newark rallied to the side of Charles I and the castle proved impregnable. Only at the king's express command did Lord Bellasis surrender, and then to march out with all the honours of war, but the castle itself was again reduced to ruin. All that is left is a mere shell. The west wall remains intact, with a tower at each end. The three large windows in the west front mark the great hall, which was much altered when the castle was used as a residence in the 15th cent. To this period belongs the beautiful oriel window, which still retains the arms of Thomas Scot, Bishop of Lincoln, and far below are the infamous dungeons to which King John once sent men to die.

The heart of Newark is the old, cobblestoned market place surrounded by many buildings of great beauty. The White Hart Inn, next to a draper's shop, is 14th-cent., one of the oldest domestic buildings in the Midlands; nearby is the Saracen's Head, where an inn of this name has existed since 1341; the hotel next door is called the Clinton Arms, formerly the Kingston Arms. In 1800 it was important enough to have stables for 90 horses. Lord Byron stayed there when he was supervising the publication of his first book of poems, and Mr Gladstone made his first public political speech from one of the windows.

The Church of St Mary Magdalen stands close to the market place and is remarkable for having a spire 30 ft greater than the length of the ground-plan. The lower part of the tower is Early English of the 13th cent. and the upper part and the needle-sharp spire with its four tiers of dormer windows are 14th-cent.

Newark is now the permanent site of the county agricultural show.

NEWCASTLE-UNDER-LYME, *Staffordshire* (8–SJ8445). This thriving industrial town, the western neighbour of the Potteries, has little to show of the castle – new in the 12th cent. – which gave it the first part of its name; no one is sure how the "under Lyme" part came into being. The most straightforward explanation offered is that it refers to the Lyme brook. King Stephen gave the "new castle" to Ranulf de Gernon, Earl of Chester, in 1149. It later reverted to the Crown, but its low-lying position led to a decline in its importance in the 15th cent., and by about 1541 it was in ruins. Only a length of its original wall, excavated in 1934, remains to be seen in what is now Queen Elizabeth Park.

Most of the town's history is to be found in the museum and art gallery in Brampton Park where seven ancient charters, dating from 1281 to 1685, are on view. The oldest public building is the Guildhall which dates from 1713 but was restored in the mid-19th cent. The Church of St Giles was founded in the 12th cent. but the present building dates from 1876, only the refaced square tower remaining of the original building. A more interesting church is that at **Whitmore,** about 5 m. SW., which is one of the few half-timbered churches in the county and has a unique timbered bell-turret dating from 1632. **Keele Hall,** 3 m. W. of Newcastle, is a happy marriage of the old and the modern for in 1949 it was converted into a university college and has now become the University of Keele.

Newcastle can claim a number of famous sons, among them Thomas Harrison, who was executed in 1660 as one of the Regicides, and Philip Astley who, in the 18th cent., gave England its first circus.

NEWPORT, *Shropshire* (8–SJ7419). This small, old market town, 13 m. W. of STAFFORD on the A518, is really one long, wide and pleasant High Street. The town is far from the sea and the "port" in the name probably has its old sense of borough or market town. At the northern end of the High Street the road divides so that the imposing Parish Church of St Nicholas, with its red sandstone tower, stands on an island site. The church contains interesting monuments, and a list of rectors back to 1100. Near the church is the Royal Victoria Hotel with its pillared entrance. Inside the foyer is displayed the shell of a large turtle, 2 ft across, which was served to celebrate the opening of the hotel, then known as the Union Hotel, in October 1830. Two years later, the then Princess Victoria visited Newport and its new hotel and, in recognition of the loyalty and warmth of her reception, she allowed the hotel to change its name.

Aqualate Park, nearby, is attractive with its herd of deer.

NEWSTEAD ABBEY, *Nottinghamshire* (13–SK5454). The famous ancestral home of Lord Byron, in a beautifully wooded park 9 m. from NOTTINGHAM. The building was founded by Henry II in 1170 as a priory of Black Canons of the Augustinian order. After the Dissolution it passed into the hands of Sir John Byron of Colwick, "little Sir John of the great beard", who at once set about converting the structure into a magnificent residence. In 1643 the family was raised to the peerage for services to the Royalist cause. The 5th Lord Byron, known as the Wicked Lord, became a recluse after killing his cousin, William Chaworth of ANNESLEY, in a duel, and allowed Newstead to fall into disrepair. He died in the scullery, the only place where the roof was watertight. He was succeeded by his great-nephew, George Gordon Noel Byron, the poet. The young Lord Byron and his mother, widow of Mad Jack Byron, were too poor to live in the abbey, but the poet was a frequent visitor and wrote *Hours of Idleness* here in 1806. He at last came to live in the home of his forebears in 1808, but after a period of acute financial distress and a disastrous marriage, resulting from his well-known eccentricity of behaviour, he left Newstead and England for ever. The property was sold a few years later to Colonel Wildman, Byron's schoolfellow at Harrow, for £100,000 and a further £¼ million was spent on restoration. Now owned by the Nottingham Corporation, it is one of the noblest houses in the county open to the public.

A long rhododendron drive leads to the dignified 13th-cent. west front, set off by a lawn and a lake with waterfalls. The monk's parlour leads directly from the entrance, the chapter house survives as a private chapel, and Byron's bedroom forms part of the prior's lodging. The grand saloon is 75 ft long, with a roof of plaster and oak of the time of Charles II. Among the pictures in this room is a portrait of Lord Byron, painted by Phillips. The bedroom and dressing-room are much as the poet left them: the original paper is on the walls, the four-poster remains where it was, and the table on which he wrote part of *Childe Harold* is still among the furnishings.

The house is also famous for its connection with David Livingstone, who wrote his journals here.

In the garden, at the extremity of the ruins of the old church, there is a monument on an octagonal pedestal panelled with white marble and surmounted by an ornately carved urn, on which is written a long epitaph to Byron's Newfoundland dog, Boatswain. In his will of 1811 Byron directed that he should be buried in the vault below the monument, near his dog; but his wish was not fulfilled.

NORTH LUFFENHAM, *Rutland* (10–SK 9303). A place of delightful views, fine limestone buildings and Collyweston slates. The 6th- and 7th-cent. finds, now in the County Museum at OAKHAM, from the excavation of an Anglo-Saxon burial ground just N. of the church, prove that North Luffenham was one of the earliest and most prosperous villages to be settled.

Luffenham Hall, E. of the church, was built by John Harington in 1538–53 and his son built the large barn, still standing and dated 1555. The Hall was greatly altered in the 17th, 18th and 20th cents., but there is still a hole in the wall flanking the church path, through which the owners used to pass food to the poor. A dry ditch also remains, part of the siege works against 200 Royalists surrounded in the Hall during the Civil War.

The founder of UPPINGHAM and Oakham schools, Archdeacon Johnson, has a brass plate to his memory on the wall of the sedilia of the late 13th- to early 14th-cent. Church of St John Baptist where he was rector. There is still ancient heraldic glass in some of the windows, which dates from the 14th cent. Especially notable is the 15th-cent. nave roof.

In Clay Lane at the west end of the village is Manor Farm, built in 1640, and there is an early 18th-cent. house opposite. Just S. of this is The Pastures, an excellent house built by C. F. A. Voysey in 1901, with a large walnut tree in the garden.

North Luffenham has a fine golf course, where leading amateur competitions are held.

NORTON DISNEY, *Lincolnshire* (13–SK 8859). A timeless village on the wooded banks of the River Witham. Nothing remains of its ancient castle nor of the manor house built from its ruins in the 17th cent., but the monuments in the wonderful old Church of St Peter continue to keep alive the name of the Disney family. From the 13th cent. until the time of James II the d'Isigny lords of the manor influenced the cultural and religious character of the small farming community here. The name changed from the Norman form to Disney, and lives in our memory of Walt Disney, who was a descendant of the junior branch. In its early days the church belonged to Sempringham Priory. It has an Early English nave of three bays, a Decorated chancel with north chapel, a Perpendicular tower, a Jacobean pulpit with canopy, and an Elizabethan screen. In the chancel is a beautiful recumbent effigy of a lady, said to be Joan d'Isigny, *c.* 1350. An exceptional late palimpsest brass set in a hinged

frame on the north side of the chapel bears a
Dutch inscription of 1518 about the founding of a
chantry in the Netherlands. The glass of the east
window commemorates the Lord St Vincent
whose title came down to him from John Jervis,
the admiral who was raised to the peerage after his
great victory over the Spaniards in 1797 near
Cape St Vincent.

NOTTINGHAM, *Nottinghamshire* (13–SK 54
40). This is a largely modern city which has
triumphed over many troubled periods in its
history to become "The Queen of the Midlands",
a prosperous centre for the manufacture of
cigarettes and tobacco, pharmaceutics, leather,
textiles, bicycles and electronic equipment, as
well as its traditional Nottingham lace. The
change from an agrarian to an industrial centre
came with the Industrial Revolution of the early
19th cent. Nottingham had long been a hosiery
town, but it was not until the power-loom and
the flying shuttle that it was truly identified with
cotton-spinning. An adaptation of the stocking-
frame quickly brought to the area the mechanized
craft of lace-making, a thriving trade which
benefited even local architecture, as may be seen
in the unique lace market occupying a large part
of the site of the medieval town.

The tempestuous story of Nottingham Castle
covers nine centuries. Edward the Elder built
fortifications on the south bank of the Trent in
920 in an attempt to prevent the Danes from
infiltrating along the waterway. To the conquering Normans the tall bluff of sandstone to the N.,
with its sheer cliff providing natural defence, was
the obvious site for a permanent fortress. William
of Normandy reached the Trent crossing in 1068
and directed William Peveril to build the first
castle on the hill. During the reign of Stephen it
was destroyed twice in internecine struggles and
rebuilt in 1154 by Henry II, who presented it
20 years later to his son John. When Richard
Lionheart became king and departed on his
crusades he left his brother John in command of
Nottingham Castle and seven others. At about
this time the legend of Robin Hood and his Merrie
Men of SHERWOOD FOREST gained its place in
local folklore: the cruelties inflicted on the
people of the Trent valley warranted opposition
and it may well have happened that supporters of
the absent king took armed refuge in the greenwood. To this day there is an inn with the crusading name of the Trip to Jerusalem built into the
cliffside, with cellars forming a labyrinth of caves
and passages in the great rock on which the castle
stands.

It is recorded that after John became king and
tried to enforce his authority on the landowners
he on one occasion held 28 Welsh boys hostage in
the castle as security against rebellion by their
chieftain fathers. When there were signs of a
rebellion he ordered all the 28 boys to be dragged
from their play and hanged from the castle walls.
Throughout the turmoil of the Wars of the Roses
the castle remained a Yorkist stronghold, until
with the coming of the Tudors it fell into disrepair;

Kenneth Scowen

Nottingham University

but it was still from here that Charles I raised
his standard and plunged the country into
Civil War in 1642. By 1651 the once proud
fortress was an uninhabitable devastation. The
ruins were bought by the Duke of Newcastle
and converted into a house for his own use, but
after many more years of political involvement the
castle was gutted by the mob during the Reform
Bill riots of 1831. Nottingham Castle is now the
property of the Corporation and is used as the
city's main museum and art gallery. It is still
possible to tour the many caves and tunnels
leading into the Castle Rock. One of the most
famous there is Mortimer's Hole, a passage

through which, it is believed, Edward III and his companions entered the castle to arrest Roger Mortimer, the adventurer who because of his influence with the Queen Mother, Isabella of France, almost became ruler of England.

The city centre is dominated by the Council House, a vast building overtopped by a dome which reaches 200 ft from the ground and is modelled on that of ST PAUL'S in London. The construction of this worthy addition to the modern development of Nottingham was completed in 1928. It contains the Lord Mayor's Parlour, the council chamber, numbers of reception rooms, and a clock with a bell named Little John after Robin Hood's outlaw companion, because of its great size. Before the Council House was built the site had for at least 400 years been the place where Nottingham's annual Goose Fair was held, an event which now takes place on the first Thursday, Friday and Saturday of October at the Forest Recreation Ground.

The University of Nottingham was established by Royal Charter in 1948, after 67 years as the University College. The University is situated in a park some 3 m. from the city centre, with the main buildings looking out across sloping lawns to a broad lake. Altogether the needs of 6,000 students are catered for. The existence of today's superb seat of learning is mainly due to the generosity of the 1st Lord Trent, earlier Sir Jesse Boot, who presented the original building. The huge firm of Boots began as a one-man business in Goose Gate, Nottingham and now employs over 1,100 men and women on research, manufacturing and administration in the Nottingham area alone. John Player & Sons, now a branch of the Imperial Tobacco Company Ltd, is another giant concern which began as a small local factory. In ironic contrast to the days when the early cotton workers had a life expectation of 20 years, the denizens of this modern city enjoy working conditions not bettered anywhere in the country. Raleigh Industries Ltd is the largest cycle factory in the world; its products are exported to over 140 countries. Output is in the region of 1,250,000 bicycles and 2,000,000 three-speed units a year.

To all this may be added up-to-date parking and garaging facilities. Trent Bridge, the ground of the Nottinghamshire County Cricket Club, is terraced on every side to accommodate as many as 40,000 spectators. The ancient inns, besides the Trip to Jerusalem, include the Salutation Inn in Hounds Gate, dating back to 1240; the Flying Horse on the site of a medieval hostelry; and The George, which shows in one of its bars the cheque with which Charles Dickens paid his bill.

The stately Church of St Mary's, which is the principal of the many fine places of worship within the civic boundaries, rises 126 ft from the heart of the Lace Market. It is a splendid example of 15th-cent. work and is richly adorned with the buttresses and panelled battlements of the period. The interior is lit by 12 great windows on each side and treasures a glorious Madonna and Child painted by Fra Bartolomeo, the pupil of Raphael. The Roman Catholic cathedral designed in Gothic Revival style by Pugin, lies near the centre of the city; and opposite it is the Playhouse, one of the best modern theatres in England with a lively repertory company.

In the fields around Nottingham there flourishes another great industry, which is the growing of tens of millions of roses. **Wollaton Hall**, a fine example of Elizabethan Renaissance architecture, on the outskirts of the city, now houses the Natural History Museum.

OAKHAM, *Rutland* (10–SK8509). The origin of the name of this pleasant county town remains obscure, but local belief maintains that there is a connection between the name Oakham and Occa, an influential Anglo-Saxon landowner of whom nothing more is known. Most certainly the manor later became the property of the Anglo-Saxon queens, and on the death of Edward the Confessor's wife, Edith, in 1075, the town, with its castle and church, as recorded in Domesday Book, was taken over by William of Normandy. By 1130 it was held by the powerful Ferrers family who built the castle, strictly speaking a fortified house, of which the surviving great hall is the finest of its kind in England. The hall, open to the public, is 60 ft long and 40 ft wide, a fascinating structure with handsome aisles and decorated doorways dating from *c.* 1180. The interior is filled from floor to roof with a remarkable collection of horse-shoes, following a centuries-old custom, perhaps starting from the time when the Conqueror's farrier lived here, of taking a token horse-shoe from every peer passing through the town. The highest ranks are represented here, including those of royalty, in a bewildering variety of horse-shoes ranging from some measuring only a few inches across to others of more than a yard. One of the shoes is said to have been given by Queen Elizabeth I. More recently, one was presented by Queen Elizabeth II on her visit to the county in May 1967.

Oakham was the birthplace, in 1619, of Jeffery Hudson, the dwarf presented in a pie to Charles I at BURLEY. Also born here, in 1649, was the infamous Titus Oates.

Oakham School was founded in 1584 by Archdeacon Robert Johnson. The original schoolhouse was restored in 1723 and is still used as a class-room. It also housed a museum of Anglo-Saxon antiquities, until the exhibits were moved into the new Rutland County Museum, which was opened in 1969 in a building originally used as an indoor riding school. Also displayed in the new museum are items showing different aspects of daily life in the county from prehistoric times to the present day.

The parish church, All Saints, has a 14th-cent. spire and south porch dating from about 1190. The font has a 12th-cent. circular bowl, and a square base which apparently belongs to the 14th cent. In the market place stands the picturesque old Butter Cross with its eight oak posts and a massive central shaft and steps. Here too are the well-worn stocks, a chilling reminder of village justice administered in a bygone age.

From Oakham to **Langham** is only 3 m. along the A606. There was probably an Iron Age settlement on Ranksborough Hill, at the east foot of which this straggling village lies. A Roman bronze statue was found there, now in the BRITISH MUSEUM.

Langham is proud of its 17th-cent. Hall and manor, but the church is the principal feature of the village. Its noble tower and spire are seen to advantage from lanes on the south side, the tower being 13th-cent. with a Decorated 14th-cent. spire added. It is spacious, with lovely windows in the chancel and the south transept by Comper. The pinnacled porch has a stone platform above, once part of an upper chamber.

OLD BOLINGBROKE, *Lincolnshire* (13–TF 3564). In the already ancient Norman castle of this historic village in the rolling foot-hills of the Wolds Henry IV was born in 1367, son of John of Gaunt and Blanche, heiress of the Earl of Lancaster, Lord of Bolingbroke. In 1643 the castle was captured by the Parliamentarians, and was reduced to ruin in the years that followed. The Church of SS. Peter and Paul stands to the N. of the castle site. It consists of the old south aisle from the 14th cent. turned into nave and chancel, a sturdy, battlemented tower, and a north aisle added in 1890. Of special interest are the two worn heads by the old doorway, believed to be John of Gaunt's parents, Edward III and Queen Philippa.

OLLERTON, *Nottinghamshire* (13–SK6567). The small mining town at the junctions of the Rivers Rainworth Water and Maun is one of the best centres from which to visit THORESBY Park and walk among the rhododendrons and stately beeches of CLUMBER PARK and the Dukeries. Ollerton Hall is built on the site of an Elizabethan mansion belonging to the Markham family, the last of whom died following the Civil War. It is a handsome, red-brick house in the late Restoration manner with projecting wings and a doorway made prominent by large stone pilasters and pediment.

OSWESTRY, *Shropshire* (8–SJ2829). Not surprisingly in view of its violent history, little remains to show that this market town on the Welsh border existed, in some form, before the Romans came to Britain. Man has lived here, in fact, for 2,500 years at least – but rarely in peace. The remains of an Iron Age Fort, dating from about 550 B.C., can be seen to the N. of the town, the earliest evidence of the need to seek security behind fortifications. The field where the Roman Catholic church now stands is believed to be the site of the Battle of Maserfield in A.D. 642, when the pagan King Penda of Mercia defeated and killed Oswald, the Christian King of Northumbria: this was the origin of the name Oswestry. The town was a frequent bone of contention between the Normans and the Welsh tribes. King John burnt it down in 1215 – and 18 years later Llewellyn of Wales did the same. Owen Glendower sacked the town and almost demolished the church in 1400; and there were three accidental but disastrous fires between 1542 and 1567.

The result of all this destruction and pillage is that Oswestry is now largely a product of the 19th cent. But odd traces remain: in the Norman foundations of the tower of St Oswald's Church; in the original buildings of the Grammar School, dating from 1407, now divided into three cottages; and in the early 17th-cent. Llwyd Mansion in the centre of the town, a well-preserved black-and-white building bearing, strangely, on its wall the double-headed eagle of the Holy Roman Empire, arms granted to a member of the Llwyd family, owners of the mansion, for distinguished service during the Crusades.

Oswestry Castle, built originally by the Normans, was destroyed on Cromwell's orders after the Civil War and today only fragments of the walls remain. But the site has been made into a public park which offers fine views from the top. King Oswald's Well, which is still in existence, is fed by a spring which, according to legend, sprang from the spot where an eagle dropped one of Oswald's limbs after the Battle of Maserfield. The Croeswylan Stone – the Cross of Weeping – can be seen in Morda Road, near the boys' secondary modern school. The stone marks the spot, then outside the town walls, where the markets were held in 1559 when the plague struck the town. Some say the hollowed-out stone was the base of a cross; others that money was washed in the "bowl" to avoid contamination.

Oswestry is a natural centre for visiting North and Central Wales as well as Shropshire.

Two famous men are natives of Oswestry. In Willow Street a plaque marks the house where Sir Walford Davies, the organist, composer and, for some years, Master of the King's Musick, was born. And Plas Wilmot is similarly commemorated in Weston Lane as the birthplace of Wilfred Owen, one of the Great War's finest poets.

OWTHORPE, *Nottinghamshire* (13–SK6733). A remote little village in a hollow of the Wolds, hard by the beautiful Vale of Belvoir. This is where Colonel Hutchinson, the Puritan governor of NOTTINGHAM, "rob'd of every thing which the neighbouring garrisons of Shelford and Wiverton could carrie . . ." paid the penalty of taking sides against his king in the Civil War. Owthorpe Hall was destroyed by the avenging Cavaliers and although rebuilt shortly afterwards is now represented only by the trees and gardens laid out by the regicide prior to his own death while imprisoned in 1664. He is buried in the Church of St Margaret, which was largely restored in 1705 and has an 18th-cent. clock which is kept going for the benefit of workers in the nearby fields.

PITCHFORD, *Shropshire* (8–SJ5303), is reckoned by experts to be the finest Elizabethan building in Shropshire. The massive black-and-white timbered Pitchford Hall is not open to the public but splendid views of it can be obtained from the road from ACTON BURNELL which runs beside the park. A closer view can be had from the Churchyard of St Michael's which stands near the house, at the end of a long drive leading off the road. From there the elaborate diagonal strutting and the star-shaped chimneys can be seen. The Hall was built by Adam Otley, a wool merchant from SHREWSBURY, between 1560 and 1570. In the grounds, in the branches of a lime tree, can be glimpsed a 200-year-old summer-house.

The church, although outshone by the Hall, is 300 years older and contains one of the most unusual church monuments in the county, an effigy in oak of Sir John de Pitchford who died towards the end of the 13th cent. The figure is 7 ft long, a knight in armour, his feet resting on a lion, his hand drawing his sword.

QUATFORD, *Shropshire* (8–SO7390). The remains of what are probably Danish earthworks, two follies and an ancient church are what this small village, 2 m. SE. of BRIDGNORTH, offers the visitor. The red-brick Watch Tower, perched on a crag to the N. of the church is one folly – but this is much overshadowed by the other, Quatford Castle. This was put up by John Smalman, a builder, for himself in 1830, complete with sham battlements. The Church of St Mary Magdalene has an impressive position, standing on a sandstone cliff approached by steps cut in the rock. The story goes that the church was built by Roger de Montgomery, the Norman Earl of Shrewsbury, to fulfil a vow made by his wife-to-be – that if she reached him safely on her journey from France a church should be built on the spot where they met. True or not the church still bears traces of its Norman foundation; and there is good reason to believe that there was a crossing of the Severn at Quatford years before Bridgnorth came into being.

QUORN, *Leicestershire* (10–SK5616). This rather industrialized village, part of what is sometimes called "the cream of the Shires", owes its fame to the non-industrial blood sport of fox-hunting. The pleasures of the chase are becoming less popular in Leicestershire, partly because of the encroachment of motor-roads across the hallowed fields, partly perhaps because the need for this sort of recreation is less urgently felt. A more placid connection with the past is the fine granite church, with its massive 15th-cent. tower and Norman doorway embellished with a double row of chevrons. It also possesses the 14th-cent. Farnham Chapel, with valuable Tudor relics which have belonged to the Farnham family for 700 years.

REDBOURNE, *Lincolnshire* (13–SK9699). The parish, lying off the continuation of Ermine Street, N. of LINCOLN, is entered by a fine stone gateway, with a lion crest and characteristic rural carvings, leading into the 300 acres of Redbourne Park. The old Hall, of which this is the setting, passed from the Carter family in the 18th cent. to the Dukes of St Albans, the lineal descendants of Charles II and Nell Gwynn. The Church of St Andrew has a lofty Perpendicular unbuttressed tower of the 15th cent., rising in four diminishing stages. Against the south wall of the chancel is an incised slab bearing the effigy of Sir Gerard Sothill, which dates from 1401 and marks the last link with Redbourne Castle. Of especial interest is the 19th-cent. east window of the church, which depicts the Last Judgment in vivid colour.

REPTON, *Derbyshire* (12–SK3026). There are few more ancient places in the county than this small town, once the capital of Mercia and now famous as the home of one of England's oldest public schools. The first monastery was founded here in A.D. 653. This was overrun by the invading Danes two centuries later but some 100 years after that, about 975, a new church was built, St Wystan's. This is the church that can be seen today, much enlarged in the 13th–15th cents. when it was given its 212-ft spire, but which still includes part of the original building. The tiny crypt, about the size of an average living-room, is among the limited number of survivals of Anglo-Saxon architecture, a priceless heritage almost 1,000 years old.

Near the church, in the 12th cent., was founded the priory which fell into ruin after the Dissolution. These ruins were eventually, in 1556, incorporated into Repton School by its founder, Sir John Port. Today the original arched gateway stands intact and parts of the priory buildings can also be seen. There is a museum in the cellars of the school, showing the history of both the village and the school, which can be viewed by appointment.

RETFORD, *Nottinghamshire* (13–SK7080), is the main market town in the N. of the county and one of the oldest chartered boroughs in the country. It is divided into two parts – East and West Retford – which are joined by a bridge across the River Idle. Its public buildings are mainly 19th-cent., though the grammar school was founded in 1552. The Church of St Swithun dates from the 13th cent., but was largely rebuilt in the 1650s. It contains Victorian stained glass.

ROTHLEY, *Leicestershire* (10–SK5812). For many centuries Rothley Temple, founded as a preceptory for the Knights Templar in the reign of Henry III, was the home of the Babington family; but it is as the birthplace of Lord Thomas Babington Macaulay, poet, historian and dramatist, that the name is best remembered. The 13th-cent. chapel, with the worn figure of a Knight Templar at the entrance, still stands at the side of the Elizabethan house, which is not, however, open to the public. The old granite church, dating from Norman times, has a massive 15th-cent.

Rudyard Lake provided the inspiration for Kipling's Christian name

tower, with nave and aisles added at a later period. In the churchyard is a weather-worn Anglo-Saxon cross, some 12 ft high, believed to be over 1,000 years old.

RUDYARD, *Staffordshire* (8–SJ9557), is a village whose name has gone round the world because Mr and Mrs Lockwood Kipling chose it for their son, later to become one of the most famous English writers of the early part of this century. The story has it that young Lockwood Kipling and Alice Macdonald frequently came to this village, about 3 m. NW. of LEEK, to walk in the woods and along the edge of Rudyard Lake – and that it was here that he asked her to marry him.

In the village itself there are some pretty houses and some prettier gardens; but the real beauty is to be found along the lake, really a reservoir constructed originally to supply the Trent and Mersey Canal. Two m. long and several hundred yards wide, the lake is now managed by the British Waterways Board and offers facilities for boating and fishing. In some places the surrounding woods come right to the edge of the lake, in others there are small cliffs of red earth; but there are also plenty of places on the lake shore for strolling and picnics.

RUFFORD ABBEY, *Nottinghamshire* (13–SK6464), 2 m. from OLLERTON, is approached by an avenue of lime trees and is set in a deer park of over 500 acres. The abbey was founded by Gilbert de Gaunt in the 12th cent. but almost all that remained after the Dissolution was the vaulted refectory which is now a hall. In the chapel in 1574 the Earl of Lennox married Elizabeth Cavendish. Rufford Abbey became the home of their daughter, Arabella Stuart, who,

because she was the niece of Lord Darnley, brother of the Earl of Lennox and close in succession to James I, died tragically in THE TOWER of London. The house now belongs to the Nottinghamshire County Council.

RUGELEY, *Staffordshire* (8–SK0418). In the churchyard of St Augustine's Church in this pleasant little town, to the NE. of CANNOCK CHASE, is a tombstone to John Parsons Cook. The simple inscription gives a date, 1855, and the statement "His life was taken away". The facts behind that relate to one of the most sensational murder trials of the mid-19th cent. when William Palmer, a Rugeley doctor born in 1824 and educated at the local grammar school, was found guilty, after a 12-day hearing, of poisoning Cook, a bookmaker to whom he owed money. Palmer was executed in public at STAFFORD, taking with him the secret of the poison he had used.

RUSHTON SPENCER, *Staffordshire* (8–SJ 9362), a small village with an unusual church, is tucked away in the north-western corner of the county, about 6 m. NW of LEEK. The Church of St Laurence the Martyr, once known as the "Chapel in the Wilderness", was originally built entirely of wood in the 14th cent. Over the years stone has replaced much of the timber but parts of the original can still be seen, including some remarkable dogtooth carving in oak, dating from the reign of Henry III, over the piers on the north side of the nave. The name of the hill near the village is The Cloud. Rising to almost 1,200 ft, it offers wide views over Cheshire and Staffordshire.

RUYTON-OF-THE-ELEVEN-TOWNS, *Shropshire* (8–SJ3922), must have one of the longest village names in England, and almost one of the longest village streets. Once, in the 14th cent., this was important enough to be a borough and the vicar still has the evidence of this, a fine silver mace more than 300 years old. The unusual name came into being in 1301 when 11 of the neighbouring townships were united into the one manor, but now even Ruyton itself is no more than a townlet.

The long street winds up from the narrow stone bridge over the River Perry at one end, along the side of a red sandstone hill. Many of the small houses and cottages are built of large slabs of the red stone. Ruyton is mentioned in the Domesday Book and its church, with its battlemented tower, dates from that time. In the churchyard are the last traces of the castle built in the early 14th cent., three fragments of the greyish-white, 8-ft-thick walls of the keep. Where the village street touches the overlooking hill at its steepest is an unusual war memorial: an alcove has been hewn out of the rock and in it stands a simple, 10-ft-tall cross, made of the local red stone, commemorating the 22 local men who died in the two World Wars.

RYHALL, *Rutland* (10–TF0311). The Church of St John the Evangelist here is traditionally associated with the legend of St Tibba, the patron saint of falconers. She was the niece of King Penda of Mercia, and is said to have lived, about 1,300 years ago, in a cell where the church now stands. In the 9th cent. her remains were transferred to the great abbey of Medeshamstede, later called PETERBOROUGH, but there is still a St Tibba's Well to be seen near the church today. The 13th-cent. tower and spire of St John's are particularly beautiful; the sedilia are 14th-cent.; in the north arcade is a crouching stone figure of St Christopher, wearing a coronet of fleurs-de-lis; the south doorway, with its border of floral moulding, is surmounted by a priest's chamber, which was once a school.

From here drive 1 m. N. up the B1174 to **Essendine,** so tucked away off the busy A-roads that you are likely to see a golden pheasant crossing unhurriedly in front of the car.

Surrounded by a moat in which water still lies are the small remains of the old home of the Cecils, a 12th-cent. castle given by Queen Elizabeth to Lord Burghley. The Church of St Mary, said to have been the castle chapel, is still substantially a Norman building, remodelled in the 13th cent. and with an especially remarkable door (*c.* 1140), which is often photographed. Note especially the tympanum decorated with a figure of Christ and two angels – more usually found in French churches. The double bellcots are typical of Rutland. SE. of the church is a 17th-cent. bridge with massive cutwaters.

Do not miss the chance of driving 1 m. N. along the B1174 to **Carlby** to see the enchanting little church with its 700-year-old spire, rescued from decay in the 1930s.

SANDON, *Staffordshire* (8–SJ9429). There are two unusual monuments to former prime ministers in this small village, 6 m. NE of STAFFORD. Both are in the grounds of Sandon Hall, the 19th-cent. home of the Earl of Harrowby: one is a 75-ft column, modelled on the Trajan Column, and set up by the 1st Earl of Harrowby in memory of William Pitt; the other is a Gothic shrine, dedicated to Spencer Perceval who was assassinated in the House of Commons. Sandon Hall itself, and its 50 acres of magnificent gardens, are open to the public on certain days. The 13th-cent. parish church contains much that is old and also something which is probably unique: on the walls are painted the family pedigree of the Erdeswicke family, long connected with Sandon. The genealogical trees, painted in 1603 and rediscovered in 1929, grow out of the family tombs below them, the trunks encircled with vine and honeysuckle.

SCRIVELSBY, *Lincolnshire* (13–TF2665). The historic importance of Scrivelsby is at once identifiable with the crowned heraldic lion surmounting the gateway to the 360-acre park, which contains the home of the Hereditary Grand Champion of England. The office of King's Champion was first conferred by William the Conqueror and together with Scrivelsby Court and the accompanying manor became the inheritance of the Dymoke family in 1350. In former times it was the duty of the King's Champion to ride, clad in full armour, into WESTMINSTER HALL during the coronation ceremony and challenge to single combat any person who dared to deny the new king's right to the throne. The privilege is now represented by the carrying of the Royal Standard. The little 13th-cent. church, with modern windows and a tower and spire dating from 1861, is filled with monuments of the Dymokes and includes two figures, of a knight in chain mail and his wife on a separate great stone in the aisle, which date from 1292.

SCROOBY, *Nottinghamshire* (13–SK6590), is a small village, which declined from some eminence in the 13th cent., but has acquired renown as the birthplace of William Brewster, one of the two leaders of the Pilgrim Fathers, who in 1620 were to sail for New England in the *Mayflower*. It is thought that he lived in what is now the manor farm-house; a tablet states that this was his home from 1588 until 1608 and was where he became Ruling Elder of the Pilgrim Church he originated. A similar claim is made for an old inn in the village street, and a cottage near the churchyard bears an inscription stating that he lived there for a time. It is certain that he and others of the Pilgrim Fathers worshipped at Scrooby church, and many of the furnishings, including Brewster's Pew, attract a large number of visitors from America every year.

SCUNTHORPE, *Lincolnshire* (13–SE8910). This large industrial town with a population of over 70,000 has evolved within a single century from a group of small villages including **Frodingham, Brumby, Crosby** and **Ashby.** This rapid growth was due to the ironstone beds discovered in about 1864 around the area, which are believed to be the most extensive in Europe. In 1967 they produced 11·8 per cent of all the ingot steel and 16·5 per cent of all the pig iron manufactured in Britain.

The centre of Scunthorpe is rather drab and uninteresting, but to the S. near the railway there has been some excellent town planning and modern building. Outstanding are the Civic Centre built in 1962 in Central Park, the Civic Theatre, and the interesting museum and art gallery in Oswald Road. The 13th-cent. Church of St Lawrence has extensive 20th-cent. additions, though the new Church of St Hugh, built in 1939 in Brumby just S. of here, is perhaps more interesting to students of architecture. Brumby Hall has a three-storied, 17th-cent. porch with a sundial dated 1637. Now a students' hostel, it was in turn the property of the Bellinghams, Fiennes and Pinders.

Two m. N. of the borough is **Normanby Hall**, built in 1825–9 by the famous Sir Robert Smirk for Sir Robert Sheffield. The reception rooms and double staircase form a setting for Regency furniture and works of art, and the house, with 40 acres of lawns and gardens, is open to the public.

SERLBY HALL, *Nottinghamshire* (13–SK 6488). In the pleasant little red-roofed village of **Harworth** Serlby Park and Hall is the residence of the Dowager Viscountess Galway. Somewhat gaunt and barrack-like, it is said to have been built by James Paine in 1760, and was considerably enlarged in the early 19th cent. It contains paintings of Henry VIII by Holbein and Charles Stuart by Van Dyck. At one end of one room, almost covering an entire wall, is a picture by Daniel Mytens depicting Charles and Henrietta Maria with two horses and dogs, and the dwarf, Jeffery Hudson, of BURLEY fame trying to quieten the dogs.

SHAWELL, *Leicestershire* (10–SP5480). A small village in a pretty valley formed by a tributary to the Avon. The chief interest of Shawell lies in the fact that Tennyson wrote much of his *In Memoriam* there after the death of his friend, Arthur Hallam. Mrs Elmhirst, wife of the rector of Shawell, had been a ward of Tennyson's father at SOMERSBY as a child, and Alfred Tennyson occasionally visited her, doing his writing in the garden summerhouse since smoking was forbidden in the rectory. The rectory had been burnt down after the Battle of NASEBY because of the strong Royalist sympathies of the rector.

From here take the secondary road which crosses the A427 going SE. to **Stanford** where the Hall built by Sir Roger Cave between 1697 and 1700 is the finest house of its date in the county and is open to the public. It stands on the Leicestershire bank of the Avon; Stanford church is on the other bank and is therefore in Northamptonshire. The house contains furniture, pictures and antique family costumes; the saloon is remarkable for its decoration, in particular the chimney-piece put in by William Smith the Younger.

A pillar set up in the meadow commemorates P. S. Pilcher who carried out flying experiments in the 1890s and was killed during an exhibition flight in Stanford Park in 1899 after rising 50 ft and travelling 150 yds. A flying machine of 1898 is exhibited among the vintage vehicles in the museum attached to the house. Traction-engine rallies take place at Stanford Hall on spring Bank Holidays. There is a pretty walled rose garden, an old forge, amusements for children and fishing.

SHELVE, *Shropshire* (8–SO3399). Looking at the scattering of cottages and the tiny church, perched more than 1,000 ft up, it is difficult to appreciate that Shelve was once a place of some importance – sufficiently so in the 12th cent. for it to be granted a royal charter to hold a market. That was in the days when the lead mines in the ridge of surrounding hills, the Stiperstones, were being worked. The derelict buildings of one of the old mines, with its ruined engine house, can be seen from the A488. The Stiperstones themselves, rising to 1,647 ft, are wild in places but offer magnificent views to those who climb them.

SHERWOOD FOREST, *Nottinghamshire* (13–SK6660). In the early 13th cent. some 100,000 acres of woodland and pasture on the outskirts of NOTTINGHAM carried stalwart oaks which were in constant demand for ship-building. Today few of these remain, although at **Bilhagh** on an open space just N. of EDWINSTOWE the Major Oak, or Queen Oak, measuring 30 ft around the trunk with an overall circumference of nearly 270 yds, is still alive and growing. Between Edwinstowe and MANSFIELD is the husk of the Parliament Oak, under which Edward I is said to have gathered his ministers in 1290. The largest tree of all is the Green Dale Oak, ½ m. S. of WELBECK ABBEY, which is at least 800 years old and perhaps as much as 1,500. In 1724 a coach road was driven through the trunk, leaving an aperture 10 ft 3 in. high and 6 ft 3 in. wide. A piece of furniture was made from part of the wood removed in the cutting and is now known as the Green Dale Cabinet. Still within the forest boundary there is another famous oak known as Robin Hood's Larder. It is believed, against all the evidence to the contrary, that Robin Hood was born in Locksley in Nottinghamshire in about 1160, and that he was in truth the Earl of Huntingdon.

Sherwood Zoo is at HUCKNALL on the A611.

SHIFNAL, *Shropshire* (8–SJ7407). This small town, mentioned by Charles Dickens in *The Old Curiosity Shop*, was once an important stopping place for coaches on the Holyhead road. A casual glance suggests the town is Georgian for there are quite a number of fine examples here of architecture of that period. But Shifnal is much older than that as the timber-framed Old Idsall House and the largely Norman Church of St Andrew prove. The explanation is that Shifnal was largely destroyed by fire in 1591 and those two buildings are the only ones of note which survived.

Shrewsbury with its two church spires piercing the skyline

The church is unusual in having in effect two chancels, one behind the other, the original Norman and the lofty 14th-cent. one. There is also a dog – a stone one lying under the feet of the stone figure of Thomas Forster, a priest who died in 1526.

In St Mary's Roman Catholic Church is a beaten silver chalice, almost 500 years old, with a curious story. It disappeared after the Reformation, was lost for hundreds of years, turned up in a Yorkshire curio shop and was returned to the church, the finder taking to heart the injunction engraved around it: "Return Mee to Sheafnall in Shropshire"

SHREWSBURY, *Shropshire* (8–SJ4912), is one of the best-preserved medieval towns in the country with much for the visitor to see.

It came into being when the inhabitants of WROXETER – the Roman town of Viroconium – were seeking a more easily defended place to live during the uneasy years which followed the departure of the Roman legions in the 5th cent. Five m. W. of Wroxeter they chose a near-island of rising ground in a loop of the Severn which met their needs; there is no doubt that they carried some of the stone from their former home to help to build the new settlement. The name Shrewsbury is believed to have come into use during the 8th cent. when the town became part of the kingdom of Mercia – and has nothing to do with the tiny mammal or a scolding woman. Scropesbyrig, or Scrobbesbyrig, the Anglo-Saxon name, probably meant the borough or fortified place of a man called Scrobb. The county name Shropshire comes from this old form.

When the Normans arrived, Roger de Montgomery was quick to appreciate that the narrow neck of land in the NE. corner, where the Severn almost knots its loop, was a natural site for a castle and there he built one. The castle remains which can be viewed today, however, date more probably from the time of Henry II, about 100 years after the Conquest; and the building was further enlarged another 100 years later by Edward I. It had fallen into grave disrepair when, in 1790, the engineer and architect, Thomas Telford, refurbished it as a private house for Sir William Pulteney. Laura's Tower, named after Sir William's wife, commemorates Telford's work; the gateway, the postern gate and the main hall pay tribute to the earlier builders.

The largest church of the Shrewsbury skyline is St Mary's and its fine stone spire is one of the three tallest in England. Built about 1200, the nave arcades, of noble proportions, the south porch and the south transept are all of that date. The beautifully carved nave roof is 15th-cent. The plentiful stained glass is reckoned the finest in Shropshire; the Jesse window in the chancel is especially rich in colour. The other major spire belongs to St Alkmund's, built in the late 18th cent. on the site of a medieval church. This, too, has good stained glass: an east window which is an adaptation by Francis Egginton of BIRMINGHAM of Reni's Assumption of the Virgin. The most unusual-looking of the town's churches is St Chad's which stands in a commanding position above the river. It has an oddly shaped tower, its top half a kind of minaret crowned with a dome; the nave is circular – one of the very few round churches in the country.

Many of Shrewsbury's old buildings have been pulled down over the years to make way for new: the railway station is a notable example of Victorian Gothic while the new Shirehall and Law Courts, opened in 1967, and the Mardol Block, housing the market hall, are interesting examples of post-war architecture. But much that is old still remains. Gullet Passage and Grope Lane exemplify the bizarre alley and street-names hereabouts and have changed little from the days of Elizabeth I: quaint, narrow passage-ways over which the leaning upper stories almost meet.

There are many fine timber-framed houses to be seen. Wyle Cop is especially rich in them – Owen's Mansion, the Plough Inn, the Cross Keys Inn and Ireland's Mansion. Another notable black-and-white structure is the Abbot's House at the top of Butcher Row, which dates from about 1450; the shops at ground level are original and retain the wide oak sills on which the medieval shopkeepers displayed their wares. Yet another is Rowley's House, situated in the centre of the bus station; it is now a museum, open to the public, housing finds from Wroxeter. Here can be seen the silver mirror once used by a Roman officer's wife, and her toilet requisites, trinkets and ornaments together with scores of other objects from the excavations at Wroxeter. The town's main museum and art gallery occupy what were the original buildings of Shrewsbury School, opposite the entrance to the castle. These buildings with an embattled tower look rather like a three-story church and date from 1598; in the garden in front is a bronze statue of one of the school's most famous old boys, the great 19th-cent. naturalist Charles Darwin. In the art gallery is a permanent exhibition of Shropshire landscapes. There is a military museum at Sir John Moore Barracks, home of the Light Infantry Brigade, which includes the county regiment, the King's Shropshire Light Infantry. Exhibits covering 200 years of military history are on view and the museum is regarded as one of the best of its kind in the country. It can be visited by appointment.

Shrewsbury School is now on the other side of the Severn in Kingsland, a residential district approached by a toll-bridge. On the town side of the river lies a park with an unusual name, The Quarry, which bears witness to the talents of that famous gardener, Percy Thrower. The splendid formal gardens of The Dingle, near the middle of the park, are Mr Thrower's great work. The Quarry is the setting for the Shrewsbury Flower Show every August.

Boats may be hired for rowing or paddling along the river to see aspects of Shrewsbury denied to the viewer on foot. Certainly the river offers the best views of the two main bridges, the English and the Welsh.

Shrewsbury in fact has a bookful of sights, and mention must also be made of the Lion Hotel, with associations with Dickens, Jenny Lind and Paganini; Pugin's fine Roman Catholic cathedral; the Lord Hill Column, just shorter than Nelson's in TRAFALGAR SQUARE; the Guildhall; the Watch Tower; and the Whitehall. From our times there is the castle footbridge of 1951, the first of its kind, concrete and cantilever, to be built in this country. Finally there is an old malting house in the suburb of Ditherington, built in 1796 and the oldest surviving iron-framed building in the world.

SHUGBOROUGH, *Staffordshire* (8–SJ9821), has been the home of the Anson family for about 350 years, has strong associations with Admiral Lord Anson, contains an important collection of 18th-cent. French furniture, and, in its grounds, has a remarkable collection of garden monuments. The mansion, near the village of Great Haywood 5½ m. SE. of STAFFORD, is now a National Trust property but is administered by Staffordshire County Council who have established the County Museum in the mid-18th-cent. stable block.

The present house was begun in 1693 by William Anson, on a small scale, and it was largely due to the efforts of Thomas Anson, his more famous brother George, the admiral, and their great-nephew Thomas William Anson, that the house was enlarged during the 18th and early 19th cents. to its present size. Samuel Wyatt was one of the architects responsible for the house as it stands today. Inside, the house is decorated and furnished in magnificent style: there is much elegant Louis XV and Louis XVI furniture, fine silver and glassware dating from the 18th and 19th cents., and pictures by such artists as Reni, Sir George Hayter, Reynolds and Nicholas Dall.

There are seven unusual monuments in the garden and grounds. The Chinese House, which was completed in 1747, doubtless owes much to the influence of Admiral Anson whose round-the-world voyage had included a prolonged call at Canton. Then there is the so-called Cat's Monument, thought for some time to commemorate the cat which accompanied the Admiral on his voyage but now believed to be in memory of one of Thomas Anson's cats. The Shepherd's Monument, erected before 1758, is something of a mystery: the name is derived from the marble relief on the monument but the inscription on the base has never been deciphered and the architect is unknown.

The other four are all the work of James Stuart who had been in Greece studying classical buildings: these structures at Shugborough are among the first in the Greek Revival style to be found in England. They are: a Doric Temple; the Tower of the Winds, a reproduction of the Horologium of Andronikos Cyrrhestes in Athens; the Lanthorn of Demosthenes, a copy of the Choragic Monument of Lysicrates in Athens; and – probably the most imposing – the Triumphal Arch, a copy of Hadrian's Arch in Athens.

The River Wye at Monsal Dale, near Bakewell   *Pix Photos*

SIBTHORPE, *Nottinghamshire* (13–SK7645), is a bare little village centred around the Church of St Peter, which has a splendid 14th-cent. chancel of the type for which Nottinghamshire is famous, and 20 1,000-year-old Irish yew trees in the churchyard. Against the north wall is one of the renowned Lincolnshire/Nottinghamshire Easter sepulchres. These are the remains of the elaborate and dramatic service which used to be performed in these churches on Easter morning. The sepulchres provided the setting for a commemoration of the Resurrection, when on Good Friday the crucifix was removed from the high altar and placed within the niche provided. From that time until Easter morning the sepulchre was attended by watchers, sometimes dressed to look like Pilate's soldiers. After the third lesson on Easter morning three priests approached the sepulchre swinging censers and wearing square pieces of white linen on their heads, to make them look like women. They then intoned the scriptural dialogue between the three women and the angel. In the Sibthorpe sepulchre the soldiers guarding the tomb are represented as sleeping while the Resurrection takes place. In later Easter sepulchres they are sometimes seen starting up in surprise as the figure of Christ leaves the tomb. Also worth looking at in the church is the excellent alabaster tomb of Edward Burnell dated "made anno domini 1590". It was erected by his widow, Barbara, who is also the third of three wives represented on the tomb of Richard Whalley at **Screveton**, just up the road, whose tomb she was also responsible for erecting.

Near the church stands a fine stone circular dovecot, 98 ft in circumference, of the early 13th cent. It contains 1,260 nesting places in 28 tiers and probably belonged to Thomas Magnus, who owned the former manor house of which only the 620-ft-long moat remains. There is a letter from Magnus to his patron, Cardinal Wolsey, who apparently asked if he could stay at Sibthorpe after his downfall, replying that his house had "but poor accommodation".

SKEGNESS, *Lincolnshire* (13–TF5663). Renowned for its bracing air, this once tiny fishing village, loved by Lord Tennyson and his brothers, is now one of the largest and best-equipped seaside resorts in Britain. There is an iron pier 1,843 ft long; one of the largest swimming-pools on the East Coast; a very popular sun castle with palm court lounge, balconies, and a Continental courtyard overlooking bowling greens; a mile-long waterway threading through the sea-front gardens planted with 100,000 flowering plants including 40,000 wallflowers in an annual spring display; a boating lake, roller-skating rink, paddling pools; a tropical plant-house, vivarium, aquarium, and jungle pavilion known as Natureland; outdoor pools accommodating sea-lions, seals and penguins; two golf courses; and entertainments including weekly bathing-beauty contests, fireworks, treasure hunts and donkey races.

The sandy beach is some 6 m. long, reaching from the holiday camp at **Ingoldmells** to Gibraltar Point where the Lincolnshire Trust for Nature Conservation have established a reserve and bird sanctuary covering an area of over 1,200 acres of sandhills, rough grazing, fresh and salt-water marshes, beach and foreshore. There is also a bird observatory at this key migration point.

Seven m. W. of Skegness on the A158 is **Gunby Hall,** a deep-plum-coloured house belonging to the National Trust and open to the public. Referred to by Tennyson as "a haunt of ancient peace", it is a William III house built by Sir William Massingberd in 1700, showing the influence of Sir Christopher Wren. There is a contemporary oak staircase and nearly every room is wainscoted. The contents include furniture, portraits by Reynolds and numerous deeds and papers. There are kitchen and formal gardens and herbaceous borders; 1,406 acres of grounds include 15 farms.

Almost next door is the little village of **Burgh le Marsh** with its five-sailed tower mill in working order and impressive church built in Perpendicular style of Portland stone. It consists of a chancel, a clerestoried nave, two fine porches and a tower surmounted by 16 iron crosses.

SLEAFORD, *Lincolnshire* (13–TF0645), is a small market town where the quiet River Slea divides into two channels. Little is known of the town itself until its emergence in the Domesday Book, but after that it became a place closely associated with the bishops of LINCOLN. The Church of St Denis, dominating the market place, has the nobility of a cathedral in the richness of its fabric, particularly on first sight of its grand west front surmounted by the sturdy tower which supports one of England's earliest stone spires; but the outstanding feature of Sleaford church is the wealth of flowing tracery that beautifies the windows beyond comparison with those of almost any parish church in the country.

Another building for which Sleaford is notable is the Carre Hospital opposite, a fine group of grey-stone almshouses founded in 1636 by Sir Robert Carre, whose family is remembered in this and the fine Sleaford Grammar School for its many works of charity in the past.

SOMERSBY, *Lincolnshire* (13–TF3472). This tiny, unremarkable village, typical of many in the wooded hollows of the Wolds, is famous as the birthplace of Alfred, Lord Tennyson. The house where he was born exists as a rambling cottage, enlarged from the original by the poet's father, the Rev. George Tennyson, to serve as a rectory. The later additions, completed early in the 19th cent., include a large dining-room with high Gothic windows and gables. The house is, however, not open to the public. The 15th-cent. Church of St Margaret safeguards a number of Tennyson memorials; many of the fine views from nearby Warden Hill are unchanged since his day.

SOUTH SCARLE, *Nottinghamshire* (13–SK 8463). This village NE. from NEWARK on the county boundary draws attention to itself

because of the magnificent proportions of its
Church of St Helen with eight-pinnacled west
tower. This, the battlemented nave, aisles and
south porch are late medieval, but inside the
church is a splendid Norman arcade, very rich
and with two bays only. A massive ladder leads
to the belfry and a figure of St Helena sits in a
niche over the 15th-cent. porch entrance.

From the edge of the village there is a fine view
of LINCOLN Cathedral. There are several brick
houses, one dated 1700 and another 1739, and a
stone dovecot with pyramidal red roof.

SOUTHWELL MINSTER, *Nottingham-*
shire (13–SK 7053). Visible across 20 m. of the
Trent Valley, dominating and dwarfing a small
town of some 3,000 inhabitants (called by Byron,
"a detestable residence" and by John Byng in
1789, "A well-built clean town such a one as a
quiet distressed family ought to retire to"), this
little-known mother church of Nottinghamshire
is worth a wide detour to visit if only for the
incredible beauty of the foliage carvings in its
chapter house. It is one of our more recent sees,
created in 1884, and its early history is mainly
based on legend.

Work on the present church began in about
1108 under Thomas, Archbishop of York, and
the minster is almost unique in this country for
retaining all three of its Norman towers, the
pyramidal roofs of two of them having been
rebuilt to the original design after a fire in 1711.
The façade, nave, crossing, crossing tower and
transepts date also from early Norman days. The
capitals of the east crossing piers have roughly
carved stories on them, Anglo-Saxon rather than
Norman. The nave has very short, thick, circular
piers, saved from being overpowering by the
elastic design of the tribune arches above, and lit
by a huge seven-light Perpendicular window at the
west end, which was unfortunately added in the
15th cent. and necessitated the destruction of
almost the entire Norman west front. The choir
was added in about 1234 and is approached
through a marvellously sculptured screen carved
with 289 small figures, dated about 1340. But it is
the chapter house most people come to see. This
was begun in 1292, built without a centrally
supporting pier, and decorated in a manner so
felicitous by an unknown artist that it is probably
the finest example of 13th-cent. stone-carving in
Britain. It is approached by a doorway carved
with oak, mulberry and maple leaves and butter-
cups. Inside are more leaves, no two alike, chief
among them oak, maple, vine, hop, ivy, rose,
whitethorn, hawthorn, ranunculus and potentilla,
copied from SHERWOOD FOREST's foliage, or
from sketches made on a possible apprenticeship
in France. The artist has managed to impart to
his work such delicacy and joy that the effect is
light rather than overwhelming. Among the
leaves are little people and animals.

The glass in the east window of the minster was
brought from the chapel of the Knights Templar
in Paris where Marie Antoinette was imprisoned.
The brass lectern was found in the pond at NEW-

National Monuments Record

Southwell: carved leaves in the minster

STEAD ABBEY – now known as the Eagle Pond –
where the monks had hidden it 300 years before
on the Dissolution. They had secreted their
ancient deeds and charters in the ball on which the
eagle stands in the hope of returning to the
monastery and recovering them. Four pieces of
sculpture are of special interest. The east end of
the choir contains the kneeling effigy in bronze
of the first Bishop of Southwell, the Right Rev.
George Ridding, who was also headmaster of
WINCHESTER College for nearly 20 years. Over
the door leading to the belfry is one of the
oldest sculptures in the Midlands, a late Anglo-
Saxon representation of St Michael with a lion, a
lamb and a very scaly and well-coiled dragon. In
the body of the church is the well-executed Elizabethan alabaster tomb of Archbishop Sandys
who died in 1588, with richly carved figures of his
wife and eight children on the front panel. And in
the corridor between chancel and chapter house
is a carving of a "secular" cleric pulling both the
ears of a "regular" monk, a reminder that Southwell was founded as a collegiate church for secular
clergy. These clergy did not live inside a monastery
but outside with their families. In a chapel off the
north transept is a more modern memorial made
of parts of aeroplanes which crashed in the First
World War. The minster itself must be the only
place of worship in which there is a notice saying
"Dogs Welcome"!

At the crossing of the main street of Southwell
is the 17th-cent. Saracen's Head where Charles I
stayed on his way to raise his standard at NOT-

TINGHAM in 1646, and again on his way back in the same year to surrender to the Scots at KELHAM. He spent his last night of freedom here before the long imprisonment which ended with his execution, and ate the last meal before his arrest in the coffee room.

On the south side of the minster is the Bishop's Palace built by Caroe in 1907–9. It borders on the remains of the Archbishop of York's monumental palace covering 1½ acres, started by Thoresby in 1360 and finished by Kemp in 1430. Wolsey, whose seat is in the choir at the minster, came here in 1530 when the clouds had already gathered about him and did not leave until he went to LEICESTER to his death. While he was there he built a unique tower still known as Wolsey's Lavatories.

On Burgage Green is Burgage Manor, where Lord Byron lived with his mother in about 1810, when he was still at Harrow. His autograph is preserved on a wall in the hall. Nearby lived his friend, Miss Elizabeth Bridge Pigot, with her mother and brother, John. Not far from the house is a rustic gate dated 1807 which led to the ill-reputed House of Correction where inmates slept in chains in a dank dungeon beneath the floors. Vicars' Close is worth inspection since it consists of the houses of the vicars choral, who did the work of non-resident canons. It was rebuilt in 1780 and makes a delightful group, with the provost's house in the middle, embellished with a porch.

At the **Easthorpe** end of Southwell, in a small garden, is a famous apple tree which began its life in about 1805 as a pip planted in a pot. By 1857 Mr Bramley, the owner of that tree, was allowing grafts to be taken on condition that his name was included in the title. Patched-up and supported, it is still on view at Bramley Tree Cottage, and is the parent of thousands of descendants in this country and overseas.

SOUTH WINGFIELD, *Derbyshire* (13–SK 3755). Just outside this village, which is about 12 m. N. of DERBY, stand the picturesque ruins of Wingfield Manor House now in the course of preservation by the Ministry of Public Building and Works with the aim of opening the manor again to the public. The tall ruins, with the main tower more than 70 ft high, stand on a small hill and can easily be seen from a considerable distance. They make a striking sight. Built by Ralph, Lord Cromwell in 1440, the manor house was once larger than HADDON HALL. It eventually passed into the hands of the Earls of Shrewsbury and one of its most famous guests was Mary Queen of Scots, imprisoned there four times between 1569 and 1584. It was the scene of much fighting during the Civil War, changing hands twice, and in 1646 the Parliamentarians made it unhabitable – and so it has remained. It is, in fact, surprising how much of it still stands – the gatehouse and barn, the banqueting hall and the crypt, and the remains of many of the ancillary buildings, including the apartments in which Queen Mary was held.

SPALDING, *Lincolnshire* (13–TF2422). More than half the acreage of bulbs grown in England, often surpassing the famous fields of Holland in a blaze of extraordinary beauty, is concentrated on an area of the Lincolnshire Fens around Spalding. The Dutch character of this important agricultural town is enhanced by the River Welland flowing through its centre like a highway. The seven bridges, principal of which is the High Bridge, rebuilt in 1838, invite pleasant walks among the many historic buildings along the river bank. One of these, Ayscoughfee Hall, dates from the early 15th cent. and now serves as a museum and recreation centre for the public. The Hall was once the home of Maurice Johnson, who in 1710 founded the Gentlemen's Society of Spalding, a social club designed to encourage the study of scientific and literary subjects and the forerunner of the Society of Antiquaries. The Spalding Gentlemen's Society, with its library and museum of antiquities, is now housed in a building in Broad Street. It also owns the Bird Museum in Red Lion Street from which many hundreds of specimens have now been transferred to the Hall. Superbly tended grounds present fine views of the Hall itself, with its long galleried porch in mellow stone and two-storied bay windows surmounted by Dutch gables. Fresh green lawns, tennis courts, aviaries and a small aquarium merge peacefully into a landscape dignified by yew hedges and a yew tunnel.

Near are several ancient inns, of which the White Horse with its bold frontage and thatched roof is the most attractive architecturally, and the White Hart the oldest, tracing its origin back to 1377. The 13th-cent. Church of SS. Mary and Nicholas is impressive and owes much to the painstaking restoration carried out by Sir Gilbert Scott. The district of which Spalding is the centre is the most fertile in England, renowned for its output of sugar beet and potatoes; above all the tulips, daffodils, narcissi and hyacinths in a vast carpet of breathtaking colour attract visitors from all parts of the world. The culminating glory is the Spalding Flower Parade, held each year at the beginning of May, when over 6 million tulip blooms are used to decorate floats.

SPILSBY, *Lincolnshire* (13–TF4066). A pleasant little market town on the edge of the Wolds and overlooking an expanse of marsh and fens towards the North Sea. The graceful market cross, with its restored centre part and 600-year-old base, denotes the town's receipt of its charter through Sir William de Willoughby in the 14th cent. With the merging of the Willoughby and d'Eresby families the parish church became for many centuries the repository of their memorials, the oldest of these being the stone tomb of John, 2nd Baron Willoughby d'Eresby, who died in 1349, three years after he had fought at Crécy. Also in the church is a tablet in remembrance of Sir John Franklin, the Spilsby-born explorer, who met his death in 1847 in the Arctic while in command of the expedition which first discovered the North West Passage. A statue of him stands in the Market Place. Much of the old church has been lost in renovations, but the unusual 15th-cent. tower in green sandstone remains.

STAFFORD, *Staffordshire* (8–SJ9223). The county town, Stafford has a history going back 1,200 years. It is mentioned in the Domesday Book of 1086 as a borough; it had a market in 1230; and it has been represented in Parliament since 1295. But its fame in the wider world rests on its being the birthplace of the world's most renowned angler, Izaak Walton. He was born here in 1593 and although he left for London to become an apprentice, he always remembered his native town. At **Shallowford**, 5 m. NE. of the town, the Borough Council have taken over the trusteeship of the Izaak Walton Cottage which was opened as a museum in 1924. This was the farm Walton left to Stafford with the stipulation that the rent should be used each year to apprentice two poor boys, provide a marriage portion for a servant girl, and pay for coal for the needy. The small black-and-white cottage has been burnt down twice since 1924, but it has been carefully restored to as near the original as possible.

Stafford has connections with another famous Englishman: playwright Richard Brinsley Sheridan was its M.P. from 1790 to 1806.

There are a number of buildings in the town which are worth a visit. The Church of St Mary in a garden of remembrance just behind the main shopping street, is striking for its unusual octagonal tower in dark grey stone. In the curiously shaped Norman font, Izaak Walton was baptized. A white bust in the north aisle is inscribed "Izaak Walton, Piscator". It was around this site, at a crossing place over the River Sow, that the town began to grow. Stafford is a contraction of Staith-ford – a ford by a landing place. The story is a shadowy one of a prince of Mercia, Bertelin, repenting of his sins and building a hermitage about A.D. 700; of a church being eventually built on the same spot, to be followed by the building of the present church late in the 12th cent.

Close by St Mary's is Stafford's oldest house, the handsome, four-story, timbered High House, where Charles I and Prince Rupert stayed for three nights in September 1642 while recruiting. The house, which is excellently preserved, probably dates from the mid-16th cent., and the beams were shaped from locally grown trees.

Stafford once had two castles. William the Conqueror built one in the north-west part of the town. One of his barons, Robert de Stafford, built his on a hill to the W. of the town, overlooking the present M6 and the A518 from NEWPORT. William's disappeared centuries ago; Robert's was rebuilt in the mid-14th cent., stood until its demolition by the Parliamentary forces when they captured it in 1643, was rebuilt once more early in the 19th cent. – and is again a ruin, its gaunt remains approachable only on foot.

Another building certain to catch the eye is the Royal Brine Baths, black-and-white but dating only from 1892. Stafford has large salt deposits, at a depth of 400 ft, found by accident during the 19th cent. when the council was searching for new sources of drinking water. The salt is extracted as brine – and the unusual amenity of brine swimming is available at these baths.

Two more of Stafford's buildings should be mentioned: the small Church of St Chad, tucked between the shops in Greengate Street, and possessing a fine Norman chancel arch; and the 17th-cent. Noel Almshouses in Mill Street. Several factories continue to make shoes, for centuries the town's staple manufacture; they have today been joined by other types of industry, such as English Electric's concrete and glass complex on the LICHFIELD road, on the outskirts of the town.

STAMFORD, *Lincolnshire* (13–TF0207). This quiet grey town, richly fashioned from mellowed local stone, is one of the finest examples of sustained architectural dignity in England. In Danish times it was selected capital of the Fens and one of the Five Boroughs of the Danelaw. Its charter was granted by Henry III in 1254, with the start of ecclesiastical building. Much damage was done during the Wars of the Roses in the 15th cent., but gradually present-day Stamford began to emerge. It has many ancient churches, Queen Anne houses and Georgian mansions, with vaulted crypts and stone-tiled roofs to mark the ages in between. Groups of almshouses, known as "callises", were founded all about the town by rich wool merchants, who traded with France through Calais. One of these old people's hospitals is the almshouse near the bridge over the River Welland, which was built by Lord Burghley in 1597; the best preserved is Browne's Hospital in Broad Street, a superb foundation endowed by William Browne in the reign of Henry VII and called the Hospital of All Saints. In the little chapel here there are a Tudor screen in excellent condition and much stained glass of considerable beauty. The audit room of the hospital contains a magnificent 16th-cent. refectory table and distinguished carved bench-ends. The oldest building in Stamford is the ruined chapel of St Leonard's Priory, founded in the 7th cent. by Wilfrid, Bishop of York.

In the 14th cent. some students quarrelled with the authorities at OXFORD and established alternative colleges at NORTHAMPTON and Stamford. When, in 1336, their differences were made up and the students returned to Oxford, they left behind them the association of names in Brasenose Hall and the impressive gateway, a pointed arch in the wall of the ancient grammar school, which still survives.

The Church of St Mary is built around a 13th-cent. tower, with a 163-ft spire added a century later. Most of the nave was rebuilt in the 15th cent. as was the notable chapel of the golden choir, so called because of the stars of gold studding the beautiful painted roof, where each star frames a laughing or grotesque face. The golden choir is completed by a modern east window ascribed to Christopher Whall and portrays the Madonna with an archangel. The two lesser lights show Adam carrying a spade and Eve a distaff. Among other churches of architectural interest is All Saints, dominating Red Lion Square, of which the great tower and spire are Perpendicular and most of the work inside is 13th-cent. The impressive timbered chancel roof is adorned with painted angels with outspread golden wings.

Daniel Lambert, the biggest Englishman ever, lies buried in the churchyard of St Martin's, near the gateway to Burghley Park. When he died in 1809, aged 39 and 5 ft 11 in. tall, he weighed nearly 53 stone. Some of his clothing may be seen by arrangement with Stamford Corporation. Sir Malcolm Sargent is also buried at Stamford.

For Burghley House see STAMFORD BARON, Huntingdonshire.

STANTON-ON-THE-WOLDS, *Nottinghamshire* (13–SK6330). Nearly deserted since the depopulation of the windswept Wolds, the tiny Church of All Saints stands alone and lost in the trees. The Norman masonry of the west side can still be seen though it is much overgrown, and there is a badly preserved Norman font.

There are grand views of the Trent Valley from the 18-hole golf course. From a house that then stood close to the church Colonel Hutchinson made a spectacular escape when surprised by a party of Royalists during the Civil War. The house belonged to William Needham, governor of LEICESTER and a colonel in the Parliamentary forces.

STAUNTON HAROLD, *Leicestershire* (10–SK3721). Approach Staunton Harold along the road giving a view from due E. The group comprising the house, chapel and lakes seen from this angle is unsurpassed anywhere else in England. The Harold in its name derives from an owner in Anglo-Saxon times and it was given by William the Conqueror to Henry de Ferrariis. It passed by the marriage of Margaret de Staunton to Ralph Shirley in 1423 into the Shirley family, but the Ferrers title was called out of abeyance by Charles II in gratitude for the family's loyalty during the Civil War. The Ferrers family have thus been the owners since the time of the Conqueror. It is one of the most beautiful country houses in Leicestershire, now a Cheshire Home for the Disabled.

The 1st Earl had 27 children, and was the patron of Robert Bakewell, who fashioned for him the magnificent wrought-iron screen at the chancel entrance to the church. The same earl also laid out magnificent formal gardens, swept away 70 years later by the 5th Earl who transformed the canal into a lake. It was also Washington, 5th Earl Ferrers, who built the present large and beautifully proportioned house. It dates from 1770 but incorporates part of the older house, a Palladian north-east front designed by Inigo Jones, probably dating from the second quarter of the 17th cent.

The church is unique and one of the most perfect things in the county. It is now the property of the National Trust and a place of pilgrimage, architecturally one of the most unspoilt buildings in Leicestershire. It was founded by Robert Shirley as an act of defiance against the Commonwealth at a time when new churches in England were rare. Over the doorway, guarded by two angels, an inscription tells the story: "In the year 1653 When all things Sacred were throughout ye nation Either demolisht or profaned Sir Robert Shirley, Barronet, Founded this church; Whose singular praise it is To have done the best things in ye worst times, and hoped them in the most callamitous." Built in the best Perpendicular style of two centuries earlier it has been little altered and retains its contemporary fittings. Since the church was not meant to be a showpiece, these are endearingly humble. Sir Robert Shirley was imprisoned in THE TOWER many times for plotting against the Commonwealth and finally died there aged only 28. He was brought back from London to be buried in the church he had built. Along the chancel is an inscription: "Sir Robert Shirley Baronet Founder of this church anno domini 1653 on whose soul God hath mercy." The church and fittings were finished nine years after his death.

STEETLEY, *Derbyshire* (13–SK5377), is a small, seemingly unremarkable village on Derbyshire's north-east boundary, almost in Yorkshire. Yet here is to be found what Sir Nikolaus Pevsner describes as "the richest example of Norman architecture in Derbyshire". Steetley Chapel is tiny, only 52 ft long by 15 ft wide, yet the quality of the 12th-cent. decoration of the interior stonework, and its lavishness, is of a kind rarely found in Norman churches in England.

STOKE DRY, *Rutland* (10–SP8597), is a hamlet with a small church set on a steep hillside. It looks over the 400-acre sheet of water opened in 1940 to make the Eye Brook Reservoir, a fine unofficial wildfowl refuge with many rare ducks and waders on passage, and in winter the heron and the Canada goose.

The Church of St Andrew is of the simple country type, but full of curious features and furnishings. Externally it is mainly 15th-cent. Perpendicular except for a 13th-cent. west tower. The interior has an early-14th-cent. arcade on the north side and an early-13th-cent. one on the south side. The mural paintings should not be overlooked and the barbaric Norman decoration on the responds of the chancel arch are worth a close examination. From the middle of the 15th cent., when Everard Digby of Tilton married the heiress to Stoke Dry, the Digby family made it their principal seat until the early 17th cent. There is a splendid alabaster table-tomb in the chancel bearing the recumbent figures of Sir Kenelm Digby (d. 1590) and his wife Anne (d. 1602). Standing against the sides of the tomb are the figures of their children, delightfully carved.

The Digby home is now no more, but it was the house of the infamous Sir Everard Digby who financed Guy Fawkes and the Gunpowder Plot. He was hanged for his part in the conspiracy and there is no memorial to him in the church.

STOKE GOLDING, *Leicestershire* (10–SP 3997). One of the villages on the edge of the famous Bosworth Field, near Crown Hill, Stoke Golding contains a very small church, with the most beautiful detail of any in the county. It is a noble edifice, with two naves of equal width, length and height, and a fine west tower and spire. Its arcade and windows are unrestored, and the clustered pillars have elaborately carved capitals thick with foliage and the heads of knights and ladies supporting the finely moulded arches. In the chancel is possibly the most beautiful of any five-light geometric window.

The fabric of the church is mainly 13th-cent. with earlier and later work. It is certainly worth a visit.

STOKE-ON-TRENT, *Staffordshire* (8–SJ 8747). The present Stoke-on-Trent came into being in 1910 when the then Stoke-upon-Trent was combined with five adjoining towns: **Tunstall, Burslem, Hanley, Fenton** and **Longton.** But long before then the area was collectively "The Potteries". Excavations in the city have established that pottery was made here during the Roman occupation: flagons, vases and platters of remarkable quality, dating from the 1st cent., can be seen in the new museum in Hanley, which also possesses one of the world's finest collections of pottery and porcelain. However, even earlier pottery has been found within the city boundary, including an Early Bronze Age (1700 B.C.) beaker and an incense-cup from roughly the same period.

Most of the great names in pottery which are famous today – Wedgwood, Minton, Spode, Coalport (originally a Shropshire firm) – date from the late 18th cent. The present factories can be visited if application is made direct to the firm concerned.

Stoke-upon-Trent was only a village round a church with 11th-cent. origins until the Industrial Revolution. The present church of St Peter ad Vincula was built between 1826 and 1830 but there is part of an Anglo-Saxon cross in the churchyard; and in the chancel a memorial tablet to Josiah Wedgwood, with a portrait medallion in high relief by Flaxman. Wedgwood is also the subject for the best known statue in the Potteries; the bronze figure of the master potter, appraising one of his own vases, greets the visitor at the railway station.

In Tunstall, most northerly of the six towns, the Primitive Methodist movement was founded by Hugh Bourne and William Clowes and the first chapel was built there in 1811, next to the present site. Bourne's home, Ford Hayes Farm, Bucknall, still stands.

Burslem was Wedgwood's birthplace, in 1730, and his association with the town is commemorated by the Wedgwood Memorial Institute, built on the site of his first factory. Burslem has had three town halls, the most interesting of which is the slightly oriental-looking second, now a public library, with its gilded angel surmounting the clock tower.

Hanley's most famous son, Arnold Bennett,

Josiah Wedgwood & Sons

Stoke-on-Trent: a statue of Josiah Wedgwood stands outside the modern factory at Barlaston

was born in Hope Street in 1867 and later lived for brief periods in Dain Street and Newport Lane in Burslem, before the family finally settled in 1880 in a house in Waterloo Road, Cobridge, the suburb which links Burslem and Hanley. The house is now the Bennett Museum, containing drawings and other personal relics. The museum supplies a leaflet which matches the fictitious names Bennett gave to the towns, villages, streets and buildings mentioned in his novels with their originals. Hanley was the birthplace of another famous Englishman, Reginald Mitchell, the designer of the Spitfire fighter, and his association with the town is commemorated by the Mitchell Memorial Youth Centre in Broad Street.

Stoke is not renowned for ancient buildings but it has one small gem: Ford Green Hall in Smallthorne, a 16th-cent. timber-framed manor house which has been restored with period furniture and domestic utensils and is open to the public.

STOKESAY, *Shropshire* (8–SO4381). The castle and the church stand side by side, separated only by the moat; at a distance the visitor could take the squat, embattled church tower for the castle. A little way off the A49, about 1 m. S. of Craven Arms, Stokesay Castle is one of the earliest fortified manor houses in England and is in a remarkable state of preservation. It can be freely visited.

The castle is approached through a black-and-white gatehouse, with gabled stone roof and overhanging story. The contrast with the main castle buildings across the courtyard, two stone towers joined by a long, gabled banqueting hall, is marked. The great hall was built towards the end of the 13th cent. and is remarkable for the size of its windows; few families risked having windows so large in those times. Also unlike most unhomely castle chambers is the gracious, oak-panelled drawing-room approached by an outside staircase. Happily the castle avoided damage in the Civil War when those garrisoning it for Charles I surrendered after brief resistance.

The church, which, with the castle, is set beside a small lake, has a Norman doorway but was largely rebuilt in the mid-17th cent. Nearby is the cast-iron bridge over the River Onny, one of Thomas Telford's minor works.

STONE, *Staffordshire* (8–SJ9034), a pleasant old town beside the River Trent, is the birthplace of one of England's most famous admirals, John Jervis, who, after helping to win the battle off the Cape St Vincent in 1797, became the Earl St Vincent. His imposing mausoleum is in the parish churchyard. Tradition has it that the town took its name from the cairn of stones erected over the bodies of two Mercian princes who were killed by their pagan father, King Wulfhere, in the 7th cent., for embracing Christianity. They are commemorated in a window in the 18th-cent. parish church.

There was an Augustinian priory at Stone in the 12th cent. and fragments of the cloisters and an arch can be seen in Abbey Street, near the churchyard. This and the pleasing long High Street apart, Stone's main interest for the visitor lies in the country on its doorstep, which includes Tittensor Chase, a stretch of heath and woodland well served with footpaths. Here, too, are the "Petrifactions"; the water of a stream which runs through a wooded hollow has a strange petrifying effect on plant life.

This is also a nursery area. One, which covers 513 acres, including 100 acres of nursery stock, is one of the largest in England. Millions of forest trees, ornamental trees, roses and shrubs are grown there – but one tree is not for sale, a huge weeping birch reputed to be more than 120 years old

STONEY MIDDLETON, *Derbyshire* (12–SK2275). One of the few completely octagonal churches in the country stands in this small village, whose other remarkable feature is its setting among the often towering limestone crags and cliffs about 4 m. N. of BAKEWELL. There are quarries here – and every tree for miles around is coated with white dust so that at night the effect is of a ghostly forest. There are two wells in the square in front of the church which are blessed and dressed each year in August in accordance with the custom peculiar to Derbyshire. The dressing, as in other villages, takes the form of an intricate reproduction in thousands of flower petals, leaves, mosses, fir cones and tiny pieces of bark of a biblical scene. Many of the pictures are as much as 8 to 10 ft tall and are the product of hours of painstaking work on the part of the villagers.

STOTTESDON, *Shropshire* (8–SO6782). Men have worshipped in the Church of St Mary in this tiny village, hidden in the lanes about 4 m. N. of CLEOBURY MORTIMER, for perhaps 900 years. And for all that time they must have gazed up at the tympanum and wondered why two of the crudely carved animals on it stand on their heads while the third stands normally. Only the Anglo-Saxon mason – or it may have been a Norman – could give the answer. The animals are actually on the stone lintel, the tympanum proper being carved with a haphazard group of saltire crosses, a bearded Norman head being at the top of the arch.

The tympanum, which is over the west doorway, now an inner doorway inside the tower, the tower itself, the arcaded nave and the font, all Norman, make this one of the most interesting churches in the county.

STOW, *Lincolnshire* (13–SK8981). An obscure, straggling village between LINCOLN and GAINSBOROUGH, occupying what is believed to be the site of the Roman station of Sidnacester. The earliest church here is said to have been built by King Ecgfrith of Northumbria in A.D. 678 to commemorate a miracle. While his wife, St Ethelreda, foundress of ELY, was in flight from him following a quarrel she stopped at this place and drove her staff into the ground, whereupon it took root and became an ash tree. King Ecgfrith on learning of this commanded that a church should be built here in respectful recognition of the event. This church was destroyed by the Danes in about 870 and remained a ruin until *c.* 1040 when it was rebuilt by Eadnoth, Bishop of Dorchester, with monetary help from Leofric, Earl of Mercia, and another determined woman, known to us as Lady Godiva, his wife. The church has been beautifully restored and is especially notable for its central tower, which springs directly from the ground to accord with the original 11th-cent. piers. The interior is a vista of great arches, the round-headed Norman alternating with the 15th-cent. pointed arches framing the original masonry.

Stow church was once the cathedral of the diocese of Lindsey, and is still known as the Dowager Minster of Lincoln.

STOWE-BY-CHARTLEY, *Staffordshire* (8–SK0027). Here, 7 m. NE. of STAFFORD, are the

Tamworth Castle stands at the junction of two rivers

ruined towers of the original Chartley Castle, now much overgrown, built in 1220 by the Crusader, Ranulf de Blundeville, Earl of Chester. A second castle here was visited by Queen Elizabeth in 1575 and was one of the places in which some years later Mary Queen of Scots was kept prisoner. This castle, and its successor, the third, was destroyed by fire. In the village of Stowe is the 12th-cent. Church of St John the Baptist, reckoned by some to be one of the best examples of the combination of ancient and Victorian architecture to be found in Staffordshire. Here, all in the one building, are a Norman chancel arch, an Early English window, a tower part 14th-, part 15th-cent. and a north aisle built less than 100 years ago.

SUDBURY, *Derbyshire* (12–SK1631), is another of Derbyshire's model villages – brick, pretty and built largely in the 17th cent. It is about 6 m. E. of UTTOXETER and here, too, is Sudbury Hall, the seat of the Vernon family which is now in the care of the National Trust. Begun by Mary Vernon in 1613, the Hall was left unfinished at her death but was eventually completed by George Vernon between 1670 and 1695. The Long Gallery is aptly named, being 138 ft long; there is much fine work to be seen including ceiling paintings by Laguerre, a staircase carved by Pierce and overmantel carvings of exceptional quality by Grinling Gibbons. Not far from the house is a strange brick structure with turrets known as "The Eye-catcher". The village church, All Saints, dating from the 14th cent., contains many monuments to the Vernon family and a stained-glass window given by Queen Victoria.

SUTTON BRIDGE, *Lincolnshire* (13–TF 4821), is a town of diminished importance

which was the point of embarkation across the Cross Keys Wash where King John lost his treasure and all his baggage in 1216. It is now an occasional port on the reclaimed marshland served by the River Nene. In 1831 a wooden bridge was built here which, with the coming of improved lines of communication, was replaced by an iron swing-bridge designed by Robert Stephenson. This gave way to the present road and railway bridge built in 1894, operated by hydraulic power. Since the collapse of faultily constructed new docks in 1881 no new plans have been adopted, so the area is largely derelict; but visitors to the scene of King John's misfortune will find an excellent nine-hole golf course on the site.

SUTTON CHENEY, *Leicestershire* (10–SK 4100), is a small village overlooking Bosworth Field. The Royal army encamped near here before the battle. The Church of St James is 13th-cent. with a 14th-cent. chancel arch, priest's doorway, east window and south aisle doorway and windows. There is an effigy of Geoffrey May, who was lord of the manor in the 17th cent. The manor has now disappeared but an Elizabethan farm-house with a stone dated 1601 set in the wall remains. Another effigy is that of Sir William Roberts (1633) with his two wives. The almshouses E. of the church were founded by Sir William in 1612. The end one of these has holes honeycombed in the gables as if the builder wished to encourage birds to nest in the roof. The third monument of note in the church is a plaque to Thomas Simpson, a local boy who became interested in astrology. Soon he became famous locally and people started to consult him, but fees were small and to keep going he married his landlady, who was 50 years old and had a son two years older than

Simpson. Finally he frightened one of his clients almost to death and had to flee to London, where he edited the first "glossy", *The Ladies' Diary*. In his spare time he studied mathematics and became a Fellow of the Royal Society and professor of mathematics at the Royal Military Academy. He was highly regarded and when he died George III awarded a large pension to his widow, who had been almost permanently drunk, and was a slut and scold into the bargain.

SWARKESTONE, *Derbyshire* (13–SK3728). The graceful bridge over the River Trent is the chief attraction for the sightseer in this small village about 4 m. SE. of DERBY. Built in the 13th and 14th cents. and much restored about 1800, its 17 sturdy old arches and the causeways stretch for three-quarters of a mile. There is also an architectural curiosity here, the so-called Summer House – also known as the Grandstand. With its two square corner towers and battlemented centre it looks like a small fort, but may well have been the grandstand in a bull-baiting arena. The enclosed area around it is known as the Cuttle.

SWINESHEAD, *Lincolnshire* (13–TF2340). The worn remains of the market cross preserved with another relic of bygone times, the old broken stocks, in the War Memorial garden here indicate that this large village was formerly a market town. It is one of the few places in England where, from October until March, the curfew still tolls at dusk. The medieval Church of St Mary, with its massive and very tall tower, is an outstanding landmark for many miles. The lower portion of this tower is 14th-cent., and the superstructure, comprising a pinnacled belfry and embattled octagon from which the spire rises a further 160 ft, dates from a century later. The interior is almost cathedral-like in its grandeur, with fine timbering and stonework providing a dignified setting for the many ancient memorials relating to the long history of the parish. A mile NW. of the village is the site of a small Cistercian abbey founded in 1148, where King John and his retinue lodged for a few days after losing their equipment at SUTTON BRIDGE while attempting to traverse the treacherous waters of the Wash. There is no foundation to the tradition, the plot of Shakespeare's tragic play, that the king was poisoned by the monks of Swineshead Abbey before meeting his end at NEWARK Castle.

SWYNNERTON, *Staffordshire* (8–SJ8435). This village, 3 m. NW. of STONE, is thought by some to be the inspiration for Longfellow's poem "Under the Spreading Chestnut Tree". Certainly there is such a tree opposite the 17th-cent. village inn, the FitzHerbert Arms; and an old smithy near at hand. Here there are thatched cottages and a fine early-18th-cent. Hall, but the oldest building is the church, which has Norman arcades and much else that is almost as old. The most striking feature in the church is the huge medieval statue of Christ.

TAMWORTH, *Staffordshire* (9–SK2004), possesses one of the two finest castles in Staffordshire – the other is at TUTBURY. Owned now by the Corporation – it was bought for £3,000 in 1897 as a memorial of Queen Victoria's Diamond Jubilee – the castle was lived in for 700 years from its erection in Norman times. But Tamworth's history goes back further than that: as long ago as 757 Offa, the Anglo-Saxon King of Mercia, had a royal palace at Tamworth but no trace of it remains. In 913, Ethelfleda, daughter of Alfred the Great, won a great battle against the Danes at Tamworth and to thwart a counter-attack built a stockade on a huge mound at the junction of the Rivers Tame and Anker. It was around this mound that Robert de Marmion, one of William the Conqueror's barons, began to build the fortress, much of which still stands today.

The Castle is, in fact, a mixture of Norman, Gothic, Tudor, Jacobean and early-19th-cent. architecture. The walls of the keep, 10 ft thick at their base, and the solid Norman tower with its dungeon, were the work of the Marmions. To the Tudor period belongs the more domestic warden's lodge and the splendid banqueting hall with its great oak-mullioned window. In the state dining-room, in the north wing – which also houses the royal bed-chamber – is a frieze of 55 oak panels painted with the arms of the lords of the castle up to 1787. There is a haunted staircase and a long gallery which is now the main museum area, where a collection of coins from Offa's Tamworth mint can be seen.

The parish church, with the rare dedication to St Editha, has one unique feature. The square tower is topped by a spire on each corner and in the south-west corner is a double-twisting staircase. There are 101 steps in the one spiral, 106 in the other, so arranged that the floor of one is the roof of the other. Climbers of one spiral do not see climbers of the other until they both reach the top. One spiral ascends from an entrance in the churchyard, the other from inside the tower.

Tamworth Town Hall is one of the prettiest in the country, built in mellow red brick with arcades at ground level, large Jacobean windows and a high-pitched roof, the whole topped with a cupola. It was built in 1701 by Thomas Guy, then M.P. for the town, whose name lives on in Guy's Hospital, in Southwark.

TATTERSHALL, *Lincolnshire* (13–TF2157). The feature of this otherwise undistinguished township is the immense castle keep built by Ralph, Lord Cromwell, in *c.* 1455, on the remains of a fortress raised by Robert de Tateshall in 1240 and acquired by the Cromwells through marriage. The building of castles solely for military purposes had reached its climax in the reign of Edward I. By the 15th cent. gunpowder superseded the old method of attack with cumbrous siege-machines, and warfare had taken to the open fields. The fortified mansion serving as stronghold and home resulted. Even so, Ralph Cromwell, Lord Treasurer to Henry VI from 1433–43, provided the castle with imposing defences of very great strength and saw to it that the basic structure was proof against the ravages of time. How well he and those who completed the work succeeded is shown in the massive remnant, now the property of the National Trust. The great quadrangled tower is one of the best examples of medieval brickwork in England, with windows, battlements and fireplaces of Ancaster stone. There are four stories, each of which has a large central room containing a fine heraldic chimney-piece and other emblems of Lord Cromwell's official standing. From the parapet wall above the gallery, and also from the top of the south-west turret, reached by a winding stairway of 181 steps, it is possible to see LINCOLN Cathedral in one direction and the BOSTON Stump in another. The guard house, set well within the periphery of the double moat, is now a museum.

Although little remains of the collegiate buildings also founded by Cromwell, the striking cruciform Church of the Holy Trinity, which he began in 1440, exists as a continuing memorial to his energy and vision. It is a remarkably beautiful edifice in durable Ancaster stone with insignia commemorating both Ralph Cromwell and William of Waynflete, Bishop of Winchester, who continued the work so ably begun.

TEALBY, *Lincolnshire* (13–TF1590). A beautiful village on the slopes of the Wolds, with the River Rase running down from Bully Hill. Across the valley once stood Bayons Manor, the house of the grandfather of Tennyson, which once belonged to William the Conqueror's half-brother, Bishop Odo of Bayeux; Bayons is an anglicized version of the title. A walk in the steps of Alfred, Lord Tennyson, is accomplished by starting in Tealby itself and setting off in a SE. direction downhill past the church to meet the bridge over the River Rase at the entrance of Bayons Park. Continue through the recently cultivated park until the track sweeps to the left. By bearing right after this, through fields and on to High Street Farm, and again at **Hainton**, with its 145-acre parkland landscaped by Capability Brown, the walk leads back through delightful scenery to cross the River Rase again and ends at Tealby. Tealby Church is an imposing building dating back in part to Norman times.

TELFORD, *Shropshire* (*see* Madeley, 8–SJ 6904). Although much work is already under way at this new town, much is still only in the planners' minds. This exciting concept for Britain's first new major city for centuries began in 1963 with a plan to develop Dawley by marrying it into one unit with **Madeley**, IRONBRIDGE and Coalbrookdale. But in 1968 the decision was made to broaden the concept and take in Wellington and Oakengates. At the same time it was decided to give the new city – for city rather than town it will be – a new name. Telford was chosen to commemorate a man whose bridges, viaducts, canals and churches can still be seen in all parts of Shropshire: Thomas Telford, 1757–1834, the

Scottish-born stone-mason, who became one of the world's most famous engineers. It is fitting that two of his major works, the Holyhead Road and the unusual octagonal church in Madeley, should be within the area of the new city which bears his name.

The plan visualizes the welding of the scattered towns of East Shropshire, with a present combined population of about 70,000, into a new, integrated city which, by the late 1980s, will be home for 220,000 people. The new city will be almost in the shadow of Shropshire's most famous hill, the 1,300-ft WREKIN, and will be flanked by the River Severn.

Building and rebuilding is going on on a vast scale. New houses by the thousand, shops, churches, factories, schools, roads and roundabouts the size of tumuli are emerging everywhere. The new city will first of all get its main artery and then its new heart. The aim of the proposed urban motorway is to join Dawley, Madeley and Stirchley in the S. with Oakengates, Trench and Wellington in the N. Then in the Malins Lee area will be built a new city centre, incorporating every modern facility and feature.

Already a new district shopping centre is under construction in Madeley and domestic building is going on apace in the Woodside area between Madeley and Coalbrookdale. But it is at Sutton Hill that the visitor can best see the physical surroundings in which people will live in the 21st cent. Here is the first completed Local Centre – scores of short terraces of modern houses grouped round a large, traffic-free precinct with lawns, shrubs and flowers. In the centre are a supermarket, other shops, the Red Admiral public house, a health clinic and surgeries, a library and church centre, and a community centre containing an assembly hall, coffee bar and children's play centre. The church, with plate-glass windows to ground level and tall, metal cross set in a courtyard, is particularly interesting.

A few miles away, just below the old village of Madeley, a huge educational and recreational centre is under construction. It is planned to include not only assembly halls but also a swimming-pool and a bowling rink. On the edge of this development stands Madeley's oldest building, Madeley Court. The Elizabethan building has lost much of its original splendour but its strange sundial, a large stone ball with holes through which could be assessed the positions of the planets and the moon, can still be seen in the garden. So future generations will be able, by a mere turn of the head, to see the buildings of the first and second Elizabethan eras.

THORESBY HALL, *Nottinghamshire* (13– SK6371). This impressive Victorian mansion near OLLERTON, 180 ft square with a great hall 61 ft long, 31 ft broad and 48 ft high, is the home of Countess Manvers and open to the public. It is the third house on the site, one of the most thickly wooded in SHERWOOD FOREST. The building, begun in 1864, was finished in 1874. The first Thoresby was enclosed out of the forest by the Duke of Kingston in 1683 and was the home of his famous daughter, Lady Mary Wortley Montagu, the greatest of English women letter writers, whose first volume of *Complete Letters* was published in 1966. In 1745 this building was destroyed by fire and replaced by a small brick mansion, the residence of the celebrated Duchess of Kingston, who was tried for bigamy in 1776. This house was described by Horace Walpole in 1772 as a place in which there was "no temptation to stop".

The present house, built when the Dukeries were fashionable, was designed by Anthony Salvin and is set in 12,000 acres. There are many magnificently furnished rooms, including the blue drawing-room and the Victoria bedroom. The principal floor contains 29 rooms and there are 78 bedrooms. The fireplace in the great hall is carved with a history of the Manvers family and there is a picture here of Lady Mary Wortley Montagu. In the library are statues of Robin Hood and Little John. Exhibitions of topical interest are held and cars may drive through the superb chestnut avenues in the park, and round the beautiful ornamental waters made by damming the River Meden. On the western extremity of the lake is a model village built in 1807 and a charming castellated folly called Budby Castle. About 1 m. E. is the village of **Perlethorpe** where Salvin built a Victorian Decorated parish church with a spire of about 130 ft.

THRUMPTON HALL, *Nottinghamshire* (13–SK5131). Built in about 1608 by the Pigots, who also gave it its massively carved wide staircase at the time of the Restoration, Thrumpton Hall is now owned by the Seymours. It is of brick with stone dressings in an H-type plan with a contemporary loggia on the garden side which was balanced with a similar loggia on the opposite side, facing a backwater of the Trent, in 1830–40.

The Church of All Saints is remarkable since it embodies the only work of restoration in the county carried out by the famous Victorian architect, G. E. Street, who designed the ROYAL COURTS OF JUSTICE in London. His work is particularly recognizable in the chancel rails and seating. Memorials to the Pigots and Emmertons are in the tower. When the pulpit was removed during the restoration it was found that a carpenter from the village had placed a board beneath it bearing the inscription: "A proud parson and a simple squire Bade me build this pulpit higher".

Thrumpton Hall, with its lovely staircase, priest's hole, carvings, paintings and gardens, may be viewed by the public at certain times.

TICKENCOTE, *Rutland* (10–SK9809). A magnet for photographers and students of architecture, Tickencote's Church of St Peter is famous for its amazing late Norman chancel arch of five orders, each carved with a different design in about 1160–70. The outer line has a unique pattern of foliage; the next a double zigzag; the third has grotesques

and foliage among which may be seen a muzzled bear, a fox's head with a monk, a green man, and two crowned heads looking opposite ways, thought to represent Stephen and Maud, rivals for the English throne; the fourth order has embattled moulding and zigzag on the soffit; and the last plain, round, stepped moulding. The sexpartite vaulting of the chancel is also late Norman; the only other occurrence of this type of vaulting is at CANTERBURY Cathedral. There is a font of 1200 and an oak effigy of a knight, possibly Sir Roland de Daneys, who died in 1363.

In 1792 the church was restored and partly rebuilt in a somewhat unattractive fashion by S. P. Cockerell.

Due N. on the A1 from here is **Stretton,** where there is another little church worth stopping to see. It has a very simple Norman south doorway and an early-13th-cent. arcade of fine design. The south transept was added in the beginning of the 17th cent., an unusual time for church building in England. Stocken Hall, about 1½ m. E., is an early-17th-cent. house with a good Georgian façade.

Continue along the A1 due N. for 1½ m. then turn right past the site of the Battle of Losecoat Field to **Pickworth,** one of the 14 Lost Villages of local lore, so called in this case because of the ravages of the plague from 1349 to the end of the 17th cent. and the disastrous event of the Battle of Losecoat Field in 1470. All that is left is one gaunt arch of the parish church standing alone in a field, a desolate monument with a beauty of its own. It was this and a few then-remaining fragments that inspired the rustic poet, John Clare, who worked as a lime-burner in Pickworth, to write the melancholy verse which made him famous.

TIDESWELL, *Derbyshire* (12–SK1575), is famous for its fine, big church, known as the "Cathedral of the Peak". This small, stone-built town lies 6 m. ENE. of BUXTON among the limestone hills of the High Peak and is dominated by its parish church, St John the Baptist, with its tall, heavy, eight-pinnacled tower, one of the earliest Perpendicular towers in England. The church was built during the 14th cent. and contains a fine collection of pre-Reformation monuments, including the best single brass in Derbyshire, that to John Foljambe who died in 1383.

About 2 m. from the town to the N. are three ancient barrows, and 3 m. to the NW. the remains of a Roman road, Batham Gate. Tideswell holds an annual Wakes Week towards the end of June and during it the well-dressing ceremony is held, and there is Morris dancing in the main street. At **Great Hucklow,** a hamlet in the hills to the N. of Tideswell, are the headquarters of the Derbyshire and Lancashire Gliding Club where instruction is given to beginners; and most surprisingly, a splendid small theatre in a barn, home of the Village Drama Players.

TISSINGTON, *Derbyshire* (12–SK1752). This exceptionally beautiful old village 3 m. N. of

ASHBOURNE is believed to have been where the Derbyshire custom of well-dressing began, as long ago as 1350. There are no fewer than five wells here and they are dressed in an interesting ceremony on Ascension Day each year. The village is a delightful ensemble with its triangular green surrounded by mellow stone houses, the church and Jacobean hall in the background. The church shows traces of its Norman origin and contains a most unusual Norman tub font carved with animals and a snake.

TITTERSTONE CLEE HILL, *Shropshire* (8–SO5878), is one of Shropshire's highest hills, 1,749 ft above sea-level. On the flat crown, an area of about 70 acres, was an Iron Age camp. Parts of the original earth and timber rampart and the rough-hewn basalt blocks used to strengthen it can still be seen.

TONG, *Shropshire* (8–SJ7907), which lies just off the A41 to WOLVERHAMPTON, about 8 m. S. of NEWPORT, has a church with one of the largest and most remarkable collections of monuments in the Midlands. The church itself, built on the foundations of an earlier one, was founded in the early 15th cent. by Lady Elizabeth Pembruge, in memory of her husband Sir Fulke, and alabaster effigies of them are among the earliest of the monuments. Many of the others are of members of the Vernon family and among the most interesting are those to Sir Richard, Speaker of the House of Commons in 1426, whose armoured figure in alabaster lies beside that of his wife; a particularly fine brass to Sir William, High Constable to Henry V; and, in an alcove, the bust of Arthur Vernon, a 15th-cent. CAMBRIDGE don. The red sandstone church itself, with its tower which starts square and then becomes octagonal, its battlements and unusual miniature stone spire, and its position on top of a small mound, cannot fail to catch the eye of anyone passing along the main road below.

In the 18th cent. George Durant bought the Vernons' castle and rebuilt it. His son, also George, put up several follies in the grounds, of which the Convent Lodge and the Egyptian Aviary remain.

TRENTHAM, *Staffordshire* (8–SJ8640), has been famous for 40 years as the site of Trentham Gardens, one of the Midlands' chief pleasure parks. But the village itself is of ancient foundation; a burial mound in Northwood Lane, excavated in 1859, is believed to date from about 1000 B.C. And as early as A.D. 660 King Wulf here, first Christian king of Mercia, had a palace near here and his daughter founded the nunnery which stood on the site of the present parish church. Trentham is mentioned in the Domesday Book and for 400 years up to the Reformation there was an Augustinian priory here. The Norman pillars of that building were incorporated into the present church which was erected in 1844.

Trentham Hall, eventually to become of palace proportions, was built in the early 17th cent. by Sir Richard Leveson whose successors the

G. Douglas Bolton

Tissington: a traditional well-dressing

Leveson-Gowers, later to become the Dukes of Sutherland, enlarged it and landscaped the estate around it so that by the mid-19th cent. Trentham was a vast Italianate mansion surrounded by formal gardens of a size and intricacy rarely found in England. Today only the ballroom and one hall of the original building remain, but the Italian garden, with its main parterre (geometric design area), can still be seen by the visitor, albeit in a simpler, less formal style.

In the grounds there is a beautiful lake, now used for boating; and on a hill-top a reminder of the former owners of Trentham – a tall, stone column on which stands a statue by Chantrey of the 1st Duke of Sutherland. Trentham can claim to have been in the "stately home" business 50 years before it became a commonplace. In the early years of this century local people were allowed to stroll through the grounds on public holidays and brass bands would play during the wakes weeks. The house has twice been described in novels: the Brentham in Disraeli's *Lothair* is Trentham, as is Sneyd Hall in Arnold Bennett's *The Card*; and in the latter, the Countess of Chell is thought to be a comic portrait of the 4th Duchess.

TUTBURY, *Staffordshire* (9–SK2129). This small, attractive old town beside the River Dove claims to have the finest Norman church in the county and, indeed, in the Midlands. The west end of the 11th-cent. building, with its doorway of seven receding Norman arches, all full of intricate and delicate carving, has a dignity which belongs to a much larger, more imposing building;

Kenneth Scowen

Uppingham: the ancient turf maze at Wing resembles certain pavement mazes in France

and inside, the thick Norman pillars frame an impressive nave. There are other treasures, too: an ancient parish chest; another Norman doorway with an Anglo-Saxon tympanum; a 13th-cent. head of Christ behind the pulpit; and the old village stocks.

Tutbury has the remains of an imposing castle; like so many in this part of the country, it was despoiled by the Parliamentarians after twice being besieged by them. Dramatically sited on an isolated rock, the castle was the final successor of a number of forts dating back to the Iron Age. Today the visitor can see John of Gaunt's gateway, built in the 14th cent.; the south tower with a winding staircase leading to an ante-chamber and the presence chamber; and the high tower where Mary Queen of Scots spent many years of her captivity. This tower has a winding staircase of 67 steps which is well worth climbing for the view it affords over Needwood Forest and into Derbyshire.

The main street of the little town is another of its charms; it is wide and gracious with Tudor, Georgian and Regency houses. Perhaps the most striking building is the black-and-white Dog and Partridge Inn, once the home of the Curzon family and later a coaching inn.

The ancient ceremony of bull running at Tutbury dates from the time of John of Gaunt, when a bull was mutilated and let loose. If the townsfolk caught him before he crossed the river he was theirs; if not he belonged to the abbot.

UPPINGHAM, *Rutland* (10–SP8699). An unhurried little town of old-fashioned, bow-fronted shops, quiet streets and sombre ironstone houses, many of them unchanged since the 18th cent. The market here was first authorized by Edward I in 1281 and a fair was granted at the same time. Great prosperity followed, reaching its height in the Elizabethan era, but today it is evident that times have changed, for little business is transacted in the market place. The prime importance of Uppingham lies in its great public school, the magnificent buildings of which occupy by far the larger part of the south-west quarter of the town. The original building, founded in 1584, accommodated no more than two dozen boarders and rated as a grammar school. In the 19th cent., under the headmastership of the Rev. Edward Thring, its increase in both size and standing can only be described as tremendous. Uppingham now has probably the biggest school playing-fields in England, a superb block of buildings, a museum, a chapel and a memorial hall in which is preserved the original charter of the school with the seal of Elizabeth I.

About 3 m. to the NE. of Uppingham is the village of **Wing,** of which the Church of SS. Peter and Paul has a Norman arcade rich with carving, and many surviving traces of 13th- and 14th-cent. stonework. Of especial interest here is the ancient turf maze, some 40 ft across, which is believed to have served as a means of doing penance.

UPTON, *Nottinghamshire* (13–SK7354). There are many fine views from this pleasant halting-place, taking in much of the countryside down to where the River Greet joins the Trent and affording a clear sight of the cathedral at LINCOLN in the distance. St Peter's Church here has an Early English arcade, a Decorated chancel and an unusual Perpendicular tower with nine instead of eight pinnacles. Also in the tower is a priest's room with a fireplace, and high in the walls are holes which show that doves were once encouraged, as was then usual, to build their nests in the stonework. Upton is the village where James Tennant was born in the 19th cent. From the humblest beginnings he went out into the world to become Professor of Mineralogy at King's College, CAMBRIDGE, and in that capacity was given the task of cutting the Koh-i-Noor diamond for Queen Victoria's crown.

UTTOXETER, *Staffordshire* (9–SK0933). The strangest thing about this small market town is its name. Today it is often called "Ucheter" or "Uxeter" and in the past it has been spelt in a variety of ways: Wotocheshede (Domesday Book, 1086), Uttokishedere (1175), Wittokeshather (1242), Uittokesather and Huttokesather (1251). It is believed to derive from a form of Witta, a man's name, and an old word for heath.

Today Uttoxeter is known mainly for its racecourse, reckoned the finest National Hunt Steeplechase course in the Midlands; and for a visit paid it about 1780 by Dr Samuel Johnson. Johnson's father was a bookseller in LICHFIELD and used to have a stall in Uttoxeter market. On one occasion, the young Samuel, too proud to stand at a market stall, refused to go with his father to Uttoxeter. Many years later, an old man near the end of his life, Dr Johnson returned – to do penance for his act of disobedience. For several hours he stood bareheaded, in the rain, on the spot in the Market Place where his father's stall used to stand: "In contrition I stood, and I hope the penance was expiatory." Today there is a substantial stone conduit here with a carving depicting the scene.

About 3 m. N. of Uttoxeter, among meadows between the Rivers Dove and Churnet, lies the village of **Rocester**. Once a Roman station, Rocester has seen much history. In the churchyard is the shaft of a 700-year-old cross, with interlaced work, said to be the best preserved example in the country; nearby are the remains of an Augustinian abbey. The visitor must look for these. He will have no need to look for Rocester's present claim to fame: the huge works of a famous firm of excavator manufacturers whose grounds are full of the "diesel dinosaurs" which have carved out the motorways.

WAINFLEET ALL SAINTS, *Lincolnshire* (13–TF4959). This small market town on the River Steeping was once a port. It is famous as the birthplace of William of Waynflete, Bishop of WINCHESTER and founder of Magdalen College, OXFORD. He founded the turreted Magdalen College School in Wainfleet in 1484.

WALL, *Staffordshire* (9–SK0906). The most complete Roman bath-house found to date in Britain was unearthed near this small village, 2 m.

S. of LICHFIELD. Wall was originally the Roman fort of Letocetum, built where Ryknild Street crossed Watling Street, and was a military centre of some importance for about three decades from A.D. 50. Excavations which eventually revealed the three baths – cold, tepid and hot – the furnace room with its floor of Roman cement and the exercise hall, were not begun until the 19th cent. The site is now in the care of the Ministry of Public Building and Works and is open to the public. A small museum has been established there containing finds made in the area, including cremation vessels.

WALSALL, *Staffordshire* (8–SP0198), is now an industrial town of a hundred trades but was once famous for only one – the working of leather. The nickname of the town's football team, the Saddlers, commemorates this connection. Today only the records remain of the town's long history: the first charter dated 1159; the Roll of Mayors back to 1377; the links with Warwick the Kingmaker, whose crest of bear and ragged staff appear in the Walsall coat of arms. The crypt of the Parish Church of St Matthew, dating from the early 13th cent., is probably the oldest building. An unusual feature of the church is the evidence in the vaulted archway beneath the high altar that a road once ran under the chancel.

Walsall's most famous son is Jerome K. Jerome, author of *Three Men in a Boat*, whose birthplace in Bradford Street is marked by a plaque. In the town centre, on The Bridge, is a bronze statue to Dorothy Pattison, known as Sister Dora, who spent 12 memorable years between 1865 and 1877 caring for Walsall's sick in an age when industrial accidents were common and smallpox epidemics not unknown.

The town, now including Willenhall, Darlaston and parts of WEDNESBURY and Bilston, has an impressive number of parks, playing fields and open spaces. The finest is undoubtedly the Arboretum, 80 acres set among trees and lakes within two minutes' walk of the town centre. For a fortnight each September the park becomes a Chinese garden of coloured lights and lanterns and rainbow fountains.

Willenhall has been turning out locks and keys for 400 years and most of those manufactured in England still originate here. Exhibits in the Lock Museum attached to the Public Library tell of the history and technical development of the lock and key.

WALTHAM-ON-THE-WOLDS, *Leicestershire* (10–SK8025). A large and pretty village standing high in the heart of the Wolds and a good place from which to explore them, Waltham-on-the-Wolds has one of the more important black smock windmills of Leicestershire, now unfortunately sailless. Most of the buildings are of the attractive, silver-grey oolitic limestone and Roman pavements and Anglo-Saxon stone coffins have been found in its soil. Most of the Church of St Mary Magdalene is very fine early 14th-cent. with many grave, gay and grotesque carvings on the nave arcade, and ten angels supporting the chancel roof, but two Norman doorways have survived – one plain and one zigzagged – and the semi-Norman font is one of the best in the county. There is a font at **Stonesby**, on the secondary road to the E., by the same artist.

WANLIP, *Leicestershire* (10–SK5910). The little church on the banks of the River Soar was entirely rebuilt in the last quarter of the 14th cent. by Sir Thomas Walsh, and Wanlip is thus worth visiting for the comparative rarity of its style in Leicestershire. The brass to its founder has the earliest prose inscription in English on any brass in the country. It tells how his wife, portrayed by his side, "in her tyme made the Kirke of Anlep and Halud the Kirkeyard". There are also some old heraldic glass shields and three medieval bells.

A legend hereabouts is that a giant named Bel vowed to reach LEICESTER from **Mountsorrel** in three leaps. He mounted his giant horse and their first jump landed them in Wanlip (One Leap). The second leap ended at **Burstall**. But the third leap was too much for them. They both fell dead a mile and a half short of Leicester and were buried in one grave – at **Bel-grave**. Possibly by the time they got to Burstall they were bursting all to get to their avowed destination.

WEDNESBURY, *Staffordshire* (8–SP0095). On its hill-top dominating this large town stands the Parish Church of St Bartholomew, reckoned one of the most beautiful Perpendicular churches in the Midlands. Parts of it date from the 12th cent.; there is some richly-coloured stained glass from the 15th cent.; a carved oak pulpit from the early 17th cent.; and a wooden lectern in the shape of a cock which is 600 years old. The town was named after Woden, the Anglo-Saxon god.

WELBECK ABBEY, *Nottinghamshire* (13–SK5674). This vast and extraordinary complex of 12th- to 19th-cent. building and subterranean labyrinth began in 1153, with the foundation of a monastic house of the order of Premonstratensian canons by Thomas de Cuckney. After the Dissolution the abbey was granted by Henry VIII to Richard Whalley, and through his heirs it eventually came into the possession of the redoubtable Bess of Hardwick. This ambitious and immensely able woman acquired incalculable wealth through successive marriages and the application of astute business acumen. Having bought Welbeck Abbey from the Whalley family she bequeathed the estate to Charles, her son by Sir William Cavendish. The son became father of another Sir William Cavendish who, because of his services to the king, was created the 1st Duke of Newcastle.

The south wing of Welbeck, built by the Duke of Newcastle in about 1630, was rebuilt in 1751 after the estate had, by several marriages, passed into the possession of the 2nd Duke of Portland, in whose family it was to remain until the 20th cent., when the greater part was put to use as an Army boarding school.

It was during the 19th cent. that the already magnificent and treasure-filled house was extended and literally undermined by the eccentric 5th Duke. This strange man was a recluse, whose morbid fear of being seen impelled him to build mile upon mile of underground tunnels and even entire suites beneath the surface. One of these consisted of three library rooms nearly 250 ft long followed by a ballroom and picture gallery measuring 174 ft by 64 ft and 22 ft high, which is described as the largest private apartment in England. After that came the Rose Corridor, a long underground conservatory with a glass roof. At the time of the 5th Duke's death in 1879 15,000 men were permanently employed on 36 different building projects in the grounds.

A disastrous fire in 1900 gutted the Oxford wing, following which considerable restoration and modernization was affected by the 6th Duke, but the great days of Welbeck Abbey were nearly over. The Army College is not open to the public.

WELL VALE, *Lincolnshire* (13–TF4574). This delightful beauty-spot on the eastern slope of the Wolds provides a perfect setting for one of the most beautiful country houses in Lincolnshire. Well Vale Hall is a fine example of early Georgian architecture, in red brick with a central pediment and an austerity of ornamentation characteristic of the period. Surrounding the house is a noble park of 170 acres, with two broad lakes fed by a chalk spring which together with the closely wooded valley gives the place its name. A few cottages, a school and a little church resembling a Grecian temple face the entrance to the Hall amid cedars, oaks and pines.

WEM, *Shropshire* (8–SJ5129), was once owned by Judge Jeffreys who was created Baron of Wem in 1685, the year he held his Bloody Assizes at which he dealt ruthlessly with those who took part in Monmouth's rebellion. This small market town 10 m. N. of SHREWSBURY was almost destroyed by a great fire in 1667, which explains why there is little pre-17th-cent. building to be seen. Today only the church and a few houses are worth a second glance. The parish church has a strong, 14th-cent. tower and inside a huge brass chandelier. The Old Hall has a pleasing black-and-white, gabled exterior. Lowe Hall, once the home of Judge Jeffreys, has a fine Jacobean interior behind a 19th-cent. façade. A little white house in Noble Street is one with interesting literary connections: it was the boyhood home of William Hazlitt, the essayist and critic. Wem gets its water from a 70-ft-deep well at nearby Preston Brockhurst; Wem ales are famous throughout the county. There could be a connection.

WEST BROMWICH, *Staffordshire* (8–SP 0091), contains four buildings which speak of its earlier history. The Manor House, now a restaurant, is regarded as a perfect example of a timber-framed manor of the late 13th and early 14th cents. Those interested can look over the great hall, the chapel, gatehouse and kitchens. A fine half-timbered building of a later period is Oak House. Built in 1450, it was given to the town by its first Mayor, Alderman Reuben Farley, and is now furnished in the style of the period and contains much handsome moulded panelling. Its tall Tudor chimneys and black-and-white "turret" give the house a striking appearance. Oak House can be viewed, as can be Asbury Cottage in Newton Road, also owned by the Corporation. This was the boyhood home of Bishop Francis Asbury, the founder of the Methodist Church in America; it has been tastefully restored.

The Parish Church of All Saints was rebuilt in the 19th cent. but the tower is 600 years old. There is a Norman oak chest, a medieval font and an oak altar dating from 1626.

WESTON UNDER REDCASTLE, *Shropshire* (8–SJ5628), is a charming, black-and-white village about 4 m. E. of WEM which gets the colourful part of its name from the adjoining **Hawkstone Park**. The Hall, in the grounds, was built in the early 18th cent. for Sir Richard Hill and later added to by his nephew Sir Rowland Hill; today it is the home of a religious foundation but can be visited occasionally on application. The park itself, once one of the wonders of Shropshire, was the brain-child of Sir Rowland and his successor, another Sir Richard Hill. It covers a long, rocky ridge with sheer red sandstone cliffs falling away along one side and isolated crags scattered here and there along it. It is a spectacular stretch of country which can be seen from the road to HODNET. Once it contained, among other oddities, a menagerie, a "Scene in Switzerland", a vineyard laid out to look like a fortress and a hermitage complete with resident hermit. Today the most obvious sights are the 112-ft obelisk, with a look-out on top, which was erected in 1795, and the Red Castle itself, built in the early 13th cent. but now a ruin strange only in its colouring.

The castle and other features of the park can be well seen from the fairways and greens of a golf course which has been laid out in part of the grounds of the park, owned by the hotel which was once the stable block for the Hall. There is a swimming-pool at the hotel and there is fishing in the nearby Hawk Lake.

A mile or two along the road towards Hodnet is what appears to be another red castle, perched on a small hill – but this is only a folly.

WHISSENDINE, *Rutland* (10–SK8214). A large, strung-out village with too many red-brick houses in it to be pretty. It is set in the middle of magnificent open hunting country with good views over Leicestershire, but its greatest attraction is the Church of St Andrew, the 14th-cent. west tower of which is one of the finest in Rutland. The exterior of the church was very badly designed at the same period on the west and south sides to accommodate a staircase, and there are also a clumsy parapet and turret pinnacles. The beautiful capitals and delicate carving in the two nave arcades are evidences of earlier building. Par-

ticularly notable, too, are the traceries of the windows, and the fine 15th-cent. nave roof and clerestory are admirable specimens of that period.

Between the transept and the aisle is the church's greatest possession, a 16th-cent. screen from St John's College, CAMBRIDGE, given by Margaret Beaufort, mother of Henry VII. When the college chapel was demolished Sir Gilbert Scott could find no place for the screen in his rebuilding, and it was acquired for Whissendine.

A walk starts from the village via Thomas Hill to Ashwell, NE. to MARKET OVERTON, then W. to **Edmondthorpe**, through the grounds of the Hall to **Wymondham**, and over Cord Hill back to Whissendine. Altogether about 12 m. and with the possibility of meeting a hunt in full cry along the way.

WHITCHURCH, *Shropshire* (8–SJ5441). Roman coins, pottery and burial urns, which can be seen in the local museum, indicate that there was a settlement at Whitchurch at least 1,800 years ago. Today this is a pleasant, mellow market town, buildings from the 16th and 17th cents. blending happily with those of more recent vintage. The original church was built here early in the 10th cent. by King Alfred's daughter, Queen Ethelfleda, who dedicated it to an early Christian martyr – and her great-great-grandfather – St Alkmund. This was replaced in the 14th cent. by another building in white stone from which the town derives its present name. This building completely collapsed on the evening of 31 July 1711, just after the congregation at Evensong had departed, and the present church still dedicated to St Alkmund, was built immediately afterwards. A painting of the famous "White church" can be seen in the vestry of the present church whose tall tower is a landmark. Here, too, is a surprising treasure, the silken arms which formerly hung behind the Speaker's Chair in the House of Commons. Under a stone slab in the church porch, in a silver urn, lies the heart of the famous John Talbot, 1st Earl of Shrewsbury, who was killed in 1453 at the age of 80 while fighting with the English army against Joan of Arc, and whose dying wish was that his heart should be buried in the church of his native town. Another famous son of Whitchurch was the composer Sir Edward German, born in St Mary's Street in 1862.

WIDMERPOOL, *Nottinghamshire* (13–SK63 27). Some of the loveliest woodland scenery in the county provides the setting for this little village in the Wolds. A leisurely walk takes the visitor to the Hall, a neo-Elizabethan house with tower and terraces, close to the Church of SS. Peter and Paul. Almost all that remains of the old church building is the 14th-cent. tower with its corner buttresses and diagonally projecting corner pinnacles; the rest was built between 1888 and 1895. Inside there is an exquisite sculpture of Harriet Anne Robertson, fashioned in white marble by an Italian artist whose work details every fold of her gown with painstaking skill.

Barnaby/Mustograph

Wirksworth: the lid of an Anglo-Saxon coffin in the parish church

WIGHTWICK MANOR, *Staffordshire* (8–SO8597), is that rarity, a house which is not yet 100 years old but which is nevertheless of great interest both for its architecture and its interior decoration and furnishings. The Manor, 3 m. W. of WOLVERHAMPTON, at a casual glance might appear to belong to the Elizabethan or Jacobean age but it was, in fact, erected in two stages, in 1887 and 1893, for Mr S. T. Mander who employed as architect the half-timber expert, Edward Ould, and for the interior used the materials of William Morris and his contemporaries in the Arts and Crafts Movement. The house and its 17 acres of grounds were presented to the National Trust in 1937 and are regularly open to the public.

Black-and-white on a red sandstone base, the house is many-gabled and has the traditional imposing Elizabethan chimneys. Inside are many fine examples of Morris wallpapers, hangings and tapestry, notable among them being his "Diagonal Trail" tapestry in the Great Parlour, the house's principal room, the "Willowbough" paper on its pale green background on the Visitors' Staircase, and the "Dove and Rose" silk and wool tapestry in the Drawing Room.

There is much else to delight the eye, including tiles designed by William de Morgan, stained glass by C. E. Kempe, drawings by Burne-Jones and pictures by such artists as Ford Madox Brown, D. G. Rossetti, Ruskin, Millais, Turner and G. F. Watts. There are also exquisite carpets and rugs, much fine furniture and china.

The gardens are a pleasing composition of the formal and the "loose landscape" with fine lawns, paths running between yew hedges, a wood and two pools. In the beds and borders are shrubs and plants from the gardens of Morris, Tennyson, Kempe, Burne-Jones and Ruskin. Among the famous people who have planted trees at Wightwick are the Duke of York, later King George V (a purple lime), Earl Attlee (a hornbeam) and Lord Samuel (an oak).

WILLOUGHBRIDGE, *Staffordshire* (8–SJ 7440). Here, in a small hamlet about 3 m. SE. of Woore, is a unique woodland garden. Set in a disused, 200-year-old gravel quarry at the top of a small hill, the garden is a fine example of marrying the natural with the cultivated. Within the framework of tall oak trees are masses of rhododendrons and azaleas of all colours, at best in May and early June; and a little earlier there is as much colour, but from banks of daffodils.

WILLOUGHBY-WITH-SLOOTHBY, *Lincolnshire* (13–TF4772). An attractive village of tree-lined roads, small cottages and flower-clustered gardens on the edge of the Lincolnshire marshland. The site was originally a Roman settlement, the mounds of what is believed to have been a Danish encampment are nearby, and traces of Anglo-Saxon masonry are to be found in the church. The village is notable for having been the birthplace of John Smith, the intrepid explorer whose discoveries established Virginia as the colony from which sprang the United States of America. It was he whose life was saved by Pocohontas, daughter of Powhattan, paramount chief of the Indians, but all that is recorded in the Church of St Helen's is the entry in the register stating that John Smith was baptized there on the 9th day of January, 1579.

WIRKSWORTH, *Derbyshire* (12–SK2854), is an attractive small old town among the hills 5 m. S. of MATLOCK. It was once the centre of the Derbyshire lead-mining industry. At the Moot

Hall can still be seen the oblong dish which was used for measuring the lead; and pigs of the mineral dating from Roman times have been found in the neighbourhood. This was the town which George Eliot used as a background for much of her novel, *Adam Bede*, and those familiar with the novel will find it an interesting exercise to try to match the places in the novel with their real-life counterparts. Other scenes in the novel were set in the village of **Roston**, about 5 m. SW. of ASHBOURNE (about 13 m. in all from Wirksworth).

There are many old buildings in Wirksworth, none older than the imposing Church of St Mary. In the church can be seen an Anglo-Saxon coffin lid, believed to have come from the stone coffin of a saint who was buried here almost 1,200 years ago. The carving on the lid is crude but quite clear and obviously depicts scenes from the life of Christ, including the washing of the disciples' feet, the raising of Jairus's daughter, and the descent into hell, as well as the symbols of the four gospel-writers. Other ancient sculpture, mainly Norman work, can be seen in the walls of the church.

Other interesting buildings include the old hospital, now a guest-house, which dates from 1588; Dale End, a gabled 17th-cent. house; Gell's Bedehouses, dating from 1584; and a number of attractive Georgian houses.

Along the road from Wirksworth to **Middleton** is some of the most spectacular scenery in the county. Here are the extensive Hopton Wood quarries with sheer walls of rock often towering impressively above the road.

WOLVERHAMPTON, *Staffordshire* (8–SO 9198). A flaming brazier and a padlock are included in the coat of arms of Wolverhampton. Today these are more obviously symbolic of this "Capital of the Black Country" than the cross, ascribed to the Anglo-Saxon King Edgar, and the woolpack, which are also in the arms and hint at Wolverhampton's beginnings. The town was first referred to as Heantun in a royal charter of 985. The name later became Wulfrunishamtun, after Wulfrun, a Mercian lady.

Most of the striking buildings to be seen here – the tower blocks of flats, the award-winning housing estates, the Mander Centre and Wulfrun Shopping Precinct – are all post-war. The outstanding exception is the Church of St Peter, in red stone, approached by a flight of wide steps, standing near the heart of the town with something of the grandeur of a small cathedral. The oldest parts are the arches under the square, 15th-cent. tower, which date from 1205. There was an earlier monastery on the site, refounded in 994 by the Lady Wulfrun, a translation of whose charter hangs in the vestry. The south chapel dates from 1350 and the nave, with its unusual double clerestory windows, from about 100 years later. The 15th-cent. carved stone pulpit, with its staircase winding round one of the nave pillars, is very rare. In the north chapel are monuments to members of the Lane family, one of whom helped Charles II escape from BOSCOBEL

House after the Battle of WORCESTER in 1651. Another monument worth seeing is the strong, bronze statue of Admiral Sir Richard Leveson, carved by Hubert Le Sueur in the early years of the 17th cent. Outside the south door of the church stands an ancient carved pillar, believed to be the remains of a column dragged from one of the nearby Roman sites by 9th-cent. Anglo-Saxons.

There are two unusual features about Wolverhampton's other town church, St John's. Built in 1760 it could be mistaken at first for ST MARTIN-IN-THE-FIELDS in London; and it has one of the most famous organs in England, built by Renatus Harris about 1683. The instrument came to St John's by accident. After being for many years in Christ Church Cathedral in Dublin, it was replaced by a new instrument. The maker of this took the old organ in part exchange and it had reached Wolverhampton on its way to London when its owner died. His widow sold it to St John's for £500.

Wolverhampton possesses a fine municipal art gallery and museum in Lichfield Street, with a good collection of English enamels and early Staffordshire pottery, and pictures by Romney, Turner and Gainsborough, among others. At Bantock House, in 43 acres of grounds 1 m. from the town centre, there are exhibits illustrating the town's industrial history: japanning, cut steel and locksmiths' work; also a collection of beautiful English porcelain.

Within reach of the town are a number of historic houses including MOSELEY OLD HALL, WIGHTWICK MANOR, **Chillington Hall** and **Himley Hall.** Chillington Hall, 8 m. N., is a fine Georgian house with gardens landscaped by Capability Brown and a magnificent avenue of trees; it is occasionally open to view. Himley Hall, owned by the Wolverhampton and Dudley Councils, is not open to the public but the extensive grounds are, including the Great Pool, in which fishing is available. Not far from Himley Hall is the village of **Wombourne;** the spired church, with a unique dedication to St Benedict Biscop, overlooks one of the few remaining walled-in cricket grounds in England.

WOODBOROUGH, *Nottinghamshire* (13–SK 6347). A village of terraced cottages, built for the 18th-cent. stocking knitters, each with its broad upper window behind which stood the frame. In 1769 a son was born to one of these hard-working families, who because of his knowledge of the Bible was later to be affectionately known as the Walking Concordance. He was George Brown, the Nottinghamshire evangelist, who devoted 50 years to preaching the gospel from house to house. This was also the home of Richard Strelley, builder of Woodborough church, with its fine windows, gabled buttresses and beautiful sedilia. Much has been added to his 14th-cent. work, particularly in sculpture and wood-carving, the latter having been executed by Mansfield Parkyns, a distinguished explorer, geographer and linguist who was also a highly talented craftsman.

WOOLSTHORPE, *Lincolnshire* (13–SK 9224). This tiny hamlet in the south-west corner of the county is famous for containing within its narrow boundaries the birthplace of Sir Isaac Newton, the supreme mathematical genius whose theory of gravitational pull revolutionized man's knowledge of astronomy. Woolsthorpe Manor, where he was born in 1642, is a small but attractive house of the 17th cent., with mullioned windows, beamed ceilings and tall, square chimneys set off by mellowing grey-stone walls. The apple orchard in the front contains a descendant of the tree which so momentously affected Sir Isaac Newton's studies. Today the whole property is in the hands of the National Trust and is open to visitors.

WOOLSTON, *Shropshire* (8–SJ3224). This hamlet is about 5 m. SE. of OSWESTRY, just off the main road to SHREWSBURY. It is unremarkable save for one building, the smallest there. At the end of a short, grassy path, set between high hedges, stands a tiny, black-and-white cottage, with musk and pink honeysuckle on the walls. This is the site of one of England's holy wells, that of St Winifred. The legend says that this is the place where a well gushed forth from the ground when the body of the saint rested there on its way from Holywell to Shrewsbury.

The cottage is built into the side of a small hill so that on its lower side there is an extra story at ground level. This looks like a large, open-fronted porch and it is here that the well emerges, bubbling up into a large, shallow stone bath with steps leading down into it. The rust-coloured water then runs down into a second, lower bath in the open air, and thence on to a small stream. Here pilgrims came to immerse themselves in the holy water. Today visitors are welcome but must not bathe. Happily the shrine is kept in good repair.

WREKIN, THE, *Shropshire* (8–SJ6208). At 1,334 ft, the Wrekin is not Shropshire's highest hill; both the Clees, Brown and Titterstone, are more than 400 ft higher. Yet on a clear day the view from the top of the Wrekin, a couple of miles S. of Wellington, is as panoramic as any in England, embracing 17 counties. This was the site of an Iron Age fort, begun about 200 B.C. Almost 1,800 years later a beacon fire blazed on its crown to give warning of the Spanish Armada. Today the visitor can climb its grassy slopes, peer into its rocky clefts, find the Gates of Heaven and Hell, the Needle's Eye, and, on the very summit, the Raven's Bowl.

WROXETER, *Shropshire* (8–SJ5608). Here, 5 m. SE. of SHREWSBURY, are the remains of what was the fourth largest town in Britain in Roman times. Wroxeter, or Viroconium, was the Roman capital of a large area of central Britain

and covered an area of 180 acres, compared with Roman London's 325 acres.

Wroxeter had a chequered history. Begun *c.* A.D. 60, it flourished for about 30 years, then relapsed until the visit to Britain of the Emperor Hadrian in 121, when it was rebuilt. For almost 150 years the city prospered and grew but with the gradual withdrawal of the Romans from Britain, Wroxeter slipped gradually into decay. By early in the 5th cent. the site was deserted and eventually it was plundered for its stone by Anglo-Saxons building Shrewsbury.

Excavation was begun in 1863 and went on at intervals until the work was taken over, in 1948, by the Ministry of Public Building and Works. The results of all that work are now there for all to see, although much is still not known. However, the visitor can walk in the forum where Roman legionaries walked 1,900 years ago, see the small market stalls where they shopped, look down into the pool where they swam, and stroll through the inter-connecting areas of the bath-house. Here were the hot, tepid and cool rooms, the furnace and the cold plunges and, all down one long side, the exercise hall, separated from the bath-house by the largest remaining fragment of the original building, part of the Roman wall, the rough stone levelled off at intervals with a course of red tiles.

At the site, too, is an excellent museum containing many of the finds made here (there are others in Rowley's House Museum in Shrewsbury). Among the exhibits are fragments of architecture and sculpture from the temple; mosaics and tiles – one bearing the clear imprint of a cat's paws; many pottery bowls and vases; bottles, flagons and perfume flasks in blue, amber and green glass; writing implements; bronze brooches, bracelets and keys; dice and counters in bone; coins; and primitive surgical instruments. But perhaps the most important exhibit is the stone inscription which was set up over the entrance to the forum on its completion in A.D. 130. Its five lines of finely chiselled lettering were cut in slabs of fine-grained sandstone almost 12 ft long and dedicate the building to the Emperor Hadrian. It must have impressed the Cornovii, the Ancient British tribe who were rulers of this area until the Romans came.

YOULGREAVE, *Derbyshire* (12–SK2164). The small, hill-top town, about 4 m. S. of BAKEWELL, is remarkable for the size of its church with its tall, imposing square tower, topped with eight pinnacles. Much of the building is Norman and the unusual, two-basin font and a sculpture of a man in a long frock also date from this period; there are also a number of interesting monuments dating from the 14th, 15th and 16th cents. The stained glass in the east window is a good example of the work of William Morris. About 3 m. W. of Youlgreave is ARBOR LOW.

Yorkshire

PHYLLIS BENTLEY

Yorkshire, 3,735,322 acres (about 6,100 square miles) in extent, is the largest county in England. It contains approximately one-eighth of the area of England, and with its four and a quarter million people, about one-tenth of England's population.

Its shape is simple: roughly a square, pulled down a little in its lower left-hand corner. Its west boundary is formed by the line north and south of the mountains of the Pennine Chain, and it stretches right across England eastwards to a slightly north-west south-east coast on the North Sea. Its northern boundary is the east-running River Tees; the southern is partly the estuary of the Humber, but further west it makes a protrusion, once very marshy, south of this line.

If its shape is simple, however, in all other respects Yorkshire is highly diversified. Geologically it is amazingly various, and this has given it not only a most delightful and refreshing variety of landscape but certain contrasts in history and economics, in dialect and ways of life, sometimes even, within a strong native similarity, in types of character.

In the north-west of the county the Pennine mountains are composed of the beautiful grey-white limestone. No heather grows on limestone; these hills are covered with short, very bright green grass, very agreeable food for sheep. Then the character of the rocks changes; south of a geological disarrangement known as the "Craven fault", which makes a gap in the chain through which the River Aire flows, the rock is millstone grit, a hard, dark, gritty rock on which grow heather and long, tough, pale grass of no great pastoral value, though even on this sheep will feed. The millstone grit is fringed, to the south-east, with coal measures, part of one of the greatest coalfields in Britain, and in these measures lie also some precious nodules of iron ore. The large central plain of the county is rich alluvial soil, which grows abundant crops and vegetables, besides providing dairy pasture. To the north-east of this the land climbs into the Hambleton Hills by the severe gradient of Sutton Bank, and from thence into the North Yorkshire Moors, composed of the considerable Cleveland Hills. North of these we find a mixture of rocks, sloping down to the valley of the Tees, amongst which is found, again, a considerable deposit of ironstone.

The county of Yorkshire is extremely well watered. Its main river system is best understood by thinking of the Humber as the wrist of a hand, the Ouse as the palm into which the tributary rivers, like fingers only more numerous, flow. From north to south these tributaries are Swale, Ure, Nidd, Wharfe, Aire, Calder, Derwent, Don. (The word *Sunwacdd* is a useful aid here to memory.) All these rivers except the last two rise in the west, in the Pennines, flow through beautiful dales, join the Ouse before or after York, and reach the North Sea through the Humber. Thus the county can show all kinds of river scenery, from the tumbling rocky mountain "beck", as Yorkshire people call their streams, to the broad smooth navigable river. Outside of this system flow the northern Tees, which directs itself due east into the North Sea, and the Ribble, which after flowing down the west side of the county has the audacity to enter Lancashire and pour itself into the Irish Sea.

Hundreds of minor tributaries in Yorkshire play a part, not only in beautifying the landscape, but in enriching, as we shall see, the economic life of the county.

There are quite a few prehistorical habitation remains to be found in Yorkshire; these will be noted as they occur, in the gazetteer. When the region emerges from the veil of prehistory we find British tribes in occupation, rebelling against Roman legions sent to keep order in this far-flung outpost of the Roman Empire. The great legacy of the Romans, here as elsewhere, was their fine road network. One great road leads north from Doncaster to Isurium (Boroughbridge) and Richmond, with branches off west and east to various camps in the Pennine Hills and signal stations on the coast. Another Roman road, Ermine Street, leads presumably to a ferry crossing the Humber to Brough, and thence proceeds along a limestone ridge which rose above the marsh, to York.

By the fifth century A.D., however, the Romans grew tired of wasting men and money on such a distant and unrewarding land as Britain. The Picts and Scots they had more or less succeeded in temporarily keeping out by building walls across the narrow neck of land between Clyde and Forth, and from Tynemouth to Solway, but the invasions of Angles and Saxons, marauding tribes from across the North Sea, had recently become a perpetual nuisance. After the Roman legions departed (c. A.D. 410) the Angles overran England and it became their country, even adopting, as we see, their name. During this period Christianity came to England, and to the North from Kent and Cornwall and from the island of Iona.

The Angles did not rule long in peace, for in the eighth and ninth centuries a fresh set of invaders poured into England – Danes and Norwegians. Vikings in their beaked ships, tall, fierce, ruthless men who, coming first to plunder and murder, presently settled in the rich lands of England and made the country into a kingdom of their own. Some sailed up the Humber; others approached by way of the west coast of Scotland, coming south thence and through the Aire gap into Yorkshire. There are many traces left in Yorkshire of our Angle and Danish conquerors. Especially is this the case with our language; innumerable dialect words today are really relics of the speech of these invaders. Place-names ending in *ham* are of Saxon origin, while *by*, *kirk*, *thorp* are Danish terminations. It was the Danes who first divided York into Ridings; the word comes from the Danish *treding*, a third part. Thus there are North, West and East Ridings, but no fourth division. (The use of "South Riding" by that fine novelist Winifred Holtby is a brilliant invention to give locality without the embarrassment of real names.) The name of York itself, after Eburach, Eboracum, and Eoforwic, gained its final form from the Danish Jorvik.

The story of the coming of our final conquerors, the Normans, is well known; it has its beginning in our county. Harold, King of England after the death of the childless Edward the Confessor, had banished his brother Tostig for ill-treatment of his northern earldom. Tostig sought help from the Norse king Hardrada, and they invaded Yorkshire. Harold marched against them, and after a brisk exchange of insults defeated them, killing both. But while still celebrating this victory he heard that William of Normandy had invaded Sussex. Marching his tired and reluctant army south through the length of the English counties, Harold met William near Hastings, and was defeated and killed there. The whole of England fell into William's hands, and he gave it away piecemeal under feudal tenancy, as rewards to his supporters and relations.

Yorkshire owes much of both good and evil to the Normans.

The evil was a massacre, outrageous even for the fierce eleventh century. The northern region rebelled three times against William the Conqueror. After the third of these rebellions William's patience was exhausted, and he harried the North with fire and sword so terribly that there was scarcely a town inhabited, a building standing, a being, animal or human, left alive in the whole stretch of land. The description of the state of Yorkshire after this harrying, by contemporary writers, is awful – corpses rotting by the wayside because there was nobody to bury them – and it was many years before the county recovered. The effects show only too clearly in the entries in Domesday Book, the account compiled twenty years later (1089) by William's orders, of every piece of land in England. After recording the size of the land in question, entry after entry in the North reads like this: *Grim* (Saxon) *held it, Ranulf* (Norman) *holds it now; T.R.E.* (in the time of King Edward) *it was worth 20 shillings, now worth five shillings and fourpence. It is waste.*

On the other hand, the Normans gave us relief from Danish invasions, increasing law and order, and many buildings of great beauty. The Norman barons built castles (twenty-two in Yorkshire before 1216) to defend themselves and their lands. Some of these have decayed, some have been destroyed, by battle or by order, but impressive remains still exist of these massive and often magnificent constructions, e.g. Scarborough, Skipton, Conisbrough, Pontefract, Richmond. The Normans also built cathedrals (such as York, Beverley) churches, abbeys, monasteries. Before Henry VIII's dissolution there were more monasteries in Yorkshire than in any other county of England, and Fountains and Rievaulx, only partly ruined, remain to show their greatness and beauty. As to parish churches, it has been said that out of eleven hundred parish churches in England, more than four hundred are in Yorkshire. They do not all exist in their entirety; but arches, doorways, pillars, remain to delight us.

England accepted, if somewhat sullenly, the Norman rule, and Yorkshire thenceforward became part of the kingdom of England and participated in the general course of English history. Its chief trouble was the Scots, who all too frequently still charged down the west side of the Pennines and crossed into Yorkshire through the Aire gap, or raided down the less hilly east coast.

A good many of the battles in the Wars of the Roses (1455–85) were fought in Yorkshire. But these did not really concern the territories of Yorkshire and Lancashire; the nobles who contested the crown chanced to hold these titles, and their men fought, not from conviction, but as their feudal allegiance required. Far different was the case during the Civil War between King and Parliament in the seventeenth century. The allegiance of Yorkshire was divided. The towns of the West Riding, and Hull on the Humber on the other side of the county, were strongly for Puritanism and Parliament; the rich central plain was for the Church of England and King Charles I. Thus already the contrasts between the Ridings show themselves.

Speaking in general terms, it may be said that the North Riding, stretching in a broad riband across the county from the Pennines to the North Sea, is pastoral and agricultural; the West Riding, shaped like a leg of mutton, nestling against the Pennines at its narrow end and spreading towards the south-east, is industrial; the East Riding, tucked between them, has a long sea coast, rich arable land, and the third port of the kingdom, Hull, on the broad estuary of the Humber.

The North Riding, including the north corner of the West, is the most strikingly beautiful stretch of the county. Fine Pennine heights – among them Ingleborough, Whernside, Pen-y-Ghent – make a superb backcloth to the landscape, and the lovely northern dales of Swaledale and Wensleydale roll away in beauty to the east. Swaledale is steep and rocky, with the marvellous castle at Richmond sitting high on its cliff; Wensleydale is serene and grassy, with Bolton Castle, where Mary Queen of Scots was imprisoned, gazing in grim strength across the broad valley. Nor must the northern Teesdale, perhaps the most rich and least bleak of Yorkshire scenery, be omitted. As the North Riding stretches east, it rises into the Cleveland Hills, which offer heather-covered slopes and some beautiful if less well known dales: Farndale, noted for its daffodils, Rosedale, Bilsdale. On the coast, at the mouth of the Tees, lies that remarkable phenomenon, the town of Middlesbrough. In 1801 only twenty people were living on the spot where the town now stands. Now, thanks to the discovery of iron ore nearby and its exploitation, Middlesbrough makes millions of tons of steel, exports it (for example, the girders for the bridge across Sydney harbour) and has a population of some 200,000.

The coast of the North Riding holds fishing villages such as Staithes and Robin Hood's Bay, and celebrated seaside resorts: Whitby, once famous for its jet, always famous for its ruined abbey and for Captain Cook; Scarborough, "queen of watering places", with its large castle and the grave of Anne Brontë on the cliff.

The West Riding has been industrial for a long time, for Sheffield discovered its iron ore and the "Little Masters" smelted it by charcoal and made steel of it in their homes as far back as the fourteenth century. We know this for certain because the Miller in Chaucer's *Canterbury Tales*, written about 1387, carried "a Sheffield thwytel in his hose". Pronounce *thwytel* as Chaucer pronounced it and you hear the origin of the word *cutlery*. Today Sheffield melts its ore, largely imported from Sweden, by coal, and though still world-famous for its cutlery, produces enormous quantities of high-quality steel in larger shapes.

The other great industry of the West Riding is the wool textile trade. Sheep and streams had always existed abundantly in the county, and from these essentials woollen cloth was made by hand in the workers' homes for many centuries, and possibly was even exported as early as A.D. 796. Edward III helped to improve this manufacture in the fourteenth century by inviting to England skilled Flemings, who taught Yorkshire folk how to spin more (and finer) yarn than previously from a pound of wool. Towards the end of the eighteenth and beginning of the nineteenth centuries it was discovered that some textile processes could be performed by simple machines run by water power. This gave the West Riding, with its abundant wealth of tumbling water, a great impetus, and the textile trade, which in its early days had flourished chiefly in a Weavers' Guild in York, gradually became the pre-eminence of the West Riding. In a few years steam was harnessed to power, and again the West Riding profited, for it had coal to raise steam, and iron to make machines, only a few miles away to the south. As a consequence of this Industrial Revolution, from hand-power to steam, the West Riding became a vast conurbation, where today thirty thousand looms continually weave cloth and 150 million pounds worth of cloth is exported yearly. Its towns are, however, agreeably separated by Pennine hills, grass or heather-covered.

May I mention that the tall mill chimneys which characterize the textile West Riding are most unjustly disliked? The smoke which they poured out (now greatly diminished) was certainly odious, but the slender circular chimneys themselves are skilful and beautiful structures.

Another beauty which the West Riding owes to the textile industry is its domestic architecture, Elizabethan and Jacobean. Sir Nikolaus Pevsner calls them "Halifax houses", these long low yeomen clothiers' houses of local stone, with their long rows of mullioned windows, and the weavers' cottages with the row of windows in the second story to lighten the loom-chamber. These houses and cottages are tucked into the hillsides, beside a stream, just below the brow. Here the textile trade began; in the valleys below, tower the huge mills of the nineteenth century.

The West Riding is not without its scenic beauty, too, for it contains the whole of lovely Wharfedale, whose mingled beauties, wood and fell and river, are a great attraction to visitors. Bolton Abbey, more correctly Bolton Priory, has an unrivalled situation on the Wharfe banks, and the rocky Strid gorge of the river is well worth visiting – but please do *not* try to jump this, it has been regularly fatal for some eight centuries. Nidderdale, another West Riding dale, is, too, very beautiful and has a unique gorge, How Stean, and a superb view down the whole dale from the upland village of Middlesmoor.

A great factor in the making of Yorkshire has been religion. Puritans in the days of Charles I, many Yorkshire people welcomed Quaker teachings in the seventeenth century, and in the eighteenth century the West Riding was strongly affected by the preaching of John Wesley, who made more than forty visits to Yorkshire. All over the Riding can be seen the chapels – some small, early, humble, some huge and proud, all without the ornament they despised – of the various nonconformist religious sects which helped to give the nineteenth century its staunch moral background.

The East Riding of Yorkshire, with the exception of its popular seaside resorts Bridlington and Filey, is perhaps insufficiently appreciated by tourists. Many fine churches enrich this flat, rich, once marshy now richly arable land. The Minster at Beverley is, by reason of the unique height and slenderness of its towers, particularly beautiful. Hull, besides being the third port of England – with vast docks, grain silos, piles of merchandise for export and import – and the centre of a large fishing fleet, holds much of interest of a historical kind. The house of William Wilberforce, the school he attended, the old fast-vanishing streets, recall days when Hull played a striking part in English history, and the branch headquarters of the Trinity Brothers, who manage our coastwise lights, is a fine building.

The striking fact about the East Riding is that its long coastline in Bridlington Bay is continually in process of erosion. Churches, houses, villages, even towns, a few hundred years ago thriving and important, now lie beneath the North Sea waves. On the other hand, the long thin sandy headland which curves round to end in Spurn Head to the south has often changed its shape by addition as well as by erosion, and there is a piece of land within its curve, Sunk Island, which has emerged from the sea, so to speak, of its own accord.

North of Holderness, as this part of Yorkshire is called, the land rises into grassy chalk wolds, which presently surge out to sea as the huge white Flamborough Head.

York, the capital city of the county, which stands at the junction of all three Ridings, belongs to none. A fortress since A.D. 71, since 1389 it has been a city with a Lord Mayor, since 1396 a county to itself, with its own Sheriff. It is, of course, a centre of government of the northern province of the Church of England, the headquarters of the Archbishop of York. With its superb Minster – the glorious elegance of the Five Sisters window must on no account be missed – its twelfth-century city walls, its innumerable old churches and streets, its ancient remains, the broad sweep of the River Ouse, the wonderful City Museum, it seems full to the brim of picturesque testimonies to English history.

The Yorkshire dialect varies between the Ridings. In the East their speech is warmer and slower than in the West. Between North and West Riding speech the

Guisborough Priory. Watercolour drawing by   *Edinburgh, National Gallery of Scotland*
Thomas Girtin, 1801

River Wharfe forms a boundary; for example, to the north *she* is *hoo*, to the south *she* is *sha*, and there are other such differences.

Yorkshire people are often vexed by the attitude of more southern counties, who seem to regard us as uncultured barbarians, as if we had not yet recovered from William's fire and sword. Let us note, then, that William Wilberforce, M.P. for Hull, initiated and saw through Parliament the Act which in 1834 terminated slavery in British possessions. Richard Oastler of the West Riding initiated the movement which forbade children to work long hours in mills. We were the first to give protection to seabirds. The first great Education Act, passed in 1870, which began to give free education to all British children, was initiated and seen through Parliament by W. E. Forster, the M.P. for Bradford (West Riding) at that time. We have today five universities: Leeds, Sheffield, Hull, York, Bradford. We are devoted to music – not, perhaps, in so poetical and inspired a style as our Welsh colleagues, but in a serious and knowledgeable fashion; music societies abound in all our towns, and the Huddersfield Choral Society is famous all over the world for its admirable performances of Handel. We love cricket, and if I may be allowed to say so, are proficient in this beautiful game. Nor are we backward in football, particularly in the game of our own invention. We play to win, but lose with stoicism. Racehorses flourish in the North Riding.

In literature we have a decidedly interesting record. We have not produced a poet of the highest class, but from the Brontës onwards clusters of novelists have recorded and enriched our scene, and today some of these have ventured into new forms of drama, both on the stage and television. In drama we have experienced with others the decay of the professional theatre, the dauntless activities of serious amateur players, and the revival of the arts under regional Art Councils.

Yorkshire is a county rich in amateur societies. There are gliding clubs, sailing clubs, literary clubs, gardening clubs, tennis clubs, science clubs and the usual Young Farmers, Women's Institutes and Townswomen's Guilds in great abundance, all democratically run by properly elected committees.

The Yorkshire people are by reputation robust in physique though not especially handsome, efficient and vigorous in their undertakings, blunt in speech and rather well satisfied with themselves. They dislike excessive expressions of emotion and are cautious with strangers, but once they accept you they are staunchly if soberly faithful. They prefer practice to theory. Above all, they are extremely independent. An Abbot of York wrote to Henry VIII: "there be such a company of wilful gentlemen within Yorkshire as there be not in all England besides". In Queen Elizabeth's days the men of Halifax were spoken of as behaving "after the rude and arrogant manner of their wilde country". It would be rash to suggest that Yorkshire folk have changed much since those days, and this applies to the women as well as to the men. A Yorkshire person has a strong backbone; lean on it but do not try to bend it.

The Strid, near Bolton Abbey. Painting by James Stark (1794–1859)   Norwich, Castle Museum

Yorkshire: Gazetteer

ELLEN WILSON

ADEL, *West Riding* (12–SE2740). Here on the NW. outskirts of LEEDS is one of the county's gems, a small Norman church dedicated to St John and built in the mid-12th cent., with few alterations imposed since. It consists of a nave and lower chancel. The two features which draw admirers are the south doorway and the chancel arch, both beautiful in design. The doorway stands under a gabled portal and is richly carved with four orders of zigzag, roll moulding, flowers and beakheads. The chancel arch is sculptured with zigzag, ladder-like moulding and picturesque heads. The capitals show the baptism of Christ on the north, and the Crucifixion on the south responds. The original bronze door ring shows a monster devouring a man, whose head alone is still visible. A memorial window and heraldic glass are by Henry Gyles, and date from 1681 and 1701.

ALDBOROUGH, *West Riding* (13–SE4065). The pretty village with a maypole on the green drowses on the site of the ancient capital of the Brigantes, largest Celtic tribe in Britain, who called it Iseur. It consisted of huts behind an earth and wood stockade when the conquering Romans came. They made it an important camp and a civilian suburb of YORK. It was known as Isurium Brigantum. It was favourably situated at the highest point for navigation up the River Ure and at the junction of important roads. The Romans circled it with a 9-ft-thick wall 20 ft high and built houses, courts, a forum and a temple here. Corn shipments were transported overland from here to the northern troops. With the withdrawal of the Romans, Aldborough fell victim to successive Angles, Scots, Danes and Normans. Under the Normans, a new bridge was built across the Ure at BOROUGHBRIDGE, less than 1 m. away, dealing the village a final blow. Part of the Roman wall, two pavements, and the museum founded in 1864 and filled with excavated objects recalling the days of Roman gracious living are in the care of the Ministry of Public Building and Works. At least 12 fine pavements were saved here, the best known being in Kirkstall Museum, LEEDS. Roman wall stone found its way into St Andrew's Church. A badly worn stone panel of Mercury is in the north aisle. The church has good woodwork and a fine brass monument of William de Aldeburgh of about 1360, the figure life-size.

AMPLEFORTH, *North Riding* (13–SE5878), is famous for its abbey and college, a Roman Catholic public school founded in 1802 by English Benedictine monks who had settled in France in 1607, then returned as refugees from the Revolution in 1793. Most of the stone-built village lies along one street on a shelf of the Hambleton Hills with the Abbey of St Lawrence and college at the east end. The view across a beautiful valley toward GILLING CASTLE is grand. The college church, designed by Sir Giles Gilbert Scott, is of greenish stone and was completed in 1961, in Romanesque style. The parish church, St Hilda's, has Norman north and south doorways and a curious stone effigy of a bearded, praying man with a woman looking over his shoulder, from about 1330. The Ampleforth sword dance has been revived by students.

AUSTERFIELD, *West Riding* (12–SK6594). William Bradford, one of America's Pilgrim Fathers, was born here in 1590 and baptized in the simple Norman Church of St Helen's. He was a member of the Brownists, an extreme separatist Puritan group, who sailed on the *Mayflower* in 1620. He was the second governor chosen in the New England colony of Massachusetts and wrote a history of it before his death in 1657. Austerfield Manor where he was born is a Tudor yeoman's house, two stories with pantile roof. The most prominent village building is the church. It has a new bellcot and windows were inserted in the 13th and 14th cents. The north aisle arcade was rebuilt in 1897 by the Society of Mayflower Descendants in honour of "the first American citizen of the English race who bore rule by the free choice of his brethren". The Norman doorway in the porch has an interesting carved arch and tympanum with a strange dragon or sea monster in relief.

AYSGARTH, *North Riding* (12–SE0088). The beautiful falls – a series of three cascades – extend for ½ m. on the River Ure in Wensleydale. The foaming waters rush over great ledges or steps between limestone walls overhung with trees and bushes, where violets and primroses thrive in season. For the Upper Falls, the approach is down a road near the youth hostel to a single-arch 16th-cent. bridge, widened in recent times, where the view is enthralling. From the next bend in the road, a footpath leads to the Middle and Lower Falls. Cars can be left in the former station yard. Aysgarth's parish church, St Andrew's, is nearly 1 m. W. of the village. It overlooks the bridge. Except for the west tower, which is medieval in its lower stages, the church is a product of 19th-

T. Parker

Aysgarth Falls on the River Ure in Wensleydale

cent. rebuilding. Two finely carved screens and a reading desk are believed to have come from JERVAULX ABBEY.

BARNSLEY, *West Riding* (12–SE3406). Few buildings here are much more than a century old and new public works are replacing some of those. Barnsley is the exact centre of the Yorkshire coalfield, the biggest in Britain, and its older streets wear the grime to prove it. There are reminders, too, of the price of coal. Silkstone church has a memorial which records that women and children were among 26 mineworkers drowned when a pit flooded in 1838. A monument on Kendray Hill commemorates the deaths of 361 men and boys in an explosion and its aftermath in the Old Oaks colliery in 1866. In the 18th cent. it was a major centre for linen weaving. The glass industry, still the second largest employer, started even earlier. The huge market, which began in 1249, is still held thrice weekly on the original town centre site and it is a major regional attraction. St Mary's Parish Church has a 15th-cent. embattled tower but the rest of the building is early 19th-cent. The 1933 Town Hall is heavily Classical. The old grammar school building in Church Street, founded in 1660, houses the free Cooper Art Gallery with its good collection of paintings and English drawings. In Cannon Hall, at Cawthorne village W. of Barnsley, the town keeps a country-house museum of decorative arts, featuring glass, period rooms and furnishings. The house is 17th-cent. with 18th-cent.

additions by John Carr. The park is a popular picnic spot. Locke Park on the south side of town was given in 1861 by the widow of Joseph Locke, an apprentice of George Stephenson, who became a famous railway builder. Near the tower, a memorial to Mrs Locke by her sister, is a view over Barnsley. On the north-eastern outskirts are the excavated ruins of MONK BRETTON PRIORY. Wentworth Castle, to the S., is a College of Education now.

BARTON-LE-STREET, *North Riding* (13–SE7274). St Michael's Church contains an astonishing amount of stone carving in the Norman style. Some of it is original and the rest was produced for an elaborate rebuilding in 1871. The quality of the Victorian contribution is outstanding and a great deal of the original fabric was re-used or reproduced. Thus this fine village church makes a fascinating study of high Norman work. The building may date from about 1160 and it shows the influence of Norman work in the area of Poitiers, although reasons for the similarity are not clear. The north porch with its handsome entrance arch of old with new work shelters a second splendid doorway, the original south doorway, moved here in the 19th-cent. rebuilding. In addition to intricate but conventional bands of ornamentation, there are studies of St Michael and the dragon on the entry arch, Samson and the lion on the doorway and numerous bizarre figures and animals. Above the doorway are scenes of shepherds in bed being visited by angels (sometimes described as a nativity with Mary in bed), the Wise Men and labours of the month. Inside the porch also, parts of the beautiful Norman corbel table are preserved, with delightful small heads in the arches linking the corbels. A Victorian Norman corbel table runs around the outside wall now. The church interior exhibits fine Norman-style carving in its chancel arch. Original work is retained in the capitals of the arch, in the corbel table in the chancel, the unusual wall frieze in the nave and in the piscina shaft.

BEDALE, *North Riding* (12–SE2688). The main street widens where the market is held then narrows at the top of the slope where the Church of St Gregory and Bedale Hall occupy opposite and commanding positions overlooking the agreeable townscape. The church tower is 14th- and 15th-cent. work and has a porch on the south side. A room on the first floor was reached by a stair guarded by a portcullis, a defensive measure in case of Scottish raids. Walls in the nave may be Anglo-Saxon in origin; the east window was possibly brought from JERVAULX ABBEY. The alabaster effigy of Sir Brian Fitzalan who died in 1306 is one of the earliest of its kind. The rear of Bedale Hall is brick and matches the rest of the Georgian-style houses in the market place, but its front faces the country and is formal, in stone, dating from about 1730. It houses the Rural District Council offices, a library and a museum. The great ballroom has a marvellous coved stucco ceiling with chubby figures fairly leaping over the cornice. The flying staircase has a bulb and umbrella balustrade. The house was built for Henry Peirse. This is splendid hunting country.

Snape Castle is 3 m. S., part ruin and part residence. The old chapel is preserved, a single room with Perpendicular windows and lively Dutch carvings of the life of Christ. Catherine Parr, sixth and last wife of Henry VIII, lived here.

BENINGBROUGH HALL, *North Riding* (13–SE5158). This early Georgian country house, 8 m. NW. of YORK at Newton-upon-Ouse, was built by an unknown architect for John Bourchier and completed in 1716. Two hundred years later it was bought by the Earl and Countess of Chesterfield and in 1959 it came from the Treasury to the National Trust in payment of death duties. On the outside, it is a simple and dignified building of small red bricks ornamented sparingly with stone quoins and sculptured pediments. The two main stories and attic are 11 bays wide. Inside, the rooms are attractive and even grand, but it is the wood-carving which will arouse the most admiration; the Hall is a storehouse of the splendid work of the York craftsmen of the day. The oak staircase, for example, has parqueted treads and a baluster so light that it seems at first glance made of wrought-iron. The stairs are supported only by fastenings in the wall. Throughout the rooms, chimney-pieces, door surrounds and friezes exhibit the artistry and tireless imagination of the wood-carvers. The Hall is open to visitors at advertised times in the summer months.

BEVERLEY, *East Riding* (13–TA0339). The capital of the East Riding is dominated by two churches, almost equally splendid. The minster is the one with two towers. There is no disputing the claim that it is one of the most beautiful churches in Europe. The Early English east end was begun in 1220 and the magnificent Perpendicular west front with its richly pinnacled towers was completed in 1420. John of Beverley built a church here in the 7th cent. and the town really grew up around the monastery that accompanied it. He became Bishop of HEXHAM and later Bishop of YORK and ended his days back here. A slab in the centre of the church marks his vault. He was canonized in 1037 and his burial place was a shrine for pilgrims. The later church erected on the site burnt down and the new minster was begun. It is in the unusual form of a double cross. Inside, amid the immense display of ornament and sculpture, the visitor may note in particular the glorious Percy Shrine – the canopy is regarded as the finest 14th-cent. work of its kind – which can be viewed best from the reredos gallery; the Frith Stool, or stone sanctuary chair; the biggest collection of misericords in England (68); and the 12th-cent. font of Frosterley marble. Nothing is left of the old monastery but a brick wall E. of the minster. St Mary's Church, hardly ½ m. away, was begun in the 12th cent. as a chapel to the minster. In rebuilding the nave in the 13th cent., the walls were so weakened that the central tower finally collapsed in 1520, killing several worshippers. In restoration, the roofs were repainted in lively medieval fashion. Also noteworthy is the minstrels' pillar in the north arcade.

Beverley is linked by river to HULL, builds trawlers, tans leather and serves as a market centre for the area. In the Saturday Market is a market cross of 1714, an open octagon on steps with pillars supporting the domed roof which displays the arms of England, France, the town and the two Members of Parliament who donated it. The Guildhall is 17th-cent. with a portico added in 1832. Beverley was protected by a ditch and five drawbridges defended by gates. Only one survives, the North Bar, brick-built in the 15th cent.

BIRKIN, *West Riding* (13–SE5226). In two directions from St Mary's churchyard on the edge of this obscure hamlet the view is now blocked by ranks of steaming cooling towers. But the church seems sublimely indifferent to change. It has been here since about 1100, looking much as it does today. Grey stone, with a plain stout tower decorated in the 15th cent. with parapet, pinnacles and gargoyles, the building invites close study. It has a rare vaulted Norman apse, a beautiful climax to the aisleless nave. A south aisle was added in the 14th cent. The south doorway, protected by a decaying wooden porch, is enriched with three orders carved with medallions, zigzag and beakheads, and faces. The tall inner arches, serving the tower and the chancel, also bear zigzag carving. A 14th-cent. stone effigy of an unknown civilian lies in a niche of the north wall of the nave. He carries his heart in his hands, his

A. F. Kersting

Beverley Minster: a detail of the Percy Shrine

character of an Elizabethan house. It is surrounded by fine gardens. The house has been used as a young ladies' academy in the past and now serves as a museum, with a permanent collection of English chairs. Plays, recitals and art exhibitions are held here. Birstall is the birthplace of Joseph Priestley (1733–1804) the dissenting theologian who was also a chemist and discovered nine gases, including oxygen. The town was "Briarfield" in *Shirley*.

BISHOP BURTON, *East Riding* (13–SE 9839), is an unforgettable village, cupped in a hollow with a large wayside pond reflecting the scene. It is a place of white-walled, red-roofed houses, trees and a grey stone village church. The village belonged for a long time to the Archbishops of YORK and one of their palaces is said to have stood in a field named Knight Garth SW. of the village. Rebuilding has left little of the original medieval All Saints Church. In the chancel is a chalice brass to Vicar Johnson, 1460, one of the earliest known examples of this kind of brass, which originated in Yorkshire. There is a bust of John Wesley carved from an elm on the green where he preached and a peace memorial cross on an island in the pond.

BOLTON ABBEY, *West Riding* (12–SE0753). The nave built by the Augustinian canons is now the parish church while the east end of the monastic house of worship is a ruined skeleton. The site is alluring near a sweeping bend of the Wharfe bordered by green pastures with wooded slopes beyond. Stepping stones cross the river. The priory was founded here in 1151 by Alicia de Romilly whose family had been granted these lands by William the Conqueror. Before that, this was the site of an Anglo-Saxon manor. With the advent of the Romillys, the centre moved to SKIPTON where the castle was built. The church is 13th-cent. with an elaborate west front and west tower unfinished by the time of the Dissolution. The ruined chancel had been built in the 14th cent. Painters have loved this scene, and Landseer made it famous with his early-19th-cent. *Bolton Abbey in Olden Time*. The rectory nearby was a free school until the later 19th cent. The priory's gatehouse is in Bolton Hall, a residence of the Dukes of Devonshire. The hamlet is known erroneously, but by long usage, as Bolton Abbey. Three m. upstream where the Wharfe narrows is the small, humped Barden Bridge and above it the ruined Barden Tower built in 1485 by Henry Lord Clifford.

BOLTON CASTLE, *North Riding* (14–SE 0391), is in the village called Castle Bolton and dominates not only the village but a lot of Wensleydale as well. The first Lord Scrope built it and Mary Queen of Scots was held prisoner here for six months in 1568–9. The Scropes had a manor house here in the 13th cent., but when given licence to crenellate in 1379, Lord Scrope put up a completely new castle. It is unusual for the size of the living-rooms, their fireplaces and privies. It

hair is carefully curled and his feet rest on a dog. An 18th-cent. wall monument records the misfortunes of one of the Thorntons who served as rectors here for 106 years. This one, Robert, came in 1612 but in 1649 he was arrested as a Royalist "tied to a horse rail and dragged to Cawood Castle" but he returned to his post 15 years later. The 18th-cent. pulpit has a finely carved tester or sounding board.

BIRSTALL, *West Riding* (12–SE2226). Oakwell Hall, now owned by the Batley Corporation, was visited by Charlotte Brontë, who thereupon used it under the name of "Fieldhead" in her novel *Shirley*. It was built by John Batt in 1583, and although later somewhat altered, retains the

suggests that some comfort was possible in a building concerned firstly with protection. It was one of the first to employ chimneys. The domestic quarters were scattered against the walls around the courtyard and in the towers. The castle was dismantled after the Civil War and lost one of its four corner towers in a storm in 1761. The Great Chamber is a Wensleydale folk museum now. The castle, village and dale were made familiar to many through the watercolours of the late Fred Lawson who came here on holiday in 1910 and stayed until his death at 80 in 1968.

BOLTON PERCY, *West Riding* (13–SE5341). This secluded village SE. of TADCASTER has an exceptional parish church, All Saints, which someone has gone so far as to call the "cathedral of the Ainsty". It was designed by Rector Thomas Parker during his incumbency here from 1411 to 1423 and completed shortly after his death. All of the details are finely attended to and the east window still has about one-half of its original glass. Two medieval altar stones and a 12th-cent. font are among the relics, and the woodwork, ranging from 15th-cent. roofs to a Georgian pulpit, is excellent. Monuments to Fairfaxes, including Ferdinando Lord Fairfax, a commander at MARSTON MOOR, are here. The shady village also has a former rectory built in 1698 and a 15th-cent. gatehouse, known locally as a tithe barn, with a good deal of carved timber work in it.

BOROUGHBRIDGE, *West Riding* (13–SE 3966). A bridge over the Ure in Norman times gave the town its start and it became an important road centre with 22 inns at one time. An impressive number of inns remain. In the 18th cent. it was a port for KNARESBOROUGH's linens. Here in 1322, Edward II defeated Thomas, Earl of Lancaster, who was followed into the church where he had taken refuge, carried a prisoner to his own castle at PONTEFRACT and beheaded. That church is no more, having been pulled down in 1851. St James's was built the next year with a few relics incorporated, including a late Norman doorway. The town's attractions include fine old houses, many trees, a cobbled square with a fanciful 1875 market cross, fishing and boating.

To the SW., behind a housing estate and on the road to Roecliffe, stand the mysterious **Devil's Arrows,** three huge weather-worn standing stones, the most famous prehistoric monuments in Yorkshire. They are probably 3,000 years old and could have been important to the Brigantes as late as Roman times. The folk story was that they were bolts shot by the Devil at ancient cities to destroy them. They stand on beds of clay and coarse stone 6 ft deep and weigh 36 tons each. They would have been quarried near Knaresborough, 7 m. away. A fourth stone was taken down and cut up for building the bridge on the small Tut long ago.

BOWES, *North Riding* (14–NY9913), gained some dubious publicity as the site of Dickens's Dotheboys Hall. He stayed at the Unicorn Inn at whose door in that day boys attending one of the several boarding schools, or "boy farms", in the vicinity were dropped by stagecoaches. Dickens's school was probably a composite of places he had visited or heard of, but by popular consent the Bowes school run by William Shaw is taken for the model, with Shaw the real-life Wackford Squeers. It is doubtful whether he merited this savage portrait, but the school had to close after the publication of *Nicholas Nickleby*. The building known as Dotheboys Hall is now a café. The Shaw family as well as the 19-year-old youth, George Arthur Taylor, whose gravestone so moved the novelist, are all buried in the churchyard of St Giles, a restored medieval building with two ancient fonts, one Norman and one early 13th-cent. The church also contains a Roman dedication stone of about A.D. 204. To the Romans, Bowes was Lavatrae: it may have been a place where baths were provided for legionaries travelling the Stainmore Road (Watling or Dere Street). Like the church, Bowes Castle used Roman stone for building. The Norman keep was the only stone building of the castle, completed in 1187, and now in the hands of the Ministry of Public Building and Works. The thick walls are still 50 ft high. It was built for Henry II by Alan Niger, Earl of Richmond.

Bowes, high on a hillside site, is 4 m. SW. of BARNARD CASTLE. The stump of the Rey Cross stands near the road, 5¾ m. W., supposedly the boundary mark in the 10th cent. between English and Danish territory and the old kingdom of Strathclyde to the NW. It is a perfect spot for moorland views. NW. looms **Mickle Fell**, at 2,591 ft, Yorkshire's highest mountain; sometimes there is snow on the top from autumn to early summer.

BRADFORD, *West Riding* (12–SE1633). The great wool town has other admirable claims to fame. It was first with a school board, school medical and dental services, school baths, school meals, a nursery school, municipal hospital, electricity department and railway – and it must be one of the first to make money extracting wool grease from its sewage and selling it in the form of lanolin and other useful products around the world.

Much of Bradford looks confidently Victorian but new building is rapidly altering the old business centre and eliminating the back-to-back housing. The residents look cosmopolitan. The city over a century has accommodated Irish, German, Eastern European, Italian and, most recently, West Indian and Asian immigrants. Their biggest employer is the wool trade, which was firmly established here in the 18th cent. Large numbers also work in engineering, chemicals and the mail-order clothing business.

Those who have not seen Bradford lately have surprises coming. Smokeless zoning already affects more than 80 per cent of the houses. The massive Gothic-style Town Hall with its illuminated campanile tower has been scrubbed and is now buff instead of black. Next to it is a new park with rose gardens, part of the city centre building and landscaping programme. There is a new entertainment centre, a new £800,000 Central Library (claimed to be the finest in Europe) and a new university, chartered in 1966, which grew out of the College of Advanced Technology. St George's Hall, highly praised for its acoustics, is once more resounding to orchestras and choirs after a bad patch as a cinema. But the house where Frederick Delius spent his early years has been replaced by a garage.

A few things do not change. The patron saint of woolcombers, St Blaise, still overlooks Market Street from the tower of the Wool Exchange where traders from the world market still gather. The cathedral is one link to the remoter past. It is late-15th- to early-16th-cent. Perpendicular with modern additions and was a parish church until 1919. The chancel contains excellent Victorian stained glass. The cathedral stands on a hillside and Church Bank runs down it into the square named after the Bradford M.P., W. E. Forster, who sponsored the compulsory education act of 1870. Another local hero is Richard Oastler, who fought the use of child labour in the mills. His statue stands in Northgate.

Two Bradford parks of special interest are Lister and Bowling, respectively NW. and SE. of the centre. Lister Park is named after the 1st Lord Masham who invented a woolcombing machine and founded a silk mill. It has a scented garden for the blind, a boating lake and a pleasant 1½-m. walk. In Cartwright Memorial Hall, built in 1904 on the site of Lord Masham's old home and named after the inventor of the power loom, is the City Art Gallery and Museum. At the park entrance is an elaborate memorial to Sir Titus Salt, who moved his alpaca and mohair mills in the 1850s to a healthier situation and built **Saltaire** near Shipley, a model village in its day.

Bowling Park spreads out opposite **Bolling Hall**, now a museum. The house includes a peel tower built in about 1400, a 17th-cent. addition and finally a wing by John Carr in 1779. The Hall was the home of Bollings, Tempests and Saviles.

A short excursion E. and S. from Bradford will take in **Fulneck**, where a Moravian settlement was established in the 18th cent.; **Tong**, for a look at an almost untouched 18th-cent. village group of hall (now a museum owned by Bradford Metropolitan District Council), church and cottages; and finally **Wyke**, a smaller Moravian settlement.

BRAMHAM PARK, *West Riding* (13–SE 4041). The small village of Bramham, S. of pleasant-looking Boston Spa, has a number of fine houses in its vicinity but easily the grandest is Bramham Park. At one time the gardens, too, were among the most remarkable in England, a rare surviving example of French-style landscaping of the days of Louis XIV. The grounds were notable for long avenues lined with towering beech hedges, with calculated vistas and ornamental buildings and ponds. A gale in 1962 destroyed 490 of the trees, including the oldest. Although the temples and obelisk were spared and the grounds have been replanted, a generation or

more must pass before they acquire their former magnificence. The gardens, however, are still unusually fine and, like the house, are open to view at advertised times. The Hon. Mrs M. A. Lane Fox is the owner today. Both house and gardens were the work of Robert Benson, the 1st Lord Bingley, who lived at YORK where he, like his father before him, was Lord Mayor and M.P. He was at one time the Ambassador to Spain and on the Continent developed a taste for the gardens of André Le Nôtre, his inspiration in planning his own park. The house and park were designed and built from about 1700 to 1710. It is believed that Benson was his own architect for the Classical buff sandstone building with its two-story centre block balanced at each side with an open colonnade and pavilion. A fire in 1828 devastated the house, and although a temporary roof was put over it, restoration did not take place until 1907. A new addition then was the horseshoe-shaped staircase copied from one at Fontainebleau. A little summer-house by James Paine (1760) at the end of the terrace was converted to a chapel. In it stands a figure of Lord Bingley. The stable block is also believed to be by Paine.

BRANDESBURTON, *East Riding* (13–TA 1147). The church, St Mary's, in an otherwise unremarkable village, is built of cobbles with a brick clerestory and south porch, and it exhibits work from the Normans to the 15th cent., when the tower was built. There is a very large piscina in the east wall of the chancel and a niche built aslant in the north. In the chancel floor is the only example of a bracket brass in the riding, a now headless memorial to Rector William Darell who died in 1364. Opposite are two brasses to Sir John de St Quintin, who died in 1397, and Lora, his wife, who died two years later. The knight has lost his head but his heart is in his hands. A greyhound lies under his feet. His wife wears a flowing tunic and the little dog at her hem has bells on his collar.

BRANDSBY, *North Riding* (13–SE5872). Here the road from YORK to HELMSLEY climbs into the wooded Howardian Hills and back over your shoulder you can see the Plain of York with the minster towers in the far-off haze. Thomas Atkinson designed both All Saints Church, completed in 1770, and the Hall, finished three years earlier. Harmonious short terraces of cottages are placed here and there on the slopes. A 16th-cent. rectory with 19th-cent. additions and a woodcarver's shop are the other village features. The church has a stone cupola on its hipped roof and this is supported inside by a pleasing arrangement of four Doric columns with cross vaults. A local man made the wrought-iron gate leading into the nave. A small crucifix is thought to be Norman.

BRIDLINGTON, *East Riding* (13–TA1766). This used to be the most "genteel" of the Yorkshire seaside resorts; it is simply one of the most popular now. Protected on the NE. by the great headland of FLAMBOROUGH, it lies near the top

Bridlington harbour

of Bridlington Bay with long stretches of fine sand both N. and S. of the harbour. A small fishing fleet still sails from here. Stones from the old priory were used to build the two harbour piers and there is some fishing-village atmosphere in the houses that cluster near the waterside. It figured dramatically in history on 22 February 1643 when Queen Henrietta Maria landed from Holland with arms for Charles I. The vessels were bombarded by Parliamentary ships. As the cannon-balls "sang merrily" around her, the Queen took refuge in a ditch, later moving on to Boynton Hall.

The great attraction of old Bridlington, 1 m. inland, is the Church of St Mary. It includes the nave of the Augustinian priory founded here in about 1119 by Walter de Gant and was saved from destruction at the Dissolution because it was already in use as a parish church. Next to BEVERLEY Minster, it is considered the finest ecclesiastical building in the East Riding. It was restored in the mid-19th cent. Portions to linger over are the richly decorated north porch, the beautiful west doorway beneath a huge window, and the 14th-cent. south aisle. The north-west tower has a plain Early English parapet but the rebuilt south-west tower has crocketed pinnacles in 15th-cent. style. Inside is a black grave slab on two low pedestals which may belong to William de Gant. It is carved with two dragons, a cat, and a fox and crane drinking from a jug. It has been used as a bread table for distributing food to the poor.

The priory's Bayle Gate across the green was built in 1388 and was, at various times, the prior's courtroom, a sailors' prison, a barracks and a school. Now it is a museum. This priory was wealthy and had several important figures, including John who worked miracles before and after his death in 1379. The last prior was hanged at Tyburn for his part in the Pilgrimage of Grace.

William Kent, the first English architect to design furniture, was born here in 1685. The 18th-cent. **Sewerby Hall**, on the cliffs NE. of the town centre, is a Corporation art gallery with interesting gardens.

Boynton, a neighbour to the NW., has pretty cottages and a Tudor hall, altered in the 18th cent. and open by appointment. The church close to the hall gates is medieval with nave and chancel rebuilt in brick in 1768 by John Carr. One Strickland family monument is attributed to William Kent. There is a choice turkey lectern.

BRIMHAM ROCKS, *West Riding* (12–SE 2165), are a collection of grotesque rock formations scattered over a 50-acre site on a heathery moor 950 ft above the Nidd valley. Found E. of PATELEY BRIDGE, they are a popular picnic spot and an endless marvel to children. The rocks are millstone grit roughly carved over thousands of years by sheets of ice, winds and frosts. The names which have been given to individuals among the weird assortment suggest their shapes: Yoke of Oxen, Pivot Rock, Chimney Rock, Baboon, Dancing Bear and Druid's Skull. An 18th-cent. visitor discovered that the stones, in some cases standing on a sort of pedestal, would rock. The 200-ton Idol Rock rests on a stem only 12 in. thick.

BROMPTON-IN-ALLERTONSHIRE, *North Riding* (15–SE3796). There are many Bromptons, but this one is near NORTHALLERTON. Here in 1867, a restoration of St Thomas's Church uncovered the best collection of Anglo-Danish hogback tombstones in the country. Six were taken to DURHAM Cathedral Library but four whole and fragments of two others are here. They are characterized by carvings of bears hugging the slabs, with strapwork in their mouths. They are probably 1,000 years old. They may have bordered a grave with crosses standing at head and foot. Portions of several fine Anglo-Saxon crosses and shafts can also be seen here.

BROUGH, *East Riding* (13–SE9326). A ferry on the YORK to LINCOLN route carried Roman soldiers across the Humber here in the days of the Roman station of Petuaria. The location was established firmly with the discovery in 1937 of an inscribed stone of about A.D. 160 recording the gift of a theatre by Marcus Ulpius Ianuarius. The station covered about 12 acres and was stone-walled. The village is now an appendage of HULL.

BROWSHOLME HALL, *West Riding* (12–SD6845). A landscaped garden and lake were created here by Thomas Lister Parker as a tribute to his good friends, the Prince Regent and Mrs Fitzherbert, and a bedroom suite with an exclusive view of his charming idea was arranged in the Hall. Parkers have been at home here since 1380.

The present Hall, near Waddington and just over the Yorkshire border from CLITHEROE in Lancashire, dates from 1507 with a new front put on in 1604 by Thomas Holt of YORK and alterations again made in 1711 and 1800. The house is of red sandstone. The oak panelling is admired.

BURNSALL, *West Riding* (12–SE0361), presents a charming picture from the grassy fells above. Its grey-stone buildings lie low amid trees and a five-arched bridge crosses the Wharfe. This is a favourite centre for Wharfedale excursions. Diversions offered include fishing for trout or grayling, boating and walking. A maypole stands on the village green where the annual feast-day games in August draw crowds to watch the amateurs compete at canoeing, tug of war, fell races, pillow fights and sprints. St Wilfrid's Church is almost entirely Perpendicular. It was "butified" in 1612, according to a plaque, at the expense of Sir William Craven. He also founded the grammar school in 1602. The building, which resembles a manor house, is now the primary school. The church treasures include an 11th-cent. font crudely carved with birds and beasts; two hogback tombstones, one showing monster heads and scales; 12 Anglo-Saxon sculpture fragments; and a lovely alabaster panel of the mid-14th cent. showing the Adoration of the Magi. To the list could be added the pretty lych-gate with its stone weights. In the churchyard are kept the village stocks. A Dawson family tombstone was designed by Eric Gill.

BURTON AGNES, *East Riding* (13–TA1063). A captivating Elizabethan great house which contains modern French paintings and a ghost is the magnet at this village. It is of mellow red brick with stone trim. The exterior is distinguished by semi-octagonal bays on the east and west sides and semi-circular bays on the south front. A gatehouse with octagonal towers, built a little later but in the same style, leads to the house, elegantly set off by the velvet lawns and almost 100 clipped yews. The house has been in the hands of the family that built it for 350 years. Sir Henry Griffith was the builder, and it was constructed between 1598 and 1610 to replace the Manor House of 1170, much of which still stands (though in an Elizabethan brick casing) under the care of the Ministry of Public Building and Works. Visitors will be hard pressed to absorb all the splendid architectural detail of the richly furnished rooms, but especially memorable are the stone and alabaster chimney-piece and oak and plaster screen of the great hall, the gilded oak panelling of the drawing-room, the massive staircase, the honeysuckle ceiling of the queen's bedroom and the beautifully restored Long Gallery. The ceiling of the gallery collapsed in 1810, and two-thirds of the room, which ran the length of the house, was converted to staff bedrooms. In 1951, the present owner, Marcus William Wickham-Boynton, began the restoration. It was a tribute to modern craftsmen that from a scrap of surviving plasterwork they could re-create the Elizabethan original.

Burton Agnes House contains a fine collection of modern French paintings

The house contains a fascinating collection of paintings which is still growing. The impressive array of French work includes Cézanne, Pisarro, Gauguin, Matisse, Vuillard, Dufy, Vlaminck and many more. The ghost is of Anne, youngest daughter of the builder, whose portrait hangs in the inner hall. She died after being attacked by ruffians at **Harpham**, and her dying wish was that her skull should remain forever in the house she loved. But her sisters buried her in the church-yard, and the place was racked with ghostly disturbance. The coffin was opened and the head found severed from her body. It was reburied in the house and each attempt to get rid of it has been followed by trouble. It is thought now to be built into a wall of the great hall. The village church, St Martin's, late Norman to Perpendicular, is found through an archway of yews and contains family tombs. At St John's Church in Harpham, ½ m. SW., there are fine 15th-cent. brasses of the St Quintin family and a rare incised alabaster slab. Harpham was the birthplace of St John of BEVERLEY.

BURTON CONSTABLE, *East Riding* (13– TA1836), the home of the Constables, whose land-holdings in the East Riding go back to the 11th cent., is open to visitors daily during the summer season. The great house is set in a 200-acre park filled by Capability Brown with oaks, chestnuts and elms, a lake with an arched bridge, an island and a bird sanctuary, and a pretty French garden. The central block and two projecting wings of the house were built in 1570, but most of the rooms were redone in the 18th cent. by such Georgian craftsmen as Robert Adam and James Wyatt. The remodelling was the work of William Constable, who collected many of the pictures which make up the excellent collection. The house interiors run the gamut from a Georgian dining-room to a Tudor Long Gallery with pendant ceiling. The east front of Burton Constable is known for its domed bays and gabled flanking ranges. The west front, where columns support the pediment and a tower stands guard at each end, measures more than 200 ft. In the stately homes competition, this one offers a zoo, model railway, collection of carriages, children's playground, camping and caravan sites. You can even tour the grounds by stagecoach.

BUTTERTUBS PASS, *North Riding* (14–SD 8795). High, wide views greet the motorist taking the road from **Hawes** N. to Thwaite over the Buttertubs Pass. It is the justly famous link be-tween Wensleydale and Swaledale, and one of the highest sections of road in the country; like all Pennine roads, it can be made hazardous by snow and ice at any time during the long winter season. It gets its name from a series of deep limestone shafts which might be said to look like buttertubs (or pots or churns, as fancy dictates). Motorists will not see them unless they get out of their cars. They are 4½ m. from Hawes and 50 to 100 ft from the side of the road on the right.

BYLAND ABBEY, *North Riding* (13–SE5478). After several unhappy moves, a Cistercian colony settled in this broad valley 2 m. NE. of COXWOLD in 1177. Here they drained the marshes, built their quarters and their church and led an uneventful life until the Dissolution. Byland is a haunting ruin now, on a bend in the road, confronting a small inn in a region that seems otherwise un-inhabited. The tall west front with its vast broken circle of a rose window and a single turret beside it

A. F. Kersting

Castle Howard is one of the most palatial country houses in England

is a telling reminder of the magnificent church that once stood here. The plan of the church and monastic buildings is easily followed on the excavated site, now in the care of the Ministry of Public Building and Works. Here you can see the green and yellow glazed tiles in geometric patterns which used to cover the nave and transept floors.

CAMPSALL, *West Riding* (13–SE5313), is known for the architectural interest of its Church of St Mary Magdalene and for Robin Hood: the legendary outlaw is supposed to have preyed on travellers passing through the Barnsdale forest which once surrounded the village. Modern housing estates are crowding the old village centre with its core of church, vicarage and hall, but the church is least affected. The Norman west tower, called by Pevsner "the most ambitious . . . in the Riding", was given battlements and pinnacles somewhat later. The west door is framed in zig-zag moulding. Over the west bay of the south aisle is a priest's room. A new south chapel uses a carved and colourfully painted stone altar by A. W. N. Pugin from the abandoned Ackworth Grange Chapel. The treasured 15th-cent. rood-screen bears a rhymed inscription. The vivid Te Deum east window was completed in 1964 by H. W. Harvey of YORK.

CARLTON-IN-CLEVELAND, *North Riding* (15–NZ5005). Under the moors S. of STOKESLEY is a village of great charm, the one-time parish of a splendid sporting parson. He was the Rev. J. L. Kyle, who came here in 1894 when the parish was under a cloud. His predecessor, George Sangar, had toiled mightily to build a new church. It was completed in 1879, and burnt in

1881. The vicar was charged with arson, but later cleared. Canon Kyle remained until his death in 1943, a hearty man who farmed, rode to hounds, kept a pub (the Fox and Hounds next to the vicarage, "to reform it"), and raised the money for the present St Botolph's Church. Both church and lych-gate were designed by Temple Moore and completed in 1897. They fit well into the village. On the main street are gracious cottages and a manor house, built after 1740, a small-scale Palladian villa with a five-bay centre block and flanking pavilions. On Carlton Bank are the remains of an alum works, which closed in 1771, and a hangar of the NEWCASTLE Gliding Club. There are two lovely runs from Carlton, SE. over the hills to Chop Gate in Bilsdale, with marvellous views all the way, or SW. to Faceby beneath Whorl Hill, a conical mound and the reputed lair of a dragon.

CASTLE HOWARD, *North Riding* (13–SE 7170). Seen against the orthodox prettiness of the Howardian Hills, the splendour of Castle Howard is all the more astonishing. This palace 6 m. W. of MALTON, the largest house in Yorkshire, has no counterpart among English country houses. It is Sir John Vanbrugh's first; his second was BLENHEIM. Castle Howard was built to replace Henderskelfe Castle which burnt down in 1693. The 3rd Earl of Carlisle chose Vanbrugh to design it, a surprise since at that time (1699) Vanbrugh was a captain of marines and successful playwright, but a complete amateur in architecture. But he in turn chose Nicholas Hawksmoor, Wren's clerk, to be his clerk of works, a partnership of brilliance and experience. The building and grounds took from 1700 to 1737 to complete at a cost of more than £78,000. By then, the earl, Vanbrugh and Hawksmoor were dead.

The west wing was added by the 4th Earl's son-in-law, Sir Thomas Robinson. The stables were designed by John Carr in 1781. With its long arched windows, pilasters, frieze, balustrade and bristling urns and statues, the great house spreads from a central block into wings, with a cupola, unheard of for houses at this date, forming a magnificent central climax. Indoors the grandeur continues with the great marble entrance hall, lit by the dome, a suitable introduction. The house has a vast treasure of statuary, furniture, china, miniatures and paintings by masters such as Rubens, Tintoretto, Van Dyke, Canaletto, and Reynolds. Perhaps its most famous picture is Holbein's Henry VIII. The house is the home of George and Lady Cecilia Howard. It has been open to the public throughout its existence. The 1,000-acre park has two lakes and many notable ornaments, including Vanbrugh's Temple of the Four Winds and Hawksmoor's Mausoleum, the size of a Wren church. The house itself is commemorated in a 100-ft obelisk on the road through the park, erected in 1714.

CATTERICK, *North Riding* (15–SE2497). The military connection goes back a long way here. The Romans had a camp they called Cataractonium to the NW. of the present village. This was probably the Catraeth that appears in an early Welsh poem telling of a doomed counter-attack by Celtic Britons against the incoming English, after the legions had gone. Catterick Camp with its monotonous buildings lies 3½ m. W. of the village and is the overwhelming presence now. According to tradition, **Hipswell** close by was the birthplace of John Wycliffe.

Catterick village used to be a major coaching stop on the Great North Road. The Perpendicular Church of St Anne is interesting partly because a contract describing the plans in detail exists for its building. A north chapel was added in 1491 and a south chapel in 1505. There are a 14th-cent. effigy of a knight and two 15th-cent. brasses among the monuments. A contract also survives to document the building of the low bridge over the Swale in 1422, 1 m. N. of the village. There has been an inn there ever since the bridge went up. Big crowds used to gather for the cockfighting. Today they come for the horse-racing.

CAWOOD, *West Riding* (13–SE5737). A tall white stone gatehouse dating from the 15th cent., and incongruously linking a brick house and a barn now, is the only physical reminder of the great palace of the archbishops of YORK which once stood here. It is an ancient site, having been used by Romans, Angles and Vikings. King Athelstan built the castle which in the 14th cent. became the palace. Seven archbishops died here and in 1465 George Neville celebrated his appointment with a gigantic feast employing 2,000 cooks for untold guests. Cardinal Wolsey had hoped to make this palace a rival to HAMPTON COURT, which he had given to Henry VIII. Wolsey was arrested here while he was ill. Cawood was taken in the Civil War and nearly demolished. With its

clustering cottages and narrow winding streets it is a pretty sight from the swing-bridge or from the churchyard. All Saints stands near the muddy banks of the Ouse. It is mainly late Norman, with a Perpendicular tower reinforced with buttresses, battlements and pinnacles. It contains a dignified monument to Archbishop Mountain who died in 1623.

About 2 m. SW. on the B1222 is the newly opened **Bishop Wood** park, part of the Forestry Commission's Selby Forest. The area is low-lying and paths may be muddy. Unlike most of the Plain of York, Bishop Wood was never reclaimed for farming so it stands as an ancient example of woodland. Poplars are a special feature and there are 300 kinds of plants and ferns, 70 species of birds, and mammals from hedgehogs to badgers to look for.

CLAPHAM, *West Riding* (12–SD7469), is the centre for potholing. Upstream a short distance is Ingleborough Cave, 900 yds into the great hill of **Ingleborough**, which was made accessible in 1857. It is a place of many eerie chambers and imaginatively named rock formations and it is open to the public. A mile further on is Gaping Gill. You can earn the freedom of Craven by descending its 378 ft, but it is necessary to go with a potholing club. A winch will lower the venturesome in 90 seconds. Gaping Gill has an underground chamber large enough to accommodate a small cathedral. The summit of Ingleborough provides far-ranging views on a good day.

Clapham itself is a tidy village of grey-stone houses and whitewashed cottages along a beck. Pretty gardens and fine trees add to the village scene. St James's Church, happily sited, was completely rebuilt in 1814 except for the Perpendicular west tower. Ingleborough Hall, developed out of a shooting lodge, is used by the West Riding County Council as a special school. The beck was dammed to create an 8-acre lake in the grounds and a waterfall spills into the ravine from it. Reginald Farrer, the botanist who introduced a hundred plants to Europe and wrote extensively on rock gardens, lived here, and the monthly magazine, *The Dalesman*, devoted to all aspects of Yorkshire country life, has been published in Clapham since 1939.

CONISBROUGH, *West Riding* (13–SK5198). The great white circular keep of the Norman castle rises dramatically above surrounding greenery high over the River Don, with a little town at its feet. The keep is 90 ft high, 52 ft in diameter and has six massive buttresses 9 ft thick. It is the oldest and best of its kind in the country and is in the care of the Ministry of Public Building and Works. The castle was founded by the de Warennes and the surviving work was by Hameline Plantagenet, who married the last of the Warenne family and took his wife's name. He built an identical keep in Normandy. This one probably dates from 1185. A narrow barbican with two turns leads inside. The tiny chapel on the third floor, built into the buttress, was the setting for a scene in Sir Walter Scott's *Ivanhoe*. From the roof is a wide view of the coalfield.

On a lesser height in the hilly town is St Peter's Church which dates from Anglo-Saxon times, with substantial parts of it constructed at the same time as the castle. The chancel arch, west tower, aisle arcades (with deeply carved capitals) and south doorway are all 12th-cent. The most important church treasure is the extraordinary Norman tomb-chest or gravestone. It is decorated all over in patterns and figures, with remarkable scenes of a man battling a dragon, two mounted knights jousting, and Adam with Eve.

COVERHAM ABBEY, *North Riding* (12–SE 1186). Coverdale is one of the smallest and quietest of the Yorkshire dales. The stream has only a short run before it empties into the Ure below MIDDLEHAM. In the valley are the slight remains of Coverham Abbey, now in the grounds of a private home. The abbey was founded by Helewisia de Glanville, wife of Robert Fitzralf of Middleham Castle, at Swainby. Her son, Ralf Fitzrobert, had many quarrels with the Premonstratensian canons and for some reason moved them to Coverdale about 1212. Relics of the abbey include portions of the arcade and transept and coffin lids, including late-13th-cent. effigies of cross-legged knights who may have been Helewisia's son and grandson. The humpbacked Coverham Bridge, the restored country church on the steep bank, the abbey mill and miller's house complete the picture in the secluded dale. Here was born Miles Coverdale who produced the translation known as the Great Bible for the common people in 1538.

COXWOLD, *North Riding* (13–SE5377), a dream of a village: a wide sloping street with broad verges, rows of honey-coloured cottages, spreading trees, and at the top a 15th-cent. church with an unusual octagonal tower. It is in the area of the gentle Howardian Hills with lovely countryside and neighbouring villages to enjoy. Despite its fame as a beauty-spot, Coxwold has managed to stay unspoilt and serene, a tribute to residents as well as the landowners, the Wombwell family.

Laurence Sterne came to Coxwold in 1760, just after he had published his first novel, *The Life and Opinions of Tristram Shandy* ("shandy" is Yorkshire for wild or eccentric). The obscure country clergyman was just becoming a social lion. He rented a rambling house N. of town, because the church had no vicarage, and named it Shandy Hall. Here he wrote at least two more volumes during a seven years' residence. He died in 1768 in London and his remains were returned to Coxwold churchyard in 1969 from a Bayswater burial ground. The Sterne Trust now owns Shandy Hall and is restoring it as a museum. The old brick farm-house has medieval timber framing, a bulky chimney and a warren of rooms.

Another notable Coxwold building is the Fauconberg Arms, 17th-cent. in its origins and restored in the 18th cent., with the family crest on the front. Under the old manorial system, the inn

is allowed the right to graze four cows on a large meadow shared by the villagers and to cut hay from two strips of the town pasture.

The church is chiefly Perpendicular but the chancel was rebuilt in the 18th cent. Pulpit, communion rail and box pews also are Georgian. There are a number of monuments of the Bellasis family, one of whom became the Earl of Fauconberg. Behind the church is Colville Hall, the former Manor House, an early 17th-cent. gabled building. Across the street is the Old Hall, formerly a grammar school and also 17th-cent.

S. of the village is **Newburgh Priory**; the pond and ornamental hedges are eye-catching features on the road. A private residence of the Wombwells, it is essentially an 18th-cent. hall. Its predecessor on the site was a house of Augustinian canons who settled here about 1150. With the Dissolution the property went to Anthony Bellasis, Henry VIII's chaplain. A Fauconberg married the daughter of Oliver Cromwell who is supposed to have brought her father's body – perhaps only the heart – back here for burial. It is thought the pitiful remains are in a bricked-up end of a small attic room.

CRAVEN, *West Riding* (12–SD9070 *around*). The district known as Craven, in the western Dales, consists of fells and peaks, nine of them more than 2,000 feet high. The best known and grandest are Whernside, Ingleborough and Pen-y-Ghent. The rivers Wharfe and Ribble, among other streams, rise in these hills. The landscape is distinguished by limestone scars and cliffs (notably MALHAM Cove, Gordale Scar and KILNSEY CRAG), underground streams, caves and potholes. Climbing and caving are naturally enough favourite pastimes in Craven. A fine example of the caverns carved by subterranean rivers is Stump Cross near PATELEY BRIDGE. Potholing requires both skill and good equipment here. Among the most explored potholes are Gaping Gill on Ingleborough and the Hunt and Hull Pots on Pen-y-Ghent. The scenery owes its dramatic appearance to the Craven Faults, giant dislocations of the Pennine rock, worked upon over the ages by wind and water. The vantage point for seeing the line of the faults is Buckhaw Brow out of GIGGLESWICK. Ingleborough was a walled stronghold of the Brigantes who resisted the Roman occupation. Collections from caves used in earlier periods can be examined at the Craven Museum, SKIPTON, and the Pig Yard Museum, SETTLE.

CRAYKE, *North Riding* (13–SE5670). You cannot miss this tiny village for it sits on a small hill on the Plain of York. On top are a church and a battlemented residence made out of the tower house of the 15th-cent. castle, and at the bottom a green and old cottages. The castle at one time was a house of the Bishops of DURHAM. Nothing remains of either the presumed Anglo-Saxon fortress or the Norman castle which came after it. St Cuthbert's Church is Perpendicular with some very good furnishings.

CROFT, *North Riding* (15–NZ2909). The village bestriding the Tees had a brief fling as a spa and even sold its bottled waters in London in the early 18th cent. But the rise of HARROGATE was the downfall of Croft. The red sandstone church at the end of the 15th-cent. bridge (widened, of course), the rambling Croft Spa Hotel and some pleasant Queen Anne and Georgian houses remind the visitor of the more important village of the past. Lewis Carroll's father, the Rev. Charles Dodgson, was vicar here for 25 years. The boy, Charles, was 12 when the big family settled into the rectory (now flats) in 1843. The long, low-lying Church of St Peter should be visited to see the 17th-cent. Milbanke pew, erected an arrogant 6 ft above the floor near the chancel. Attained by a staircase and resting upon Tuscan columns, the pew is 15 ft long. Lord Byron and his bride probably sat in it when visiting at Halnaby Hall, once the home of the Milbankes, Lady Byron's family, but now demolished.

DANBY-IN-CLEVELAND, *North Riding* (15–NZ7007). The classic account of moorland life is still *Forty Years in a Moorland Parish* by Canon John Christopher Atkinson, who spent 53 of his 86 years at St Hilda's Church here and was buried in the churchyard in 1900. The village, also called Dale End, is at the head of Danby Dale which runs S. into the moors. The church is 2 m. from the village, with the rectory halfway between. The church has a Perpendicular south porch and a fragment or so of other old stone, but is chiefly an 18th-cent. nave on a 19th-cent. chancel. One m. SE. of the village is the ruin of 14th-cent. Danby Castle, now built into a farmhouse. Catherine Parr's second husband, Lord Latimer, owned it in those days. After his death she married, and survived, Henry VIII. Near the castle is the packhorse Duck Bridge, built around 1386. On the 1,000-ft Danby Beacon, 1½ m. NE. of the village, stands a radar station. Danby Dale is a beautiful broad valley of the Esk, with many ancient cairns. Much scenic beauty awaits you if you cannot resist the names of Little Fryup and Great Fryup.

DENT, *West Riding* (12–SD7087). The only town in Dentdale has a narrow cobbled main street which no one who has driven or walked over will soon forget. Dent is picturesque in a wholly natural, effortless way. It lies deep in the valley cut by the Dee, unspoilt, unimportant, unhurried. Grey-stone cottages, many now painted white, are what the visitor remembers of the town. Against one rests a slab of Shap granite that forms a drinking fountain memorial to a famous 19th-cent. local man, Adam Sedgwick, the vicar's son who became a pioneer geologist. There was a move in his day to change the name of a Dentdale hamlet from Cowgill to Kirkthwaite, because it was thought seemlier. Sedgwick is remembered locally for his *Memorial* in defence of the homely old name which was confirmed by Act of Parliament.

Dent has lost many of its old activities, such as making cheese, or hay rakes and butter boxes. In the 18th cent. people here turned out hand-knitted garments so rapidly that they were known as the "terrible knitters of Dent". Marble quarried in the upper valley for more than a century was made into countless tombs, fonts, tables and stairs. It is almost entirely a farming economy now, with an inflow of townsfolk and holiday-makers partly offsetting the loss of other vocations. The steep slopes of Whernside, Great Coum, Middleton Fell and Rise Hill which form the dale walls tempt walkers.

DONCASTER, *West Riding* (13–SE5803). The classic St Leger has been run since 1776, although it was not given the name of its founder until two years later. Thus it is four years older than the Derby. The grandstand designed by John Carr in 1776 and enlarged in the early 19th cent. is an attractive component of the Doncaster racing scene which goes back 400 years. Dickens came to the races in 1857, stayed at the then relatively new New Angel Hotel and commented acidly on the "horse-mad, betting-mad, drunken-mad, vice-mad" crowds. Doncaster was the site of a Roman station, Danum, with extensive iron and pottery works. It was also known to Anglo-Saxons and Normans. Although the charters date back to 1194, it is a modern town, transformed from an agricultural to an industrial centre by the arrival of the railway in 1848 and a carriage works in 1853. The surrounding coalfield is today the basis of the economy: Doncaster is ringed by mining villages. The National Coal Board's 10-story office block is one of the buildings in the new Civic Centre, Glasgow Paddocks.

The Museum and Art Gallery, completed in 1964, is in Chequer Road and contains relics from the Roman station, fossils from mines, and British birds. Paintings and sculpture are mainly by British artists. Fabio Barraclough and Frantz Belsky did the sculptures on the exterior.

Among older buildings, two churches and the Mansion House stand out. The Mansion House, the pretty pride of Doncaster, is in the High Street and was completed in 1748. James Paine's plan included two supporting wings but these were never built. A third story was added in 1801, in place of the original pediment, for the mayor's use but the building has not been a mayoral residence for 140 years. It is used for civic and social occasions. The façade has first-floor Corinthian columns and a lovely Venetian window which lights a handsome ballroom with stucco work by Joseph Rose and two fireplaces probably by Robert Adam.

St George's Parish Church is on almost cathedral scale and it replaced a medieval church burnt in 1833. It was designed by Sir George Gilbert Scott and completed in 1858. It is 170 ft long and its massive tower stands 170 ft high. The exterior bristles with pinnacles. Scott also designed the Doncaster Grammar School for Boys, 1864. Christ Church in Thorne Road was designed by William Hurst and completed in 1829. It has a steeple and octagonal lantern.

G. Douglas Bolton

Dent: the Adam Sedgwick memorial in the village street

On Hall Cross Hill is the monument rebuilt by the corporation in 1793 to replace a cross originally in Hall Gate which commemorated Ote de Tilli about 1182.

Doncaster manufactures wire and wire rope, brass fittings, nylon yarn, agricultural equipment and the famous butterscotch.

At the South Yorkshire Industrial Museum in Cusworth Hall on the outskirts, an absorbing hour or two can be spent among exhibits tracing the social history of mining and manufacturing in this area.

EASBY, *North Riding* (15–NZ1800). An ancient church and picturesque monastery ruins await the traveller who takes the footpath from RICH-MOND station along the River Swale or turns his car off the B6271 SE. of Richmond. St Agatha's Church is much older than the religious house, though mainly 13th- and 14th-cent. as it now stands. Rather plain and low, the church contains three features of special interest: a Norman font; a cast of the very early-9th-cent. Easby Cross (the original is in the VICTORIA AND ALBERT MUSEUM); and wall paintings of the mid-13th cent. The cross is the best Anglo-Saxon sculpture in Yorkshire and depicts birds and beasts on the back with Christ and the Apostles on the front. Scrolls and foliage are carved on the sides and borders. The wall paintings in the chancel are fairly well preserved and tell the story of man from the creation of Eve through the expulsion from Eden, the Annunciation, Nativity and Entombment. In the splays of the windows are the homely labours of the months: hawking, digging, pruning and sowing, all delightfully drawn. Portraits of archbishops are visible on the sedilia.

The extensive remains of the monastery are crowded on the bank of the Swale on the strip of land which rises towards Easby Hall, a Georgian mansion. The abbey was founded for Premonstratensian canons about 1155 by Roald, Constable of Richmond Castle. It suffered at the hands of both English and Scots and was greatly damaged in 1346 when the English army was billeted here. It was acquired by the Scrope family in the same cent. The Ministry of Public Building and Works is the guardian now. The highlight of a tour in the ruins probably will be the splendid windows of the great refectory, where the walls still stand almost to their full height. There is a fine east window here and windows along the south wall, with beautiful tracery. The 14th-cent. gatehouse remains but there is little left of the church, though enough to recapture the sense of this medieval community.

ECCLESFIELD, *West Riding* (12–SK3393). This steel town has a large and handsome parish church, St Mary's, which is chiefly Perpendicular in style with traces of earlier work. An unusual feature are the small flying buttresses which link the buttresses and pinnacles to the church body. The windows contain an assortment of 19th-cent. stained glass and there is good 16th-cent. woodwork. The parish was once exceptionally large and the church was known as the "Minster of the Moors". It had one vicar for 63 years, Alfred Gatty, who served here until the age of 90. His wife wrote children's books, as did their daughter, Juliana Heratia Ewing. The Rev. Joseph Hunter, the 19th-cent. Yorkshire historian who traced the names and towns of the people who sailed for America on the *Mayflower*, is buried in the churchyard. A cell of the Benedictines was established here and some remains of their priory are now in the house called The Priory, N. of the church. Whiteley Hall, in the valley ¾ m. NW., was built in 1584 with a wing added in 1683. Later alterations were made to front and rear. It is a horticultural centre now.

EGGLESTONE ABBEY, *North Riding* (14–NZ0615). A pastoral setting on a knoll beside the Tees 1½ m. S. of BARNARD CASTLE gives the abbey ruins their quiet charm. The river is crossed here by a single-arch stone bridge with a battlemented parapet, built in 1773. This is the place to enjoy the river view. Over Thorsgill Beck, which the monks employed in their drainage system, stands an old packhorse bridge. Woods and running waters combine here to create a memorable scene. The abbey was founded for Premonstratensian canons from EASBY by Robert de Malton in about 1196. It was neither large nor important when it surrendered in 1540. Robert Strelley acquired it in 1548 and converted a range of buildings on the east side into a house. The ruins are chiefly of the cruciform church. The Ministry of Public Building and Works is in charge. There are pleasant walks to and from Barnard Castle.

EGTON, *North Riding* (15–NZ8006). High in the moors, this village overlooks the Esk and is noted for salmon fishing and a Gooseberry Fair in August. Bronze and jet ornaments have been found in ancient graves in the vicinity. St Hilda's, the parish church, was rebuilt in the 1870s in the Norman style. Below at leafy Egton Bridge is St Hedda's Roman Catholic Church built a decade earlier. This was a Catholic stronghold and near here lived the last of the English martyrs, Father Nicholas Postgate. He was finally arrested after baptizing a child, tried at YORK, and hanged at the age of 83 in 1679.

ESCRICK, *East Riding* (13–SE6243). A substantial village near enough to YORK for its residents to work there, Escrick has a lovely Victorian church, St Helen's, built in 1857 and designed by F. C. Penrose in 14th-cent. style. It makes colourful use of marble in the semi-circular west-end baptistry where the vaulted brick roof is supported by red and black marble pillars. The font is the work of Giovanni Tognoli of Rome and consists of a translucent white marble basin upheld on the heads of two standing cherubs. Pink stone is used in the body of the church which has a fine barrel-vaulted roof. A legless effigy by York craftsmen is of Sir Thomas de Lascelles who died in 1324. An 1868 marble effigy of the 1st Lady Wenlock by Count Gleichen shows her as an old lady in a lace shawl. Escrick Park was the home of Sir Thomas Kynvet who discovered the gunpowder hidden by Guy Fawkes (a York lad) in the HOUSES OF PARLIAMENT. The hall has been converted to flats.

FILEY, *East Riding* (13–TA1180). Filey Brigg is a mile-long rocky reef jutting out from the Carr Naze headland at the top of Filey Bay. Half of the brigg is under water and the rest gives anglers, picnickers and geologists endless happy hours. It is a coralline oolite ridge topped with boulder clay. Weather and erosion have carved it into ledges, coves, caves, cliffs and pools. The waves hammer it mercilessly in stormy weather, sending up seething clouds of spray. The Romans left traces and it may have provided them with an anchorage. From it you can look S. to FLAMBOROUGH Head and N. to SCARBOROUGH Castle. It forms a natural pier and breakwater for Filey part old-world fishing village and part modern holiday resort with promenade, gardens and long sandy beach. Most of the town stands on the cliff top with a fine outlook over the crescent bay. Wooded Church Ravine runs up from the sea and above it stands St Oswald's Church which belonged until 1537 to the Augustinian canons of BRIDLINGTON. Its oldest parts date to the late 12th cent. There is a fishermen's memorial window to those lost at sea and a "weatherfish" on the heavy square tower. The Roman Catholic Church of St Mary is in the form of an ancient basilica with an altar in 6th-cent. Italian style and a mosaic on the east end. Charlotte Brontë often stayed at Cliff House, now a café.

FLAMBOROUGH, *East Riding* (13–TA2570). The chalky cliffs of Flamborough Head jut out of the Yorkshire coast where the wolds plunge into the sea. The promontory forms the "nose" on the bearded profile of the Yorkshire map. Ships have often foundered here and in 1779 people watched John Paul Jones win a sea fight with two English men-of-war. The area was taken by Vikings 1,000 years ago and is still sometimes called "Little Denmark". The South Landing offers a view of BRIDLINGTON while on the North Landing you can watch the cobles hauled up by engine and the crab pots unloaded on a beach embraced by cliffs. Flamborough village is 2 m. inland from the lighthouse, a straggling place with a much restored church, St Oswald's. It has a fine 16th-cent. rood-screen and a rare loft, monuments to Constables and Stricklands, and a pair of white paper gloves such as were worn at a maiden's funeral. The monument to Sir Marmaduke Constable who died in 1520 shows him with bared heart, a reference to the gruesome story that his heart was eaten by a toad he had swallowed.

The wind- and wave-sculptured cliffs, 300 to 400 ft high, between Flamborough and Bempton are the best and largest mainland breeding ground for sea birds in England, with numbers at their peak in the first half of July. The only mainland gannet colony in Britain is slowly increasing here and there are numbers of kittiwakes, herring gulls, guillemots, razorbills and some puffins. At times in the past the birds have been shot for food or feathers and crowds used to come to watch the climmers, as they are called here, risk their necks to plunder nests for eggs to sell the spectators. That trade was stopped by Act of Parliament in 1954.

J. K. St Joseph, Cambridge University Collection

Fountains Abbey preserves the plan of a medieval monastery almost intact

FOSTON, *North Riding* (13–SE6965). In Sydney Smith's church here a bronze wall tablet pays tribute to him as "the faithful friend and counsellor of his parishioners; a fearless advocate of civil and religious freedom; a seeker and ensuer of peace; a wit who used his powers to delight and not to wound. One of the founders and first editor of *The Edinburgh Review*." The great cleric and reformer served this parish as rector, doctor and magistrate from 1809 to 1829. St Paul's Church, up a cobblestone path lined with yews, was consecrated in 1290, the church notes tell us, but it must be even older in light of the sumptuous Norman south doorway. Sheltered by a timber-framed porch, it has a series of medallions on the hood mould with such scenes as the Last Supper, St George and the Dragon, David with a harp, and various angels, beasts and humans. There is a lesser Norman doorway on the north wall, reset in the aisle added in 1911, and a Norman pillar piscina. Pink roses nod over the wall of the churchyard in this hamlet. A friendly note pinned to the visitors' book in the church invites all callers to a cup of tea at the rectory in Flaxton. The rectory that Sydney Smith built, a long pink-brick classically Georgian house, is about 1 m. away near Thornton-le-Clay and open to visitors on summer Sundays.

FOUNTAINS ABBEY, *West Riding* (12–SE 2768). The incomparable ruins of the greatest abbey in England stand in the lovely valley of the River Skell 4 m. SW. of RIPON. The amazing thing is how much is left. Partly this is due to William Aislabie, owner of adjoining STUDLEY ROYAL, who acquired Fountains in 1768 and, continuing the landscaping hobby of his father, "gardened" the ruins. The story of the abbey is one of humble beginnings, a rise to power, and eclipse. The prior and several monks at St Mary's Abbey, YORK, disapproved of the laxity which had overtaken their house and with the help of Archbishop Thurstan left to make a new beginning. They adopted the Cistercian rule and began building. They grew in property and recruits but unfortunately the estates outstripped the number of lay brothers and the monks had to let their farms and employ workers. Their huge wool clips paid for the building programme. Power and the display of wealth had replaced the reformist zeal by the time of the Dissolution. Fountains was a great prize, and Henry VIII sold it to Sir Richard Gresham in 1540.

The ruins give a comprehensive picture of life in a medieval monastery. The church extended 360 ft with a 168-ft tower added just before the end. The east window and Chapel of the Nine

G. Douglas Bolton

Fylingdales: the radomes of the Early Warning Station are designed to detect ballistic missiles

Altars are special points of interest. The cellarium with its double row of arches is outstanding among the features of the monastic quarters. Near the West Gate, Fountains Hall was built in 1610 by Sir Stephen Proctor who helped himself to abbey stone for the purpose. The house is a Jacobean triumph, built on a hillside and five stories tall. It is furnished in the style of the period. The banqueting hall has a minstrel gallery and an oriel window contains fine heraldic glass. Among the many treasures kept here is the foundation charter for Fountains. Today the abbey, Hall and grounds are owned by the West Riding County Council and cared for by the Ministry of Public Building and Works.

FYLINGDALES, *North Riding* (15–SE9199). Since 1961, the empty moor inland from ROBIN HOOD'S BAY has had a focal point – the radomes of the Air Ministry's Ballistic Missile Early Warning Station. Visible for miles, the three giant white globes have an unearthly look. Their intrusion into the NORTH YORK MOORS NATIONAL PARK was much regretted by many people but to Pevsner they represent "the geometry of the space age at its most alluring and most frightening".

GIGGLESWICK, *West Riding* (12–SD8163). The village with the infectious name enjoys spectacular upland scenery in its nearby Giggleswick Scar and the heights of Ingleborough and Pen-y-Ghent (2,273 ft) to the N. The well-known public school occupies grey-stone 19th-cent. buildings to the W. of the village, with its chapel under a copper dome, now turned green, standing conspicuously above. The school was founded here in 1553. The parish church is dedicated to St Alkelda, an obscure Anglo-Saxon saint said to have been martyred by the Danes, and is wholly Perpendicular. It contains excellent 17th-cent. furnishings including a pulpit, reading desk, communion rail and poor box. It also has a battered effigy of a knight, Sir Richard Tempest, who was buried in 1488 with the head of his favourite horse. The village itself is pleasantly old-fashioned

with market cross, stocks and tithe barn near the church and period cottages. Near the foot of the Scar is the Ebbing and Flowing Well, an oddity which behaves as its name suggests. It is beside the steep Buckhaw Brow road to CLAPHAM.

GILLING CASTLE, *North Riding* (13–SE 6277), at Gilling East between the Hambleton and Howardian Hills, was built on a steep rise above the village. The house is a fascinating study for its mixture of building styles, its beautiful chimney-pieces, panelling and heraldry, and for its gardens. It stands on three sides of a courtyard. The central block is Tudor and was built on medieval foundations of a 14th-cent. tower house of Thomas of Etton. The wings are 18th-cent. for the most part. Vanbrugh, Wakefield and Gibbs have all been mentioned as possible architects. The castle was occupied by Fairfaxes and their successors from 1492 until 1930. Precious parts were sold in 1929. The wall panelling and heraldic glass of the Great Chamber, for example, were bought by William Randolph Hearst, the American publisher. After Hearst's death in 1951, these were found still in packing cases and re-purchased for the castle. The Long Gallery sold at the same time is at the Bowes Museum, BARNARD CASTLE. AMPLEFORTH College bought the castle as a preparatory school in 1930, preserving the rest. It is open to visitors. The Great Chamber is a stunning room built in 1575–85 with its restored stained-glass windows and painted frieze above the panelling showing family trees bearing 370 coats of arms. The ceiling has a pattern of ribs and pendants. The lofty entrance hall has Corinthian columns and stucco work by Cortese.

GOATHLAND, *North Riding* (15–NZ8301). Tourists and sheep occupy the residents of this big, breezy village, an ideal centre for the North York Moors. It spreads around a very large green. Among the mixed old and new inns and houses, St Mary's Church, built in the 1890s to a plan of W. H. Brierley, fits pleasantly. It has a stone roof and a low oblong tower between the chancel and the nave. An early stone altar and font link it to the past. A path leads off the green to Mallyan Spout, a 70-ft waterfall, one of several in the neighbourhood (Nellie Ayre, Thomason and Water Ark being among the better known). A waterfall is known as a foss in these parts; the word is one of many reminders of Danish settlement. Two m. S. of Goathland station is a mile-long section of the Roman road, kept by the Ministry of Public Building and Works. The road probably dates from the 1st cent. and crosses Wheeldale Moor, part of Wade's Way from MALTON to WHITBY. On special occasions, men and boys perform the ancient longsword and plough stots dances here. Stots is the name for bullocks and here applies to the men who drag the plough around to collect donations for a merry celebration on Plough Monday. Goathland's famous hunt dates from 1750.

GOODMANHAM, *East Riding* (13–SE8842). The village NE. of Market Weighton in the good farmland of the East Riding is one of the oldest as well as most evocative religious sites in the county. Bede's *History of the English Church and Nation* relates the conversion of King Edwin to Christianity in 627 and tells how the high priest, Coifi, also renounced his pagan beliefs. But not content with words, Coifi borrowed arms and a horse from the king and smashed and burnt his own temple, where Goodmanham church now stands. This church is All Saints, commendable for its simplicity and its age. Parts are Norman – the lower part of the stubby tower and the nave – while the north aisle was added and the chancel rebuilt in the 13th cent. In the 15th cent., the tower was given a belfry and battlements. Two unusual fonts are owned by the church. A 15th-cent. octagonal one 5 ft tall is heavily sculptured. The other, well worn from use as a horse trough, could be Anglo-Saxon.

GOOLE, *West Riding* (13–SE7423). Fifty miles from the sea is this busy port, established as the terminus of the Aire and Calder canal from Knottingley in 1826. The canal company sought to improve navigation to the Ouse to speed the export of Yorkshire coal and textiles. At this point, the Don and Ouse rivers meet by way of the "Dutch River", so named because it was cut by Cornelius Vermuyden, a Dutch engineer, in the days of Charles I to drain the Hatfield Chase marshes. The area around Goole, low and watery, does have a Netherlandish feeling. The red-brick town is visible for some distance across the flat land, its high points being two water towers, the church steeple and the dockside cranes. Town life centres around the busy docks, with municipal and harbour offices sharing the Bank Chambers, built in 1892. The port handles two million tons of cargo a year, its inland position making it handy for the coalfields and industrial areas. Nearly all of Goole was built after 1820. The Lowther Hotel, Georgian, is the oldest standing building. The larger water tower was once

reckoned to be the biggest in England, able to hold 750,000 gallons. St John's Church, completed in 1838 by the navigation company, is Perpendicular in style. It is close to the dock sheds and contains memorials to ships as well as seamen. The Garside local history collection is in the new Public Library and museum building in Carlisle Street.

GRASSINGTON, *West Riding* (12–SE0064). This Wharfedale village is one of the most appealing in the dales; its buildings crowd around a small market place paved with cobblestones and along irregular passages. The river is crossed by a stone bridge placed there in 1603 and widened in the late 18th cent. One of the houses, the Old Hall, dates in part from the 13th cent., and 17th-cent. cottages are fairly common. It has been a centre for lead-mining but today is largely dependent upon the visitors' trade. Fishing and walking are two popular diversions. River paths lead to BURNSALL and BOLTON ABBEY or up into the moors. Grassington has always appealed to people, it seems, for the area has numerous prehistoric sites. An especially good one is Lea Green, a pasture reached from Chapel Street, where an Iron Age village stood. Grass Woods nearby is a nature reserve.

GREAT AYTON, *North Riding* (15–NZ5510). Approaching from the SW., the visitor first sees the obelisk to Captain James Cook, famed navigator and explorer, standing boldly on Easby Moor. To this village he was brought at the age of eight from his birthplace at **Marton-in-Cleveland** NW. of here. His baptism is entered in the parish register at Marton and a granite vase marks the site of his birth in 1728. A piece of sandstone with dogtooth carvings, saved from the rebuilding of Marton's church, is cherished in the church at Gisborne, New Zealand, near the spot where the captain landed. At Great Ayton, the boy studied his lessons in the Old School, 18th-cent. and of course new in his time. The red-brick Cook cottage was taken down in 1934 and re-erected in Australia, but a marker records its site. In the upper room of the school is a museum of Cook mementoes. At 13, the boy was apprenticed from here to a grocer at STAITHES.

Outstanding in the great range of the Cleveland Hills hereabouts is cone-shaped Roseberry Topping, a pinnacle preserved from erosion by its sandstone cap. It makes a delightful landmark. There are grand views from the Cook monument, at 1,064 ft, and better ones from Roseberry Topping, 1,057 ft. Revealed from here are the North Sea, the industrial area of Teesside and the hill country. It is an ancient beacon site and Bronze Age implements were found here.

GREAT DRIFFIELD, *East Riding* (13–TA0257). This brisk market town on the edge of the Yorkshire Wolds was more important perhaps a century ago than it is today, but it still serves as the focal point for its area. One of its most admired possessions is the tower of the predominantly Early English All Saints Church. The tower is a remarkably handsome 15th-cent. conception with panelled and graduated buttresses, parapet and eight crocketed pinnacles combining to suggest grace and nobility. The tower has been credited to human frailty: a Hotham, whose family arms share a place on the western face of the tower with those of six other important families, is by tradition believed to have paid for the tower to absolve himself from a vow, made during a serious illness, to undertake a pilgrimage to the Holy Land. (Another version has him paying the price for absolution of immoral conduct.) Driffield is known to anglers for its trout streams, which pour out of the Wolds to form the River Hull. Barges and houseboats moor along its 18th-cent. canal. It is 1 m. from Little Driffield where King Aldred of Northumbria is said to be buried under the chancel. At **Kirkburn**, 4 m. SW., the church vies with NORTH NEWBALD as the best of the Norman style in the East Riding. The font is of Conquest date with animal motifs carved in the lower tier and scenes from the life of Christ above.

GRETA BRIDGE, *North Riding* (14–NZ0813). In spite of some ravages of time, this is still a lovely and romantic spot where the bridge built in 1776 crosses the Greta, a tributary of the Tees. The view painted by John Cotman of the bridge has been spoilt by a new steel span to the N. Nevertheless, this gateway to Teesdale deserves a second glance. The Morritt Arms on the site of a Roman fort is at one side of the bridge and opposite is the entrance to Rokeby Park. It is privately owned but permission can be obtained to follow the Greta through the estate to the Meeting of the Waters which J. M. W. Turner painted. Sir Walter Scott was a frequent guest at Rokeby Hall and wrote his poem of the same name there. His host arranged a writing desk for him in a cave in the secluded woods overlooking the river.

GUISBOROUGH, *North Riding* (15–NZ61 15). One of the last quiet spots before the north-bound traveller plunges into the industrial turmoil of Teesside, Guisborough is a busy market town with a motley collection of buildings. It is distinguished by its ancient priory which lifts its broken east end most evocatively above the trees and roofs now crowding in upon it. It is owned by Lord Gisborough and is in the grounds of Gisborough Hall though it lies close to the parish church. The Ministry of Public Building and Works cares for it. The priory belonged to the Augustinian canons and was founded by Robert de Brus (Bruce) about 1120. It became very rich. The great east end, late 13th-cent., and the 12th-cent. gatehouse and dovecot are, however, the only standing remains. St Nicholas's Church is strikingly low, about 1500 in date, and in it is the Brus cenotaph, a good 16th-cent. work, formerly in the priory. Carved upon it are 10 knights from the English and Scottish branches of the family. The town itself looks friendly and well-used. It accommodates Teesside workers now and has a

quarry and tailoring factory among its own industries. There is a very long main street, with a widened market place where cars can be parked on the cobbles.

GUISELEY, *West Riding* (12–SE1941). St Oswald's Church is an interesting building with Norman features (the south doorway and south arcade), fine 13th-cent. south transept and a splendid 15th-cent. tower. In the 20th cent., there was extensive rebuilding of the nave and chancel in Perpendicular style under the direction of Sir Charles Nicholson. Near the church is the charming rectory, dated 1601, with mullioned windows and a three-story porch. It stands in park-like ground and was built on the site of a medieval moated house. The market place has a village cross and stocks but the village has changed into a lively market and manufacturing town. It clings to tradition, however, with an annual Pageant of St Oswald in the rectory grounds in August. Patrick Brontë, a poor curate at Hartshead at the time, and Maria Branwell, were married here on 29 December 1812, and founded the most remarkable literary family in English history. The grandfather of the American poet Henry Wadsworth Longfellow emigrated from Guiseley and Longfellows are buried in the churchyard.

HALIFAX, *West Riding* (12–SE0825). Motorists have good reason to know Halifax for here Percy Shaw in 1934 produced the first of the reflecting roadstuds (cats' eyes) that now guide them through fog or darkness. English toffee also was invented in Halifax, which further claims to be the home of the world's largest building society. Other important products are carpets and yarns. But Halifax was built on the cloth trade as far back as the 13th cent., and it is still a major producer of cloth. The Piece Hall, an Ancient Monument, was completed in 1779 with 315 rooms around a quadrangle for cloth traders' displays. It has three stories and is used now for a vegetable market. Until the mid-17th cent. there was a gibbet law under which a theft of cloth valued at 13½*d*. or more was punishable by beheading, hence the Beggar's or Vagrant's Litany: "From Hull, Hell and Halifax, good Lord deliver us." The 50th and last victim of the guillotine-like gibbet was executed in 1650. The site of the gibbet is still visible in Gibbet Street.

The town in the Pennine foothills has a spectacular setting. It rises on steep hills from Hebble Brook. Like other West Riding industrial centres it is largely 19th-cent. in appearance. The Town Hall of 1863 was designed by Sir Charles Barry in more or less Italian style with a tall clock tower. Wainhouse Tower is the most familiar landmark, an octagonal stone 270-ft chimney built in 1871 to serve a dye-works but never used. Up 400 winding steps there is a panoramic view. Another fine viewpoint is Beacon Hill, 850 ft high.

St John's blackened parish church, once the centre of the old town, now has factories, the railway station and a viaduct for company. It dates from the 12th cent. but is mainly, in its present form, of the 15th and 16th cents. It has excellent woodwork, including ceilings, font cover, stalls, communion rail and pews, also fine windows of Commonwealth glass. Beside the poor box is a life-size figure known as Old Tristram, supposed to have been modelled on a local beggar, dated 1701. All Souls Church, Haley Hill, built to serve the model suburb of Akroydon, was completed in 1859 and Sir George Gilbert Scott called it "on the whole, my best church".

The Old Cock Hotel in South Gate has a handsome 16th- or 17th-cent. oak-panelled room. Shibden Hall, a splendid 15th-cent. timbered house with 17th- and 19th-cent. additions, belongs to the corporation and contains period furnishings. Its outbuildings house an unusual folk museum. The Bankfield Museum occupies the Italian-style mansion of the Akroyd family. The major historical collection here is of textile machinery, fabrics and costume, including Balkan peasant dress. The museum has the *Young Actress* by Halifax's famous artist-son, Sir Matthew Smith. Mendelssohn in 1842 and John Joubert in 1968 composed for the Halifax Choral Society. Halifax is the birthplace and home of the novelist Phyllis Bentley.

Luddenden, in a glen 2 m. NW. of Halifax, recalls the atmosphere of an upland weaving hamlet with its 17th-cent. buildings and tricky steep and narrow streets.

HARDRAW SCAUR, *North Riding* (14–SD 8891). Fossdale Beck, a tributary of the Ure, rises on Great Shunner Fell and drops over a limestone scar or cliff 2 m. N. of **Hawes** as a force nearly 100 ft high. The cliff projects so that you can walk behind the waterfall. Hardraw Force as it is called is reached through the grounds of the Green Dragon Inn. The glen used to be a popular place for brass band contests because of its splendid acoustics. Some of the thinnest and smoothest stone slates for traditional Dales roofs have come from here for centuries. Fell-climbing is popular around Hawes, the last town as you travel westwards up the dale; Wensleydale cheese is made at factories here. Great Shunner is the highest of the nearby fells, at 2,340 ft, with Dodd Fell and Lovely Seat not far short of this. To the SE. over Wether Fell lies a lonely tarn, **Semer Water**, approachable by a steep narrow road from **Bainbridge**, E. of Hawes. There are two Roman camp sites near this epitome of a Dales village.

HAREWOOD HOUSE, *West Riding* (12–SE3144). This opulent 18th-cent. mansion, planned by John Carr and largely decorated by Robert Adam, is beautifully sited for views over the rolling countryside. Capability Brown landscaped the grounds in 1772 and his achievement survives despite a 1962 storm that destroyed thousands of trees. The house was built by Edwin Lascelles in 1759 with stone quarried on the grounds. It succeeded Gawthorpe Hall, the Gascoigne mansion demolished in 1771, and the even earlier

Harewood Castle of the 12th and 13th cents., the ruins of which can be seen from the road. Lascelles' father, Henry, having made his fortune in the West Indies, had bought the estate in 1738. The new house cost, reportedly, £100,000. In the 1840s, a third story was added and Sir Charles Barry redesigned the south front and added the grandiose terraces.

Room after room reflects the exquisite crafts-manship of the 18th cent., with Adam-designed stucco work carried out by Joseph Rose and William Collins and decorative painting by Bagio Rebecca, Angelica Kaufmann and her husband, Antonio Zucchi. Harewood offers many examples of Adam's passion for designing rooms as a whole, including ceilings, chimney-pieces, mirrors and carpets. He even designed furniture for the master, Thomas Chippendale, to make.

Harewood also has a notable collection of paintings with works by El Greco, Tintoretto, Veronese, Titian, Bellini, Turner, Sargent and Munnings, among others.

Edwin Lascelles also had Harewood village moved out of the grounds and replanned by John Carr in long terraces extending from the main gates. All Saints Church was left behind in the park, in a clump of trees. Of 15th-cent. origin, with alterations in the 18th and mid-19th cents., it has six impressive 15th-cent. monuments of the Redmans, Rythers, Gascoignes and Nevils.

HARROGATE, *West Riding* (12–SE3055). The demand for spa cures may be dwindling but the appetite for conferences is not, and Harrogate adapts to modern ways more easily than some towns. Attractive in itself and handy for some of the best scenery of Yorkshire and the North, Harrogate is becoming Britain's convention centre. It is a stately place, with numerous dig-nified hotels and houses built of dark stone in the late 19th cent. when respectability was taken seriously. But the effect is softened by the high, airy location, spacious parks, great abundance of trees and lavish flower-beds, especially in Harlow Car Gardens. Famous for its toffee, it is a town for fine shopping and rich teas, and is also a dormi-tory town for LEEDS and BRADFORD.

Harrogate's mineral springs were discovered by William Slingsby in 1571. He was a travelled man and he knew the water from Tewit (local name for lapwing) Well tasted like waters he had drunk abroad. A temple has since been erected over this well on the wide Stray.

In the early spa days, people bathed in or drank waters brought to their lodgings in barrels. The first public baths went up in 1842, the Royal Pump Room, now a museum. The town became very popular in the 18th and especially the 19th cent. when London society came for relaxation and treatment for gout, rheumatism, lumbago, the liver or jangled nerves. In 1840, the Duchy of Lancaster began to develop the town in earnest. In 1949, the cure was nationalized and patients were treated under the National Health Service.

In 1969, however, the Royal Municipal Baths were closed.

Harrogate features French and Italian weeks and puts on an annual festival of arts and sciences. To look at all of it properly, you should climb the observatory tower, built in 1829 on Harlow Hill in Otley Road. The tower overlooks Harlow Moor and a lot of Yorkshire.

Three m. SE. of Harrogate is **Rudding Park**, open to the public at advertised times in the summer seasons. A fine example of Regency building, it was designed by James Wyatt.

HAWNBY, *North Riding* (13–SE5389). The road to this Hambleton Hills village from RIEVAULX is crowded with choice views; another beautiful run through sheep and heather carries you on over the moors towards Osmotherley. The small grey-stone village clings to a hillside above the Rye, with All Saints Church below near the stream. Originally a Norman church, it has been considerably refashioned, with nave, chancel and bell-turret added in the 14th and 15th cents.

HAWORTH, *West Riding* (12–SE0337), thrills some visitors and depresses others. It was, of course, the home of the amazing Brontë family. Not everyone is prepared to find it a small manufacturing town in a Pennine area of industrial valleys separated by brief stretches of sombre moor on which people still can get lost. The village is all grey-stone houses, slate roofs and smoking chimneypots. It still carries on the spinning and weaving tradition and is about the same size as it was when the Brontës lived here from 1820 to 1861. But there is a whole new industry in tourism. Haworth, 4 m. SW. of **Keighley**, is out-ranked in pilgrims only by STRATFORD-UPON-AVON as an English literary shrine.

The main street paved with stones struggles up an incredibly steep bank. Near the top the street widens into a little square with the Black Bull Hotel, where Branwell Brontë drank away the hours, on the left. A winding lane leads higher to the Church of St Michael and All Angels and finally, past a gloomy graveyard, to the parsonage, now the Brontë Museum. Behind the parsonage lies moorland and a hint of that windswept isolation which so vividly recalls the writings of the talented sisters, Charlotte, Emily and Anne.

The Brontë Society was founded in 1893 and for some time operated from rooms above the Yorkshire Penny Bank. Then in 1926, Henry Houston Bonnell, an American publisher, be-queathed his extensive collection to the Society. Sir James Roberts bought the parsonage for it. Like much of the town it overlooks, the parsonage is a grim, blackened and plain 18th-cent. sand-stone building. Inside, the rooms are furnished with family articles restored to the house over the years, including the sofa on which Emily died in 1848; Mr. Brontë's Bible and spectacles; the children's pencil drawings; some of the tiny home-made books of their childhood writings; Branwell's portraits of his sisters; and Charlotte's work-box. The Bonnell collection of letters, manu-

G. *Douglas Bolton*

Haworth: a corner of the moorland village

scripts and first editions is available to scholars.

The church has nothing but the west tower remaining of the building the Brontës knew, having been rebuilt in 1880. It contains a brass plaque and chapel in memory of the family and a 19th-cent. stained-glass window given "in pleasant memory of Charlotte Brontë by an American citizen" (Thomas Hockley of Philadelphia).

Keighley, to which the girls used to walk to shop and borrow books, is a pleasant, open 19th-cent. town with a variety of local industries. In the museum at Cliffe Castle there is a large collection of Victorian bygones and the loom of the last weaver to work at a handloom in England. One m. E. is **East Riddlesden Hall**, a National Trust property consisting of a 1692 manor house with 17th-cent. furnishings and one of the finest medieval barns in the North.

The Keighley and Worth Valley Light Railway has been preserved by enthusiasts and offers trips up and down its line from Keighley to Oxenhope. Its workshops and museum at Haworth station are open to visitors.

HEBDEN BRIDGE, *West Riding* (12–SD 9927). Together with its higher neighbour, **Hep-tonstall**, Hebden Bridge illustrates the story of the Industrial Revolution in the narrow West Riding valleys. And the illustration in this case is ex-ceedingly picturesque. First there was Hepton-stall, a village of stone weavers' cottages and crooked streets that grew up on a moorland ridge. There was a 15th-cent. church, dismantled in 1854

Helmsley is an attractive market town

with the ruins of the tower, porch and double nave left standing in the churchyard next to its successor. An octagonal Wesleyan chapel was built in Northgate in 1764 and the 17th-cent. grammar school, lately an old people's club, was nearby. When the village was young, the weavers worked in their homes. With the coming of steam power, mills were set up lower down the valley and this was Hebden Bridge. Terraces of workers' cottages with a boss's house at the end of each row crowded on to the hillsides. These are often of several stories, the top ones entered from the upper level of the hill, the lower ones from below. A modern road, painfully steep, connects the two communities; the old packhorse track called the Buttress, was even steeper. The pine-clad **Hardcastle Crags** in a glen 3 m. NW. provide a fine bit of rocky scenery and are sometimes known as "Little Switzerland". A reservoir is to be constructed in the upper glen.

HEDON, *East Riding* (13–TA1828). The "King of Holderness" is St Augustine's Church here (the "Queen" is in PATRINGTON), with its 129-ft pinnacled central tower which calls attention boldly to an otherwise dowdy town. The church building began in the mid-12th cent. when Hedon was at its peak as a trading centre. Although 2 m. inland from the Humber, it had, through Hedon Haven and a system of canals, become a major port. By the time the church was finished (it took over 300 years to complete) HULL had created port facilities that far outstripped its small neighbour. The church has a particularly striking original north front with lancet windows and doorway ornamented with well-carved dogtooth design. Church Lane leads into a small green beside the church which gives something of the old atmosphere of the early village in the shadow of the great church. Some interesting-looking houses are, however, going to ruin hereabouts. In the Town Hall is a mace said to be the oldest in England. It dates from Henry V.

HELMSLEY, *North Riding* (13–SE6183). One of the North Riding's prettiest market towns, Helmsley lies in a hollow of the River Rye, an excellent entrance to Ryedale and the Yorkshire Moors. The view, dropping into it from the S., takes in the red-roofed houses, the spacious market square, the pinnacled church tower and the gaunt bones of Helmsley Castle. The square has a stately Victorian monument to the second Lord Feversham, a modest early-20th-cent. Town Hall and several inns, one of which, the Black Swan, spreads over two Georgian houses and an adjoining 16th-cent. timber-framed house. Off one corner is All Saints Church, rebuilt in the 1860s. It keeps some features of its predecessors, including the Norman south doorway and chancel arch. Murals in the north aisle were completed in 1909 to picture the development of Christianity in the area with Helmsley as the tree from which branches grew. Canon's Garth nearby was built originally for priests of KIRKHAM appointed vicars here.

Helmsley Castle, just off the town centre, had a rather pacific history. It was started by Walter L'Espec in the 12th cent. but the oldest part of the ruins date from 1200 or later. The castle surrendered after a three-month siege in the Civil War in 1644, and was partly repaired. But when Sir Charles Duncombe, a London banker, bought Helmsley in 1689 he had Duncombe Park built by Sir John Vanbrugh and the castle fell into disuse. Duncombe Park is now a school and the castle is in the care of the Ministry of Public Building and Works. It is remarkable for its earthworks, the deep double ditch which surrounds the curtain wall, towers and keep. A domestic range of the 16th cent. has some oak panelling and plaster frieze work.

HEMINGBROUGH, *East Riding* (13–SE67 30). The grandeur of St Mary's Church contrasts sharply with the simplicity of the village. The great cruciform church was built of white Tadcaster stone chiefly in the 13th and 15th cents. The feature that draws the traveller to it across the Plain of York is the 120-ft needle-sharp spire set on a squat 60-ft tower. A close look can just make out the worn row of washing tuns or tubs carved in the tower moulding: a pun on Prior Washington who built the tower. This church was made collegiate with the founding by the Prior of DURHAM in 1426 of the College of the Blessed Mary, the last church in the North to which the system was applied. Very interesting woodwork here: the fine Perpendicular screens and surviving stalls of that date; the restored bench-ends in the nave (note the carvings of a jester in belled cap with a dragon underneath on one, the bust of a young man and grotesque mask on another); and a four-panel carving carelessly hung in the south transept showing a monkey or dog with its paw in a dragon's mouth, two beasts in combat, a two-headed dragon, and a female figure crouching under a man in a tree (an Adam and Eve perhaps?). A painted panel hung in the south aisle describes the church's famous peals of bells and the bell-ringers who performed them on special occasions from 1909 to 1919.

HOLME-UPON-SPALDING-MOOR, *East Riding* (13–SE8138). A memorable sight in the Vale of York is All Saints Church crowning this island hill (the meaning of holme) in the flat former marshland. The stiff climb or easy drive up is worth it for the expansive view. The steadily growing town is some distance W. and the church site encourages a sense of rural detachment. Trees and gravestones crowd the churchyard. The building itself is a time-worn patchwork of 15th- and 16th-cent. stone with 17th-cent. brick parapets and porch. The walls inside are plastered now, and their white sets off the good woodwork: medieval screen, Jacobean pulpit, 18th-cent. gallery and dark roof. Holme Hall, of late a convent, stands out in the view from the hill-top.

HORNSEA, *East Riding* (13–TA2047). The largest freshwater lake in Yorkshire – a placid 467 acres – is only ¾ m. from the North Sea and the wonder of this small town in Holderness. The lake was formed by glacial deposits and it has wooded banks, two small islands and wildfowl sanctuary. Herons, geese, swans, grebes, cormorants, teal, and goldeneye are seen here. There are also rare plants. The lake has a sailing club. Boating and angling can be arranged for visitors. The mere belongs to a descendant of the Constable family who lives at Wassand Hall. For about 20 years in the 13th cent. it was the object of bitter dispute over fishing rights between the abbots of St Mary's, YORK, and Meaux. They decided to settle it with a duel and engaged champions. The contest lasted all day and, apparently without bloodshed, St Mary's knight won. A public footpath allows you to make the 5-m. walk around the lake. Building hides the mere from the main street which winds through the holiday town, but it is found easily enough by a lane. The old village has extended itself to the sea, where there are boarding houses, sandy beaches and bracing views. A small museum of Roman and Anglo-Saxon relics can be visited in the Town Hall. St Nicholas's Church was built of cobbles in the 14th and 15th cent. The spire fell from its battlemented tower in 1733.

HOVINGHAM, *North Riding* (13–SE6675). This restful village of substantial stone cottages clusters around Hovingham Hall, designed and built around 1760 by Sir Thomas Worsley, Surveyor-General under George III. It is of local yellow limestone and is entered in an unusual manner through the vaulted archway of a gatehouse which is really a riding school – a place to exercise the horses under cover. In latter years, the riding school has been the scene of music festivals. On the west lawn of the Hall is the village cricket ground. Cricket festivals have brought in many notable players. The Hall is the home of Sir William Worsley, father of the Duchess of Kent. It is close to the village green on which stands the Georgian Worsley Arms. All Saints Church has a late Anglo-Saxon west tower and west doorway with thick roll moulding, but basically the present building dates from 1860. In it is a carved Anglo-Saxon slab, possibly from an altar, a cross head and several other early fragments. When the grounds of the hall were landscaped, relics of a Roman villa were found, including part of a bath-house and two tessellated pavements.

HOWDEN, *East Riding* (13–SE7428). Written descriptions do not prepare the visitor for the startling sight of this magnificent church framed in its own ruins just off a small market place. Lordly St Peter's today consists of a living part – the nave and transepts with tower between them; and an empty shell – the ruined east end, chancel and chapter house. The tower rises in splendour over the little town and makes the church seem very close to all that goes on. A walk through the churchyard is the quickest way to get from the market place on the E. to a similar centre on the W. Terraces of pleasingly proportioned but now deteriorating houses of the last two centuries surround the church closely. All that is needed is some active restoration to transform Howden into a charming place. Perhaps the people now moving in from GOOLE will make the "discovery".

The church has ancient roots. It was raised by the Prior of DURHAM to collegiate status in 1267. Most of the present church is of late 13th- to early 14th-cent. construction. As the work progressed westwards from the tower, the 107-ft-long nave beautifully illustrates the change from Early English to Decorated styles, with the crowning touch on the west end where the great window is set off by four octagonal turrets, pierced and pinnacled with crocketed spires. The chancel, 110 ft long, continued this style and was finished in 1335. Towards the end of the 14th cent., the beautiful octagonal chapter house was built by Bishop Walter Skirlaw in Perpendicular style with 30 seats, each backed by a carved panel in deep relief quatrefoil design. To keep up this magnificence after the Dissolution was a great burden and by 1609 the parishioners were using only the nave, as now. The lead was taken from the chancel roof to repair the nave and in 1696 the chancel collapsed in a thunderstorm. The chapter house, similarly neglected, fell in 1750.

The church contains a wealth of interesting detail and fine objects, such as the 1480 brass portrait of a knight in the Lady Chapel near a 1340 stone statue of the Annunciation showing a dove on the shoulder of the Virgin; the tomb effigies of the 14th cent. in the Saltmarshe Chapel; and the three heavy churchwardens' chests, one roughed out of a single tree trunk.

A path beside the church leads to the playing fields past the old bishop's palace, now a private residence.

HOWSHAM, *East Riding* (13–SE7362). George Hudson, the YORK draper who became a great railway tycoon of the 19th cent., was born in this tiny village in 1800. He was a yeoman farmer's son and was apprenticed after his father's death. He made good as a draper and then, with an inheritance, plunged into railway promotions. By 1848, he controlled nearly one-third of all the lines in the kingdom. He was thrice Lord Mayor of York and M.P. for SUNDERLAND. Then the boom ended amid charges of financial wrong-doing. Broken, he ended his days on the charity of friends. His village, 7 m. SW. of MALTON, is tucked away on a wooded bank of the River Derwent. The toffee-coloured stone cottages run down the slope towards Howsham Hall. Halfway down is St John's Church, designed by G. E. Street and built in neo-Gothic style in 1860. A tall bell-turret on one side and the steep roof blend with the hilly surroundings. The Hall, an elegant grey stone Elizabethan manor with Georgian interiors, is a preparatory school and open to visitors in May and June.

HUDDERSFIELD, *West Riding* (12–SE1416), means music and worsted. The town sponsors several concert series in the Town Hall, featuring visiting artists as well as local choirs and soloists. The hall is packed out, as a rule, except for the occasional jazz concert. Choir and organ programmes in the municipal series are inexpensive and lunchtime concerts are free. The Huddersfield Choral Society's performance of Handel's *Messiah* is an institution rooted in the tradition of choral singing in the Pennine valleys and Nonconformist churches.

As for cloth, Huddersfield has been the centre of textile production for centuries and its special reputation was built on fine wool worsted. At first the cloth was woven in homes, and houses with many mullioned windows are still to be seen in the villages at the edge of the Pennine moors which have gradually been absorbed into the town. The first market was **Almondbury**, in the 13th cent., the oldest and still the prettiest of these villages. Until the Huddersfield market was established in 1672, cloth was traded there in the parish church-yard with gravestones for tables. The mills grew up along the river and introduction of machinery brought violent Luddite protest in the early 19th cent. Today the major textile industry relies heavily on women workers brought in daily by coach from surrounding areas. Huddersfield makes, among other things, dyestuffs, detergents, pickles and footballs.

The town is extremely hilly and it covers a spectacular site in the Colne valley on the edge of the Pennines. It climbs 1,000 ft from the east to the west sides of town. Since 1920, it has owned all of its centre and it is carrying out what is regarded by experts as an enlightened plan for redevelopment and rebuilding. Older buildings are chiefly 19th-cent., including the Italianate Town Hall and Gothic Revival Market Hall of the 1870s. The parish church, St Peter's, was rebuilt in 1834–6 by J. S. Pritchett of YORK on the Norman foundations. The huge block of the modern public library houses a periodicals room stocked with the European and Indian languages press, a local history room, and an art gallery which has a good permanent collection (Henry Moore, L. S. Lowry, Stanley Spencer, Ben Nicholson, Ruskin, Turner, Constable, Gainsborough etc.) and 15 exhibitions a year. The noted College of Technology has added virtually a new plant, two seven-story blocks and a single-story workshop for textile and chemistry laboratories, and is scheduled to become a polytechnic. The Huddersfield College of Education is one of four in Britain that trains teachers in technical education.

Ravensknowle Park and Hall, 1½ m. from the centre, were given to the town by Leigh Tolson in memory of two nephews lost in the First World War. The Hall, an 1860 residence, is now the Tolson Memorial Museum, with interesting collections, among them the Foggitt herbarium of British plants, restorations of early Christian monuments, dolls and doll furniture, the kitchen of a weaver's cottage, and early weaving machines and relics of the Luddite riots.

Huddersfield's railway station, completed in 1848, has an impressive portico with Corinthian columns and long colonnaded wings.

At Almondbury, All Hallows Church is chiefly Perpendicular, with an Early English chancel and battlements and pinnacles added in the 19th cent. The ceilings are particularly handsome and the 15th-cent. font cover one of the county's best. Wormall's Hall nearby is dated 1631 and consists of a stone ground floor with black-and-white timbered overhanging upper story. It is now a clubhouse. Weavers' cottages with the long upper windows for lighting the work are in Lumb Lane.

On Castle Hill are the remains of an important Iron Age camp, later partly obscured by a stone keep. The hill-top is crowned by the 1897 land-mark of Victoria Tower with a heady view.

Prime Minister Harold Wilson was born here.

HULL, *East Riding* (13–TA0929). Almost a new town since the Second World War, when Hull was the hardest hit of any place in the North. Modern, if unexciting, new buildings have sprung up in the centre where the lawns, flower-beds and pools of Queen's Gardens cover the site of the first (1778) dock. The city is very proud of its tidy flower-beds. The third largest port in the kingdom, it has docks running for 7 m. on the north bank of the Humber and the country's largest fishing operation. It handles cargoes valued at more than £600 million a year and 160,000 passengers annually travel to and from Rotterdam and Gothenburg. Hull also manufactures oilcake, metal boxes, plastic bags, excavators and cara-vans. The growing University of Hull and the Colleges of Technology are part of a lively scene.

There was a small settlement at this junction of the Hull and Humber rivers in the 12th cent., acquired from the Abbot of Meaux by King Edward I in 1293, when it took the name of Kingston-upon-Hull. (Today it is officially accept-able to call it simply Hull.) The port began to flourish when the patronage of William de la Pole, the biggest merchant of the day, was switched from HEDON. He became the first mayor.

What is now called the Old Town is the section which was bounded by the Hull on the E., the Humber on the S., and a moat on the W. and N. Docks were built in the moat later. Surviving in the area today are Holy Trinity Church, of the 13th to 15th cents. with an unusual early brick chancel and seats for 2,000 in the nave alone; a lane called Land of Green Ginger; and Ye Old White Harte Inn, the house where the Governor and others decided not to let King Charles into the city in 1642.

The poet Andrew Marvell was brought to Hull from nearby Winestead at the age of three. Later he represented Hull in Parliament for 18 years. In a town of museums, one of the most interesting is in the old High Street, where William Wilberforce was born in 1759. A wealthy young man about town, he was elected to Parliament at 21 and his monument was the 1833 Act abolishing slavery throughout the Empire. He was known as "the nightingale of the House of Commons". His home now contains relics of the slave trade, the appro-priately furnished room of his birth and other historical mementoes. The Maister's House across the street is another Georgian dwelling, with a splendid staircase. It is used for offices but owned by the National Trust. At the Transport Museum in High Street you can see the excellent archaeo-logical collection, including mosaic paving from a Roman villa at RUDSTON. A Maritime Museum of Shipping and Fisheries is in Pickering Park. The Hull Trinity House was built in 1753, the headquarters of the guild which in early days controlled pilotage in the Humber and in later times supported a navigational school and welfare services for seamen and their dependants.

Do not look for red telephone kiosks in Hull. Since 1904, it has owned its own telephone system and is the only municipality in Britain to do so. You can dial for recipes, pop record releases, bedtime stories and Santa Claus at Christmas time.

HUTTON-LE-HOLE, *North Riding* (15–SE 7090). The red-roofed stone houses are widely dispersed around an irregular green which is divided by Hutton Beck, with small white bridges crossing the stream. Weekenders and retired people make up much of the resident population of this best-known Yorkshire Moors beauty-spot. Here is the peace of bright gardens and browsing sheep, but it is a peace shattered all summer by streams of motorists. Hutton-le-Hole does not have a long history. Quakers settled here in the 17th cent. In the 18th cent., its people worked in small-scale coal-mining on the moors and in the 19th cent. they worked in local iron-stone mines and wove linen. The earliest building is the 1695 Quaker Cottage, associated with John Richardson, a missionary to America, who became a friend of William Penn, founder of the State of Pennsylvania. Brookside Cottage is on the site of the Quaker Meeting House which had a stable below and the meeting room above it. The Hammer and Hand, so named for the motto carved on the lintel ("By Hammer and Hand All Arts Do Stand"), was built in 1784 and once served as an inn. The school went up in 1875, the church in 1935 and the village hall in 1939. The Ryedale Folk Museum near the Crown Inn is worth a visit. It occupies a range of farm buildings and is filled with local farming and household bygones. The idea, the nucleus of the collection and the building came from the late R. W. Crosland and the plan was carried out by his friend Bertram Frank.

The road to **Gillamoor** brings sweeping views across the moors, superb when the heather is in bloom. Both villages are to the S. of **Farndale**, the beautiful valley cut by the River Dove, famous for its profusion of wild daffodils and now a nature reserve.

ILKLEY, *West Riding* (12–SE1147). This spa in the moors gave Yorkshire its national anthem, "On Ilkla Moor baht 'at", a ballad about the uselessness of it all, set to a hymn tune. The town is not like that, however. It is a lively tourist

T. Parker

Ingleton: the summit of Ingleborough seen from the pavement of limestone on Twisserton Scar

and shopping centre as well as a health resort. Situated on the Wharfe, a safe distance from the industrial grime of the LEEDS–BRADFORD area, Ilkley is a favoured place of residence. On first glance it is thoroughly modern, its chief public buildings and hotels having been put up in the late 19th or early 20th cent. There are some houses of earlier date, for example, the 16th-cent. Manor House, now a museum, or the 18th-cent. Box Tree Cottage, now a restaurant. The spring waters here were found to have medicinal value in the 1840s and hydrotherapy was introduced. The older part of town is near the parish church, All Saints, which is Ilkley's most obvious link with the past. The south doorway here is 13th-cent., enriched with mouldings and dog-tooth carving. The tower is of the 15th cent. and much of the rest reflects the 19th-cent. restorations and alterations. There are three Anglo-Saxon cross shafts in the churchyard. Bronze Age carvings in considerable number have been found in the area and some cup-and-ring examples are exhibited in the gardens opposite the church. The Manor House Museum, too, displays prehistoric and Roman relics from the locality. A popular walk from Ilkley leads west up the valley and up Heber's Ghyll to the Swastika Stone on the moor. It is the only one in Britain, and like other ancient markings, full of mystery. It may have been used in fire worship.

INGLEBY GREENHOW, *North Riding* (13–NZ5806). Set beautifully on the edge of the Cleveland Hills, the village boasts a Norman church "barbarized and rebuilt" (says Morris) in 1741. The barbarians, however, left the chancel and tower arches and north arcade at St Andrew's for antiquarians to puzzle over the carvings on the capitals – foliage, heads, dragons, pigs and other grotesques included. Two good but not well preserved effigies show a 13th-cent. priest and a 15th-cent. knight. Ingleby Moor rises nearly 1,300 ft above, and across it to the SE. is Burton Howe with four large Bronze Age cairns, one 50 ft in diameter and 8 ft high.

INGLETON, *West Riding* (12–SD6972). This is a one-industry town and the industry is tourism. The main street is solidly lined with shops and cafés and the pavements thronged with fell-walkers, climbers and potholers. Signs of Ingleton's small-scale industrial past are blurring. Coal workings established it in the first place, and cotton mills and lime kilns kept it going. But the railway from SKIPTON in 1849 made Ingleton a tourist centre for the ruggedly beautiful terrain of the far West Riding. The little town clings to the hillside above the junction of the Twiss and Doe rivers which thereafter become the Greta. There is a beautiful 4-m. walk up the Twiss valley, across the moors and down the Doe with views of the renowned waterfalls. For climbers, **Ingleborough** summit at 2,373 ft is less than 4 m. by a good path. A long ridge walk (some 7 m.) leads to the top of **Whernside,** 2,414 ft above sea-level. For those fascinated by caves, there are the popular **White Scar Caves**, open to the public, with their intricate rock formations, stalagmites and stalactites, underground river and lake, and Skirwith Cave with its waterfall.

JERVAULX ABBEY, *North Riding* (12–SE 1785). The Cistercian abbey ruins SE. of MIDDLE-HAM are privately owned, but open to the public on an honour system of admission. Although the remains are rather sparse, the site is charming. It has not been tidied up completely, and shrubs and trees are allowed to grow among the ancient stones in a romantic fashion. The ground plan can be seen very well and the best feature is the wall of the monks' dormitory with a fine row of lancet windows high up. The monastery was founded in 1156 and 15 different mason's marks are still discernible on the building fragments. The order was not supposed to eat meat except in illness, but lots of bones were found here. The last abbot was executed in 1537 for taking part, albeit unwillingly, in the Pilgrimage of Grace, and the abbey was destroyed.

KILBURN, *North Riding* (13–SE5179). When Yorkshire people see hand-made oak furnishings, they search for the mouse, the signature of Robert Thompson of Kilburn. He was born here in 1876, son of the local joiner, and here he realized his dream of carving in oak. One of his first assignments was furniture for AMPLEFORTH College, 7 m. away. The mouse adorns pieces in more than 700 churches as well as homes, schools and offices in Britain and abroad. Thompson said he got the idea for the mouse when, as he carved a beam on a church roof, a companion muttered something about their being poor as church mice. "On the spur of the moment I carved one. Afterwards I decided to adopt the mouse as a trade mark, because I thought how a mouse manages to scrape and chew away the hardest wood with his chisel-like teeth, and it works quietly; nobody takes much notice. I thought that was maybe like this workshop hidden away in the Hambleton Hills." Since Thompson's death in 1955, his workshop has carried on with his grandsons and some 30 craftsmen. It is the major industry in this village of snug stone houses strung out along a beck. The Mouseman's Cottage is a rambling brick and timbered building near the centre. An annual quoits competition is held on the green. Six hundred ft above the village rises Roulston Scar with its familiar white-horse landmark. It was dug out in 1857 and covered in white stone by the village schoolmaster, Thomas Hodgson, and a swarm of boys. The horse is 314 ft long and 228 ft high.

KILNSEY CRAG, *West Riding* (12–SD9767). This famous limestone scar juts out in Wharfedale, dwarfing the village near it and providing an imposing landmark for travellers. On the meadow between the precipice and the river, the annual Upper Wharfedale show is held and young men who are fit enough compete in the Crag Race to the top of the hill and back. The village is of ancient origin and was given to FOUNTAINS ABBEY in 1156. It became the monks' headquarters for manor courts and sheep-shearing. Mastiles Lane, an old drovers' road, gives walkers a good route to MALHAM.

KIRBY MISPERTON, *North Riding* (13–SE7779). **Flamingo Park Zoo** has taken over the park and 18th-cent. Hall here in the heart of the Vale of Pickering.

KIRKBYMOORSIDE, *North Riding* (13–SE6986). An unexciting small market town but an agreeable starting point for explorations of the moors. It is just off the PICKERING–HELMSLEY road and the main street climbs steeply towards the hills. On Vivers Hill behind the church are the sketchy remains of a Norman castle. The Black Swan Inn has a timber porch from 1634. In the building called Buckingham House near the top of the street, George Villiers, 2nd Duke of Buckingham, a great wit and friend of Charles II who had fallen from favour, died after a fall while hunting. The town has an unusual number of blacksmiths.

KIRKDALE, *North Riding* (13–SE6885). The little church 1½ m. W. of KIRKBYMOORSIDE, once the minster church of St Gregory, has an Anglo-Saxon sundial over its south doorway with an Old English inscription which translated says "Orm, the son of Gamal, bought St Gregorious' Minster when it was all broken and fallen and he let it be made new from the ground in Edward's days the King, and Tosti's days the Earl", which puts its date of rebuilding at 1060. Of the same period is the chancel arch but the church was largely rebuilt again in the 19th cent. There are two Anglo-Saxon coffin lids, one 11th- and the other 7th-cent., it is believed. Kirkdale Cave, discovered in quarrying operations in 1821, held the bones and teeth of hundreds of hyenas and their victims – rhinoceros, mammoth, tiger, bear, bison and others – and the pygmy flints of the Mesolithic hunters.

KIRKHAM PRIORY, *North Riding* (13–SE 7565). Secluded in an entrancing site on the River Derwent 5 m. SW. of MALTON are the ruins of this priory. The lawns stretch gently to the river and thick woods cover the opposite bank. This was a house of the Augustinian canons, founded about 1125 by Walter L'Espec, according to legend in memory of an only son killed in a riding accident near the fragment of a cross at the entrance to the monastery. Visitors will want to study at least two features: the 13th-cent. gatehouse and the handsome lavatorium. The gatehouse has a good deal of fine sculpture, including figures (from the top down) of Christ seated, St Philip and St Bartholomew in niches and St George and the Dragon opposite David and Goliath. There are also 10 carved heraldic shields. In a corner of the cloister, near the fine Norman doorway leading into the refectory, is the lavatorium where before meals the monks washed in leaded troughs under a beautiful late-13th-cent. arcade. The priory was working in the 13th cent. on a great enlargement of its Norman church but apparently ran out of money after the presbytery and choir were built, so the nave and transepts are on the smaller earlier scale.

KIRKLEATHAM, *North Riding* (15–NZ5921). S. of REDCAR is this astonishing piece of 17th-cent. philanthropy, Sir William Turner's Hospital, possibly England's most impressive almshouse. The U-shaped range of buildings has for its showpiece a chapel, flanked by what were two charity schools. The wings extending forward to the road contained the apartments of the deserving 10 men and 10 women. The place had markedly declined by the time of the death of the last owner in 1948. There were only eight residents and almost no modern conveniences. A kind of revival followed the 1951 Act of Parliament permitting the institution to continue under the Charity Commissioners after the sale of the Kirkleatham estate. It is fully occupied now. School rooms were converted into flats to help support the place and the chapel is open to the public. Briefly, the hospital was founded in 1668 and built in 1676 by Sir William, a self-made woollen draper who became Lord Mayor of London. He was a friend and financial supporter of Charles II, who gave him his knighthood. He was also acquainted with Sir Christopher Wren, being on the Building Committee for the re-building of St Paul's Cathedral. The elegant chapel is very much in the style of Wren's pupil, James Gibbs, whose *Book of Architecture*, 1728, inspired Gibbsian buildings all over England. How much responsibility for the building was

actually taken by Gibbs is uncertain, but it is said that he was responsible for the beautiful Venetian window behind the altar, which is probably the work of Sebastino Ricci. The right-hand window depicts Turner in his mayoral robes (and an extraordinary death mask of him stares from a glass case at the rear). The chapel was completed in 1742 with heavy exterior additions in 1820. Noteworthy are the fluted Ionic columns, decorated arches, wrought-iron railings, mahogany pews facing the centre, baroque gilt chandelier and gilt chairs probably made by William Kent.

Kirkleatham Hall stood a short distance away. It is gone and a modern school occupies the site. The old stables and fine gateposts remain. Across the road is St Cuthbert's Church, 18th-cent., and thought to be designed by John Carr. Its distinguishing feature, and jarring note, is the octagonal baroque mausoleum to Turner, who died in 1692, designed by James Gibbs. It has heavy rusticated foundations and odd pyramid top. A prettily garlanded doorway leads into its stern interior from the chancel and it holds the Classical Turner family monuments. In the chancel are two interesting brasses to a four-year-old girl, Dorothy, who died in 1628 and Robert Coulthirst buried in 1631 aged 90. At the back is a large iron-bound 14th-cent. chest carved with monsters and tracery.

KNARESBOROUGH, *West Riding* (13–SE 3557). The most picturesque town of the Riding covers a bluff on the Nidd with a pleasant jumble of buildings that lie in irregular tiers above the riverside. The town has England's oldest linen mill and once employed weavers in cottages for miles around. Today it is chiefly a market town.

Knaresborough is picturesquely situated on the River Nidd

Kenneth Scowen

The ruins of the castle stand on a strategic height and from them you can get a heady view of the town and the river gorge. A Norman castle was built here by Baron Serlo de Burg but the existing remains date from 1310 to 1340. They include some curtain wall with towers, the rectangular keep of three floors and a basement, and a 14th-cent. gatehouse. Near the entrance is the old Court of Knaresborough with a 14th-cent. lower story and 17th-cent. upper. The ground floor of the castle keep is a museum, among its items being armour worn at MARSTON MOOR. History did not pass Knaresborough by. The murderers of Thomas à Becket hid out for three years and Richard II was imprisoned here on his way to death at PONTEFRACT. The castle was sacked by the Scots and thoroughly "slighted" by Parliament after the Civil War.

Halfway up the hillside between Waterside and High Street is St John's Parish Church whose central tower is crowned with a little spirelet. The church is mainly of 13th- and 14th-cent. date with some rebuilding in the 15th. Furnishings include a poor-box of about 1600 shaped like a clock. There are three noteworthy 17th-cent. monuments to Slingsbys, including a standing figure of Sir William Slingsby in an arched niche. He died in 1634 and is partly remembered for discovering the mineral springs at HARROGATE.

St Robert's Chapel in Abbey Road is named after Robert Flower (1160–1218), its fanatical founder. It is tiny but ornamented with primitive colonettes, a vaulted roof and carved faces. At the entrance stands the 16th-cent. larger-than-life figure of the hermit saint, drawing his sword. Dropping Well is a petrifying spring whose limestone content solidifies objects which fall into it. It is near Low Bridge and not far off in a cave once lived Mother Shipton, a prophetess of the 1500s who forecast motorcars, aircraft and other strange things.

Knaresborough boasts the oldest chemist's shop in England, in the Market Place. The Old Manor House, now a restaurant, is a medieval building with chequerboard walls, built originally around an oak tree. It was a royal fishing lodge given by James I to his son, and Cromwell slept here. Among other buildings of special interest are Knaresborough House, a Georgian mansion now used for council offices; Conyngham Hall, another 18th-cent. house whose grounds are a public park and zoo; and Fort Montague built into the cliff above the cave chapel. Knaresborough is a good starting point for Dales tours. Boats and punts can be hired on the river, which is spanned by High and Low bridges on either side of the towering railway viaduct.

Schoolchildren know all about Blind Jack Metcalf of Knaresborough, born in 1717, who in 93 years of vigorous living was a violinist, soldier, forest guide, and major roadbuilder.

LASTINGHAM, *North Riding* (15–SE7290). The precious 11th-cent. crypt beneath St Mary's Church is a complete little church in itself, with a vaulted roof borne on thick low columns, a chancel, nave and aisles. It was built between 1078 and 1085 as a shrine for St Cedd. According to Bede's history, Bishop Cedd came to this remote edge of the moors to found a monastery for King Ethelwald. He died of the plague in 664. In the 9th cent. the monastery was destroyed by the Danes. In 1078 Abbot Stephen of WHITBY began the restoration by building the crypt for the remains of the founder. In 1086, Stephen moved on to YORK to establish St Mary's Abbey. The church contains some 11th-cent. work with later work concluding in the 15th-cent. tower. From the unusual size of an Anglo-Saxon cross head here, the original cross must have been more than 24 ft high. There are other early carved stones, including a hogback tombstone with a bear on it. The village is comfortably sheltered in a dip of the ridge between Rosedale and Farndale.

LEEDS, *West Riding* (12–SE3034). When Dickens visited Leeds he decided "you must like it very much or not at all". If you like it very much you will be attracted by a town that is big (over 500,000), bold in replacing old buildings with brash new ones, and brisk. Leeds works at an enormous variety of manufacturing activities, is the ready-to-wear capital of the country, and a centre of coal and iron industries. Iron forging began with the monks of **Kirkstall Abbey** in 1200. The cloth trade was firmly established by the 17th cent., and the first wholesale clothier began in 1856.

Leeds spreads over a large and hilly area with a town centre on Victoria Square. Here the Town Hall, a famous and architecturally successful example of Classic revival, was built in a great burst of civic confidence in the 1850s and opened by Queen Victoria. On that occasion, the streets were lined with palm trees and triumphal arches. Eighteen thousand Sunday-school children sang the national anthem as she passed. The immense building, brown stone then and now recently cleaned, was designed by a young HULL architect, Cuthbert Brodrick. Giant columns line the façade and the 225-ft clock tower is the symbol of Leeds. The building is guarded by white lions, cut out of Portland stone which is more resistant to grime. Its ornate Victoria Hall is the scene of the famed triennial music festival.

Brodrick planned some other major buildings which give Leeds a strong Victorian flavour: the public baths and Civic Theatre in Cookridge Street and the oval Corn Exchange in Duncan Street, for example. One of the newer streets, Headrow, opened the centre considerably. A principal shopping street is Briggate, off which are examples of the typically Leeds arcades, delightful glass-roofed passages lined with shops. One has a clock with revolving figures from Scott's *Ivanhoe*. The City Market was enclosed in 1904 giving the city a dashing new roofline of towers and spires.

Leeds is one of the few places where it is worth noting the warehouses, although the bulldozers are moving in fast. Eighteenth-cent. gentlemen designed their country houses after the Classical themes they admired on the Grand Tour; 19th-cent. industrialists put these ideas into their mills. One Leeds chimney was a brick version of Giotto's campanile in Florence, and an Egyptian temple was the model for a mill.

City offices now occupy the Civic Hall opened in 1933 in Calverley Street, a noteworthy building with columned portico, pediment and slender towers. New buildings have gone up for the Central Colleges (of education, technology, art, commerce and home economics) and the University, which covers a hill-top overlooking the centre. The university began in 1904, growing out of the Yorkshire College of Science. Its old buildings are red-brick, its more recent ones ponderous stone. The blocky tower of the Parkinson administration building, opened in 1950, is a landmark.

There are no medieval churches in central Leeds. One that is architecturally important is St John the Evangelist in New Briggate, completed in 1634 and a rare example of early-17th-cent. ecclesiastical work. It has twin naves, a plaster-work ceiling and an excellent Jacobean screen across the whole width. Another is Holy Trinity, Boar Lane, completed in 1727, whose charming spire ornaments the commonplace shopping area.

The Yorkshire County Cricket Club grounds at Headingley need no introduction. The largest park is Roundhay, an open space of lake and woodland bought in 1872. The City Art Gallery near the Town Hall has a good permanent collection of painting and sculpture and a print room and library for scholars. The gallery was a first patron of Castleford-born Henry Moore, who, like Barbara Hepworth, born at WAKEFIELD, trained at Leeds School of Art.

Visible efforts are being made to clear slum housing and derelict factory areas. When the Quarry Hill estate flats were built in 1935, they were the largest public housing project in England.

The corporation owns two remarkable places of special historical interest: Temple Newsam, a great country house, and Kirkstall Abbey, both in easy reach of the centre. Temple Newsam was started by Thomas Lord Darcy before 1521. It was modernized and enlarged in the early 17th and late 18th cents. A splendid mansion, it contains a superb collection of furniture, paintings, ceramics and porcelain. The original park has suffered from opencast mining, but the grounds contain two golf courses and the gardens are noted for roses, azaleas and rhododendrons.

Kirkstall Abbey was founded in 1152 as a daughter house of FOUNTAINS and much of the building was completed by 1175. The chapter house, cloisters and abbot's lodging are outstanding.

The Abbey House Museum in the 12th-cent. gatehouse has re-created three streets of Victorian shops.

LEVISHAM, *North Riding* (15–SE8390). The isolated moorland village overlooks Newton Dale ½ m. off the WHITBY–PICKERING route. The road plunges downhill to the station, a watermill and a church on Levisham Beck. St Mary's has the marks of antiquity in its Anglo-Saxon chancel arch and a fragment of an Anglo-Danish gravestone, carved with a dragon. A 19th-cent. church, St John's, stands in the village above. Interesting explorations include the **Hole of Horcum**, at the head of the beck, the largest hollow in Yorkshire. It is a natural amphitheatre carved by glaciers and springs. It is carpeted with meadow and once supported a small settlement. Only one family still lives there. There is a good footpath over the moor. A 5½-m. Newton Dale drive was opened in 1969 by the Forestry Commission. It starts at Levisham station and carries on to the Mauley Cross and Stape village. There are picnic spots, views, and you might see deer. The **Bridestones** to the E. are strange rock formations and they, together with 870 acres, belong to the National Trust.

LEYBURN, *North Riding* (15–SE1190). Take the corner near the Bolton Arms to get on to the Shawl, a broad mile-long terrace shaded with evergreens, oaks and sycamores which allows entrancing views over Wensleydale. Among other landmarks will be two castles, BOLTON and MIDDLEHAM. Tradition says that this was where Mary Queen of Scots was recaptured after an escape from Bolton Castle which lasted a brief two hours. Leyburn's wide sloping market place is filled on Fridays with traders and shoppers from up the dale.

For a higher vantage point, take the steep road up to Preston Scar.

LINTON-IN-CRAVEN, *West Riding* (13–SD9962). Linton Beck which divides the village green can be crossed in a number of ways: by clapper bridge, packhorse bridge, ordinary road bridge, stepping stones or ford. At one end of the green stands the little community's largest gift, the Georgian hospital – seven almshouses endowed by Richard Fountaine in 1721 for poor women. It is still in use, but by both sexes. Beside the green, the old rectory is now a youth hostel. Linton has been called the prettiest village in the North. It is nearly hidden in trees. A mile away on the Wharfe is St Michael's Church which serves four parishes. It is charming in both its structure and its setting. There are some Norman features but chiefly it is a 14th-cent. building with later restorations.

LITTLEBECK, *North Riding* (15–NZ8707). This hamlet may be found S. of WHITBY and W. of the SCARBOROUGH or E. of the PICKERING roads, if you are willing to risk the descent of the twisting road leading into the narrow valley. The approach is slightly easier from the Scarborough road side. You will find a few cottages, farms, a chapel, village hall and the workshop of wood-carver Thomas E. Whittaker, who signs his oak pieces with a gnome. Nearby are a hermit's cave, a small waterfall called Falling Foss and a number of wooded walks and picnic spots.

LONDESBOROUGH, *East Riding* (13–SE 8645), is a placid Yorkshire Wolds village now but it has seen some stirring days in the past. By tradition this was the site of the summer palace of King Edwin of Northumbria and the place where he was converted to Christianity. From here the Anglo-Saxon priest, Coifi, rode forth to destroy his own temple at GOODMANHAM in that same year, 627. Londesborough is thought to have been on the Roman map of Britain (a bit of a Roman road was seen when the lake in Londesborough Park was drained in 1895). Here the boy Henry Lord Clifford was hidden for a time among the shepherds to evade the Yorkists. Later he went to Cumberland, staying in hiding until 1485 when, aged 30 and illiterate, he returned to his station in life and became an astronomer. All Saints Church at the park gates has an ancient sundial above the Norman doorway, a brass inscription to the Shepherd Lord's mother and four funeral banners of the Earls of Burlington. The 3rd Earl laid out the park with an avenue of elms planted in memory of his friend, David Garrick, who on one visit coached the local parson in effective reading of the Bible. This earl also planted the circle of trees known as Londesborough Clump and visible for miles. The 6th Duke of Devonshire pulled down the old hall in 1812, and regretted it later. However, he managed to sell the property to the railway king, George Hudson, for £470,000. Hudson routed the YORK – Market Weighton line past his gates where he had a private station.

MALHAM, *West Riding* (12–SD8963). The hamlet of stone cottages and a humped bridge is surrounded by moorland, high and wild, and some spectacular limestone scenery is within easy reach. Malham Cove is ¾ m. N., a curving sheer white cliff about 240 ft high of the Great Scar Limestone created by the Craven Fault. The River Aire steals out from its base. Above the rock stretches the dry valley along which, before the Ice Age, the Aire used to flow, plunging over the Cove in a great waterfall. It is a 2-m. walk up the valley to Malham Tarn (also accessible by road from Malham), a 150-acre natural lake formed by a dam of glacial moraine, on which there is skating in winter. Tarn House, the lake and 2,000 acres between Ribblesdale and Wharfedale now belong to the National Trust. The house is used by the Field Studies Council. It is said that Charles Kingsley, while staying at Tarn House, humorously explained the dark marks on the Cove as made by a chimney sweep falling over, and from this was born *The Water Babies.* Two m. NE. of Malham is **Gordale Scar,** also part of the CRAVEN Fault. It is possible to drive to within a quarter of a mile of this winding gorge with its splendid series of cascades.

MALTON, *North Riding* (13–SE7871). Too many remember Malton as a traffic bottle-neck on the way to or from SCARBOROUGH, but there is more to it than that. It is in fact two places, Old Malton and New, with the site of a Roman station between them. New Malton was built after the old

Malham Cove was the site of a great waterfall before the Ice Age

village was burnt down in 1138 to drive out the Scots. It is a teeming market town for a large farming district and its big irregular square is full of activity. St Michael's Church competes for attention in the middle of things. It is a sturdy-looking Norman church with a 15th-cent. tower and not too successful 19th-cent. additions. The spire on Church Hill belongs to St Leonard's Church, now redundant, and the subject of proposals for transfer to the Roman Catholics. It is Norman in character with a Perpendicular tower and 19th-cent. spire. It contains an amusing monument to an iron-founder, Arthur Gibson, who died in 1837. Of metal entirely, it carries a brass plate showing the deceased in prayer and at drink. He designed it himself. The Town Hall around the corner from the square is 18th-cent. and a plaque on it records that Edmund Burke was Malton's M.P. from 1780 to 1794. Among buildings of interest in the centre is the Cross Keys Inn in Wheelgate which has a medieval crypt, possibly from the former Hospital of St Mary Magdalene here.

Old Malton is on the road to PICKERING, with old-fashioned cottages and inns. Its Church of St Mary is built in part from the church of the Gilbertine priory founded in c. 1150.

There is little to see on the site of the Roman station in a pasture called Orchard Field but finds from excavations can be examined in the Roman Malton Museum in the market place.

MARKENFIELD HALL, *West Riding* (12–SE3066). This is one for collectors of out-of-the-way places. It is a remarkable example of a fortified manor house and, given persistence, you will find it at the end of a long lane which leaves the HARROGATE road about 3 m. S. of RIPON. The owners do not believe in signs although visitors are welcome at advertised times during the summer season. The lane is surfaced and there are plain stone gate piers where it begins on the right-hand side of the main road, if approached from Ripon. After a mile and two gates, the visitor will be in a farmyard staring in amazement across a moat at the protective grey walls of the manor house.

The Hall was built by John de Markenfield in 1310 and except for the addition of domestic ranges in the 17th cent., it has suffered little change. The original Hall is L-shaped and it faces the gateway across the courtyard. The moat is crossed now by a small stone bridge to the 16th-cent. gatehouse. The Hall has battlements and an outside turreted staircase. In its first days, it had a hall on the upper floor with kitchens and cellars below and a chapel in the wing.

The Markenfields forfeited the Hall after supporting Mary Stuart's claim to the throne and Queen Elizabeth gave it to Lord Chancellor Ellesmere. It has not apparently been used as a home since, although the outbuildings are occupied.

MARSTON MOOR, *West Riding* (13–SE 4853). The battle of 2 July 1644 was fought N. of the road that connects the villages of **Long Marston** and Tockwith. It was the turning point in the Civil War, a clear victory for the Parliamentary forces under the Yorkshire Fairfaxes and Cromwell over those of Charles I. The field today is marked by an obelisk near the intersection of the road with a track. Royalist YORK was under siege 7 m. W. when word came that Prince Rupert, nephew of the king, was coming from Lancashire with 20,000 Royalist troops. The Parliamentary force moved out to Marston Moor to prevent the prince joining forces with the Marquess of Newcastle in the city. The tactic failed and Rupert entered York on 1 July. But the next day he and Newcastle left York for Marston Moor. The Parliamentary army had started to retreat to better ground at TADCASTER, but turned and the two armies lined up on opposite sides of a ditch running parallel to the present road. After a fierce battle of varying fortunes, in which Sir Thomas Fairfax showed great valour, Cromwell charged at 7 p.m., when the opposing commanders, by some accounts, were at supper. He was wounded and at one point appeared to have lost the battle, but recovered the initiative and by 10 o'clock had won. In this three-hour engagement of 40,000 troops, 4,000 Royalists and 300 Parliamentarians died. It was another four years before the war was over.

The parents of General James Wolfe, who defeated Montcalm on the Plains of Abraham before Quebec and won Canada for England, were married in All Saints Church at Long Marston.

MASHAM, *North Riding* (12–SE2280). Just off the main road is the shady market square with a maypole and cross, but the market for which the village was chartered in 1250 has long since ceased to be held. Here the River Ure has left Wensleydale and is crossed by a four-arched bridge built in 1754. St Mary's Church at the corner of the square has a Norman tower on which a 15th-cent. spire was raised. In the churchyard is the treasured circular shaft of an Anglo-Saxon cross, probably 9th-cent. work. It shows four tiers of figures. Across the river in Swinton Park, part of the castle is used for a Conservative College.

METHLEY, *West Riding* (13–SE3826). Monuments in St Oswald's Church impressed the young Henry Moore, born at Castleford not far away to the E. The church does contain a rich collection of sculpture. The oldest is the tomb-chest with alabaster effigies of Sir Robert Waterton (who died in 1424) and his wife, elaborately and delicately carved. Another alabaster tomb-chest bears the effigies of Lionel Lord Welles (who fell at Towton in 1461) and his first wife. Two stone figures, originally part of this monument, now occupy recesses in the aisles. A tall black-and-white marble tomb-chest of the early 17th cent. honours Sir John Savile, his son, Sir Henry, and Henry's wife, whose son sits at her feet. The figure of Charles Savile (who died in 1741) reclines on another monument with his bereaved wife shown at his feet. A later 18th-cent. monument to John Savile, 1st Earl of Mexborough, who died in 1778, and a 19th-cent. tablet with draped figures and a relief of the resurrection of Lazarus, erected to Sarah Dowager Countess of Mexborough who died in 1821, complete the array of major memorials. The church was rebuilt in the 12th cent., but the oldest visible work now dates to the 14th and 15th cents. The excellent woodwork includes an Elizabethan font cover, a pulpit of 1708, 17th-cent. screen and an ornate 16th-cent. eagle lectern, probably Dutch, with niches and statues in the pedestal.

MIDDLEHAM, *North Riding* (12–SE1287). The monks of JERVAULX ABBEY probably started the horse-breeding and training that made this a racing centre before NEWMARKET. The former capital of Wensleydale is only a village now, but a pretty one. The castle that led to the settlement is now a ruin in the care of the Ministry of Public Building and Works. The Nevilles got it through marriage in the 13th cent. and made it the "Windsor of the North". Richard III acquired it in 1471. His son was born here. The castle was dismantled in 1646. The keep, built in the 1170s by Robert Fitzralf, survives nearly to its full height. The 13th-cent. chapel and 14th-cent. gatehouse are still to be seen. The Church of SS. Mary and Alkelda is mainly 14th-cent. It contains a 10-ft-high Perpendicular font cover.

MIDDLESBROUGH, *North Riding* (15–NZ 4920). Since 1968 this has been the administrative centre of **Teesside,** the county borough with a population of nearly 400,000, created in the great and growing complex of industrial towns and villages on the Durham and Yorkshire banks of the Tees. Middlesbrough is a latecomer among them. It was a dying village in 1831 when the backers of the STOCKTON and DARLINGTON railway bought land here to augment facilities for coal export at Stockton. Ten years later the first ironworks were started. The phenomenal growth came with the discovery in 1850 of iron ore in the Cleveland Hills. In 1875 came the move to steel. Teesside now has Europe's largest petro-chemical industry and is a leading contender in steel, iron and engineering. It is an area of hard work, strong beer and sport. The shopping centres, especially Middlesbrough's, are rebuilding at a great rate and housing estates multiply as fast as factory chimneys. Just about all that is left of Middlesbrough in ancient times is a Norman font, recovered from a farmyard, and placed in the new (1840) St Hilda's Church. The town has a large Roman Catholic population and a Catholic cathedral, red-brick St Mary's, was built in 1872. Still the most fascinating structure in Middlesbrough is the gaunt iron Transporter Bridge, built in 1911 and a wonder of its time. It was designed by the Cleveland Bridge & Engineering Co. of Darlington to replace a ferry. It is the largest of its kind in the world. It carries 10 vehicles and 600 passengers in the travelling cable car.

The 18th-cent. **Ormesby Hall,** 3 m. SE. of Middlesbrough and a National Trust property, has exceptionally fine interior work, including stucco, chimney-pieces and staircase. It was built by the Pennymans, whose village of Ormesby is nearly swallowed now by urban development.

MONK BRETTON PRIORY, *West Riding* (13–SE3607). With the coalfield in the distance and a modern housing estate at its gates, Monk Bretton comes as a surprise 2 m. NE. of BARNS-LEY, just off the junction of the A633 and A628. Here are the ruins of an important Cluniac house, much admired for its well-preserved drains. The monastery was founded about 1154 by Adam Fitzwane whose father had been a benefactor of the Cluniac priory at PONTEFRACT. There were vigorous – even violent – disputes over supervision and appointments between the two houses and in 1281 it was agreed that Monk Bretton should be an independent Benedictine priory visited by the Archbishop of YORK.

At the Dissolution, the prior and some half a dozen monks here decided to continue as a community so they bought the monastery library (148 books) and went to live at Worsborough. In 1589 after the lead had been stripped from the church, the bells sent to London and parts of the stone sold, the property was purchased by the Earl of Shrewsbury who gave it to his son Henry Talbot. The prior's house was converted to a residence. The site was excavated after it was bought by Henry Horne in the 1920s and later acquired by the Borough of Barnsley which put it in the care of the Ministry of Public Building and Works. Visitors will be interested in the 15th-cent. gatehouse, the 13th-cent. guest-house or administrative building in the outer courtyard, and the remains of the late-12th-cent. church. The drainage system devised for kitchens and dormitories is particularly easy to see here.

MOUNT GRACE PRIORY, *North Riding* (15–SE4498). In spring, the lawns around the ruins of this country's finest example of a Carthusian monastery are strewn with daffodils. It is a lovely site, tucked under the protective moors N. of **Osmotherley** and just off the A19 below its junction with the A172. Mount Grace was established in 1398 by Thomas Holland, Duke of Surrey, the last monastery founded in Yorkshire. He lost his dukedom when Richard II (son of his grandmother, the Fair Maid of Kent, by a second marriage) was deposed and the priory had a great deal of trouble holding on to its endowments. Thomas later rebelled against King Henry IV and was beheaded and buried here. With the Dissolution, the last prior, John Wilson, was granted the Chapel of Our Lady and a dwelling house on the steep bank above the priory. Called the Lady's Chapel, it is still in use, and the view from it is extensive.

The Carthusians, a contemplative order reacting against the laxity of many monasteries, lived as hermits within their communities and the remains at Mount Grace give a vivid picture of

English Life Publications

Newby Hall: the Tapestry Room

their establishment and rule. Each monk had a little house or cell, 27 ft square, consisting of a bedroom, living-room, study and lobby on the ground floor and a workshop above. Each house opened into a walled garden with a lavatory at the bottom of it. There was a dog-leg hatch in the front wall through which food was passed. The monks ate together only on Saturdays. The cells surrounded a large cloister and the plain, rather small church. One cell has been restored. Cook-house, granaries, guest-house and stables were built on the outer courtyard. In 1654, Thomas Lascelles, then the owner, converted the buildings to the left of the gate into a private residence, still lived in. The property belongs to the National Trust and is cared for by the Ministry of Public Building and Works.

Near the market cross at Osmotherley, there is a heavy stone table which John Wesley used as a pulpit. One of the first Methodist chapels was built here in 1754.

NEWBY HALL, *West Riding* (12–SE3467), illustrates the finest work of Robert Adam. Located between RIPON and BOROUGHBRIDGE at the hamlet of Skelton, Newby Hall was started in 1705 for Sir Edward Blackett, whose wealth came from the mines. In the mid-18th cent. the new owner, William Weddell, made the Grand Tour and in Italy acquired a splendid collection of sculpture. He employed Adam to redesign and enlarge his home especially to house his new

treasures. The work was under way from 1765 to 1783. The house and gardens – 25 acres of beautifully laid out shrubberies, flower-beds and rock gardens sloping down to the River Ure – are now held by R. E. J. Compton. The house is open four days a week and the gardens daily. The house is, of course, famous for its Roman sculpture galleries, which Adam created as two rectangular rooms linked by a rotunda with a Roman bath of white and purple marble as a final touch. The most notable piece of statuary displayed is the Venus from the Barberini Palace. Hardly less renowned is the Tapestry Room hung with a complete set of Gobelin tapestries designed by Neilson and Boucher. The room as planned by Adam has harmonizing carpet and furnishings and the plasterwork ceiling has inset paintings by Antonio Zucchi. The Adam entrance hall has a particularly rich ceiling reflected in the design of the Sicilian marble floor, again the Adam method. Adam and Thomas Chippendale made much of the furniture.

The ornate village church of Christ the Consoler in the grounds was completed in 1872 as a memorial of Lady Mary Vyner to her son. It has, in Pevsner's view, "uncommonly excellent" Victorian stained glass designed by F. Weeks and made by Saunders & Co.

NORTHALLERTON, *North Riding* (15–SE 3793), is another of those old posting towns still generously endowed with inns. Strong ale and dear prices seem to be the thing travellers of old remembered to jot down about it. There is a long, curving street to which most of the town is attached. This street broadens near the centre for a busy market place and narrows at the north end near the Parish Church of All Saints. This is the capital of the North Riding and county offices are housed in a dignified but ornamental building of brick and stone which went up in 1906. The Town Hall is older, 1873, and on an island site in the centre. There is a good deal of Georgian work about. Imposing All Saints overlooks a triangular green with several old houses grouped around it. Its Perpendicular, pinnacled tower is set off by trees. Much of the structure is earlier, the nave dating to before 1200. The chancel was rebuilt in Perpendicular style in 1885. There are some Anglo-Saxon and Danish carved stone fragments inside.

NORTH NEWBALD, *East Riding* (13–SE 9136). There are no less than four Norman doorways to examine in St Nicholas's Church, often thought of as the best Norman church in the Riding. The most elaborate of the quartet is the south entrance with four orders of arches beautifully enriched with zigzag and cable, and foliage embellishing the capitals. An oval niche above the door houses Christ in Majesty. The other Norman doors lead into the transepts and vestry. The central tower is Norman in its lower parts, with an Early English belfry. The battlements and rebuilt chancel are 15th-cent. The church dates from 1151 but is so well kept that it defies its age. Other points of interest: the medieval iron handle on the priest's door and the consecration cross and mason's mark on the right-hand jamb; the font carved in bands of leafy scroll in the late 12th or early 13th cent.; the four fine round arches in the crossing with their chevron markings. The town around is as neat as its parish church and stone-built, with a small sloping green.

NORTH YORK MOORS NATIONAL PARK, *North Riding* (15–NZ7010). A great area of heather-covered moorland is included in the 550 sq. m. of the park designated in 1952 in the North Riding. In August, the moors are purple. In October, the bracken turns dark gold. The park includes Pickering Forest District along the southern border, where tree planting began in 1921. Several drives and nature trails are available now to visitors. The **Cleveland Hills** form the highest range in the park, rising to 1,400 ft. The series of four heights, Hasty Bank, Cold Moor, Cringle Moor and Carlton Bank, is a familiar landmark. Deep valleys break into the uplands. The park reaches from the **Hambleton Hills** to the North Sea coast above SCARBOROUGH and includes moorland villages, old fishing ports, abbeys, prehistoric and Roman remains, early Christian crosses and some of the loneliest countryside in this crowded island.

NOSTELL PRIORY, *West Riding* (13–SE 4117). Nothing remains of the Augustinian priory founded in the 12th cent., but the Georgian mansion on its site, 6 m. SE. of WAKEFIELD,

exhibits side by side the work of James Paine and Robert Adam. Paine was only 19 when Sir Rowland Winn commissioned him to build this house in 1733. He planned the stone structure in the Palladian style and intended four pavilions to be built, but only one was completed. The house was redesigned 30 years later by Robert Adam, who also planned the stable block. Rooms on the south side are mainly as Paine would have them while those in the north range are in Adam style. Adam engaged such masters of interior decoration as Joseph Rose for stucco work and Antonio Zucchi and Angelica Kaufmann for painted murals. The house contains a good deal of furniture made to order by Thomas Chippendale whose accounts are also on view. In the park are a lake, a bridge, a herd of deer and the parish church of **Wragby**, St Michael's, a large Perpendicular building. The windows contain hundreds of panels of Swiss glass collected by one of the family and ranging from the early 16th to the mid-18th cent. Nostell Priory is the home of the present Rowland Winn (Lord St Oswald) who gave it to the National Trust in 1953. A vintage motorcycle museum is on the premises.

NUN MONKTON, *West Riding* (13–SE5057). The tranquil village at the end of Pool Lane near the meeting of the Rivers Nidd and Ouse, has all the charm of a rural retreat and with it the hint of a greater past. There is a large green, bordered by brick cottages, with a maypole. An avenue leads to the Church of St Mary which is partly obscured by an old weeping beech. Nearby is the Hall, built in 1690. This house is believed to stand on the site of the Benedictine nunnery which was founded here by William de Arches in about 1150. A prioress and 12 nuns inhabited it, but nothing remains save the late-12th- or early-13th-cent. nave of the nuns' chapel which is now the parish church. Worthy of special note are the fine west doorway and front and the handling of the lancet windows with tall arcades in the upper nave. The east end was redone in the 1873 restoration and in the three lancet windows of the east wall is what has been called the finest stained glass in the West Riding, by William Morris.

OTLEY, *West Riding* (12–SE2045). This Wharfedale town lies at the foot of the Chevin, a 900-ft-high hill with a superb view at the end of the path leading from the station. It serves the agricultural area as a market town and manufactures printing machines. Thomas Chippendale was born here in 1718 but his birthplace has been supplanted by the building bearing a memorial plaque. J. M. W. Turner painted many scenes in the area when he was a guest at nearby Farnley Hall. The town has a maypole, old inns, a rebuilt medieval bridge and a bevy of antique shops. The Museum of the Liberty of Otley, in Queen's Place, has a local history collection. All Saints Parish Church has a Norman north doorway and long chancel windows, while the rest of the building is of 14th- and 15th-cent. work. It contains 17 sculptured fragments of four Anglo-Saxon crosses from the 9th to 11th cents. There is also part of a grave-slab with Viking ornament. The Lyndley and Palmes, Fairfax and Fawkes families are remembered in monuments. The Otley agricultural show each May is claimed to be the oldest of its kind.

Bramhope Chapel, in the grounds of Bramhope Hall SE. of Otley, is Puritan, of 1649 date, with box pews grouped around a three-decker pulpit. It was recently restored by the Wharfedale Rural District Council and is frequently open to visitors.

PATELEY BRIDGE, *West Riding* (12–SE 1565). Upper Nidderdale, which contains the noted How Stean gorge, is easily explored from Pateley Bridge, the ancient centre of the dale. It has a narrow, plunging High Street. Well above the town are the ruins of the medieval St Mary's Church with distant views of the moors from the churchyard. This has been a market town since the 14th cent. The Romans worked the lead deposits in the vicinity. Flax and linen industries once flourished in this remote and beautiful setting. In steep Greenhow Hill are the **Stump Cross Caverns** with a quarter mile of strange rock formations.

PATRINGTON, *East Riding* (13–TA3122). The "Queen of Holderness" (the "King" is at HEDON) is St Patrick's here, and it is an incomparable parish church. It is well worth a detour to this flat peninsula close to the mouth of the Humber. A cathedral in miniature, it is utterly beautiful in a pale, serene way, a masterpiece of the Decorated. The building seems all of a piece with restrained use of exquisite but imaginative carving for decoration. The church has been associated with Robert of Patrington, who became master mason at YORK Minster in the later 14th cent. St Patrick's was built rather quickly, most of it done between 1310 and 1349, although parts were not finished until 1410 because of the blow to all activity dealt by the Black Death. The later – and lesser – work includes the chancel and Perpendicular tracery in the east window and west windows of the nave aisles.

In the north wall of the sanctuary is a splendid Easter sepulchre showing at the bottom, in deep relief, three nodding soldiers, and above the chamber for the host and cross, the Lord rising from his coffin with angels swinging censers on either side.

The spire which soars 189 ft serves as a beacon to Holderness and Lincolnshire as well. It is set in a corona which rests on the central tower. The gargoyles at Patrington are unusually fierce but four on the south transept are not of traditional subjects. Instead they represent two musicians and two saints.

The village that produced this magnificent building was once a fairly important market town. The archbishops of York were lords of the manor. They liked to leave the doldrums of York for the bracing air of the Holderness. Shipping in the Humber estuary can be watched from the churchyard.

PICKERING, *North Riding* (13–SE7983). Neat terraces of stone cottages lead into a town which is visually far more rewarding than it may at first appear to a traveller hurrying between SCARBOROUGH and HELMSLEY. Narrow up-and-down streets lead off in all directions and above the piles of red-tiled roofs there are glimpses of the spire of the Church of SS. Peter and Paul. At one end of the town lies a ruined castle. The market place straggles along the hilly main street. This is both a trading and a tourist centre for the Vale of Pickering and the North York Moors. Visitors short of time will concentrate on the church and castle. The former, medieval and much restored, has one of the most complete series of early wall paintings in England and present-day visitors are lucky to be seeing them. They were discovered under whitewash in 1851 by a vicar who regarded them as "purely ridiculous" with a "tendency to excite feelings of curiosity and distract the attention of the congregation". He ordered them whitewashed once more. But 25 years later they were restored under a more appreciative incumbent. Although considerably touched up, the paintings show how a medieval church must have looked. The basic colours are black and reddish. Crude and compelling, the murals are thought to have been done by a travelling artist in the late 15th cent. They cover the walls of the nave with imaginative recollections of the lives of saints.

The castle ruins peer above the treetops on a hill near the stream which runs through town. A castle was founded here by William the Conqueror but the standing buildings date from a later period. Some of the curtain wall with towers, the shell keep on a 43-ft-high motte, two halls and a chapel survive. The castle was badly damaged in the Civil War. It belongs to the Duchy of Lancaster and is in the care of the Ministry of Public Building and Works.

At the end of the low partly medieval bridge, tall trees shade Beck Isle, an interesting Georgian house which now contains a voluntarily assembled and staffed local folk museum. The house belonged to William Marshall, an 18th-cent. pioneer of modern farming who in 1818 altered the house (the long Gothic windows left of the porch were added) to use it as a college of agriculture. It is not certain whether it was actually used as a teaching centre for he died that year. Marshall travelled the country to collect the best information on farming practice and his dream was to disseminate this knowledge. He introduced the idea of a ministry of agriculture.

Beyond Beck Isle, on Potter Hill, is the newest of the three influential Primitive Methodist chapels Pickering has had. Further on, St Joseph's Roman Catholic Church and hall form an attractive composition designed by Leonard Stokes in 1911. The church contains a sculptured font by Eric Gill, made in 1910.

POCKLINGTON, *East Riding* (13–SE8048). Beyond the red roofs of this homely market town lie the Yorkshire Wolds. All Saints Church is the chief legacy from the Middle Ages, a large cruciform structure of the 13th and 15th cents. which replaced a Norman one. Among many interesting details are the grotesque carvings on the 13th-cent. north arcade, a beautifully sculptured cross head (on modern base) with Crucifixion scenes on both north and south sides and a stone credence table or gospel lectern in the sanctuary. William Wilberforce, the abolitionist, went to the grammar school here. It was founded in 1514 by Archdeacon John Dolman.

One of the finest collections of water lilies in Europe (more than 50 varieties) is in bloom from May to October in the gardens of **Burnby Hall** on the outskirts of the town. The gardens and an astonishing array of souvenirs housed in a new exhibition hall were given to Pocklington by the late Major P. M. Stewart. The gardens and collection are open at advertised times in the summer. Burnby Hall now houses local council offices. The water gardens were started by the Major, an ardent angler, as trout ponds. The water-lily beds were planted in 1935. The Stewart collection reflects the donor's favourite pastimes – hunting and fishing – with trophies brought back from frequent expeditions around the world. He also acquired objects of art and household use and weapons, all of which are also on view. Major Stewart was a Cambridge tutor before he settled down on estates near Pocklington in 1904. He died in 1962.

PONTEFRACT, *West Riding* (13–SE4522). The liquorice for the famous Pontefract cakes is no longer grown here though once a field of it filled the ruined castle precincts. The Romans chewed the sweet roots, and cakes of liquorice were made for medicinal purposes early on. But not until 1760 did George Dunhill, a local chemist, add sugar and start the production of the sweets known today. Five firms now make them here. The best viewpoint for a survey of the town and collieries is the castle keep, part of the sparse ruins which stand in a public park on a rocky hill. Pontefract Castle, built by Ilbert de Lacy in the late 12th cent. and later strengthened, figured largely in history. One owner, Thomas Earl of Lancaster, was brought home in chains after the Battle of BOROUGHBRIDGE in 1322, found guilty of treason and beheaded. Richard II was a prisoner here in cold and misery until his murder. The castle also imprisoned James I of Scotland. Charles Duke of Orleans was held here for many years; he was captured at Agincourt. It was a place of execution in the War of the Roses. No wonder Shakespeare called it "bloody Pomfret". A Royalist stronghold in the Civil War, it was surrendered in 1648. The townspeople petitioned that it be pulled down and in 10 weeks it was in ruins.

The castle stood just above All Saints Church which was damaged in the Civil War and only repaired in 1838 when the crossing and transepts were restored to use. The nave was extended recently. The revived church is within its ruins, a curious sight.

There are some good 18th- and 19th-cent. buildings here. The Town Hall of 1785 faces the Market Place where there also is a 1734 butter cross, a round-arched, hipped-roof arcaded stone shelter. The red-brick Red Lion Hotel was remodelled in 1776 by Robert Adam. St Giles's Church, which originated in the 14th cent. became the parish church in 1789.

Below the hospital in Southgate is the 14th-cent. Hermitage carved out of stone by Brother Adam de Laythorpe. It has two chambers and an underground spring.

RALPH CROSS, *North Riding* (15–NZ6802) This is one of the more noticeable of about 30 surviving wayside crosses that dot the North York Moors and which, like the occasional line of shooting butts, provide small points of interest in the vast rolling sweep of heather and bracken. Not much is known about them but they are usually on some ancient track or crossroads and may have been set out by monasteries to guide pilgrims. Sometimes they were boundary posts. Ralph Cross is about 9 ft high, an 18th-cent. replacement of the original, with a hollow on top for coins for poor passers-by. It is on Castleton Rigg in Westerdale Moor at a spot where many tracks meet at 1,409 ft. A few hundred yards W. is Young Ralph and down the ROSEDALE road is Fat Betty (White Cross). Lilla Cross on FYLINGDALES moor may be the oldest. It is a memorial to a thane of King Edwin of Northumbria who died saving the king from assassination in about 626.

REDCAR, *North Riding* (15–NZ6024). The "poor fysher-toune" of the 16th cent. has turned into a holiday resort for Teesside. Coatham, now part of Redcar, was the more significant port in medieval times, manufacturing salt by boiling sea water and later turning to alum burning. Redcar has three beaches and three long rocky reefs, called scars, running out to sea which are left bare, but for seaweed, in low tides. These form a breakwater which has also been a hazard to shipping throughout history.

REETH, *North Riding* (14–SE0499). This was a market town in the 17th and 18th cents., a lively centre for lead-miners in the 19th (the area once produced a large percentage of the national tonnage). Reeth today serves the holidaymakers in Swaledale. It is on the hillside where Arkengarthdale and Swaledale join. Beside Arkle Beck is a miller's house with small millstones set over the windows. High Row, the western border of what is perhaps the best green in this part of Yorkshire, is lined with 18th-cent. inns and shops. Walkers and motorists have many scenic routes to choose from. The road to RICHMOND has been described as the most beautiful in England. The road W. from Reeth leads to some of the wildest country in the Dales. To the NW. beyond Arkengarthdale is **Tan Hill** and England's highest inn.

The parish church stands across the valley at Grinton. People used to bear their dead on wicker biers over rough tracks to its churchyard.

Noel Habgood

Richmond is dominated by the keep of the Norman castle

from the far-flung corners of the parish, which before its subdivision stretched some 20 m. to the Westmorland border.

RICHMOND, *North Riding* (15–NZ1701). An early visitor, given to understatement, observed, "This towne standeth on unequal grounde": Richmond's setting at the entrance to steep-sided Swaledale can hardly be matched, even in a region of dramatic sites. Looking at the town across the river, the viewer is first struck by the strength of the ruined Norman fortress on its sheer rock. The castle was begun by Alan Rufus in 1071, when the border of newly conquered England ran not far to the NW. It is distinctive for having its keep at the gate, a handsome 100-ft tower built in the 12th cent. From its top is the best viewpoint, over the market place, the old town about it, the Swale – the fastest-flowing English river – and the moors. The castle still has two of its towers on the curtain wall and, in Scollard's Hall, built in 1080, it has perhaps the oldest domestic building in Britain. Splendid as it is, the castle was never completed and had little part in history, but it claims one of those unlikely legends of Arthur and his knights asleep until the country needs them. Another story tells of an underground passage to EASBY Abbey, down which a ghostly drummer boy can be heard. The castle is in the hands of the Ministry of Public Building and Works now and is open to the public.

The market place is large, sloping and cobbled. An easy blend of Georgian and Victorian stone buildings surrounds it. The Town Hall on the south side was built in 1756. The obelisk near Holy Trinity Church was put up in 1771. The medieval church itself is a curious assemblage of the ecclesiastical and secular, shops and offices having been built into it; this undermining by commerce at one time threatened the tower.

Friars Wynd leads off to the perfect Georgian Theatre Royal. It was built in 1788 and is one of only two theatres of the period left, the other being at BRISTOL. It closed in 1848. After a long interval as an auction room, corn-chandler's shop, furniture warehouse and salvage depot, it was restored and reopened in 1962. The audience crowds close to the little stage, watching the action from the original pit, boxes and gallery.

Across Queen's Road is Greyfriars Tower, 15th-cent. relic of the Franciscan church. A walk along Frenchgate, leading NE. off the market place, passes some of the finest early residences.

I'Anson Road commemorates Frances I'Anson, the "Lass of Richmond Hill" to whom the famous song was dedicated in 1785. LEYBURN-born, she spent her girlhood here at Hill House.

St Mary's, the parish church on steep ground overlooking the Swale, was extensively restored by Gilbert Scott in 1859–60. In the chancel are 12 medieval canopied stalls from Easby, with some fascinating carvings under the seats. The church contains the memorial chapel of the Green Howards, whose regimental museum in Gallowgate is open to the public.

Lewis Carroll attended for a time the Grammar School opposite, a foundation much older than its Elizabethan charter, when his father was vicar of CROFT.

RIEVAULX ABBEY, *North Riding* (13–SE 5785). Walter L'Espec, the founder of KIRKHAM PRIORY, granted this site in the wilderness to a band of 12 Cistercians in 1131, and thus began an exceptionally prosperous house. Its grandeur is indicated by the ruins here of buildings mostly completed before the end of the 12th cent. Under the third abbot, the great Aelred (1147 to 1167) there were 140 monks and more than 500 lay brothers. The abbey was too large by the 15th cent., however, and parts of the chapter house, warming house and dormitory were taken down. By the Dissolution in 1539 there were only 22 monks. The site, now tended by the Ministry of Public Building and Works, is one of the loveliest in England. It is in the Rye valley 3 m. NW. of HELMSLEY, marvellously secluded, sheltered from the moors which rise above it, and filled with beautiful trees. Rievaulx was the first Cistercian abbey in Yorkshire. There are considerable remains of the lofty church and the extensive monastic quarters. The church nave dates from about 1135. The choir is a particularly fine example of 13th-cent. work.

The long curving terrace which overlooks Rievaulx affords the most satisfying vantage point. This gem of 18th-cent. landscaping belongs to Duncombe Park. When it was laid out, the gentry would drive over to enjoy the views of the desolate abbey and the wide sweep of Yorkshire beyond the valley. At one end was built an oblong Ionic temple, richly decorated and furnished, for hunting parties. At the other end there is a small round Doric temple for solitude. Along the easy stroll between them are openings in the forested slope, cleverly cut to show Rievaulx from interesting angles. These are the views that held Dorothy Wordsworth spellbound, that Turner painted and that made Cowper wish to stay forever. The terrace is reached by a side lane from the Helmsley road.

RIPLEY, *West Riding* (12–SE2860). One wide street and a small cobbled square make up the village remodelled by one of the Ingilbys of Ripley Castle in 1827 to resemble an Alsatian community. Bypassed by the RIPON-HARROGATE road, Ripley offers motorists who stray from the main route an old church and a weeping cross, claimed to be the only one in the county, as well as the castle. All Saints had to be rebuilt after the River Nidd undercut its site in about 1395. A clerestory and upper part of the tower were added in the 16th cent. and there have been 19th-cent. restorations, with much Victorian glass put in. Its oldest monument is a 14th-cent. effigy of Sir Thomas de Ingilby and wife with their children lining the sides of the chest. A stair turret climbs the tower and there is a priest's room above the south chapel. The weeping cross is in the churchyard, with shaft and head missing. What remains is the base with eight niches in which to kneel and repent. It may be 2nd-cent. There are stocks in the square and the village cross. The castle is open on Sundays throughout the summer and the landscaped grounds with lake and walled garden are open on Saturdays as well. The 15th-cent. gatehouse leads into a courtyard where a tower from the original castle now joins a late-18th-cent. hall. Both James I and Cromwell stayed here, the latter, it is said, watched throughout the night by Lady

Ingilby armed with pistols. In the library you ca see the foundation charter for MOUNT GRAC PRIORY.

RIPON, *West Riding* (12–SE3171), is a sma market town with a great cathedral and a Horr blower in three-corner hat who nightly sounds horn at the market cross and in front of th Mayor's house, carrying out a tradition said to b 1,000 years old.

An Anglo-Saxon church destroyed in 95 stood where the relatively small but impressiv cathedral now stands. Building took place main in the 12th and 13th cents. but important change were made in later centuries, including a 19th cent. restoration. The oldest part, and one of th oldest Christian shrines in England, is the cryp all that remains of the original Church of S Wilfrid and very like the crypt from his church c the same period at HEXHAM. It lies below th central tower. The west front is exceptionall beautiful Early English work. Among notabl furnishings are a late 15th-cent. screen and miser cords of the same period by the local carvers guild, among them delightful versions of Samsor Jonah, a pelican, fox and geese, pigs, an owl an an angel.

The heart of the town is the rectangular marke place with its dominating 90-ft obelisk raised i 1781 to William Aislabie of STUDLEY ROYAL the M.P. for 60 years. The Town Hall, designe by James Wyatt in 1801, faces the square, and th medieval Wakeman's House is near one corner The house was built in the 13th cent. and th Wakeman, or night watchman, lived there. householders who had paid for his services wer robbed, the Wakeman paid the loss. Under 1604 charter, Wakemen were replaced by mayors Hugh Ripley was last Wakeman and first Mayor The house is now a café and a museum.

The town museum is in Thorpe Prebend Hous in St Agnesgate, rebuilt in the 17th cent. Ripo was a clothmaking centre in the Middle Ages but by the 16th cent. the trade was moving t towns in the W. of Yorkshire. This also was lacemaking centre, the only one in the county Probably the craft was started by refugee monk or nuns. By 1862, only one lacemaker was left Ripon was also famous for its spurs.

The city motto is inscribed on the Town Hall i glittering letters: "Except ye Lord keep ye cittie ye Wakeman waketh in vain."

ROBIN HOOD'S BAY, *North Riding* (15 NZ9505). On the top of the cliffs are run-of-the mill houses but down the ravine towards the shor is an old fishing village. There is a tangle o houses, cafés, shops and inns, many all too pre cariously perched on their rocky ledges and ofte connected by narrow passages or a flight of steps The village is sought out by artists as well a holidaymakers. Many of the red-roofed cottage are done up in bright paint and flowers. The village is near the north end of a sweeping ba which extends from the cliffs of Ravenscar on th S. to the jutting headland of Ness Point on the N nland stretches FYLINGDALES Moor. Strange things happen here. Every house used to have a hiding place for contraband in the 18th cent. The bowsprit of a stranded ship once pierced the window of an inn. Rocks frequently, but cottages rarely, fall into the bay, yet erosion has claimed at least two rows of houses and a road in the last 100 years. It is not clear why it was named after the legendary outlaw, but it adds to the romance of the place. One story is that Robin Hood came here to get boats ready for an escape to the Continent. The old Fylingdales parish church, St Stephen's, rebuilt in 1822, is interesting for its box pews and three-decker pulpit.

ROCHE ABBEY, *West Riding* (13–SK5489). This Cistercian house founded in 1147 lies in ruins ½ m. SE. of Maltby. Its founders were Richard de Bully, Lord of TICKHILL, and Richard son of Turgis, owners of the land on either side of the stream. The monastery here was colonized by Newminster near MORPETH. It got its name from a rock formation which bore some likeness to a cross and was an object of pilgrimage. When the property was surrendered in 1538 it was plundered by the neighbourhood. The site was granted to Thomas Vavasour and William Ramsden in 1554. Eventually it came into the hands of the 10th Earl of Scarbrough who put the ruins in the care of the Ministry of Public Building and Works.

The great charm of Roche today is its position, sheltered by cliffs overgrown by trees and shrubs and standing on a grassy valley bottom landscaped by Capability Brown. The buildings were constructed on both sides of the stream which formed a natural drain, with the water supply controlled by a dam. The area is entered by a fine vaulted gatehouse, partly rebuilt in the 14th cent. The east walls of the transepts of the church still stand, and the outlines of the rest of the buildings are substantial.

ROMALDKIRK, *North Riding* (14–NY9921). The village takes its name from the Church of St Romald, which is derived from the name of St Rumwald and is perhaps the only dedication to this prodigious infant saint. The church is cruciform and the fabric spans the ages from the late-12th-cent. arcades and south doorway to the 15th-cent. tower. It contains a Norman font carved with rows of foliage in circles and a 14th-cent. effigy of Sir Hugh Fitzhenry in the act of drawing his sword. The church, the irregular green, the scattered houses, a stream, almshouses and the fragments of stocks and a pound for stray cattle all give the village a beguiling air: most visitors find it one of the prettiest in Teesdale.

ROSEDALE ABBEY, *North Riding* (15–SE 7296), is a sturdy hamlet in the middle of Rosedale, largest of the moorland valleys. There is a steep drop down to it on the W., past the landmark chimney of the old ironworks, and a nearly equally steep climb out. A Cistercian nunnery was established here in the mid-12th cent., but it was demolished by the Scots in 1322. Much of the stone went into various village buildings. A few carved stones and fragment of a turret stair survive in the new (1839) Church of SS. Mary and Lawrence. The church has an interesting angel lectern, probably 17th-cent. Dutch. The Milburn Arms Hotel has been the social centre for over 500 years. BYLAND ABBEY made iron here from the mid-13th to the 16th cent.

ROTHERHAM, *West Riding* (13–SK4492). A close neighbour to SHEFFIELD, Rotherham, too, is chiefly a child of the Industrial Revolution. Its coal-mines, iron, steel, brass and glass works dominate its situation in the Don valley. Like other towns of its generation, Rotherham has been rebuilding in recent years, but some of the medieval street plan remains. With the founding of the College of Jesus in 1482 by Archbishop Thomas Rotherham of YORK, the town became an important centre of learning. The college ended with the Dissolution.

The town's showpiece, All Saints Church, succeeded Anglo-Saxon and Norman churches on its site. Its pinnacled tower, 1409, is the earliest part and the remainder is almost entirely 15th-cent. There are some finely carved bench ends and stalls. It was restored in 1875.

The other medieval survivals in the town are the Chapel of Our Lady and the four-arched bridge at which it stands. The only other bridge chantry in the county is at WAKEFIELD. This one was built in 1482 and after the Dissolution served successively as an almshouse, a prison and a tobacconist's shop. It was restored in 1924. The old bridge, returned to its 15-ft width, was scheduled as an Ancient Monument when the new Chantry Bridge was completed in 1930.

Modern growth began with the establishment of the first ironworks in 1746 by Samuel Walker, a former schoolmaster. John Wesley often visited Rotherham and Nonconformity became firmly established, especially after Walker built the Independent Chapel in 1763. He died 20 years later and his mausoleum is in the chapel graveyard. His son, Joshua, was at the time of his father's death building Clifton House, with John Carr of York as his architect. The house is now the local museum, notable for remains from the excavated site of the Roman fort of Templeborough, 1½ m. SW., and for a remarkable collection of Rockingham china, including tea services and ornamental ware. The china used to be made at nearby Swinton.

A favourite outing is to ROCHE ABBEY, 8 m. E. **Wentworth Woodhouse,** which is really two 18th-cent. houses facing in opposite directions, is 4 m. from the town centre and home of the West Riding County Council's Lady Mabel Training College. It has the longest frontage (600 ft) of any country residence in England. The park is open to the public. In the grounds are three follies: Hoober Stand, built in 1748 by the Marquess of Rockingham; Keppel's Pillar, a huge Doric column erected in honour of Admiral Keppel; and the Needle's Eye, a pyramid pierced by an arch, built in 1780.

Kenneth Scowe

Scarborough: the harbour

RUDSTON, *East Riding* (13–TA0967). Another uncanny monolith, but larger than the Devil's Arrows at BOROUGHBRIDGE, stands in the church-yard. It measures 25 ft 4 in. high, 6 ft wide and 2 ft 3 in. thick at the base. It may be as deep into the ground as it is high, but this is a guess. Since the nearest quarry would be 40 m. away, it is believed that the stone was deposited here by glacial action and then erected on this hill by prehistoric men for reasons not now discoverable. The circular churchyard encloses All Saints, which surveys the Yorkshire Wolds 5 m. W. of BRID-LINGTON. It has a thick west Norman tower with most of the fabric Decorated, and restored in 1861. The Norman font is circular with diaper pattern carving. SW. towards Kilham, the site of a Roman villa was uncovered by a ploughman in 1933. Three fine tessellated pavements from here are now in the HULL Transport Museum. The largest is 13 ft by 10 ft 6 in. and shows a bulging Venus with flying hair holding an apple and a mirror, the artist's conception of Venus at her bath. Leopards, hunters and birds are arranged around her. The stone, the pavements and the church speak of occupation stretching over thousands of years. Winifred Holtby, the novelist and journalist, was buried here in 1935. Her *South Riding* was the East Riding.

SCARBOROUGH, *North Riding* (13–TA03 88). It is easy to enjoy this big breezy North Sea resort which combines castle ruins, a fishing village, a working port, luxury hotels, boarding houses, sands, terraced gardens, long wave-swept promenades, views, walks, and carnival-style amusements of all descriptions. Scarborough holds an annual cricket festival. It also puts on an annual Continental festival in a bid to attract visitors from those parts. According to the sagas, the town was founded by a Norseman. It cele-brated the 900th anniversary of its burning by another one, Harald Hardrada, in 1066 with th friendly co-operation of modern Norsemen This was a stylish spa in the 17th and 18th cents and it is still a popular place for retirement or second home or flat.

Scarborough is built below and on top of a cliff, with steep streets, footpaths and lifts con necting the parts. To the W. stretch new suburbs The interest for the visitor is concentrated near the sea. The castle ruins stand on a narrow headland which was earlier an ancient British camp and a Roman signal station. The approach is by a 13th cent. barbican which leads to the shell of th square keep, built about 1160. The curtain wall was the first feature of the castle, probably built 30 years earlier. Remnants of three medieval chapels and a house survive. The site is 300 f above the sea and covers 19 acres. The castle looks down upon the medieval red-roofed town around the harbour. Here stand the 18th-cent Customs House, King Richard III House (now a café), old pubs, gaudy arcades and souveni shops. Hotels, including the monumental Grand and terraces of houses line the banks. The valle separating the southern parts of town is crossed by high bridges and was landscaped in the 19th cent. Villas were built along its steep sides, fo the Victorians did not wish to face the sea. Three of these houses, all in The Crescent, are now th Natural History Museum, Art Gallery and Medical Baths. The museum occupies Woodend the 1840 seaside home of the Sitwells.

The splendid Marine Drive and promenade completed in 1908 after repeated delays due to gales, follows the base of the castle promontor and the wide curve of North Bay. Some fin walks run along the cliffs above South Bay. Ther is a matchless view from Oliver's Mount, th 500-ft-high hill with a war memorial obelisk.

Anne Brontë is buried in the hillside church-yard of St Mary's below the castle. St Mary's was built in the early 12th cent. but rebuilt into the 15th, by which time it was a large cruciform building with three towers. It was severely damaged in the Civil War and the central tower rebuilt at the east end, with the chancel abandoned. There is an interesting row of 14th-cent. chapels on the south aisle.

SEDBERGH, *West Riding* (14–SD6592). There are two points of interest in this hill town in a north-west corner of Yorkshire. The noted boys' school was founded by Roger Lupton, a canon of WINDSOR and provost of ETON, in 1525. A new school built in 1716 is now the library and museum and most of the present buildings, extending to the S., are late 19th-cent. An early and successful headmaster had the unlikely name of Posthumous Wharton. The Quaker meeting house was built in Brigflatts, just over 1 m. SW., in 1675. White-walled and furnished in utter simplicity, it keeps a fragment of a yew tree under which George Fox preached. The parish church, St Andrew's, is chiefly 13th-cent. work with some 18th-cent. furnishings. Sedbergh's setting, below the slate Howgill Fells, is more like the Lake District just over the border than the Yorkshire Dales to the S. and E. These are huge smooth hills with rich grass cover. A busy market town, Sedbergh has to handle heavy traffic on its narrow main street.

SELBY, *West Riding* (13–SE6132). The abbey in 1969 celebrated its 900th anniversary. It was founded by Benedict of Auxerre who was directed in a vision to go to "Selebaie" in England. Discouraged by his superiors, he fled, taking St Germain's finger with him. As he sailed up the River Ouse, three swans settled in the water where Selby now stands. This he took as a sign of the place in his dream. He planted a cross and built a hut. He had trespassed on royal property, but with the approval of the Norman governor and the assent of King William, Benedict was made an abbot and given the land.

The present abbey was begun in about 1100. The nave took 100 years and with its absorbing development from Norman to Early English styles as building progressed from east to west it is, perhaps, the greatest attraction of this noble building. The chancel was built between 1280 and 1340 and includes an east Jesse window of about 1330 with roughly one-fourth of its original glass. Worshippers enter the nave through two magnificent doorways: the Norman west doorway with its beautifully carved five recessed arches or the equally handsome north doorway within a 13th-to 15th-cent. porch. The abbey has withstood several disasters, but rebuilding and restoration have left an unusually complete abbey church. In the Dissolution, it became the parish church. In 1690 the central tower fell and in 1906 a great fire swept the building. The last work was completed in 1935.

Selby is believed to be the birthplace of Henry I, only son of William the Conqueror to be born in England. Small boats still come up the Ouse to unload and load at the modest dock and motor traffic crosses by an 18th-cent. wooden toll-bridge. The abbey, in its railed lawn, faces the most attractive part of the town, the broad Market Place. Outer Selby is dominated by flour and cattle-feed mills but fortunately none is so close to the heart of the town as to lessen the joy of seeing the beautiful white towers of the abbey rising from their surrounding trees.

SETTLE, *West Riding* (12–SD8263). A picturesque centre for touring in an area of great limestone hills and crags, across the Ribble from GIGGLESWICK. Narrow streets, tiny courtyards, and good Georgian houses contribute to an interesting townscape. In the Market Square are the Elizabethan-style Town Hall built in 1832 and the 17th-cent. Shambles, with living-quarters opening on to a gallery above the filled-in arcade. The large stone town house built in 1679 by Thomas Preston is known as The Folly because he lacked the money to finish it. Lovers of panoramas will toil up Castleberg Crag that stands 300 ft above the town. The Pig Yard Club Museum has many of the weapons, bones, tools, ornaments and coins found in Victoria Cave, discovered in 1838 at Langcliffe, NE. of Settle. The cave is 1,450 ft above sea-level, and it had through the ages been a hyena den, a hunters' refuge and a place of concealment during the troubled days of the later Roman occupation. Benjamin Waugh, the founder of the National Society for the Prevention of Cruelty to Children, was born in Settle. So, too, was Dr George Birkbeck who founded the mechanics' institutes and whose name is remembered in Birkbeck College, London.

SHEFFIELD, *West Riding* (13–SK3587). The steel capital of Britain has the best of two worlds. It is a thriving industrial centre but it is not stifled by its factories. It holds a happy situation on three hills at the meeting of two rivers, the Don and Sheaf. The Pennines, castles, priories and abbeys are only a short distance away. Civic planning by a forward-looking authority, smoke-less zoning, and outstanding modern architecture have improved appearances in recent years. Sheffield was famous for cutlery as early as the 14th cent. (there is a famous reference in Chaucer's *Canterbury Tales*) and it began to specialize in such tools with the arrival of Flemish immigrants in the 16th cent. Steel products followed the invention of the crucible process by Benjamin Huntsman in 1740. At about the same time Thomas Boulsover found out how to fuse silver to copper ingots and roll the silver plate by which Sheffield is known the world over.

It was not always such a stimulating place to visit, but damage suffered in the Second World War forced rebuilding of the grimy centre, and under the guidance of City Architects J. L. Womersley and L. L. Clunie, buildings worthy of their sites began to rise. There is little building older than Victorian left, except for part of the

Henk Snoek

Sheffield University Library

cathedral and a handful of houses. The Town Hall, opened in 1897, towers over the city centre with a statue of Vulcan, appropriately, on the very top. The Cutlers' Hall of 1832 stands nearby. The Master Cutler is second only to the Lord Mayor in Sheffield. The hall contains a fine collection of silver from 1773 to the present. The city's major social event, the Cutlers' Feast, is held annually in the banqueting hall, a 350-year-old tradition.

The City Museum near the University in Weston Park has an unmatched collection of cutlery from the 16th cent. and the world's largest array of Sheffield plate. The University of Sheffield, chartered in 1905, specializes in applied sciences. It has a red-brick core and some striking new buildings, including a library rated the best 20th-cent. building in town. A low, square structure with bands of glass and stone, it is connected by a bridge to the 19-story glass Arts Tower. Another institution, Sheffield Polytechnic in Pond Street, occupies a 12-story slab-like building with two low wings close to the railway and bus stations and car parks.

Sheffield has been daring in its treatment of both shopping and housing. The Castle Market, on the site of vanished Sheffield Castle, opened in 1959 as a roofed shopping centre. There is street access from three floors because of the hilly terrain. Multiple stores and shops are connected to the market by covered galleries.

Housing here became famous with the Park Hill development on a derelict area above the Sheaf. Huge blocks of flats, 4 to 14 stories high, were built in polygonal shapes so that there would be a variety of views. The units open on to wide decks that serve as internal streets and are reported to be socially successful. This is part of an even larger scheme, Hyde Park, to the E. The largest Sheffield housing estate is at Gleadless Valley where three neighbourhoods with 17,000 people were established.

The Cathedral Church of SS. Peter and Paul, across from Cutlers' Hall in Church Street, dates

from about 1435, and is Perpendicular in style with a crocketed spire. The building has been extensively altered and enlarged with, among other changes, a new glass and steel entrance, modern tower and lantern. Visitors will want to look at the Shrewsbury Chapel monuments and the stained-glass windows by Christopher Webb relating local history, and to linger over his Chaucer window in the chapter house.

There are two art galleries, the Graves on the top floor of the Central Library with a fine collection of Chinese ivories, and the Mappin Art Gallery in Weston Park, featuring English art. Persons interested in industrial antiquities should contact the City Museum for permission to visit the Shepherd Wheel in Whiteley Woods, the only known working water-powered grinding wheel and, at the new Abbeydale Industrial Hamlet, a scythe-works of the 18th and 19th cents.

Sheffield and its neighbours strongly back the Sheffield Repertory Company and a £900,000 theatre is opening in 1971 to replace the present Playhouse.

Sheffield relishes its reputation as a city without rigid class barriers, of friendly and city-proud residents.

A round walk of 10 m. will take visitors around the town on public parks property through shady suburbs, woods and fields. The Civic Information Service in the Central Library can provide details. The walk passes **Beauchief Abbey**, founded in 1175, of which only the west tower stands. The Church of St Thomas in this former village was built with abbey stones in the 17th cent. and has fine contemporary furnishings, including box pews. The walk also leads through Graves Park from which there is an overall view of this surprising city.

SHERIFF HUTTON, *North Riding* (13–SE 6566). The village is easily spotted by the broken towers of Sheriff Hutton Castle, the backdrop for a farmyard today, but at one time the centre for great intrigues and deeds of violence in the Wars of the Roses. The village stands on a rise above the Plain of York and you can see YORK Minster's towers from it. The once-mighty fortress was built in the 14th cent. replacing an earlier 12th-cent. castle put up by Bertram de Bulmer, Sheriff of Yorkshire, after whom the village took its name. In the medieval Church of St Helen and Holy Cross with its low Norman west tower are several interesting monuments. The worn alabaster effigy of a boy is supposed to represent Edward Prince of Wales, the son of Richard III, who died in 1484 at the age of 11 at MIDDLEHAM Castle. A cross-legged knight effigy with two angels near the pillow is of Sir Edmund Thweng who died in 1344. There is also a brass memorial to two babies, Dorothy and John Fenys, who died in 1491 and are shown in swaddling clothes. The church is furnished with box pews and a Jacobean communion rail.

SKIPSEA, *East Riding* (13–TA1655). The earthworks of a Norman castle outside the old village constitute the best feudal relic in the Riding. The large circular motte or mound is separated from the bailey by an area once covered with water known as Skipsea Mere. A causeway crossed it. This part of the lowland of Holderness was granted by William the Conqueror to Drogo de Brevere, a "Flemish adventurer", who had married a relative of the king. According to a medieval historian, Drogo killed his wife and obtained by a ruse enough money from the king to finance an escape to the Continent. His lands and Skipsea Castle were of course seized. Later a centre for rebels, the castle was demolished by Henry III about 1220. From the top of the motte there is a view of the sea N. to FLAMBOROUGH. The unpretentious parish church, All Saints, was built, mainly in the 13th cent., of cobbles in a lively zigzag pattern.

SKIPTON, *West Riding* (12–SD9851), has its mills (it makes among other things mercerized thread), but it still has the feel of a country town in a green setting and this contributes to its popularity as a good gateway to the Dales. It is easily accessible today, even by canal, although in 1747 John Wesley complained that it was so "pent up" in its valley that "you can expect little company from without". Skipton contains charming old houses, courtyards, an old toll-booth and stocks in Sheep Street, a 16th-cent. grammar school, a Palladian (1862 vintage) Town Hall, and a simple 1693 Friends Meeting House. But its focal points are the castle and the church, both located where the High Street fans out at the top. The first castle was built by Robert de Romille, but only one gateway of this Norman fortress survives. The present castle dates from the time the Cliffords took possession in the 14th cent. The last Clifford to own it was Lady Anne, who died in 1676. The castle had been partly demolished in 1649 and she reconstructed it. One of her additions was the balustrade over the gatehouse incorporating the family motto "Desormais"

(henceforth). On either side of the gatehouse are massive round towers. Lawns and cobbles inside the walls set off the main buildings and towers. Conduit Court is particularly lovely, shaded as it is by an ancient yew. Among parts of the castle open to the public are an 18th-cent. room lined with pearly shells and the dungeon. This castle is one of the most complete and well preserved in the country.

Holy Trinity Church was extensively restored also by Lady Anne. Among its older parts are the 12th-cent. font, with a superb spire-like Jacobean font cover; the 14th-cent. sedilia with four seats; and the early-16th-cent. screen. There are several impressive Clifford tombs. Skipton was the sheep town (Sceptun) of the Angles and it still has a sheep and cattle auction.

SLEDMERE, *East Riding* (13–SE9364). The house is interesting but the family a Yorkshire institution. Much of what attracts the traveller in the Yorkshire Wolds is their doing. Sir Christopher Sykes transformed the open fields of the area into the splendid agricultural area it still is. Before his death in 1801 he had planted trees and hedgerows, built new roads with wide verges for ordinary folk to graze their cattle on, and pioneered in growing grain for the newly popular wheaten bread. In 1823, the title went to his second son, Sir Tatton, a legend in his own time. He was famous for farming, hunting, racing, boxing, building schools, breeding sheep and establishing the Sledmere stud. He married at 50 and died at 91. His son, also Sir Tatton, was a shy man who spent £2 million rebuilding and restoring churches between the 1860s and his death in 1913. He passed his summers here, taking daily walks for which he would start swaddled in waistcoats. As the day advanced he would peel them off, to be collected by a footman in the rear. His son, Col. Mark, was a soldier and scholar who raised the Yorkshire Waggoners in 1912 and died in 1919. Today Sledmere House is the seat of Sir Richard Sykes and is open daily in summer except Mondays and Fridays. The 1787 mansion was burnt in 1911 and was rebuilt in the same handsome style. It is beautifully set in a park arranged by Capability Brown. Sir Richard, when at home, plays the organ during the Sunday afternoon "viewings".

The church within the park is counted among the loveliest modern parish churches in England. The tower is old, the rest rebuilt by Temple Moore in 1898, one of that Sir Tatton's works. A staircase leads to a small study furnished with the favourite books of the late Col. Mark Sykes. There are far more noticeable monuments in the almost-too-tidy village. A fascinating one was designed by Col. Mark and built after his death to the Waggoners. The panels of low relief carvings on it show these Yorkshire farm boys in driving competitions, at work, joining up, saying good-bye, on the sea, disembarking, and putting the Germans to flight. A canopied well was erected to Sir Christopher by his son and a 60-ft-high cross is the local war memorial. It would be quite at home in a city. On Garton Hill just outside the village is a great spire honouring the most celebrated Sir Tatton. He is pictured on horseback in a carving on the front. The view from here displays the full glory of the Wolds.

SPOFFORTH CASTLE, *West Riding* (13–SE3650).

The castle, a 14th-cent. fortified manor house, is a ruin but with hall and solar wing standing. Its licence to crenellate was granted Sir Henry Percy and the house was wrecked by his enemies after his death at Towton in 1461. It was dismantled almost completely in 1650. Built against the natural rock, the house had an outside door leading directly into the upper floor with its great hall and other main rooms. The vaulted basement and kitchen were below. The Ministry of Public Building and Works maintains the site. All Saints Church here has a 15th-cent. tower and the rest of the building is Norman revival of 1855. Some traces of original work survive, including beakhead and zigzag ornament and 12th-cent. capitals. There is a fragment of an Anglo-Saxon cross shaft and a badly worn 14th-cent. figure of a cross-legged knight, Sir Robert de Plumpton III. The rectory stands behind a medieval gateway.

STAITHES, *North Riding* (15–NZ7818).

As many as 400 fishermen sailed from this small harbour in the old days, and even in the early 19th cent. it was a principal centre for cod, haddock and mackerel. WHITBY nearby was specializing in whaling and the coastal trade. Three fish trains a week left Staithes when the railway came. But with the growth of Whitby and the arrival of steam trawlers, Staithes fell into decline. The village is said to have begun when a shipwreck cast many Frenchmen ashore and they remained. Smuggling was a local industry in the 18th cent. and alum and jet were mined in the area. As at Whitby, the women then – and some now – wore frilled cotton bonnets and the men navy blue granzies (jerseys). The only road into the village is extraordinarily steep, even by North Riding standards, and the houses in every shape and size cling to the slope at all levels. At the bottom is the Cod and Lobster Inn. It does not look very picturesque, but then it has been washed away three times, and each time rebuilt. It is the village social centre and here the menfolk still sing hymns over their pints. Two famous names: Dame Laura Knight lived and painted here for 18 years, and James Cook, born at Marton-in-Cleveland, was apprenticed to a grocer around the corner from the inn. Fishermen's tales or the stern treatment of his master encouraged the boy to run away to Whitby and sign on as a cabin boy. He is supposed to have taken a shilling from the till to finance the flight which was to lead him to fame as a navigator. Two m. N. is **Boulby Cliff** which, at 666 ft, is the highest coastal point in England.

STAMFORD BRIDGE, *East Riding* (13–SE7155).

This was a famous victory in 1066, but this is England and so it is not as well known as the defeat at HASTINGS. Here on the Derwent 8 m.

E. of YORK Harold of England decisively defeated Harald of Norway and saved his kingdom for a while. The invaders, after harrying the coast, had sailed up the Humber and Ouse, landed at Riccall and taken York. King Harold hastened north with what forces he could muster. The Norse king went to Stamford Bridge, a road centre from Roman times, to receive tribute and hostages from local leaders, but the English king pounced and the unprepared Norsemen, many of whom had shed their armour in the heat, were slaughtered. Two tales emerge: of the Norse warrior who held the wooden bridge for hours until he was speared from beneath by an Englishman floating downstream in a tub; and of a parley in which King Harold, asked what terms he would offer his enemy, replied, "Six feet of English earth – or say he is a giant, seven". This was all on 25 September. On 14 October, a weary King Harold met the Norman invaders at Hastings with dire results. The present (1727) narrow arched bridge is of stone and it stands above the flats where the battle was fought. The women here occasionally bake the spear pies that used to be a traditional September dish, recalling how the bridge was taken. There is a stone marker on a weedy green. The village is something of a dormitory for York now, with little of the picturesque about it.

STANWICK FORTIFICATIONS, *North Riding* (15–NZ1813).

From these impressive earthworks, King Venutius of the Brigantes led the last serious battle against the conquering Romans in A.D. 74, and was defeated. The defences are reached from Forcett village 6½ m. N. of RICHMOND. Venutius was the great organizer of resistance to the Romans, while his wife, Cartimandua, sided with the invaders and, with their protection, sought to stop the guerilla attacks. These defences were built from about A.D. 69 to 72, first as a bank and ditch surrounding a 17-acre site and then expanded to enclose 850 acres in all. The place chosen to make the stand was a prominent point, Toft Hill, on a crossroads. The excavated section is carefully preserved.

STILLINGFLEET, *East Riding* (13–SE5940).

The Norman south doorway of St Helen's Church makes this insignificant hamlet a place of pilgrimage. There are five orders arching over the entry, a geometrical design, beakheads, two rows of zigzag, and a combination of beasts, medallions and heads. The oak doorway itself may be original and the ironwork is a delight. There are two C-hinges, a small pair of gesturing figures at the top left and, near the centre, a (possibly Viking) ship. These could be the fragments of a larger design which related a story. The churchyard is entered through a fine lych-gate and a gravel walk leads through aged holly, yew and conifers. The Moreby Chapel, founded about 1336, has its old piscina, two Jacobean screens and the 14th-cent. figure of a knight. There is a second Norman doorway in the north wall of the nave, with zigzag and ball moulding.

STOKESLEY, *North Riding* (15–NZ5208). The immediate charm of this market town at the foot of the Cleveland Hills arises from its wealth of early houses, mainly brick, around an irregular and spacious centre. The scale is small and harmonious. The River Leven runs along one side with many little footbridges across it. There are frequent narrow cobbled passages between houses. At either end of the long market place are the East and West Greens. On an island in the middle, more or less, stands the straightforward 1853 stone Town Hall. Many buildings – both houses and commercial places – have been lovingly kept or restored, but others, regretfully, are in danger of being lost altogether or brutally altered, which will be a great loss. Facing the Town Hall across the market place is the former Manor House, now the Rural District Council offices. It is a simple, three-story stone composition of the 19th cent. with a wing to the right.

Nearby is the Church of SS. Peter and Paul with its low battlemented tower and small chancel, both Perpendicular, connected by a broad nave of 1771. The path through the churchyard leads across the Leven into a lovely tree-shaded walk which follows the stream as it skirts the town centre, passing modest but interesting houses of the last three centuries. A plaque commemorates Miss Jane Page, a Stokesley native who in 1836 became the first white woman to settle in Victoria, Australia, and in whose memory the trees on Levenside were planted 100 years later. The packhorse bridge is locally thought to be either of 1640 or an 1850 imitation. Near the iron bridge further on, Levenside widens with pretty cottages on either side of the stream. Behind is the well-kept 19th-cent. Union Mill and a former home of a candle factory. West Green has many pleasant houses with bay windows and also the imposing Handyside, red brick trimmed with stone, now the home of the Bishop of WHITBY. Behind the neglected Stone Hall, with its Classical 18th-cent. façade, is the old Wesley Chapel of 1812, now a brewery. A major agricultural show and fair fills the town centre each September.

STUDLEY ROYAL, *West Riding* (12–SE 2768). The beautiful parkland adjoins, and provides a superb entrance to, FOUNTAINS ABBEY. The entrance gates stand near a group of pretty cottages known as Studley Roger. Inside the park is the Church of St Mary, a William Burges creation of the 1870s, very rich, with good Victorian glass and much use of marble from faraway places: Purbeck, Sicilian, Belgian, Tennesseean and Californian. The house burnt down here in 1945 and the owner lived in the High Stables, built about 1720, until the property was sold to the West Riding County Council. The fine stone buildings enclose a courtyard. A large herd of deer shares the park with various livestock and is usually visible from the drive. The grounds were laid out by John Aislabie in the leisure following his forced retirement as Chancellor of the Exchequer. William Fisher was his landscape gardener and the work was spread over

Staithes was an important harbour in the 18th cent.

Noel Habgood

G. Douglas Bolton

Thornton Dale is one of the prettiest villages in the North Riding

the years 1720 to 1740. The climax was the "pleasure grounds" which begin at the lake (the weir end) and lead on a half-mile or so through the valley to the abbey. This is a pure 18th-cent. conception, making delightful scenic use of woods, walks, towers, temples, ponds, a canal, statuary and "surprise" views. Truly a setting to dawdle in.

SUTTON BANK, *North Riding* (13–SE5383), is one of the most famous viewpoints and one of the toughest road ascents in the county. From Sutton-under-Whitestone Cliffe, the road twists and climbs 500 ft in half a mile. It is 960 ft high at the top. An escarpment of the Hambleton Hills E. of THIRSK, the great Sutton Bank is a landmark for miles across the level plain below it. To the right of the sheer cliff is Roulston Scar on which the white horse of KILBURN was cut in 1857. There is space to park for viewing across the Vale of York to the Pennines. Below to the NW. is Gormire, a natural lake where a landslip formed a kind of dam. Roulston Scar is headquarters of the Yorkshire Gliding Club.

TADCASTER, *West Riding* (13–SE4843), has been brewing beer since the 18th cent. and the breweries are the most conspicuous objects on its landscape today. St Mary's Church has traces of

Norman work inside, but it is mainly Perpendicular, a fine white stone building which was taken down between 1875 and 1877 and reconstructed 5 ft higher up to protect it from River Wharfe floods. Its exterior is livened with pinnacles and gargoyles. It has fine modern woodwork. The Wharfe bridge is early 18th-cent., later widened, with seven arches. Above it stands the "virgin viaduct", built in 1849, but the railway that should have used it was never built. Tadcaster was a Roman outpost for YORK and known then as Calcaria. The Ark Museum, built near the church in the 15th cent. and used as a meeting place by Dissenters in the 17th, is maintained by a brewery and open at advertised times. Tadcaster is 2 m. N. of **Towton**, a hamlet near which a bloody battle of the Wars of the Roses was fought in a snowstorm on 29 March 1461. A cross near the road to Saxton marks the field where 50,000 men fought, said to be the largest number ever engaged on English soil, and thousands died.

THIRSK, *North Riding* (13–SE4282), is a thriving market town and convenient stop at a major crossroads. You can hurry through the newer part of town on one main road or crawl through the crowded market square on another. The square, still cobbled, is surrounded by old shops and inns. This was an important posting station in the 18th and 19th cents. The Three Tuns is the oldest inn, an 18th-cent. front with a fine staircase inside. The Fleece, also Georgian, was once the main coaching inn. It has horse paintings and a coaching clock by Palliser. The Crown Inn dates from 1682. St Mary's Church may well be the best example of Perpendicular work in the county, a notable dark stone building with fanciful openwork parapet outlining walls, tower and porch. The tower is braced by stepped buttresses; 15th-cent. details include the door in the porch, the barrel roof of the nave and some glass. The church was begun in 1430 and completed in the early 16th cent., with 19th-cent. restoration. It was based on a chantry founded by Robert Thirsk who died in 1419. His small brass memorial is inside. Thirsk Hall, a handsome 18th-cent. brick house, stands across from the church.

THORNTON DALE, *North Riding* (13–SE 8383), often earns plaudits as prettiest or tidiest village. On the main PICKERING–SCARBOROUGH road, it is strung out along a stream crossed by little bridges. At the central crossroads are a market cross and stocks. Stone cottages and houses all seem to have pretty gardens. Alms-houses and a grammar school were 17th-cent. benefactions. Thornton Hall, with parts dating to Tudor times behind an 18th-cent. façade, is now a hotel. All Saints Church was rebuilt in the 14th cent. and has a large chancel from 1866. A stone effigy of a woman has been dated to the early 14th cent. and the font assigned to 1200. At Low Dalby, 1 m. N., you can now stretch your legs on the **Sneverdale Nature Trail** in Allerston State Forest. A mile's walk from the car park will take you to the forest nursery. A 3-m. hike will reveal the whole story of how the forest grows.

TICKHILL, *West Riding* (13–SK5892). A pleasant change in a colliery area, this was never more than a village although it had one of the most important castles in the North, now in very sketchy ruins, and a splendid parish church. Richard Lionheart licensed the castle for tour-neys, and it was demolished by Cromwell's men. The remains, in the grounds of a modern house at the edge of the village, include the 75-ft mound on which the keep stood, some curtain wall and the roofless 12th- and 15th-cent. gatehouse. St Mary's Church, considered one of the finest in the West Riding, has a 124-ft tower noted for its graceful arcades and pinnacles. The church is of the 13th to 15th cents. with many beautiful details and furnishings. A tomb-chest with effigies of Thomas Fitzwilliam, who died in 1478, and his first wife is dated about 1530 and follows the Italian Renais-sance style. It was formerly in the Friary, at the west end of town, once part of the Austin Friars house founded in the 13th cent. St Leonard's Hospital, a fine 1470 timbered house, is now the parish room. The Maison Dieu almshouses were believed founded by John of Gaunt. In the market place is a 1766 cross consisting of a dome over eight columns on steps.

WAKEFIELD, *West Riding* (12–SE3320). An important weaving and dyeing centre as far back as the 13th cent., Wakefield did not grow quite so highly industrialized as other south Yorkshire towns. In the mid-19th cent. it was the chief grain market (the Corn Exchange, built in 1838, was reckoned the best building in town, but was demolished in 1963 just the same) and it also became the administrative headquarters of the West Riding. Wakefield builders have been fond of towers and turrets, which give the place an interesting skyline as it spreads up the hillsides from the River Calder. The Cathedral Church of All Saints, completed in 1329, then pulled down and rebuilt in the 15th cent. (and altered again in the 19th and 20th), added its 247-ft spire, the highest in Yorkshire, in 1861. The clock tower on the 1880 Town Hall on Wood Street rises 200 ft and the County Hall, opened in 1898, has a 130-ft dome. The city centre is the Bull Ring, re-developed with modern shops and flower-beds. The cathedral towers overhead. Kirkgate leads to the Old Bridge, a nine-arch stone structure with a tiny chantry chapel, St Mary's, the best example in England. Traffic now flows over the New Bridge of 1933. The chapel is 14th-cent. and was heavily restored by Sir George Gilbert Scott. The original west front was removed and now stands in the Kettlethorpe Hall grounds. The chapel has lovely traceried windows, pinnacled buttresses and an embattled turret.

Some good Georgian houses remain, for example those on South and West Parades behind Kirkgate on a green square and in the northern parts of the city. In 1954, the city bought New-millerdam, a suburb to the S. with a lake noted for bird life. The grassy mounds marking the site of the castle at Sandal are now part of the city, too. St Helen's Church nearby is chiefly 14th-cent.

Three estates have been combined to give Wakefield a central 130-acre park with a chestnut-lined drive, 6,000 roses and an alpine garden near Holmefield House which now includes a licensed café. The Art Gallery in Westworth Terrace has a large collection of drawings of Yorkshire and fine modern sculpture.

Only a mile from the city centre is Heath Common, a rough open space around which were loosely gathered three houses of major archi-tectural importance, one Elizabethan and two Georgian. **Heath Hall,** however, is the only one to get needed attention. It was rescued after 50 years of neglect by Mr and Mrs Muir M. Oddie and is open to visitors at intervals. The central part of the handsome grey stone block was built in the early 18th cent. and then incorporated into a much grander design of John Carr in the 1750s. As completed, it is 11 bays wide with detached pavilions on either side. Among the finely restored rooms, the drawing-room is the most elaborate with its dashing stucco work. The Hall was once the home of the eccentric Charles Waterton.

John Carr, the son of a mason, was born in 1723 at **Horbury,** SW. of Wakefield. He designed and built the church there, and paid for it, in 1794. He died in 1807 and is buried in the churchyard.

Whitby is still an active fishing port

WENSLEY, *North Riding* (12–SE0989), has given its name to a dale (the other Yorkshire dales are named after their rivers) and a cheese. Wensleydale is a large and fertile valley drained by the River Ure, and Wensley, now a small village, was once its market town. It has a gentle valley site. Houses, church and the gates to Bolton Hall, a mile away through the park, all face the sloping green. Holy Trinity Church has been called the best in the dales. It is chiefly 13th- and 14th-cent. Among its possessions is an old chest, possibly a reliquary from EASBY Abbey which may have held the bones of St Agatha; a finely carved roodscreen, quite likely from the same source, which is now situated behind the Bolton box pew; and a late 14th-cent. brass to a priest, Sir Simon de Wenslaw.

WHITBY, *North Riding* (15–NZ8911). The sound of gulls, the smell of fish, the sight of red roofs up the steep banks from the quay and above the ruin of the abbey on the cliff – this is Whitby. The River Esk, emptying here into the North Sea, divides the town. The older part is on the East Cliff, under the abbey. The West Cliff is a 19th-

cent. development along the sands, and connected to the harbour by the romantically named Khyber Pass cut through solid rock. Whitby is still a port and fishing town – fishermen still mend their nets by the harbour – but it reached its seafaring peak with the whaling in the 18th cent. Although it is increasingly a holiday town, it still has little of the artificial feeling of resorts with no other industry and little history; there is character here and an exhilarating sense of place. Whitby's story probably goes back to a Roman signal station and certainly dates to 657 when St Hilda founded the abbey for King Oswy of Northumbria in thanks for his victory over the heathen Penda of Mercia. The Synod of Whitby of 664 committed the English Church to the Roman instead of the Celtic rite. Both men and women lived in the early monastery, a renowned centre of learning. This is where the herdsman Caedmon was inspired to sing of Creation. The abbey was destroyed by the Danes in 867 and not refounded until 1078 by the Benedictines. It flourished then until its surrender in 1539. The property went to the Cholmley family. The Ministry of Public Building and Works has had custody since 1921. The monastic buildings have virtually disappeared but the church was not so much pulled down as blown away. The lead was taken from the roof but the building left as a seamark, familiar to sailors. In its cruelly exposed position, it could not last. Nave, south transept, west front and central tower had collapsed by 1830, and in 1914 came a final indignity – shelling by the German fleet.

St Mary's Parish Church is at the top of 199 steps near the ruins. It is a large medieval church with a low Norman tower, but drastically altered by the Georgians. It is full of galleries and box pews, with a three-decker pulpit presiding.

The 1788 Town Hall, off Church Street, has its ground floor open for traders, behind Tuscan columns. The home of the great navigator, Captain James Cook, is marked by a plaque in Grape Lane. The handsome Georgian Mission to Seamen is in Haggersgate and the Museum and Art Gallery in Pannett Park contains one of the country's finest fossil collections. More jet, or fossilized wood, is found in the Whitby area than anywhere else in Britain. It was especially popular with Victorians and in 1873, 200 workshops were kept going here. A few craftsmen still work in jet.

YARM, *North Riding* (15–NZ4112), has a strong 18th-cent. feel, perhaps rightly so since that was its greatest period. Today's small market town and gateway to the North Riding on the River Tees is up until two centuries ago the main port of Teesside, busily exporting corn and lead. It was displaced by STOCKTON in the 18th cent. Granaries close to the river are one of the few reminders of this past. It was also prominent as a coaching stop and in 1848 it had 16 inns and public houses. There are still eight in the High Street. The oldest is the Ketton Ox, possibly 400 years old, and named after a shorthorn reared near DARLINGTON which weighed 220 stone when it was slaughtered in 1801. This inn was known for cockfighting. The cockpit was in a second-floor room. When the sport was made illegal in 1849, another room was used with a trap door to permit escape if the place was raided. At another inn, the George and Dragon, the first meeting of promoters for the Stockton and Darlington railway was held in 1820.

The bridge which links Yarm and County Durham was built in 1400 by Bishop Walter Skirlaw and quite naturally has been much repaired. Another connection is the 43-arch railway viaduct designed by Thomas Grainger in 1849. Yarm's High Street is wide and cobbled, with tall terraces of brick houses bordering it. The Town Hall was built in 1710 and two of the churches date from that building period. St Mary Magdalene was rebuilt in 1730 and still has a Norman west front and tower. Its interior is Victorian except for a stained-glass window by William Peckett and the Venetian east window. The octagonal Wesleyan Chapel in Capel Wynd was built in 1763, and Wesley himself pronounced it very elegant.

YORK (13–SE6052). The fascinating townscape of this walled city illustrates much of its nearly 2,000 years of history. Although York possesses in its minster the largest medieval church in northern Europe, the general scale of its buildings is small and human. York lies at the juncture of the three Ridings but belongs administratively to none. Historically it has been similarly independent, acting as a regional capital more often than as a county one and bypassed almost entirely by the Industrial Revolution. Even today York seems more medieval than almost any other English town. The compact core is a treasure-house for anyone interested in history, architecture or ancient crafts, and it is best seen on foot. For a good introduction, join one of the 1½-hour walks, led by a voluntary guide, which start twice a day in summer from the City Library.

The Romans, who called the place Eboracum, built a fort in A.D. 71, the headquarters for their campaigns in the unruly North for three centuries. Constantine the Great was proclaimed emperor here in 306. York has been a garrison town ever since – it is now the headquarters of Northern Command. For the sightseer, a multi-angular tower remains from Roman York, the west corner of the Roman fortress. The inside of this fine ruin can be seen beside the City Library (and Information Centre) in Museum Street and the outside from Museum Gardens. The Museum of Natural History at the top of the gardens and the Hospitium down the slope contain important relics of Roman occupation, including a superior statue of a legionary and the hair of a Roman lady.

Under the Angles, York was capital of their Kingdom of Deira; King Edwin was baptized here by Paulinus, who became the first Archbishop of York in 634; and a grammar school was founded by the great Alcuin. The Danes captured and burnt York in 867 and it was their capital in England for nearly 100 years; they called it Jorvik and it is from this that the present name derives. Anglo-Saxon and Danish York left nothing to see, but the use of "gate" for street is a reminder that the Danes settled here; Goodramgate has been said, but not proved, to be named after Guthrum, the Danish leader defeated by Alfred. The Normans found a thriving little trading centre and burnt it in 1069, during their frightful ravaging of the North, and then rebuilt the walls, expanding them to take in the present 263 acres. They erected two castles. The Norman period saw the founding of most of the institutions which flourished through the Middle Ages, but the existing remains of them are chiefly of later date. There is a partial Norman house off Stonegate, however, newly restored. In Gray's Court, now part of St John's College, the original Treasurer's House was built.

Medieval York is everywhere, not least in the web of narrow streets. The Shambles and Stonegate are two of the best preserved examples. But the minster is the city's chief glory, appropriate to the dignity of an archbishopric. Built between 1220 and 1470, at least the fourth church on that site, it is a textbook of Early English, Decorated and Perpendicular styles. Since 1967, it has been

J. Allan Cash

York: (above) *a view of the minster from the city walls;* (below) *the Merchant Adventurers' Hall*

G. Douglas Bolton

the object of a £2 million rescue operation to strengthen the foundations and prepare it for another few centuries. It contains England's greatest concentration of medieval stained glass, principally from the 13th and 14th cents. The two most famous windows are the Five Sisters and the magnificent 15th-cent. east window, largest in the world. The minster's length is 518 ft and it is 241 ft wide at the transept. The central tower rises 198 ft and is the largest lantern tower in Britain. The 14th-cent. chapter house, with seven lovely window walls, has no central support for its conical roof, just the great buttresses on the eight sides. Rebuilding the present minster, around its Norman predecessor, began with Archbishop Walter de Gray, who was responsible for construction of the transept in the new Early English style in the mid-13th cent. It was so vast that the nave was enlarged by the mid-14th cent. This was followed by the chapter house around 1340. The choir was completed by 1400 and its great climax, the east window, with 2,000 sq. ft of ancient glass by John Thornton of COVENTRY, was finished in 1408. The massive towers came last.

To the E. of the minister is the half-timbered St William's College, the 15th-cent. home of the chantry priests, now the headquarters of the Northern Convocation. In the Civil War, it was the location of a Royalist printing press. From the 11th cent. onwards, some 40 parish churches sprang up in York. An embarrassing number (considering the upkeep problems) survive. Each has a particular interest but the visitor unfortunately short of time might well choose 15th-cent. All Saints, North Street, and its unique windows and medieval woodwork. Three of the nine guildhalls survive, and the Merchant Adventurers' in Fossgate, dating from the 14th cent., gives perhaps the clearest picture of how powerful these institutions were.

The scant 13th-cent. remains of St Mary's Abbey form a backdrop in Museum Gardens for the triennal performance of the York Mystery Plays, and the abbot's house is the nucleus of the rambling King's Manor facing Exhibition Square. This is one of York's most fascinating buildings, restored now by the university, after many years as a school for the blind. It was the seat of the Council of the North after the Dissolution and in its patchwork fabric records many chapters of civic history. Above all, the city walls are medieval, rebuilt on the old Roman and Norman foundations in the 13th cent. A 2½-m. footpath on the walls gives a circular tour (with a few gaps) of the city, passing the four remaining "bars", Micklegate, Bootham, Monk and Walmgate.

In the Middle Ages, York was England's second city, a great religious and commercial centre, fattening on the wool trade. The economic impact of the Dissolution was cushioned by the establishment here of the Council of the North. When this was abolished in the 17th cent., York declined. It revived in the 18th cent. as a social centre for county families. The race-course on the Knavesmire and the Theatre Royal both opened in the 18th cent., and continue to be magnets

today. York saw a great burst of new building in the 1700s, and a whole school of craftsmen made the city known.

Georgians left a pronounced impression on York, particularly in the former town houses along such streets as Micklegate and Bootham. Notable public buildings of the 18th cent. include the Mansion House, Assembly Rooms, Judge's Lodgings, and Assize Courts. The early 18th-cent. Debtors' Prison and the later Female Prison, almost equally grand, now house the justly famous Castle Museum with its period rooms and streets. The Mansion House is the official residence of the Lord Mayor, but can be seen (along with the exceptionally large collection of civic plate) by arrangement. Just behind it is the 15th-cent. Guildhall, bombed in 1942 but restored in 1960.

Victorian York saw the start of the confectionery industry, now the biggest employer, and the establishment of the railway centre here thanks to its enterprising citizen, George Hudson. The station is a superb example of graceful iron construction and the Railway Museum nearby has 12 famous locomotives that children can clamber on.

The City Art Gallery in Exhibition Square, of 1878 vintage, contains a good collection of old masters and work by William Etty, a York man, famous for his nudes in the 19th cent.

The University of York opened in 1963, taking over an Elizabethan manor house and estate at Heslington village where a completely modern complex has grown up around an artificial lake. The university is a collection (five at present) of colleges each with teaching and residence facilities. Economics, English, history and education are major departments. The music department with its own fine concert hall offers an extensive public programme.

At **Bishopthorpe**, 2½ m. S. of York, is the Archbishops' palace, which includes traces of an Early English structure. Excursion boats from York's Lendal Bridge take visitors past the palace on the River Ouse.

YORKSHIRE DALES NATIONAL PARK, *North and West Ridings* (12–SD9080). Some 680 sq. m. of the two Ridings were set aside in 1954 as a National Park. High fells, moors of heather and bracken, limestone screes, scars and outcrops, richly wooded dales, swift becks, tumbling forces and unpretentious grey-stone villages all combine to produce truly refreshing landscapes. First-time visitors will be nervous about the drystone walls that so closely border the twisting roads in many places. There are steep gradients and upland sheep abound. It is not much use planning for average speeds above 20 to 25 m.p.h. The park takes in much of the central Pennines and the **Pennine Way** from Derbyshire to Scotland passes through it. Fishing, nature and archaeological studies, potholing, walking, ponytrekking and just plain viewing are the natural activities for the Dales. There is an information centre at the Reading Room in CLAPHAM.

The North-East

Durham   Northumberland

THOMAS SHARP

Northumberland and Durham are more than merely two neighbouring counties. Physically they are a kind of north-eastern "peninsula" of England. Some hundred miles of sea constitute their eastern boundary. On the north the broad Tweed and the mass of the Cheviot Hills cut them off from Scotland in a fifty-mile stretch crossed by only half a dozen roads. Down the west, forty miles of Pennines crossed by five mountain roads and one valley road separate them from the similar "peninsula" containing the two neighbouring north-western counties. Only at the southern boundary, where the lowland country of south Durham shades into the North Riding of Yorkshire, is the physical form of the "peninsula" open enough to give it a firm regional attachment to the rest of England.

Physically isolated in this way, the two counties have had close historical associations. From Roman times onward Northumberland was the frontier land of England's northern boundary, defended first by the legionaries of the Roman Wall and then later, through medieval times, by the Prince Bishops of Durham, whose jurisdiction extended, indeed, to detached pockets of Northumberland itself in the palatinate areas around Norham and Bedlington. Then, later, the winning of coal and the industrial development subsequently associated with it brought something like economic and social unification to at least their adjoining lowland areas. So today the close past and present relationship is expressed, among other ways, in the existence of such bodies as the Durham and Northumberland Miners Association, the Northumberland and Durham Association, the Northumberland and Durham Travel Association, and so on.

Yet, associated though they are in these many ways, the two counties have their marked individual characteristics and qualities. Even their historical development, though related, differed markedly – and indeed inevitably – because of the relationship itself. County Durham, secure behind the defensive works and the frontier lands of its northern neighbour, and under the control of its Prince Bishops, was settled and peaceful centuries before Northumberland achieved that condition. It was the need for peace and security that drove the early saints and scholars down to Durham from that great cradle of early Christianity in England at Holy Island. And it was the combination of the affairs of church and state-defence that established the Prince Bishops in the Durham palatinate after the Norman Conquest. Here they ruled like the kings themselves, and in their name. They had their own parliament, their own coinage. They gave licences to crenellate castles. They bade their subjects to military service, levied taxes, administered their own laws. So they continued all down the medieval centuries; the palatinate, with its powers slowly reduced over the years, continuing, indeed, until comparatively recent times, and not being finally abolished until 1836, with vestiges of it continuing even today.

Under the comparative peace of this protected part of the frontier, agriculture developed, inclosure proceeded; and County Durham got the landscape pattern it shows today in its small-to-medium-sized fields, hedged in its lowland parts, stonewalled in its hill country, together with the frequent villages and the small market-towns of a settled moderately-populated countryside – to which, of course, over the last century, has been added, in the coalfield which occupies much of its lowland area, the thickly scattered villages and half-towns, and the other physical appurtenances, of mining.

Northumberland was still wild and unsettled hundreds of years after County Durham was more or less secure. The raiding, pillaging and murder that for centuries had ravaged the county as far down as the Tyne valley, officially ended with the Act of Union between England and Scotland in 1707: but, even for some time following that, raiding by the county's own moss-troopers and rival families was not unknown. Against this war and raiding the powerful families lived in great castles and the lesser gentry in peel-towers, where the humbler folk took refuge, if they could, while their huts were being burned and their cattle and horses carried off. A catalogue of 1541, covering only part of the county, listed no less than 120 castles of various types. Under conditions of that kind there could be little agricultural development. It was not until well into the eighteenth century that Northumberland was brought into settled agricultural use. Then the making of roads, the draining of moorland farms, the planting of woods and the inclosure of the waste lands began to bring the countryside towards the appearance that it is seen in today. Late though the beginning of that transformation was, it was long in completion. Even as late as the 1770s, at least half the county was still in a waste state: and it was not until well into the nineteenth century that the transformation of all the cultivable lands from waste to cultivation was accomplished. So it is probably true to say that in large part the agricultural landscape of Northumberland is the newest (or the least old) of any in England. And, even so, transformation in some parts goes on again today, in the ecological-economic revolution that the Forestry Commission is making in the planting of its great new hill-country forests – the most extensive in the country.

This fashioning of the Northumberland landscape did not come about solely out of the opportunity afforded by settled conditions. The manner in which the opportunity was taken had a decisive effect on the special scenic character that the landscape developed. Its character over large areas even today is of landowners' landscape. Many of the old landowners of the great castles played their part in its creation. But newcomers also moved in to take over some of the old estates, particularly those which were confiscated from supporters of the Stuart cause. These newcomers were people who had made their fortunes in the coal and shipping trades of Tyneside and the developing industries associated with them. So the improvement of the rest of the Northumbrian countryside was largely created out of the spoliation of one small corner of it.

The landscape that resulted from these changes is very different from the landscape of the neighbouring county. Whereas the feeling of the Durham countryside, even in the mining areas, is of medium-sized hedged fields with hedgerow trees (small and stunted as they often are), or of stone-walled fields in the hill country, that of Northumberland is much more open – often, indeed, wide-open – with large fields and relatively fewer trees, except in the river valleys or in the parklands of the mansions and castles. There is still a strong feeling of feudalism in the Northumbrian countryside – not of feudal landscape, of course, but a sense and an evidence of large estates seen not only in the parklands and in glimpses of castles and large country houses, but in the number of hamlets at or near park-gates – tidy groups of estate-cottages that have a character of their own. And the sense of quiet and remoteness which still characterizes the county (away, at least, from the main roads) must arise out of this combination of conditions that brought it into being in its present form – the sparseness of its population in the lawless times and the manner of its establishment through the agency of large estates. For Northumberland, outside the industrialized corner of Tyneside, is still the quietest and most sparsely populated county in England. In all that wide area there are only five or six small towns and less than a dozen substantial villages. For the rest, such population as there is is either gathered into insignificant hamlets or thinly scattered in isolated cottages and farm-houses.

This past history has been described at some length because here, more than in most parts of England, it illuminates the striking differences of the effect of human exploitation in two neighbouring counties that are historically closely associated. The combination of this human exploitation and the physical terrain upon which it has been imposed creates the individual kinds of countryside in which the counties show their differences.

Leaving aside the industrial areas for the moment, it can be said that there are some six or seven distinctive kinds of scenery here. The two coasts themselves differ. Between the level lands and the wide sandy beaches at the estuaries of the Tees, the Wear and the Tyne, the 25-mile-long Durham coastline is of low cliffs with few appreciable bays. It is not naturally very interesting, and the industrial additions to it have not made it more attractive. The Northumberland coastline is generally lower, except at the one or two places where the Whin Sill that slashes across the county ends in iron-hard dolerite cliffs, as at Cullernose, Dunstanburgh and Bamburgh. Most of it is pitched up into sandhills; there are miles of splendid accessible sands running down to the sea; and the succession of large and small bays, headlands with castles, and offshore islands with lighthouses on them, makes it a coast that has a good deal of incident and variety.

Back from the sea, right up from Tyne to Tweed and almost as far west as the Great North Road, there is a low-lying coastal plain. It is bleakly industrialized for the first dozen miles from Tynemouth; with, further on, scattered collieries and (in the late 1960s) occasional heavy disturbances by open-cast coal-workings – which will no doubt be restored when the available coal has been won. But beyond Warkworth it is land of a very special quality, land which is considered by many people to be the richest fattening ground in England. Here, and back some way towards the hills, in the cattle-sheep-and-barley country of highly-mechanized mixed farming, farms are large (750 acres not being considered a particularly big farm there), and the countryside tends to be wide and somewhat open, though well hedged and diversified with hedgerow trees and patches of woodland.

Back from the coastal plain, between Alnwick and Chollerford, is a large triangle of upland-feeling country, rather bare-seeming for much of the year, with fewer trees, and those mostly late-leafing ash. And then, for the rest of this part of Northumberland (by far the greater part), as far down as where the South Tyne valley constitutes the Tyne Gap, there are the hills – the wide rolling lonely range of the Cheviots.

Something like two-thirds and more of the two counties is hill country – hill country of two distinct kinds. These Cheviots are not moorlands in the ordinary sense, nor whale-backed hills. They are more bumpy, with individual summits; and there is not much heather on them. More generally (except now in the large areas of Forestry Commission plantations) they are covered with the fine bent grass that takes changing colour from varying wind, sun and cloud. The highest

Barnaby/Mustograph

The Cheviot Hills

of them, Cheviot itself, though impressive with its 2,678 feet of height, is perhaps lumpish rather than of fine outline. But others have more peak-like outlines among the general wave-like crests, like Yeavering Bell, Hedgehope and Peel Fell. And the subsidiary range of the Simonsides especially has a pronounced wave-like character.

The lesser rivers of the northern Cheviots, College Burn, Harthope Burn, the Breamish and others, run in narrow dales. And so does the Coquet in its upper reaches. But the more substantial rivers, the Rede, the North Tyne, and the South Tyne as far up as Haltwhistle where it turns in from the south, run in wider more open-sided valleys rather than true dales. The true dales belong to the other type of hill country, where again a difference in the two counties is shown.

Not that Northumberland has no Pennine country. As has been indicated, it has a very substantial knob of it southwards of the main South Tyne valley. There, and over the whole of the western half of County Durham, the whale-backed Pennine moors are for the most part heather-covered, and are deeply indented by narrower dales. The Northumberland dales of this part, those of the South Tyne, the West Allen and the East Allen, are richly wooded in their lower reaches towards the main Tyne valley, and bare in their upper miles. The Durham dales of the Wear and

Crown Copyright

Hadrian's Wall at Housesteads in Northumberland

the Tees are rather more open and have more of the typical patterns of stone-walled fields which give such individuality to Pennine country.

Those are the main types of landscape in the two counties. There remains a smaller lowland countryside of mixed farming in south Durham between the mining area and the lower Tees valley. And, as well as that, the mining and industrial areas themselves.

These, too, differ between the two counties. In Northumberland the nearly-twenty-mile stretch along the Tyne from Heddon-on-the-Wall to Tynemouth constitutes a practically continuous urban sprawl. And it is much the same on the Durham side of the valley from Blaydon to South Shields. But the mining areas behind these show some differences in kind. On the level Northumberland land the pit villages seem to stretch out and run together more than those south of the river. The Durham coalfield extends further back into the county (though in the south-western part mining is now almost completely dead). Its surface, right back from the coast, is more broken, has a more upland feeling. Its pit villages are somewhat less contiguous, and many of them are centred on the older villages and hamlets of the earlier-settled countryside. But in both counties these industrial districts have the sad and forlorn ugliness that characterizes all the older indus-trialized areas of England, though perhaps here it is less oppressive than in most.

Except for some most notable examples, as in a few still comparatively un-corrupted old towns, building in the two counties is not of any very high quality. Durham city, Berwick, Alnwick, Hexham still have an attractive general character; and the Grainger-built section of Newcastle is an example of central city planning and building that is unique in Britain. But most of the older places are sadly corrupted – Stockton, whose wide High Street must once have been especially pleasant; Sunderland become nondescript; Darlington ditto; Old Hartlepool a ruin; North Shields almost derelict; Morpeth vulgarized. Few even of the small towns and older villages off the coalfield have kept their character unblemished – industrial corruption spreads all too easily beyond its own boundaries. In Northumberland, in any case, because of its late settlement, some of the few villages and most of the scattered hamlets have little obvious historical character. They are apt to be somewhat dour and hard-faced. Many, perhaps most, even of the churches – country as well as town churches – are late and austere; nineteenth-century-new in Northumberland because of the late settlement; nineteenth-century-restored-and-rebuilt or newly built in County Durham because of the rapidity of the industrial expansion of that time. Perhaps the most consistently attractive district of buildings in relation to landscape is the Teesdale area of County Durham – and that due to a policy of estate management rather than architectural quality. There, on the Raby estates and in their neighbourhood, running up from east of Staindrop to the hill country of the county boundary, groups of white- or cream-washed farm-houses and farm buildings delightfully enliven and humanize the landscape – an effect charmingly seen in small unfrequented Langleydale immediately west of Staindrop, as well as in Teesdale itself.

In spite of the moderate quality of most of its ordinary buildings, the genius of the county seems to lie in the invention and making of things rather than in the pursuit of any of the creative arts. Invention in building, too, at an earlier time: for it was in Durham Cathedral that the first developments were made towards the Gothic style of architecture which came to characterize so many of the cathedrals and churches of western Europe. But mainly it has been in machines and utilities – for the winning of coal to begin with, and its transport by sea and land. Colliers for bearing the sea-coal down to London; and, from that, ship-building, with the invention of the first steam turbine. Railways, first for getting the coal to the sea-ports; then, in the Darlington and Stockton railway (the first of its kind in the world), for the carrying of passengers. And, along with these, other engineering inventions: the first large-scale cast-iron bridge (the High Level) at Newcastle; Armstrong's hydraulic engines and armaments; Swan's electric bulb; the first dynamo; and so on through things like the first self-righting lifeboat at South Shields and the first friction matches at Stockton. And invention has lain not only in inanimate things but in living ones, too: the famous Durham Ox, bred by Charles Colling at his farm near Darlington, the father of the whole short-horn breed throughout the world; the dairying rather than the beef-producing type of that animal developed by Thomas Bates at Halton in the Tyne valley; the Cheviot sheep (the unconscious instrument of the Highland clearances) developed in the hills by a farmer called Robson; and, more domestically, that canine curiosity, the woolly-coated terrier named after Bedlington.

They are mixed counties, these. Town building at its best (in Newcastle) and near its worst in scores of industrial places concentrated in a comparatively small fraction of the whole. History visible everywhere, even in the industrial areas themselves: but especially in the wide countrysides; in the different agricultural landscapes there as well as in the castles and the battlefields. And, after the stormy history, a peace and a calm now such perhaps as cannot be got in any other part of this country. Here, away from the industrial areas, in these lowlands, these dales, on these remote far-ranging hills and moors, is the widest and least populated, and one of the quietest (as well as one of the most individual) regions in the whole of England.

The North-East: Gazetteer

ELLEN WILSON

ALLENDALE, *Northumberland* (14–NY8455), claims to be the geographical centre of Great Britain. True or false, this is a splendid centre for getting to know the beautiful scenery of the moorland district watered by the East and West Allen Rivers and Allendale to the N. where the two streams meet. Allendale once was the market town for an important lead-mining area. Today it lives on hill farming and holiday-resort business. It is 1,400 ft above sea-level and offers a variety of sport including trout fishing and skiing. Allendale keeps a pagan New Year's Eve custom, well attended by outsiders. Twenty-four masked men, or guisers, march behind a band round the town, carrying barrels of blazing tar on their heads. A fire is lit in the large market place and the tar barrels are thrown upon it. Then the marchers and townspeople dance until midnight, when "first footing" begins. Described in the late 19th cent. as a "straggling, dreary looking place", Allendale in recent years has spruced itself up and repeatedly won county contests for the best-kept village.

ALNHAM, *Northumberland* (14–NT9910). A few scattered houses, a castle site, a fortified former vicarage and an appealing little church make up the hamlet of Alnham today. Three hundred years ago it was an important place at the crossroads of many packhorse and drovers' tracks and at the south end of Salter's Road from Scotland. The vicarage, which dates from 1541 and incorporates the old peel-tower, has been converted into a handsome residence. The grassed-over remains of Alnham Castle, demolished or burnt in 1532, are opposite the church. In the hills round about are several Ancient British camps and earthworks. St Michael and All Angels, standing in a tree-bordered churchyard, has a snug and earthy quality and it retains a sense of age despite several restorations which rescued it from ruin as late as the mid-1960s. A broad (12th-cent.) round arch leads into the chancel, where a fine oak-timbered ceiling adds to the feeling of strength. Four medieval tomb lids have been set in the chancel floor. Near the 1664 font is an unfinished monument. The mason, in 1611, must have grown weary, or bored, when filling the slab with the history and virtues of one George Adder for, about three-quarters of the way down, he decided he had done enough and ended abruptly "and so forth". The River Aln rises near here.

ALNMOUTH, *Northumberland* (15–NU2410). From the WARKWORTH road, there is a striking view of this small red-roofed town piled beside the estuary where the Aln flows into the North Sea. Once an important grain-shipping port (and smugglers' haven, reputedly) it is now a holiday resort with yachting, good sands both N. and S., and one of the oldest golf courses in England. A pleasant walk on the sands leads 3 m. S. to Warkworth past a pile of rocks called Birling Carrs. Alnmouth was the port for ALNWICK in the late 12th cent., and in the early 19th cent. it was still exporting considerable amounts of corn and importing Norway timber. Ships were built here. Some of the granaries were later converted to houses. In a terrible storm on Christmas Day, 1806, the crashing seas broke through the north-east bank of the river and the Aln changed course, pouring into the sea through the new opening on the north side of Church Hill. The harbour was left on the south side where it gradually silted up. Church Hill is the site of an Anglo-Saxon church and the ruins of the later Norman church were finally destroyed by the 1806 gale. Alnmouth is the probable site of the great synod of 684 in which Cuthbert was chosen Bishop of Lindisfarne. The little town witnessed several naval encounters in the 18th-cent. war with France and in 1779 it was itself bombarded. The American John Paul Jones, who had been cruising along the coast, fired a cannon at the old church. He missed, and the cannon-ball, weighing 68 lb, hit the ground, bounced three times and crashed into the end of a farm-house. Beacon Hill N. of the town is an Ancient British camp.

ALNWICK, *Northumberland* (15–NU1912), still looks like a stronghold of the Earls and Dukes of Northumberland. You may enter from the S. through a narrow medieval arch of Hotspur Tower and within moments confront the great barbican guarding the gateway to Alnwick Castle. From the Lion Bridge on the N. the castle appears all-powerful and brooding. Within the town, age speaks from the narrow streets, cobblestones, passageways, sturdy grey buildings and monuments. Alnwick is 4 m. from the coast and on the A1 almost exactly halfway between NEWCASTLE-UPON-TYNE and BERWICK-UPON-TWEED, a convenient centre for touring and a destination in its own right. It grew up on the River Aln beside the great border castle whose walls enclose 7 acres. Below and around the castle are grounds landscaped in 1765 by Capability Brown, forming a beautiful park. The Pastures, the riverside section of the castle grounds, has a footpath

Noel Habgood

Alnwick Castle has hardly changed outwardly since the 14th cent.

leading from the 18th-cent. Lion Bridge to the CRASTER road, with views of the castle along the way.

The castle was begun by the de Vesci family in the early 12th cent. The last of the legitimate line died in 1297 leaving the castle in trust for a natural son. The trustee was the Bishop of DURHAM, who sold the castle to Henry Percy in 1309 and, it is said, pocketed the money. The castle was elaborated and strengthened during the years of border warfare, then stood a ruin for nearly 200 years. The 1st Duke of Northumberland restored it in the 18th cent. with James Paine and Robert Adam. In the mid-19th cent., the 4th Duke employed Anthony Salvin to make extensive changes in the interior. Most of the Adam work was removed and an Italian Renaissance style adopted. Outwardly, however, the castle has not altered much since the 14th cent. The great walls, huge keep and flanking towers make it one of the more spectacular sights in the country. The exceptionally fine barbican, topped with figures which look as if they had just raced there to take up their guard duties, now leads into the present ducal residence and a teachers' training college. Visitors are admitted at advertised times to such apartments as the armoury in Constable's Tower, the museum of British and Roman antiquities in Postern Tower, the keep, and many splendidly furnished rooms including the library, largest room in the castle, and grand staircase.

In the town, a broad main street, with sloping, tree-shaded cobblestone parking space alongside, passes near a market square. A free-standing 18th-cent. hall has an arcade for shops in the ground floor and assembly rooms upstairs.

The first object to greet the traveller arriving from the S. is the Percy Tenantry Column, an 83-ft fluted monument erected in 1816 by grateful tenants because their rents had been reduced during a period of agricultural depression. A Percy lion with straight, stiff tail stands majestically on the top. The column is sometimes known as "The Farmers' Folly" because, so the story goes, the duke was surprised to find his tenants were rich enough to afford such a tribute and raised their rents again.

On the other side of Alnwick is St Michael's Church, said to be the most important 15th-cent. work in Northumberland. It stands on a hillside overlooking the river. The battlemented tower is stoutly buttressed in steps and the church is wide, with aisles running the full length of nave and chancel. Among the interesting contents are two 14th-cent. tombs with figures of a man in a tunic and a lady, a third medieval figure which appears to be a cleric, and a handsome 14th-cent. Flemish carved chest.

In a town so dominated by its castle, two well-known schools are named, appropriately, the Duke's School and the Duchess's School. An Old Ragged or Industrial School Foundation still educates needy boys and girls. The Bondgate Gallery regularly exhibits the work of living artists. Fishing tackle is manufactured here.

The remains of HULNE PRIORY are 3½ m. NW.

ALWINTON, *Northumberland* (15–NT9206). An unusual split-level church with a tall west end and pointed bell turret stands on a hillside S. of this hamlet tucked into a hollow of the CHEVIOT HILLS where the Alwin and the Coquet rivers meet. The Church of St Michael has remnants of its original fabric dating from the late 11th cent., but most of it is 13th-cent., considerably restored in the 19th. The chancel is 10 steps above the nave, and a crypt housing Selby family tombs is under the elevated portion. Clennell table tombs are in the north aisle. The path leading to the church door is paved with interesting gravestones and it leads through a well-kept churchyard with a good view of the gently rounded hills. Near the gate is a little stone-roofed stable where the parish hearse is stored. It was bought in 1840 for £9 and is rarely used today for lack of horses strong enough to pull it. The handsome wooden body surmounted by an urn stands on wheels large enough to pass through fords or deep snows. There is good angling and walking in the vicinity, and the Coquet river-bed has been known to yield agates, cornelians and pebble crystals. One walk follows old Clennell Street, the drovers' road, to the Scottish border at Russell's Cairn on top of Windy Gyle, 2,034 ft high. The cairn is named after Lord Francis Russell who was murdered by Scots at a border meeting in 1585. Sir Walter Scott stayed at the Rose and Thistle in Alwinton when he was working on *Rob Roy*. Alwinton has a famous sheep show and hound trials each October. There are remains of prehistoric camps and earthworks in the area.

AYCLIFFE, *Durham* (15–NZ2822). An ancient church is the chief reminder of the long history of this limestone quarry village N. of DARLINGTON. The future doubtless will centre at Newton Aycliffe nearby, a new town for workers from a trading estate which was developed out of a wartime munitions works. St Andrew's Church has interesting relics of its Anglo-Saxon foundation, although most of the present structure is 12th- and 13th-cent., partly rebuilt in 1882. There are remains of two Anglo-Saxon cross shafts, one with crucifixion scenes, which probably were gravestones in the 10th cent. An early 14th-cent. tomb lid with birds and oak leaves is in the north aisle floor and there are attractive 17th-cent. furnishings.

BAMBURGH, *Northumberland* (15–NU1834). No castle could look more imposing than Bamburgh, a magnificent red sandstone mass which presents a startling sight whether approached from N. or S. The road takes the motorist directly under its walls on its land side, while on the other it towers over the sea from a 150-ft precipice. Bamburgh was founded in 547 by King Ida who built a wooden fortification here. It was given by his grandson, Ethelfrith, to his wife Bebba and became known as Bebbanburgh, from which the modern name derives. Although the seat of the government of Northumbria moved in the mid-8th cent. to CORBRIDGE, Bamburgh remained a

royal residence. It was rebuilt in Norman times and by then included a keep, chapel, living quarters and enclosures for the garrison and for prisoners. Much of the castle was restored and altered in the 18th cent. by trustees of Lord Crewe, Bishop of DURHAM, who had acquired the property after marrying into the Forster family. They added a long range of domestic buildings. During the late 18th cent., out of Lord Crewe's beneficence, the castle was used as a boarding school to train servant girls, as a surgery and dispensary for the poor, as the site of a windmill to grind corn for those in need and as a haven for shipwrecked sailors. In 1894, the 1st Lord Armstrong bought the castle and it was again extensively restored. It is open daily and from the upper terraces where the guns still point out to sea, there is a celebrated view of the FARNE ISLANDS.

The castle rises boldly at the apex of a triangular wooded green which is the centre of a still unspoilt and – despite the endless streams of Sunday motorists – peaceful village of soft grey stone. St Aidan's Church is mainly 13th-cent. with a fine and large chancel. During work in 1837, an unusual 13th-cent. crypt was discovered. In it were coffins of the Forster family, who owned Bamburgh and BLANCHLAND. The crypt may have been built originally for relics of St Aidan.

In the churchyard is an over-elaborate monument to the 19th-cent. heroine of the village (and the country) Grace Darling. She was born here in 1815 in the house which is now the post office and she died at the early age of 27, but not before she had engraved her name in the hearts of her own and later generations. She was the daughter of the lighthouse keeper on Longstone Light. On 7 September 1838, the *Forfarshire* was wrecked in a gale. Grace and her father rowed out in the storm to rescue nine survivors. The coble they used and other souvenirs of the heroic event are in the Grace Darling Museum of the Royal National Lifeboat Institution which stands opposite the church.

BARNARD CASTLE, *Durham* (14–NZ0516). Here, on a cliff above the Tees, is a picturesque centre for discovering the delights of Teesdale. The castle was founded by Guy de Bailleul and rebuilt by his nephew, Bernard Balliol, after about 1150. Its ruins cover 6½ acres. The chief survival is the Round Tower, mostly 14th-cent., offering a splendid view which inspired Sir Walter Scott when he was writing *Rokeby*.

The town which grew up outside the castle has two broad main thoroughfares today: Galgate, leading up to the Methodist church and castle entrance, and Market Place, at a right angle to it, with a cobblestone car park and, at the bottom, an octagonal, two-tiered Market Hall or Cross built in 1747. There used to be a lock-up in the centre, shelter for butter-sellers in the colonnaded veranda and an administrative hall upstairs. Charles Dickens stayed at the King's Head Hotel in 1838 while writing *Nicholas Nickleby*. At a corner of the Market Place is St Mary's Church, largely

Norman and Transitional. The west tower is a replacement of 1874. Inside, the 15th-cent. chancel arch, leading into the raised chancel, rests on the head of Edward IV on the left pillar and that of Richard III, who obtained Barnard Castle by marriage, on the right.

Descending The Bank from the Market Cross, the visitor comes to Blagraves House, now a café, a narrow, four-story gabled Tudor house in which Oliver Cromwell may have been entertained with mulled wine and shortcake in 1648. Thorngate still has some interesting 18th-cent. houses. Their long top-floor windows used to light weaving lofts. On the riverside are disused sandstone factories which recall the days when the town was important as a textile and carpet manufacturing centre. It lives now on the work provided by a penicillin factory, on tourism and as a shopping centre. There are lovely riverside walks here, especially to EGGLESTONE ABBEY on the Yorkshire side.

The **Bowes Museum** W. of the town is a surprise however many times you see it. It is a massive 19th-cent. French château designed by Jules Pellechet for John Bowes, son of the Earl of Strathmore, and his wife, a French actress and artist. The couple collected paintings, furniture and ceramics. Both had died by the time their dream of a museum was realized in 1892. The museum was run by trustees until the Durham County Council acquired it in 1956. It stands in a 21-acre park with gardens, bowling green and tennis courts. It claims to house 10,000 beautiful things in 22 exhibition rooms. Notable are paint-ings by El Greco, Goya, Boucher, Courbet, Sassetta and Tiepolo; French 18th-cent. furniture, tapestries, period rooms and a children's room with dolls and doll's houses.

BEADNELL, *Northumberland* (15–NU2329). The harbour walls were built in the drystone wall way, probably in the 1790s when the lime kilns which stand nearby were also constructed. The kilns, a relic of the days when Beadnell shipped coal and lime, belong to the National Trust. There is some crab and lobster fishing and a good holiday trade here. The sandy beaches are excellent and there is safe yachting in the wide Beadnell Bay. A large caravan park shelters behind the dunes. The Craster Arms is built round a 1460 defensive peel-tower. The 1740 church was restored in pseudo-Gothic fashion with an odd pierced octagonal stone screen placed round its short spire in 1860.

BEDLINGTON, *Northumberland* (15–NZ 2581). The Northumberland miners' picnic is held here annually in June in Attlee Park, with march-ing bands, juvenile jazz bands, a beauty contest and an array of politicians. Bedlington was the capital of a shire attached to the Palatinate of DURHAM until 1844. The church's dedication to St Cuthbert refers to the night in 1069 when the Durham monks, carrying the saint's coffin and in flight from the Normans, stopped on their way to Lindisfarne. In 1669 a resident named Cuthbert Watson, locally renowned as a sleepwalker,

Barnard Castle: the Bowes Museum houses a magnificent collection of paintings and works of art

Barnaby/Mustograph

Bellingham stands on the edge of the moors

climbed a buttress, was awakened by a passer-by and fell to his death. A stone inscribed "Watson's Wake" was placed in the north aisle to mark the event. A plaque on the King's Arms hotel marks the birthplace of Sir Daniel Gooch, born in 1816, who laid the Atlantic cables in 1865 and 1866. The extinct Bedlington Iron Works produced the first rolled iron rails, used by George Stephenson's locomotives. Bedlington terriers were bred here for badger baiting. The broad Front Street leads downhill to the River Blyth.

BELFORD, *Northumberland* (15–NU1033). This small town on the A1 has long been a coaching stop for travellers. The centre of Belford climbs a long southward-looking slope off which run streets of stone houses and cottages with a good deal of modern housing growing up around the edges. Entering from the S., the visitor sees on the E. the large park and honey-coloured façade of Belford Hall, designed by James Paine in 1756 for Abraham Dixon, manufacturer and merchant. It was partly remodelled by John Dobson in 1818. Further on, the long, low ivy-covered brick front of the old Blue Bell Inn encloses the view. Belford had a difficult history. It suffered repeated border raids, which accounts for the fact that most of its buildings are relatively modern. As late as 1639 it was described as "the most miserable, beggarly town, or town of sods, that ever was made in an afternoon of loam and sticks". The houses were described as hovels with roofs of heather or sod. Later it became a fox-hunting centre and now it is a market town. To the SW., Belford Moor on the way to WOOLER provides splendid views towards the CHEVIOT HILLS on one side, and the coast on the other.

BELLINGHAM, *Northumberland* (14–NY 8383). People here still like to draw water from St Cuthbert's Well which is supposed to have healing powers (and which is reached by a winding path behind the churchyard towards the North Tyne). The big attraction for many visitors, however, is the curious pack-shaped tombstone in the church-yard, associated with the Legend of the Long Pack. It is told that a pedlar called one day at Lee Hall, the Georgian riverside mansion of a Col. Ridley who had made his fortune in India, and asked for a night's lodging. The colonel was not at home and the maid, Alice, refused the request. But she allowed the man to leave his heavy pack in the kitchen. Some time later she saw the pack move and called for help. A ploughboy fired a shot into the pack and blood poured out. Inside was the body of a young man. The servants realized that a raid was imminent, mustered help and then blew the silver horn found on the body. When the robbers came they were met with force, and fled. The man in the pack was buried, unidentified, in the churchyard.

Bellingham may be plain, as many a border town preferred to be in the days of marauding neighbours, but it is a friendly and accommodating spot and a gateway to the great moors and forests of this area. A special point of interest is St Cuthbert's Church which has a weighty and unique stone roof, well restored in recent years. It is barrel-vaulted with hexagonal stone ribs about a yard apart. The building had to be buttressed in the 18th cent. to counteract the thrust of the roof. The stone slabs were laid after two fires had destroyed wooden roofs. The church has whitewashed walls, narrow deep-splayed windows, a chastely restored and furnished chancel and an air of fortitude. The churchyard overlooks the river and here you can rest in view of the 1835 stone bridge and in sound of the running waters.

The market place is ornamented with a dainty Boer War memorial and handily situated just behind the village hall with its wooden cupola and clock. Next to the hall is a Chinese gingall (a mounted musket) taken in 1900 and presented by Cdr E. Charlton of H.M.S. *Orlando*. The name recalls the town's long prominence as a haunt and target of such rival graynes or clans as the Charltons, Armstrongs, Dodds, Milburns and Robsons in the days when the frontier was in turmoil.

A popular agricultural show is held in September.

BELSAY, *Northumberland* (15–NZ1078). Travellers on the A696 must often wonder about the unusual and attractive sandstone arcade of shops that sets Belsay apart from other villages along the busy NEWCASTLE to Carter Bar route. These Italianate buildings were designed by Sir Charles Monck, assisted by the architect John Dobson, when the village was re-created in the early 19th cent. Nearby, but no longer open to the public, is Belsay Hall, built by Monck in the style of a Grecian temple. The beautiful park includes the ruins of the 14th-cent. Belsay Castle, said to have been the finest English tower house in the North. Stone for the hall was quarried on the grounds and the quarries were later transformed into gardens.

BERWICK-UPON-TWEED, *Northumberland* (14–NT9953). Somewhat seedy, but highly picturesque, Berwick is the northernmost town in England, steeped in history, and fascinating to explore on foot. It is built mainly of stone in grey or pinkish-brown. The roofs are mostly red-tiled and many a street is cobbled. The harbour has swans. The town is piled upon a peninsula at the mouth of the Tweed and it faces the river, rather than the sea. Three great bridges connect it with Tweedmouth on the south side of the estuary: the low stone bridge with 15 arches of varying height and width, completed in 1634; the 1928 concrete span known as the Royal Tweed which carries the heavy vehicular traffic now; and the railway's Royal Border with its 28 soaring arches, completed in 1850. The town is an entrancing sight from the Tweedmouth bank or the railway bridge.

Berwick's well-worn appearance seems to suit its historical rôle as a buffer town. It was an important trading centre and international port and was captured or sacked 13 times before 1482 when it was finally made English. But almost until the Union of the Crowns in 1603, it was regarded on both sides of the border as an English outpost. Until 1746, Berwick had a special status as a free borough and was mentioned separately in Acts of Parliament. (So far as records show, it is still at war with Russia in the Crimea, having been specifically listed as declaring hostilities in 1854 and having been left out of the 1856 peace treaty.) Berwick was part of the ransom paid by the

captured William the Lion of Scotland to Henry II in 1147. It was sold to the Scots by Richard I to get money for his Crusade. It was destroyed in 1216 by King John in person. When William Wallace was executed in 1305 in London, one quarter of him was displayed here as a warning to other rebels. The Countess of Buchan, who had crowned Robert Bruce King of Scotland, was caged for six years in the castle yard from 1306.

Berwick has had two sets of protecting walls and the remains of the later ones give visitors their most interesting circuit of the town. The first walls were completed in the reign of Edward II and little is left of them. The town was then fortified by Elizabeth, starting in 1558, on the new Italian design with great emphasis on effective use of artillery. The Berwick walls are the only example of this style in Britain and among the earliest of the type in Europe. Three of the projecting bastions, shaped like flat arrowheads, remain. Cowport is the only surviving original gate. The high ramparts of earth and stone include Meg's Mount with its superb view of the town, the river and the sea.

In the late 18th cent., the medieval riverside walls were rebuilt with gun emplacements overlooking the river mouth. Most of the old guns were turned into scrap for the Second World War. A pleasant walk along the Quay Walls passes a number of interesting looking buildings, including the Customs House.

The Town Hall, built in the 1750s, is possibly the handsomest building, facing and dominating broad Marygate. Of rich brown stone in a Classical design, it has a grand portico with giant Tuscan columns and a tall spire. The bells of the Town Hall ring for Holy Trinity Church as well as the town curfew. The top floor used to be a gaol and prisoners were aired on the balcony around the roof. The restoration of the hall, which reinstated the butter market in the colonnaded rear ground floor and brought in a coffee bar and small shop, won a Civic Trust award in 1969.

Holy Trinity Parish Church in Wallace Green, which has no bell-tower, was completed in 1652 under Colonel George Fenwick, the Puritan governor, and is one of the few examples of its period. The Barracks were built between 1717 and 1721 in response to town objections to billeting soldiers in public houses. Their design is attributed to Vanbrugh. They contain the museum of the King's Own Scottish Borderers, open to the public.

Little is left of the ancient castle, except for a small ruin of the watch-tower on the riverside near the railway bridge and a length of wall which guarded a flight of steps up the steep bank. Much of the castle stone went into the railway bridge and the station occupies the castle site.

Berwick cockles are an old-fashioned peppermint sweet. Modern industries include the manufacture of puff pastry and components (such as doors and windows) for houses.

BILLINGHAM, *Durham* (15–NZ4624), was transformed from a sleepy village into a thriving industrial complex on Teesside when the chemicals industry, dominated now by Imperial Chemical Industries, developed here after the First World War. The need to produce homemade explosives and fertilizers had been underlined by the German blockade and this location was conveniently near a coalfield and the sea. Looking at the practically all new town, it is hard to think of it as 1,000 years old, but it was founded in the 10th cent. by Edgar, father of Ethelred II. In 1801, its population was only 335; today it is 35,000. The chemicals industry employs some 15,000 highly skilled workers and it has been said that Billingham has a record number of graduates per acre. There is almost an industrial forest of plant, pipe and retort here. The showpiece is the new town centre, with its hotel, shops, offices, library, car park and £1 million Forum, said to be unique in Europe, which provides indoor iceskating, swimming, squash, badminton and a theatre. St Cuthbert's Church symbolizes the marriage of old and new. It was founded in 860 and has a tall, square Anglo-Saxon tower, a long, narrow Anglo-Saxon nave, altered in the 12th cent., and a broad, light chancel completed in 1939.

Billingham was incorporated in the county borough of Teesside in 1968.

BISHOP AUCKLAND, *Durham* (15–NZ 2029). Although the busy commercial and social centre of the south-west Durham coalfield, Bishop Auckland is much older than the Industrial Revolution and has not lost all of its country charm. It is fortunate in having a beautiful open space on its edge. This is Bishop's Park, which surrounds the castle, official residence of the Bishops of DURHAM for more than a century. The bishops had a country residence here from the 12th cent. onwards, and the town grew up round a market at its gates. The 800-acre park, entered through an imposing 1760 gatehouse off the market place, has winding walks, lovely trees and lawns and two small streams, the Gaunless and Coundon Burn. It is open to the public as is the 18th-cent. deer shelter within it. The castle and its splendid chapel, however, are open to visitors only about once a year. Inside the gate, a screen wall designed by James Wyatt about 1800 divides the public park from castle and gardens. The residence began as a Norman manor house and was castellated about 1300. Extensive alterations were made in the 18th cent. The chapel of St Peter is considered an architectural treasure and should not be missed. This was the former banqueting hall. Bishop Cosin converted it into a chapel after 1660 because the original chapel was pulled down by a previous occupant to erect a new mansion on the site. The chapel is late 12th-cent., with tall, wide arcades, shafts of Frosterley marble and limestone, handsome marble arches and mouldings. The elaborate roof and screens are 17th cent. Bishop Cosin died in 1672 and is buried here as he wished under a marble slab in the nave.

St Andrew's Church, well out of the town itself, at South Church, is a choice example of Early English architecture and the largest parish church in the county. It has an Anglo-Saxon cross relic from about 800 with interesting eastern motifs, a holy-water stoup made from a Roman altar, and effigies and a brass of the 14th cent.

Bishop Auckland is seeking new industries to provide alternative employment for displaced miners, and industrial and housing estates are rising everywhere. The urban district includes St Helen's and West Auckland, which are today mainly continuations of the mother town, strung out along a busy road. The largest new trading estate is at **St Helen's Auckland,** a former mining village. It is worth pausing here to visit the church. Small, grimy and yet appealing, it squats beside the road in an overgrown churchyard with a sprawl of commercial development and council houses nearby. It is almost entirely late 12th- and early 13th-cent. with simple round-arched arcades in the nave and small round-headed clerestory windows. St Helen Hall, beside the main road, is an interesting house of the 17th and 18th cents. The one or two other interesting-looking old houses in the neighbourhood seem neglected and doomed.

West Auckland is an old spoiled village round a large green.

BISHOP MIDDLEHAM, *Durham* (15–NZ 3231), was the site of a favourite manor house of the Bishops of DURHAM, and two of them died in it in 1283 and 1316. But by the end of the 14th cent. they preferred BISHOP AUCKLAND. All that is left of the former residence are the grassy mounds S. of the church, St Michael's, which itself is nearly all 13th-cent. It has a large original font of Frosterley marble and an inscription to Robert Surtees, the county historian, who lived at Mainsforth Hall nearby. Surtees' grave is in the churchyard. He died in 1834 and his massive *History and Antiquities of the County Palatine of Durham* was published between 1816 and 1840. Shortly after his death, the Surtees Society for publishing historical works of the North of England was founded as a memorial. Surtees, a kindly country gentleman, was a talented antiquary and scholar. He also had lighter moments. A friend and correspondent of Sir Walter Scott, he once sent the latter a ballad which he claimed to have heard from an old countrywoman. Scott printed it, quite unaware that it was Surtees' own invention. The village today is a centre for farming and quarrying. Outside the Dun Cow Inn at the bottom of Church Street hangs a stone sign, an interesting piece of 18th-cent. folk art.

BLANCHLAND, *Northumberland* (14–NY 9650), has been called one of the most perfect villages of England, and few travellers who drop from the wild moorland around it down into this wooded glen of the Derwent would dispute the label. A medieval gatehouse bars the HEXHAM road and a 19th-cent. stone bridge carries the road out on the opposite side of the village. Charming houses of warm stone surround the L-shaped centre, probably once the outer yard of the old monastery. The Lord Crewe Arms includes parts of what was the abbey guest-house and the later residence of the Forster family. Blanchland, named for the Premonstratensian white canons, dates to the founding of the monastery by Walter de Bolbec in 1165. After the Dissolution, Blanchland fell into decline. The estate was owned first by the Radcliffes and then bought in 1623 by the Forsters of BAMBURGH. It probably was used as a hunting box. A Dorothy Forster in 1699 married Lord Crewe, Bishop of DURHAM, who bought the debt-ridden estate here in 1704. Lady Crewe's niece, the second Dorothy Forster, helped her brother, Thomas, escape from Newgate after he was taken in the Jacobite rising of 1715. She became the heroine of Sir Walter Besant's novel, *Dorothy Forster*, and many of the scenes were laid here and in Bamburgh.

When Lord Crewe died, he left his estates to trustees with the income to go to OXFORD and various schools and almshouses. The Crewe trustees are still in charge. It was they who in the mid-18th cent. used the abbey ruins to rebuild the houses and create the model village seen today. Most of the inhabitants in those days worked in the nearby lead mines. The trustees also rebuilt the abbey church chancel of the 13th cent. as a parish church. This was restored later, in the 19th cent. Three medieval coffin lids in the transept floor are interesting. Two are of abbots and are marked by a pastoral staff and a host and chalice, and the third is of an abbey huntsman, Robert de Eglyston, who was buried under a slab carved with a horn, sword and arrow.

BLYTH, *Northumberland* (15–NZ3181). One of the oddities here is an 18th-cent. lighthouse, once on the shore, and now stranded in the rear of a terrace of houses. Blyth rose to prominence as a coal-shipping port and ship-building centre in the late 19th cent. It never became a seaside resort like some of its northern neighbours, although it has developed a 3-m. stretch of sands which, in 1795, accommodated 7,000 horse and foot soldiers in a fine parade inspected by the Dukes of York and Gloucester under the eyes of 30,000 spectators. With collieries closing down, Blyth of late has sought new industries, and residents are now engaged in manufacturing ladies' underwear, cosmetics, tractors and electronic equipment. They also, of course, work on the docks, and in the remaining pit. Ship-building ended but the production of bridges and industrialized housing began. Two power stations are located here. Blyth got additional encouragement when Alcan Aluminium (U.K.) Ltd began to build its £60 million smelter and power station at **Lynemouth** to the N. and to improve harbour facilities at Blyth for handling alumina cargoes. Lynemouth, with Ellington colliery 6 m. N., forms the largest undersea mine in the world. The Royal Earsdon Sword Dancers of Blyth perform the "rapper" or short sword dance adapted from a Viking rite. Rappers were used in the early coal-mines and the five dancers, fiddler and two clowns dress somewhat like pitmen of 150 years ago.

BOLAM, *Northumberland* (15–NZ0982). It is hard to believe that this was once a village of 200 houses with a market, a fair, a school and an inn. Now there are only a church, a rectory, a few cottages and Bolam House. But Bolam Lake, designed by John Dobson, remains a beauty-spot, with a great variety of flowering shrubs, trees, birds and waterfowl to be enjoyed on a walk round it. St Andrew's Church is mainly Norman, but it has a late Anglo-Saxon tower with triangular-headed belfry windows. It was bombed by a German aircraft during the Second World War. From the churchyard there is a good view of the SIMONSIDE HILLS. Bolam took its name from the Baron de Bolam, the first owner of record in the 13th cent. Stone from the original tower house went into Bolam House. Within walking distance W. are the **Shaftoe Crags**, with a remarkable punch-bowl hollowed out of the flat sandstone rock. Legend describes the Romans making celebratory drinks in it.

BOTHAL, *Northumberland* (15–NZ2386). This pretty Wansbeck hamlet has two points of special interest: the castle and the Church of St Andrew. The small castle is now owned by a BEDLINGTON manufacturer of electrical components and used for entertaining business guests. It was built in 1343 by Robert Bertram. It is the surviving gatehouse, with its twin towers facing the hamlet, which was converted into a residence. Below the castle is the 13th-cent. church which was altered and enlarged in the 14th cent. It has a notable bell turret with three oblong openings. Inside is an angel roof and the worn but impressive alabaster tomb of Ralph Lord Ogle, who died in 1516, and his wife.

BRANCEPETH, *Durham* (15–NZ2238). St Brandon's Church is the place to see "Cosin style" woodwork at its finest. John Cosin, later Bishop of DURHAM, was the rector from 1626 to 1644. He was responsible for the restoration of many parish churches after the Commonwealth, and the carving here, by Robert Barker, is outstanding in the pews, pulpit, screen, choir stalls, font cover and roof. Pevsner calls the Cosin style with its "fully conscious Gothic revival" plus contemporary 17th-cent. elements "one of the most remarkable contributions" of County Durham to English architecture. The church stands in the grounds of Brancepeth Castle and both date from the late 12th cent. The village consists of a few Georgian and later houses at the gates of the castle. From the S., especially, the castle provides a splendid view. Close up, it turns out to be mainly 19th-cent. work, some of it "remarkably incorrect" in the expert view. The castle passed through several families including the Nevilles before it was bought in 1796 by William Russell, a wealthy Sunderland banker who made a fortune from mines. He and his son, Matthew, started rebuilding in 1817 at vast expense. The castle ceased to be a residence in 1922 and today it is a research centre for the Pyrex company in SUNDERLAND.

BRANXTON, *Northumberland* (14–NT8937). S. of St Paul's Church is the historic battleground of Flodden. There on a small knoll in a field stands a plain granite cross erected in 1910 to honour "the brave of both nations". The battle occurred on 9 September 1513, between Scottish and English armies. It was a fierce engagement, and it settled nothing. The Scots were defeated and the losses, by various estimates, were from 9,000 to 16,000 men. Among the slain was James IV of Scotland who had led his troops here to help create a diversion for the French who were under attack at home by Henry VIII and the bulk of the English army. A northern army led by the ailing Earl of Surrey was hastily recruited to meet him. The cross is supposed to mark the spot where James fell. A line of pylons marching in the distance mars the scene today, but inside the small church, the past can be summoned. With its blue painted walls and lino down the aisle it is a homely enough place, but in it one can still imagine the refuge it must have seemed the night James's body was carried in. The corpse next morning was borne to BERWICK to be embalmed, encased in lead and taken finally to London. The slightly pointed arch is the only survival of the original 12th-cent. church structure. The building was virtually re-created in 1849, in a heavy Norman style. The altar rails are of oak taken from a ship which foundered off the FARNE ISLANDS.

BRINKBURN, *Northumberland* (15–NZ1198). One of the loveliest spots in the county is the site of Brinkburn Priory church which, since its 19th-cent. restoration by Thomas Austin of DURHAM, has been called probably Northumberland's best Gothic church. Found SE. of ROTHBURY in a loop of the River Coquet, it is now in the care of the Ministry of Public Building and Works. The church is all that is left of the Augustinian priory founded about 1135 by William de Bertram. It is noteworthy for its spaciousness, lancet windows, stone-vaulted roof and numerous splendid details. During the days of the border troubles, the priory often was disturbed by raids, and on one occasion the monks, believing they had escaped the Scots, rang the bells in jubilation. The joyful peal guided the raiders to the densely wooded and secluded spot which they had inadvertently missed. They threw the bells into a deep pool of the Coquet where they are supposed to lie to this day. A ruined watermill is just E. of the church. There is a tradition that a shady green spot nearby is the burial place of Northumbrian fairies, among the foxglove, woodruff, figwort and other flowers they loved. The Hall, near the church, is in a ruinous state.

BYWELL, *Northumberland* (14–NZ0461), on an enchanting site on the River Tyne, is a village no longer. But here, in witness to a livelier past, are two fine churches, a vicarage, an empty castle, a hall, a medieval market cross and a farm – all framed in trees and meadowland. The story goes that two quarrelling sisters, owners of adjacent manors, founded rival churches within a few yards of each other. But there is nothing to substantiate this account and it is more likely that the manors built neighbouring churches to give the clergy companionship. St Andrew's Church, the "white" church, belonged to Premonstratensian canons of BLANCHLAND. It has the county's best Anglo-Saxon tower, according to Pevsner. It is tall, unbuttressed and has round-headed windows. The body of the church dates from the 13th cent. and the chancel is longer than the nave. Medieval tombstones have been built into the north wall exterior. The larger St Peter's Church has Anglo-Saxon and Norman traces with 13th- and 19th-cent. changes. It is the "black" church because it was served by Benedictine monks of DURHAM. The vicarage is a late 17th-cent. building. The Hall is dated 1760 and was designed by James Paine. The castle is a fine tower house with four turrets from the 15th cent. Bywell in 1570 had 15 shops and was a centre of ironwork, particularly famous for making harness and other gear for the border horsemen. A hundred years later, a visitor reported that the inhabitants rode small horses, wore long beards and dressed with cloaks and swords. By the 19th cent. hardly a handful of houses remained.

CALLALY CASTLE, *Northumberland* (14–NU0509). The present mansion, representing Classical styles from about 1675 to 1835, incorporates a 15th-cent. peel-tower and can be visited on weekends and Bank Holidays. Only three families – Callalys, Claverings and Brownes – have owned the estate 2 m. from WHITTINGHAM since Anglo-Saxon times. The south-west corner includes the medieval tower but it is thoroughly disguised by later building work. According to legend, the Lord of Callaly wanted to build his tower on Castle Hill ½ m. SE. but his wife preferred the sheltered valley. As work began at his choice of site, the determined spouse engaged the steward to pull down every night what the masons had put up by day. Her lord finally decided to sit up all night to find out what or who was responsible. His wife dressed the steward as a wild boar and instructed him to dance wildly around, pulling down the stones and singing a ditty to the effect that only a tower erected where she had wished it would ever stand. The thoroughly frightened lord gave in. Italian stucco artists from WALLINGTON HALL did the plasterwork in the showpiece drawing-room, possibly to the design of James Paine. The first hall was built just E. of the tower in 1619. Robert Trollope of NEWCASTLE designed the late-17th-cent. changes. There were other alterations and additions in Georgian and Victorian times. A false flue in the drawing-room chimney was prepared by the Catholic Claverings for use as a priest's hiding hole.

CAPHEATON, *Northumberland* (14–NZ0380). The road leading off the A696 to the village is lined with magnificent trees and known as Silver Lane. In its vicinity in 1747, a group of workmen found a hoard of Roman coins and silver dishes.

A. F. Kersting

Chillingham church: the Grey monument

Capheaton Hall, which is not open to visitors, was designed by Robert Trollope of NEWCASTLE and built in 1668; it is historically a building of architectural importance. The village, consisting chiefly of a row of low cottages with overhanging front eaves, has a good view over the park with its shallow lake. Swinburnes have lived at Capheaton since the 14th cent. The present hall was built by Sir John Swinburne, whose grandson Algernon Charles spent his holidays here. At WALLINGTON HALL, the future poet met John Ruskin and Dante Gabriel Rossetti and other literary lights.

CHESTER-LE-STREET, *Durham* (15–NZ 2751).

Very old, and not much to show for it. This was the site of an important Roman military station on the River Wear. The church stands where the remains of St Cuthbert rested in a little wooden Anglo-Saxon church from 882 to 995, before they were taken by the monks from Lindisfarne first to RIPON and finally to DURHAM. For these 113 years, the town was the centre of a large diocese. The present church, St Mary and St Cuthbert, was begun in the early 11th cent. and rebuilt in the 13th and 14th. The octagonal tower dates from about 1400. A small stone cell for an anchorite huddles against the north wall of the tower, with a narrow squint into the church. It became an almshouse after the Reformation. Inside on a stone bench along the wall of the north aisle are squeezed 14 effigies of members of the Lumley family, put there in 1594 by John Lord

Lumley. LUMLEY CASTLE is 1 m. E. The town is now a market place for the area. **Lambton Castle**, 1½ m. NE., is a romantic reproduction of a medieval castle, turrets, curtain wall and all. The original was dismantled in 1797 and replaced by a hall which in 1833 was enlarged and castellated. Almost wrecked in 1854 by mining subsidence, it was altered again in 1875. It is now the County Council's adult residential college.

CHEVIOT HILLS, *Northumberland* (14–NT 81).

The great bald domes of the Cheviots are among the most pronounced and the most memorable landmarks in the county. They lie in the north-west corner and form a barrier to Scotland. They offer some of the grandest scenery to be found anywhere. The hills cover 200 sq. m. of Northumberland and spill over another 100 sq. m. into Roxburghshire. The chain extends 35 m. in length. The Cheviots make up the northern third of the NORTHUMBERLAND NATIONAL PARK. The highest among them is Cheviot itself, 2,676 ft above sea-level. The summit here is level and some 50 acres in extent, most of it peat bog. It can be climbed in 1½ hours from Langleeford SW. of WOOLER. But many prefer Hedgehope, 2,348 ft high, which can be climbed in about an hour from Langleeford and rewards the visitor with marvellous views in all directions. Other main hills are Comb Fell, Bloodybush Edge, Windy Gyle, the Schil and Black Hag. The Cheviots look gentle because of their rounded shapes and seemingly smooth, grassy surfaces and they do in fact provide unrivalled walking. But ramblers are warned not to attempt long outings in bad weather and to wear brightly coloured garments to aid searchers, if a search proves necessary. The range is thinly populated, mainly with hill farmers, and there is only about one person to each 350 acres around Cheviot. This is sheep country with a distinctive breed of white-faced sheep. The Cheviots were carved out of one huge mountain by the streams that rise on Cheviot and radiate from it – the Rivers Breamish and Coquet, and the Harthope and College Burns. The waters attract many anglers, and archaeologists are drawn by numerous ancient remains.

CHILLINGHAM, *Northumberland* (14–NU 0625).

A small herd of white cattle, descendants of prehistoric wild oxen, inhabit the wooded park of Chillingham Castle. They are under the watchful care of the Chillingham Wild Cattle Association and can be visited by the public. There were 34 in 1969, surprisingly near the 28 in the herd in 1692 when records began. It is believed that the herd was trapped here when the 600-acre park was walled in 1220. The cattle are small and creamy white. Their crescent-shaped horns are tipped in black and they have black muzzles. They are fleet and shy (but they sent Thomas Bewick, the engraver, up a tree when he was sketching for his Chillingham Bull study).

The castle, home of the Earl of Tankerville, is not open to the public. It was fortified in 1344 and consists of four square angle towers linked by a curtain wall, with domestic buildings added at various later dates. The grand entrance was built in the 17th cent. The grounds were laid out by Sir Jeffry Wyatville, who did WINDSOR Castle, in the early 19th cent.

Chillingham church is a much restored building of 12th-cent. origin with an exceptionally interesting monument. On a sandstone altar tomb lie alabaster figures of Sir Ralph Grey, who died in 1443, and his wife Elizabeth. The sides are richly carved with niches and canopies and contain 14 figures of saints alternating with angels bearing shields. Unlike many others, this tomb escaped injury in the 16th and 17th cents. and Pevsner regards it as an important example of dated sculpture of about 1450.

CHOLLERFORD, *Northumberland* (14–NY 9372). One of the most interesting and accessible forts of HADRIAN'S WALL stood on the bank of the North Tyne in this wooded valley. It was **Chesters (Cilurnum)**. It housed 500 troops and guarded the west side of a bridge. It covered 5¾ acres, which made it the largest fort in Northumberland. It is now in the custody of the Ministry of Public Building and Works. Excavation on the beautiful site has revealed a great deal about the life of the fort. Its rectangular wall was 5 ft thick with an earth bank behind and a ditch in front. There were six gatehouses with guard chambers. Spring water was brought in to a settling tank by aqueduct. Refuse reveals that the soldiers managed to get quantities of oysters, mussels, cockles and limpets though 30 m. from the sea. Layers of debris pointed to three destructions of the fort, which was each time rebuilt. The visitor can marvel here at the "modern" conveniences the Roman forces provided. A commandant's house has underfloor heating. The regimental bathhouse, between the fort and the river, is a most imposing ruin, with round-headed niches or cupboards, latrines, and provision for hot or cold, dry or steam baths.

An abutment of the Roman bridge is reached by crossing the present bridge near the George Inn and taking a footpath along the former railway line on the east bank of the river.

The fort site was in the park of Chesters, an 18th-cent. mansion, whose owner, John Clayton, a Classical scholar, was the first to examine the Roman remains systematically. He died in 1890, and the preservation of the surviving Wall owes much to his work and concern. The museum at Chesters was built in his memory.

CONSETT, *Durham* (15–NZ1150). The steaming chimneys, furnaces and roofs of the giant Consett Iron Co. fill the horizon on the high ground between the Derwent and Wear rivers. This great complex of quarries and brickworks, engineering shops and slag-heaps seems all the more overpowering to the traveller for looming on its own in a rural landscape. The company dates from 1840, but iron was being produced as far back as Roman times at **Ebchester**, 3 m.

away. The limestone and coal needed to manufacture steel still come from local sources, but all of the iron ore is now imported. Consett has some other industries, including a new man-made fibres plant. The first Salvation Army band in the world was organized here in 1879. Anyone can buy a meal at the Trade Union Memorial Hall.

CORBRIDGE, *Northumberland* (14–NY9964), with its lofty trees and charming stone-built houses, is steadily becoming more attractive the more it is "discovered" by Tynesiders. It is on the River Tyne, 16 m. W. of NEWCASTLE, and at many times in its long history has been of considerable importance. The town probably grew out of its proximity to the Roman camp at **Corstopitum** and the later presence of an Anglo-Saxon monastery. In its medieval heyday, Corbridge had four churches, two peel-towers, a mint and two burgesses in the first English parliament. It was burnt three times in the period of border clashes. In the 18th-cent., travellers reported that it was filthy and populated by half-fed, sallow people. But by the 19th cent. it had recovered enough to be considered a bracing health resort.

St Andrew's Church is the most important Anglo-Saxon survival in the county after the crypt at HEXHAM across the river. Lower parts of the slender tower are dated before 786 and there are two Anglo-Saxon windowheads in the nave. A few Norman features are evident, but most of the present building dates to the 13th cent. An interior tower arch is a Roman gateway, transported intact.

Low Hall at the east end of the main street has a peel-tower of about 1500 in a later house. Opposite is Monks Holme, a former inn said to be on the monastery site. The fortified vicarage near the churchyard dates to 1318. Other interesting domestic buildings are the 17th- to 18th-cent. Angel Inn and the 1700 Heron House, now an art gallery.

The seven-arch bridge was built in 1674. It was the only bridge to withstand the great Tyne flood of 1771. The good footing on this stretch of the river probably accounts for the location of Corstopitum here.

A walk 1½ m. NE. takes the visitor to **Aydon Castle,** a choice example of a medieval fortified manor house now belonging to the Ministry of Public Building and Works. **Dilston Castle** is 1½ m. to the SW., a ruin in a delightful wood.

Corstopitum, ½ m. to the W., was at the junction of the Roman roads Dere Street, running N. from YORK, and Stanegate, joining with CARLISLE. It was 2½ m. S. of HADRIAN'S WALL. The site was first excavated in 1201 by King John's men, searching for treasure. The first systematic examination of the site was in 1906–14 and work resumed in 1934. The Ministry now has custody.

The camp served successively as a fort, supply base for actions against the Picts, and an arsenal with a large civilian settlement. The excavated portion discloses the foundations of the headquarters building, two military compounds, two temples, granaries, a spring-fed fountain, and an imposing storehouse. A museum contains many post-1906 finds, including inscriptions. The most famous of the objects is the Corbridge Lion, shown by the sculptor feeding on a stag.

CRAGSIDE, *Northumberland* (15–NU0702). The grounds of the Armstrong estate just outside ROTHBURY are open to the public for walks or drives, and they are famous for rhododendrons, azaleas and rock gardens. Lord Armstrong, the great inventor (of the hydraulic crane and first rifled gun) was regarded also as the "great magician" when he transformed a barren hillside on the River Coquet into a magnificent setting for his Wagnerian mansion by Norman Shaw, begun in 1863. The house is set in an estate of 14,000 acres. Here Lord Armstrong planted 7 million trees, diverted streams and created lakes, a waterfall, terraces, winding paths, gardens and orchards. Lord Armstrong's was the first house in England completely fitted out with electric light in 1880. The power came from a stream on the grounds. He also introduced "communication by means of the telephone" to his shooting box on the moors.

CRASTER, *Northumberland* (15–NU2519). This tiny fishing village is still famous for its oak-smoked kippers but the fish nowadays are imported from North Shields. Crab and lobster are still caught by local boats. Until the nearby quarry closed in 1939, Craster shipped whinstone. The harbour was built in 1906 by the Craster family as a memorial for a brother who died in Tibet. Craster Tower, the family home, is an 18th-cent. residence incorporating a 15th-cent. tower. There is an easy walk by path along the sea 1½ m. N. to DUNSTANBURGH CASTLE.

CULLERCOATS, *Northumberland* (15–NZ 3571), is a suburb of TYNEMOUTH, and still a fishing village. Its red-roofed houses cluster on a cliff with a fine sandy beach around the bay. In the last century, Cullercoats attracted many artists, including Winslow Homer. The village once exported salt, grindstones and coal, but the last ship to clear the harbour was the *Fortune of Whitby*, loaded with 21 tons of salt, in 1726. St George's Church, a large Early English, stone-vaulted edifice, was built in 1882–4. It has been described as a 13th-cent. ideal rarely achieved in the 13th cent. In the days when some 50 fishing cobles worked out of Cullercoats, the women played a key rôle in the local industry. They prepared bait, carried gear to the boats and hawked the catch on Tyneside. The fishwives' distinctive costume of blue serge jacket, full skirt, large apron and black straw bonnet is a museum piece now. The Dove Marine Laboratory, part of the University of NEWCASTLE, has an aquarium open to the public. The Watch House on the Bank Top is a good place to meet the locals.

DARLINGTON, *Durham* (15–NZ2914), the "cradle of railways". In Bank Top station are *Locomotion Number One*, George Stephenson's early engine, standing on two original rails, and the 1845 model locomotive, *Derwent*. John Dobbin's painting of the opening of the first public railway, the Darlington and STOCKTON-ON-TEES, on 27 September 1825 hangs in the Art Gallery. Stephenson's genius and the financial backing of Edward Pease, a public-spirited Quaker businessman, made Darlington the important rail centre that it was. British Rail closed the locomotive engineering shops in 1966, thus ending a historic chapter in the town's life. Originally an Anglo-Saxon settlement on the River Skerne, it became a lively market town with a textile industry even before the railway age dawned. Today, its diversified industries range from iron-founding, heavy engineering, spinning, wire rolling and the manufacture of agricultural implements to the production of knitting wools. Darlington pioneered nursery education and double the national average of pupils leave its secondary schools each year for universities.

Darlington's skyline is now dominated by bulky cooling towers but it presents an attractive and busy face to visitors. The Town Hall clock tower, given by Edward Pease, rises over the sloping market place. On the opposite side is the spire of St Cuthbert's, sharp as a needle. This is one of the most important Early English churches in the North. It was built by Bishop Pudsey about 1192 and, except for the early 14th-cent. aisle windows and crossing tower, exhibits little of a style later than 1250. The woodwork includes medieval stalls with misericords alive with heads, angels, monsters and branches. This is the home of the *Northern Echo*, the first halfpenny paper in England when it began publication in 1869. Its most famous editor was W. T. Stead, who was in charge from 1871 until 1880.

DODDINGTON, *Northumberland* (14–NU00 32). The peel-tower here was built in 1584 and is one of the last to be constructed for defence before the union of England and Scotland. A ruin, it is now enclosed in a farmyard in the village. The Church of SS. Mary and Michael is 13th-cent., restored and rearranged in the late 19th cent. Its Norman font has a massive carved round bowl. The watch-house was built in the churchyard in 1826 to guard against body-snatchers. Dod Law, which rises 654 ft on the S., has two early British forts, hut circles and rocks with cup and ring markings. Within a 5-m. radius of Doddington are said to be more of these mysterious markings than in any comparable area in Britain. Typically they consist of a cup-shaped design surrounded by one or more concentric rings. They are found in high places but their purpose is obscure. Dod Law provides wide views of the CHEVIOT HILLS. On the south side of the hill is a cave known as Cuddy's Cove where St Cuthbert is supposed to have sheltered when he was a shepherd. Above it is a stone block on which the devil is supposed to have hanged his grandmother. Rowting Linn camp, 3½ m. N., is another earthwork. It is near pretty falls and has unusual cup and ring markings above it.

DUDDO, *Northumberland* (14–NT9342). On a
knoll in a field 1 m. NW. of this hamlet stand the
remains of a red sandstone circle which may have
marked an Ancient British burial place. There are
five stones, 5 to 10 ft high, with worn channels on
their tops. They form the best megalithic monument in Northumberland.

DUNSTANBURGH CASTLE, *Northumberland* (15–NU2523). The eerie skeleton of Dunstanburgh Castle seen through a sea fret is one of the
spectacular sights of the Northumberland coast.
It is the county's largest castle site, its walls
having enclosed some 9 acres on the outcrop of the
Great Whin Sill. There is little left, but the jagged
remains of curtain wall, towers and gatehouse
have not undergone modernization or restoration
(beyond strengthening) and they furnish plentiful inspiration for a romantic imagination.
Turner painted the castle three times. It is reached
by footpath from EMBLETON or CRASTER. Since
it was given to the nation by Sir Arthur Sutherland, the shipowner, in 1929 it has been in the care
of the Ministry of Public Building and Works.

Dunstanburgh seems to hold an invincible
site on the basalt crag rearing up more than 100 ft
from the sea. It is believed to have been a site for
Roman and British strongholds but the existing
castle was built in the 14th cent. by Thomas Earl
of Lancaster who was executed for treason in
1322, nine years after he started the castle. It may
have been intended originally as a fortified port.
The castle then went to John of Gaunt who added
the surviving gateway. During the Wars of the
Roses, the castle changed hands five times,
suffering great damage from bombardment. By

1538 it was in ruins. Crops of hay and corn were
harvested inside the walls.

Tomlinson notes that the castle had no significant rôle in history but that four persons
connected with it were canonized or revered as
saints: Queen Margaret, Simon de Montfort,
Thomas of Lancaster and Henry VI.

Dunstanburgh diamonds, little coloured quartz
crystals, are found in the cracks of the crag here.
A fascinating feature on the shore is the "Rum-
bling Churn", a cavern in the rocks into which
waves rush causing a great noise, by rolling stones
about, and sending up sprays of water.

DURHAM, *Durham* (15–NZ2742). It is not
necessary to be a student of architecture or a
lover of history to be thrilled by Durham. It is one
of the most visually exciting cities in Britain. The
magnificent Norman cathedral and the castle
which form the centrepiece stand proudly on a
sandstone bluff almost enclosed, as by a moat, in a
steep-banked, wooded bend of the River Wear. It
is a scene worth gazing upon from every vantage
point. The best views are obtained from the
railway station, Prebends' Bridge, South Street,
Gilesgate, the south end of Church Street and
finally at Palace Green, close up.

The Green, in fact, is a logical place from
which to start an exploratory walk along the
streets, footpaths and alleys of the ancient town.

The castle was built in 1069 after the North
had rebelled against the Norman conquerors. It
was sited at the top of Palace Green where it
could guard the northern neck of the peninsula.
The curfew instituted then still rings on weekdays
at 9 o'clock. A small town grew up under the

Durham University: the bridge and Dunelm House

castle walls between two river crossings, Elvet and Framwellgate bridges.

The cathedral was founded as a shrine for the body of St Cuthbert. When Viking raids forced the monks on Lindisfarne to flee in 875, they carried with them the body of the saint. They first found their way to CHESTER-LE-STREET and then to RIPON before they reached Durham in 995. Here the coffin became rooted to the ground and the spot for the new shrine was revealed in a vision. This must have seemed a safe place to the wanderers, almost a natural fortress. By 998 they had built their church, of which no trace is left. It quickly became, and long continued to be, a place of pilgrimage. Pilgrims' offerings made the town prosper and enabled the bishops to build on a far grander scale.

Durham's prince bishops had unique powers. They were lay rulers as well as religious leaders. As a palatinate, Durham could have its own army, nobility, coinage and courts. These privileges ended in 1836, though vestiges remain. Around Palace Green are various 15th- to 20th-cent. buildings which originally housed courts, hospitals, almshouses or residences and most of which are now used by the university.

The present Cathedral Church of Christ and Blessed Mary the Virgin was built between 1093 and 1133 to a plan of Bishop William of Calais. He died and was succeeded in the course of the building by Bishop Flambard, who saw the work completed. This is undoubtedly the finest Norman building in Europe. Only two significant additions were made, both highly successful. Bishop Pudsey built the Galilee Chapel (the Lady Chapel oddly placed at the west end of the nave), between 1170 and 1175. Its roof is supported by slim clusters of Purbeck marble and stone and with its remarkably light, airy feeling gives a quite different impression from the rest of the church. At the opposite end, the Chapel of the Nine Altars, or eastern transept, was added between 1242 and 1280. Here are the pointed arches and richly carved capitals of the Early English style. St Cuthbert's body was brought to his shrine behind the high altar in 1104.

Almost no amount of time is too long to spend in Durham Cathedral and visitors probably will want to provide themselves with a detailed guide, but some of the other features to look for on a first visit may be mentioned here. The impression of strength and antiquity begins with the bronze knocker on the broad Norman north door. The ferocious beast's head has lost its enamel eyes but it still clenches the great ring which gave sanctuary to anyone who grasped it in the Middle Ages. A sanctuary book records that 331 criminals sought refuge here between 1464 and 1524, most of them murderers.

The cathedral was the first in northern Europe to be covered with stone-ribbed vaulting and it has the earliest pointed transverse arches in England. It was also the first European church to decorate the aisle walls with an arcade of arches. The nave is lined with massive compound piers alternating with circular ones which are deeply carved in geometric designs. The round pillars have an equal height and circumference – 22 ft.

There are few monuments because of a long-held rule that no one should be buried in the shrine of St Cuthbert. The first layman to lie here was Ralph Lord Neville, commander of the English army which defeated the Scots at Neville's Cross at the edge of the city in 1346. There is also the tomb of his son, John, who gave the cathedral the splendid stone screen behind the high altar. The 107 statues that once adorned it and all the stained glass were destroyed either in the Dissolution or during the Commonwealth. The cathedral was used by Puritan soldiers to hold Scots prisoners.

The choir stalls are fine 17th-cent. work as is the font at the west end of the nave. In front of the font is a line of Frosterley marble, the nearest women were allowed to get to the altar. Bishop Hatfield's throne of the 14th cent. is the highest known. He prepared his own tomb under it.

From the south aisle a door leads to the cloisters and the monks' dormitory, a great timbered hall 194 ft by 39 ft where some of the cathedral's prized possessions can be seen. They include relics of St Cuthbert, illuminated manuscripts and a collection of crosses.

The keep of the Norman castle was rebuilt in 1840 to house students and the moat has been filled in. Here the visitor can see the tiny Norman crypt chapel, Bishop Cosin's black staircase of 1662, the great hall of 1284 and the 15th-cent. kitchens. The castle was the bishop's official residence and the key to the town's early defences. Durham University was created as the third university in England by Act of Parliament in 1832, and the castle was turned over to University College by Bishop van Mildert in 1836. He was the last count palatine. New university colleges, now totalling 14, have grown up E. and S. of the peninsula. The expansion of the university in this historical setting has been a challenge to architects and one of their most successful creations is the bridge (by Ove Arup) from the Palace Green across the river to Dunelm House, on the far bank. The university uses the Victorian Shire Hall in Old Elvet for administrative headquarters.

Durham is still small (just over 24,000 population); it is a centre for local government and education and its chief industrial concerns are a carpet factory and two organ-building firms. The generally admired new county buildings on the north part of the city form a complex which includes an open-air museum, police headquarters, council chambers and school.

The old city centre is now the traffic-choked market place where municipal offices and banks predominate. In Saddler Street leading out of the market place, the world's first ground mustard was prepared. Production of Durham mustard has now ended. The North and South Bailey which run from the market place along the east side of the cathedral still have many 18th-cent. town houses now used by the university. There are good 18th-cent. houses in Old Elvet and South Street.

Boating is a popular recreation here, and a regatta, claimed to be the oldest in Britain, is held in June. The Durham miners' gala on the third Saturday of July still fills the streets with bands and marchers.

The Gulbenkian Museum of Oriental Art and Archaeology in Elvet Hill Road is unique in Britain. Its collections include Egyptian art and tomb furnishings, Chinese and Japanese jades, ceramics, sculptures and bronzes, and Chinese and Tibetan paintings. A museum of relics and trophies of the disbanded Durham Light Infantry opened in the County Hall grounds in 1969. The jutting concrete building includes an art gallery.

From the village of **Shincliffe**, 1 m. SE. of the city, a beautiful view of the cathedral and castle can be had from the bank top across the Wear valley. The walk to the village passes an old gravel working where in 1940 remains of a Roman farm were found, confirming for the first time the activities of Roman civilians in the county. The village itself is pleasant, with trees and a roadside green.

EASTGATE, *Durham* (14–NY9538), and **Westgate**, 3 m. W., were entrances to the Old Park, hunting grounds of the Bishops of DURHAM. Today Eastgate is a hamlet near Low Linn Falls, where Rookhope Burn tumbles over a horseshoe of rocks. The stream attracts geologists and botanists alike. There is a large new cement works in the valley, but this will not deter holiday visitors in search of fine moorland scenery. The large All Saints Church, an 1887 gift to the community, has a massive font of Frosterley marble. Westgate also has a 19th-cent. church and an old watermill. It was once a cockfighting centre. The site of the bishops' hunting lodge has been excavated and the only medieval thimble ever found was brought to light.

EDLINGHAM, *Northumberland* (15–NU11 08). Little St John's Church is so plain and sturdy that it is easy to mistake it for a farm building when it is viewed across the valley from the scenic ALNWICK road. It stands in trees on the hillside just above the ruins of a 14th-cent. castle, and both stand apart from the small village further up the slope. The church is mainly Norman, with a square tower and slit windows. It must have afforded protection in the days of border raiding. The first church on the site was probably wooden and built in the 8th cent. The stone building began in about 1050 and the west wall of the nave dates to this time. The wide round chancel arch, the chancel itself and the beautiful north aisle arcade are 12th-cent. Fragments from earlier times include part of a sculptured cross in a recess below the pulpit and the base of the font.

Edlingham was the home of an alleged witch, Margaret Stothard, in the 17th cent. She was never punished, perhaps because the charges against her were so flimsy. In 1879 the vicarage burglary brought other notoriety to the village. Two men were wrongly convicted and served 10 years in prison before the real culprits were brought to justice. The case inspired the novel, *The Massingham Affair*, by John Grierson.

EDMONDBYERS, *Durham* (14–NZ0149). Isolated high in the moors, this is a popular centre for hiking and bicycling holidays. The village has an appealing little church founded in 1150 and a youth hostel. With its neighbour, **Muggleswick**, it lies just N. of Muggleswick Common where Hise Hope, Smithyshaw and Waskerley reservoirs attract fishermen and picnickers. A giant reservoir has been built on the River Derwent on the Northumberland border N. of both villages. It covers 1,000 acres.

EGGLESCLIFFE, *Durham* (15–NZ4213), faces the town of YARM in Yorkshire across the River Tees. The towns are connected by a stone bridge that dates from 1400 (the medieval work is still visible on the Yorkshire side) but has since been widened and mended. A 43-arch brick railway viaduct of 1849 marches majestically across the river nearby. The village, expanding now with modern houses along the riverside, was built originally around a sloping green. At St Mary's Church, a Norman south doorway is the oldest important feature. The building also has a 15th-cent. battlemented tower, a 13th-cent. chancel arch built of alternating red and white stone, an oaken barrel roof, fine 17th-cent. furnishings, and two well-worn 13th-cent. sandstone cross-legged knights. The church has two chained books, Bishop Jewell's *Apology* and *Eikon Basilike*.

ELSDON, *Northumberland* (14–NY9393). There is still a gibbet 2 m. SE. of Elsdon and the official guidebook to the area begs that "overseas visitors should note that gibbets in Britain are long since disused". But it fits in with the atmosphere of this isolated – and captivating – moorland village. This was a lawless area not so very long ago, the gathering place and market centre for the Redesdale clans. The wide-open village green, ringed with houses, covers 7 acres. During times of danger or in severe weather the cattle were herded here. The stone-walled pound for strays is still in use. In the last century, Elsdon folk often took their herds to the upland pastures and lived in huts through the summer. Those were also the days when cattle were driven through a midsummer bonfire in a rite passed down from pagan times.

An unsightly coalyard spoils the entrance from the W. to the village but at the NE., across the pretty burn, are two interesting mounds, sometimes called mote hills, 70 and 63 ft high. They were some sort of fortification, and probably an 11th-cent. motte and bailey castle.

St Cuthbert's Church lies low among the trees in a walled yard. As it stands now, it is mainly a 14th-cent. building with an odd heavy bell-turret decorated with stone knobs. Three horse skulls were found there in 1877, thought to be protection against lightning or an aid to acoustics, but one historian at least has hinted they might

G. Douglas Bolton

Escomb has one of the most complete Anglo-Saxon churches in England

have come from victims of some ancient sacrificial rite performed when the church was built. Worse, a mass grave was found in 1810 under the north wall of the church. More than 100 human skulls were found, probably English soldiers killed at OTTERBURN. In the church is a Roman tombstone erected to a commandant by his wife. It was found at High Rochester.

The 14th-cent. vicar's peel is part of a handsome residence on high ground behind the church.

A former café, marked by a sculpture of Bacchus over the door, now houses a crafts studio.

EMBLETON, *Northumberland* (15–NU2322). The village consists of unpretentious old cottages and streets of new houses on the outskirts. It lies 1 m. inland from the sea with a striking view across the meadow to DUNSTANBURGH CASTLE on the southern tip of Embleton Bay. There is an 18-hole golf course between the village and the shore. Holy Trinity Church is medieval but considerably altered in the 19th cent. The ground floor of the 12th-cent. tower is tunnel-vaulted with stone arches. The vicarage includes the typical Northumberland peel-tower dated about 1415. One notable Embleton vicar was the Rev. Mandell Creighton, later Bishop of Peterborough and London, who wrote *History of the Papacy*. Memorials to the Greys of Falloden are contained in the church. Embleton in 1849 was the birthplace of W. T. Stead, the doughty editor. On the 1½-m. walk to Dunstanburgh Castle you can see Saddle Rock, a strange limestone outcrop.

ESCOMB, *Durham* (15–NZ2029). One of the most complete small Anglo-Saxon churches in England is found here at the bottom of a steep road leading through a former pit village about 2½ m. from BISHOP AUCKLAND. It has probably survived because it was so obscure and unimportant. For a short period in the mid-19th cent., St John's was unused and partly roofless. It was only in 1875 that its true character was recognized and reported by the Rev. R. E. Hooppell and a public appeal launched to repair it. The building, its stone now blackened, stands rather sternly in a leafy churchyard enclosed by a circular wall. The key can be had from the house facing the entrance. No one knows exactly when the church was built but it is contemporary with those of the 7th cent. at JARROW and MONK-WEARMOUTH, and may even be older. The porch was added in the 12th cent. and five larger windows inserted in the 13th and 19th cents., but these alterations do not detract from the church's appearance of great antiquity. Above the porch and to the right is a sundial, part of the original fabric, and probably the oldest in the country. The dial is a raised semi-circle with a serpentine border. All but the upper parts of the walls are built of stones from the former Roman fort at Binchester and the Roman tool-marks are easily seen. On the north wall is embedded a small raised rosette which may have been a sacrificial stone and, under a projection, there is an upside-down inscribed stone marked LEG VI, for the 6th Roman Legion. The serenity of the interior is a tribute to the care with which the recent

G. Douglas Bolton

The Farne Islands are an important bird sanctuary

restoration was done. The walls are white. Both the new and the old windows are of clear glass through which the branches of the trees outside wave a pattern. The modern oak furnishings are simple and unobtrusive. The long, narrow nave culminates in a small square chancel. There are two small round-headed windows and two square-headed ones with another tiny original window high in the gable end. But the most striking feature is the slim, round-headed chancel arch. It has the remains of a 12th-cent. painting on the underside of the curve. The arch is believed to have been taken intact from Roman Binchester and put here. A patch of the original cobble-stone floor is preserved near the font. Behind the altar table is a pre-Norman carved stone cross.

The village of Escomb is being attractively rebuilt.

ETAL, *Northumberland* (14–NT9339). A street of thatched cottages with a manor house at one end and a crumbling castle ruin at the other gives Etal its own distinctive aspect among the county's villages. New slate roofs over new stone houses are appearing, but efforts are clearly made to keep the additions in harmony with the past legacy. The cottages are set behind flower gardens and trees shelter the site on the River Till. The manor house is not open to the public. It was built for Sir William Carr in 1748 and enlarged a few years later. In its grounds stands the Church of the Blessed Virgin Mary, designed by William Butterfield in 1850 for Lady Augusta FitzClarence in memory of her husband and child. All that remains of the castle is the south-east gate-tower and a portion of curtain wall with parts of two other towers. It was built about 1342 for Sir Robert de Manners and destroyed in 1496 by James IV of Scotland. The village's most charming building is the thatched and white-washed Black Bull Inn.

FARNE ISLANDS, *Northumberland* (15–NU 2337). Best known as a bird sanctuary, the Farne Islands number about 25, are of basaltic rock and lie from 2 to 5 m. off the Northumberland coast. They are visited by boat from BAMBURGH or SEAHOUSES. The favoured time (for bird-watching) is late May or early June. The islands, virtually uninhabited, are the property of the National Trust and administered by a joint committee of the Trust and the Farne Islands Association. The largest and nearest is the Inner Farne (or House Island) which covers 16 acres and has cliffs 80 ft high. A peel-tower built in 1500 by Prior Thomas Castell of DURHAM has been converted into the headquarters of the Farne Islands bird observatory. During migration seasons, it is manned around the clock. The tower was used for warning lights to mariners until a lighthouse was established on Longstone Island. It was from the latter that Grace Darling and her father set forth in a gale in 1838 to rescue survivors of the *Forfarshire* which had run aground on Big Harcar Rock. On these bleak outcrops is seen a great variety of bird life: eider ducks, cormorants, shags, fulmars, oyster catchers, ringed plovers, guillemots, razor-bills and puffins, four species of terns, herring gulls and kittiwakes. The islands are the only east-coast breeding place of the grey seal.

The first recorded visitor to the Farnes was St Aidan, Bishop of Lindisfarne (HOLY ISLAND), who came here to meditate in 635. St Cuthbert in 676 built a hermitage on Inner Farne. It had no window openings save a hole in the roof through which he could see heaven. He lived here till 684 when he was persuaded to become bishop. Two years later he resigned his high office to return to the hermitage, but he died only three months afterwards. His cell and well may have been on the site of the later tower, where there is the only well now. A chapel to St Cuthbert was built in 1370 and in an 1848 restoration it was fitted out with 17th-cent. panelling and pews from Durham Cathedral.

FELTON, *Northumberland* (15–NU1800). The barons of Northumberland met at Felton Park on 22 October 1215 to transfer their allegiance from the English King John to Alexander of Scotland. The following year King John burnt down the village. Few other historic events disturbed the village. Thomas Forster managed to raise 70 horsemen here in the 1715 Jacobite uprising. The Duke of Cumberland stopped in 1745 on his way to victory at Culloden. In 1766, John Wesley preached but "very few seemed to understand anything of the matter". N. of the village and away from the road is a Nelson monument erected in 1806 by a friend, Alexander Davison, an army clothing contractor. Two bridges, medieval and modern, span the Coquet River here. St Michael's Church, W. of the village, has been altered so often that it is difficult even for experts to work out its dates. It probably is a 13th-cent. heritage, with aisles added in the 14th.

FINCHALE PRIORY, *Durham* (15–NZ29 47). Set in a loop of the Wear NE. of DURHAM are the ruins of the 13th-cent. Finchale Priory, now an Ancient Monument. Their story begins with St Godric, a pedlar and shipowner who later became a hermit. He built a hut a short distance upstream in about 1110 in response to a vision. Later a stone chapel and living quarters were constructed on the priory site. St Godric lived here until he died in 1170 at the age of 105. Durham Priory took over the chapel and in the 13th cent. it was considerably enlarged. Later it became a kind of holiday resort for monks from Durham. Traces of the first chapel can be detected in the chancel wall, and a cross marks St Godric's grave. The ruins include four piers of the central tower of the church, most of the transept walls and a little of the cloister, chapter house, refectory and prior's house.

FORD, *Northumberland* (14–NT9437). A ponderous model village of the mid-19th cent., Ford could be a prosperous suburb instead of the adjunct to an ancient castle. Ford Castle, owned by Lord Joicey and used as an educational and cultural centre by the Northumberland County Council, was started in 1287 by Odenel de Forde and crenellated in 1338. It was demolished by the Scots in 1385 and attacked again in 1549. It was in the style of four corner towers with a curtain wall, and three of the original towers survive. The castle was extensively restored and altered in both the 18th and 19th cents. St Michael's Church in the castle grounds dates from the early 13th cent. with a thorough 19th-cent. restoration.

Ford village as seen today is the work of Louisa, Marchioness of Waterford, who did it over as a memorial to her husband who suffered a fatal fall from a horse in 1859. Tastes may differ about the result (to the 19th-cent. historian Tomlinson there was "no sweeter village outside Arcadia") but her Biblical paintings in the former village school are a memorial that requires no defence. Lady Waterford was a talented artist in the pre-Raphaelite style. She spent 22 years (from 1860 to 1882) on this series of watercolours on paper which was applied to canvas and then fitted into the walls and gables of the long school hall. Residents who attended classes there tell how the Bible lessons were drawn from Lady Waterford's pictures. She used villagers for models and paid the children sixpence and a "gilly piece" (bread and jelly) for their sittings. A surprising number of descendants of those models visit Ford to see the paintings.

FROSTERLEY, *Durham* (14–NZ0237). Churches throughout County Durham exhibit fonts, pillars and memorials in Frosterley marble, actually a grey limestone full of fossils which becomes black when polished. In the 13th cent. it was as greatly prized here as Purbeck marble in the South. The Weardale village, originally Forest Lea, has working quarries still but Frosterley marble, which occurs in thin bands between courses of limestone, is now only produced for special orders. In St Michael's Church, built in 1866, a beautiful sample of the marble is mounted near the door with the tribute: "This Frosterley marble and limestone, quarried for centuries in this parish, adorns cathedrals and churches throughout the world."

GAINFORD, *Durham* (15–NZ1716). One of the loveliest villages in southern County Durham, Gainford lies round a large and tranquil green between the A67 and the Tees. The Georgian flavour predominates, but the houses fronting the green or crowded into the narrow streets round it offer a variety of style and colour. Probably the most striking domestic building is the Hall, built in 1603 by Vicar John Cradock and now a farmhouse. It has 11 chimneys rising from the middle of the three-story stone structure. A big circular stone dovecot stands nearby. St Mary's Church at a corner of the green is almost all excellent 13th-cent. work with a west stair and turret added in 1786. Within the porch is a collection of tomb lids and carved stones. According to Sir Timothy Eden this is the church where, on three successive days, the vicar married a Pigg, christened a Lamb, and buried a Hogg.

GATESHEAD, *Durham* (15–NZ2562). Fine views from here of the five famous Tyne bridges linking Gateshead to NEWCASTLE-UPON-TYNE. Dr Johnson once referred to this place as "a dirty lane leading to Newcastle", but in its own right Gateshead is a major town, third largest in County Durham. The name means "goat's headland". At the start of the 19th cent. it was still little more than a village with numerous oak trees and 11 windmills, now all gone. In the beginning, the protection of the Bishops of DURHAM, and later the grit of the citizens kept

Gateshead from becoming a suburb of bigger, richer Newcastle. Today it is nearly all modern; a great fire in 1854 took most of the historical buildings. Its famous residents have included Sir Joseph Swan, inventor of the incandescent lamp in 1878, Thomas Bewick, the great engraver, and in modern times, Alex Glasgow, the composer, singer and writer. Daniel Defoe is said to have written *Robinson Crusoe* here. New houses and blocks of flats are replacing rows of 19th-cent. workers' dwellings. The Team Valley Trading Estate, begun in 1936 to relieve unemployment, is considered a model of industrial planning. Saltwell Park, high on the bluffs, provides the town with a central recreation ground, gardens and lake. Its large pavilion café is owned by the Corporation. Near it are the Shipley Art Gallery, the library and an industrial museum. The gallery has a varied permanent collection and loan exhibitions nearly every three weeks. St Mary's Church near Tyne Bridge is the oldest ecclesiastical building. It dates from the 12th cent. but was almost completely rebuilt in 1855. The earliest feature is the south doorway. The body of the church is mainly 14th-cent. and it has an 18th-cent. tower. An anchorage rebuilt in the 18th cent. is attached to the north aisle and serves as a vestry. Gateshead workers are engaged in engineering, brass and iron-founding, and the manufacture of paper, glass, hawsers, hemp, oils, paints and enamels.

GIBSIDE CHAPEL, *Durham* (15–NZ1758). The 18th-cent. estate SW. of GATESHEAD is in ruins, but the classical chapel, originally a mausoleum and designed by James Paine about 1760, is exquisite and open to visitors since the National Trust restored it. It stands on a terrace at the end of an avenue of trees. The grounds were landscaped by Capability Brown. The chapel takes the shape of a Greek cross with a shallow dome over the centre. Four Ionic columns guard the portico. Inside, the altar is placed under the central dome. The furnishings, including a three-decker pulpit and box pews, are all in cherrywood and mahogany. On a 140-ft Tuscan column NE. stands a British Liberty statue, 12 ft high, erected by George Bowes in about 1750.

GREATHAM, *Durham* (15–NZ4927). Brine pumped from salt beds 1,000 ft below ground at Greatham yields the greater part of the salt for British tables. "Salt de Gretham" has been known from the 15th cent. The industry grew out of the early custom of slaughtering and salting meat in early November for a winter-long supply. Most of the town will not long delay visitors but the Hospital of God, the Blessed Mary and St Cuthbert, N. of the churchyard, is well worth a second glance. Founded in 1272 by Bishop Robert de Stitchill, it was re-established in 1610 and rebuilt in part in the late 18th and early 19th cents. It is single storied with an octagonal bell-turret above the clock tower. Almshouses for 13 men and six women were provided in the wings. The much grander master's house, Greatham Hall, was built in 1725. The Church of St John the Baptist dates

from the 12th cent. but was rebuilt and enlarged in the 18th, 19th and even 20th cents. It has its original round Norman nave arcades, a Norman font and a medieval altar of Frosterley marble.

HADRIAN'S WALL, *Northumberland* (14–NY6367 to 15–NZ1366). An amazing fortification, 73½ m. long, in Roman days divided the difficult province of Britain from unoccupied Caledonia, from Wallsend on the E. to Bowness on the W. The finest stretch of the surviving wall is in the NORTHUMBERLAND NATIONAL PARK between the North Tyne River and GILSLAND. The ruins constitute a unique monument of the Roman Empire and they are found, in places, among some of the most dramatic scenery in Britain.

The wall was built after a visit to Britain by the Emperor Hadrian in A.D. 122. He decided a permanent barrier was required for defence against the unsubdued Caledonian tribes. It was planned first as a series of signal stations but in the end it consisted of 17 forts (permanent quarters for garrisons) with mile castles every Roman mile for patrols, and turrets or signal towers between, all linked by a curtain wall. There was a ditch on the N. as added protection against the Picts, and a broad vallum, or flat-bottomed trench, at the southern boundary of the military zone. The giant project was probably finished by A.D. 138. Legionary soldiers were responsible for the building and the wall was garrisoned by some 5,500 cavalry and 13,000 infantry. The wall stood perhaps 20 ft high, to the top of the parapet, and 8 to 10 ft broad, but the highest remaining portion is about 9 ft. The work consumed one million cubic feet of stone.

The wall suffered destruction during three periods of civil disorders and in each case was rebuilt by the Romans. Uprisings in continental Europe caused the reduction of Roman forces in Britain in the 4th cent., and by the early 5th cent. the remaining token force of troops, or farmer-soldiers as many were by now, merged with the native tribes, allies of Rome. The wall became a vast quarry for building stone. Its greatest destruction occurred in 1751 when Parliament ordered a new road between NEWCASTLE and CARLISLE. For much of the way this was built on and with material from the Wall.

It is thanks to scholars and antiquaries that anything is left to see today. The Wall was described as early as 1599 and the first accounts of the whole line came in the early 18th cent., notably by the Rev. John Horsley of MORPETH. William Hutton of BIRMINGHAM, at 78, walked it from end to end in 1801 and wrote a history. Near Planetrees Farm, the old man's tears persuaded one Henry Tulip, then building a house, not to tear down a fine section of wall. The Rev. John Hodgson's *History of Northumberland* was the first to date the vallum with the Wall. Since 1851, J. Collingwood Bruce's *Handbook to the Roman Wall* has been the standard guide. The first accurate survey was made in the 1850s and a special Ordnance Survey map came out in 1964.

A special debt is owed to John Clayton (1792–1890) of Chesters (site of Cilurnum) who inherited or acquired five wall forts and did the first systematic excavations.

For non-specialist visitors, the best sense of the original Wall will come with time spent at such sites as those at CHOLLERFORD, HOUSESTEADS and CORBRIDGE and from a walk along some of the line, perhaps the superb and wild stretch between Housesteads and the Once Brewed youth hostel and Park Information Centre.

HALTWHISTLE, *Northumberland* (14–NY 7064). A small market town for a large rural district, Haltwhistle makes a good jumping-off point for visits to HADRIAN'S WALL which lies to the N. The town is tucked into the juncture of Haltwhistle Burn and the South Tyne. Its area has turned from coal-mining to light industry, including paint manufacturing, and quarrying. Holy Cross Church, towerless and almost hidden in trees, is regarded as an unusually good example of Early English architecture. On the north bank of the river about 3 m. away is **Featherstone Castle**, a 14th-cent. peel-tower to which a Jacobean mansion was attached. Part of it is now in use as a young people's holiday centre. Another peel-tower forms part of the Red Lion Hotel. Haltwhistle Castle, a fortified house, has been demolished.

HAMSTERLEY, *Durham* (15–NZ1131). A thousand acres of Hamsterley Forest have been opened as a park, giving additional access to the most beautiful woodland in the county. The new road, which is open to motorists but not to heavy coaches, crosses streams and is crowded with beauty-spots. There is a forest trail for children with a printed guide available to help them identify plants and animals. This State Forest contains conifers and broad-leaved trees and already has a popular picnic area at **Bedburn**. The village of Hamsterley overlooks Bedburn Beck. There is a restored 13th-cent. church to one side. Some carved medieval monuments have been built into the church walls. One m. N. of Bedburn are **The Castles**, remains of a stone-walled British camp built after the Roman occupation. On the other side of the road by the church is a series of Anglo-Saxon or medieval fields stepping down the hillside.

HARBOTTLE, *Northumberland* (14–NT9304). This ancient village, deep in Coquetdale, used to be known for its good health, having one of the lowest death rates known. The fragmentary remains of Harbottle castle are on a hill at the north-eastern outskirts of the village. It was the second castle on the site, built about 1160, but by 1541 it was a ruin. Here in 1515 Queen Margaret of Scotland gave birth to a daughter who was to become mother-in-law of Mary Queen of Scots and grandmother of James I. Further along the road, a footpath on the left leads up to the dramatic rock formation known as the Drake (or Dragon) Stone. It is 30 ft high, rising above Har-

bottle Crag. It was the scene of Druidic rites, and well into the 19th cent. sick children were passed over it to be cured. In a lonely lake near it, black-headed gulls breed. The modern Harbottle Castle was designed by Dobson in 1829 and includes 17th-cent. work. A private residence, it also houses a crafts centre.

HART, *Durham* (15–NZ4735). Here, NW. of HARTLEPOOL, is the town's mother church. It stands on a slanting street from which the North Sea can be seen. St Mary Magdalene is built of grey stone rubble with larger stones for quoins. Its aisle-less nave suggests its Anglo-Saxon origins which were confirmed during a restoration in 1885. Several carved stones were found in the walls, notably a semi-circular sundial now built into the west wall of the south aisle. The low tower is Norman. Most of the windows were replaced in the 17th and 18th cents. and the chancel was rebuilt and restored in the 19th. There are two fonts, one simple, square and Norman, and the other 15th-cent. and richly carved all over the eight-sided bowl and shaft. The village once was owned by the Bruce family and by tradition this is the birthplace of Robert the Bruce.

HARTBURN, *Northumberland* (15–NZ0886). The Church of St Andrew probably began with a free-standing tower built or taken over by monks from TYNEMOUTH Priory in the 11th or 12th cent. But most of what stands today dates from the 13th cent., with many repairs and alterations in all the centuries since. The small, heavily buttressed tower is attached to a square nave with aisles which, in turn, leads into a long narrow chancel. Among many interesting furnishings are four wooden collection boxes. Two are plain and crude, dated 1721 and 1725, and the two others are elegantly carved at a later date. Also on view is a Cromwellian money box and a carved oak plaque of Adam and Eve. Florentine brass lamps hang in the chancel. The Rev. John Hodgson, the county historian, was vicar here when he died in 1845. A crenellated school was built in Hartburn by Dr John Sharp when he was vicar from 1749 to 1796.

HARTLEPOOL, *Durham* (15–NZ5032), is an ancient seaport and county borough which merged with its Victorian neighbour, West Hartlepool, in 1967. It was really a reconciliation, since West Hartlepool was built by Ralph Ward Jackson in the 1830s partly in protest against coal shipment charges at the senior port. Recorded history begins in the early 7th cent. when the Bishop of Lindisfarne authorized a religious house on the Heugh, the headland N. of the harbour. Its second abbess was St Hilda who later founded WHITBY Abbey. The establishment was completely destroyed by the Danes. The harbour had seen the assembly of a Crusader fleet before King John gave the town a charter in 1201. The town was walled in the Middle Ages, and a 600-yd relic can be seen on the south side of the headland. In the Napoleonic wars, says a legend, a French ship

was wrecked offshore and the loyal Hartlepool
fishermen hanged its only survivor, a monkey.
This is commemorated in the emblem of the local
Rugby Union football club tie. The town was
shelled by German warships in 1914, 128 people
being killed and 400 wounded.

Such rapid development has taken place that
half the buildings in Hartlepool are new. It is still
a major port, but its last shipyard closed in 1962.
Since then, the town has concentrated on diversified industry, and among its products are telecommunications equipment, vacuum flasks,
knitwear, crankshafts, anchor chains and marine
engine controls. It makes refractory magnesia
from sea-water and salvages pure tin from waste.
Its port operates two systems: tidal, for the
coastal coal trade and for handling iron ore, other
ocean cargoes and liquefied chemicals; and enclosed, where the large timber import trade is
centred. There is a modern fish quay and a marina
for pleasure sailors. Although coal exports have
declined here as elsewhere, the port still handles
close to two million tons a year. Construction has
begun on a £125 million nuclear power station S.
of **Seaton Carew**, within the county borough.

The College of Art, for years the only separate
art college in the North-East, is putting up a new
building which will include a theatre workshop,
cinema and exhibition hall. The most important
historic building is St Hilda's Church, founded in
1129 on the site of the much older monastery, and
now in a rundown neighbourhood on the headland. Its architecture is early Early English, later
restored, with exceptionally large buttresses supporting a massive tower. "Pillow stones" from
the Anglo-Saxon burial-ground discovered in
1833 can be seen inside. Christ Church, near the
railway station, with its strange tower and spire,
was built in 1854 from limestone quarried by
Jackson for West Hartlepool docks. For fun, the
people of Hartlepool have, among many choices,
the seaside resort of Seaton Carew with some of
the most golden sands in Britain, a week-long
August fair on the Town Moor, and a "floral
mile" in Burn Valley Gardens. Sir Compton
Mackenzie was born here.

HAUGHTON-LE-SKERNE, *Durham* (15–
NZ3015). Now a suburb of DARLINGTON, this
village has the visual attractions of fine 18th-cent.
houses, a principally Norman church, and the
long green typical of County Durham. The
furnishings of St Andrew's Church are in the late
17th-cent. style identified with Bishop Cosin's
restoration work. Here they are unusually complete, and include box pews, panelled walls,
pulpit, lectern, font cover and two armchairs. The
village can claim an important rôle in the Industrial Revolution in that flax was first spun by
machinery here, by John Kendrew at his mill.

HAYDON BRIDGE, *Northumberland* (14–
NY8464). The South Tyne divides this quiet stone-
built village. The bridge, rebuilt in 1773, had to be
chained and barred in the more turbulent days of
Scottish raiding parties. Of special interest is the

Reece Winstone

Hexham: the Frith Stool

Old Church, standing apart from the village on a
hillside. Its nave was pulled down in the late 18th
cent. to build the new church in the centre. But in
the late 19th cent. it was repaired. Much of the Old
Church was of stone from nearby Roman sites.
In its abbreviated form today, it consists of a
Norman chancel and a 14th-cent. chapel. The
east window is a triplet of lancets only 7 in. wide.
The font was once a Roman altar.

About 1½ m. SW. is **Langley Castle**, a fine
example of a 14th-cent. battlemented tower house,
restored in 1900. Its walls are 6 ft thick. Now it is
used by a girls' school. **Staward Pele** is 4 m. SW., a
ruin on a steep and rocky bank of the Allen River.
The tower is at least 14th-cent., and its occupants
have included an 18th-cent. outlaw, Dicky of
Greenwood. The **Allen Banks**, 3 m. W. of Haydon
Bridge where the Allen joins the Tyne, are
National Trust property. Here are 185 acres of
hill and river scenery to walk in.

HEDDON-ON-THE-WALL, *Northumberland* (15–NZ1366). A splendid fragment of
HADRIAN'S WALL can be seen alongside the road
7 m. from NEWCASTLE and just below this hill-
top village. The visible portion, 100 yds long and
from four to seven courses high, is more than 10
ft wide. From high ground above the wall it is
possible to see the defensive ditch and vallum
which completed the wall complex. The village is

where a mile-castle stood. In 1796 the government allotted cottages built for the miners of Heddon colliery, but never used by them, to refugee French royalist priests; this was the origin of their name, Frenchman's Row. The priests left in 1802. Crowning the hill is St Andrew's Church with several traces of its Anglo-Saxon origins in the fabric. That first church was rebuilt in early Norman times and altered again in subsequent centuries. A good deal of the Roman wall went into the church building.

HEIGHINGTON, *Durham* (15–NZ2522). This hillside village in the form of an irregular square has a particularly large and spacious green in a county noted for long greens. On its north side stands the important St Michael's Church, Norman except for the 13th-cent. south aisle, 19th-cent. north aisle and 15th-cent. tower. The singular chancel arch is Norman. The church's rarest article is said to be its pre-Reformation oak pulpit with six traceried linenfold panels and an inscription beseeching prayers for the donor, Alexander Flettcher and his wife Agnes. Beside the B6275, 2½ m. W., stands a railed-in piece of stone shaft known as **Legs Cross**. It affords a panoramic view of the Tees valley. Its origin and purpose are obscure: suggestions include a Roman milestone, a marker for the 10th Roman Legion (LEG X), an Anglo-Saxon cross or a reminder of a stop made by James I, on his way to London for his coronation, who sat cross-legged on a stone here to admire this "bonny, bonny land".

HEXHAM, *Northumberland* (14–NY9364). Hexham is endowed with a beautiful setting on the Tyne. It is convenient for exploration of HADRIAN'S WALL and a major social and shopping centre (even drawing housewives from NEWCASTLE). It has three steeplechase meetings a year. Hexham's historical associations have left some delightful street names, for example, Priest-popple, Hencotes, Quatre Bras and St Mary's Chare. Modern developments (the cinema being one of the most obvious) have spoilt some of the visual charms of the town but it remains a very attractive and lively place. The abbey church makes Hexham an important place, but it also has other rewards: the market square beside the church has a small colonnaded shelter put up in 1766; the Moot Hall, or council chamber, was the 12th-cent. gatehouse of a castle; the 14th-cent. Manor Office was the gaol until 1824; the grammar school was founded in 1599; and a pretty park crossed by a burn lies next to the abbey church. Another park is laid out on The Seal, a hill which affords an excellent view of the town.

The first church in Hexham was founded by St Wilfrid on land given him by Queen Etheldreda. It was completed in 678. St Wilfrid was the queen's spiritual adviser and such an influential one that he persuaded her to leave her husband and became a nun.

Stone for that first church came from the Roman camp of Corstopitum near CORBRIDGE.

It was said to have been a magnificent building for its day, but only the crypt now remains – the finest Anglo-Saxon crypt in England. It may have housed relics of St Andrew to whom the church was dedicated. Two stones in the crypt have Roman inscriptions.

The Anglo-Saxon Frith Stool (St Wilfrid's chair) in the chancel marks the site beneath the Anglo-Saxon apse. The stone chair, believed used for Northumbrian coronations, in later days gave sanctuary to anyone who sat in it, as its name implies. The font bowl, also Anglo-Saxon, was carved from a Roman stone.

The church standing now was begun by the Augustinians in the 12th cent. The beautiful choir is 13th-cent. with a 15th-cent. roof. The transepts, also 13th-cent., include on the west wall the strikingly broad and worn Night Stair which once led from the monks' dormitory. The nave was partly in ruins before its rebuilding in the early 20th cent. by Temple Moore in 14th-cent. style.

Hexham's church is especially rich in furnishings. A notable ornament is the Anglo-Saxon Acca cross, set up in 740 at the grave of Bishop Acca. Another is the Roman monument to Flavinus, showing the Roman standardbearer riding over a crouched Briton who is armed with a dagger. There are three other Roman altars in the church and many carved Roman and Anglo-Saxon stones in the rebuilt wall of the nave.

There are 38 splendid medieval misericords, screens and rare painted panels. Benches and bench-ends were sold in 1858 for firewood. Prior Rowland Leschman's 15th-cent. chantry includes intriguing stone caricatures by local masons of St Christopher, St George and dragon, musicians, a fox preaching to geese, a jester and representations of vanity, piety, purity, gluttony and other human attributes.

HIGH FORCE, *Durham* (14–NY8828). During or just after a rainy period is the best time to see England's highest waterfall in all its fury. Here the Tees drops 70 ft over a huge black cliff of the Great Whin Sill. There is a second channel on the Yorkshire side, and in flood times even the central rock between the two may be briefly covered with water. The Force freezes in hard winters. The falls plunge into a deep pool which is enclosed by rocks and shrubs. A wooded path leads down the bank to the falls from an entrance opposite the High Force Hotel on B6277, which winds past many beauty-spots and whitewashed stone cottages. High Force is 5 m. NW. of MIDDLETON-IN-TEESDALE. The Tees has another spectacular offering, and one even preferred by some, about 6 m. upstream. This is **Caldron Snout**. It is a little harder to reach. The visitor turns off B6277 at Langdon Beck, drives about 2½ m. and then walks along a track for another mile. Caldron Snout is a great cascade where the river tumbles some 200 ft down a dolerite staircase. The water feeding the falls comes out of a deep winding pool known as the Weel. This is to become a reservoir behind the new Cow Green dam. Between High Force and

High Force on the River Tees is England's highest waterfall

Caldron Snout there is a small area of slate with the ruins of a mill where slate pencils were made for much of the 19th cent. Good walking hereabouts: this is where the famous walk to Dufton begins.

HOLY ISLAND (LINDISFARNE), *Northumberland* (15–NU1342), is famed as the birthplace of English Christianity. It is reached from **Beal** on the A1. A 3-m. causeway connects the island to the shore at low tide and can be travelled during six-hour periods between tides. Despite a rather dull appearance from afar, Holy Island makes a fascinating place to visit, with an invincible atmosphere of age and the lure of all island communities. It has a population of some 250 mostly engaged in fishing or tourism. The island even produces souvenirs in the form of mead, honey and liqueur.

In A.D. 635, St Aidan came on the invitation of King Oswald from Iona on the west coast of Scotland to teach Christianity to the Angles of Northumbria. Lindisfarne monastery was established and the first English diocese founded. The sixth bishop was St Cuthbert, who came to the island in 664 and was buried here until the monks of the time fled with his coffin ahead of the invading Danes in 875. The Danes destroyed the abbey and the island lay deserted until a priory was founded by Benedictines from DURHAM in the early 11th cent. The picturesque remains of this red sandstone building are now in the care of the Ministry of Public Building and Works. They exhibit some of the same Norman features as Durham Cathedral, including carved pillars and zigzag ornament. There is a museum here. Near to the priory ruins are those of the old parish church, built about 1140 but with the surviving fabric mainly of late-12th- and early-13th-cent. date.

On a small pyramid of rock overlooking the

tiny harbour is the castle, built about 1500 and restored as a private dwelling for Edward Hudson by Sir Edwin Lutyens in 1902; it now belongs to the National Trust. Stone from the monastery went into the castle.

HOLYSTONE, *Northumberland* (14–NT9502). A path behind the Salmon Inn leads to the spring-fed Lady's Well which dates at least to Anglo-Saxon times. Now a National Trust property, it feeds a railed-in pool in the shadow of tall beech trees. Here Paulinus is supposed to have baptized 3,000 persons at Easter in 627, but historians have no evidence to support the tale. Missionaries of those days may, however, have preached at a "holy stone" here. There was an Augustinian nunnery here before 1124 and the village church probably was built out of its chancel.

HORNCLIFFE, *Northumberland* (14–NT92 49). A shallow crossing of the River Tweed is spanned by the Union Bridge, the first important suspension bridge in Britain. It is 432 ft long and 69 ft above the water, and links Northumberland to Scotland. Sir Samuel Brown designed it – and later the chain pier at BRIGHTON. The village of red sandstone houses is on the cliff to the S.

HOUGHTON-LE-SPRING, *Durham* (15–NZ3450). Historical interest is concentrated around the church in this bustling mining town. St Michael and All Angels is large, impressive and, as it stands today, largely 13th-cent. with traces of earlier work. The south chancel wall with eight lancet windows is noteworthy. A small detached two-story building in the corner between the chancel and south transept was put up in the 15th cent. for the Guild of Holy Trinity. A chantry priest lived upstairs. A passage leads into the church. Monuments include the great tomb chest of Bernard Gilpin, the kindly, generous evangelist known as the "Apostle of the North". Gilpin was rector here from 1556 until his death in 1583. It was the richest living in England in those days, and he shared it widely. He fed two dozen poor men every week and held open house for all comers on Sundays. He completely supported and educated 24 boys. It was said that if a horse were turned loose anywhere in the county, it would make its way to the rectory stables. Gilpin refused a bishopric to carry on his ministry here, among a notoriously wild and lawless people. He died at 66 after being knocked down by an ox in DURHAM market. His tomb is decorated with panels carved in circles and squares. Buildings of the Kepier Grammar School which he founded with John Heath, a wealthy Londoner and Durham landowner, in 1574 are at the north-east corner of the churchyard, with 18th-cent. additions. The Davenport almshouses, founded in 1668 by Rector George Davenport, are at the south-east corner. The rectory, a stone battlemented house, medieval in origin but rebuilt later, now contains council offices. The garden is a public park. Houghton Hall, the manor house of the old village, was built about 1600 and is now a YMCA centre.

The town was popular with wealthy Georgians, drawn by the pure spring waters, and many of their pleasant houses remain. The market place is surrounded by new council houses. The shopping centre has been redeveloped and major road re-alignments have altered the face of the town. A noticeable secular building is the old four-story brewery, not now in use.

HOUSESTEADS, *Northumberland* (15–NY 7868). The Roman fort here is considered the finest on HADRIAN'S WALL and it occupies the highest ground, on a ridge N. of the military road 8 m. W. of CHOLLERFORD. The Roman name of the fort is not known, but **Borcovicium** has been suggested. A footpath over hilly pastures leads to it from the roadside car park. The site was bought by the late Professor G. M. Trevelyan in 1930 and given to the National Trust; the Ministry of Public Building and Works cares for it. Housesteads has the typical Roman rectangular walls with rounded corners and it accommodated 1,000 infantrymen in its 5 acres. It guarded the gap where Knag Burn runs through the Wall by means of a Roman culvert. The fort stands on a cliff with a superb view of the Wall snaking over the hills. There is a museum here and a good deal to see on the actual site: walls 12 courses high, gateways, the foundations of the headquarters, comman-dant's house, hospital, granaries, barracks and officers' baths (supplied by rainwater). Outside the south gate, by which visitors usually enter, are the unusual indications of a large civil settle-ment, including an inn, a shop and the "murder house", where skeletons of a woman and a man with a sword in his ribs were found.

A short distance W. of the fort, the visitor can see a substantial ruin of a mile-castle. In this direction, too, is a thrilling walk along or on top of the Wall which follows the crags, overlooking Greenlee Lough and beautiful Crag Lough.

HOWICK, *Northumberland* (15–NU2517). Howick Hall gardens and woods about ½ m. from the tiny village are open to the public each after-noon during the summer. From the park im-mediately around the house, the visitor can walk along a little burn 1½ m. to Howick Haven cove on the North Sea shore. The variety of plantings is great, from the kitchen and flower gardens to the Silver Wood (planted on a silver wedding anniversary). Howick Hall has been the home of the Grey family since 1319. The house was built for Sir Henry Grey in 1782 and rebuilt in 1926 after a fire. St Michael's Church in the grounds was rebuilt in Norman style in 1849. It contains many Grey monuments including one to the 2nd Earl Grey, who died in 1845 and who pushed through the Reform Bill, and another to the 4th Earl, a Governor-General of Canada.

HULNE PRIORY, *Northumberland* (15–NU 1615). The ruins of what may be the earliest Carmelite establishment in Britain are 3 m. NW. of ALNWICK, in the park of Alnwick Castle. The priory was founded about 1240 by William de Vesci. It is said that a de Vesci Crusader found a Northumbrian knight, Ralph Fresborn, living in a monastery on Mount Carmel and encouraged him to return home and found the priory here. Other accounts say that Fresborn was so impressed with the monks of Mount Carmel when he visited them that he brought them here and made himself their first abbot. These white friars kept a severe discipline. Each had a coffin in his cell and every morning each dug a shovelful of earth for his grave. They slept on straw and ate sparsely of vegetable foods but their services were unusually splendid. The ruins, including part of their church, are in a lovely setting on a hill above the River Aln. The best of the remains is the tower built in 1488 to protect the friars when beset by Scottish raiders. The only other English monastery which had such a refuge was HOLY ISLAND (LINDISFARNE). In the 18th cent., the Duke of Northumberland did quite a lot of building on this romantic site, adding a Gothic-style summer-house on the west side óf the cloister and a house, now in ruins, to the tower. Two 18th-cent. cottages are still used. The priory is enclosed by its original 12-ft-high wall. The walk along the river to the priory takes the visitor past the lesser remains of Alnwick Abbey, founded in 1147 by the de Vesci family for the Premonstratensian canons. A 14th-cent. gatehouse with four square towers and battlements marks the site. **Brizlee Hill**, 2 m. NW. of Alnwick, reminded the friars of Mount Carmel. On its top is the 1781 tower designed by Robert Adam, circular and 78 ft high – a matchless viewpoint.

HURWORTH, *Durham* (15–NZ3010). Off the beaten track, and lying along a green, is this brick-built village with several fine Georgian houses. It was the birthplace and lifelong home of William Emerson, an 18th-cent. mathematical genius and eccentric, whose tomb is in the churchyard. Emerson, the son of the local schoolmaster, was a rough, unkempt character with an encyclopedic knowledge. His odd ways and talents made the villagers think him a kind of wizard and it enraged him when they sought his advice. He liked his ale and it seems fitting that his birthplace is now a pub, the Emerson Arms. All Saints Church has a 15th-cent. tower but the rest was thoroughly restored and rebuilt twice in the 19th cent. Two mutilated cross-legged knight effigies in Frosterley marble lie in niches at the end of the nave. Both are 14th-cent. and may have come from Neasham Priory.

HYLTON CASTLE, *Durham* (15–NZ3558). Experts disagree as to whether this ancient monument just outside SUNDERLAND is a gatehouse, a castle or a keep, and the Ministry of Public Building and Works resolves the dispute by calling it a "keep gatehouse". It was built by William de Hylton in the early 15th cent. and wings were added in the 18th and 19th cents. It guarded a ford on the Wear against the Scots. Pevsner believes it was built about 1400 and is a complete castle of the tower-house type. There is a curious detached chapel of the 15th cent., which may have been used for domestic purposes at a later date.

INGRAM, *Northumberland* (14–NU0116). A NORTHUMBERLAND NATIONAL PARK information centre and the park's only camping site, 400 acres in extent, are on the outskirts of this village in the broad Breamish valley where the river flows over a stony bed. It is a popular weekend destination for the citizens of NEWCASTLE. St Michael's Church which stands opposite the information centre, has parts dating from the 11th to the 19th cent. The oldest survival may be the plain and heavy tower arch and the tower itself is of Norman date, later restored. The church was burnt by Scots raiders in the late 13th cent. and the lead roof stripped off by another party in 1578. By the mid-17th cent. the church was in ruinous condition, and little wonder. In Ingram church, the relics include tombstones in the chancel floor and a carved fragment, the feet, of an effigy of a cleric. Upstream the Breamish valley narrows and fills with heather, bracken, birch and hawthorn trees. Many prehistoric earthworks can be found hereabout. The prehistoric village of **Greaves Ash** is near **Linhope Spout**, a 56-ft waterfall $1\frac{1}{2}$ m. uphill from the hamlet of Linhope, which is $3\frac{1}{2}$ m. upstream from Ingram. The falls are on private land but may be visited.

JARROW, *Durham* (15–NZ3265). Modern Jarrow is known as "the town that was murdered" by readers of Ellen Wilkinson's 1939 book which described the intense poverty that followed the closing in 1933 of the Charles Palmer shipyards. The desperate hunger march warned the rest of Britain of the dangers of depending upon a single industry within one area. Jarrow is still part of the teeming industrial Tyneside. It lies at the Durham end of the Tyne tunnel. New houses and blocks of flats are replacing some of the rough slums and a traffic-free shopping centre has been built, which has a C. M. Davidson sculpture of two spindly-legged Vikings. Many small factories, turning out metal goods, furniture and pharmaceuticals, have been introduced to prevent another civic murder. But visitors will be more interested, probably, in St Paul's Church, one of the most important of Christian shrines and the "cradle of English learning".

It was part of the monastery where the Venerable Bede passed almost all of his productive and scholarly life. The church where he worshipped is next to the very few remains of the religious establishment where he came at the age of about seven and remained until his death in 735. The church's site seems incongruous today, with a new trading estate in one direction, the mudflats of the estuary (Jarrow Slake) in another and the busy Tyne beyond. It probably was built within an earlier Roman fort. It was founded by Benedict Biscop in 681, seven years after MONKWEARMOUTH. It was twice sacked by the Danes in their attacks on the Northumbrian kingdom and razed by William the Conqueror only to be rebuilt in

1074. But not long afterwards, the monks of Jarrow moved to DURHAM. The original Anglo-Saxon church nave is now the chancel, with a Victorian nave added. The fine masonry is believed to be the work of stonemasons imported from France by Biscop. Original round-headed windows and doorways exist along with window additions of the late 13th and 14th cents. The tower may date from the 11th-cent. rebuilding. The original dedication stone of 685 has been set above the chancel arch. The modern east window by L. C. Evetts shows Bede in a blue robe with a book in his hand, together with the crucifixion and St Peter with a sword. "Bede's chair", a battered relic, probably dates from the 14th cent. The church is still in use and an annual Bede lecture has been instituted there. Looking at the modest remnant, it is hard to imagine Jarrow's importance in Bede's time. There were 600 monks here and at Monkwearmouth. The 79 books Bede wrote for his students represented the collected knowledge of his time in science, literature, philosophy and the arts. His most famous book is the *Ecclesiastical History of the English People*. He made the first translation of St John's Gospel into English.

KIELDER, *Northumberland* (14–NY6293). The Border Forest National Park, largest forest area in Britain, covers some 200 sq. m. and has significantly altered the look of the countryside since planting of spruce, pine and larch began in 1926 in a previously nearly treeless area. In recent years, the Forestry Commission has developed public access to many sections of the forest, thus creating a new and delightful recreation ground. The **Pennine Way** crosses the forest and camping, caravan and picnic sites have been established. Permits can be obtained for deer stalking and trout fishing. There are a few observation points from which visitors can watch or photograph wild life, including the increasing number of roe deer. The country's first trailside museum is situated near the Lewisburn camp site. Kielder Castle and Lewisburn forest trails have been laid out and helpful printed guides for them make it easier to enjoy the outings and to identify the trees, plants and bird or animal life encountered along the route. (Information on public facilities is available from the Forestry Commission headquarters at Kielder Castle, BELLINGHAM, or H.M.S.O. shops and other booksellers.) Kielder (from the Old Norse *kelda* or spring) is one of the forest villages built to house the workers in this new industry. The castle, standing above the meeting of the North Tyne River and Kielder Burn, is the administrative headquarters for one forest area and a social club for the workers. It was built in 1775 as a shooting box by the Duke of Northumberland. Early visitors told of the inhabitants indulging in a riotous folk dance in which the men drew their dirks and appeared, all things considered, "scarcely less savage than the Indians of California". Kielder viaduct was purchased in 1969 by the Northumberland and Newcastle Society to preserve "the finest example of Victorian railway architecture in Britain".

KIRKHARLE, *Northumberland* (14–NZ0182). Capability Brown was born in this hamlet in 1716, and it has been suggested that the place deserves more visits. But finding it in this county, where off-the-beaten-track signposting is fairly whimsical, is the problem. After leaving the A696, you pass through an unmarked white farm gate, across a pasture and through another gate to reach the church in the farmyard. St Wilfrid's Church has no memorial to Brown but many to the Loraine family who were here for about 400 years. The church was rebuilt in 1336 and has a fine triple sedilia and a pretty fluted piscina. The font, which seems too monumental for the little parish, dates from 1500 and came out of All Saints Church in NEWCASTLE. Carved around the bowl are the arms of various Northumberland families and these are repeated in brass at the base. A reminder of turbulent days comes from a stone erected by a descendant in 1728 to Robert Loraine who died in 1483 at the hands of a party of Scots raiders.

KIRKNEWTON, *Northumberland* (14–NT91 30). The panorama of hills, the presence of ancient ruins or the Church of St Gregory might cause visitors to call at this remote village in the Cheviot foothills. The highest point in the vicinity is **Yeavering Bell,** 1,182 ft high, 2 m. to the SE., which provides a viewpoint near the traces of a large ancient camp. At the nearby place called Yeavering, a mile or so E. of the church, it is believed that King Edwin of Northumbria had a palace. He married the Christian Ethelburga here. Beside a particularly beautiful stretch of the B6351 stands a cairn, erected in 1964, marking the royal township known of old as Gefrin. "Here the missionary Paulinus in A.D. 627 instructed the people in Christianity for thirty-six days and baptized them in the River Glen close by", the plaque records. The church has been rebuilt several times and probably dates to the late 12th or early 13th cent. The present comfortable structure reflects the work of John Dobson in the 19th cent. for the most part, but remnants of earlier times provoke considerable curiosity. Both the chancel and the south transept are tunnel-vaulted. In the chancel the side walls are less than 3 ft high and extremely thick. In the transept there is no vertical wall, the vaulting starting from floor level. Both could have been part of a defensive building or one used for refuge, during the border troubles. Behind the lectern is a primitive carving of the Adoration of the Magi. It shows a stiff-armed Virgin greeting the three Wise Men. Each of the bearers of gifts seems to be dressed in a kilt and each has both knees bent to the mother and child. Experts differ on its date, but the charming though primitive work may have survived from a previous Anglo-Saxon church here. Some believe it to be 12th-cent. Josephine Butler, the great social reformer, is buried here. She died in 1906.

KIRKWHELPINGTON, *Northumberland* (14–NY9984). This pastoral village near the

River Wansbeck has cottages of a tawny stone around a small, low-walled meadow opposite the church. Rolling farmlands seem to seal the village off from the bustle of the nearby road to Carter Bar. An early 19th-cent. bridge spans the Wansbeck. One of the vicars at St Bartholomew's Church was the Rev. John Hodgson who wrote most of his *County History of Northumberland* while he was here. The church has a generally make-do-and-mend air (for example, a plain Georgian window is stuck into the chancel wall). It is a puzzle as to dates but is basically 13th-cent. in style with later alterations. A monument to Gawen Aynsley, who died in 1750, and his wife should give pause to all who take the trouble to read it. They were, it reports: "Kind to their children. Humane to their servants. Obliging to their neighbours. Friendly, just, and courteous to all. Religious without superstition. Charitable without ostentation. Lovers and practisers of virtue." The churchyard contains the grave of Sir Charles Algernon Parsons, inventor of the steam turbine, who died in 1931.

LANCHESTER, *Durham* (15–NZ1647). The Roman fort of Longovicium was ½ m. SW. of Lanchester but it is now grassed over. The most the visitor will see here of that period in history now is the assortment of Roman relics incorporated in the church. The fort, 560 by 485 ft, was built about A.D. 122, destroyed in 197 and restored about 240. It then remained in use by some 1,000 men until the end of the 4th cent. It guarded the route from YORK to HADRIAN'S WALL. All Saints Church has a Roman altar, dated 244, in its south porch. The 15th-cent. tower has Roman stones, and Roman pillars are used in the north aisle arcade. The rest is Norman or Early English. The sculpture is of particular interest, and it includes head corbels used as candle brackets. Recesses in the side walls of the chancel were made to allow room for stalls for vicars choral when the church was made collegiate in 1283.

LUMLEY CASTLE, *Durham* (15–NZ2851). This splendid castle E. of CHESTER-LE-STREET now belongs to University College, DURHAM, but it was for generations the seat of the Lumleys, Earls of Scarbrough. It is built on four sides of a courtyard with bold buttressed and crenellated towers in the angles. It appears now much as it did when new, in the late 14th cent. John Lord Lumley, who was responsible for the row of family effigies in the church at Chester-le-Street, began his genealogical hobby here by adding a display of shields in the courtyard about 1580. He also contributed a huge fireplace with classical columns to the hall. In the early 18th cent., Sir John Vanbrugh designed a library and made other alterations.

MARSDEN ROCK, *Durham* (15–NZ4064). On the coast S. of SOUTH SHIELDS is this offshore mass of weathered limestone rock pierced by an arch through which boats may pass at high tide. It is a haunt of kittiwakes, fulmar petrels and cormorants. Let into Marsden Cliff is a lift which will take visitors down to the beach and to Marsden Grotto, an inn in a cave, from which they can watch the birds outside and fish in glass tanks inside. Further S. is Souter Point lighthouse.

MIDDLETON-IN-TEESDALE, *Durham* (14–NY9425). The Quaker-run London Lead Co., which developed the lead-mines in Teesdale in the mid-18th cent., continued until it closed in the early 20th cent. to be a strong influence in this area. Its imprint, and its concern for the well-being of its workers, is clearly seen in the substantial stone buildings in Middleton, in the snug miners' cottages in the villages throughout the valley, and even in the road system. Its headquarters here at Middleton House on Hude Hill is used today for private shooting parties and Middleton itself is a convenient centre for upper Teesdale holidays. The town is built in terraces along the road as it climbs up from the river. Outside the churchyard is a spot where the visitor can join the locals, sitting and watching the traffic, or examine the old cross which also once marked the village stocks. Inside the churchyard railings, a 13th-cent. window has been planted in the grass. This, the piscina in the vestry and the font pedestal are nearly the only reminders of the church which preceded the present St Mary's, built in 1876. A dozen interesting fragments of medieval grave covers, mouldings and other stone carvings have been mounted attractively in the white wall of the north aisle. The tomb lids have such symbols as spades, hoes, crosses and swords to indicate the life's work of the deceased. A feature of this church is the stubby stone bell-tower, completely detached, which dates from the 16th cent. One of its three bells is dated 1558. In the town centre further up the hill is a Victorian cast-iron fountain, painted in cheerful blue and white, with a cherub.

MITFORD, *Northumberland* (15–NZ1685). The Wansbeck valley is at its most charming around Mitford, 2 m. W. of MORPETH. The village once was more important than Morpeth and numbered among its attractions a snuff factory. Today it is an insignificant hamlet except for its proximity to the castle, manor house and St Mary Magdalene Church. The castle, long in ruins on the rocky river bank, was built in the 12th cent. by William Bertram. By 1323 it was useless, the victim of repeated assaults and seizures. Mitford Hall was designed in 1828 by John Dobson to replace the 17th-cent. manor house of which only a battlemented gatehouse survives. It is a private residence. The church was extensively restored and rebuilt in 1875, when the steeple and spire were added, but it has a splendid Norman south arcade and 13th-cent. chancel.

MONKWEARMOUTH, *Durham* (15–NZ39 58). This is the old portion of SUNDERLAND (originally known as Wearmouth), lying N. of the River Wear. Like the church at JARROW, St Peter's here is a cherished link with early Christianity.

and it, too, must now be sought in an unlovely industrial scene. This church was part of a monastery established shortly before Jarrow (in 674) by Benedict Biscop, the Anglian nobleman educated in France, who had returned to his native Northumbria. His two establishments had 600 monks at one time. Only the west wall and the tower remain here of the original church, and the tower has been heightened. Anglo-Saxon baluster shafts in their original position can be seen in the doorway of the vaulted porch. Above, over a window, there are traces of a large sculptured figure, the earliest major sculpture in England. A collection of important Anglo-Saxon carvings is exhibited in the church, including two stones with lions. Biscop is believed to have imported craftsmen from France for his building, and excavations here have indicated that these buildings had windows of glass made on the site. This makes St Peter's the first English church to use glass.

MORPETH, *Northumberland* (15–NZ2085), is a very old place with little visible history but travellers find it useful as a shopping centre and a gateway to the moors, hills and coast of Northumberland. It is an attractive town in a U-shaped bend of the River Wansbeck with plentiful trees and parks, including the 400-acre Common with its golf course. In Carlisle Park are formal flower-beds, tennis courts and bowling greens. It is the scene of the annual miners' gala. On quaintly-named Ha' Hill overlooking the park were found early remains of a fortification. The remnants of Morpeth Castle are on a steep bank S. of this hill. A restored 15th-cent. gatehouse is the chief survival. A good view of the town can be had from the path E. of the castle.

The Parish Church of St Mary is on the southern edge of the town, a 14th-cent. building with later restoration. The east Jesse window contains the most important 14th-cent. glass in the county. An 1831 watch-house guards the churchyard against body-snatchers. In the Presbyterian Church of St George near the Telford Bridge (1861) is a memorial to Dr John Horsley, "father of British archaeology", who died here in 1732, the year his *Britannia Romana* was published. Opposite this church is the former All Saints chantry chapel, which marked the river crossing in the 13th cent. and in the 16th cent. became part of a grammar school. The west porch and the north wall are all that remain of the original and the building is now a soft drinks factory.

The south entrance to Morpeth passes a huge battlemented tower which turns out to be the courthouse and police station (1822, by Dobson) with the gatehouse for a gaol. In the Market Place stands the Town Hall, designed in 1714 by Sir John Vanbrugh and rebuilt in 1870. The hall opening into the street was the butter and egg market. The 15th-cent. clock tower with later additions is planted sturdily in the middle of Oldgate. It was the house of correction at one time and its bells still ring a curfew. Further along the street on the north side is the late Georgian Collingwood House, which once belonged to Admiral Collingwood.

Until the railway made it unnecessary, there was a weekly market in the Market Place, Bridge and Newgate Streets for cattle and sheep from the whole of the North of England and Scotland, with buyers from as far away as the North Riding of Yorkshire. There is still a weekly mart.

A walk 1½ m. W. brings you to Newminster Abbey, a 12th-cent. Cistercian monastery site. It was the daughter of FOUNTAINS ABBEY and the mother of ROCHE.

NEWBIGGIN-BY-THE-SEA, *Northumberland* (14–NZ3188). Just a few of the many brightly coloured cobles, the characteristic inshore fishing-boats of the North-East, that used to cover the shore of Newbiggin bay still fish off here today. The old Herring House, where the daily catch was washed and sold, is gone, too. The men of the sea now work in the neighbouring mines or new industries, or cater for the visitors who seek sea air here. The sands have suffered from wave action and industrial pollution at Lynemouth and BLYTH above and below on the coast. But Newbiggin offers a promenade, a golf course and a caravan site near the Town Moor. St Bartholomew's Church, with its landmark of a 14th-cent. stone spire, stands dangerously close to the cliffs on the north-eastern tip of the bay. It goes back to the 13th cent. At some later date both aisles were removed. The north aisle was restored about 1910. Several medieval tombstones have been set in the north wall. In the Second World War, mines exploding on the rocks below damaged the roof and windows, since repaired.

NEWCASTLE-UPON-TYNE, *Northumberland* (15–NZ2464). Approach this impressive regional capital, if you can, from the S. for a quick survey, from one of the five bridges that reach across the Tyne, of the city packed on the steep north bank. It is a complex scene of blackened masses of old building, tall new blocks, the ornamental crown of St Nicholas Cathedral, the pretty spire of All Saints, the square-shouldered castle keep, the quays, warehouses and industry. The city holds up, upon scrutiny, to the first impression of a rather special place, particularly in the area of most concern to visitors, the square mile between the riverside and the Town Moor.

Newcastle began as a minor fort and bridge on HADRIAN'S WALL, which started from neighbouring Wallsend, the ship-building town on the E. Westgate Road now follows the line of the wall and vestiges can be seen along it. A causeway crossing the vallum and relics of a temple can be found in residential Benwell, rather comically surrounded by tidy brick houses. After the Romans came an obscure religious colony known as Monkchester and then the Normans, who in 1080 established the "new castle" on the Roman site. A stone castle replaced the wooden one from 1172 onwards. Of this, the very complete keep and 13th-cent. fortified Black Gate survive as museums now hemmed in by railway lines and the High Level Bridge. The restored battlemented roof of the keep is a good place from which to look at the Tyne.

Medieval Newcastle was a base for the continuous warfare with the Scots. It lay inside 2 m. of city wall begun in 1280. A part of the restored West Wall can be seen in Bath Lane. The Plummer Tower in Croft Street now houses 18th-cent. furnishings from the Laing Art Gallery; the Sallyport or Wall Knoll tower at the top of Causey Bank Steps, off City Road, has been restored by the Corporation for meeting rooms.

Newcastle established itself as a market town and seaport because of the surrounding coalfield, one of the first to be worked in England and the first to export coal. But the 19th cent. brought the greatest growth and firmly established the city as a major heavy engineering centre. The key industries continue to be ship-building and repair and the manufacture of marine engines, ship fittings, generators and transformers, but the city also now makes scores of other products including detergents and flour. Most of the city seen today dates from this expansive period. One way to explore it is from the riverside up the hill, roughly the way it grew.

Of the great bridges that overshadow the waterfront, the High Level for rail and road traffic was earliest, flung across the Tyne gorge by Robert Stephenson in 1849. The Swing Bridge designed by the inventive Lord Armstrong replaced a medieval span in 1876. The King Edward, now the main railway bridge, opened in 1906 and the Redheugh and Tyne road bridges are 20th-cent. Near the Swing Bridge is the 17th-cent. Guildhall with a 1796 façade, that has been renovated. The centre of local affairs until the 19th cent., it is still used by the freemen. Merchants lived in timbered houses in Sandhill and from No. 41, Bessie Surtees in 1772 eloped with the man who became Lord Eldon and Chancellor of England. A popular Sunday morning market is held on Quayside where an obelisk marks the spot on which John Wesley first preached in 1742. Trinity House in Broad Chare is the ancient headquarters of the mariners. St Nicholas's Church became a cathedral in 1882. A mainly 14th-cent. building with rare 15th-cent. crown and spire supported by delicate arches, it is richly endowed with monuments, fine woodwork and a charnel chapel or crypt discovered in 1824. All Saints was designed in 1788 by David Stephenson and survives as a beautiful example of a rare elliptical style. It contains the largest memorial brass in England, to Roger Thornton who died in 1429. Redundant, but with prospect of becoming a concert hall, the church is the focal point of a Quayside redevelopment plan. Keelmen's Hospital, built in 1701, is off City Road not far from Holy Jesus, the important 17th-cent. hospital for aged and impoverished freemen which is being restored as a museum after years of neglect.

Richard Grainger, with John Dobson as his architect, and John Clayton, the Town Clerk as his supporter, were the courageous planners responsible for the sense of order and space in the present commercial centre which they thoroughly

reconstructed between 1835 and 1840. Grey Street is their masterpiece, with its curve of gracious façades culminating in the stately Theatre Royal, by Benjamin Green, sweeping uphill to Grey's Monument. Their Grainger Street leads into broad Neville Street with Central Station, also by Dobson, behind a grand-scale portico. Covered markets are a city centre feature.

The sparkling new Civic Centre at Barras Bridge dominates an interesting precinct of the city which was rural land when the 19th-cent. planners were at work. Cool white office blocks and a mushroom-capped round chamber bring Newcastle well into the 20th cent. The centre was designed by City Architect George Kenyon. The main 12-story block is capped by a copper lantern and beacon with three gold castles from the coat of arms 250 ft above the street. A carillon in the tower plays Tyneside tunes four times a day. Impressive use is made of modern sculpture with, most noticeably, a 16-ft-long River God Tyne by David Wynne.

In the neighbourhood are the proliferating buildings of the University of Newcastle; the Hancock Natural History Museum famous for amphibian fossils; and three other museums connected with the university: the Greek Museum, the Hatton Art Gallery, and the Museum of Antiquities with one of the most important collections of Roman inscriptions and sculpture in the country and a reconstructed Temple of Mithras. The Laing Art Gallery, with a fine permanent collection of British art, is near the new Central Library in New Bridge Street and the Municipal Museum of Science and Industry is in Exhibition Park.

Foremost of Newcastle parks is the vast Town Moor which gives this highly industrial city its unique breathing space in 927 windswept acres on which freemen can – and do – pasture cows. The country's biggest fair or "hoppings" is held there in June.

NORHAM, *Northumberland* (14–NT9047). The pinkish castle rises high on rocks above the River Tweed and the view of it from the riverside near the bridge was the one chosen by Turner to paint. The ruin, in the care of the Ministry of Public Building and Works, is what remains of a major border stronghold. It was built about 1160 by Bishop Pudsey of DURHAM as the capital of Norhamshire, part of the Durham palatine. Its keep was one of the best of its period in Britain. Alterations were made into the 16th cent. and the ruins were partially restored in 1900. The road from BERWICK now runs through what was the castle moat. The village with its large triangular green is one of the oldest on the border and it suffered all of the usual vicissitudes. St Cuthbert's, a plain church which faces the castle across the green, once was held as a fortress for a year by the Scots. It is early Norman in its foundation although Christianity was practised here in the 7th cent. around a preaching cross. At midnight on 14 February each year the vicar blesses the nets to open the salmon fishing.

Kenneth Scowen

Newcastle-upon-Tyne: a view of the bridges over the river

NORTHUMBERLAND NATIONAL PARK, *Northumberland* (14–NY8595). Most of the county's fine wild uplands are within the 398 sq. m. of the park, designated in 1956. It runs from the CHEVIOT HILLS in the N. to HADRIAN'S WALL in the S. and forms an eastern boundary to the Border Forest National Park. It takes in the SIMONSIDE HILLS. The variety of landscape is wide, with mountains, moors, forests and river valleys. The park is dotted with the sites of Ancient British tribes and evidences of Roman occupation, as well as with survivals of border defences. Many places are associated with early Christianity. The **Pennine Way** enters the park near Greenhead and leaves some 60 m. further N. near the Roman camps of Chew Green on the Scottish border. Information centres with exhibits of the geology, history, flora and fauna of the park area are maintained at INGRAM and near the Once Brewed youth hostel. A 40-m. stretch of the coast, from WARKWORTH to near BERWICK was in 1958 declared an area of outstanding natural beauty.

NORTON, *Durham* (15–NZ4421), is a Georgian suburb which first catered for merchants from STOCKTON-ON-TEES and now is taking the well-off overflow from the newer BILLINGHAM chemical industry as well. Yet it has managed to main-

tain its village tranquillity. The tree-shaded High Street leads to a green bordered with numerous fine houses, including a handsome 1762 vicarage. Once Norton eclipsed Stockton in importance. The Norton Iron Co. in 1856 made the first bell for Big Ben. But it cracked when tested, and the contract went to another firm. The ironworks closed in 1916. St Mary's Church is the only cruciform Anglo-Saxon church in the North. The crossing tower, with eight triangular-headed windows, has a battlemented top of later date. The rest of the church has been altered at various times. There is an excellent 14th-cent. effigy of a knight in chain mail, bare-headed and cross-legged. At his feet are a lion and a dog, and a small figure reading prayers. A comical head peers over his shield. In the churchyard is the grave of John Walker who invented matches (or friction lights as he called them).

With Stockton and Billingham, Norton was incorporated in the county borough of Teesside in 1968.

OTTERBURN, *Northumberland* (14–NY8893). The battle of Otterburn (better known in song as Chevy Chase) was fought in August 1388. Historically it may have settled nothing but it achieved fame through the best known of border ballads. It was fought between soldiers led by the

Earl of Douglas and Sir Henry Percy. The Scots won the moonlight affray but Douglas was killed on the battlefield about $1\frac{1}{2}$ m. NW. There is a memorial at Bennetsfield. Otterburn is a sleepy kind of place on the River Rede on the NEW-CASTLE–Carter Bar road. This route, which crosses the CHEVIOT HILLS, offers immense blue vistas. The Otterburn Towers Hotel occupies the battlemented mansion which was built on to a medieval peel-tower. The Otterburn Mill, still using an old water-wheel, produces widely known tweeds and rugs, and visitors may see them made.

OVINGHAM, *Northumberland* (14–NZ0863), and **Prudhoe** occupy opposite banks of the River Tyne, with a narrow iron bridge connecting them across the wide river bottom. Ovingham is known for Thomas Bewick who was born at Cherryburn House across the river in 1753. He taught himself to draw and when every inch of his books was filled, he drew on the church floor and grave-stones. The only paintings he knew were the pub signs. He was apprenticed to Ralph Beilby, a NEWCASTLE engraver, and went on to become one of the great artists of that and later days. His best works were a history of quadrupeds and British birds. He died in 1828 and a monument in the chancel here pays tribute to the local boy "whose genius restored the art of engraving on wood". The church has a large late Anglo-Saxon west tower, dated 1050, probably originally defensive. Roman stone went into the church building; most of the present fabric is 13th-cent. in origin. The vicarage is partly 14th-cent.

Prudhoe is the bigger and more industrial community. It consists mostly of long terraces of houses on the steep river bank as well as much new housing. But on a wooded spur overlooking the Tyne, is Prudhoe Castle. It has been taken over from the Duke of Northumberland by the Ministry of Public Building and Works and is to be opened to the public. Prudhoe (proud hill) was built by the d'Umfravilles as an earthwork defence about 1150, with a stone curtain wall and keep added in the late 12th- cent. It was strengthened further in the 13th cent. and came into the hands of the Percys in 1381. Its substantial remains include an almost perfect 14th-cent. barbican, a long stretch of curtain wall and a splendid gatehouse. Above the latter is a chapel with the oldest oriel window in England, it is believed. A second-story chamber has its original chimney and battlements. The castle never fell until Oliver Cromwell knocked down the tower with cannon fire.

A Georgian house was built in the inner court-yard. There is a legend that a lady walks in the corridors, but the caretaker has never seen her. There is another that Prudhoe is connected to BYWELL Castle, miles away, by a secret under-ground passage.

PENSHAW MONUMENT, *Durham* (15–NZ 3253). This notable landmark on the A183 SW. of SUNDERLAND was erected to honour the Earl of Durham, first to bear that title and first High Commissioner for Canada, in 1844. It stands on Penshaw Hill in the form of a roofless Doric temple. The National Trust owns it now. Visitors will be rewarded with a splendid view of north Durham, collieries, quarries and all.

PETERLEE, *Durham* (15–NZ4440). The most distinctive of Durham's new towns, Peterlee was established near Easington to accommodate some 30,000 people, to provide a shopping and re-creational centre for many more, and to attract industry employing women into the south-eastern part of the county. The last objective had to be revised to give priority to jobs for displaced colliers as pits in the area closed down. The Victor Pasmore houses of timber panels and brick in a white and dark grey-blue colour scheme surround a modern centre with two-tier shops, car parks, blocks of flats, civic offices and places of enter-tainment. So far, the new town has acquired firms producing such things as clothing, potato crisps, zip fasteners, wall coverings, fire surrounds, lingerie, kitchen units and machine tools. Inter-national Business Machines is setting up a centre for research into management science and com-puter application which, the developers hope, will bring other laboratories and institutes here and make Peterlee the "intellectual powerhouse" of its region.

Peterlee has what most new towns can only dream about – a nature reserve of its own. **Castle Eden Dene**, now owned by the development corporation, is one of the last unspoilt wood-lands in eastern Durham. It runs about 3 m. to the North Sea. Hundreds of species of flowers, grasses, ferns, trees and shrubs as well as bird, animal and insect life have been identified here. In the tiny village at the head of the dene is Castle Eden Castle, an 18th-cent. mansion now the property of the National Coal Board. In the 1764 church, a rich stained-glass window by L. C. Evetts commemorates the last survivor of the Burdon family which held the manor from 1758.

Peterlee is named after Peter Lee who died in 1935. He started work in the pits at 10 and rose to become president of the Miners' Federation and first chairman of a Labour county council. He was also a Methodist preacher.

PIERCEBRIDGE, *Durham* (15–NZ2115), was built inside the nearly 11-acre area of a Roman fort which guarded Dere Street where it crossed the Tees. It was the largest fort in the county, and could have accommodated 1,000 cavalry. The fort was constructed about A.D. 297 and the only remaining evidence of it is some turf-covered mounds and part of the drainage system in the north-east corner. The most picturesque part of the village is the rectangle of white-washed and red-roofed cottages round the broad green. The village museum has some of the relics excavated on the fort site. A three-arched, 18th-cent. bridge, recently widened, now spans the river. On the Yorkshire side is the old George Inn where the clock that inspired the song "My grandfather's clock" stands in a passage.

PITTINGTON CHURCH, *Durham* (15–NZ 3245), is originally Anglo-Saxon, was dedicated to St Lawrence, and worth seeing for the 12th-cent. north arcade, consisting of six round arches with bold zigzag carving. The eight-sided pillars have alternating square and round reeding and the circular ones a dashing spiral motif, both in high relief, and similar to, though livelier than, those in DURHAM Cathedral. Many other features will repay close study. In the jambs of the Anglo-Saxon windows are traces of 12th-cent. red paintings, depicting the consecration of St Cuthbert and his vision in WHITBY Abbey. There is a Norman font, a 13th-cent. cross-legged knight in Frosterley marble and a 13th-cent. foot-long monument to two boys, with two toy swords carved on it. An 1183 tombstone to "Christian" may mark the grave of Bishop Pudsey's master mason during the great period of church building in Pudsey's long reign from 1153 to 1195 as bishop.

ROKER, *Durham* (15–NZ4059). With **Seaburn,** Roker is the pleasure ground of SUNDERLAND. Within 10 minutes of the city centre on the north shore, tired workers can find every sort of recreation from angling and archery to tenpin bowling and tennis. There are parks, a 1½-m. promenade, sandy beaches, car parks and picnic areas. In Roker Cliff Park, a memorial cross to the Venerable Bede was erected in 1904. St Andrew's Church (1906) is a successful example of neo-Gothic architecture. Its modern fittings, including tapestry, carpets, furniture and glass, also are admired. On the sea-front can be seen the unique "cannon-ball" rocks, formed from the underlying limestone bed.

ROMAN WALL, *see* HADRIAN'S WALL.

ROS CASTLE, *Northumberland* (14–NU0725). Many a native Northumbrian will insist that the view from Ros Castle surpasses all others in this county of splendid views. This is a 1,000-ft height overlooking CHILLINGHAM. It has easy access, for the motorist can drive from the A1 to within a 10-minute climb to the top. The outlines of an ancient fort can be traced on the summit. But visitors are chiefly rewarded with a sweeping picture which embraces to the E. the FARNE ISLANDS, BAMBURGH and DUNSTANBURGH castles on the shore and to the W. the CHEVIOT HILLS. Just below lies Chillingham Park with an occasional glimpse of its herd of wild white cattle. This was a favourite spot for Viscount Grey of Falloden and 7½ acres on the crest were given to the National Trust in his memory. Ros Castle was doubtless a beacon hill in prehistoric times and in the days of border fighting, too.

ROTHBURY, *Northumberland* (14–NU0601). Few villages in the county have a longer history than Rothbury, which can trace its origins to long before the Norman Conquest. It spreads over the banks along the narrowing Coquet valley and makes an ideal centre for touring, walking, or fishing for trout and salmon. It is convenient for visits to the CRAGSIDE gardens and BRINKBURN PRIORY. The SIMONSIDE HILLS stretch to the S. The ruins of Cartington Castle stand 3½ m. to the NW. Across the river is Whitton where a peel-tower has been converted into a children's convalescent home. Other such fortifications stand at Tosson and Hepple. Lordenshaws Camp, a well-preserved hill-fort, is also nearby. Rothbury has a cheerful atmosphere suitable to its reputation as a healthful summer resort. The main street, lined with sycamores, cuts through a sloping green with shops and houses above and below it. Visitors are welcomed at all local dances, concerts, matches, and sports clubs, although officials admit most of those who come are apt to be solitary anglers or walkers. To the W. of town, a row of benches beside the road encourages travellers to linger over the view across the Coquet to the Simonsides. Lord Armstrong, the inventor and engineer who died at Cragside in 1900, is commemorated in the chancel screen of the parish church.

RYTON, *Durham* (15–NZ1564). This former colliery village, always one of Tyneside's attractions, made such a good readjustment after its five famous pits closed that it won a Britain in Bloom trophy in 1968. After the first mine opened in 1800, the industry grew rapidly here. Then 10 years ago, the pits were shut down. Ryton's determined citizens removed the pit-heads and heaps and introduced modern light industries on landscaped sites. The fine 18th-cent. buildings on the wooded, sloping green are now shown to even better advantage. Many residents work in NEWCASTLE-UPON-TYNE. The 13th-cent. broach spire of Holy Cross Church rises 120 ft. Among its possessions is a 13th-cent. Frosterley marble effigy of a deacon holding a book, resting his head upon a cushion.

SEAHAM, *Durham* (15–NZ4250). Lord Londonderry hired John Dobson of NEWCASTLE-UPON-TYNE to design a port to ship his coal. Operations began in 1828 amid the firing of cannon and the cheers of 5,000 people. There is nothing picturesque about it; it is just a workaday outlet for colliery wastes and a declining coal trade. The promenade on the sea-front to the N., however, is good for views. On the limestone cliffs above is St Mary's Church, in the old village, an interesting small and low building with aisleless nave and chancel, dating from Anglo-Saxon times. Some Roman stones were used in the walls. Over the double piscina, a carved hand seems to be raised in blessing. There is an early 13th-cent. font and a 16th-cent. pulpit.

Seaham Hall was the scene of the unfortunate marriage of Lord Byron and Anne Isabella Milbanke in 1815. Byron, we are told, loathed Seaham and wrote to a friend, "Upon this dreary coast we have nothing but county meetings and shipwrecks; and I have this day dined upon fish, which probably dined upon the crews of several colliers lost in the late gales."

Seaton Delaval is a masterpiece in the Palladian style by Sir John Vanbrugh

SEAHOUSES, *Northumberland* (15–NU2232). Boat trips to the FARNE ISLANDS start from this busy little port. The village grew up in the late 19th cent. when the harbour here was built to serve North Sunderland inland. A small fleet of fishing-boats still works out of Seahouses but the chief reason for existence now seems to be summer visitors. The village centre is a car park and new houses fill the perimeter. Excellent sandy beaches stretch S. towards BEADNELL and EMBLETON bay.

SEATON DELAVAL HALL, *Northumberland* (15–NZ3075), is held by many to be Vanbrugh's masterpiece. No other work of the architect is so "mature, so compact and so powerful", Pevsner says. No expense was spared when Admiral George Delaval commissioned a new mansion that would compare with CASTLE HOWARD or any other great house. It took 10 years and was finished in 1728, five years after the admiral's death from a fall from his horse. His nephew, Captain Francis Blake-Delaval, inherited. He had a family of eight sons and five daughters and they led a gay and spendthrift life.

The house, said a visitor, was "an Italian palace, and the grounds were a perfect fairyland". The Delavals loved entertainments and on one occasion borrowed Drury Lane Theatre for their own production of *Othello*. The House of Commons adjourned two hours early to attend. The captain's son, Sir Francis, was fond of practical jokes, such as suddenly lowering the beds of guests into cold baths in the middle of the night. He was also, it should be added, an M.P. of talent.

Built in the Palladian style, Seaton Delaval consists of a central block with a great entrance flanked by huge Tuscan pillars and dominated by a lofty portico. On either side are long wings. Visitors can tour the uninhabited main block with its statuary, spiral staircases and room of historic documents; the modernized west wing, now the family residence of the owner, Lord Hastings, and the stables in the east wing. The 18th-cent. gardens have been restored.

The hall was burnt twice, stood without a roof for 50 years and was used by the military in both World Wars. It was nearly derelict when the restoration work began more than 20 years ago. Medieval banquets with traditional entertainments, costume and pageantry are held here for the public most evenings.

In the grounds is the tiny Norman church, consecrated in 1102 as a family chapel, and made into a parish church in 1891. The nave has its original west door and broad arch with zigzag ornament leading into the chancel. There are two 13th-cent effigies of a knight and a lady.

Seaton Sluice is the harbour built by Sir Ralph Delaval in the early 17th cent. at the outlet of Seaton Burn. It was a flourishing port for two centuries.

SEDGEFIELD, *Durham* (15–NZ3528), has been an active market town since the 14th cent. St Edmund's Church has 17th-cent. carved oak woodwork in the style of Cosin comparable with that at BRANCEPETH. It is by the same craftsman, Robert Barker, who lived here. The church building is mainly 13th-cent., with a particularly beautiful nave and a 15th-cent. tower rising 90 ft and topped with battlements and pinnacles. The Cooper almshouses date from 1703 and the rectory from 1792. The spacious Georgian manor house is now the headquarters of the Rural District Council. A Shrove Tuesday football match has been played on the green here since the 12th cent. This old game of "pila" originated in CHESTER-LE-STREET and is played between tradesmen and countrymen. The game can last for hours and get rather rowdy. The object is to "alley" the ball – get it into the part of the village defended by the other side. It is said to have started from a quarrel between Chester-le-Street apprentices and a retainer at LUMLEY CASTLE, and the first football used was the latter's head. Sedgefield is a centre for fox hunting and its racecourse has six steeplechase meetings yearly. Hardwick Hall, 1 m. W., is a fine 18th-cent. mansion which in recent years has been a workers' training centre and a maternity hospital. Now it is a hotel. Several ornamental but deteriorating outbuildings are attributed to James Paine. They are an octagonal temple, a banqueting house and a sham gatehouse.

SIMONBURN, *Northumberland* (14–NY8773). A green surrounded by low cottages, many of them white-washed, friendly gardens, and tall trees: that is all there is to Simonburn, but it is enough to make it lovely. There is a fragmentary ruin of Simonburn Castle within short walking distance. The last attack on it is said to have been by villagers searching for a hidden treasure which reputedly was so great it could buy all of Northumberland. On the crags nearby is a circle of four standing stones known as the Goat Stones. St Mungo's Church is a handsome buff stone building of 13th-cent. origin with rebuildings in 1762 and 1863. The floor slopes from W. to E., in harmony with the site, or perhaps because the chancel was once a few steps down from the nave. Portions of ancient carved stones are attractively set in a niche in the porch. An original double piscina is in the sanctuary wall. Near the wooded churchyard stands the 18th-cent. rectory.

SIMONSIDE HILLS, *Northumberland* (ROTHBURY: 14–NU0601). The sharp outline of this range of hills in the centre of Northumberland suggests a series of steps or breaking waves, and offers a notable contrast to the great domes of the CHEVIOTS to the N. The Simonsides are rocky and heather-clad, good to look at and to climb for justly famous views. The centre for the sandstone range is ROTHBURY. The highest peak is Simonside, 1,409 ft, which can be climbed from Great Tosson, a hillside village SW. of Rothbury. The view from this summit encompasses the whole Northumberland coast, in fine weather. Access to the Simonsides is somewhat restricted by forestry plantations and the Redesdale All Arms Range. The Grasslees Valley divides the Harbottle from the Simonside hills.

SOUTH SHIELDS, *Durham* (15–NZ3667), was established by the Romans about A.D. 80 but their real interests lay up the Tyne at NEWCASTLE, and South Shields never caught up with its neighbour. Nevertheless, through the centuries, it has been important for saltworks, glass-making, coal-mining, shipping, ship-building, engineering, electronics and the manufacture of such items as cigarette filters, women's clothes, meat pies and metal tanks. Recently a large chain of northern night clubs was launched here. The port runs from Jarrow Quay to Souter Point 3 m. S. and the great Tyne Dock handles iron ore for the works at CONSETT, as well as other cargoes. The town gives a strong impression of pulling down and putting up as dreary terraces yield to modern housing. Like several other Durham industrial areas, South Shields has its breezy escape, in this case to a variety of sea-front parks, long sandy beaches and a broad grassland known as the Leas along the Coast Road. There is a thoughtfully planned garden for the blind with flowers chosen for their scent and shrubs labelled in Braille. The Marine and Technical College is a notable centre for the study of marine engineering and navigation. The Museum exhibits the original model of the first self-righting lifeboat, invented by William Wouldhave in 1789. A memorial to him and Henry Greathead, the shipbuilder, stands at the sea end of Ocean Road. The world's first lifeboat service began here in 1790. Ocean Road-King Street cuts through the northern tip of the town. At the Tyne end is the small square 1768 Town Hall, with an arcade round the ground floor and an upper room ornamented by Venetian windows. Twice-weekly markets are held in the large Market Place outside, near the rail, bus and North Shields ferry terminals. Also nearby is a late-18th-cent. church, St Hilda's. The 20th-cent. Baroque municipal buildings in Westoe Road have been called "the most convincing expression in the county of Edwardian prosperity". An island of good Georgian and Victorian houses survives in Westoe Village, on either side of a long green. No visit is complete without a call at the Roman fort, Arbeia, on the Lawe at the north end of Baring Street. Although surrounded by houses and a

school, it is quite possible to imagine from the excavated evidence the great supply base this was in the early 3rd cent. There were nine large well-ventilated graneries, an imposing headquarters, barracks and offices. In the 4th cent., four granaries were converted to quarters for the garrison which now included experienced Tigris lightermen. They took ship cargoes by boat upriver to Wallsend and beyond. In the museum on the site, see the two famous tombstones. One commemorates Victor, a 20-year-old Moor and ex-slave of a Roman trooper, pictured in paradise being handed a cup of wine. The other depicts Regina, a native Briton who was enslaved then freed and married by a Syrian soldier. She is shown in a wicker chair with her jewel box and sewing basket to hand. For a good view of water-front activity, take the River Drive curving NE. from the Market Place.

STAINDROP, *Durham* (15–NZ1220). St Mary's is an exceptionally interesting church and not solely because of the many monuments to the Neville family of nearby **Raby Castle.** The blocked round-headed windows in the upper nave walls indicate an earlier Anglo-Saxon church. The west tower is Norman and the aisles and arcades were added in about 1170. A century later, the north transept was added, with a two-story priest's dwelling, now the vestry, and the east chancel. The south aisle and porch were built in 1343. In the 15th cent. the tower was heightened and clerestory and flat nave roof added. It is an architectural text spanning some six centuries. The church has the only pre-Reformation screen in the county. Among the numerous effigies is a battered alabaster tomb-chest of 1425 bearing the figures of Ralph Neville and two wives. Other monuments, which overflow into a mausoleum, date from the 13th to 19th cents. The village grew up beside the castle and has a single street with a very long green between two lines of houses, some 18th-cent. and earlier.

The full splendour of a medieval stronghold can be seen in the castle, the seat of the Nevilles for two centuries and in the hands of the Vanes since the early 17th cent. It is open two afternoons a week. It stands superbly in a great park of 270 acres with gardens, deer and two lakes. The fortress is built round a courtyard and encircled by a moat. Its notable features include the Neville gateway, which allowed carriages to drive inside and stop near an inner stair, and the nine distinctive towers. The highest of these is the Clifford, 80 ft high, and the others are known as Joan, Kitchen, Bulmer, Watch, Chapel, Raskelf, Keep and Neville. Although it existed as early as 1016, and has been altered in later years, the castle looks essentially 14th-cent. Much history was made here. In the vast Baron's Hall, the Rising of the North, intended to put Mary on the throne in place of Queen Elizabeth, was planned on 13 November 1569. It failed, and the castle was forfeited to the Crown. In addition to portraits by Lely, Reynolds, Kneller and others, the castle contains interesting furniture and ceramics. The

octagonal drawing-room is said to be the finest Victorian drawing-room in the country. The kitchen has a smoke-driven spit and the stables house a fine array of carriages.

STAMFORDHAM, *Northumberland* (14–NZ 0772). Recent additions do not detract from the 18th-cent. feeling of the village with its rows of houses confronting each other across a long, bare village green. Between them is the plain little 1736 market cross. St Mary's Church, the oldest structure here, has a tower, chancel and priest effigy (possibly the oldest in Northumberland) all dating from the 13th cent. Interesting parts of medieval coffin covers are inserted in the porch. The church had extensive work done on it in 1848.

STANHOPE, *Durham* (14–NY9939), the "capital" of Weardale, lies high in the moorland with fells reaching more than 2,000 ft towards the SW. Weardale is a quiet holiday haven, an old lead-mining centre which is now more concerned with farming, quarrying and visitors. The area, still rich in beauty-spots, walks and drives, once provided good hunting for medieval knights and princes of the Church. There are plentiful caravan and camping sites. Stanhope itself is memorable for its lime trees, the Old Rectory, which was built in 1697 and rebuilt as it was in 1821, the 18th-cent. castle, and St Thomas's Church, with the market cross at its gate. The church dates from 1200. In the sanctuary hang two interesting Flemish carved oak plaques (one showing Adam and Eve and the other Christ baptizing St Peter) and a painting, probably also Flemish. The old stone font is thought to be Anglo-Saxon. The Victorian font is of Frosterley marble and local marble also borders the altar dais. Stanhope Castle, fronting the market place, was rebuilt in 1798 on a medieval foundation. It is now an approved school for boys. A Roman altar discovered in the 18th cent. on Bollihope Common is in the choir vestry. The giant stump of a fossilized tree can be seen through a gap in the churchyard wall. At the west side of town, a path up Stanhope Dene leads through a wooded gorge to **Heathery Burn Cave,** where in 1843 men building a tramway for a limestone quarry broke into a cave from which a remarkable collection of Bronze Age tools and weapons was taken in the next few years. The finds are now in the British Museum. They are believed to be relics of a wealthy family which took refuge in the cave and was drowned when the waters rose rapidly. Among the articles found were spearheads, axes, a gold bracelet, a bronze bucket, and cheek pieces and a bit which pointed to the first use of domesticated horses and wheeled vehicles in Britain.

STOCKTON-ON-TEES, *Durham* (15–NZ 4419), since 1968 administratively part of Teesside, is famous for an open-air market which started in 1310. It is still held on Wednesdays and Saturdays in the broadest High Street in England. There are some 175 open-air stalls and 75 more in a covered market building called the Shambles.

Stanhope: lies in the high moorland country of Weardale   Kenneth Scowen

On an island in the street is the 18th-cent. red-brick Town Hall. History was made in Stockton when the world's first railway passenger train steamed in on the afternoon of 27 September 1825. The same century saw its development as a ship-building and engineering centre. Its factories have diversified in the 20th cent. St Thomas's Church, a spacious red-brick edifice built in 1710–12, is supposed to have had the benefit of Sir Christopher Wren's advice. It was here that John Walker, a chemist, invented the friction match in 1827. He made and sold them at his shop for a couple of years and then left the exploitation of his idea to others. Thomas Sheraton was born here in 1731, but he made his name after he moved to London.

SUNDERLAND, *Durham* (15–NZ3957). The county's largest town (pop. 220,000) grew out of three settlements at Wearmouth: MONKWEAR-MOUTH, N. of the river under the monks of DURHAM; Bishopwearmouth on the south bank, which belonged to the Bishop of Durham; and Sunderland to the E., which had been "sundered" from the monastery founded in 674. Although its origins are ancient, the town achieved size only with the Industrial Revolution and it is today undergoing another kind of renewal. It claims, for example, to have built more new houses per head of population than any county borough in Britain since the Second World War. The visitor can read the story in the new estates forming a wide outer fringe and the belt of dingy commercial and domestic building surrounding the old centre. This has been a ship-building and coal-exporting town since the 14th cent. Glass-making became the first other industry in the 17th cent. The 18th cent. brought potteries, a theatre and the Wear-mouth Bridge (replaced in 1929). This was one of the first cast-iron bridges, and the biggest, with a span of 236 ft. It was originally designed by Thomas Paine, author of *The Rights of Man*, for Philadelphia, Pa. The 19th cent. was one of rapid growth and booming trade with new docks, the railway, the development of marine engines, and the erection of numerous undistinguished public buildings. It is famous today for a first division football team, but it lives on its ship-building, marine engineering and great variety of new manufacturing. It still makes traditional stained glass but also modern ovenproof glassware. It has created a new shopping centre with a hotel, walkways, car parks, offices and flats. Sir Basil Spence designed the £3 million new civic centre near Mowbray Park.

Sunderland prides itself on a reputation for friendly, civic-minded and forward-looking people. It pioneered in developing the Empire Theatre (now leased to a private operator) as a social service to bring the arts to the people, with opera, films, ballet and drama, drawing large audiences. Its technical college was the first in the country to offer sandwich courses. The Museum contains an important collection of local pottery and glass, including the Rowland Burdon collection of Sunderland lustre ware. There is also the James Wilson Collection of English silver from the 15th to the 19th cent. Models, paintings and prints of locally built ships are also on display. Other exhibits call attention to the inventions of native sons: Dr William Reid Clanny's miners' safety lamp and Sir Joseph Wilson Swan's electric lamp. To see Sunderland as a whole, go to Mow-bray Park in the centre where, near the bronze statue of General Sir Henry Havelock, hero of the Indian Mutiny (who was born at Ford Hall nearby), there is a panoramic view of town, docks and sea. ROKER and Seaburn on the northern edge of modern Sunderland give the populace its own seaside resort area.

TWIZEL, *Northumberland* (14–NT8743). Some 5 m. S. of NORHAM, a historic bridge in a wooded setting marks the confluence of the Rivers Till and Tweed. The bridge is thought to be 15th-cent. It is narrow and unusually high (46 ft) with a 90-ft span. High up on the bank are the pathetic ruins of an 18th-cent. folly, Twizel Castle, with its back in a ploughed field. Sir Francis Blake began to build his medieval fortress about 1770. In 1812 it was five stories high but never finished. Much of its stone has gone into another house.

TYNEMOUTH, *Northumberland* (15–NZ 3468). A walk along the ¾-m. North Tyne Pier has been called a trip to sea without leaving land. It is an excellent vantage point for ship-watching or for viewing the priory ruins and the coastline. Tynemouth occupies the cliffs on the north side of the river mouth and it has been known as a seaside resort for at least 200 years. It had a rapid growth in the 19th cent. The haunting intermingled ruins of Tynemouth Priory and Castle stand on the crag above the North Tyne Pier. The surviving parts date from the 11th and 14th cents. and are in the custody of the Ministry of Public Building and Works. The priory succeeded an earlier 7th-cent. Anglo-Saxon monastery which was destroyed by the Danes in 865. Benedictines founded the later house. Visitors pass through the ruined gateway at the end of Front Street to reach the site where there are parts of the curtain wall, church nave and chancel.

Sheltered by the pier and the headland where the priory stands is Prior's Haven, a sandy cove used for sailing, boating and fishing. On the road above is the Tynemouth Volunteer Life Brigade headquarters and Watch House, containing a collection of relics from 19th-cent. wrecks. The country's first volunteer life brigade was established here in 1869. Near the Watch House is the huge Collingwood Monument, with a highly rewarding view from the top. It was erected in 1845 to Admiral Lord Collingwood who led the British fleet into battle at Trafalgar.

Tynemouth boasts that its Long Sands are one of the finest stretches of beach in the country. They are overlooked by a well-developed amusement centre and park.

Harriet Martineau lived at 57 Front Street from 1840 to 1845 and entertained there the literary lights of her day.

Durham Cathedral   Pix Photos

Industrial Tynemouth is concentrated in **North Shields**, and the two towns are visually almost inseparable. North Shields has a very long history of trades connected with the sea. The port activities of today include ship repairing, coal bunkering, and passenger services to the Scandinavian countries. The fish quay and market attract many visitors. In Northumberland Square is a life-size figure of a CULLERCOATS fishwife known as Wooden Dolly. John Dobson, the NEWCASTLE architect, was born at North Shields in 1787.

USHAW, *Durham* (15–NZ2143). The Roman Catholic St Cuthbert's College stands on a 600-ft hill W. of DURHAM. It was opened here in 1808 by refugees from the seminary founded in Douai in 1568 and destroyed in the French Revolution. Most of the 400 students in residence are training for the priesthood. Francis Thompson, the poet, attended the college. The first buildings were classical in design. Numerous changes and additions in the later 19th cent. were in the neo-Gothic style. The chief architects were A. W. N. Pugin and his son, and Joseph and Charles Hansom. The main buildings surround a quadrangle and include the elaborate and colourful Chapel of St Cuthbert. There is a large library and cloisters and several smaller chapels are also provided. The community is virtually self-sufficient, supplying much of its own food, quarrying its own stone and making its own furniture. Visitors may see it by arrangement.

WALLINGTON HALL, *Northumberland* (14–NZ0384). In the Wansbeck valley, about 1 m. below the pretty village of **Cambo**, stands Wallington Hall, a late 17th-cent. mansion. Together with 13,000 acres and most of the village it was given to the National Trust in 1941 by Sir Charles Trevelyan. It is one of the most distinguished and probably the most popular of the Northumberland stately homes open to the public. The hall was preceded by a border castle and then a 15th-cent. house which was pulled down by Sir William Blackett, a NEWCASTLE merchant, when he built the present elegant buff sandstone residence in 1688. Forty years later, Sir Walter Blackett devoted himself to improving the house and its unprepossessing and largely treeless neighbourhood. He planted woods and hedges and built roads and bridges. He enhanced the hall with staircases and beautiful plasterwork, done by a resident team of Italian *stuccatori* whose masterpiece is the great saloon with its deep coved ceiling. He added stables, cottages and the clock tower to the estate. The gardens were designed by Capability Brown, who began his professional career as a gardener here. Sir Walter died in 1777 and the hall went to his sister, a Trevelyan by marriage.

The next great changes came in 1855 when Pauline Lady Trevelyan, who had made the hall a gathering place for the literary and artistic figures of the day, was persuaded by John Ruskin to cover the central court for a picture

gallery, lighted through a glass roof. The arcading formed recesses in which William Bell Scott, a Newcastle pre-Raphaelite, painted the story of Northumberland: the building of the Roman wall; St Cuthbert; the death of Bede; the invasion of the Danes; the legend of the spur in the dish; Gilpin as the North's apostle; the heroism of Grace Darling; and the final (1861) entrance of the coal and iron age. The hall contains a number of important paintings, including one of Luther by Cranach, and family portraits by Sir Joshua Reynolds and Gainsborough; a collection of Chinese porcelain and a fine library collected by Sir George Otto Trevelyan, the statesman and historian. Also here are books of his uncle, Lord Macaulay, and the latter's writing table. Macaulay wrote much of his *History of the American Revolution* at Wallington.

Appropriately for a seat of a family with a long tradition of public service and learning, the hall has been used for many weekend schools and had the county's first youth hostel.

Cambo on the ridge-top was created as model village in 1740 and is almost unchanged. Its oldest building is the post office-general store which includes a medieval fortified vicarage. Capability Brown, born at KIRKHARLE, went to school here. The church was built in 1842. It has a slender spire and several window memorials to Macaulays and Trevelyans.

A charming arched bridge across the Wansbeck beyond the hall was designed by James Paine about 1760.

WARK-ON-TYNE, *Northumberland* (14–NY 8576). A great horse chestnut tree stands in the centre of the green in this pleasant village on the North Tyne. It was a larger place at one time and can trace its history at least to 788 when it is believed to have been the scene of the murder of the "just and pious" King Alfwald of Northumbria. The Normans had a castle here but only a turf-covered earthwork remains on the river bank. The village itself is particularly charming when seen as a huddle of roofs from the narrow iron bridge that crosses the stream. On the east side of the river, 1½ m. from the village, Chipchase Castle can be seen from the road. The present mansion consists of a 1621 building added to a medieval tower. When it was the capital of Tynedale, Wark (meaning work or earthwork) was the scene of courts held by Scottish kings.

WARKWORTH, *Northumberland* (15–NU 2306). The castle dominates the town from a hill up which the main road angles and climbs. When traffic entered from the N. through a narrow medieval bridge and gatehouse arch, the effect was even more dramatic than today when a new bridge over the Coquet sweeps motorists easily into the centre. The 14th-cent. bridge is now for pedestrians only. The village itself is of interest with terraces of 18th- and 19th-cent. houses built in grey stone with red roofs. It still looks as if it were clinging to the protection of the great stronghold. It is, in fact, tightly packed on a

Seahouses: the harbour   *Kenneth Scowen*

Warkworth Castle was one of the most important in the north of England

peninsula of the river, with the castle guarding the neck and the sea within earshot. St Laurence's Church is the only fairly complete Norman church in the county. It has five Norman windows in the nave, a highly decorated chancel arch and vaulted chancel ceiling, and a rare 14th-cent. stone spire. There is a 15th-cent. priest's room over the porch. The church has a well-preserved effigy of a cross-legged knight of about 1330.

Warkworth, near the mouth of the Coquet, has a sandy beach only 1 m. away and fishing and boating in the river. You can travel by boat from the castle (or follow a shady path) upstream to the Hermitage, an unusual refuge dug into the face of the bluff by some hermit in the 14th cent. Not much is known about him, but he hollowed out a chapel and two living chambers on two floors connected by steps. Hermits lived here into the 16th cent. The hermitage belongs to the Ministry of Public Building and Works as does the castle. Coquet Island offshore was also supposed to be the retreat of solitary monks.

The castle is the most splendid ruin of its type in Northumberland. It has not been extensively restored as were the castles at BAMBURGH and ALNWICK. The first fortification on the site was probably in 1139, with a curtain wall added in the early 13th cent. The chief building period came in the late 14th and early 15th cent. and a good deal remains from this, including the highly impressive keep. The castle came into the hands of the Percys in the 14th cent. and remained theirs for some 600 years.

WASHINGTON, *Durham* (15–NZ3056). A new town is rising upon this former colliery village. Streets of old miners' houses have been demolished, pit-head buildings converted to a museum, and the pit heap moved away. The population eventually will be 80,000. All this is taking place round the original town centre where stands the Old Hall, a medieval building greatly altered in the 17th cent. It housed the ancestors of George Washington, first president of the United States. The Washingtons, under many spellings of the name, were lords of the manor here from 1183 to 1376, when they moved to Sulgrave in Northamptonshire. Their arms, three stars and two stripes, provided the inspiration for the American flag. Gifts from America helped restore the hall, a National Trust property, which is open daily and also serves as a centre for local social events.

WHALTON, *Northumberland* (15–NZ1281). This is the only community in the county known to keep the ancient rite of the bale fire on 4 July, the old Midsummer Eve. The tradition has been observed here for probably 1,400 years, since the Angles originated it. "Bale" is from an Anglo-Saxon word for great fire. It is thought to have been the custom to drive cattle through the fire to purify them or rid them of vermin and at one time the villagers themselves used to jump into the flames. Within living memory, people carried burning branches from the fire around the fields to protect against blight and around houses to fend off witches. Some took home the ashes from the fire for good luck.

Whalton is an exceptionally pretty and well-kept village, laid out along a broad street with stone houses and bright gardens on either side. At the east end is the Manor House, which was four village houses until they were combined and converted by Sir Edwin Lutyens in 1909. The gardens there are sometimes open to visitors.

St Mary Magdalene Church, S. of the main street, although much restored in modern times, retains some interesting early-13th-cent. features. One is a square pier in the north chancel arcade which is made up of four shafts with huge segments of dogtooth carving running vertically between them.

WHITBURN, *Durham* (15–NZ4061). An old custom here, but reported, alas, to be dying out, was the offering of a "hot pot" composed of mulled ale and spirits to newly married couples as they left the parish church. The church itself, a coastal landmark, is early 13th-cent., but with heavy-handed Victorian restoration. The village lies between SUNDERLAND and SOUTH SHIELDS, and has a pleasant sycamore-shaded green. Whit-burn Hall is a rambling building with parts attributed to the 17th and 19th cents. Whitburn House, 19th cent., has a Perpendicular window from St John's Church, NEWCASTLE-UPON-TYNE, in the garden.

WHITLEY BAY, *Northumberland* (15–NZ 3572). Most of the beaches on Northumberland's lovely coast are lightly used and stretches often lie empty, but not so at Whitley Bay, the most popular of the resorts. It is too close to industrial Tyneside, in easy reach for a day's outing. The beach with its grassy banks runs the length of the town. Among the entertainments provided for holidaymakers are one of the North East's biggest amusement parks, a children's sandpit and pool, an ice-skating rink, a bowling club and two miniature golf courses. A full-size golf course has been built over the site of an opencast working. The sea-angling festival here each autumn is the largest in Europe. St Mary's Island lying off the north end of the bay can be reached by foot at low tide or by boat otherwise. Its white lighthouse is a seamark.

WHITTINGHAM, *Northumberland* (14–NU 0611). This inviting village is divided by the River Aln and connected by a fine stone arch for motorists and a pretty footbridge for pedestrians. It was, in olden times, the location of a famous fair (and still holds a games day near 24 August, St Bartholomew's day). On one side of the village is St Bartholomew's Church, where in 1840 an Anglo-Saxon tower was destroyed to make way for one in the Gothic fashion. It has some surviving interior Norman and 13th-cent. features. On the opposite side of the Aln is a peel-tower dating from the 15th cent. Its battlemented top overlooks a new housing estate. Unused now, the tower belonged to Lord Ravensworth of Eslington and existed as early as 1415. In 1845 the tower long used by villagers for refuge "in times of rapine and insecurity" was converted by Lady Ravensworth into an almshouse. There Henry Ogle, inventor of the reaping machine, was born in 1765. He died in ALNWICK workhouse in 1848. Attractive stone houses and shops enclose a small tree-shaded green. CALLALY CASTLE is only 2 m. away.

WINSTON, *Durham* (15–NZ1416). To walk into the shady churchyard of St Andrew's standing on an airy height above the Tees, is to enter an earlier, more peaceful world. The church is a little apart from the village proper. It dates from 1254, with changes made in 1848. There is a small bell-turret, but no tower. Inside is a wide, light chancel with lancet windows, and a trefoiled piscina with nutmeg ornament. Two other interesting windows also light this area, one round-headed and the other slightly pointed, both narrow and both with mouldings around them. The 13th-cent. circular stone font deserves a close look. The date of the carving puzzles experts. The subjects shown are two Celtic-headed dragons biting each other, a flower and oak leaves.

WITTON-LE-WEAR, *Durham* (15–NZ1431). Witton Castle outside the village is almost best known as the home of Sir Thomas Lawrence's painting of Master Lambton, *The Red Boy*. The castle was erected by Ralph de Eure in the 15th cent. and although much altered by rebuilding in the 18th and 19th cents., still presents a romantic front from its valley site, well framed in trees. The castle grounds have become probably one of the county's prettiest caravan and camping places, with woods and stream to give a sense of solitude. The castle was crenellated in 1410. In 1689 it was partially dismantled and the material auctioned. In the early 18th cent. it was rebuilt only to suffer some time afterwards a disastrous fire that took all but the outer walls, tower house and turrets. The living quarters were rebuilt once more.

There is a good view of the castle from the triangular village green which occupies a hillside above the River Wear. Here the Church of SS. Philip and James, of Norman foundation, was rebuilt in 1902. On the north side of town is Witton Tower, a private residence, which incorporates a medieval tower house and even older chapel.

WOLSINGHAM, *Durham* (14–NZ0737). To travellers approaching from the E., Wolsingham is the entrance to some of the finest Weardale scenery. It is sturdily built of stone with a rather prim town hall standing on its own in a small market place. Its chief industry is the large steelworks on the outskirts. This is a good walking centre and Tunstall Reservoir on Waskerley Beck to the N. is a good hunting-ground for birds and flowers. The Parish Church of SS. Mary and Stephen has a late-12th-cent. west tower with the rest 19th cent., in pseudo-Early English style. The sanctuary and chancel are marble-floored, partly in the Frosterley marble of Weardale. The church owns three chained books (not on display). The Grammar School on the west side of town opened in 1911. In Chapel Garth are the bare remains of a moated residence, Chapel Walls.

WOOLER, *Northumberland* (14–NT9928), is a workaday town, but a welcome sight to travellers in the thinly populated Glendale district it serves. It has an unusual number of shops, some 50 for a population of 2,000, since it is the market place for a large sheep-farming and forestry area around. The natural centre for exploring or angling in the CHEVIOT HILLS, it is a breezy place, nicely set above the Milfield plain with the great Cheviot in its background. The town suffered frequent raids in the Middle Ages and destructive fires in 1722 and again in 1862, so there are few buildings of much age. The oldest church building is Presbyterian, founded in 1700. At one time there were three Presbyterian churches at Wooler. It has always been a grey-stone town and it must be said that newer buildings of pantile roofs, stucco and smooth red brick strike a jarring note.

There are many fine walks from Wooler. One of 2½ m. leads to the prehistoric Kettle's Camp and the wishing well, Pin Well, S. of it. The Happy Valley along Colegate Burn involves a 6-m. return walk. Many visitors like to climb Humbleton Hill, just 1 m. away, to see the terrace fortifications, cairn and fine view.

A plaque on Victoria Villas in Queen's Road records the death here in 1906 of Josephine Butler, fighter for women's education and legal rights, who is buried at KIRKNEWTON.

WORM HILL, *Durham* (15–NZ3053). Near Fatfield, just off the A182 S. of WASHINGTON, is a small mound near a bridge, associated with the most famous of the many "loathly worm" legends in County Durham. There is a little war memorial there now, but the mound recalls, for those who enjoy folk tales, the story of the heir of the Lambtons who, while fishing in the Wear, hooked a small worm and threw it into a nearby well. There it grew to enormous proportions, and then spent part of its time coiled (nine times) round Worm Hill and part of the time wound round a crag in the river. Unless it were daily fed the milk of nine cows, it would devour any living creature it could find. The young Lambton returned from the Crusades to find the countryside terrified. He tried to kill the worm by cutting through it, but the worm had the knack of joining its parts as new. Finally, the young man decided to consult a wise woman who told him to don a coat of mail covered with razors and await the worm on its river crag. The worm soon wrapped itself round Lambton and was cut to bits, which drifted away in the water before they could be reunited. In return for the advice, Lambton had promised to kill the first thing he saw after the slaying. He had arranged with his father to send a dog out to meet him at his signal. But the father, happy at his son's success, rushed out himself. Lambton did not carry out his pledge, and the wise woman decreed that for nine generations no Lambton would die in his bed. And none did. "Worm" here seems to have its old meaning of serpent or dragon. The tale may hark back to pagan Anglo-Saxon or Norse dragon-slaying legends which later become localized and acquired Christian elements.

WYLAM-ON-TYNE, *Northumberland* (15–NZ1164). New housing for the workers of NEWCASTLE 8 m. away is filling the outskirts of this village on the last rural stretch of the River Tyne. It goes into history because it is the birthplace of the famous engineer and railwayman, George Stephenson. The 18th-cent. miner's cottage in which he was born in 1781 (and where he lived as a child) was given to the National Trust by the North-East Coast Institution of Engineers and Shipbuilders, but it is not open to the public. The house, known as High Street House, stands beside a line which, in Stephenson's time, was a waggon-way carrying coal waggons on wooden rails from the local colliery. In 1813 on this line William Hedley tried out his pioneer locomotive and namesake, Puffing Billy.

Barnaby

Witton-le-Wear: a view of the river

The North-West

Cheshire   Lancashire   Westmorland   Cumberland

PETER FLEETWOOD-HESKETH

England's North-West comprises the counties of Cheshire, Lancashire, Westmorland and Cumberland. Each has its history and individuality, upon which rests the loyalty of its people. Those who would arbitrarily redraw the boundaries of these ancient territories may not realize what they would be destroying or how bitterly such tampering would be resented and resisted.

The entire region is bounded on the east by the Pennine Chain and on the west by the hills of North Wales and the Irish Sea. Between these are smaller ranges of hills in central Cheshire and Lancashire, and the larger Cumbrian group in the north, which includes Sca Fell Pike (3,210 feet), the highest point in England. The rest is relatively low-lying country, mostly in the south, becoming extremely flat along the Lancashire coast.

The principal rivers of the North-West, from south to north, are the Dee, Mersey, Ribble, Lune and Eden. The Mersey separates Cheshire from Lancashire, but through both now passes the M6 motorway, revealing their landscape to great advantage and leading northwards to the mountainous Lake District which is shared between Lancashire, Westmorland and Cumberland. Of the many lakes in this region Ullswater is the most spectacular, Derwentwater the most picturesque, Wastwater the most sombre, and Windermere the most frequented.

Agriculturally, Cheshire is both pastoral and arable, Lancashire mainly arable in the south, becoming more pastoral towards the north, where it meets Westmorland and Cumberland, which are both predominantly pastoral. Forestry on a large scale is now an important industry in all four counties.

Throughout the North-West stone is the traditional building material in the hilly country – red sandstone in the south and north, millstone grit in the east, and limestone in the centre. In the flat country timber was the basic building material until the introduction of brick in the sixteenth century.

Of the ancient capitals and county towns, Chester and Carlisle retain their cathedrals (the latter much reduced in the Civil War), while Lancaster and Appleby are still dominated by their somewhat remodelled medieval castles.

Modern industry is mainly concentrated in the southern part of the region, where coal has been mined in Lancashire from very early times and salt in Cheshire. Among the Pennine Hills the cotton industry developed logically from the wool trade. Some of the earliest developments of the Industrial Revolution were born north and south of the Mersey, eventually to form an industrial band from Yorkshire to the Irish Sea, with the great cities of Manchester in the east and Liverpool in the west. The Weaver Navigation scheme was undertaken in the eighteenth century to provide an outlet to the Mersey for the salt, mined in central Cheshire, while soon afterwards the Sankey (1755–60) and Bridgewater (1759–65) Canals, the earliest of modern canals, were constructed to serve a similar purpose for the Lancashire coalfields. Here, too, we find the world's first great railway, from Manchester to Liverpool, opened in 1830.

Yet this industrialized region possesses numerous examples of the finer arts: two fine monuments by the younger John Bacon in the parish church of Runcorn, signed and dated 1792 and 1796; and, at Widnes, others by Chantrey and Tenerani in Farnworth church; or Alkrington Hall, four miles north of the centre of Manchester, recently identified as an authentic work of the Venetian architect, Giacomo Leoni.

Cheshire is a county of prosperous farms and large estates. Its roads are good, but inadequately signposted. Chester, of ancient origin, is the capital. It stands on the Dee, near the Welsh border, and its buildings range from the medieval city walls and cathedral, timber-framed Tudor houses and those of Georgian brick, to the great sandstone castle, rebuilt about 1800 in Classic style by Thomas Harrison, who later bridged the Dee here with a single arch of 200-foot span; the handsome Italianate railway station; a fine Gothic town hall of 1869 and the later Victorian work of John Douglas. Threading through the two main streets are the "Rows" – covered footways at first-floor level.

Birkenhead is a modern seaport (though it has an ancient priory) on the flat Wirral peninsula separating the Dee from the Mersey, on whose opposite bank is Liverpool. Crewe, in the south, is also modern, an important railway and industrial town. Among the older, smaller towns, Frodsham, Tarporley and Malpas are as well endowed as any with their legacy of inherited charm.

Cheshire is remarkable for its handsome churches, of which there are many, its ancient castles such as Beeston and Halton – both of them spectacular ruins perched high above the surrounding country – and some great houses. Dunham Massey, near Altrincham, and Lyme, high up on the edge of the Derbyshire moors, are quadrangular Elizabethan houses remodelled (the former almost rebuilt) early in the eighteenth century. Adlington, near Macclesfield, is also an ancient quadrangle with a fifteenth-century timber hall and brick Georgian additions. Doddington, Tabley and Tatton are later Georgian, and there are similar and smaller houses of that era. Peckforton and Cholmondeley are grand nineteenth-century castles; Hawarden Castle is of various dates, while Capesthorne is an early Victorian-Jacobean rebuilding of a burnt Georgian house. Grandest of all, but now largely demolished, is Eaton Hall, built in 1870–82 for the 1st Duke of Westminster by Alfred Waterhouse in robust Victorian Gothic.

In north-east Cheshire there are prosperous suburbs of Manchester at Altrincham and Hale, and beyond Stockport a tongue of hilly, romantic and half-industrial country forming a wedge between Lancashire, Derbyshire and the West Riding of Yorkshire. Lower down the Mersey, at Runcorn, is some of Cheshire's finest scenery. Resembling a miniature Mont Saint Michel, the village of Halton clusters round its lofty ruined castle, its high-roofed Victorian church and eighteenth-century court house. The noble water-tower at Norton stands like a temple on the skyline; and in the west the rugged escarpments of Frodsham and Helsby Crag stand out against the western sky. But at the moment of writing this landscape is being bulldozed out of existence to make way for Runcorn New Town. Twenty-seven good Cheshire farms are disappearing in the process.

At this point we may pass from Cheshire into Lancashire by crossing the magnificent new bridge which brings us over the Mersey into Widnes. North-east from the bridge can be seen the immense new power station at Fiddler's Ferry – an industrial building of vast dimensions, symmetrical in design and perfectly composed from every angle, which retains its elemental beauty through every change of light and shadow.

Kenneth Scowen

The Lake District: the River Derwent in Borrowdale

Lancashire has upwards of a hundred miles of coastline, of which at least thirty have been developed as holiday resorts – Southport, Blackpool, Fleetwood, Morecambe and Grange, to name only the chief ones. A further seven miles comprise the Liverpool docks.

Industry and commerce are mainly in the south of Lancashire, with Liverpool and Manchester as the principal centres. The latter is virtually joined to the East Lancashire manufacturing towns of Oldham, Rochdale, Bury, Bolton and Salford, which are interspersed with innumerable smaller ones. Blackburn, Accrington, Burnley, Nelson and Colne form the northern fringe of industrial Lancashire. Liverpool is almost joined to St Helen's, the seat of the glass-making industry.

The development of the Lancashire coast for recreation began in the eighteenth century, Southport and Blackpool being among the earliest places of resort. The latter was already popular locally in 1730. By 1788 it had fifty houses and four hundred visitors from Manchester at the height of the season. In Southport the first house was built in 1792 but the place did not receive its name till six years later, from Dr Barton of Hoole at a public dinner held there.

These remain the largest of the Lancashire coastal resorts, but many others have since grown up and indeed joined up, all providing for the recreational needs not only of Lancastrians from the more industrial districts but for visitors from elsewhere. To Southport, the first "Garden City", soon was added Birkdale and then Ainsdale, to form a quiet, dignified and rather opulent town largely used by commuters with business in Manchester and Liverpool. Its wide streets are well laid out as tree-lined avenues. The sea, however, has tended to withdraw from this part of the coast as much as it has tried to erode further north.

Blackpool fulfils a rather different rôle, and though it has its permanent popula-

G. Douglas Bolton

A great house in Cheshire: Lyme Hall was remodelled in the 18th century

tion, its prosperity depends largely upon its enormous holiday trade, as well as great political conferences. The sea air at Blackpool is strong and invigorating – somewhat flavoured with fish and chips – in marked contrast to the more relaxing air and genteel atmosphere of Southport.

Now practically joining Blackpool southwards are St Anne's, Fairhaven, Ansdell (named after the Lancashire painter who lived there) and Lytham, an older place, more dignified and less pretentious than some of its neighbours. North of Blackpool is Fleetwood, founded in 1836 to provide a rail and sea link with Ireland and Scotland, and a seaside resort for industrial East Lancashire. It is now chiefly known for its fishing fleets, and might be called the Grimsby of the West Coast. Further north still is Morecambe, whose chief asset is its magnificent view over the Bay to the fells of Cartmel and Furness. On the other side is Grange-over-Sands, a pleasant place of Victorian retirement.

From south to north through Lancashire, along the old Roman road, stand the ancient towns of Warrington, Wigan, Preston (the capital) and Lancaster (the county town). M6 runs close to this route to a point north of Carnforth where it rejoins the old road to Kendal. West of the motorway the land flattens out towards the sea, while to the east it rises gently to the Pennine Chain which forms the frontier with Yorkshire.

North-west, over Morecambe Bay, is the detached part of Lancashire comprising Cartmel and Furness, formerly connected by the coach route over Cartmel Sands. This is the most picturesque part of the county and forms a large part of the Lake District, including the lake of Coniston and its fell, called the "Old Man" – the highest point in the county (2,633 feet) – and more than two-thirds of the shores of Lake Windermere. In the Furness peninsula are the old towns of Ulverston,

The River Mersey at Liverpool

Dalton and Broughton, and the modern ship-building port of Barrow.

Of Lancashire's ancient towns, Lancaster, with its castle, priory church and Georgian streets, is the only one that can claim consistent over-all beauty, though Clitheroe and Broughton-in-Furness have the same quality in a lesser degree. Other towns, however, have buildings or groups of buildings of very high quality that make some compensation for their shortcomings. Liverpool possesses two buildings – the town hall and St George's Hall – which rank among the most beautiful in the world in the Classic tradition, which is magnificently continued in Preston's Harris Library, Museum and Gallery (1882–93). The town halls of Manchester and Rochdale represent the height of Victorian Gothic, while that of Warrington is a perfect Georgian house designed by James Gibbs.

The most important monastic remains in Lancashire are the abbeys of Furness and Whalley, and the priory church of Cartmel, its greatest parish church. Great houses include Towneley Hall, now a museum, Stonyhurst, a public school since 1794, and Hoghton Tower. These are mainly pre-1600. Later in their present form are Croxteth and Knowsley. The castles of Thurland and Hornby are of ancient foundation, though both considerably rebuilt. Among Victorian houses the most important architecturally is Scarisbrick, remodelled in the Gothic style by the Pugins for Charles and Anne Scarisbrick between 1836 and 1870; and Holker is perhaps the most charmingly situated. Both incorporate parts of earlier houses, while Leighton Hall, near Carnforth, a house of many dates, with its "Gothick" front of white stone and mountainous background, provides a piece of breath-taking scenery that has no rival in the county.

Besides these, Lancashire still has a number of lesser country houses – "semistalelies" and even the occasional "mini-stately" – but their number has diminished as the families which were their *raison d'être* have died or departed. Like Cheshire, Lancashire has some important timber-framed houses, of which Speke Hall (1500–98), near Liverpool, is one of the most complete, while Rufford Old Hall has the finest fifteenth-century open-roofed great hall.

Westmorland embodies both banks of the Leven estuary, thereby separating Cartmel and Furness from the rest of Lancashire. It includes a large part of the Lake District, with all the mountains and fells from Windermere to Ullswater, while high rolling country stretches away eastwards to make a long frontier with Yorkshire and a short one with Durham. Appleby, in the north-east, is the county town. It has a pleasant wide main street leading up to the gates of the castle, which retains its Norman keep but was otherwise rebuilt in the seventeenth century. It was one of several owned by Lady Anne Clifford (1590–1676), whose tomb and that of her mother are in the church. Kendal (the capital) is a much larger place – the metropolis of the Lake District. It is ancient but has a strongly Georgian flavour, and the ruins of a castle that was probably the birthplace of Catherine Parr. Here the country of Wordsworth and George Romney is entered, through Windermere and Ambleside to Grasmere. As everywhere in this northern region, the farm-houses are low and long and cling to the hillsides.

South of Kendal are the ancient houses of Levens Hall and Sizergh Castle. Near Milnthorpe is Dallam Tower, which is early Georgian. At Shap are the ruins of a medieval abbey and at Lowther the shell of an early nineteenth-century castle that remains a picturesque and commanding feature in a noble landscape. To the south is the eighteenth-century "model" village, well laid out but unfinished. A little to the north is the county boundary.

In Cumberland the first town reached by this route is Penrith, in open rolling country with views of the fells west and south, flattening out northwards to Carlisle, the capital. Westwards from here is the coast on the Solway Firth, and further south the coastal towns of Maryport, Workington and Whitehaven – the chief port in the north-west until overtaken by Liverpool, and an early coal-mining centre where some of the mines ran several miles under the sea. The north of Cumberland is relatively flat, but the south includes some of the most spectacular and magical scenery in the mountain group it shares with Westmorland and Lancashire.

Cumberland's greatest legacy from antiquity is, perhaps, the remains of the Roman Wall which was built in the second century A.D. and restored in the third. It crosses from west to east a little to the north of Carlisle. Next in antiquarian interest are the peel-towers, of which a number survive. Of the ancient religious establishments, Lanercost Priory and the ruins of Calder Abbey are the most important.

Naworth, near Brampton, is possibly the best-preserved ancient castle, and Muncaster, largely rebuilt by Salvin in the nineteenth century, the best situated. Among other castles, Dacre comprises an ancient keep; Greystoke near Penrith is chiefly remarkable for the follies that were built to enliven the views from its windows; Highhead was rebuilt in Georgian days and has recently been burnt; while Dalemain is a fine early Georgian house. Hutton-in-the-Forest is a highly romantic house of three main periods, romantically situated as its name suggests. And among the more picturesque smaller houses are Moresby Hall, north of Whitehaven, and Dalegarth, with its waterfall, in Eskdale. Irton Hall is built round a peel-tower in some of the loveliest country in West Cumberland.

The North-West: Gazetteer

J. B. WILLAN AND BETTY JAMES

ACTON, *Cheshire* (12–SJ6253), is in the neighbourhood of NANTWICH and has fine views over the countryside. St Mary's Church is mainly 13th- and 14th-cent., and its tower, rebuilt in the 18th cent., dominates the village. There are several monuments, including a knight in armour, and a beautiful 17th-cent. screen with rich gates.

ADLINGTON HALL, *Cheshire* (12–SJ8880). This magnificent old house, part Elizabethan timber-and-plaster and part brick from its restoration and enlargement in 1757, is sited on a pre-Norman hunting lodge built between two giant oak trees, the roots of which still support the east end of the 15th-cent. great hall. For 600 years the house has been in the hands of the Legh family, one of the oldest in Cheshire. Sir Uryan Legh, whose smiling portrait may be seen with others of the family collection, was knighted for his services under the Earl of Essex during the siege of Cadiz in 1596. A ballad of the time records that he captured a Spanish lady while he was there and treated her with such courtesy that she declined to be released and insisted on returning to England with him. How Sir Uryan resolved this difficulty is not known, but the gold chain she gave him as a memento of the encounter is included in the portrait. During the Civil War the Hall was strongly besieged for a fortnight and eventually taken by the Roundheads, leaving scars on the exterior apparent to this day. The older part of the house is beautiful for its black-and-white timbering. The gables and porch, the latter dating from 1581, face a wide courtyard and the open roof is mounted on hammer-beams decorated with angels. The Hall is still partly surrounded by an old moat, the whole structure standing in a fine park with one of Cheshire's noblest chestnut avenues. It is believed that Handel once played the organ which stands in the great hall and composed his *Harmonious Blacksmith* when a guest at the house. The organ was the work of Bernard Smith, or Schmidt, in *c.* 1670. Enlarged in the 18th cent., it was put out of action by children about 1800 and restored in the 1950s. Adlington Hall is open to the public.

ALSTON, *Cumberland* (14–NY7146). At Townfoot in Alston the milestone shows a height of 921 ft above sea-level, and not far up the main road it is 1,000 ft. This is the highest market town in England, and although Alston stands in the valley of the South Tyne it is almost surrounded by the highest fells of the Pennine Chain. Five roads converge: NEWCASTLE (A686), CARLISLE, PENRITH, the B6277 from Scotch Corner, and the B6293 from Weardale. Alston is a holiday centre, offering numerous walks in the sweeping moorland scenery. Variations of hardness in the limestone layers produce several waterfalls, such as Ashgill Force.

This was one of the richest mineral areas in Britain until the early 19th cent., with lead and silver, iron, zinc and copper ores and fluorspar. The only workings now are small anthracite drifts. Two Middle or Late Bronze Age barrows were found at Ayle; N., and near it the Roman mounds and ditches of Whitley Castle can be clearly seen. Some old buildings date from the late 17th and early 18th cents., when there was a renewal of mining operations, such as Church Gaytes House (1681) and the Quaker Meeting House (1732–59). The parish church, St Augustine's, built in 1869, is the third on the site and has records from 1154. The 1765 Market Cross, replacing an earlier one, has been knocked down by a lorry. Also of architectural interest are Kirkhaugh Church near Alston, and the Old Manor House on the HEXHAM road. Just W. of Alston runs the **Pennine Way**. It passes through Garrigill (to the SE. near the B6277), which may pre-date the earliest settlement in Alston. Eastward on the B6293 is Nenthead, 1,415 ft, the highest village in England. The Penrith road climbs SW. from Alston on **Hartside Height** to 1,903 ft, offering a panoramic view over the Eden valley: it ranges from Lakeland fells to Scottish hills, with the Solway Firth like a golden ribbon at sunset. Cross Fell, to the SSE., at 2,930 ft is the highest point of the Pennines. The road drops down Hartside with awe-inspiring zigzags to Melmerby.

The Hartside route is not one to choose in ice or snow. Winter is a time when the tourist may be unable to see Alston. He may reach only the north or east edges of the great white waste, since the famous Helm Wind from Cross Fell may have piled snow 15 ft or higher round the isolated town.

ALTRINCHAM, *Cheshire* (12–SJ7687). An industrial and residential centre close to MANCHESTER, but still retaining its own individuality. The town was first granted borough status by Hamon de Massey, Lord of Dunham, in 1290, implying partial relinquishment of the traditional powers of the lord of the manor. It is recorded that since 1452 more than 500 mayors have been elected to office here. Today Altrincham is often

Kenneth Scowen

Ambleside: the Bridge House

chosen as the starting-point for visits to the many beauty-spots in the neighbourhood. Within walking distance of the town, towards the SW., are picturesque villages, ancient churches, and broad stretches of placid water reaching for miles across the countryside. In the environs is Dunham Massey park, where some of the trees in the beech avenue are said to be over 250 years old and a herd of deer roams as it has for centuries past. Dunham Massey Hall, seat of the Earls of Stamford and their ancestors the Booths, is a fine, mainly 18th-cent. quadrangular house of brick and stone.

At **Ringway**, about 4 m. SE. of Altrincham, is Manchester Airport.

AMBLESIDE, *Westmorland* (14–NY3704), is, like KESWICK, a principal tourist centre in Lakeland, particularly for the more southerly areas. The town lies on the main north and south through route, the A591, close to WINDERMERE. Being protected by mountain groups from north and east winds, and open to warmer air from the S., Ambleside claims an equable temperature and, for the Lakes, a comparatively low rainfall, probably due to the fact that the nearest peaks to the SW., the CONISTON fells, are about 3 m. away. The town has many hotels and guesthouses, especially in the newer part, W. of the division made by the main road. Shops offer a variety of holiday equipment, gifts and souvenirs. A pottery shop is called Ruskin House; Ruskin

had close associations with the Lakes, especially Coniston.

In Borrans Park and owned by the National Trust, where the River Brathay enters Windermere, are remains of the Roman fort of Galava, probably built between the 2nd and 4th cents., and of an earlier one believed to be of about A.D. 79 during Agricola's campaign. The Roman road from Ravenglass on the west coast, via HARD-KNOTT, passed near Borrans Field and then over the ridge of High Street mountain range to BROUGHAM. Discoveries in the 21-acre field (open to the public) are in the museum at the Armitt Library. The library itself was endowed by Miss Mary Louisa Armitt, who left her books to it, and opened in 1912. It received the balance of funds of the old Ambleside Book Society (founded in 1828) to which Wordsworth belonged. There are now over 6,000 books and pamphlets in the library, many from donors, of literary, scientific and antiquarian value. The Ambleside Ruskin Library is also housed here.

The former parish church, now used as a parish hall, is of a typically primitive Lakeland type. Attractive old houses are perched around it on the hillside. The present parish church, St Mary the Virgin, on the W., was erected in 1854 to the design of Sir Gilbert Scott. He gave it a steeple – unusual in the Lakes – a handsome feature to be seen across the old roofs of the houses. There is a fine marble reredos. Memorial windows to

Wordsworth and his family are in the Wordsworth Chapel. The Bible on the lectern was given by Mrs Wordsworth. On the west wall a mural (1944) by Gordon Ransom depicts the ancient rush-bearing ceremony. The bearings are now crosses and designs in flowers and rushes, carried by children in a procession to St Mary's in late July. Owen Lloyd, a friend of Hartley Coleridge who was the son of Samuel Taylor Coleridge, composed the rush-bearing hymn which is sung in the Market Place. This ceremony, which has continued for centuries, is believed to derive from the annual renewal of rushes on the church floor in the Middle Ages, or to be a mixture of something like the Roman *floralia* and of a thanksgiving and merry-making to mark the safe gathering of the hay. At GRASMERE there is a similar ceremony, and both have been recorded by Wordsworth.

The tiny Bridge House is a curiosity, only a few yards long, which in the 18th cent. was probably a summer-house for Ambleside Hall. There are two rooms, and the house is now an information centre for the National Trust which bought it by subscription in 1928. The story is told that a Scotsman built this rough stone structure on its arch over the little river so that he could avoid paying ground rent!

Ambleside has many literary associations. The Wordsworths lived at nearby Grasmere and RYDAL, and besides Ruskin and the Coleridges, authors who visited or stayed in the area include Keats, Southey, De Quincey, and Mrs Humphrey Ward. Harriet Martineau, who died in Ambleside in 1876, lived at the Knoll, which is outside the town on the Keswick road. She was visited there by Charlotte Brontë and George Eliot. Along the River Rothay is Fox Howe, the summer residence of Dr Thomas Arnold, the headmaster of RUGBY School and father of Matthew Arnold. Nearby are the much photographed stepping stones across the river. Loughrigg Holme was the house of Wordsworth's daughter, Dora.

The town has sporting facilities, and in August the Ambleside Sports and the internationally famous sheepdog trials are held in Rydal Park. At Waterhead on the N. of Windermere is one of the great boating centres of Lakeland, with a car park. Other lakes within walking distance are ELTERWATER, RYDAL WATER, and Grasmere. There is a variety of routes to explore on foot. STOCK GHYLL is in the park, to the E. Signs from Waterhead lead to Jenkin's Crag with excellent views of Windermere and the mountains. For Loughrigg, *see* Grasmere. Sweden Bridge and Skelwith Force are other walks, as are Nab Scar and Fairfield (2,863 ft), both on the N. Besides the north and south roads for Keswick and WINDERMERE TOWN, other motoring routes are to the NE. for ULLSWATER (the direct route from Ambleside to the KIRKSTONE PASS is not advised for towing caravans), or W. for the LANGDALE PIKES, WRYNOSE PASS, or Coniston.

APPLEBY, *Westmorland* (14–NY6820), is the county town. It is set in the pleasant Eden valley, sheltered from much of the western rains by the LAKE DISTRICT mountains, on a well-drained site in a loop of the river by the A66. To the NE. the Pennines run like a wall for about 30 m. The area is rich in flora and fauna, and geological formations are diverse. Appleby has been an inhabited site for over 1,000 years but has none of the more ancient British remains whose builders, unlike the Anglo-Saxons and Vikings, seemed to prefer the higher land, such as around CROSBY RAVENSWORTH. Traces of the Roman road (BROUGH to KIRKBY THORE) can be seen on the E. but the first evidence of settlers is that of Norsemen in the 10th cent. The town was transferred from Scotland to England only in 1092; but suffered Scottish attacks later, culminating in that of 1388, which laid it waste.

The castle is a motte-and-bailey type of the 12th cent., the main eastern part having been rebuilt by Lord Clifford in 1454. A later member of his family, Lady Anne Clifford, dismantled and restored the castle (now a private residence) in the mid-17th cent. She became an important figure in the history of this part of Westmorland, and rebuilt her family's castles at Brough, BROUGHAM, and Pendragon (KIRKBY STEPHEN), as well as restoring churches in these places and in Appleby, building bridges and endowing almshouses.

Lady Anne's tomb is in St Lawrence's Church. This, the parish church, was rebuilt in the late 12th cent. after the Scots had burnt the earlier one. From that rebuilding there remains the tower's lower story, with its small original window, and the base of the chancel's east wall. There was more rebuilding in the 13th cent., the 15th, and by Lady Anne in the 17th. Most of the clerestory and upper walls are 15th-cent. The organ, formerly in CARLISLE Cathedral, is one of the three oldest in the country. St Michael's has Appleby's oldest stone monument, a Scandinavian hog-back gravestone, built into its north wall. Lady Anne also did much to restore this church.

The main street, Boroughgate, has old houses, mainly Georgian in the upper part. The hospital has old carvings. The grammar school succeeds an earlier building on another site, which has a record of a headmaster as far back as 1478. The school had a number of famous men as pupils, including the Dean of Lichfield (1632–1703), who was the father of Joseph Addison the essayist (1672–1719), and John Langhorne, the translator of Plutarch's *Lives*, published in 1770. The Moot Hall, with one stone dated 1596, is another historic building. The annual fair, traditionally the horse fair, is in June.

There are various pleasant country walks in the neighbourhood, including that to High Cup Nick where a beck flows in unusual Pennine formations.

ARLEY HALL GARDENS, *Cheshire* (12–SJ6565). Arley Hall gardens (open to the public) lie 6 m. from KNUTSFORD on the west side of the M6. These large and old-established gardens are in the estate of Arley Hall (not open), the private residence of Viscount and Viscountess Ashbrook.

The hall has been well known as the seat of the Warburtons since the period of Henry VIII. Teas are provided in the 16th-cent. barn, which is of historic and architectural interest. The gardens have a topiary with roses, rhododendrons, azaleas and a herbaceous border.

ARMATHWAITE, *Cumberland* (14–NY 5046), lies about 2 m. E. of the A6 and SE. of CARLISLE. An old bridge crosses the River Eden and beside the river stands the small Chapel of Christ and St Mary, set in pleasant scenery. The chapel consists of a chancel, a nave, a wooden roof and a small bell-turret. The original 12th-cent. building fell into ruins and was used to house cattle, but was rebuilt in the 17th cent. In 1914 Morris and Co. made the east window.

ASHTON-UNDER-LYNE, *Lancashire* (12–SJ9399). The Church of St Michael, though completely restored, is on a site that has held a church since the 13th cent. St Michael's is noteworthy for its stained glass of about 1500 portraying the Assheton family, and there are also five windows depicting the history of St Helena and her discovery of the True Cross. Sir Ralph Assheton was known as the Black Knight from the colour of his armour and Sir Thomas fought at the battle of Nevilles Cross, DURHAM.

Medlock Vale, 1½ m. NE. of the town, is on the banks of the Medlock with Hen Cote Cottage at Daisy Nook. It is a rural refuge in an industrial area, and comprises 15½ acres of National Trust property, bought in 1944 and 1951.

ASTBURY, *Cheshire* (12–SJ8461). The old church here is mainly of the 14th and 15th cents. and those parts of it still identifiable with that era are excellently preserved. There are two towers, the more ancient, of Norman foundation, being linked on to another built 300 years later and carrying an imposing spire dating from 1823. Several stones from the original structure were employed in the walling of the chancel, some showing fragments of Norman and Anglo-Saxon carving. Grotesque faces peer down from the stonework, and over the door of the west tower porch is a weathered figure with four stone minstrels, one with bagpipes. The south porch has a priest's room and some fine windows, while the church interior has a Jacobean nave roof and massive clustered pillars lending great dignity to the whole structure. During the Civil War Sir William Brereton and his followers made Astbury their headquarters in the siege of BIDDULPH Hall and stabled their horses in the pews, damaging the woodwork and many of the windows and screens. They also dismantled the church organ and buried it in a field which was afterwards known locally as Organ Close. Astbury church contains memorials connected with many of the powerful Cheshire landowning families, the Moretons, Davenports, Venables, Mainwarings, Shakerleys, Breretons, and Wilbrahams, from whom any account of the history of the county is inseparable.

AUGHTON, *Lancashire* (12–SD3905). At Aughton, SW. of ORMSKIRK, is the garden of Cranford (open to the public). It covers half an acre and is of unusual design, with shrubs, roses and rare trees. St Michael's Church is a mixture of styles. The tower has a square base and an octagonal upper part below the Decorated spire. The north aisle is 16th- or 17th-cent., and a north window is dated 1623. There is a Westmacott memorial to a rector. In 1829 the low church building was repaired and pointed.

BACUP, *Lancashire* (12–SD8622), is a town in the Irwell valley, surrounded by stretches of moorland close to the Yorkshire border, with a textile manufacturing background. The Natural History Society Museum has collections of natural history, geology and old household items.

Rawtenstall, on the W., also has moorland scenery. The Museum and Art Gallery is in Whitaker Park. There is a fine art collection, and the museum, although small, has interesting displays of natural history and curiosities and crafts of the area.

BADDILEY, *Cheshire* (12–SJ6049), is a quiet village with the small Church of St Michael, reached by a winding route. The nave lacks aisles and the chancel is built of brick and timber. There is painted work dated 1663 of the Creed, the Commandments, the Lord's Prayer and a coat of arms. There are also box pews and a large monument.

BAMPTON, *Westmorland* (14–NY5118), is a village about 2 m. NE. of the foot of HAWES WATER, in an agricultural area. The Church of St Patrick was founded in 1726 and has timber arcades. There are remains of ancient British settlements in the neighbourhood. In this quiet village the grammar school was founded in 1623 and a number of its pupils reached distinguished positions in various parts of the country. The free library, founded by Lord Lonsdale in 1710, was one of the first in Britain.

BARROW-IN-FURNESS, *Lancashire* (12–SD1969). Although this county borough is better known as an industrial and ship-building town, with acres of docks and quays, there are beaches here. The long stretch of Walney Island shuts off the Irish Sea to enclose the dockyards. On Piel Island the rebuilt castle is a link with the monks of FURNESS ABBEY. The Council runs the town's museum in Ramsden Square. This includes some discoveries from prehistoric sites, mainly Bronze Age, and models and exhibits relating to the area.

BASSENTHWAITE *Cumberland* (14–NY2332). This village lies near the north end of the lake of the same name; to the east side of the A591, and somewhat remote from the Lakes area generally. Its people must have been remote, too, for centuries. There were Norse settlers here: "thwaite", so common in Lakeland and Yorkshire Dales place-names, is from the Norse word for cleared land. In the Middle Ages a church was built beside the village, and in the 19th cent. the Church of St John. During the coaching era Bassenthwaite was on the route to CARLISLE. Armathwaite Hall, before it became a hotel, included among its owners the Speddings (*see* BASSENTHWAITE LAKE), the Vanes, and a family of ironmasters from BECKERMET. The folk hereabouts are said to live long.

BASSENTHWAITE LAKE, *Cumberland* (14–NY2332). Bassenthwaite is a beautiful lake, lying between the smaller peak of Lord's Seat on the W., and the bulk of SKIDDAW on the E. Everyone sees it from the busy route that runs along its west shore between KESWICK and COCKERMOUTH and the Cumberland coast, from which Skiddaw is also prominent, but it is worth going round the N. of the lake and coming S. on the A591 past the wooded reaches of Dodd Fell for the view of the DERWENTWATER valley opening out with Keswick nestling at the head of its lake. It is perhaps passed by more often than visited, because considerable stretches of the lakeside are private property, and so not easy for the tourist to reach. As the most northerly of the Lakes, Bassenthwaite lies in a direct line between breeding grounds of wildfowl at MORECAMBE Bay and the Solway Firth, and is visited by many varieties of migrating birds. Bassenthwaite is usually called a lake, not a "water" or "mere" like the others, and has the largest catchment area of any of them. Counting the stretch from BORROWDALE, it also has the longest valley. Boats can be hired near Piel Wyke.

A mile or so before the south end of Bassenthwaite is the small Church of SS. Bridget and Bega between A591 and the lake. The church is late 12th- to 13th-cent., restored in the 19th cent., and has a Norman chancel arch and Early English features. It is one of two dedicated to St Bega, the other being at ST BEES. Wordsworth and other Lake Poets knew this lakeside church, and Mire House nearby, owned by the Spedding family, also has literary associations. James Spedding, the biographer of Francis Bacon, was visited there by Tennyson, Edward FitzGerald and Carlyle.

Above the main road, near the south end of the lake's 4-m. stretch, is the white rock called the Bishop; there are various stories about its name, some saying a bishop rode up to it. Castle How at the N. (near Piel Wyke) has some traces of an ancient fort, and the early British Embleton Sword was found and sent to the BRITISH MUSEUM.

BECKERMET, *Cumberland* (14–NY0207), is a village S. of EGREMONT, between the A595 and the coast. It has two parts – St John and St Bridget Beckermet – in an old iron-ore producing area. St John's Church has a good site near where two becks meet (hence the village name) and was rebuilt during the 19th cent. It is small but well-designed, with a bell and clock tower. The interesting collection of carved stones dates from before

the Norman Conquest. St Bridget's has two shafts of ancient crosses.

BEETHAM, *Westmorland* (14–SD4979). This village lies off the A6, with two old mills, a waterfall, and a riverside mansion. Beetham Hall was originally a peel-tower and in the Middle Ages became a castle; but it is now a farm-house and the 14th-cent. great hall is a barn. The original Church of St Michael was early Norman, but the present structure shows a mixture of Gothic styles. It is approached under a pergola of rambler roses.

BILLINGE, *Lancashire* (12–SD5300). St Aidan's Church stands on fairly high ground near the south end of the straggling village, and its 18th-cent. structure is in a curious mixture of Classical and medieval styles. It has a clock-turret over the west door and a bell in a cupola above. The small transepts are modern, built in the Gothic style, and the nave arcades have Doric columns. There is a fine two-tier chandelier. The chancel apse has black-and-white marble paving and a domed roof. There are no pews. The old west gallery has extensive panelling.

On Billinge Hill a square stone beacon was put up in 1780 and this site gives a view over the countryside towards the Irish Sea.

BIRKENHEAD, *Cheshire* (12–SJ3188). Birkenhead Priory existed before there was any town of Birkenhead as such. It was founded in the mid-12th cent. when land was granted to a Benedictine order, the Black Monks, who may have come from CHESTER. They favoured this secluded spot near the head of the Wirral peninsula where their priory was screened by forests on the landward side. There was a ferry-boat point nearby over which the monks later gained rights, granted by a charter from Edward III. The remains of the priory were acquired by Birkenhead Corporation in 1896. The Wirral area was less troubled by the strife of the post-Dissolution period than places further inland, and even up to the 19th cent. Birkenhead remained a quiet hamlet. St Mary's was built from 1819 to 1821 as the parish church, in Victorian Gothic style on a cruciform plan. In 1817 the steam ferry began to operate and this encouraged people from the north side of the Mersey to settle in Birkenhead. From 1824 William Laird began to buy land, and established a boiler works and then ship-building yards. The first docks opened in 1847, and from then on the two major industries of ship-building and docks were the decisive influences in the steady growth of the town. Its links with the north side of the Mersey were further improved by the opening of the Mersey rail tunnel in 1886, and the **Mersey Tunnel** in 1934 for road traffic.

In 1826 Hamilton Square was laid out by Gillespie Graham like an Edinburgh square, with the support of William Laird. Originally residential, it is now mainly business premises, and has a public garden. The handsome town hall was built in 1887. Several sites have been used for the Central Library, and the present building was opened in 1934. The large entrance portico is in a dignified Classical style, decorated with marble: grey travertine with a black inlay for the floors, door architraves and wall pilasters and golden travertine marble for the columns. The imposing Williamson Art Gallery was specially designed for its purpose and opened in 1928. English water-colours are a special feature, and there are many English oils of the late 18th and early 19th cents. and some of the 20th cent. The Knowles Boney Collection of Liverpool porcelain may be the largest of its kind in the country. Other ceramics include Japanese, Persian, early Viennese, Vene-tian, Dresden and French pottery, and examples of Crown Derby and Staffordshire work. In 1962 the Shipping Gallery was added which, with models and other material, it illustrates the work of the town and its port. Considerable residential and shopping development has taken place in recent years in Birkenhead and in the outlying districts of Oxton, Claughton and Prenton.

Arrowe Park, which the corporation acquired in 1927, contains 425 acres of fine woodland and a bird sanctuary. There is also a golf course and various playing fields. Arrowe Hall is an 1835 building in Elizabethan style.

Men associated with the town include Lord Birkenhead, better known there as F. E. Smith, who was born at 8 Pilgrim Street; J. L. Garvin of the *Observer* who was born at 117 Anne Street; and Wilfred Owen, the poet, who was born at OSWESTRY, went to Birkenhead in 1900 and died in France a week before the 1918 armistice. At the Y.M.C.A. hall in Whetstone Lane is a tablet that commemorates the inauguration of the Boy Scout movement in Grange Road Hall by Baden-Powell in 1908. Nathaniel Hawthorne lived at Rock Ferry and became American consul at Liverpool in 1853.

Bidston Hill on the NW. is the oldest of the town's open spaces, and the old windmill is a well-known landmark. There is a direction indicator for the extensive views from the top of the hill. Liverpool University has an observatory and Tidal Institute on the hill, which provides meteorological information and makes tidal pre-dictions for some 160 ports throughout the world. Bidston Old Hall, which became a farm-house, is believed to have been rebuilt in 1620 by William, 6th Earl of Derby, and looks down on Leasowe Castle (WALLASEY), another residence of the Stanleys, the Earls of Derby (*see* KNOWSLEY HALL and CHESTER).

BIRTLES, *Cheshire* (12–SJ8574). This is fine walking country, with miles of lanes and tracks inviting exploration of the undulating heights and woodland glades. The hamlet of Birtles, too small to appear on all but the most detailed of maps, offers access to Alderley Park, a beautiful stretch of the central Cheshire uplands containing all that remains of the ancestral home of a junior branch of the Stanley family. The 19th-cent. church, with its octagonal tower and unusual porch, has many attractive roundels in its 16th-and 17th-cent. windows, the dominant colours

employed by the Flemish craftsmen being blue and red.

Birtles Hall is a handsome Georgian house.

BLACKBURN, *Lancashire* (12–SD6827). The town's museum has collections of local geology, mineralogy and natural history, with a small archaeological and Egyptian section, some medieval manuscripts and early printed books, coins (including Roman), porcelain, pottery and glass. The art gallery has oil paintings, 18th- to 20th-cent. English watercolours, Japanese prints and examples of industrial art.

An aspect of the town's industrial background is shown in the Lewis Textile Museum which traces the development of the spinning and weav-ing industries and contains early examples of machinery. James Hargreaves, who was born near Blackburn about 1720, invented a carding machine in 1760 and the spinning-jenny about 1764. These were among the developments which led to the Industrial Revolution. They came at a time when labourers' living standards were affected by bad harvests and the Corn Laws, and there were riots in Lancashire by those who saw their livelihoods further threatened by the intro-duction of machines. Hargreaves' inventions were smashed more than once, and in 1768 he moved to NOTTINGHAM. Richard Arkwright of PRESTON also removed to avoid such attacks. Later these inventions, as at BOLTON, led to enormous expansion of the Lancashire cotton industry.

Blackburn has in recent years seen considerable development and re-planning. Modern industries now range from valve-making to heavy engineer-ing. The town has six parks, and is also within reach of the Ribble and Hodder Valley moorlands.

BLACKPOOL, *Lancashire* (12–SD3035). If there is a form of holiday entertainment that Blackpool cannot provide it is difficult to think of. The town stretches along the Lancashire coast with a resident population of some 152,000, annually swollen by the hordes of people lured to this metropolis of pleasure packed with all the elements of a vast fun-fair. Yet beside the strident and overcrowded entertainments, there is another and a quieter Blackpool – a resort of spacious parks and bowling greens for those who prefer their recreation in a more individual form. The town claims to have everything for holidays, from old-style tram rides along the sea-front to remedial and sauna baths. It also has the Grundy Art Gallery, in Queen Street, with a permanent collection of 19th- and 20th-cent. British artists.

The tower is Blackpool's great landmark. This showpiece and engineering feat is well worth inspection. Except in windy weather, the lift carries passengers to a height of 518 ft for the breathtaking view from the top. Housed in the tower is a fine aquarium, a zoo, a circus, a ball-room and the well-known organ. The promenade runs for 7 m. and most of it is traversed by the trams. Stanley Park has Italian-style gardens, a huge boating lake, and bowls, tennis and golf.

Blackpool: the Tower and the beach

Its rose garden displays some 30,000 blooms, and in the conservatories is a "living museum" of 700 species of chrysanthemum. Blackpool has 26 municipal bowling greens, two 18-hole golf courses, 16 children's playgrounds, three piers, a winter garden and a waxworks. Among its annual events are the Lancashire Agricultural Society show, the veteran car run from MANCHESTER, and the "milk race" (the cycling tour of Britain). The famous illuminations are a great attraction from early September to late October, when 6 m. of promenade, the tower and the pleasure beach are lit up. Spectators can also travel in the illuminated trams.

BLACKSTONE EDGE, *Lancashire* (12–SD 9717). E. of Littleborough the route of the old Roman road goes steeply up to the borders of Yorkshire. It ran originally all the way from MANCHESTER to ILKLEY, it is believed, but much of it has been obliterated. At Blackstone Edge, however, a lengthy stretch, probably the best surviving section of Roman road in the country, demonstrates an engineering feat of nearly 2,000 years ago; the solid foundations have kept the paving in place against all the moorland storm and frost. Some difference of opinion exists about the depression in the middle, as to whether it held turf for the horses to get a grip or was worn down by the chariots.

BOLTON, *Lancashire* (12–SD7108). Bolton is a busy Lancashire industrial town. There is an imposing town hall in Classical style by William Hill, 1873, and the civic centre houses an aquarium, the museum and the art gallery. Museum collections include geology, botany, zoology, ornithology, archaeology and an Egyptian collection. The art gallery has English paintings, English 18th-cent. pottery, and English and European sculpture with an Epstein collection.

Bolton's history goes back to before the Conquest but the town became prominent with the development of the cotton industry. It has grown into one of the largest boroughs in Lancashire, although many old mills are now devoted to other manufactures. During the Civil War the town was the scene of a massacre committed by Royalists, and James Stanley, Earl of Derby (*see* ORMSKIRK) was beheaded in retaliation by Cromwell. In one of the ancient streets, Churchgate, is Ye Old Man and Scythe, dated 1251, with a statement that in this hostelry Stanley passed his last few hours before execution. At a cottage in Firwood Fold, off Crompton Way on the north-east edge of Bolton, is the birthplace of Samuel Crompton, the inventor of the spinning-mule (*see* HALL I' TH' WOOD, his residence). Crompton's tomb is in the parish churchyard. The town was also the birthplace of William Hesketh Lever (1851–1925), who became the 1st Viscount Leverhulme. Lever, whose father was a Bolton grocer, began to make soap at WIGAN in 1886. He founded Lever Brothers (which became Unilever Ltd after his death) and his Sunlight Soap became well known. Lever bought and restored Hall i' th' Wood; and then, in 1902, presented it to the town, of which he was mayor in 1918. He was Liberal M.P. for the Wirral Division (1906–10), and he built the model village and fine art gallery of PORT SUNLIGHT. Bolton also has one of Lancashire's oldest manor houses, SMITHILLS HALL. The arts are well represented by a variety of cultural organizations, using lecture rooms at the Central Library; and by the highly successful Octagon Theatre. Built only a few years ago, it is a source of civic pride to the inhabitants of Bolton, and has become a theatrical centre for the North West.

Besides St Saviour's in Bolton, there is St Mary's Church at **Deane**, nearby. It is in the Perpendicular style with a Decorated west tower. The nave and chancel have a continuous roof dated 1570.

BOLTON, *Westmorland* (14–NY6323), is a village on the west side of the River Eden. Its small church, All Saints', has ancient stonework. There is a Norman nave and two Norman doorways. Above the north doorway is an interesting small medieval carving of knights jousting. The west turret, built in 1693, has two bells. The chancel screen with open tracery is probably late 18th-cent.

E., beyond the main road, are the Pennine villages of Dufton and Knock, an area of narrow roads leading past Milburn's medieval streets to Skirwith and **Kirkland**, which lies below the 2,930 ft of **Cross Fell**, the highest point of the Pennines. At Kirkland is the curious formation of ground called the Hanging Walls of Mark Anthony.

BOOT, *Cumberland* (14–NY1700). You can drive to this village from either direction on the road through ESKDALE; or, in the summer at least, you can travel there on the miniature railway from **Ravenglass** on the coast. The line was laid in the last century to carry ore from the mines at Boot, and soon carried passengers, too, later adding other freight when the mines closed, and stone from a quarry. Dalegarth Force and Birker Force are high waterfalls near Boot. Dalegarth Hall, which became a farm-house, is an old seat of the Stanley family, dating from the 16th cent. "Owd Ratty" is the nickname for the miniature railway, so called after the original contractor, Ratcliffe. Its popularity increases, and it is one of the institutions of Lakeland. There is nothing "owd" (old) about the equipment which is specially built. The latest diesel locomotive, with a rare drive system, can haul 21 coaches up to **Dalegarth** (the actual terminus) on the 7 m. of 15-in. gauge. A private company runs the system and has even made innovations which have been adopted on full-scale railways. Saloon coaches are available in case of wet weather. The company also operates cafés, shops and car parks, with a games and picnic field at Dalegarth.

BOOTLE, *Lancashire* (12–SJ3394), is a thickly populated industrial town at the mouth of the River Mersey. It adjoins LIVERPOOL and is very much a continuation northwards of its larger neighbour's dockland. The Bootle Museum and Art Gallery in Oriel Road is administered by the Corporation and contains the Lancaster collection of English figure pottery and the Bishop collection of Liverpool pottery. Various art exhibitions are held there.

BORROWDALE, *Cumberland* (14–NY2514), is often described as the most beautiful valley in the Lakes, and is one of the great centres of attraction for climbers. It is the southward continuation of the valley where DERWENTWATER lies and the River Derwent flows down the **Seathwaite** branch of Borrowdale; various parts of it are owned by the National Trust. At **Grange**, S. of Derwentwater, the roads round each side of the lake join to enter the well-known Jaws of Borrowdale. This entry is formed by Grange Fell on the E. and Scawdel close by on the W. The village of Grange is in a beautiful spot beside the old bridge over the river and backed by mountain views. Although so well known because of its site, Grange is a tiny place. It once had connections with FURNESS ABBEY.

The Bowder Stone is below Grange Fell. This huge boulder (National Trust) is metamorphic rock, estimated to weigh about 2,000 tons, and can be ascended by ladder despite its apparently precarious balance. Castle Crag is further in through the Jaws, W. of the river. It gives a view of Derwentwater, and on its summit is the site of an ancient British fort. Further up the valley, and 6 m. from KESWICK, is ROSTHWAITE. Like Borrowdale village a little to the S., it is beloved of walkers and climbers. The Borrowdale Yews are higher up the Derwent valley, near Seathwaite, and were celebrated by Wordsworth before a storm destroyed most of them. Seathwaite (not the one in DUDDON VALLEY) is situated just off the B5289. It has the highest average rainfall in England. The road peters out beyond this village, one track going over Sty Head Pass beside GREAT GABLE (2,949 ft) on the SW., and another to Esk Hause, high in the knot of peaks of the SCA FELL and BOW FELL group. These wild and lofty regions offer magnificent views but are only for experienced climbers, and even they should avoid them if the weather is not clear. Glaramara (2,560 ft) divides Seathwaite from Stonethwaite, the east valley of Borrowdale, where Stake Pass leads to the LANGDALE valleys.

An industrial footnote: Seathwaite once mined the graphite for Keswick pencils.

BOSLEY RESERVOIR, *Cheshire* (12–SJ 9165). A beautiful sheet of water, of about 120 acres, with an island on which grows a clump of Scots firs. It is backed by high hills on the N. and E. and may best be viewed from the heights of Bosley Cloud, at the far end of which are the remains of an ancient Roman fort. The village and reservoir are close beside the River Dane, which here forms the boundary between Cheshire and Staffordshire, flowing under Hug Bridge, the

Bramall Hall

scene of an early battle between the men of the district and the invading Danish forces. The church nestling among the trees was restored towards the end of the 18th cent. but still has its early 16th-cent. tower with strange figure carvings weathered by time. It is said that Bosley was the birthplace of Raphael Holinshed, upon whose *Chronicles* Shakespeare drew heavily for his historical plays.

BOW FELL, *Cumberland* (14–NY2406). Bow Fell towers over Great LANGDALE in the wild region that lies in the heart of the Lake District. It is at 2,960 ft the highest point in the eastern range of the central knot of peaks. Between Bow Fell and the western part of this group lies the head of ESKDALE and Esk Hause, the highest pass for climbers and fell-walkers where tracks from WASDALE, BORROWDALE, and Langdale meet. Bow Fell is often climbed, along with Crinkle Crags to the S.

BOWNESS, *Westmorland* (14–SD4097), is on the shore of WINDERMERE and virtually a continuation of WINDERMERE Town, but its centre is off the main (A591) road. It lies roughly midway on the E. of the lake, and its proximity to the Windermere railhead has established it as the vital link in the lake's transport system, both between the north end at Waterhead (for AMBLESIDE and centres northward) and the south end at Lake Side (for ULVERSTON and the western areas); also for the west shore of the lake by the car ferry service, which runs just S. of Bowness and cuts out a long drive round the $10\frac{1}{2}$-m. lake to reach HAWKSHEAD and CONISTON. In the season, Bowness pier is busy with passengers using the summer service of British Rail motor vessels to travel to either end of the lake, and with those using them for pleasure trips throughout its length. Besides this steamer pier are other, public, piers, and facilities for hiring all manner of craft, from rowing boats to high-powered launches and cruising

vessels with sleeping accommodation. The lake has been a water highway for centuries, and it is now the greatest centre in the Lakes for cruising and for every kind of water sport: water-skiing, underwater swimming, or yachting. It is well provided with boat builders, boat repairers and equipment suppliers. It is also the headquarters of the Royal Windermere Yacht Club and their sails are a familiar sight on the water. A favourite excursion is by the ferry to see Beatrix Potter's house at Sawrey (ESTHWAITE WATER).

Users of the lake must remember that the rules of conduct are mandatory, and that the lake patrol, there to help in emergencies, will also enforce the rules (*see* WINDERMERE).

St Martin's Church at Bowness is the parish church of Windermere. It has been the site of a religious foundation for over 1,000 years; the old structure was burnt and was rebuilt in 1484, with restoration in 1870. Its east window contains 14th- or 15th-cent. glass from CARTMEL Priory. There are mural inscriptions, some chained books, a "Breeches" Bible, an ancient font and a monument by Flaxman.

BRAITHWAITE, *Cumberland* (14–NY2323), is about $2\frac{1}{2}$ m. W. of KESWICK at the entry to WHINLATTER PASS. From it several roads lead S. along the west side of DERWENTWATER. The village is the starting point for climbing Grisedale Pike, one of the northern peaks in the Grasmoor group of mountains. It lies near the edge of the plain N. of Derwentwater, and from here you can drive along a beautiful alternative route on the west side of BASSENTHWAITE LAKE.

BRAMALL HALL, *Cheshire* (12–SJ8984). This may well be the finest surviving black-and-white house in England. It dates from the 15th cent., the manor having passed by marriage from the ancient Bramhale family to the Davenports, who held it for 500 years. Considerable rebuilding was carried out by Sir William and Dame

Dorothy Davenport in about 1600, but in 1819 the whole of the west side of the structure was taken down and the remainder shaped into its present form. The Hall has now been acquired by the local Urban District Council and is open to the public all through the year at advertised times. A spiral stairway of solid oak leads from the ground floor to a beautiful Elizabethan drawing-room, notable for its superb ceiling, oriel window and vast fire-place. The banqueting hall has a roof of great arched timbers believed to have been set in position in an even earlier building of the 14th cent., but the outstanding feature of the house is a tapestry representing the Fall of Man. This magnificent example of 17th-cent. craftsmanship was the work of Dame Dorothy Davenport and took 36 years to complete.

BRIDESTONES, *Cheshire* (12–SJ8964). This is the principal megalithic monument in the county, lying just within the boundary line that divides Cheshire from Staffordshire, and must in some way be connected with the adjacent earthworks believed to be of Roman or even much earlier origin. The Bridestones consist of a number of rough-hewn blocks arranged in the semblance of an uncompleted box, with two tall uprights standing at the open end. The whole is believed to be the remains of a prehistoric burial chamber and was formerly covered with a mound of earth. The indication is that the sepulchre may have been raised by people who were contemporaries of the builders of STONEHENGE, as a last resting-place for some important tribal chieftain; but local legend holds to the more romantic theory that a Viking nobleman married an Anglo-Saxon girl from BIDDULPH and that both are buried here.

BROTHERS' WATER, *Westmorland* (14–NY4012), is a lonely place, set below the north end of the KIRKSTONE PASS and its sweeping sides, with the hard volcanic crags and black fissures of the HELVELLYN range high up to the W. Dovedale, on this side, is one of the steepest valleys, with an overhanging crag. On the east side, next to ULLSWATER, is Place Fell, 2,154 ft, and lesser slopes S. of it. But the lake itself lies in a pleasant pastoral plain. The water is only about ¼ m. wide. It is alleged that the reason for changing its name from Broadwater was because two brothers were drowned there. Although it is so quiet now, the valley must have been busier once, for there are remains of lead-mines, of old habitations and of a cornmill. A farm, Hartsop Hall, is included in land given by the Treasury, which had accepted these properties in lieu of death duties, to the National Trust – the first property so acquired. This land includes the lake itself.

BROUGH, *Westmorland* (14–NY7914). The history of this small town goes back almost 2,000 years. It was a coaching town in the last century and still holds a horse fair at the end of September. Brough is at the foot of the long ascent (difficult in winter) over Stainmore where the A66 follows the route of the old Roman road most of the way across the moors to the E. The castle probably dates from the 11th cent. but the keep was added between 1175 and 1200. The south-east round tower, gatehouse and curtain are probably of the early 13th cent. Lady Anne Clifford (*see* APPLEBY and BROUGHAM) repaired the castle in the late 17th cent. It is an Ancient Monument (open to the public), and lies in the northern part of the Roman fort of Verterae, where the Roman road continued to KIRKBY THORE. St Michael's Church is mainly Early English and Perpendicular, with a 17th-cent. stone pulpit. Musgrave Fell, to the N., a limestone pavement area for plants, is protected by the National Trust.

BROUGHAM, *Westmorland* (14–NY5228). Brougham Castle (open to the public) is an extensive and important military survival. This ruined but imposing building is on the banks of the River Eamont near where it joins the River Lowther, about 1 m. S. of PENRITH on the APPLEBY road. The earliest part, the keep, was built *c.* 1170–80 and much of the curtain wall in the 13th cent. In 1202 it passed from Gospatrick to the Viponts, and later by marriage to the Cliffords, who made additions. It was here that Thomas, Lord Dacre, carried off the heiress, Elizabeth, from the care of the Cliffords.

Against the castle the outlines of the Roman fort of Brocavum are to be seen. This was an important site where two Roman roads joined, from Ravenglass via HARDKNOTT and from the S., as well as from KIRKBY THORE on the E.

The Church of St Ninian, in a dale by the River Eamont, is known as "Nine Kirks", and an Anglo-Saxon church once stood on the site of the present Norman one. This remains as it was rebuilt by Lady Anne Clifford of Brougham Castle in 1660, with its contemporary furnishings. St Wilfrid's Chapel nearby was restored, by Lady Anne Clifford in the 17th cent., and again in the 19th cent. The plain building belies the rich interior which is full of finely carved oak, a 15th-cent. altar-piece and carved scenes on the church walls.

BROUGHTON-IN-FURNESS, *Lancashire* (12–SD2087). In this old market town, less than 1 m. E. of the River Duddon, the historic charter is still proclaimed each August in the market square. The DUDDON VALLEY, on which Wordsworth wrote a series of poems, can be explored from here, and for climbing there is Black Combe (1,969 ft) on the W. The Church of St Mary, in the Early English style, was largely rebuilt in 1873, but parts may date from the 12th cent. and a fine Norman south doorway remains. Of the old castle of the Broughton family the tower and the dungeons are all that remain. A modern mansion built round the tower is a school for delicate children. **Swinside Stone Circle** is 5 m. W. and 20 minutes' walk from the road. Over 50 stones, many fallen, make a circle roughly 100 ft across. It is 2,000 to 3,000 years old, and called Sunken-kirk but its purpose is unknown.

BUDWORTH, *Cheshire* (12–SJ6677). At **Great Budworth** is the Church of St Mary and All Saints which, with its imposing tower, dates from the 14th and 15th cents. The interior has some of the original roofing, and there are medieval stalls, which may be 14th-cent., a 15th-cent. font and many monuments, including those of the Leycester and Warburton families.

Budworth Mere is one of a number of meres in this part of the country. The village of **Nether Tabley**, which is 2½ m. from KNUTSFORD, and W. of the M6, has the fine estate of the Leycester-Warrens. The ruined Old Hall stands on an island in the lake. It was built originally by Sir John Leycester; the new frontage is of 1671. Tabley House (open to the public occasionally), standing in an estate of 800 acres, dates from 1760 and was built by Carr of YORK.

BUNBURY, *Cheshire* (12–SJ5658). This village with its old cottages and pleasant lanes has the interesting Church of St Boniface, a large collegiate church of the 14th cent. with additions in the 15th. It has 16th-cent. oak doors, and memorials of Sir George Beeston, who fought against the Armada, and Sir R. Egerton, standard-bearer to Henry VIII. Bunbury has a strong Methodist tradition, and John Wesley preached here.

Peckforton village, to the W. of Bunbury, has some half-timbered cottages. N. of the village is the imposing castle, the seat of the Tollemache family, set on a lofty site. It is 19th-cent. and designed by Salvin, one of his best works.

BURNLEY, *Lancashire* (12–SD8332). The name of Burnley can be traced back two centuries before the Norman Conquest, and the history of St Peter's Church is believed to go back to the 12th cent. The history of the Towneley family, conspicuous in Burnley, started about the beginning of the 13th cent. when land was granted by the Normans. The woollen industry began in the late 13th cent., and Burnley grew as a market town; the Industrial Revolution brought great expansion due to the cotton-spinning industry which preceded the present emphasis on engineering.

Towneley Hall (open to the public) is to the SE. of Burnley. Its 6-ft-thick walls have undergone so many alterations that it is difficult to decide on the hall's original character. The south-east wing was probably begun in the mid-14th cent. as a two-story building. The central part and the north-west wing were probably built about a century later on three sides of a square, as they stand today. The square was completed later, but a variety of alterations followed, including removal of this fourth side; and in the 19th cent., with the additions to the north-west wing, and the castellations and turrets, the hall's exterior assumed its present form. In 1725 Richard Towneley began alterations to the central hall, then decorated in neo-Classical style by Vassali, the Italian plaster sculptor. Other rooms contain an Adam-style fireplace and a hiding place for priests. Old

English vestments of cloth of gold, 17th-cent. panelling and a Spode dinner service are on display. Paintings include oils by Constable, Peter Lely and Fantin Latour, and watercolours by Gainsborough, Prout, de Wint, Turner and Cox. The John Zoffany oil of *Charles Towneley and his friends* has been widely exhibited and reproduced. Notable rooms are the bedrooms off the 85-ft Long Gallery, the dining-room, servants' dining-room and the chapel. A triumph of the Libraries and Arts Committee of Burnley Corporation, which bought the Hall in 1901, was to buy back the altar-piece. This has fine Netherlandish wood sculpture, probably early 16th-cent., in the oak reredos with scenes of the life of Christ. The altar itself is of later production, possibly late 17th cent., with three panel scenes. It was retrieved from the Convent of Notre Dame in Sussex, and in 1969 was replaced in the chapel where Charles Towneley (1737–1805), the art collector, had placed it. He brought to England a collection of Greek and Roman art, later bought by the BRITISH MUSEUM. Other Towneleys include Christopher (b. 1603), the Lancashire antiquary, and John (b. 1697), the translator into French of *Hudibras*. Besides being the town's art gallery, the hall is also a museum of geology, archaeology and natural history.

On the road to Padiham is **Gawthorpe Hall** (open to the public after restoration) the home of the Shuttleworth family since 1330. The present mansion was built round an earlier house about the beginning of the 17th cent., and elaborated by Sir Charles Barry in 1850. It is a fine specimen of the architecture of its period. It has many displays of textiles and other crafts in a collection established by the late Hon. Rachel Kay Shuttleworth.

BURTON, *Cheshire* (12–SJ3174). Charles Kingsley's poem beginning "Mary go and call the cattle home . . . Across the sands of Dee", refers to the wide stretches of tidal sand which grew over the centuries as the Dee became silted up. As a result, the village of Burton lost its status as a port for Ireland. It is one of the most charming villages in the Wirral. Bulley's Gardens, originally belonging to A. K. Bulley, a LIVERPOOL cotton merchant, were handed on for public use by his daughter. Mr Bulley himself gave to the National Trust the area of Burton Wood, 20 acres of Scots pines above the village. The cottage where Bishop Thomas Wilson was born in 1663 is preserved by the council. He was famous in the locality as a writer and benefactor, and became Bishop of Sodor and Man. The Parish Church of St Nicholas, on a fine site, was rebuilt in 1721 and has 17th-cent. altar rails, and old relics. There is evidence of a church on the site in Norman times.

Ness, to the N., is where Nelson's Lady Hamilton was born. She was much painted by Romney (*see* DALTON-IN-FURNESS) and others.

BUTTERMERE, *Cumberland* (14–NY1815), is a lake set among some of the most beautiful scenery in the LAKE DISTRICT. It is an ideal centre for climbing the peaks. Sour Milk Gill

British Travel Association

Carlisle: a misericord in the cathedral showing a man in a kilt being swallowed by a dragon

originates in Bleaberry Tarn, set 1,600 ft up among the slopes of Red Pike and High Stile on the W. and comes rushing down in milk-like spray to Buttermere. Walkers and climbers may come in from various directions. The motorist can choose only from three, for the High Stile range blocks his access on the W.: he can enter from the N. beside CRUMMOCK WATER, from the E. by **Newlands Pass** (with care down the last mile), or from the S. by HONISTER PASS. Crummock Water is often considered the most pleasant approach, with the magnificent Fleetwith Pike S. of Buttermere.

The latter is hemmed in by mountains, those of Robinson and Hindscarth on the E. being lower than High Stile (2,644 ft), Red Pike and High Crag opposite. There is pleasant pastureland N. and S. of the lake, joined by an attractive path along the west side. Buttermere is noted for its fishing, and rods and boats are let by the National Trust which owns the whole lake and 94 acres of plantations on the south shore.

BUTTERMERE (VILLAGE), *Cumberland* (14–NY1717). This is a small village and is roughly halfway between the north end of Buttermere and CRUMMOCK WATER. The road from **Newlands Pass** descends steeply to the village, joining the one that runs from HONISTER PASS N. to Crummock Water. The village is popular with walkers and climbers as a centre for excursions in the Cumbrian mountains, and has hotels, guest-houses and an old church.

Wordsworth includes the local tale of the Maid of Buttermere in Book VII of *The Prelude*. She was the daughter of the landlord of the Fish Inn and had the misfortune to marry a man who proved to be a forger and bigamist and was later hanged. She later moved to CALDBECK.

CALDBECK, *Cumberland* (14–NY3239). Caldbeck lies at the northern edge of the LAKE DISTRICT National Park. The Church of St Kentigern is 12th- to early 16th-cent., but mostly of the latter period, when it was partly rebuilt. Various windows are later still: one has unusual columns below the wooden lintel.

In the churchyard the Maid of BUTTERMERE was buried. Better known is that tireless pursuer of foxes, John Peel, born at Greenrigg nearby, whose 1854 gravestone is decorated with a horn. His friend, J. W. Graves, wrote the song during the huntsman's lifetime.

CALDER ABBEY, *Cumberland* (14–NY0307), is E. of Calder Bridge (A595) in a fine situation beside the River Calder. The site, open to the public at advertised times, is administered by the Ministry of Public Building and Works. The ruins that remain include the nave, the church aisles and parts of the cloister. The abbey was founded in 1135 by the Savignac Order from FURNESS ABBEY, which later became Cistercian. The earliest parts of the ruins are 12th-cent., and the latest part, the chapter house, is late 13th- or early 14th-cent.

Ponsonby Hall is a fine 18th-cent. house built by the Stanleys.

CAPESTHORNE, *Cheshire* (12–SJ8372). This is the seat of the Bromley-Davenport family, who for many centuries have exerted their influence in Cheshire affairs. The old hall was burned down in 1861 and a large, impressive Victorian building by Anthony Salvin took its place, incorporating parts of the earlier house in the wings. The chapel adjacent to the new hall was built in 1722 in the Classic style and restored in 1888. The most attractive feature of the area is Redes Mere, a beautiful sheet of placid water over 60 acres in extent. Many of these lakes to the W. of MACCLESFIELD were formed from the marl-pits dug in the meadows during the 13th cent. The one here came more recently as the result of silica sand excavations and has become the haunt of waterfowl. There are many delightful walks for nature-lovers among the giant oaks and beeches with which the estate abounds.

CARLISLE, *Cumberland* (14–NY3955), is the county and principal town of Cumberland. Its previous Celtic settlement is undated. The Roman period began under Agricola about A.D. 80. The Romans called it Luguvallium. Later HADRIAN'S

WALL was built, passing just N., and when Stanwix fort was placed there it left Carlisle as a civic centre for administering the whole western area of the Roman frontier. The town held this role for 250 years, benefiting from Roman civil organization. But the apparent security was breached by raids, and Picts and other tribes over-ran the Roman sites in 181, and again in 367. The Vikings sacked the town in 875. It was added to England after the Norman Conquest; William Rufus claimed it in 1092 and it was then that the city walls, castle and priory were begun. But for nearly seven centuries after that Carlisle could change little in size and shape owing to its un-certain position: there were frequent border raids, and the town became a shuttlecock passed be-tween England and Scotland. The longest siege was in 1644–5 when Royalist Carlisle fell to the Scots. It fell to them again when it surrendered to Bonnie Prince Charlie in 1745 as he set out on his march into England that was only halted at DERBY. In the last two centuries, the city has had a chance to settle down, after 1,700 years of warfare, struggle or family feuds – probably the longest period of strife known by any English town.

The first Town Hall, apparently built in Eliza-bethan days, was succeeded by another in 1717, partly on the same site; with the 14th-cent. Guild Hall nearby, it was the town's governmental centre for nearly six centuries. Much plate from the eight trade guilds is in the City Museum. The Town Hall had two bells: the one that, from 1584 until the mid-19th cent., announced the opening of the market, and the "muckle town bell", whose alarm warning could be heard for 11 m. Both are in the museum. The two round towers that are so prominent at the city centre, above the railway station, represent the citadel, and are a recon-struction (1807) of the original citadel built in 1541–3, which was a second defence in case the castle fell. The present citadel was built in 1807 by Sir Robert Smirke, who designed the BRITISH MUSEUM. At the west tower of the original was English Gate (or Botchergate), and the other two gates in the city walls were Scotch Gate on the E. and Irish Gate on the W. They were slammed at dusk: after that, let no Scot dare to move about inside. Carlisle Cross (1682) stands in English Street on the site of the traditional town centre where Bonnie Prince Charlie made his proclama-tion in 1745. The old town hall faces it but is dominated by the 1964 civic centre to the N., with an elaborate octagonal council chamber. Beyond it is a modern square office block, incongruous in the old city.

The small cathedral was finished in 1123 as the Church of the Blessed Virgin Mary and became an Augustinian priory. The priory church became the cathedral when the diocese of Carlisle was founded in 1133. The nave then became the parish church. A larger choir was made but was destroyed by fire in 1292. The monks did more building later, including the magnificent Decor-ated east window, 58 ft high and 32½ ft wide, which has original 14th-cent. glass at the top. The tower was added about 1401. After the 1644–5 siege General Leslie tore down about two-thirds of the nave (in ruins since the Dissolution) and much of the cloisters and other buildings to obtain stone for repairing city walls and castle. Only about 1853 was serious restoration work begun. There is a fine 15th-cent. fratery and traces of other monastic buildings. About 39 ft of the original 140 ft of the Norman nave remain. Sir Walter Scott was married in it in 1797; he had many associa-tions with the Border country. There are 15th-cent. paintings on the backs of the choir stalls in the north aisle and interesting misericords, a Renaissance screen and a carved head, probably of Edward I.

Tullie House Museum was originally a Jaco-bean mansion and the southern façade has orna-mented fall pipes dated 1689. The original staircase with oak banisters remains. Various public rooms were added after the building was acquired in 1893 as a cultural centre, and it now houses an art gallery, a library and a museum. There is a gallery containing geological specimens, a Roman gallery with material from Hadrian's wall, and a natural history section.

The bluff where the castle was built N. of the medieval city was probably the site of an ancient British camp or caer, a term preserved in the name Carlisle. The castle, which is open to the public, was founded in 1092 and enlarged later. The existing keep, built at some time in the 12th cent., has been considerably altered. It is now a museum of the history of the Border Regiment. The castle was badly damaged when taken by the Scots in 1216, and fell into disrepair, subsequently to be rebuilt and strengthened at various periods. The badge of Richard III can be seen on the Tile Tower and the arms of Elizabeth I near the keep. The apartments where Mary Queen of Scots was imprisoned have gone, but Queen Mary's Tower remains, as does the 14th-cent. main gate.

At **Burgh-by-Sands**, 6 m. NW. of Carlisle, St Michael's is a strongly fortified church, built almost entirely from Roman stones. Edward I, who died on his way to attack the Scots, lay in state there and a monument to him stands near the village.

CARNFORTH, *Lancashire* (12–SD4970). Nearby are two old houses of interest, open to the public: **Borwick Hall** and **Leighton Hall**, Borwick, about 2 m. NE., stands among fine gardens. It is an Elizabethan manor house, and has not been altered since it was built round an earlier structure in 1595. Leighton Hall occupies a fine site in extensive grounds about 3 m. N. of Carnforth via Yealand Conyers. It has belonged to the Gillow family for many generations and has good early furniture and pictures. The façade of the hall is Gothic, of *c*. 1800–20, superimposed on a Classical building.

S. of Carnforth is **Halton** village on the River Lune, E. of the M6. The churchyard cross is 11th-cent. and its original shaft carved by Norsemen shows a combination of Christian and pagan symbolism. The cross head was added in 1890.

Ullswater   W. A. Poucher

CARROCK FELL, *Cumberland* (14–NY3334), is not easily accessible to the motorist, although a road N. from the A66 to the E. of KESWICK runs below the fell. Thereafter a steep climb leads to the remains of a hill fort. Its unknown builders added to the deterrent of the steep slopes a stone wall surrounding five acres of land. It is possible that it dates from the Early Iron Age, although the fort-dwellers could have been following the earlier Bronze Age mode of life. To the N. are various cairns, similar to one in the enclosure, which may be of the Bronze Age. Do not try the ascent in bad weather, as Dickens and Wilkie Collins are said to have done.

CARTMEL, *Lancashire* (12–SD3778). The village is 2 m. W. of GRANGE-OVER-SANDS, below the high limestone ridge of Hampsfell. The gatehouse and the church are the only two remaining parts of Cartmel Priory. The gatehouse, overlooking the village market cross, is a picturesque building over the street, dating from about 1330. From 1624 to 1790 it was used as a grammar school and is now an artist's studio. It is National Trust property. The Priory Church of St Mary the Virgin, in Transitional style, was founded in 1188. Its square central tower, 15th-cent. in the upper part, is set diagonally on its base. By 1618 the roof had gone, the priory having apparently decayed since the Dissolution, although not destroyed then. George Preston of Holker carried out restoration from 1618, erecting the stall canopies and the superb Renaissance screens. Notable are the stained glass and the carved misericords on the choir stalls. The chancel arcades are round, but the central arches and those in the aisles and the triforium are pointed. The east window is Perpendicular. There are many memorials, including the 14th-cent. Harrington monument with recumbent effigies, and brass chandeliers. Among the many treasures of the priory is a first edition of Spenser's *Faerie Queen*.

The Church of St Andrew at Cartmel Fell, to the N., built about 1503, has roughcast walls and a low tower. It contains screened pews, a three-decker pulpit, good medieval stained glass, and a carved pre-Reformation figure of Christ, a rare specimen, although much damaged.

CASTLE ROCK, *Cumberland* (14–NY3121). Castle Rock is in St John's Vale, and the latter runs N. after the junction of the B5322 and A591 near the north end of THIRLMERE. St John's Beck flows out of Thirlmere, through the vale, and down to the River Greta near THRELKELD. E. is Great Dodd (2,807 ft) and just S. of this is Watson's Dodd, a lower peak which has, jutting up below it, Castle Rock. This is Sir Walter Scott's rock in his poem, *The Bridal of Triermain*, and it is also called the Rock of Triermain. This crag has climbing routes and some are classed as very severe.

Further N., on the west side of the vale, is High Rigg with the Church of St John's-in-the-Vale on its northern slopes. The church was built there in the 19th cent. It seems an unusually high position for a church, but it is believed there was a hermitage of St John there in the 13th cent.

CATON, *Lancashire* (12–SD5365). Caton is famous because of its association with Turner who painted its celebrated Crook O' Lune. This beautiful curve of the Lune's course is best seen in spring, when it is covered with bluebells. St Paul's Church in the hamlet of **Brookhouse** has been entirely rebuilt apart from its 500-year-old tower. The Norman doorway has fragments of an Adam and Eve carving.

Claughton, about 5 m. E. on the A683, has a Tudor house, Claughton Hall, most of which has been moved uphill from its old site. The church, renewed in the last century, has a bell marked 1296, one of the oldest dated English bells.

St John the Baptist's Church (formerly St Michael's), Perpendicular with large buttresses, is at **Tunstall**, further NE. on the A683. When the Brontë sisters were at **Casterton** (*see* KIRKBY LONSDALE, Westmorland) they had to attend this church – the Brocklebridge of *Jane Eyre*. Since then the 500-year-old glass of the east window has been brought from Belgium and a Roman altar stone found.

Thurland Castle nearby has been rebuilt since the destruction of the interior in the Civil War.

CHEADLE, *Cheshire* (12–SJ8788). A pleasant residential area some 7 m. SE. of MANCHESTER but with little left to show of its early history. There is evidence that the Romans maintained a fortification here and that the Anglo-Saxons set up a stone cross on the south bank of the Mersey dedicated to St Chad, from whose name Cheadle is derived. With the coming of the Normans the place had identity enough to be listed in the Domesday Book. The first church at Cheadle was built in about 1200 but burnt down in 1520. Only a few fragments of glass and two old monuments remained for incorporation in the 16th-cent. rebuilding, but the 16-windowed clerestory lighting the nave, with its two chapels, and the three stone monuments of knights in armour, together with the many sculptured figures projecting from the exterior are points of unusual interest.

Moseley Old Hall, at the end of Cuthbert Road off Stockport Road, is a half-timbered building bearing the date 1666. It has been much restored in recent times, although a large fire-place and part of a staircase remain unchanged.

CHESTER, *Cheshire* (12–SJ4066). A combination of Roman and medieval relics, as well as many fine timber-framed buildings, makes Chester, the city of Deva, one of England's most interesting old cities. It also contains the architecturally important work of Thomas Harrison, who rebuilt the castle and constructed a single-span bridge here in the early 19th cent., as well as some excellent examples of Victorian black-and-white buildings. It has been chosen for government conservation studies, which will perhaps ensure the survival of its historic monuments.

Little Moreton Hall is an outstanding example of black-and-white architecture   *G. Douglas Bolton*

Roman occupation in the later 1st cent. made Chester an important military point, with a fortress on a sandstone hill at the head of the estuary. During most of the Roman occupation it was the headquarters of one of the three Roman legions of Britain. The first defences were turf ramparts with wooden gates. After the 1st cent. there was a stone wall with four stone gates and 26 stone towers, and on the north and east sides of the city, from St Martin's Gate to Newgate, the present city wall follows the line of the Roman wall, incorporating parts of it. The west and south sides of the old stone wall were later destroyed and the walls extended over a wider area, including that of the castle. It is not certain whether the extension was made by Romans or Anglo-Saxons, and it could even have been as late as the 12th or early 13th cent. Roman remains were found in the Eastgate when it was rebuilt in 1769. Near steps leading down to Frodsham Street are the lower parts of the Roman wall and the foundation of a 13th-cent. drum tower. Between King Charles' Tower and Northgate are two stretches of Roman wall as much as 17 ft high. The foundations of the Roman gate were found when Northgate was rebuilt in 1808. The open space of the Roodee is where the Romans had a harbour and a large section of their quay wall stands on the race-course below the city walls. The south-east angle of the Roman wall meets the medieval wall near the Wolfe Gate with the lower Roman courses visible. The most important Roman area is the amphitheatre, E. of Newgate. It is the largest Roman amphitheatre so far discovered in Britain, built of stone, covering an area of 314 ft by 286 ft, with an arena 190 ft by 162 ft. The street plan of the city originated with the Romans, and inside the walls the four main streets today follow their plan: Eastgate Street, Watergate Street, Bridge Street and upper Northgate Street. There were Roman roads to London and YORK below Lower Bridge Street and Foregate Street. A Roman hypocaust is in the basement of Quaintways Café, Northgate Street, and on the opposite side, in the cellars of No. 23, are bases, shafts and a capital from the Roman headquarters.

The Roman legion probably abandoned Chester before the early 5th cent. and the fortress was then deserted for hundreds of years. By late Anglo-Saxon times the city was important enough to produce coins at its own mint, and it was four years after the Conquest before the city gave way to Norman rule. The 13th and early 14th cents. were a period of great importance, when the port had become prominent and traded with Ireland, Scotland and parts of the Continent. Like York, Chester had medieval mystery plays, presented at Abbey Square, then the outer court of the Abbey of St Werburgh, and in the streets. In the 15th cent. the city had a military quarrel with the Welsh, but a greater problem was the silting-up of the River Dee, which choked the trade of the port, whereas in Roman times the tower at the north-west corner had stood in the water. This impoverished the city as did the siege in the Civil War which interrupted commerce on land that was never subsequently regained.

The remarkably well-preserved walls, with their medieval reconstruction, provide an interesting walk and cover a circuit of 2 m. There was further re-fortification of the walls in the Tudor and Civil War periods, from which some of the present towers date. The Eastgate with a large 1897 clock is the main entrance. King Charles' Tower (NE.) is said to be where Charles I watched the defeat of his forces by the Parliamentarians after the city had been more or less besieged for two years. The tower has a Civil War exhibition. West of Northgate tower is Morgan's Mount, which was violently bombarded during the Civil War. St Martin's Gate, further W., was built in 1966 to allow the ring road to breach the walls. The Goblin Tower dates from 1702 and 1894. Bonewaldsthorne's Tower is at the north-west corner, connected to the Water Tower which the recession of the Dee left high and dry. The Water Tower built in 1322 is substantially unaltered and contains an exhibition of medieval Chester with dioramas. Watergate, on the west side, was once controlled by the Earls of Derby who charged a toll on goods taken through. Their kinsmen, the Alderley Stanleys, owned Stanley Palace (1591), a fine half-timbered building. By the 16th cent. the city was a well-known centre of drama with Whitsuntide and midsummer festivals; some researchers have suggested that Shakespeare lived in Chester, or even that the author of his plays was not Shakespeare but William Stanley, 6th Earl of Derby. William was brother to the 5th Earl, Ferdinando, who was a patron of actors, including Shakespeare. Bridgegate (S.) is 18th-cent. and replaces a medieval gate. Newgate is modern (1938), built to give more space than the old Wolfe Gate nearby.

The Rows, a unique feature of the city, can be found in Watergate Street, Eastgate Street and Bridge Street. You can inspect modern shops in the appropriate stretches of these streets, take the first flight of steps you find between shops and find yourself walking on the roofs of the shops beside another row of shops set further back; an interesting form of "pedestrian precinct" that surpasses the modern type.

The Cathedral was designed as an abbey church and the buildings round the cloisters were the monks' living-quarters. On this site there was a church or minster founded in the 10th cent. to hold the body of St Werburgh. In 1092, Hugh Lupus, the Norman Earl of Chester, made it an abbey of Benedictine monks, and for five centuries this monastery was powerful and owned much land. After the Dissolution the abbey became a cathedral and bishopric. The consistory court has woodwork and a screen of the 17th cent. The nave was begun in the 14th cent. but not completed until the 16th. In the north aisle of the choir parts of the 12th-cent. abbey church were incorporated in the foundations built some two centuries later. There are remarkable late 14th-cent. carvings on the choir stalls, including a Tree of Jesse with the genealogy of Christ. The

Chester has many good examples of black-and-white buildings, both medieval and Victorian

south transept is 14th-cent. and was once the Parish Church of St Oswald. There is a fine stone pulpit in the refectory, and the chapter house has early MSS. and printed books.

The Grosvenor Museum has two important Roman galleries, the Newstead and another with an unrivalled collection of inscribed material. A third gallery has coins from Chester mint. An early 18th-cent. house attached to the museum holds costumes, a Victorian room, period furniture, natural history, and watercolours and drawings of the locality.

Chester Zoo, to the N., is famous. Its aim is to show animals, birds, reptiles and fish in conditions as much like their natural environment as possible, and bars and cages are minimized. Gardens are an integral part of it, and there is a special tropical house.

CHIPPING, *Lancashire* (12–SD6243). This charming village has beautiful scenery around, with moorland on the N. It lies in an agricultural area with some old industry. The Church of St Bartholomew is mainly early 16th-cent. with 19th-cent. restoration, but traces survive of all periods from the 12th cent. onward. There is a 12th-cent. piscina.

At **Bleasdale,** NW. of the village, an important discovery was made of wooden posts in a circular area similar to Woodhenge, and relics of human occupation were also found. The posts were intact at a certain distance below ground level but threatened to decay after exposure to the air. They were removed to PRESTON Museum and concrete posts substituted to mark the site.

CHOLMONDELEY, *Cheshire* (12–SJ5351). The large early-19th-cent. castle lies in a 500-acre deer park, between MALPAS and NANTWICH, and is the private residence of the Marquess of Cholmondeley. On the estate, which has close historical connections with Malpas, is a 13th-cent. chapel, rebuilt in the 18th cent. It contains 17th-cent. box pews, a large family pew, altar rails and a fine screen.

CHORLEY, *Lancashire* (12–SD5817). Chorley, with its grim industrial atmosphere, is the indirect source of a great art collection: Henry Tate, founder of the sugar firm, was born here in 1819, and with the fortune he made, he endowed London's TATE GALLERY.

After five minutes' walk from Union Street car park you escape through the big gates of Astley Hall into spacious and peaceful parkland. It takes three or four times as long to stroll across to the Hall (open to the public). This Renaissance structure is superbly set beside placid water. The oldest part dates back to the 16th cent., the main front having been rebuilt in the 17th. The entrance leads into the great hall with its wooden panel portraits, including those of Drake and Columbus. The drawing-room has a fantastically decorated ceiling and tapestries with scenes from the story of the Golden Fleece. Astley Hall's many interesting features and fine furniture include the long gallery's shovel-table, $23\frac{1}{2}$ ft long. In one bedchamber is a bed Cromwell is said to have slept in after the battle of PRESTON. An upper room has been converted into a modern art gallery.

Miles Standish of the *Mayflower* was born at

Duxbury Hall, now demolished, 1½ m. S. of Chorley.

CLIFTON, *Westmorland* (14–NY5326). This was the scene of the last battle on English soil (between English forces and the Jacobites): in 1745, on his retreat from DERBY. Bonnie Prince Charlie had a minor success here before Butcher Cumberland ended his hopes at Culloden. The dead were buried in Clifton churchyard; it was in a sense the last chapter in the long border warfare that had plagued this part of the country (formerly the old Celtic kingdom of Strathclyde), and which is indicated by all the fortified houses and churches and peel-towers, such as those at DACRE, GREYSTOKE or GREAT SALKELD.

Clifton is on the A6, like **Eamont Bridge** whose triple-arched medieval bridge has for long carried trunk road traffic into PENRITH. Just S. of Eamont Bridge is **King Arthur's Round Table**. This prehistoric earthwork about 300 ft across is roughly circular and surrounded by a ditch. **Mayburgh** is nearby to the W., another circular structure, wider than the table and with a single standing stone remaining in the centre. Bronze and stone axes were found at Mayburgh.

CLITHEROE, *Lancashire* (12–SD7441), is a very old Ribble Valley town, now an industrial centre but with a pleasant country atmosphere and delightful walks in the locality. The town is the second oldest borough in Lancashire (WIGAN is the oldest) and gained its charter in 1147. Traces of the Roman road from RIBCHESTER to Yorkshire can be seen. Pendle, the 1,831-ft hill on the E. is the reputed old haunt of witches (*see* WHALLEY). The castle on its limestone crag in the town is a dominant landmark. It was built in the 12th cent. before LANCASTER castle; held first by Roger de Poitou, then the de Lacys until 1311, it was a Royalist stronghold in the Civil War and then had various owners. In 1920 it was bought for the town and now much of the 16-acre grounds is a recreational area. Little remains apart from the keep with its 9-ft walls, of interest as one of the oldest stone structures in Lancashire and as the smallest keep in England. St Mary Magdalene Church, on a lesser knoll, has been the site of a church for more than 800 years. In the early 19th cent. the church was dismantled and rebuilt, a twisted spire being added later. The bells were recast in 1658. The Town Hall has the sculpted arms of the de Lacys (the Lords of Lancaster), and carving by a local craftsman inside. An attractive building is the Royal Grammar School; it was founded in 1554, but there is evidence that a school existed as far back as the 13th cent. A notable headmaster was the Rev. T. Wilson, who in the 18th cent. compiled the *Archaeological Dictionary* and dedicated it to Dr Johnson, receiving a flattering acknowledgment. Low Moor, now closed, was a large Lancashire mill built by the Garnett family of Waddow Hall. They built a little self-contained township round the mill, and were connected with the foundation of the *Manchester Guardian*.

Stonyhurst, to the SW., formerly the seat of the Shireburne family, has since 1794 been a Roman Catholic public school, with a library of over 40,000 books. Among its treasures are works printed by Caxton, a copy of the Gospel of St John with a 7th-cent. binding judged to be the oldest in England, and what is believed to be the Book of Hours owned by Mary Stuart at her death. There are paintings attributed to Rubens and Murillo. Arthur Conan Doyle was a pupil here.

Browsholme Hall, NW. of Clitheroe and reached by minor roads, actually stands in beautiful surroundings in Yorkshire. It contains considerable art treasures, and house and gardens are open to the public at advertised times.

COCKERMOUTH, *Cumberland* (14–NY 1230), can be used as a base for motoring tours into the LAKE DISTRICT. It is among the 51 towns recommended by the Council for British Archaeology for preservation. This confluence of the Rivers Cocker and Derwent was a strategic point for the Romans, and stone from their fort at Papcastle was used in 1134 by Waltheof of Dunbar to build a castle. It was partly destroyed by Robert the Bruce, and after various other attacks and sieges was partly dismantled after the Civil War. The present ruins (open to the public) are said to be 13th- and 14th-cent. Cockermouth was a busy market town in the 16th cent., and the county's commercial centre by the mid-17th. It was one of the oldest parliamentary boroughs in the country. The statue in the pleasant wide main street is of Earl Mayo, one of its Members of Parliament. In 1568 Mary Queen of Scots was received at Cockermouth Hall after her flight from the Battle of Langside via WORKINGTON.

Cockermouth was the birthplace of several famous people, including John Dalton, formulator of the atomic theory, and Fletcher Christian, leader of the mutiny on the *Bounty*. The house where Dalton was born is at Eaglesfield, 3 m. SW., and bears a commemorative plaque. Christian was born in 1764 at Moorland Close, a farmhouse near the southern boundary of the town beside the A5086.

But the great figures of Cockermouth, of course, are the Wordsworths, and Wordsworth House (open to the public) is internationally known as one of the two principal residences of the poet to visit in the Lake District, the other being Dove Cottage at GRASMERE. That at Cockermouth is on the north side of Main Street, near the west end, and was acquired by the National Trust in 1938 after a public appeal. It is a handsome house built in 1745 and became the home of William's father in 1766 when he was made steward to Sir James Lowther. William was born here in 1770, and Dorothy in 1771. It is a house with many windows, and the original staircase, fire-places and panelling are to be seen. A reception book holds the names of famous visitors from many parts of the world. William spent some time at a PENRITH school, but when he was only eight, his mother died and he went to HAWKSHEAD. In *The*

Prelude he recalls the garden behind the house, and Dorothy mentions the house in her Journals.

The 19th-cent. Church of All Saints, S. of the market place, has a memorial stained-glass window to Wordsworth, and his father's grave near the east end. He and Fletcher Christian also attended the grammar school, formerly on the site in the churchyard where the church rooms now stand. At Pardshaw the Society of Friends has one of its oldest meeting houses. George Fox preached at Pardshaw Crags in 1657 and 1663.

COLNE, *Lancashire* (12–SD8839), is an old market town, with mixed industries. Beyond it is the moorland country of the Brontës. The Romans had a chain of forts in Lancashire, linked by military roads, and their road from MANCHESTER ran through Colne and on to Yorkshire. The roads in this area, as in other parts of England, were used for centuries after the Romans left; they later carried the produce of hand-loom weaving. The Church of St Bartholomew has Perpendicular features (but was probably begun in an earlier period) and a 16th-cent. roof. There are monuments by Sir Robert Taylor. The town's museum includes collections of geographical, historical, geological and natural history material. Wycoller Hall, E. of Colne and now in ruins, is the house that Charlotte Brontë made into Ferndean Manor in *Jane Eyre*.

CONGLETON, *Cheshire* (12–SJ8562). An important cattle market and Cheshire's second silk town, more concerned today with manufacturing for the general textile trade. At one time there was a minor Roman settlement at the crossing-point on the River Dane where the town now stands, but most signs of early habitation have been swept away in the waves of prosperity that followed. In 1035 it was part of the extensive possessions of Earl Godwin, Harold's father, and was recorded in the Domesday Book of 1086, by which date it had become one of the properties of the great Norman family of de Lacy. In 1272 Henry de Lacy procured a charter freeing Congleton from feudal tolls and conferring the right to hold fairs and a weekly market. During the 13th cent., various trade guilds were formed. It was during this period that Congleton's long association with the production of leather gloves and laces began. After a calamitous flooding of the River Dane in the reign of Henry VI, the king gave permission for the course of the river to be diverted and in addition granted the town a royal mill. The latter events made for a long run of prosperity, lasting until the terrible plague epidemics of 1603 and 1641 wiped out almost the entire local population.

The most prominent citizen in the history of Congleton was the Cromwellian fanatic John Bradshaw, a native of STOCKPORT, in his capacity as Mayor. Bradshaw later became High Steward, Lord Chancellor, and finally Lord President of the High Court when he was to be a key figure in the trial and execution of Charles I. The seals of office he used are kept with other relics of Congleton's past in the present Town Hall, a fine Victorian building, in the Venetian Gothic style, conspicuous by its 110-ft clock tower. Also to be seen here are records of the appointment and activities of various town officers, with the intriguing titles of ale taster, swine catcher, and chimney looker. An interesting oddity is a leather belt, fitted with three bells called St Peter's chains, which was used to proclaim the chimney sweep's holiday in the days when most of this dangerous work was carried out by boys small enough to clamber up the inside of the stack. It was the custom for three priests or acolytes to dance with these belts on the Eve of St Peter's Day, a link with pagan times when it was believed that the ceremony would drive away evil spirits. Another item in the collection is one of the old branks, or scold's bridles, with a chain by which nagging wives could be attached to a wall in the market place.

St Peter's Church is a plain 18th-cent. structure, unremarkable except for its profusion of massive woodwork in the interior, which includes a Jacobean pulpit and a fine lectern decorated with four apostles and an angel. On one of the walls is a memorial to Sir Thomas Reade, who was a member of the Governor's entourage at St Helena when Napoleon was a captive there and in another connection became famous for having persuaded the Bey of Tunis to abolish slavery as long ago as 1849. Of the few half-timbered houses still standing in Congleton, three are inns: the curiously-fronted White Lion Hotel; the Swan and Lion, which dates from the 15th cent.; and the Bear's Head Hotel, named after the medieval sport of bear-baiting which flourished longer in Congleton than anywhere else in the country.

CONISTON, *Lancashire* (14–SD3097). This village lies on the west side of CONISTON WATER, and is accessible from AMBLESIDE, N., from BROUGHTON or Lowick Bridge, S., or from BOWNESS ferry, E. Along the NW. of the village run the Coniston Fells, dominated by Coniston Old Man, with the DUDDON VALLEY behind them. Coniston is the centre for ascents of this range. In the churchyard is the cross commemorating Ruskin (*see* CONISTON WATER). Of hard green local stone, the cross is carved on four sides, one of them showing an artist drawing with the sun rising above pine trees. The small Ruskin Museum in Yewdale Road illustrates the life and work of the critic and writer, together with material relating to the locality. On view are handbells with which he made musical experiments, specimens of his mineral collection (he presented the Edwardes Ruby to the NATURAL HISTORY MUSEUM, London), his paintbox and sketch books, and drawings and books.

Tarn Hows, celebrated for its beauty, is NE. of the village and near the road, surrounded by areas of National Trust property. It is a favourite place for excursions, and from the slopes above there are magnificent views of mountains that include Red Screes, Fairfield, the HELVELLYN range and

LANGDALE PIKES. Yewdale Tarn is near, and W. lies the Tilberthwaite valley with a series of waterfalls.

CONISTON WATER, *Lancashire* (14–SD 3094), is about 5½ m. long, with tree-lined bays, and its background of wooded hills and mountains on the W. make a striking picture. The Coniston Fells run along the north-west side of the lake, rising to 2,633 ft at the summit of Coniston Old Man. Beyond them Grey Friar and Dow Crag look down on the DUDDON VALLEY. There are continuous ridges leading to several connected heights on the Coniston range. Old Man is a well-known peak for climbers and walkers, but its east side particularly, and other parts of the range, have been defaced by old quarries and copper mines; these should be avoided for safety reasons. Around the lake most place-names have Norse origins, as elsewhere in Lakeland. There is fishing, boating and swimming on the lake. It was here that Donald Campbell died in 1967 in an attempt to break the water speed record.

Brantwood (open to the public) is on the east side. John Ruskin bought this house in 1871, and died there in 1900. Ruskin insisted on the value of hand-made as against machine-made goods, and preached the gospel of beauty. He could read and write at the age of four, at six began trying to write books and at seven poetry. Volume I of his *Modern Painters* (arising from his spirited defence of Turner) made him famous as an art critic at 24. He championed the Pre-Raphaelites, and opened a window on the beauty of Italian art. A passionate campaigner, he spent most of his father's legacy of £157,000 on educational work, gifts and attempts to improve working-class conditions. While at Brantwood Ruskin attempted one of his industrial experiments, a revival of the old hand-made linen industry at ELTERWATER; and at KESWICK his work is also remembered. In CONISTON village the museum and churchyard cross are a reminder of the man who believed that the gentleman should labour and the labourer should exercise mind and soul. Brantwood is kept by the Education Trust as a memorial. It contains some 250 paintings by Ruskin.

Another old building is Tent Lodge, where Tennyson once stayed. Monk Coniston Hall is a National Trust property that is let to the Holiday Fellowship. Among various routes for walks are those towards Walna Scar, Broughton Mills, the Grizedale Forest (*see* HAWKSHEAD, nature trail), and W. of Water Yeat and Blawith. **Tarn Hows** to the N. gives good views along Coniston Water.

CROSBY GARRETT, *Westmorland* (14–NY 7309), near KIRKBY STEPHEN, has a group of ancient village settlement sites. They comprise three lying roughly in line over about 1,000 yds, the south-west one being largest. It has remains of a large rectangular hut and smaller ones. The other two sites are similar but smaller. Around them are the traces of boundaries and pathways.

The Church of St Andrew at Crosby Garrett village is mainly Norman.

CROSBY RAVENSWORTH, *Westmorland* (14–NY6214), E. of SHAP, is a village in an area of great antiquity. On a 2- or 3-m. stretch of moorland about 1 m. SW. are some 90 sites of prehistoric village settlements. One of them, Ewe Close, has walls about 6 ft high, and covers more than an acre roughly square in shape where there are also traces of banks and ditches. It is believed to date from the Iron Age and also to have been occupied in Roman times. Another, Burwens, has the remains of a hut, 25 ft across, inside an enclosure of about 1 acre with a causeway outside it. The picturesque village has the Church of St Lawrence, of the 15th cent. or earlier, the origins of which were 11th-cent.

CROSSCANONBY, *Cumberland* (14–NY 0739), lies N. of the A596 about 3 m. from MARYPORT. The Church of St John the Evangelist is a 12th-cent. structure with later additions, but it made use of Roman stones in its early stages. There is a carved hog-back tomb, some interesting Anglo-Saxon and early Norman carving, and some early 18th-cent. woodwork. In 1880 C. J. Ferguson of CARLISLE made a conscientious restoration.

CROSTON, *Lancashire* (12–SD4818), stands in the valley of the twisting River Yarrow. The Royal Umpire Museum and Carriage Exhibition (open to the public) is on the CHORLEY to SOUTHPORT road. This is one of the country's best collections of old carriages and coaches, and it includes vintage cars. Other attractions of the museum are relics from old Croston Hall, a replica of an 18th-cent. village, and a monk's cell. There is also an aviary, a children's playground and a lake and waterfall.

A church was on the site of St Michael's in the reign of the Conqueror; it is supposed to have been rebuilt in 1577 and was restored in 1866–7.

CRUMMOCK WATER, *Cumberland* (14–NY1519). Like BUTTERMERE to the S., Crummock Water has the road (B5289) along its east side. It must be approached (by road) from either the north or south end, and lies in the same valley as Buttermere, to which it was probably joined once. Crummock is a fairly large lake, 2½ m. long, and has Grasmoor, 2,791 ft, E. of its northern end and S. of it is Whiteless Pike. An impressive sight on the W. of the lake is Mellbreak; it is only 1,668 ft high but below its top lie the screes. A path lies along the lake below Mellbreak, between the Buttermere end and a subsidiary road from the village of LOWESWATER at the N. On the W. of the main road and just N. of the lake is Lanthwaite Hill. It is only 674 ft high and well worth climbing for a fine view along the lake towards GREAT GABLE beyond Buttermere. Coming down to Crummock Water S. of Mellbreak is Scale Force, the highest waterfall in the Lakes. It drops more than 100 ft, and after rain

Noel Habgood

Coniston Water from Tarn Hows

is even more striking. Crummock Water, owned by the National Trust, is a good area for walking, climbing and fishing.

DACRE, *Cumberland* (14–NY4526). A few miles W. and N. of PENRITH a number of fortifications, such as peel-towers, were built against Scottish raiders who, in the 14th and 15th cents., often came south through what was then the Royal Forest of Inglewood. *See* GREYSTOKE (church and castle).

Dacre Castle, 14th-cent., was one stronghold which later became a farm-house. Hutton-in-the-Forest is a romantic house consisting of a 14th-cent. peel-tower with 17th-cent. and later additions. The house and gardens, laid out in the 17th cent., are open by appointment. Hutton John is a peel-tower near Dacre (open by appointment), where a manor house was added later.

Dacre's church, St Andrew's, has 9th- or 10th-cent. cross shafts and an Early English chancel. Bede's ecclesiastical history mentions a monastery at Dacre in the 7th cent. It was here, according to tradition, that the Scots met King Athelstan of England to sign a treaty in the 10th cent. Dacre Castle may be on the site of this meeting.

DALTON, *Lancashire* (12–SD4907), is a small village about 5½ m. NW. of WIGAN, where the River Douglas winds along on the N. In this stretch of fertile farmland, which contrasts with the busy towns it supplies with its crops, is Ashurst Hill. The old beacon on top of the hill is a prominent landmark with its pointed top which from a distance looks like a church steeple. It was built of strong masonry, with nothing inflam-

mable, in the Napoleonic war, and was intended as one of that chain of beacons right across England which would blaze to raise the alarm when invasion was imminent. In this neighbourhood was built a curious structure called Parbold Bottle, looking like a large beehive, which is said to commemorate the Reform Act of 1832.

DALTON-IN-FURNESS, *Lancashire* (12–SD2374), was the old capital of the Furness district. Its castle, of which the 14th-cent. tower remains in the main street, was the Court House of the Abbot of St Mary, but after the Dissolution the district's trade gradually passed to ULVERSTON. During the 19th cent. Dalton became important again while its iron-ore mines were busy, but did not regain its position as the market town of Furness. George Romney, the portrait painter, was born in a house called Beckside nearby in 1734, and worked with his father, a cabinet-maker, at a house at High Cocken. He was apprenticed to Steele, an artist, at KENDAL, before achieving fame in London, particularly with portraits of Emma Hart, later Lady Hamilton. The NATIONAL and TATE galleries have works by Romney. He died at Kendal in 1802 and was buried at Dalton, in the parish churchyard.

Urswick, to the E., has the Church of St Mary where a rush-bearing ceremony is still performed. Three dolorosas on the west wall were almost completely destroyed by Cromwellians. There is an organ-grinder and monkey carved in wood, a well-carved font top, a three-decker pulpit, fragments of a 9th-cent. Anglo-Saxon cross, and a Viking cross with runic inscriptions. The church has a massive tower as well as box pews.

DARESBURY, *Cheshire* (12–SJ5782). The parsonage, now demolished, in this village was the birthplace, in 1832, of the Rev. Charles Lutwidge Dodgson, poet, mathematician and author. He took deacon's orders in 1861. He became famous under his pen-name of Lewis Carroll when he published *Alice's Adventures in Wonderland* in 1865. He also wrote on mathematics, and lectured for 20 years on the subject at OXFORD. The Daresbury church is the delight of all children (and not a few adults) for its memorial window depicting the Cheshire Cat, White Rabbit and other characters. Daresbury Hall is a fine brick Georgian house.

DERWENTWATER, *Cumberland* (14–NY26 21). The lake is oval in shape, 3 m. long and ½ m. to 1¼ m. wide. Round most of the lake the rounded forms of the mountains are due to the effect of weathering on the SKIDDAW slate. The grass-covered slopes are broken here and there by sharper screes where the brittle rock has fallen away. But the eastern crags, and especially the heights piled beyond the south end of Derwentwater, through BORROWDALE up to SCA FELL, are composed of hard volcanic blocks. The only break in the encircling slopes is to the NW., where the longest Lakeland valley, beginning in Borrowdale below the central cluster of peaks, carries the River Derwent out through BASSENTHWAITE LAKE. The vast bulks of Skiddaw (3,054 ft), fourth highest of the LAKE DISTRICT mountains, and SADDLEBACK, lie across the north, sheltering KESWICK. The roads to PENRITH and GRASMERE climb out of Keswick at the lake's northeast corner. Contours rise to Bleaberry Fell and High Seat (1,996 ft) to shut in the lake along the east side. Across the S. is the glorious sight of the opening of Borrowdale beyond the lakeside road, through the Jaws of Borrowdale, beyond which Castle Crag stands, with the rugged Glaramara, and BOW FELL and Sca Fell, further S. The Dale Head group of peaks come down the west of Borrowdale to the south-west corner of Derwentwater at Manesty Park, and near here is Brackenburn, the house where Hugh Walpole lived. His *Rogue Herries* series of novels covers various Lakeland scenes, as at WATENDLATH. This valley, an offshoot to the E. of Borrowdale, is approached by a road leaving the lakeside route and crossing **Ashness Bridge**, a noted beauty-spot overlooking Derwentwater. Just W. of this area and behind the Lodore Hotel are the well-known Lodore Falls, cascades in Watendlath Beck. To complete the scene on the lake's west shore is the lower but graceful shape of Cat Bells, followed by Swinside.

Below Cat Bells are the 108 acres of Brandelhow, the first property acquired by the National Trust in the Lake District. The Trust protects for the public many acres of beauty around the Derwentwater area. Among them are Castle Head, which gives a good view of the lake on the NE.; and below this Friar's Crag, another famous vantage point, notable for the Ruskin memorial; as well as St Herbert's, Lord's, and Derwent islands. On St Herbert's Island are traces of the home of St Herbert, a disciple of St Cuthbert in the 7th cent., although these traces could be of a later structure. Lord's Island was the residence of the Earls of Derwentwater.

As well as fishing and swimming facilities there is a motor launch service and motor boats and rowing boats can be hired. You can also drive all the way round this, the widest of the Lakes.

DORFOLD HALL, *Cheshire* (12–SJ6352). This handsome Jacobean country house (open to the public) is 1 m. W. of NANTWICH on the road to TARPORLEY. The hall dates from about 1616, and is noted for the fine plasterwork decoration of its ceilings and its panelling. It was for long the home of the Wilbraham family, well known in Cheshire. During the Civil War Dorfold Hall was captured by the Royalists who used it as a site from which to attack Nantwich. The hall stands in a large park with fine gates and is approached along an avenue of trees.

DUDDON VALLEY, *Cumberland* (14–SD 1988). The River Duddon rises near Three Shires Stone at the top of WRYNOSE PASS. At the stone you can step through Cumberland, Westmorland and Lancashire within a few seconds. The river descends through Wrynose Bottom, dividing Cumberland on the W. from Lancashire on the E. And from here, where it leaves the road that begins (at Cockley Beck Bridge) to climb HARDKNOTT PASS, the river is the county boundary to the sea. A road follows the Duddon's east side through Seathwaite (not the BORROWDALE one) and Dunnerdale villages, crosses to Ulpha in Cumberland, and returns to the east side to join the A595 at Duddon Bridge. The CONISTON range is on the E. At Ulpha you can turn NW. to reach ESKDALE without surmounting Hardknott Pass. The lower area of Duddon is also called Dunnerdale.

The river inspired 35 of Wordsworth's sonnets; his Notes on the Duddon series commemorated the Rev. Robert Walker–"Wonderful Walker"–of the now rebuilt Seathwaite church. The poet's "Kirk of Ulpha", built in local stone, is still there.

EASEDALE, *Westmorland* (14–NY3008). This is a small dale on the north-west side of GRASMERE. The walk up and down it from Read's bookshop in the town covers 4 m. and includes a rise of about 700 ft. It is approached by crossing the KESWICK road and entering Easedale Tarn Road. After passing through several gates, you begin to climb more steeply, beside Sour Milk Ghyll (the same name as the one in BUTTERMERE), which forms some fine waterfalls. At the top of the rise you turn left on to a level stretch and then climb to the ruins of a refreshment hut and to the tarn. W. are High Raise and Sergeant Man peaks, both over 2,000 ft. The dale is rocky in places.

ECCLES, *Lancashire* (12–SJ7798), is 4 m. W. of MANCHESTER, and its south boundary lies along

T. Parker

The Duddon divides Cumberland from Lancashire

Eccles is famous for its cakes

British Travel Association

the Ship Canal with which the town's more modern growth has been associated. On the River Irwell medieval villages developed into towns, including Patricroft and Ellesmere Park, which eventually became part of the borough of Eccles. This is in a busy part of Lancashire, with the M62 motorway at the west side, but nevertheless has some pleasant countryside beyond the motorway. The central library contains microfilm records of local history and special collections dealing with Harold Brighouse, the dramatist, Lettice Cooper, novelist, and James Nasmyth, the inventor of the steam hammer. Monk's Hall is the oldest secular building; it dates from the Tudor period, with early 19th-cent. additions. The hall was a farmhouse during the 17th, 18th and early 19th cents., then became a residence; it was bought by the corporation, and opened as a museum and art gallery in 1961. Machine tools made by Nasmyth at his Bridgewater foundry are on show, as well as monthly night sky charts; there are permanent collections of art and pottery, as well as temporary exhibitions. In the 1862 restoration of St Mary's, the parish church, Norman masonry was found, but it is thought that there was an earlier Christian church on the site in Anglo-Saxon times. In the 13th cent. there was a church comprising a chancel, a nave without aisles, and a tower. Various alterations and additions were made during the next two centuries. The Boothe chantry chapel is 14th-cent. and in the 15th a clerestory and the handsome panelling were added. Until 1939 curfew was rung by St Mary's. Near the pulpit is part of the shaft of a pre-Conquest cross. The oak south door is 14th-cent. and there is some 16th-cent. Flemish glass.

Having inspected ancient and modern features, and noted that the aeronautical pioneer Sir Alliot Verdon-Roe was born at the house named The Poplars, visitors may recall another tradition: Eccles cakes. A shop in Church Street still makes them from the original recipe, and was rebuilt in the 19th cent. on the site of their first production.

ECCLESTON, *Lancashire* (12–SD5218), a village on the western boundary of ST HELENS, that was the birthplace of Richard Seddon, who became Prime Minister of New Zealand. Christ Church is a massive 19th-cent. building in red sandstone with a spire and high pinnacles. It was designed by Samuel Taylor. Inside are an oak gallery and hammer-beam roof. There are lavish carvings of fruit, flowers and foliage. Panels from New Zealand include a memorial to Seddon.

EGREMONT, *Cumberland* (14–NY0110), on the A595, near the more pleasant area of ST BEES, is an industrial town producing plastic and leather goods, and with a grimy air due to the reddish iron ore with which it has been particularly associated. But even here Wordsworth found inspiration. In 1806 he wrote "The Horn of Egremont Castle", ". . . which none could sound . . . Save He who came as rightful Heir". This castle, of the House of Lucie, was built about 1140 to uphold Norman rule, but was destroyed in the

16th cent. and is now a ruin. St Mary's is on the site of a church believed to date from the 12th cent. It is late 19th-cent. but includes early features.

ELTERWATER, *Westmorland* (14–NY3204). This small lake, not easy of access on its shores, is at the entrance to the LANGDALE valleys. There was formerly much slate production in the area, and some is still carried on today. Varied species of bird frequent this lake. On the River Brathay, which flows from the SE. of Elterwater, there is the charming waterfall of Skelwith Force before the river reaches Skelwith Bridge. A path leads to the fall from near this bridge. At Neaum Crag is the caravan, chalet and camping site run by the Lake District Planning Board. The site covers 18 acres of fell and woodland, with good views from the higher part. White Craggs Rock Garden (open to the public), at the junction of the A593 and B5343, has a colourful display of rare shrubs, azaleas and rhododendrons; it also has parking space. Near Elterwater village, at the late 17th-cent. St Martin's Farm, John Ruskin (*see* CONISTON WATER) established a centre for the revival of the hand-made linen industry.

ENNERDALE WATER, *Cumberland* (14–NY1015). It is impossible to approach this lake by road except from the W., and it is the most westerly of all the lakes. Near the west end of the lake the track becomes very rough and you must proceed on foot or not at all. From there the dale stretches SE. for about 8 m. and near its head Black Sail Pass leads to the SW. into WASDALE for WASTWATER. The pass is only a track, of course, 1,800 ft up in the wild and very isolated region of Ennerdale that is a favourite with rock-climbers. The High Stile range lies along the north-east side of the dale with BUTTER-MERE beyond. On the south-west side is the Pillar group of peaks with the formidable-looking Pillar Rock dominating the view of precipices; Pillar itself is higher (2,927 ft) and further back. Then beyond Black Sail Pass and Kirk Fell the dale is closed by the majestic GREAT GABLE.

The National Trust owns many acres of land stretching over into Stockdale and Wasdale. But the approach to Ennerdale by road has less in common with the peaceful solitude of these acres encompassing or adjoining the mighty peaks; it is more akin to the Cumberland coastal stretch and the decayed industrial atmosphere of Cleator Moor. There are various old iron mines, and the iron ore was known in Roman times. A mile or so W. of the lake is the small village of Ennerdale Bridge. Its churchyard was the setting for Wordsworth's poem, "The Brothers".

ESKDALE, *Cumberland* (14–SD1599), can be reached either up the extremely steep HARDKNOTT PASS from the E., or from the W. The west end is reached by various roads from the coastal area, and one crossing over the Esk from further down the DUDDON VALLEY. In summer, as a change from driving, you can take the miniature railway from **Ravenglass** as far as BOOT. The lower

reaches, green with farmland, have occasional houses dotted about and footpaths near the River Esk. Beyond the villages of Eskdale Green and Boot the valley turns towards the N., leaving the road before Hardknott, and rises into the wild regions between the two SCA FELL peaks (both over 3,000 ft) and BOW FELL (nearly 3,000 ft). At the end is Esk Hause, where the Sca Fell and Bow Fell tracks join at the watershed above BORROW-DALE. Around the hause is a conjunction of tracks well known to climbers – those from WASDALE, from Borrowdale and from LANGDALE. At 2,490 ft, this is the highest pass in Lakeland.

ESTHWAITE WATER, *Lancashire* (14–SD 3596), is a beautiful small lake only about 1½ m. long. Small roads surround the lake, there are fells in the distance, and nearby are the wooded areas that lie between CONISTON WATER and WINDERMERE. Historic HAWKSHEAD is close to the N. of the lake and Ruskin's home, Brantwood, is beside Coniston Water. Rowing boats can be hired on Esthwaite, which has trout and perch, and birdlife around its quiet recesses.

Wray Castle is NE., near Windermere. It is a mansion built in early Victorian times in the medieval style. It is National Trust property and the grounds are open to the public. Esthwaite Hall, on the west side of its own lake, is a historic house which became the home of the Sandys family. Edwin Sandys was Archbishop of YORK in the 16th cent.

Hill Top, a house popular with visitors, is E. of Esthwaite Water, in Near Sawrey, a village which, like Hawkshead, can be reached by the ferry from BOWNESS across Windermere. In 1944, under the will of Beatrix Potter, the National Trust acquired about half the village, including Hill Top and Castle Farm, cottages, Town Bank estate and a field. The 17th-cent. house (open to the public) contains Beatrix Potter's furniture, china, pictures and some of her drawings and is full of the atmosphere of characters from her books such as Jemima Puddleduck and Tom Kitten. She invented the Peter Rabbit character earlier, and was able to buy Hill Top, and there continued her series of children's books.

EUXTON, *Lancashire* (12–SD5518). With the River Yarrow nearby on the S., and on a site some 2 m. W. of CHORLEY, Euxton has a little church that seems to have lost the record of its dedication. It consists of a 14th-cent. nave without aisles, and has the date of 1513 on the south wall. Rebuilt about 1724, and enlarged in the 19th cent., the church has a good roof, which has been reinforced, and an old sundial.

FARNWORTH, *Lancashire* (12–SJ5187). This village adjoins Widnes, the industrial port on the Mersey. The Church of St Luke, of 12th-cent. origin, retains its 14th-cent. tower and south arcade. It was restored later. It has Tudor wood ceilings in the south transept and the chancel. The chapel of the Bold family was rebuilt about 1855. There are interesting monuments.

FLEETWOOD, *Lancashire* (12–SD3247), faces into MORECAMBE Bay at the mouth of the River Wyre. On a clear day you can see from the Mount Pavilion, above the Marine Hall and gardens, across the bay to the LAKE DISTRICT fells and inland to the Lune valley and the Pennines.

Fleetwood was originally the northern terminus of the railway from Euston, with connections by sea to Scotland and Ireland. In 1847 Queen Victoria first set foot in Lancashire at Fleetwood on her return from Scotland.

Fleetwood is a fishing port and a resort, bounded by the sea on three sides. It has a fine promenade and spacious sea-front gardens, a marine pool and an amusement park. Pleasure cruises cross Morecambe Bay and there is a hovercraft service.

The town was founded in 1836 by Sir Peter Hesketh-Fleetwood of Rossall Hall, 2 m. to the S., which became a public school in 1844. Decimus Burton laid out the town, but did not complete the plan. His buildings include the North Euston Hotel, Queen's Terrace, both lighthouses and the lodge to the Mount Pavilion.

FORMBY, *Lancashire* (12–SD2907). The sea was here once and there was a fishing village on the shore, but the sea has receded as on various parts of the west coast. At Formby it is a mile or so away, beyond extensive sandhills. The National Trust control 400 acres of sand dunes and fore-shore W. of the town. These were bought by public subscription in 1967 as part of Enterprise Neptune, and constitute the nearest unspoilt coastline to the centre of LIVERPOOL. The Church of St Peter of brick and stone was built in 1736. It has a bell-turret, large windows with round tops and clear glass. A chancel and side chapel were built in Gothic style in 1873.

FOXDENTON HALL, *Lancashire* (12–SD 9005), is in Foxdenton Park, Chadderton, about 4 m. NE. of MANCHESTER, and owned by the Chadderton Urban Council. This Stuart mansion (open to the public) was restored in 1965. The present structure dates from the beginning of the 18th cent., when it was erected on the base of the 1620 hall which was partly demolished. There had been an earlier hall owned by the de Trafford family.

FURNESS ABBEY, *Lancashire* (12–SD2271), lies NE. of BARROW-IN-FURNESS in a narrow, thickly-wooded valley. Its red sandstone ruins are an Ancient Monument, open to the public, and show the great size of this rich and powerful religious house. Savignac monks founded the abbey in 1127. When the parent house at Savigny in Normandy adopted the Cistercian rule about 1147, the Furness monks followed suit. King Stephen endowed the abbey with nearly all the Furness area, later kings adding large estates in other parts of Lancashire and in Yorkshire. The Abbot of Furness ruled the district as a feudal lord from an abbey that was richly decorated and had well-equipped domestic buildings. The monks

administered the area until the Dissolution, and built a castle on Piel Island as a refuge from Scottish raids.

The parts of the church nave and transepts that remain date from the 12th to 13th cents. Notable features include the late Norman arches of the cloisters; three fine Transitional arches on the east of the north transept; the Early English chapter house, an extension of the south transept; and the good carved work of the sedilia and piscina. Among other remains are the infirmary and the abbot's lodging.

GAWSWORTH, *Cheshire* (12–SJ8869). An enchanting village, set among forest, parkland and ornamental ponds. The beautiful timber-framed Gawsworth Old Hall was the seat of the Fytton family from the time of building in the 16th cent. until it was taken over by the Main-warings. The house is notable for its black-and-white gable and great windows overlooking spacious lawns and gardens embellished with five lakes. In the grounds are the traces of one of the finest tilting arenas in England, 200 yds long and over 60 yds wide. That it should have been here was fully in character with the reputation for aggressiveness which caused the Fytton family to be known as "The Fighting Fyttons" among the chroniclers.

At the end of an avenue of elms is the Old Rectory, with its black-and-white medieval walls dating from 1470. The building encompasses a gracious central hall with an open roof and carved timbers, the whole fronted by a window made up of scores of diamond panes. The church is mainly a 15th-cent. Perpendicular structure, on Norman foundations, and stands near two of the Gaws-worth lakes in company with yews which may well have supplied the Cheshire archers with bows in the 12th cent. Gargoyles and other carvings enrich the tower, matching their oddity with heraldic shields and canopied niches ornamenting the buttresses. A Tudor doorway leads from the neat stone porch to the nave, with its 400-year-old font bowl and delightful painted roof. In the chancel are the tombs of the Fytton family, one of whom, Sir Edward Fytton, married Anne Warburton when he was only 12 years of age and she a month younger. They lived together for 34 years in uninterrupted harmony and had 15 children. A son, also Sir Edward, born in 1550, became Lord President of Munster and died in London in 1606. His monument is at Gawsworth church without his effigy, but his wife and children are represented in stone at the side of the space it should have occupied. One of the daughters in the group attained the distinction of being accepted as a favourite maid of honour by Elizabeth I, but was soon in disgrace following an affair with the Earl of Pembroke. It is of particular interest that she is now thought to have been the Dark Lady of Shakespeare's sonnets.

Near the church is a wood in which may be seen the tomb of "Maggotty Johnson", sometimes called "Lord Flame" after the leading character in one of his operas. He was by profession a fiddle-player and stilt-walker, who had begun life as a dancing-master, and is remembered more for his eccentricity as a person than as a playwright. The opera was called *Hurlothrumbo* and ran for a month, encouraging Johnson to write three more plays in expectation of a London production, but this time he failed to arouse any interest and returned, chastened, to the village. He died in 1773, aged 82, and was buried in the place of his own choosing.

The new Hall, much larger than the old one, was built early in the 18th cent. by Lord Mohun, whose duel with the Duke of Hamilton in KENSINGTON GARDENS resulted in both their deaths. The duel, which arose from differences connected with the disposal of the estate, became the subject of a chapter in Thackeray's *Henry Esmond*. The new Hall is now a home for the aged, but Gawsworth Old Hall is open to visitors.

GILSLAND, *Cumberland* (14–NY6366), is about 1 m. N. of the A69 from CARLISLE and is a small village at the edge of the county where the River Irthing flows down from almost deserted land stretching to the Scottish border. A good section of HADRIAN'S WALL extends to Gilsland from the E. Part of Poltross Burn milecastle is in the railway embankment, and a stretch of wall is in a garden E. of the school. There are Roman inscriptions on two altars. The Wall continues W. It was in Gilsland that Sir Walter Scott met Charlotte Carpenter, and they were married in Carlisle. Several years after their marriage, they revisited the wells of Gilsland, to spend a few days among the scenes where they had first met. Whilst they were at the spa, the invasion was signalled by beacon-flares on hill-tops and Martello towers spread across England. Scott immediately set off on horseback to volunteer to fight Napoleon, and rode a hundred miles into Scotland in twenty-four hours; only to find that it was a false alarm.

Birdoswald, close to Gilsland, has the remains of a 5-acre Roman fort, comprising walls and east gateway.

Brampton, W., is a pleasant market town. The Written Rock of Gelt, a rock inscribed by a Roman standard bearer, is on the River Gelt 1½ m. S. of Brampton.

Bewcastle, a Roman site, is 11 m. N. of Brampton and has some remains of a castle. The famous Bewcastle Cross, the only one of its kind in England, is in the churchyard. It is a shaft, dating from the late 7th cent., classed as an Ancient Monument. St John the Baptist, Christ, and a "falconer" (St John the Evangelist? or Alcfrith?) are shown, with Runic inscriptions and decorations.

GRANGE-OVER-SANDS, *Lancashire* (12–SD4178). Backed by wooded fells, Grange is a fine seaside resort, sheltered and with a mild climate, overlooking MORECAMBE Bay. It has a promenade free of traffic, good sands, a bathing pool and tennis and golf. There is pony-trekking to CARTMEL (2 m.). The Lakeland Rose Show is held annually at the beginning of July. The town's parks are noted for flowering shrubs, alpine and rock plants and herbaceous plants. Many species of bird have been noted, and sometimes the rare golden eagle at WITHERSLACK. The Nature Conservancy has a research station at Merlewood. Nearby Hampsfell (750 ft) has an indicator and view of LAKE DISTRICT mountains.

Lindale, 2 m. N., has a monument to John Wilkinson, the 18th-cent. ironmaster, who launched the first iron ship, on the River Winster.

GRASMERE, *Westmorland* (14–NY3307). This tranquil little lake is famous above all as Wordsworth's home from 1799 until he moved to RYDAL in 1813. Dove Cottage, where he lived for nine years, is open to the public. The site of his Wishing Gate is on the old road, which gives fine views of the lake running behind the main road along the east shore. There is a little island of which Coleridge wrote, "We drank tea the night before I left Grasmere, on the island in that lovely lake, our kettle swung over the fire, hanging from the branch of a Fir-tree". Rowing boats can be hired.

The area around village and lake is notable for the scenery along various walking routes. The strikingly shaped Helm Crag lies NW., Rydal Fell and Nab Scar lie E., and Yew Crag and Silver Howe W. Apart from the main road, the only motoring exit is SW. past the lake to Red Bank where the road forks right for ELTERWATER and the LANGDALE PIKES, and left to pass Loughrigg. From the top of the steep bank the path of Loughrigg Terrace on the left gives fine views of the lake. There is little parking space at Red Bank, and cars are better left at the village or White Moss Common in order to cross the Rothay footbridge and come up at the middle of the Terrace. This continues E. above RYDAL WATER, and past a huge cave left from an old quarry which can be penetrated by the light from the entrance. Other walks are to Helm Crag, to Grey Crag and Alcock Tarn, to Silver Howe, to Dow Bank, and to Swinescar Hause. To reach the tops of Helm Crag, the Howe and Swinescar, however, you must climb over 1,000 ft.

GRASMERE (VILLAGE), *Westmorland* (14–NY3307). Placed just W. of the main road to the N. of GRASMERE (LAKE), the village can be missed by the motorist. Grasmere village and its offshoot to the S., the tiny group of houses of Town End, are not particularly notable in themselves; it is their setting below Helm Crag and Nab Scar, above the lake, which provides the attraction. Wordsworth pronounced it "the loveliest spot that man hath ever found", and Thomas Gray called it "this little unsuspected paradise".

At Town End is Dove Cottage (open to the public), the home of Wordsworth where he lived with his sister, Dorothy, from 1799 to 1808. He brought his bride, Mary, to Dove Cottage in 1802. What is often regarded as his best work was written at this small house, a former inn, and probably built in the 17th cent.; and it was a meeting point for famous literary figures – Coleridge, Southey, de Quincey and others. It is preserved almost as it was when Wordsworth lived there, by the Dove Cottage Trust, and holds many relics. Coleridge followed Wordsworth to the Lakes in 1800 and lived at Greta Hall, KESWICK, until 1804. He returned to the Lakes in 1808 and lived for two years at Wordsworth's next home, Allan Bank. Later, de Quincey lived in Dove Cottage for 26 years from 1809. The Wordsworth Museum nearby contains MSS. and other important items.

Allan Bank, Wordsworth's next home, is just NW. of the village. Owned by the National Trust, it is private, but visitors may view it from the drive. While there from 1808 to 1811, the poet wrote most of *The Excursion*. He then lived at the old rectory, opposite St Oswald's Church, before moving to RYDAL in 1813.

In *The Excursion* he gives a description of St Oswald's, which he attended during his life at Grasmere. In the churchyard are the graves of Wordsworth and his wife, his sister, his daughter Dora and her husband, and of Hartley Coleridge. It is believed that there was a 12th-cent. church on the site, of which parts may be incorporated in the present one. It contains the 17th-cent. manor pew of the Le Fleming family, with other monuments. A Wordsworth plaque, a pitch pipe, old chairs and alms box can be seen. An annual rush-bearing festival is held, similar to the one at AMBLESIDE.

The Grasmere Sports is famous and traditionally is held on the Thursday nearest to 20 August. Up to 20,000 spectators gather in a large field to watch the Cumberland and Westmorland wrestlers, the hound trail, the athletes who race to the top of Butter Crag, and other events.

The Swan Hotel, an old coaching inn, appears in Wordsworth's poem *The Waggoner*. At the bottom of the south slope of Helm Crag is Lancrigg, the house where Wordsworth composed much of *The Prelude*, walking to and fro on a garden terrace as his sister took it down.

The 1970 Wordsworth Bi-Centenary Celebrations, supported by Mr Richard Wordsworth, great-great-grandson of the poet, and Cecil Day-Lewis, the Poet Laureate – with the inclusion of the world première of Wordsworth's only play, "The Borderers" – underline the importance of his Grasmere period. It was appropriate to arrange these events in the village, a place Wordsworth always valued for the inspiration such an environment gave "to see into the heart of things".

GREAT GABLE, *Cumberland* (14–NY2110). This is the seventh highest Lake peak and is 2,949 ft high. Its majestic bulk makes it a favourite subject for photographs. Although the north and south sides are very precipitous, the stony wilderness at the top is reached frequently by climbers, who have given various names to its features, such as Moses' Sledgate or Moses' Trod. This is a route made by quarrymen and supposed to have been used by Moses the smuggler; it comes from HONISTER PASS quarries. Great Gable is the highest of a group of peaks, among which are Kirk Fell, above ENNERDALE, to the W., and Fleetwith to the N. SW. is WASTWATER and S. is SCA FELL.

GREAT SALKELD, *Cumberland* (14–NY55 36), is NE. of PENRITH. The massive fortified tower of St Cuthbert's Church is a reminder of the many Scottish raids into Cumberland. It was added to the Norman nave in the 14th cent. The south doorway is notable. **Long Meg and her Daughters**, near Little Salkeld, are standing stones in a ring about 350 yds in circumference, with resemblances to STONEHENGE. Long Meg is a stone about 18 ft high. The Little Meg circle is nearby at Maughanby. Both may date from the Bronze Age.

GREAT SANKEY, *Lancashire* (12–SJ5688). This small village and church lies W. of WARRINGTON in an old agricultural area. St Mary's was said to have been built by subscription in the reign of Charles I, but little used. After the Restoration it continued in use as a Presbyterian chapel until, in 1728, it was handed to the Church of England by the Atherton family. It was rebuilt in the later 18th cent. and consecrated in 1769. The brick building contains marble tablets.

GREYSTOKE, *Cumberland* (14–NY4330). On the A66, about 5 m. W. of PENRITH, Greystroke has the interesting Church of St Andrew, one of the largest in the diocese. The earliest part is 13th-cent. and later the church became collegiate. Most of the structure is 15th-cent., when it was considerably rebuilt. The tower and the sacristy have battlements. Notable is the east window with very fine stained glass of the 15th cent. or earlier, inscribed brass, two effigies (probably 14th- and 15th-cent.), stalls with misericords, and a chancel screen with a carved rood-loft.

The castle is the residence of the descendants of Thomas Howard, Duke of Norfolk in the reign of Elizabeth I, and was restored in the 19th cent. by Anthony Salvin. It is remarkable for the follies built to enhance the view from the windows.

GRISEDALE, *Westmorland* (14–NY3715). The lovely valley of Grisedale descends from the SW. to the upper end of ULLSWATER, following the course of Grisedale Beck, and is a magnificent area for walking. The A592 crosses the beck near the lake, just N. of PATTERDALE. And from this end you can mount towards impressive views on the eastern slopes of the HELVELLYN range, from which the famous Striding Edge juts out to the N. of Grisedale. The path rises between the Edge and St Sunday Crag (2,756 ft) to the S., leading to Grisedale Tarn, 1,768 ft above sea-level and S. of Dollywagon Pike (2,810 ft), ascended by a path. From the tarn a path covers 6 m. to GRASMERE, first surmounting Grisedale Pass at 1,929 ft between Sea Sandal on the W. (2,415 ft) and Fairfield on the E. (2,863 ft). Not

T. Park

Hardknott Pass, with a flock of the tough Herdwick sheep

far from the tarn the path passes Brothers' Rock, sad memorial of the last time that Wordsworth saw his brother John, who was drowned at sea in 1805.

HADRIAN'S WALL, *Cumberland* (14–NY 2363–14–NY6366).

The Emperor Hadrian, on a visit to Britain in A.D. 122, decided to build a wall as a permanent defence against Pictish invaders, and to mark the northern limit of the Roman Empire. Aulus Platorius Nepos supervised the building from 122 until at least 126, but final completion was not until after 130. It ran for 73 m. from Wallsend to the Solway Firth.

The Wall was more than a wall: it was more elaborate than Roman demarcations of the same nature on the Continent. In front, on the northern side, ran a ditch, averaging about 27 ft wide and 9 ft deep, except where the wall was above the sea or some steep edge. The wall itself was about 7½ ft thick, and the part to walk on is supposed to have been about 15 ft above ground with the breastwork above that. The military way was behind, and the vallum behind that again, the latter having subsequent alterations, but being originally about 20 ft wide and 10 ft deep. Forts adjoined the south side of the wall at intervals, the smaller type holding 500 infantry and the larger having 1,000 infantry or 500 cavalry. There were milecastles, usually at a Roman mile apart, and two turrets between each pair of milecastles. One theory advanced for the vallum was that it was a defence against attack from the rear by the Brigantes, whose territory ranged over the whole north from what is now Lancashire and Yorkshire into the area beyond the wall. They never became so reconciled to Roman rule as tribes further south. About 140 the Romans built another wall between Forth and Clyde – probably this was stretching their lines of communication too far, and after the troubles they had from 155 to 181 it was abandoned.

The Romans held Hadrian's Wall through various disasters, but after 383 it lost its impor tance for them.

A good section of wall extends into Cumber land from the E. at GILSLAND, where part of Poltross Burn milecastle is in the railway embank ment, and a stretch of it is in a garden E. of Gils land school. Willowford is the east abutment where the Roman bridge crossed the Rive Irthing, and 1,000 yds of wall run W. to the abut ment. Across the river the wall continues W. from Harrow's Scar milecastle. This is where th original turf wall, on a slightly different route began – replaced with a stone one which goes W to **Birdoswald**. Here the east gateway and walls of a 5-acre fort are preserved. The wall can be fol lowed for some distance W. to LANERCOST. Stan wix, just N. of CARLISLE, was the largest an most important fort. Rich Roman discoverie have been made in these two areas: *see* Tulli House Museum, Carlisle. The wall ended a Bowness-on-Solway. But to prevent its end bein turned, there were Roman defences S. along th West coast including Beckfoot, MARYPORT Burrow Walls and Moresby. Cumberland S. o the wall was linked by various forts (and roads such as **Ravenglass** (under MUNCASTER), HARD KNOTT and BROUGHAM.

HALL I' TH' WOOD, *Lancashire* (12–SD 7512).

The Hall (open to the public) is on the Breightmet–Astley Bridge Road, N. of BOLTON It is a half-timbered manor house, built in 1483 with a stone wing of 1591 and alterations of 1648 Mr W. H. Lever, later 1st Viscount Leverhulme (*see* Bolton) bought and restored the Hall, an presented it to the Corporation in 1902. Between 1758 and 1782 part of it was inhabited by Samue Crompton, who invented the spinning-mule i one of the rooms. The Hall is now a folk museum

At Tonge Moor Road, Bolton, is the Tong Museum, where a collection of historic textil machinery can be seen, including Hargreaves spinning-jenny (about 1764), Arkwright's spin ning-frame (1769) and Crompton's spinning-mule (1779). Crompton (1753–1827) was born in a house to be seen at Firwood Fold, off Crompton Way, and his tomb is in the parish churchyard. The "mule" he invented was an improved version of Hargreaves' spinning-jenny for fine cottons, and a cross between that and the Arkwright frame. The Lancashire cotton industry had formerly been limited to hand-production, and the advent of machinery was to have widespread repercussions. The Industrial Revolution increased cotton production fourfold, but brought with it "dark Satanic mills" and appalling working conditions. In a sense, the whole technological evolution of the present era can be traced back to these primitive looms.

HALSALL, *Lancashire* (12–SD3713). This West Lancashire village has a very fine church. The tower is 15th-cent., an octagonal shape on a square base. Nave and chancel have steep and beautiful roofs. In the north wall is a Decorated doorway with the original oak door. Inside, this wall has a finely ornamented tomb recess, probably of the 14th cent. The chancel is notable for rich carvings in wood and stone and sculptured figures. Effigies of the Halsall family are in the church.

HARDKNOTT PASS, *Cumberland* (14–NY 2101), is well named. Whether it is approached from the E., from the GRASMERE, AMBLESIDE or CONISTON areas, or from the W. up ESKDALE, matters little, except that from the E. the WRYNOSE PASS will provide a foretaste of what is to come. The Hardknott is nearly the highest – 1,291 ft at the summit – and certainly the most difficult motoring road in Lakeland. It is surfaced but narrow, and there are gradients of 1 in 3 with bends. The vehicle should be in first-class condition – and the driver, too. It would be wise to avoid being on the pass after dark.

Hardknott Castle is N. of the road at the west end of the pass, where you can stop to inspect this fort the Romans used in the 2nd cent. A.D. It covers more than 2 acres, has ramparts 20 ft thick, walls and gateways. It was on the route of the Roman road from Ravenglass on the coast, through Ambleside, and over High Street mountain to PENRITH.

HAWES WATER, *Westmorland* (14–NY4713), is no longer a lake but a reservoir like THIRLMERE, and is not only the most easterly of Lakeland waters, but also one of the most difficult to reach from the central areas. The widespread High Street group of peaks prevents all access for vehicles from the W., as do continuations of this group into the SHAP fells across the S. This combined knot of mountains in the western part of Westmorland leaves only the KIRKSTONE PASS and Shap Fell roads as north and south routes on each side of it. Hawes Water, lying inside the angle of this L-shaped knot, can be reached by car only from its east end. The Romans, however, had a road right along the High Street ridge, close

to its 2,718-ft summit, which came up from AMBLESIDE and went down to the PENRITH area. There are plenty of tracks for climbing up to this ridge, and cars can get below it by the road along the south-east side of Hawes Water that begins at BAMPTON. The road ends in the Mardale area, where Mardale village was submerged by the MANCHESTER waterworks scheme that raised the level by some 90 ft. The road along the other side of the lake was submerged, but a footpath remains. High up in a recess on the slopes of High Street the tarn of Blea Water stands at over 1,500 ft; it is more than 200 ft deep – the deepest tarn in Lakeland. Some unsightly concrete was laid to link it with waterworks schemes. At the northwest corner of Hawes Water, above the footpath, are the Standing Stones, one of several groups of remains of ancient communities in the area.

HAWKSHEAD, *Lancashire* (14–SD3597), lies near ESTHWAITE WATER and was formerly a market centre. It is one of the most delightful villages in Lakeland, with old cottages and narrow alleyways and courtyards. It was here that Wordsworth went to school when he was sent from COCKERMOUTH at the age of eight after his mother died.

The Grammar School is at the south end of the village. It was built in 1585, and is an interesting structure with old mullioned windows, and a door with large corbels supporting a pediment over which is a big sundial. The school is now a museum and library (open to the public), and many people go to see the desk on which Wordsworth carved his name. He attended from 1778 until shortly before he went to CAMBRIDGE in 1787. "And has the sun his flaming chariot driven", is among the early verse he wrote at this period. Wordsworth lodged at Anne Tyson's Cottage while at the school.

The Courthouse (open to the public) stands at the north end. This pre-Reformation building is historically connected with the monks of FURNESS ABBEY and in 1932 was given to the National Trust. It is now a folk museum, housing a collection from Abbott Hall, KENDAL, arranged by the Lake District Museum Trust. The National Trust also has four cottages in Vicarage Lane near Wordsworth's lodging, and 10 other properties around the village.

St Michael's Church was built in the late 15th cent. on the site of a 12th-cent. or earlier church or chapel. The modest tower is in rough stonework. In Wordsworth's time the exterior was whitewashed. The arcades inside have short, thick pillars that lack both base and capital and there are restored mural paintings. There are wall monuments to Thomas Bowman and Daniel Rawlinson, both connected with the grammar school, and to Edwin Sandys who became Archbishop of YORK. The ancient Quaker Meeting House is at Town End nearby. The medieval gatehouse and part of one wing, now a farm-house, survive of Hawkshead Hall, an old manor house. At Hawkshead Hill is the Baptist chapel (1678).

There is a 4-m. walk, as an alternative to

driving, between Hawkshead and the ferry at WINDERMERE. A Nature Trail can be followed for an hour, starting at the car park 1 m. from Satterthwaite. This is arranged by the Forestry Commission (at Grizedale) which has an information room, a wildlife centre and a forest nursery. There are photographic facilities on the trail. Another trail runs from the Claife shore of Windermere.

HESWALL, *Cheshire* (12–SJ2682), is a residential area on the main road running along the W. of the Wirral peninsula. It stands on the highest part of the peninsula and there are good views across the Dee estuary to the Welsh hills. Reaching from WEST KIRBY almost to Heswall is a line of cliff, interesting geologically as it is believed to be a relic of the Ice Age.

At **Bebington,** E. across the peninsula, the Mayer Free Public Library was founded by Joseph Mayer, the Liverpool goldsmith who helped to found the City Museum, LIVERPOOL.

Parkgate, S. of Heswall, was once a busy port, but the water has receded with the silting-up of the Dee, as at CHESTER. Handel stayed at the George Inn (Mostyn House school) when waiting to sail to Ireland in 1741 for the great Dublin performance of the *Messiah* that made London reverse its attitude to the composition. John Wesley sailed many times from Parkgate.

HEVERSHAM, *Westmorland* (14–SD4983), is an attractive village on a hill with an old hall, and a grammar school founded in 1613. The church was originally Norman but was altered in the 14th and 15th cents. and considerably rebuilt in the later 19th. There are fragments of an Anglian cross.

HOLKER HALL, *Lancashire* (12–SD3677), is 4 m. W. of GRANGE-OVER-SANDS. This former home of the Dukes of Devonshire is still owned by the Cavendish family. The house, open to the public at advertised times, is famous for the local craftsmanship shown in the interior wood-carving. A 17th-cent. structure, it was partly rebuilt in 1873, after a fire, with additions from local material and timber on the estate. The collection includes period furniture and paintings. It was the favourite seat of William Cavendish, the 19th-cent. 7th Duke, the agriculturalist and patron of science and industry. The grounds, on the edge of MORECAMBE Bay, have a 200-acre deer park with one of the oldest and largest herds of fallow deer in the country, and extensive gardens.

HOLME CULTRAM ABBEY, *Cumberland* (14–NY1750), in Abbey Town, is the remains of a Cistercian abbey founded about 1150. The 12th-cent. nave survives, used as the Parish Church of St Mary, with the west porch built by Abbot Chamber in the early 16th cent. The abbey underwent many restorations in the 17th and 18th cents. The fine arches of the nave were filled in to make the outer walls.

Silloth, to the NW., is a small port and coastal resort on the Solway Firth.

HONISTER PASS, *Cumberland* (14–NY 2214). This famous pass is not the steepest road in the Lakes, but it is probably the most dramatic pass for the motorist. To obtain the striking view of Honister Crag, with the valley of BUTTER MERE opening far beyond the tiny ribbons of road and beck that fall towards it, you should enter Honister from the BORROWDALE end. There is a 5-m. drive to Buttermere, from Seatoller where the pass begins suddenly, on a twist to the right with an unexpectedly steep gradient of 1 in 4. At the hause, or summit (1,190 ft), there are youth hostel and quarry buildings. Behind is a fine view over Borrowdale with HELVELLYN in the far distance. To the right is Dale Head (2,473 ft) whose ridge is joined by that of Grey Knott (2,287 ft on the S.) where the hause lies. Hind scarth and Robinson peaks extend NW. from Dale Head. And dominating the view down the pass ahead is the mighty sweep of Honister Crag on the left of the road, jutting out from Fleetwith These gigantic slopes were carved millions of years ago by the grinding might of natural forces, volcanic eruptions followed by the tremendous weight of the Ice Age glaciers. Many ages later came the men who opened the quarries to extract the slate of the Honister area that became noted as Buttermere green slate.

From its top, the pass falls about 500 ft in the first $\frac{1}{2}$ m., and then becomes a steadier descent below the towering mountain walls as it emerges into the rich beauty of Buttermere valley.

HOOLE, *Lancashire* (12–SD4623), near the Ribble estuary, was the home of a pioneer English astronomer, Jeremiah Horrocks, the curate or Hoole church, who is reputed to have lived at the 17th-cent. Carr House. He studied Kepler's works and in 1639 caught the silhouette of Venus on the sun's disc which he projected through his telescope on to a piece of paper – the first time the transit had been observed. St Michael's Church, Toxteth, LIVERPOOL, has a monument to him The Church of St Michael at Hoole was rebuilt in 1628. In 1720 the stone tower with battlements was added, and the chancel in the 19th cent. There are box pews and a two-decker pulpit of 1695 Horrocks's observation of Venus is commemorated in a window.

HORNBY, *Lancashire* (12–SD5868). There is a striking view of Hornby Castle and its tower on the road NE. from CATON and Scott paints a romantic portrait in *Marmion* of Sir Edward Stanley (1460–1523), the knight who built this keep. As a thank-offering for his safe return from Flodden Field, Stanley built the octagonal tower of St Margaret's Church. There is a new nave and a modern reredos. Dr John Lingard (d. 1851) the Roman Catholic historian, is commemorated by a memorial on the wall. The base of an Anglo-Saxon cross is in the churchyard.

Also in this area is **Castle Stede,** a Norman

Camera Press

odrell Bank radio telescope

arthwork, and **Melling-with-Wrayton** church, a
medieval structure on a steep site above the River
une.

HOYLAKE, *Cheshire* (12–SJ2189). This is a
combination of residential and seaside resort with
good beaches, a 4-m. promenade and the links of
the Royal Liverpool Golf Club at the corner of
the Dee estuary. Once it was a hamlet used as a
port of embarkation for Ireland, and then became
a fishing village. The small **Hilbre Islands** lie off
this coast and at one time were used by Benedictine monks. The islands have a considerable
variety of bird-life.

HUXLEY, *Cheshire* (12–SJ5061). Huxley Lower
Hall, W. of TARPORLEY and near the village of
Huxley, is a 17th-cent. manor house (open to the
public) with richly decorated plaster ceilings and
a moat. In the Civil War the hall was involved on
the Parliamentarian side. It was the home of
ancestors of Professor Thomas Henry Huxley,
the famous scientist.

INGS, *Westmorland* (14–SD4498), is a place
little known to the average tourist, by the main
road between WINDERMERE TOWN and KENT-
MERE valley. The Church of St Anne was built in
the 18th cent. by Robert Bateman, a local man,

and contains Wordsworth's epitaph to him in
brass. The church is in Renaissance style with a
marble floor.

JODRELL BANK, *Cheshire* (12–SJ8071). This
tiny spot just off the A535, between Holmes
Chapel and Alderley Edge, is internationally
famous as the site of the giant steerable radio
telescope, built by MANCHESTER University and
put into service in 1957. It has a 250-ft reflector
with a beam width of 12 minutes of arc. Radio
waves of much longer wavelength than light are
constantly being detected by this sensitive re-
ceiver, with its special aerial systems, and the
information used to record the movement of
extra-terrestrial bodies.

A settlement on Tunstead Hill, near the village
of **Withington**, is known to have existed in
pre-Anglo-Saxon times. Old Withington Hall is
a large mansion situated in a fine open park of
112 acres with a lake; and Welltrough Hall, a
farm-house in what was formerly called Lower
Withington and is now part of Chelford parish,
was at one time a seat of the Davenport family.

KENDAL, *Westmorland* (14–SD5192), is an
ancient town: there is some evidence of early
British settlement on the site of Castle How, and
there was a Roman camp at Watercrook which
was part of the road system connected with
HADRIAN'S WALL. Later there was the Anglo-
Saxon occupation. But most of Kendal's recorded history dates from the time of the Conqueror, who gave land to his Norman henchmen.
Richard I made the town a barony in 1189, and
Richard II made divisions in this barony, of which
one passed to Sir William Parr, an ancestor of
Catherine Parr. There were Scottish raids – even
as far south of CARLISLE as this – particularly in
1210; and fires and floods. Later came the Black
Death, but by 1331 the woollen industry had
begun. Edward III authorized John Kemp of
Flanders to establish Flemish weavers in the town,
and the woollen industry flourished for six centuries. Hence the Latin motto on the town's coat
of arms, *Pannus mihi panis* (Wool is my bread).
The town was noted for the production of
"Kendal Green", a green woollen cloth, mentioned as the clothing of archers by Shakespeare
in *Henry IV* and Scott in *The Lay of the Last
Minstrel*. Since then other industries have superseded woollen manufacture, such as footwear,
hosiery, carpets, engineering and insurance.

"The Auld Grey Town", so called because of its
many grey limestone buildings, is the largest and
most important in Westmorland. It lies in the
valley of the River Kent, with six bridges (three
of them good stonework), the A6 road and the
main railway for Scotland; it is the centre of communications and the market town for the surrounding agricultural area. Market days have
been held since the market charter of 1189. Off
the main streets are the old yards with narrow
pavements, probably designed for easy access to
the main streets and the river for handling the
wool. Kendal lies just outside the Lakeland

National Park, the Lake District proper. But it is the gateway to the Lakes from the SE., by way of the A591, the through road that leads first to WINDERMERE TOWN, only 8 m. away, and the M6 extension is not far E. of Kendal. The town's own surroundings are attractive, however, with a backcloth of Westmorland fells on three sides. The approach from Sedbergh on the E. is over a switchback moorland road offering glimpses of groups of Lakeland peaks. Kendal is well enough equipped with hotels to make it a centre from which to visit the Lakes, or the local countryside, and GRANGE and MORECAMBE are not far off.

Abbot Hall Art Gallery was opened in 1962 in a country mansion built in the town in 1759 by John Carr of YORK, adjoining the parish church and surrounded by gardens. The original carving and panelling on the ground floor has been restored. The gallery has permanent and changing displays of 18th-cent. furniture, paintings, silver, porcelain and glasswork. Other cultural activities are pursued at this centre. The Borough Museum has collections dealing with natural history and the history of the area as well as items of general interest.

The Parish Church of the Holy Trinity, in Kirkland, is one of the largest churches in England, a Gothic structure of the 13th cent. It is built on the site of an earlier church, and is unusual in having four aisles. The interior is a complicated arrangement of pillars and arches within the building's wide rectangle. Above the rather squat roofs is the square tower, 80 ft high. Some parts of the church date from about 1200, and there were 19th-cent. restorations. Chapels of the Parr, Bellingham and Strickland families of Kendal have various arms and monuments. A sword and helmet are traditionally associated with "Robin the Devil", Major Robert Philipson, the Royalist, who was besieged on Belle Isle, WINDERMERE, by Colonel Briggs, the Roundhead. After the siege Philipson is said to have ridden into Kendal church on horseback in a vain attempt at revenge on Briggs who was attending a service. Scott made this exploit one of the adventures of the hero in the poem *Rokeby*.

The ruined Norman castle apparently decayed some time after 1586, when it was pronounced by Camden, the historian, as being ready to drop with age. Catherine Parr, the last, and surviving, wife of Henry VIII was born there; she was the daughter of Thomas Parr, the lord of the castle. Her prayer book is on show in the Town Hall; it is bound in solid silver, has fine lettering, and cost £500 when it was bought by public subscription in 1936. The castle dairy (open to the public) in Wildman Street is a well-preserved example of Tudor domestic architecture with richly carved oak beams. It was rebuilt in 1564 by Anthony Garnet. The Town Hall is comparatively modern. Its tall clock tower has a carillon of bells which, on different days of the week, chooses in turn one of seven tunes, from English, Scottish, Welsh and Irish sources, to be played six times in the day. Seven paintings by George Romney adorn the Town Hall. Romney, associated with DALTON-

IN-FURNESS, served his apprenticeship in Kendal left in 1762 to achieve fame in London, but returned to Kendal and died at Romney House in Kirkland in 1802. The house where he was an apprentice was in a yard W. of Stricklandgate. Sandes Hospital, near the Town Hall in Highgate, was built in 1659 by the Sandes, cotton manufacturers. The Call Stone, formerly in the Market Place, is before the Town Hall and is the traditional stone for proclaiming English monarchs. Near the G.P.O. in the house now occupied by the Y.W.C.A. Prince Charlie stayed on his march to DERBY and again on his retreat; two nights after that his pursuer, "Butcher" Cumberland, slept at the same house in the same bed. The Old Grammar School was founded in 1525.

There are several parks and open spaces, such as Castle Hill and Serpentine Woods, and sport facilities, including golf. The town also holds music festivals. Joan Littlewood's Theatre Workshop became noted while it was in Kendal. Many areas exist for excursions beyond the town, including Skelsmergh, Longsleddale and Bannisdale.

KENTMERE, *Westmorland* (14–NY4504), is entered by the road turning N. from the KENDAL to WINDERMERE route. But this dale is not enhanced by its industrial developments. The lake was drained in the 19th cent., disclosing deposits of diatomaceous earth for insulating material. Since then a Viking spearhead and medieval canoe have been found. Near the village of Kentmere is Kentmere Hall where in 1517 Bernard Gilpin was born; he became Archdeacon of DURHAM and was known as the Apostle of the North. The road ends above the village; there is water beyond but it is a reservoir. Higher still, the foot-track goes over Nan Bield Pass, one of the wildest in Lakeland, and over 2,000 ft high. Harter Fell and Ill Bell that enclose this way to HAWES WATER rise about 500 ft above the pass.

KESWICK, *Cumberland* (14–NY2723). Keswick, the northern centre of the Lakes, lies in a beautiful position below the towering bulks of SKIDDAW and SADDLEBACK. It has a remote and almost magical quality.

Its beauty has made the town a mecca for poets, artists and visitors from all over the world. The town is attractive in itself, with intriguing narrow streets and buildings of old grey stone; a natural convergence of roads makes it an excellent centre for tours to other parts of Lakeland. Every type of accommodation can be found, from luxury hotels to guest-houses and private homes, but in the busy season the tourist who has no reservation may have difficulty in finding a room. At such times driving cars is a problem and the town is best seen on foot. A short walk takes one down the pleasant road below The Heads to the edge of DERWENTWATER, where the landing stages cater for cruises, motor boats and rowing boats on this, the "queen of the English lakes" (*see* Derwent water).

T. Parker

Kirkby Lonsdale: the Devil's Bridge

disciple of Ruskin, and Vicar of Crosthwaite, who was also one of the founders of the National Trust (*see* THIRLMERE). John Ruskin (*see* CONISTON WATER) once had a branch of his hand-made linen industry at Keswick, as he had at ELTERWATER.

Crosthwaite church, on the north-west side, is dedicated to St Kentigern. In this saint's time Cumberland was in the Kingdom of Strathclyde, ruled by the pagan Morken, from whom Kentigern fled to erect his cross in this "thwaite". The church is said to have been founded in the 12th cent. Its present form, which makes it the oldest structure in the valley, is a rebuilding, probably of 1553. It has a rare set of old consecration crosses and a 14th-cent. font and 15th-cent. effigies. In 1844 the church was restored by Gilbert Scott. It has a memorial effigy to Southey.

The tiny moot hall with its one-handed clock dates from 1813.

Special facilities are offered to visitors by the Public Library (St John's Street), which has a large collection of material on Keswick and the Lake District. Sporting facilities include golf, and there are numerous well-known walks to be taken. One is to **Friar's Crag** on the lakeside, the scene of much photographed views across the water, described by Ruskin as one of the earliest memories of his life. It is National Trust property, bought as a memorial to Canon Rawnsley, and also has a stone memorial to Ruskin. Inland beyond the lakeside road is **Castle Head**, 20 acres of National Trust woodland, where a point over 500 ft high gives a panorama of peaks identified on the indicator.

Castlerigg Stone Circle is an Ancient Monument (National Trust), 2 m. E. of Keswick. It is also called the Carles and the Druids' Circle, and is about 100 ft in diameter, formed of 38 megalithic stones. Inside this oval ring there is an oblong space of 10 more stones. From this prehistoric site there are excellent views.

Coleridge came to live at Greta Hall, behind the school, in 1800, pursuing his friendship with William and Dorothy Wordsworth who were already settled at GRASMERE village. Southey followed Coleridge in 1803. Charles Lamb came to Keswick for holidays, and Shelley resided there for a time after his marriage. Southey lived at Greta Hall for many years after Coleridge left Keswick in 1804. The Royal Oak Hotel was patronized by Scott, Tennyson, R. L. Stevenson and Wordsworth, and visited by the Southeys and Coleridge.

The Fitz Park Museum and Art Gallery has a large and famous collection of MSS. by Robert Southey, as well as those of Wordsworth, Coleridge's son, Hartley, and Hugh Walpole, six MSS. of whose novels it contains. There is a small collection of letters by John Ruskin. One of his paintings, together with works by Turner and others, is in the art gallery. Tunes can be played on the "musical stones" in the museum. There is a scale model of the Lake District, and a large collection of mineral and rock specimens of the geology of the area, as well as specimens of birds, butterflies and fossils. Fitz Park itself includes a recreational area and a children's playground.

The School of Industrial Arts was founded in 1883 by Canon H. D. Rawnsley, the friend and

KIRKBY LONSDALE, *Westmorland* (14–SD 6178), is easily missed from the E., being hidden behind the junction of the A65 and the A683. The Devil's Bridge over the River Lune, an Ancient Monument of obscure origin, is probably 13th-cent. and considered one of the finest ancient English bridges. Turn N. from the main road to enter this charming old town of narrow streets and Georgian buildings.

A good centre for visiting the unspoilt Lune valley, the town is a market and social centre for the surrounding agricultural area which, like much of the north-west region, has relics of the long Roman occupation. There are some good, small shops, particularly the bookshop. Restaurants are few, but there are several residential hotels and guest-houses. The motorist can park in the little Market Square (with the still smaller Horsemarket beyond), or in car parks uphill from it, and walk N. along the main street and then left, past old inns like the Sun, with its stone columns. At the church gates is the notice pointing to the place, the view from which Ruskin described as "one of the loveliest in England and therefore in the world". A plaque on the wall at Church Brow, quotes "Fors Clavigera", his monthly letter to "the workmen and labourers of Great Britain", and marks the spot where Turner (whom Ruskin so strongly championed) painted a picture of the Lune.

St Mary's Church is Norman, built on an Anglo-Saxon site, and the earliest of the churches in the valley. It has been developed and added to rather haphazardly, the remaining parts of the Norman period being the three westernmost arches and piers of the nave's north arcade, and the south and west doorways. The mosaic reredos, iron screen, attractive stained glass, choir seats and encaustic floor tiles are all Victorian. The six-sided pulpit is 17th-cent. There are various 18th-cent. mural tablets, and a font that came from the 14th-cent. Killington chapel.

Casterton, about 1½ m. N., is on the route of a Roman road. The well-known Casterton Girls' School (the Clergy Daughters' School) was formerly at Cowan Bridge, where four Brontë sisters were pupils, and may be the original of "Lowood" in *Jane Eyre*.

KIRKBY STEPHEN, *Westmorland* (14–NY 7708). Largely consisting of its main street, this old picturesque market town lies among the moors. The Church of St Stephen dates from Anglo-Saxon times and parts, including the impressive nave, are in the Early English style. The west tower has battlements. Carvings and memorials commemorate the Musgrave and Wharton families. One of the old buildings, now called the Fountain Café, dates from about 1650, and is listed as a building of historical interest. It has provided hospitality in some form for travellers during most of its 300 years' existence.

Wharton Hall, an Ancient Monument which is now a farm-house, is about 1¾ m. S. of the town, and the name of this family has a long association with Kirkby Stephen. It is a hall with two cross wings, built in the late 14th or early 15th cent. A new great hall was added by Thomas, Lord Wharton, in 1540; he founded a grammar school in Kirkby Stephen in 1566, and the 4th Lord Wharton a Bible Trust. The gatehouse and north-west part of the hall were added about 1559, and the original block was restored in 1785.

Further S. is Mallerstang Common, a fertile valley where the River Eden begins, with Wild Boar Fell on the W. This valley has been occupied from the Bronze Age onward. Part way up is **Pendragon Castle**, and to the E. Mallerstang Edge marks the Yorkshire border. There is a tradition that Pendragon was built by the father of King Arthur. It is certainly one of those castles that later belonged to the Clifford family and which were rebuilt by the energetic Lady Anne Clifford of APPLEBY and BROUGHAM. Recent excavations have yielded pottery in the ruins.

KIRKBY THORE, *Westmorland* (14–NY 6325). This was the site of the Roman fort and settlement of Bravoniacum, and the junction of

Roman roads. One came from E. over the moors via BROUGH on the way to BROUGHAM, and another came from Whitley Castle near ALSTON to the N. of Kirkby Thore. Roman relics have been found during building operations. The church, St Michael's, is 12th- to 14th-cent., with 17th-cent. altar rails and pulpit.

KIRKOSWALD, *Cumberland* (14–NY5541). This small village is up the Eden valley above ARMATHWAITE. The Church of St Oswald, from which the village derives its name, has a 19th-cent. tower standing apart 200 yds away uphill. The chancel is 16th-cent., and other parts range from the 12th to 14th cents. A spring flows below the nave and emerges at the west.

Kirkoswald also has a ruined castle, of which dungeons and one turret remain, and a private house, the College, with 16th- and 17th-cent. features.

KIRKSTONE PASS, *Westmorland* (14–NY 4008). This is the longest and the highest of all the LAKE DISTRICT motor passes, and its summit is 1,476 ft above sea-level. It is part of the A592 linking ULLSWATER and PENRITH in the N. with WINDERMERE (and AMBLESIDE) to the S. It is the only motor route between the Fairfield and HELVELLYN range on the W. and the High Street group of peaks on the E. Beyond High Street the mountain area reaches to SHAP Fell, making this part of Westmorland impassable for drivers just as the SCA FELL group does in Cumberland. The pass has gradients of up to 1 in 4, and needs much care and patience; it "lengthens" the 12 m. between Windermere and PATTERDALE. The Kirkstone Pass Inn is at the top, commanding good views; there is a parking space. At this area a branch of the pass comes twisting up from the SW. on the slopes of Snarker Pike (2,096 ft) – a direct route from Ambleside (instead of the main road from Windermere via TROUTBECK) but not practicable for caravans. Red Screes (2,541 ft) lies to the W., Caudale Moor to the E., and BROTHERS' WATER to the N.

KNOWSLEY HALL, *Lancashire* (12–SJ4493). In a park of some 2,000 acres W. of ST HELENS, surrounded by a wall about 12 m. long is Knowsley Hall, the private residence of the Stanley family, the Earls of Derby. The Stanleys are prominent in Lancashire and their history is interwoven with that of England. This site has been theirs for some six centuries, and the oldest part of the present mansion dates from the 15th cent. It contains old masters and family portraits. The park is one of the largest in the county. A portion of the Hall that was prepared for the reception of Henry VII was rebuilt in 1820. On the gateway to the deer park are carved the words: "Bring good news and knock boldly". Thomas, 1st Earl of Derby, married Margaret Beaufort, Countess of Richmond and mother of Henry VII. Sir Edward Stanley, of HORNBY Castle, was the fifth son of the 1st Earl. Henry, the 4th Earl, was one of the commissioners who tried Mary Queen of Scots in 1586. One member of the family, Ferdinando, Lord Derby, better known as Lord Strange, appears in our literary history. He was a patron of players, including Shakespeare, and had a book dedicated to him by Robert Greene, the poet, and panegyric by Spenser. The wife of the 7th Earl, Charlotte Stanley, held Lathom House near ORMSKIRK against the Parliamentarians in 1644. In 1780 the 12th Earl instigated the Derby horse-race. The 14th Earl, Edward Stanley, was a Classical scholar and statesman. As colonial secretary he carried out the emancipation of the West Indian slaves. He was three times Prime Minister. He published a translation of the Iliad into blank verse in 1864. The 15th Earl was also a distinguished Liberal politician. He was offered the crown of Greece in 1863, but he declined it.

Rainford, a village NE. of Knowsley Hall, is in pleasant farming country, much of it owned by the Stanleys and Pilkingtons. Between Rainford and BILLINGE is **Crank**, on a ridge of higher land with some interesting caves where it is believed that Roman Catholic priests hid from persecution.

KNUTSFORD, *Cheshire* (12–SJ7578).

Knutsford is a pleasant town with an old-world atmosphere and with good hotels and guest-houses from which to explore the countryside or the great TATTON HALL estate to the N. MANCHESTER is accessible by road or a quick rail service. Knutsford is essentially residential and has interesting associations and buildings. It makes a special event of May Day celebrations, which are among the oldest in the country and on two occasions have had Royal patronage. A procession precedes the crowning ceremony, with such characters as "Highwayman Higgins" and "Jack-in-the-Green". Carriages carry the May Queen, with the Lord Chamberlain, judge and courtiers. A sedan chair is carried by chairmen in livery. The queen is crowned on the heath, where there is dancing round the may-pole.

Tradition links Knutsford with King Cnut, or more strictly with Knut, another Dane said to have forded the stream. It has had a charter since 1292 and was once the capital of mid-Cheshire. For the last two centuries it has had associations with many interesting people. Edward Penny, R.A., a founder member of the Royal Academy and its first professor of painting, was born in Silkmill Street in 1714. In about 1760, Thomas Gaskell, maker of the famous long-case clocks, had premises in King Street. Sir Henry Holland (1788–1873), physician to William IV and Queen Victoria and also a writer, was born in the house that is now a stationer's shop, opposite the Royal George Hotel. His sisters, the Misses Mary and Lucy Holland, were the originals of Miss Deborah and Miss Matty Jenkyns, the heroines of *Cranford*, written by Knutsford's greatest figure, Mrs Gaskell. Sir Henry's son, Henry Thurston, became the 1st Lord Knutsford, and later Secretary of State for the colonies. Frank Boyd Merriman, who became Solicitor-General, was born in Knutsford in 1880 and it was his father who bought from the Hollands Church House, asso-

ciated with Mrs Gaskell's book, *Wives and Daughters*. It was while Sir Henry Royce was living in Legh Road in 1904 that he met Charles Stewart Rolls, a meeting which led to the great Rolls-Royce partnership.

Knutsford is very proud of Mrs Gaskell (1810–65), *née* Elizabeth Cleghorn Stevenson. Her mother, one of the Hollands, died a few months after Elizabeth was born and the girl lived with an aunt in what is now 17 Gaskell Avenue, Knutsford. In 1832 she married William Gaskell at the parish church, and they lived in Manchester. But the names of Mrs Gaskell and Knutsford became inseparable, and *Cranford* is considered a portrayal of the town and its personalities. Mrs Gaskell was a close friend of Charlotte Brontë, whose biography she wrote. The Unitarian chapel in Knutsford is where Mrs Gaskell taught in the Sunday School, and she and her husband were buried in the chapelyard. Edward Higgins, the highwayman, lived at 19 Gaskell Avenue; he appears in Mrs Gaskell's *Squire's Tale* and in De Quincey's *Reminiscences*. In Mrs Gaskell's *Wives and Daughters* Tatton Hall appears as Cumnor Towers, and in *Cranford* she mentions the Royal George Hotel. This is the town's chief hotel, an ancient hostelry that was once the White Swan.

Drury Lane, Legh Road and the King's Coffee House were designed by Richard Harding Watt. He was influenced by continental travels and his Ruskin Rooms show Italian influences in the tiled roofs and little tower. The Coffee House is a striking building with a principal tower and a subsidiary tower. Round a pillar are inscribed names and dates of English monarchs. The parish church, 1744, is early Georgian and replaced earlier chapels of ease. Parochial registers go back to 1581. Princess Street runs parallel with the trunk road on the edge of the town, and is interesting architecturally. King Street has a number of timbered buildings of historic interest, some well-preserved, and in parts of this narrow street old porches and steps cover the pavement.

LAKE DISTRICT, THE, *Cumberland* (14–NY1740),

is a heading that applies equally to Westmorland and northern Lancashire from a descriptive point of view. But if the Lake District National Park is taken as the area that defines the District, Cumberland contains rather more of it than the other two counties. The Lake District is quite small and compact: some 30 m. across. The only way really to absorb the beauty of this unique area is to go on foot. The views from a moving vehicle are no substitute and however busy the main traffic routes may be, the walker can, in many parts of Lakeland, soon reach areas remote from crowds and the hum of modern life.

For motorists, gradients on the main routes present no great difficulty. But roads squeezed between mountain bases in remote areas demand constant alertness for abrupt corners, bridges and similar hazards, not to mention sudden confrontations with large motor coaches, for which such conditions were never designed. The wise driver ensures that his vehicle is in good order before approaching the mountain passes. Those who tow caravans are advised to verify that their proposed routes are suitable. The western road passes, except possibly the WHINLATTER, are not suitable for caravans, nor is the direct route between AMBLESIDE and the KIRKSTONE PASS (well named The Struggle). For the more difficult passes, see WRYNOSE and HARDKNOTT. About caravan sites, as well as general information on walking routes, historic sites, buildings and gardens, literary associations, advice for fell-walkers, exploring North-West England by car, nature trails, riding, books and maps, consult The Lake District National Park Information Service, District Bank House, High Street, WINDERMERE, Westmorland. The Lake District has been a National Park since 1951, administered by the Lake District Planning Board. In 1966 the Board bought Brockhole, a country house halfway between Windermere and Ambleside on the main road, and established the Lake District National Park Centre, the first of its kind. The centre (open to the public) has information rooms, educational facilities including a lecture room, a unique exhibition tracing the physical and human development of the District, and a tea-room. The 32 acres of grounds have a car park, refreshment and picnic areas, formal gardens, a putting green and a jetty. Other important organizations for information are The English Lakes Counties Travel Association, Ellerthwaite, Windermere, Westmorland, for general and local brochures, and the area office of The National Trust, Broadlands, Borrans Road, Ambleside, Westmorland. The Trust has done much to protect amenities (see THIRLMERE).

No single area of natural beauty in England has such a wealth of literary associations as the Lake District. It was visited at various times by Sir Walter Scott, Tennyson, Hazlitt, Shelley, Charles Lamb and Carlyle; and John Ruskin (see CONISTON WATER), De Quincey and Hugh Walpole lived there. It is, of course, particularly associated with the Lake Poets – William Wordsworth, the Coleridges, and Robert Southey, who were connected with KESWICK among other places. Wordsworth (see particularly COCKERMOUTH, PENRITH, HAWKSHEAD, GRASMERE (village), and RYDAL) made an important contribution to the national idea of the Lake District. Topographical references are scattered through numerous poems, and he wrote a whole series on the DUDDON VALLEY. From his peaceful contemplation of the peaks and lakes he derived his idea that Nature is our great source of solace and strength, from the spirit that lies behind its outward manifestation. "I sit upon this old grey stone, And dream my time away", he said, and the visitor who spends his limited time at a single lake will better appreciate the atmosphere than those who try to cover the whole area in a single visit.

LANCASTER, Lancashire (12–SD4761). The history of this town goes back more than seven and a half centuries. There were various early occupations of Castle Hill, where prehistoric flint implements were found, and its vicinity. There was a Roman camp by the River Lune (or Loyne) It is supposed that before the Romans came the river flowed on the S. of Castle Hill instead of the N. as now, and attempts have been made to establish its exact course. Little is known of the Anglo-Saxon period: some survivals of this are in St Mary's Church. William I bestowed Halton Manor, which included Lancaster, on Roger de Poitou. The latter built the first fortifications of the Norman castle on Castle Hill, the site of a Roman military station, in the 11th cent. The great square Norman keep was built about 1170, and this, still to be seen, is 78 ft high with walls 10 ft thick. King John built a curtain wall with round towers, and a massive gateway, round the keep, enclosing a roughly circular area 380 ft by 350 ft; and also built Hadrian's Tower, which still remains (it was drastically restored in the 18th and 19th cents.). In 1322 Robert Bruce burnt most of the town but made no impression on the castle. Edward III's son, John of Gaunt, was much associated with the castle; he is "Time-honour'd Lancaster" in Shakespeare's depiction. But John of Gaunt paid only brief visits to his castle. On the keep a turret named after him was used as a beacon to signal the approach of the Armada. The lower parts of the gateway were added to in the 15th cent.; begun by King John, this, like his Well Tower, is still to be seen. There was repair work by Elizabeth I, shown by her initials on the castle. It was a Parliamentary stronghold in the Civil War, and later George Fox, founder of the Society of Friends, was twice imprisoned there. The castle is used as the gaol and for assize and other courts (it is open to the public subject to court requirements).

The Shire Hall is within the castle and has an impressive display of heraldry with the coats of arms of all sovereigns from Richard I.

Lancaster is the county town and has many fine buildings. The Priory and Parish Church of St Mary is particularly interesting. There was first a church on this site built by the Romans, probably before the end of the 2nd cent. Part of its east end was discovered in 1912, and Roman lamps with Christian marking were found in the vicarage garden. The converted Anglo-Saxons built a church on the site, and its remains are a small square-topped doorway and part of the west wall. A rare type of early Anglian cross with runic inscriptions was found in the churchyard and sent to the BRITISH MUSEUM. Roger de Poitou gave St Mary's to a Benedictine abbey of Normandy, which founded a small monastery at the end of the 11th cent. There is no record of a Norman church, but, E. of the Roman section choir walls in the Transitional style came to light. The south-west doorway is in the same style, so there may have been a 12th-cent. church almost as large as the present one. It was probably destroyed when the town was twice burnt by the Scots or during the Black Death of 1349. Rebuilding began before the end of the 14th cent. In the 1414 suppression of foreign priories the Lancaster one was given to the

Noel Habgood

The Lake District: a view of Derwentwater

Brigitine Convent of SYON (Middlesex). In 1430 St Mary's became the parish church of Lancaster, but its fabric is largely that built by the nuns of Syon, including its main features: the great east window, the windows of the north and south walls, and the clerestory. The church contains outstanding Decorated choir stalls of about 1340, possibly brought from FURNESS ABBEY. John Ruskin considered the carved work of their canopies to be the finest in England. The carved oak two-decker pulpit is early 17th-cent., as is the font cover; the font itself is early 19th-cent. The colourful stained glass is mid-19th-cent. One of many wall tablets is by Fisher of YORK, and another by L. F. Roubiliac. The previous Gothic tower was replaced by the present one, built in 1759 to the design of Henry Sephton.

The handsome old Custom House has graceful Ionic columns at its front, each carved from a single block. It was built in 1764 to the design of Richard Gillow, of the family whose Lancaster furniture factory became famous for nearly three centuries. The Friends' Meeting House, founded in 1690, is associated with their leaders, including George Fox. It is now a modern school, of high educational standards. The old Town Hall has fine proportions and dates from 1781–3. It houses the Regimental museum and the Lancaster museum, the latter illustrating the history of Lancaster from the Stone Age to modern times. The Storey Institute holds the art gallery. The new Town Hall, by E. W. Mountford, who also designed THE OLD BAILEY, was given by Lord Ashton in 1909. It is a dignified Classical building, with a marble staircase and two stained-glass windows, containing handsome plate and historic charters. There is a domed council chamber, and seating for 1,300 in a large concert hall. Lord Ashton also gave the town its dominant

landmark, the Ashton Memorial which, with its green dome, overlooks the city from Williamson Park. The memorial's higher galleries give a panorama of BLACKPOOL, MORECAMBE Bay, the LAKE DISTRICT hills, the Lune Valley and Ingleborough in the West Riding.

The Roman Catholic cathedral was erected in 1859. It has a chancel with a gilded roof, and brilliant frescoes of saints, kings and angels. The Last Supper is carved in relief. The reredos has gilded canopies and the windows stained glass. There is a prominent statue of St Peter. Each chapel has a well-decorated altar, and the Hardman baptistry has fine stone vaulting.

In St Leonardgate is the Grand Theatre, listed as a building of architectural and historic interest. On its site was the old Athenaeum where Mrs Siddons acted. The city has some fine Georgian mansions with good hooded doorways. The Royal King's Arms, where Dickens stayed, replaced in Victorian times the original inn of 1625. Prince Charlie, on his southward march in 1745, stayed in the house which is now the Conservative Club. Skerton Bridge, crossing the Lune, was built in 1783–8 by Thomas Harrison. Modern buildings include the new Lancaster University, developing on a campus basis to the S.

Lancaster is a good tourist centre for the Lake District some 35 m. N. and for some of the loveliest moorland, where Lancashire and Yorkshire meet across the **Trough of Bowland**. Most north-west coastal resorts are easily reached, and HEYSHAM is a port for Northern Ireland.

LANERCOST PRIORY, *Cumberland* (14–NY5563), was founded about 1144 as an Augustinian priory by William de Vaux. The buildings date from the 12th to 13th cents. There is a gatehouse in which Edward I was received by the monks. Queen Eleanor, the Scottish King David, and Robert Bruce are others associated with the priory's history. The nave and north aisle were restored in the last century and subsequently used as the parish church. There are fine clerestory arches, the Lanercost Cross of 1214, a bold recessed doorway in the west front, the old monastic building called Dacre Hall, cloisters and interesting memorials and tombs.

LANGDALE PIKES, *Westmorland* (14–NY 2707). Here is scenic splendour on a grand scale, ranging from the two rugged pikes piled up like gigantic sculpture in rock to the green dales with their tarns. You can approach from GRASMERE, AMBLESIDE or CONISTON. Beyond ELTERWATER there are the two Langdale valleys: Great Langdale on the N. and Little Langdale on the S.

Along the north side of Great Langdale the land rises from Silver Howe and Yew Crag past Stickle Tarn to the two pikes. First is Harrison Stickle, 2,403 ft, and then Pike o' Stickle, 2,323 ft, both rising steeply from the valley; Dungeon Ghyll begins in their cleft and flows SE., with the celebrated Dungeon Ghyll Force within walking distance of the road where it passes the New Hotel. The Force was depicted by Wordsworth and Coleridge. The Old Dungeon Ghyll Hotel is National Trust property and beyond it are the roadless Mickleden and Oxendale branches of the valley. Mickleden leads NW. to Stake Head Pass, for the Stonethwaite branch of BORROWDALE, and Rossett Gill Pass, for the SCA FELL group. Across the ends of both Langdale valleys are BOW FELL on the N., nearly 3,000 ft, and Crinkle Crags S. of it.

The WRYNOSE PASS rises steeply out of the west end of Little Langdale, for the DUDDON VALLEY or HARDKNOTT PASS. The road from Wrynose descends Little Langdale beside the River Brathay (which is the North Lancashire boundary), and this was the route of the Roman road from Hardknott and the west coast. E. of the Pike of Blisco, which is below Crinkle Crags, is the pleasant dale with Blea Tarn where a steep road joins the two Langdale valleys. This dale is the scene of The Solitary in Book II of Wordsworth's *The Excursion*, and the poet also knew Blea Tarn House, a farm N. of the tarn. The Little Langdale road passes Little Langdale Tarn, Birk Howe (a 17th-cent. farm-house bought by the National Trust) and Colwith Force, another waterfall accessible on foot.

Both Langdale valleys are well worth exploring on foot, and are also favoured by rock-climbers.

LEVENS HALL, *Westmorland* (14–SD4886), is a beautiful Elizabethan mansion (open to the public at advertised times in the summer), at Levens Bridge on the River Kent. Among its important features are the plasterwork ceilings, fine oak chimney-pieces, Spanish leather panelling and – outside the house – the particular attraction of the topiary gardens. These were designed by Monsieur Beaumont, the man who remodelled the gardens of HAMPTON COURT for

James II. They retain their original plan of 1689. This estate was occupied by the Redmans in 1188, the Bellinghams in 1489, the Grahames and Howards from 1688 to 1885, and the Bagots from 1885. In the 14th cent. the Redman family built a peel-tower; portions of it are incorporated in the present house, which is mainly of about 1585. Up the river there is a well-wooded park. Down stream is Nether Levens Hall, a 14th-cent. peel tower developed into a 16th-cent. farm-house.

LITTLE MORETON HALL, *Cheshire* (12–SJ8558). This magnificent 16th-cent. moated manor house, 2 m. S. of CONGLETON, on the A34, is unquestionably one of the finest specimens of black-and-white architecture in England. It is approached on the south side by way of an arched stone bridge and high timbered gatehouse, with rooms above the entrance, leading into a cobbled courtyard of great beauty. The house itself is built on three sides of the quadrangle, the fourth side having been cleared at one period of restoration to provide a vista of perfectly kept gardens sweeping down to the tall green mound where once the watch-tower stood.

At Little Moreton Hall the upper story is reached by three or four narrow stairways emerging from the gatehouse, and the stately rooms in the body of the house are entered after passing through a series of small panelled apart-

Langdale: the Little Langdale valley

T. Parker

ents. One of them contains a sliding panel
iving access to a secret room behind the chimney-
reast. This secret chamber may have been
esigned to be discovered without much difficulty,
ecause far below the moat, at the end of a tor-
uous underground passage, there is a tiny cell
which in time of danger served as the real hiding-
lace. The wainscoted long gallery, 68 ft by 12 ft,
s superbly representative of Elizabethan England.
ts immense fire-places are decorated with the
Royal Arms of England and France, the roof is
plendidly beamed in oak, and the fine leaded
rt. The retiring room of the long gallery has a fire-
lace with a carved stone coat of arms of the
Moreton family. The exact date of construction
s not known, although an inscription on one of
he window beams states that "Richard Dale,
Carpeder", made them in 1559. The entire
uilding is very slightly tilted, and has, in fact,
een discreetly strengthened by steel and concrete
upports behind the panelling. Many of the old
urnishings remain in their original setting. The
uge kitchen serving the banqueting hall contains
25 spice drawers in a chest, an oak table, quan-
ities of pewterware, and a fire-place large enough
o roast an ox.

Moreton Old Hall, as it is also known, is now
he property of the National Trust and is open to
he public.

Liverpool: the Roman Catholic cathedral

LIVERPOOL, *Lancashire* (12–SJ3591). The
waterfront of Liverpool, dominated by the big
buildings of Liver, Cunard and the Docks
Board claims to be Europe's greatest Atlantic
seaport. Seven m. of docks are packed along this
waterfront; and it has the world's largest floating
landing stage, about $\frac{1}{2}$ m. long, and adjustable, to
move up and down with the tide. Liverpool began
as a fishing village in the 13th cent., and its
present, comparatively modern, form derives
from its rapid growth during the 18th cent. Now
it concerns itself with many more industries than
shipping, but in spite of its transformation the
city retains distinctive landmarks, has many
cultural features and a flourishing musical and
artistic life.

Just above the waterfront stands the fine 18th-
cent. *Town Hall* (normally open to the public for
a week in August). It was designed by John Wood
of BATH and completed in 1754. The interior was
rebuilt (after a fire) between 1795 and 1802, by
John Foster, under James Wyatt, who added
the dome in 1802, with Felix Rossi's figure of
Minerva, and the portico in 1811. The mirrors in
the small ballroom came from Lathom House
(ORMSKIRK) and are probably early 18th-cent.
Italian. The Hall's furniture harmonizes with its
architectural period. Then comes the entrance
to the **Mersey Tunnel**, which traffic approaches
through an elaborate central traffic scheme,
and above this are St George's Hall, the City
Museums, the Central Libraries, and Walker Art
Gallery.

St George's Hall, with its 60-ft-high Corinthian
columns, concert hall and law courts, was designed
by Harvey Lonsdale Elmes. It was begun in 1838
and finished by C. R. Cockerell in 1854, seven
years after Elmes's death. The Great Hall is 151
ft long, richly finished, and contains a magnificent
organ which was rebuilt in 1957 after its war-time
destruction.

The City Museums owe their foundation to the
13th Earl of Derby, who bequeathed his natural
history collection, and Joseph Mayer, a Liverpool
goldsmith, who gave his archaeological and
ethnographical collections; Liverpool became
famous for its ivories, gold and jewelry, plant
collections, fossils, and the Derby collection of
birds. The original museum building perished in
flames in May 1941, with valuable material.
Fortunately much had been sent for safe storage.
The first part of the rebuilding plan has provided
an aquarium, and galleries dealing with prehistoric life, shipping, local history and applied
and decorative arts. The second stage aims to
restore the main museum completely, and to
include an astronomy gallery and planetarium.

The Central Libraries comprise the Picton,
Horn and Brown buildings. Picton has the
reference library, with some 92,000 books, and
holds regular exhibitions of its treasures. On the
ground floor is the international library (100,000
books), which also has regular exhibitions.
Hornby has first editions, prints and fine bindings,
permanently displayed. Brown has scientific and
technical sections; visitors are welcome.

The Walker Art Gallery, endowed by Sir Andrew Barclay Walker, could well claim the best provincial collection in England. Its early Italian and Flemish works are especially notable. Simone Martini's *Christ Discovered in the Temple* (14th-cent. Sienese) is a work that influenced the "international Gothic" style, and a beautiful *Pietà* by Ercole de' Roberti represents the 15th-cent. school of Ferrara. There are the *Portrait of a Young Man* from the Giovanni Bellini studio, an attribution to Basaiti, and a Bonifazio Veronese (*Virgin and Child*). From Veronese's studio is *The Finding of Moses*. Besides one painting attributed to Francesco Bassano and another from his studio, there is a Jacopo Bassano work (*Country Scene*), and two Guardis. The *Portrait of a Young Man* by Jan Mostaert is noteworthy and there is an outstanding mature work by Rubens, the *Virgin and Child with St Elizabeth and the Child Baptist*. Among the Dutch paintings is a river scene by Ruysdael. The most famous picture here is Rembrandt's early work, *Portrait of the Artist as a Young Man*. From Germany there is a Cranach the Elder, and from Spain a Murillo. British portraits include Kneller and Hogarth, and British landscape is well represented by works by Richard Wilson, Cox, Turner, Constable and Stubbs. There are Pre-Raphaelite works by Millais, Rossetti and Burne-Jones. French paintings include a Poussin, a Fragonard, an early Cézanne, a Monet, a small Seurat and a Matisse. Henry Moore and Victor Pasmore are among the gallery's increasing number of 20th-cent. acquisitions. The Sudley Gallery, in a 19th-cent. house in Mossley Hill Road, has a large British collection including two Turners. The house and its contents were bequeathed by Miss Holt.

Liverpool (Anglican) Cathedral soars superbly on its lofty site. It was the life work of Sir Giles Gilbert Scott who died in 1960 in his 80th year, still supervising it. When complete (1975?) it will be second in size only to St Peter's in Rome. Sir Giles's conception is generally Gothic but not really classifiable. The decoration in red sandstone is an integral part of the fabric. A special feature is that the aisles are built as tunnels in the walls. The nave, not yet completed, and the choir lie at opposite ends of what, with the under-tower and transept crossings, is called the central space. The central tower, across the full width of the nave, rises 331 ft above floor level. The vast scale creates an atmosphere of peace and grandeur. Notable are the font, the stained glass in all windows, and the sandstone reredos and sculptured panels.

The Roman Catholic Cathedral is completely different. The foundation stone was laid in 1933 but the design has been completely changed, and its final form, designed by Sir Frederick Gibberd, is a total departure from the original plan by Sir Edwin Lutyens. The building is circular, round the focal point of the high altar; this circle is surmounted by a conical roof capped with a tower of coloured glass by John Piper and Patrick Reyntiens, which throws a pool of light on the altar. The cathedral itself is raised on an upper level, on a concrete base above the crypt completed by Lutyens. Below, the approach road runs right through, with a car park under the nave.

The Philharmonic Hall, home of Liverpool great orchestra, is on the site of the "Old Phil" which fire destroyed in 1933. Its acoustics are among the best in Britain. A financial arrangement with the corporation gives the orchestra security. About 75 public concerts are given annually in the hall, and the orchestra appear about 55 times outside Liverpool and gives about 60 concerts to schools. The Royal Liverpool Philharmonic Society is at the head of the city musical fame.

Bluecoat Chambers, originally the Bluecoat School, in the shopping centre is a Queen Anne building, which is now a centre for the arts, and open to visitors.

Liverpool has many and varied churches. St Agnes, Sefton Park, is by J. L. Pearson, 1883–, with a reredos in cream, red and gold. All Hallows, Allerton (1872–6, by Grayson and Ould), has a fine set of Burne-Jones glass made by William Morris. All Saints, Childwall, is mediæval with a tower erected in 1810 and an ancient font. The 19th-cent. St Bridget at Wavertree is graceful and has a Last Supper in mosaic. Also at Wavertree, Holy Trinity is good Georgian, its classic steeple a landmark, at present awaiting rebuilding. St Mary's, Edge Hill, is neo-Gothic, with clustered columns and handsome doors. St Michael, Toxteth, is also 19th-cent., and has a monument to Horrocks, the HOOLE astronomer.

Theatres include the well-known Playhouse and the Everyman. Besides having so many cultural amenities, Liverpool has a large, steadily developing civic university. There are ample facilities for entertainment and sport, and **Aintree** is 6 m. N. The city is ringed by parks and open spaces, led by Sefton, its "HYDE PARK".

The shopping centre represents a commercial aspect as important, or more so, as the industrial one. Well defined and compact, the main shopping area is Castle Street, Dale Street, Lord Street, Church Street with offshoots, and Bold Street. It has customers as far as the Lakes, the Isle of Man and Ireland, and Liverpool is called the shopping capital of North Wales. The city's airport is Speke, 6 m. SE., which claims to be the most modern in the country. Also there is SPEKE HALL run by Liverpool Corporation for the National Trust.

Within reach of the city are golf courses, the Lancashire coastal resorts, the Wirral Peninsula and historic CHESTER. Liverpool calls itself the gateway to the world, with its passenger liners and some 30 million tons of cargo handled annually. And it looks to the future: to an underground railway linking the main city stations and to an internal motorway, among many other plans for development.

LOWER PEOVER, Cheshire (12–SJ7474). A tiny village of thatched and timbered cottages, an old water-mill, an inn and a 17th-cent. school.

ouse, surrounded by quiet fields and woodlands of the fertile Cheshire Plain. The outstanding feature is the richly handsome church, with its overhanging eaves and startling black-and-white gables. Some of the great oak beams are believed to date back to 1296, when the church was a chapel of ease to Great BUDWORTH 5 m. to the NW. The stone tower is 16th-cent., but the nave and chancel are of 14th-cent. timber and plaster-work in the prevalent style of the period. Inside are massive pillars with plain capitals supporting a raftered roof of singular beauty, and the splendid woodwork is continued throughout the composition of the church. Of special note are the strange old box pews with narrow doors raised high above the floor to keep out draughts. Wooden shelves on one of the pillars were meant to carry charity loaves to be given to the poor every Sunday. In the chapel hangs a curious wooden hand, thought to have been exhibited outside the church in medieval times to show that buying and selling might be carried out at fair-time. Here, too, is a vast oaken chest, of which local legend has it that unless a girl could lift the lid with one hand she was not fit to be a farmer's wife. In the side chapels are monuments to generations of the Cholmondeley, de Tabley and Shakerley families, one of which commemorates Sir Geoffrey Shakerley who fought for Charles I and distinguished himself at the battle of Rowton Heath.

At the side of the church stands the ancient and famous Warren de Tabley Arms Hotel, a fine hostelry more generally known as the Bells of Peover.

LOWESWATER, *Cumberland* (14–NY1421). This is the last lake in the NW. of the Lake District. Beyond it Lakeland proper ends towards the A5086 connecting COCKERMOUTH and Cleator Moor. But it is precisely from this end that the approach to the small lake is more interesting, showing how the character of the countryside changes from the coastal plain to the grandeur of the mountain groups. Thus beyond and to the E. of Loweswater the great peak of Grasmoor can be seen, followed by Whiteless Pike. Further S. are Robinson, Dale Head and Fleetwith. Opposite Grasmoor is Mellbreak, with its impressive screes, on the west side of CRUMMOCK WATER. The road is narrow and leads to the village of Loweswater, which lies halfway across the plain towards Crummock Water. After the village the main road turns NE. towards the Vale of Lorton to skirt the end of Crummock Water, but there are some smaller roads between the two lakes, and a foot-path goes along the south-west side of Lowes-water. This lake, with Holme Wood where the footpath runs, is National Trust Property.

LOWTHER, *Westmorland* (14–NY5223). Lowther Castle was one of the great baronial houses of England which once entertained royal and foreign guests, including Mary Queen of Scots, and was the home of the Earls of Lonsdale until 1936. It stands in a 3,000-acre park just W. of the A6. It had magnificent proportions, of which the preserved frontage gives some idea, although it was rebuilt at various times in its history. The huge park contains beautiful country-side and also Lowther church, dedicated to St Michael. The church pillars and arches date from the 12th or 13th cents. but the walls were rebuilt in 1686. Outside it is the mausoleum of the Lowthers, the Earls of Lonsdale. The home of the present Earl is **Askham Hall,** a 14th-cent. forti-fied tower. It is to the W. across the River Lowther, at the entrance to the picturesque village of Askham. The name of Lowther figures in Wordsworth's history. His grandfather, Richard Wordsworth, became superintendent to the Lowther estates about 1725, and lived at Sock-bridge near PENRITH. The poet's father, John, became chief law-agent to Sir James Lowther, later the 1st Earl of Lonsdale. Wordsworth's poem, "To the Earl of Lonsdale", welcomes a legal vindication of the character of William Lowther, Sir James's successor, who discharged to Wordsworth the debt which the late earl had owed John Wordsworth but had refused to pay.

The village of Lowther lies on the east side of the park, with interesting old cottages. At nearby Hackthorpe, Lowther Wildlife Park is an interest-ing experiment in presenting in a natural setting various species of deer, cranes and other animals and birds. They are free to wander in more than 100 acres of parkland (open to the public). Visitors are encouraged to establish friendly relations with the animals.

LYME PARK, *Cheshire* (12–SJ9784). The house is of Elizabethan origin, but was provided with an impressive Palladian exterior in the 18th cent. It was the home of the Legh family for 600 years and is now owned by the National Trust. It contains some elaborate Jacobean rooms and carvings by a student of Grinling Gibbons. The extensive park contains a herd of red deer. The entrance to the park is on the western outskirts of Disley, through which the **Peak Forest Canal** runs through beautiful country to its terminus at Whaley Bridge.

LYTHAM AND ST ANNE'S, *Lancashire* (12–SD3328). Of quite a different character from its larger neighbour BLACKPOOL on the N., Lytham and St Anne's has a charm of its own. Some half-timbered buildings mingle pleasantly with a scene of peaceful parks and gardens, with their floral displays. A promenade borders 1½ m. of coast along part of the town, and in one area encloses Lytham Green, with its old windmill on the lawns and the church steeple and houses behind. In all there are 6½ m. of sandy beaches and dunes. Ashton Gardens are a minute's walk from the busy little shopping centre, with tree-lined paths, rose garden, water-course and bowling green. Lowther Garden has sweeping lawns and trees, with areas for bowls, tennis, putting and crazy golf. The Alpine Gardens with their little bridges are pleasant for gentle strolls. Fairhaven Lake offers sailing dinghies, rowing boats, motor boats and water skiing. There is also a separate boating lake, and a pool for children to paddle and sail model yachts. The Ribble Cruising Club has its headquarters on the promenade and organizes regattas and weekend races. Beach chalets, and both open-air and indoor swimming-pools are available, as is horse-riding in the country lanes. The combined borough of St Anne's with Lytham has excellent golf links. The visitor can use four championship courses: the Royal Lytham and St Anne's, St Anne's Old Links, Fairhaven and Lytham Green Drive.

John Carr of YORK built Lytham Hall in c. 1760, incorporating part of an earlier house.

MACCLESFIELD, *Cheshire* (12–SJ9173). The emergence of Macclesfield as one of the leading silk manufacturing towns in England has given it an interesting architectural legacy of good 18th- and early 19th-cent. mills. They contribute to the town's character. Macclesfield is mentioned in the Domesday Book as having formed part of the demesne of Edwin, Earl of Chester, before the Norman Conquest. In 1261 a charter granted by Edward, Prince of Wales and Earl of Chester, constituted Macclesfield a free borough. In 1278 Edward I and Queen Eleanor founded the Parochial Chapel of Macclesfield, dedicated to All Saints. At some unknown date in the 18th cent. the church was re-dedicated to St Michael and All Angels. Very little remains of Queen Eleanor's chapel, the church having been rebuilt twice, in 1739 in the Classical style and again between 1898 and 1901. St Michael's may either be entered from the level of the wide market place or by climbing 108 steps from below. The newly pinnacled west tower rises high and contains in its walling many carved fragments from the medieval foundation. Over the south door is a stone anointed by the bishop conducting the first service 700 years ago. There is a fine hammer-beam roof to the chancel, a superb clerestory, and among the multitude of scenes depicted in the windows is a glorious Ascension designed by Burne-Jones and made by his friend William Morris. On the east wall of the Legh Chapel, which survives from the earlier building, there is a tablet to the memory of John Brownsword, a grammarian and poet who is believed to have been a master at STRATFORD-UPON-AVON at a time when William Shakespeare could have been one of the pupils. The epitaph of another master of the school, William Legh, is inscribed on brass in the church and dated 1630. The Savage Chapel was built by Thomas Savage, who became Archbishop of York in 1501, with the intention that it should serve as a college, but instead it became the mortuary chapel of his family. Of special interest here is the Legh Pardon Brass of 1506, encased in a wooden frame. It shows Roger Legh kneeling with his six sons below the vision of Pope St Gregory, the inscription recording that, as a reward for good works and prayers, pardon had been offered to him and his family for 26,000 years and 26 days. The Savage Chapel is reached from the south aisle through a doorway guarded by two unicorns and an angel, and from the south

tower below a delicate oriel window. Marb tombs and effigies fill the church.

Macclesfield's Town Hall is a good Georgia building. The market cross, now removed to th West Park, once stood in the centre of the mark square, and it was from here that proclamatior were read out to the townspeople, as when th yeomen and archers of the borough mustered t march to Bosworth Field and again to Flodde Field in 1513. In West Park can also be seen som old iron stocks in an excellent state of preserva tion and a 30-ton boulder believed to have bee brought from Cumberland by Ice Age glacier Here, too, is one of the largest bowling greens i the North of England (crowned, as is usual in th North), covering approximately 1 acre, and at th gates of the park itself is a museum and a gallery.

Macclesfield Forest, 5 m. E. of Macclesfiel on the A537, is a tiny village on the edge of wide stretch of wild country presenting magnif cent views across crags and narrow valleys tc wards the Peak District. The Forest Chapel here originally built in 1673, was largely rebuilt in 1834 The ancient ceremony of the rush-bearing service at which the floor is covered with rushes as of old is held every August and attended by larg numbers of people from all over the county Two m. further along the road is Cheshire's mos famous inn, the Cat and Fiddle, 1,600 ft up an one of the highest licensed houses in England From this remote point close to the count boundary the vista is remarkable. Whetston Ridge, 1,795 ft high, rises to the S. directly i front of the inn, with many other summits o over 1,000 ft on every side. In the past this was region of turbulence to match the rugged grandeu of its scenery. The Davenports of CAPESTHORN were the hereditary sergeants of the forest, whos duty to the king was to keep the 4,000 acres i readiness for hunting parties and prevent band of outlaws from killing for the pot deer that wer meant to provide royal sport. Lawlessness thrive until well beyond medieval times. Gangs o robbers, poachers and cut-throats made travel s hazardous that merchants dared only cross th area in the often questionable protection o professional guards. The wildness of Macclesfiel Forest is reflected today in some of its names Cat's Tor, Wolf's Edge, Dane's Moss, an Wildboarclough.

MAIDEN CASTLE, *Cheshire* (12–SJ5053) an ancient earthwork on the east side of th A41, is thought to date from the Iron Age. lies on top of a small hill and on the south-eas side, where it joins the main hill, there is a shallov ditch between two banks. The other sides face ou above the slopes of the hill. The earthwork ha stone and timber banking up the interior.

MALPAS, *Cheshire* (12–SJ4847), is one of th pleasantest old towns in Cheshire, with rows o timbered houses and cottages, some of which ar good examples of medieval brickwork. There is a block of old almshouses, and many old inns, on of which has an oak chair said to have been used by James I. Visitors can regale themselves with the famous Cheshire cheeses – red Cheshire, white Cheshire and the coveted "Old Blue" – for Malpas is set in rich farming land where dairy farms are a speciality. The farming community is very strong in the town and has its own club and social centre. Formerly Malpas was a market town but now it is mainly a shopping centre for the surrounding villages. It is set on a hill-top, 2 m. from the road between CHESTER and the West Midlands, and is a junction for various local routes. This makes it an excellent centre from which to tour south-west Cheshire, the Dee valley, northern Shropshire and the Wrexham area of Wales.

Although it is an old town not much of its early history is recorded. A mound on the Bickerton Hills indicates a castle, possibly Norman, which served to repel Welsh invaders from the other side of the River Dee which winds only 4 m. away. In the 14th cent., it is said, Malpas people hardly dared to go out to church for fear of being attacked by Welshmen. There was an attempt to get the chapel on the estate at CHOLMONDELEY, 4 m. NE., raised to church status as it would have been a safer place for worship. The Civil War caused much damage and the beautiful church was used as sleeping quarters for Parliamentarian troops. A battle was fought at Oldcastle Heath nearby in 1643. Today, Malpas, which is well equipped with shops, is developing as a residential area for business people of Merseyside.

The town's treasure is the spacious and well-proportioned Church of St Oswald. It was built mainly in the 14th and 15th cents., and by the late 15th was practically complete in its present form. It is built of red sandstone and the external walls of the aisles with the clerestory above have good examples of medieval work: windows with rich tracery, castellations and pinnacles. Above each buttress is a set of gargoyles of various creatures. The tower is in keeping with the craftsmanship of the rest. Inside, a high tower arch and a broad, low chancel arch set off the nave, which has slender, clustered columns. Panelled roofs complete the nave and chancel. The long chest in the south aisle, companion to another in the crypt, has ironwork dating from the 13th cent. There are four sedilias, one of which, carved with grinning faces, is 600 years old. Two windows are of Flemish medieval glass. The east window commemorates Bishop Heber, a friend of Tennyson, who became Bishop of Calcutta, and wrote many hymns that are used today, including *Greenland's Icy Mountains* and *Holy, holy, holy*. There are monuments to the Cholmondeley family, of the nearby estate, and the finely sculpted tomb of Randolphus Brereton dressed in the armour of a Tudor knight. The Breretons, one of the great Cheshire families, were prominent in Malpas, and their seat, the 16th-cent. Brereton Hall, is one of the county's finest mansions. Sir Randle Brereton was a patron of Malpas, and founded a grammar school in 1528, endowed a hospital, presented a bell in the church tower and founded a chantry of St George.

Around Malpas are several interesting places to visit, such as Peckforton Hills, TARPORLEY, the Delamere Forest, Shocklach, Tilston and Tushingham.

MANCHESTER, *Lancashire* (12–SJ8397), may claim to be the country's second city, but the radical innovations for which its history has been notable have often placed the city not second, but first. It is also the capital of the North: far enough south of the bulk of the western Pennines that compress Lancashire's northern area and far enough into their recess where the county widens to be a natural centre of communications. There Manchester sprawls across an area that is about 12 m. from N. to S. and between 3 and 5 m. from E. to W., the great hub in a conglomeration of other towns whose divisions are difficult to distinguish. Within a ring 5 m. from Manchester's centre, one million people live, and within 10 m. there are two and a half million. It is one of the most thickly populated areas of England. Among the traffic noise below Manchester's vast buildings, the constant millions of transactions and the daily hordes of people, in the air that is Mersey-grey or humidly tinted by the sun, there hang memories of causes lost or won beyond counting. Much redevelopment is foreseen, with planning schemes that seem designed to sweep away many of the present central buildings and leave the cathedral dwarfed among square blocks. As part of these developments the Mancunian Way swings across the city – a modernistic road on stilts. Piccadilly, the large square which forms the centre of Manchester, has also been extensively redeveloped, with new parades of shops and the towering Piccadilly Hotel, designed to equal the large London hotels with facilities for an international clientele.

Manchester's site has been important since Roman times, with several river crossings and easy access from other parts of the country. Later came the exploitation of the coal supplies, and the water power and the humid air helped the development of the textile industries. The fairly flat land favoured transport by railways and canals. Thus circumstances combined to encourage the rapid development of commerce and industry in the 19th cent. The social and political struggles this engendered was the background for the radical ideas for which Manchester became prominent. In the earlier part of that century there was appalling squalor, moral degradation and poverty among people living under vile conditions in congested districts of the city, described by James P. Kay, the physician (later Sir James Kay-Shuttleworth). Workers, a third of them women, worked for 12 hours a day in mills. There were many strikes, food riots and machine smashing. Eventually discontent brought the notorious mass meeting, nicknamed Peterloo, when troops rode into the crowd with slashing sabres; there were 11 deaths and hundreds of injuries. This was a set-back for the working-class part of the Radical movement, but it strengthened the hands of middle-class Radicals,

Manchester: the John Rylands Library

who finally achieved a measure of reform in the Factory Acts.

The Peterloo Chartists also wanted parliamentary reform, and a middle-class Radical, John Edward Taylor, founded the *Manchester Guardian* in 1821, two years after Peterloo, to support constitutional reform. The *Guardian* became outstanding under the driving force of great editors and its influence for reform was felt on a national scale. The greatest of these editors was C. P. Scott, LL.D., and the art gallery has a bust of him by Epstein. Leading Manchester men founded the Anti-Corn Law League, which from 1838 had its headquarters in the city, with John Bright and Richard Cobden among its leaders. The Free Trade Hall was built as the League's headquarters in 1840. A great engineering feat was the building of the Ship Canal, which opened in 1894. Industry had tended to move to the ports, so the great spinners and merchants solved the problem by making Manchester an inland port. This helped to obviate dependence on the cotton trade, by bringing in raw materials for other industries. Thus Manchester is the third port of England. It is also the second most important commercial, financial and banking centre. It is still the country's second centre for newspapers, having not only its own newspapers but being the northern centre for editions of national papers. The Manchester Press Club is the oldest in the country.

The Cathedral stands on what was the old centre of the town. Largely a 15th-cent. structure, it was the parish church, and became the cathedral when the Manchester diocese was created in 1847. Chapels added to the outer north and south aisles make it one of the widest churches in the country. Cleaning has revealed the original sandstone. A special feature is the 30 choir stalls with canopies, all in intricately carved wood.

The galleries and museums comprise the *City Art Gallery* and six branches. As they hold some 23,000 items, not all collections can be shown at once and what is currently on view is indicated on the City Gallery notice boards. The best of the foreign collection is permanently shown at the City Art Gallery, designed by Sir Charles Barry, where Italian works include a Piero di Cosimo, four works of the Lo Spagna school and a Matteo di Giovanni. North European works include an early Flemish *Madonna and Child*, a *Holy Family* by Van Dyck, a seascape by Ruysdael, and landscapes of Teniers the Younger and Cuyp. Later European exhibits are mainly 19th-cent. French from the Barbizon and Impressionist schools including works by Corot, Millet and Fantin Latour; and Pissarro, Gauguin, Sisley, Renoir and Vlaminck, among others. British works form the largest part of the collection, covering the better known artists mainly from the mid-18th cent. onward. There are works by Hogarth, Gainsborough and Reynolds and a unique set of 18 idealized portraits by Blake. Notable are Turner's *Heidelberg Sunset* and Constable's *Hampstead*. Important Pre-Raphaelite works include *Autumn Leaves* by Millais, *Hireling Shepherd* by Holman Hunt, and several by D. G. Rossetti. Their associates are well represented by numerous works by Ford Madox Brown and Burne-Jones. Later British painters displayed include Sargent, Sickert, John, Orpen, Nevinson, Paul and John Nash, the Spencers, Lowry, Piper, Sutherland and Pasmore. The Athenaeum Annexe, adjacent to the City Gallery, has pottery and porcelain from early times to the 19th cent.

Queen's Park Art Gallery has important sculptures by Rodin in bronze, and by Epstein, whose large male figure, *Youth Advances*, was made for

he Festival of Britain exhibition. It also displays
ictorian painting and sculpture.

Heaton Hall, like the other outlying galleries,
tands in its own grounds. The former home of
he Earls of Wilton, it was built in 1772 to the
esign of James Wyatt, and has period collections
f paintings, watercolours, furniture, ceramics,
ilver and glass.

The Gallery of English Costume, in the fine
Georgian mansion of Platt Hall, Rusholme,
ormer seat of the Worsley family, has one of the
nost comprehensive collections in the country.

The Fletcher Moss Museum is housed in the Old
Parsonage at Didsbury. This has the best of the
watercolour collections, including works by Turner, David Cox and Paul Sandby, with early
9th-cent. silver and porcelain.

Wythenshawe Hall is a half-timbered house
built in the 16th cent. with later additions. It is
devoted to collections of Elizabethan furniture,
Staffordshire ware, English delft pottery and
English and European paintings. There are also
displays illustrating various aspects of daily life
n the past and of Chinese porcelain of the 17th
and 18th cents.

Whitworth Art Gallery, run by the University in
Oxford Road, displays English watercolours,
European prints and engravings from the 15th
cent. to the present and textiles and embroideries.

Manchester Museum, also in Oxford Road, has
a large collection of geology, botany, zoology,
archaeology and anthropology. There is also the
famous Lloyd Japanese collection and an
aquarium.

The John Rylands Library holds a multitude of
treasures, and is of world importance for its col-
ection of medieval jewelled bindings. As a whole,
this library (open to the public) is the most
notable of English provincial endowed libraries.
It is remarkable that it arose from the industry of
one man, Rylands, who was a weaver in WIGAN.
From his legacies, his widow founded the library
as a memorial and bought many rare books and
manuscripts for it; two such purchases alone
(Earl Spencer's Althorp collection and the famous
Crawford MSS.) cost half a million pounds. The
library opened in 1900 in a fine neo-Gothic building by Basil Champneys. The Printed Book Department has the earliest dated Western print (St
Christopher, 1423), the Gutenberg Bible, valuable editions of English and foreign classics, works
of art from 16th-cent. scholar printers and from
de-luxe printers of the 17th and 18th cents. – in all
over 3,000 incunabula from the leading English
and Continental presses. The department has
exceptional facilities for specialists in fields such as
Egyptology, archaeology, French Revolution
broadsides, select editions and foreign periodicals.
The Manuscript Department has records on clay,
bark, bamboo, papyrus and parchment, representing over 50 cultures and languages from the
3rd millennium B.C. onward, with some 250,000
documents from the 11th to the 20th cent. Its
treasures include the earliest known manuscript
of a New Testament book (a fragment of St
John's Gospel, written before A.D. 150).

The Chetham Library (open by arrangement)
was founded in 1653 and was the first free public
library in Europe. Its founder, Humphrey Chetham, provided parish libraries in Manchester and
BOLTON and was a merchant, who at one time
owned TURTON TOWER. Chetham's is still housed
in its old collegiate building, and has 100,000
books and MSS.

The Central Library has, in its fine circular
building by Vincent Harris, 1930–4, a Shakespeare
hall and a huge window that depicts the playwright surrounded by many of his famous characters. The building contains one of the greatest
reference libraries in England. It is also unusual in
that the basement houses a fully equipped theatre,
naturally called the Library Theatre.

Other theatres of note include The Opera
House, which receives such distinguished visiting
companies as the London Festival Ballet and
GLYNDEBOURNE Opera Company, the Stables
Theatre Club, a platform for prospective television drama, and the University Theatre which
provides a mixture of professional and student
productions.

Anyone approaching the centre of Manchester
along Oxford Road will see the large number of
university buildings on either side, and there are
many more situated off the main roads. Redevelopment on this long road is extensive and
many new university buildings are rising from the
stretches of waste ground.

The Hallé arose from the Art Treasures Exhibition of 1857; Charles Hallé founded the concerts as a private venture in the following year, and
Manchester's love of music developed along with
this famous orchestra. After Hallé's death the
Hallé Concerts Society was founded in 1898, and a
series of distinguished conductors followed. Prominent among them was Sir John Barbirolli, who,
during his leadership of the orchestra in the last
two decades, was largely responsible for establishing the international reputation which the
orchestra today enjoys.

The Free Trade Hall was first a wooden building
built in 1840 as the headquarters of the Anti-Corn
Law League, followed by the brick one of 1843,
which served the League until the repeal of the
Corn Laws in 1849. Later users of the hall included the Athenaeum Society, of which Dickens
was chairman at the first meeting, and later chairmen included Disraeli and Ralph Waldo Emerson.
The third hall, built in 1856, was the best known
building in Manchester, and the Hallé concerts
started there. The hall was destroyed by fire
bombs in 1940, but the Peter Street and South
Street façades survived with damage. It was the
Palladian style of these façades that Professor
Reilly described as the greatest architecture in
Manchester. The reconstruction (completed in
1951) by Mr Leonard C. Howitt, architect to the
corporation, which became owners of the hall in
1921, preserved them and completely restored the
vaulted arcade adjoining Peter Street, although
the Windmill Street façade is in a simplified
modern style. The hall is still the home of the
Hallé and also provides some of the finest Folk

and Jazz concerts in the country. It stands on part of the site of the Battle of Peterloo, which is depicted in a mural. (Open to the public at times.)

The Town Hall (open to the public) is a Gothic-style building completed in 1876, one of the most important works of Alfred Waterhouse. It has statues of various historic figures outside. Inside are those of John Bright and Richard Cobden, John Dalton, Gladstone, Sir Charles Hallé and others. The large hall has Ford Madox Brown's 12 mural paintings depicting scenes of local history. Notable are the fire-place in the reception room, the conference hall, the valuable collection of civic plate and the insignia.

Belle Vue is the great entertainment, concert and exhibition centre, along with one of Britain's largest zoos. There is a vast amusement park, a boating lake and a model village. The stadium can hold 25,000 spectators for speedway and sports events. Hallé concerts take place in Kings Hall, as well as sports events and ice shows. Among other features are three halls for trade fairs and exhibitions, and extensive catering facilities.

MARYPORT, *Cumberland* (14–NY0336). The shipping of coal and the iron industry were once the most important activities of Maryport. Now the harbour is closed to shipping and other industries have been developed, including plastics, clothing, engineering and chemicals. But Maryport is also a coastal resort with a good stretch of sands. Mote Hill is a vantage point from which to watch the blaze of colour made by the sunset across the Solway. **Allonby,** further N. on the coast, is an old and pretty little resort with good sands. Romans built a fort at Maryport, one of their chain of defensive points along the coast as a precaution against northern tribes turning the flank of HADRIAN'S WALL, which ended at Bowness on the Solway. The Maryport fort was called *Alauna*, and important discoveries of Roman altars and other relics have been made. The town has a golf course and fishing facilities.

MIDDLETON, *Lancashire* (12–SD8606), is about 6 m. from MANCHESTER's centre and near OLDHAM. Silk and cotton were its staple products, but the emphasis now is also on things like chemicals, plastics and engineering. St Leonard's Church was rebuilt in the 16th cent. and the tower has a curious wooden belfry cap with gables, added later. There is a Tudor screen, and brasses to the Assheton family. The stained glass is interesting, and a window depicts Sir Ralph Assheton's archers who fought at Flodden Field. The Boar's Head Inn is a 17th-cent. black-and-white building.

MIDDLETON, *Westmorland* (14–SD6286). Middleton Hall (a farm) is N. of KIRKBY LONS-DALE. The hall was the home of an important family through several centuries from Edward III to Charles I. With its walled courtyards it is a good example of 15th-cent. manor house domestic architecture. A Roman milestone, erected in recent times on a nearby field, indicates the 53rd

Roman mile from CARLISLE along an old Roman road which ran in this area. The Standing Stone of Whelprigg, an ancient cross, is in the vicinity.

At Firbank Fell to the N., the founder of the Society of Friends, George Fox, preached to a large crowd on Trinity Sunday, 1652.

MIDDLEWICH, *Cheshire* (12–SJ7066). The second oldest of the Cheshire salt towns, thriving today on an industry having its beginnings in Roman times. A collection of Stone Age tools and weapons and fragments of Roman pottery recently found in the area is on display in the town. One of the many encounters between Royalists and Parliamentarians took place here in 1642, resulting in the total defeat of a party of Royalist troops attacked while plundering the town. There are associations with violence of another sort; Middlewich was one of the last outposts of bear-baiting in the country.

The parish church here is mainly Perpendicular in style and contains some interesting old chairs and settles in wood together with memorials of the Venables family that date from the 17th cent.

MILLOM, *Cumberland* (14–SD1780), is in the south-west tip of the county, not far from the DUDDON VALLEY. It has the remains of a 14th-to 15th-cent. castle that became a farm, and the Church of the Holy Trinity near it. The church has Norman work: a doorway and piers in the nave. There is a beach at nearby **Haverigg.**

MOBBERLEY, *Cheshire* (12–SJ8081), has some half-timbered houses. The National Trust owns 20 acres to the N. of Mobberley, given to it by the Cheshire County Council and local residents to protect the church, St Wilfrid's. A public footpath leads from the S. of the church, which is mostly late medieval, with a good rood screen of *c.* 1500, a tower screen dated 1683, and some old stained glass. There are some wall paintings, one of them of St Christopher. A modern window commemorates George Mallory, born here in 1886, who was last seen when he and Irvine began the final stage of the climb to the top of Mount Everest in 1924.

MORECAMBE AND HEYSHAM, *Lancashire* (12–SD4364). Morecambe was originally Poulton-le-Sands, an ancient fishing village mentioned in the Domesday Book, and became popular as a holiday resort about half a century ago, following the construction of the railway. In the Town Hall grounds is a gateway from Old Poulton Hall, which was on the site of the present open-air market and which belonged to the paternal ancestors of George Washington. Growth of the town as a resort necessitated the building of a new port at Heysham between 1900 and 1904. Now the M6 which passes only 4 m. to the E. makes access still easier. Morecambe Bay is vast, and it is possible to walk across the sands to GRANGE-OVER-SANDS, but *not*, the council rightly insists, without the safety of an official

Nantwich: a bedroom in Churche's Mansion

guide. These official walks take three hours and may be cancelled if rainfall has endangered the channels. Moored off the central promenade is *Moby Dick*, the famous sailing ship.

New Heysham Head Entertainments Centre is a major attraction which cost almost £500,000. Its Bird House has some rare species. The centre has tea-gardens, a children's zoo, an Old World Village and go-kart racing. The other major feature is Marineland – the first oceanarium built in Europe, the town claims. Its special event is the summer circus, in which dolphins perform. There are also sea-lions, chimpanzees and a well-stocked aquarium. Other attractions include the swimming stadium, the ballroom, variety shows, ice-skating, a model railway, a yachting slipway, boating pools, water-ski facilities and the notable autumn illuminations.

Heysham is a very old village. There is evidence that its church was built by the Angles in the 7th cent. Dedicated to St Peter, the church is modelled on the ruins of St Patrick's Chapel which a previous generation of Angles destroyed. The chancel was added in the 14th cent., making the original church into the present nave. The south aisle was built on in the 15th cent., and lengthened in the 17th. The north aisle was added in 1864.

Several of Peter Scott's books on wild birds deal partly with Morecambe Bay, which has various winter migrant flocks, and breeding grounds in the area. The eider and sheld-duck are notable.

MOW COP, *Cheshire* (12–SJ8557). A stark limestone ridge rising well over 1,000 ft above the Cheshire Plain and the lowland towns of CONGLE-TON and ASTBURY, it is in fact the last escarpment of the Pennines in their southward sweep from the Peak District. The climb to the top provides a rewarding view in all directions, of undulating hills and contrasting sweeps of broad fertile valley. It was here at the summit that a beacon tower was raised in the days of the Armada to signal news of invasion. The beacon is gone, but in its place stands a sham ruin, built in 1750 by Randle Wilbraham on a rock called "The Old Man of Mow" and known as Mow Cop Castle to hosts of summer picnickers. On this site, too, in 1807, the Primitive Methodists held their first meeting. Mow Cop covers six acres of country and is owned by the National Trust.

MUNCASTER, *Cumberland* (14–SD1096). Muncaster Castle (A595) is near **Ravenglass** and the Esk estuary. The castle (open to the public) is the seat of the Pennington family and this site has been theirs since the 13th cent. The original castle was built then or earlier, and the later 19th-cent. reconstruction by Anthony Salvin incorporates an ancient tower. The valuable collection of furniture and other items includes the "Luck of Muncaster", a bowl presented by Henry VI, who took refuge there after his defeat at Hexham in 1464, to ensure prosperity for the family. The flowering gardens and views from the castle terrace are famous. The church in the grounds contains Pennington family monuments and ancient stones.

At Ravenglass are the important Roman ruins known as Walls Castle (Clanoventa), remarkable in being one of the best preserved Roman sites in the N. From here the Roman road ran over HARDKNOTT PASS to PENRITH. In summer at least, the miniature railway train (*see* ESKDALE) carries passengers for some 7 m. from Ravenglass to BOOT, a pleasant way to see the countryside.

NANTWICH, *Cheshire* (12–SJ6552). This is a pleasant old market town on the River Weaver. It was once a busy salt-producing town and still has facilities for brine-bathing, the brine springs having been noted in Roman times. Nantwich is surrounded by a rich agricultural area that produces Cheshire cheese. The town suffered a disastrous fire in 1583 when most of the buildings were destroyed. Rebuilding gave it a wealth of Elizabethan structures, and the Crown Hotel is an example of that period. There are at least a hundred buildings of architectural interest, including some of the Georgian period. There were about 400 salt works in the town in the reign of Henry VIII, but the industry had dwindled by the mid-19th cent. Nantwich was harassed by Welsh raids in earlier days, and during its Parliamentary allegiance in the Civil War was severely besieged by the Royalists. There is a group of almshouses built in the 17th cent. The stone bridge over the Weaver was built in 1803, replacing one of 1663.

Churche's Mansion is a fine half-timbered Elizabethan merchant's house built in 1577 that survived the fire. The fine oak panelling was revealed during restoration. The large grammar school is also a 16th-cent. foundation.

St Mary's Church, one of the best in Cheshire, is a handsome structure in red sandstone with Decorated and Perpendicular work and a central octagonal tower. The church had considerable restoration in 1885, but there is a fine vaulted chancel of the 14th cent. with magnificent carved choir stalls. The font, the stone pulpit and the stone chancel screen are of note. Among the old window glass decoration is a Tree of Jesse.

The large industrial town of **Crewe** is close to Nantwich and a great contrast to it. Crewe, of course, is always associated with its great railway junction, and it was from its importance in this connection, and its spread of railway workshops in the 19th cent., that Crewe developed out of a combination of two villages. Railway engineering is still important among the town's industries, but other factories now employ a similar number of people and include the production of Rolls-Royce and Bentley cars. Crewe has seen considerable housing developments and has a modern town centre. Its theatre was saved from closure by being administered as a trust. There are golf and fishing facilities, and motor racing at **Oulton Park** 10 m. to the NW.

NAWORTH CASTLE, *Cumberland* (14–NY 5662), is just N. of the A69 about 3 m. E. of **Brampton**. It is owned by the Earl of Carlisle and parts of it are open by arrangement. The castle is 14th-cent. (1335), with alterations in the early 16th and 17th cents. It was restored by Anthony Salvin after a fire in 1844. It is built round a central courtyard and has a great hall, oratory and rich tapestry furnishings. In the park is a ruined 16th-cent. house with cattle sheds on the ground floor and living quarters above.

NEW BRIGHTON, *Cheshire* (12–SJ3093), is only 15 minutes by ferry from LIVERPOOL. Sea trips are a feature of this resort in summer. There are two-hour pleasure cruises, giving fine views of the ever-changing shipping scene along the Mersey waterfronts to the entrance of the MAN-CHESTER Ship Canal. The resort also has sea trips to Ireland and Llandudno. There are 7 m. of coastline and ample parking facilities on its King's Parade promenade. The town has good sports facilities, with a sports festival in June that covers some 20 different activities, numerous public tennis courts and bowling greens and three first-class 18-hole golf courses run by the WALLASEY, Leasowe and Bidston clubs. Vale Park near the New Brighton seafront has a bandstand, and other attractions are Tower Grounds, the Floral Pavilion and Marine Park. The extensive Marine Lake offers boating, and the bathing pool can accommodate 4,000 bathers and 10,000 spectators. There is also the indoor New Palace amusement park. Three m. of the promenade from New Brighton to Seacombe are prohibited to vehicles and children can roam freely.

NEWBY BRIDGE, *Lancashire* (12–SD3685), is a charming village on the River Leven where it leaves WINDERMERE. There is an unusual stone bridge with arches of unequal size and the pretty Swan Hotel. This is a convenient centre from which to explore the Furness district, Windermere, or CONISTON WATER, and with walking routes along the Leven, in Grizedale or in the CARTMEL area. Lake Side is the pier for the motor vessel service on Windermere, with a park for 350 vehicles. British Rail closed the passenger line from Lake Side to ULVERSTON in spite of this being a much-used connection with the lake vessels. The alternative motor-coach service adds to road congestion.

NORTHWICH, *Cheshire* (12–SJ6573). For centuries the chief concern of Northwich was getting salt. There was formerly a museum of the history of the salt industry, but it was closed several years ago. Ludwig Mond with J. T. Brunner founded an alkali works at Winnington nearby, which was eventually to grow into the vast I.C.I. There has been some replanning in the town and a modern shopping precinct has been built. Subsidence caused by old salt workings can still take place today; its occurrence in the past has left some walls out of true. A number of the black-and-white buildings here are modern. VALE ROYAL is a few miles SW.

OLDHAM, *Lancashire* (12–SD9305), is a big and important town in Merseyside's northern area. Arkwright's spinning-frame and James Watt's steam engine boosted the town's cotton industry in the early 19th cent., work which continues with the addition of textile engineering today. The Town Hall is in Classical style. Early English watercolours are a notable feature of the art gallery, which also exhibits British paintings of the 19th and 20th cents. The watercolours include works by Sandby, Cozens, Girtin, Turner, Constable, Prout and Cox. The Werneth Park Study Centre has a natural history collection.

ORMSIDE, *Westmorland* (14–NY7017). In an area of country roads and wild flowers W. of the A66 is the little village of Ormside where St James's Church overlooks the River Eden. The Black Prince made a will here, which the vicar witnessed, perhaps on his way to the Border. In 1823 the churchyard yielded the Ormside Cup, of Anglo-Saxon workmanship in gold and enamel, now at YORK. The church is mainly Norman, with an Anglo-Saxon tower that was probably used for defence. The chancel roof is 16th-cent.

ORMSKIRK, *Lancashire* (12–SD4107). The Church of SS. Peter and Paul has both a tower and a separate spire, the tower of about 1540 and the spire being earlier. The church, partly rebuilt in 1729, is largely Perpendicular; the tower was probably added to house bells brought from Burscough Priory after the Dissolution. The church also has effigies of the 1st Earl of Derby and his wife, also from the priory, the ruins of which are nearby, and early memorials of the Scarisbrick family.

The Stanley family, the Earls of Derby from KNOWSLEY HALL, were long associated with the Ormskirk area, and were also the ancient kings of the Isle of Man. The 7th Earl, James Stanley, was a rich landowner and raised a Royalist army in the Civil War. His French wife, Charlotte, held out for months (in Stanley's absence) against Cromwell's forces at Lathom House, until the besiegers retreated before the approach of Prince Rupert. Stanley was later beheaded at BOLTON by Cromwell.

ORTON, *Westmorland* (14–NY6208), is a small village N. of TEBAY with some old buildings and, on its N., Orton Scar. From this, just above the road, there is a good view over the village towards the upper reaches of the River Lune and Tebay Gorge. All Saints' Church at Orton is mostly late medieval with a nave roof of the 15th cent. In many areas of north-western England the Society of Friends has always been strong. In this peaceful village George Whitehead, a man who influenced the Society's growth, was born in 1636. He joined the Society at the age of 14, became an itinerant Quaker preacher in many parts of the country and suffered imprisonment, but improved the legal status of the Friends by interviews with successive sovereigns.

OVER DENTON, *Cumberland* (14–NY6065), near GILSLAND, is an interesting small church of an early type, thought to have been built by Anglo-Saxons using stone from HADRIAN'S WALL. There are new windows from 1881 restorations but a small Anglo-Saxon window remains. An unusual feature is the arch in the chancel, which is believed to be a rebuilt Roman arch, with stones possibly brought from **Birdoswald**.

PATTERDALE, *Westmorland* (14–NY3915). This small village is a well-known vantage point at the head of ULLSWATER. The visitor who comes here over the great height of the KIRKSTONE PASS on the S. finds Patterdale superbly placed among fields beside the lake and hemmed in by mountains on all sides except the north. To the E. the High Street group continues northward to Place Fell (2,154 ft), which rises steeply above the village and the lake. On the other side of the descent from Kirkstone are the slopes below St Sunday Crag; and beyond these the great eastern bulks of the HELVELLYN range stretch away to the N. Only a mile or so along the west shore of Ullswater is Glenridding, from which motor-vessel services traverse the lake to the other end, at POOLEY BRIDGE. According to tradition, St Patrick, patron saint of Ireland, preached at Patterdale; the church is dedicated to him. This village is a good centre for exploring the Ullswater area. The A592 runs northward along the whole length of the lake, but only beyond Glencoyne Park do any other roads lead away from it.

PENRITH, *Cumberland* (14–NY5130), is an ancient and historic town. There are indications of Celtic occupation in about 500 B.C. First the Romans, who built a road through it, and then Norsemen and Angles came to the area. In the 9th and 10th cents. the town was the capital of Cumbria, a semi-independent state in the Kingdom of Strathclyde. For nearly three centuries up to 1603 Penrith was plagued by Scottish raids and was sacked twice. Penrith Castle, now in ruins (open to the public), was built as a defence against the Scots, the original tower being erected in 1397–9. Later owners included the Earl of Warwick, the "King-Maker". The castle was enlarged by the Duke of Gloucester, who became Richard III.

St Andrew's, the parish church, in the town centre stands on a site that is believed to have been a place of worship for more than 1,500 years; the present church was established before 1133, although there has been rebuilding since, including that of the nave in 1719 and 1722. Parts of the church are Norman: the strong tower with 6-ft-thick walls built by the Nevilles which bears the arms of the Earls of Warwick. It contrasts with the classical Georgian architecture which is seen to advantage since the 1951 interior re-decoration which restored the chancel and the sanctuary to their original style. There are two Hutton family effigies, and in the chancel arch a wall painting by Jacob Thomson frames the east window. This has some interesting 15th-cent. stained glass: a portrait said to be of Richard II or III, and two others formerly believed to be of Richard, Duke of York, and Cecily Neville, the parents of Edward IV and Richard III, but now thought to be of Cecily Neville's parents, Ralf Neville, 1st Earl of Westmorland, and his wife Joan, daughter of John of Gaunt.

The Giant's Grave is a popular sight in the churchyard, and is supposed to be of Owen, or Owen Caesarius, King of Cumbria in 920–37. But the two stone crosses and the four hogs-back stones are probably separate memorials from different periods of the 10th cent. Nearby is the "Giant's Thumb", possibly dated as early as 920, also connected with Owen Caesarius. It was once surmounted by a wheel cross but the upper arms are missing. A number of interesting gravestones have regrettably been removed in recent years, including that of "a straw-bonnet maker". By the church is a 16th-cent. building which was formerly the Queen Elizabeth Grammar School, believed to be founded in 1340 and re-established in 1564.

Wordsworth had connections with Penrith. His paternal grandfather lived at Sockbridge nearby. William's father, after moving to COCKERMOUTH, was married in Penrith to Ann Cookson, the daughter of William Cookson, a Penrith mercer, shown in the parochial register of 1766. William and Dorothy paid visits from Cockermouth to their grandfather Cookson. At one period, 1776–7, they attended Dame Birkett's infant school, which was possibly in the building overlooking St Andrew's churchyard. At the same time Mary Hutchinson, daughter of a prominent Penrith tobacconist, and William's future wife, attended the same school. The Cookson house was on the site of Messrs. Arnison, drapers. About 2 m. S. of Penrith at Yanwath on the A592 is to be seen the house, The Grotto, where Wordsworth often visited Thomas Wilkinson, his Quaker friend, as did Clarkson, who worked with Wilberforce against the slave trade, and Charles Lloyd, the friend of Lamb and Coleridge. The house was also known to De Quincey, Scott and Coleridge. The Penrith Town Hall is formed of two houses built in 1791 and designed by Robert Adam. One was the residence of Wordsworth's cousin John.

The Gloucester Arms hotel, one of the oldest inns in England, dating from 1477, is said to have been the residence of Richard III and bears his coat of arms. The Two Lions hotel building dates from 1584. The mansion of Carleton Hill was built by Mrs Frances Trollope, mother of Anthony, the novelist. Up the hill on the NE. is the famous Penrith Beacon. This was built in 1719, but the site was used long before that to flash warnings. Sir Walter Scott was in Cumberland in 1805 when it flashed the warning of Napoleon's expected invasion, and he dashed back to Scotland. The Luck of Edenhall, a medieval glass goblet in the VICTORIA AND ALBERT MUSEUM, came from the now demolished Eden Hall near Penrith. The goblet may date from about 1240 and was possibly brought back by one of the Musgrave family from the Crusades. The clock tower in the centre of Penrith is a Musgrave monument.

The town has golf and many other sports facilities. It is a touring centre for the pleasant Eden Valley, for ULLSWATER and for the Pennines.

PEOVER HALL, *Cheshire* (12–SJ7674). The hamlet of Over Peover, sometimes called Peover Superior, or Higher Peover, and recorded as Pevre in the Domesday Book, is historically important only because it contains within its manorial boundaries the great house which was for many generations the property of the Mainwaring family. Peover Hall, originally a timber building, was rebuilt by Sir Randle Mainwaring in 1585, largely in brick, and restored many times in later centuries. Above the main door appears the date 1654, the year in which Ellen, the wife of one of Sir Randle's sons, built the remarkably fine stables of which the carved Jacobean woodwork and ornamental plaster ceilings survive. The Hall has several tall gables and delightful mullioned stone window frames, the whole being surrounded by a moat. The Tudor part retains a long dining-room above the huge kitchen with its complicated timber roof.

Through the stableyard leading from the back of the building is the church with its two chapels dedicated almost solely to the Mainwarings. The church itself was originally built in the reign of Edward III, in the style of the period, and rebuilt in brick in 1811, while still retaining its old font, its perfect Jacobean pulpit and a chair said to have been made from a still earlier pulpit of some 400 years ago by one of the Mainwaring family.

The two chapels contain splendid tombs and are well preserved. An American flag and plaque have been placed in the church to commemorate the fact that General George S. Patton and his staff of the American Third Army worshipped here while occupying Peover Hall during the Second World War.

POOLEY BRIDGE, *Westmorland* (14–NY 4724), is on the A592 beside the River Eamont where it flows out of the east end of ULLSWATER. This small village is a good starting point from which to see this fine lake; the scenery becomes more impressive as you go W. along the lakeside road, passing the area of Wordsworth's daffodils (*see* Ullswater) and reaching the far end where PATTERDALE is hemmed in by high fells. A pleasant alternative is to take one of the passenger vessels which sail regularly in summer. There are boats for hire at Pooley Bridge. The village is also a good centre on this eastern fringe of Lakeland for exploring the Eden Valley or PENRITH. Near the village, at Eusemere, lived Thomas Clarkson, the abolitionist, who was visited by Wordsworth and other men of letters; and it was along the Pooley road that Coleridge walked from GRASMERE to find the Penrith printer, Brown, who afterwards printed "The Friend" for him.

There is a road part way along the south-east side of Ullswater and into **Martindale.** Here the 19th-cent. Church of St Peter, built in the Early English style, stands on a steep and isolated slope. It has 17th-cent. woodwork, and occupies the site of 11th- and 17th-cent. churches. Also in Martindale is the deer forest, the home of wild red deer.

PORT SUNLIGHT, *Cheshire* (12–SJ3483). It is well worth turning W. from the main road S. of BIRKENHEAD to visit Port Sunlight. This is the model village built for his employees by the 1st Viscount Leverhulme, the great benefactor. He was William Hesketh Lever, born in BOLTON in 1851, who began to make soap at WIGAN in 1886 and whose Sunlight Soap became famous. The centre-piece of the village is the Lady Lever Art Gallery and Museum. Its 31 rooms contain a magnificent collection of works of art collected by its founder over half a century. The gallery was designed as a memorial to Lady Lever and was opened in 1922.

British painters are strongly represented. There are many Pre-Raphaelite works, including Holman Hunt's *The Scapegoat* and *May Morning on Magdalen Tower,* Ford Madox Brown's *Cromwell on his Farm* and Rossetti's *Blessed Damozel* (1879). There are various works by Millais, including *Sir Isumbras at the Ford.* Mostly they are of the period of this and later pictures, when he was moving away from Pre-Raphaelite principles. Works by the Victorians Lord Leighton and Alma-Tadema are included: two small works by the latter, and *Garden of the Hesperides* and *Daphnephoria,* a large-scale representation of a Greek procession at Thebes, finished to the last detail, by the former. The portraitists shown include Hoppner, Reynolds, with several works including *Elizabeth Gunning*, Gainsborough, with *Mrs Charlotte Freer*, and Romney. Burne-Jones's *Beguiling of Merlin* is included. There are landscapes by Richard Wilson, Constable's *Gamekeeper's Cottage* and Turner's *Falls of Clyde*. As well as a set of Turner drawings there are English watercolours of the late 18th and 19th cents. In the north Sculpture Hall the marble *Antinoüs* is shown to advantage in the centre; it was found in the ruins of Hadrian's Tivoli villa. The so-called Gladiator in polished black marble, probably of the 2nd cent., is a Roman copy of an earlier Greek bronze.

The gallery also has Epstein's *Deirdre* in bronze and works by Nollekens and Flaxman. The bust of Ferdinando de' Medici is by Giovacchino Fortini of Florence. It contains one of the best English collections of furniture, mostly of the second and third quarters of the 18th cent. A rosewood dressing table and a mahogany bookcase may have come from the workshop of Thomas Chippendale the Elder. Various period rooms show work from Tudor and Stuart times up to Wedgwood. There are important collections of Wedgwood pottery, Carrara marble mantlepieces and interesting old clocks. Chinese pottery and porcelain are a special feature, including Han, T'ang, Sung and Ming works.

POULTON-LE-FYLDE, *Lancashire* (12–SD 3439), is an old market town. Its Church of St Chad has an early 17th-cent. tower in the Perpendicular style. The rest of the church was rebuilt in stone in 1752–3. The Romanesque chancel was added in 1868. There are Doric doorways with pediments, and a Georgian interior. A staircase leads to the galleries, which have square pews with the original candle sockets. There are wall monuments to Fleetwoods and Heskeths and a vault dated 1699. The baptistry has a 17th-cent. screen, and there is a carved Jacobean pulpit.

PRESTBURY, *Cheshire* (12–SJ8976). Lying 2½ m. NW. of MACCLESFIELD, Prestbury has a strong claim to being the prettiest and most visited town in Cheshire. The attractive appearance of so many timbered cottages, each differently presented in a frame of trees and flowered gardens, might well be qualification enough; but to this is added a wealth of ancient buildings of great interest.

The earliest relic is an Anglo-Saxon cross, about 4 ft in height, which is made up of fragmented carvings at least 1,200 years old. It stands, encased in glass, in the churchyard of the beautifully restored and enlarged 13th-cent. church adjacent to a Norman chapel and in company with two fine yew trees planted here 600 years ago. The church, dedicated to St Peter, is in styles of architecture from Early English to Perpendicular. The oldest part is the chancel, dating from *c.* 1220. The pillars on the north side of the nave are 13th-cent. and those on the

south side probably a century later. Among the memorials on the north wall of the chancel is a monument to Reginald Legh, of 1482, who was concerned in the building of the tower. This tower, with its rows of faces and grotesques, still stands, the massive base forming a porch. Also in the chancel is the armoured figure of Sir Edward Warren and on the south side are the figures of Robert Downes and his wife. Another elaborate sculpture, of Jasper Worth with his wife and three children, is affixed to the wall of the Tytherington Chapel, and at the east end of the north aisle is the Legh Chapel where several members of this family are buried. Great antiquarian interest will attach to the sanctuary chair, the oak screens and the two old chests, one of which is 8 ft long, all originals of the Jacobean period. The churchyard, already mentioned, contains several other curiosities. One is the grave of Paul Mason of Rainow, who, when he died in 1752 at the age of 95, was the father or grandfather of 94 children. Another is that of Sarah Peckford "who died a bachelor in the 48th year of her life". The third is a 19th-cent. inscription to Maria Rathbone, a child who lost her way home and whose body was found 25 days later as the result of a dream by a complete stranger.

The Norman chapel next door is kept bare and plainly furnished in simulation of its appearance when its first worshippers attended here more than 750 years ago. The doorway is the oldest in a neighbourhood famous for ancient buildings. The arch above it is carved with zigzags and strange beaked heads, opening into a further Norman arch leading to the chancel. Only the roof had to be made new in the restoration work carried out two centuries ago.

Opposite the churchyard is the handsome black-and-white Priest's House, probably 14th-cent., with gables and diamond-paned windows. During the days of the Commonwealth a parson ejected from the church used to preach from a gallery over the door. This superbly maintained and rare building is now the property of the District Bank. At the far end of the town is a Reading Room, built in 1720 and endowed by Anne Whittaker for "promotion of a schoolmaster to teach ten of the poorest children in the township of Prestbury from the Primer to the Bible". Today this is used as a branch of Williams Deacons Bank, with other sections appropriately housing a library and the parish council chamber. Still another link with the past has been effected by restoring the old village stocks to their original site after they were found to have been serving as a farmyard gate in 1934.

The amenities of Prestbury include one of the best golf courses in the county, several restaurants, and three fine inns in late Tudor style: the Unicorn, the Admiral Rodney and the Legh Arms.

PRESTON, *Lancashire* (12–SD5329). It was at the Battle of Preston in 1648 that Cromwell inflicted a decisive defeat on the Royalist forces. Milton, devout propagandist of the Lord Protector, mentions the event at the River Darwen, "with blood of Scots imbrued". In the 18th cent. Preston was associated with another kind of battle – the Industrial Revolution's consequences. The introduction of machinery lessened the demand for hand-labour and, combined with bad harvests and the Corn Laws, brought riots and demands for the destruction of machinery. Richard Arkwright, who was born at Preston in 1732, invented the spinning-frame (1769) to cheapen cotton production but had to remove to NOTTINGHAM first to avoid the attacks that drove Hargreaves out of Lancashire. Another northerner, John Horrocks, set up the first cotton mill in Preston, and the town became an important centre of the industry. Local history is told in the exhibits of the Harris Museum, which also has burial urns and wood timbers from **Bleasdale**, a unique wood circle (*see* CHIPPING), as well as other archaeological relics, pottery, porcelain, glass and costumes. There is material relating to Francis Thompson, the poet, who was born at Preston in 1859; his birthplace is 7 Winckley Street. The art gallery is in the same building as the Harris museum, a fine late Classical building, built 1882–93, to the design of James Hibbert, architect and alderman of Preston. The gallery has a special collection of works and relics of the Devis family, and works by 19th- and 20th-cent. painters and sculptors. St George's Church is early 19th-cent. and was rebuilt in 1884. St Peter's was designed by Rickman in 1832–5 in Gothic style, with the spire added later. It has flying buttresses outside and many cusps in the interior design.

Hoghton Tower is about 5 m. SE. of Preston, but is a private residence. For long the home of the de Hoghton family, the tower has mementoes of a visit by James I; he is said to have "knighted" a piece of beef as "Sir Loin", creating the word sirloin, but the veracity of this episode is dubious.

PUDDINGTON OLD HALL, *Cheshire* (12–SJ3273), is above the Dee between BURTON and SHOTWICK. Now privately owned, it has been involved in much of Cheshire's history as the home for seven centuries of the de Masseys, a family known all over the county. The Hall was also called The Priest's House because of the Catholic faith of its owners, and was suspected of being the centre of plots and conspiracies. In the hysteria of Titus Oates' "popish plot", Father Plessington of Burton, the chaplain of the Masseys, was seized, and slaughtered at CHESTER, in 1679. The last of the Masseys, William, fought in the battle of PRESTON as a Jacobite in 1715. He escaped after the battle but was caught at Puddington and died in Chester Castle dungeon. The great Cheshire families were seriously perplexed over their loyalties in the Jacobite uprising; the meeting of the Ten Cheshire Gentlemen after the battle of Preston finally decided to cast their lot with the King and not the Old Pretender. Their portraits can be seen at TATTON HALL.

RAVENSTONEDALE, *Westmorland* (14–NY7203), is a village set below Ash Fell, SW. of

KIRKBY STEPHEN, in pleasant moorland. St Oswald's Church is 18th-cent. but includes portions of an older structure. Sections of the congregation sit facing each other and the pulpit is on three levels. Ash Fell rises to 1,185 ft and gives a good view of the dale, in which rises the River Lune.

RIBCHESTER, *Lancashire* (12–SD6435), is a village with an ancient history 10 m. NE. of PRESTON; the Romans were followed there by Anglo-Saxon settlers and then by Norman conquerors. It was listed in the Domesday Book. A Royalist outpost, it was the site of several battles in the Civil War. It has pleasant houses, and an old bridge over the Ribble where there was a Roman ford; this area was the scene of some most important Roman discoveries. The Church of St Wilfrid is probably 13th- or 14th-cent. Two pillars fitted to hold the organ loft are believed to come from the Roman site.

The Ribchester Museum of Roman Antiquities has remains from Bremetennacum, the great Roman fort covering about six acres. An excavated area adjoining the museum shows the foundations of two granaries built by Agricola about A.D. 80. Among objects found were Samian pottery, coins and inscribed stones. A Roman helmet with a visor was sent to the BRITISH MUSEUM. Even wheat from the granaries was found, which crumbled when exposed to the air. The museum was bought by the National Trust in 1912, and the foundations were given to the Trust in 1922. The site is scheduled as an Ancient Monument and is of great archaeological importance. Roman roads led from here to MANCHESTER and E. through the Pennines, others to the Lune valley, LANCASTER and Preston.

Stydd church, near Ribchester, is believed to have been built in the reign of Stephen and to be the oldest church in the Ribble valley. It has neither tower, turret nor belfry. Many original features remain, and an old gritstone font with crude carvings.

The White Bull Inn, Ribchester, has Doric pillars supposed to be of Roman origin. There are pleasant picnic spots on the river banks, and the area has a number of old manor houses.

RIVINGTON, *Lancashire* (12–SD6214), lies to the SE. of CHORLEY, between a reservoir and the moorland where Rivington Pike rises to 1,190 ft. The Pike is the site of an old tower, dated 1733, said to be used as a beacon, and from here there are extensive views. The Lever Park at Rivington of about 400 acres was presented to the public by the 1st Lord Leverhulme, who was born at BOLTON (*see also* HALL I' TH' WOOD). The Hall in the park, rebuilt in 1744, is now a museum. The small Church of Holy Trinity was built about 1540 by the Pilkington family, of whom there is a genealogical picture. The church was re-modelled later and has an unusual belfry standing apart from the church. The pulpit has linenfold panels. See also the Unitarian chapel, scarcely altered since its erection in 1703.

Rosthwaite lies in the valley of Borrowdale

ROCHDALE, *Lancashire* (12–SD8913). This old mill town, 400 ft up near the Pennine moors, evokes memories of women spinning cotton, of John Bright, of Gracie Fields, of 19th-cent. economic struggles and of the little co-operative store opening in Toad Lane. Rochdale became so well known as a cotton town that people forget its original source of industrial prosperity, which was based on wool, for woollen textiles were the main local industry until the end of the 18th cent. The town's history can be traced back for very many centuries before that. A considerable collection of flints and Bronze Age implements were gathered for the Rochdale Museum, showing that the area was inhabited since prehistoric times. A Roman road is believed to have run to the town from MANCHESTER, and a remarkably well-preserved stretch of it can be seen up in the moors at BLACKSTONE EDGE where it crosses into Yorkshire. Rochdale was in King Athelstan's West Saxon kingdom, was listed in the Domesday Book, and was one of the largest manors in medieval times in the Hundred of Salford. It has had a weekly market charter from 1251, and since that time the wool industry developed from the moorland sheep. But by the end of the 18th cent. cotton was beginning to replace wool, and many mills sprang up. The industry suffered depression at various times, and severe conditions led a little band of Rochdale men to make a co-operative effort by establishing their own shop and dividing the surplus for mutual benefit. They met with hostility and suspicion, but finally set up their shop in 1844 as the Rochdale Society of Equitable Pioneers. The co-operative movement was developing simultaneously elsewhere, but Rochdale is generally regarded as the first; and its old "co-op" store is still there as a museum for visitors. Varied new industries now supplement textiles, and square blocks of flats are dominant.

The borough has a handsome town hall, completed in 1871, in Gothic style by W. H. Crossland, with a frontage of 264 ft. There is a hammer-beam roof of a single span over its Great Hall of 90 ft by 58 ft. *The Signing of Magna Carta,* a fresco by Henry Holiday, covers the east wall. The exterior of the Parish Church of St Chad is in Perpendicular style, and in the 19th cent. much of the interior was restored, but there are 13th-cent. arcades, and carved 16th-cent. screens. The art gallery contains works in oils and watercolour. Archaeological and geological material is stored in the museum, with new premises under development. Among special sections in the central library are the Ember Collection dealing with cricket, works on the co-operative movement, and the John Collier Collection. Collier, the painter and earliest of the Lancashire dialect poets, wrote as Tim Bobbin. The most famous 19th-cent. citizen of Rochdale, John Bright, was born here in 1811; he is best known as an opponent of the Corn Laws, and a bronze statue of him stands in Hillside Gardens. Gracie Fields was also born in Rochdale, and was made a Freeman.

The art gallery at **Bury,** W., contains the Wrigley Collection which includes works by Constable, Turner, Crome, Cox, de Wint, Canova and Epstein. Thomas Wrigley (portrayed by G. F. Watts), a 19th-cent. paper-maker and pamphleteer, formed the collection. Bury was the birthplace of Sir Robert Peel, whose statue is in the market place. Kay Gardens commemorates John Kay, inventor of the flying shuttle.

Radcliffe, SW. of Bury, has a local history museum, covering the district from prehistoric times, and the remains of Radcliffe Tower (*c.* 1403).

ROSTHWAITE, *Cumberland* (14–NY2514). This is a small village, but it lies in a setting that amply repays the visitor's journey. It is surrounded in almost every direction by the magnificent peaks and fells of BORROWDALE. It is 6 m.

Rydal church from Dora's Field

S. of KESWICK, centrally placed in the valley, and is a good departure point for walking or climbing in such areas as Dale Head, Langstrath, Sty Head or GREAT GABLE, Greenup and WATENDLATH. Seatoller and HONISTER PASS are SW., and the Seathwaite and Stonethwaite areas lie to the SW. and SE.

RUFFORD, *Lancashire* (12–SD4515), NE. of ORMSKIRK on the main road, has Rufford Old Hall (open to the public) on a site of 14½ acres owned by the National Trust. The building is one of the best remaining examples of a late medieval timber-framed hall with plaster panels. It was built by the Hesketh family in the 15th cent., with wings added in 1662 and 1821. The great hall is notable for its ornate hammer-beam roof, and for a rare type of 15th-cent. movable screen with rich panels. The property was given to the Trust in 1936 by the 1st Baron Hesketh with an endowment; one wing, containing the Philip Ashcroft folk museum, with collections from surrounding areas, was given in 1946. The hall has fine displays of 17th-cent. furniture, 16th-cent. arms and armour, old English coins and tapestry, and Roman relics.

Rufford's church, St Mary's, is an 1869 building with a spire and succeeds an earlier church on the site. There is interesting window glass and carving on the capitals of pillars. A chapel is devoted to the Hesketh family of Rufford. The memorials (some of them from the older church) include a marble carving by Flaxman, and a wall tablet to Sir Thomas Hesketh with a verse by William Cowper.

RYDAL AND RYDAL WATER, *Westmorland* (14–NY3606). On 23 April 1850 William Wordsworth died at Rydal. He was born on 7 April 1770 at COCKERMOUTH. In a life of 80 years Wordsworth changed in his outlook from youthful ardour for the French Revolution ("Bliss was it in that dawn to be alive") to conservatism; his work at Rydal, during which he became Poet Laureate, shows a corresponding change of emphasis from that of the great period of the "Lyrical Ballads" and GRASMERE. Nevertheless, he continued to work unceasingly in his last 37 years, which he spent at Rydal Mount after moving there in 1813. The house is up the hill on the left, on the road for Rydal Hall.

Below Nab Scar is Nab Cottage, off the main road by Rydal Water, where De Quincey lived and later Hartley Coleridge, when De Quincey moved to Dove Cottage, Wordsworth's former home, in 1809. Behind Nab Cottage runs a path, one of Wordsworth's routes between Rydal Mount and Grasmere. Dora's Field is also on the north side of the main road opposite the lake. Wordsworth bought the field in 1826, and his grandson, Mr Gordon Wordsworth, gave it to the National Trust in 1935. St Mary's Church, 19th-cent., has a memorial window to Dr Thomas Arnold, his wife, and their son Matthew, the poet. Dr Arnold lived at AMBLESIDE.

Rydal Water is a small but beautiful lake sheltered by Rydal Fell, 2,000 ft high on the north side. Round either end of the lake you can walk to Loughrigg Terrace (*see* Grasmere) on the S. Rydal Water is one of the first lakes to freeze in winter and then becomes a popular skating resort.

SADDLEBACK (BLENCATHRA), *Cumberland* (14–NY3227). The name derives from the saddle-shaped hollow between Foule Crag and the main summit. The alternative name of Blencathra is a reminder that this was Celtic territory before the English inroads from the E. and Norse settle

ient from overseas. THRELKELD, about 4 m. E.
f KESWICK, is below Saddleback, and the climb
from here is more severe than by routes from
cales, further E. A series of peaks joined by
ollows form a ridge in which Saddleback itself is
,847 ft high. Along the top from E. to W. there
s more than a mile of good views. To the S. is the
HELVELLYN range, SE. the High Street group
above HAWES WATER, and more to the W. are
GREAT GABLE and SCA FELL. To the W. of
DERWENTWATER lie the beautiful smaller peaks
of the Catbells, and to the N. is a wild region
imilar to that beyond SKIDDAW.

ST BEES, *Cumberland* (14–NX9611), is a
mall coastal resort, about 4 m. S. of WHITE-
HAVEN. The town lies mainly inland but has a good
beach. Nearby is St Bees Head in fine red sand-
tone – the most westerly point of Cumberland.

The Church of SS. Mary and Bega belonged
to a Benedictine priory of the 12th cent. and is
one of the most outstanding in Cumberland. St
Bega is believed to have come from Ireland in
about A.D. 650 to found a nunnery that preceded
the priory, and the other church dedicated to
her is at BASSENTHWAITE LAKE. St Bees Church
has work of Norman and later periods; there
has been much restoration and the central tower
vas altered in the 19th cent. by Butterfield.
The fine Norman doorway should be noted. An
impressive carved stone in the churchyard wall
shows St Michael fighting a dragon. It is thought
to be 8th-cent. and may have survived from the
nunnery.

St Bees grammar school was founded in the
16th cent. and is now a public school.

ST HELEN'S, *Lancashire* (12–SJ5094). This
industrial centre has since the 18th cent. gained a
world-wide reputation for its production of glass.
In Prescot Road is the Pilkington Glass Museum
(open to the public), displaying English and
Continental examples of the craft. There is also a
tiny figure from Egypt of the god Bes, and a
George IV glass decanter. Ample supplies of
almost uniform sand grains has helped glass-
making at St Helen's.

The Gamble Institute houses the library, the
art gallery, with periodic exhibitions, and a
museum dealing with natural history, glass and
folklore.

Prescot, to the SW., has the Church of Our
Lady, with the tower and spire added by Henry
Sephton in 1729, above a notable black-and-white
Jacobean roof. The spire was later rebuilt after
lightning had struck it.

Rainhill, to the S., has an ancient stone cross,
a 19th-cent. church with a hollow spire, and a
Grecian-style Roman Catholic church.

SALFORD, *Lancashire* (12–SJ7796), is more
or less joined to MANCHESTER and its docks.
Salford developed as a cotton-spinning town, and
the industry continues today, together with
important rubber and waterproofing industries;
there has been considerable re-planning. The

museum and art gallery is at Peel Park. A feature
of the museum is Lark Hill Place, a reconstruction
of a street in a 19th-cent. northern industrial town.
The art gallery is notable for its L. S. Lowry
collection. At Buile Hill Park is the science
museum, containing exhibits of mammals, local
natural history, coal-mining and general science.
Ordsall Hall is a medieval manor house, formerly
the home of the Radcliffe family.

Sir Charles Hallé, the conductor, is buried at
Salford.

SAMLESBURY, *Lancashire* (12–SD6231), in
the Ribble valley has the Church of St Leonard
standing on a low site near the river. A stone
church, it was rebuilt in the 16th cent., of which
period is the nave with its clerestory and aisles.
The tower is of about 1900. There are 17th- and
18th-cent. box pews, a two-decker pulpit, a plain
Norman font, and Jacobean altar rails. Memorials and relics include those of the Southworth
family.

Samlesbury Hall (open to the public on Sundays
in summer) is on the PRESTON TO BLACKBURN
road within five minutes of the M6, and has an
ample car park. The building dates mainly from
the 15th and 16th cents., but was considerably
altered in the 19th. Some of the windows in
the later parts of the Hall were acquired from
nearby WHALLEY Abbey after the Dissolution.
There are nearly 100 pictures on view, including a
collection of watercolours, specially painted for
the Hall by Sir Charles Holmes, showing local
Lancashire scenes. There are also 50 European
and oriental casks and cabinets of various ages on
display. A previous fortified house was destroyed
by the Scots after Bannockburn, and the present
mansion was owned by the Southworth family,
to which John Southworth, the Jesuit martyr,
belonged. The Hall is now in charge of the
Samlesbury Hall Trust.

SANDBACH, *Cheshire* (12–SJ7560). A small
town of considerable industrial importance,
which still preserves many interesting features
connected with its long history. The winding
streets, the cobbled market place and the rows of
old timbered houses show connections with past
ages of prosperity, but the outstanding historical
possession of Sandbach is the pair of Anglo-
Saxon crosses on a stone platform in the square.
The taller of these is over 16 ft high and the
shorter nearly 12 ft. It is believed that they were
put here some 1,300 years ago to commemorate
the conversion to Christianity of Paeda, the son of
Penda, King of Mercia. After the Reformation
the crosses were broken up and the pieces distri-
buted about the area for use in building. In 1816
Dr Ormerod, the Cheshire historian, collected
most of the fragments and had them restored to
their original position. The weathered carvings
are in rough bas-relief and depict Biblical scenes.
These monuments are certainly among the
earliest of their kind left in England.

Sandbach was once a salt town and later became
the centre of the silk trade. Both of these industries

Southport: one of the handsome shopping boulevards

continue to flourish under modern conditions, in the company, since 1901, of the giant Foden's Motor Works, whose prizewinning band is well known to brass bandsmen everywhere.

SCA FELL, *Cumberland* (14–NY2006), is described as the highest mountain in England, and it is in the sense of giving its name to the group which includes the real summit, Sca Fell Pike, 3,210 ft, Sca Fell itself being 3,162 ft high. This dominating group is like a giant knot near the geographical centre of Lakeland, as if a mighty convulsion had thrust it up and thrown the main lakes outward from it. Sca Fell, Glaramara and BOW FELL, with the flanking groups of GREAT GABLE and the Pillar group on the NW., and the LANGDALE PIKES on the E., force motoring routes to keep to the N. and S.; even the road via WASTWATER near Sca Fell can be reached only from the W. The stony crags of this volcanic range are a scene of grandeur, but they are no place for inexperienced climbers.

SCARISBRICK HALL, *Lancashire* (12–SD 3713). This attractive building is worthy of inspection by those interested in architecture. It stands 3 m. SE. of SOUTHPORT, on the site of a 13th-cent. dwelling, and has 150 rooms. The fine setting is in a private estate protected by a preservation order, for the hall is officially listed as a building of special architectural interest. The wide expanse of woodland and pasture, with pleasant gardens, orchard and lake, create an atmosphere of peaceful grandeur. The present hall was remodelled by John Foster in 1814 and by Augustus Welby Northmore Pugin in 1836–45; it was added to (including the tower, now minus its wrought-iron cresting) by Edward Welby Pugin in 1860–70. It is a handsome example of neo-Gothic residential architecture. Inside are elaborate oak carvings, panelling and finely decorated ceilings. A fine collection of 17th-cent. oak carvings of Flemish craftsmanship, in the oak room, provide a wealth of pictorial scenes and decoration. The Kings' Room has 27 oil paintings of royal personages set in panelled walls, and a finely carved ceiling.

In 1946 the Scarisbrick family left the hall and the estate was bought by the Church of England Commissioners. With Ministry of Education aid, the building was equipped as a modern teachers' training college at a cost of £250,000, which included making it structurally sound and adding central heating and hot-water systems, laboratories, an art room and playing fields. New buildings were added to provide a chapel, a sanatorium, dormitory wings, a dining hall, kitchen and gymnasium. In 1963, the hall and 38 acres of the estate were bought by Mr Charles A. Oxley, sometime housemaster in Alexandria, Egypt, and principal of Tower College, LIVERPOOL. He has established an independent school for boys, Christian but inter-denominational, run as a non-profit-making company with strong emphasis on academic attainment along with outdoor and voluntary activities.

SEASCALE, *Cumberland* (14–NY0301). This small resort stands on a pleasant stretch of coast with good sands and a golf course. S. is Ravenglass Gullery Nature Reserve (entry by permit) at Drigg Point with the largest colony of black-headed gulls in Europe. Seascale is convenient for reaching WASTWATER. About 2 m. N. are Windscale and Calder Hall atomic stations. It was Windscale, in 1957, that had the leakage into the atmosphere of radioactive iodine which necessitated the banning of milk sales over 200 sq. m. for six weeks.

Forces of a different kind contended 1,000 years ago at **Gosforth,** 3 m. to the E. The famous 14½-ft Gosforth Cross combines Christian and pagan symbols. The representation on this cross of the Norse god Loki and his wife Sigun, and other figures who may be Baldur and his unwitting slayer, or Heimdal, or Odin who gave an eye for wisdom, shows how shallow-rooted the new faith then was among these early settlers and how they preferred to take no spiritual chances. St Mary's Church, rebuilt in the 19th cent., is probably on the site of a Norman, or earlier, structure. There are several ancient relics besides the Gosforth Cross, including two hog-back carved tombstones and cross shaft.

SEFTON, *Lancashire* (12–SD3500), is a little village on the coastal plain, N. of LIVERPOOL, and its Church of St Helen has been called the queen of Lancashire churches. An outstanding feature is the 16th-cent. carved woodwork of the rood-screen with its canopy (restored in the 19th cent.), the screens north and south of the chancel, and the screens in two chapels. The fine carved pulpit and its canopy (1635) and the screen of Lord Sefton's pew should be seen. The church has a lofty 14th-cent. spire but the rest of the building dates from the early 16th cent. There is also a notable series of monuments and brasses to the Molyneux family, including a knight in armour.

SHAP, *Westmorland* (14–NY5615). Shap Summit is, at over 1,300 ft, the highest point of the A6. One of the wildest-looking English main roads, it is often blocked when snow falls. The north-ward continuation of the M6 route approaches further E., avoiding the KENDAL route. Shap village, N. of the summit, is nearly 1,000 ft above sea-level. The parish church was restored in the 19th cent. but may have origins older than Shap Abbey. The Shap granite works are near the summit, but the abbey is hidden in a valley W. of the village. The Ministry of Public Building and Works has charge of the abbey (open to the public), which was founded about 1191 by Premonstratensian canons. Most of the ruins date from the early 13th cent. when the church was begun, but the tower is early 16th-cent. Keld Chapel nearby, administered by the National Trust, is a small pre-Reformation building.

SHOTWICK, *Cheshire* (12–SJ3371), is a very quiet village, although not far from an ironworks and an atomic factory. The River Dee, which once washed the edge of Shotwick, is now nearly 2 m. away. There was a ford here as a route to Wales, no doubt much used by armies to attack the Welsh. The battlements of St Michael's Church are a reminder of troubled times at this strategic point. The old church retains a Norman doorway and some interesting stained glass which may be 14th-cent. There is a three-decker pulpit, box pews, a churchwarden's seat with a canopy and a low arcade. The Elizabethan Shotwick Hall became a farm-house. To the S. is the site of the former castle, supposed to have been built by Hugh Lupus, Earl of Chester.

SIZERGH CASTLE, *Westmorland* (14–SD 4988), is 3 m. S. of KENDAL on the road to LANCASTER. This site has been the home of the Strickland family for 700 years, whose chapel is in the parish church of Kendal. The castle (open to the public at advertised times) is a peel-tower, built about 1340; additions – including that of the Tudor great hall – and alterations were made in the 15th, 16th and 18th cents. There is some fine Tudor panelling, furniture, 17th-cent. Flemish tapestry, and Stuart and Jacobite relics, as well as decorated plasterwork on ceilings and a portrait collection. A bell beaker was found in a cairn on Sizergh Fell and preserved. The castle stands in 1,556 acres and, with the estate, was given by the Stricklands with an endowment to the National Trust in 1950. E. of the castle is a panorama of countryside rising to the Pennines.

SKIDDAW, *Cumberland* (14–NY2629), dominates the Skiddaw group of fells, and at 3,054 ft is overtopped in the Lakes only by the two SCA FELL peaks and HELVELLYN. But Skiddaw is a favourite because it is what climbers call an easy ascent; however, those unaccustomed to the lengthy exercise involved should allow most of the day for the task so as to have intervals for rest. The north side slopes down through the wilds of Uldale Fells. Eastward is SADDLEBACK; and to the S. are magnificent views over DERWENT-WATER and KESWICK, with Helvellyn and BOR-ROWDALE. W. of Derwentwater are Causey Pike, Grisedale Pike, Lord's Seat and BASSENTHWAITE. Occasionally Ireland can be seen.

SMITHILLS HALL, *Lancashire* (12–SD70 12). This Hall (open to the public) is one of the oldest manor houses in Lancashire, and is a good specimen of English domestic architecture. It lies in parkland 2 m. NW. of BOLTON on the slopes of the moors overlooking the town. Various parts of the Hall are of the 14th and 15th cents. Certain rooms were added in Tudor times. The great hall is timbered, and there is a withdrawing room with fine panelling. The house has had restorations and additions, and has been the home of such families as the Radcliffes, Bartons, Byrons, Shuttleworths, Belasyses and Ainsworths, until acquired by Bolton Corporation in 1938. Smithills is scheduled as an Ancient Monument, and contains furniture mainly of the Stuart period.

SOUTHPORT, *Lancashire* (12–SD3316). Southport is a pleasant resort most notable for Lord Street, a handsome boulevard, lined with trees and elegant shops which runs parallel to the coast for 1½ m. with its continuation, Albert Road. Marine Lake and Princes Park lie outside the promenade. Beyond, Marine Drive runs right along the seafront, passing the municipal golf links on the N. and Victoria Park and its esplanade on the S.

Southport Flower Show is a famous annual event, with horse-jumping trials as an added attraction. Other special events include county cricket, lawn tennis, golf tournaments, a music festival and a stage dancing festival. The Royal Birkdale Golf Club is well known, and the Ryder Cup Competition has been held there more than once. Marine Lake has 91 acres of water for sailing yachts and other boats. Besides its 6 m. of sandy beach, Southport also has a miniature model village. Conferences are catered for in two halls. In Lord Street the art gallery has a permanent collection of British art over the last 300 years. The museum, in the botanic gardens, includes a Victorian period room and a display of 18th-cent. Liverpool porcelain.

St Cuthbert's is the parish church of **North Meols**. It was rebuilt in 1730 and the spire is dated 1739. Enlargements and additions were made by Isaac Taylor in 1908. There is a Nollekens monument, and carving by Richard Prescot of about 1704. Holy Trinity Church is 19th-cent., rebuilt by Huon Matear, 1903–14. Its high tower is a landmark in the town; its pinnacles were restored with fibreglass. The interior has a ribbed barrel vault, and flamboyant stone tracery in the chancel roof.

SPEKE HALL, *Lancashire* (12–SJ4383), is one of the best half-timbered houses in the county. In a rural setting in 35 acres of land near the Mersey sheltered by trees, it would be peaceful indeed but for the roar from LIVERPOOL airport close by. The Norris family built Speke Hall round a square courtyard during the 16th cent. Sir Edward Norreys completed it in 1598 and an inscription on the north front records that this was his work. The hall was for long the ancestral home of the family. There is a wainscot which was said to have been brought from Holyrood Palace, Edinburgh, by Sir William Norreys (who fought at Flodden Field), and which Sir Edward inherited. A red sandstone bridge crosses the hollow that was formerly the moat, and leads to a series of small rooms, some of which conceal secret chambers. The interior has rich decoration and furnishings, including Mortlake tapestries, and other fine antiques. There is elaborate 16th- and 17th-cent. plasterwork in the great hall, and a fine plastered ceiling and carved chimney-piece in the great parlour. The kitchen has stone mullioned windows and a display of polished brass and copper.

Hale, about 3 m. E., was called by Jane Carlyle, wife of Thomas Carlyle, the "beautifullest village in all England". It has old cottages and flowers, and an 18th-cent. church with a 500-year-old tower. In the churchyard was buried the Childe of Hale, John Middleton, said to have been over 9 ft tall. There are many tales of this giant who visited the court of James I and defeated his wrestler. S. of the village is the southernmost tip of Lancashire, and E. of it a ford where Prince Rupert is said to have escaped into Cheshire after the Battle of MARSTON MOOR.

STALYBRIDGE, *Cheshire* (12–SJ9698). The name of this small manufacturing town on the River Tame probably derives from that of the Stayley or Stavelegh family, who were prominent landowners in the district from the 14th cent. The present Stayley Hall was constructed in 1580 on the site of an earlier building of 1343. It is said that

The British Tourist Authority

Speke Hall

John Wesley preached here in 1745. Stalybridge reached its full stature early in the 19th cent. as a cotton town, having been one of the first to employ steam power in the mills, but with the decline of cotton local enterprise was largely deflected into light industry. The amenities of the borough include Cheetham Park, with its colourful bird sanctuary, and the beautiful Stamford Park of 60 acres surrounding a large boating lake.

STAND, *Lancashire* (12–SD8007). The lofty Church of All Saints with its tower and pinnacles was built between 1822 and 1826 to a neo-Gothic design by Sir Charles Barry.

STANDISH, *Lancashire* (12–SD5609). The church has an imposing steeple rebuilt in 1867, which is a landmark for miles. In the churchyard to the left of the main entrance lies a boulder about 4 ft high, found buried 11 ft deep in 1895 according to its inscription, and presumably from the Ice Age. The Church of St Wilfred is a curiosity: late Gothic (1582–4) in general form – it has Classical details. Where the nave and chancel meet are two domed turrets with stairs inside them. Of note are the roofs, font, pulpit, tombs and monuments. The rich stained glass is Victorian, and a modern vestry was added in 1913.

STOCK GHYLL, *Westmorland* (14–NY3804). Stock Ghyll Force is about 1 m. from the centre of AMBLESIDE. You leave by Stock Ghyll Road (E.) beside the River Stock and enter Stock Ghyll Park, where there is an old bobbin mill and its dam which interested Dickens. The mill obtained its timber from ample woodland in the neighbourhood. The way to the Force, which becomes audible as you approach, is along the path by the stream. Set among trees, the torrent leaps down some 75 ft. It rises in Red Screes 4 m. above the Rothay.

STOCKPORT, *Cheshire* (12–SJ8989). This county town was a market centre with its own bridge across the Mersey in the 13th cent. In the street called Great Underbank stands a timber-framed hall, believed to have been built in the late 15th cent., which was occupied for three centuries by the Arderne family who claimed kinship with Shakespeare through Mary Arden. It contains an 18th-cent. oak staircase. The house, excellently preserved, is now a branch of the District Bank. A few doors away is the White Lion, the town's oldest hostelry.

Stockport, however, is largely the product of the Industrial Revolution and the railway age. There are mills and great chimneys, and a fine 19th-cent. railway viaduct, over 100 ft high, dominates the town. The parish church, dedicated to St Mary the Virgin, is also 19th-cent., having been rebuilt in the Perpendicular and Decorated styles between 1810 and 1817, but some 14th-cent. fragments remain in the finely restored chancel. There is a modern brass here to the memory of John Wainwright, who composed the hymn "Christians Awake". The church stands at one end of the market place, believed to be the site of a 12th-cent. Norman castle built over a Roman fortification of A.D. 79. A Victorian iron-framed covered market occupies a large part of the area. On market days the stalls spread colourfully into the surrounding streets.

The town has an interesting piece of early 20th-cent. civil engineering: the Mersey is covered over here by a road built along its course.

About ½ m. from the market place, in the direction of the river, is Vernon Park Museum, beautifully situated on a high point affording fine views of the hills in the background and the river far below. In addition to its comprehensive coverage of local fauna, flora and geology, the museum is notable for an unusual window made up of some 250 pieces of fluor-spar from the Blue John Mine at CASTLETON. One room is set aside for an impressive bird collection, and another for items connected with local history, of which a particularly barbarous scold's bridle is a disconcerting example.

STYAL, *Cheshire* (12–SJ8383). A picturesque little village of Cheshire "magpie" inns, white cottages, a valley and an old mill, all now administered by the National Trust. The 18th-cent. cotton mill still stands, where the River Bollin flows swiftly through a deep wooded glen. The great mill-wheel has gone, but the original sluice and tunnel remain, with the rest of the structure, much as they would have appeared in the days when the employment of child labour was accepted as normal practice. Below the mill is Norcliffe Hall, a modern mansion built in Elizabethan style, where Audubon, the famous American naturalist, used to stay as a guest of the Greg family. He says in his reminiscences that

about here he saw the finest cattle in England. In the woods of the ravine are some very tall trees planted by Robert Hyde Greg in 1838 from cuttings taken from Wellingtonias (*Sequoiadendron gigan-teum*) in California. These parent trees are 3,500 years old and have attained a height of 350 ft, as one day may their offspring.

SWINTON AND PENDLEBURY, *Lanca-shire* (12–SD7802). These two towns have become a joint modern borough lying about 5 m. NW. of MANCHESTER. With a coal-mining background, it is an industrial area for textiles and engineering products, but the borough is also a residential district. Replanning has provided a modern town hall combined with a recently developed civic centre which includes a library and civic hall, and also shopping precincts. Pendlebury's Church of St Augustine is in brick, a Gothic masterpiece by Bodley and Garner. Nearby is Warke Dam, shared with WORSLEY.

TARLETON, *Lancashire* (12–SD4420), is a village by the River Douglas. St Mary's is an early 18th-cent. brick church; a stone turret and a cupola were added in the 19th cent. It has square pews, original benches and clear glass windows. Carr House to the NE. near Bretherton is a 17th-cent. house formerly containing Barry Elder's Doll Museum, a collection of dolls and tapestries.

TARPORLEY, *Cheshire* (12–SJ5562). This old town with gabled houses stretches along the A51 (A49). The Church of St Helen is medieval in origin, but considerably restored so that most of it is now 19th-cent. work. It has a handsome tower, long gables and great width. Notable are the monuments to the Done family, a historic name in these parts. A large marble monument depicts Jane Done (died 1662) and her sister, Mary Crewe. Another is the tomb of Sir John Crewe. There is some colourful stained glass.

The 13th-cent. **Beeston Castle** is about 3 m. S., ruins on a steep rock that gives a magnificent view. The castle was destroyed after the Civil War. It stands in the park of Peckforton Castle, one of Salvin's best works (*see* BUNBURY).

TARVIN, *Cheshire* (12–SJ4867), is beside the A51, the Roman Watling Street, and 5½ m. E. of CHESTER. It is a small, old village that was of strategic importance in the Civil War when it was a garrison for the Parliamentary side. Where the A51 leaves for TARPORLEY stands the 14th-cent. Perpendicular Church of St Andrew. It has a square tower and the doorway is decorated with angels and the parapet with gargoyles. There are grotesque figures on the north wall. Six dormer windows light the nave and chancel, and the south aisle has a fine roof. The screen is massive.

Duddon, 2¼ m. to the SE., is a tiny village, with old farm-houses and black-and-white cottages.

TATTON HALL, *Cheshire* (12–SJ7582). Although Tatton Park abuts on the north side of

KNUTSFORD, the entrance for motorists is further round the estate, by the Rostherne gates. It claims to be the most visited house owned by the National Trust. The building is of excellent proportions, exquisitely furnished and in perfect order; it also has a wide range of pictures. Tatton was built soon after the end of the 18th cent. but the architect, Samuel Wyatt, elder brother of James, died in 1807 before it was complete, and his nephew, Lewis Wyatt, took over the design. Likewise the owner, William Egerton, died before completion, and his son Wilbraham worked with the new architect. A former hall stood on the estate held by the Egertons since 1598, when Sir Thomas was prominent at the court of Elizabeth I. A later relative, Samuel Hill, an art collector, secured the apprenticeship of his nephew, Samuel Egerton, to Joseph Smith, later the consul at Venice who patronized Canaletto and shipped art works for young Englishmen making the Grand Tour. Thus it was probably Samuel Hill who commissioned the two works by Canaletto now in the drawing-room, and other Italian works no doubt arrived by arrangement with Consul Smith. One of Canaletto's two Venice scenes includes the Doge's Palace and the other the Grand Canal. The third most important painting is Van Dyck's *Martyrdom of St Stephen*, painted in Rome about 1623. Other works include those by followers or imitators of Titian, Rubens, Poussin and Jacopo Bassano, a Veronese studio work, an attribution to Domenico Tintoretto, a portrait begun by Lawrence, a Murillo and a Chardin.

There are Italian Renaissance chests, a Boulle bookcase, Chippendale ladder-back chairs, a French Boulle clock (Louis XV), Adam-style chairs, and a fine collection of china, silver and glass. The library has an impressive collection, begun in the 18th cent. on foundations laid in the 16th and 17th cents. There are important works on architecture with collections of engravings, and on travel, husbandry, horticulture and estate management, and also atlases. A table is set with fine silver and glass in the dining-room, below the large 18th-cent. cut-glass chandelier. Upstairs are the portraits of the Ten Cheshire Gentlemen (*see* PUDDINGTON). After the sumptuous bedrooms and the 17th-cent. oak staircase, the kitchens and the Tenants' Hall laid out as a museum by Maurice, the last Lord Egerton, should be seen. The last Egerton was a many-sided character, a big-game hunter, a pioneer in motor travel with his Benz of 1900 (on view), a pioneer aviator and a friend of Orville Wright. As a young man he disappeared, and was found living with a tribe in the Gobi desert; he even tried to stake gold in the Yukon.

Humphry Repton laid out the 54 acres of formal gardens and woodland. Oranges and lemons grow in the orangery and there are exotic plants. A classical temple is based on the Choragic Monument of Lysicrates in Athens. Nearby is the Japanese Garden where a Shinto temple stands on an islet in the Golden Brook. The temple is said to have come from Japan and to have been erected by Japanese workmen. The mere, in the park of over 1,000 acres, is about a mile long and the home of many wildfowl. The grounds can accommodate huge numbers of visitors, but, if necessary, entrance to the building is regulated so that visitors can proceed at leisure. There are some catering facilities. The hall and grounds were both opened to the public only in 1962, and by 1967 the millionth visitor had passed through.

About $\frac{1}{2}$ m. N. is **Rostherne**, an attractive village which has a large mere and a church with monuments.

TEBAY, *Westmorland* (14–NY6104), is a village among high fells at the north end of the Lune Gorge, which· has traces of Roman occupation. Down the gorge the River Lune flows S. on its way to the Irish Sea past CATON and LANCASTER. The impressive landscape of the gorge has been long known to travellers on the main-line railway, but now it is also the route of the M6 extension. The fells stretch E. to RAVENSTONEDALE and NW. to the SHAP Fell area.

TEMPLE SOWERBY, *Westmorland* (14–NY6127), a pleasant village SE. of PENRITH, has a village green, an old church and a four-arch bridge, and prides itself on being Queen of the Westmorland Villages. To the N. is Acorn Bank or Temple Sowerby Manor, a red-sandstone house, mainly 18th-cent., but with some 16th-cent. work. It is National Trust property; its famous rose gardens are open to the public, but not the house.

THIRLMERE and HELVELLYN, *Cumberland* (14–NY3116). The Thirlmere of today is not the one Wordsworth knew. In the days of the Lake Poets it was a smaller area, comprising two natural lakes which were almost joined. There were about 14 farms around the Dalehead and Armboth end of the valley, often on the sites of earlier, Norse dwellings. Along the west shore was the main coach road from GRASMERE to KESWICK, and at the south end the community's centre, Wythburn. The Wordsworths often rested or met Coleridge at the village's oldest inn, the Cherry Tree, and it appears in Wordsworth's Poem, "The Waggoner". In the later 19th cent. MANCHESTER secured the water for its growing population, but only in the teeth of a raging controversy over industrial progress versus conservation. Thirlmere became a reservoir, with a dam at the N. raising the level 50 ft; Hawes How and Deergarth How became islands; all farms in the valley itself were submerged or demolished except two; and the remainder of Wythburn was cut off from the burn. The 17th-cent. church mentioned by Wordsworth survives, but not the Cherry Tree. At Thirlspot, about 3 m. N. of Wythburn and also on the east side, the Wordsworths sometimes visited the King's Head Inn, which is still there.

It was out of such controversy as that over Thirlmere that the National Trust was born. In

1895 it was founded by Miss Octavia Hill, Sir Robert Hunter, and Canon H. D. Rawnsley, the vicar of Crosthwaite (*see* Keswick) and a writer and poet. In the Trust's words: "Each had realised that the growth of population, the spread of industrialisation and a lack of planning were rapidly spoiling much of the beauty of England. To halt this uncontrolled destruction, to educate public opinion and to give people access to the countryside, they agreed to set up a body of responsible private citizens who would act as trustees for the nation in the acquisition and ownership of land and buildings worthy of permanent preservation." The Trust's first acquisition in the Lakes was Brandelhow (DERWENT-WATER) in 1902; now it owns 72,884 acres in the district, 14,188 of them protected, and 14,710 sheep, all these properties being in the National Park.

Helvellyn is 3,118 ft high and the third highest Lakeland peak. It stands towards the southern end of a long series of fells that reach about 9 m. from Dollywaggon Pike on the S. to Clough Head on the N., and measure about 5 m. across their widest part. Slopes are steeper on the W. and often have spectacular crags and valleys on the E. Until the 18th cent. Helvellyn itself was believed to be the highest peak in England, but SCA FELL PIKE and Sca Fell precede it by a few score feet. Helvellyn is probably the most popular mountain for ascents in the Lakes, being within reach of various main resorts and with the A591 along its base. Two favourite routes are from Wythburn and Thirlspot; they are shorter than those from PATTERDALE or Grasmere but are fairly steep. There is some parking space at Wythburn and Thirlspot. Those climbing from the former place follow the footsteps of Wordsworth, Sir Walter Scott and Humphry Davy who went up together.

There are extensive views from various points on the top of this range, such as over Red Tarn, the famous Striding Edge, Swirrel Edge, and, in clear weather, as far as Scotland.

Dunmail Raise is on the A591, a pass just S. of Thirlmere where the road climbs up from Grasmere. It is not very steep. A cairn on the west side of the summit is alleged by tradition to be the burial place of Dunmail, King of Cumbria, who was killed here in a 10th-cent. battle with Edmund, King of the English, who gave Cumbria to Malcolm of Scotland.

THRELKELD, *Cumberland* (14–NY3225), is a small village about 4 m. to the E. of KESWICK. SADDLEBACK (Blencathra) towers above Threlkeld to the N. and the village is a centre for climbing this range. St John's Vale is S. (*see* CASTLE ROCK) and the slopes of Great Dodd, beginning of the HELVELLYN range.

TORPENHOW, *Cumberland* (14–NY2039), is E. of the A595, about 8 m. from COCKERMOUTH. St Michael's Church was built about 1170. Its Norman door, arches, chancel arch and font still remain. There is a painted deal ceiling with flowers and gilding, added in the late 17th cent. The church is unspoilt, without restorations. The site gives good views towards the Solway Firth and the beginnings of the Lake District hills.

TORVER, *Lancashire* (14–SD2894), lies on the main road, about 1 m. W. of CONISTON WATER. As it lies close to the Coniston range of peaks, the village affords excellent views of them. Walna Scar and Dow Crag are nearer summits, and further N. is the 2,633-ft Coniston Old Man. Ascents of the Old Man often start from the village. The church is 19th-cent., but one of its records, a paper of consecration signed by Cranmer in 1538, showed that there was an earlier church on the site. A curiosity is a chest made from a hollowed-out single log, and there is an ancient font. On the slopes of Bleaberry Haws, to the W., are lines of ancient fortifications. At **Lowick Bridge**, S. beyond the lake, Arthur Ransome lived at Lowick Hall; some think that the setting of his children's book *Swallows and Amazons* was based on WINDERMERE.

TROUTBECK, *Westmorland* (14–NY4103). This is a wild and beautiful valley, with a stream and a village of the same name. The beck flows down from the mountainous area E. of the KIRKSTONE PASS into WINDERMERE, and the main road for ULLSWATER climbs up to the pass from the A591, N. of WINDERMERE TOWN. A tradition of the ancient village is that it once had a race of giants or strong men. Townend is National Trust property and open to the public. Its house, built about 1626, was the home of a yeoman family, the Brownes, who lived there for three centuries. Their furniture and possessions, and carved woodwork, are preserved. The house stands in 776 acres of farmland, at the south end of the village.

TURTON TOWER, *Lancashire* (12–SD7315). The house is 4½ m. N. of BOLTON, near Turton village, and its history goes back some 800 years. There are three sections of the building: the peel-tower itself, the east wing (with the present entrance hall and flanking rooms), and the north-east wing. The tower itself was probably begun in the 12th cent. as a simple defensive structure, with a vault below to house cattle. In the 15th cent., windows, instead of mere slits, were made in the three lower stories, and the present top story was added in the late 16th cent. The east wing was built in the early 16th cent., two stories high; another story, with heavy mullioned windows, the entrance hall and the adjoining rooms were added to it in about 1596. The north-east wing is also early 16th-cent., but its north and east sides, and third story were built in 1844 in the Jacobean style. Much of the gabling is also 19th-cent.

The manor of Turton belonged in the 12th cent. to Roger Fitz-Robert and to Henry, Duke of Lancaster. The Orrell family had the house in the 16th cent., and in the 17th cent. it was acquired by Humphrey Chetham (founder of the Chetham Library, MANCHESTER). In the 19th cent. it passed to James Kay who saved the building by carrying out restoration work, though not always in keeping with its character. Until this time, it was probably the north-east wing, and not the tower itself, that was used as a residence. Turton Tower was sold in 1903 to the Knowles family, who gave it to Turton Urban District Council in 1930.

The stone walls behind the panels in the dining-room are probably original 12th-cent., and the upper lights of the large window have early 17th-cent. Swiss glass. The morning-room is mainly early 16th-cent. The drawing-room of 1596 is now the council chamber of Turton Council. The grandfather clock may have been made by Samuel Crompton (*see* HALL I' TH' WOOD). Among the interesting items to be seen are the arms and armour in the entrance hall, cradles, old furniture (including Early English inlaid work) and paintings in the Ashworth Room, and a carved oak tester bed in the Bradshaw Room. The Chetham Room (1596) has old furnishings, arms, fire-place and kitchen implements, and a candelabra made from stags' horns. The house, which is unusually well documented and has housed a folk museum in the upper story since 1952, is well worth visiting. It is open to the public at advertised times.

ULLSWATER, *Cumberland* (14–NY4220). There are four main routes to this lake: from the S. via the KIRKSTONE PASS, from the N. by leaving the A66 at TROUTBECK station, or from the E. either from PENRITH or via POOLEY BRIDGE. Between the Troutbeck and Penrith routes are several smaller roads; but the north and south approaches are the only roads in their areas. The Kirkstone road is the A592, a main north and south through road for the Lakes. It gives magnificent views over PATTERDALE, but probably the best way to see the lake itself is to approach from its lower, Pooley Bridge and Penrith end, where the River Eamont runs out. The Cumberland and Westmorland border runs through Ullswater, but the A592 goes along the Cumberland side, the NW. There is a road from Pooley Bridge part way along the other side but it ends in the Martindale area, and the circuit of the lake can be completed only on foot. Ullswater is over 7 m. long and second in size only to WINDERMERE.

Gowbarrow Park, 4 or 5 m. from the east end of the lake and beside the A592, should be seen in spring for its daffodils immortalized by Wordsworth. He knew this area well: "List, ye who pass by Lyulph's Tower", he wrote at the beginning of *The Somnambulist,* and also refers to Aira Force, the fine waterfall away from the road, on Aira Beck. Lyulph, or L'Ulf, is said to have been the baron or chieftain who built a tower on this site (the present tower is modern), and Ullswater may be derived from his name. The National Trust owns most of this area, as well as some land at the head of the lake on the east side of Stybarrow Dodd, one of the peaks of the range of HELVELLYN mountains. Wordsworth climbed Helvellyn from the west side with Scott and Humphry Davy in 1805. There are paths up this range from the Ullswater side, including Striding Edge, which juts out towards the lake. GRISEDALE comes down between this range and St Sunday Crag, 2,756 ft. which is SW. of the lake; a path goes up Grisedale to Dollywaggon Pike. **Glenridding** is a hamlet by the lake, N. of Grisedale. Opposite across the head of the lake is Place Fell, over 2,000 ft.

This stretch of the water is one of three which mark Ullswater's length, and their changes on direction alter the view considerably as you proceed. E. of Place Fell and the Martindale area the High Street range, with its highest peak well to the S., slants northward towards the Pooley Bridge end of the lake. All these lofty peaks ranging round the south, west, and east areas of Ullswater make an impressive background to the quiet lake scene. In summer there is a regular service of motor vessels along the lake between Pooley Bridge and Glenridding, passing, towards the south end, the island of House Holme that is associated with legends of King Arthur. The full trip, either way, takes about an hour, and is especially for drivers, a relaxing means of seeing the lake. Boats can also be hired.

ULVERSTON, *Lancashire* (12–SD2878), is a market town for the district, and lies between green fells and the sea. The lighthouse on The Hoad is a monument to Sir John Barrow (1764–1848, founder of the Royal Geographical Society), and Barrow Sound is named after him. Swarthmoor Hall was the home of Margaret Fell. She was the wife of Judge Fell (died 1658) and was converted to the Quaker faith by George Fox, its founder. Margaret Fell opened her house to the Society of Friends' preachers, became one of their leaders, and was imprisoned after her husband's death. She married George Fox in 1669 and died in 1702. She is buried nearby at **Sunbrick,** together with some 200 other Friends. The Quaker Meeting House at Rake Head was given by George Fox. St Mary's Church is supposed to have been founded in 1111 but has been much rebuilt since. The Norman doorway is the oldest part, but has a modern porch. The tower was built in Tudor times. **Bardsea** is a village on the coast road 3 m. from Ulverston; a lane leads up to the Stone Circle on Birkrigg Common, where Bronze Age implements were found. **Colton** is a tiny village N. of Ulverston. Its church has a bell more than 500 years old and a silver paten dated 1671. Below the church is the holy well of St Cuthbert where this 7th-cent. missionary is said to have won converts and baptized children.

UPHOLLAND, *Lancashire* (12–SD5105). The Church of St Thomas in this small town occupies a high site at the top of a curve of the main road. The tower is square and squat, but the 14th-cent. church is fairly massive as it incorporates the remains of an earlier Benedictine priory. The priory chancel, with soaring arcades and arch, became the nave. The colourful stained glass came from the priory.

UTKINTON, *Cheshire* (12–SJ5564). This small

Noel Habgood

e Vale of Newlands

lage is near the road that rises through a cut in
e rock NE. of TARPORLEY. Utkinton Hall, now
arm-house, was formerly the seat of the Dones,
family that had branches in other parts of
heshire – the Dones of Flaxyards, of Crowton,
Duddon and of Oulton. The Utkinton Dones
ere Chief Foresters for the king at Delamere
orest in the days when the sovereign visited
ALE ROYAL for hunting. The last of the male
le was Sir John Done who was knighted by
mes I. Family monuments can be seen in St
elen's Church, Tarporley.

ALE OF NEWLANDS, *Cumberland* (14–
Y2422). From the KESWICK side the approach
via Portinscale or BRAITHWAITE up to the tiny
lage of Stair. This faces S. up Newlands
lley proper, down which the Newlands Beck
ns from Dale Head, a peak 2,473 ft high. The
lley is roughly parallel with DERWENTWATER
t ends a good deal further S. For motorists,
wever, the route runs SW. from Stair over the
m.-long **Newlands Pass** (1,096 ft) leading via
eskadale to BUTTERMERE VILLAGE. For about
m. the pass is a reasonably steady ascent to its
p, with craggy heights all around, but once
yond that the driver faces a descent of about
0 ft in 1 m. to Buttermere.

ALE ROYAL, *Cheshire* (12–SJ6369). Vale
oyal of England was the old name for the area,

and Vale Royal is the great hall that stands there
in the heart of Cheshire, not far from the Delamere
Forest. The estate is SW. of NORTHWICH, and
the easiest way to reach it is to turn S. from the
A533 near its junction with the A556. The drive
from the road leads under a lofty archway of
trees through beautiful parkland to the hall
which stands near the River Weaver. It is strange
to think that in this quiet spot there was once a
huge Cistercian abbey, of which Edward I laid the
foundation stone in 1277. The traces of the foundations remaining after its destruction in the
Dissolution indicate a larger size even than
FOUNTAINS ABBEY. The hall stands on the site.
Its old wing was built by the Holcrofts in the
16th cent. and the Cholmondeleys of CHOL-
MONDELEY made alterations at various times.
James I stayed at Vale Royal to hunt in Delamere
Forest with John Done of UTKINTON, whom he
knighted. The hall has had various owners in
recent years.

WALLASEY, *Cheshire* (12–SJ2992), is a county
borough in the north-east corner of the Wirral
peninsula, of which NEW BRIGHTON forms a
part. The ferry crosses from LIVERPOOL to
Wallasey in 7 minutes. As well as being a holiday
resort Wallasey is a residential area. Wallasey
beach overlooks the Irish Sea and from New
Brighton along the King's Parade promenade is
a pleasant walk. Wide stretches of sand continue

to the borough boundary at HOYLAKE. These are used for motor-cycle races in spring and autumn. Wallasey offers yacht sailing, the Derby and Guinea Gap bathing pools and an 18-hole minia-ture golf course. With the sandhills and Moreton Common, the beach provides nearly 3 m. of unspoilt coastline.

Leasowe is an area of natural sandhills W. along the coast. The castle here was built in 1593 by Ferdinando, 5th Earl of Derby, a member of the Stanley family of KNOWSLEY HALL and patron of Shakespeare and actors. The castle was apparently a summer residence, and probably it was also a convenient spot on the way to the Stanley family estates in the Isle of Man. The castle became known as Mockbeggar Hall when it fell into ruin during the vicissitudes of the Stanleys after the Civil War (the 7th Earl was executed by Cromwell and the family lost much of its estates). More recently it became a con-valescent home.

WARBURTON, *Cheshire* (12–SJ7089). The main attraction of this 700-year-old village on the banks of the MANCHESTER Ship Canal is the old church built on the site of an earlier one founded by the daughter of Alfred the Great. The timber-framed structure, common to many churches in 14th-cent. Cheshire, was considerably renovated with brick and stone some 300 years later and remains today a building of oddity and charm. The beams and rafters of the roof interior are said to be secured with deer horns and the pillars of the nave are of time-hardened oak as enduring as stone. The brick tower is curiously placed in the E., and the north wall is wooden with wattle-and-daub plasterwork. In the village a fine yew tree and the old stocks lend extra interest to the medieval character of the area.

WARRINGTON, *Lancashire* (12–SJ6088), is a town with locks on the MANCHESTER Ship Canal. It is an industrial town, in which clock-making has played a part, and is a gateway to Cheshire. Nearby, the Romans had a ford across the Mersey at Latchford. Warrington was the scene of many battles from Roman times until 1648, when Cromwell entered after his victory at PRESTON. His statue stands near the bridge. The town was the first in the country to have a public library supported from the rates (1848). St Elphin's Church has a large 19th-cent. spire and a 14th-cent. chancel. Memorials include those of the Botelers and the Pattens. Holy Trinity is a fine church of the 18th cent. probably built to the designs of James Gibbs, the architect of Bank Hall (1750), the seat of the Patten family and since 1872 the Town Hall. The municipal museum and art gallery is in Bold Street. Museum collections include natural history and anthropology. The gallery has English watercolours and glass.

To the SW., across the border into Cheshire, towns such as **Runcorn**, **Halton** and **Frodsham** are not without their own charm and are situated in attractive landscape, though the New Town at Runcorn is destroying some pleasant scenery.

WARTON, *Lancashire* (12–SD4972). Church of St Oswald or Holy Trinity is 15th-ce and has been restored. On the tower are the ar of the Washington family (ancestors of Geo Washington) who lived in the area for ma generations. Thomas, last of the Washington Warton, was parson at the church, 1799–18 To the NW. is **Silverdale**, where the Natio Trust owns many acres that give a panorama with MORECAMBE Bay. This village has associatic with Mrs Gaskell, who lived at a house where was often visited by Charlotte Brontë. W. Ril author of the *Windyridge* novels, also lived at village.

WASTWATER and WASDALE, *Cumb land* (14–NY1505). Wastwater is the deep English lake, reaching nearly 260 ft in places, a is also the most rugged and spectacular in setti It is about 3 m. long, but narrow. The Scree forbidding wall of rubble, line the steep drop alc most of its south-east side. Motorists can re the lake only from the W., and can follow north-west side as far as a parking place in W dale (or Wastdale), the nearest point accessible car to the majestic SCA FELL peaks which, at o 3,000 ft, wall in the Sty Head Pass against GRE GABLE on the N. The pass winds at 1,600 ft lik rock ladder between the eastern ramparts of W dale. SE. is Esk Hause, the great crossroads climbers from Wasdale, from BORROWDA from ESKDALE and from LANGDALE. Motor should follow at least part of the lakeside rc on foot fully to appreciate the stern beauty of scenery. The north-west wall of the valley beg with smaller hills but mounts to Yewbarrow a Kirk Fell, both over 2,000 ft, before Great Gat

Wasdale Head is a hamlet where many climbe stay; some of the graves in its churchyard are the of climbers who have died in the fells.

WATENDLATH, *Cumberland* (14–NY271 is sometimes grouped with BORROWDALE, bu more an offshoot to the E., quiet, remote, and c that has been called a secret valley. It is a place great charm, deserving the regard in which it held, and is easily reached from DERWEN WATER. The route leaves the road going S. on east side of the lake and goes uphill to **Ashn Bridge**, also a notable Lakeland scene. There i narrow old packhorse bridge over the beck, whe the bend and the width can easily be misc culated. Higher up a good view of the lake can had, and from High Crag, higher still, an impr sive sight of the lake landing stage far below. Ne is Shepherd's Crag, but this has to be climbed foot to see the view.

Watendlath itself is a hamlet, its houses bu and roofed with stone. The entire hamlet, exce for one dwelling house, is fortunately protect by the National Trust which also owns the ta and the surrounding land. Thus the character the place is preserved as it ought to be. This *Rogue Herries* country, for Hugh Walpole la the scenes of these novels in the countrysi round Borrowdale and KESWICK. Watendla

T. Parker

astwater and Wasdale seen from Great Gable

itself is introduced into *Judith Paris*.

The tarn is fed from Blea Tarn higher up, in the slopes of Ullscarf. Where the Watendlath tarn flows out, it forms the curious Churn, or the Devil's Punch Bowl. The peak on the E. of the valley is High Seat, 1,996 ft high.

WEST KIRBY, *Cheshire* (12–SJ2181). This residential and seaside resort adjoins HOYLAKE to the N., but enjoys a more sheltered climate because of its site just inside the Dee estuary, with the ridge of the Grange and Caldy hills behind it on the E. It was one of the oldest places of settlement in the Wirral peninsula, and was granted a charter by the Conqueror although its history pre-dates his period. There is a marine lake of over 30 acres, and pleasant beaches.

There are three areas of National Trust property in the vicinity: Caldy Hill, 1 m. SE., Harrock Wood, E. of Irby, and Thurstaston Common, 2 m. SE. of West Kirby. Caldy and Thurstaston give fine views over the Dee estuary. The road from West Kirby climbs steadily up to the plateau of Thurstaston Common, where you can park in pleasant picnic areas.

WETHERAL, *Cumberland* (14–NY4654). A Benedictine priory was founded in Wetheral, which is about 5 m. E. of CARLISLE, but only the 15th-cent. gatehouse remains. Near the river are caves said to have been the cell of St Constantine.

The Gothic Church of the Holy Trinity is 15th-cent., but has undergone considerable alteration. Apart from the stained glass, the most interesting feature is a large monument by Joseph Nollekens, 1789, to Lady Maria Howard of Corby. The figure of Religion points to heaven beside a young woman with a baby.

Corby Castle, built mainly in the 17th cent., stands by the River Eden. The grounds (open to the public) were laid out by Thomas Howard before 1740.

WHALLEY, *Lancashire* (12–SD7335). Whalley is an interesting village on the River Calder, about 12 m. ENE. of PRESTON on the A59. The Ancient Monument of Whalley Abbey (open to the public) is the ruin of a Cistercian house that was partly rebuilt. The monks who founded it came from Cheshire in the 13th cent. Among notable features of the remains are the north-east and north-west gateways, the chapter house, the abbot's lodging and the kitchen. Parts of the structure were made into a residence for the Assheton family in the late 17th cent.

The parish church, St Mary's, is mainly 13th-cent., with a 15th-cent. tower and clerestory. There are very fine wood carvings, including the stalls. The screened pews are 17th- and 18th-cent. work. An organ of 1729 came from LANCASTER parish church.

The village is associated with the witches of Pendle, whose misfortunes are described in Harrison Ainsworth's *Lancashire Witches*. Roger Nowell, a magistrate, and member of the Read Hall family, began enquiries into witchcraft that

Barnaby/Mustogr.

Wigan pier

led to a group of unfortunate women being tri at Lancaster in 1612; most were executed. Now quarrelled with the Whalley church authoriti over a specially large pew he wanted to install emphasize his importance. There was a con impasse when the church would not admit it a Nowell would not withdraw it; the pew ended a barn and it was 70 years before it was fina put into the church.

WHINLATTER PASS, *Cumberland* (14–N 1924), is, at its highest point, 1,043 ft high. It is t best road for driving over any of the Lakela passes as its bends are not excessively sharp. Fro KESWICK you take the road round the nor end of the lake through the little village Portinscale, and then the B5292 through BRAIT WAITE. The road climbs soon after that affor ing views of SKIDDAW and BASSENTHWAI below. The peak of Whinlatter lies N. (1,696 and Grisedale Pike to the S. (2,593 ft). the other end of the steep-sided pass the ro descends into the Vale of Lorton and goes N to COCKERMOUTH. After High Lorton one c turn S. and return to Keswick via CRUMMOC WATER, BUTTERMERE, HONISTER PASS a BORROWDALE.

WHITEHAVEN, *Cumberland* (14–NX971 This was previously a hamlet, but in 1690 Sir Jo Lowther began the work that eventually trar formed it into a seaport and coal-mining town. development was fostered by Sir James Lowth (1736–1802), the 1st Earl of Lonsdale, who bu Whitehaven Castle (now a hospital) in 1769. T Friends' Meeting House, the lighthouse, the ne quay, and St James's Church were built in the 18 cent. There are also Georgian houses in Lowth Street. Whitehaven is now an industrial area b can be used as a centre for visiting the weste lakes and is the nearest important town ENNERDALE.

Paul Jones attacked Whitehaven in 1788 and a ærman U-boat shelled it in 1915.

IGAN, *Lancashire* (12–SD5805), is some-mes dismissed as an industrial town of little terest, with memories of *The Road to Wigan er*. The pier was so named from the wharf made the canal cut in the 18th cent., one of many aking Lancashire towns for the transport of ods. The first industries were pewter, brass, ll-founding, clock-making, cotton, coal-mining, n and clothing; now Wigan relies more on ings like light engineering, plastics, coach-ilding and container-making. But Wigan is also historic town, with names of Norse, Celtic and xon origin, and relics of Roman occupation. It d a charter as far back as 1246 and its coat of ms is unusual for the privilege of bearing royal mbols. Wigan was Royalist in the Civil War d James Stanley, 7th Earl of Derby, was uted there (*see* ORMSKIRK and KNOWSLEY ALL). He was later executed at BOLTON. In igan Lane is the monument marking the spot here the earl's general, Tyldesley, was killed.

Haigh Hall (open to the public), about 1½ m. E. of Wigan, is the former house of the Earls of rawford, a family who collected thousands of ooks and manuscripts. With the plantations of ver 200 acres, the hall and grounds were acquired om the Earl of Crawford by the corporation in 947 at a generously low price. It houses a local istory museum, containing archaeological and dustrial exhibits, and certain rooms are used for hibitions. Wigan's library has a Public Record ffice with 60,000 MSS. of archives for the area. here is also a Little Theatre, a Historic and ntiquarian Society and several organizations atering for music and drama. The Parish Church f All Saints is Gothic in style, largely rebuilt. An scription on the churchyard wall is dated 1683. mong monuments is that to Sir William Brads-aigh and his wife. According to legend she elieved her husband dead after several years of is absence, and married a Welsh knight; on his eturn she walked barefoot in penance once eekly for a year from Haigh to Mab's Cross (in tandishgate). It was in Wigan that William lesketh Lever (of Bolton and PORT SUNLIGHT) egan making soap in 1886.

VILMSLOW, *Cheshire* (12–SJ8580). Here is a mall town which is outwardly a modern shopping-entre and also a dormitory area for MAN-HESTER, but behind the appearance of modernity here is much that connects Wilmslow with the ast. Intolerance of one kind or another was a haracteristic of Cheshire people for centuries and he Quaker Meeting House in the town was often he scene in the 17th cent. of cruel persecutions gainst a sect which refused to conform to the stablished church. Wilmslow is also the town of amuel Finney, the portrait painter who became special favourite of Queen Caroline. In his *Historical Survey of the Parish of Wilmslow* he ailed against the drunkenness and disorder which vas prevalent there in the 18th cent. Later, when

he became a magistrate, he put down hooliganism with such firmness that Wilmslow has wryly claimed a reputation for respectability ever since.

An object of really unusual interest to visitors is the green-and-white gypsy caravan at Parkway, which is carefully preserved as a memorial to the celebrated naturalist and broadcaster "Romany of the B.B.C.", in private life the Rev. G. Bram-well Evans, who spent the last years of his life here.

Wilmslow lies in a deep valley of the Bollin river which has its source near Shuttlings Low and flows through some 20 m. of extremely beautiful country before eventually finding its way into the Mersey near Heatley. On the banks of the river is Wilmslow church with its fine tower and sombre walls dating mainly from the 16th cent., as does the splendid oak roof of the chancel. Under two arches are monuments to Humphrey Newton and his wife, which have been here for 400 years, and the brass in front of the altar, a memorial to Robert Booth of Dunham and his lady, is the oldest in Cheshire.

WINDERMERE, *Westmorland* (14–SD3995). This is the largest lake in England. It covers 10½ m. from N. to S., and in that distance its sur-roundings change in character from the milder countryside at the south end, to the mountainous scenery at the north where the lake reaches almost to AMBLESIDE. But it is not really a mountain lake, having no high peaks rising beside it. The shores are thickly wooded, so that when driving round Windermere, you often have only restricted views of the water from the road.

Ambleside was on the route of the Roman road from Ravenglass and HARDKNOTT to PENRITH, and the Roman fort of Galava stood between Ambleside and the lake. Roman remains have also been found on Belle Isle. Norsemen settled here in the 10th cent. Windermere was a forest belonging to the lords of KENDAL in the 11th cent. and was included in the manor of Strickland Ketel, which changed hands at various times: like other parts of the North of England, it was held by the Scots at one period. In the reign of Henry II it passed to the Lancasters, and in the 13th cent. a Lancaster nephew founded a hermitage on the island of Ladyholme. Belle Isle became the home of the Philipson family and one of them was besieged there by the Roundheads. From far back in history Windermere has been constantly used by boats of various kinds, serving as a water high-way for the transport of goods to the lakeside communities.

Since the 19th cent. Windermere has become noted for its sailing clubs and its yacht racing; it is the country's greatest inland water centre for sailing and boating. A wide variety of craft can be hired, from rowing boats to cabin cruisers with sleeping accommodation. The lake has the head-quarters of the Royal Windermere Yacht Club at BOWNESS Bay, the South Windermere Sailing Club at Fell Foot, and the Windermere Motor Boat Club at Broad Leys. In summer the pas-senger vessels ply from end to end of the lake. There is a public pier for visiting vessels at

Louis and Daphne P

Windermere from Ambleside at sunset

Bowness Bay and similar ones at Parsonage Bay and Waterhead. At the height of the season there can be as many as 1,500 boats using the lake, besides the increasing number of underwater swimmers. It became necessary to make a code of conduct if all users of the lake were to enjoy its facilities with safety, and a Collision Rules Order was established. This is outlined in the Council's booklet, *Chart of Lake Windermere*, containing information for all who use the lake. A chart shows the position of rocks and shallow areas, fairway markers, submarine contours and so on. The booklet gives information on angling, swimming and yachting. Lake wardens patrol the lake during the season in a motor launch, specially equipped for emergencies, which keeps in touch with a police patrol boat by radio. Observance of the lake rules is compulsory.

The passenger vessels are a traditional means of transport for holidaymakers arriving from WIN-DERMERE TOWN railway station: the boats take them either to the Ambleside end of the lake for bus services to KESWICK, or to Lake Side for services to ULVERSTON. But a trip on one of these boats – or a craft from the various boating companies – is an admirable way of seeing the lake. The passenger boats take 1¼ hours to cover the length of the lake, including the busy stop at Bowness; S. of here there is also a ferry across the lake, for HAWKSHEAD and CONISTON.

Pony-trekking is an enjoyable activity in the countryside, and at Windermere it is organized by the Central Council of Physical Recreation (Storrs Hall).

The widest view around the lake is from Orrest Head, on the N. of Windermere town, where there is a chart to indicate the peaks. Across the lake, beyond the woods of Claife Heights, is Coniston Old Man, and N. of it are Carrs and Wetherlam with the DUDDON VALLEY hidden behind them.

Then there are Crinkle Crags with Pike of Blis in front and SCA FELL behind, BOW FEL GREAT GABLE, and the LANGDALE PIKES. T view N. shows the TROUTBECK valley and Hig Street, and SE. are the Ingleborough moors Yorkshire. The National Trust owns variou properties around the lake, including Clai Cockshott Point, Ladyholme island, and Que Adelaide's Hill. Cockshott and Adelaide a among vantage points for views.

WINDERMERE (TOWN), *Westmorla* (14–SD4198). The town's rise to importance dat from the introduction of the railway in 184 before that it was merely a village called Birt waite. The town is now administered jointly wi BOWNESS, which is on the lakeside. The wo Windermere used alone really denotes the lak The railway meant an influx of holidaymakers one of the few points in the LAKE DISTRICT th could be reached by rail. The station is linked Bowness by a bus service so that passengers ca use the summer motor-vessel services to both en of the lake, and from these travel to other parts Lakeland. Thus the town is largely a mode development in its present form; but various o Westmorland families have been prominent in t area for centuries, and as far back as the 11th cer the lake was part of a manor called Stricklar Ketel, which later passed through various han in the barony of KENDAL or Kentdale.

The town is one of England's most importa holiday centres and is easily accessible from t M6. It lies on the A591, between Kendal to t SE. and AMBLESIDE, GRASMERE and KESWIC to the N. It offers a wide range of accommodatio from first-class hotels to quiet guest-houses ar caravan sites; it has garages and boat-builder In or near the town are ample facilities for go tennis, fishing, water-skiing, pony-trekking, ar very form of water sport. Sheepdog trials are held on Applethwaite Common, to the N., in August.

Orrest Head is a well-known vantage point on the north side with an extensive view of Lakeland peaks (*see* previous entry). Other views can be had from Queen Adelaide's Hill, National Trust property, 1 m. W. of Windermere station.

WINSFORD, *Cheshire* (12–SJ6565). This is a small industrial region comprising the townships of Over, Swanlow, and Wharton, all of which are linked by a modern bridge across the River Weaver. The whole of the area is utilized for the production of salt and chemicals and this largely determines its appearance. Winsford has a fine grammar school, founded in the last century by Sir Joseph Verdin, but its main function, apart from industry, is as a dormitory for LIVERPOOL and MANCHESTER. The urban district of Over is the reputed birthplace of Robert Nixon, "the Cheshire Prophet", an illiterate ploughboy whose predictions were to earn him a place in Cheshire folklore. The square-towered Church of St Chad, about 1 m. from the town, was rebuilt in 1543, restored in 1870, and considerably altered since.

WINWICK, *Lancashire* (12–SJ6094). This little village with the Church of St Oswald lies between WARRINGTON and M6. As evidence of a long history it contains an inscription which records the attachment to this church of Oswald, King of Northumbria, who died fighting against the pagan King Penda of Mercia. Centuries later the Royalists were defeated here in two engagements of the Civil War in 1643 and 1648. Presumably there was an earlier church on this site as St Oswald's is partly 14th-cent. Two chantry chapels have memorials to the Legh and Gerard families. A. W. N. Pugin designed the chancel, 1847–8. The churchyard has part of a fine large wheel cross, possibly of Anglo-Saxon workmanship.

WITHERSLACK, *Westmorland* (14–SD4384). St Paul's Church, NW. of the A590, has a restrained Classical interior with four pillars and 17th-cent. woodwork. It was endowed and built by John Barwick, who became Dean of ST PAUL'S, in 1664–9. There were alterations in the 18th cent.

WOODPLUMPTON, *Lancashire* (12–SD 4934), is the birthplace of Henry Foster, the 19th-cent. navigator, who was drowned in the Gulf of Mexico in 1831. The Church of St Anne has a memorial to him. A low building in warm-coloured stone, St Anne's has a belfry with an octagonal dome. It is 15th-cent., apparently re-erected in 1630, and with further rebuilding work in 1748. There are three aisles under separate roofs, and interesting stained glass.

WORKINGTON, *Cumberland* (14–NX9928), was Gabrosentum in Roman times and the site of a fort. Anglian invaders settled at some stage of the Anglo-Saxon conquest. In the 9th cent. the

Lindisfarne monks, fleeing from the Danes on the north-east coast of England tried to sail for Ireland from Workington, and the Lindisfarne Gospels (BRITISH MUSEUM) were washed overboard. The Curwen family, claiming descent from Malcolm II of Scotland and Ethelred the Unready, built Workington Hall (not in use now) in the 14th cent. Mary Queen of Scots spent a night there in 1568 after fleeing from the battle of Langside. The Helena Thompson Museum exhibits costumes, ceramics, glass and local objects. There is a civic theatre. St Michael's Church, largely rebuilt in 1887 after a fire, is late Decorated Gothic. Cross fragments indicate use of the site from the 8th cent. St John's (1823) has a Classical exterior, a replica of St Paul's, COVENT GARDEN. Sir Ninian Comper designed the painted interior with its golden columns in 1931. The town's main industry is steel.

WORSLEY, *Lancashire* (12–SD7400), lies between the MANCHESTER Ship Canal and BOLTON. Several old houses have been demolished but Worsley Old Hall, former seat of the Earl of Ellesmere which is now offices, and the 16th-cent. Wardley Hall remain. Sir Geoffrey de Massey of Worsley was the founder of the Trinity Chapel in St Mary's Church at ECCLES in 1454. Worsley was a centre for coal-mining in the time of the ironworks of James Nasmyth of Eccles, and the Duke of Bridgewater built the canal in 1759–65 to take coal from his mines at Worsley to Manchester. A Tudor-style building, the Aviary, is modern. The golf club at Monton Green has an 18-hole course of 6,429 yds founded in 1894. A pleasant spot is Warke Dam, shared with SWINTON AND PENDLEBURY.

WRENBURY, *Cheshire* (12–SJ5947). St Margaret's Church is early 16th-cent. Its pleasant renovated interior has a west gallery and box pews, and monuments include one to Sir Stapleton Cotton, one of Wellington's generals. **Combermere Abbey**, S. of Wrenbury, stands in a large park with a mere and was the former home of the Cotton family. **Audlem**, SE. of Wrenbury, has a number of timbered buildings. The Gothic church has a handsome oak ceiling.

WRYNOSE PASS, *Westmorland* (14–NY 2602–3105). Its eastern ascent is in Westmorland, but the descent at the south-west end is just on the Lancashire side of the River Duddon, which to the SW. marks the border with Cumberland (*see* DUDDON VALLEY). Near the top of the pass Three Shires Stone marks the junction of the three counties. The pass reaches 1,270 ft, and can be approached only from the E. (GRASMERE or AMBLESIDE areas) or from the W. (up the Duddon valley or the notorious HARDKNOTT PASS). Wrynose has gradients of up to 1 in 4 on its narrow road, which, though surfaced, must be treated with caution. There are wide sweeps of moorland on each side, with the Pike of Blisco (2,304 ft) to the N. and the beginning of the CONISTON range to the S. – a wild, lonely area.

A Brief Bibliography

GUIDE BOOKS

In the space available it is impossible to list under each area the many admirable local guide books or studies of special areas that are available Booksellers mostly stock such standard series as Methuen's Little Guides Benn's Blue Guides, Robert Hale's County Books, and Arthur Mee's The King's England (Hodder & Stoughton). A series of great value and authority as regards architecture, listing as it does the more important buildings of each parish, is Sir Nikolaus Pevsner's *Buildings of England*, of which some 36 volumes have been published so far by Penguin. The Shell County Guides so far published (Faber) are:

Cornwall: *John Betjeman*   Derbyshire: *Christopher Hobhouse*
Devon: *Brian Watson*   Dorset: *Michael Pitt-Rivers*
Essex: *Norman Scarfe*   Gloucestershire: *Anthony West, David Verey*
Herefordshire: *David Verey*   Isle of Wight: *J. Pennethorne Hughes*
Leicestershire: *W. G. Hoskins*   Lincolnshire: *Henry Thorold, Jack Yates*
Norfolk: *Wilhelmine Harrod, The Rev. C. L. S. Linnell*
Northamptonshire: *J. Smith*   Northumberland: *Thomas Sharp*
Oxfordshire: *John Piper*   Rutland: *W. G. Hoskins*
Shropshire: *John Piper, John Betjeman*
Somerset: *C. H. B. & Peter Quennell*   Suffolk: *Norman Scarfe*
Wiltshire: *David Verey*   Worcestershire: *J. Lees-Milne*

The following is a short list of books for further reading on the subjects of the introductory chapters.

THE BEGINNINGS

ATKINSON, R. J. C. *Stonehenge*. Hamish Hamilton, 1956
CLARK, Grahame. *Prehistoric England*. Batsford, 1962
CLARKE, Rainbird. *East Anglia*. Ancient People and Places Series, Thames & Hudson, 1960
FOX, Aileen. *South-West England*. Ancient People and Places Series, Thames & Hudson, 1964
GRINSELL, L. V. *Ancient Burial Mounds of England*. Methuen, 1956
HAWKES, Jacquetta. *Guide to the Prehistoric and Roman Monuments of England and Wales*. Chatto & Windus, revised edition, 1954
HAWKES, Jacquetta. *A Land*. Chatto & Windus, 1951
STONE, J. F. S. *Wessex*. Ancient People and Places Series, Thames & Hudson, 1958
THOMAS, Nicolas. *A Guide to Prehistoric England*. Batsford, 1960

THE AGRICULTURAL HERITAGE

ERNLE, Lord. *English Farming, Past and Present* (ed. Fussell and
O. R. Macgregor). Cassell, 6th edition, 1961
FUSSELL, G. E. *Farming Technique from prehistoric to modern times.*
Commonwealth Library, Pergamon Press, 1966
HARTLEY, Dorothy. *The Countryman's England.* Batsford, 1935
HOSKINS, W. G. *The Making of the English Landscape.* Hodder &
Stoughton, 1955
STAMP, L. Dudley. *Britain's Structure and Scenery.* Collins, 1946
STAMP, L. Dudley. *Types of Farming Map of England and Wales.*
Ministry of Agriculture, 1941 etc.

TREES AND WOODLANDS

BRIMBLE, L. J. F. *Trees in Britain.* Macmillan, 1946
EDLIN, H. L. *Know Your Broadleaves.* Forestry Commission, 1968
EDLIN, H. L. *Know Your Conifers.* Forestry Commission, 1966
EVELYN, John. *Sylva.* Various publishers
HADFIELD, Miles. *British Trees.* A Guide for Everyman, Dent, 1957
HADFIELD, Miles. *Landscape with Trees.* Country Life, 1967
MAKINS, F. K. *The Identification of Trees and Shrubs.* Dent, 1948
RODGERS, J. *The English Woodland.* Batsford, 1942
STROUD, Dorothy. *Capability Brown.* Country Life, 1950
TANSLEY, A. F. revised by M. C. F. Porter. *Britain's Green Mantle.*
Allen & Unwin, 1968
WOOD, R. F. and ANDERSON, I.A. *Forestry and the British Scene.*
Forestry Commission, 1968

THE VILLAGE

FINBERG, J. *Exploring Villages.* Routledge, 1958
HOSKINS, W. G. *The Making of the English Landscape.* Hodder &
Stoughton, 1955
MUNRO CANTLEY, H. *Suffolk Churches and their Treasure.* Batsford, 1937
'MISS READ'. *Village School.* Michael Joseph, 1955
The Legacy of England (anthology). Batsford, 1935

THE TOWN

DALE, A. *The History and Architecture of Brighton.* Bredon &
Heginbotham, 1950
DYOS, H. J. *Victorian Suburb.* Leicester University Press, 1961
ISON, W. *The Georgian Buildings of Bath.* Faber, 1948
ISON, W. *The Georgian Buildings of Bristol.* Faber, 1952
LITTLE, B. *The Buildings of Bath.* Collins, 1947
SUMMERSON, Sir John. *Georgian London.* Pelican, revised edition, 1962

THE COUNTRY HOUSE

DUTTON, Ralph. *The English Country House*. Batsford, 1950

HILL, Oliver, and CORNFORTH, John. *The English Country House: Caroline, 1625–85*. Country Life, 1966

HUSSEY, Christopher. *The English Country House: Early Georgian, 1715–60*. Country Life, 1955

HUSSEY, Christopher. *The English Country House: Mid-Georgian, 1760–1800*. Country Life, 1956

HUSSEY, Christopher. *The English Country House: Late Georgian, 1800–40*. Country Life, 1958

LEES-MILNE, James. *The English Country House: Baroque, 1685–1714*. Country Life, 1970

LLOYD, Nathaniel. *A History of the English House*. Architectural Press, 1949

SUMMERSON, Sir John. *Architecture in Britain, 1530–1830*. Penguin, 1953

WOOD, Margaret. *The English Mediaeval House*. Phoenix House, 1965

Historic Houses, Castles and Gardens in Great Britain and Ireland: Published annually by Index Publishers, giving days and times of opening throughout the year

The National Trust's List of Properties. Published biennially, free to members

CATHEDRALS AND CHURCHES

BATSFORD, H. and FRY, T. *The Cathedrals of England*. Batsford, 1936

BATSFORD, H. and FRY, T. *The Greater English Church*. Batsford, 1940

BETJEMAN, John (editor). *Guide to English Parish Churches* (2 vols). Collins, 1958

BETJEMAN, John and CLARKE, B. *English Churches*. Studio Vista, 1964

BOND, F. *Introduction to English Church Architecture* (2 vols). Humphrey Milford, 1913

COOK, G. H. *The English Cathedral through the Centuries*. Phoenix House, 1957

COOK, G. H. *English Collegiate Churches of the Middle Ages*. Phoenix House, 1959

COOK, G. H. *The English Medieval Parish Church*. Phoenix House, 1954

COX, J. C. and FORD, C. B. *Parish Churches*. Batsford, 1961

CROSSLEY, F. *English Church Craftsmanship*. Batsford, 1941

CROSSLEY, F. *English Church Monuments*. Batsford, 1920

ESDAILE, Katherine. *English Church Monuments, 1510–1840*. Batsford, 1946

HARVEY, John. *The English Cathedral*. Batsford, new edition, 1961

HUTTON, Graham and SMITH, Edwin. *English Parish Churches*. Thames & Hudson, 1952

PEVSNER, N. *Buildings of England series*. Penguin Books, 1951–

WHIFFEN, Marcus. *Stuart and Georgian Churches*. Batsford, 1947–8

FOLLIES

JONES, Barbara. *Follies and Grottoes*. Constable, 1953

MACAULAY, Rose. *Pleasure of Ruins*. Weidenfeld & Nicolson, 1953

THE INDUSTRIAL HERITAGE

BARTON, D. B. *The Cornish Beam Engine*. D. Bradford Barton, 1965

HADFIELD, E. C. R. *British Canals*. David & Charles, 1962

KLINGENDER, F. D. *Art and the Industrial Revolution*, second edition edited by Sir Arthur Elton. Evelyn, Adams & Mackay, 1968

RICHARDS, J. M. and DE MARE, Eric. *The Functional Tradition*. Architectural Press, 1958

ROLT, L. T. C. *Victorian Engineering*. Allen Lane, the Penguin Press, 1970

SIMMONS, Jack. *The Railways of Britain*. Routledge, 1965

There are also two series of books on Britain's Industrial Archaeology. One is published by David & Charles and volumes covering the following districts are currently available: Bristol Region, Dartmoor, Derbyshire, East Midlands, Hertfordshire, Lake Counties, Lancashire, Scotland, Southern England, The Tamar Valley. The series published by the Longman Group is on a subject basis and the four following titles have been published so far: *Navigable Waterways, Roads and Vehicles, Iron and Steel, The Textile Industry*.

MOUNTAIN, HILL AND MOORLAND

BLACKSHAW, A. *Mountaineering*. Kaye & Ward, 1968

BYNE, Eric and SUTTON, G. *High Peak: the story of walking and climbing in the Peak*. Secker & Warburg, 1966

CLARK, R. C. and PYATT, E. C. *Mountaineering in Britain: a history from earliest times to the present day*. Phoenix House, 1957

CROSSING, W. *Guide to Dartmoor*. Macdonald, 1965

EDWARDS, K. C. *The Peak District*. Collins, 1962

HARVEY, L. A. and ST LEGER GORDON, D. *Dartmoor*. Collins, 1953

MARRIOTT, M. *The Shell Book of the Pennine Way*. Queen Anne Press, 1968

NATIONAL PARKS COMMISSION and DARTMOOR NATIONAL PARK COMMITTEE. *Dartmoor*. H.M.S.O., 1957

NATIONAL PARKS COMMISSION. *North York Moors*. H.M.S.O., 1966

P.P.P.B. *Peak District*. Bakewell P.P.P.B., 1960

PEARSALL, W. H. *Mountains and Moorlands*. Collins, 1950

PEEL, J. H. B. *Along the Pennine Way*. Cassell, 1969

POUCHER, W. A. *The Lakeland Peaks*. Constable, 2nd edition, 1962

PYATT, E. C. *A Climber in the West Country*. David & Charles, 1968

PYATT, E. C. *Mountains of Britain*. Batsford, 1966

PYATT, E. C. *Where to Climb in the British Isles*. Faber, 1960

UNSWORTH, W. *The English Outcrops*. Gollancz, 1964

WAINWRIGHT, A. *Pennine Way Companion*. Kendal, Westmorland Gazette

SEASCAPE

ADDISON, W. *Thames Estuary*. Hale, 1954

ADLARD COLES, K. *Creeks and Harbours of the Solent*. E. Arnold, 1959

ADMIRALTY, Hydrographic Department. *North Sea Pilot, Channel Pilot, Bristol Channel Pilot, Northern Irish Sea Pilot*. H.M.S.O.

ARNOTT, W. G. *Alde Estuary.* Norman Adlard, 1954. Also *Suffolk Estuary* and *Orwell-Estuary*

BELLOC, Hilaire. *The Cruise of the Nona.* Constable, 1925

BENHAM, Hervey. *The Last Stronghold of Sail.* Harrap, 1949

DAVIES, G. M. *The Dorset Coast.* Black, 1956

JESSUP, R. F. and F. W. *The Cinque Ports.* Batsford, new edition, 1956

PHILLIPS-BIRT, Douglas. *Waters of Wight.* Cassell, 1967

POOLEY, D. J. *West Country Rivers.* Yachting Monthly, 1957

WENTWORTH DAY, James. *Coastal Adventure.* Harrap, 1949

STEERS, J. A. *The Coastline of England and Wales.* Cambridge University Press, 1946

RIVERS

CHALMERS, Patrick R. *The Angler's England.* Seeley Service, 1938

COOTE, J. H. *East Coast Rivers.* Yachting Monthly, 1956

GIBBINGS, Robert. *Sweet Thames Run Softly.* Dent, 1940

GIBBINGS, Robert. *Coming Down the Wye.* Dent, 1942

GIBBINGS, Robert. *Till I End my Song.* (The Thames) Dent, 1957

GOODSALL, R. H. *The Medway and its Tributaries.* Constable, 1955

HILLS, J. W. *A Summer on the Test.* Bles, 1946

WATERS, Brian. *Severn Tide.* Dent, new edition, 1963

WENTWORTH DAY, James. *A History of the Fens.* Harrap, 1954

PLUNKET-GREENE, H. *Where the Bright Waters Meet.* Witherby, new edition, 1969

WILLIAMSON, Henry. *A Clear Water Stream.* Faber, 1958

THE ENGLISH GARDEN

CLARK, H. F. *The English Landscape Garden.* Cresset, 1949

FAIRBROTHER, Nan. *Men and Gardens.* Hogarth Press, 1956

HADFIELD, Miles. *A History of British Gardening.* Revised edition, Spring Books, 1969

HUNT, Peter (editor). *The Shell Garden Book.* Phoenix House and Rainbird, 1964

HYAMS, Edward. *The English Garden.* Thames & Hudson, 1964

TAYLOR, Geoffrey. *The Victorian Flower Garden.* Skeffington, 1952

An essential guide to the larger gardens, including many National Trust properties, is *Historic Houses, Castles and Gardens in Great Britain and Ireland.* For gardens open for charity, see *Gardens of England and Wales Open to the Public Under the National Gardens Scheme,* obtainable from 57 Lower Belgrave Street, London S.W.1, and *Gardens to Visit,* from Mrs K. Collett, White Witches, Claygate Road, Dorking, Surrey.

Index

s provides an index to all the places mentioned in the Gazetteers, either as main entries or as sub-entries. In cases
re these places are also referred to in the Introductory Essays, these page references are printed in italic type. When
re than one place of the same name is referred to, the names of the counties in which the places lie have been added.

aps

end

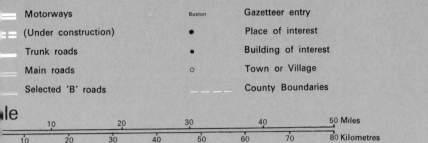
le

Scale bar: 10 20 30 40 50 Miles
10 20 30 40 50 60 70 80 Kilometres

p Pages

● Counties and sections

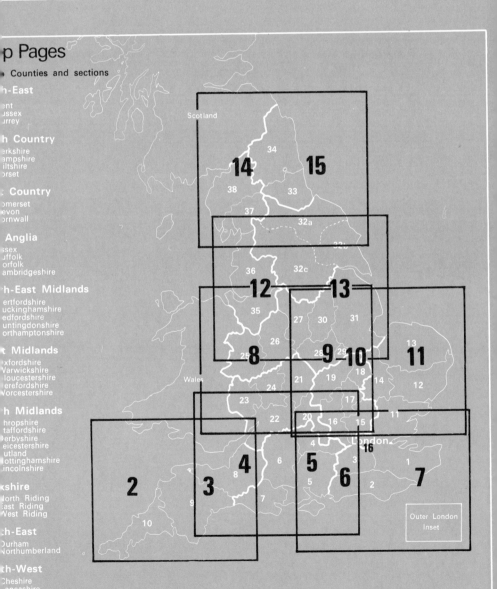

2

LUNDY

BAR

HARTLAND POINT

Hartland

Morwenstow

Kilkha

Stratton

Penfound
Manor

Boscastle

Tintagel

Delabole

St Clether

Laun

St Endellion   Port Isaac

Altarnun

St Kew

Padstow

St Merryn

BODMIN MOOR

Blisland

Wadebridge

BEDRUTHAN STEPS

St Neot

St Clees

St Mawgan-in-Pydar

Bodmin

Liske

St Columb
Major

Landydrock
House

Newquay   C   O   R   N   W   A

St Cubert

Roche

Lostwithiel

St Keyne

Perranporth

Luxulyan
Valley

Lerryn

Lanteglos-
by-Fowey

Loo

TREVAUNANCE
COVE

St Austell

Fowey

Polperro

Probus

Truro

St Michael
Penkevil

Mevagissey

St Ives

Veryan

Redruth

ROSELAND

Zennor

Camborne

St Just-in-Roseland

Chysauster

St Mawes

St Just
in Penwith   Penzance

Lanyon Quoit

Godolphin House

Falmouth

Newlyn

Breage

Glendurgan
Gardens

Mousehole

Helston

ST
MICHAEL'S
MOUNT

St Antony in Meneage

LAND'S END

Helford

Porthcurno

GOONHILLY
DOWNS

Gunwalloe

Mullion

Coverack

KYNANCE COVE

LIZARD POINT

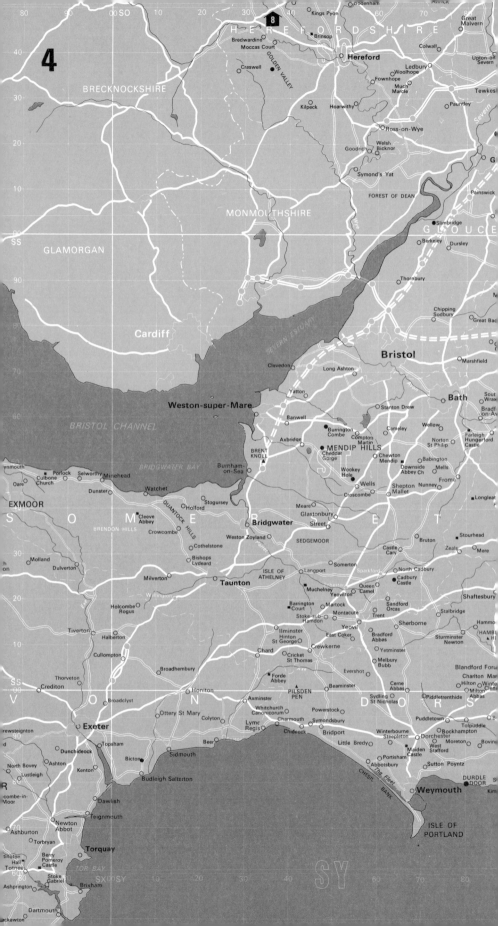

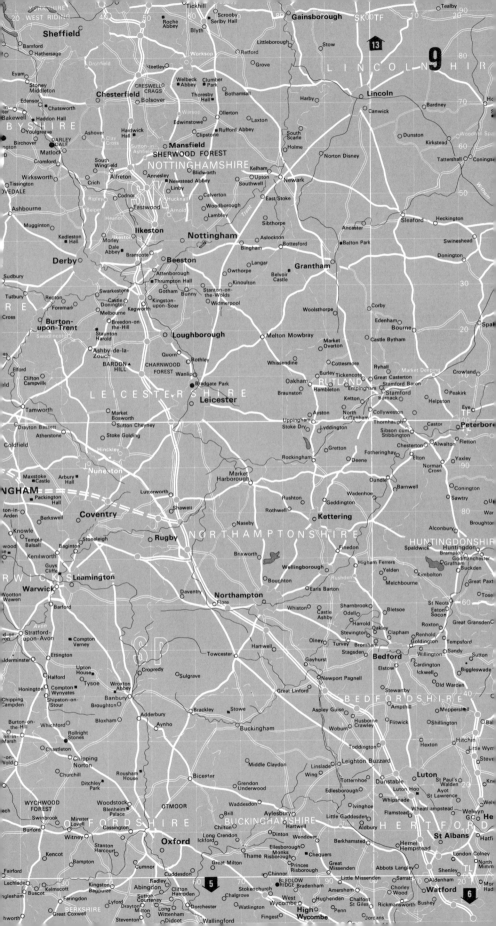

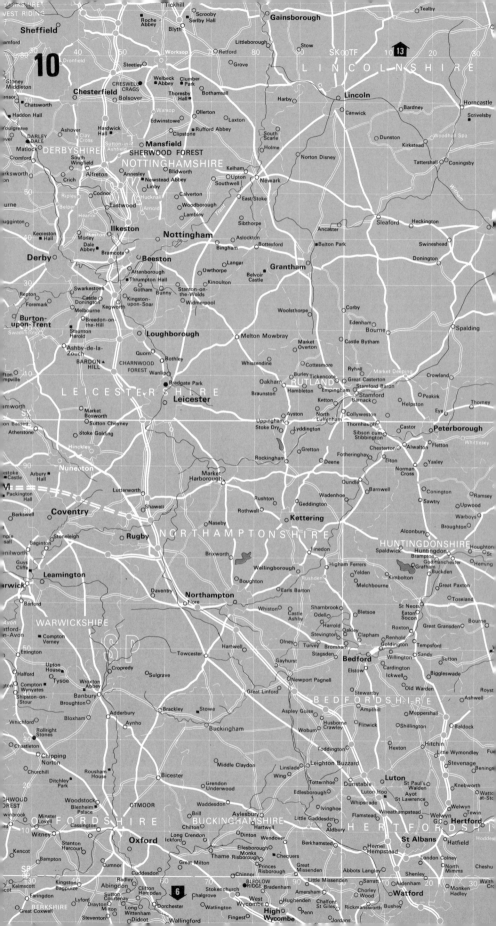

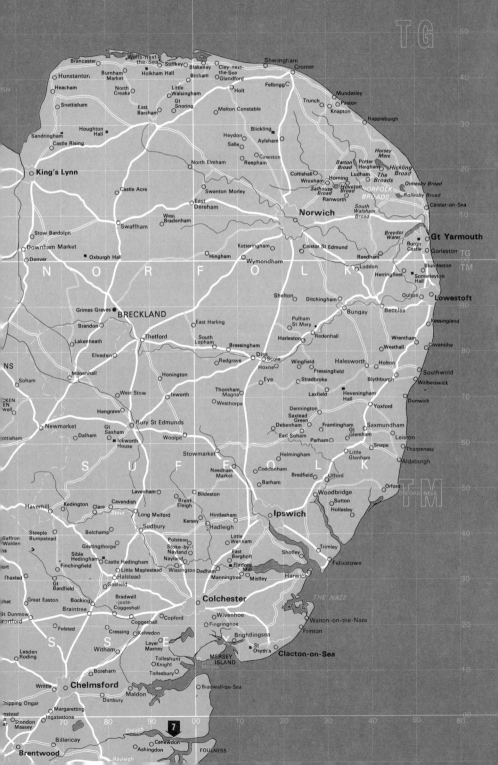

NU

NU OO OQ

ND

burgh

FARNE ISLANDS

Seahouses

Beadnell

eton

Dunstanburgh
Castle

Craster

Howick

wick

Alnmouth

North Sea

kworth

on

D

Lynemouth

Bothal

Newbiggin-
by-the-Sea

lington

Blyth

Seaton Delaval

nd

Whitley Bay

Cullercoats
Tynemouth

Newcastle-
upon-Tyne

South Shields

Jarrow MARSDEN
ROCK

Gateshead

Whitburn
Roker
Monkwearmouth

de

Hylton
Castle

Washington

Sunderland

nley

WORM
HILL

Penshaw
Monument

NZ

Chester-
le-Street

Lumley
Castle

Houghton-
le-Spring

aster

Finchale
Priory

Seaham

y

Pittington

Durham

Peterlee

eth

Hart

A

M

Spennymoor

West Hartlepool

Wear

Bishop Middleham

Hartlepool

Bishop
Auckland

Sedgefield

Greatham

Shildon

Billingham

Redcar

Aycliffe

Norton

ington

Kirkleatham

Staithes

d
Piercebridge

Stockton-
on-Tees

Middlesbrough

Loftus

rlington

Haughton-le-
Skerne

Egglescliffe

Guisborough

Whitby

Hurworth

Yarm

Croft

Stokesley

Great
Ayton

NORTH YORK MOORS
NATIONAL PARK

Egton

Littlebeck

Robin Hood's
Bay

asby

Carlton-in-
Cleveland

Ingleby
Greenhow

Danby-in-
Cleveland

Catterick

Ralph Cross

Goathland

RTH

Brompton-in-
Allertonshire

Mount Grace
Priory

Rosedale Abbey

FYLINGDALES

Northallerton

RIDING

Bedale

Lastingham

Levisham

Hawnby

Hutton-le-Hole

rvaulx Abbey

Kirkbymoorside

Scarborough

Masham

Thirsk

Rievaulx
Abbey

Kirkdale

Sutton Bank

Helmsley

Pickering

Thornton Dale

Filey

Kilburn

Byland
Abbey

SE

Ampleforth

Kirby
Misperton

Coxwold

Gilling
Castle

Hovingham

SH

Brandsby

Barton-le-Street

Ripon

Studley Royal
Fountains
Abbey

Newby
Hall

Boroughbridge
Aldborough

Crayke

Castle Howard

Malton

FLAMBO

y Bridge

Markenfield
Hall

Sheriff Hutton

Kirkham
Priory

I

Rudston

Bridlington

Brimham
Rocks

Foston

R

Sledmere
House

Ripley

SE OO TA

Howsham

EAST RIDING

Burton Agnes

TA

NG

Knaresborough

Nun
Monkton

Beningbrough
Hall

SE OO TA

Great
Driffield

Stamford